PHILIP'S

NAVIGATOR BRITAIN CAMPING & CARAVANNING

T0301047

The Camping and Caravanning Club

The Friendly Club

www.philips-maps.co.uk

First published in 2014 by Philip's,
a division of Octopus Publishing Group Ltd
www.octopusbooks.co.uk
Carmelite House
50 Victoria Embankment
London EC4Y 0DZ
An Hachette UK Company
www.hachette.co.uk

Fifth edition 2023
First impression 2023

ISBN 978-1-84907-628-9

Cartography by Philip's
Copyright © 2023 Philip's

This product includes mapping data licensed
from Ordnance Survey®, with the permission of
the Controller of His Majesty's Stationery Office.
© Crown copyright 2023. All rights reserved.
Licence number AC0000851689

Data for the caravan sites provided by
The Camping and Caravanning Club.

Information for the selection of Wildlife Trust nature reserves
provided by The Wildlife Trusts.

Information for National Parks, Areas of Outstanding Natural Beauty,
National Trails and Country Parks in Wales supplied by the
Countryside Council for Wales.

Information for National Parks, Areas of Outstanding Natural Beauty,
National Trails and Country Parks in England supplied by Natural
England. Data for Regional Parks, Long Distance Footpaths and
Country Parks in Scotland provided by Scottish Natural Heritage.

Information for Forest Parks supplied
by the Forestry Commission.

Information for the RSPB reserves provided by the RSPB

Gaelic name forms used in the Western Isles provided by
Comhairle nan Eilean.

Data for the National Nature Reserves in England provided by Natural
England. Data for the National Nature Reserves in Wales provided
by Countryside Council for Wales. Darparwyd data'n ymwneud â
Gwarchodfeydd Natur Cenedlaethol Cymru gan Gyngor Cefn Gwlad
Cymru.

Information on the location of National Nature Reserves in Scotland
was provided by Scottish Natural Heritage.

Data for National Scenic Areas in Scotland provided by the Scottish
Executive Office. Crown copyright material is reproduced with the
permission of the Controller of HMSO and the Queen's Printer for
Scotland. Licence number C02W0003960.

Photographic acknowledgements
Front cover and title page:
Wensleydale, North Yorkshire. Wayne Hutchinson / Alamy Stock Photo
Back cover middle: Camping and Caravanning Club

Printed in China

CONTENTS

II Key to map symbols

III Our great camp sites, your great experiences

VIII Route planning maps

XIV Distances and journey times

1 Road maps of Britain

315 Urban approach maps

315 Bristol *approaches*
316 Birmingham *approaches*
318 Cardiff *approaches*
319 Edinburgh *approaches*

320 Glasgow *approaches*
321 Leeds *approaches*
322 London *approaches*
326 Liverpool *approaches*

327 Manchester *approaches*
328 Newcastle *approaches*
329 Nottingham *approaches*
330 Sheffield *approaches*

331 Town plans

331 Aberdeen · Aberystwyth · Ashford · Ayr · Bangor · Barrow-in-Furness · Bath · Berwick-upon-Tweed
332 Birmingham · Blackpool · Bournemouth · Bradford · Brighton · Bristol · Bury St Edmunds
333 Cambridge · Canterbury · Cardiff · Carlisle · Chelmsford · Cheltenham · Chester · Chichester · Colchester
334 Coventry · Derby · Dorchester · Dumfries · Dundee · Durham · Edinburgh · Exeter
335 Fort William · Glasgow · Gloucester · Grimsby · Hanley · Harrogate · Holyhead · Hull
336 Inverness · Ipswich · Kendal · King's Lynn · Leeds · Lancaster · Leicester · Lewes
337 Lincoln · Liverpool · Llandudno · Llanelli · Luton · Macclesfield · Manchester
338 London
340 Maidstone · Merthyr Tydfil · Middlesbrough · Milton Keynes · Newcastle · Newport · Newquay · Newtown · Northampton
341 Norwich · Nottingham · Oban · Oxford · Perth · Peterborough · Plymouth · Poole · Portsmouth
342 Preston · Reading · St Andrews · Salisbury · Scarborough · Shrewsbury · Sheffield · Southampton
343 Southend-on-Sea · Stirling · Stoke · Stratford-upon-Avon · Sunderland · Swansea · Swindon · Taunton · Telford
344 Torquay · Truro · Wick · Winchester · Windsor · Wolverhampton · Worcester · Wrexham · York

345 Index to town plans

361 Index to road maps of Britain

402 County and unitary authority boundaries

Road map symbols

M25	Motorway
16 17	Motorway junctions – full access, restricted access
	Toll motorway
Pease Pottage Services	Motorway service area
	Motorway under construction
S	Primary route – dual, single carriageway, services – under construction, narrow
Cardiff	Primary destination
25 26	Numbered junctions – full, restricted access
	A road – dual, single carriageway – under construction, narrow
	B road – dual, single carriageway – under construction, narrow
	Minor road – dual, single carriageway
	Drive or track
	Urban side roads (height, weight and width restrictions not shown)
12'9 6'6 12.5	Height restriction, width restriction – feet and inches
	Tunnel, weight restriction – tonnes
2	Distance in miles
Toll	Roundabout, multi-level junction, Toll, steep gradient – points downhill
CLEVELAND WAY	National trail – England and Wales
GREAT GLEN WAY	Long distance footpath – Scotland
YATTON	Railway with station, level crossing, tunnel
ROPLEY	Preserved railway with level crossing, station, tunnel
	Tramway
	National boundary
	County or unitary authority boundary
	Car ferry, catamaran
	Passenger ferry, catamaran
	Hovercraft
V P	Internal ferry – car, passenger
	Principal airport, other airport or airfield
MENDIP HILLS	Area of outstanding natural beauty, National Forest – England and Wales, Forest park, National park, National scenic area – Scotland, Regional park
	Woodland
	Beach – sand, shingle
KENNET AND AVON CANAL	Navigable river or canal
6	Lock, flight of locks, canal bridge number
	Caravan or camping sites – CCC* Club Site
	– CCC Certificated Site, Listed Site
	*Categories defined by The Camping and Caravanning Club of Great Britain
P&R ▲965	Viewpoint, park and ride, spot height – in metres
	Linear antiquity
29 SY 70/80	Adjoining page number, OS National Grid reference – see page 402

Road map scale

1:100 000 • 1cm = 1km • 1 inch = 1.58 miles

0 1 2 3 4 5 km
0 1 2 3 miles

Road map scale (Isle of Man and parts of Scotland)

1:200 000 • 1cm = 2km • 1 inch = 3.15 miles

0 1 2 3 4 5 6 7 8 9 10 km
0 1 2 3 4 5 6 miles

Tourist information

BYLAND ABBEY	Abbey or priory		Marina
WOODHENGE	Ancient monument	SILVERSTONE	Motor racing circuit
SEALIFE CENTRE	Aquarium or dolphinarium		Nature reserves
CITY MUSEUM AND ART GALLERY	Art collection or museum	HOLTON HEATH	– National nature reserve
TATE ST IVES	Art gallery	BOYTON MARSHES	– RSPB reserve
1644	Battle site and date	DRAYCOTT SLEIGHTS	– Wildlife Trust reserve
ABBOTSBURY SWANNERY	Bird sanctuary or aviary		Picnic area
BAMBURGH CASTLE	Castle	WEST SOMERSET RAILWAY	Preserved railway
YORK MINSTER	Cathedral	THIRSK	Racecourse
SANDHAM MEMORIAL CHAPEL	Church of interest	LEAHILL TURRET	Roman antiquity
SEVEN SISTERS	Country park – England and Wales	THRIGBY HALL	Safari park
LOCHORE MEADOWS	– Scotland	FREEPORT BRAINTREE	Shopping village
ROYAL BATH & WEST SHOWGROUND	County show ground	MILLENNIUM STADIUM	Sports venue
MONK PARK FARM	Farm park	ALTON TOWERS	Theme park
HILLIER GARDENS AND ARBORETUM	Garden, arboretum		Tourist information
ST ANDREWS	Golf course – 18-hole	NATIONAL RAILWAY MUSEUM	Transport collection
TYNTESFIELD	Historic house	LEVANT MINE	World heritage site
SS GREAT BRITAIN	Historic ship	HELMSLEY	Youth hostel
HATFIELD HOUSE	House and garden	MARWELL	Zoo
CUMBERLAND PENCIL MUSEUM	Museum	SUTTON BANK VISITOR CENTRE	Other place
MUSEUM OF DARTMOOR LIFE	– Local	GLENFIDDICH DISTILLERY	of interest
NAT MARITIME MUSEUM	– Maritime or military		

Approach map symbols

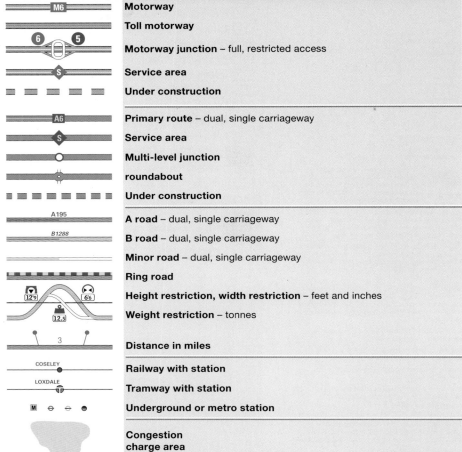

M6	Motorway
	Toll motorway
6 5	Motorway junction – full, restricted access
S	Service area
	Under construction
A6	Primary route – dual, single carriageway
S	Service area
	Multi-level junction
	roundabout
	Under construction
A195	A road – dual, single carriageway
B1288	B road – dual, single carriageway
	Minor road – dual, single carriageway
	Ring road
12'9 6'6 12.5	Height restriction, width restriction – feet and inches
	Weight restriction – tonnes
3	Distance in miles
COSELEY	Railway with station
LOXDALE	Tramway with station
M	Underground or metro station
	Congestion charge area

OUR CAMPSITES, YOUR GREAT EXPERIENCES

The
Camping and
Caravanning
Club
The Friendly Club

campingandcaravanningclub.co.uk

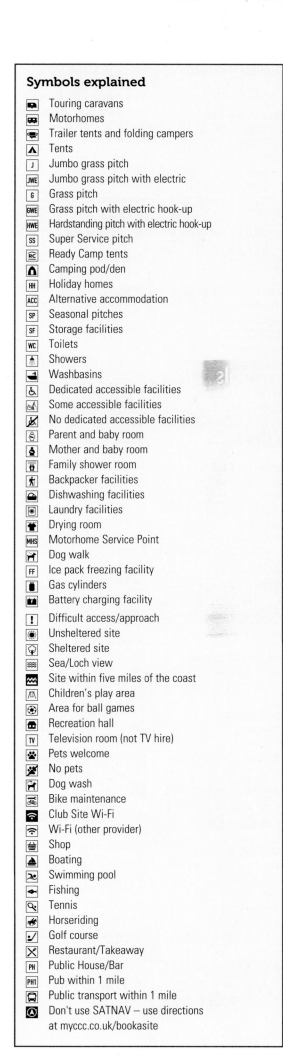

Symbols explained

🚐	Touring caravans
🚐	Motorhomes
🚐	Trailer tents and folding campers
⛺	Tents
J	Jumbo grass pitch
JWE	Jumbo grass pitch with electric
G	Grass pitch
GWE	Grass pitch with electric hook-up
HWE	Hardstanding pitch with electric hook-up
SS	Super Service pitch
RC	Ready Camp tents
🏠	Camping pod/den
HH	Holiday homes
ACC	Alternative accommodation
SP	Seasonal pitches
SF	Storage facilities
WC	Toilets
🚿	Showers
🚰	Washbasins
♿	Dedicated accessible facilities
♿	Some accessible facilities
♿	No dedicated accessible facilities
👶	Parent and baby room
👶	Mother and baby room
🚿	Family shower room
🚶	Backpacker facilities
🍽	Dishwashing facilities
🧺	Laundry facilities
👕	Drying room
MHS	Motorhome Service Point
🐕	Dog walk
FF	Ice pack freezing facility
⛽	Gas cylinders
🔋	Battery charging facility
!	Difficult access/approach
☀	Unsheltered site
🌴	Sheltered site
〰	Sea/Loch view
〰	Site within five miles of the coast
🎠	Children's play area
⚽	Area for ball games
🎱	Recreation hall
TV	Television room (not TV hire)
🐾	Pets welcome
🐾	No pets
🐕	Dog wash
🚲	Bike maintenance
📶	Club Site Wi-Fi
📶	Wi-Fi (other provider)
🛒	Shop
⛵	Boating
🏊	Swimming pool
🎣	Fishing
🎾	Tennis
🐎	Horseriding
⛳	Golf course
🍴	Restaurant/Takeaway
PH	Public House/Bar
PH1	Pub within 1 mile
🚌	Public transport within 1 mile
⚠	Don't use SATNAV – use directions at mycccc.co.uk/bookasite

Map Key

● Club Site

Philip's Map Key to Sites

Club Site – we have nearly 100 campsites across the UK. See them listed over the next 3 pages and within the map pages.

Certificated Site – over 1,200 smaller campsites, exclusively for Club members. Space permitting, they accept up to 5 caravans or motorhomes, plus tents.

Listed Site – these can range from huge holiday parks with entertainment to quiet commercial sites. The Club does not approve or recommend any of these sites.

SCOTLAND

Culzean Castle Club Site
Culzean, Maybole, Ayrshire
KA19 8JX
Tel: 01655 760627
Map reference:
Pg: 256 Grid Ref: G6
Open: 31 Mar – 30 Oct 2023
Pitches: 90

Dingwall Club Site
Jubilee Park Road, Dingwall,
Highland IV15 9QZ
Tel: 01349 862236
Map reference:
Pg: 300 Grid Ref: D5
Open: 31 Mar – 23 Oct 2023
Pitches: 75

Dunbar Club Site
Oxwellmains, Dunbar,
East Lothian EH42 1WG
Tel: 01368 866881
Map reference:
Pg: 282 Grid Ref: F4
Open: 31 Mar – 30 Oct 2023
Pitches: 115

Glencoe Club Site
Glencoe, Ballachulish, Argyll
PH49 4LA
Tel: 01855 811397
Map reference:
Pg: 284 Grid Ref: B5
Open: 31 Mar – 23 Oct 2023
Pitches: 100

Inverewe Gardens Club Site
Poolewe, Achnasheen, Highland
IV22 2LF
Tel: 01445 781249
Map reference:
Pg: 307 Grid Ref: L3
Open: 31 Mar – 23 Oct 2023
Pitches: 54

Jedburgh Club Site
Elliot Park, Jedburgh, Borders
TD8 6EF
Tel: 01835 863393
Map reference:
Pg: 262 Grid Ref: E5
Open: 31 Mar – 30 Oct 2023
Pitches: 45

Lauder Club Site
Carfraemill, Oxton, Lauder,
Borders TD2 6RA
Tel: 01578 750697
Map reference:
Pg: 271 Grid Ref: E10
Open: 31 Mar – 30 Oct 2023
Pitches: 60

Loch Ness Shores Club Site
Monument Park, Foyers, Inverness
IV2 6YH
Tel: 01456 486333
Map reference:
Pg: 300 Grid Ref: G4
Open: 31 Mar 2023– 3 Jan 2024
Pitches: 99

Milarrochy Bay Club Site
Milarrochy Bay, Balmaha,
Nr Drymen, Glasgow G63 0AL
Tel: 01360 870236
Map reference:
Pg: 277 Grid Ref: C8
Open: 31 Mar – 30 Oct 2023
Pitches: 150

Moffat Club Site
Hammerlands, Moffat
DG10 9DY
Tel: 01683 220436
Map reference:
Pg: 248 Grid Ref: C3
Open: All year
Pitches: 150

Nairn Club Site
Delnies Wood, Nairn, Inverness,
Morayshire IV12 5NX
Tel: 01667 455281
Map reference:
Pg: 301 Grid Ref: D8
Open: 31 Mar – 30 Oct 2023
Pitches: 75

Oban Club Site
Barcaldine by Connel, Argyll
PA37 1SG
Tel: 01631 720348
Map reference:
Pg: 284 Grid Ref: C3
Open: 31 Mar – 30 Oct 2023
Pitches: 70

Rosemarkie Club Site
Ness Road East, Rosemarkie,
Fortrose, Highlands IV10 8SE
Tel: 01381 621117
Map reference:
Pg: 301 Grid Ref: D7
Open: 31 Mar – 23 Oct 2023
Pitches: 67

Scone Club Site
Scone Palace Caravan Park,
Scone, Tayside PH2 6BB
Tel: 01738 552323
Map reference:
Pg: 286 Grid Ref: E5
Open: 3 Mar 2023 – 3 Jan 2024
Pitches: 120

Skye Club Site
Loch Greshornish, Edinbane,
Isle of Skye IV51 9PS
Tel: 01470 582230
Map reference:
Pg: 298 Grid Ref: D3
Open: 20 Mar – 31 Oct 2023
Pitches: 105

Speyside Club Site
Archiestown, Aberlour,
Moray AB38 9SL
Tel: 01340 810414
Map reference:
Pg: 302 Grid Ref: E2
Open: 31 Mar – 2 Oct 2023
Pitches: 75

Tarland by Deeside Club Site
Tarland by Aboyne,
Aberdeenshire AB34 4UP
Tel: 01339 881388
Map reference:
Pg: 292 Grid Ref: C6
Open: 3 Mar – 23 Oct 2023
Pitches: 50

NORTHERN IRELAND

Delamont Country Park Club Site
Downpatrick Road, Killyleagh,
Northern Ireland BT30 9TZ
Tel: 028 4482 1833
Map reference:
Pg: N/A Grid Ref: N/A
Open: 3 Mar – 30 Oct 2023
Pitches: 70

NORTHERN ENGLAND

Barnard Castle Club Site
Dockenflatts Lane, Lartington,
Barnard Castle, County Durham
DL12 9DG
Tel: 01833 630228
Map reference:
Pg: 223 Grid Ref: B10
Open: 3 Mar – 30 Oct 2023
Pitches: 90

Beadnell Bay Club Site
Beadnell, Chathill,
Northumberland NE67 5BX
Tel: 01665 720586
Map reference:
Pg: 264 Grid Ref: D6
Open: 31 Mar – 30 Oct 2023
Pitches: 150

Bellingham Club Site
Brown Rigg, Bellingham, Hexham,
Northumberland NE48 2JY
Tel: 01434 220175
Map reference:
Pg: 251 Grid Ref: G8
Open: 1 Mar – 30 Nov 2023
Pitches: 70

Boroughbridge Club Site
Bar Lane, Roecliffe,
Boroughbridge, North Yorkshire
YO51 9LS
Tel: 01423 322683
Map reference:
Pg: 215 Grid Ref: F7
Open: All year
Pitches: 95

Bowness on Windermere Club Site
Glebe Rd, Bowness-On-Windermere, Cumbria LA23 3HB
Tel: 01539 442177
Map reference:
Pg: 221 Grid Ref: F7
Open: All year
Pitches: 74

Braithwaite Village Club Site
Keswick, Cumbria CA12 5TF
Tel: 01763 778343
Map reference:
Pg: XX Grid Ref: XX
Open: All year
Pitches: 90

Clitheroe Club Site
Edisford Road, Clitheroe,
Lancashire BB7 3LA
Tel: 01200 425294
Map reference:
Pg: 203 Grid Ref: E10
Open: 17 Feb – 30 Oct 2023
Pitches: 65

Derwentwater Club Site
Crow Park Road, Keswick,
Cumbria CA12 5EN
Tel: 01768 772579
Map reference:
Pg: 229 Grid Ref: G11
Open: All year
Pitches: 55

Dunstan Hill Club Site
Alnwick, Northumberland,
NE66 3TQ
Tel: 01665 576310
Map reference:
Pg: 264 Grid Ref: E6
Open: 31 Mar – 30 Oct 2023
Pitches: 150

Haltwhistle Club Site
Burnfoot Park Village,
Haltwhistle, Northumberland
NE49 0JP
Tel: 01434 320106
Map reference:
Pg: 240 Grid Ref: E5
Open: 31 Mar – 30 Oct 2023
Pitches: 45

Kendal Club Site
Millcrest, Shap Road, Kendal,
Cumbria LA9 6NY
Tel: 01539 741363
Map reference:
Pg: 221 Grid Ref: G10
Open: 31 Mar – 4 Dec 2023
Pitches: 50

Keswick Club Site
Crow Park Road, Keswick,
Cumbria CA12 5EP
Tel: 01768 772392
Map reference:
Pg: 229 Grid Ref: G11
Open: All year
Pitches: 250

Ravenglass Club Site
Ravenglass, Cumbria CA18 1SR
Tel: 01229 717250
Map reference:
Pg: 219 Grid Ref: F11
Open: 31 Mar – 30 Oct 2023
Pitches: 70

Scarborough Club Site
Field Lane, Burniston Road,
Scarborough, North Yorkshire
YO13 0DA
Tel: 01723 366212
Map reference:
Pg: 227 Grid Ref: G10
Open: 31 Mar – 30 Oct 2023
Pitches: 290

Sheriff Hutton Club Site
Bracken Hill, Sheriff Hutton,
North Yorkshire YO60 6QG
Tel: 01347 878660
Map reference:
Pg: 216 Grid Ref: F2
Open: 31 Mar – 30 Oct 2023
Pitches: 85

Slingsby Club Site
Railway Street, Slingsby,
North Yorkshire YO62 4AN
Tel: 01653 628335
Map reference:
Pg: 216 Grid Ref: D4
Open: 31 Mar – 30 Oct 2023
Pitches: 55

Windermere Club Site
Ashes Lane, Staveley, Kendal,
Cumbria LA8 9JS
Tel: 01539 821119
Map reference:
Pg: 221 Grid Ref: F9
Open: 10 Mar 2023 – 15 Jan 2024
Pitches: 215

WALES

Bala Club Site
Crynierth Caravan Park,
Cefn-Ddwysarn, Bala,
Gwynedd LL23 7LN
Tel: 01678 530324
Map reference:
Pg: 147 Grid Ref: B9
Open: 31 Mar – 30 Oct 2023
Pitches: 45

Cardigan Bay Club Site
Llwynhelyg, Cross Inn, Llandysul,
Ceredigion SA44 6LW
Tel: 01545 560029
Map reference:
Pg: 111 Grid Ref: F7
Open: 31 Mar – 30 Oct 2023
Pitches: 85

Llanystumdwy Club Site
Tyddyn Sianel, Llanystumdwy,
Criccieth, Gwynedd LL52 0LS
Tel: 01766 522855
Map reference:
Pg: 145 Grid Ref: B9
Open: 31 Mar – 2 Oct 2023
Pitches: 60

Rhandirmwyn Club Site
Llandovery, Carmarthenshire
SA20 0NT
Tel: 01550 760257
Map reference:
Pg: 94 Grid Ref: C5
Open: 31 Mar – 30 Oct 2023
Pitches: 80

St David's Club Site
Dwr Cwmwdig, Berea, St David's,
Haverfordwest, Pembrokeshire
SA62 6DW
Tel: 01348 831376
Map reference:
Pg: 90 Grid Ref: E6
Open: 31 Mar – 2 Oct 2023
Pitches: 40

Wyeside Club Site
Rhayader, Powys LD6 5LB
Tel: 01597 810183
Map reference:
Pg: 113 Grid Ref: D9
Open: 31 Mar – 30 Oct 2023
Pitches: 60

CENTRAL ENGLAND

Alton, The Star Club Site
Cotton, Stoke-on-Trent,
Staffordshire ST10 3DW
Tel: 01538 702219
Map reference:
Pg: 169 Grid Ref: F9
Open: 3 Mar – 30 Oct 2023
Pitches: 180

Bakewell Club Site
Hopping Lane, Youlgreave,
Bakewell, Derbyshire
DE45 1NA
Tel: 01629 636555
Map reference:
Pg: 170 Grid Ref: C2
Open: 31 Mar – 30 Oct 2023
Pitches: 100

NO TOILETS OR SHOWERS

Blackmore Club Site
No.2, Hanley Swan,
Worcestershire WR8 0EE
Tel: 01684 310280
Map reference:
Pg: 98 Grid Ref: C6
Open: All year
Pitches: 190

Cannock Chase Club Site
Old Youth Hostel, Wandon,
Rugeley, Staffordshire WS15 1QW
Tel: 01889 582166
Map reference:
Pg: 151 Grid Ref: G10
Open: 31 Mar – 30 Oct 2023
Pitches: 50

Chipping Norton Club Site
Chipping Norton Road,
Chadlington, Chipping Norton,
Oxfordshire OX7 3PE
Tel: 01608 641993
Map reference:
Pg: 100 Grid Ref: G6
Open: 31 Mar – 30 Oct 2023
Pitches: 90

Clent Hills Club Site
Fieldhouse Lane, Romsley,
Halesowen, West Midlands B62 0NH
Tel: 01562 710015
Map reference:
Pg: 117 Grid Ref: B9
Open: 31 Mar – 30 Oct 2023
Pitches: 90

Conkers, National Forest Club Site
50 Bath Lane, Moira, Swadlincote,
Derbyshire DE12 6BD
Tel: 01283 224925
Map reference:
Pg: 152 Grid Ref: F6
Open: All year
Pitches: 100

Crowden Club Site
Woodhead Road, Crowden,
Glossop SK13 1HZ
Tel: 01457 866057
Map reference:
Pg: 185 Grid Ref: B9
Open: 31 Mar – 30 Oct 2023
Pitches: 45

Delamere Forest Club Site
Station Road, Delamere,
Northwich, Cheshire CW8 2HZ
Tel: 01606 889231
Map reference:
Pg: 183 Grid Ref: G8
Open: All year
Pitches: 80

Drayton Manor Club Site
Drayton Manor, Nr Tamworth,
Staffordshire B78 3TW
Tel: 01827 260617
Map reference:
Pg: 134 Grid Ref: C3
Open: 3 Feb – 30 Oct 2023
Pitches: 90

Ebury Hill Club Site
Ring Bank, Haughton, Shrewsbury
SY4 4GB
Tel: 01743 709334
Map reference:
Pg: 149 Grid Ref: F10
Open: 31 Mar – 30 Oct 2023
Pitches: 110

MINIMAL FACILITIES SITE

Hayfield Club Site
Kinder Road, Hayfield, High Peak,
Derbyshire SK22 2LE
Tel: 01663 745394
Map reference:
Pg: 185 Grid Ref: D8
Open: 31 Mar – 30 Oct 2023
Pitches: 80

NO CARAVANS PERMITTTED

Hereford Club Site
The Millpond, Little Tarrington,
Hereford HR1 4JA
Tel: 01432 890243
Map reference:
Pg: 98 Grid Ref: C2
Open: 17 Mar – 5 Nov 2023
Pitches: 102

Kingsbury Water Park Club Site
Bodymoor Heath Lane, Sutton
Coldfield, West Mids B76 0DY
Tel: 01827 874101
Map reference:
Pg: 134 Grid Ref: D3
Open: All year
Pitches: 150

Leek Club Site
Blackshaw Grange, Blackshaw
Moor, Leek, Staffordshire ST13 8TL
Tel: 01538 300285
Map reference:
Pg: 169 Grid Ref: D8
Open: 31 Mar – 30 Oct 2023
Pitches: 75

Mablethorpe Club Site
Church Lane, Mablethorpe,
Lincolnshire LN12 2NU
Tel: 01507 472374
Map reference:
Pg: 191 Grid Ref: E7
Open: 31 Mar – 30 Oct 2023
Pitches: 110

Oxford Club Site
426 Abingdon Road,
Oxford OX1 4XN
Tel: 01865 244088
Map reference:
Pg: 83 Grid Ref: E8
Open: All year
Pitches: 90

Winchcombe Club Site
Brooklands Farm, Alderton,
Nr Tewkesbury, Gloucestershire
GL20 8NX
Tel: 01242 620259
Map reference:
Pg: 99 Grid Ref: E10
Open: 3 Mar 2023 – 3 Jan 2024
Pitches: 80

Wolverley Club Site
Brown Westhead Park, Wolverley,
Worcestershire DY10 3PX
Tel: 01562 850909
Map reference:
Pg: 116 Grid Ref: B6
Open: 3 Mar 2023 – 3 Jan 2024
Pitches: 105

Woodhall Spa Club Site
Wellsyke Lane, Kirkby-on-Bain,
Woodhall Spa, Lincolnshire
LN10 6YU
Tel: 01526 352911
Map reference:
Pg: 174 Grid Ref: C2
Open: 31 Mar – 30 Oct 2023
Pitches: 90

EAST ANGLIA

Cambridge Club Site
19 Cabbage Moor, Great Shelford,
Cambridgeshire CB22 5NB
Tel: 01223 841185
Map reference:
Pg: 123 Grid Ref: G9
Open: 31 Mar – 30 Oct 2023
Pitches: 160

Kessingland Club Site
Whites Lane, Kessingland,
Suffolk NR33 7TF
Tel: 01502 742040
Map reference:
Pg: 143 Grid Ref: F10
Open: 31 Mar – 2 Oct 2023
Pitches: 85

Norwich Club Site
Martineau Lane, Norwich,
Norfolk NR1 2HX
Tel: 01603 620060
Map reference:
Pg: 142 Grid Ref: B4
Open: 31 Mar – 30 Oct 2023
Pitches: 50

Sandringham Club Site
Coach Road, The Sandringham
Estate, Sandringham, Norfolk
PE35 6EA
Tel: 01485 542555
Map reference:
Pg: 158 Grid Ref: D3
Open: 10 Feb 2023 – 3 Jan 2024
Pitches: 270

St Neots Club Site
Hardwick Road, Eynesbury,
St Neots, Cambridgeshire PE19 2PR
Tel: 01480 474404
Map reference:
Pg: 122 Grid Ref: F3
Open: 31 Mar – 30 Oct 2023
Pitches: 175

West Runton Club Site
Holgate Lane, West Runton,
Cromer, Norfolk NR27 9NW
Tel: 01263 837544
Map reference:
Pg: 177 Grid Ref: E11
Open: 31 Mar – 30 Oct 2023
Pitches: 180

SOUTH EAST ENGLAND

Adgestone Club Site
Lower Road, Adgestone,
Isle of Wight PO36 0HL
Tel: 01983 403432
Map reference:
Pg: 21 Grid Ref: D7
Open: 21 Apr – 2 Oct 2023
Pitches: 270

Canterbury Club Site
Bekesbourne Lane, Canterbury,
Kent CT3 4AB
Tel: 01227 463216
Map reference:
Pg: 55 Grid Ref: B7
Open: All year
Pitches: 180

Chertsey Club Site
Bridge Road, Chertsey, Surrey
KT16 8JX
Tel: 01932 562405
Map reference:
Pg: 66 Grid Ref: F5
Open: All year
Pitches: 159 (70 in winter months)

Chichester Club Site
345 Main Road, Southbourne,
Hampshire PO10 8JH
Tel: 01243 373202
Map reference:
Pg: 34 Grid Ref: F3
Open: 3 Feb – 13 Nov 2023
Pitches: 55

Crowborough Club Site
Goldsmith Recreation Ground,
Eridge Road, Crowborough, East
Sussex TN6 2TN
Tel: 01892 664827
Map reference:
Pg: 52 Grid Ref: G4
Open: 31 Mar – 30 Oct 2023
Pitches: 90

Folkestone Club Site
The Warren, Folkestone,
Kent CT19 6NQ
Tel: 01303 255093
Map reference:
Pg: 55 Grid Ref: F8
Open: 31 Mar – 30 Oct 2023
Pitches: 60

NO CARAVANS PERMITTED

Graffham Club Site
Great Bury, Graffham, Petworth,
West Sussex GU28 0QF
Tel: 01798 867476
Map reference:
Pg: 34 Grid Ref: D6
Open: 31 Mar – 30 Oct 2023
Pitches: 90

Hertford Club Site
Mangrove Road (Not Ball Park),
Hertford, Hertfordshire SG13 8AJ
Tel: 01992 586696
Map reference:
Pg: 86 Grid Ref: C4
Open: All year
Pitches: 245

Horsley Club Site
Ockham Road North, East
Horsley, Surrey KT24 6PE
Tel: 01483 283273
Map reference:
Pg: 50 Grid Ref: B5
Open: 31 Mar – 4 Dec 2023
Pitches: 120

Kelvedon Hatch Club Site
Warren Lane, Doddinghurst,
Brentwood, Essex CM15 0JG
Tel: 01277 372773
Map reference:
Pg: 87 Grid Ref: F9
Open: 31 Mar – 30 Oct 2023
Pitches: 90

Normans Bay Club Site
Normans Bay, Pevensey,
East Sussex BN24 6PR
Tel: 01323 761190
Map reference:
Pg: 37 Grid Ref: F11
Open: 31 Mar – 30 Oct 2023
Pitches: 200

Slindon Club Site
Slindon Park, Nr Arundel,
Sussex BN18 0RG
Tel: 01243 814387
Map reference:
Pg: 35 Grid Ref: F7
Open: 31 Mar – 2 Oct 2023
Pitches: 40

NO TOILETS OR SHOWERS

Theobalds Park Club Site
Bulls Cross Ride, Waltham Cross,
Hertfordshire EN7 5HS
Tel: 01992 620604
Map reference:
Pg: 86 Grid Ref: E4
Open: All year
Pitches: 75

Walton on Thames Club Site
Fieldcommon Lane, Walton on
Thames, Surrey KT12 3QG
Tel: 01932 220392
Map reference:
Pg: 66 Grid Ref: F6
Open: 31 Mar – 30 Oct 2023
Pitches: 120 (Members only site)

NO TOILETS OR SHOWERS

SOUTH WEST ENGLAND

Bude Club Site
Gillards Moor, St Gennys, Bude,
Cornwall EX23 0BG
Tel: 01840 230650
Map reference:
Pg: 11 Grid Ref: C9
Open: 21 Apr – 2 Oct 2023
Pitches: 100

California Cross Club Site
Modbury, Ivybridge, Devon
PL21 0SG
Tel: 01548 821297
Map reference:
Pg: 8 Grid Ref: E4
Open: 21 Apr – 2 Oct 2023
Pitches: 80

Charmouth Club Site
Monkton Wyld Farm, Scotts Lane,
Nr Charmouth, Dorset DT6 6DB
Tel: 01297 32965
Map reference:
Pg: 16 Grid Ref: B2
Open: 10 Feb – 6 Nov 2023
Pitches: 180

Cheddar, Mendip Heights Club Site
Mendip Heights, Townsend,
Priddy Wells, Somerset
BA5 3BP
Tel: 01749 870241
Map reference:
Pg: 44 Grid Ref: C4
Open: 17 Mar – 27 Nov 2023
       26 Dec 2023 – 2 Jan 2024
Pitches: 85

Dartmouth Club Site
Stoke Fleming, Dartmouth,
Devon TQ6 0RF
Tel: 01803 770253
Map reference:
Pg: 9 Grid Ref: F7
Open: 31 Mar – 30 Oct 2023
Pitches: 90

Devizes Club Site
Spout Lane, Nr Seend, Melksham,
Wiltshire SN12 6RN
Tel: 01380 828839
Map reference:
Pg: 62 Grid Ref: G2
Open: All year
Pitches: 115

Lynton Club Site
Lydiate Lane, Caffyn's Cross,
Lynton, Devon EX35 6JS
Tel: 01598 752379
Map reference:
Pg: 41 Grid Ref: D8
Open: 31 Mar – 2 Oct 2023
Pitches: 105

Minehead Club Site
Hill Road, North Hill, Minehead
Somerset TA24 5LB
Tel: 01643 704138
Map reference:
Pg: 42 Grid Ref: D3
Open: 21 Apr – 2 Oct 2023
Pitches: 50

NO CARAVANS PERMITTED

Moreton Club Site
Station Road, Moreton,
Dorchester, Dorset DT2 8BB
Tel: 01305 853801
Map reference:
Pg: 17 Grid Ref: D11
Open: 31 Mar – 30 Oct 2023
Pitches: 120

Salisbury Club Site
Hudson's Field, Castle Road,
Salisbury, Wiltshire SP1 3SA
Tel: 01722 320713
Map reference:
Pg: 46 Grid Ref: G6
Open: All year
Pitches: 150

Sennen Cove Club Site
Higher Tregiffian Farm, St Buryan,
Penzance, Cornwall TR19 6JB
Tel: 01736 871588
Map reference:
Pg: 1 Grid Ref: D3
Open: 31 Mar – 30 Oct 2023
Pitches: 75

Slapton Sands Club Site
Middle Grounds, Slapton,
Kingsbridge, Devon TQ7 2QW
Tel: 01548 580538
Map reference:
Pg: 8 Grid Ref: G6
Open: 31 Mar – 30 Oct 2023
Pitches: 105
Note: Member-only caravans

Tavistock Club Site
Higher Longford, Moorshop,
Devon PL19 9LQ
Tel: 01822 618672
Map reference:
Pg: 12 Grid Ref: G6
Open: All year
Pitches: 80

Tregurrian Club Site
Nr Newquay, Cornwall TR8 4AE
Tel: 01637 860448
Map reference:
Pg: 4 Grid Ref: B6
Open: 31 Mar – 30 Oct 2023
Pitches: 90

Umberleigh Club Site
Over Weir, Umberleigh,
Devon EX37 9DU
Tel: 01769 560009
Map reference:
Pg: 25 Grid Ref: C10
Open: 31 Mar – 2 Oct 2023
Pitches: 65

Verwood Club Site
Sutton Hill, Woodlands,
Wimborne, Dorset BH21 8NQ
Tel: 01202 822763
Map reference:
Pg: 31 Grid Ref: F9
Open: 31 Mar – 30 Oct 2023
Pitches: 140

Veryan Club Site
Tretheake, Veryan, Truro,
Cornwall TR2 5PP
Tel: 01872 501658
Map reference:
Pg: 5 Grid Ref: G8
Open: 31 Mar – 2 Oct 2023
Pitches: 145

MORE THAN JUST GREAT CAMPSITES

The Camping and Caravanning Club
The Friendly Club

Become a Club member
and enjoy so much more...

- Exclusive access to over 1,300 member-only sites

- Up to 30% saving on Club Site pitch fees

- An extra 25% off for over 60s

- Great savings on ferry crossings and Eurotunnel

- Discounts with retailers, on days out and attractions

- Specialist insurance and breakdown cover

- Friendly support and expert advice

- Award-winning monthly magazine

Membership from just £45* | Join and book at **campingandcaravanningclub.co.uk**

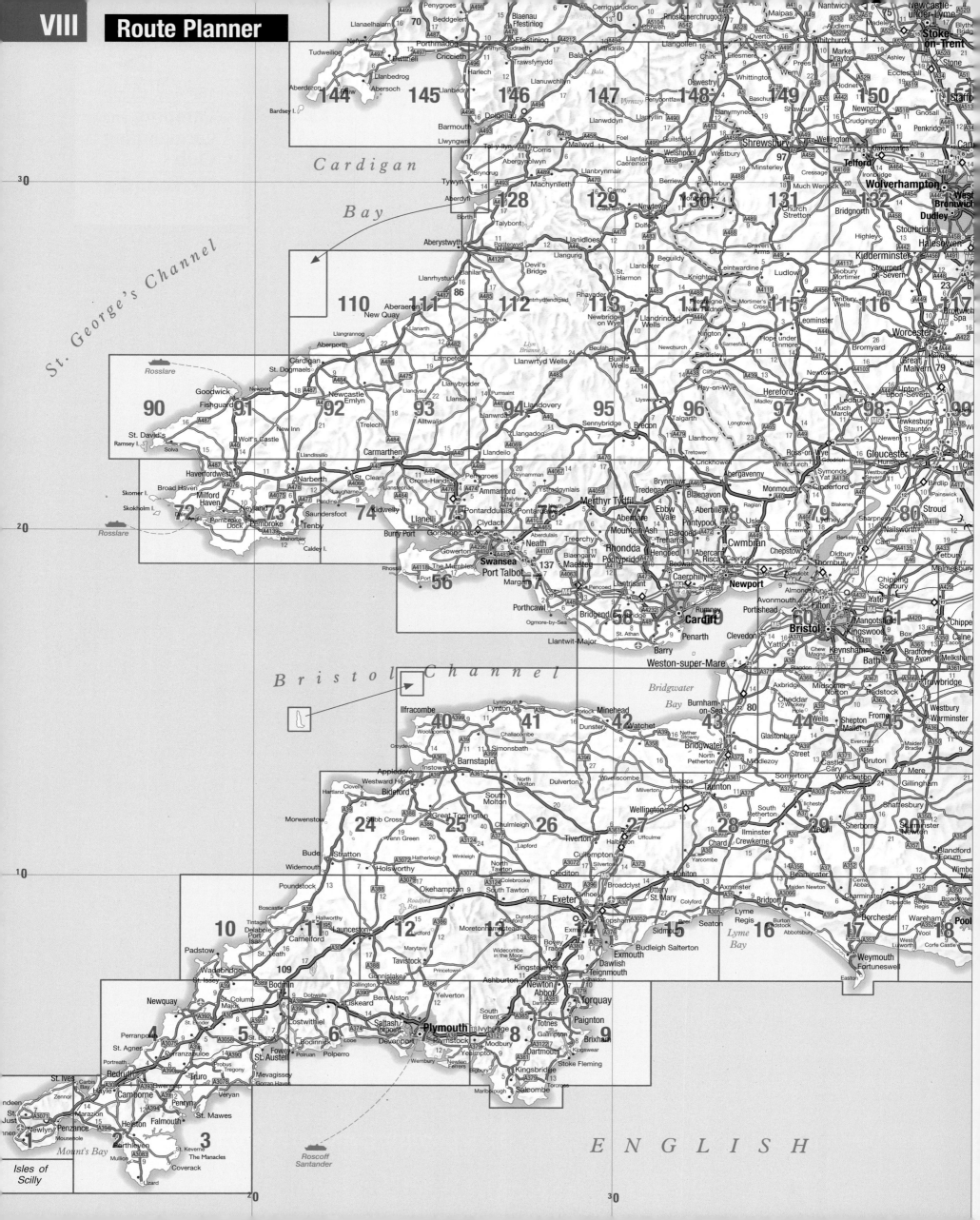

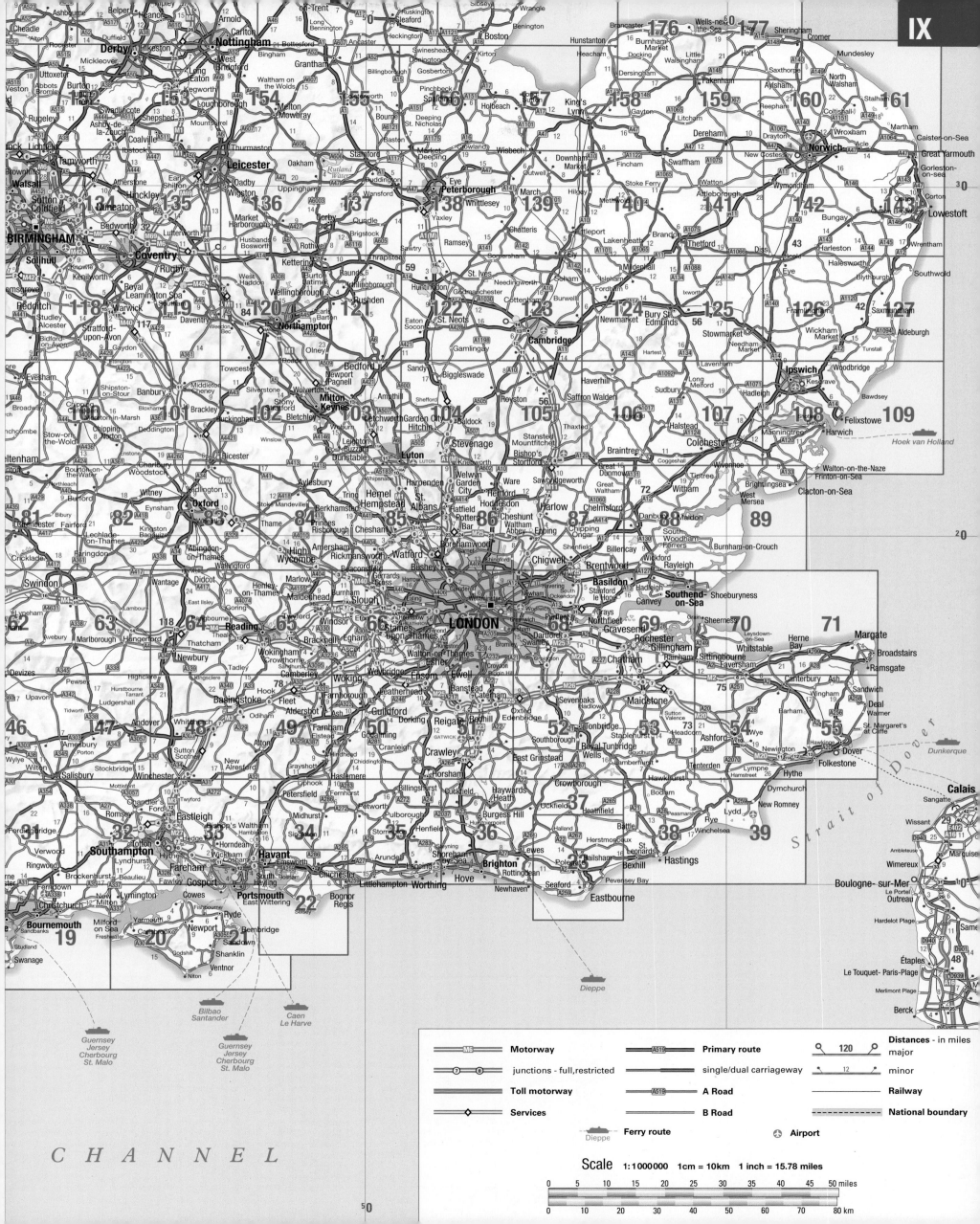

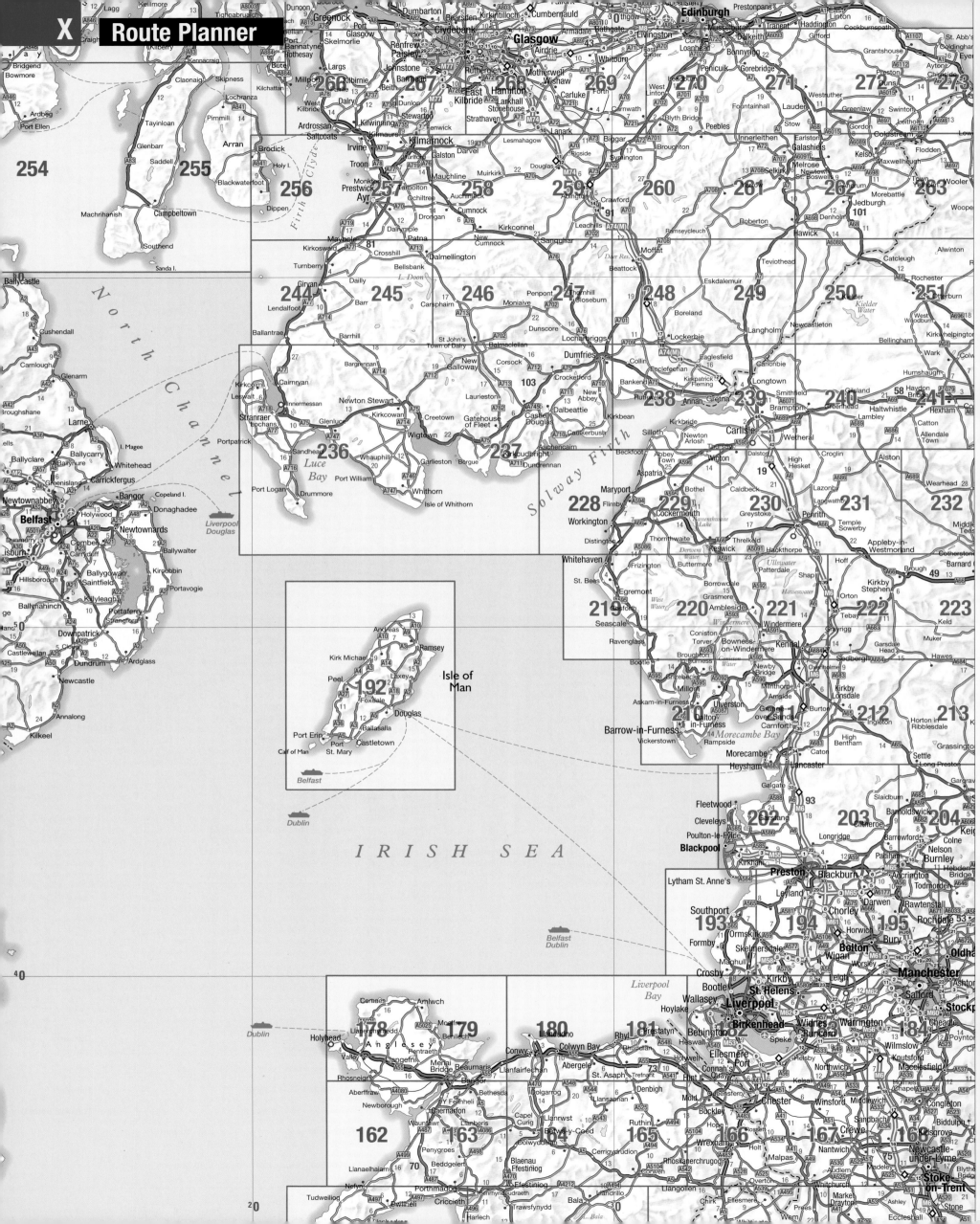

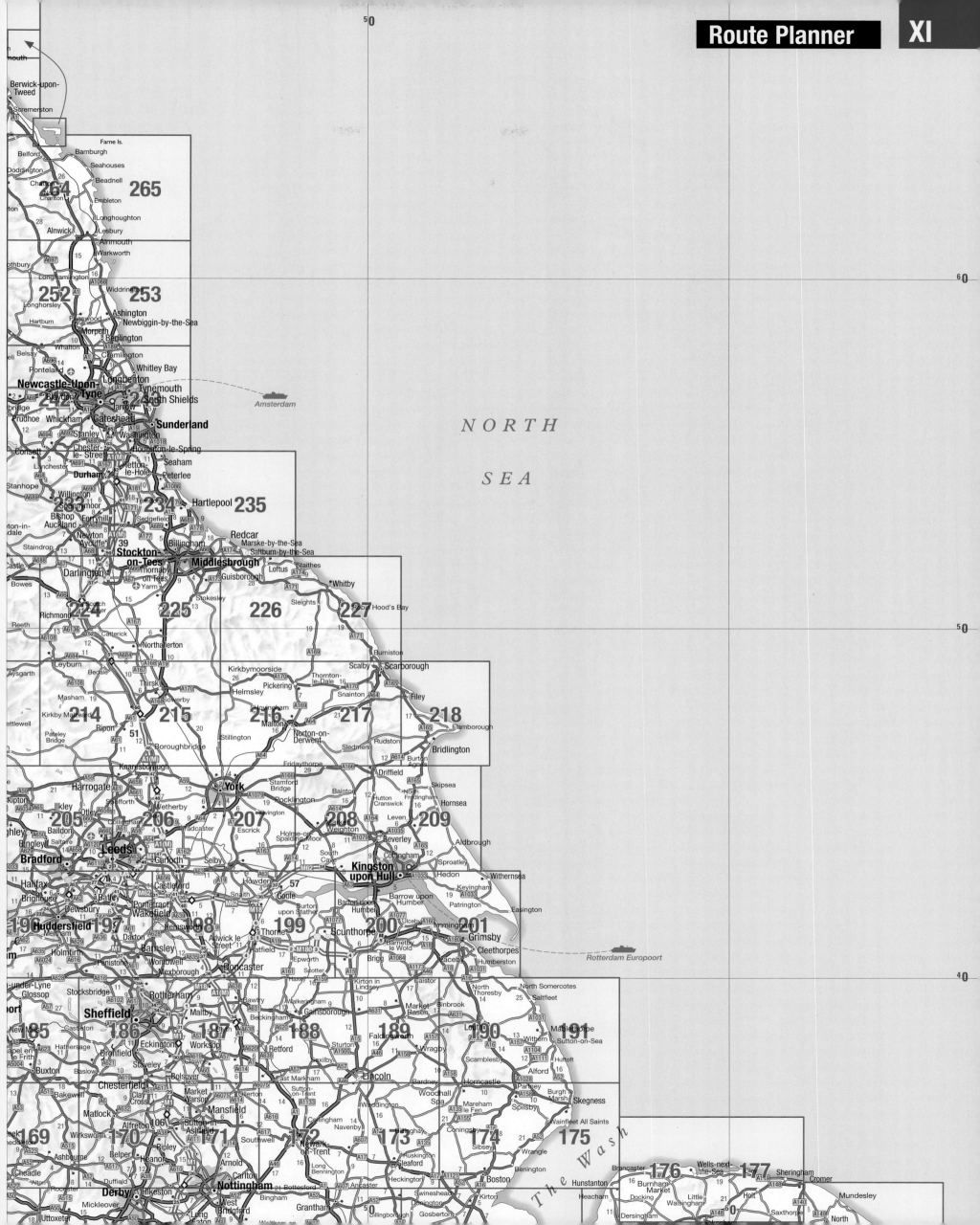

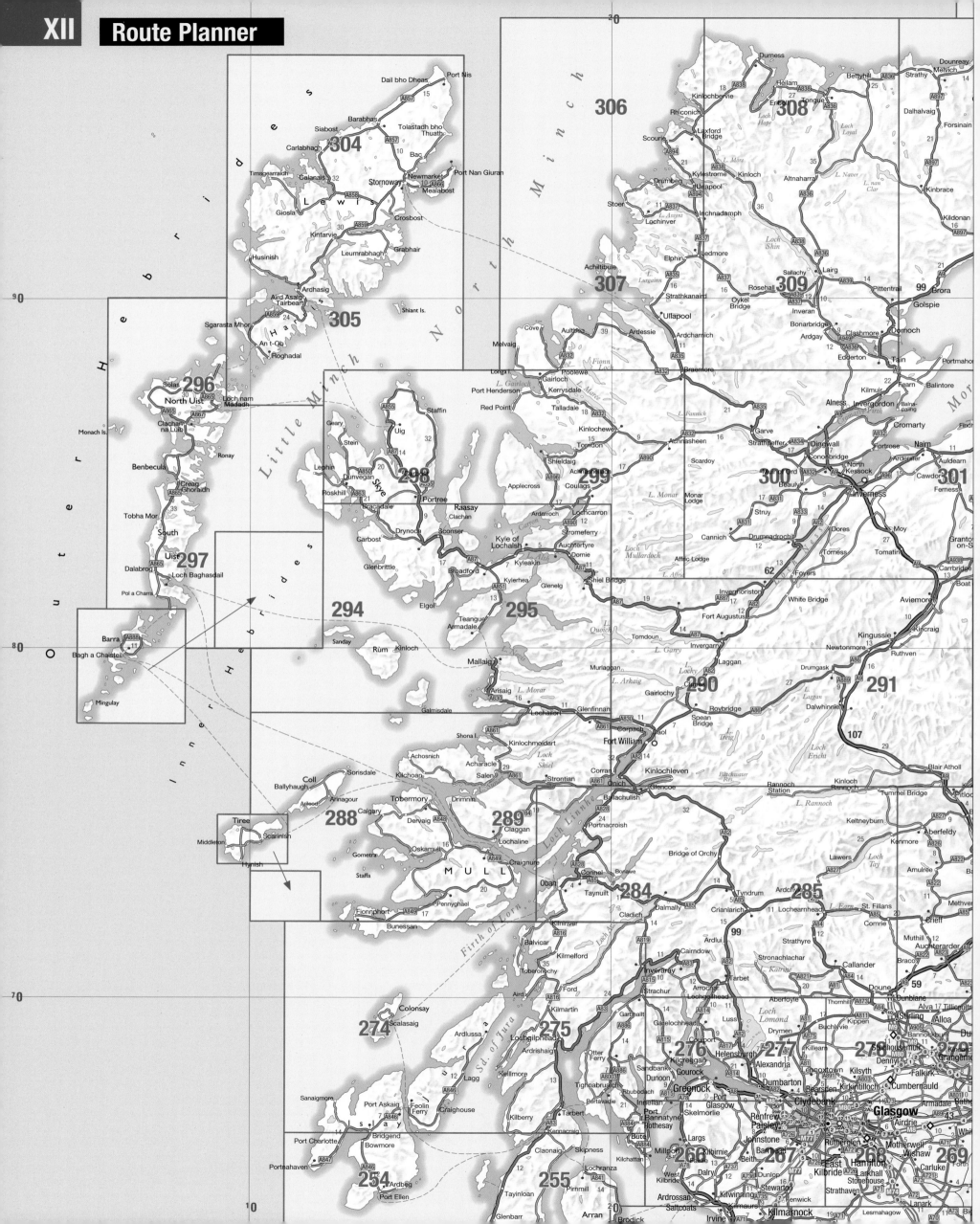

Distances and journey times

How to use this table

Distances are shown in miles and, in italics, kilometres with estimated journey times in hours and minutes.

For example, the distance between Dover and Fishguard is 331 miles or 533 kilometres with an estimated journey time of 6 hours, 20 minutes.

Estimated driving times are based on an average speed of 60mph on Motorways and 40mph on other roads. Drivers should allow extra time when driving at peak periods or through areas likely to be congested.

Supporting

THINK!

Travel safe –
Don't drive tired

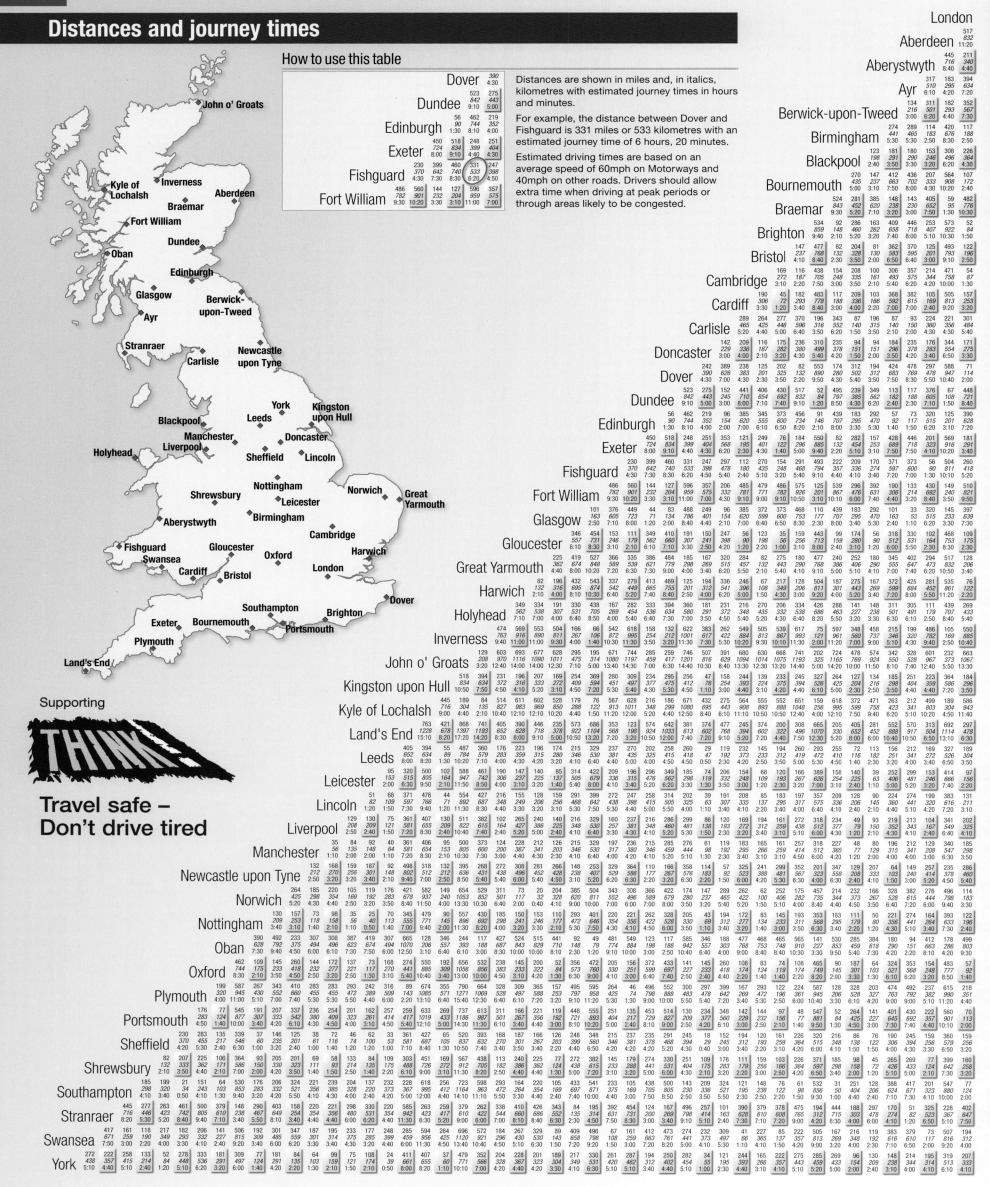

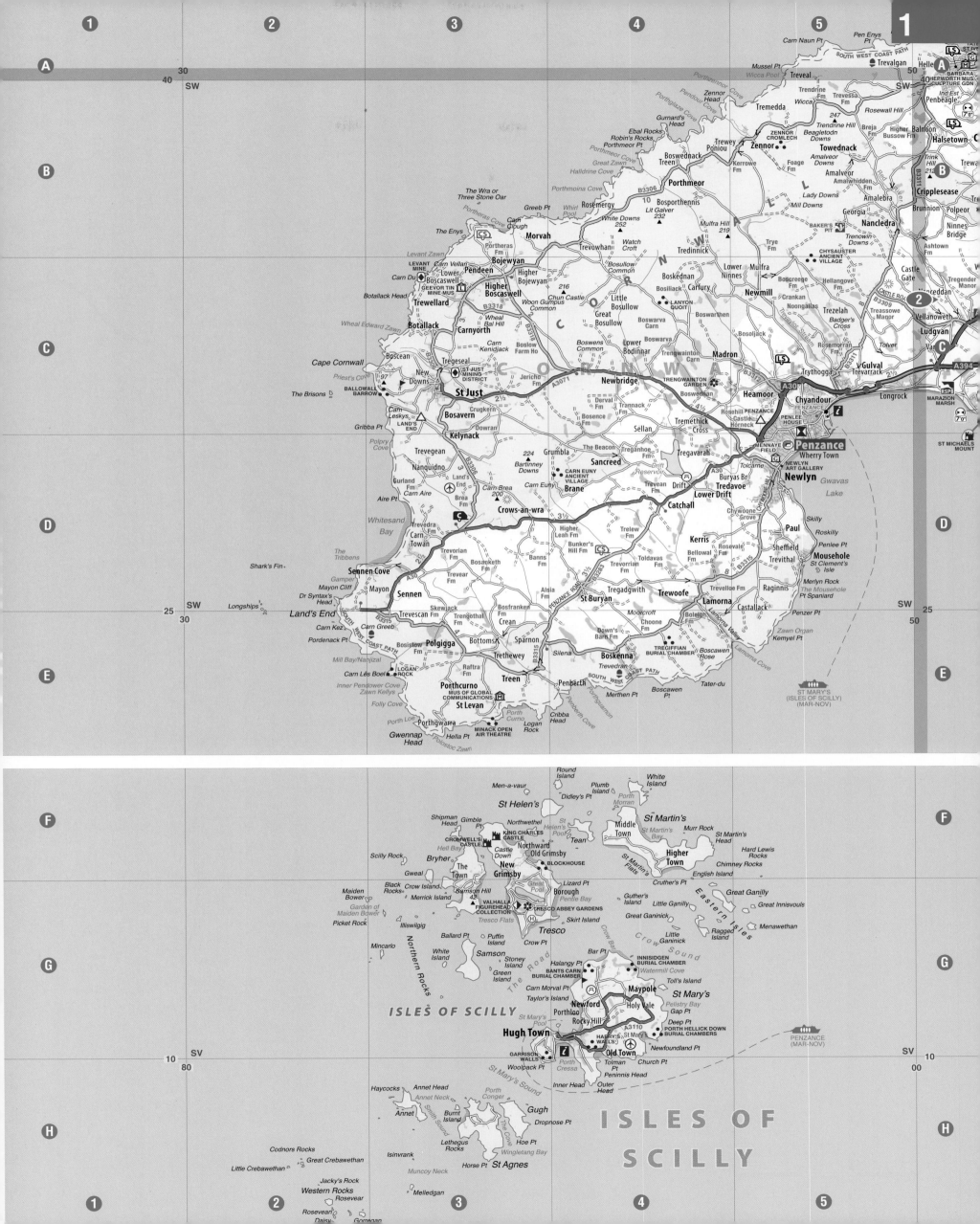

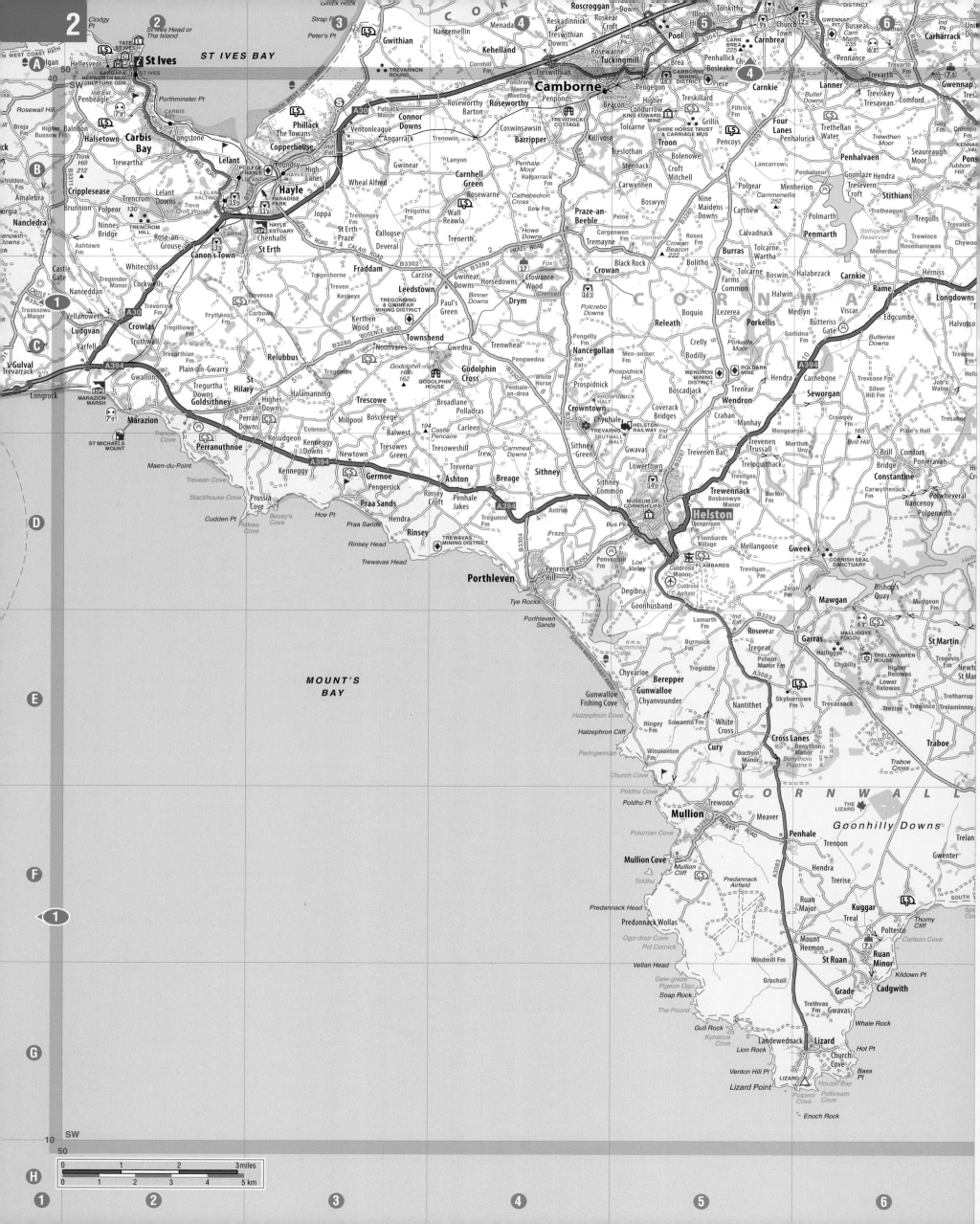

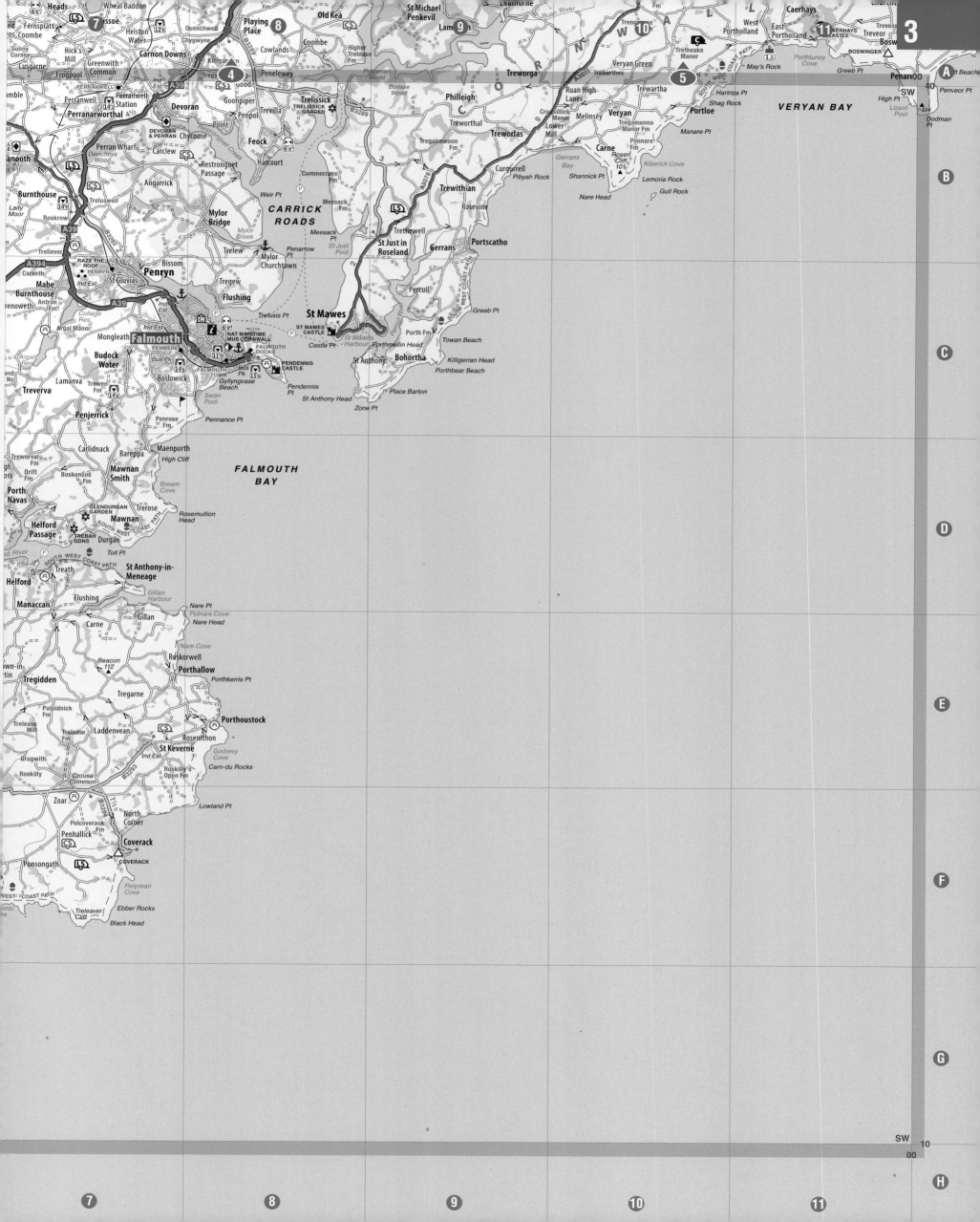

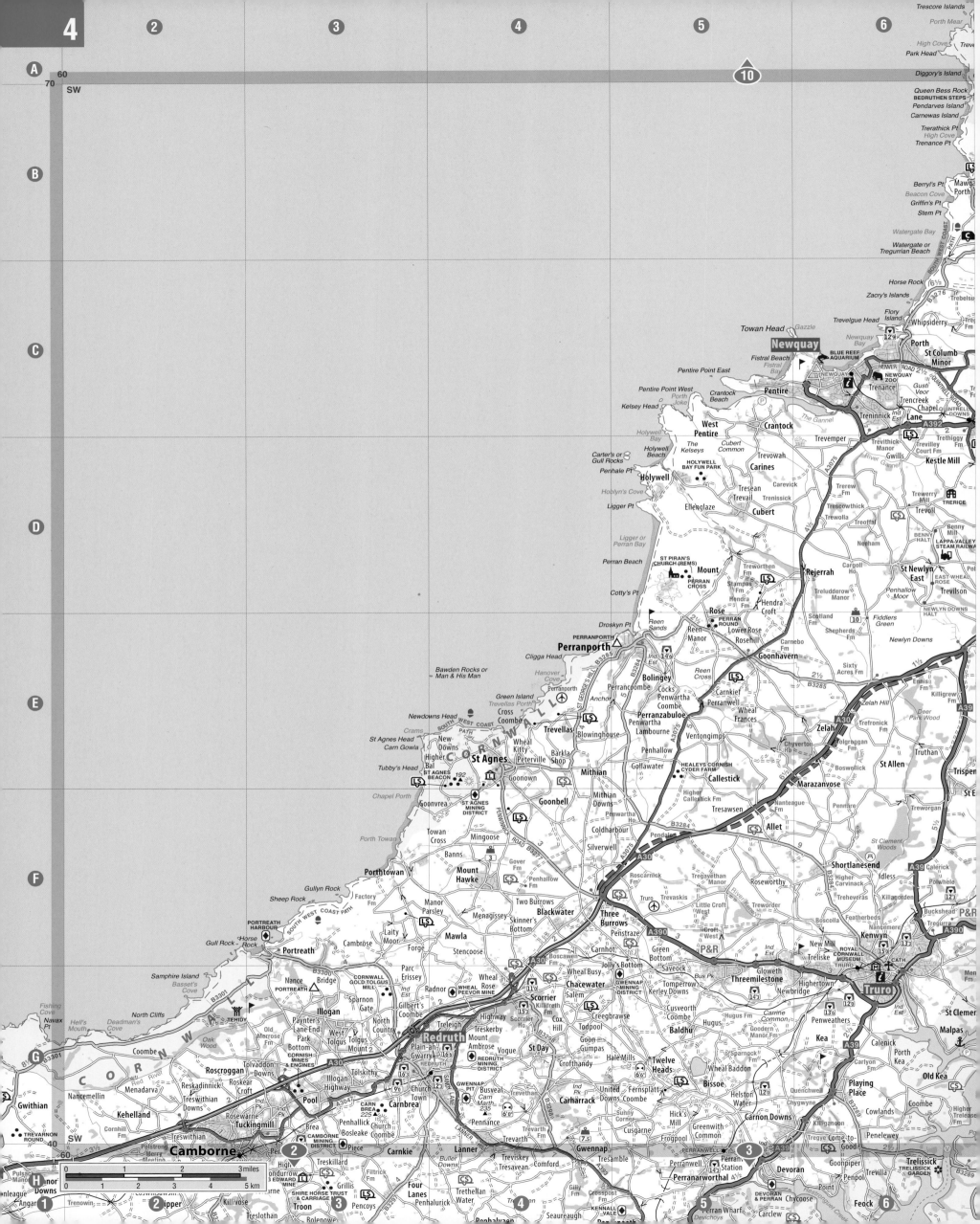

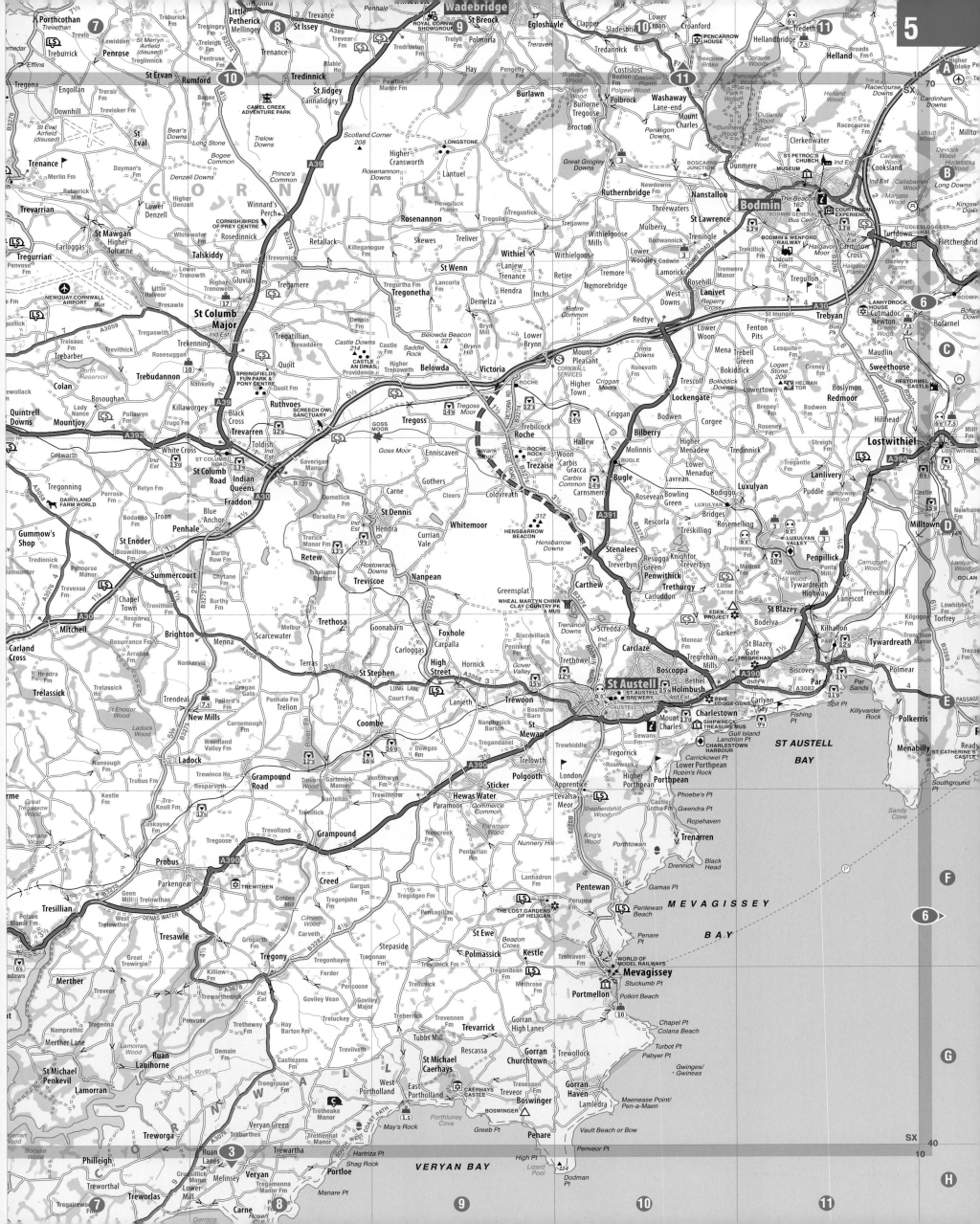

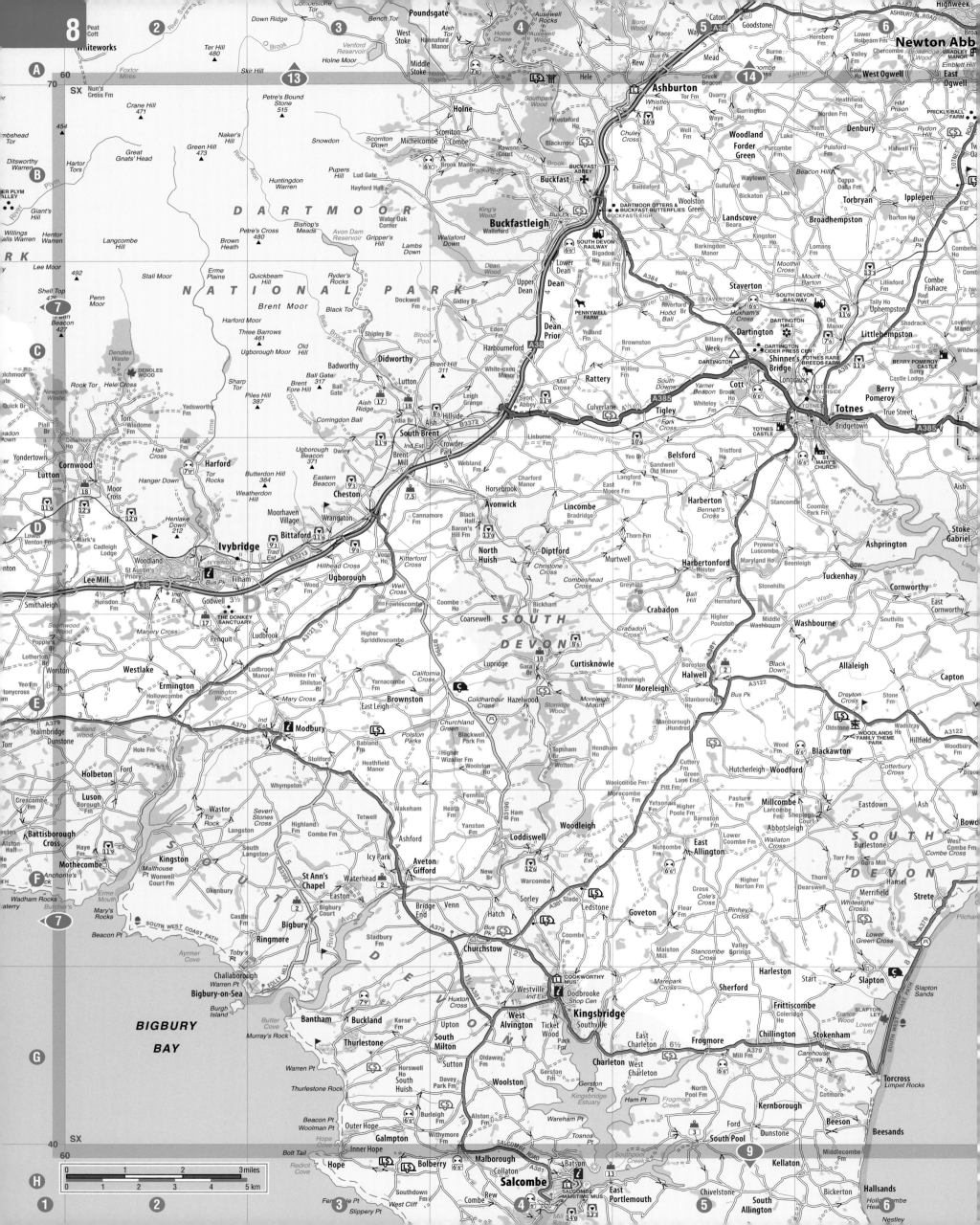

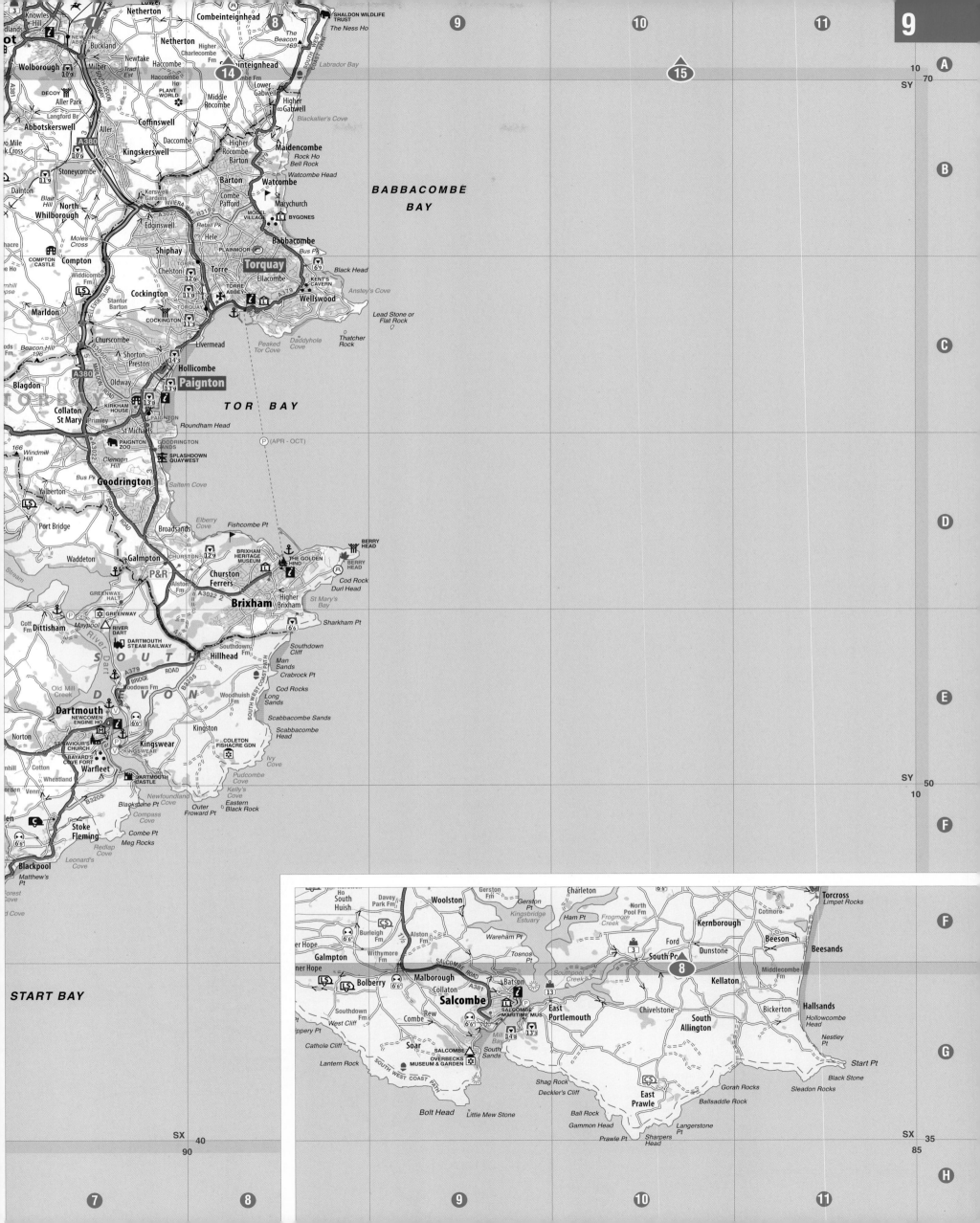

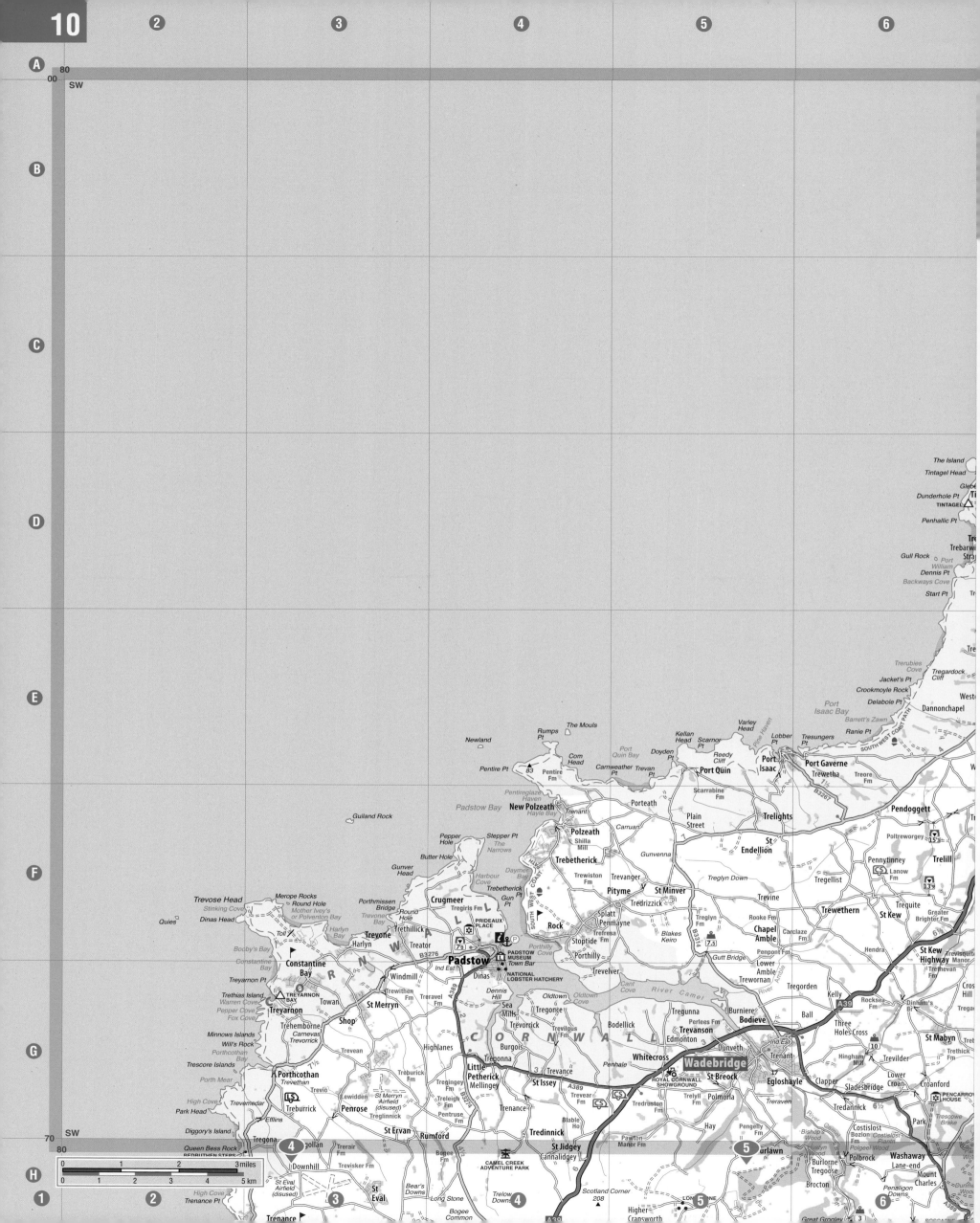

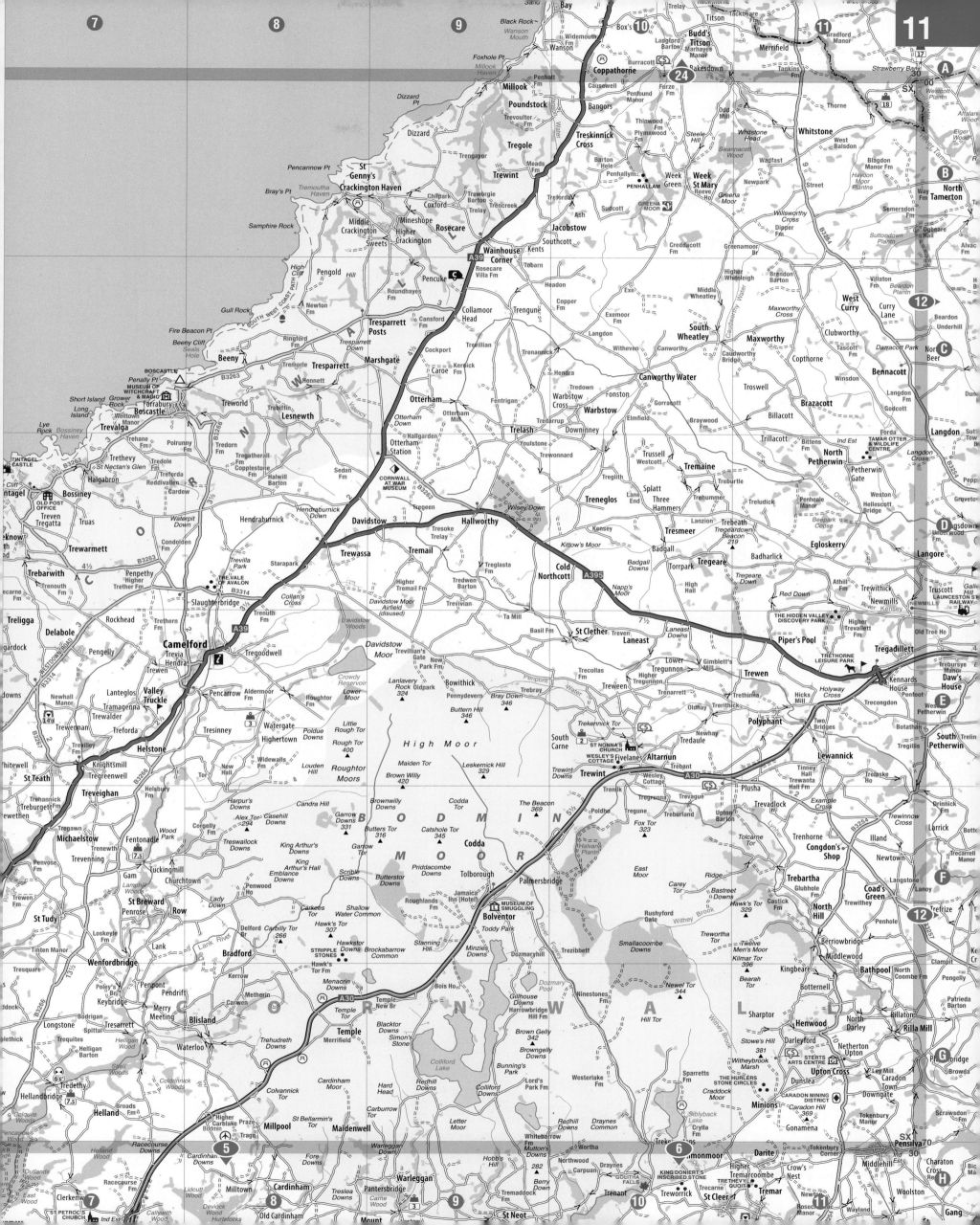

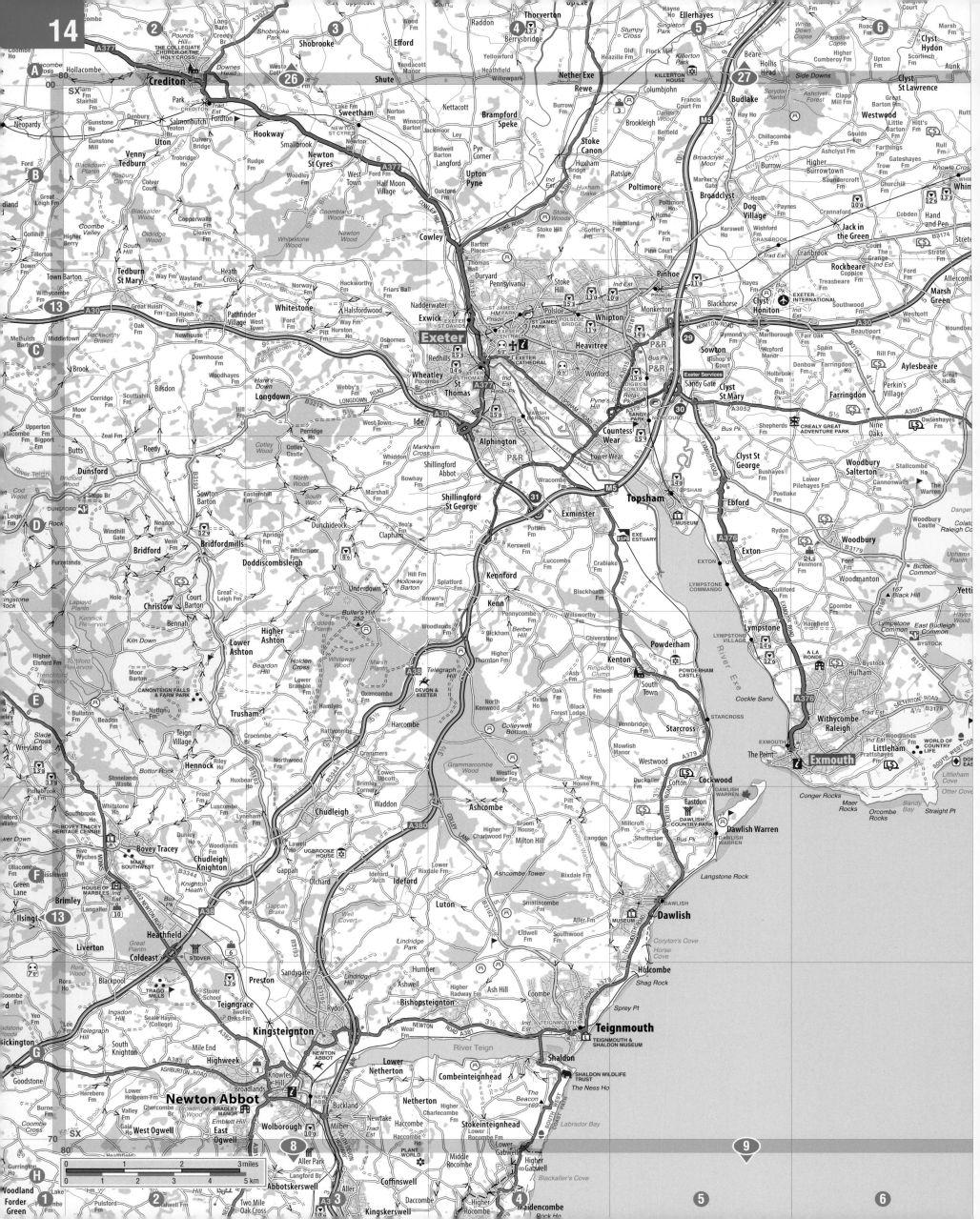

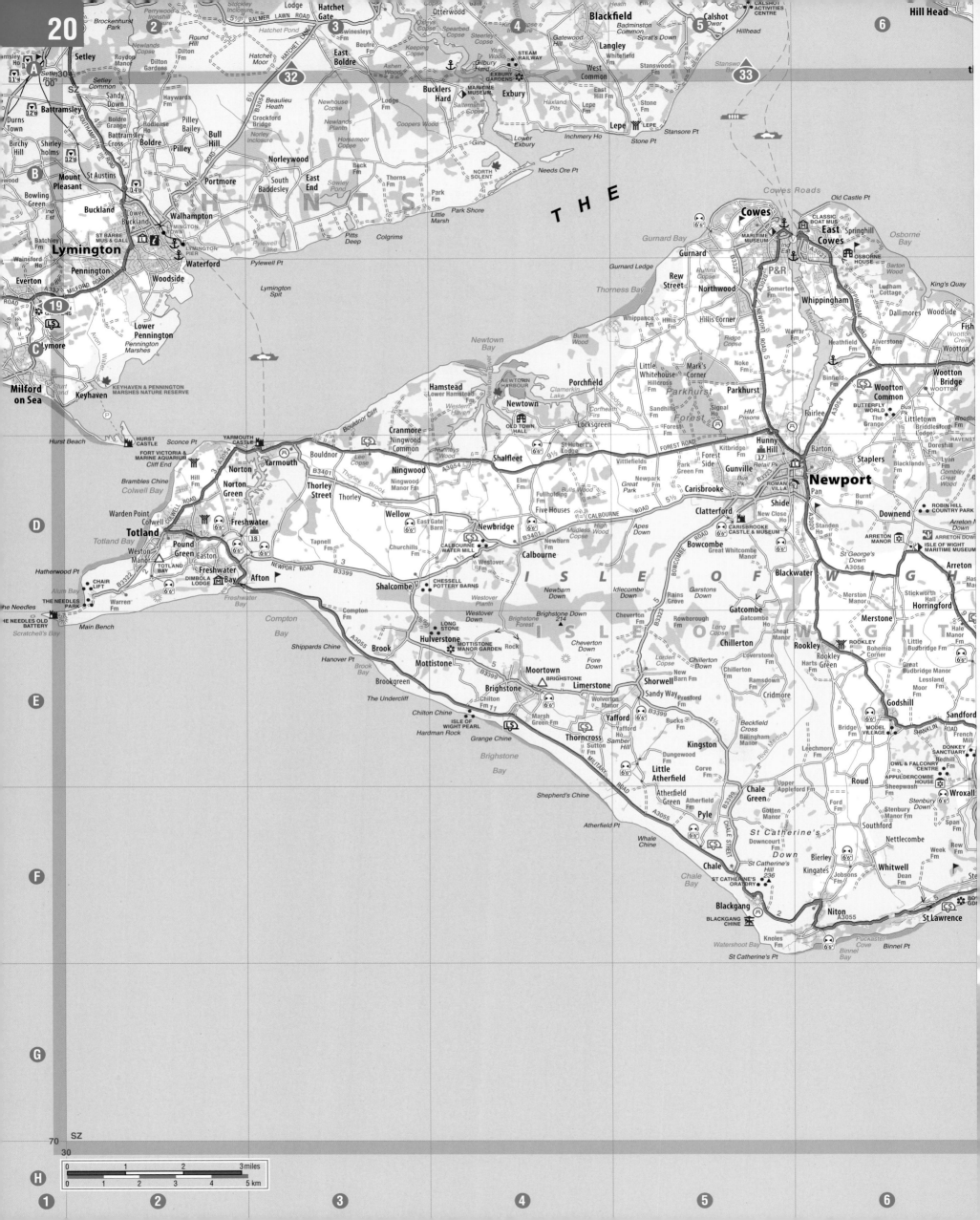

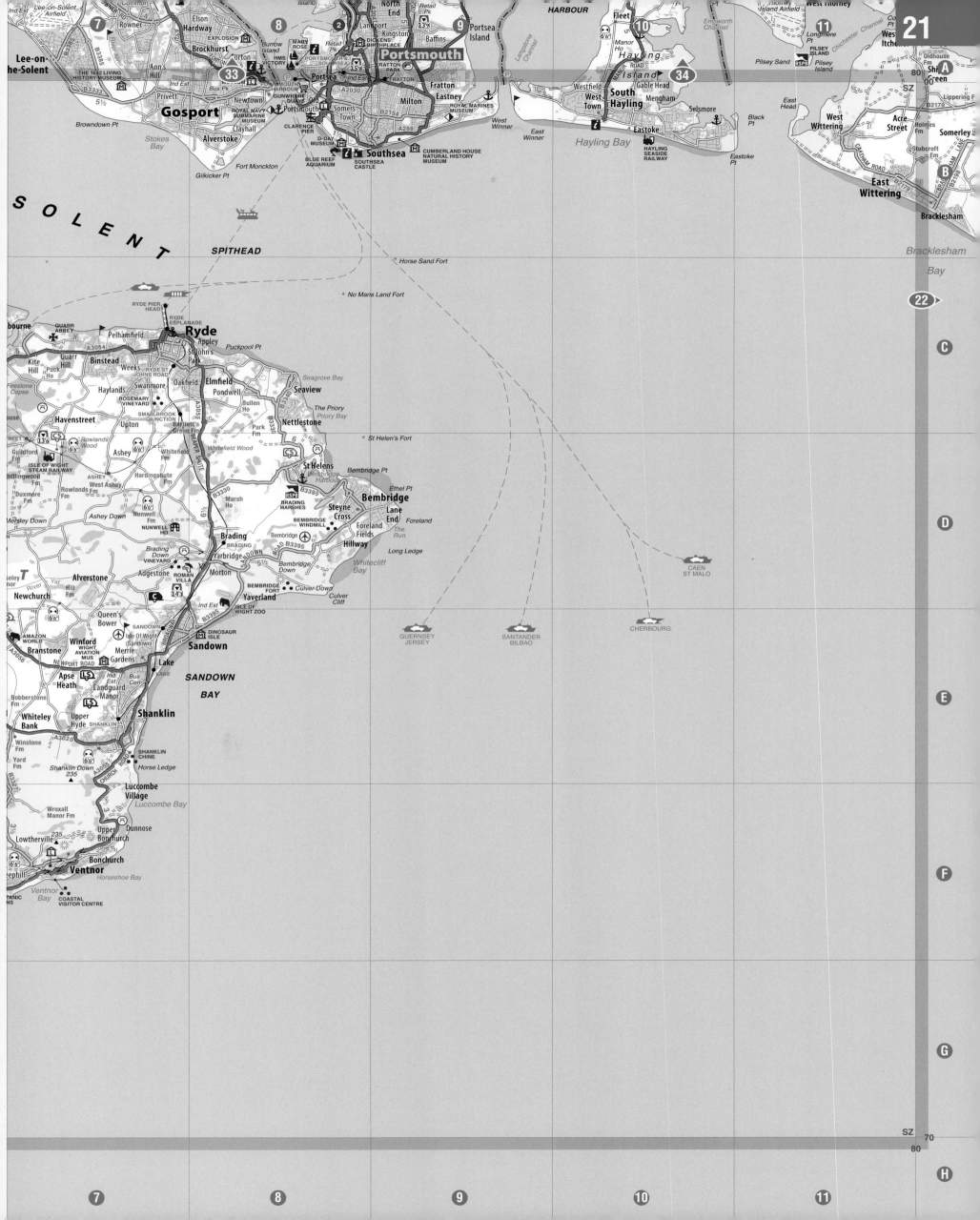

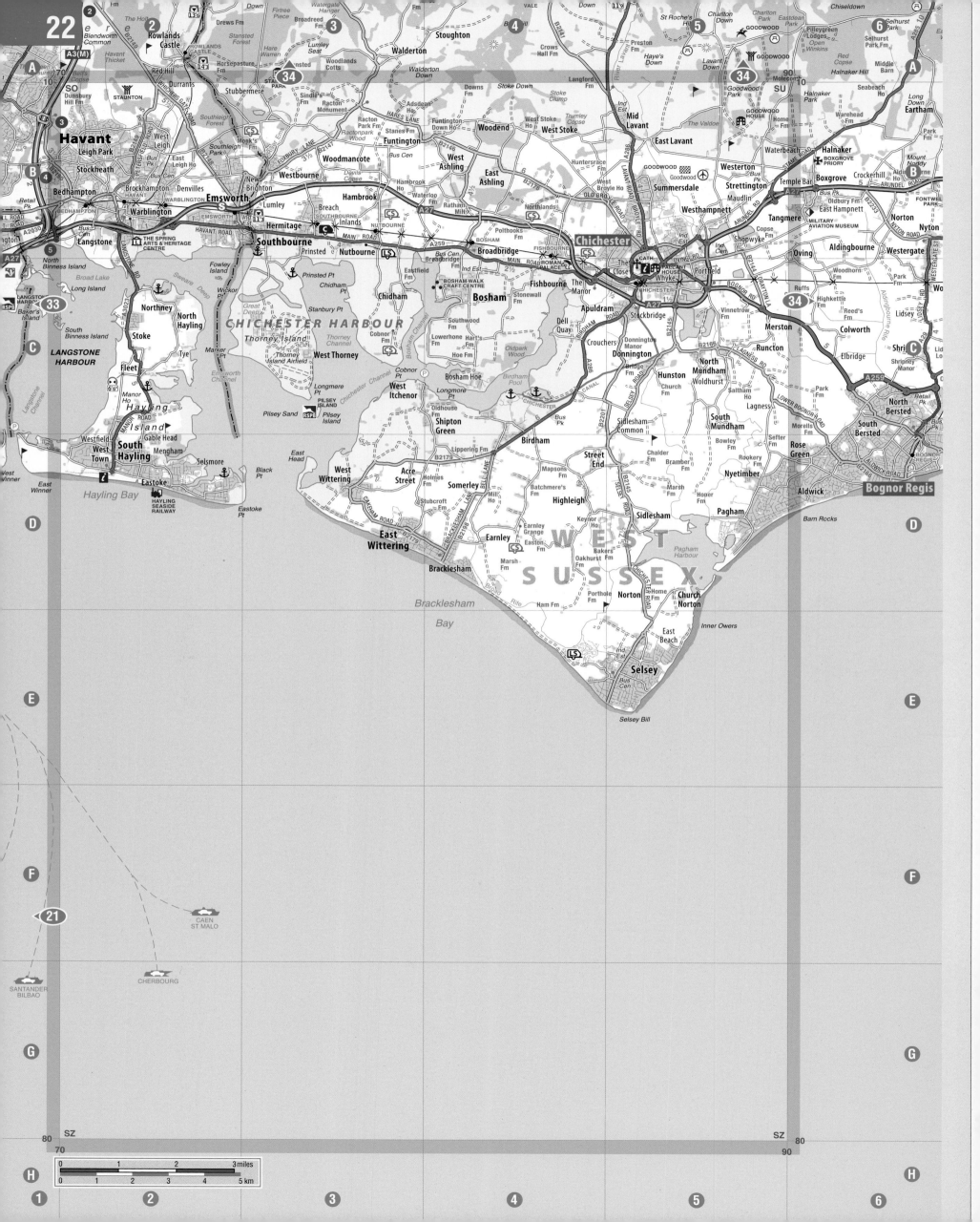

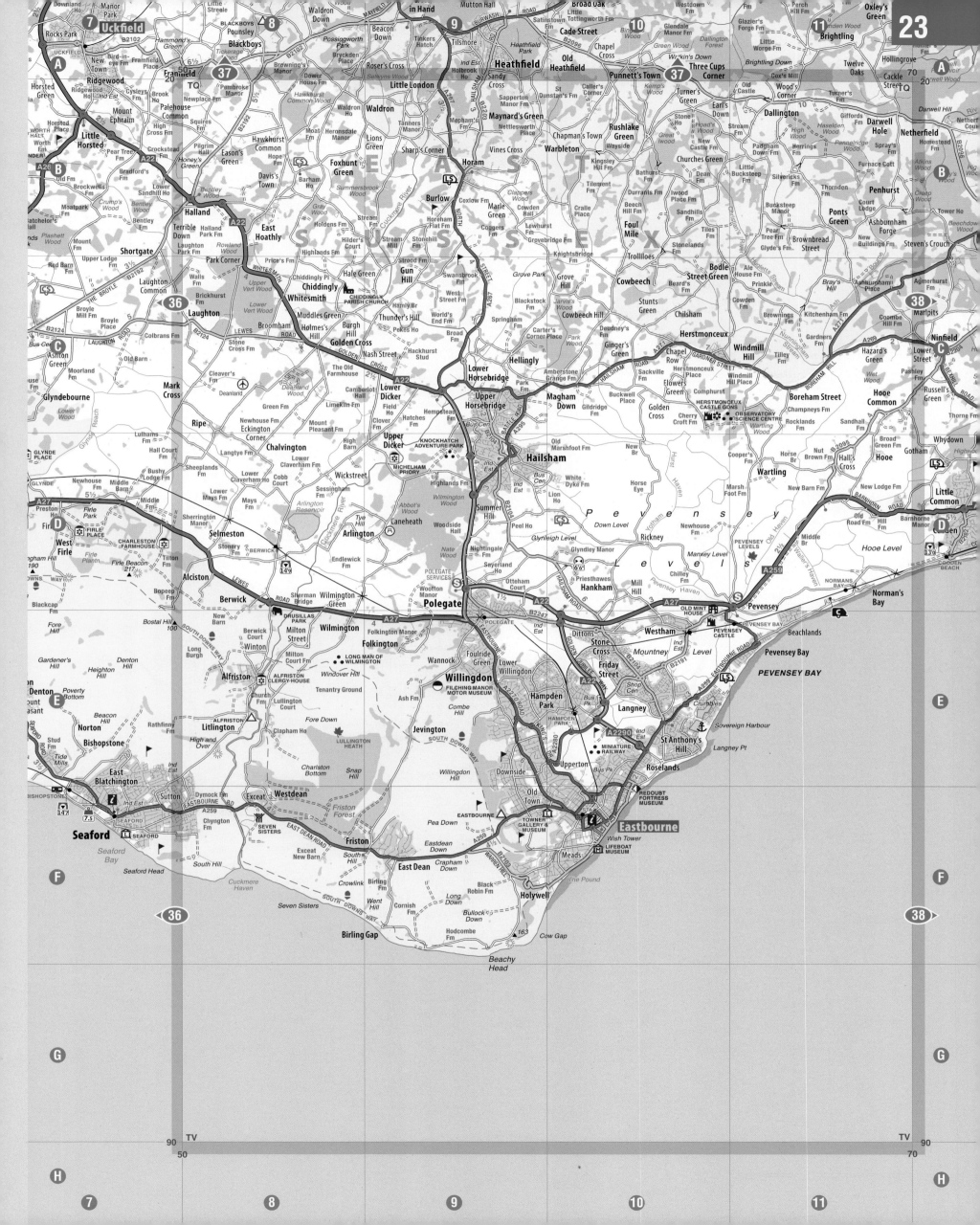

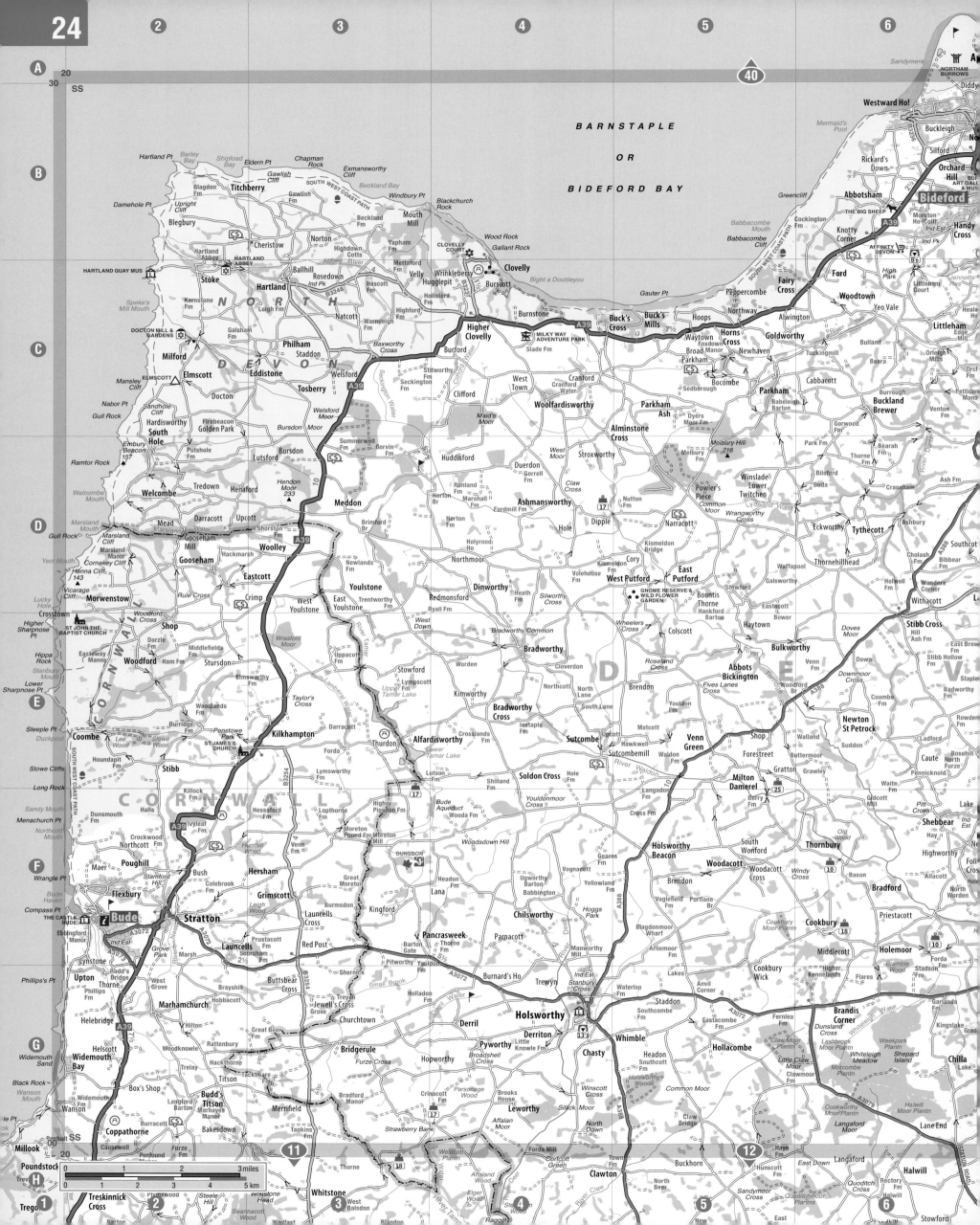

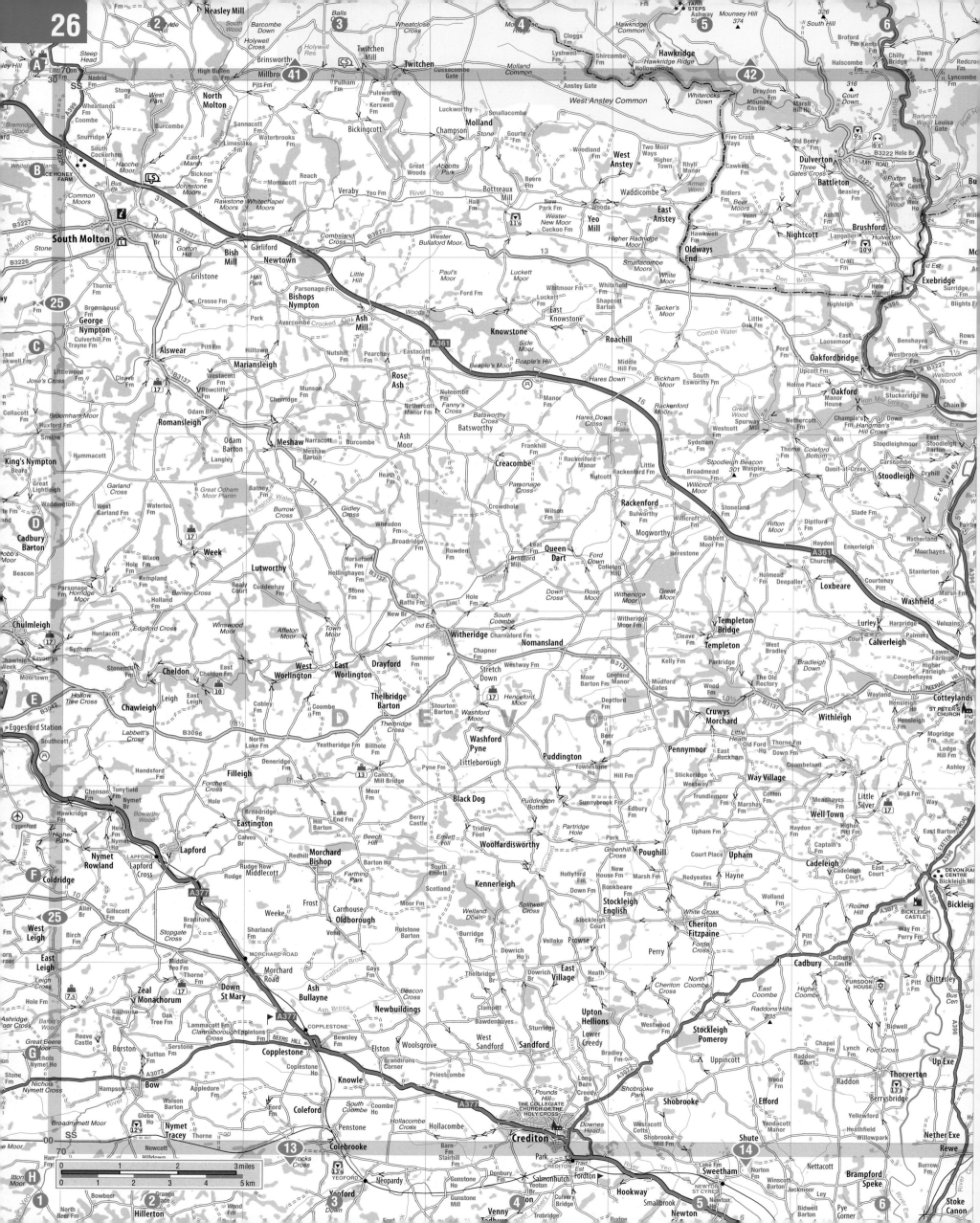

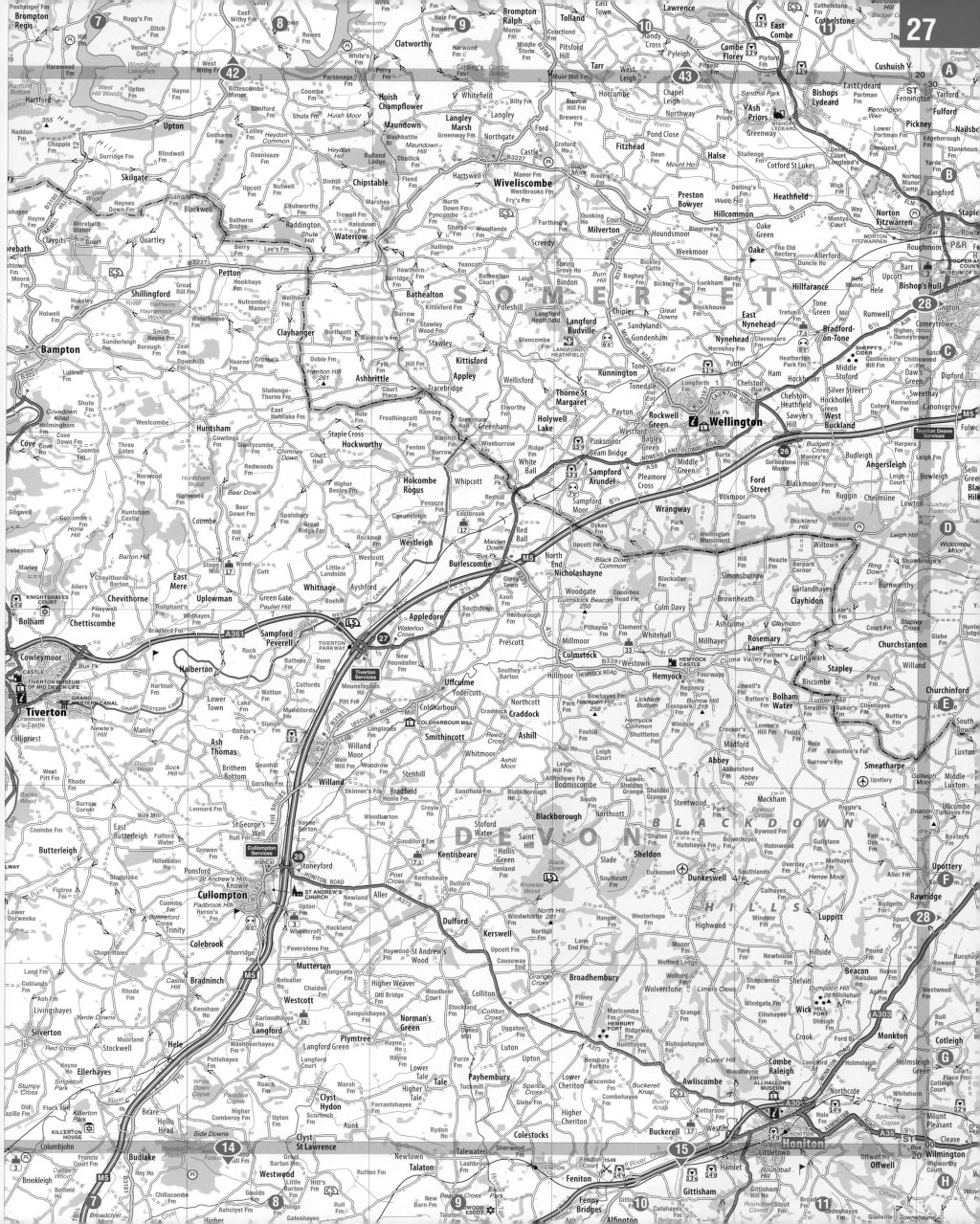

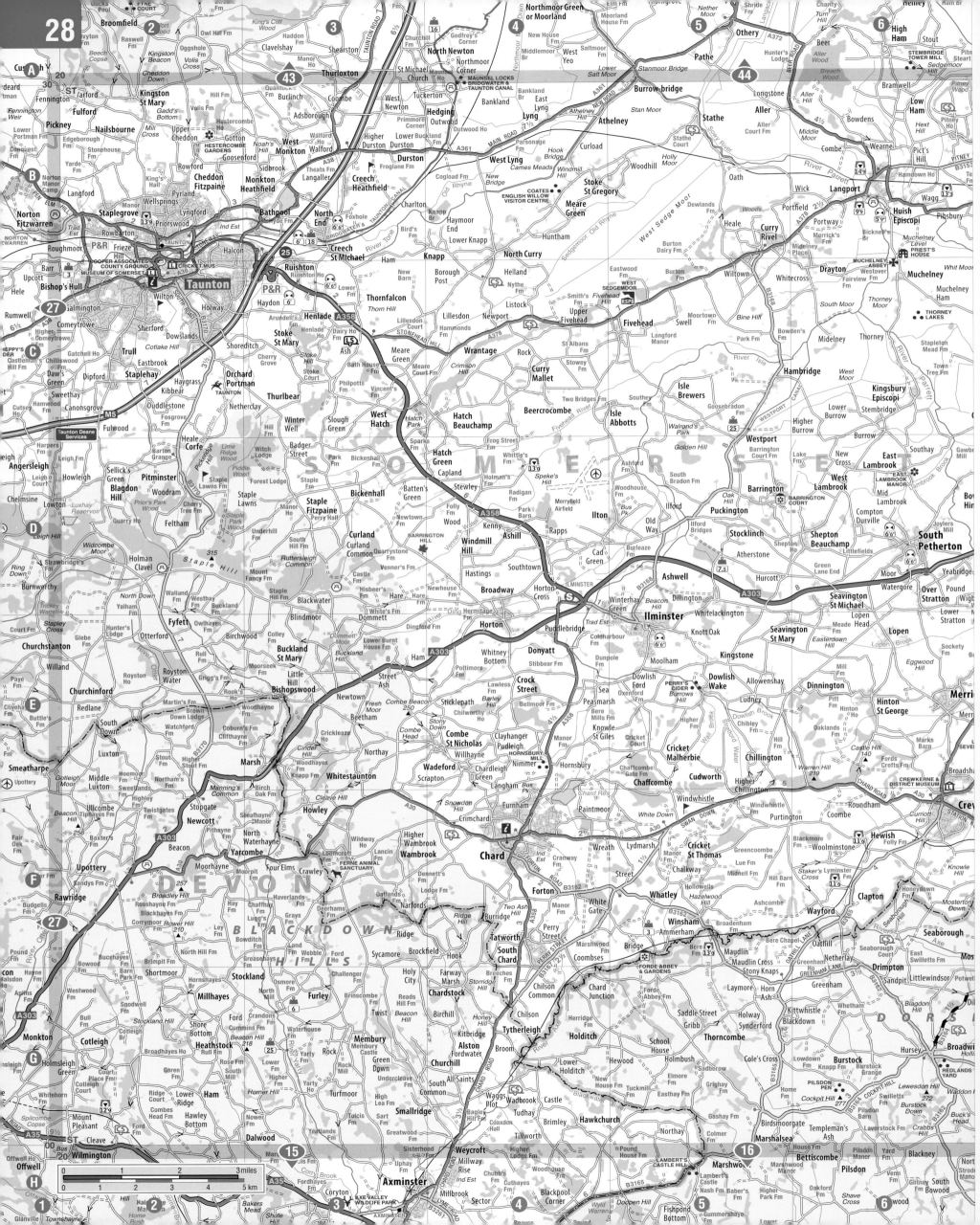

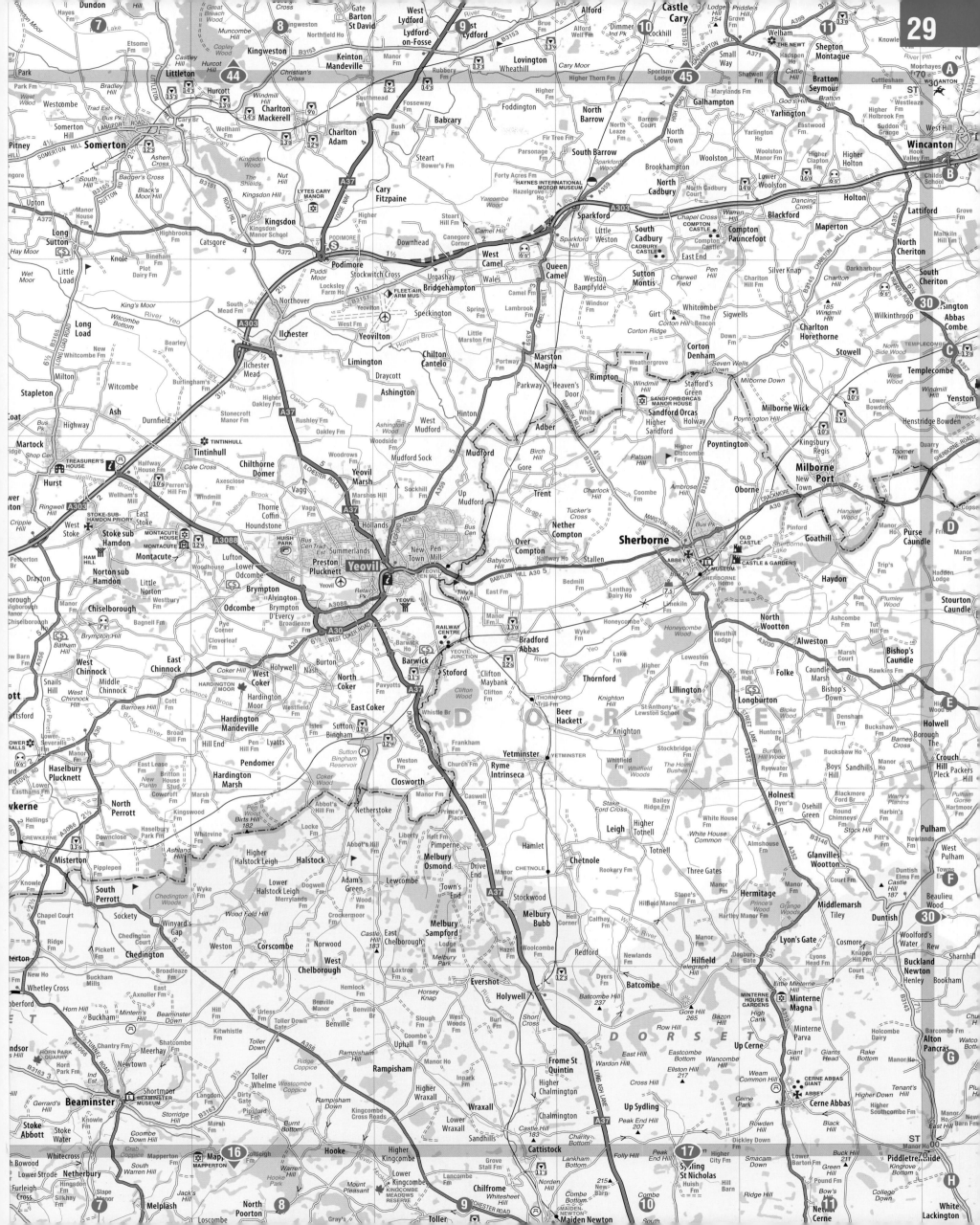

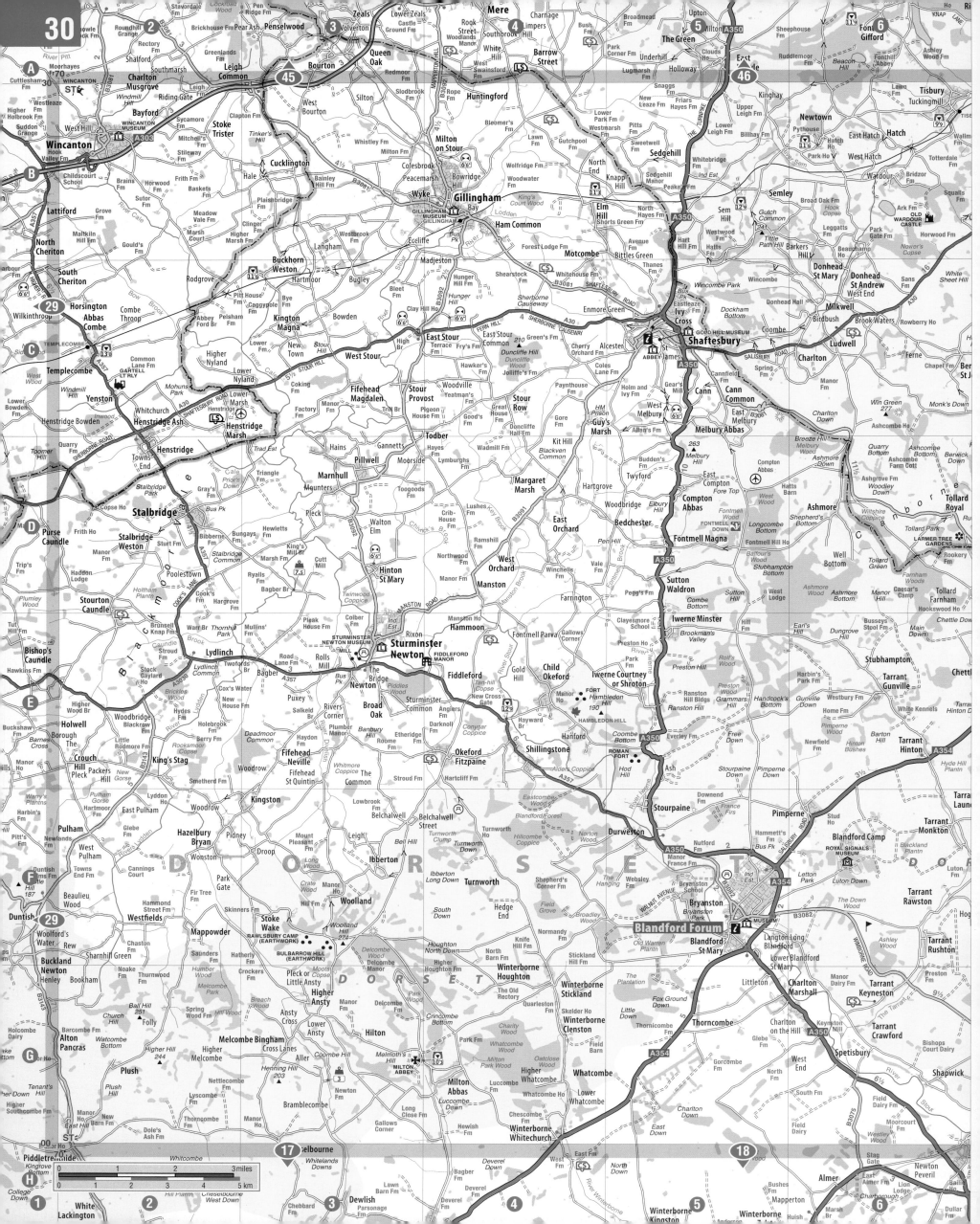

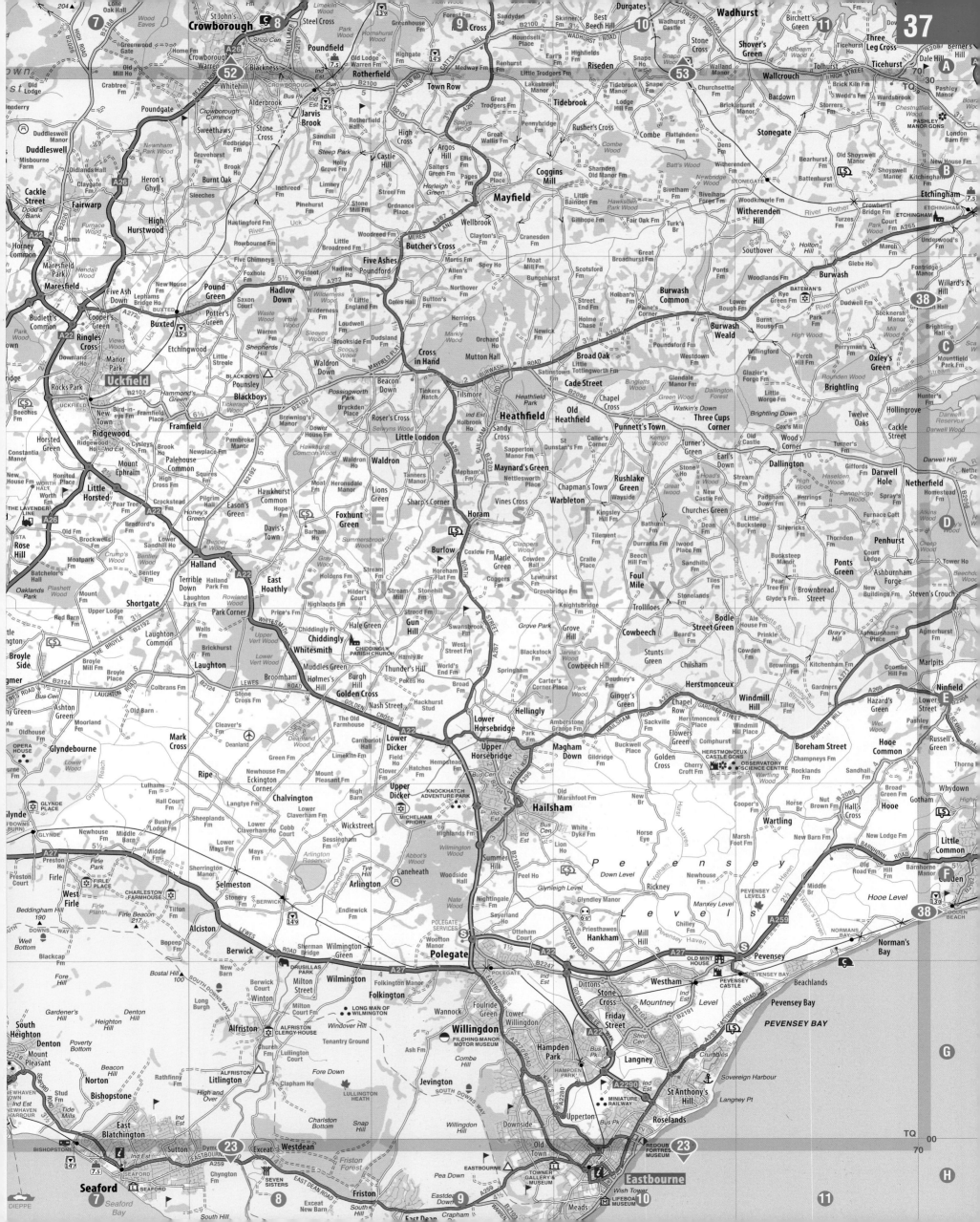

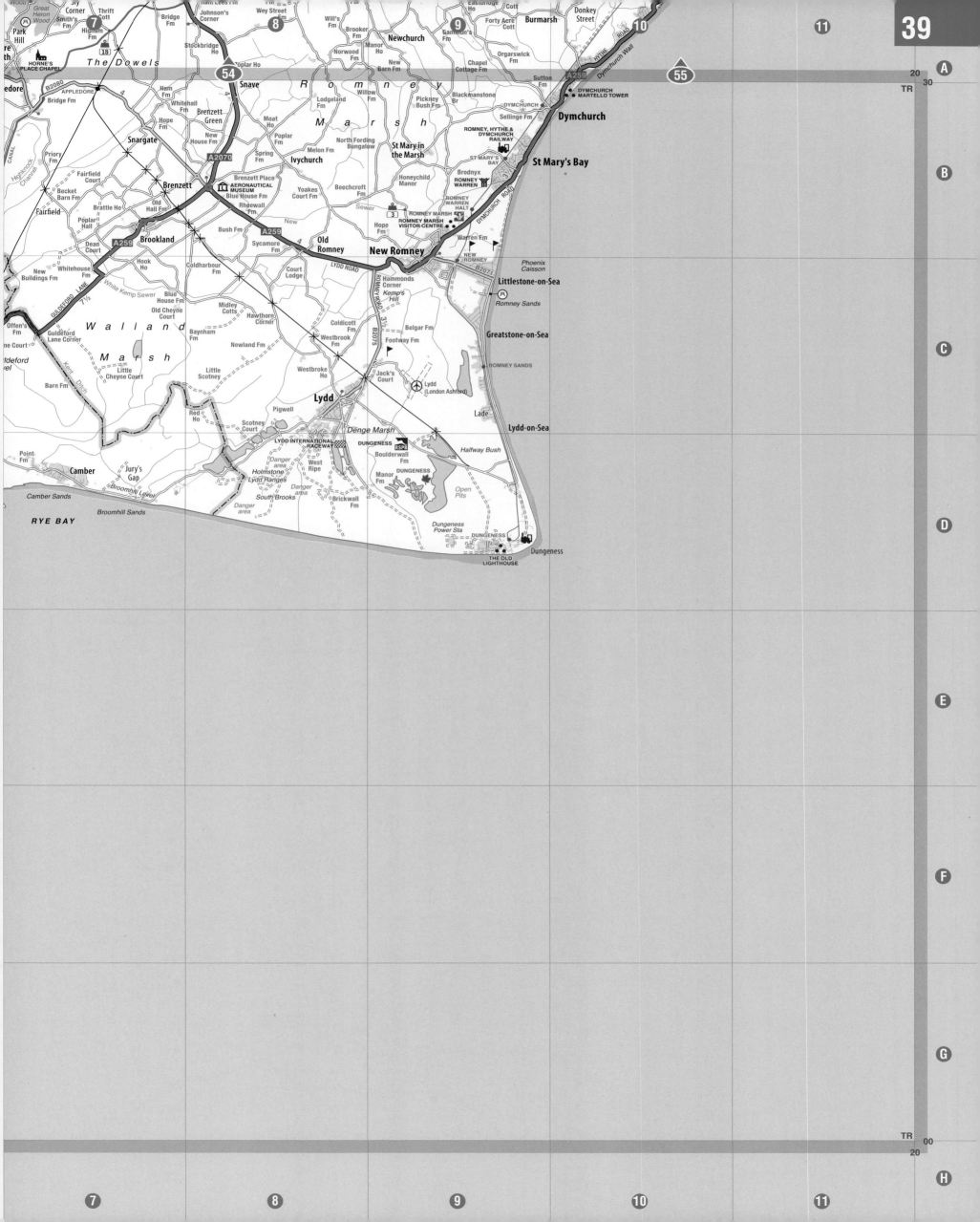

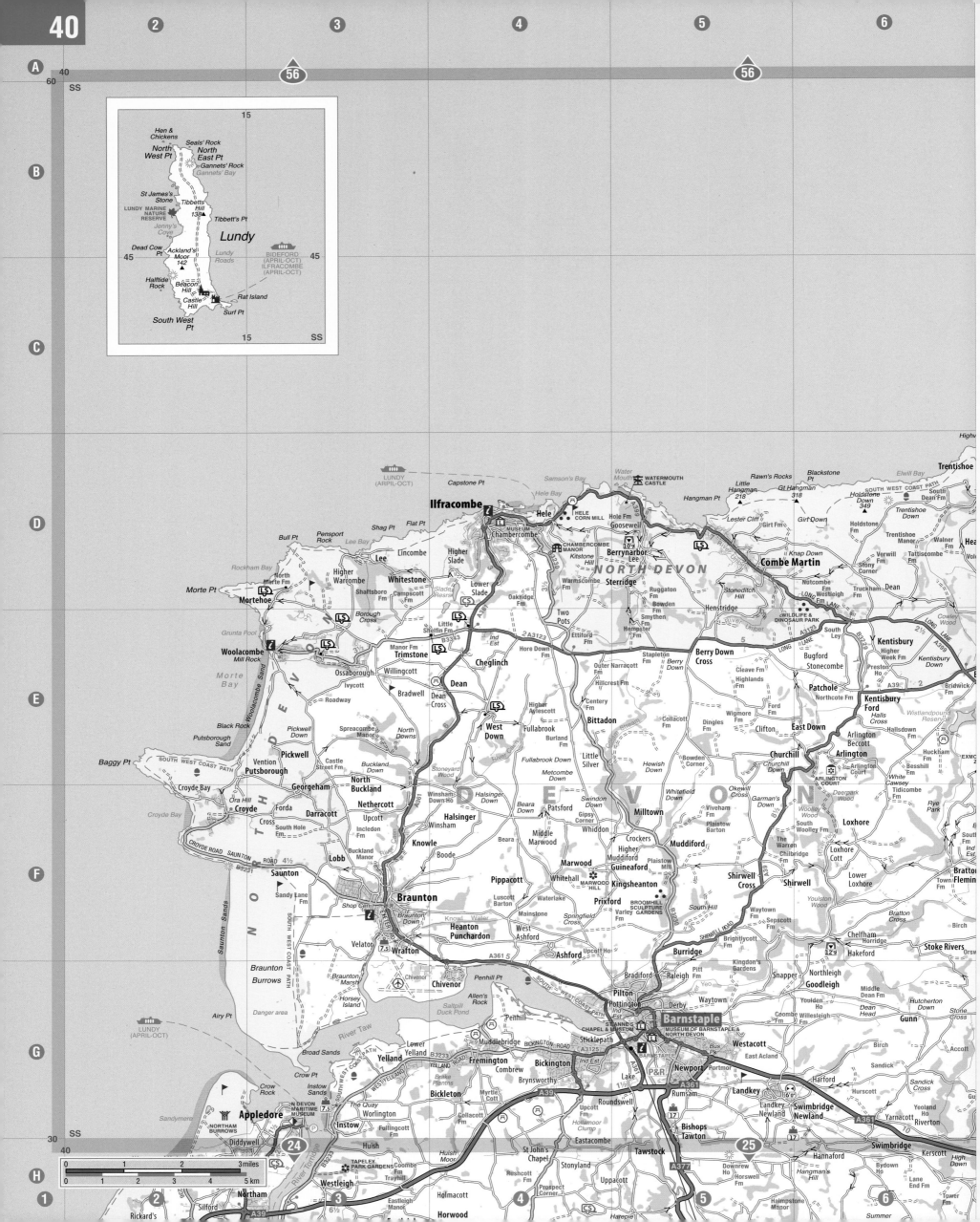

Inset map (Lundy)

Lundy

Hen & Chickens
Seals' Rock
North West Pt
North East Pt
Gannets' Rock
Gannets' Bay
St James's Stone
Tibbetts Hill 138
Tibbett's Pt
LUNDY MARINE NATURE RESERVE
Jenny's Cove
Lundy Roads
BIDEFORD (APRIL-OCT)
ILFRACOMBE (APRIL-OCT)
Dead Cow Pt
Ackland's Moor 142
Halftide Rock
Beacon Hill
Castle Hill
Rat Island
South West Pt
Surf Pt

Main map

LUNDY (APRIL-OCT)
Capstone Pt
Samson's Bay
Water Mouth
WATERMOUTH CASTLE
Rawn's Rocks
Blackstone
Elwill Bay
Trentishoe
SOUTH WEST COAST PATH
South Dean Fm
Hele Bay
Little Hangman 218
Gt Hangman 318
Holdstone Down 349
Trentishoe Down
Ilfracombe
Hele
HELE CORN MILL
Hole Fm
Goosewell
Hangman Pt
Lee
Holdstone Down
MUSEUM
Chambercombe
Hole Fm
Lester Cliff
Girt Fm
Girt Down
Holdstone Fm
Bull Pt
Pensport Rock
Lee Bay
Flat Pt
Shag Pt
CHAMBERCOMBE MANOR
Kitstone Hill
Berrynarbor
Lee
Combe Martin
Knap Down
Verwill Fm
Stony Corner
Trentishoe Manor
Tattiscombe Fm
Walner
Hea
Rockham Bay
Higher Warcombe
Whitestone
Higher Slade
Lower Slade
Slade Resrs
NORTH DEVON
Warmscombe Fm
Sterridge
Ruggaton Fm
Bowden
Smythen
Stonedicth Hill
Henstridge
WILDLIFE & DINOSAUR PARK
Cowley Wood
Morte Pt
North Morte Fm
Shaftsboro Fm
Campscott Fm
Oakridge Fm
A399
Two Pots
Ettiford Fm
Hampster
Stapleton Fm
Berry Fm
Berry Down
Berry Down Cross
South Ley
A3123
Bugford
Stonecombe
Preston Ho
Kentisbury
Higher Week Fm
Kentisbury Down
Mortehoe
Borough Cross
Little Shelfin Fm
B3343
Ind Est
A3123
Hore Down Fm
Outer Narracott Fm
Hillcrest Fm
Cleave Fm
Highlands Fm
Wigmore Fm
Ford Fm
Northcote Fm
Kentisbury Ford
Halls Cross
Hallsdown Fm
A39
Bridwick
Woolacombe
Mill Rock
Manor Fm
Trimstone
Willingcott
Cheglinch
Ossaborough
Ivycott
Dean
Dean Cross
Higher Aylescott
Fullabrook
Bittadon
Centery Fm
Collacott Fm
Dingles Fm
Clifton
East Down
Arlington Beccott
Huckham Fm
Besshill Fm
Morte Bay
Roadway
Bradwell
West Down
Burland Fm
Little Silver
Bowden Corner
Churchill
Churchill Down
Arlington
ARLINGTON COURT
White Cawsey
Tidicombe Fm
Rye Park
Black Rock
Pickwell Down
North Downs
Spreacombe Manor
Buckland Down
Stoneyard Wood
Metcombe Down
Hewish Fm
Whitefield Down
Okewill Cross
Garman's Down
Deerpark Wood
Woolley Wood
EXMO
Putsborough Sand
Pickwell
Vention
Putsborough
Castle Street Fm
North Buckland
Fullabrook Down
Beara Down
Swindon Down
Viveham Fm
Plaistow Barton
South Woolley Fm
Loxhore
Baggy Pt
SOUTH WEST COAST PATH
Ora Hill
Forda
Winsham Down Ho
Halsinger Down
Patsford
Gipsy Corner
Whiddon
Milltown
Waytown Fm
Sepscott Fm
The Warren
Chilbridge
Loxhore Cott
Croyde Bay
Croyde
Georgeham
Darracott
Upcott
Incledon
Halsinger
Beara
Middle Marwood
Crockers
Muddiford
Higher Muddiford
Plaistow Mill
South Hill
Shirwell Cross
A39
Shirwell
Lower Loxhore
Bratton Fleming
Cross
South Hole Fm
Nethercott
Winsham
Knowle
Boode
Beara
Marwood
Whitehall
Guineaford
Kingsheanton
MARWOOD HILL
Youlston Wood
Croyde
SAUNTON ROAD 4½
B3231
Saunton
Sandy Lane Fm
Lobb
Buckland Manor
Pippacott
Prixford
BROOMHILL SCULPTURE GARDENS
Varley Green
Brightlycott
Chelfham Horridge
Stoke Rivers
Bratton Fleming
Birch
Sandy Lane Fm
Shop Centre
Braunton
Luscott Barton
Waterlake
Mainstone
Springfield Cross
South Hill
Waytown Fm
Burridge
Pitt Fm
Kingdon's Gardens
Hakeford
Town
Orsw
Braunton Burrows
Braunton Down
Heanton Punchardon
West Ashford
Knowl Water
Ashford
Upcott Ho
Northleigh Fm
Youlden Ho
Dean Fm
Middle Dean Fm
Goodleigh
Hutcherton Down
Stone Cross
Velator
Wrafton
7.5
A361
Chivenor
SOUTH WEST COAST PATH
Bradiford
Raleigh
Yeo
Waytown
Derby
Coombe Willesleigh
Birch
SOUTH WEST COAST PATH
Chivenor
Penhill Pt
Allen's Rock
Pilton
Pottington Ind Est
Snapper
Coombe Willesleigh Fm
Braunton Marsh
Horsey Island
Saltpill Duck Pond
Penhill
ST ANNE'S CHAPEL & MUSEUM
Barnstaple
MUSEUM OF BARNSTAPLE & NORTH DEVON
Westacott
Gunn
Birch
Airy Pt
Danger area
River Taw
Airy Pt
Sticklepath
Bus Pk
East Acland
Accott
Sandick
Broad Sands
Muddlebridge
BICKINGTON ROAD
Bickington
Ind Est
Newport
P&R
Harford
Portmor
Sandick Cross
Crow Rock
Instow Sands
Yelland
Lower Yelland
B3233
Fremington
Combrew
Brynsworthy
Lake
A361
Rumsaa
Landkey
Landkey Newland
Hurscott
Birch
WEST YELLAND
Crow Pt
Bickleton
Myrtle Cott
Roundswell
A39
1½
A361
Swimbridge Newland
Yarnacott
Riverton
Yeoland Ho
24
N DEVON MARITIME MUSEUM
7.5
Appledore
The Quay
Worlington
Collacott
Upcott Cross
Hollamoor Clump
Bishops Tawton
17
25
Swimbridge
High
NORTHAM BURROWS
Instow
Fullington
Huish
St John's Chapel
Eastacombe
Roundswell
A377
Tawstock
Hannaford
Kerscott
Sandymere
Diddywell
Northam
Silford
Huish
Huish Moor
Coombe Trayhill
Stonyland
Uppacott
Downrew Ho
Horswell Fm
Hangman's Hill
Bydown Ho
Tower Fm
Lane End Fm
TAPELEY PARK GARDENS
Westleigh
Holmacott
Prospect Corner
Hampstacombe Fm
0 1 2 3 miles
0 1 2 3 4 5 km
Rickard's
Silford
Horwood
Eastleigh
Manor
Harepie
Summer
A39

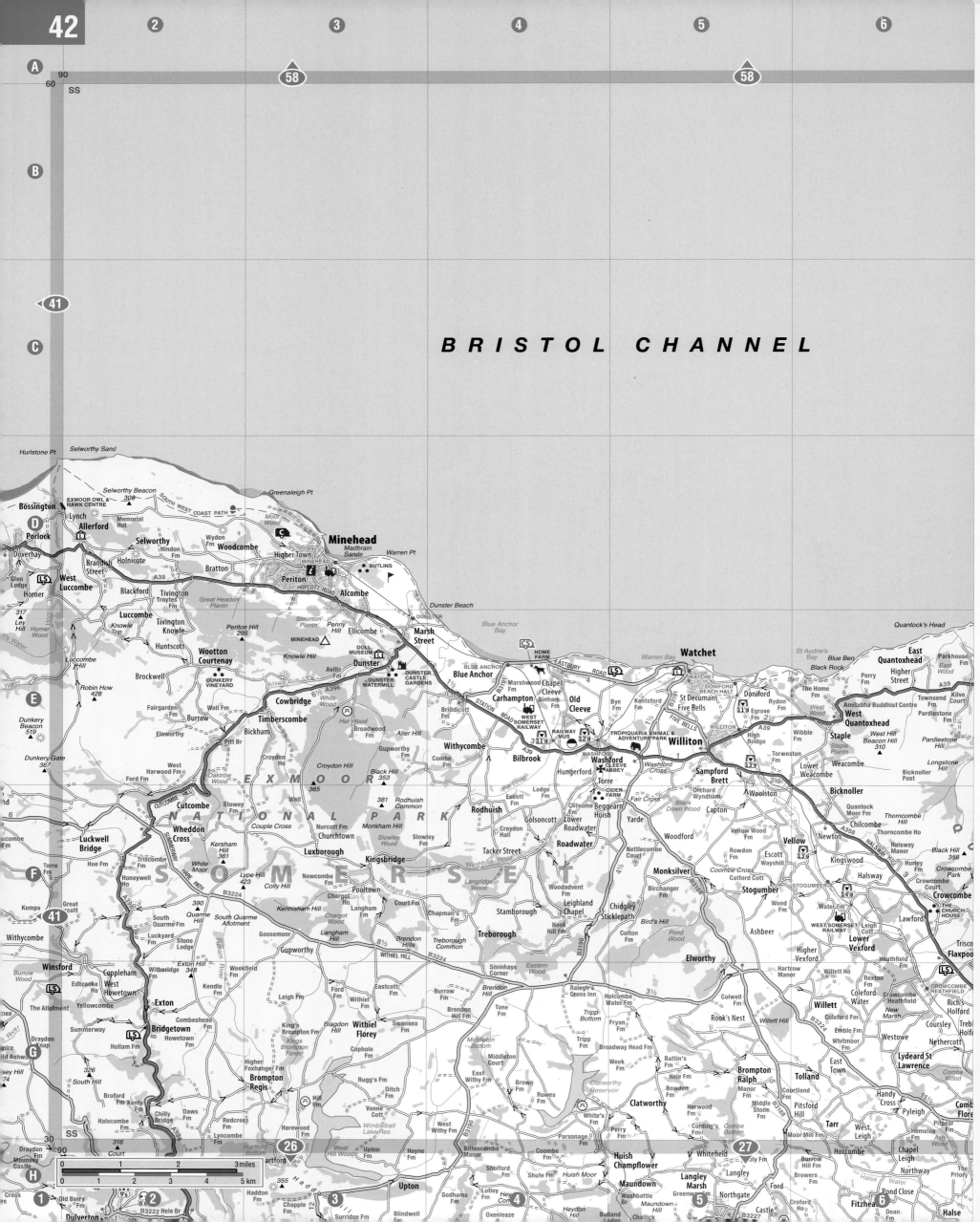

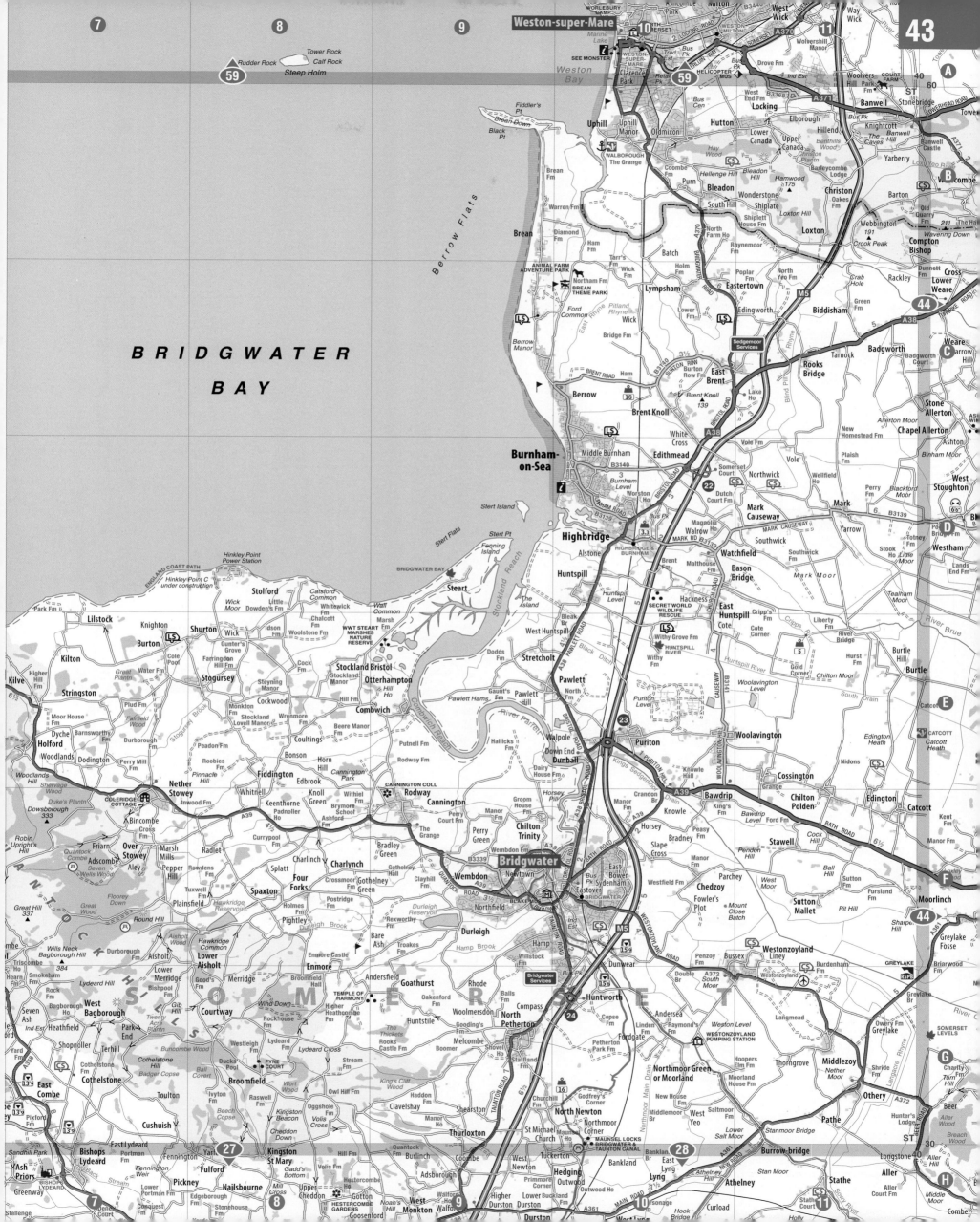

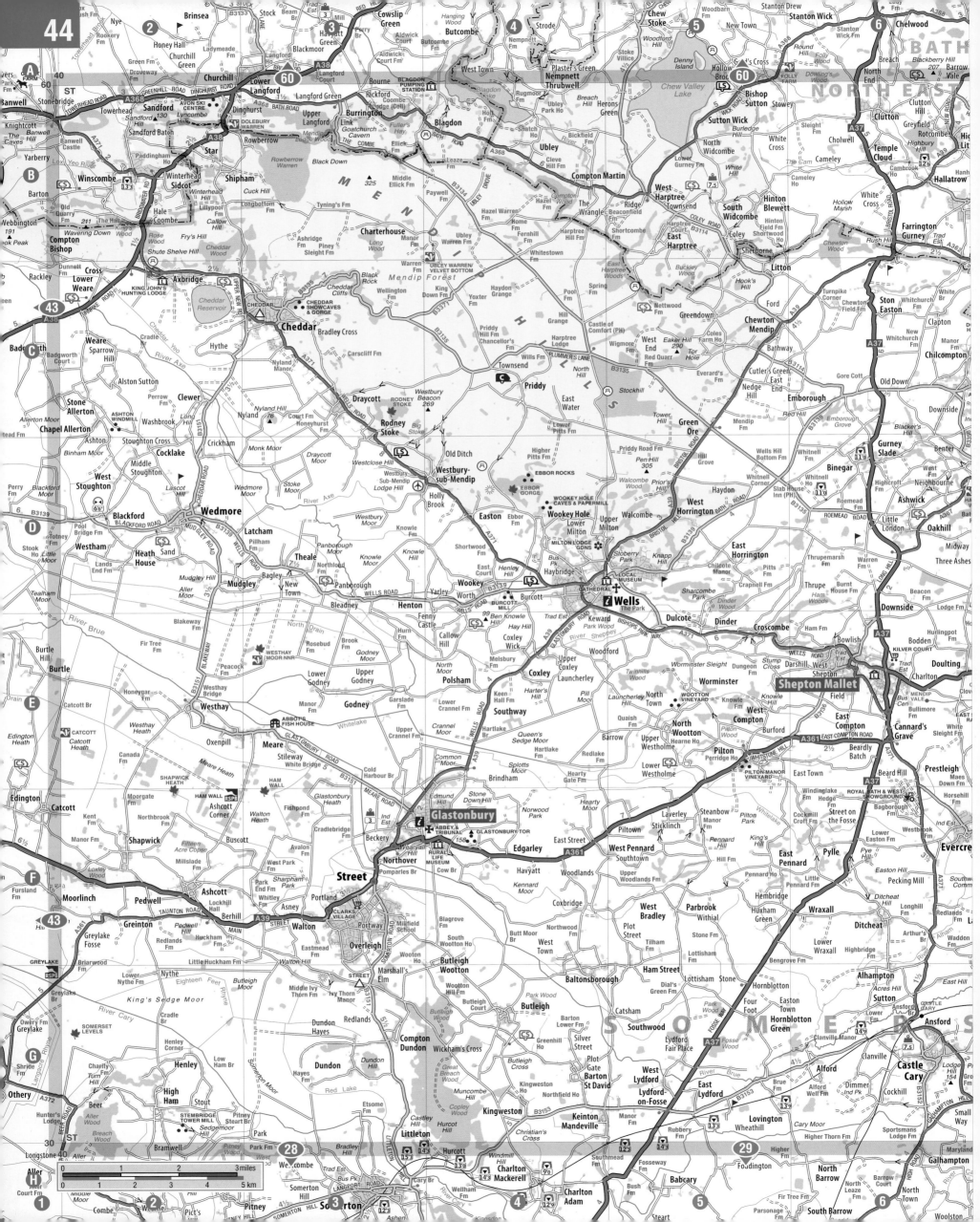

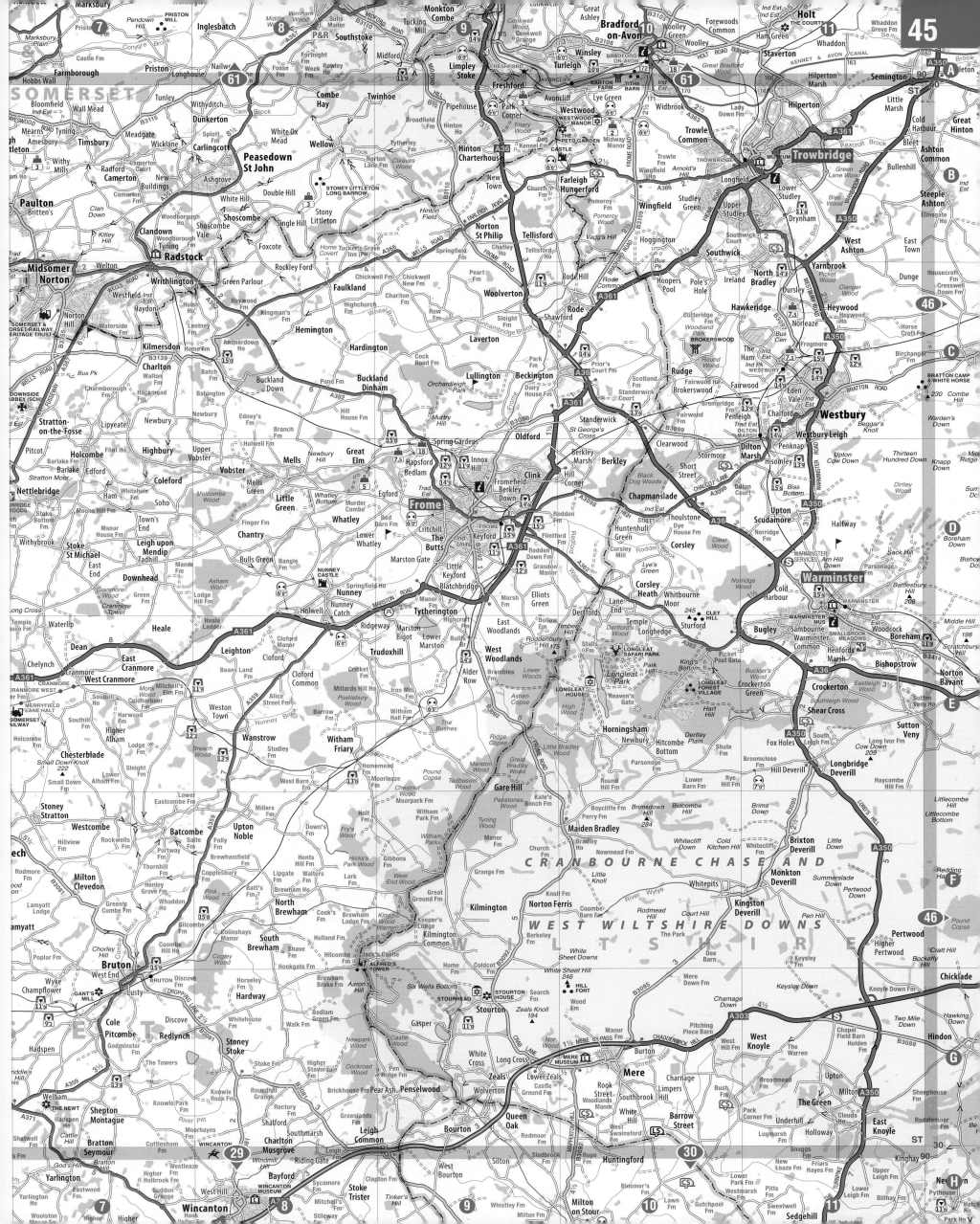

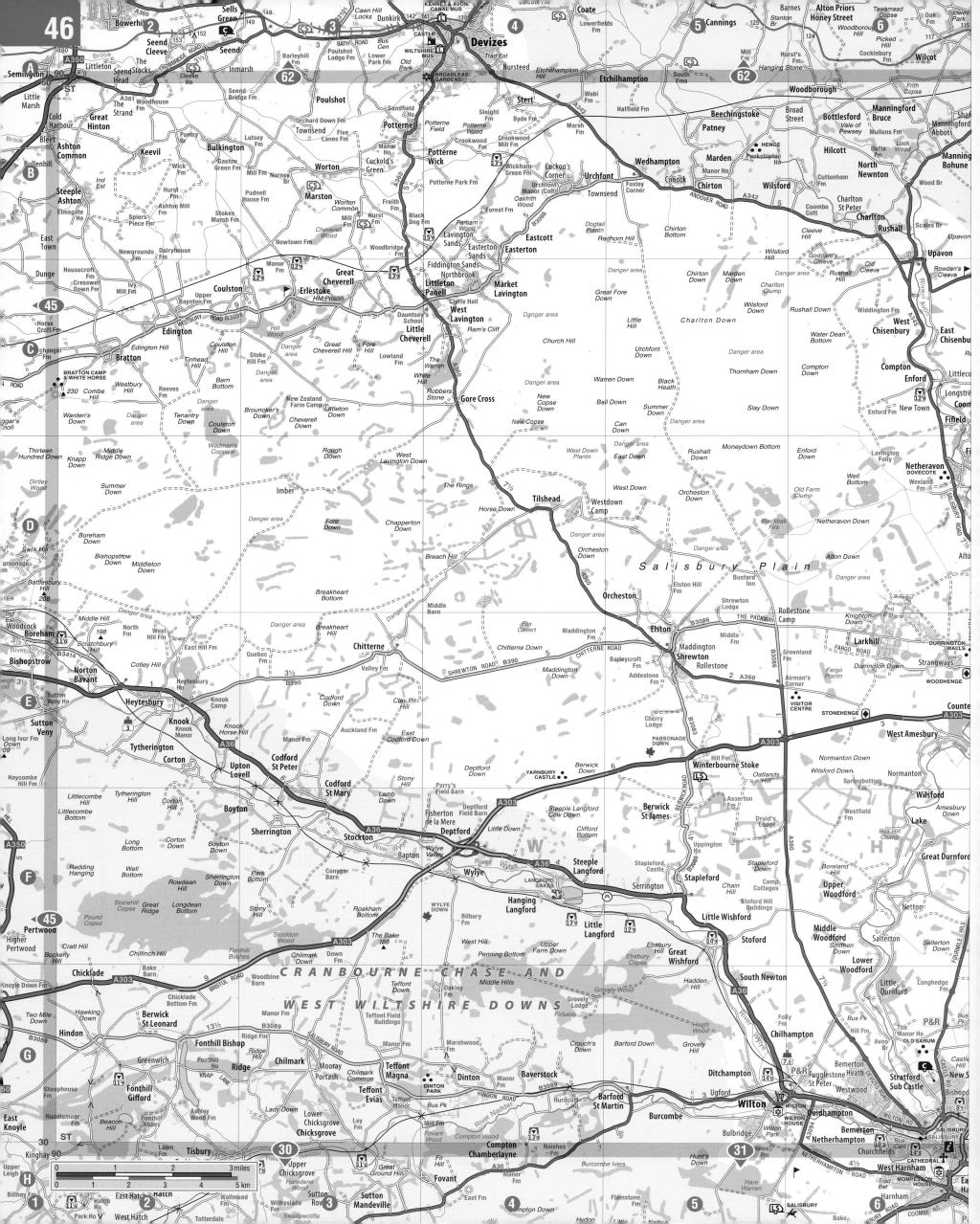

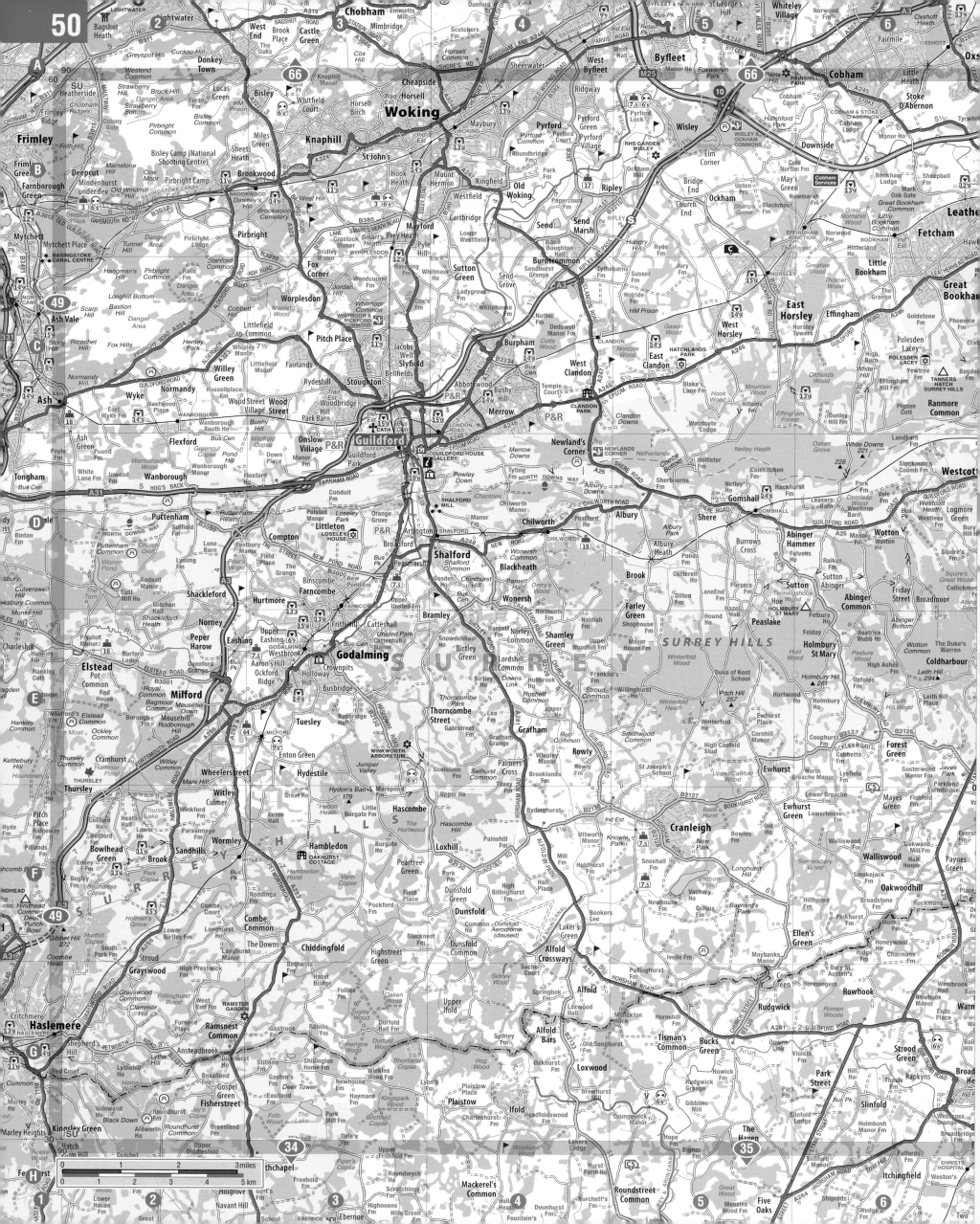

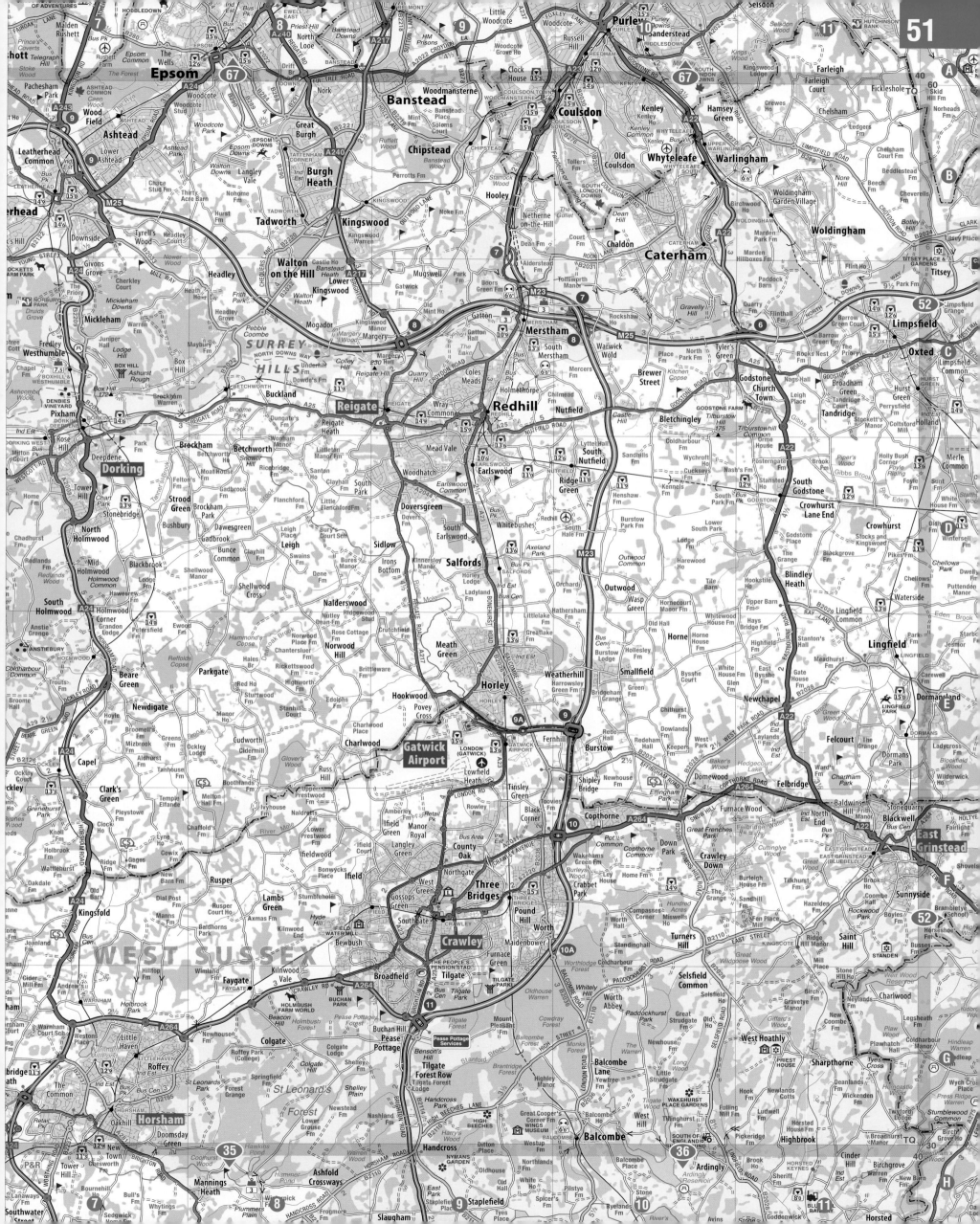

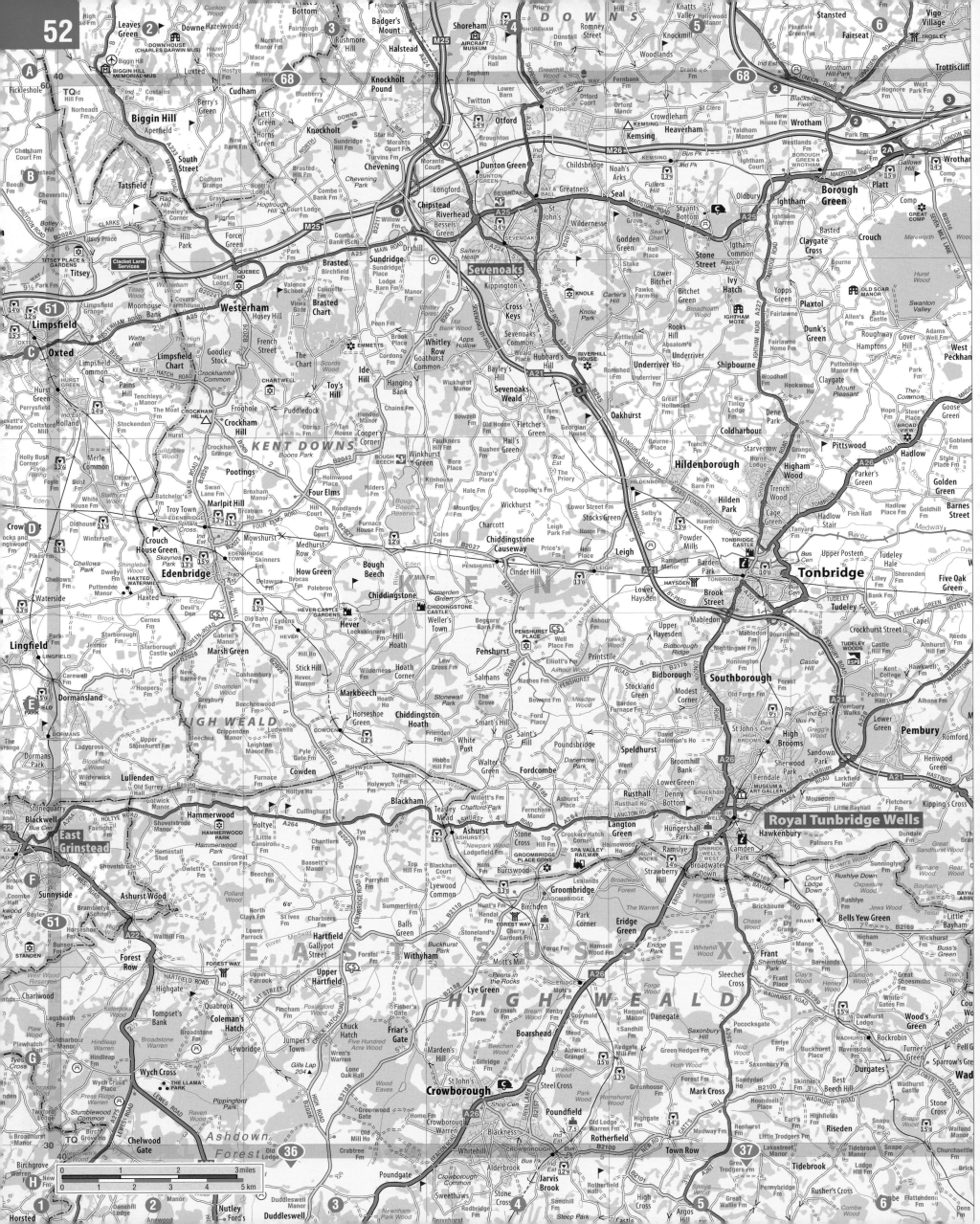

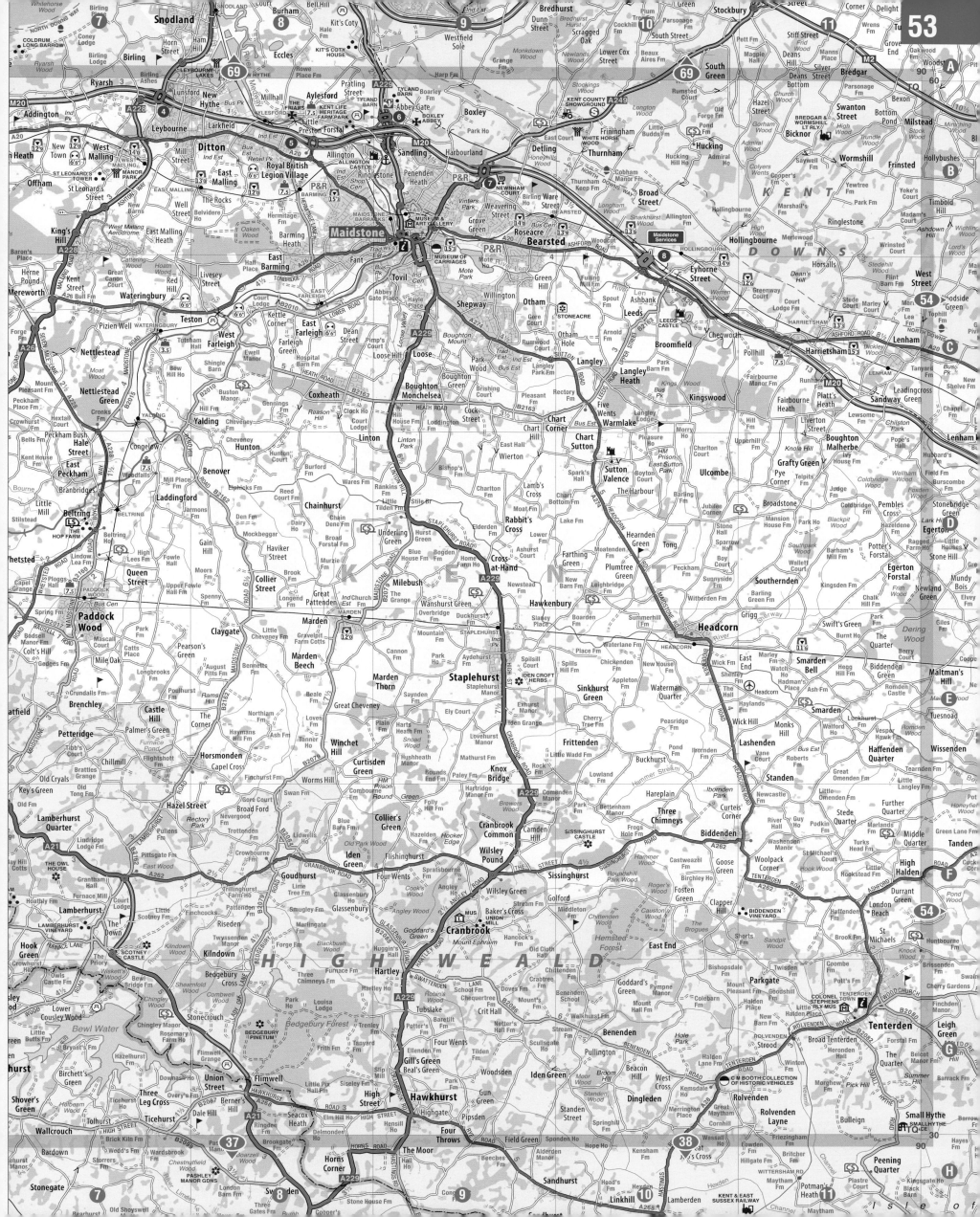

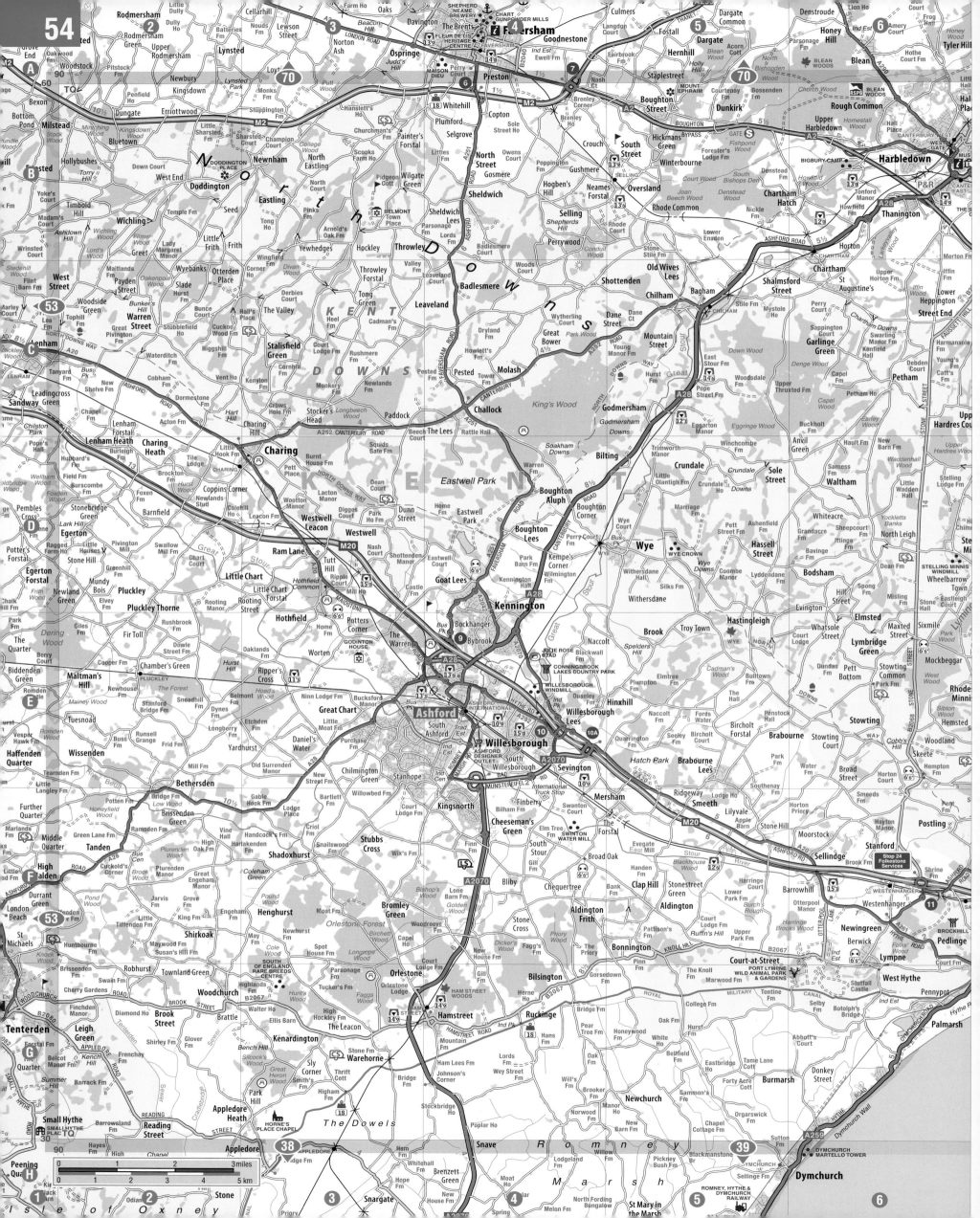

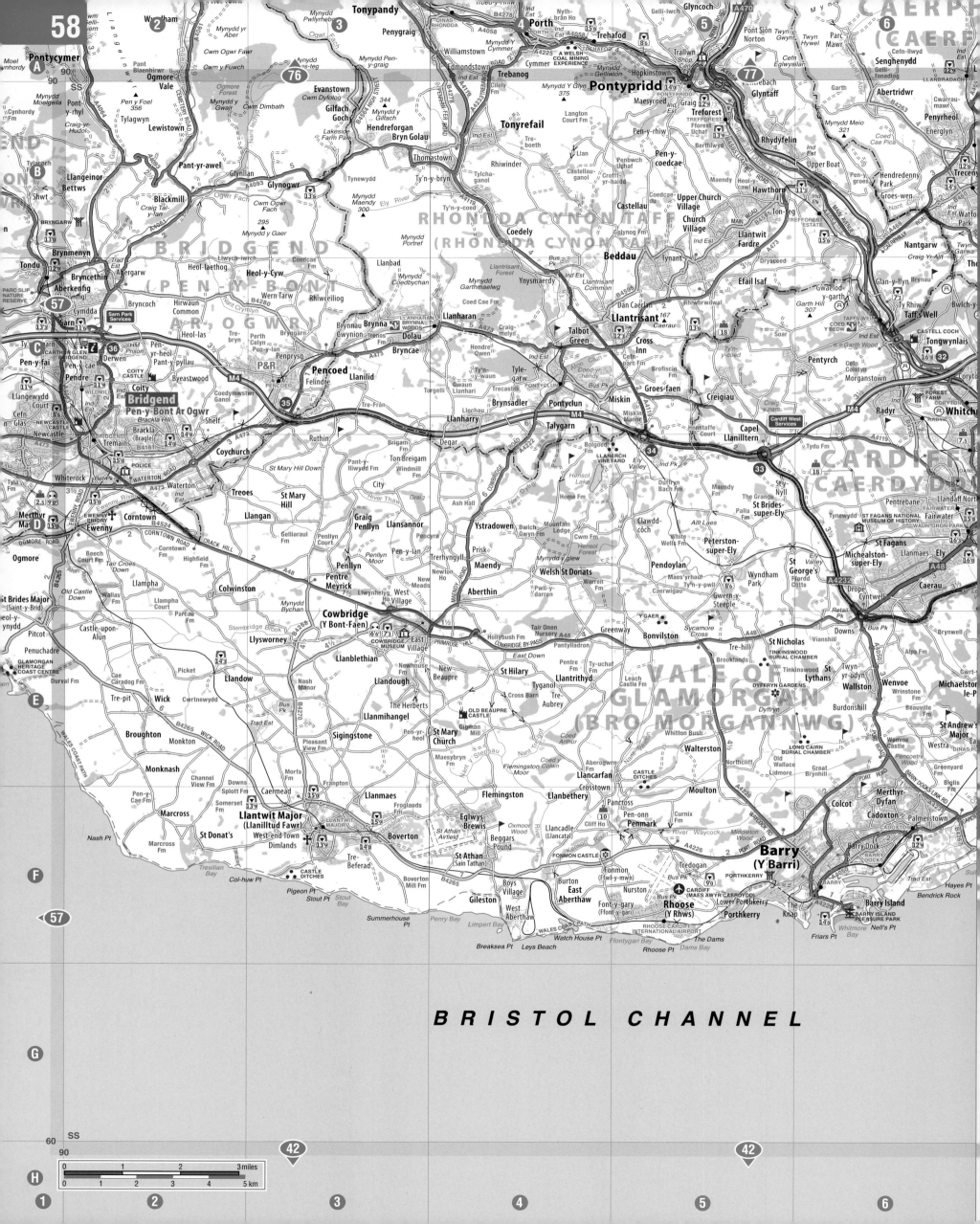

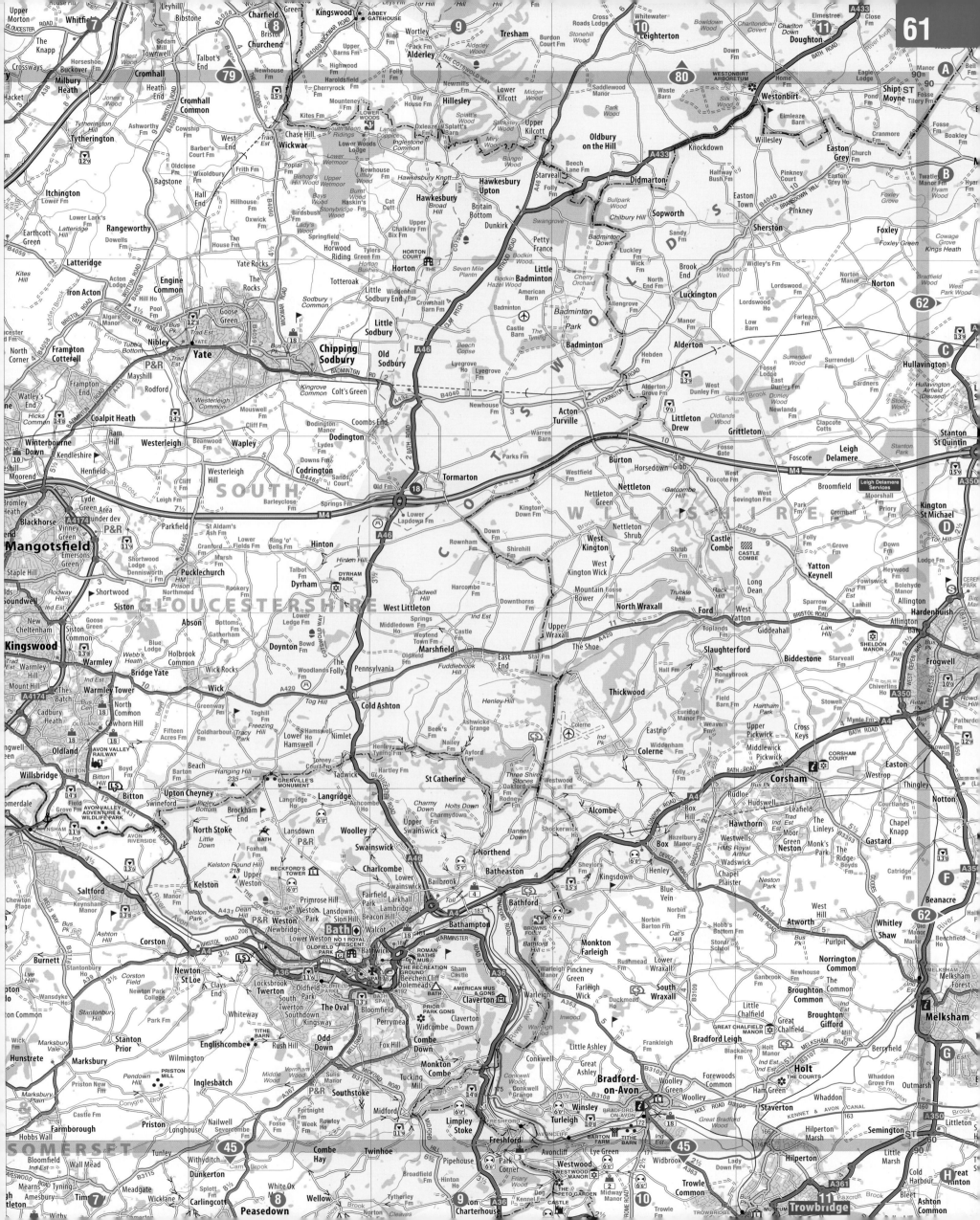

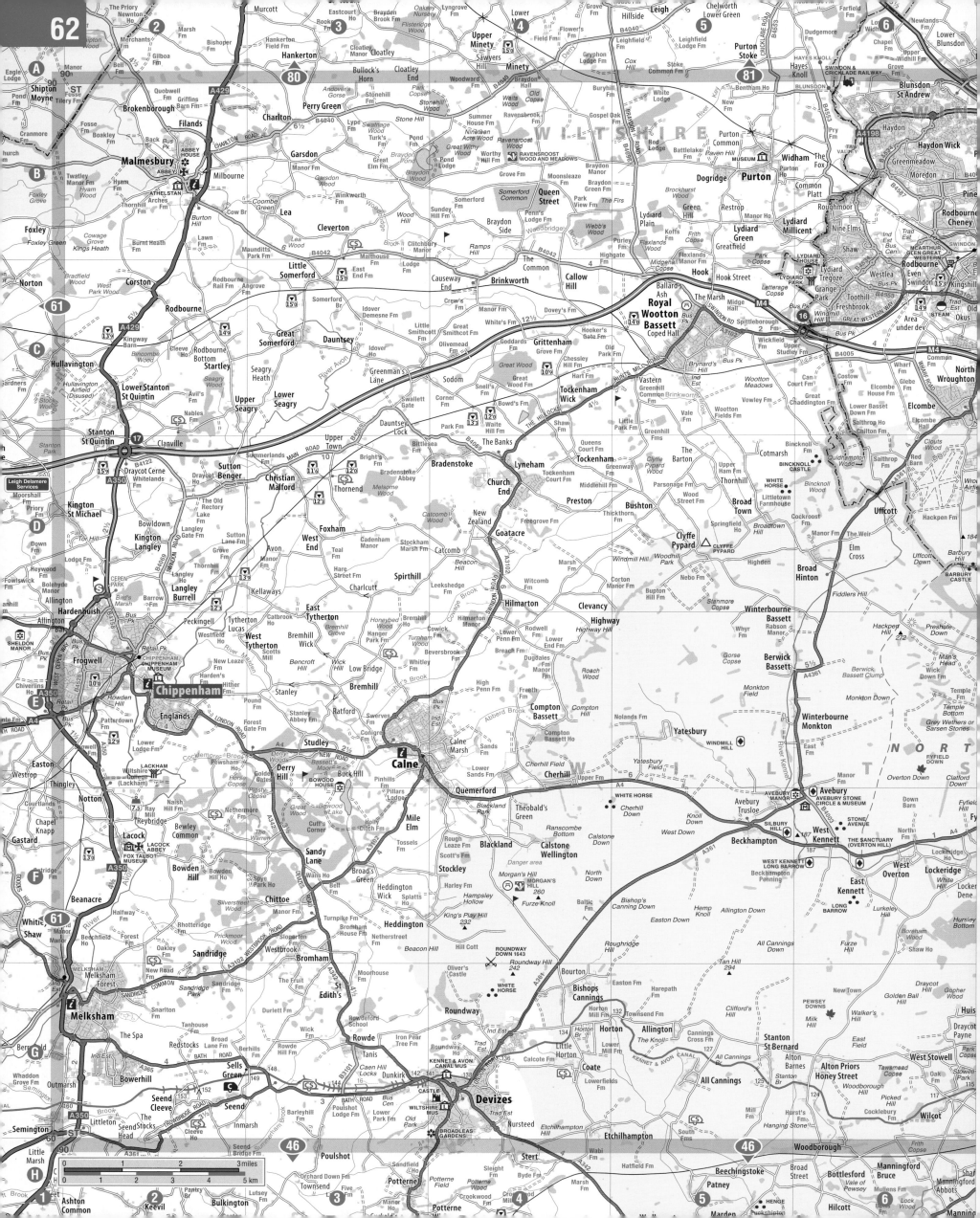

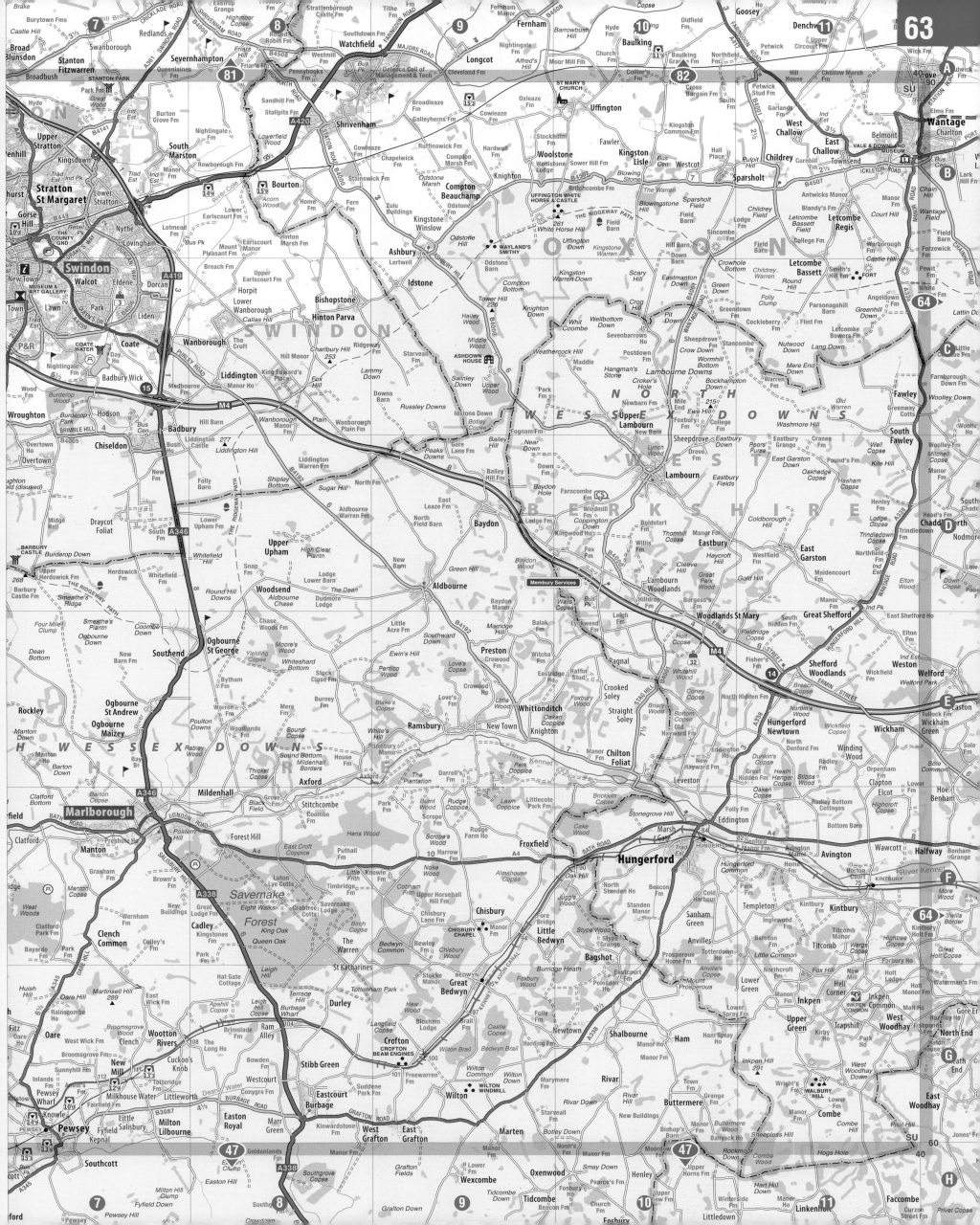

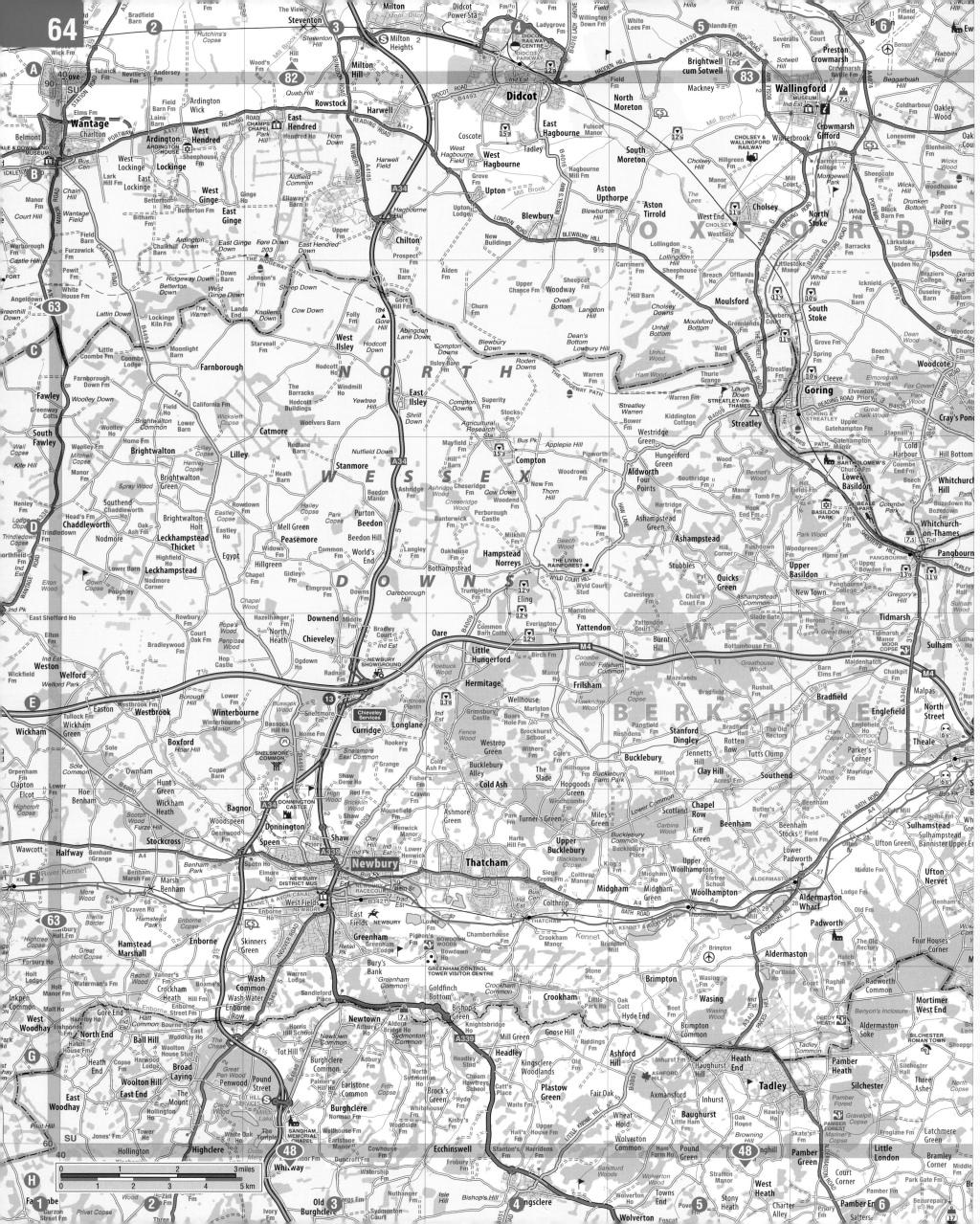

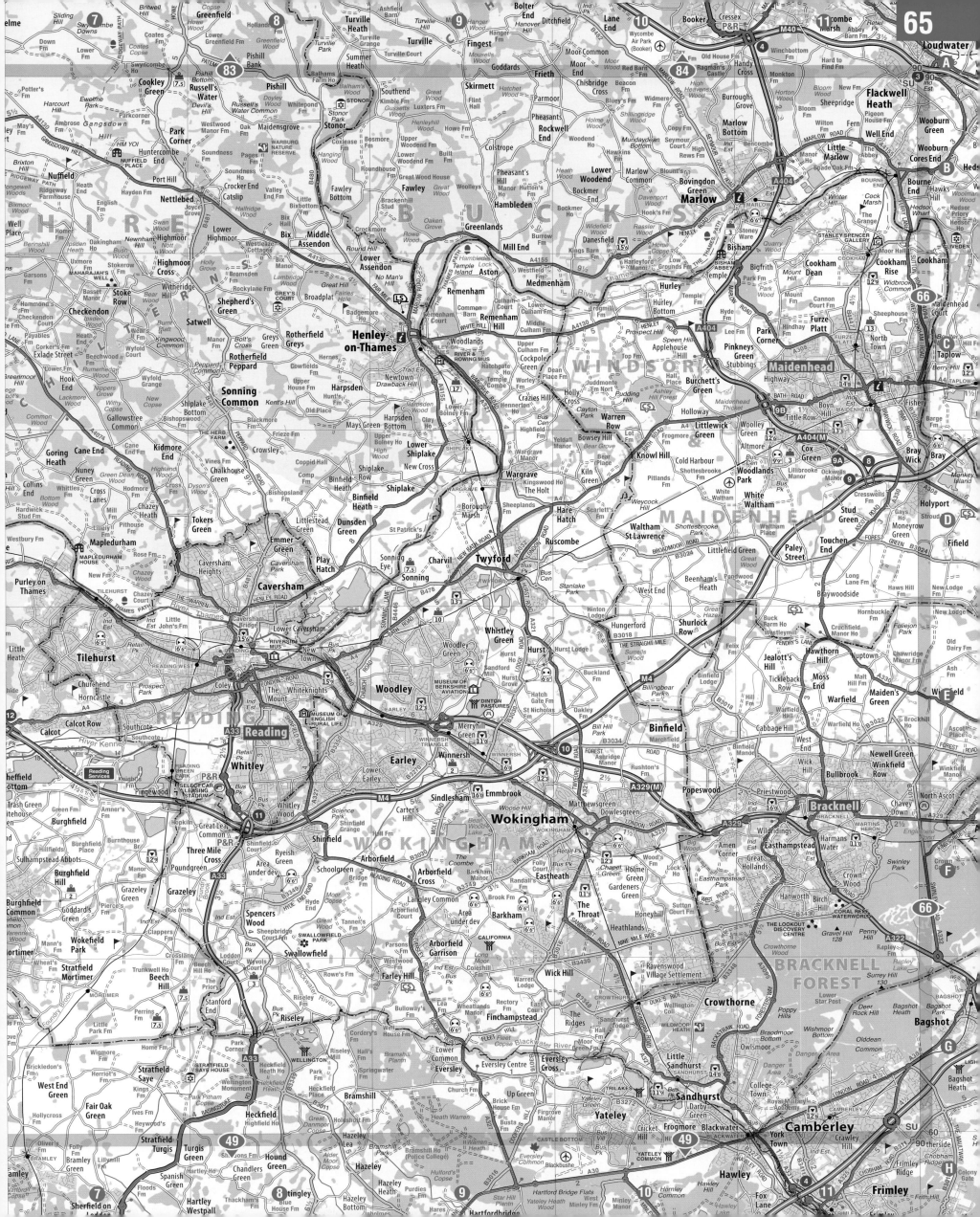

ST BRIDES BAY

BAIE SAIN FFRAID

PEMBROKESHIRE COAST

NATIONAL PARK

PEMBROKESHIRE

COAST NATIONAL PARK

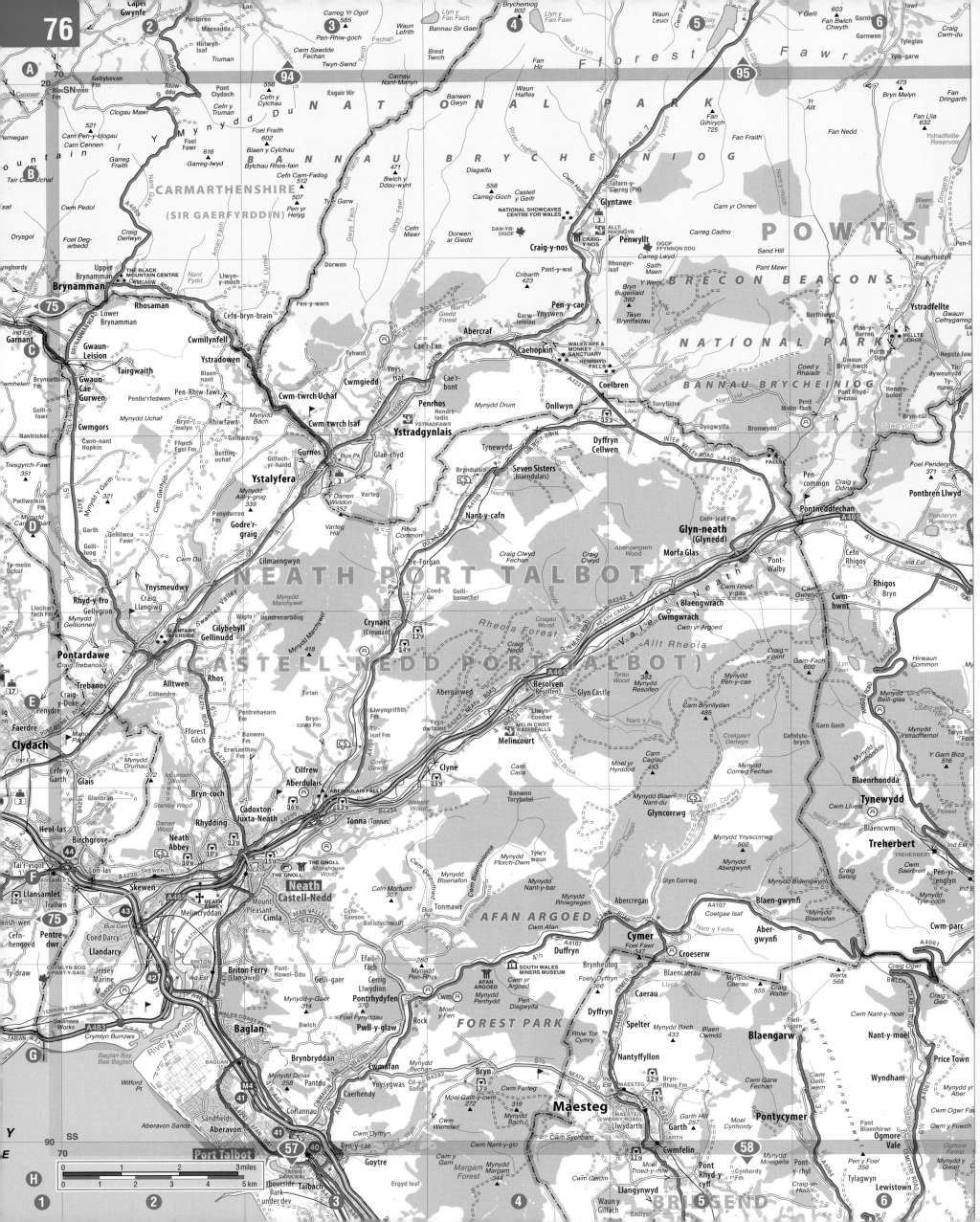

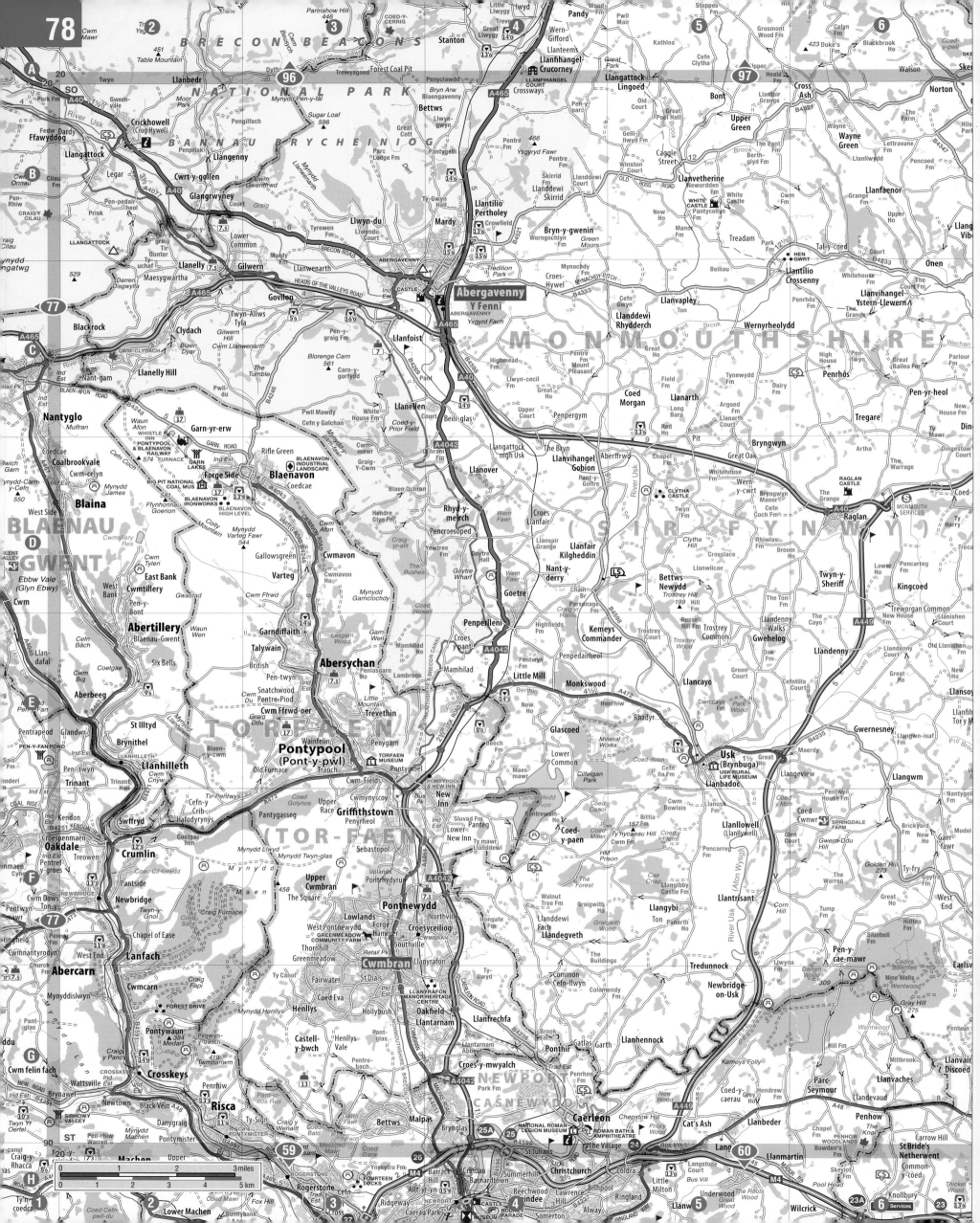

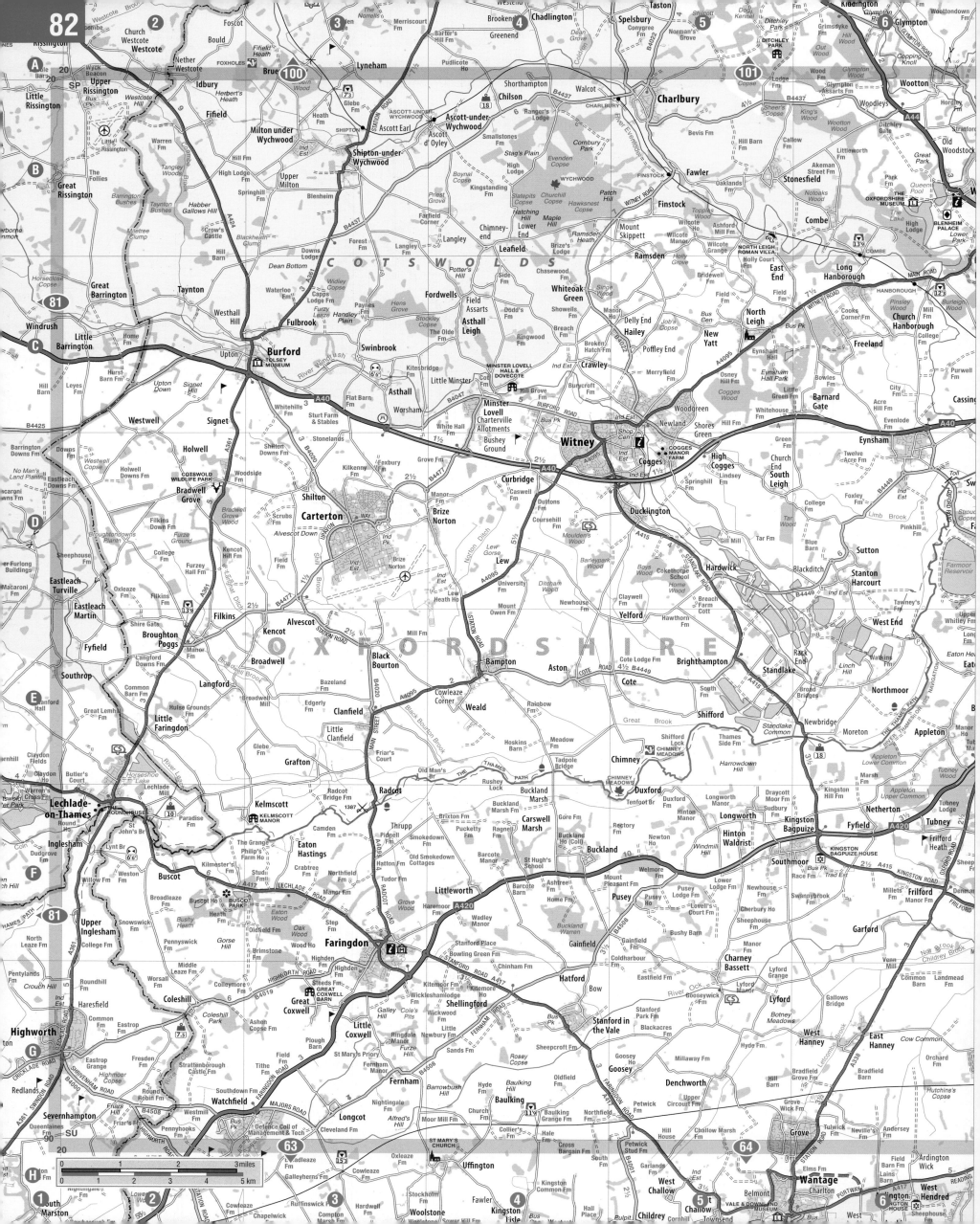

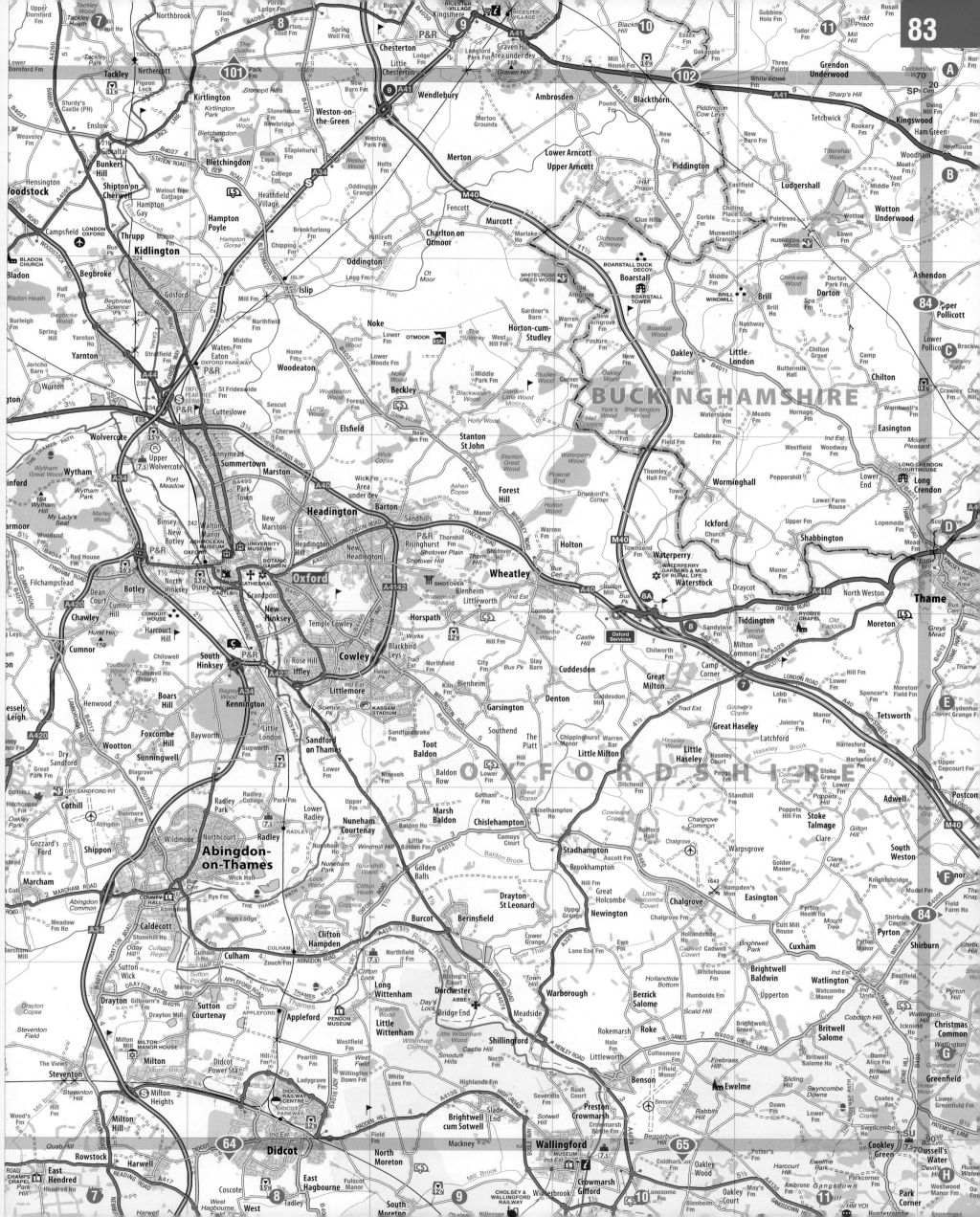

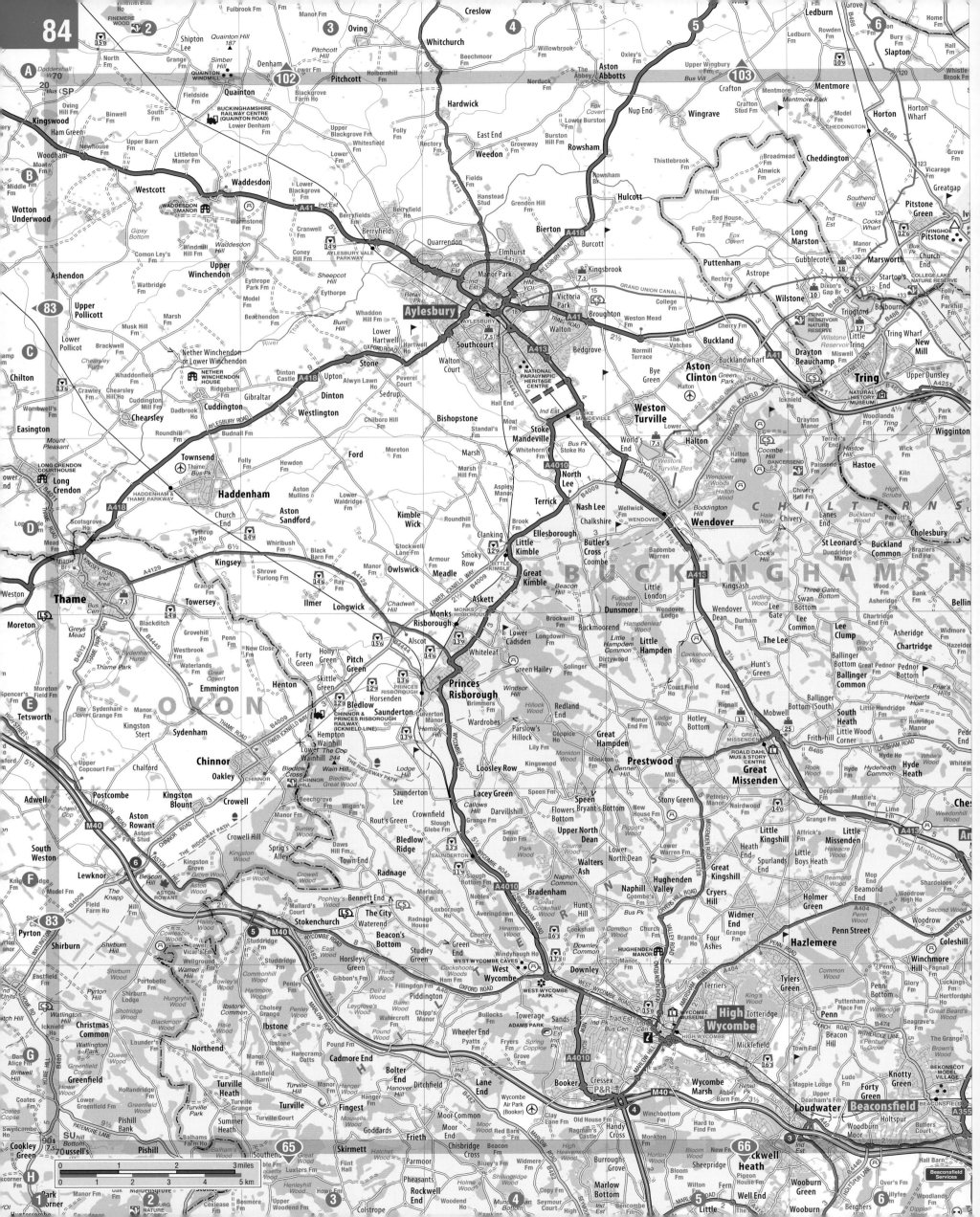

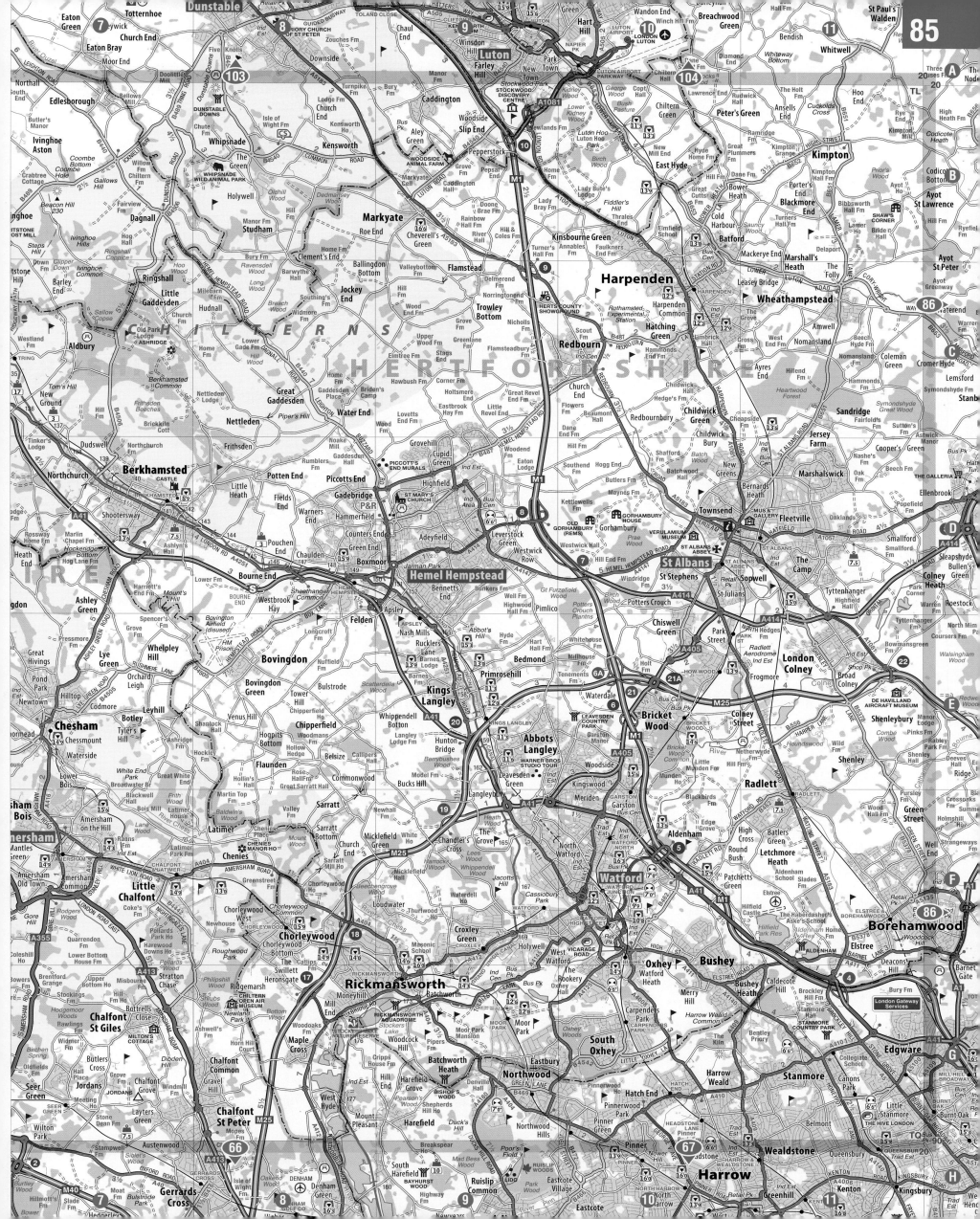

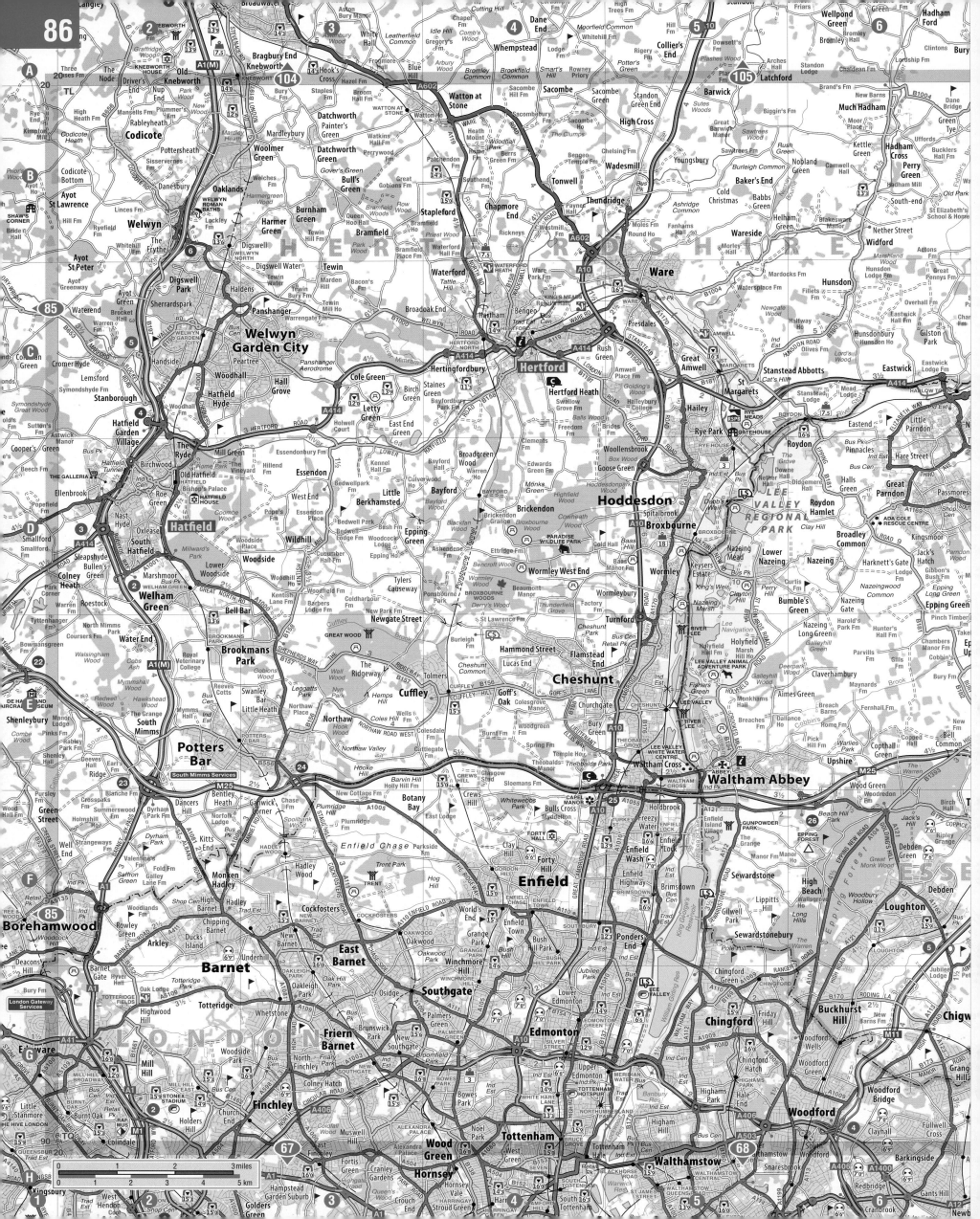

A
60
50
SM

B

C

D

IRISH SEA

MÔR IWERDDON

E

F

G

20 SM
60

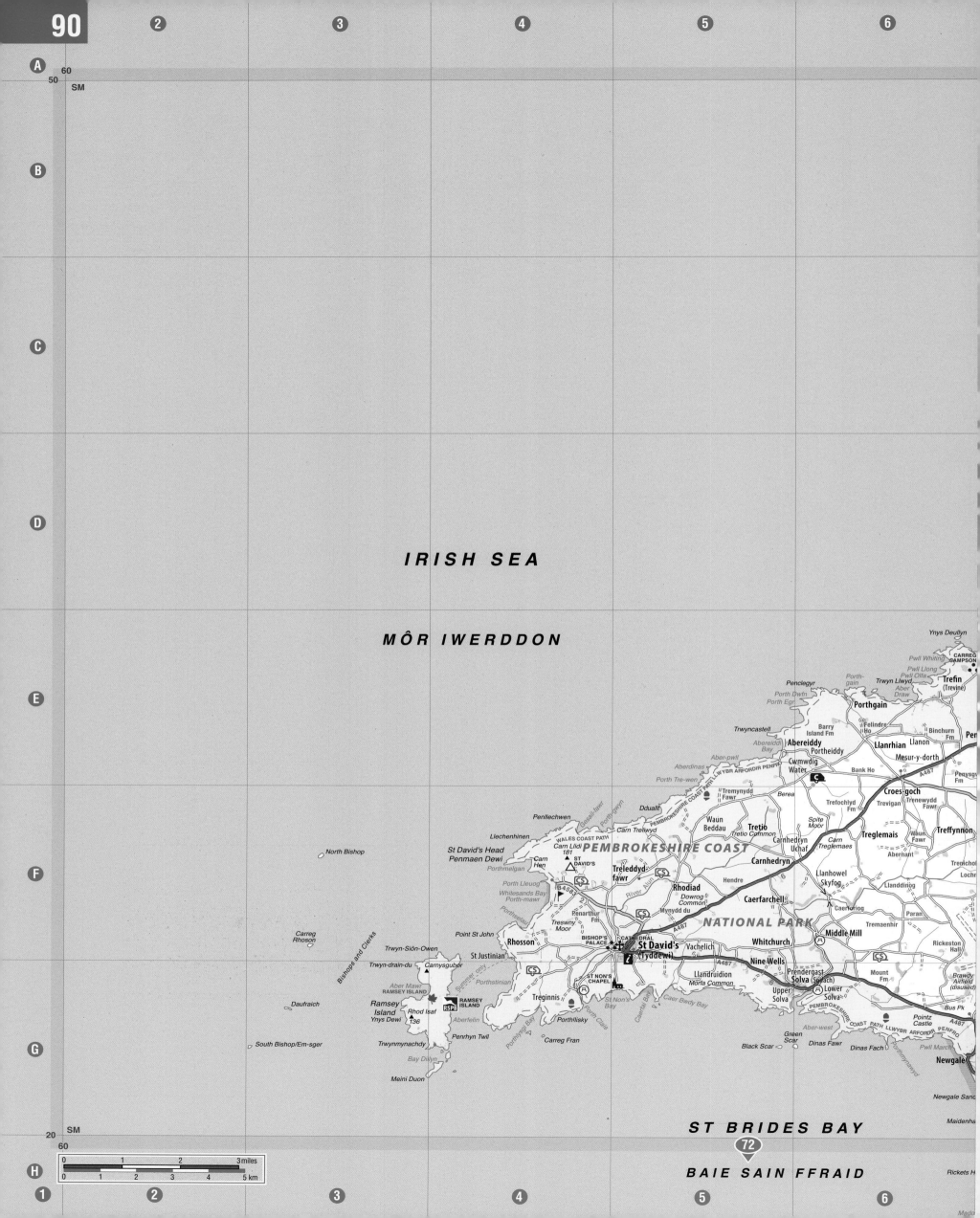

ST BRIDES BAY

(72)

BAIE SAIN FFRAID

Ynys Deullyn
Pwll Whiting
CARREG
SAMPSON
Pwll Llong
Pwll Olfa
Trwyn Llwyd
Trefin
(Trevine)
Penclegyr
Porth-gain
Porth Dwfn
Aber Draw
Porth Egr
Porthgain
Trwyncastell
Barry
Island Fm
Felindre
Binchurn
Fm
Llanon
Pen
Abereiddi
Bay
Abereiddy
Portheiddy
Llanrhian
Aberdinas
Cwmwdig
Water
Mesur-y-dorth
A487
Peqysg
Fm
Porth Tre-wen
PEMBROKESHIRE COAST PATH LLWYBR ARFORDIR PENFRO
Tremynydd
Fawr
Bank Ho
Croes-goch
Penllechwen
Dduallt
Berea
Trefochlyd
Fm
Trevigan
Trenewydd
Fawr
Llechenhinen
Carn Treliwyd
Waun
Beddau
Tretio
Tretio Common
Spite
Moor
Carn
Treglemaes
Treglemais
Waun
Fawr
Treffynnon
North Bishop
St David's Head
Penmaen Dewi
Carn Llidi
181
ST
DAVID'S
PEMBROKESHIRE COAST
Carnhedryn
Uchaf
Carn
Fawr
Abernant
Carn
Hen
Porthmelgan
**Treleddyd
fawr**
Carnhedryn
Tremichol
Llanhowel
Skyfog
Llanddinog
Porth Lleuog
Whitesands Bay
Porth-mawr
B4583
Rhodiad
Hendre
Caerfarchell
Paran
Porthsefin
Dowrog
Common
Mynydd du
Caeriog
Tremaenhir
Carreg
Rhoson
Point St John
Penarthur
NATIONAL PARK
Rickeston
Hall
Rhosson
BISHOP'S
PALACE
CATHEDRAL
St David's
(Tyddewi)
Vachelich
Whitchurch
Middle Mill
Twyn-Siôn-Owen
St Justinian
i
Treswny
Moor
Nine Wells
Twyn-drain-du
Carnysgubor
Summer only
Porthstinian
ST NON'S
CHAPEL
Prendergast
Solva
(Solfach)
Mount
Fm
Brawdy
Airfield
(disused)
Daufraich
Aber Mawr
RAMSEY ISLAND
RAMSEY
ISLAND
Llandruidion
Morfa Common
**Ramsey
Island**
Ynys Dewi
Rhod Isaf
136
RSPB
Aberfelin
Treginnis
St Non's
Bay
Caer Bwdy Bay
**Upper
Solva**
**Lower
Solva**
PEMBROKESHIRE
Bus Pk
A487
South Bishop/Em-sger
Trwynmynachdy
Penrhyn Twll
Porthlysgi
Porth Clais
COAST PATH LLWYBR ARFORDIR
Pointz
Castle
PENFRO
Bay Dillyn
Carreg Fran
Porthlysgi Bay
Aber-west
Black Scar
Green
Scar
Dinas Fawr
Dinas Fach
Pwll March
Meini Duon
Newgale
Newgale Sand
Maidenha
Rickets H
Mada

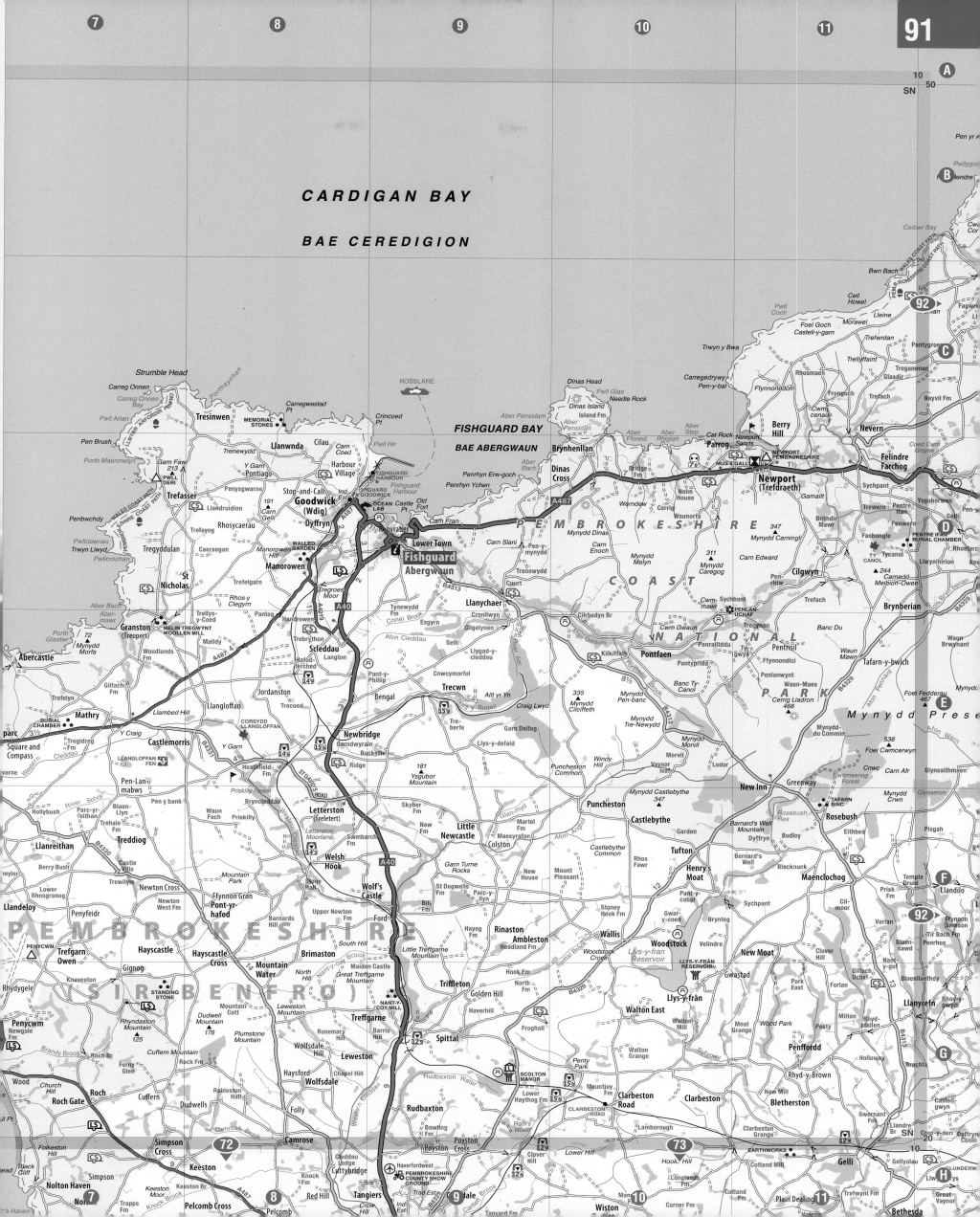

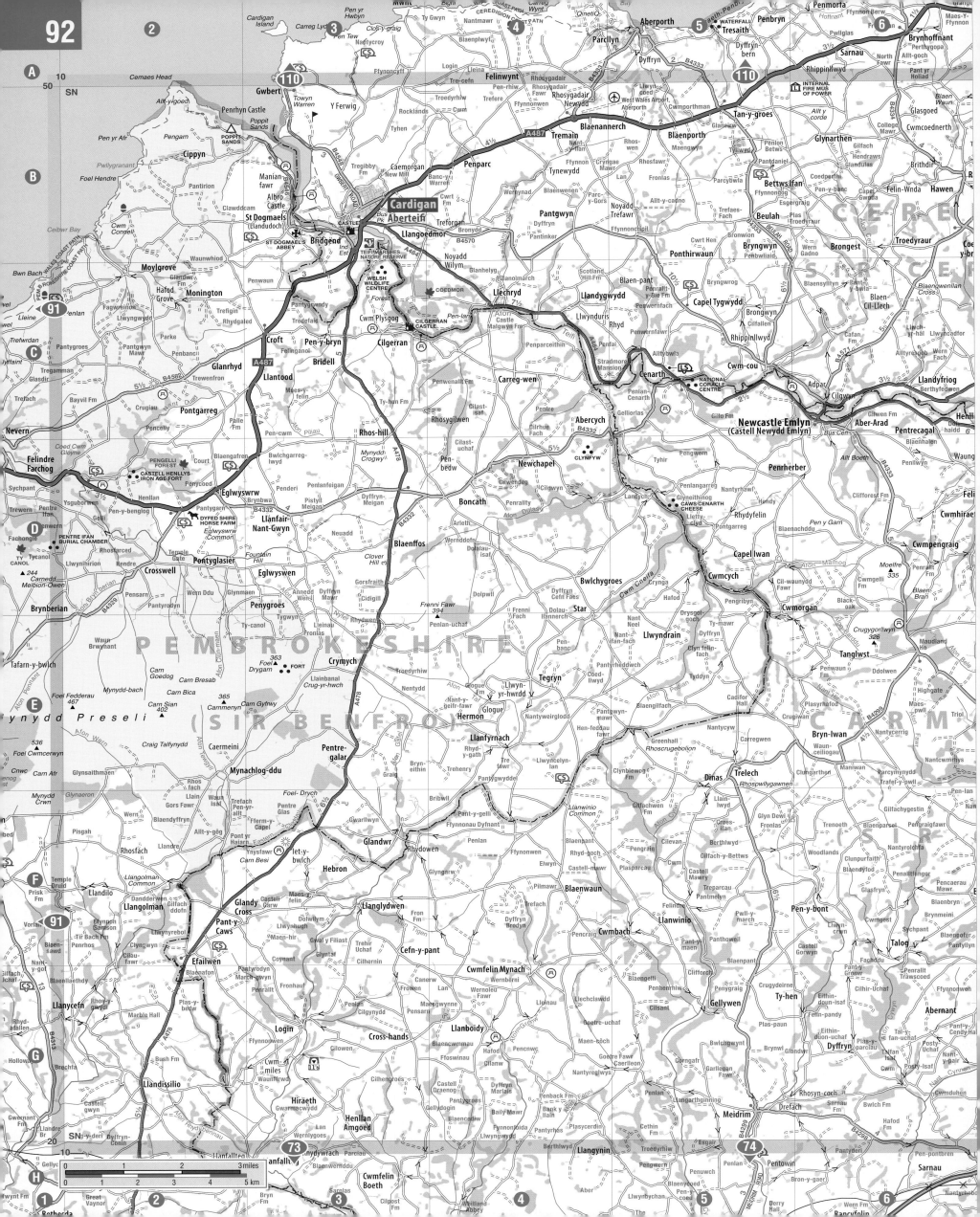

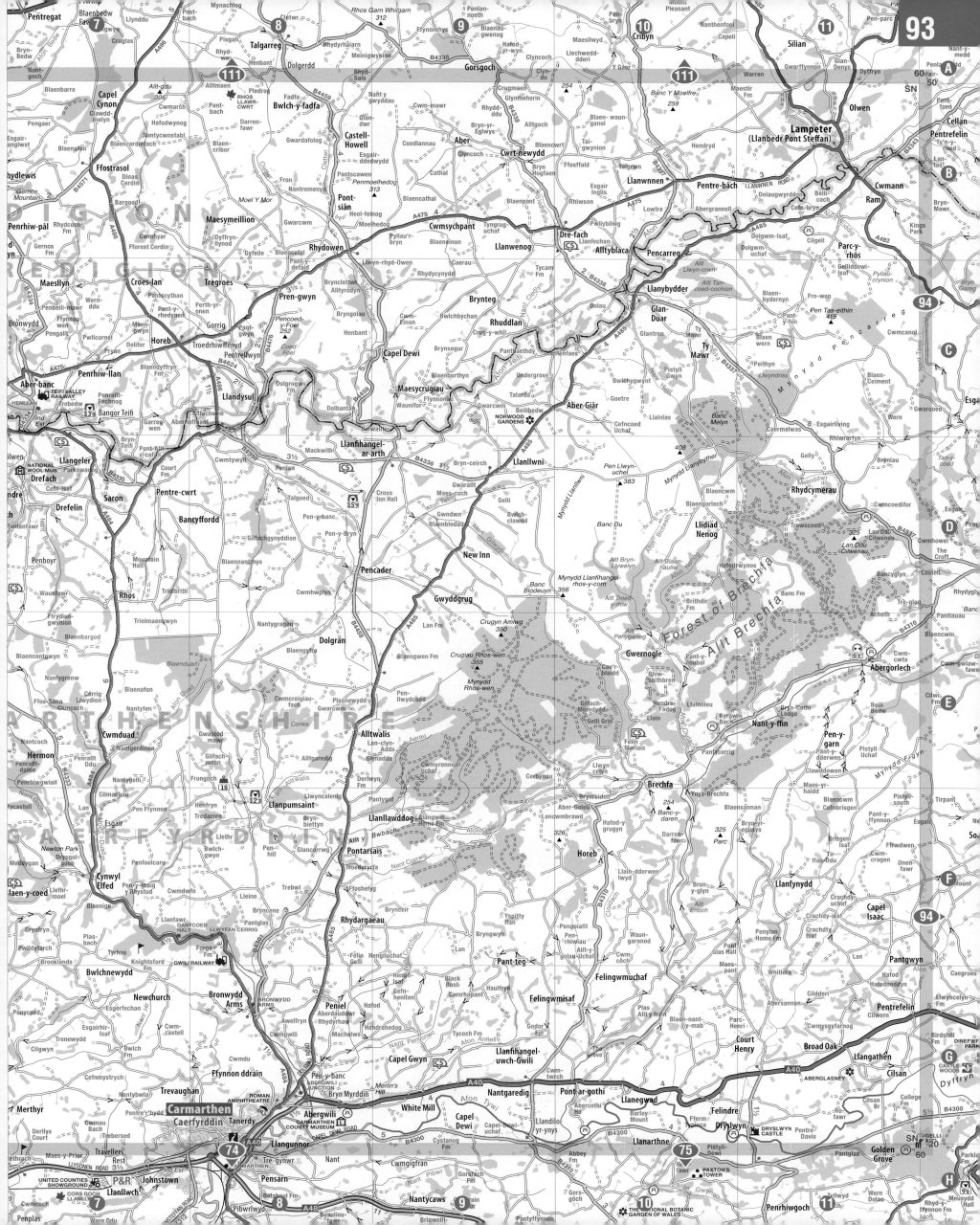

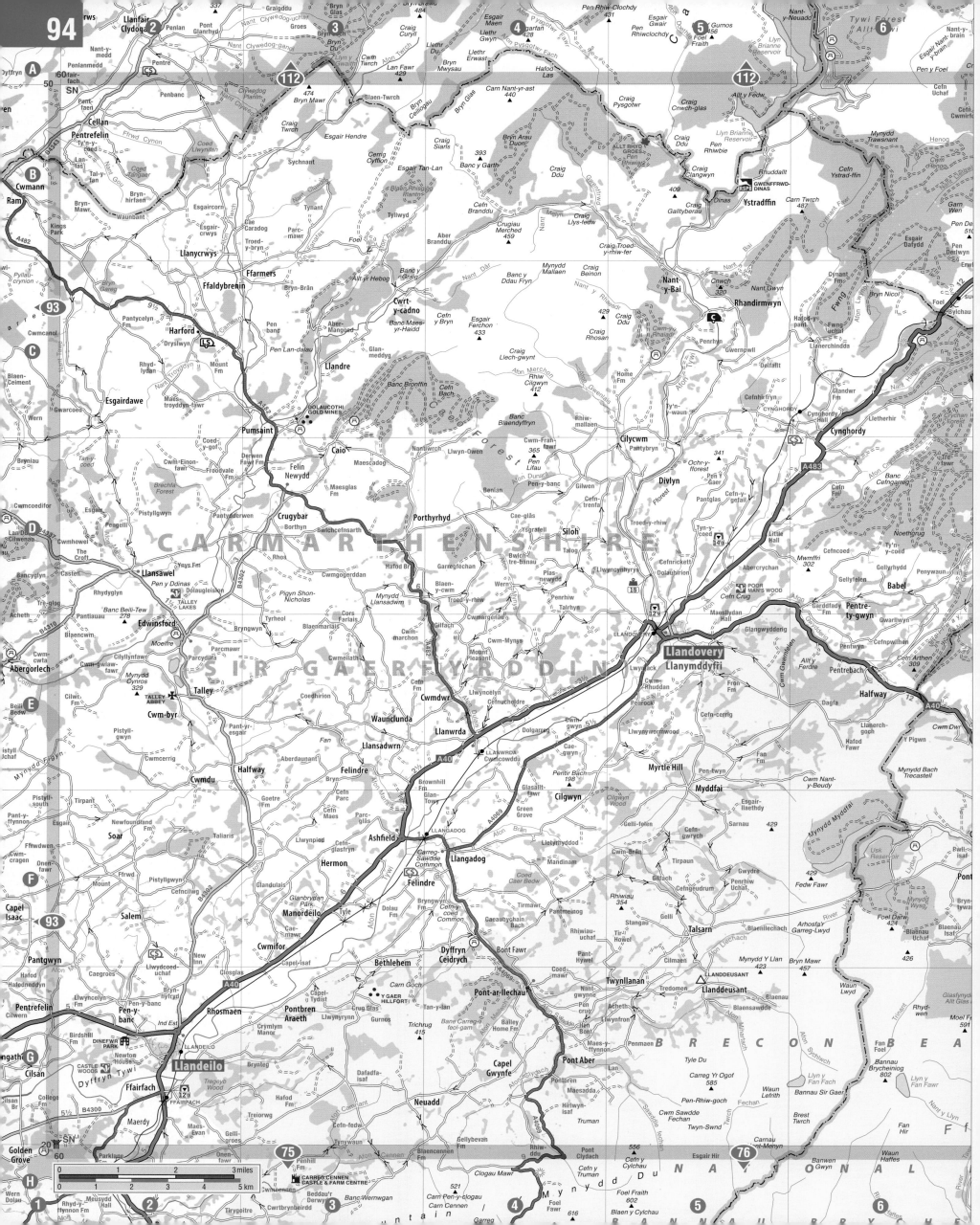

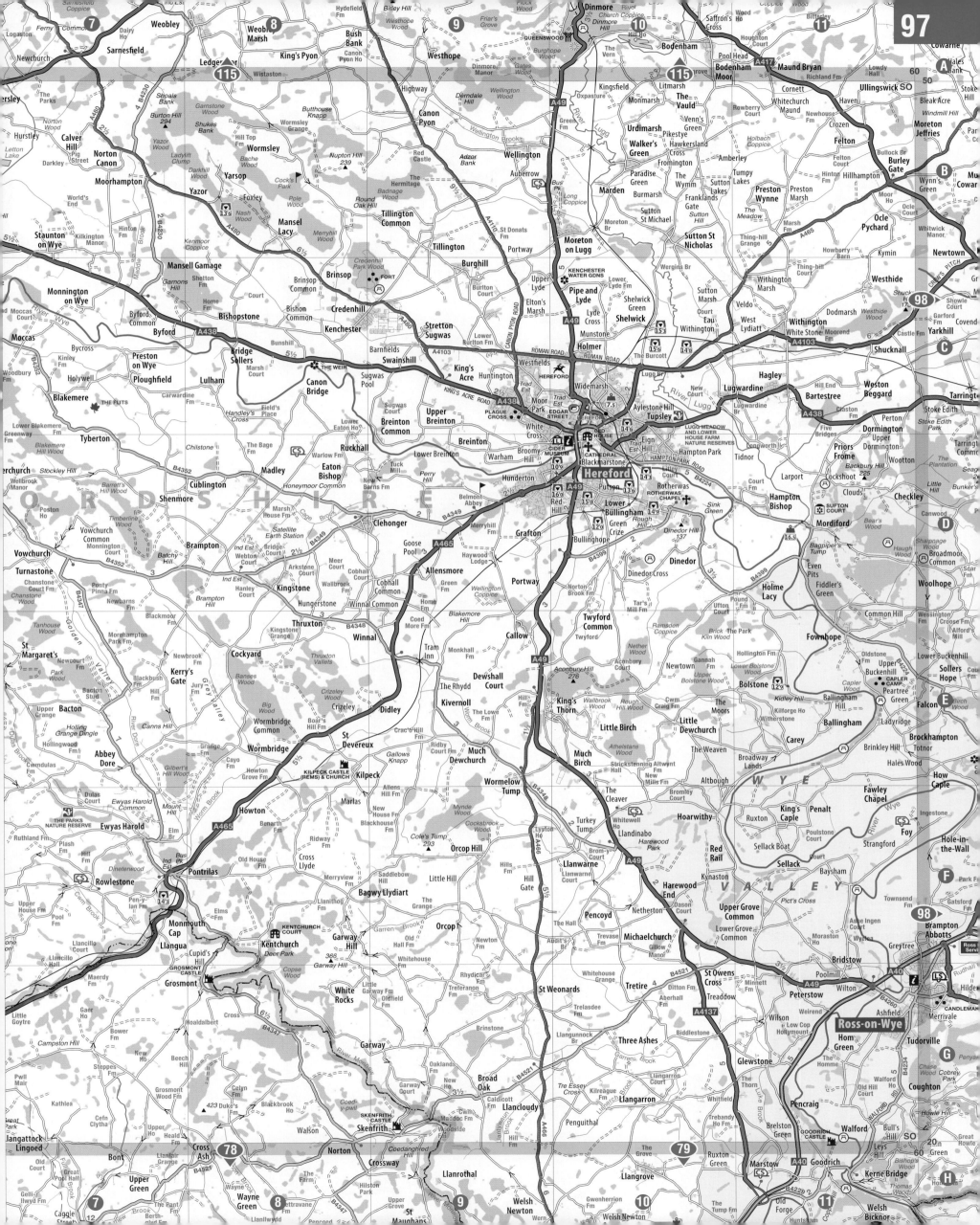

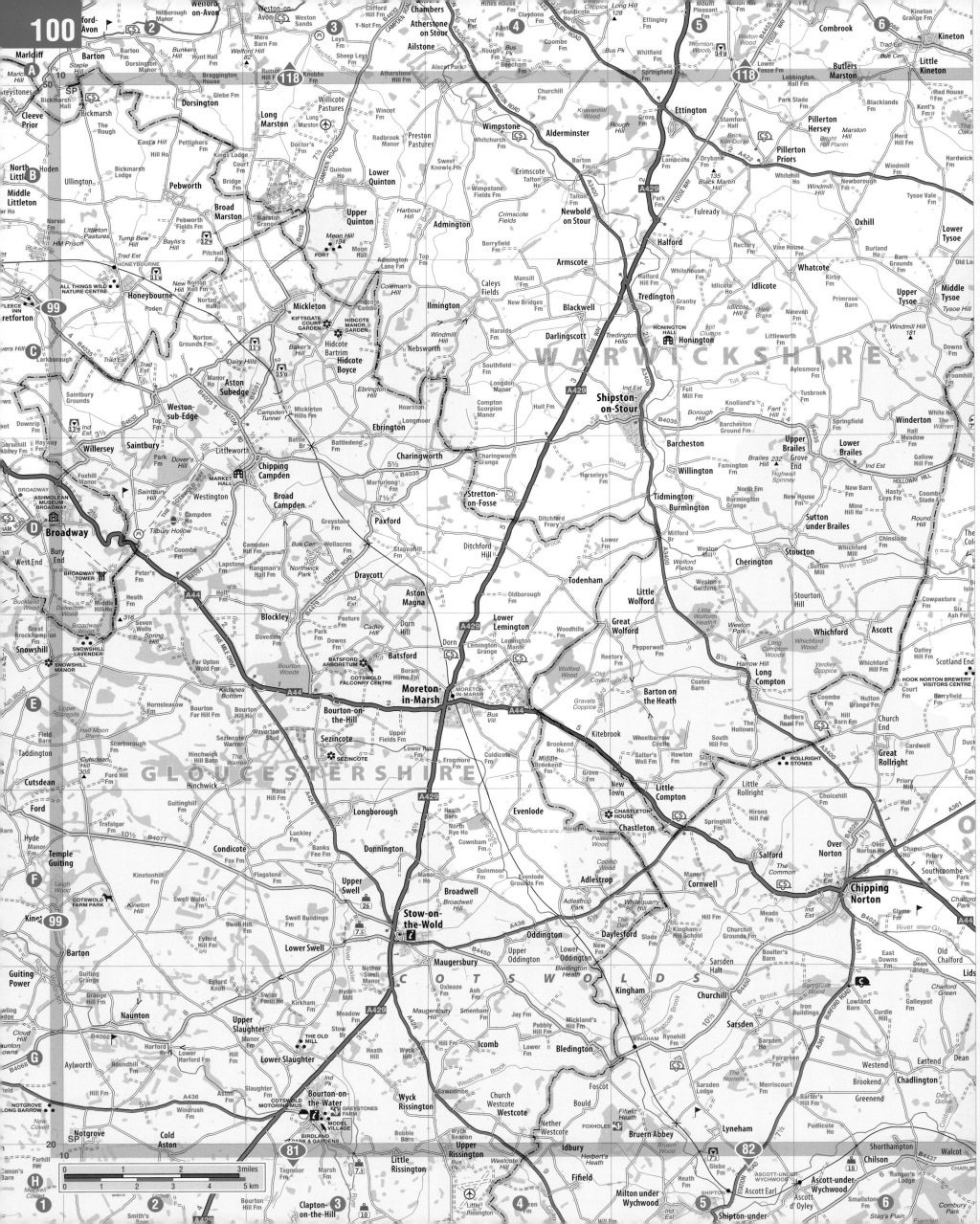

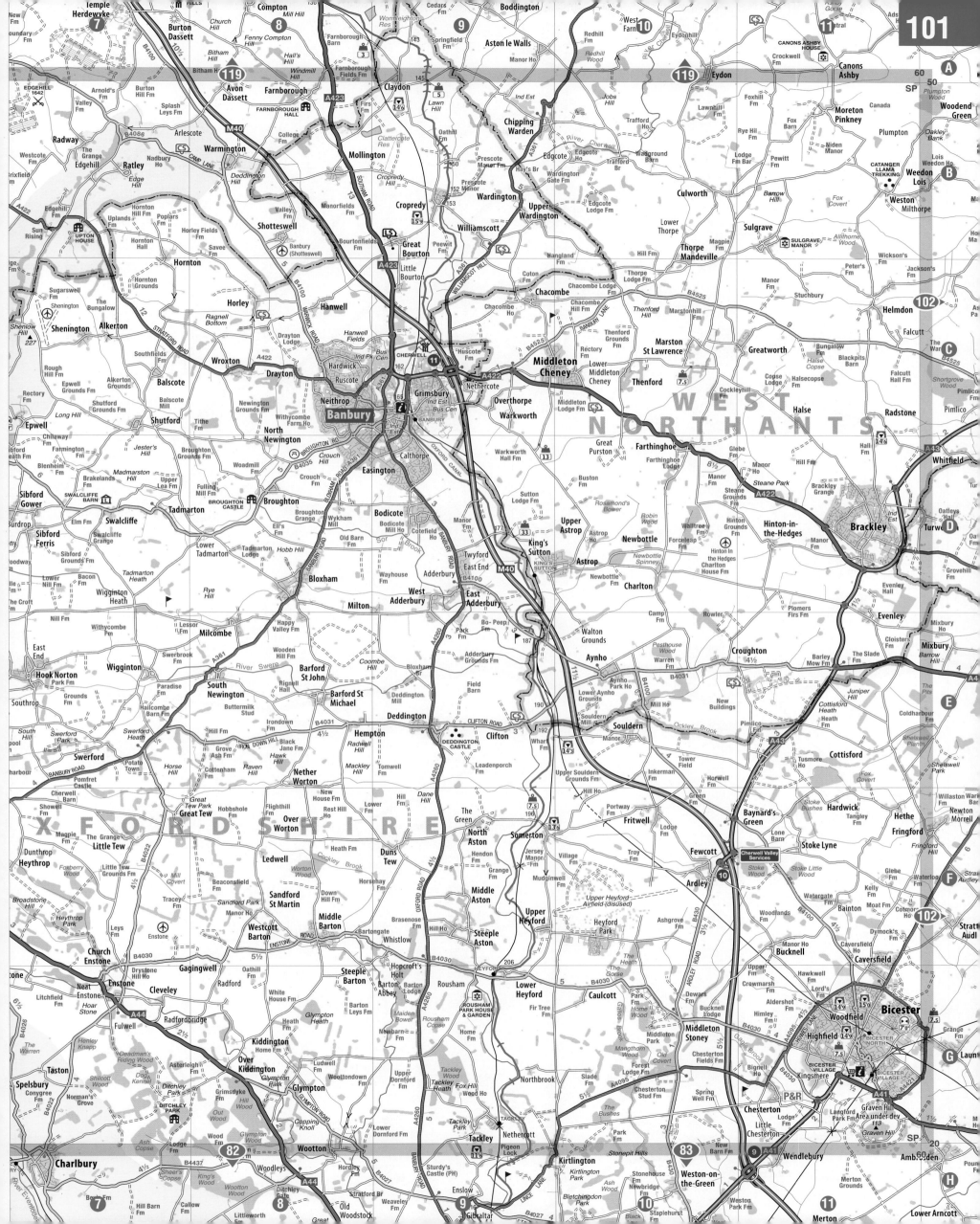

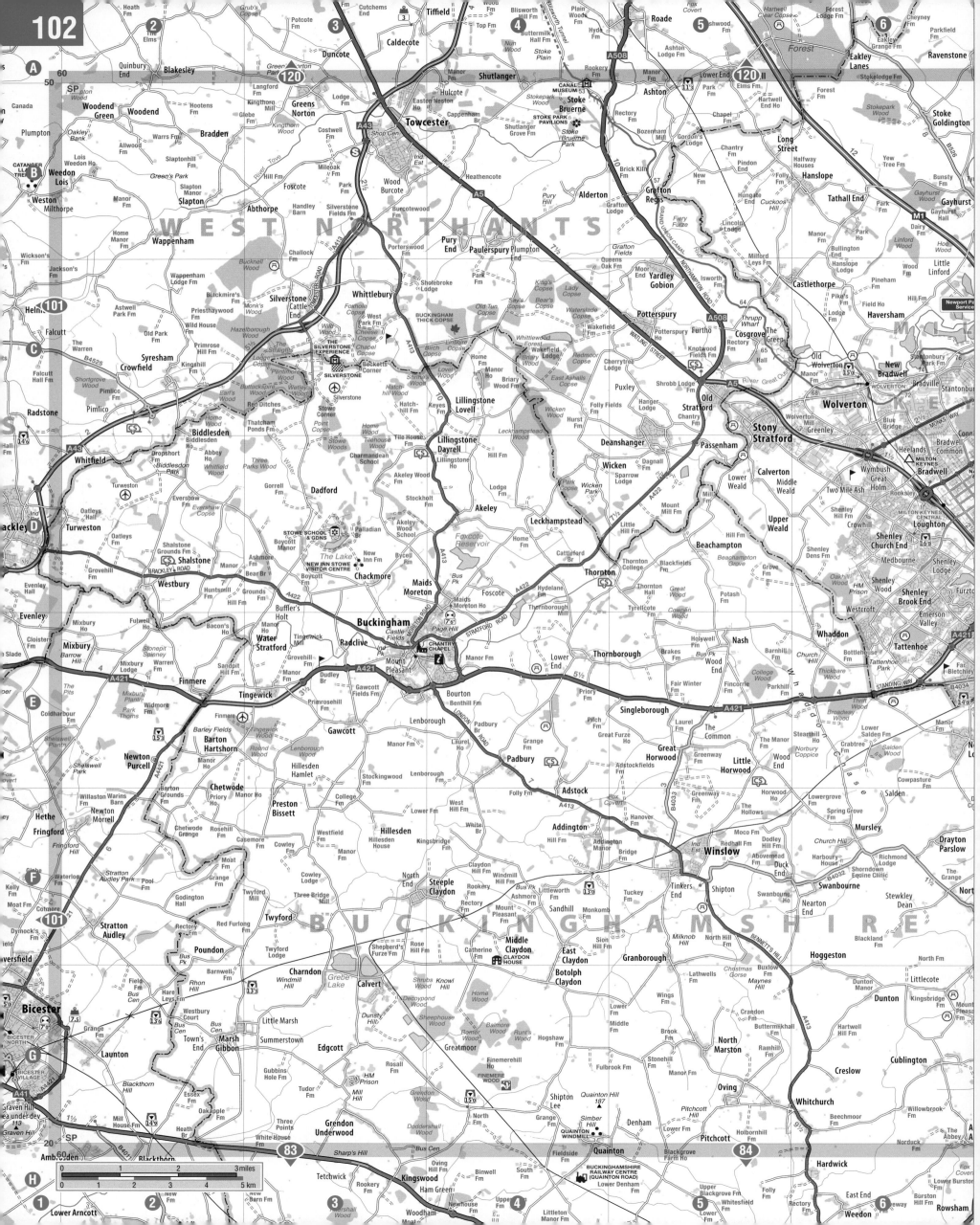

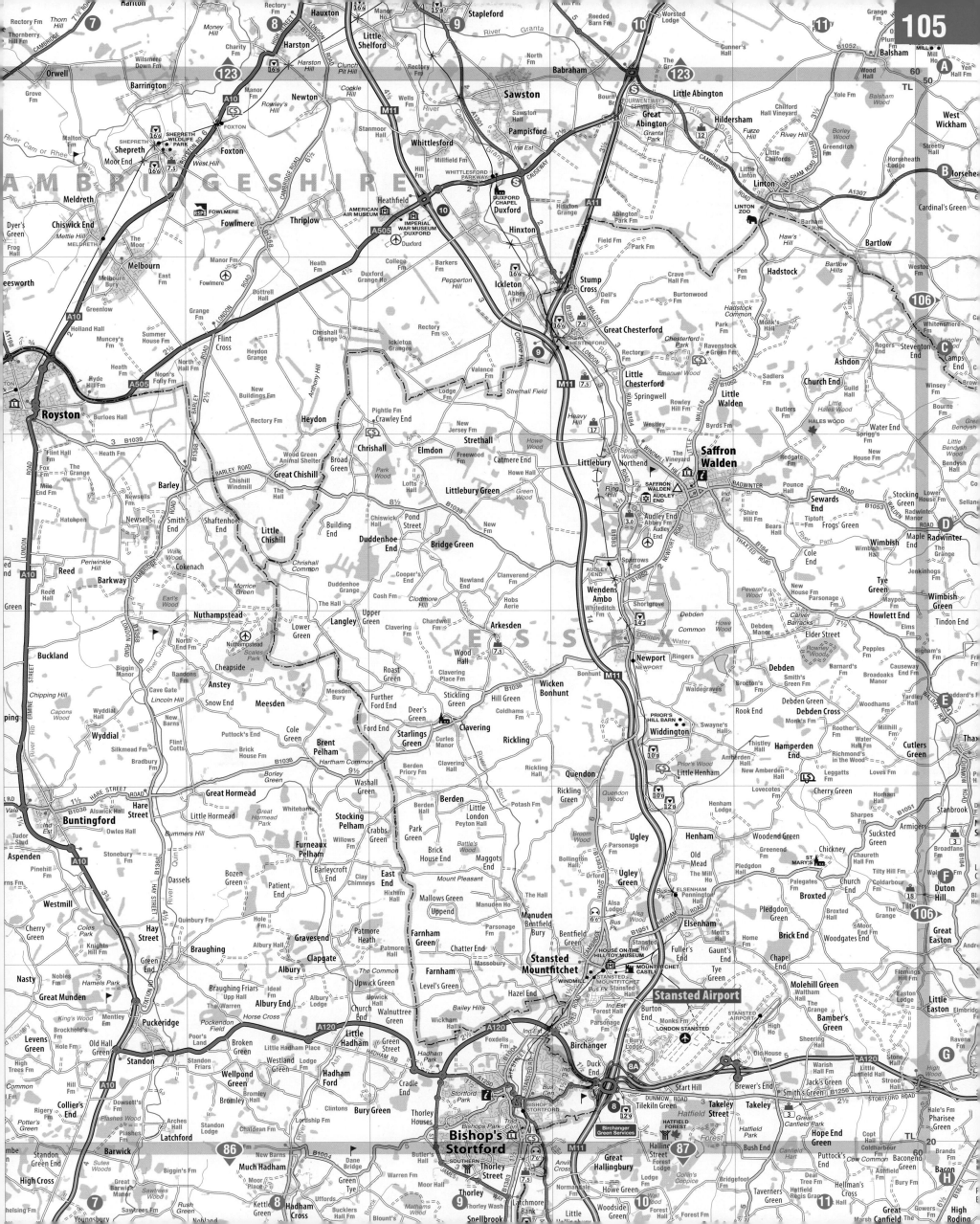

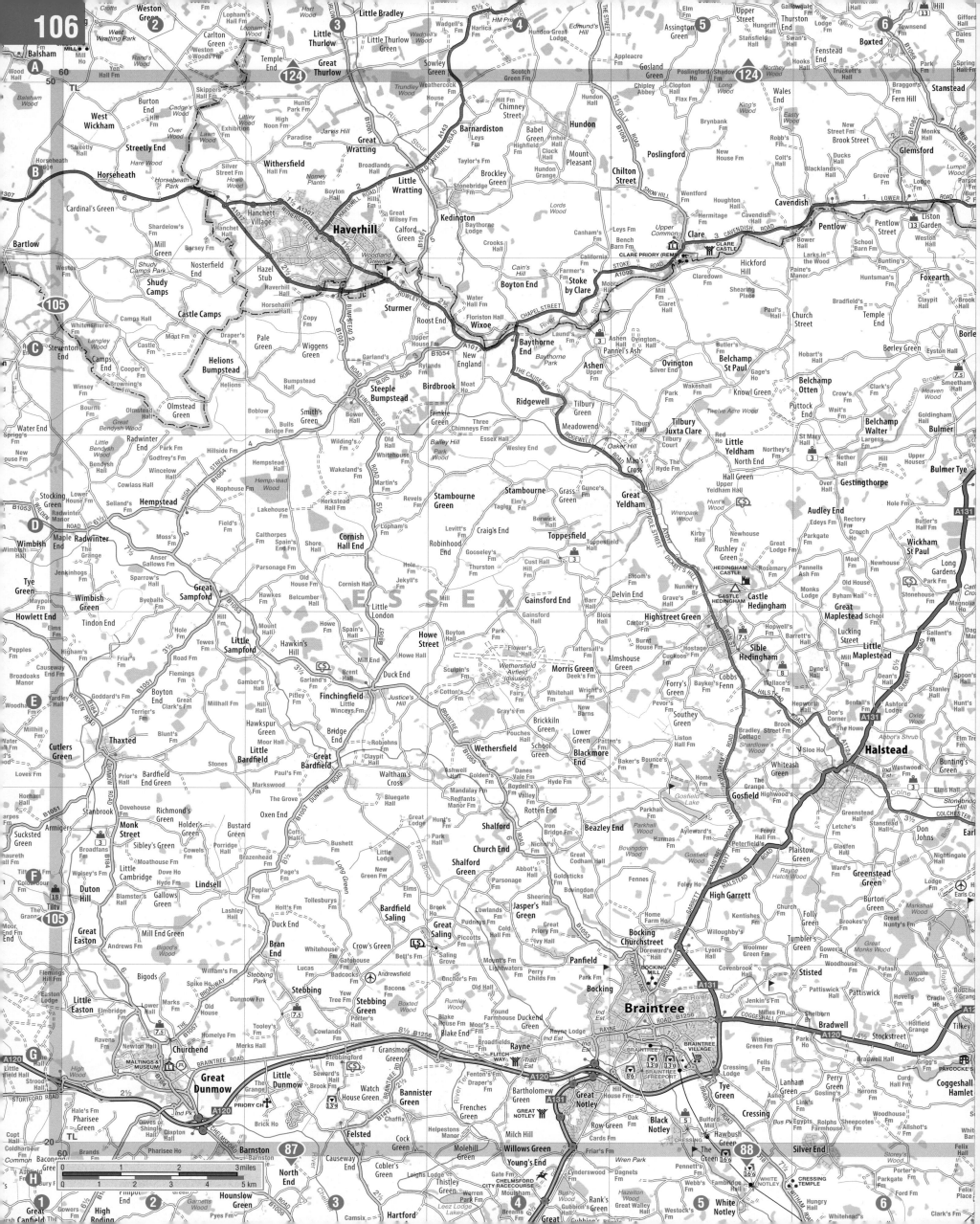

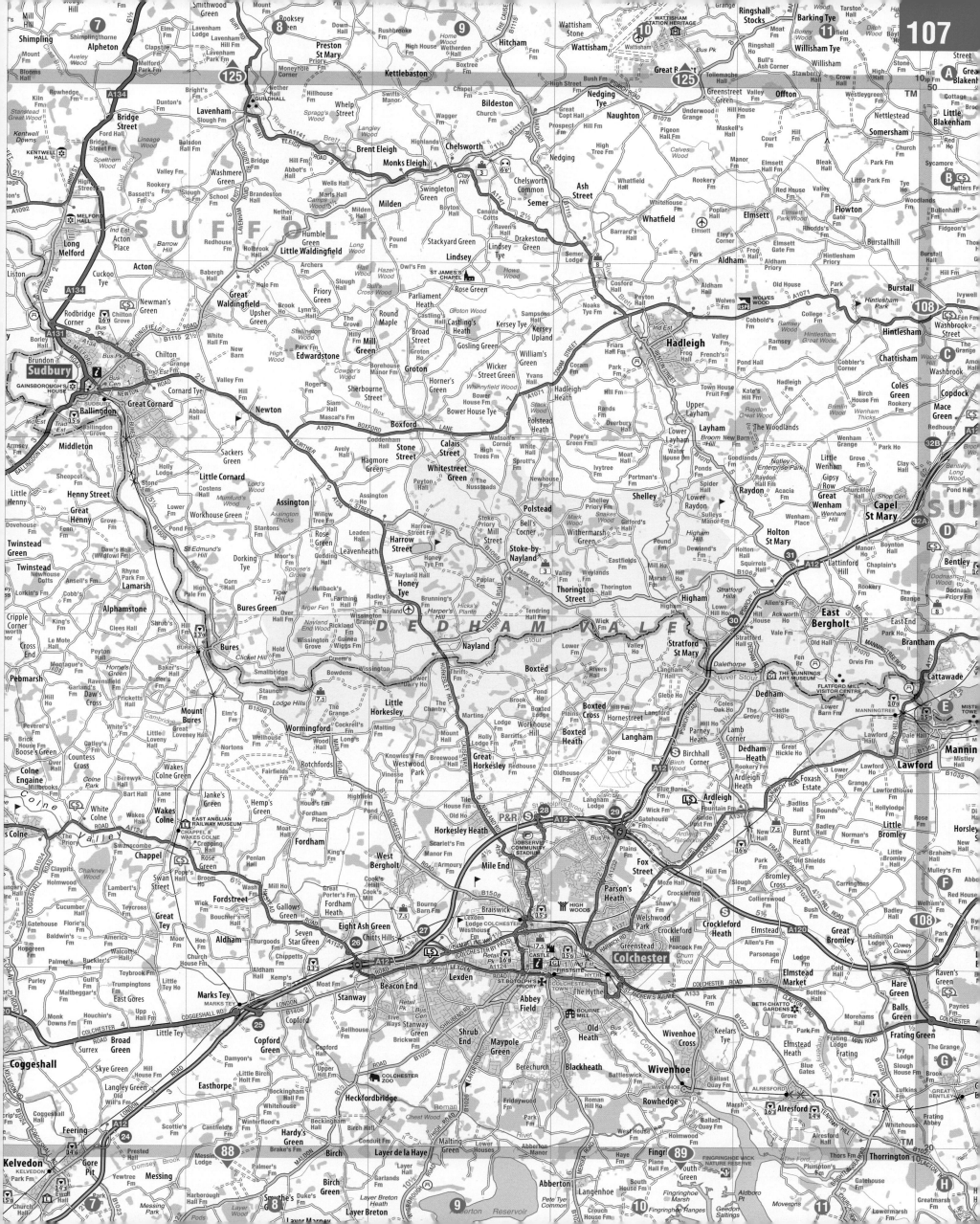

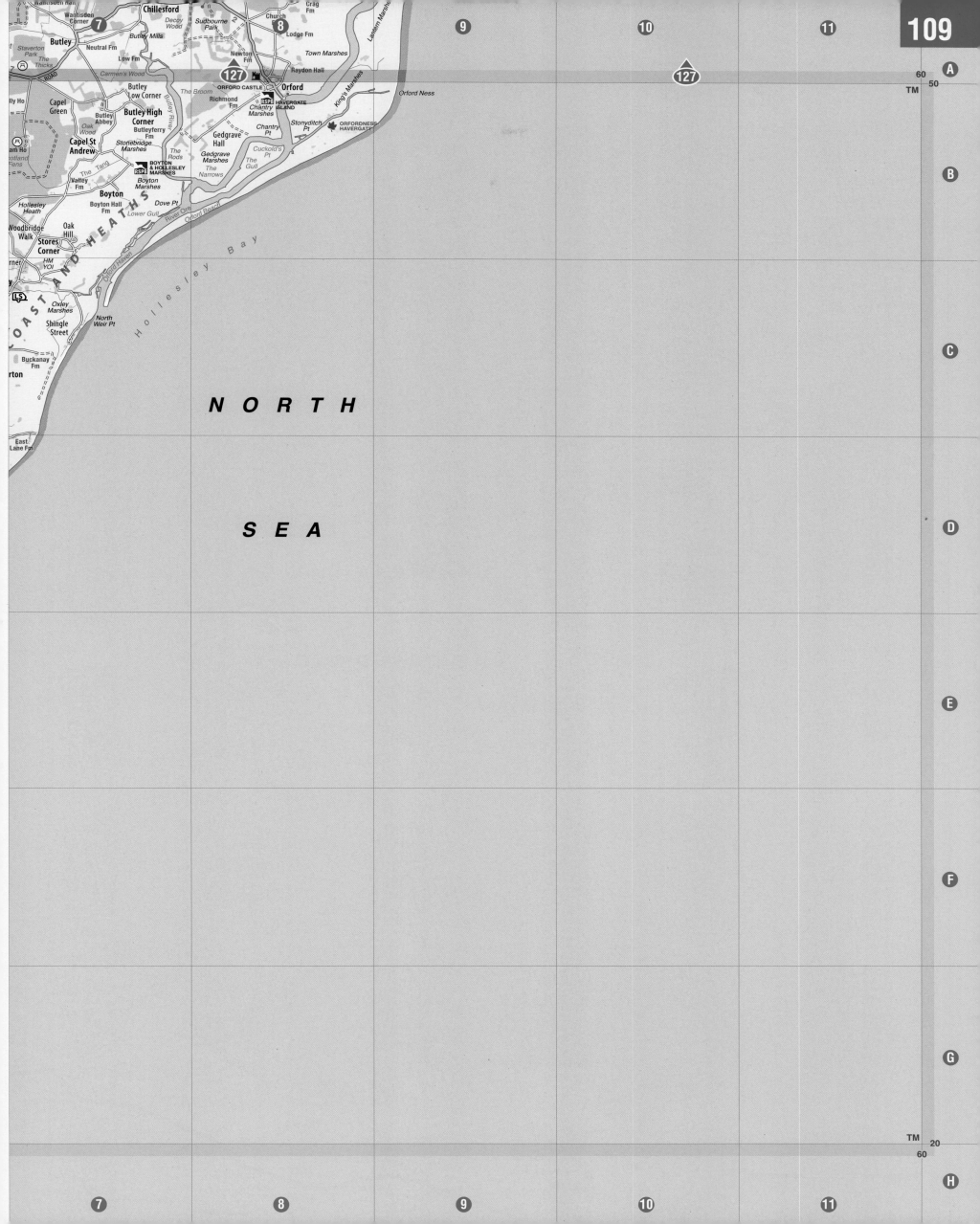

NORTH

SEA

Chillesford

Butley

Orford

Orford Ness

Hollesley Bay

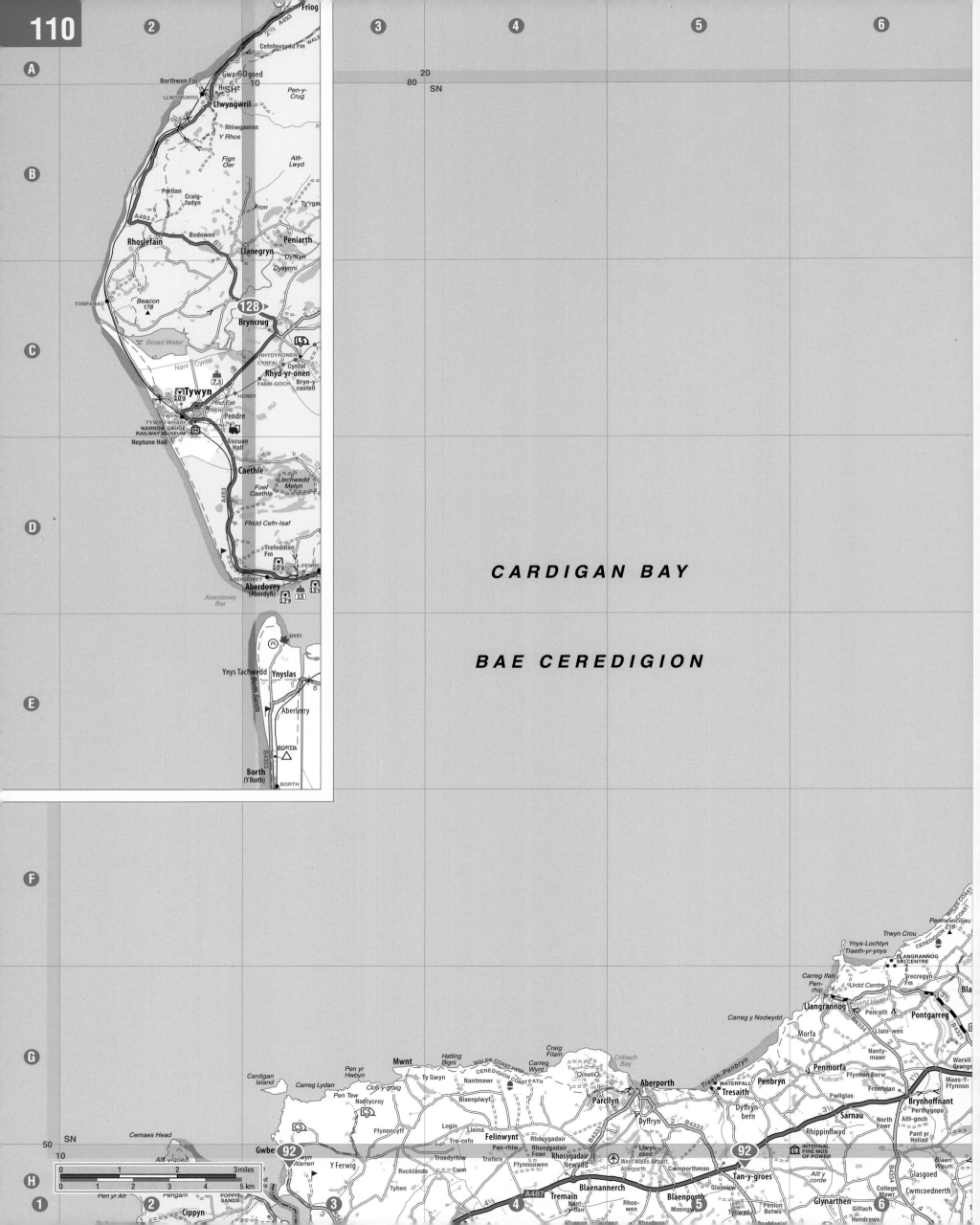

CARDIGAN BAY

BAE CEREDIGION

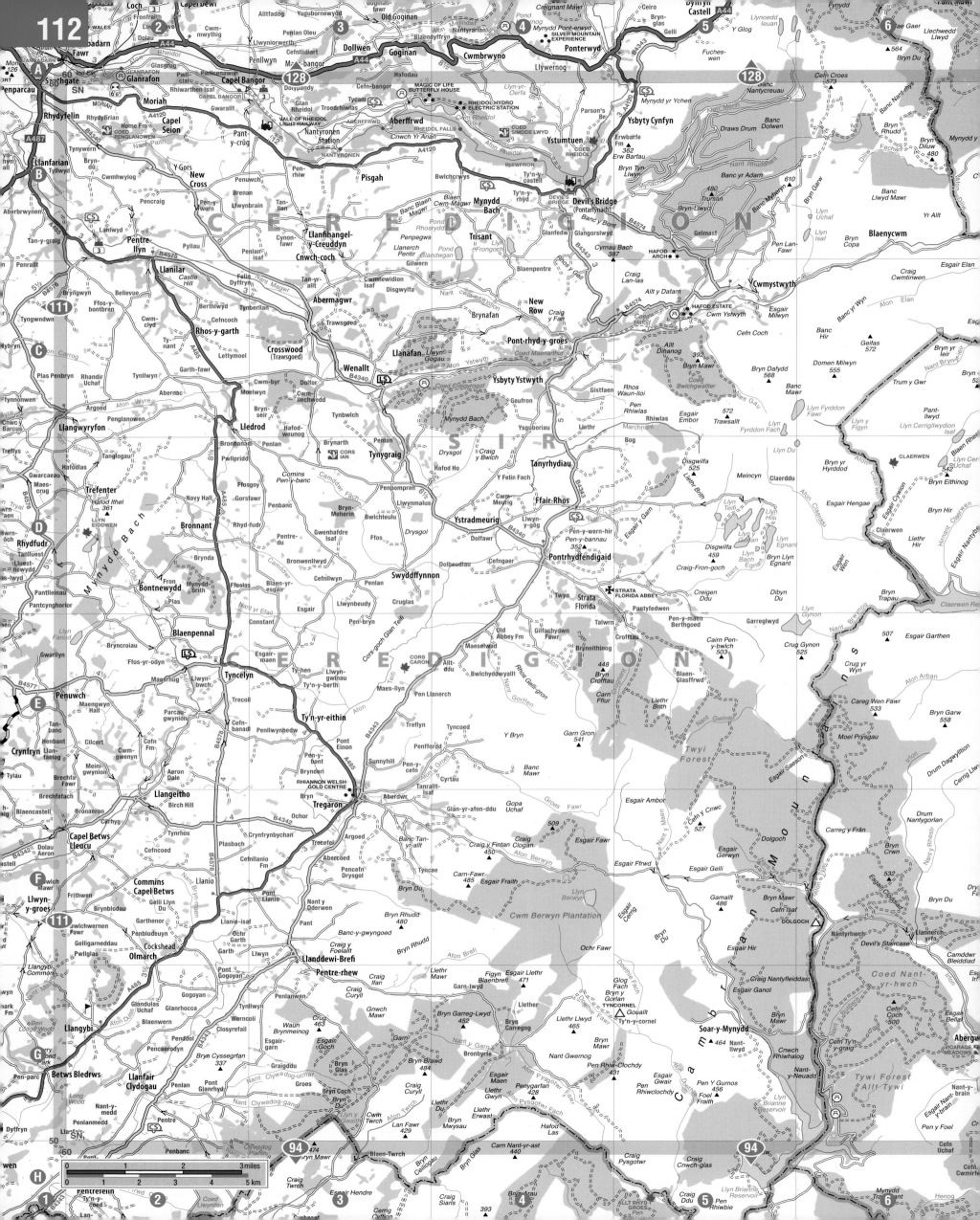

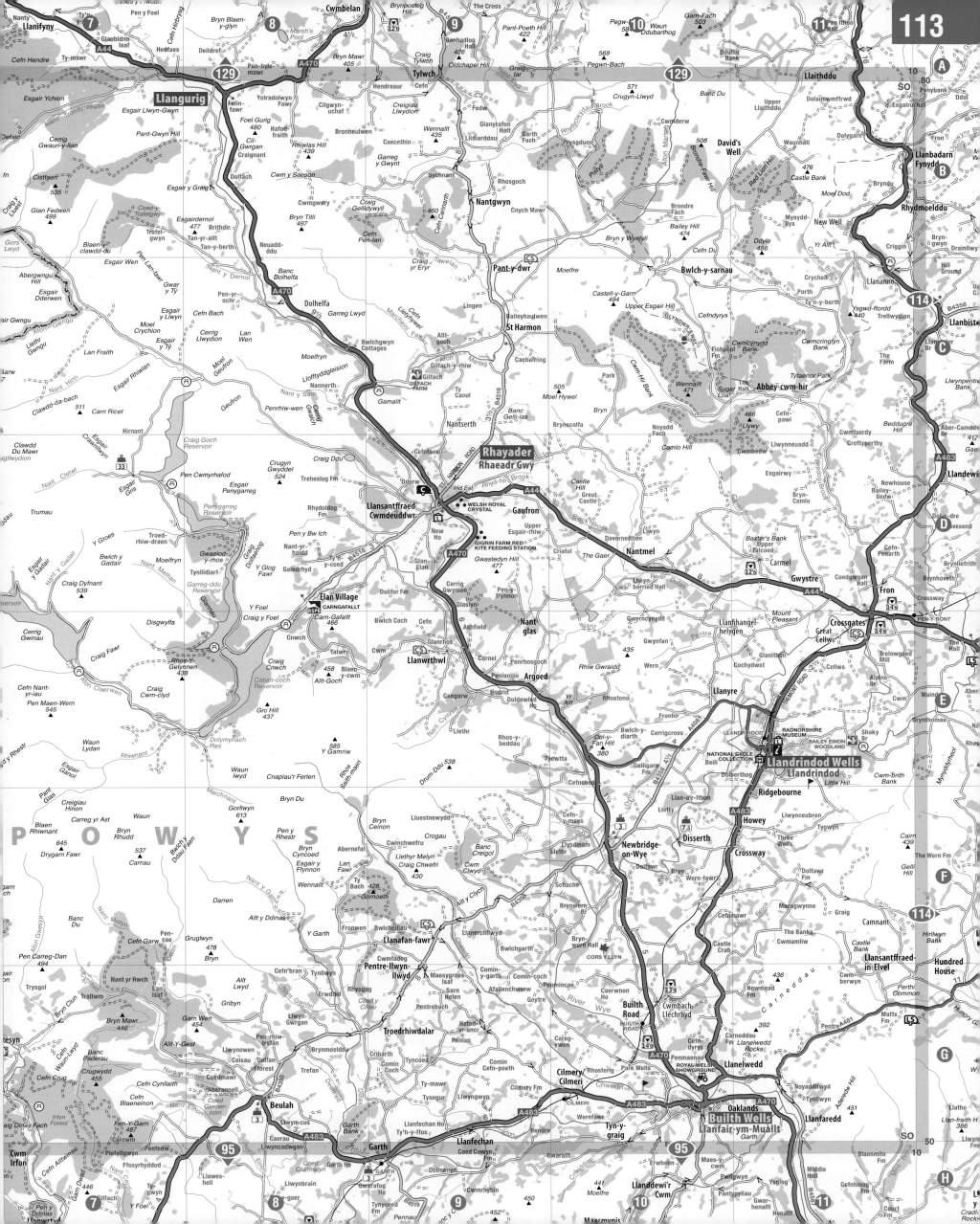

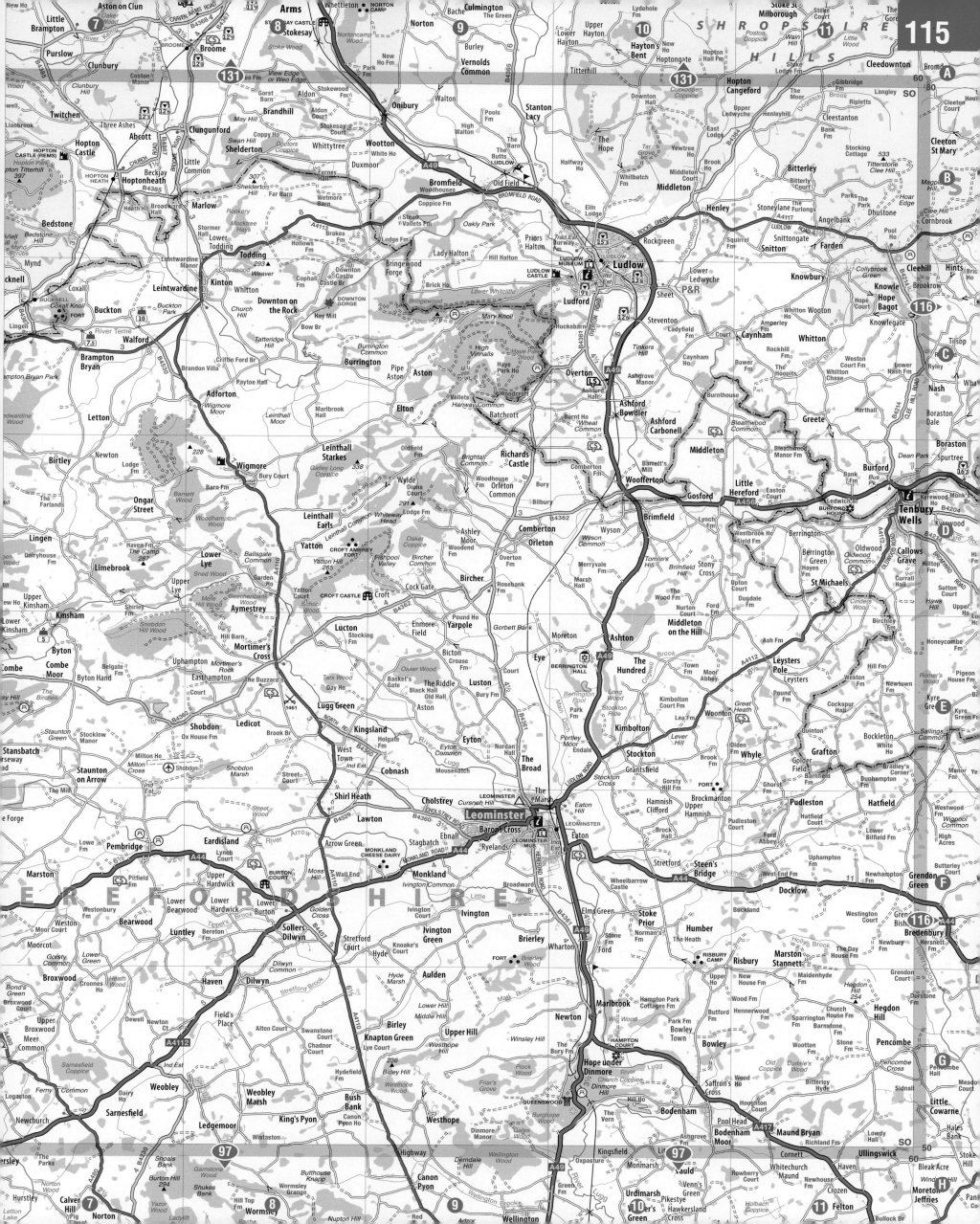

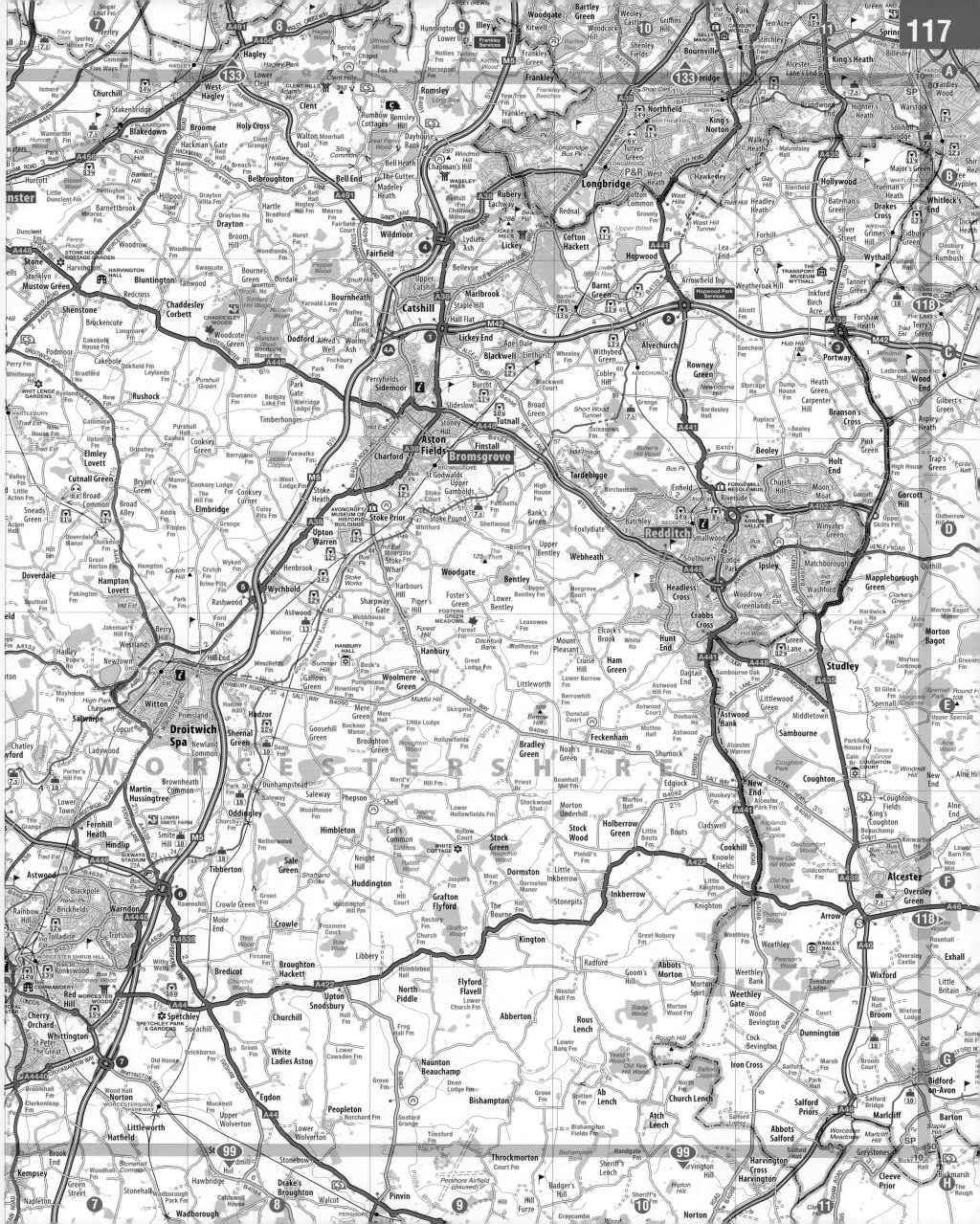

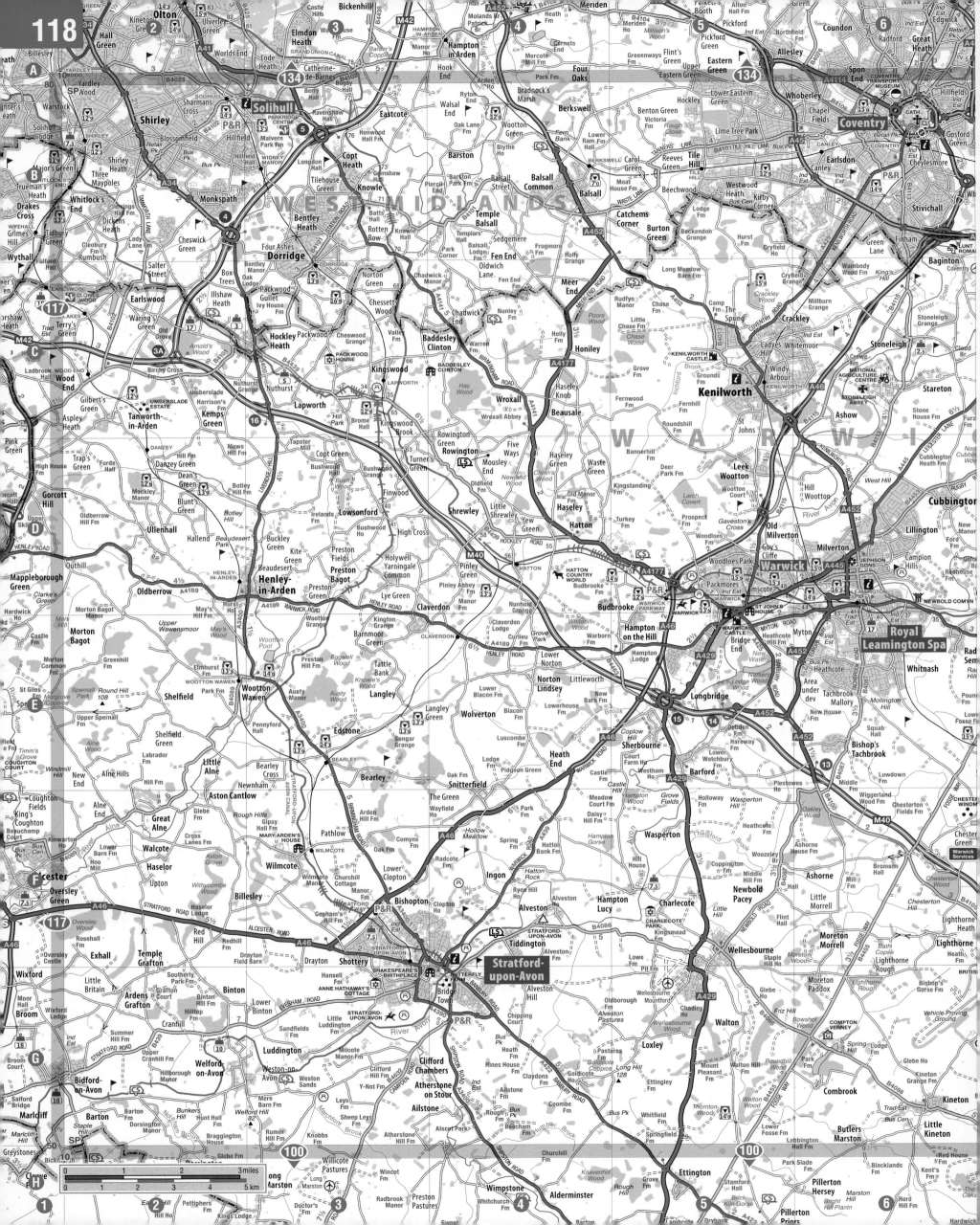

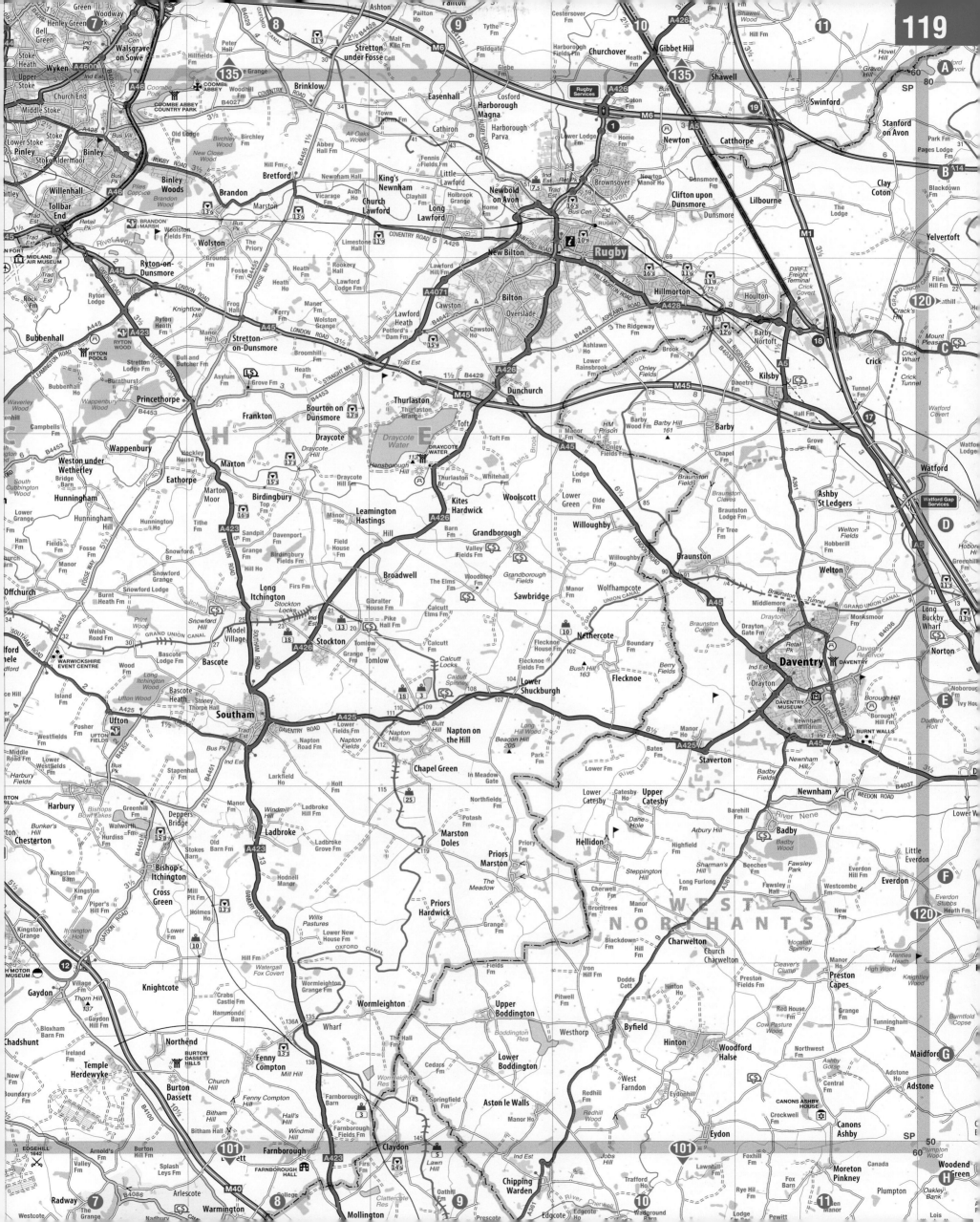

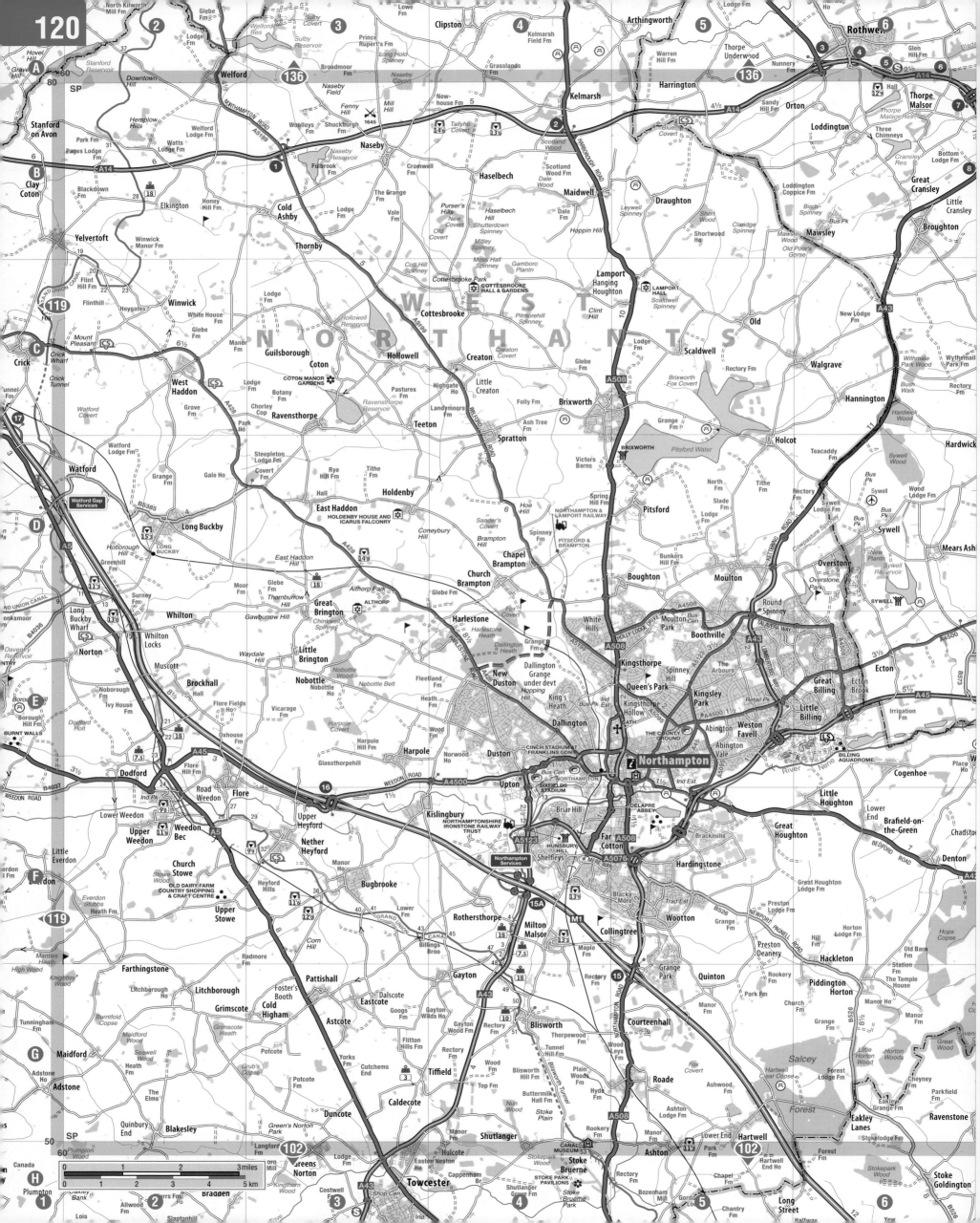

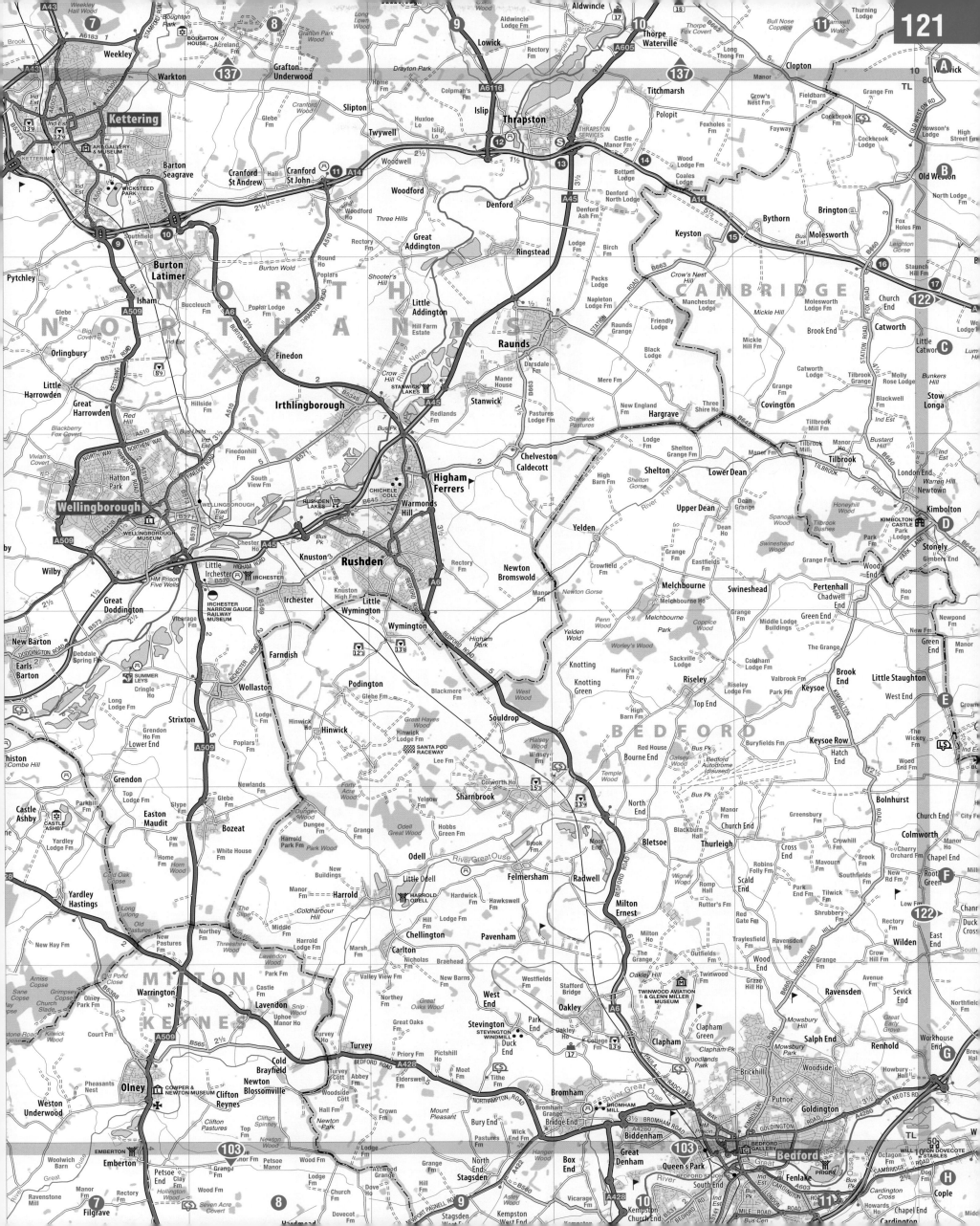

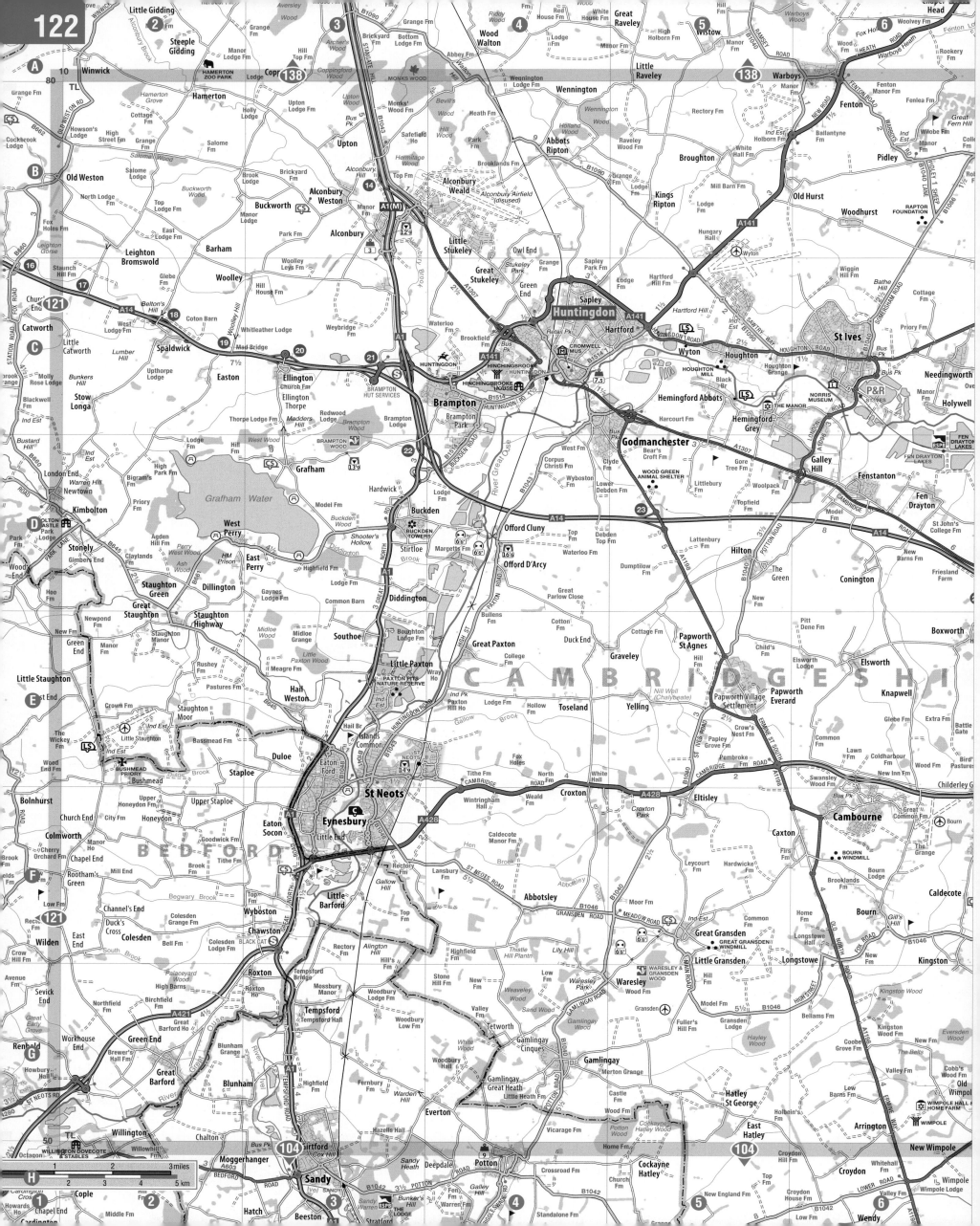

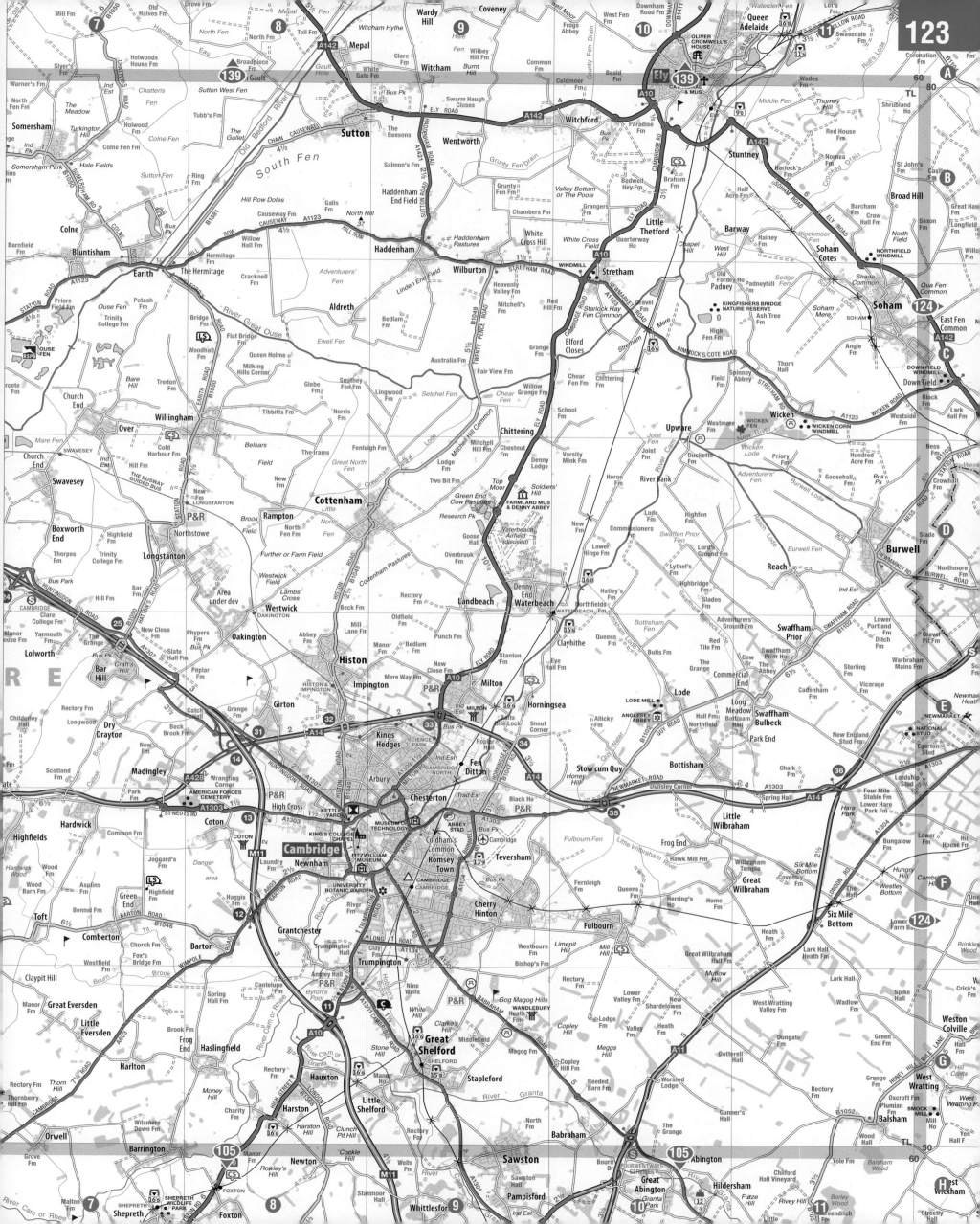

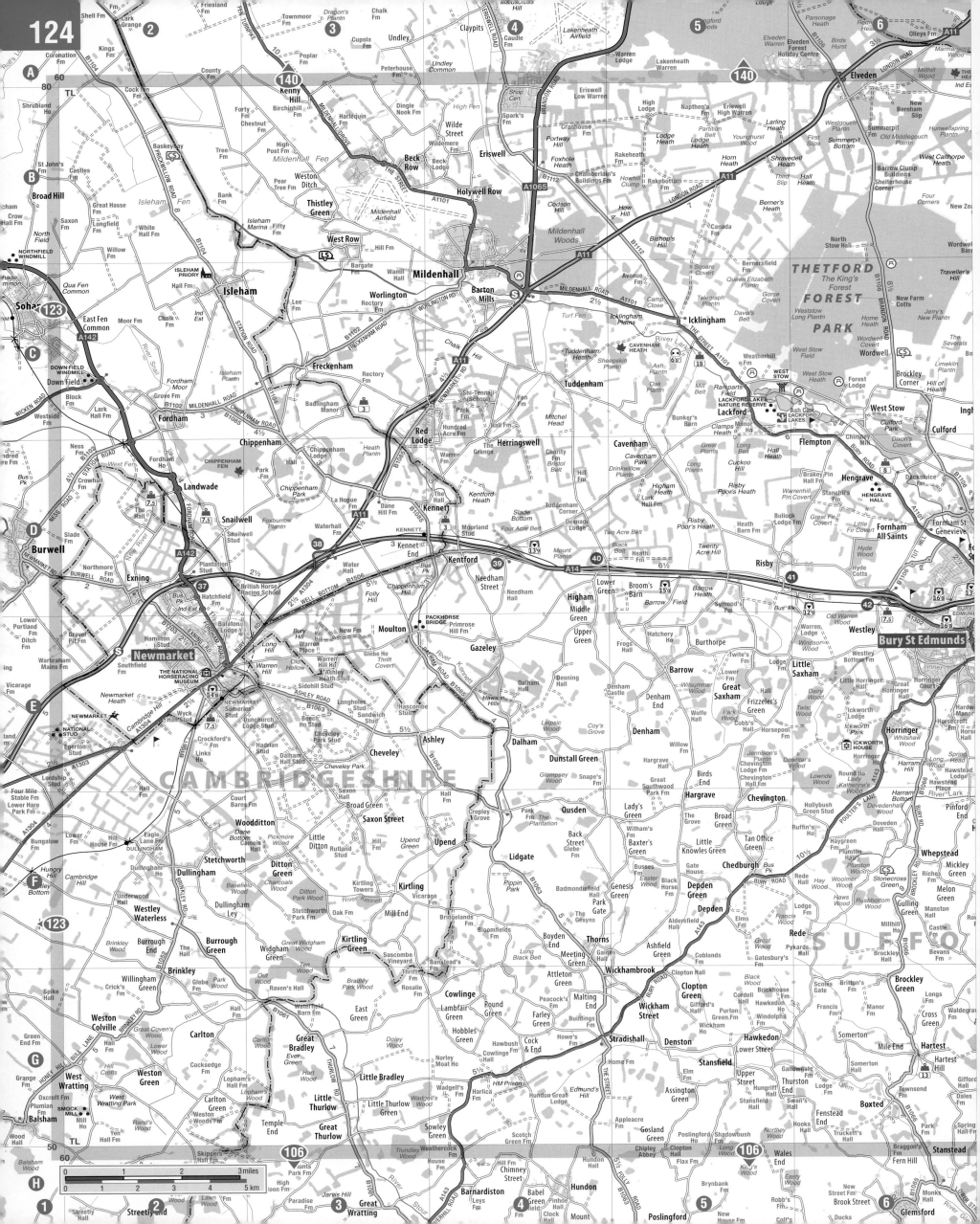

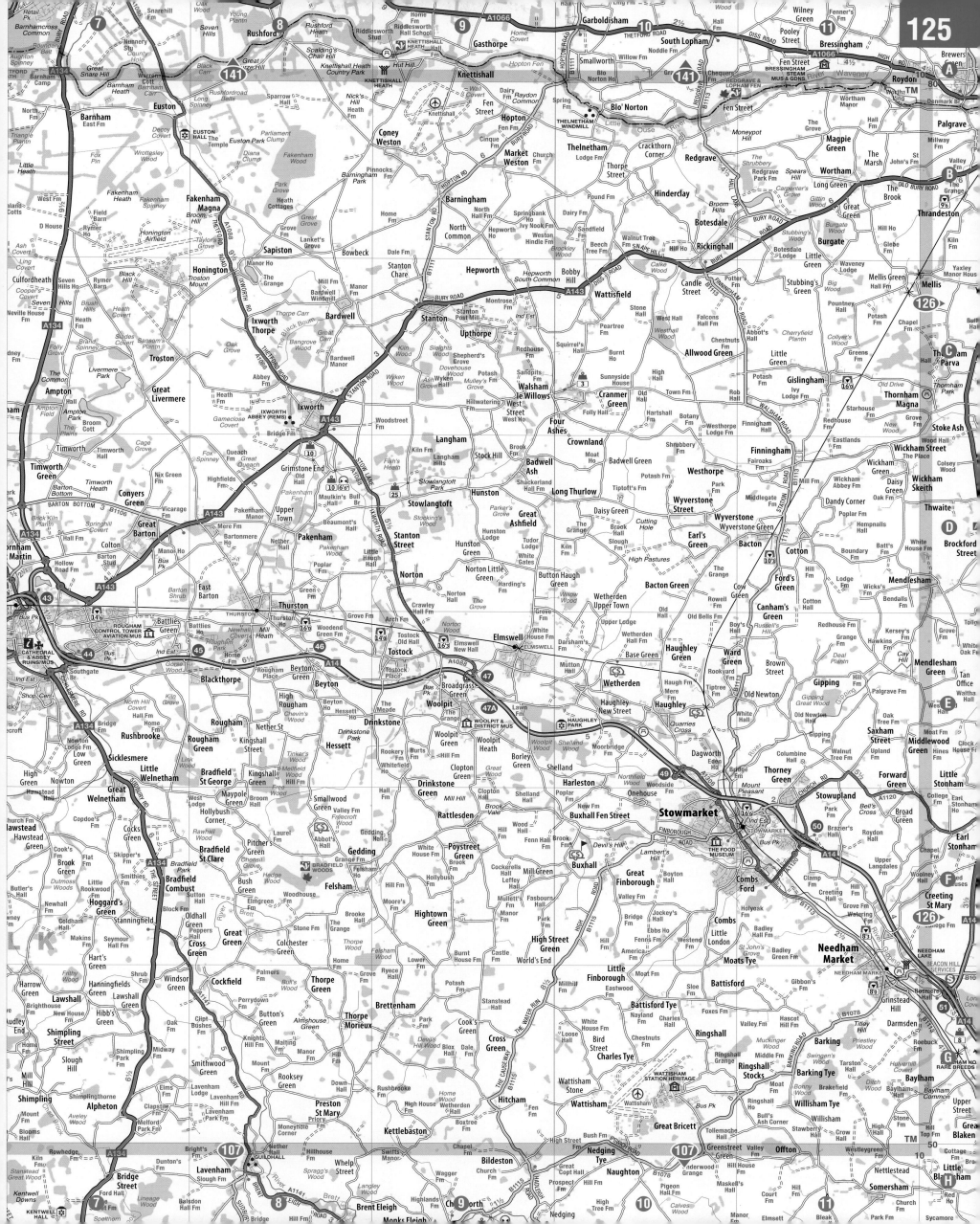

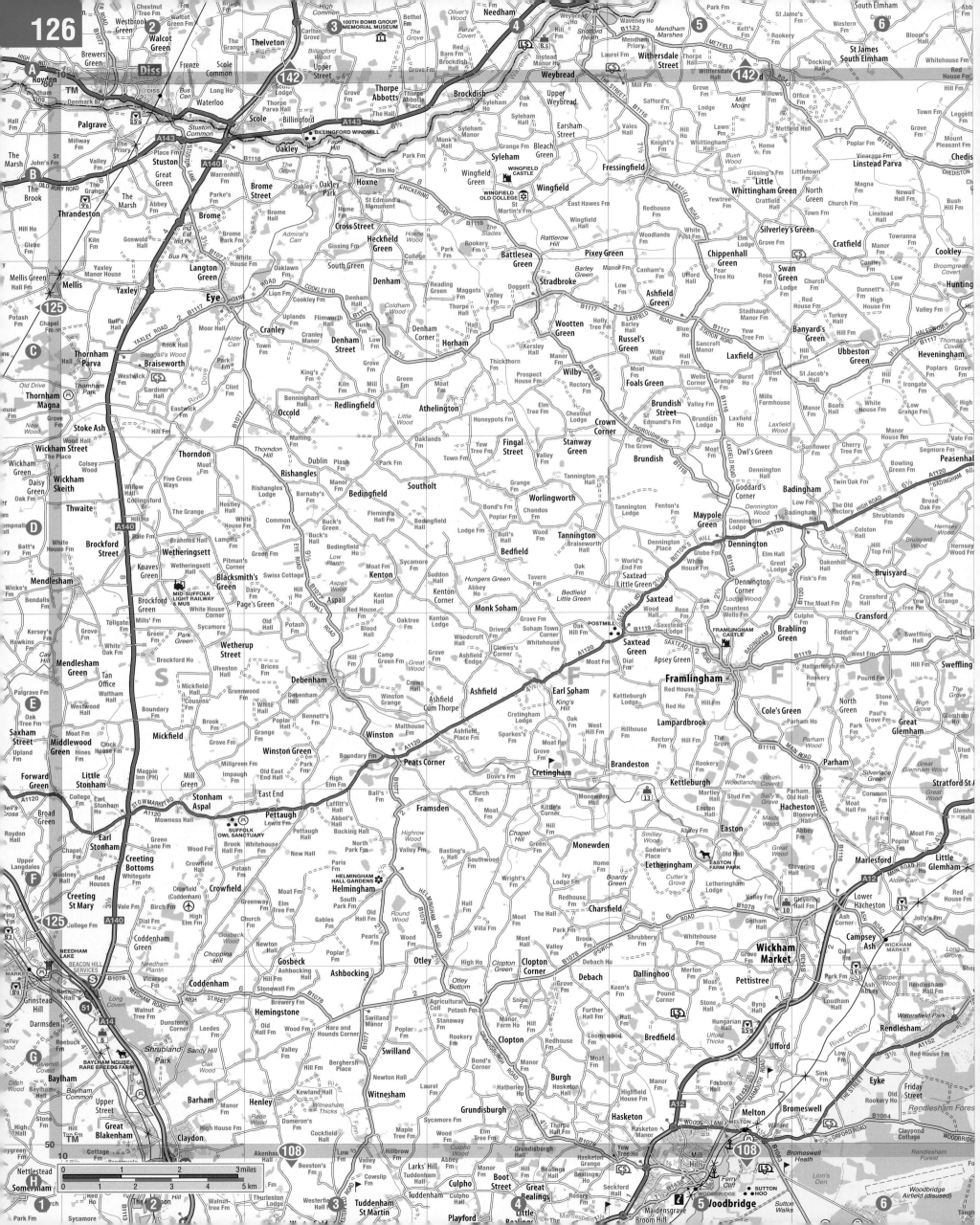

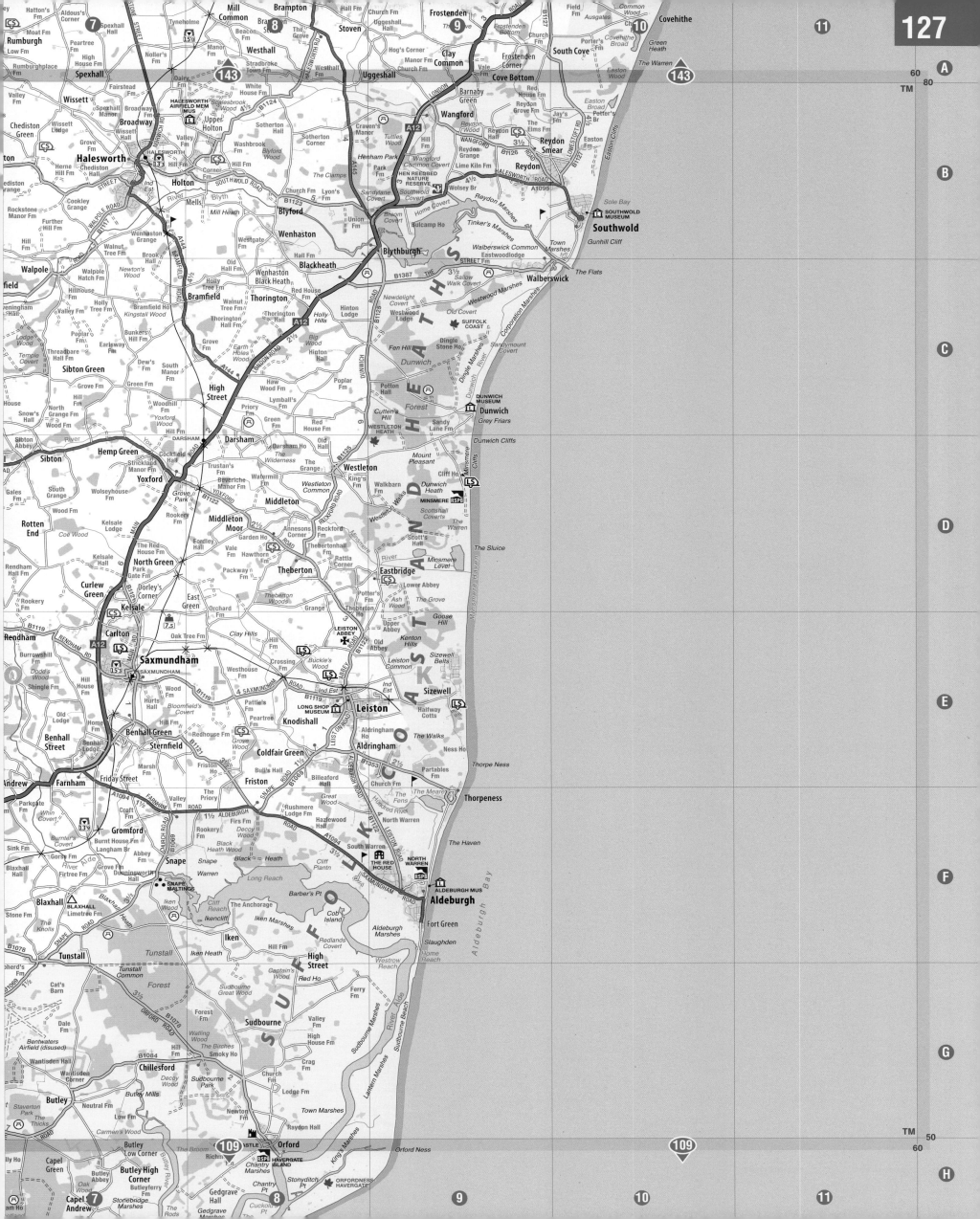

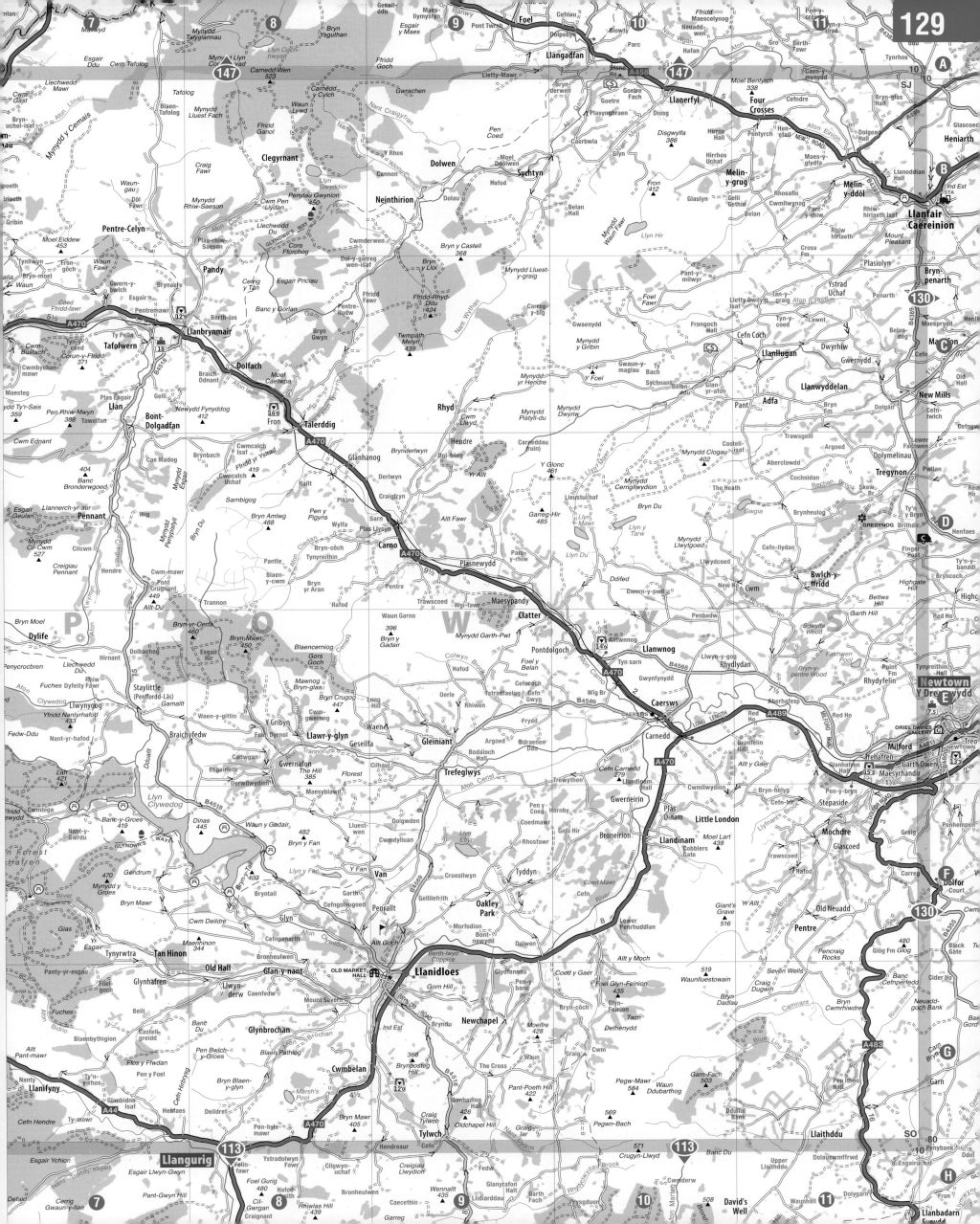

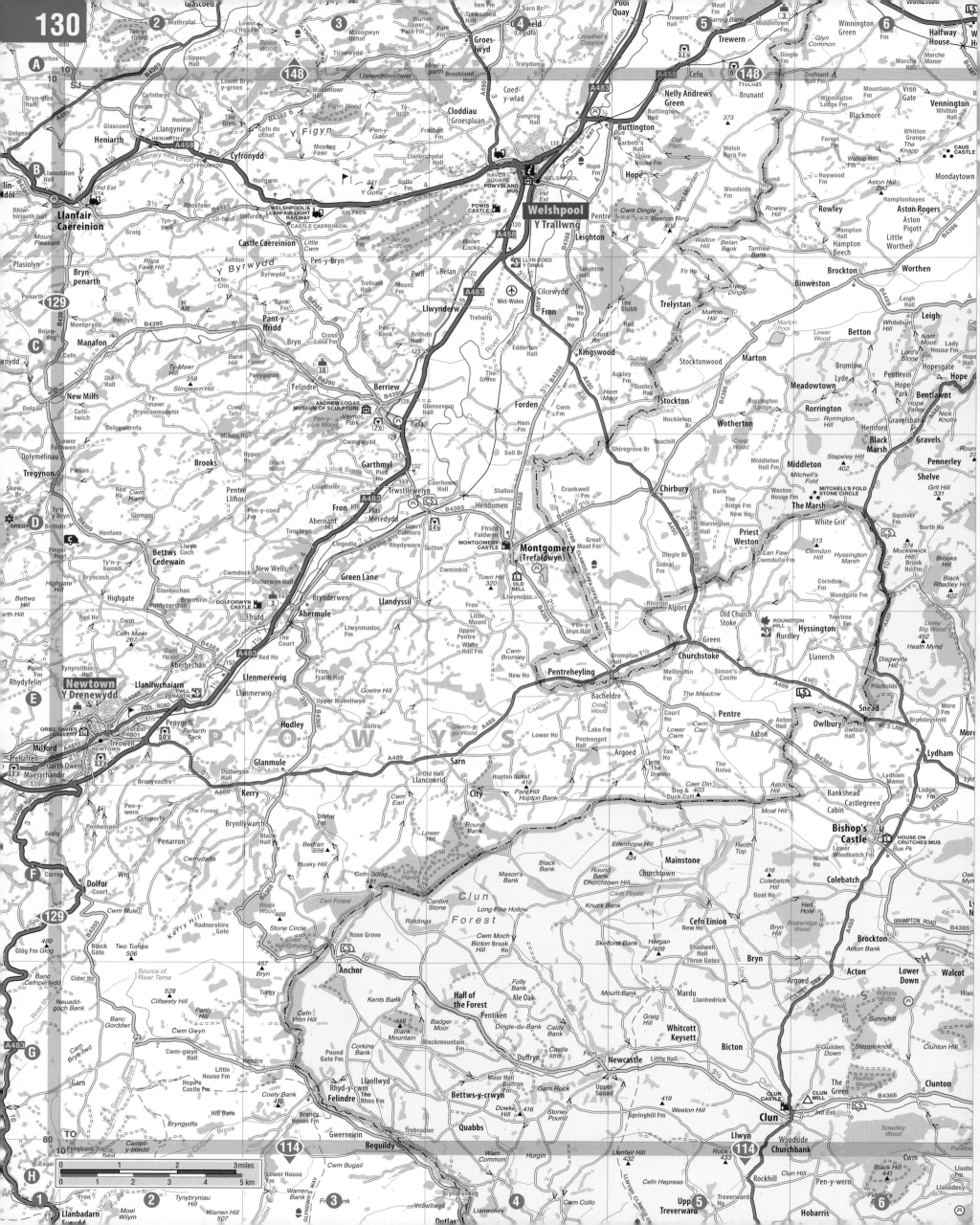

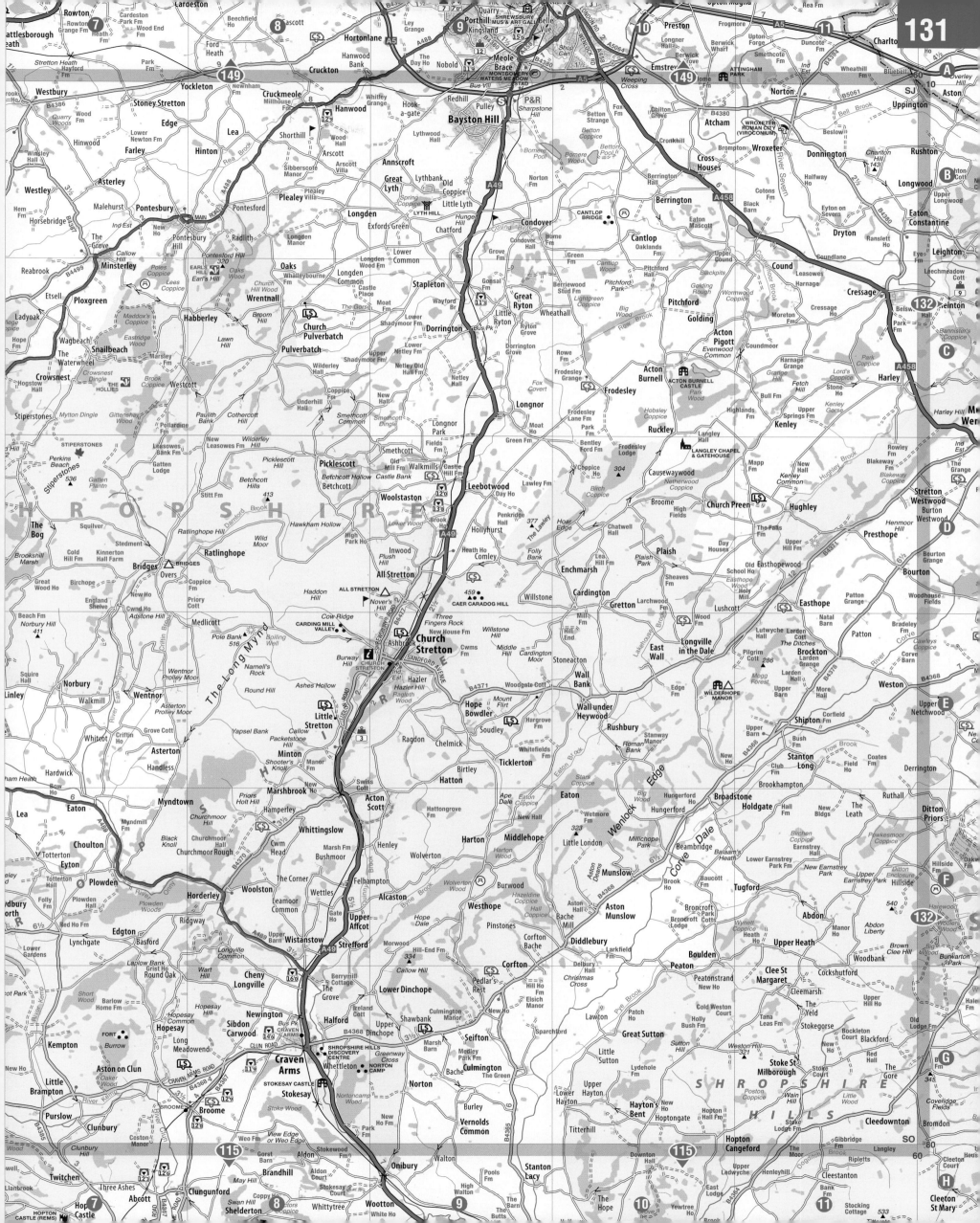

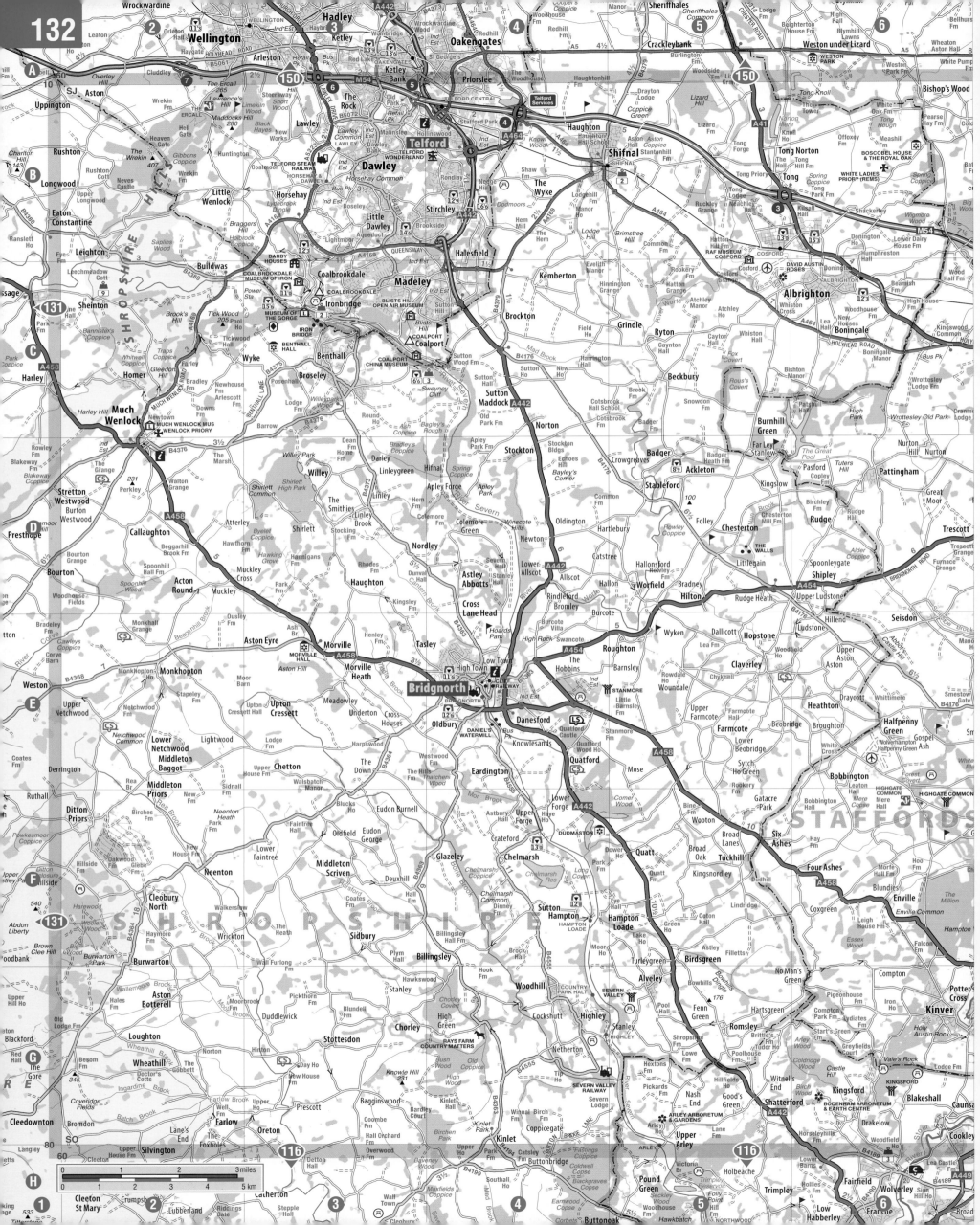

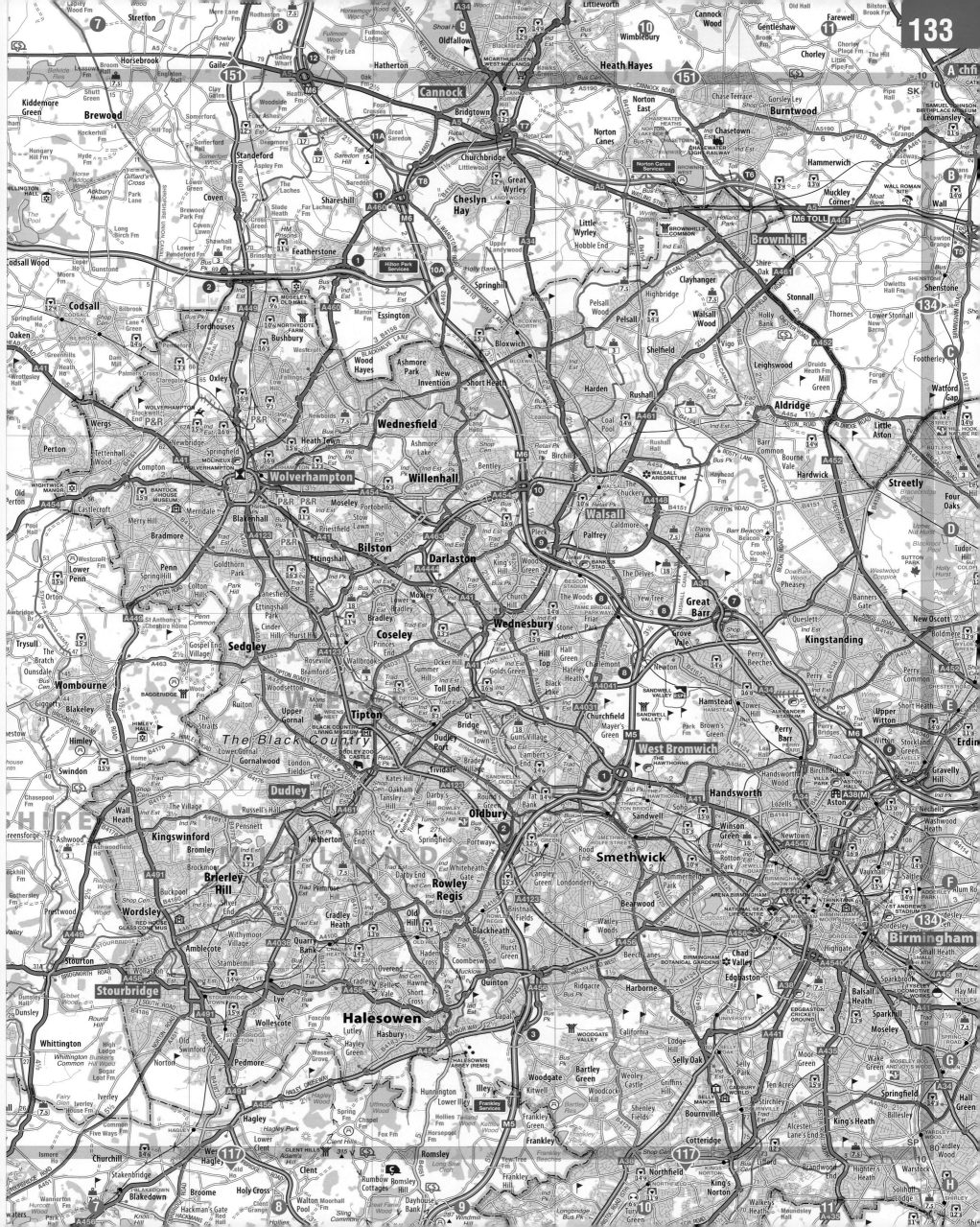

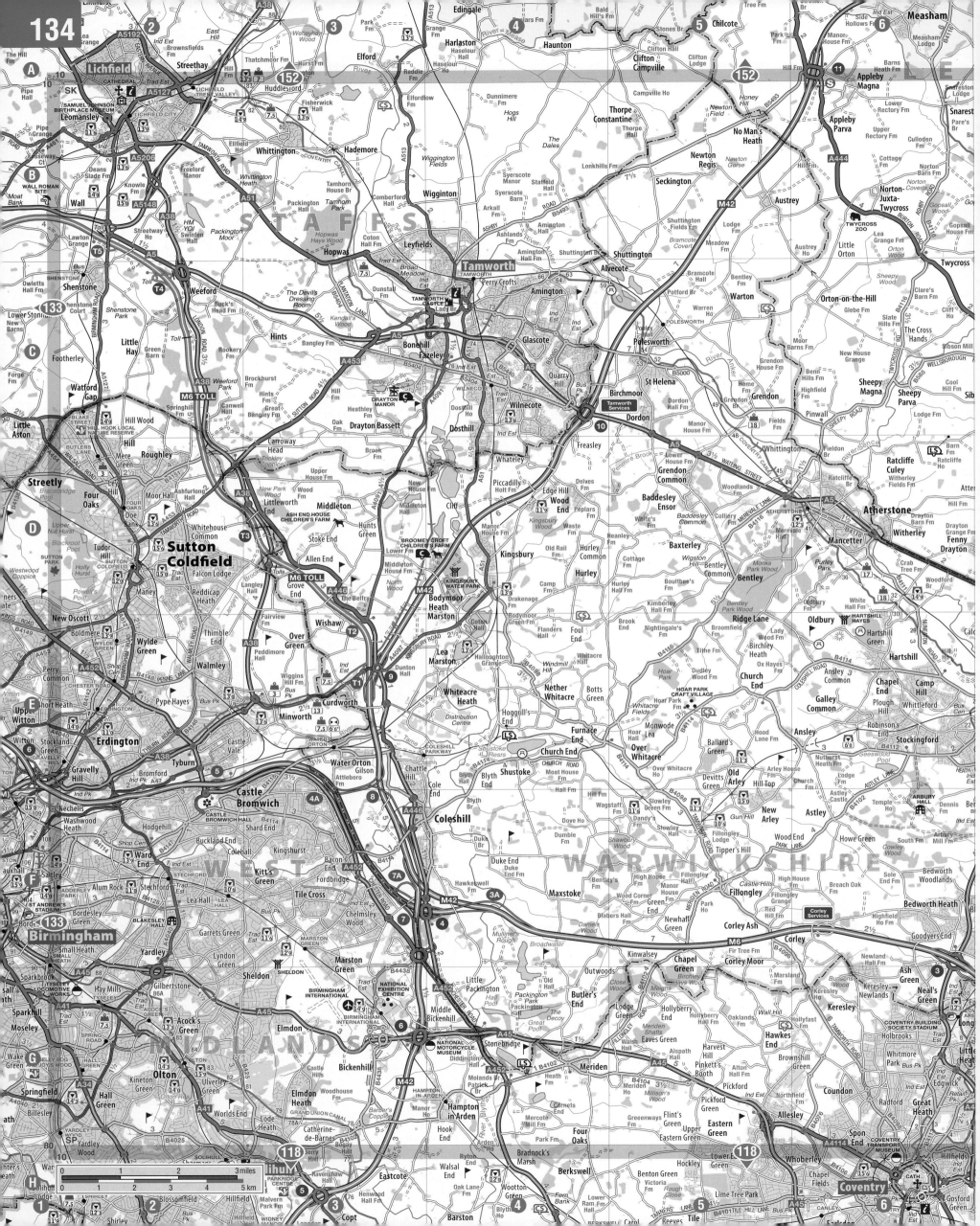

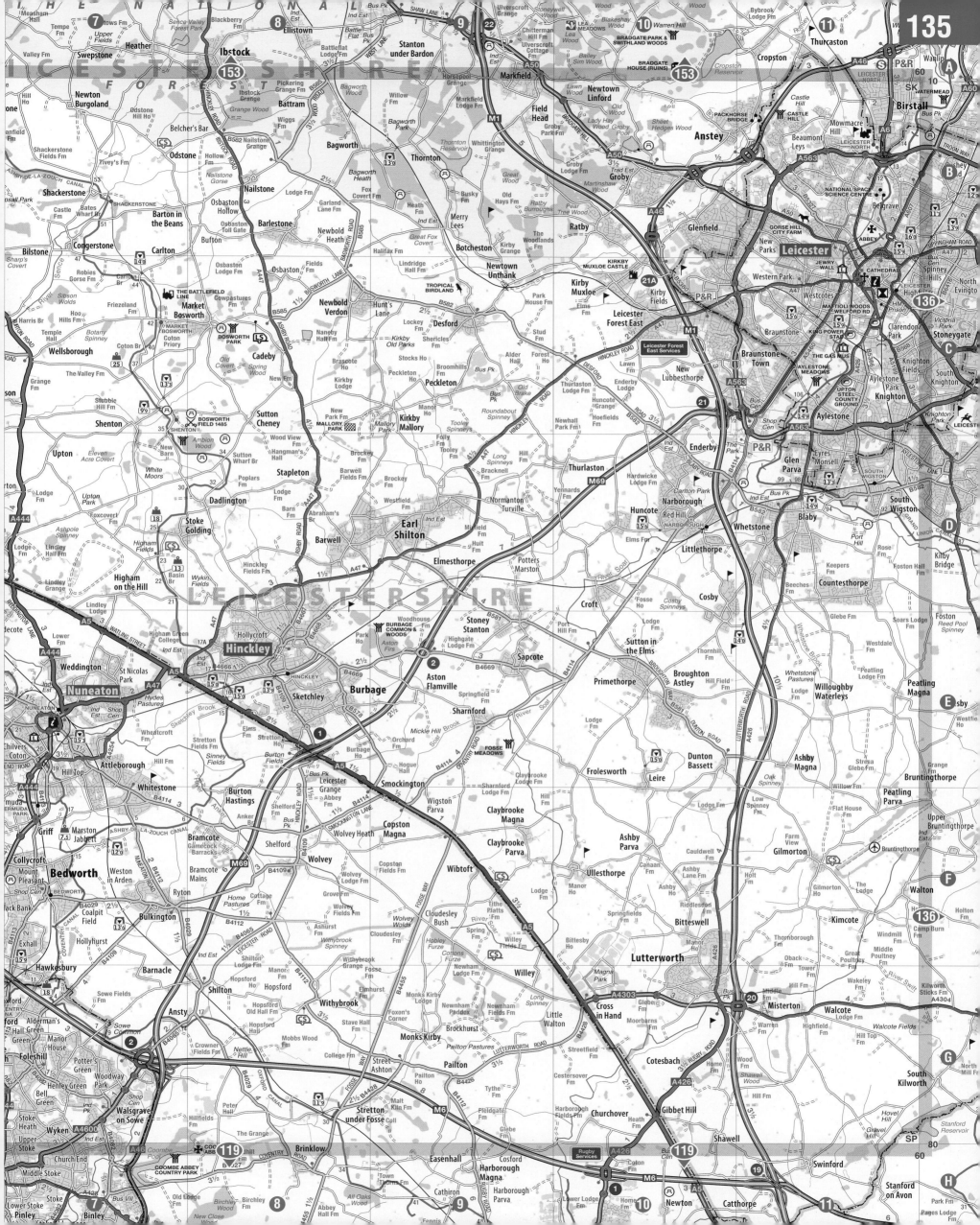

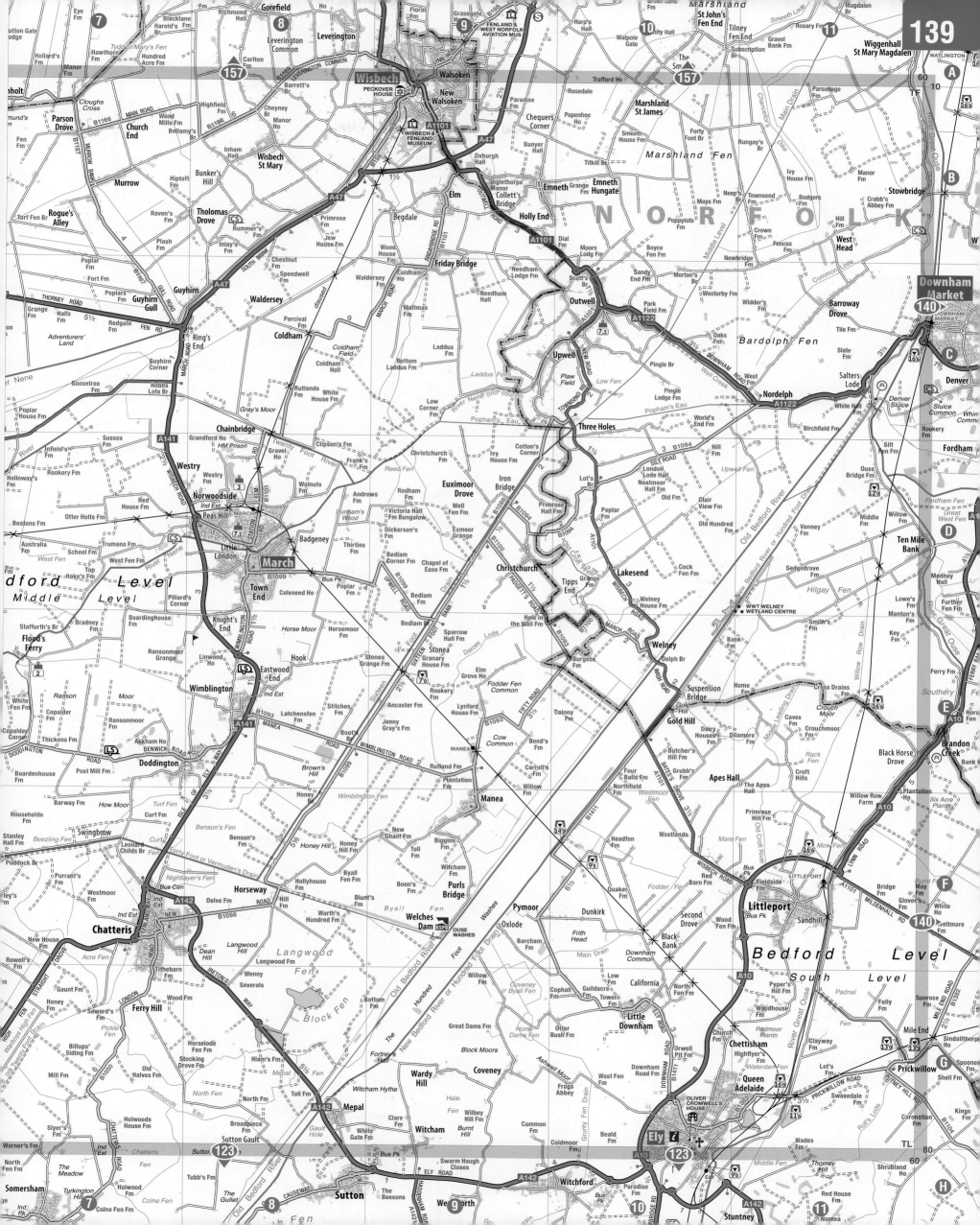

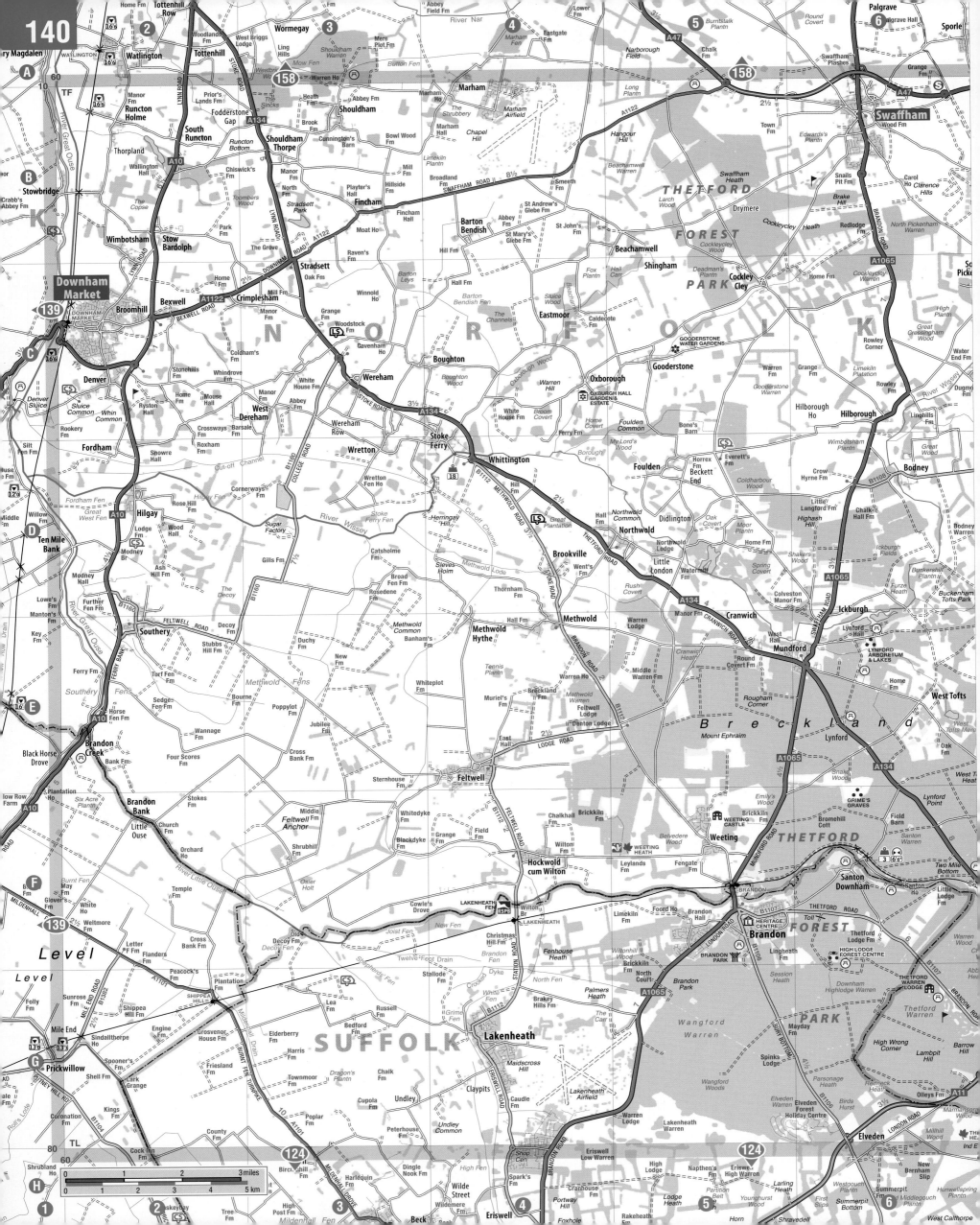

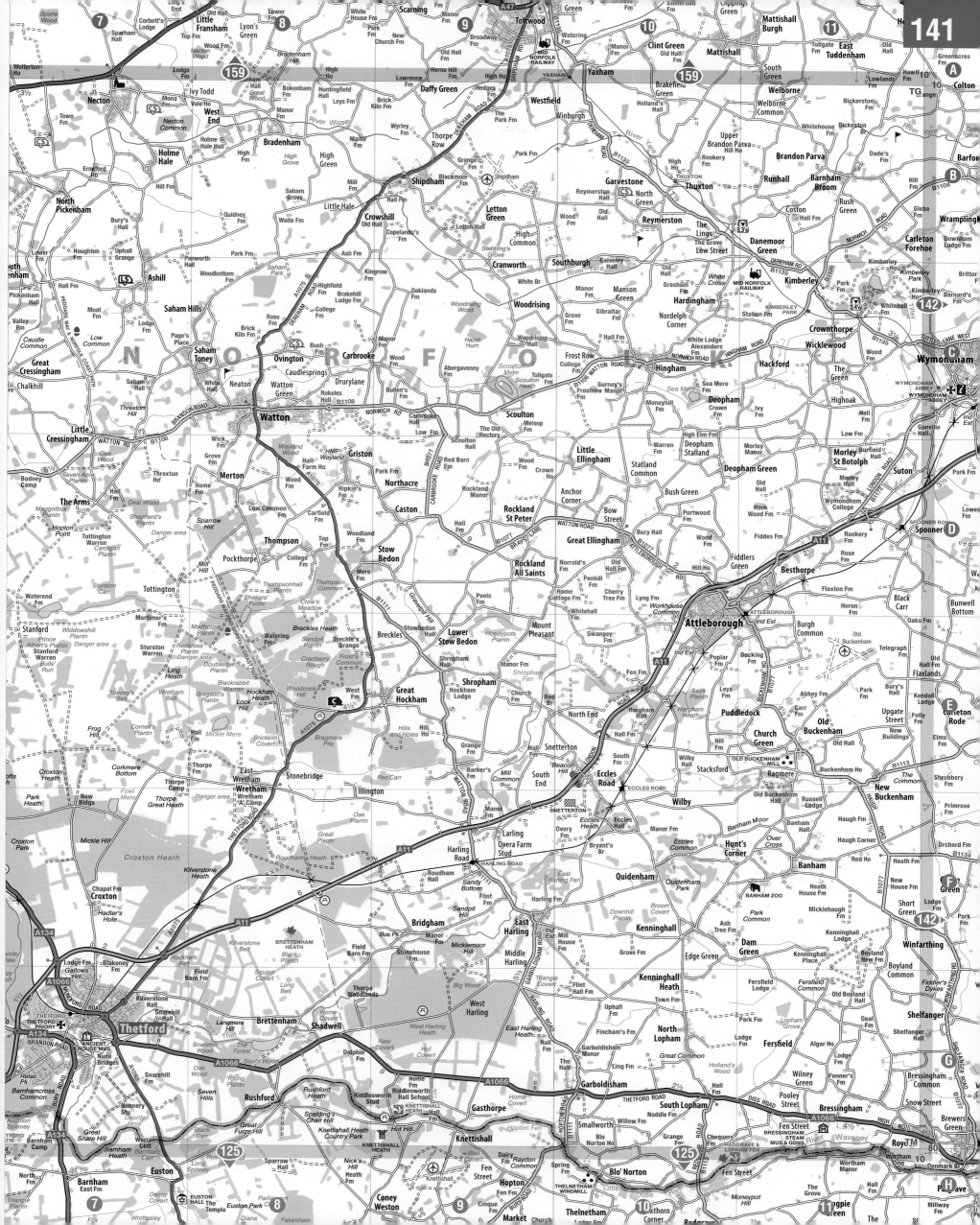

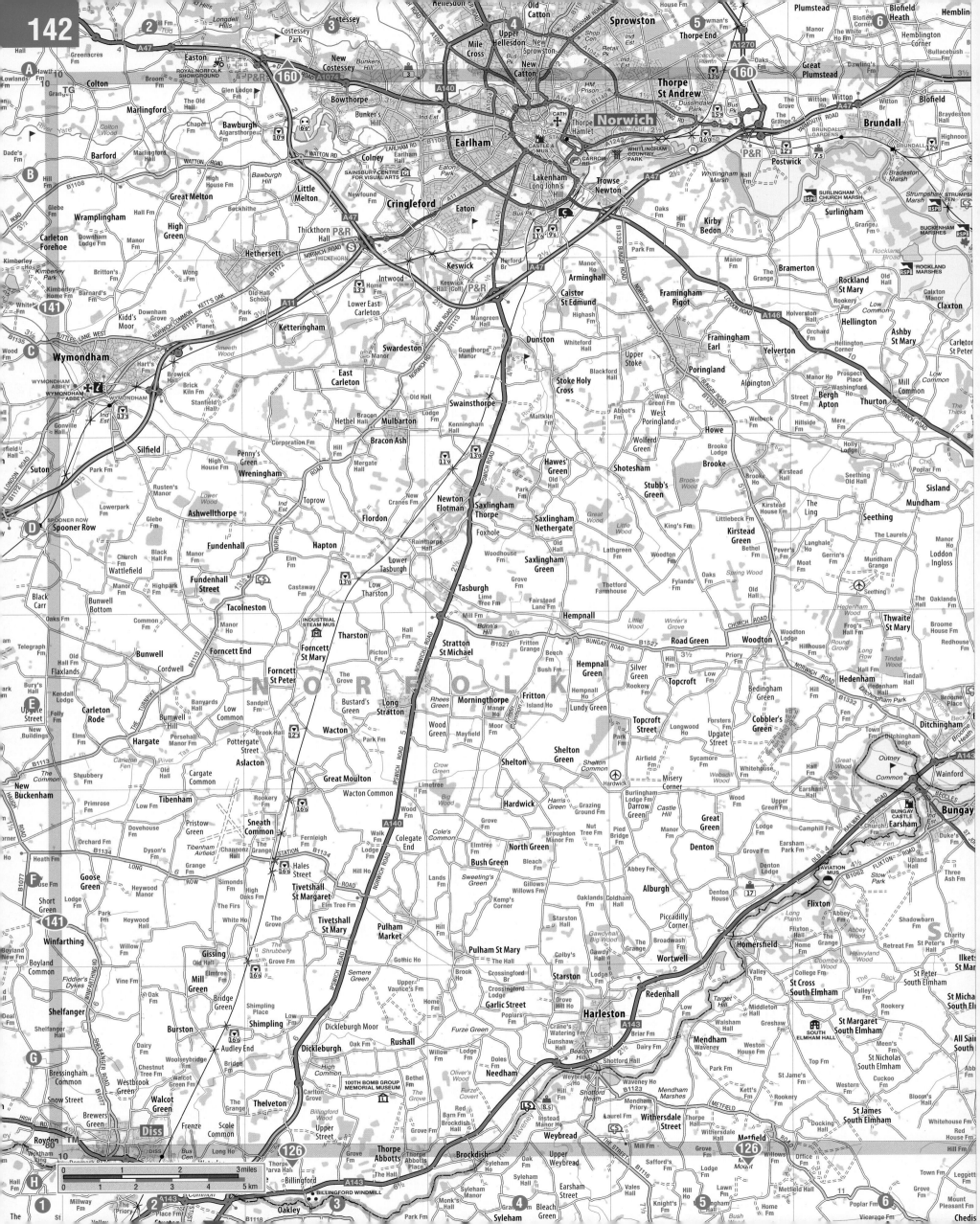

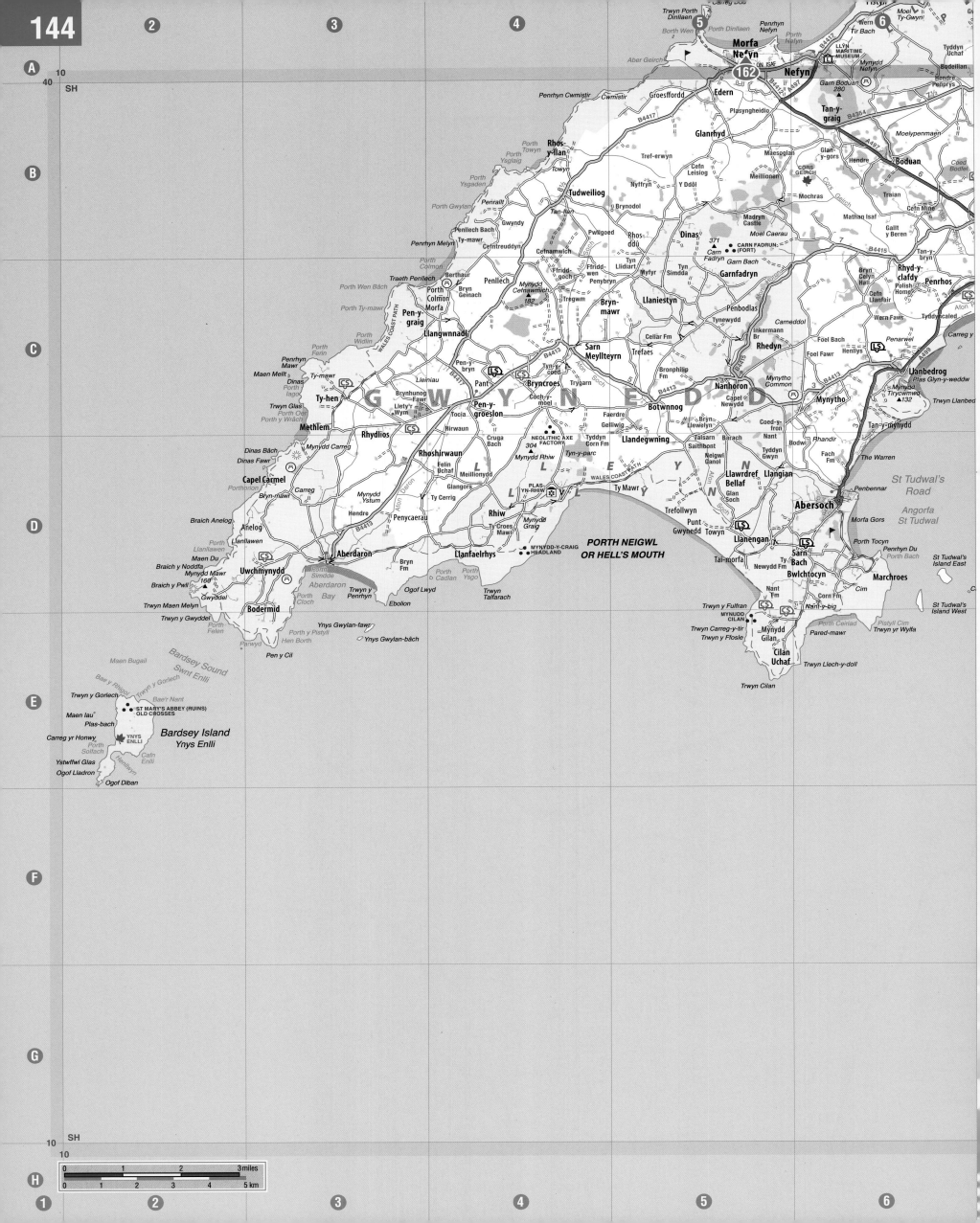

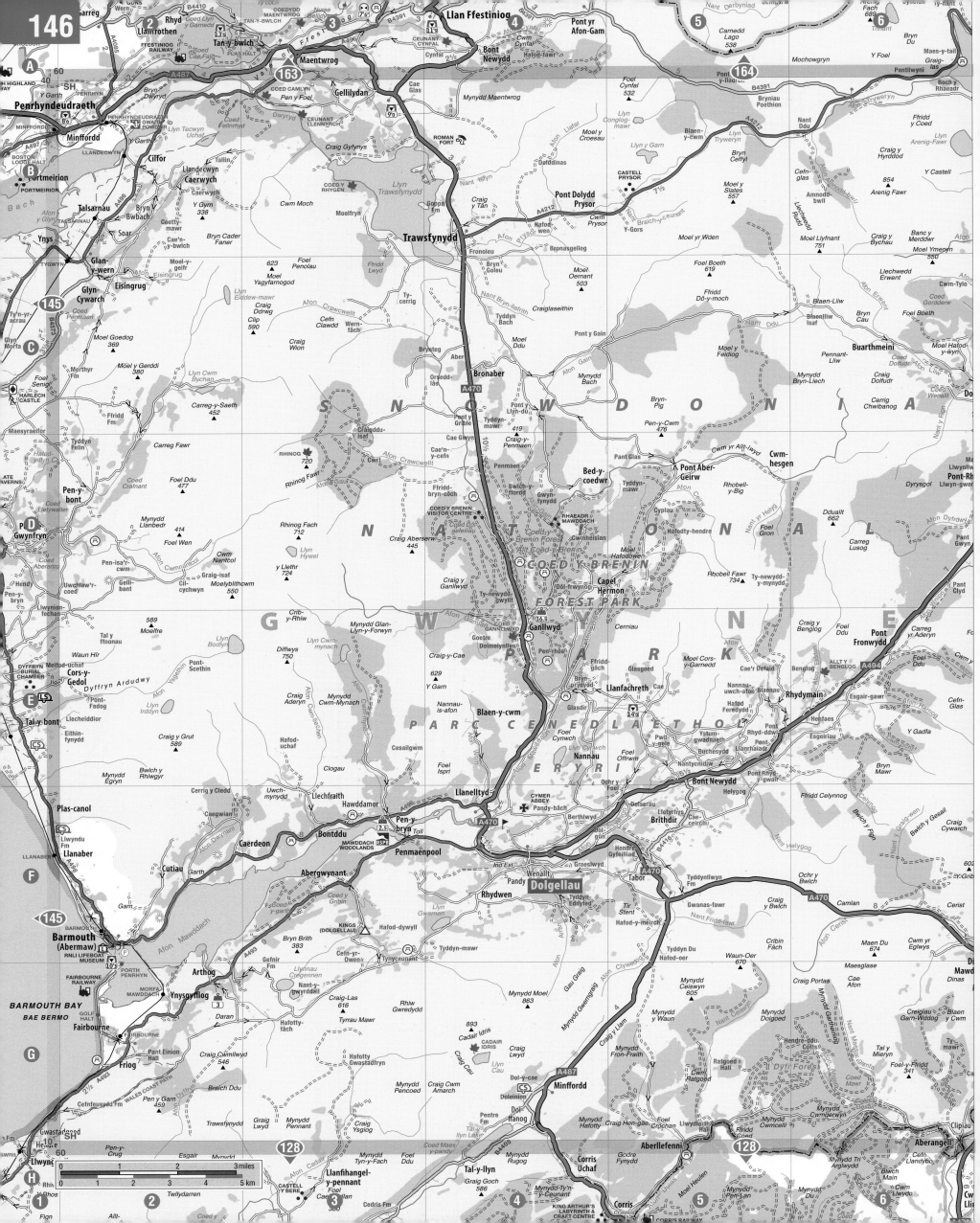

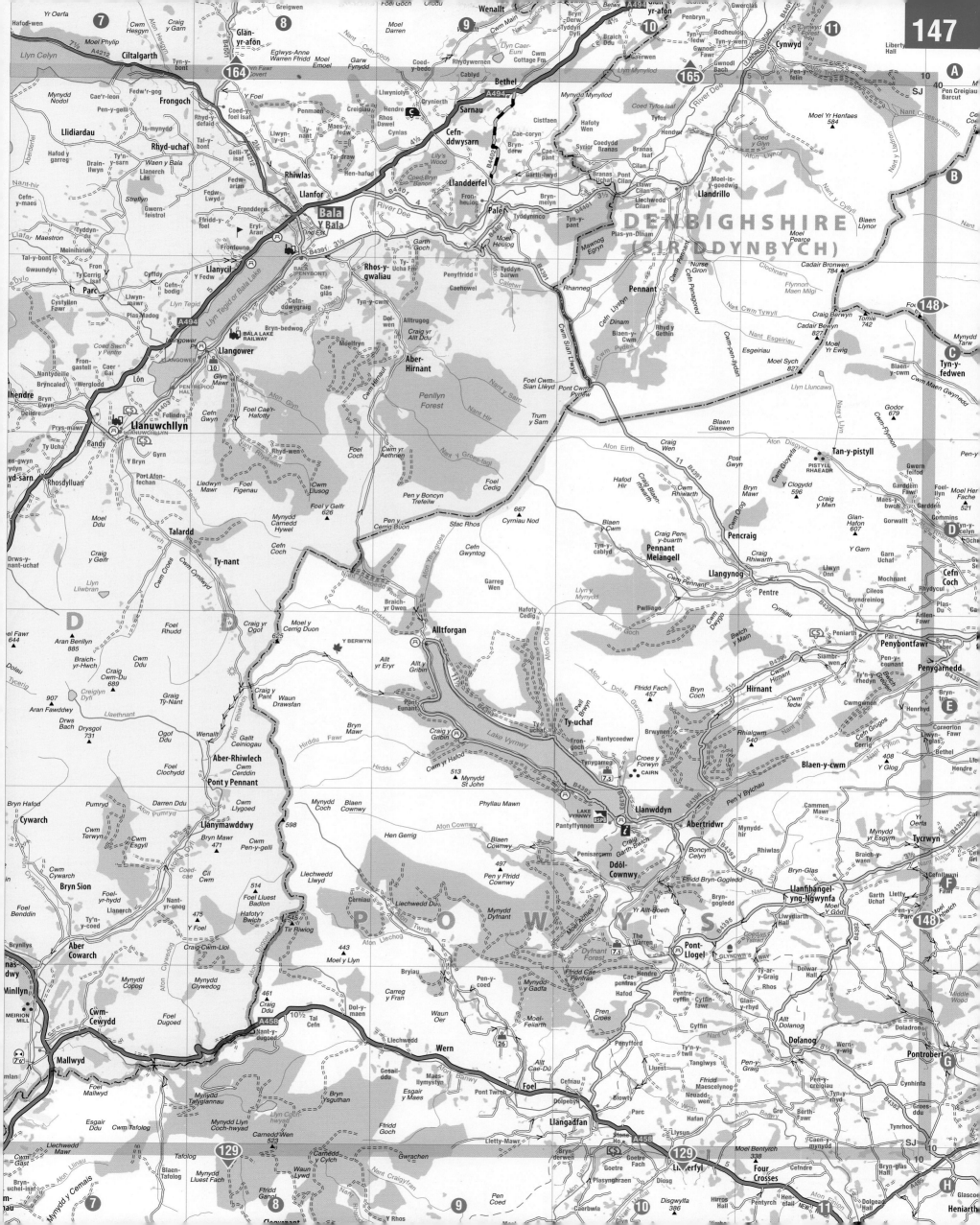

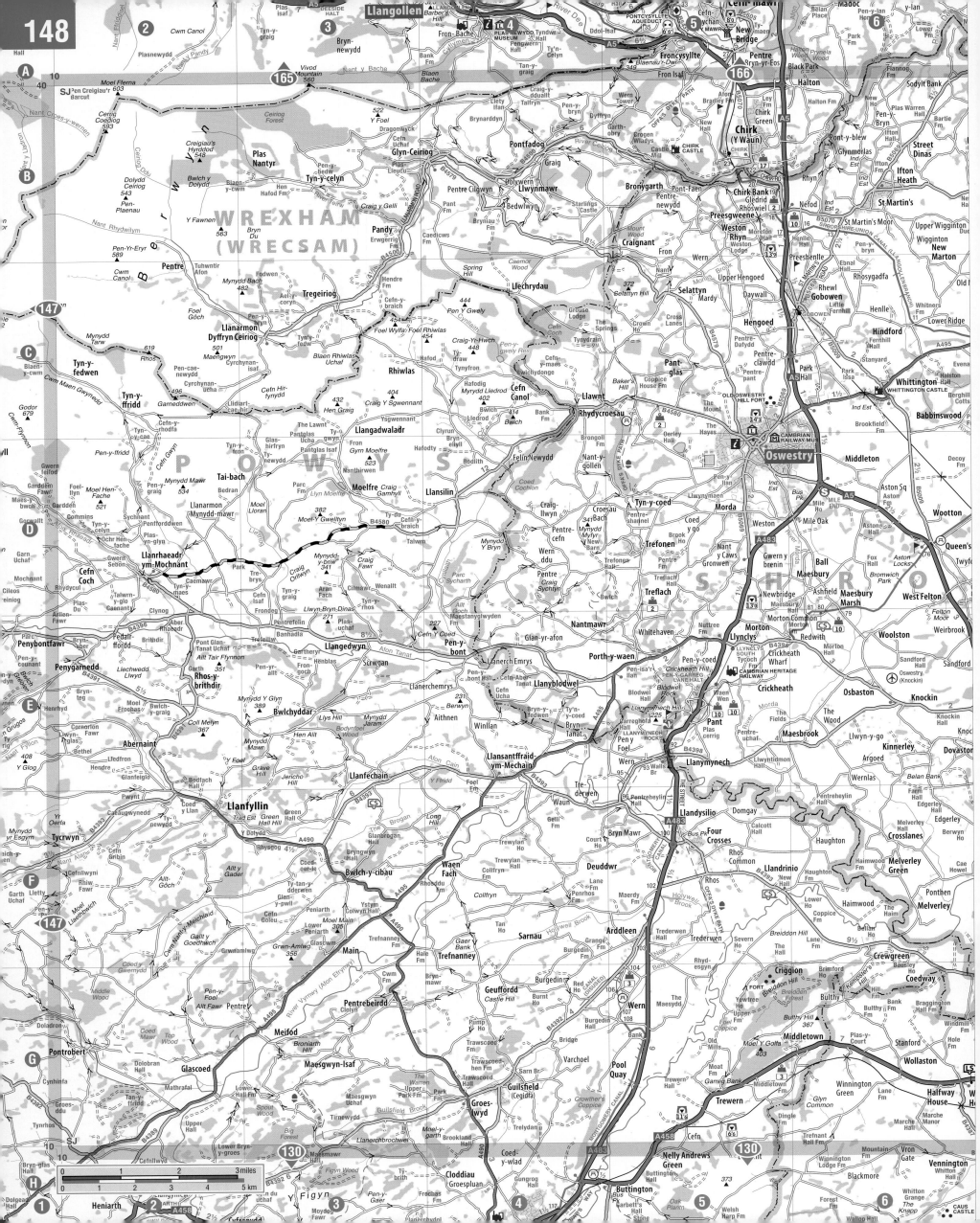

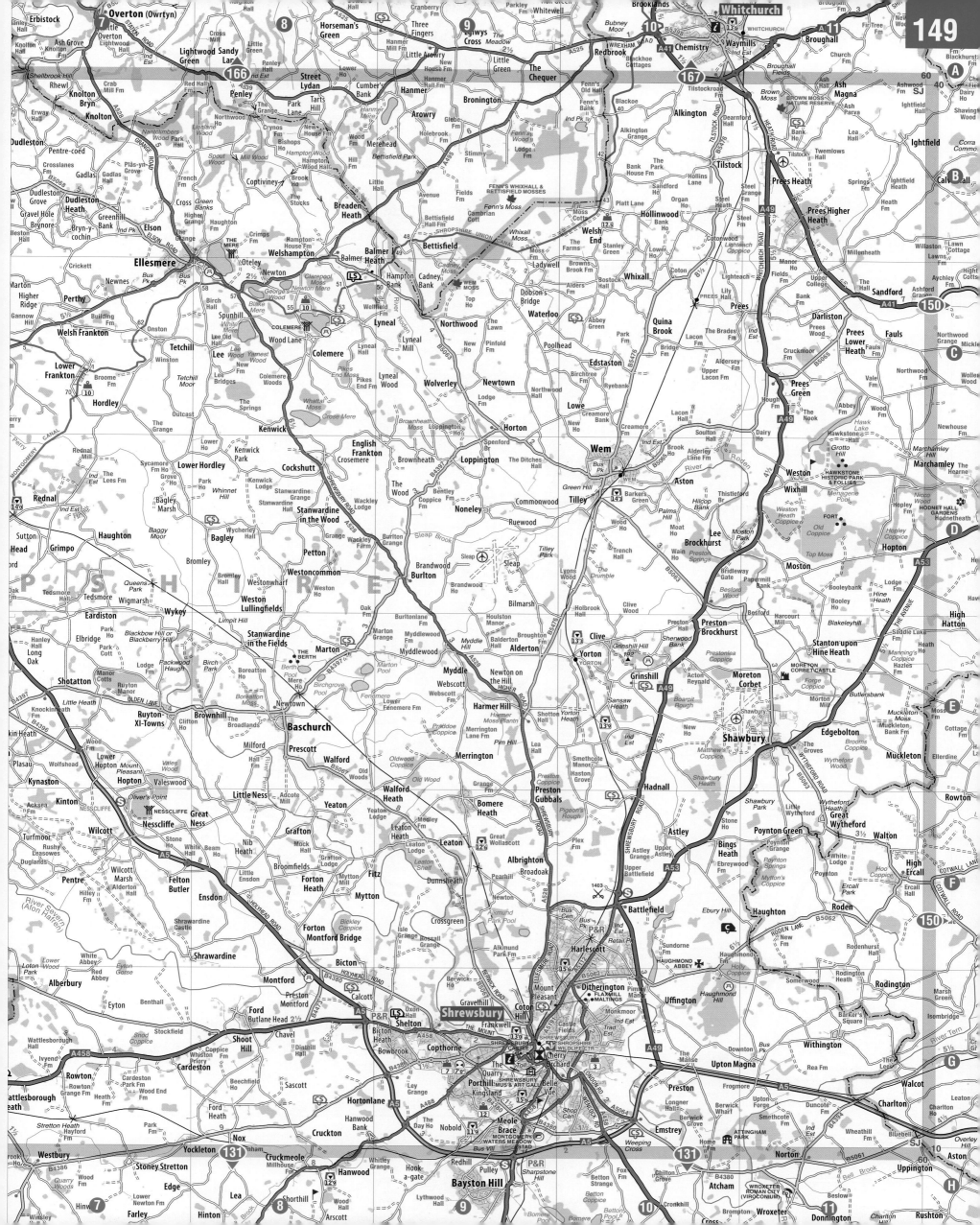

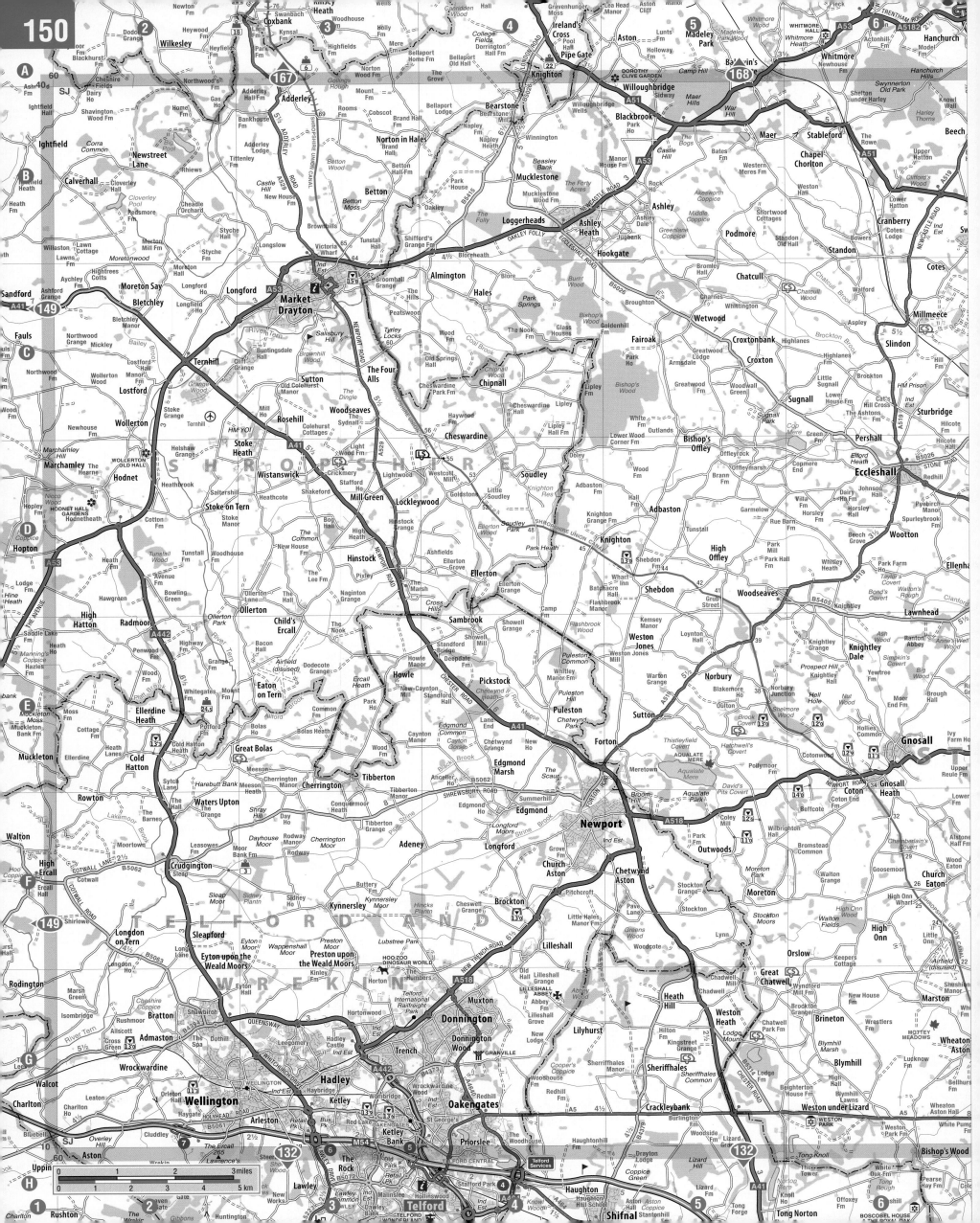

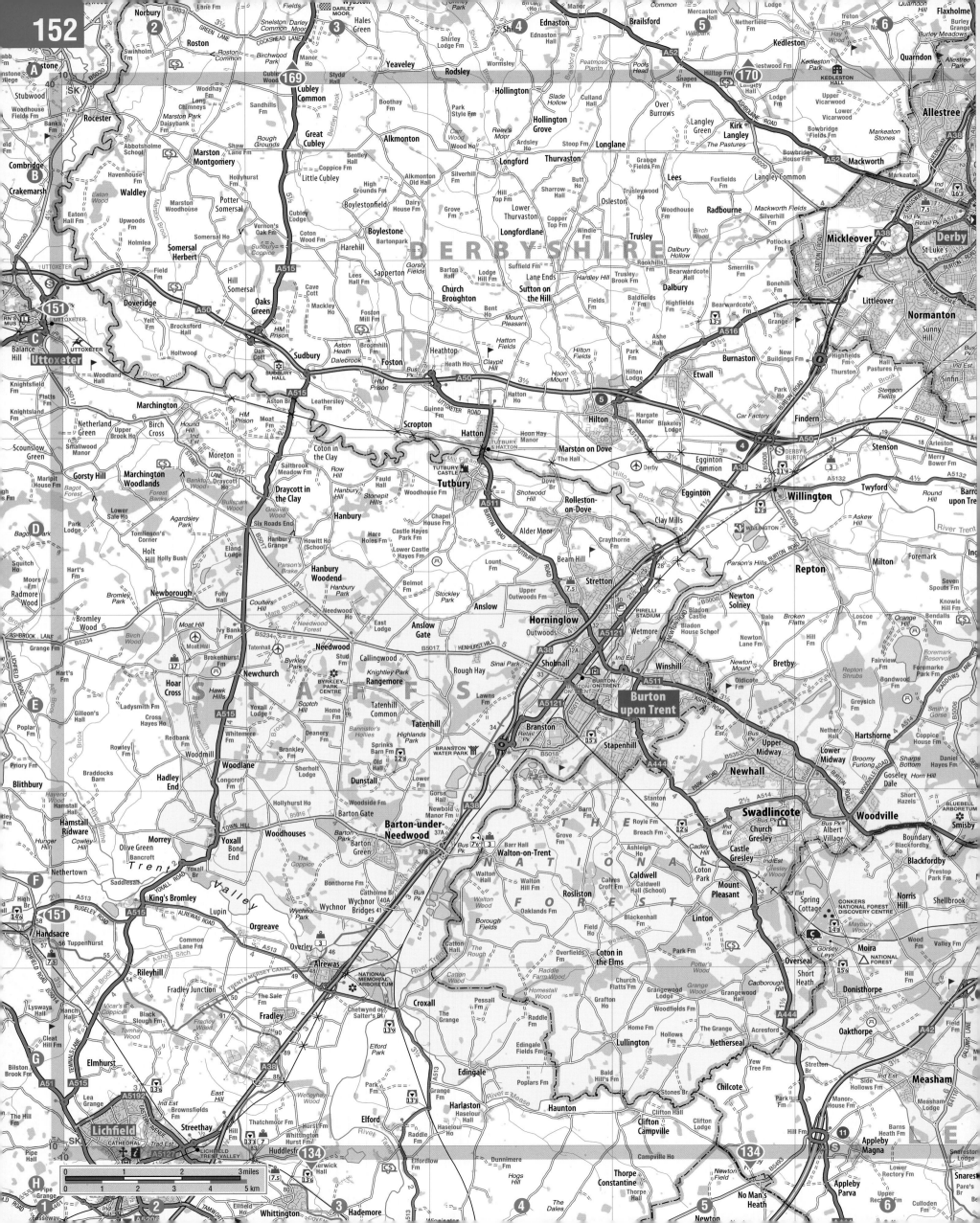

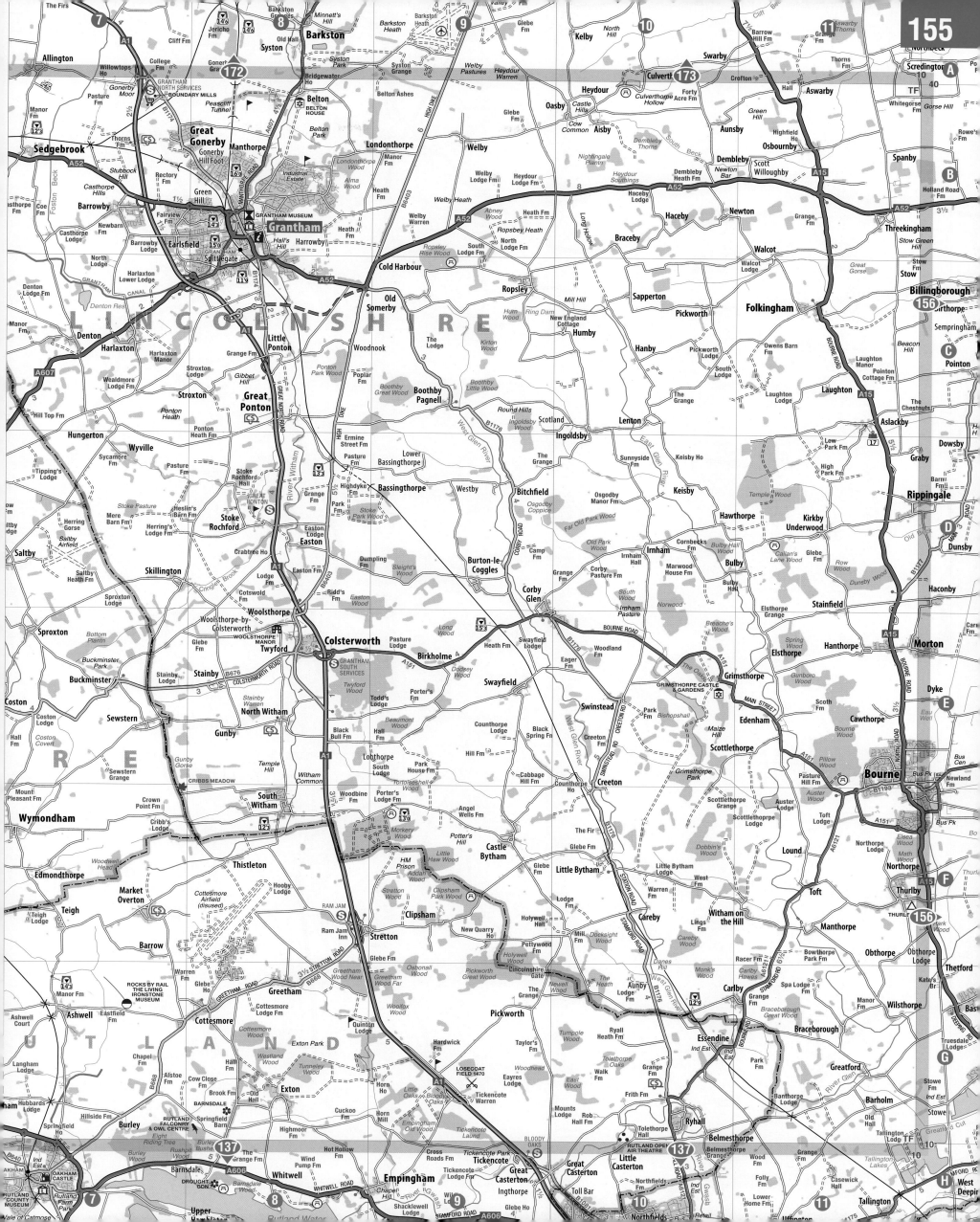

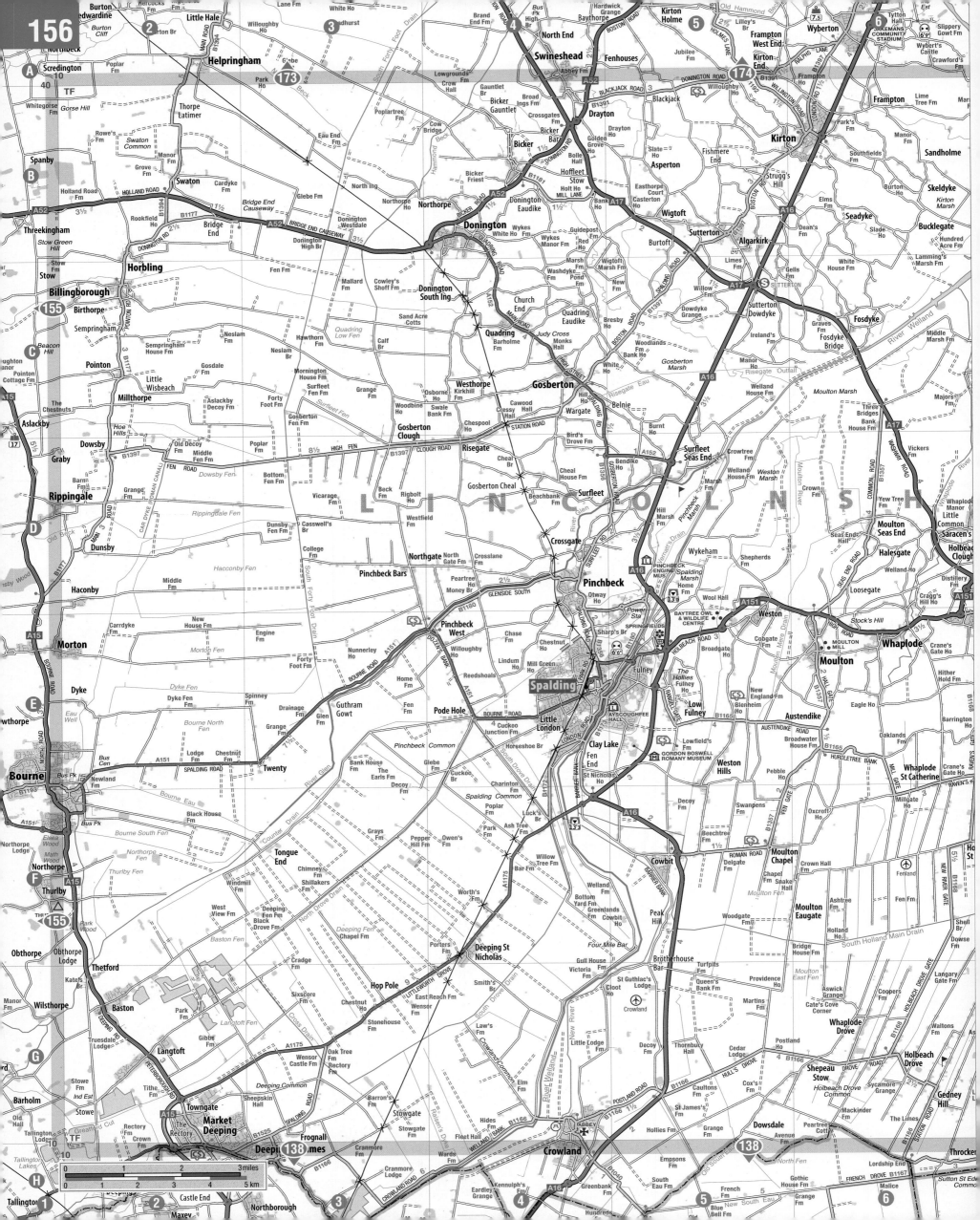

THE WASH

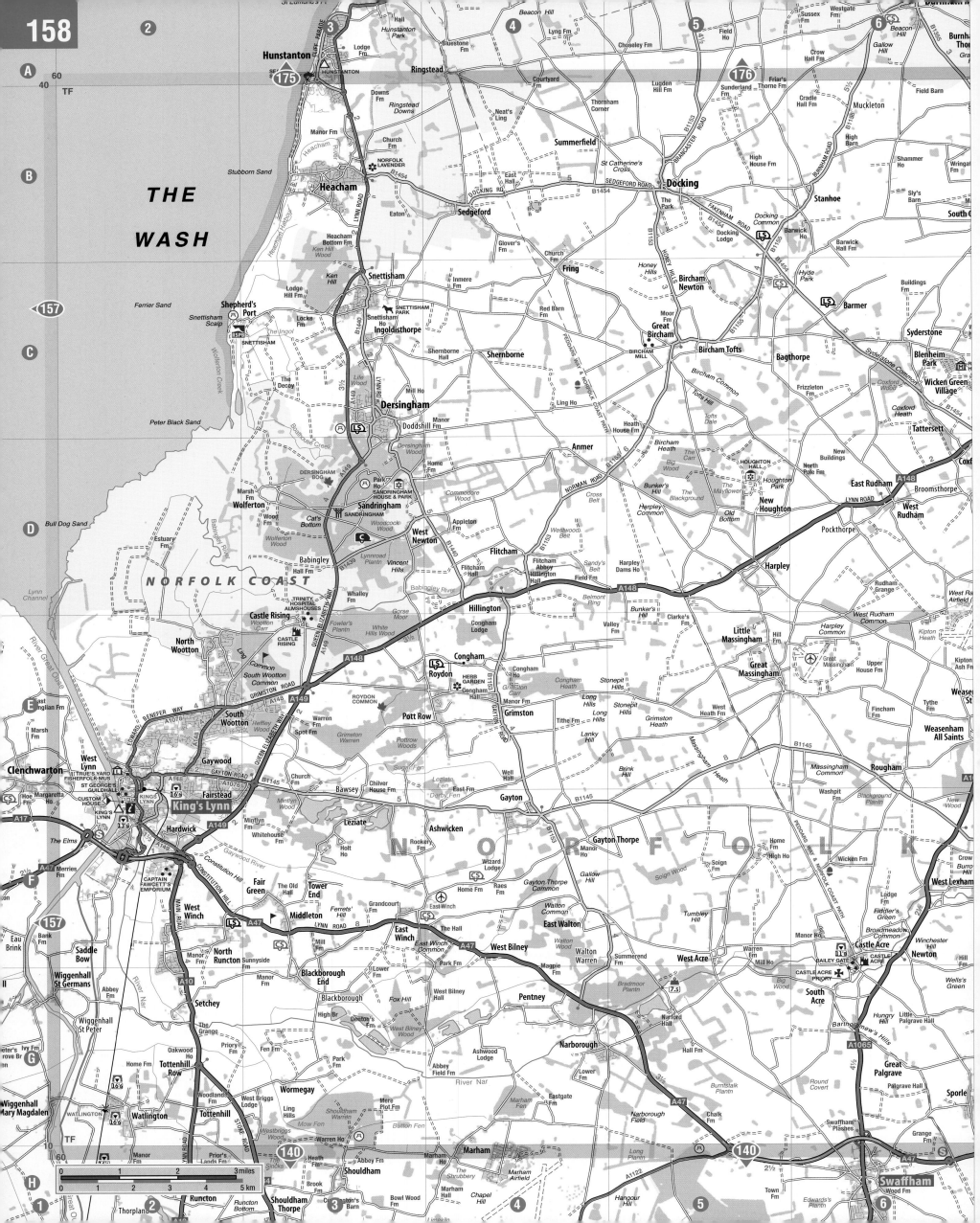

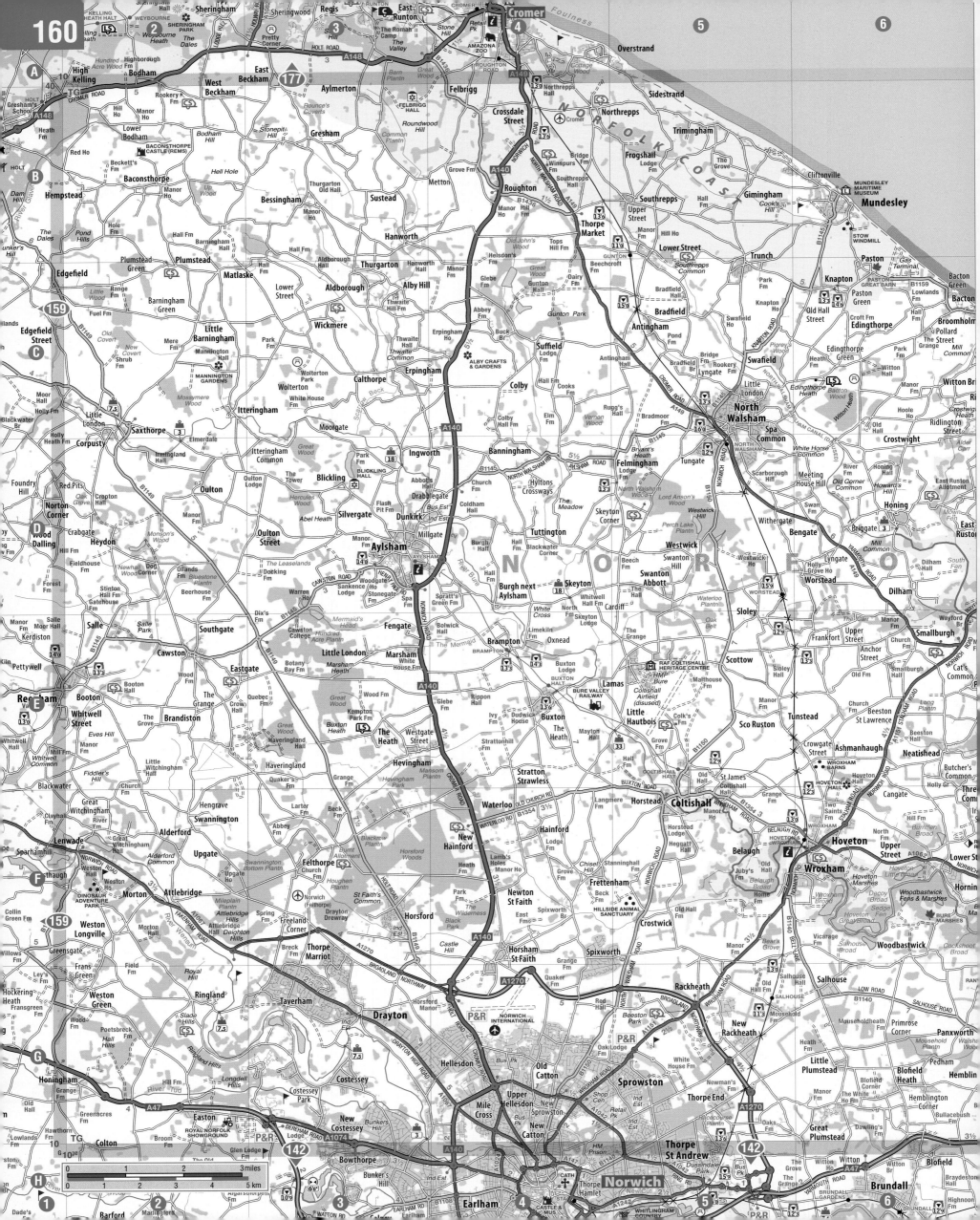

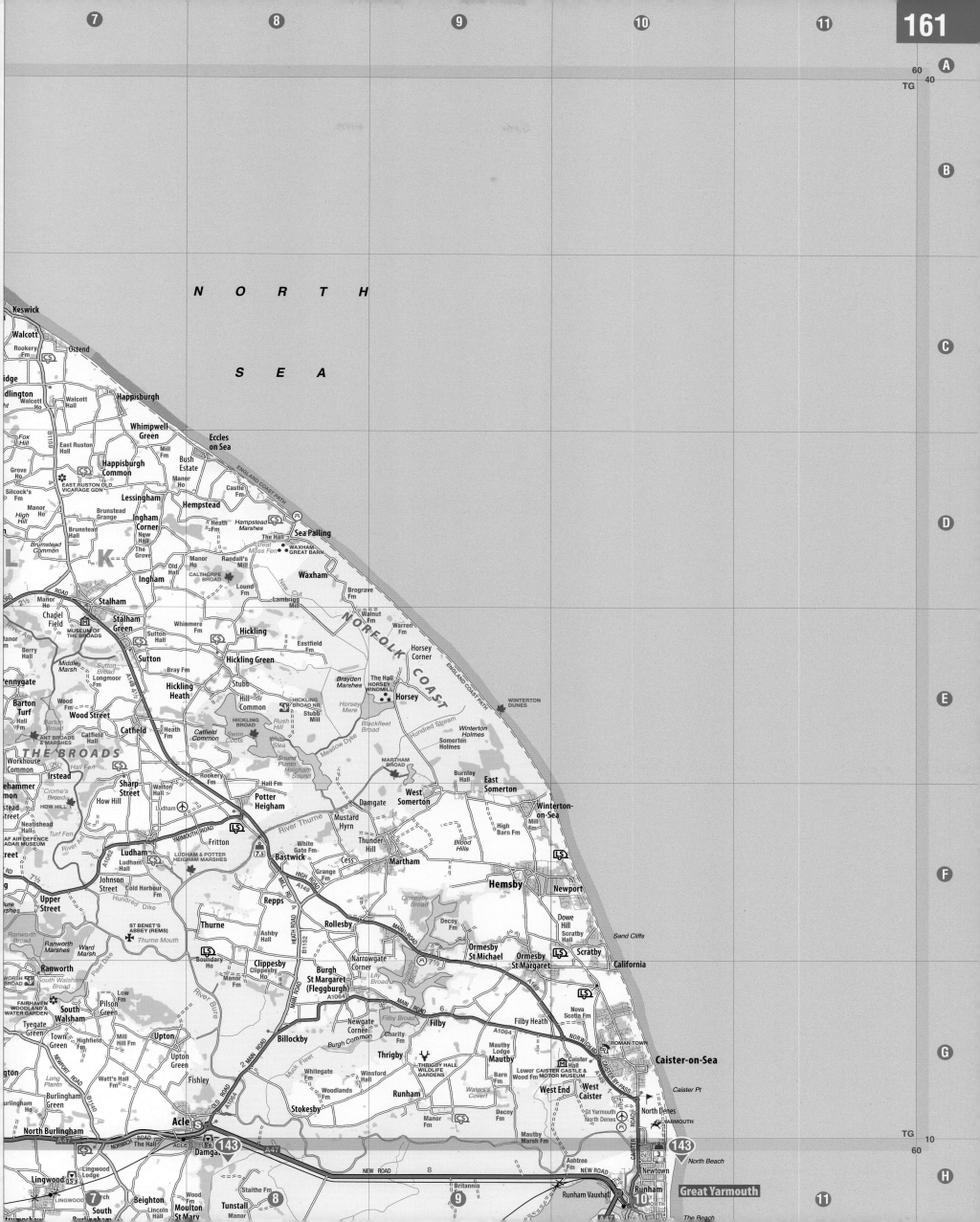

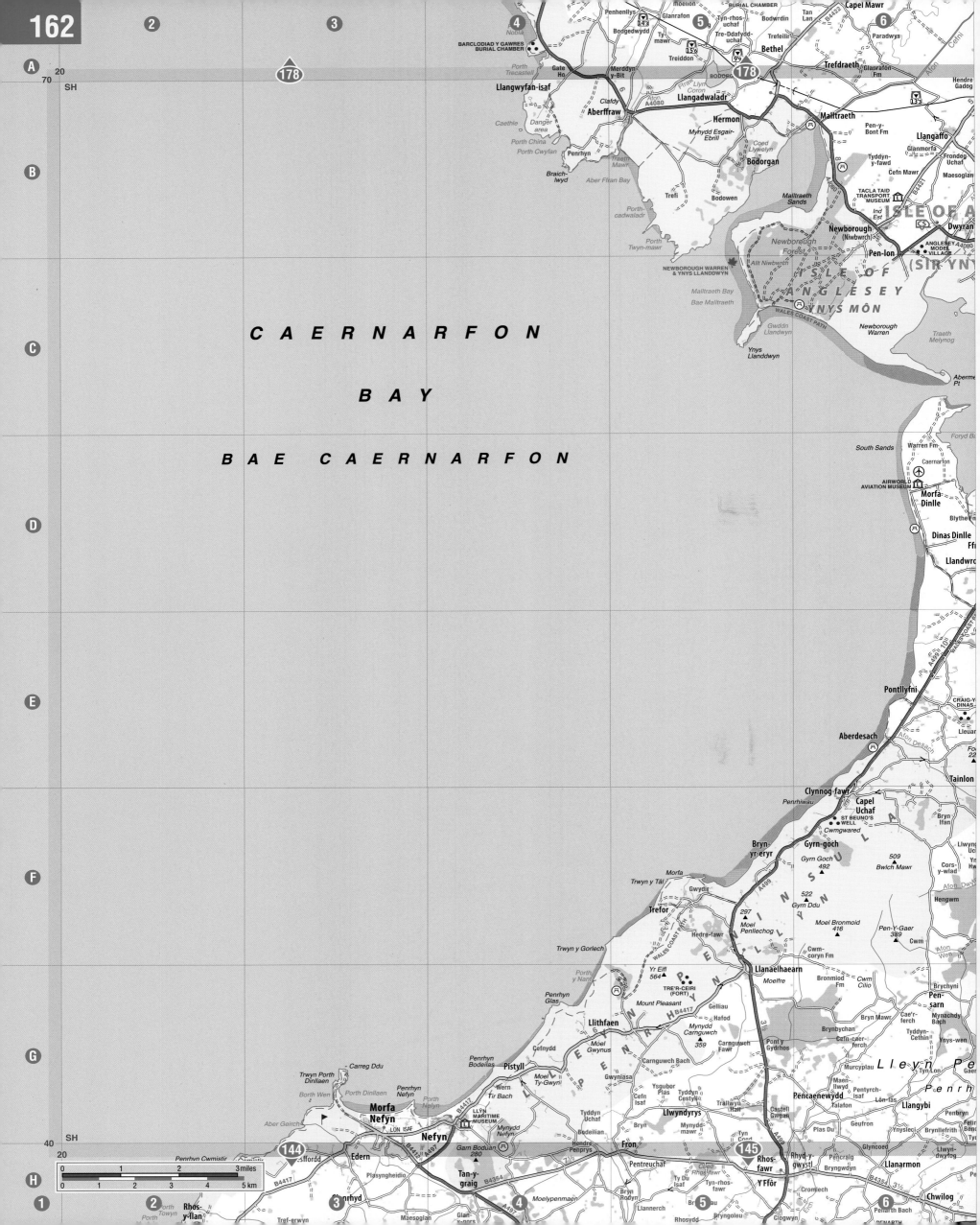

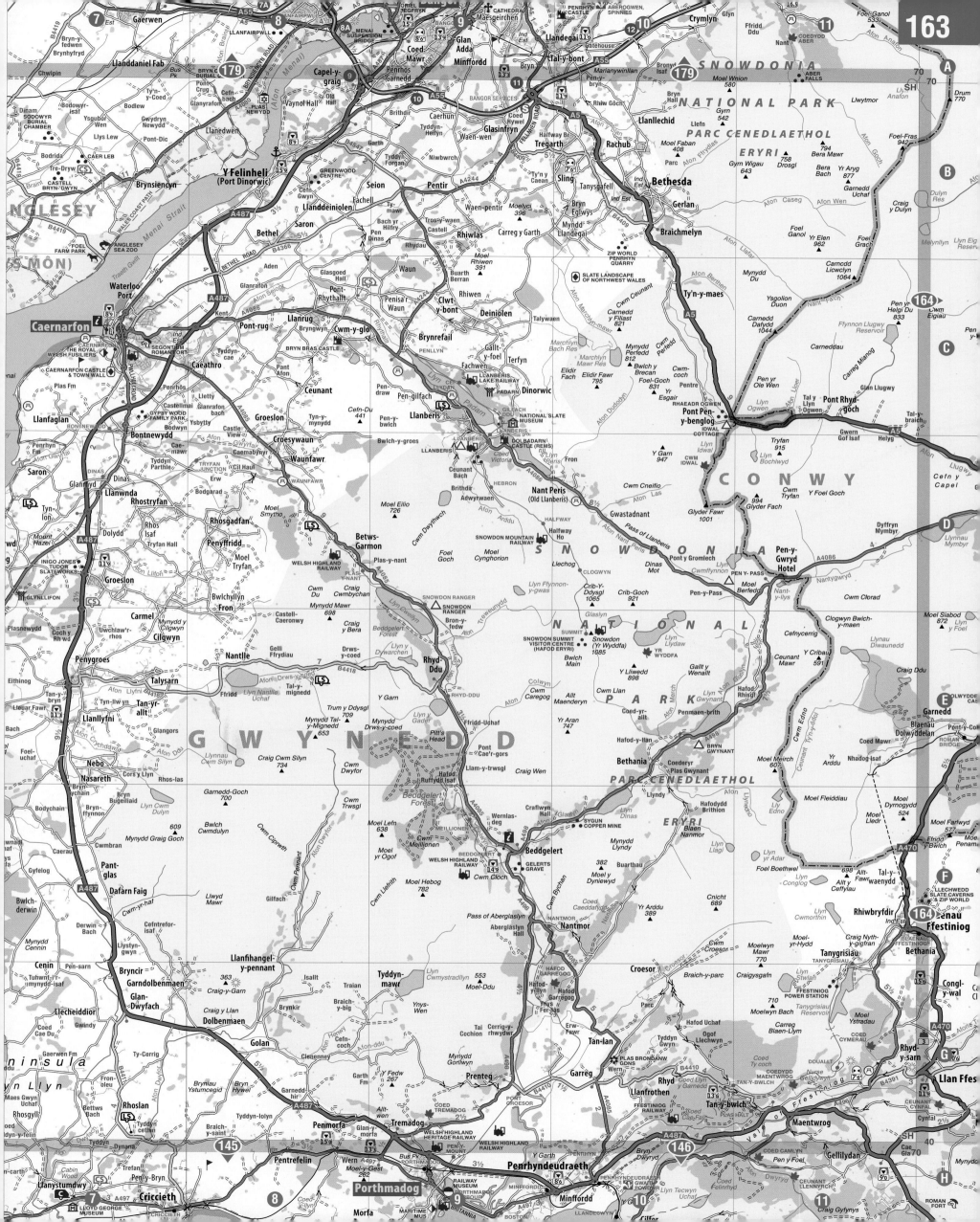

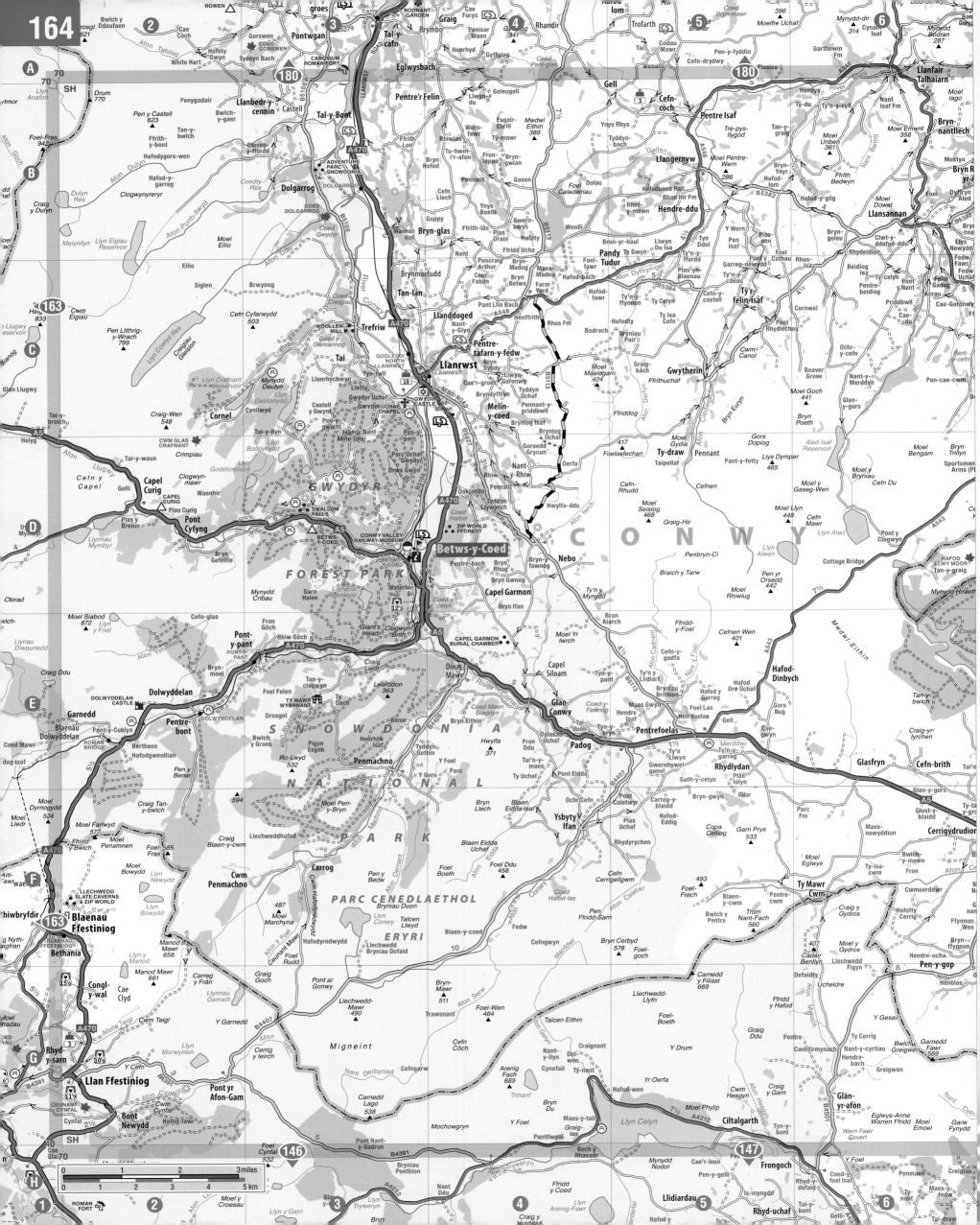

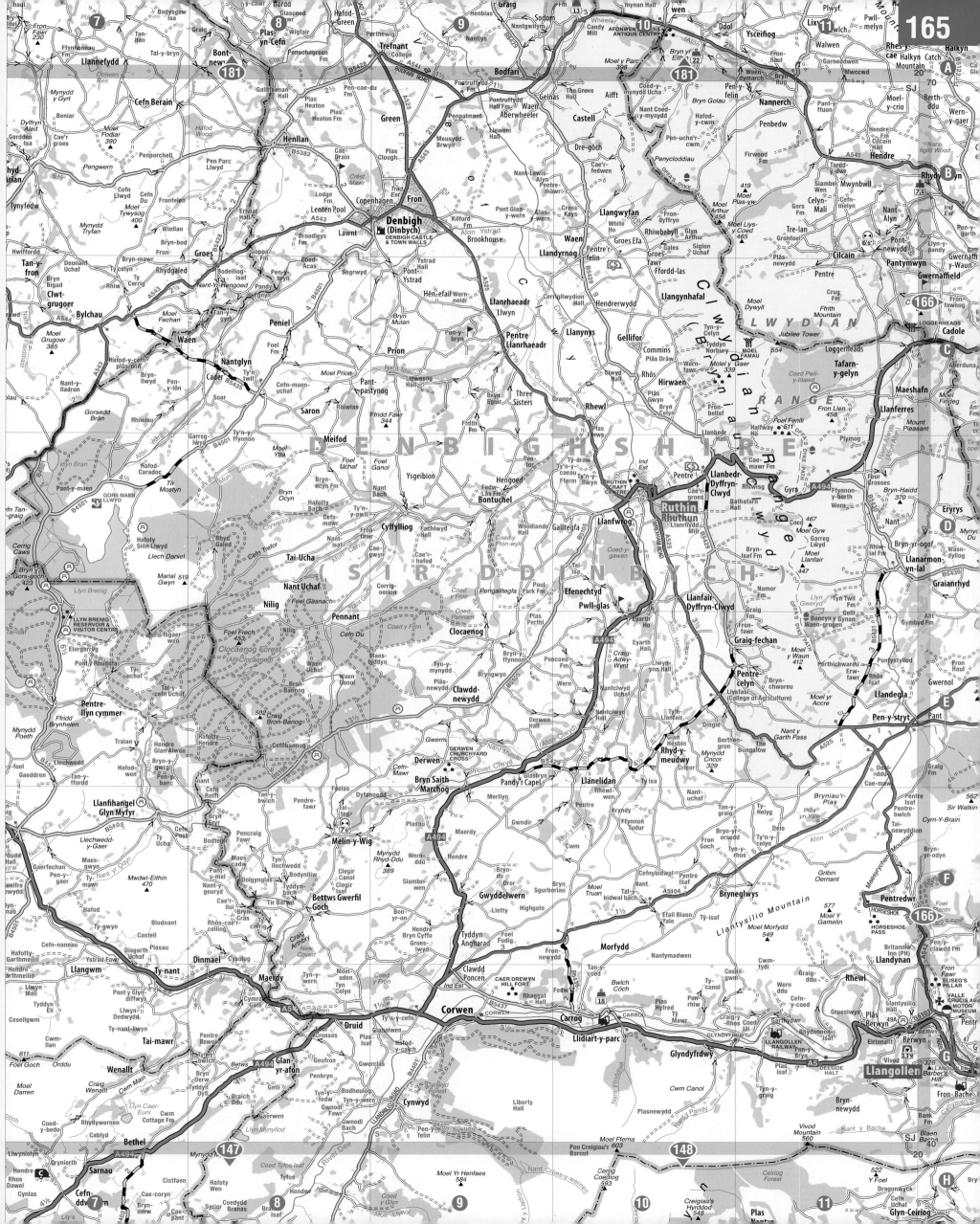

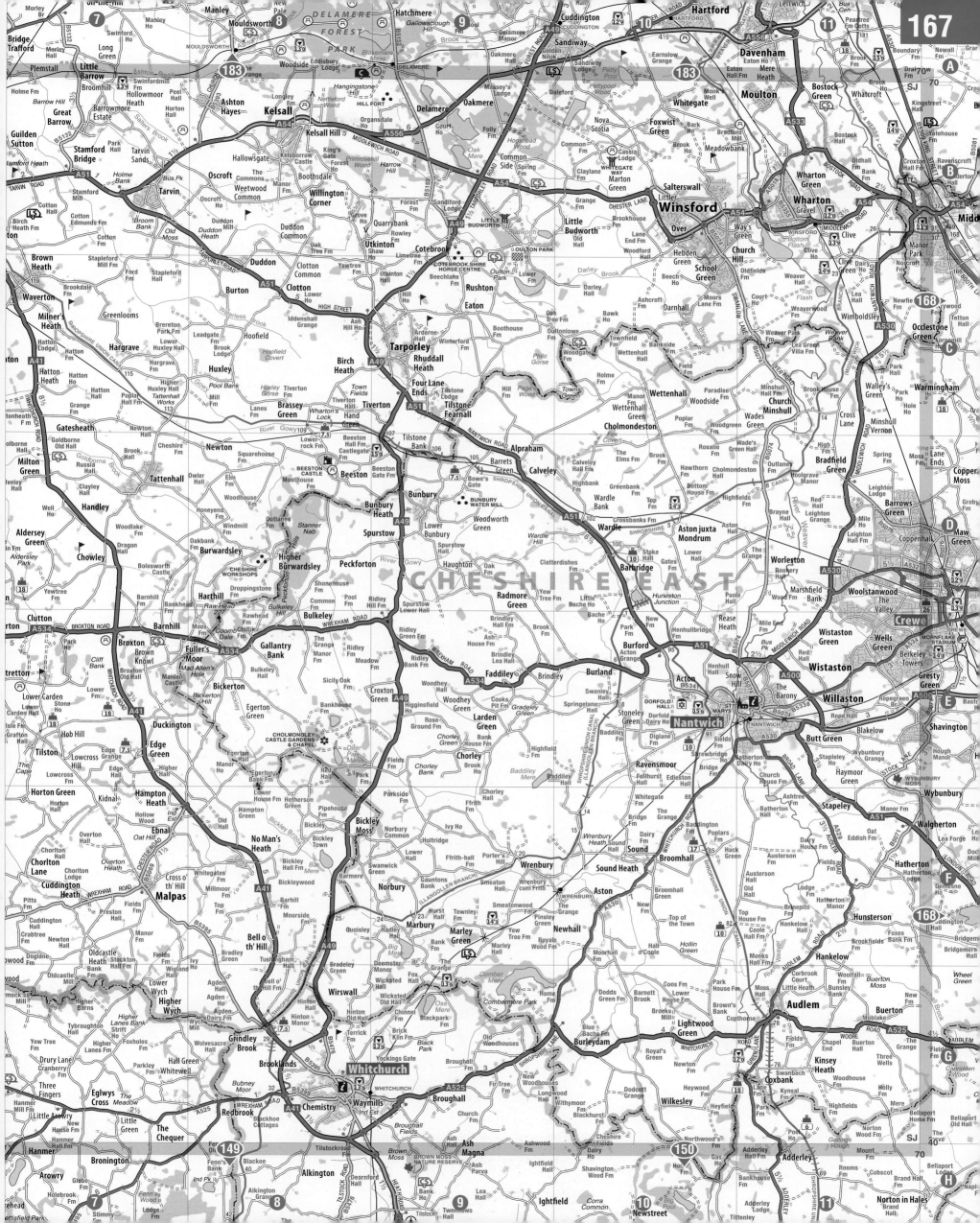

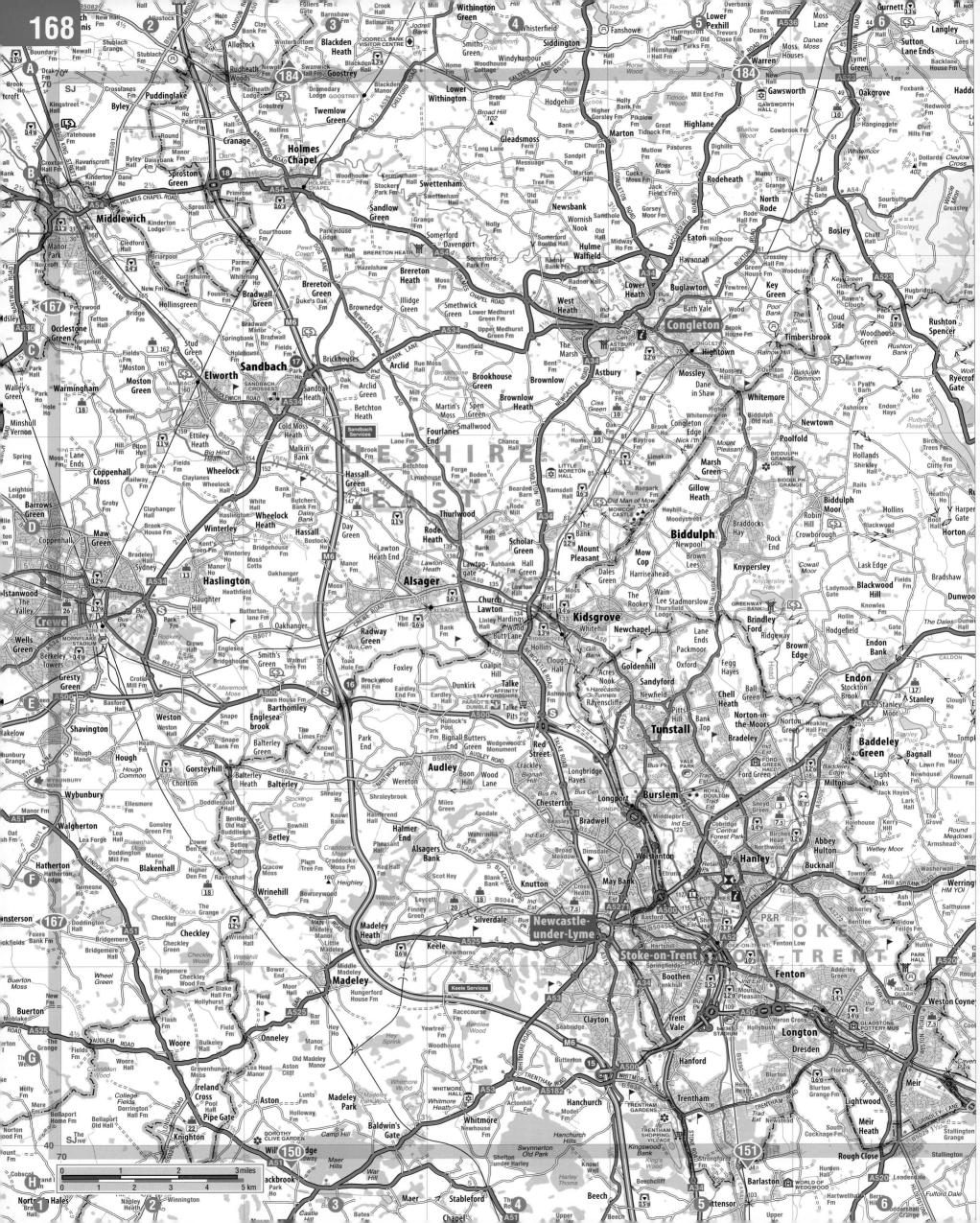

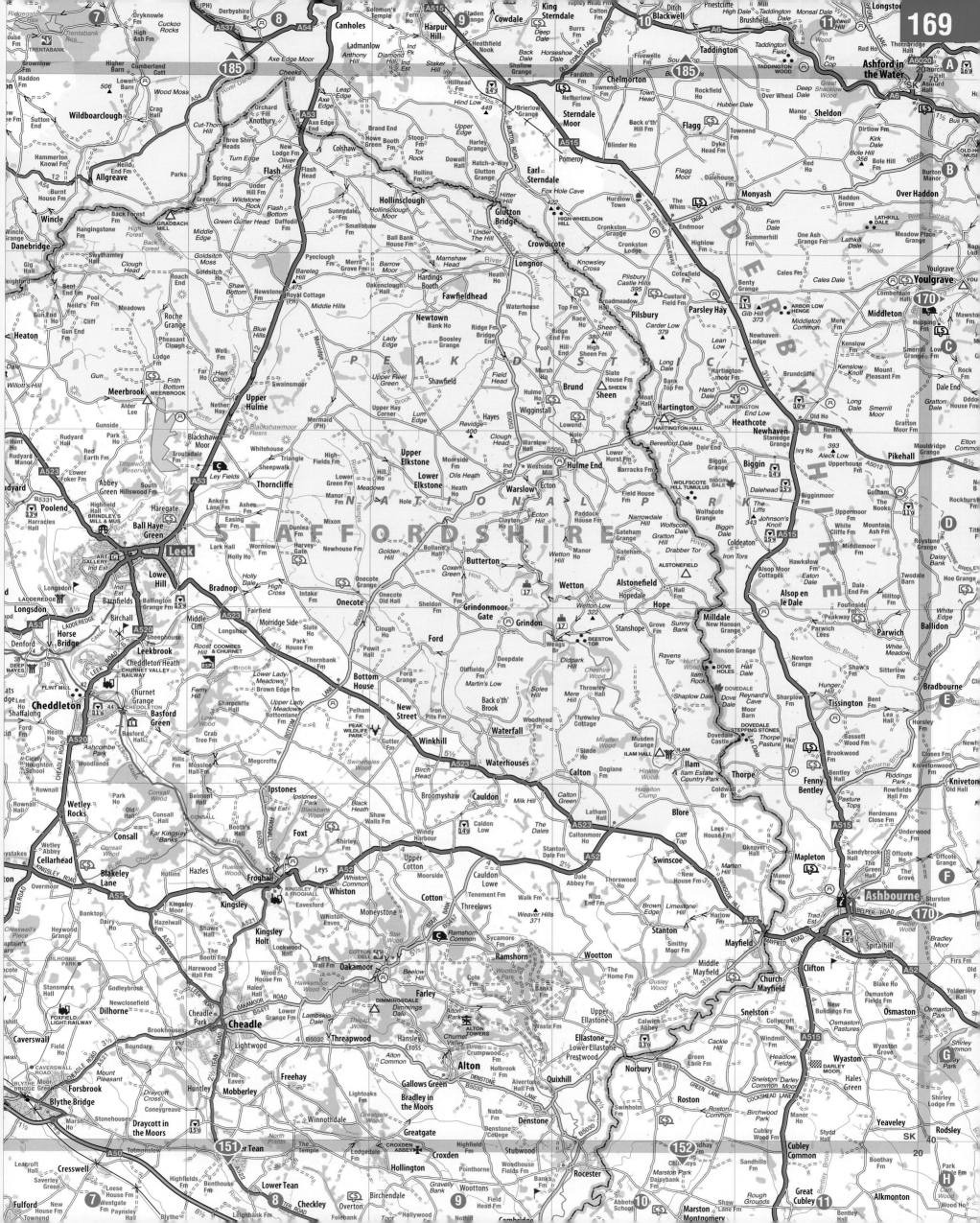

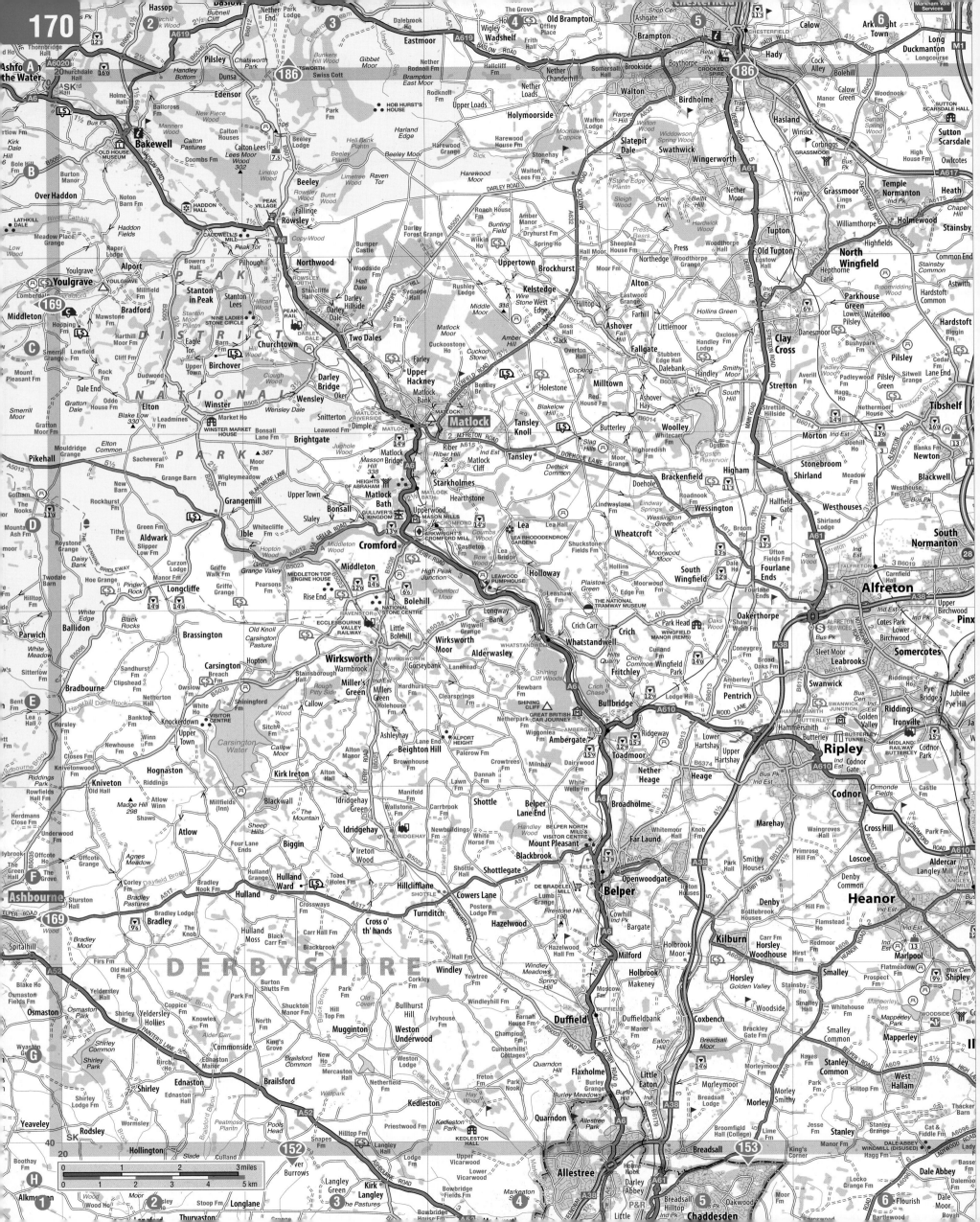

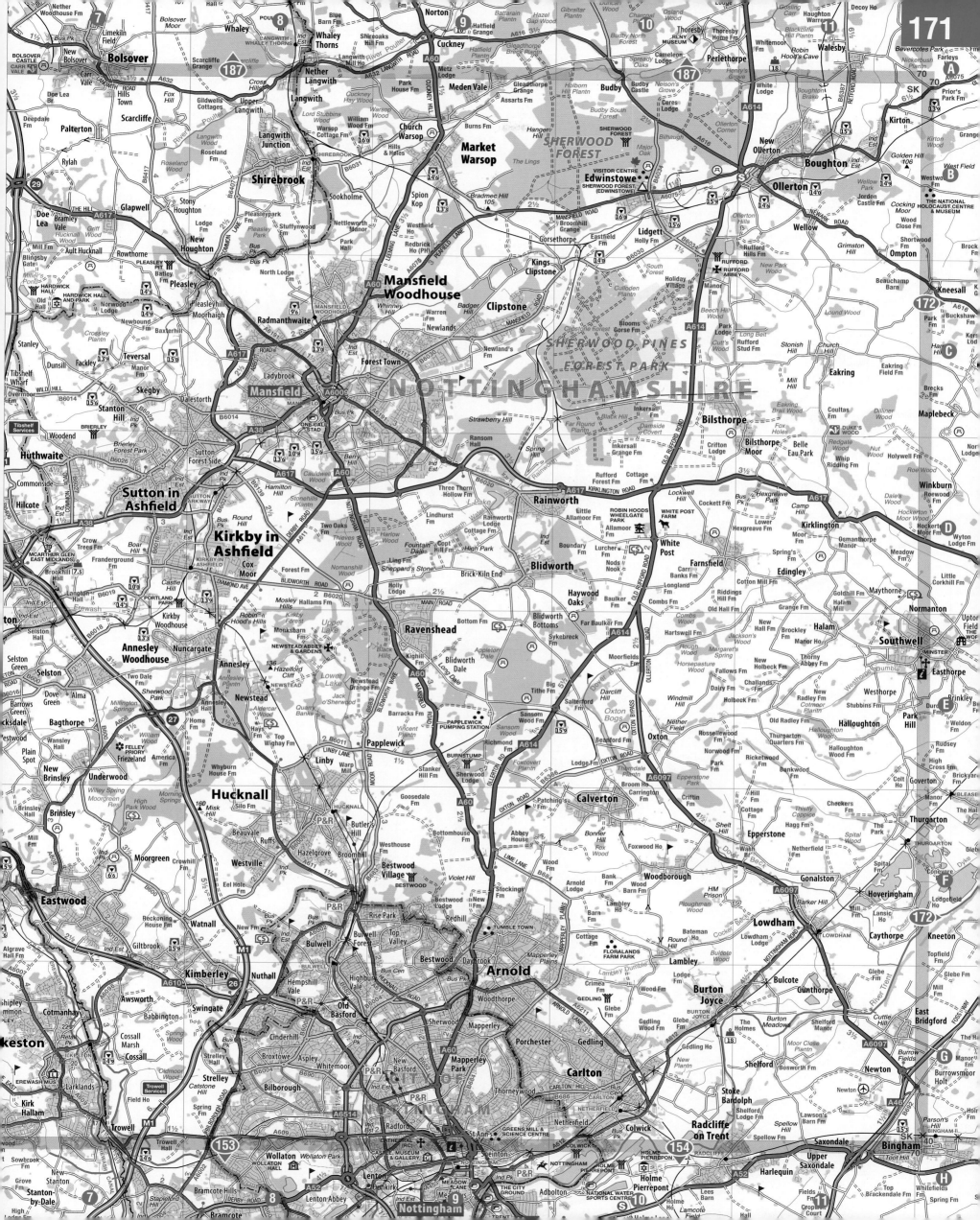

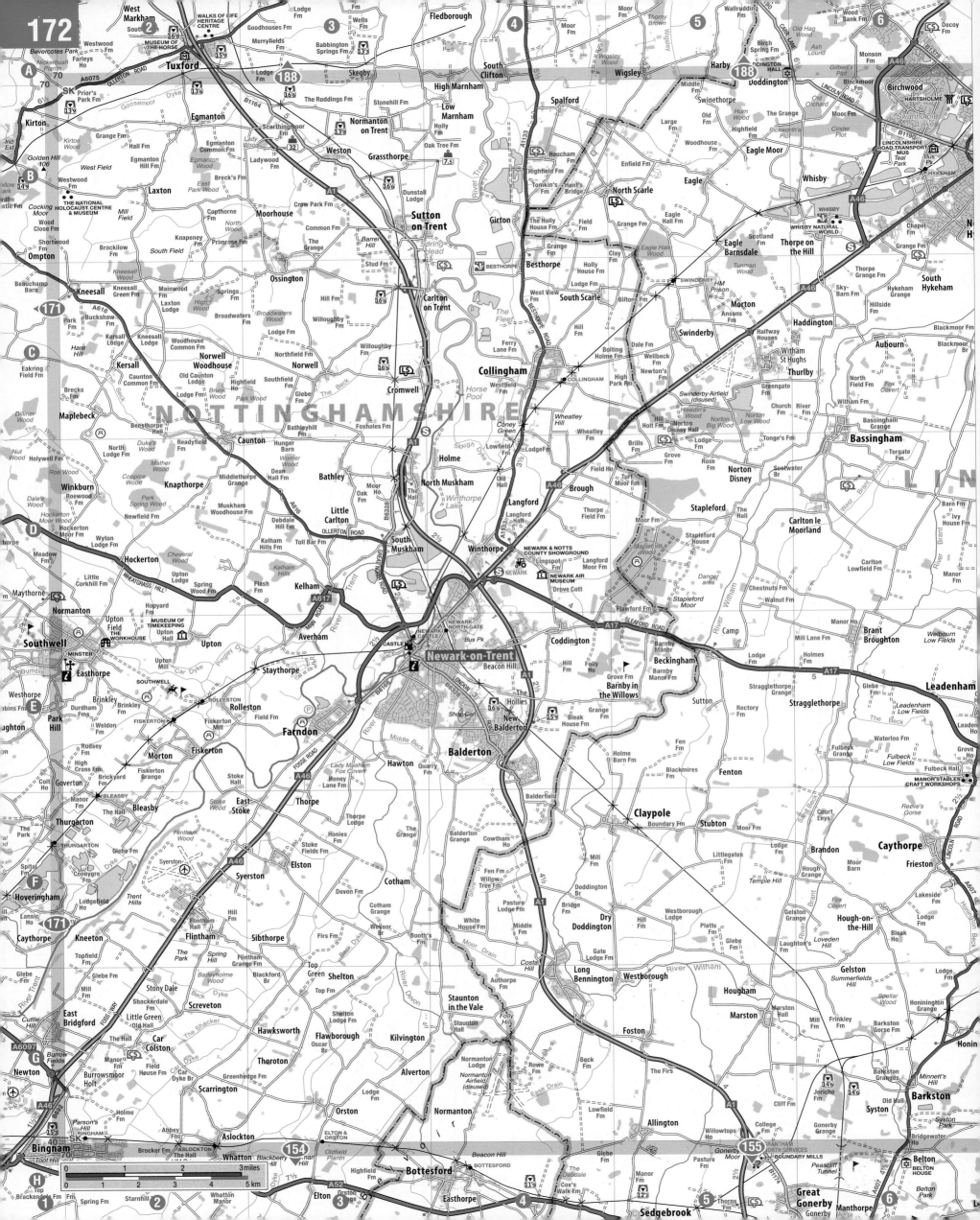

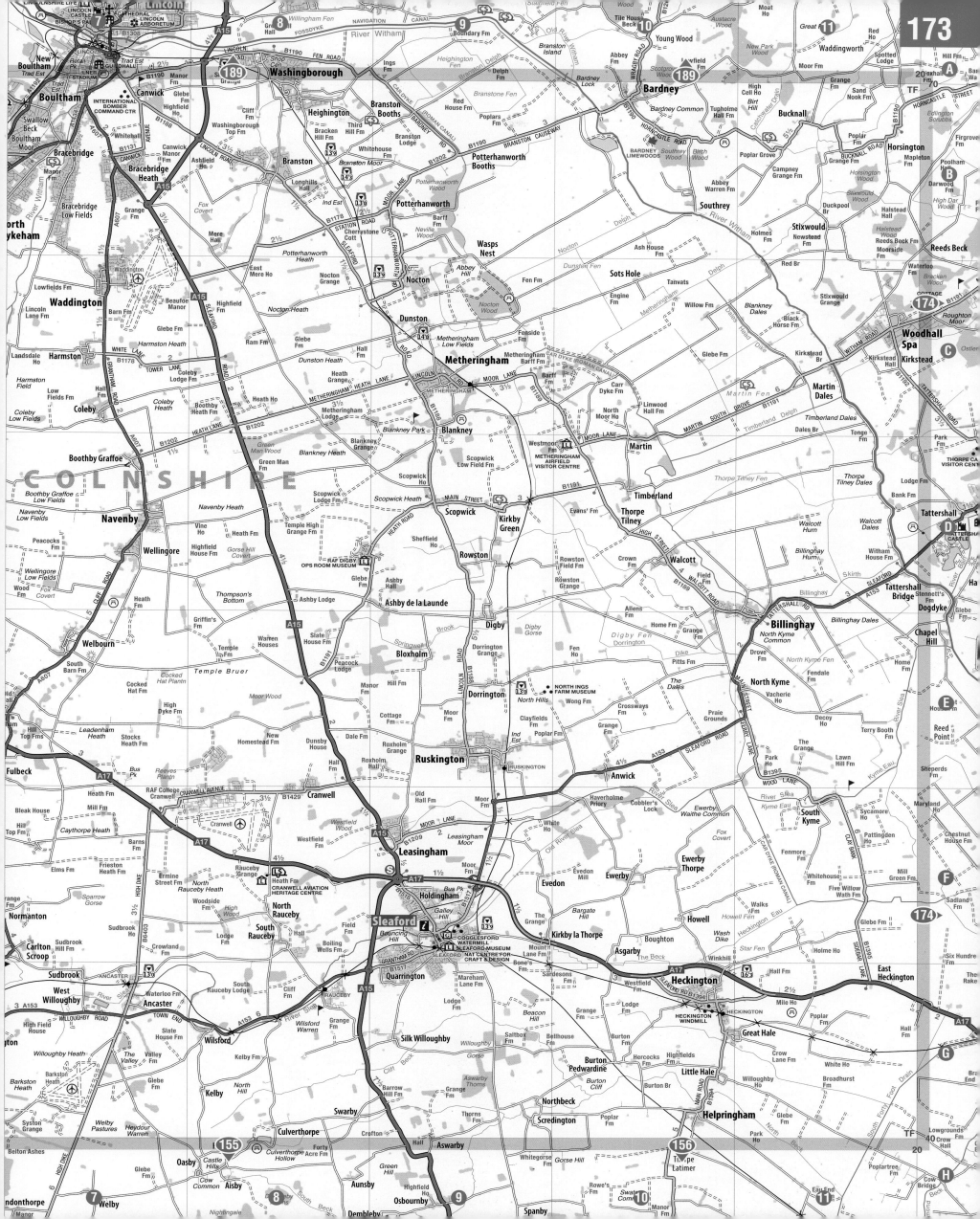

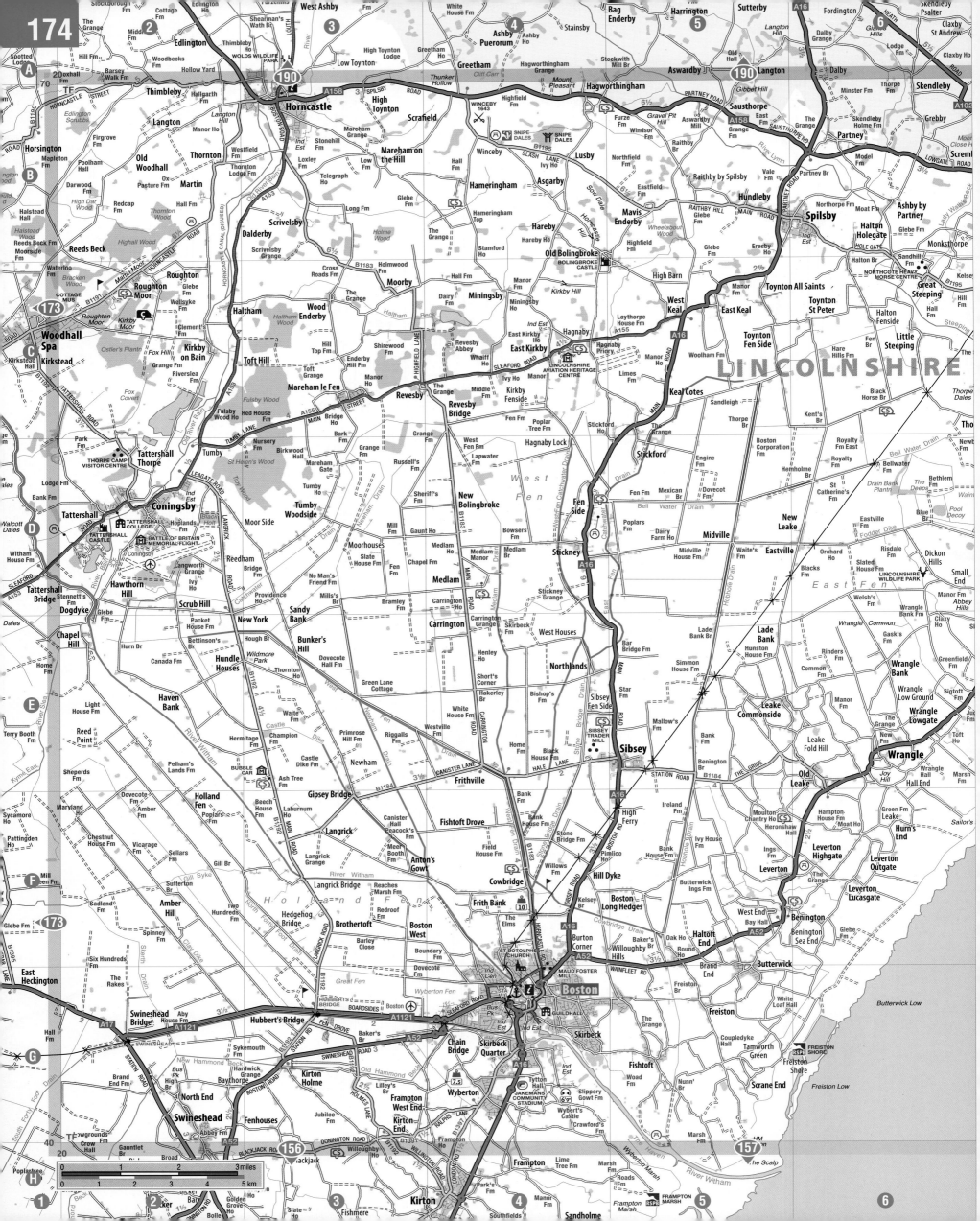

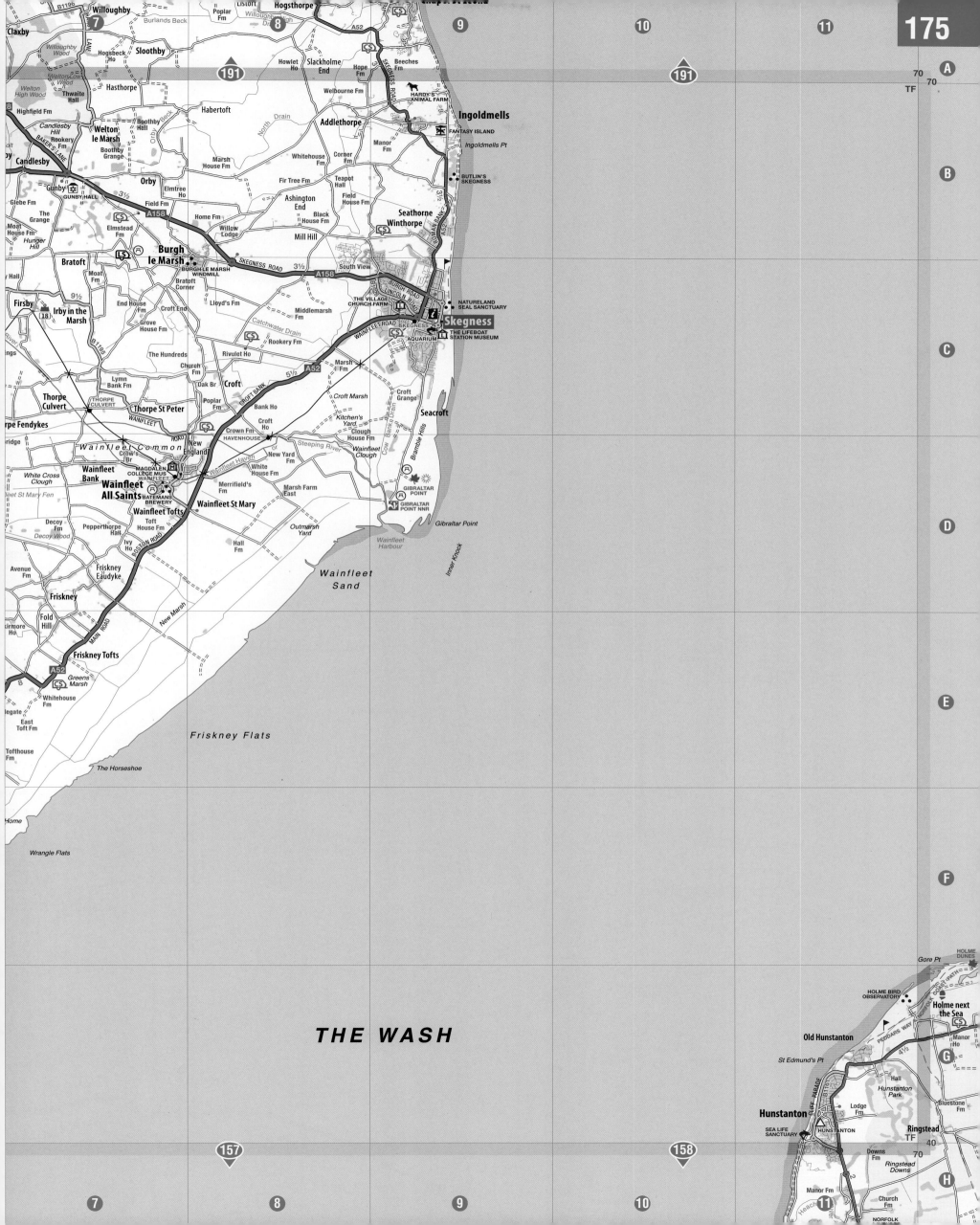

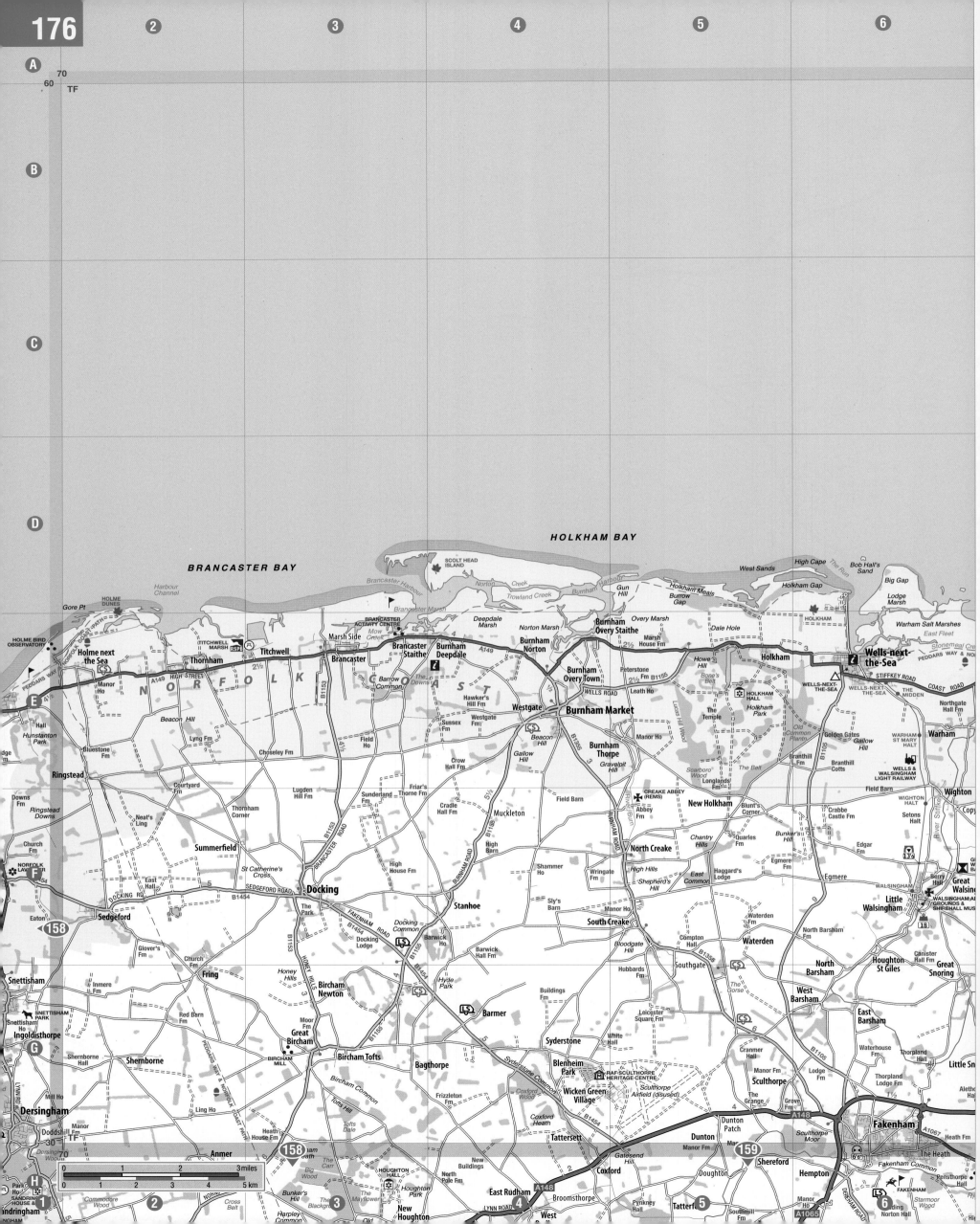

BRANCASTER BAY

HOLKHAM BAY

Scolt Head Island

Gore Pt
HOLME DUNES
Harbour Channel

Holme Bird Observatory
Holme next the Sea
Thornham
Titchwell Marsh RSPB
Titchwell
Marsh Side
Brancaster
Brancaster Staithe
Burnham Deepdale
Burnham Norton
Burnham Overy Staithe
Burnham Overy Town
Holkham
Wells-next-the-Sea

NORFOLK COAST

Ringstead
Hunstanton Park
Beacon Hill
Lyng Fm
Choseley Fm
Westgate
Burnham Market
Burnham Thorpe
Wells & Walsingham Light Railway
Warham
Wighton

Church Fm
Ringstead Downs
Summerfield
St Catherine's Cross
Docking
Muckleton
North Creake
New Holkham
Wighton Halt
Great Walsingham

Snettisham
Ingoldisthorpe
Sedgeford
Fring
Bircham Newton
Great Bircham
Stanhoe
South Creake
Waterden
North Barsham
Little Walsingham

Dersingham
Shernborne
Bircham Tofts
Bagthorpe
Blenheim Park
RAF Sculthorpe Heritage Centre
Wicken Green Village
Syderstone
Sculthorpe

Anmer
Houghton Hall
East Rudham
Coxford
Dunton
Shereford
Hempton
Fakenham

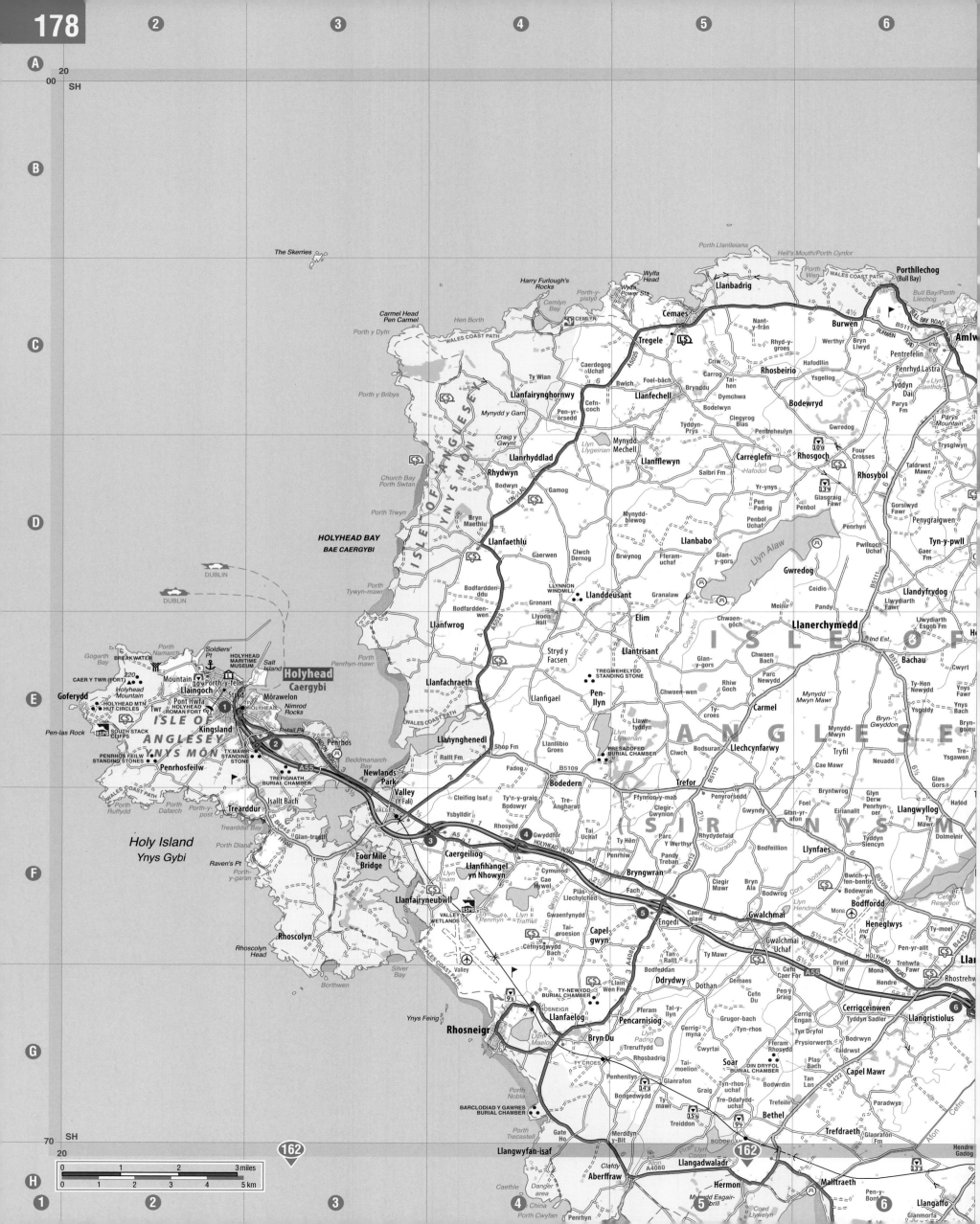

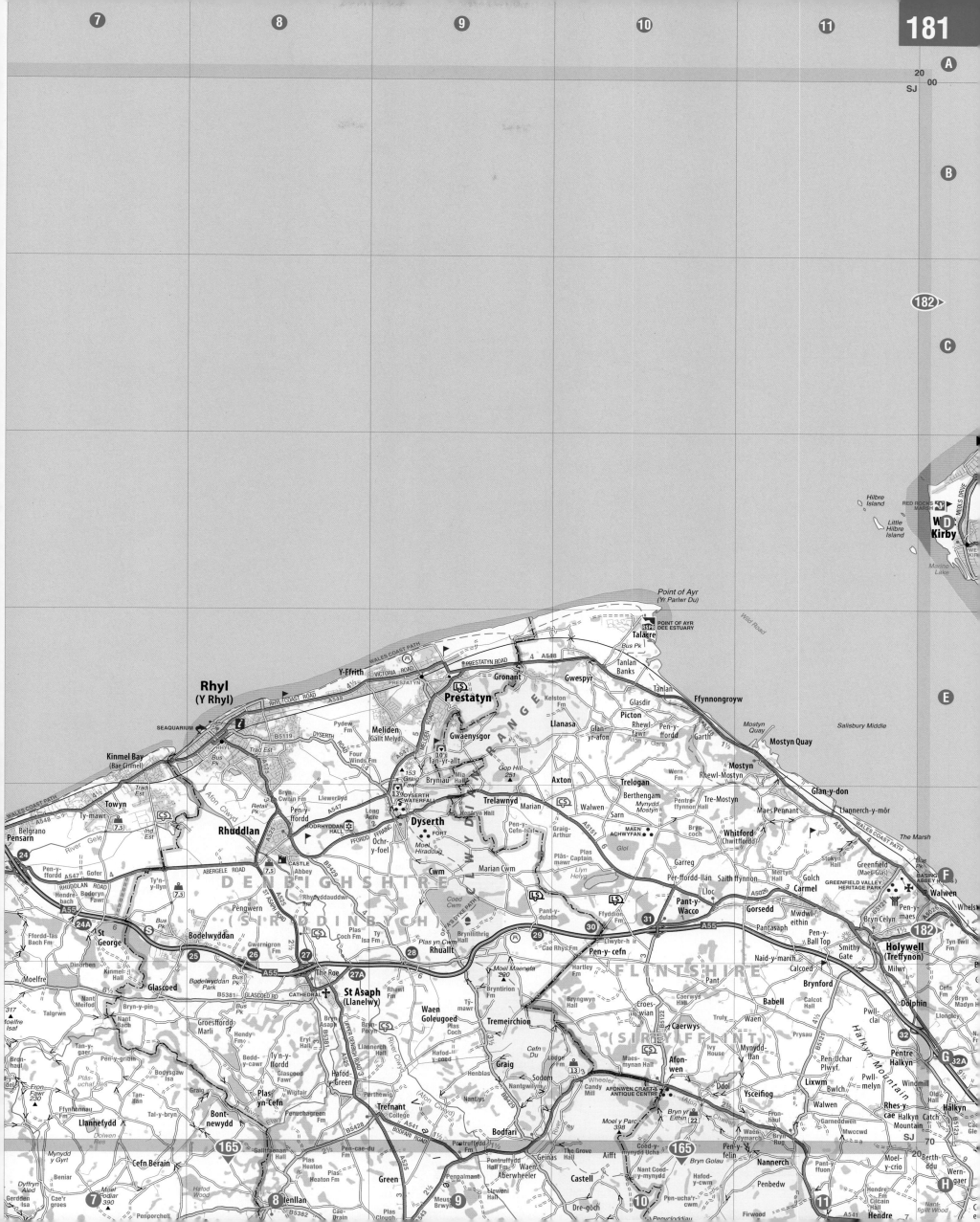

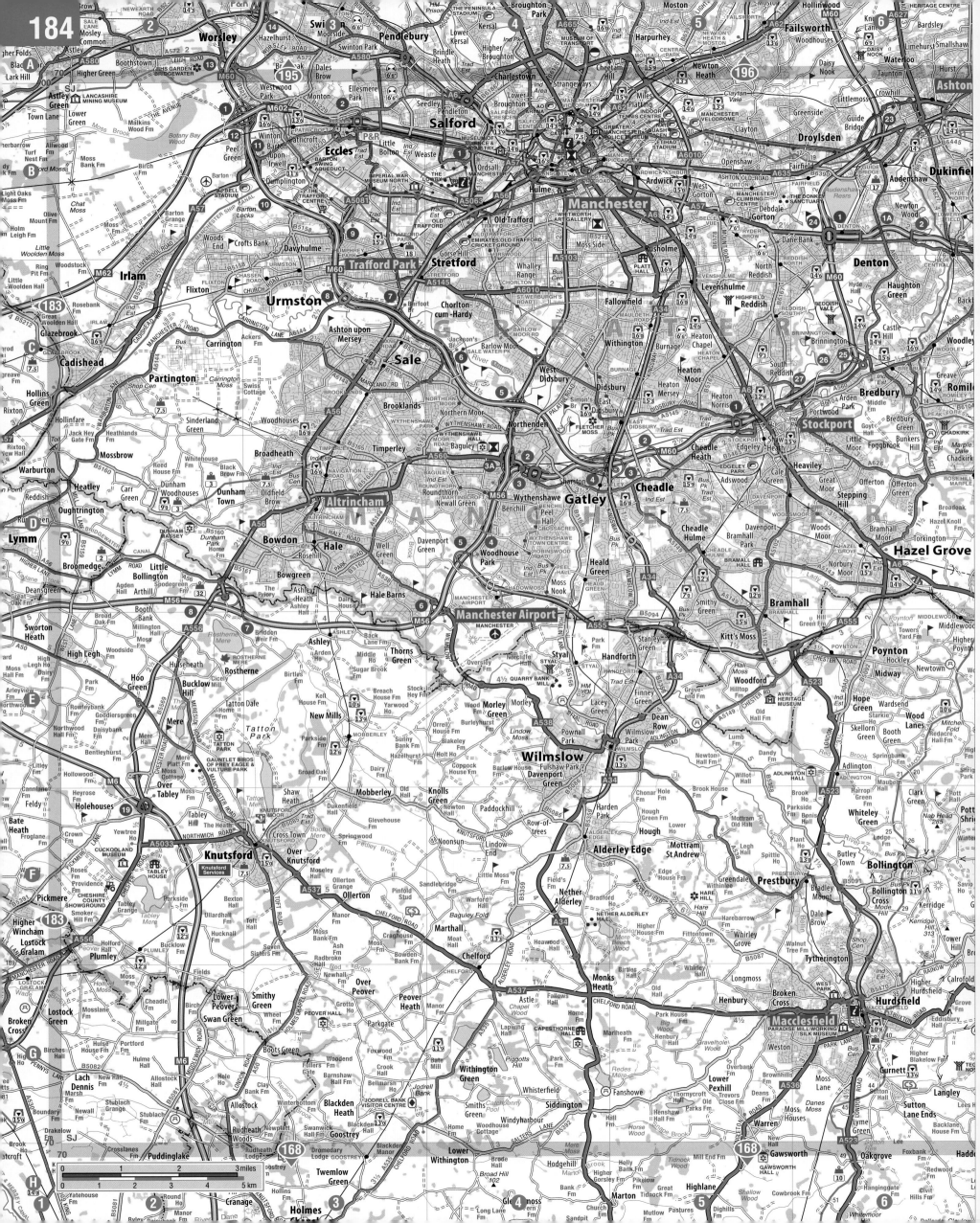

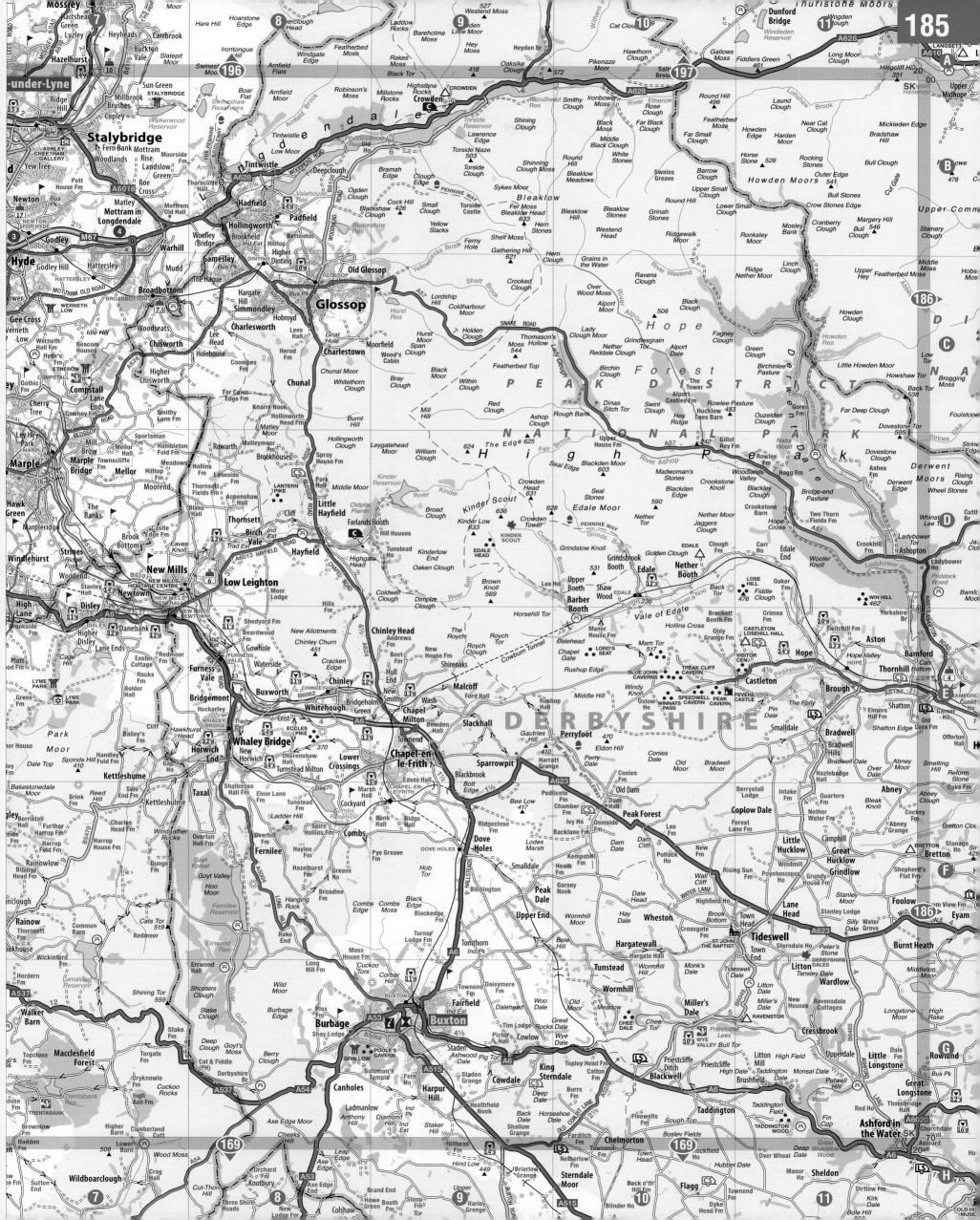

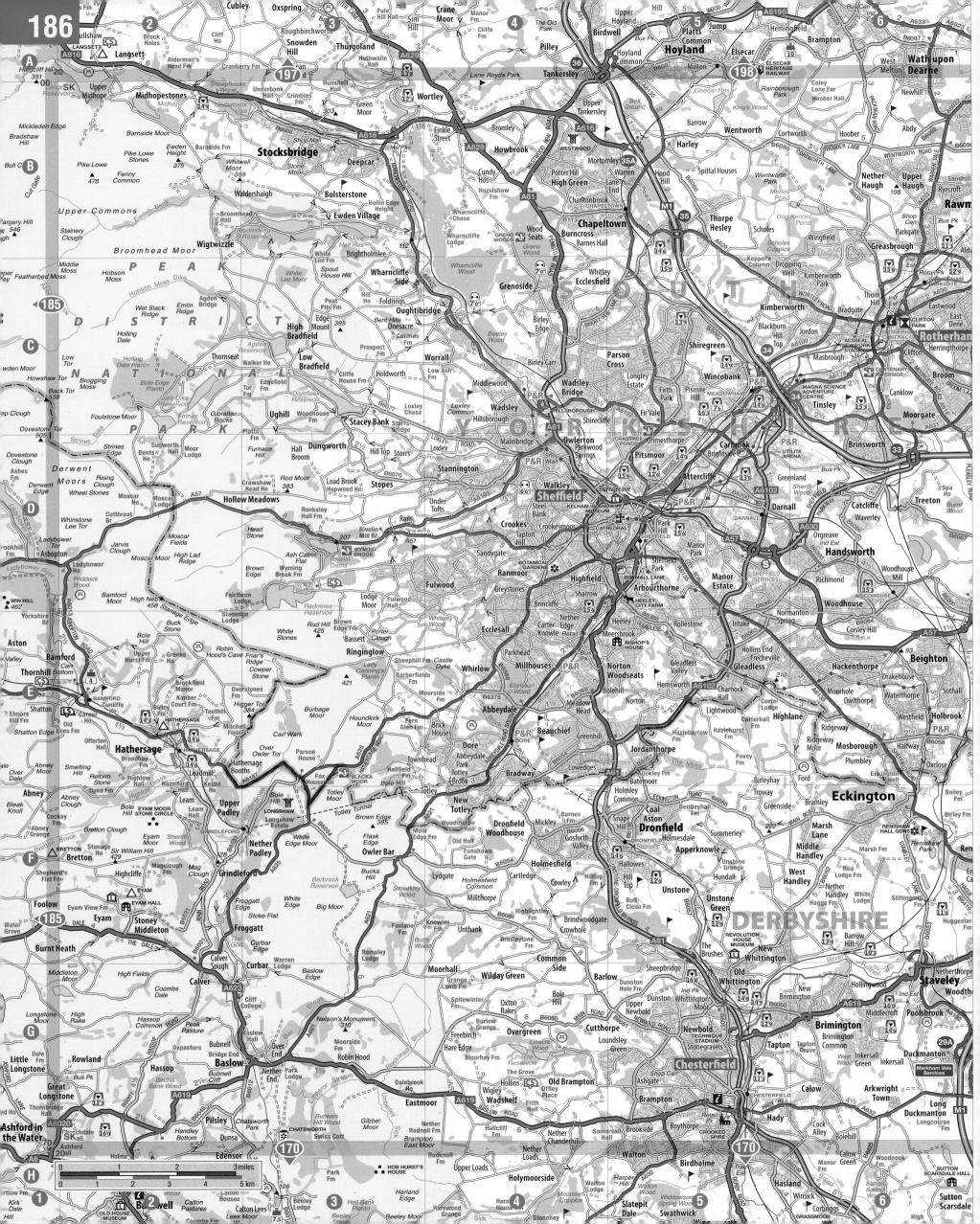

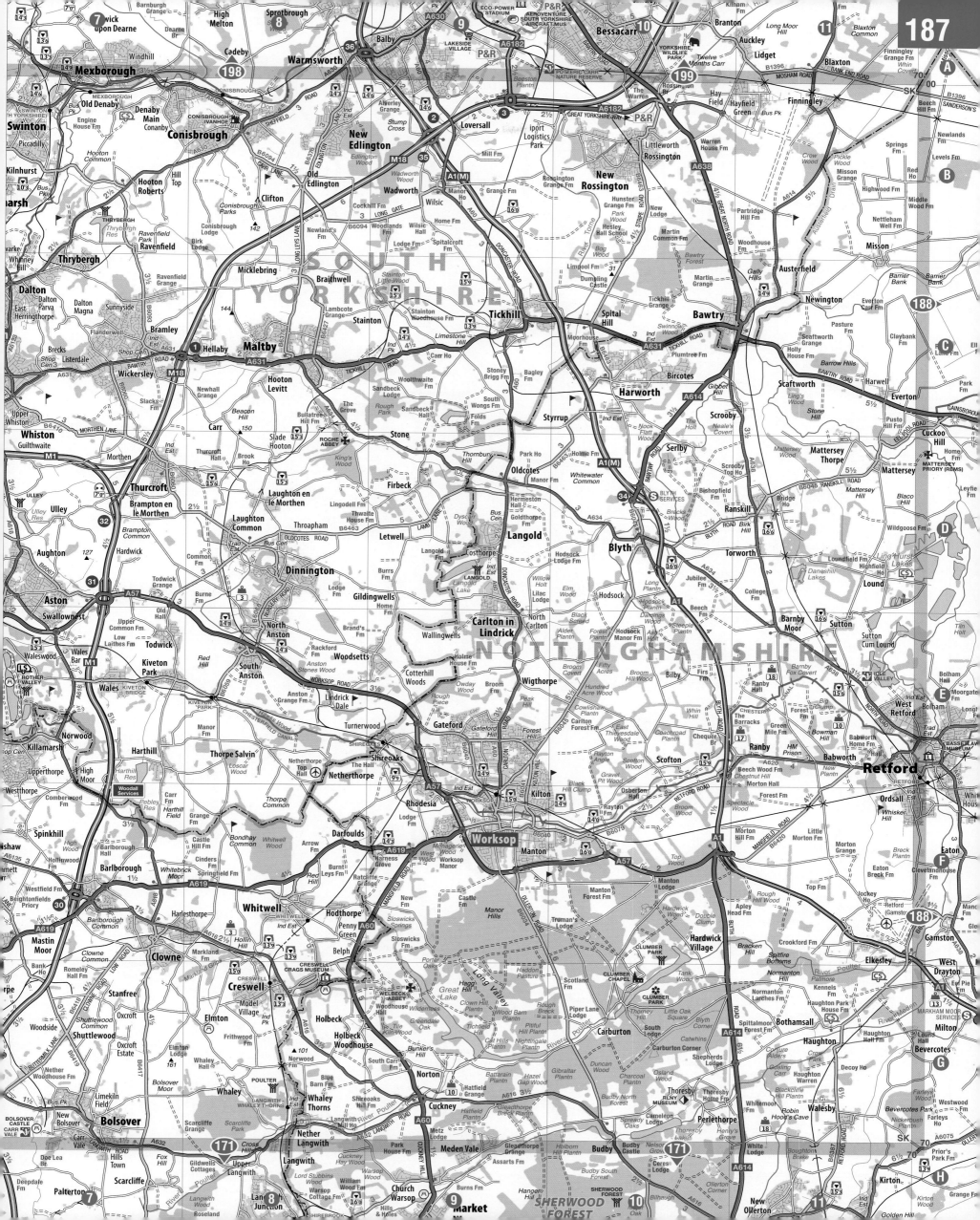

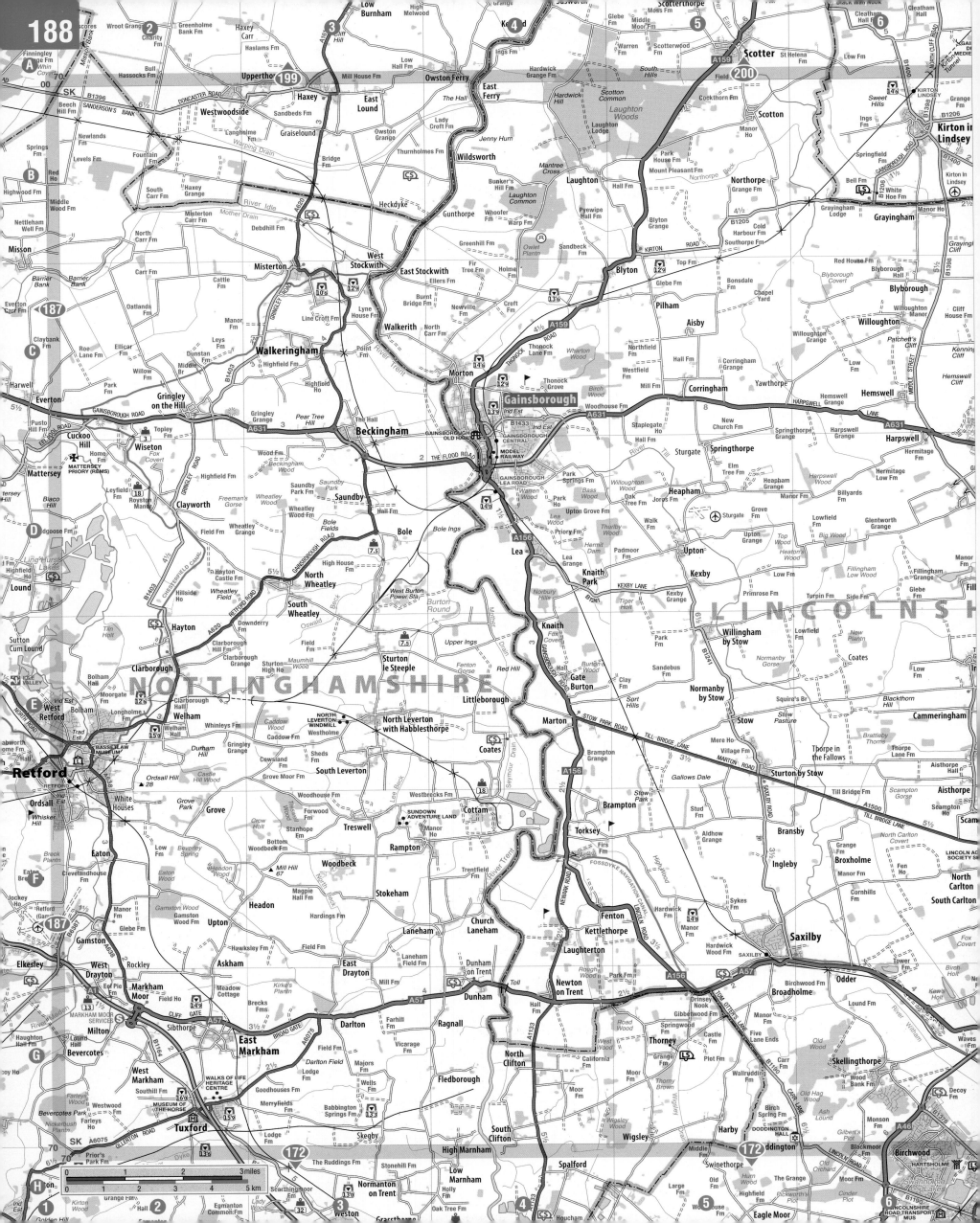

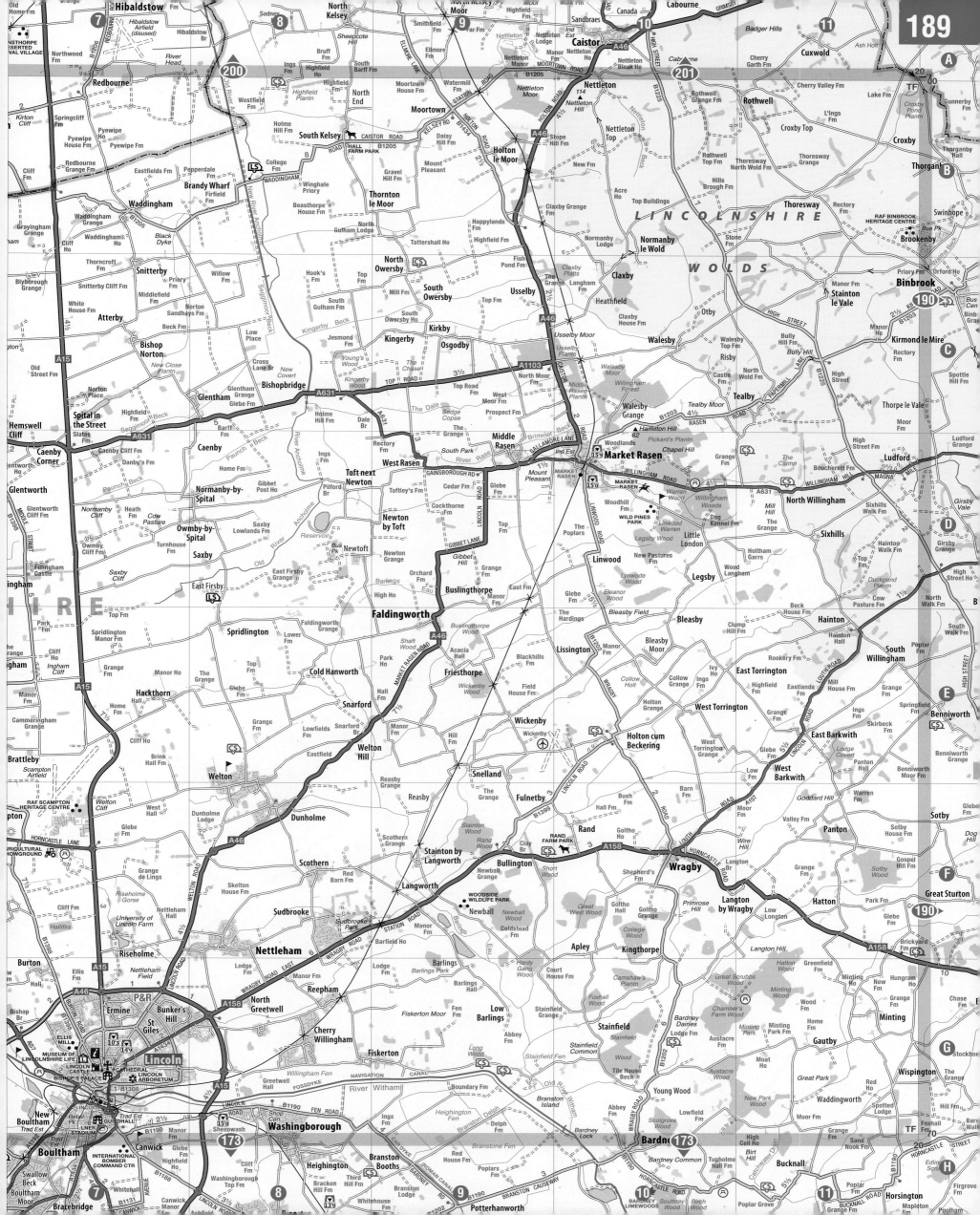

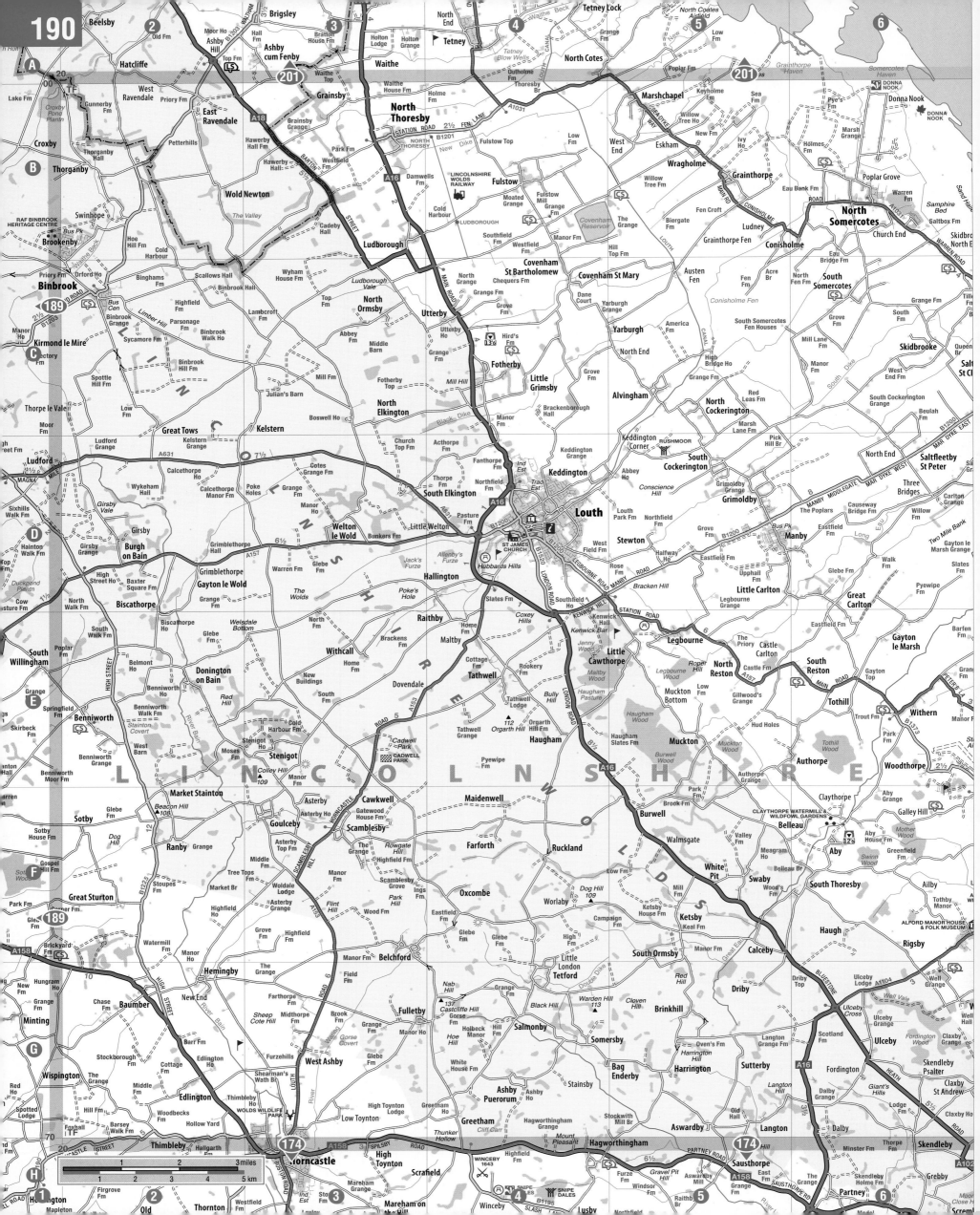

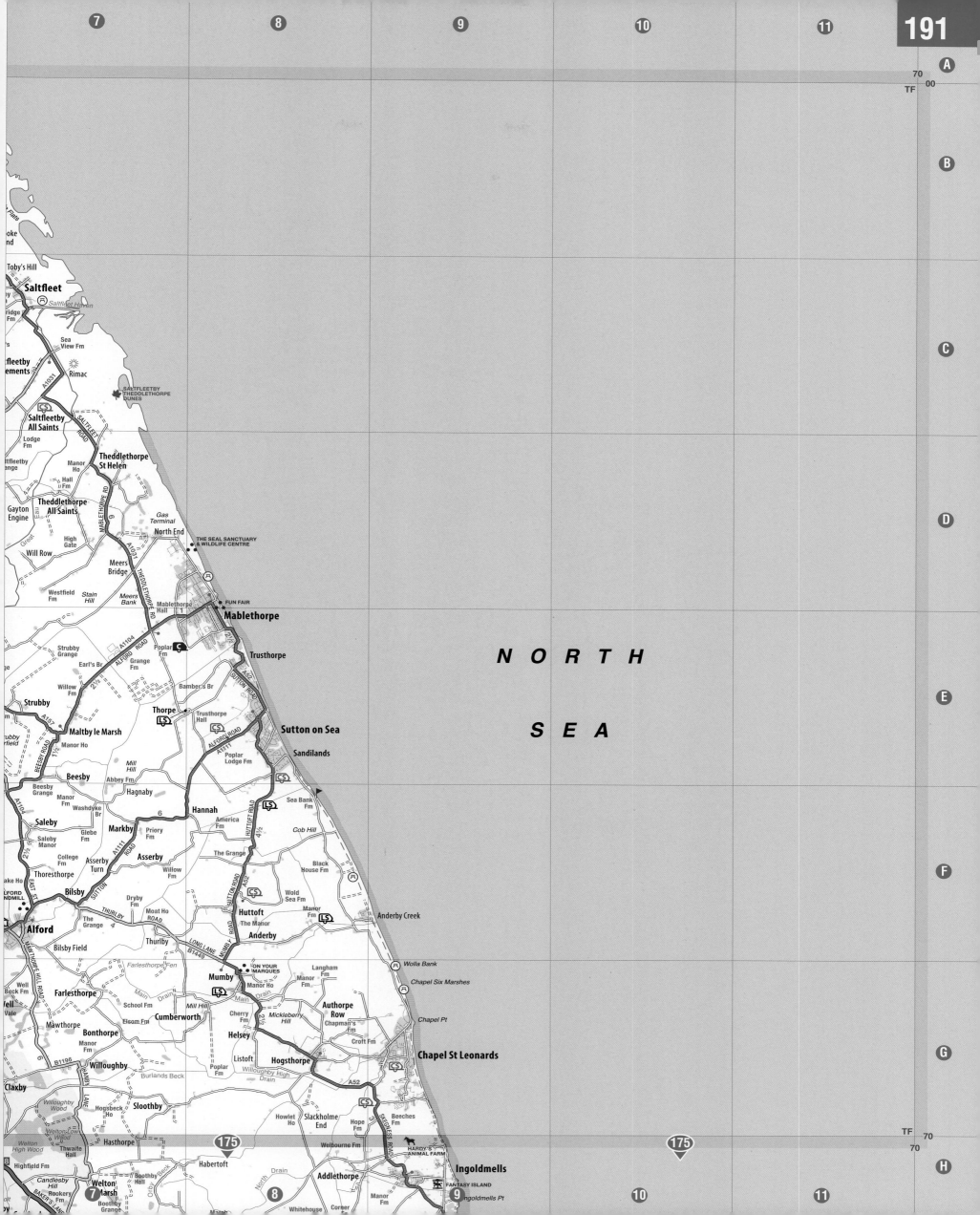

A

70
00
TF

B

C

Toby's Hill
Saltfleet
Saltfleet Haven
Sea View Fm
Rimac
A1031
Saltfleetby
tlfleetby
ements
SALTFLEETBY
THEDDLETHORPE
DUNES

Saltfleetby
All Saints
Lodge Fm
Manor Ho
Hall Fm
Theddlethorpe
St Helen

SALTFLEET ROAD

Theddlethorpe
All Saints
Gayton Engine
High Gate
Will Row

MABLETHORPE RD

A1031

Gas Terminal
North End
THE SEAL SANCTUARY
& WILDLIFE CENTRE

D

Meers Bridge
Westfield Fm
Stain Hill
Meers Bank
Mablethorpe Hall 1

THEDDLETHORPE RD

FUN FAIR

Mablethorpe

Strubby Grange
Earl's Br
Grange Fm
Poplar Fm
CS

A1104
ALFORD ROAD

Trusthorpe

Willow Fm
2½
Bamber's Br

SUTTON ROAD

N O R T H

Strubby
Thorpe
LS
Trusthorpe Hall
CS
Sutton on Sea

A157
Maltby le Marsh
Manor Ho

ALFORD ROAD
A1111

Sandilands

S E A

E

Beesby
Mill Hill
Poplar Lodge Fm

11½

BEESBY ROAD

Beesby Grange
Manor Fm
Washdyke Br
Hagnaby
Abbey Fm
CS

A1104
Hannah
America Fm
LS
Sea Bank Fm

Saleby
6
Cob Hill

Markby
Priory Fm

HUTTOFT ROAD

4½

Saleby Manor
Glebe Fm
The Grange

College Fm
Asserby
Willow Fm
Black House Fm

F

A1111 ROAD

Thorsthorpe
Asserby Turn

Dryby Fm
Wold Sea Fm

Bilsby
Moat Ho Fm
A52
Manor Fm
LS

ake Ho
FORD
NDMILL
The Grange
4

SUTTON ROAD

Huttoft
The Manor
Anderby Creek

Alford
THURLBY

Bilsby Field
Thurlby
Anderby

Farlesthorpe Fen

HUMBY ROAD
LONG LANE
B1449

Wolla Bank
R

Well Beck Fm
Mumby
ON YOUR MARQUES
Manor Fm
Langham Fm
Chapel Six Marshes
R

Farlesthorpe
Manor Ho
LS
Main Drain

ell
Vale
School Fm
Mill Hill
Cherry Fm
Mickleberry Hill
Authorpe Row
Chapel Pt

Mawthorpe
Cumberworth
Elsom Fm
2½
Chapman's Fm

Bonthorpe
Helsey
Croft Fm

G

Manor Fm
B1196

Listoft
Poplar Fm
Hogsthorpe
Chapel St Leonards

Willoughby
Willoughby High Drain
A52
CS

Claxby
Burlands Beck

HAMBY LANE

Willoughby Wood
Hogsbeck Ho
Sloothby
Howlet Ho
Slackholme End
Hope Fm
Beeches Fm

Welton Low
TF
70
70

Welton High Wood
Hasthorpe
175
Welbourne Fm
175

Thwaite Hall
HARDY'S ANIMAL FARM

Highfield Fm
Habertoft

H

Candlesby Hill
Rookery
Welton Marsh
7
Addlethorpe
Ingoldmells
FANTASY ISLAND
Ingoldmells Pt

Boothby Hall
8
9

Boothby Grange
Manor Fm

7   8   9   10   11

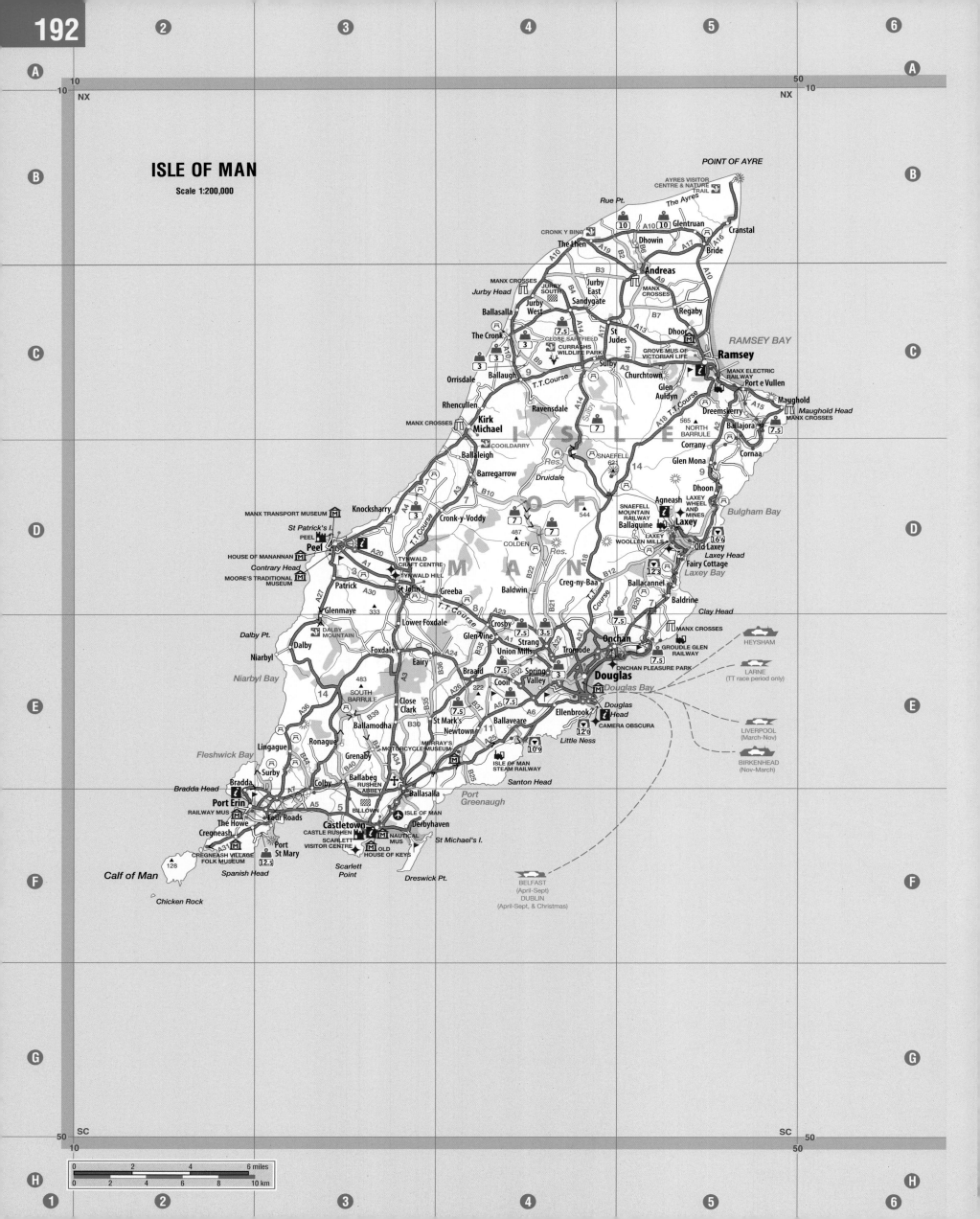

ISLE OF MAN

Scale 1:200,000

POINT OF AYRE

AYRES VISITOR
CENTRE & NATURE
TRAIL

Rue Pt.   The Ayres

CRONK Y BING   A10   10   Glentruan   Cranstal
                            Dhowin
The Lhen   A19   B2   A17   Bride
A10   B6   A16
                    B3   Andreas   A9   A10
MANX CROSSES   Jurby   A9
Jurby Head   JURBY   East   MANX CROSSES
          SOUTH   Sandygate   B7   Regaby
Ballasalla   Jurby   B4   Dhoor
          West   A14   A13
The Cronk   CLOSE SARTFIELD   St
                    3   Judes   RAMSEY BAY
          3   CURRAGHS   B14
                    WILDLIFE PARK   Sulby   GROVE MUS.OF
          3   VICTORIAN LIFE   Ramsey
Orrisdale   Ballaugh   B9   Port e Vullen
                    9   Sulby   Churchtown   MANX ELECTRIC
                    T.T.Course   Glen   RAILWAY
Rhencullen   Ravensdale   Auldyn   Maughold
                    A14   7   Dreemskerry   Maughold Head
MANX CROSSES   Kirk   565   A18 T.T.Course   MANX CROSSES
          Michael   NORTH   7.5
                    COOILDARRY   BARRULE   Ballajora
          Ballaleigh   622   Corrany   Cornaa
          Barregarrow   SNAEFELL   Glen Mona
                    Res.   14   9
                    Druidale   Dhoon   Bulgham Bay
MANX TRANSPORT MUSEUM   B10   SNAEFELL   Agneash   LAXEY WHEEL
Knocksharry   7   544   MOUNTAIN   AND MINES
          3   RAILWAY   Laxey
St Patrick's I.   Cronk-y-Voddy   7   Ballaquine
PEEL   487   LAXEY   Old Laxey
House OF MANANNAN   COLDEN   WOOLLEN MILLS   16
Peel   A20   Res.   Fairy Cottage
          TYNWALD   B2   12   Laxey Bay
Contrary Head   CRAFT CENTRE   Ballacannel
MOORE'S TRADITIONAL   3   A1   B12
MUSEUM   TYNWALD HILL   Baldrine
          Patrick   St John's   Greeba   Baldwin   B20
Glenmaye   A30   333   Creg-ny-Baa   Clay Head
          T.T.Course   A23   MANX CROSSES
Dalby Pt.   Lower Foxdale   Crosby   B21   7.5
          Dalby   7.5   3.5   GROUDLE GLEN
DALBY   Glen Vine   Strang   RAILWAY   HEYSHAM
Niarbyl   MOUNTAIN   A24   Onchan   7.5
          Foxdale   Eairy   Union Mills   Tromode
Niarbyl Bay   483   A5   Spring   3   LARNE
          SOUTH   B35   Braaid   7.5   Valley   Douglas   (TT race period only)
          BARRULE   A26   Cooil   ONCHAN PLEASURE PARK
          14   Close   222   Douglas
                    Clark   St Mark's   7.5   Head   LIVERPOOL
Fleshwick Bay   Ballamodha   B30   Newtown   Ballaveare   Ellenbrook   (March-Nov)
          Ronague   11   A25   Douglas
Lingague   B39   MURRAY'S   Little Ness   Head   BIRKENHEAD
          Surby   MOTORCYCLE   12   CAMERA OBSCURA   (Nov-March)
          Colby   MUSEUM   10
Bradda Head   Ballabeg   ISLE OF MAN
          Bradda   RUSHEN   STEAM RAILWAY
Port Erin   ABBEY   Santon Head
RAILWAY MUS   Four Roads   BILLOWN   Port
          The Howe   A5   Ballasalla   Greenaugh
Cregneash   5   ISLE OF MAN
          Port   Castletown   Derbyhaven
Calf of Man   St Mary   CASTLE RUSHEN   NAUTICAL   St Michael's I.
          CREGNEASH VILLAGE   SCARLETT   MUS
          FOLK MUSEUM   VISITOR CENTRE   OLD
          12.5   HOUSE OF KEYS
          128   Scarlett   Dreswick Pt.
Chicken Rock   Spanish Head   Point   BELFAST
                              (April-Sept)
                              DUBLIN
                              (April-Sept, & Christmas)

0   2   4   6 miles
0   2   4   6   8   10 km

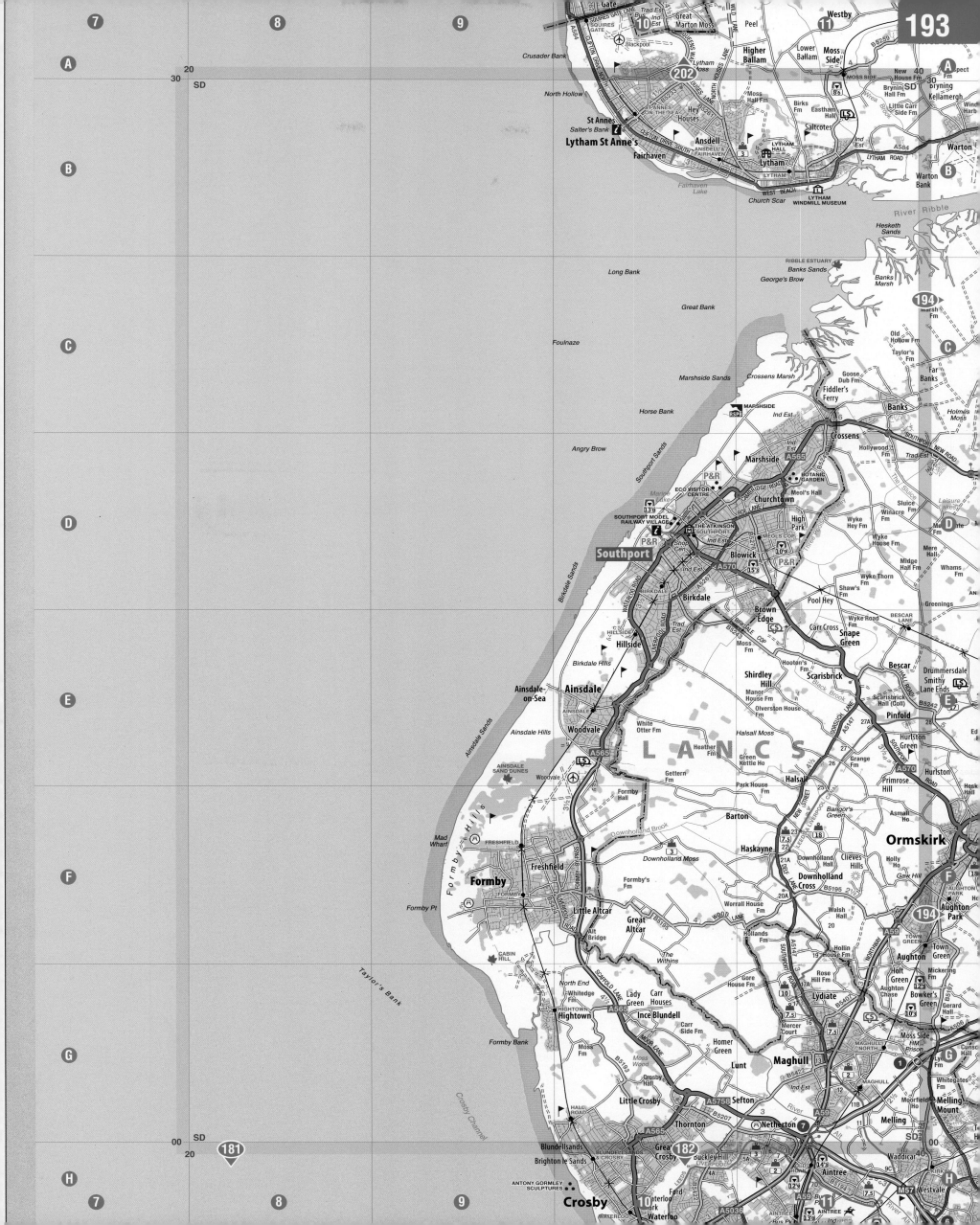

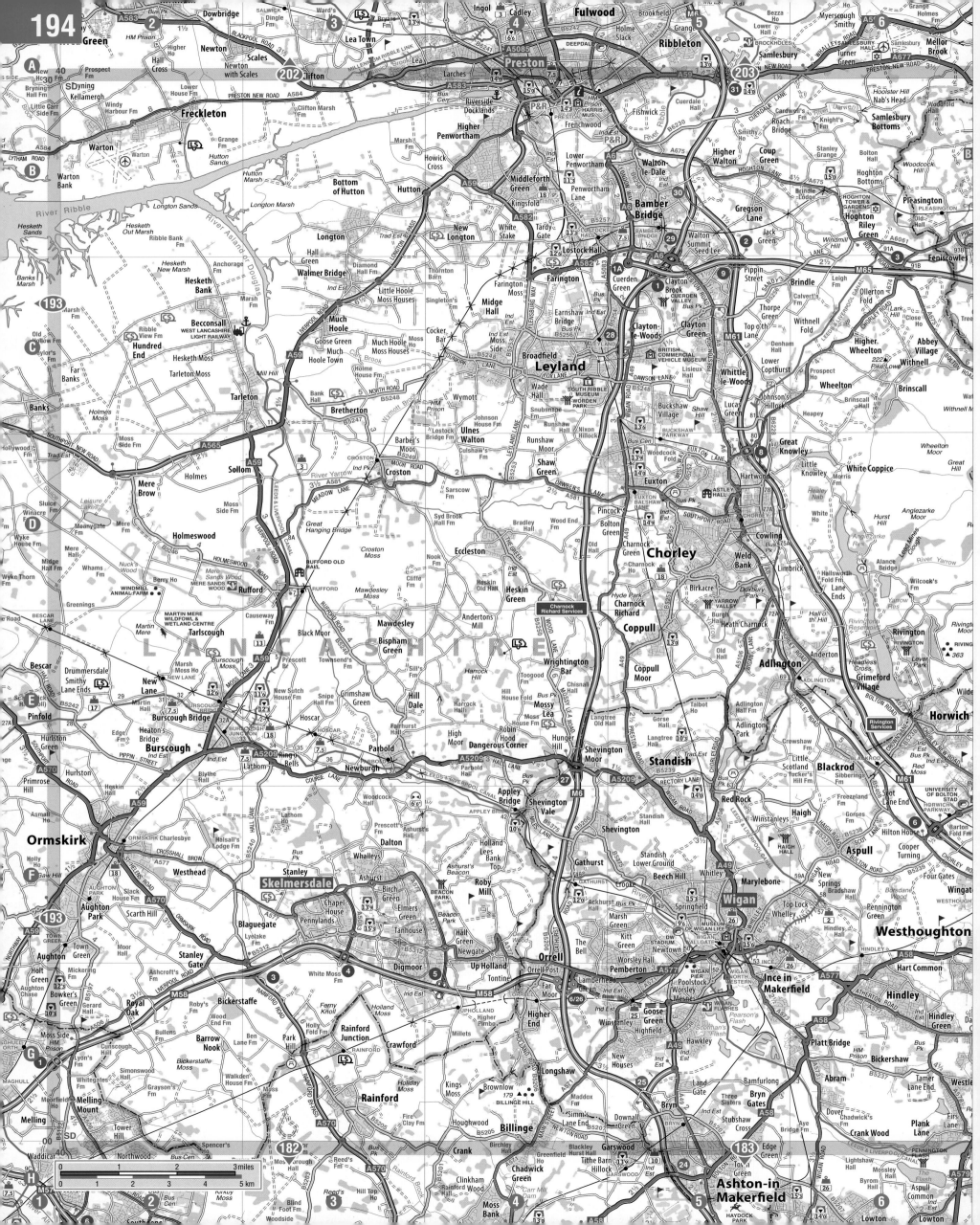

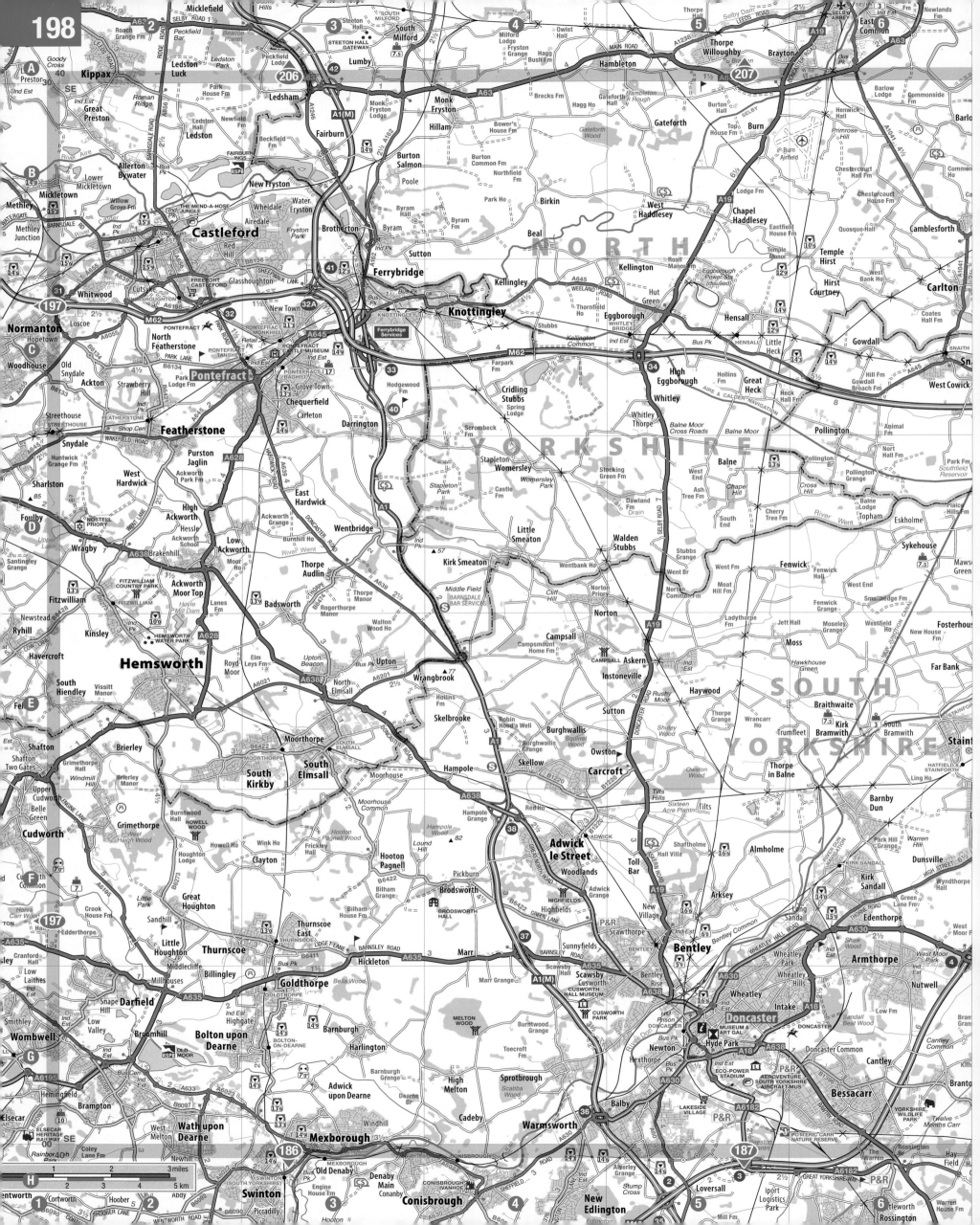

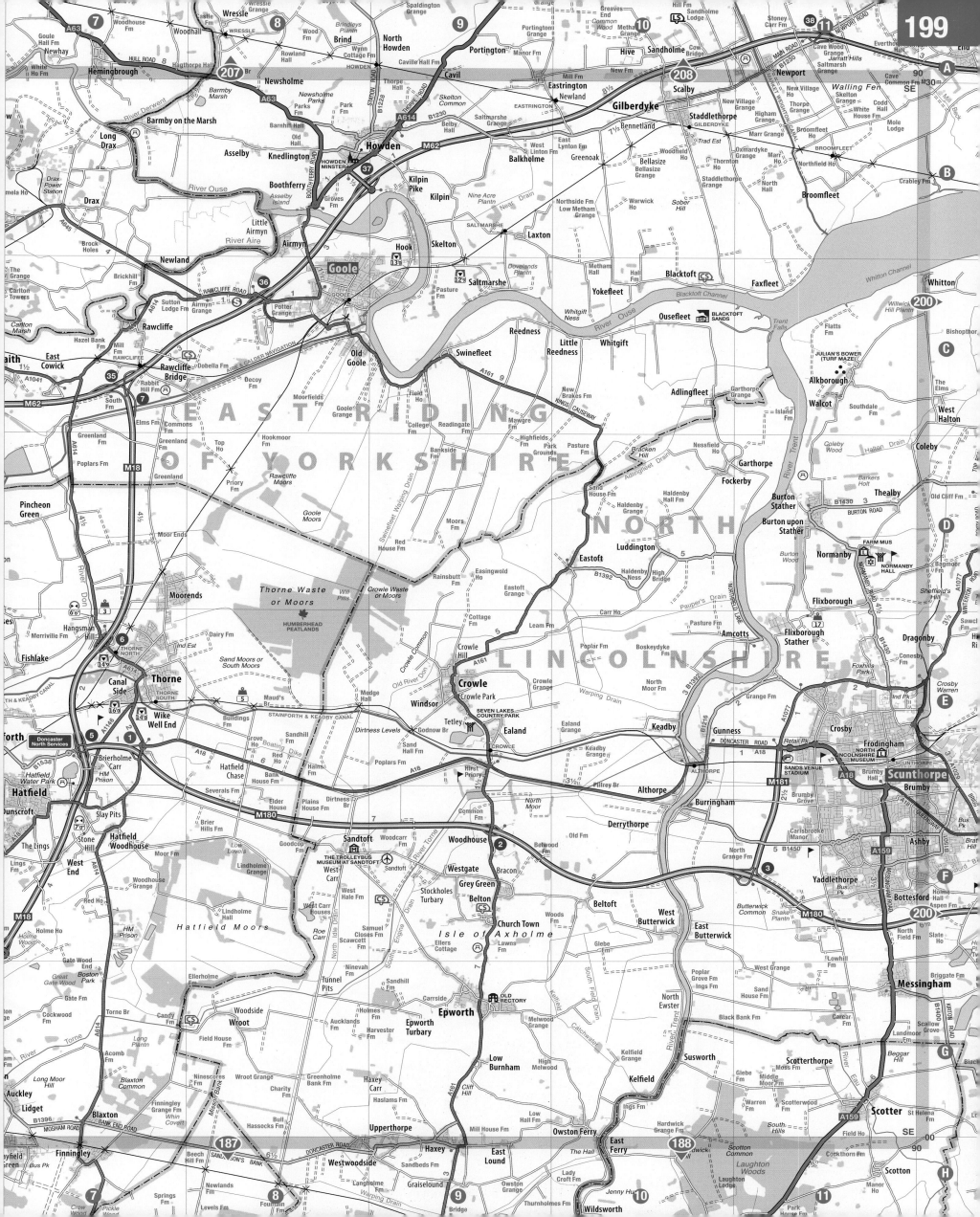

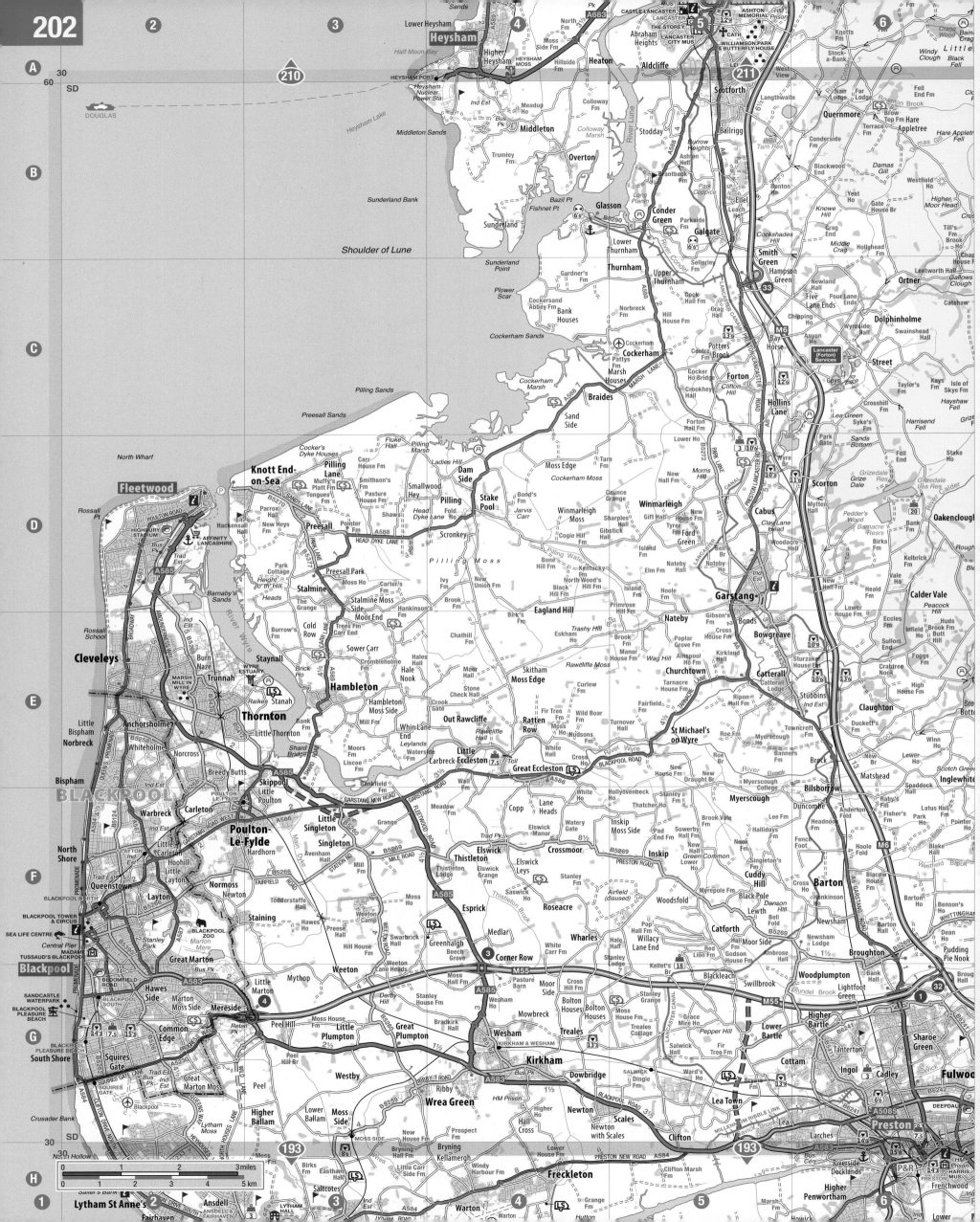

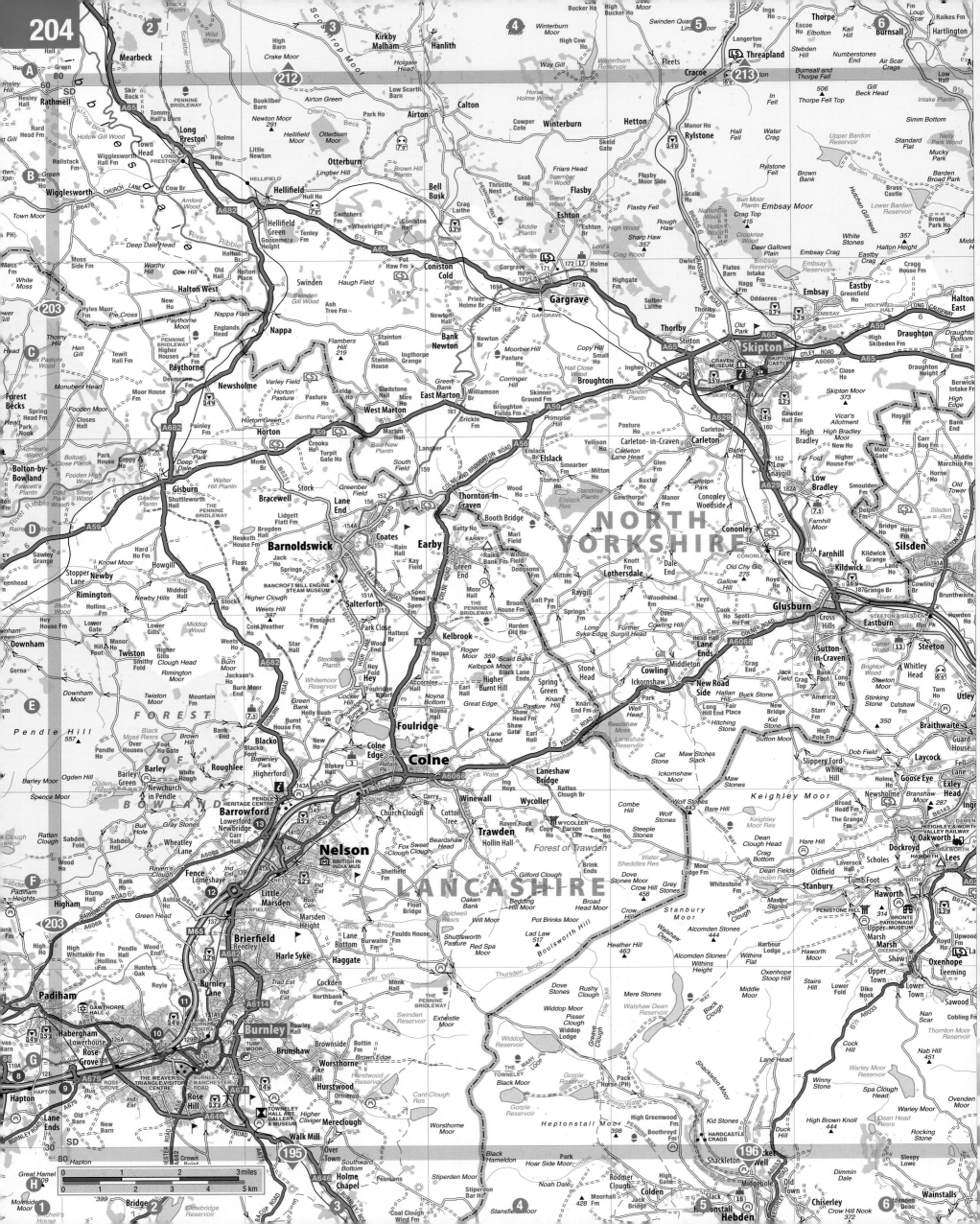

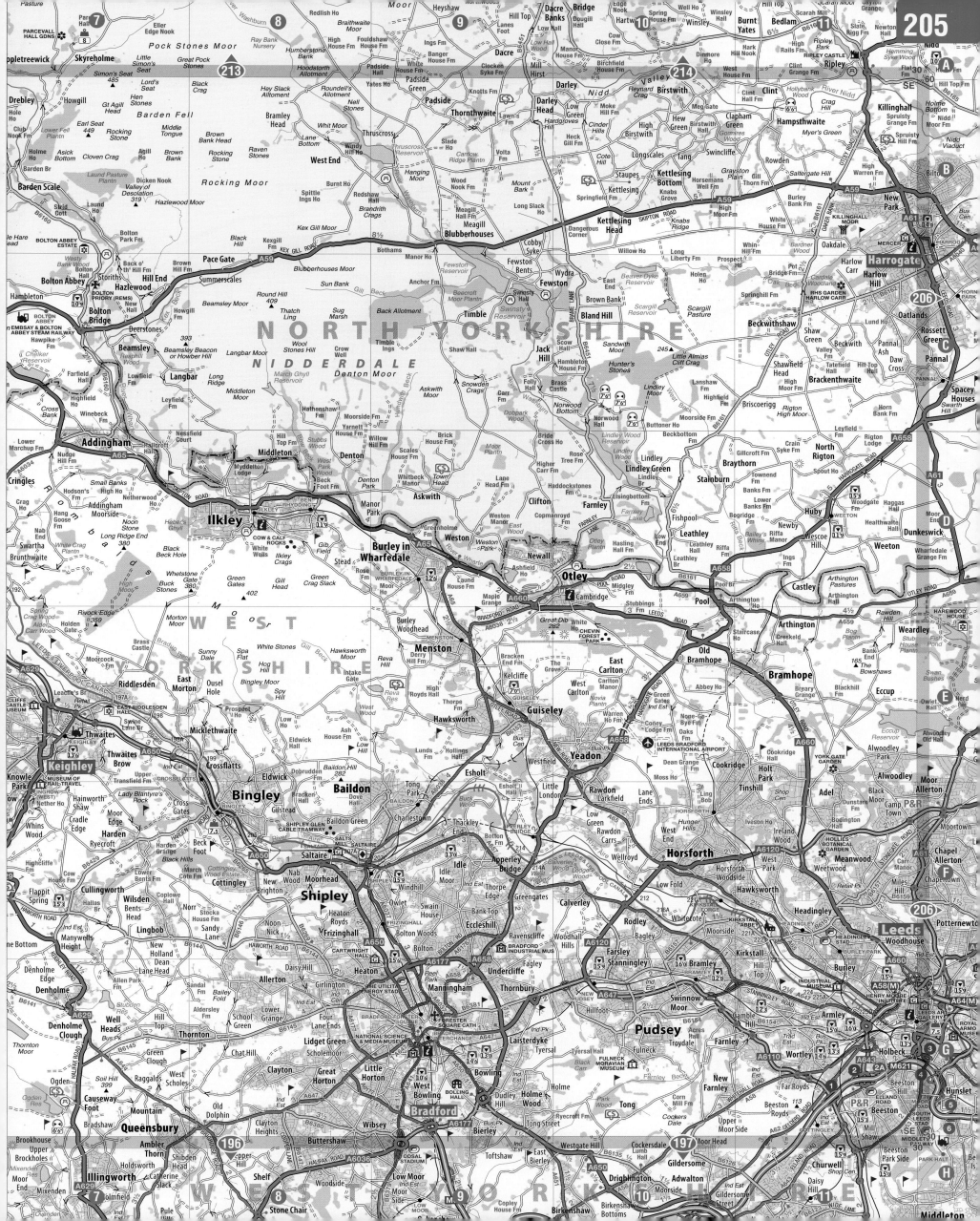

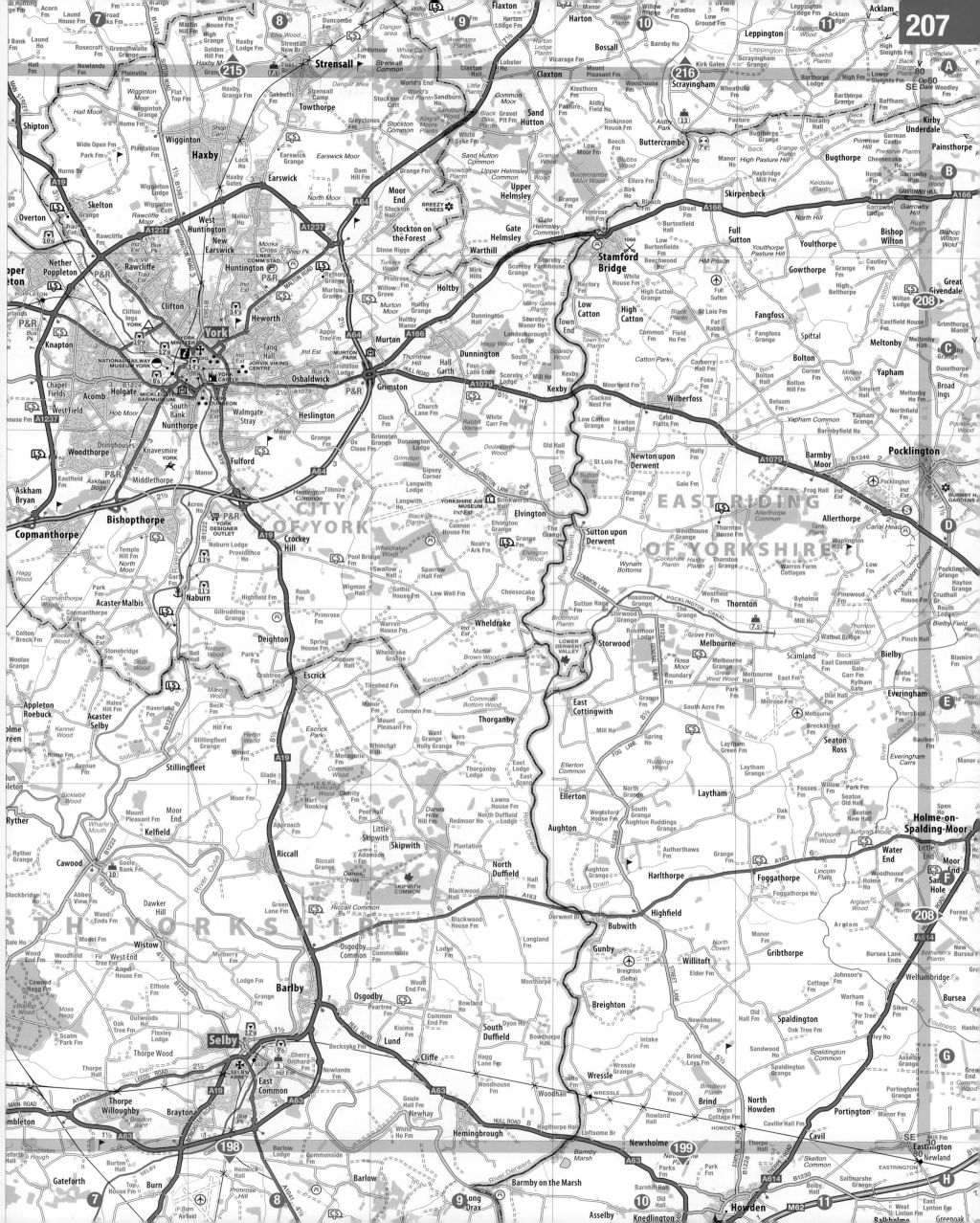

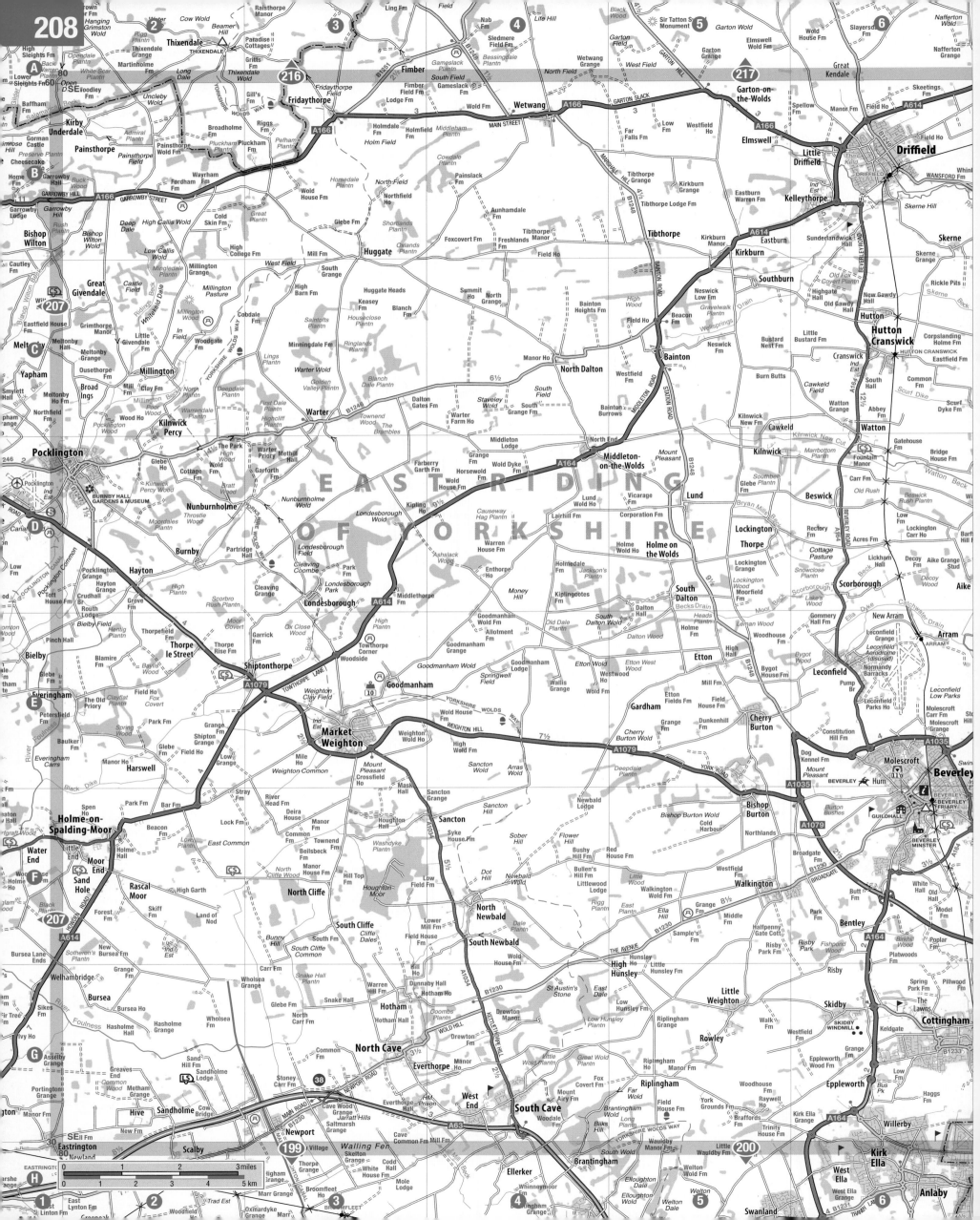

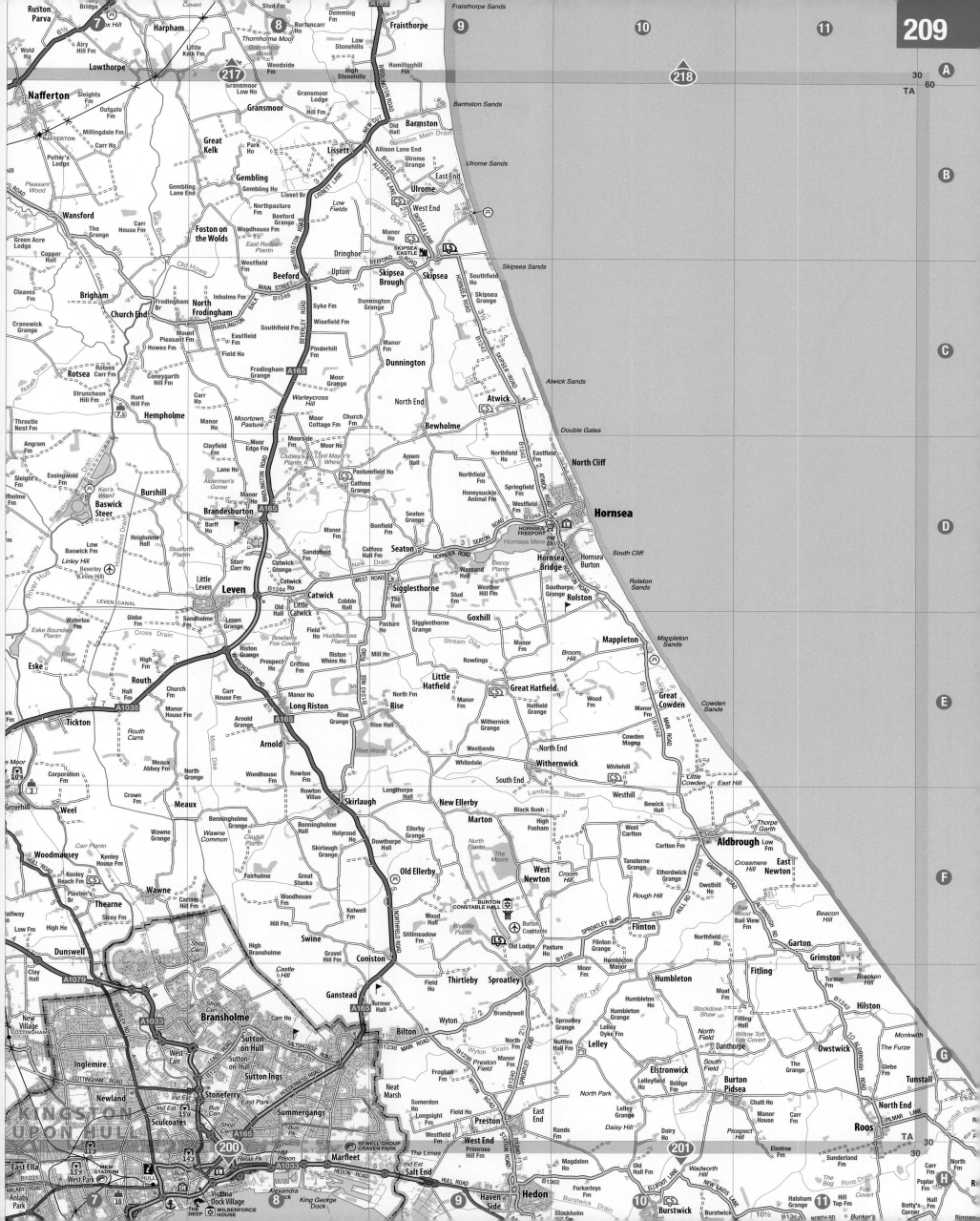

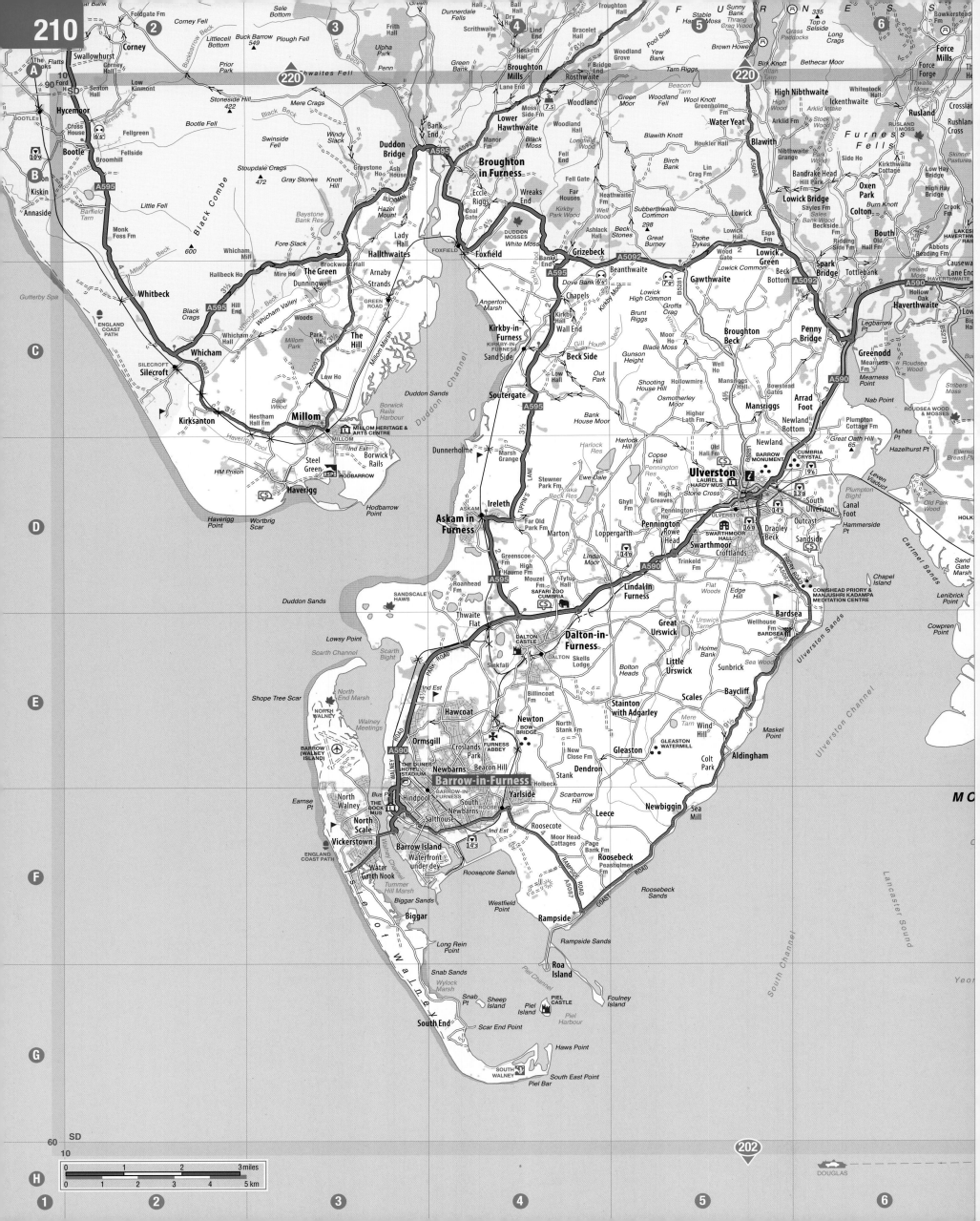

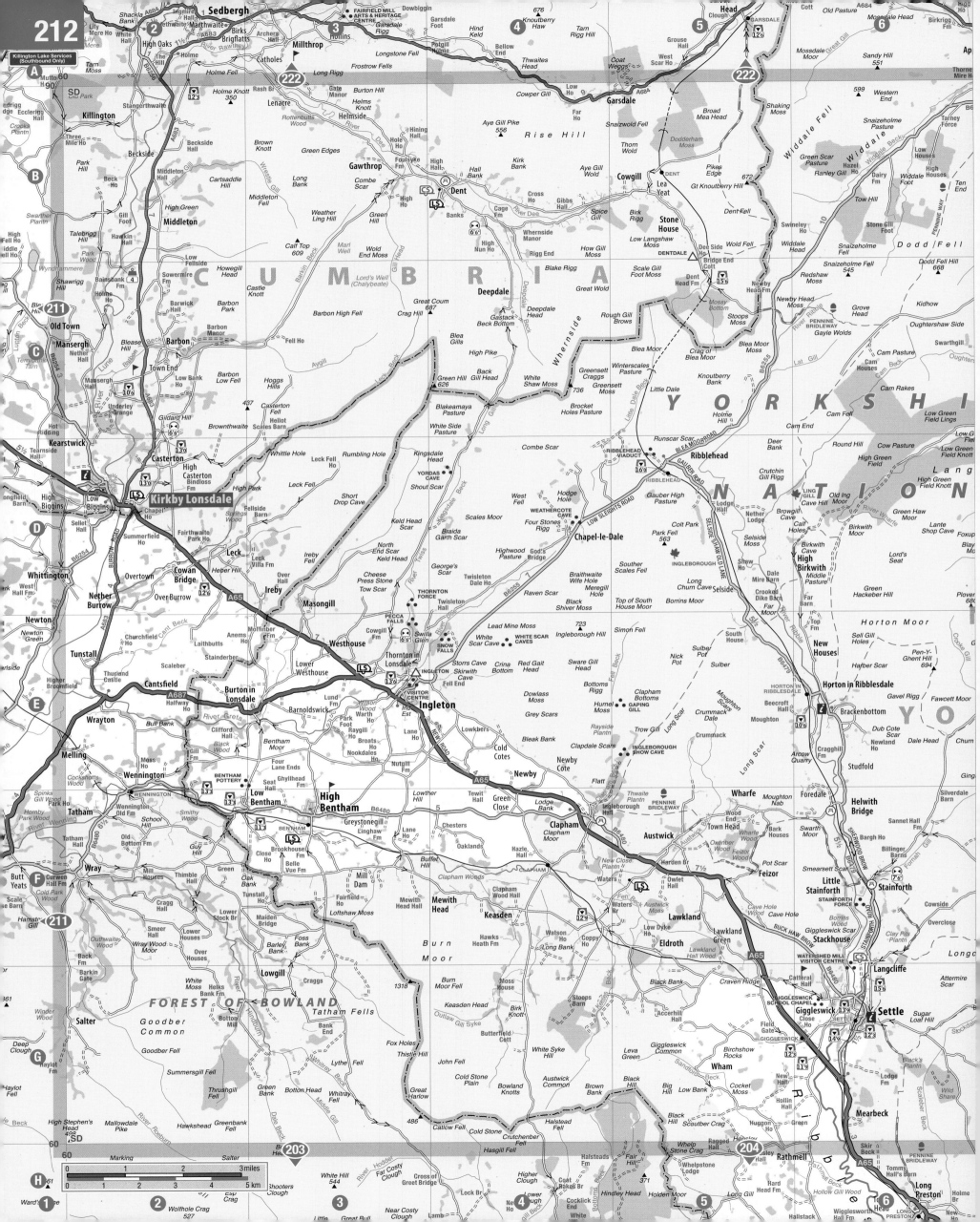

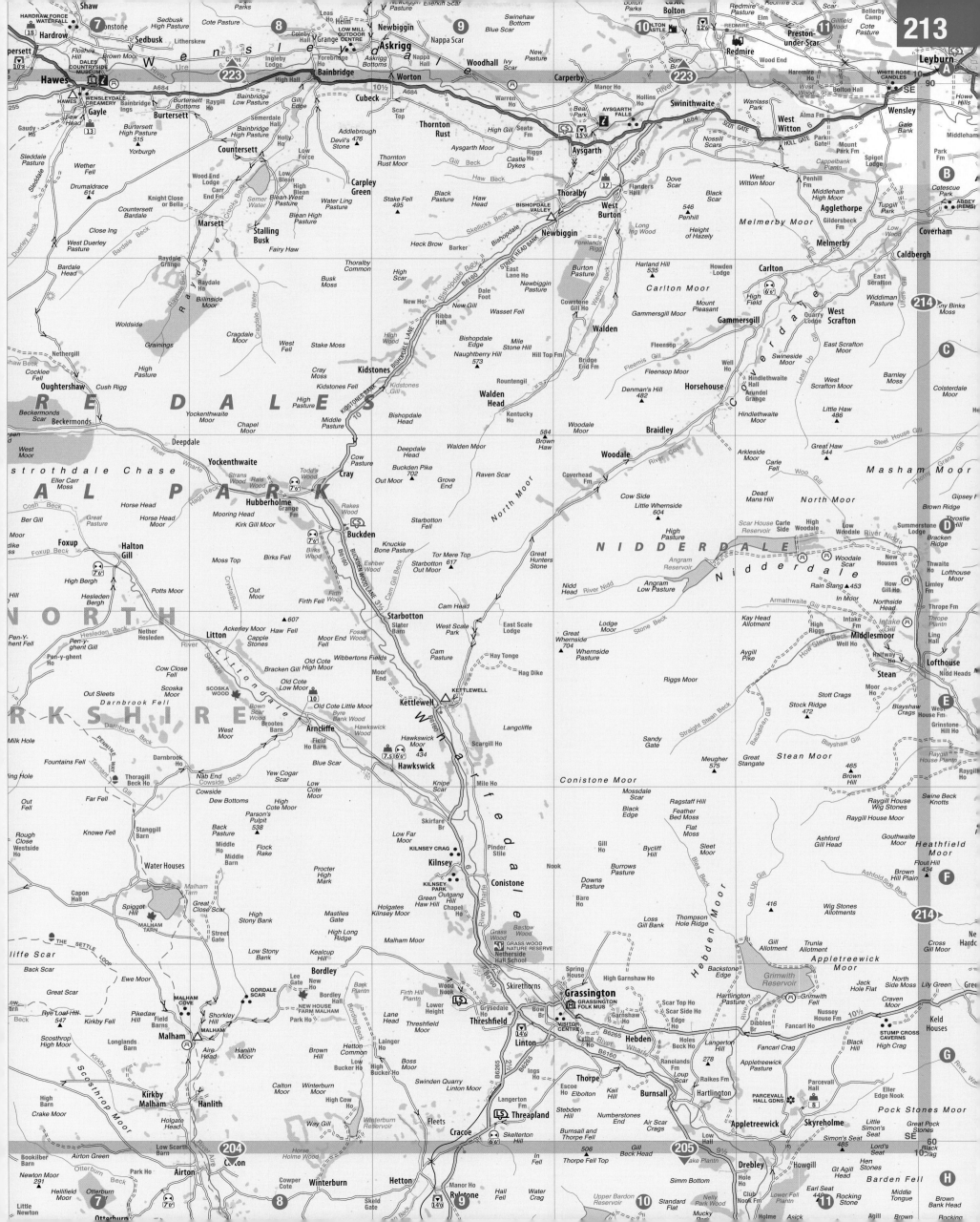

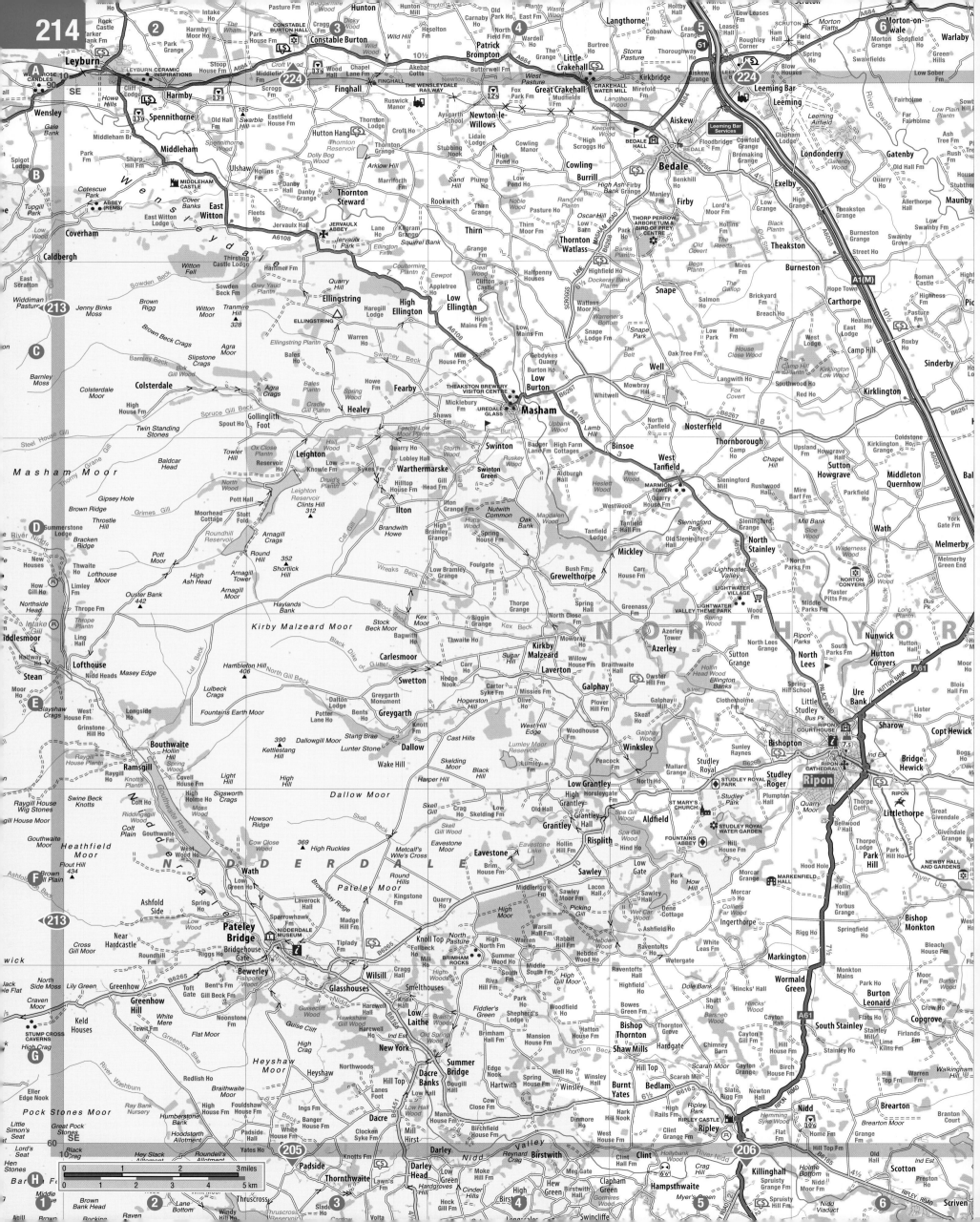

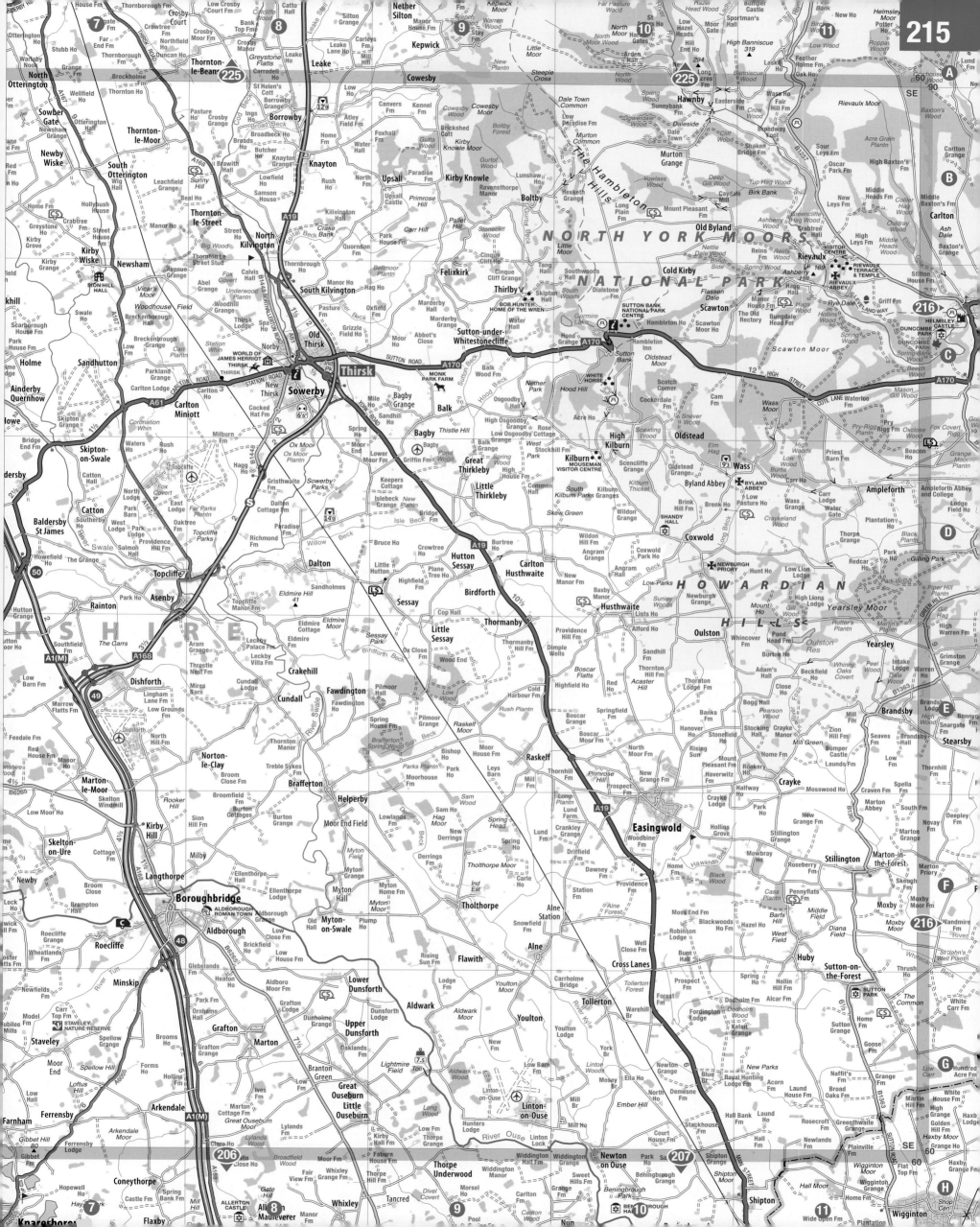

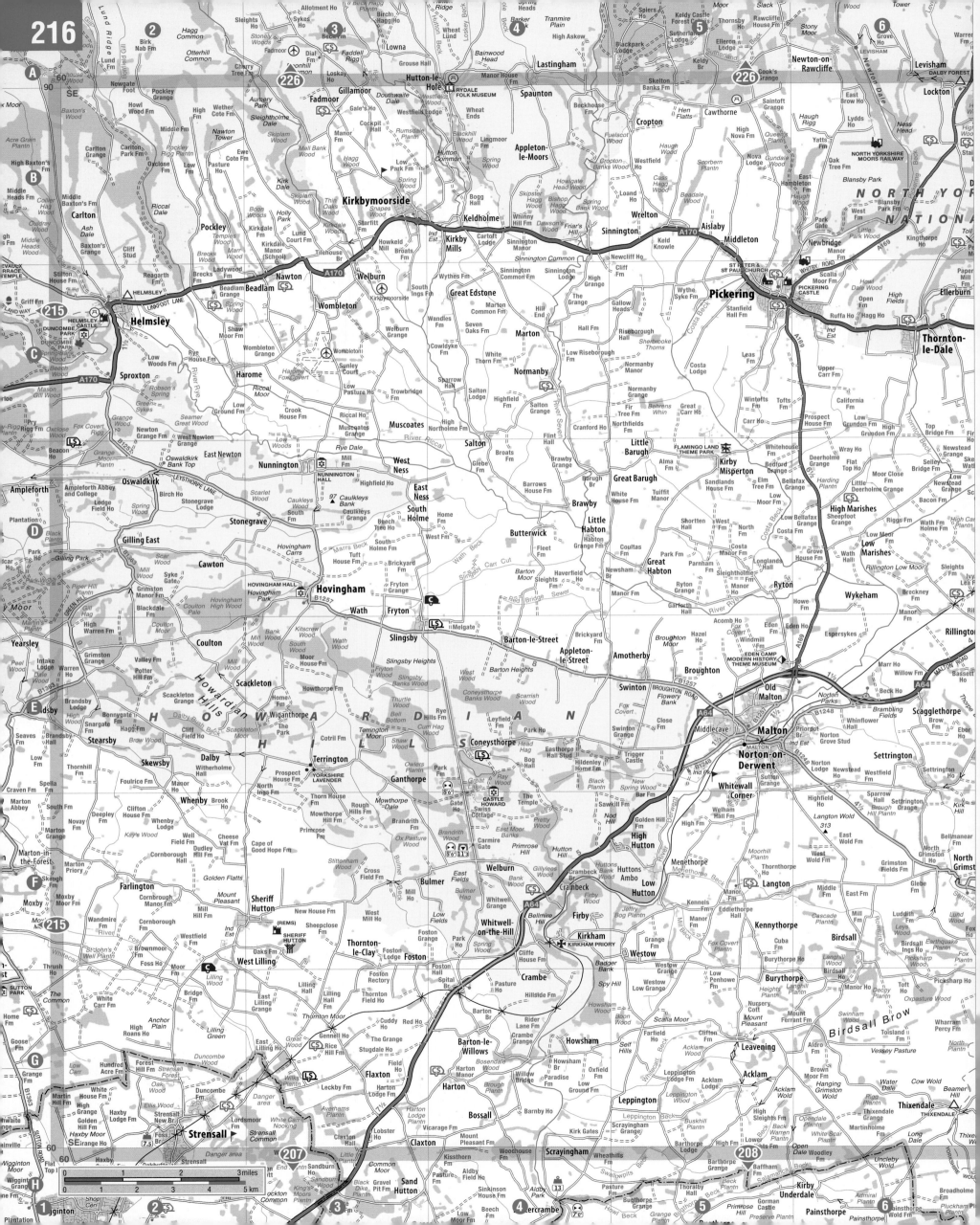

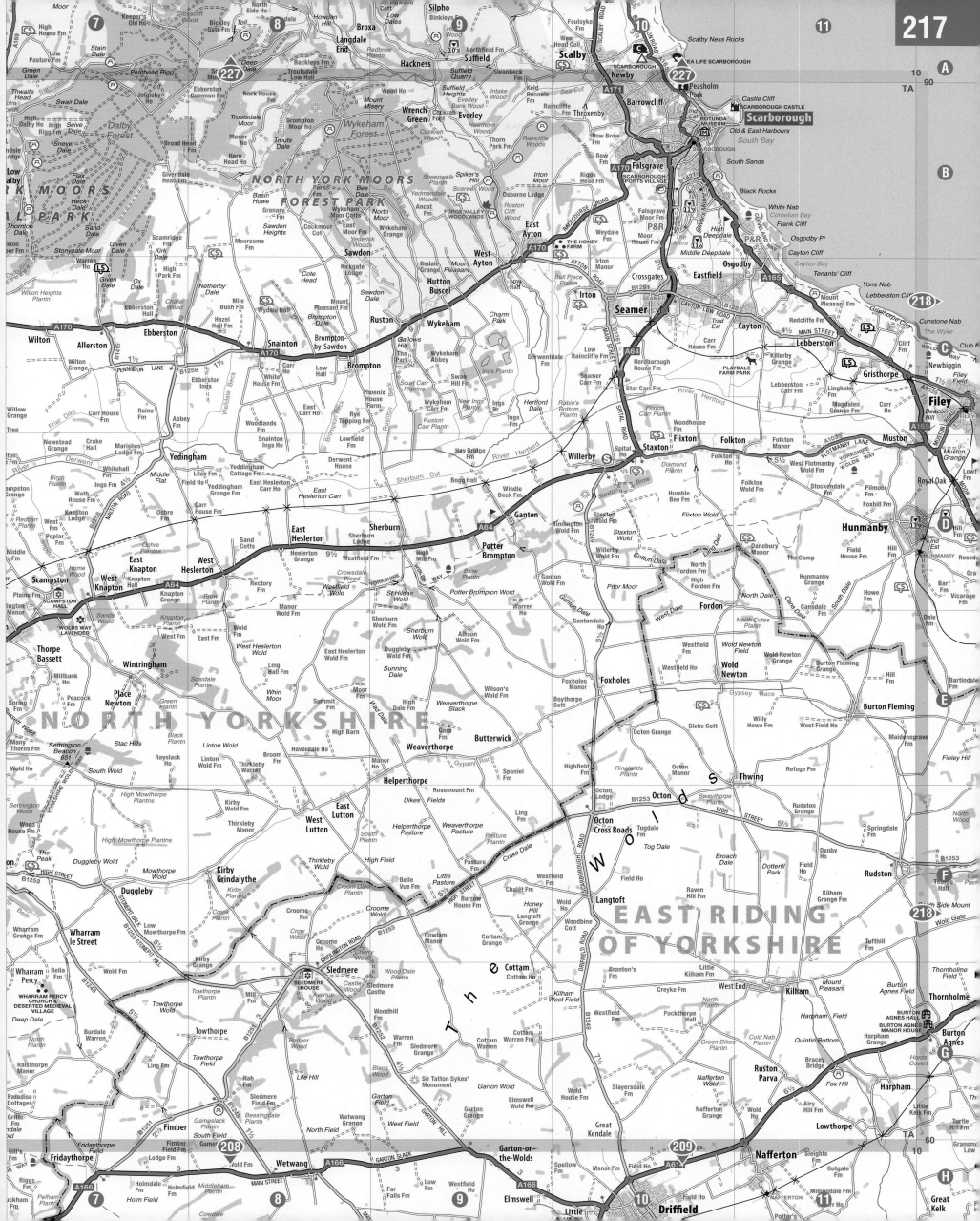

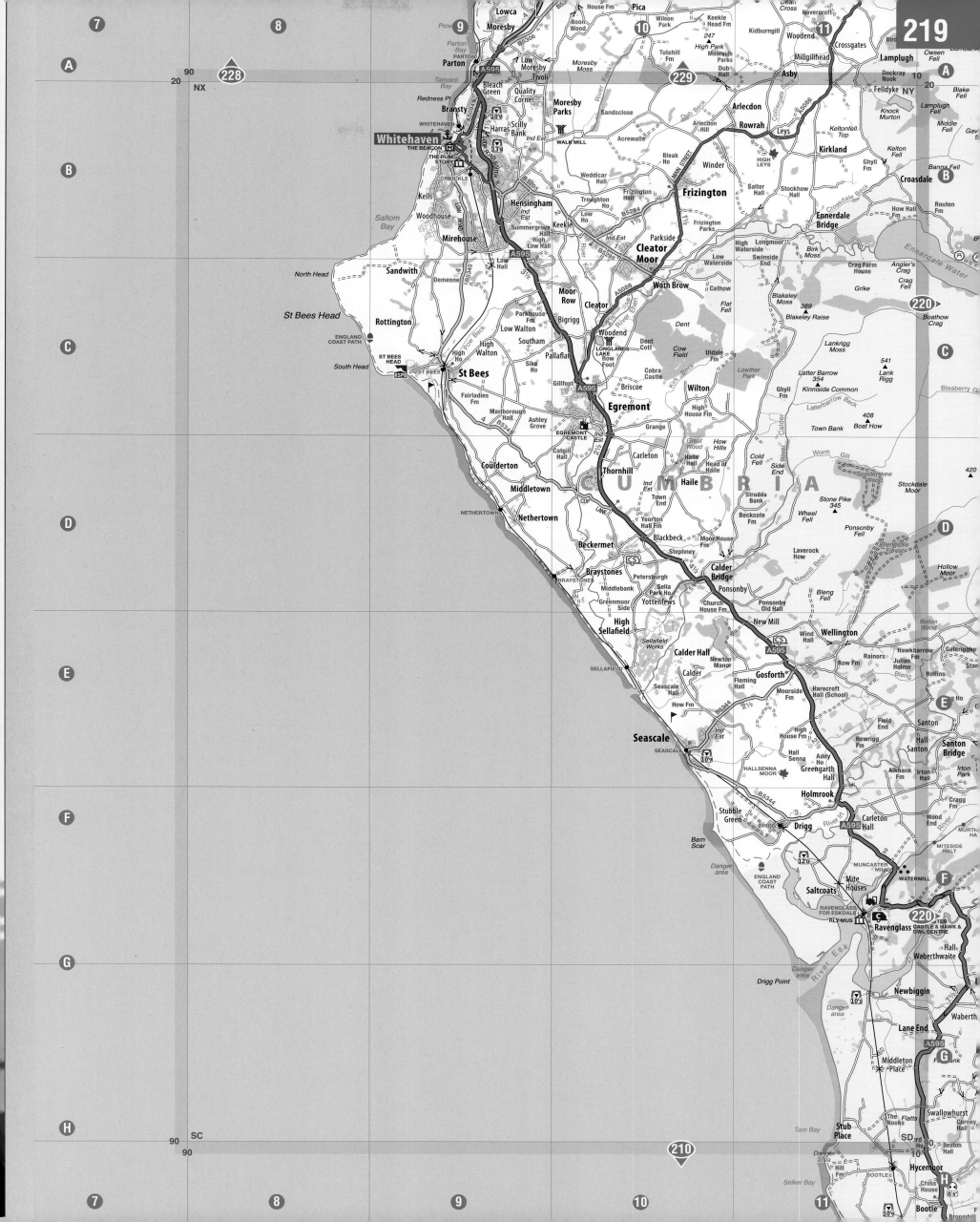

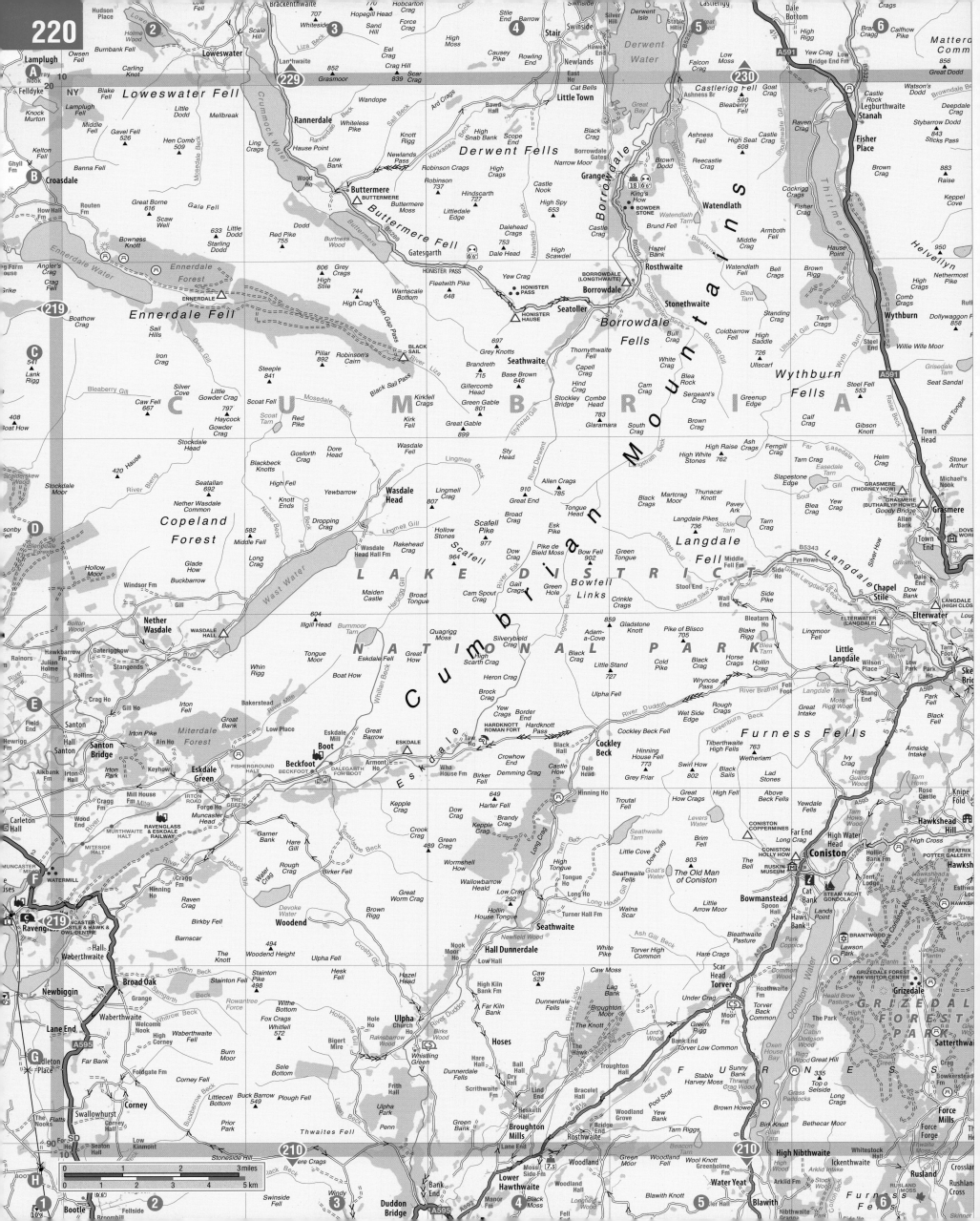

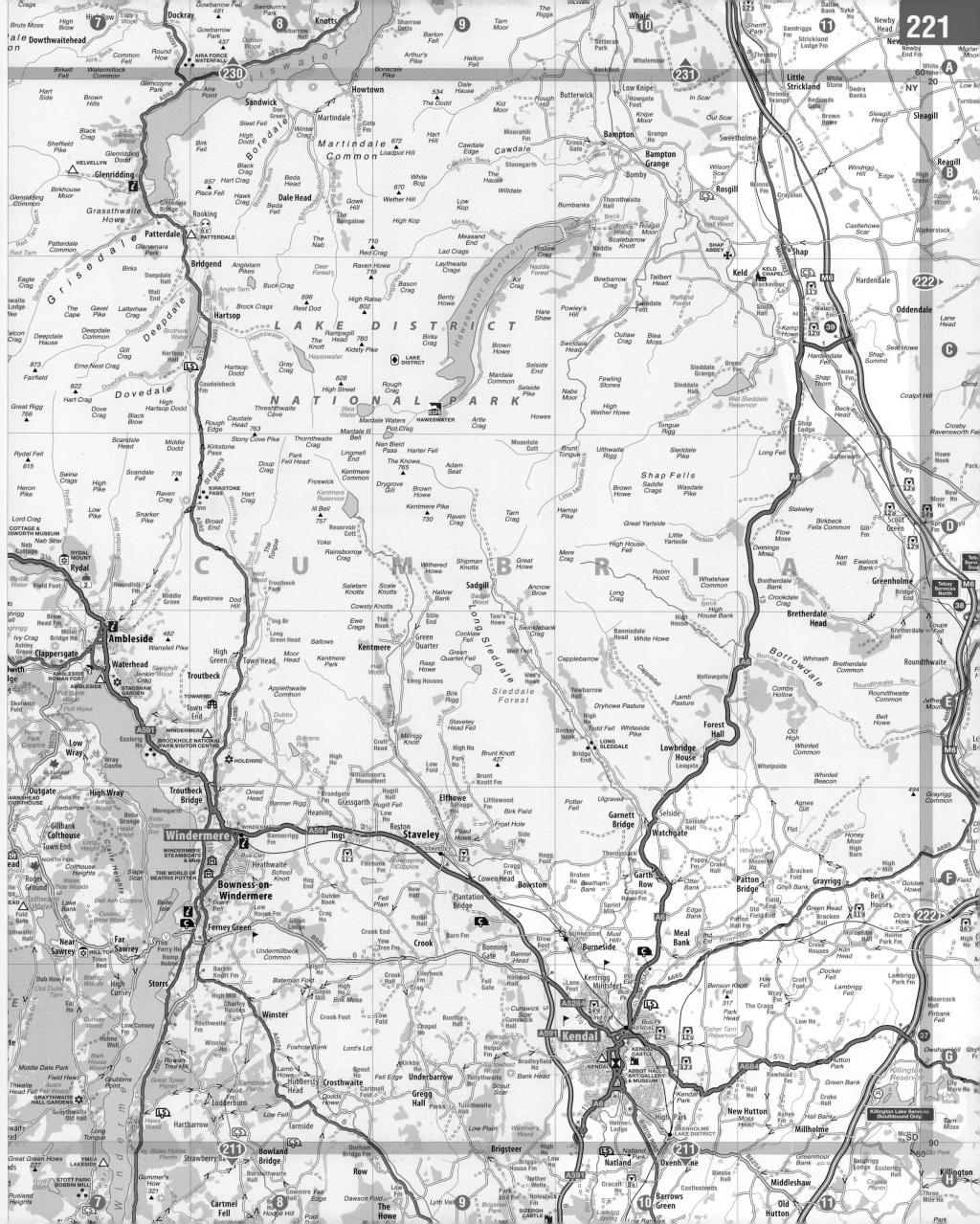

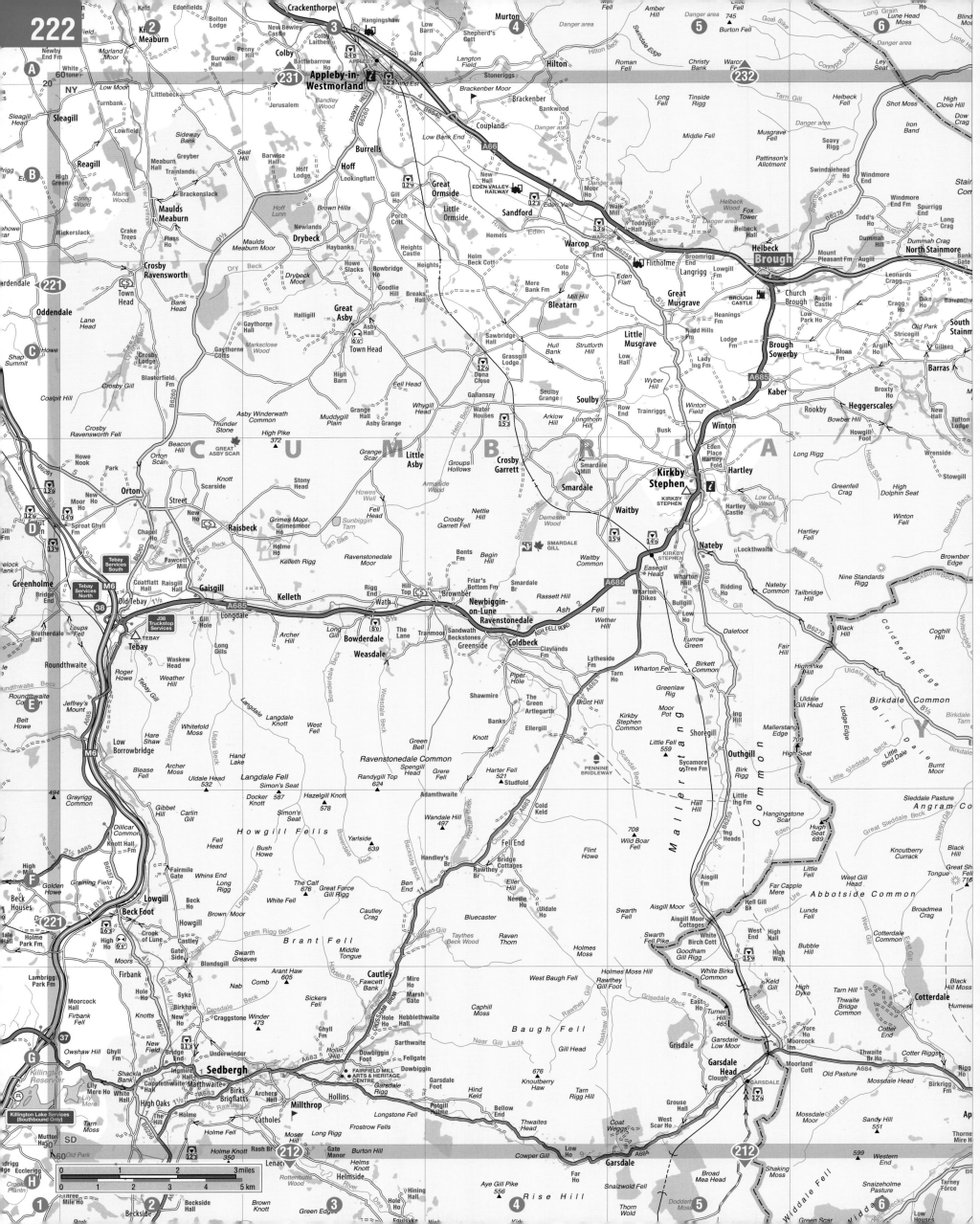

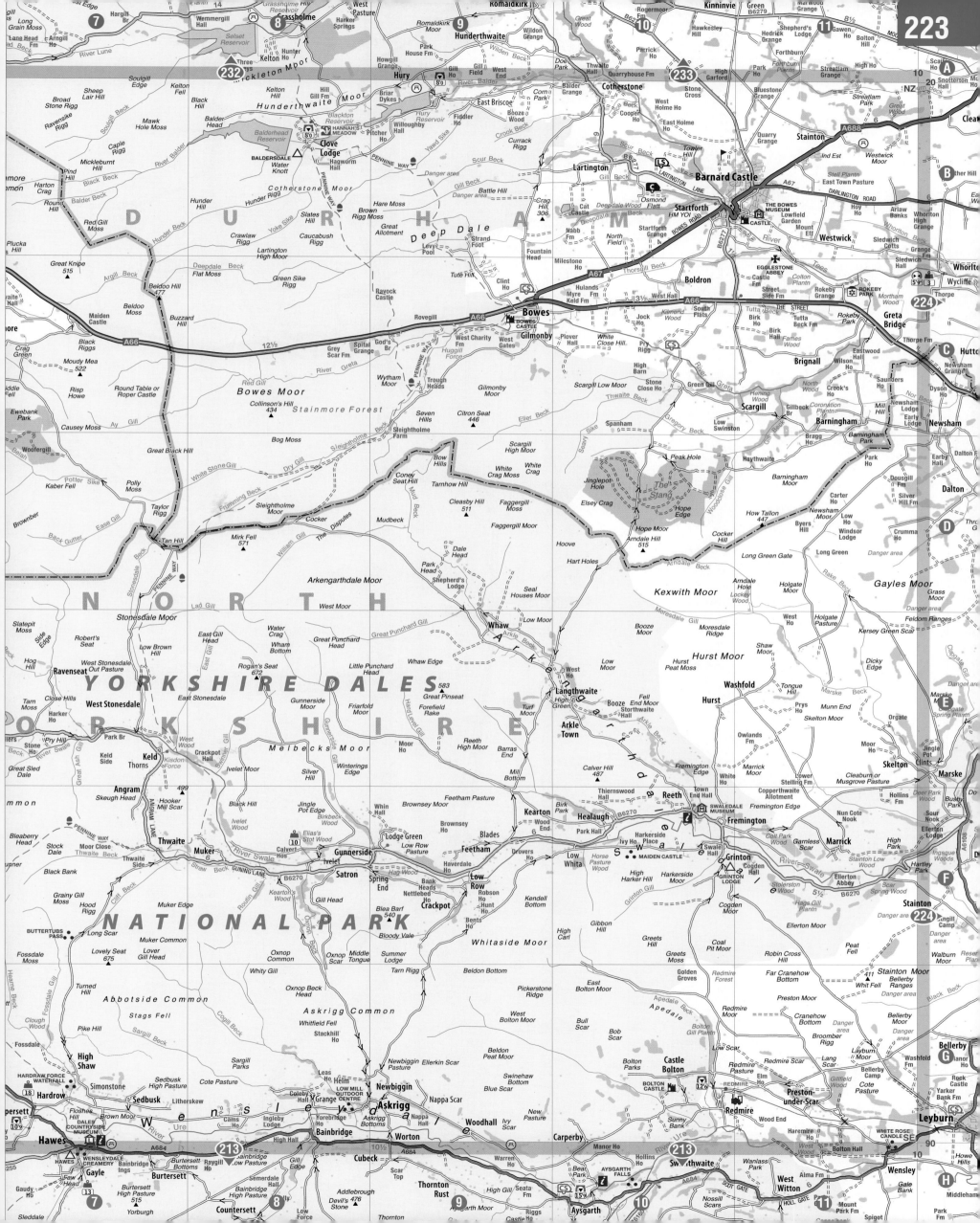

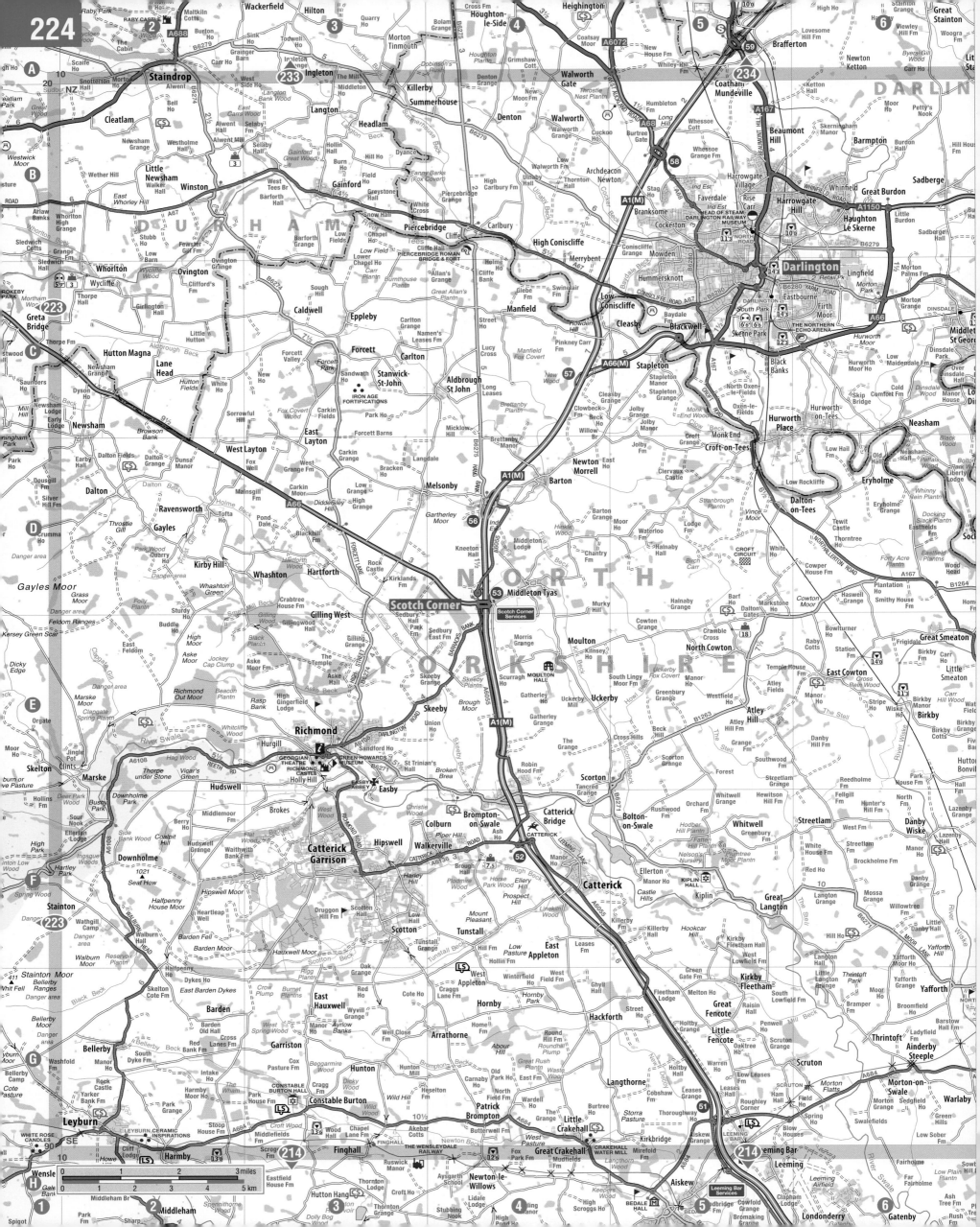

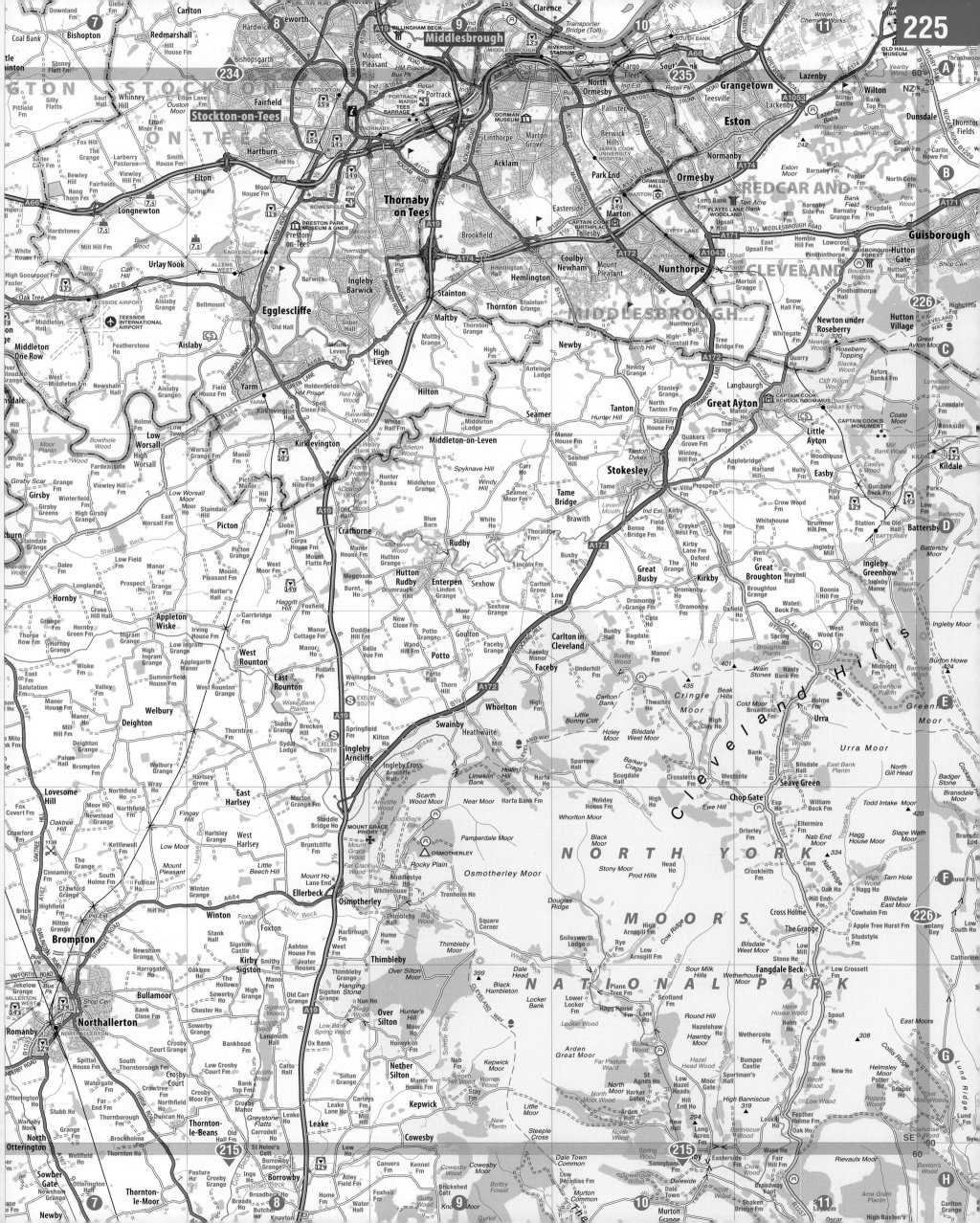

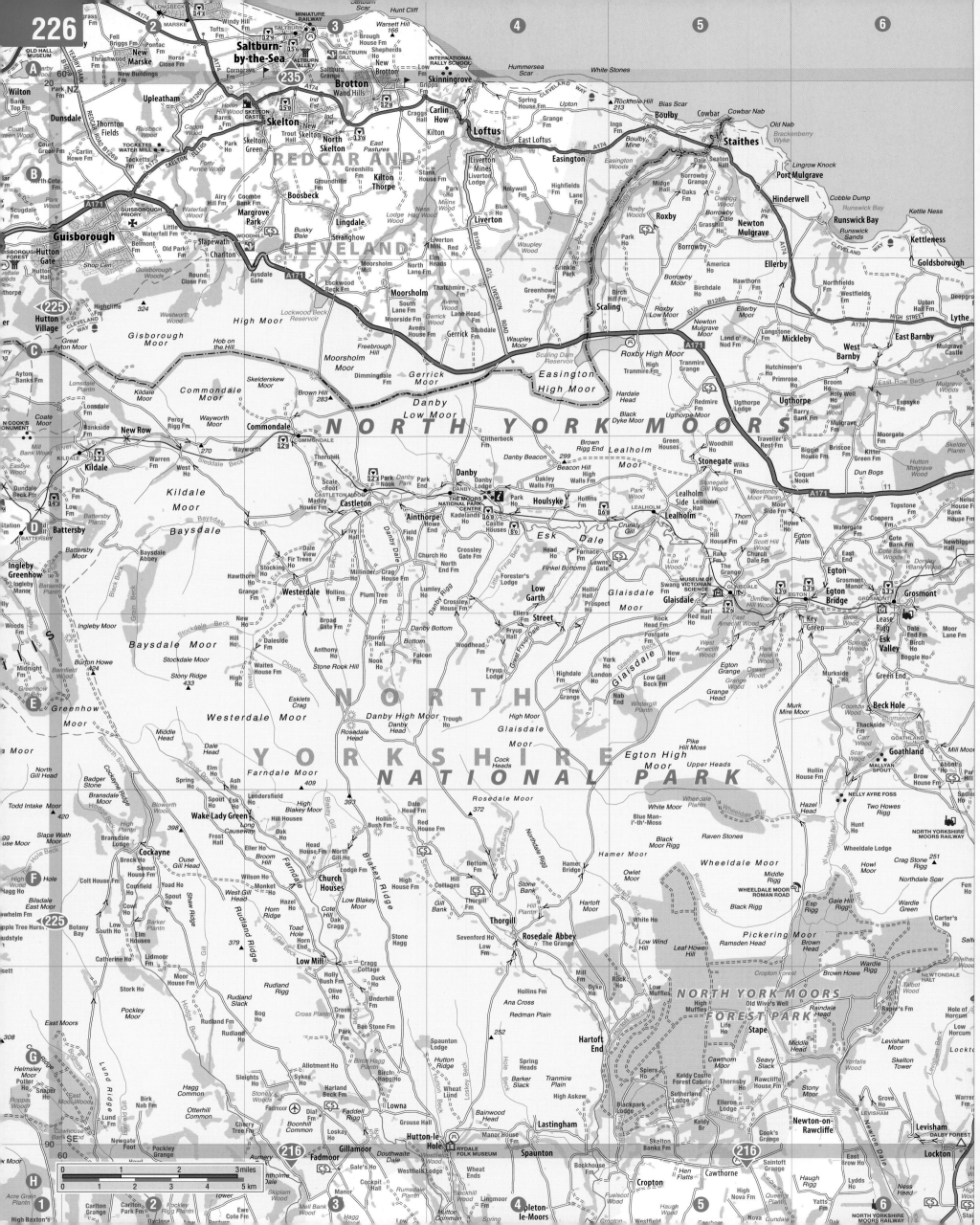

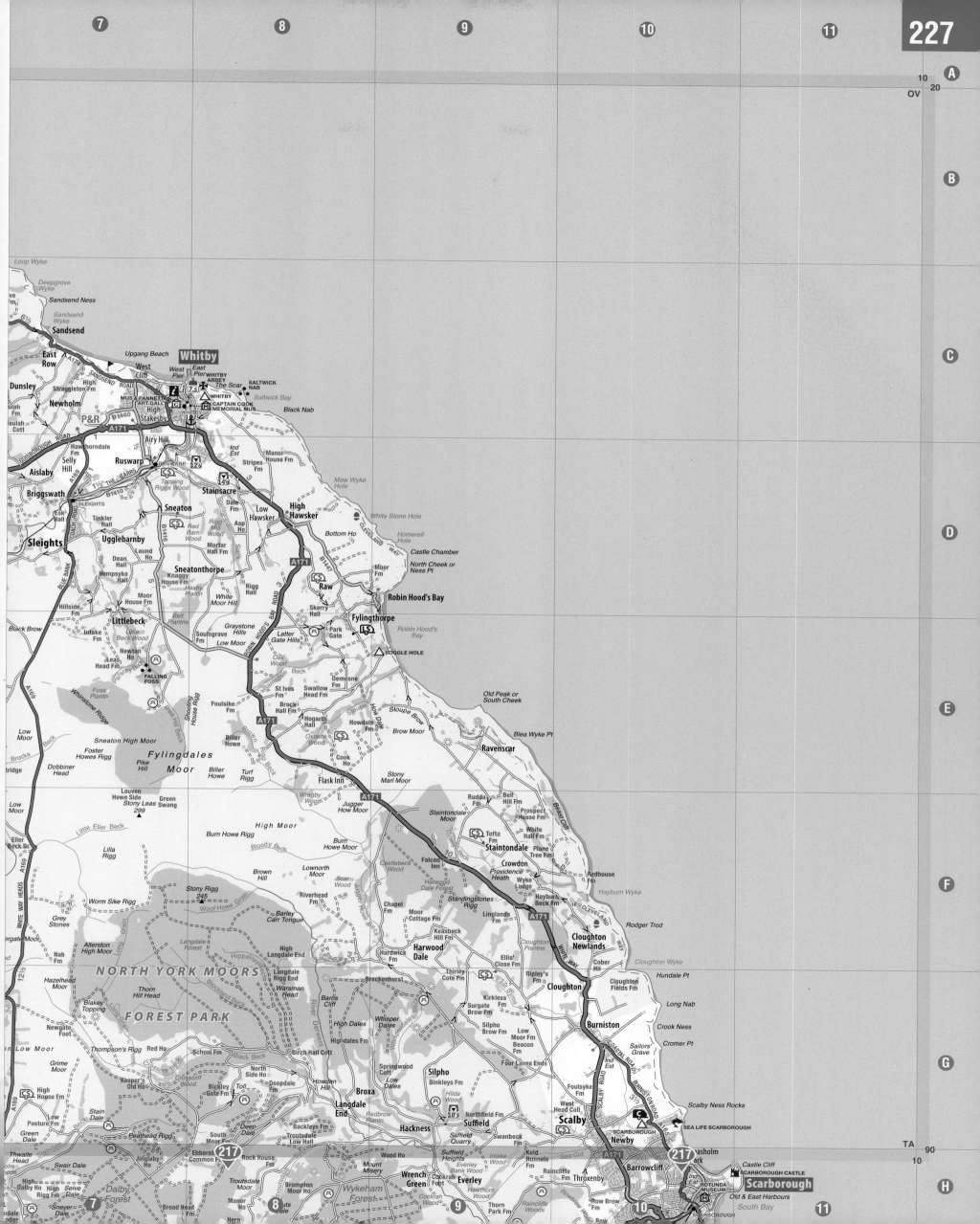

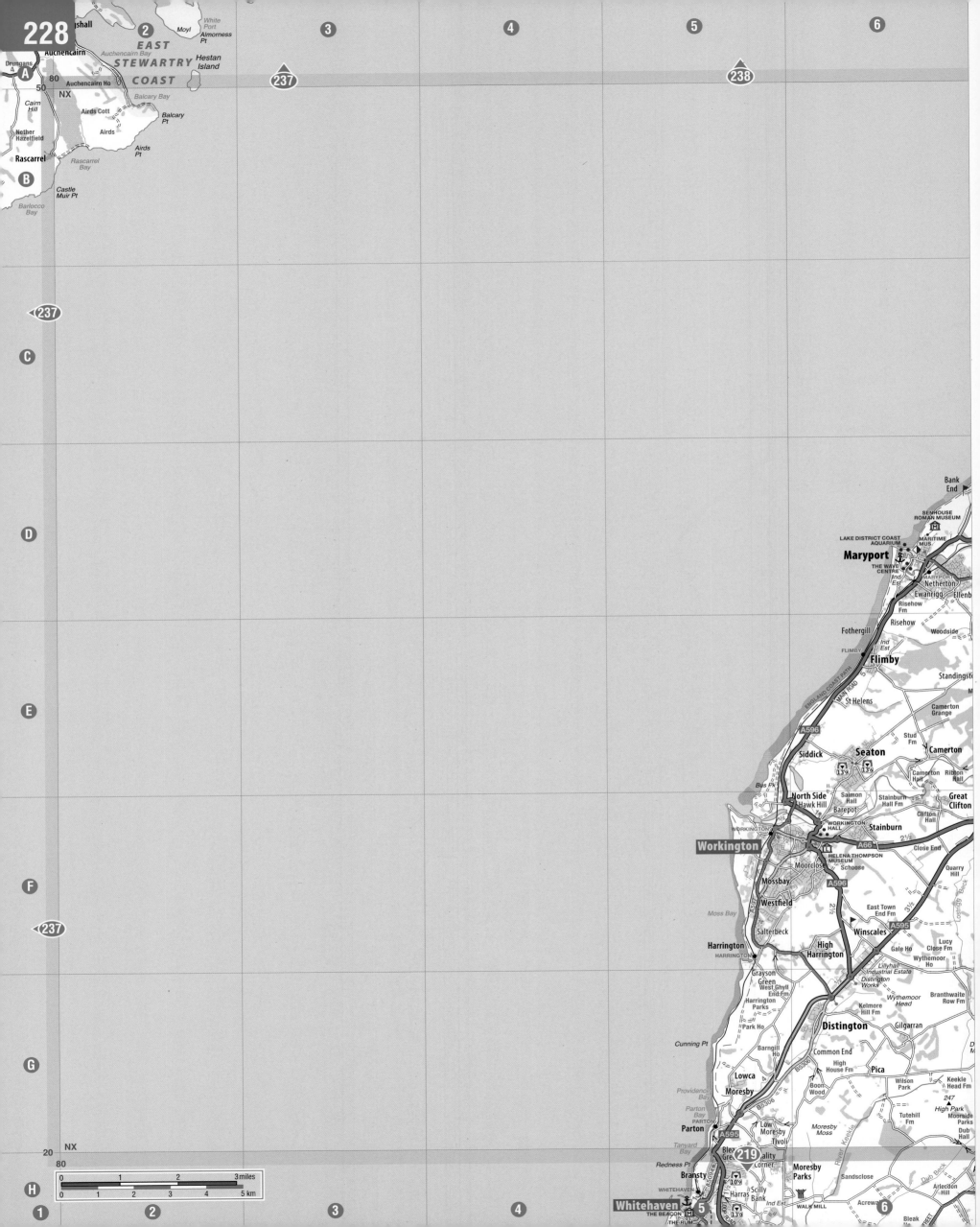

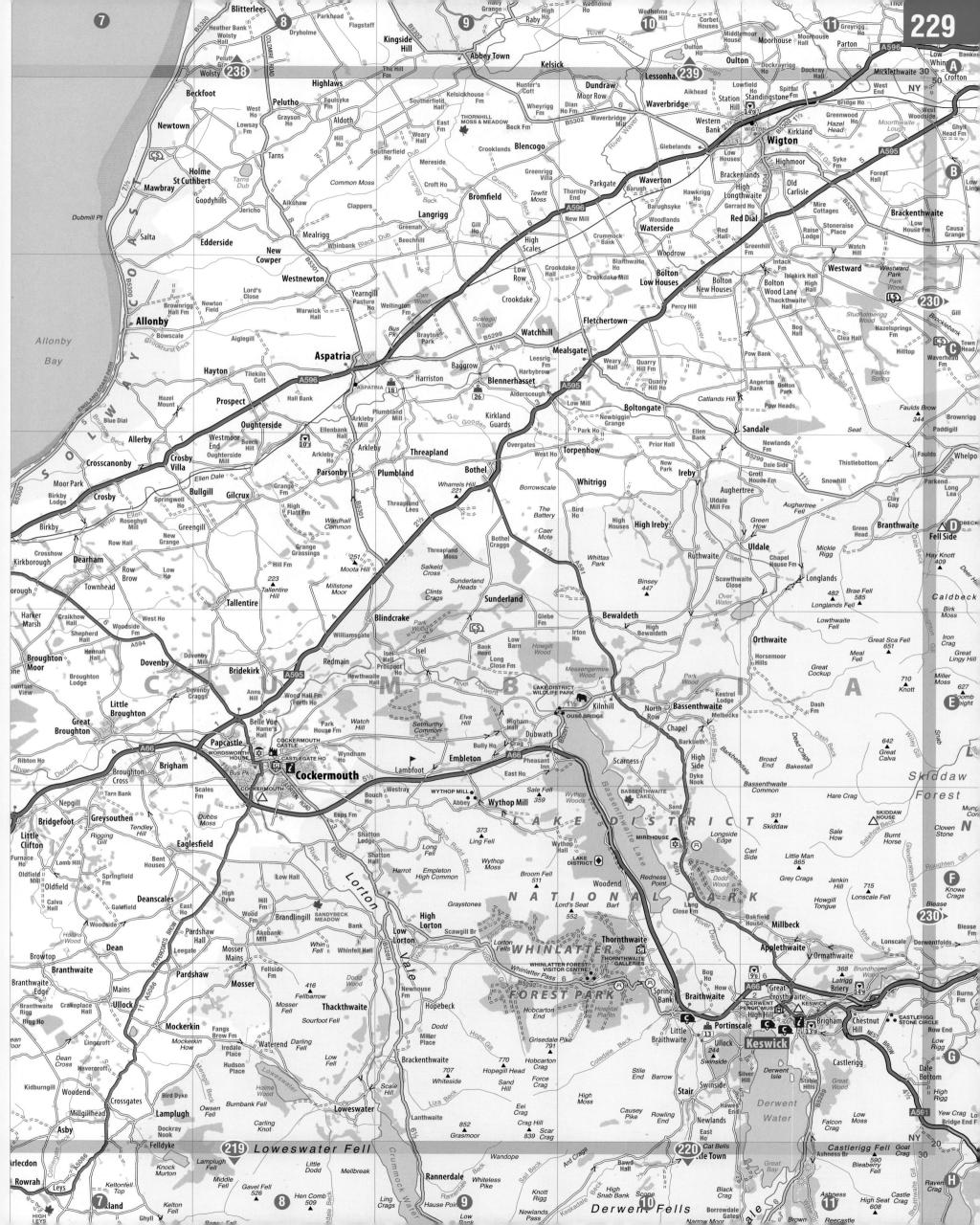

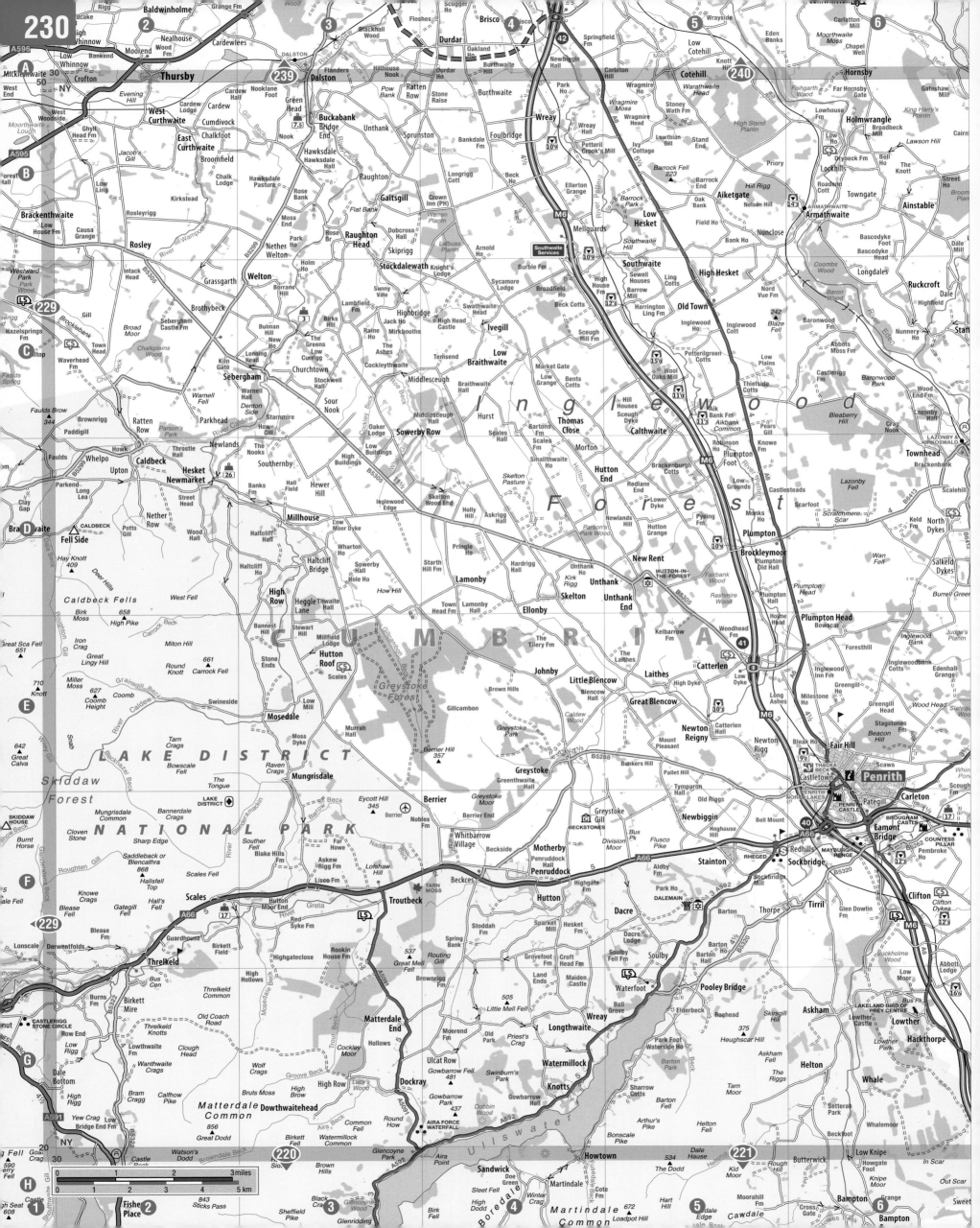

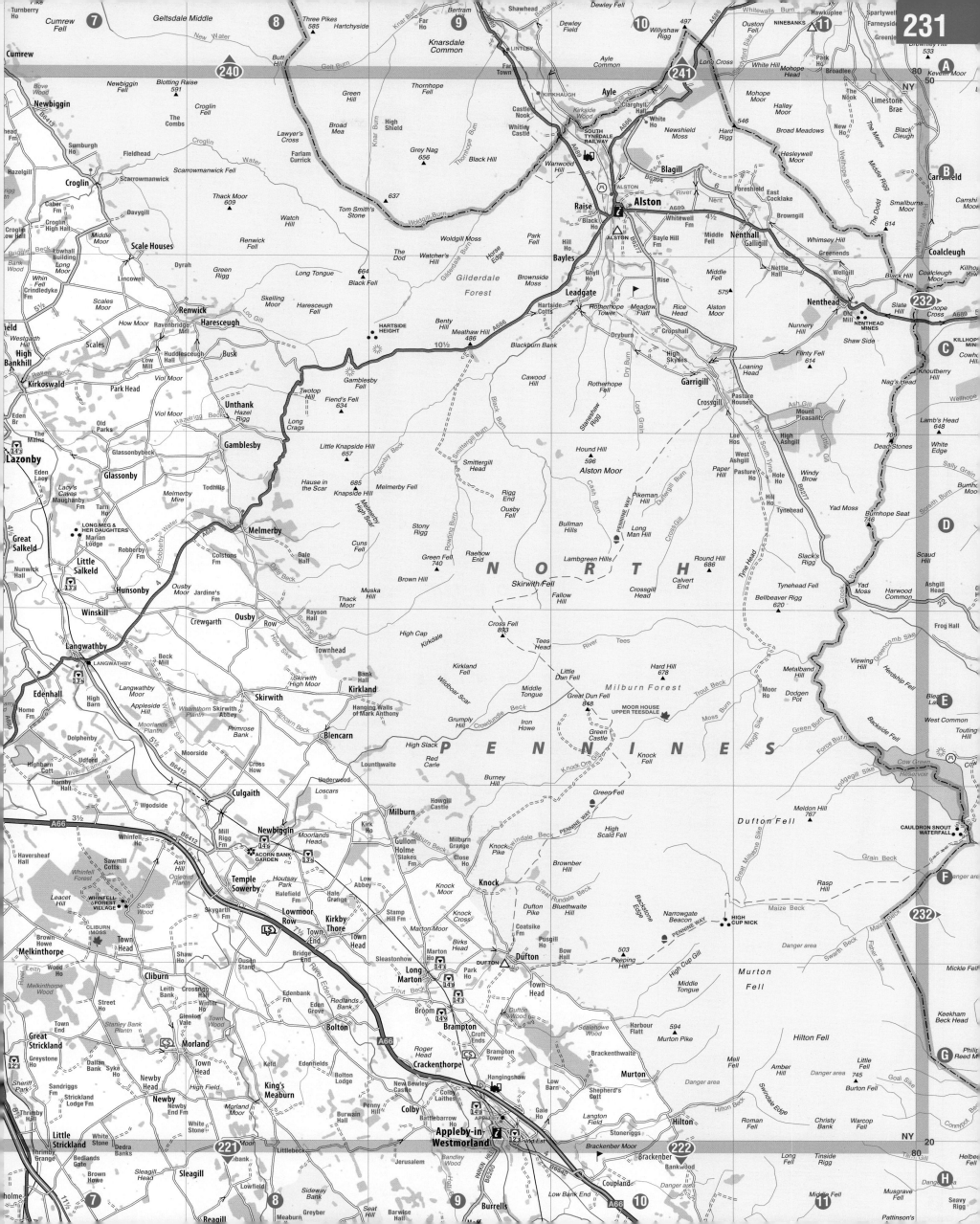

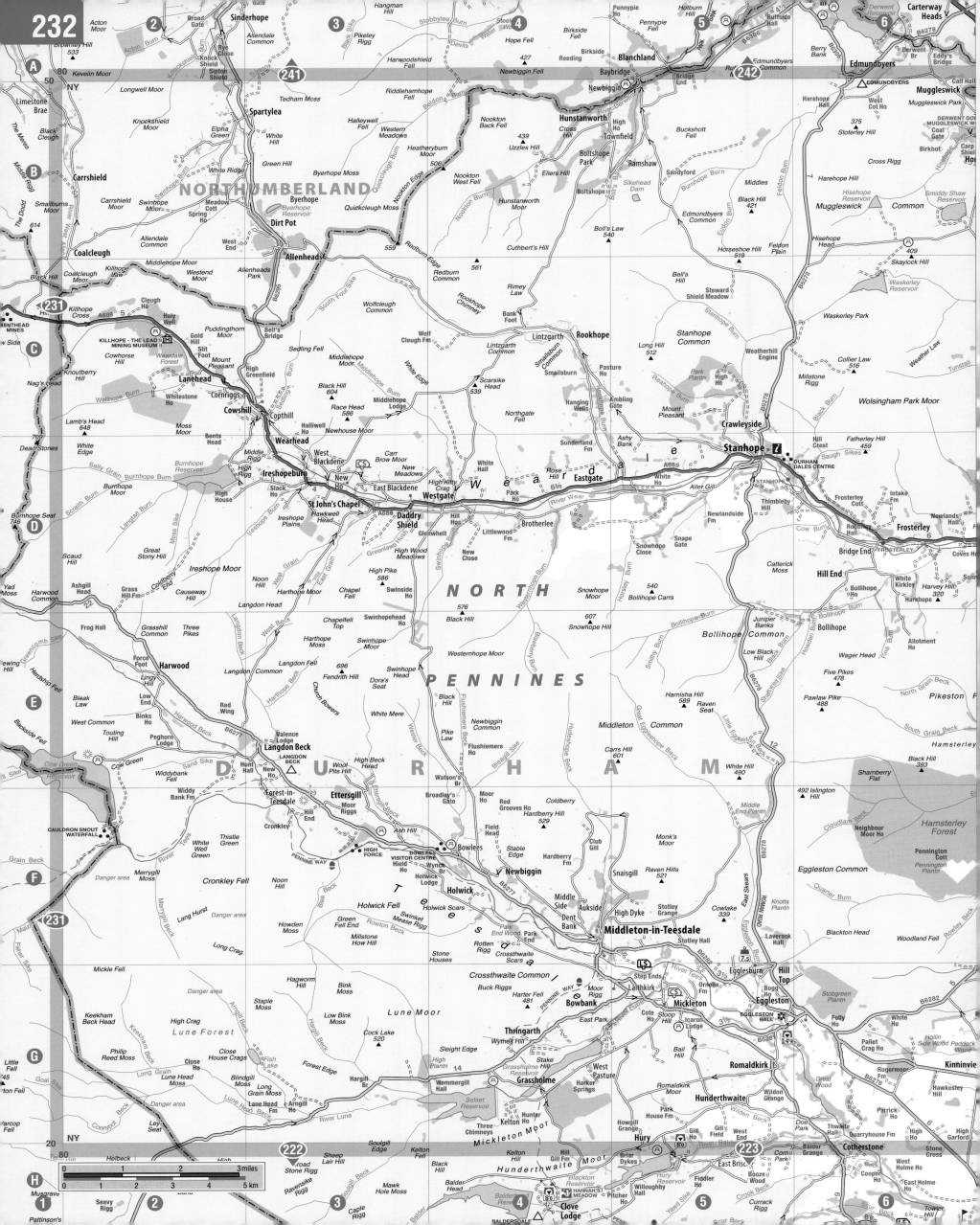

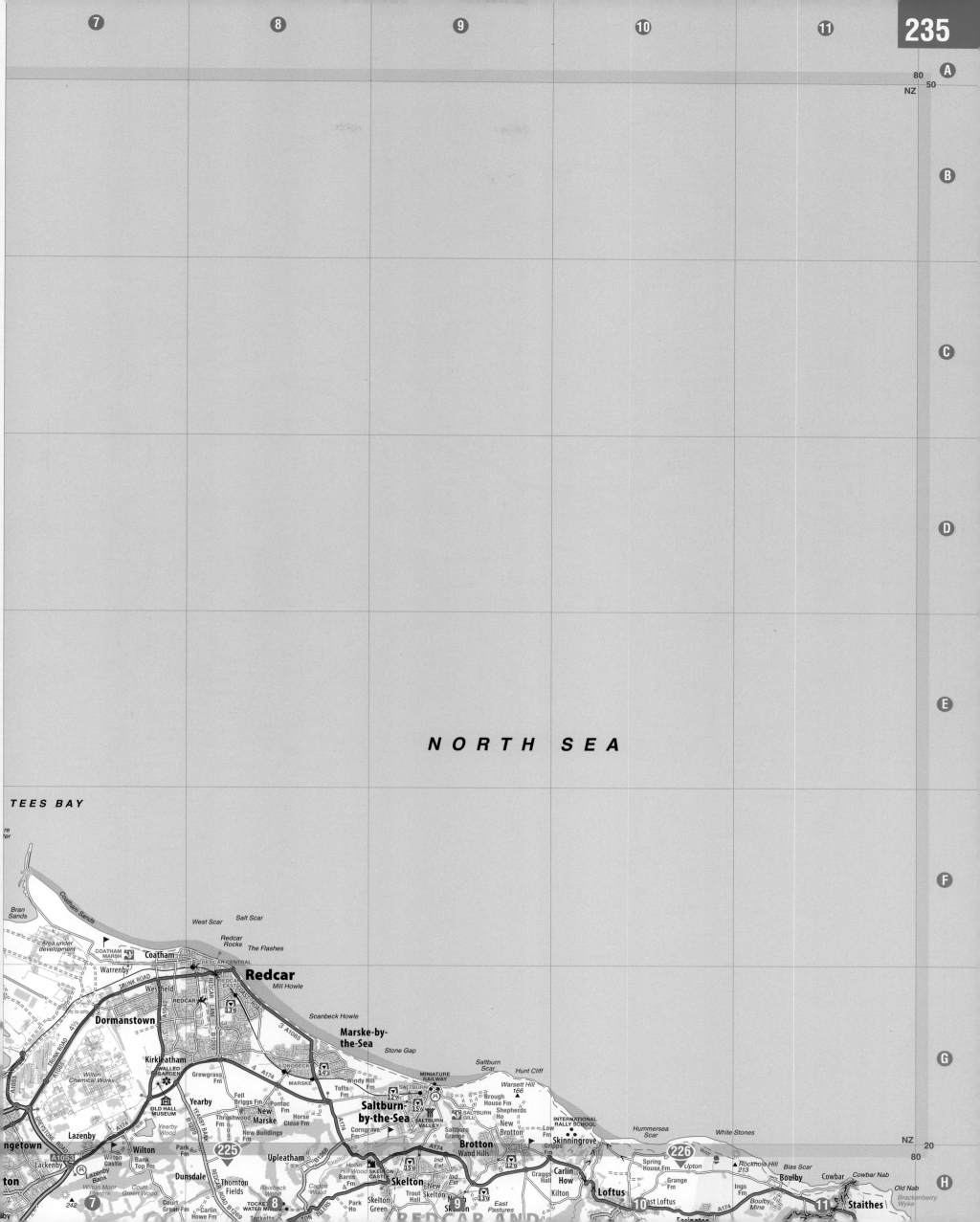

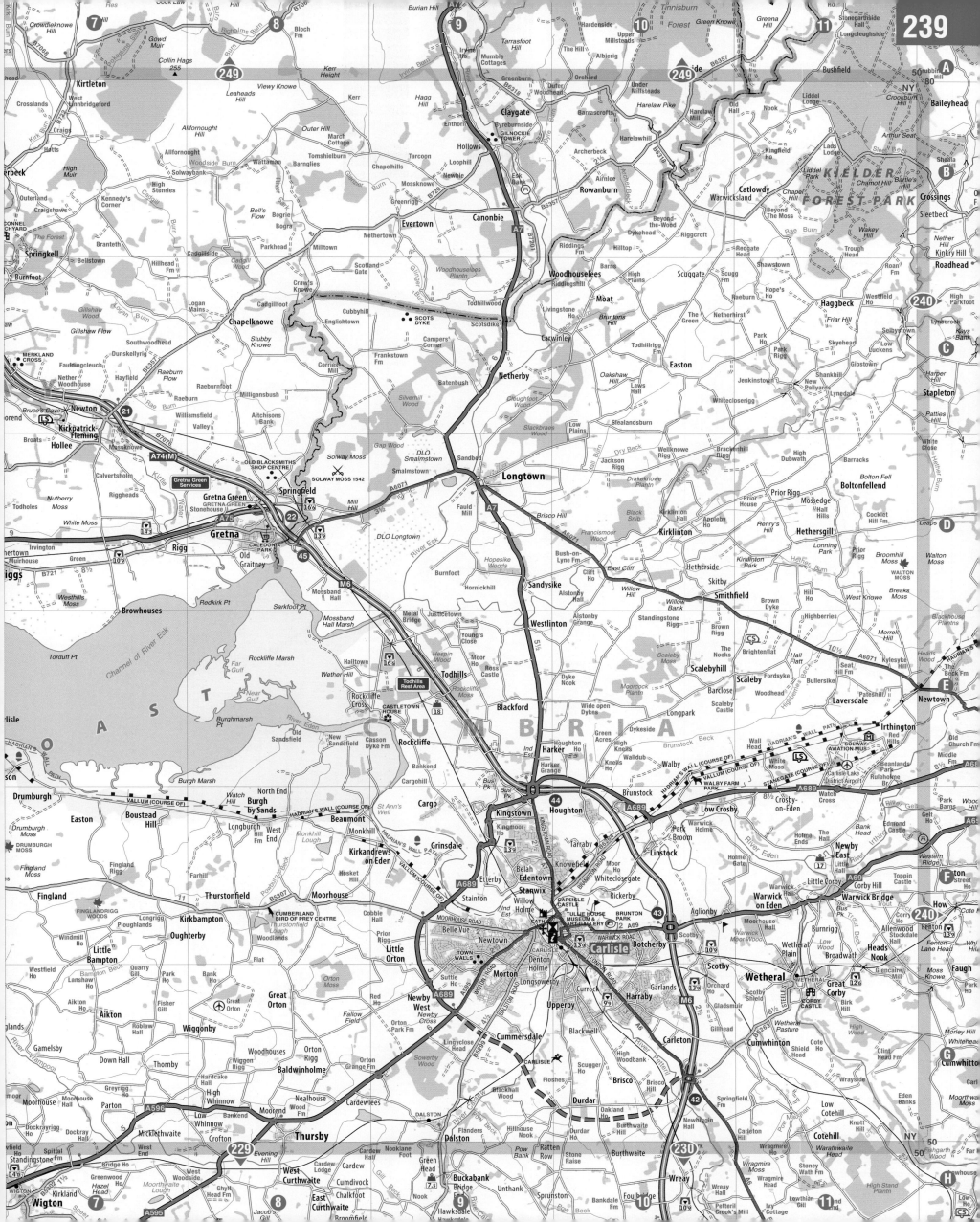

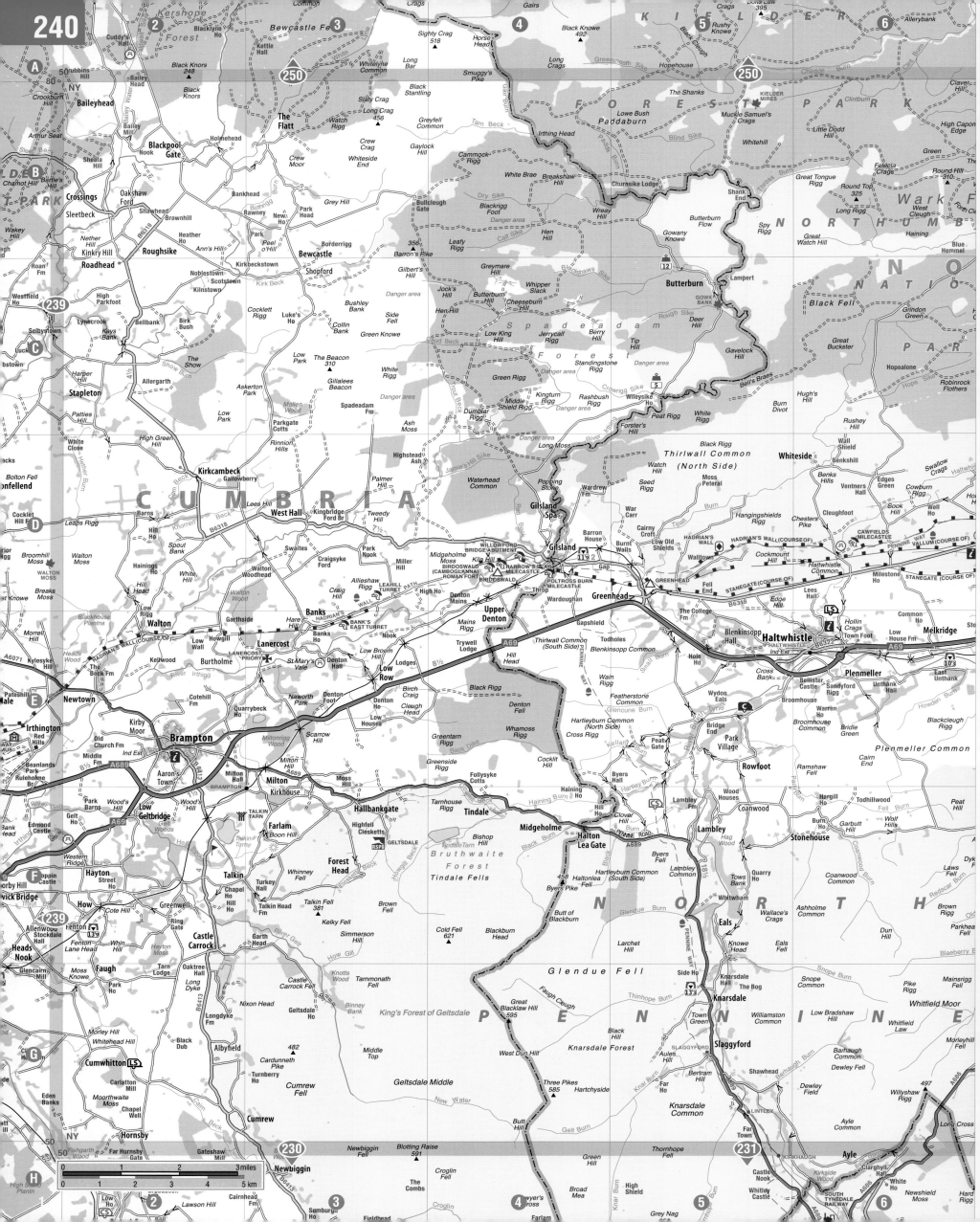

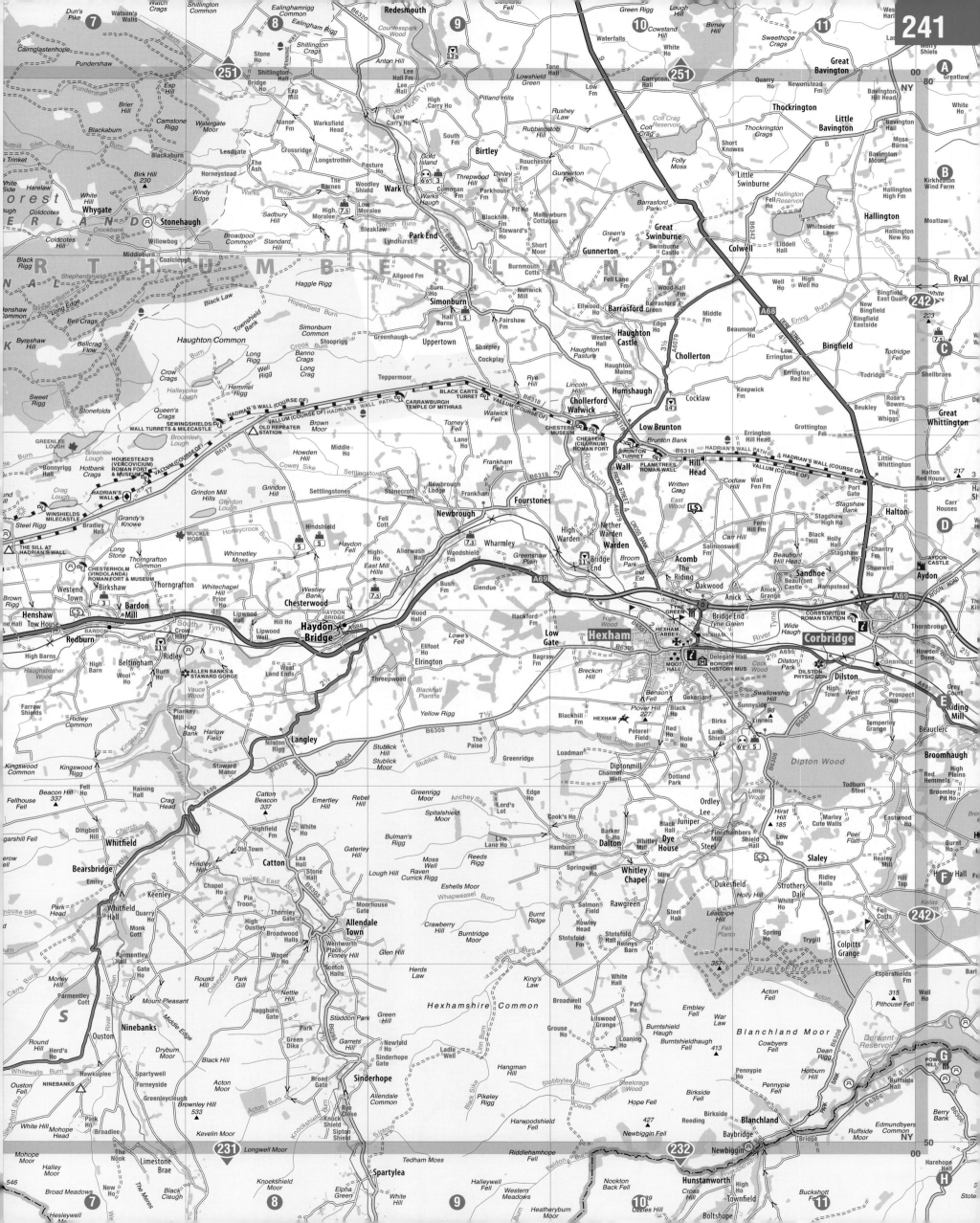

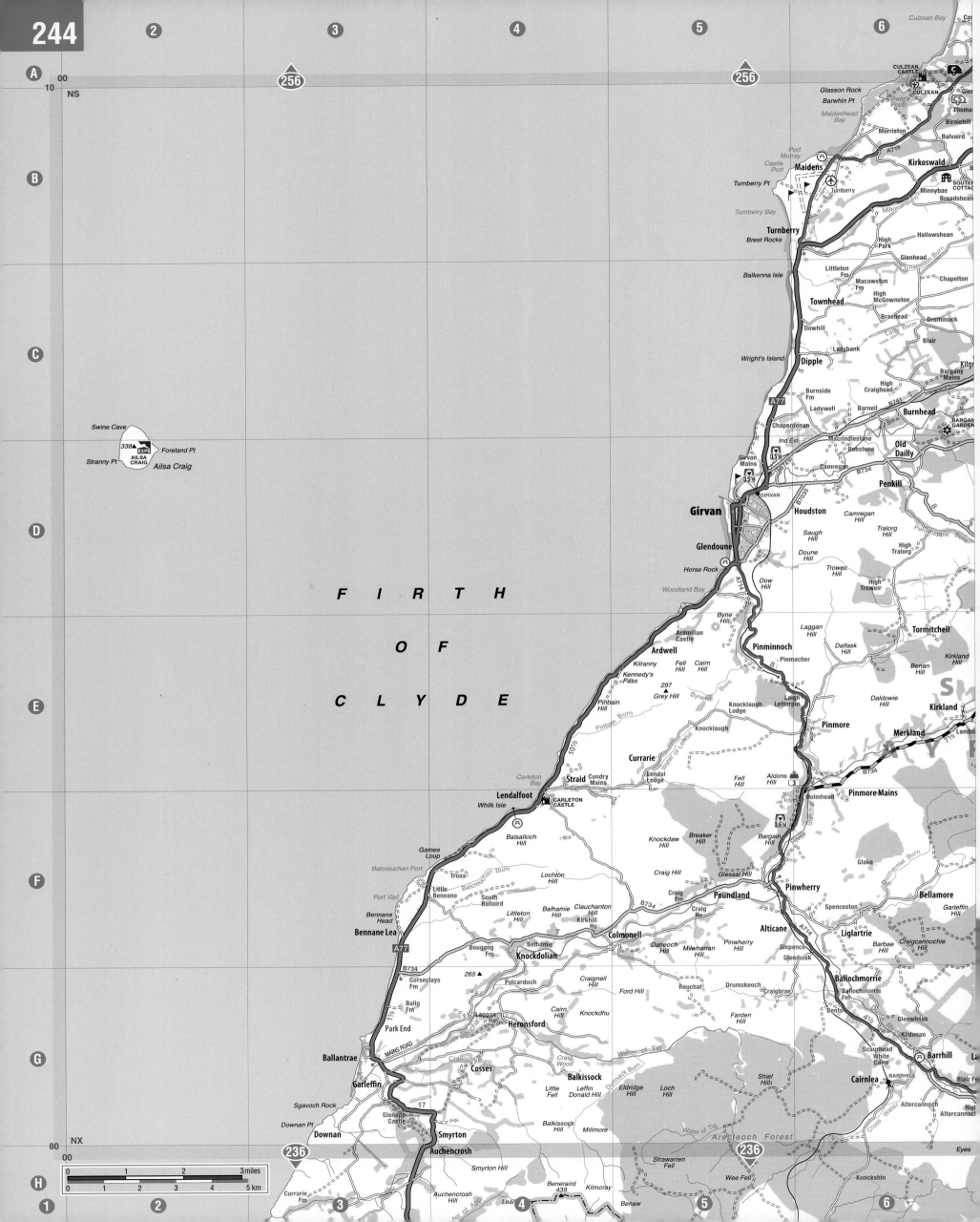

FIRTH

OF

CLYDE

Ailsa Craig
338▲ AILSA CRAIG
Swine Cave
Stranny Pt
Foreland Pt

Kirkoswald
Maidens
Turnberry Pt
Turnberry
Brest Rocks
Balkenna Isle
Townhead
Dowhill
Ladybank
Dipple
Wright's Island
Chaperdonan
Girvan Mains
Girvan
Glendoune
Horse Rock
Woodland Bay
Byne Hill
Ardmillan Castle
Ardwell
Kilranny
Kennedy's Pass
Pinbain Hill
Pinbain Burn
297 ▲ Grey Hill
Fell Hill
Cairn Hill
Bynehill
Knocklaugh Lodge
Knocklaugh
Currarie
Carleton Bay
Straid
Cundry Mains
Lendal Lodge
Fell Hill
Aldons Hill
Lendalfoot
CARLETON CASTLE
Whilk Isle
Balsalloch Hill
Games Loup
Balcreuchan Port
Troax
Port Vad
Little Bennane
South Ballaird
Littleton Hill
Lochton Hill
Balcreuchan Burn
Balhamie Hill
Clauchanton Hill
Kirkhill Ho
Bennane Head
Bennane Lea
Bougang Fm
Bethamie Fm
Knockdolian
265 ▲
Corseclays Fm
Balig Fm
Park End
Ballantrae
MAINS ROAD
Garleffin
Cosses
Laggan Ho
Heronsford
Polcardoch
Craigneil Hill
Ford Hill
Cairn Hill
Knockdhu
Little Fell
Leffin Donald Hill
Balkissock
Eldridge Hill
Sgavoch Rock
Downan Pt
Glenapp Castle
17
Downan
Smyrton
Balkissock Hill
Millmore
Auchencrosh
Smyrton Hill
Currarie Fm
Auchencrosh Hill
Beneraird 439
Kilmoray
Benaw

CULZEAN CASTLE
CULZEAN
Culzean Bay
Glasson Rock
Barwhin Pt
Maidenhead Bay
Morriston
Birniehill
Balvaird
SOUTER COTTAGE
Minnybae
Broadshean
High Park
Hallowshean
Glenhead
Littleton Fm
Macawston Fm
High McGownston
Chapelton
Braehead
Drummuck
Blair
High Craighead
Kilgr
Bargany Mains
Burnside Fm
Ladywell
Barneil
Burnhead
BARGAN GARDEN
Macrindlestone
Bobstone
Old Dailly
Camregan
Penkill
Ind Est
Houdston
Camregan Hill
Tralorg Hill
Saugh Hill
Doune Hill
High Tralorg
Troweir Hill
High Troweir
Dow Hill
Laggan Hill
Tormitchell
Dalfask Hill
Pinmacher
Pinminnoch
Benan Hill
Kirkland Hill
Daldowie Hill
Kirkland
Laigh Letterpin
Pinmore
Merkland
Lambd
Bargain Hill
Holmhead
Pinmore Mains
Knockdaw Hill
Breaker Hill
Glake
Craig Hill
Glessal Hill
Docherneil Burn
Craig Fm
Poundland
Pinwherry
Bellamore
Craig Ho
Dalreoch Hill
Milwharran Hill
Pinwherry Hill
Spenceston
Garleffin Hill
Alticane
Liglartrie
Barbae Hill
Craigcannochie Hill
Glenduisk
Sixpence
Ballochmorrie
Drumskeoch
Craigbrae
Reuchal
Farden Hill
Bents
Glenwhask
Scaurhead White Cairn
Kildonan
Barrhill
Cairnlea
Blair F
Shiel Hill
Altercannoch
Cross Water
Strawarren Fell
Wee Fell
Eyes
Knockshin

A77
A719
A77
A714
B741
B734
B7035
B7023

FIRTH OF CLYDE

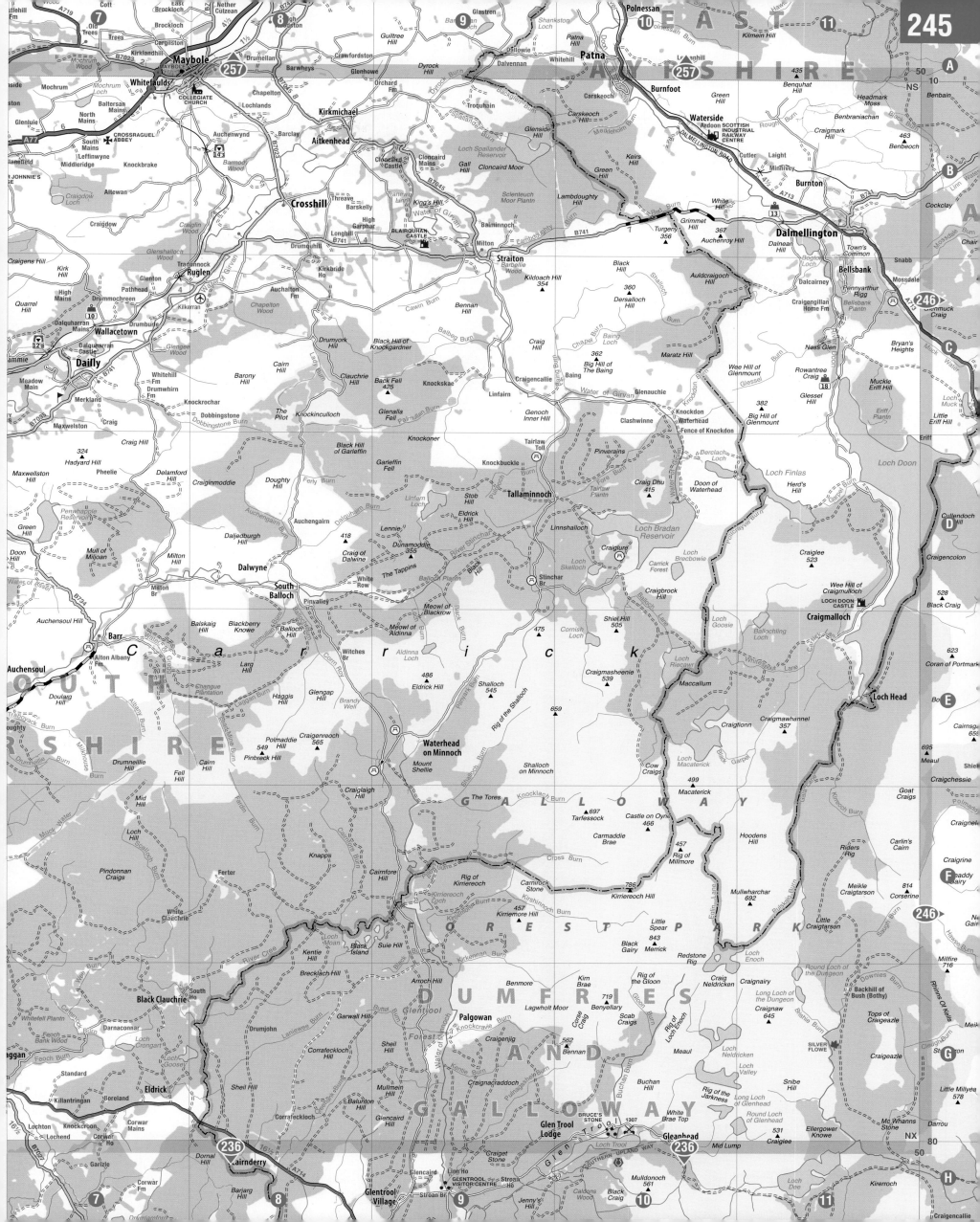

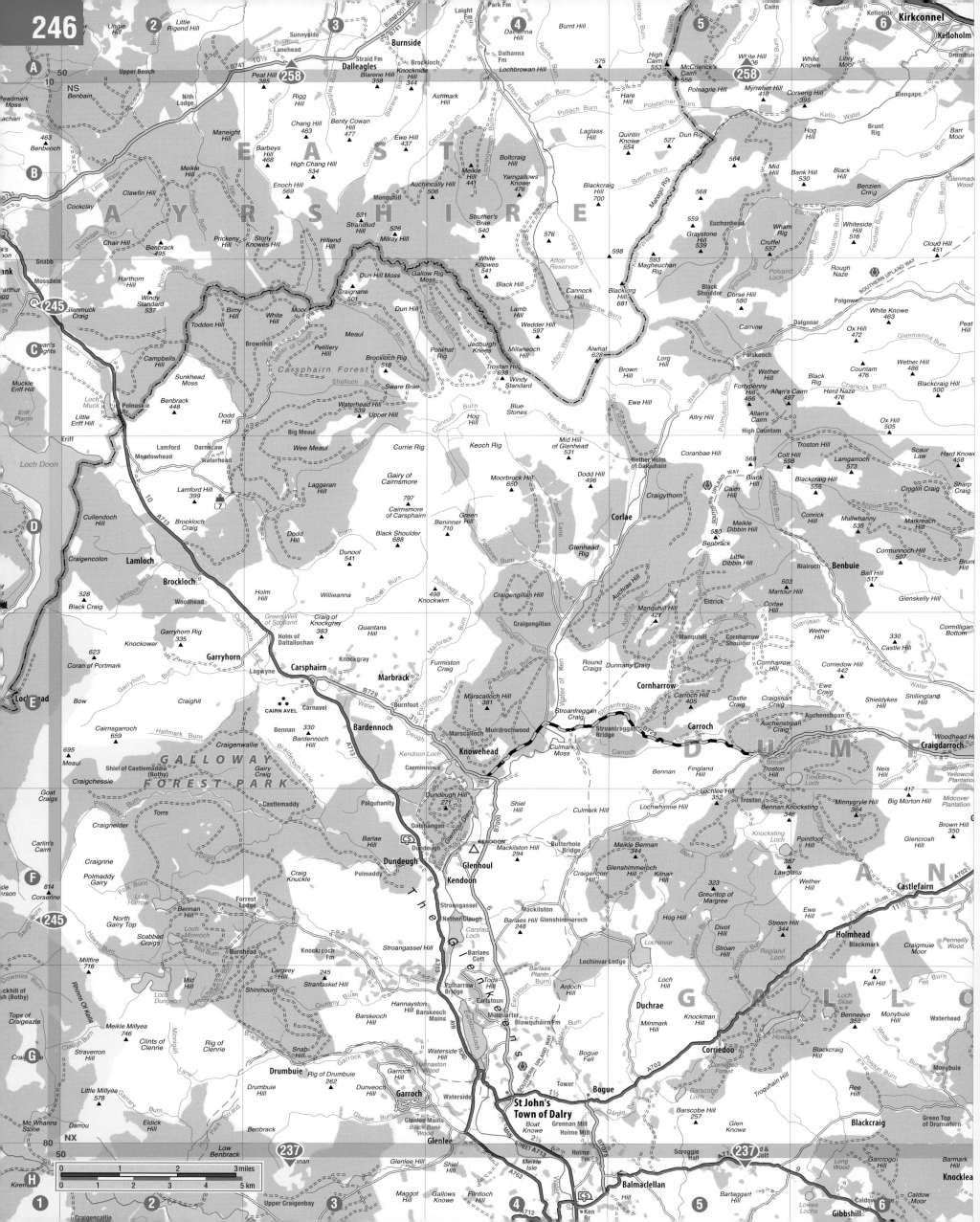

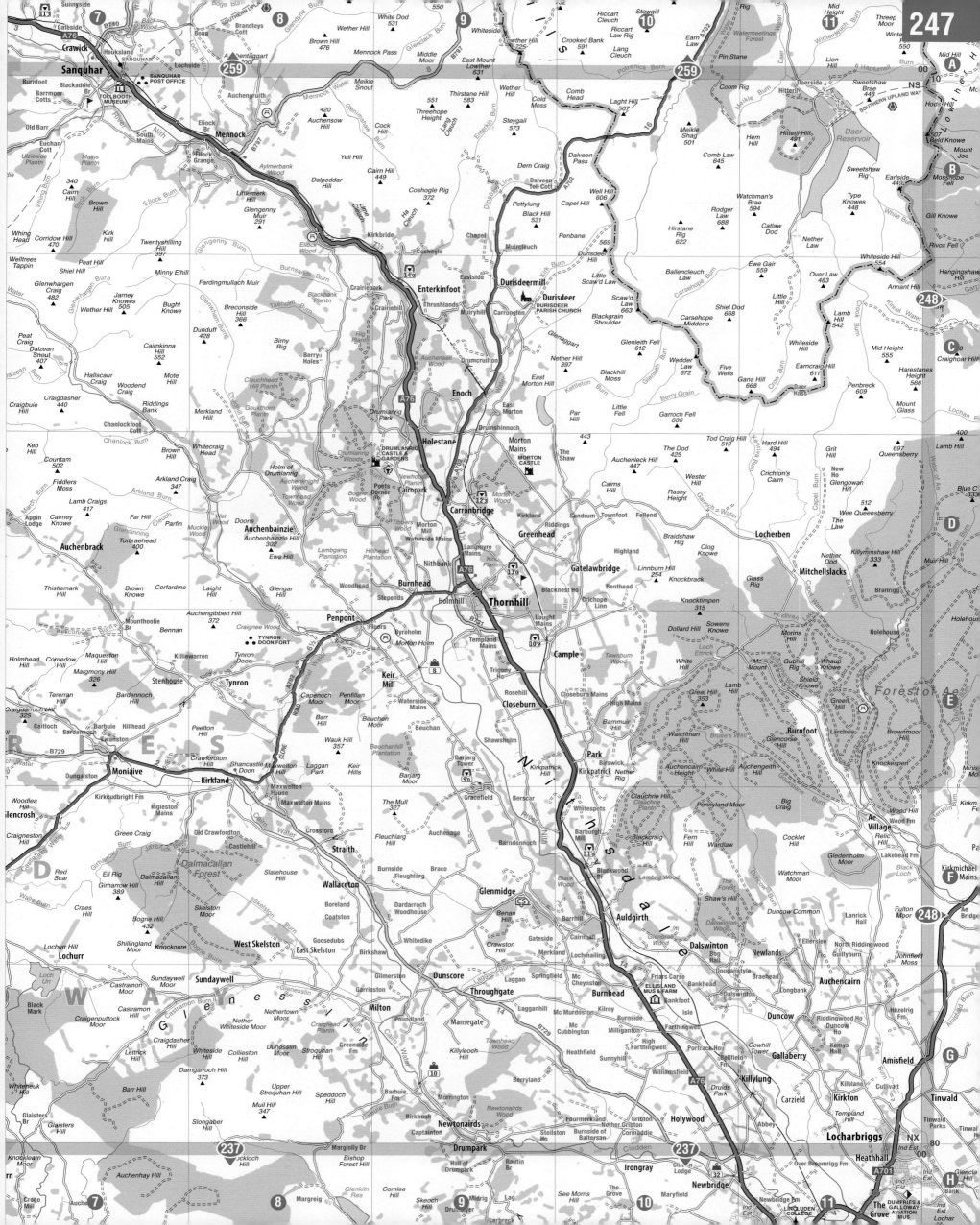

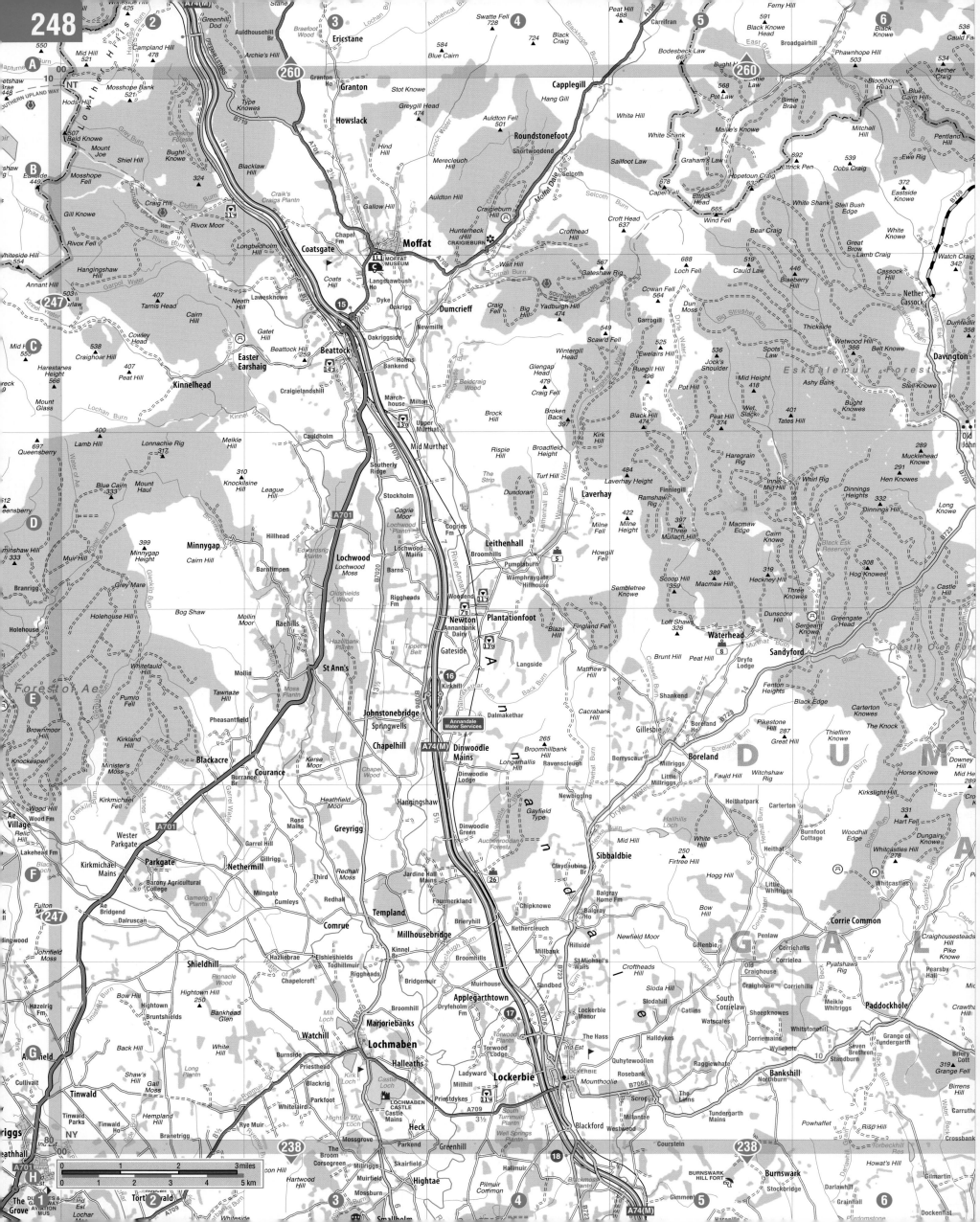

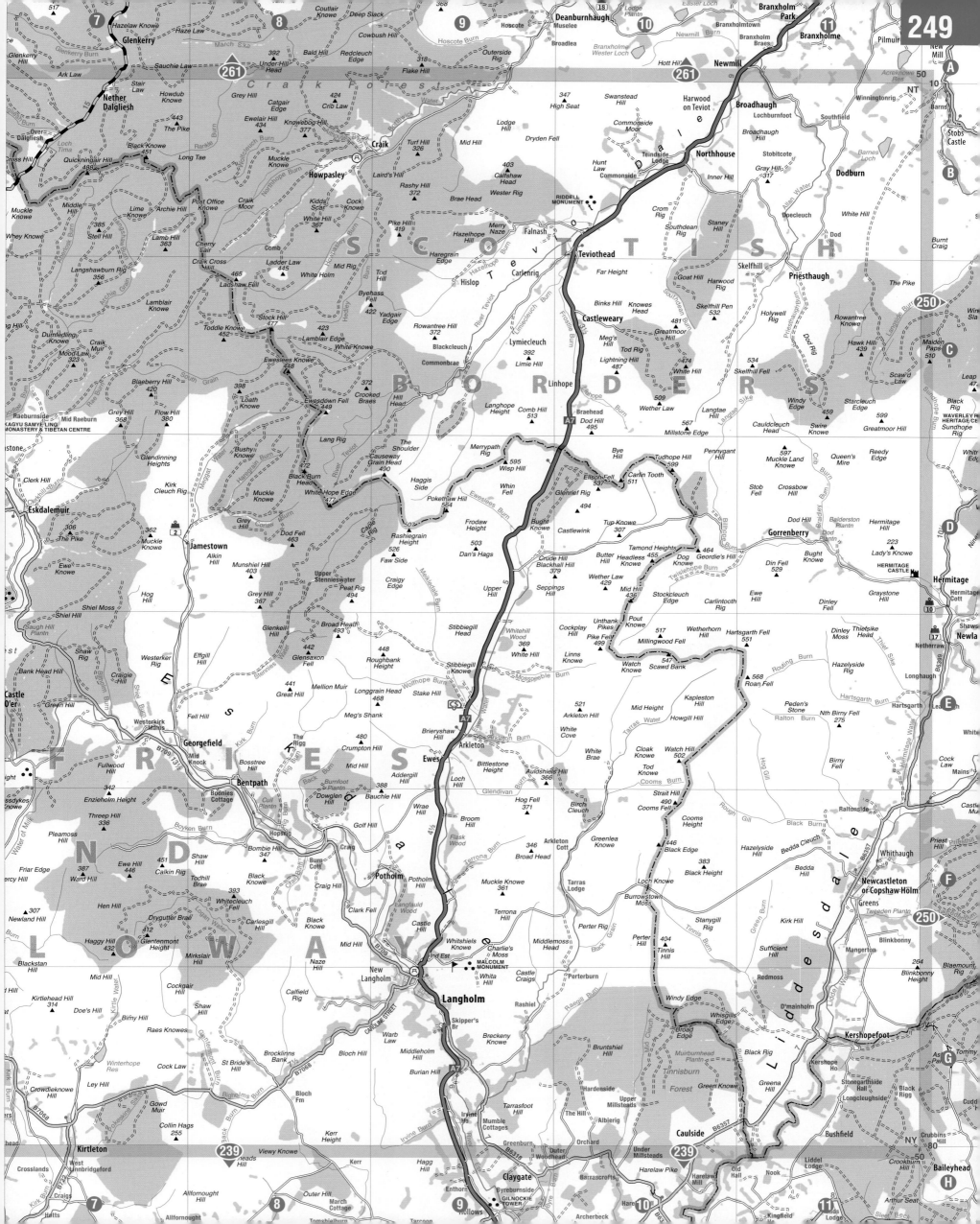

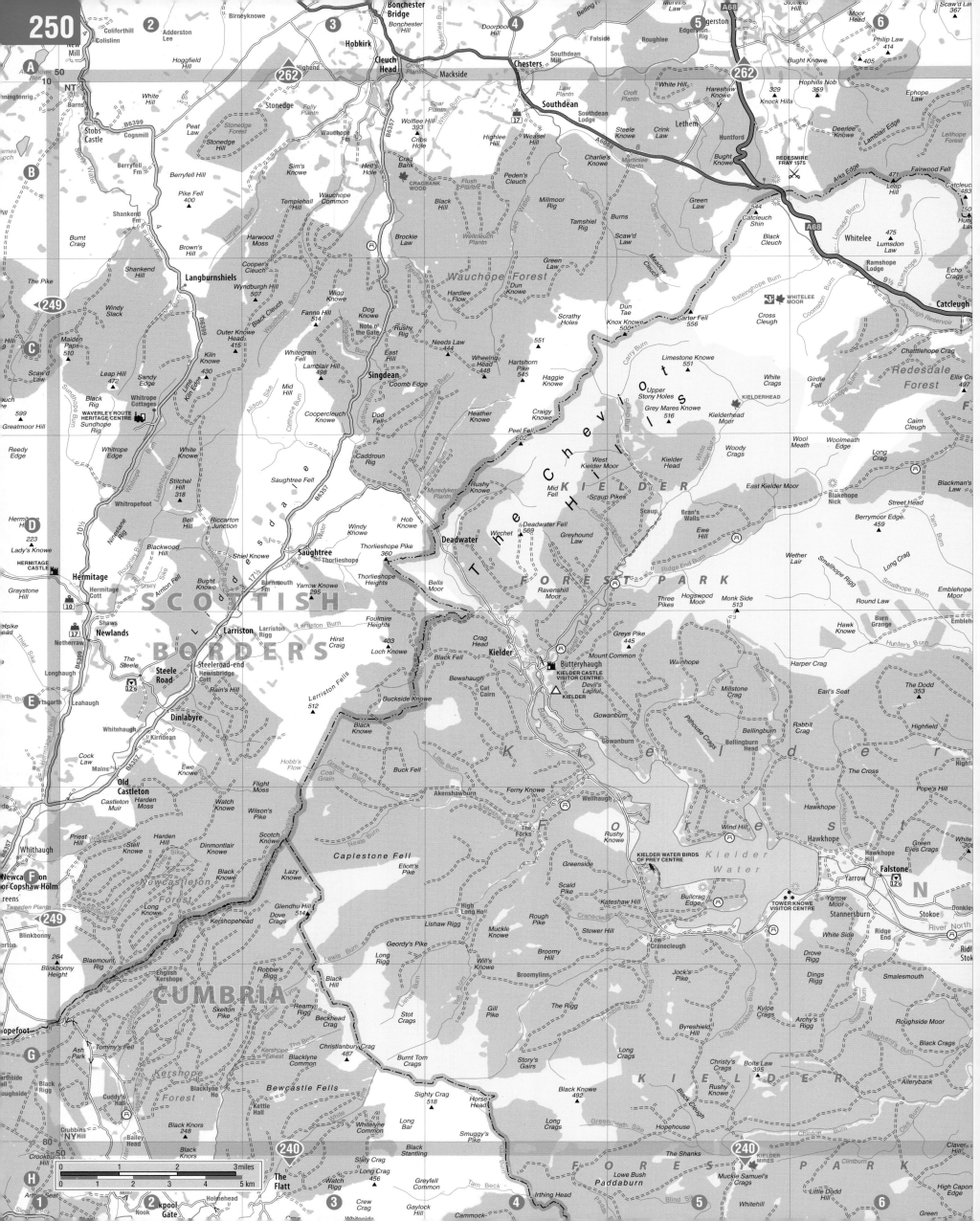

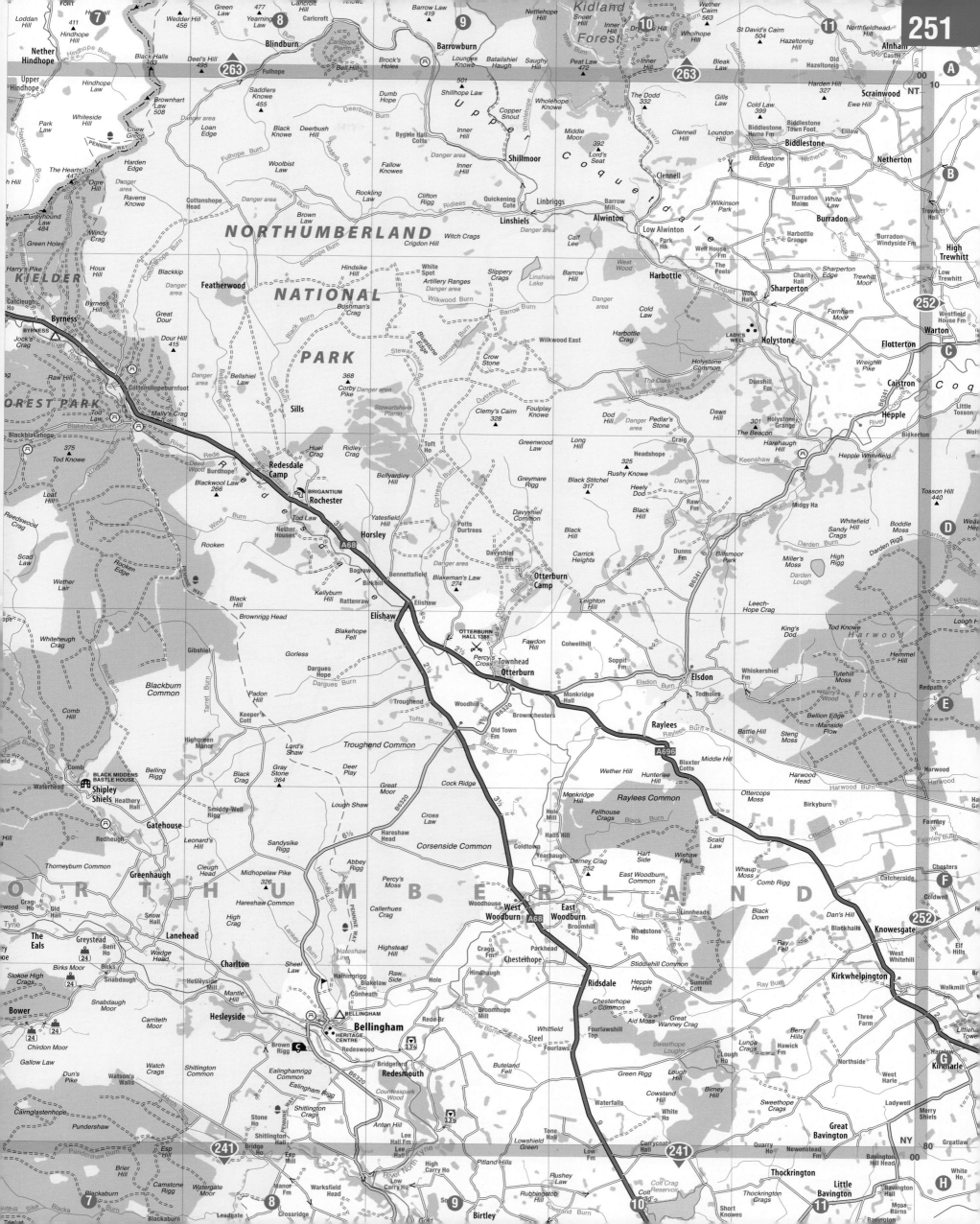

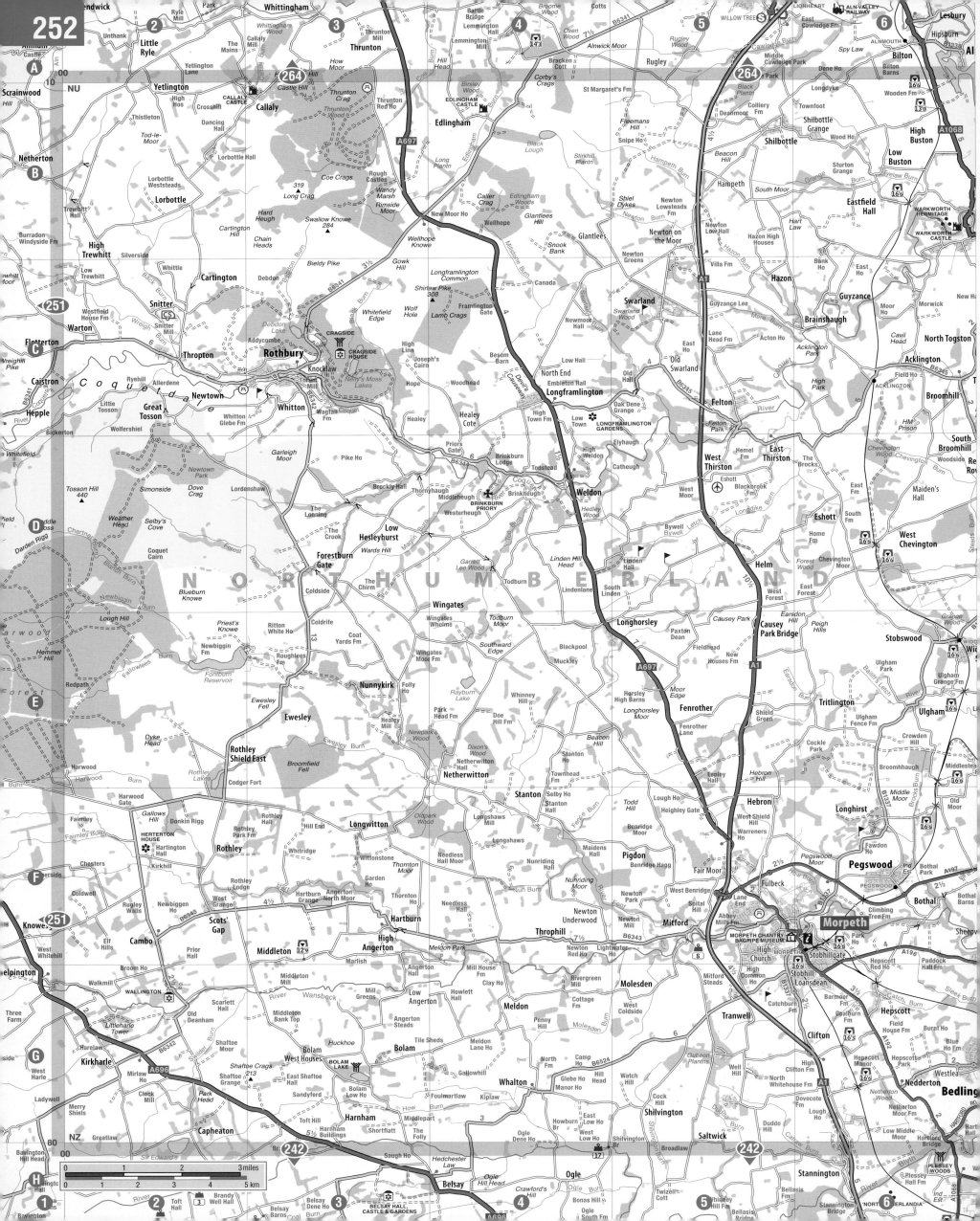

NORTH SEA

Marden Rocks

nmouth

Alnmouth Bay

265

265

Birling

Warkworth

Pan Pt

Wellhaugh Pt

Coquet Island

Gloster Hill

Amble

Moorhouse Fm

High Hauxley

Togston Hall

Radcliffe

Low Hauxley

HAUXLEY

Togston Barns

A1068

Togston East Fm

ogston

Danger area

Ladyburn Lake

Hadston

DRURIDGE BAY

Druridge Bay

Whitefield Ho

Chibburn Fm

High Chibburn

Widdrington

Hemscott Hill

A1068

RINGTON

ddrington Station

Highthorn

Cresswell

Warkworthlane Cott

Hagg House

North nton Fm

Ellington

Cresswell Home Fm

Linton

Lynemouth

East Moor Fm

Potland Fm

Works

QUEEN ELIZABETH II

Woodhorn

A189

WOODHORN MUS

Bus Cen

Woodbridge

A197

Ashington

Newbiggin-by-the-Sea

Hirst

North Seaton

Newbiggin Bay

WANSBECK

North Seaton Colliery

Stakeford

Wansbeck

wash

West Sleekburn

Guide Post

Scotland Gate

Bomarsund

Bus Cen

Cambois

Choppington

East Sleekburn

Bedlington Station

Mount Pleasant Fm

North Blyth

BEDLINGTON

STEAD

Bebside

COWPEN ROAD

Cowpen

A193

Blyth

Isabella Pit

ton

Humford Mill

A189

HORTON

South Beach

East Hartford

243

South Newsham

est Hartford

New Delaval

Laverock Hall

Gloucester Lodge Fm

Shankhouse

A192

LAVEROCK HALL ROAD

Meggie's Burn

Newsl

A1061

Stickley Fm

ISLAY

Coul Pt.
Foreland Ho
Lyrabus
Esknish
Knocklearoch
Cabrach
Strone

Sunderland
Blackrock
Redhous
Daill
BEINN DUBH
Camas an
staca

Kilchoman
Gortan
Islay
Ho
Som
Am Fraoch
Eilean
Rubha na Tràille

Conisby
Bridgend
Brosdale I.

Machir Bay

A
10
60
NR
Kilchiaran Bay
Bowmore
McArthur's Hd.
PORT ASKAIG

MUSEUM OF ISLAY LIFE
BOWMORE ROUND CHURCH

Tormisdale
RHINNS
PORT CHARLOTTE
Mulindry
Cattadale

Port Charlotte
15

Lossit
232
Gartbreck
Laggan
BEINN BHAN
BEINN BHEIGEIR
Carraig Mhór

Lossit Pt.
Kelsay
Bridge Ho
471
491
Ardtalla

B
Nerabus
Laggan Pt.
Duich
13
Loch Beinn Uraraidh
Claggain Bay

ISLAY
Laggan
Torra

Rubha na Faing
Claddach
ISLAY
B8016
Kintour

Portnahaven
Easter Ellister
LAGGAN
Glenegedale
Kildalton
Ardmore Pt.

Port Wemyss
Wester Ellister
BAY
ISLAY
Castlehill
KILDALTON CHURCH AND CROSSES

Orsay
Rinns Pt.
Arivoichallum
347
Eilean Craobhach

BEINN SHOLUM
Eilean a'Chuirn

Port Alsaig
Machrie Hotel
Leorin
Eilean Bhride

Rubha Mór
Kintra
Ardbeg Distillery
Kildaton Ho

Cornabus
Kilbride
Lagavulin

C
Lower Cragabus
Imeraval
Port Ellen
Ardbeg
Eilean Imersay

Dùn Mór Ghil
THE OA
152
LAPHROAIG DISTILLERY
LAGAVULIN DISTILLERY

Lower Killeyan
Risabus
Laphroaig
Texa

Upper Killeyan
THE OA
Kinabus
Inerval
ARGY

AMERICAN MONUMENT
Mull of Oa
202

Rubha nan Leacan

AN

D
BALLYCASTLE
BUT

E

Earadale Pt.

F

Rubh'a'Mharaiche

NORTH CHANNEL

G
Rathlin Island
MULL OF KINTYRE

60
NR
10
Bushmills

H
0   2   4   6 miles
0 2 4 6 8 10 km
Ballycastle Bay
Ballycastle

1   2   3   4   5   6

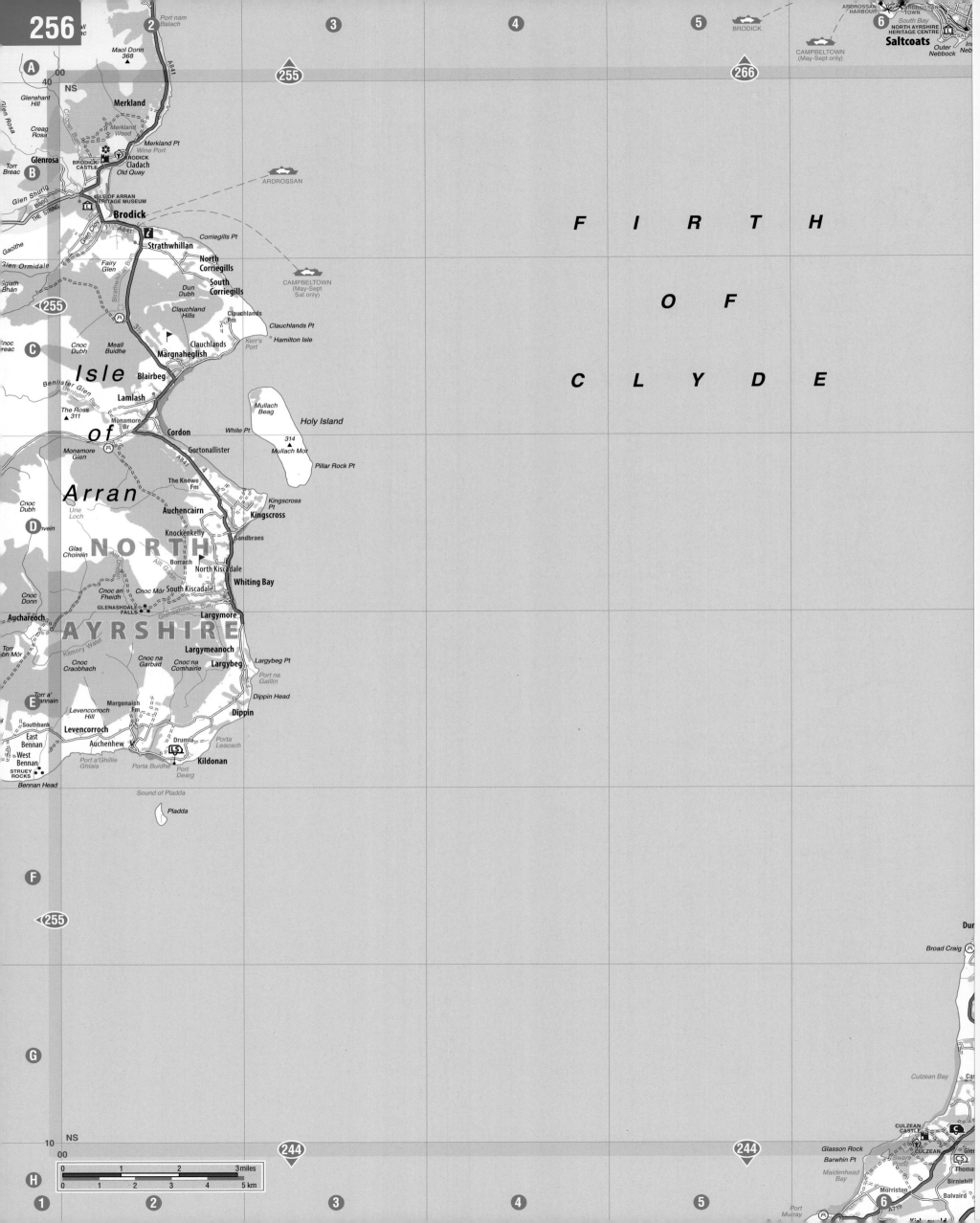

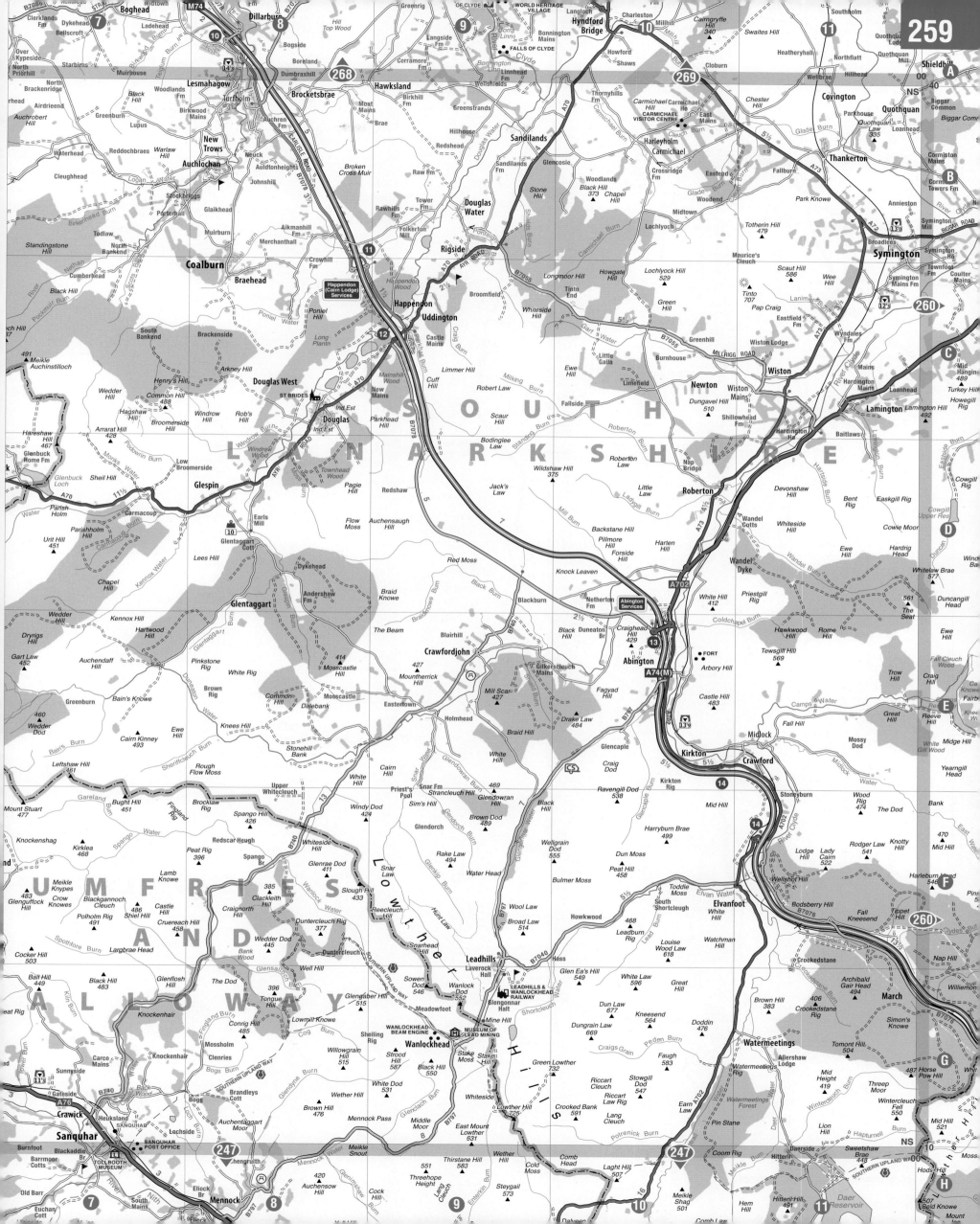

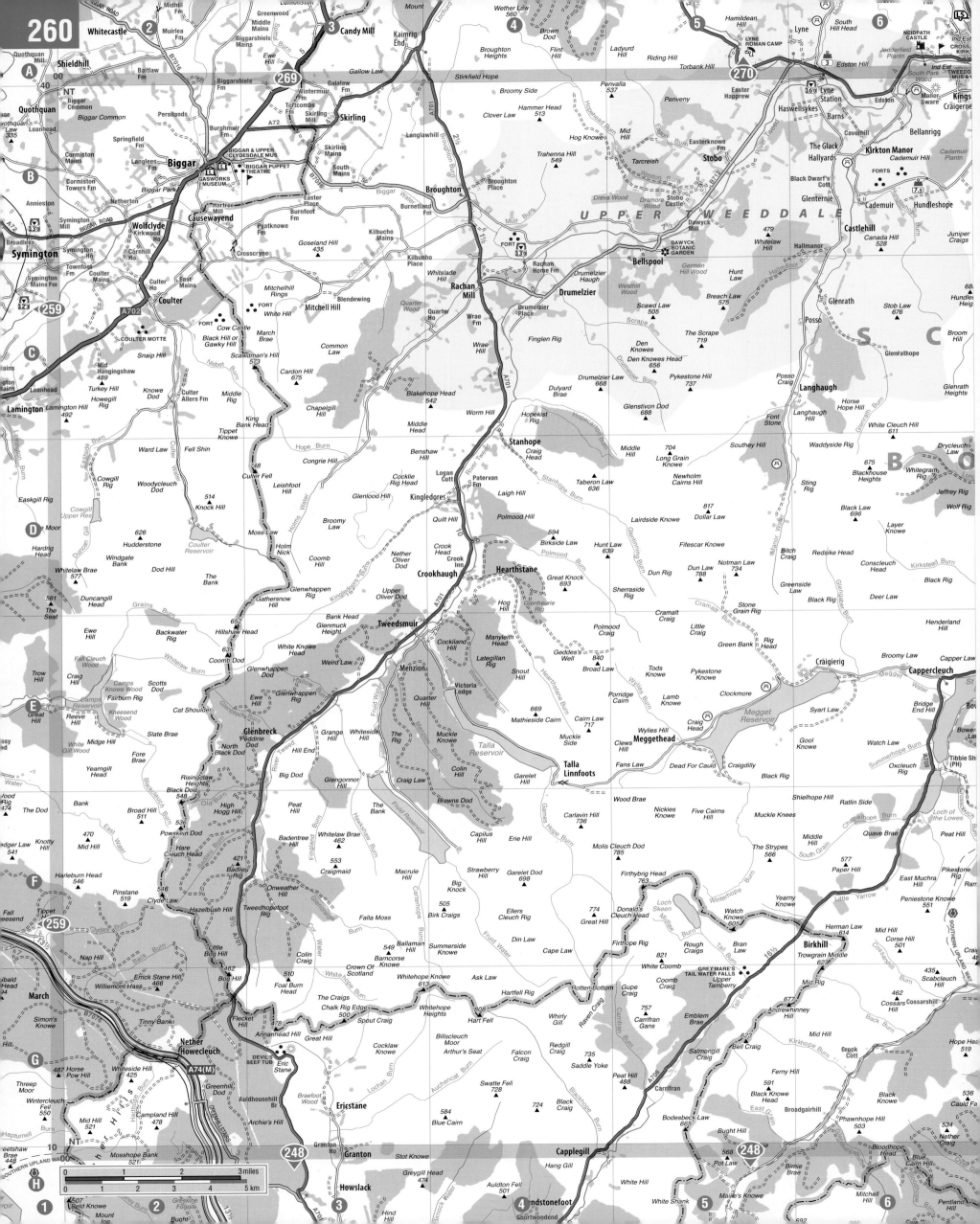

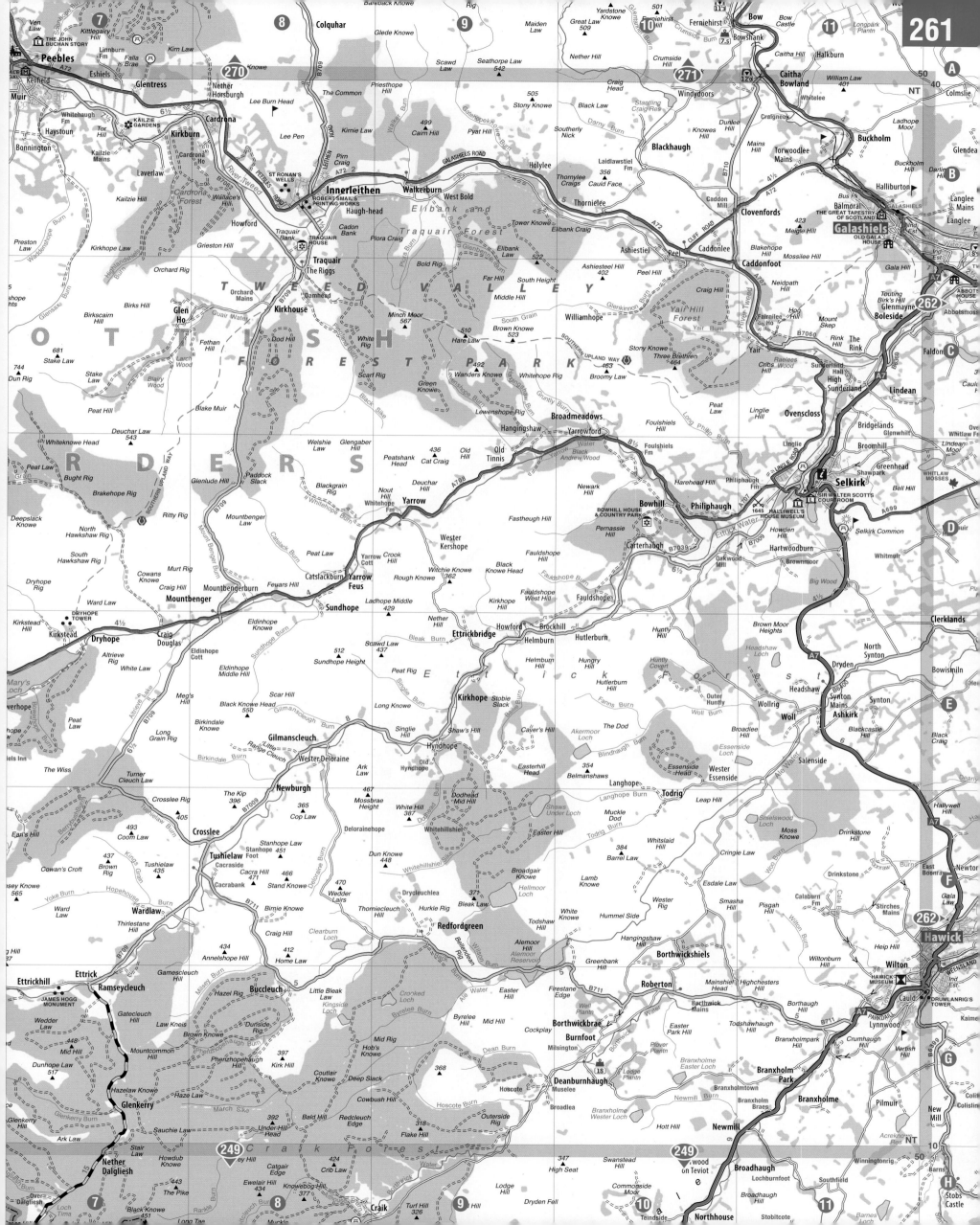

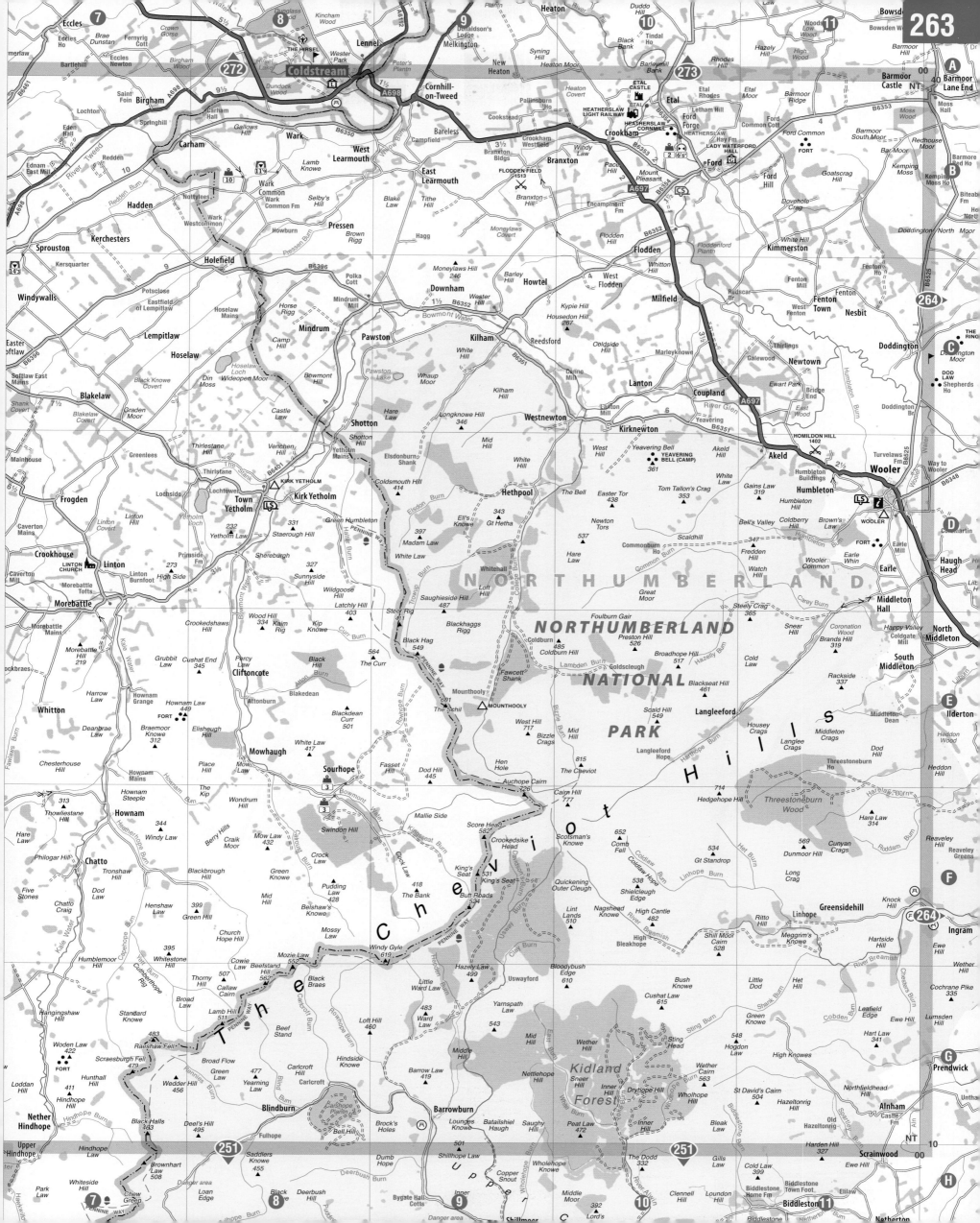

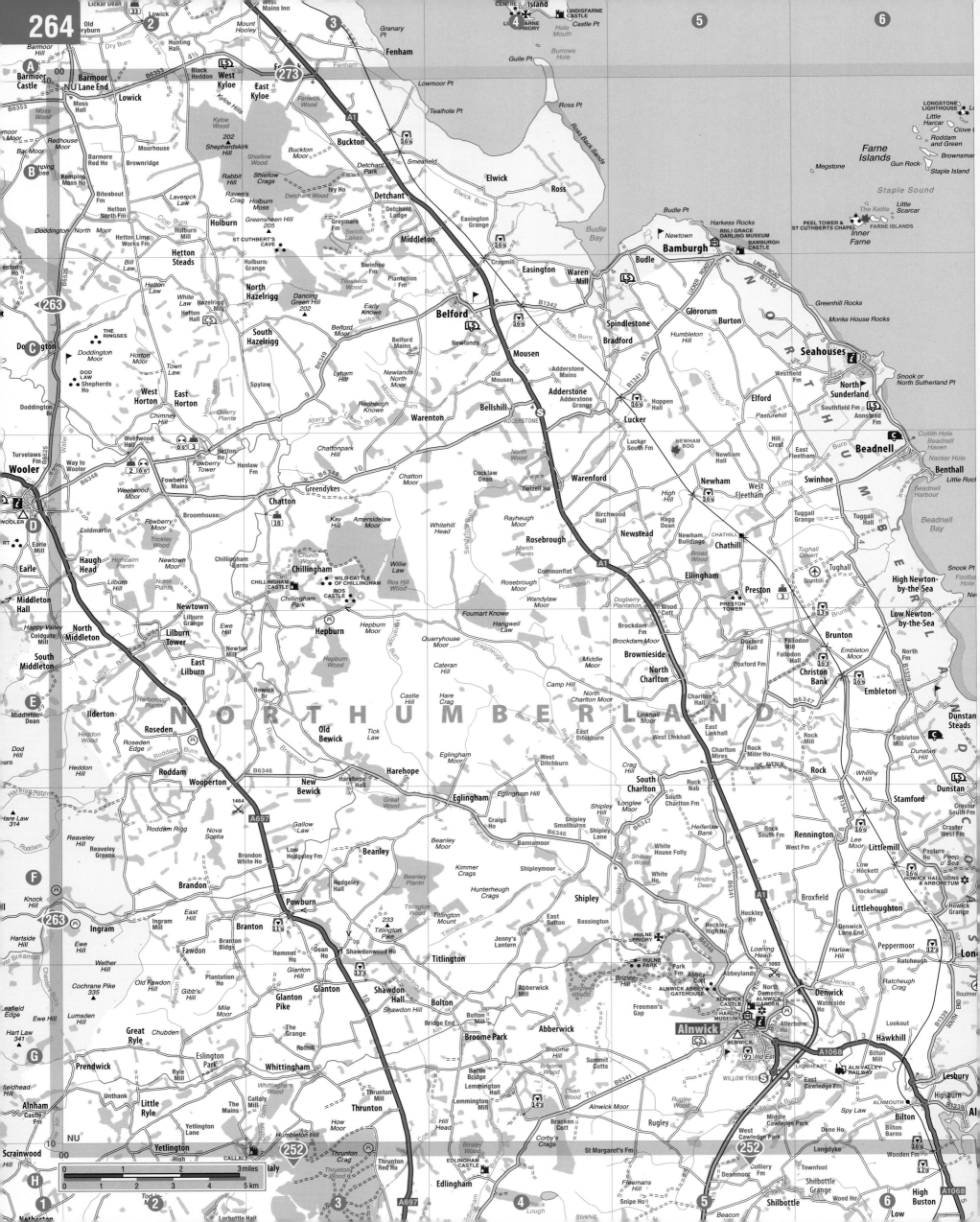

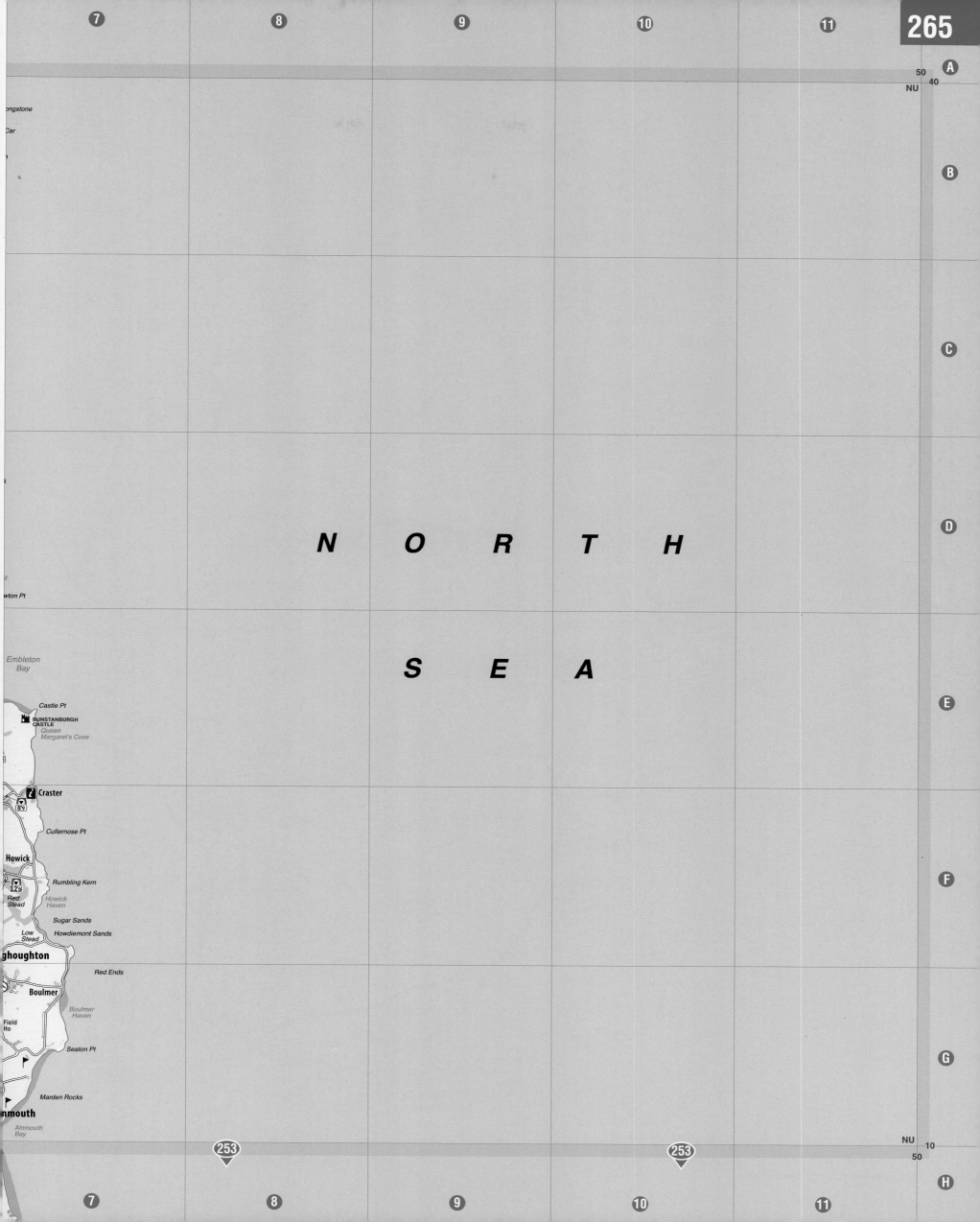

N O R T H

S E A

Embleton
Bay

Castle Pt
DUNSTANBURGH
CASTLE
Queen
Margaret's Cove

Craster

Cullernose Pt

Howick

Rumbling Kern
Howick
Haven
Red
Stead

Sugar Sands
Howdiemont Sands
Low
Stead

ghoughton
Red Ends

Boulmer
Boulmer
Haven
Field
Ho

Seaton Pt

Marden Rocks

nmouth
Almouth
Bay

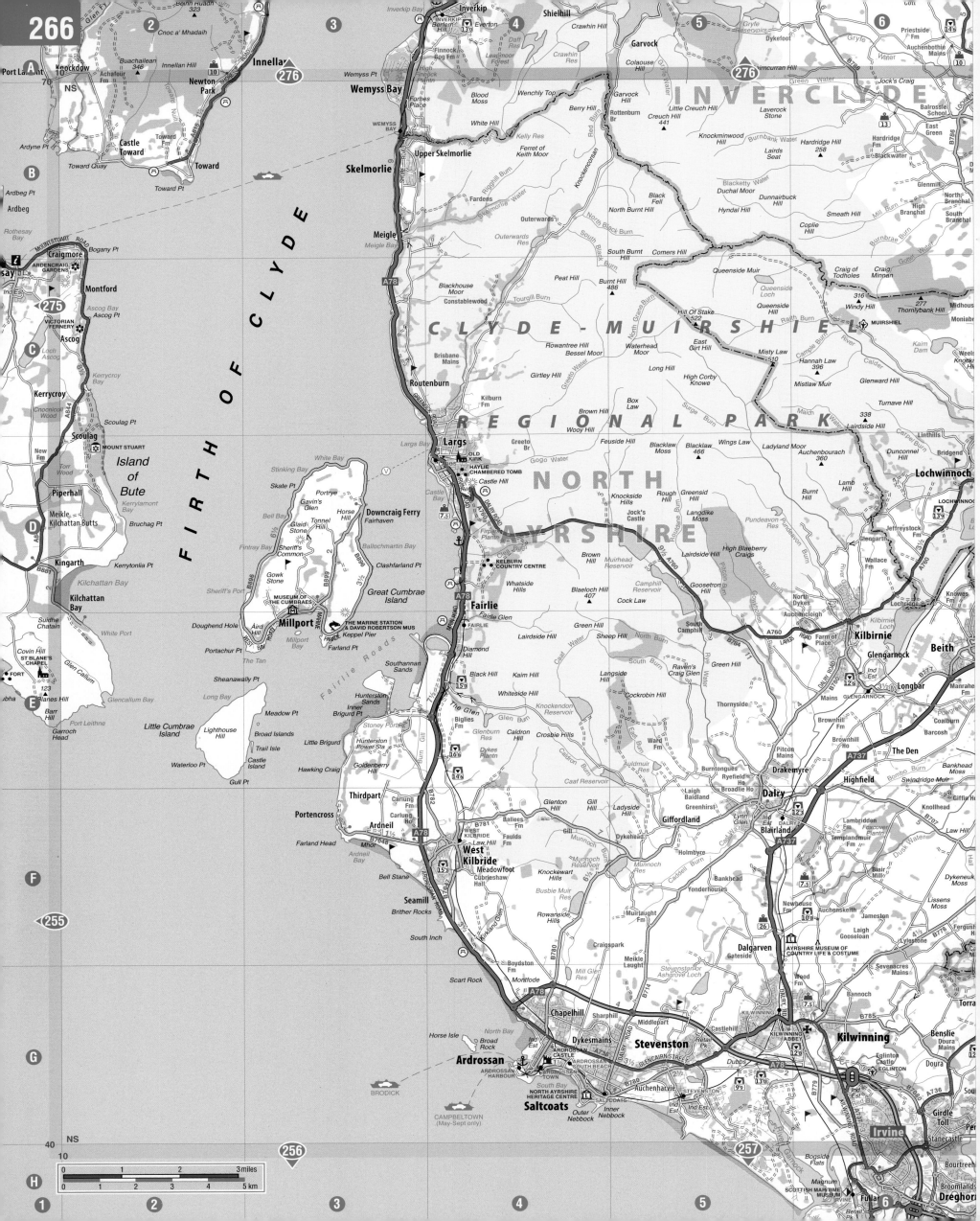

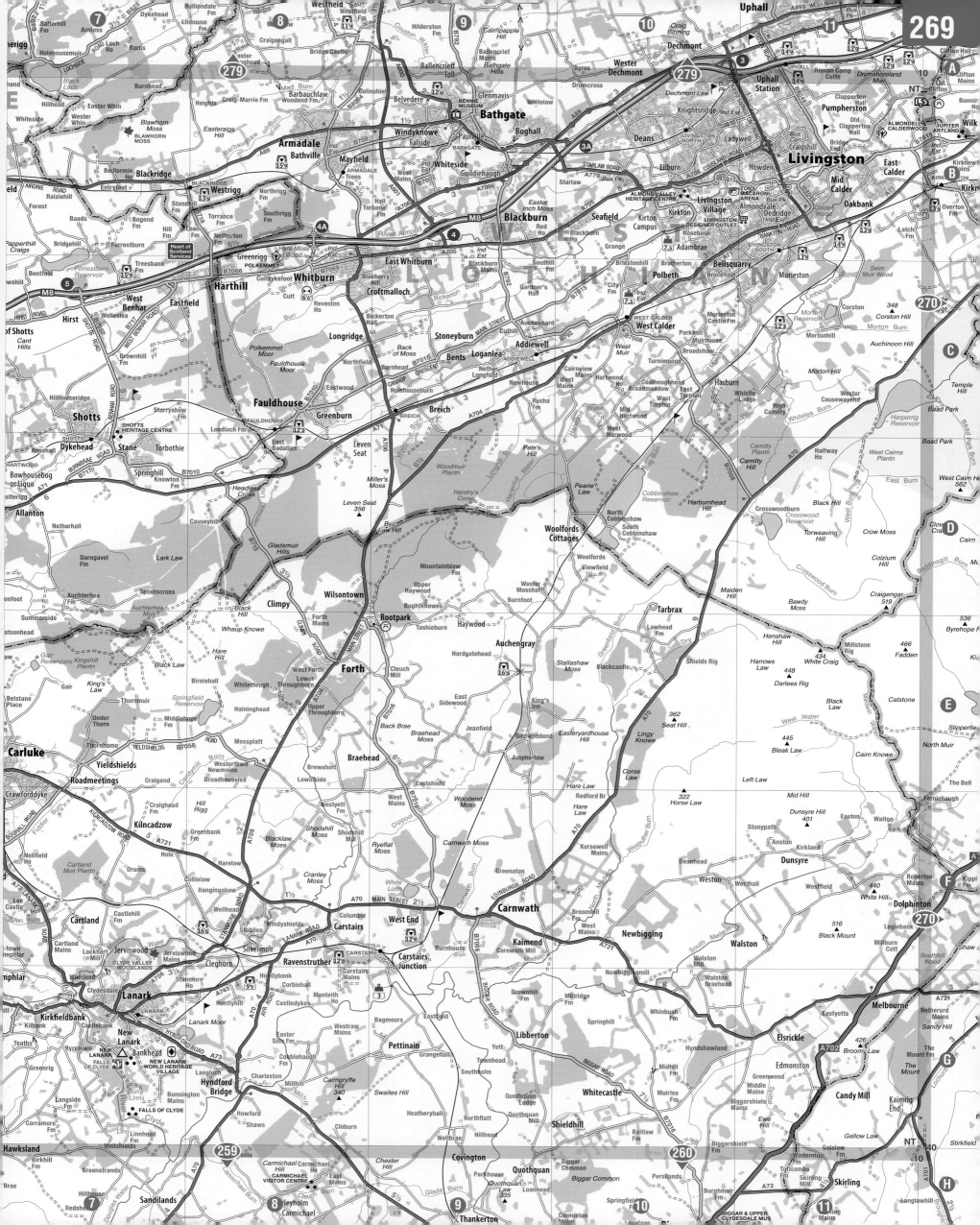

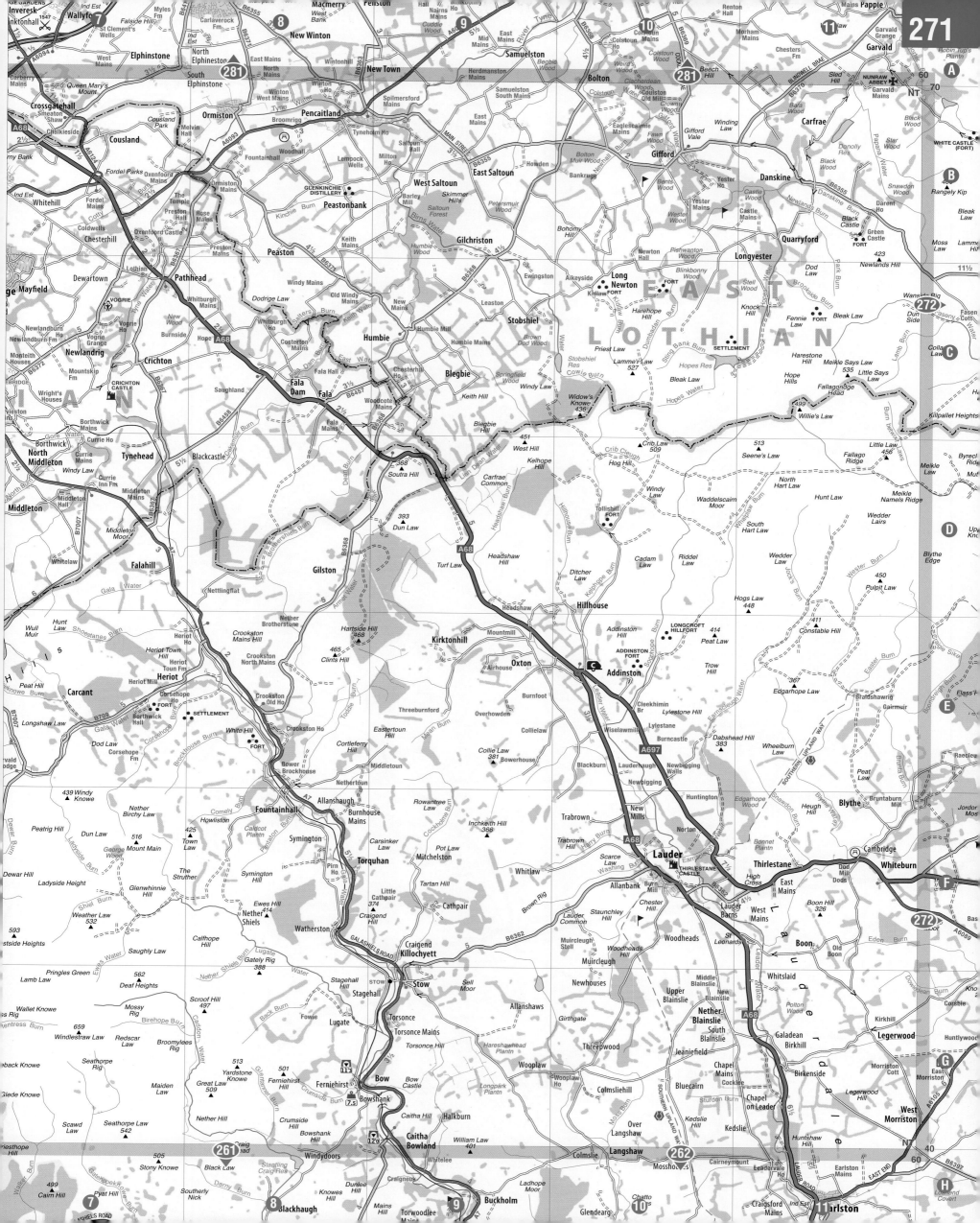

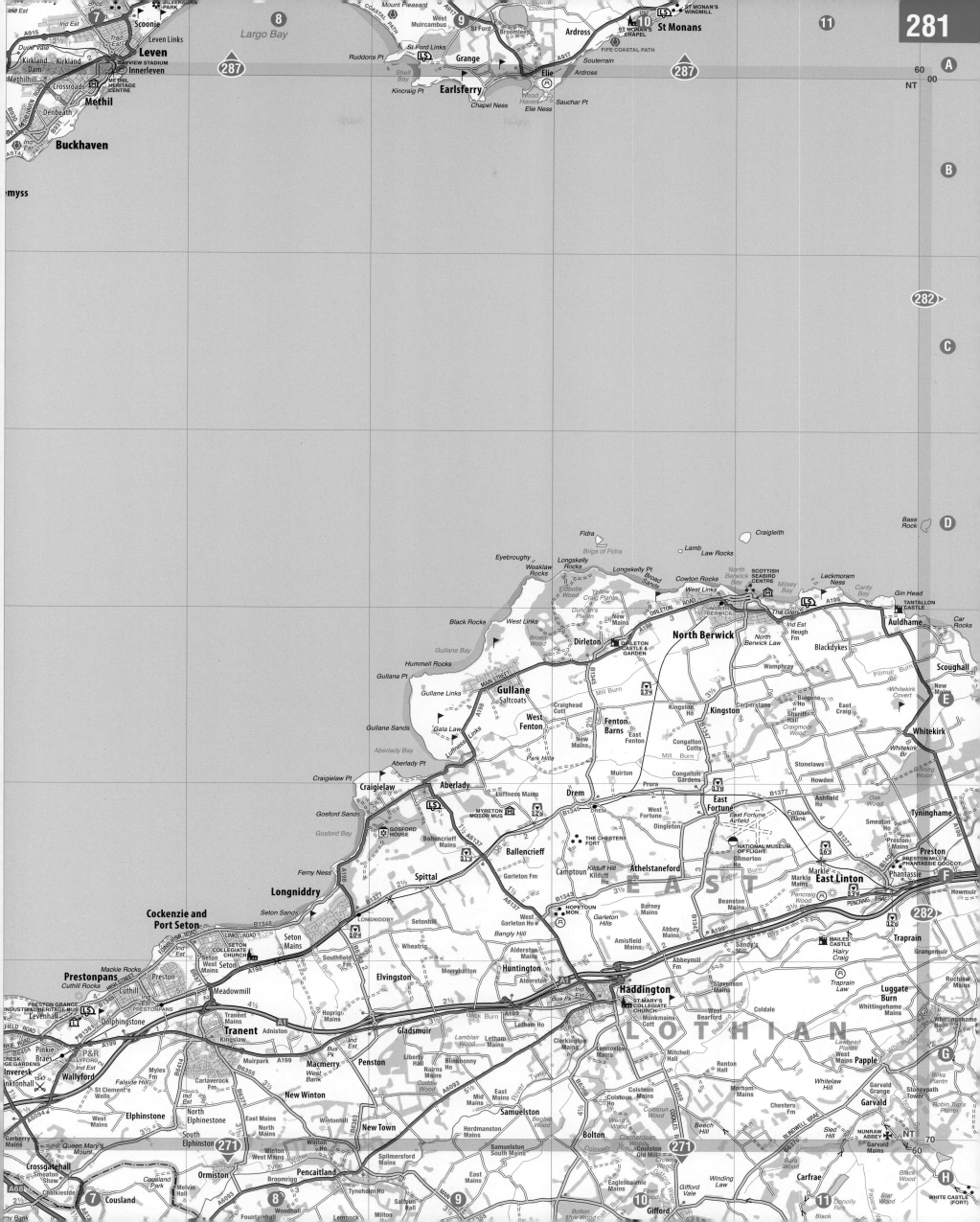

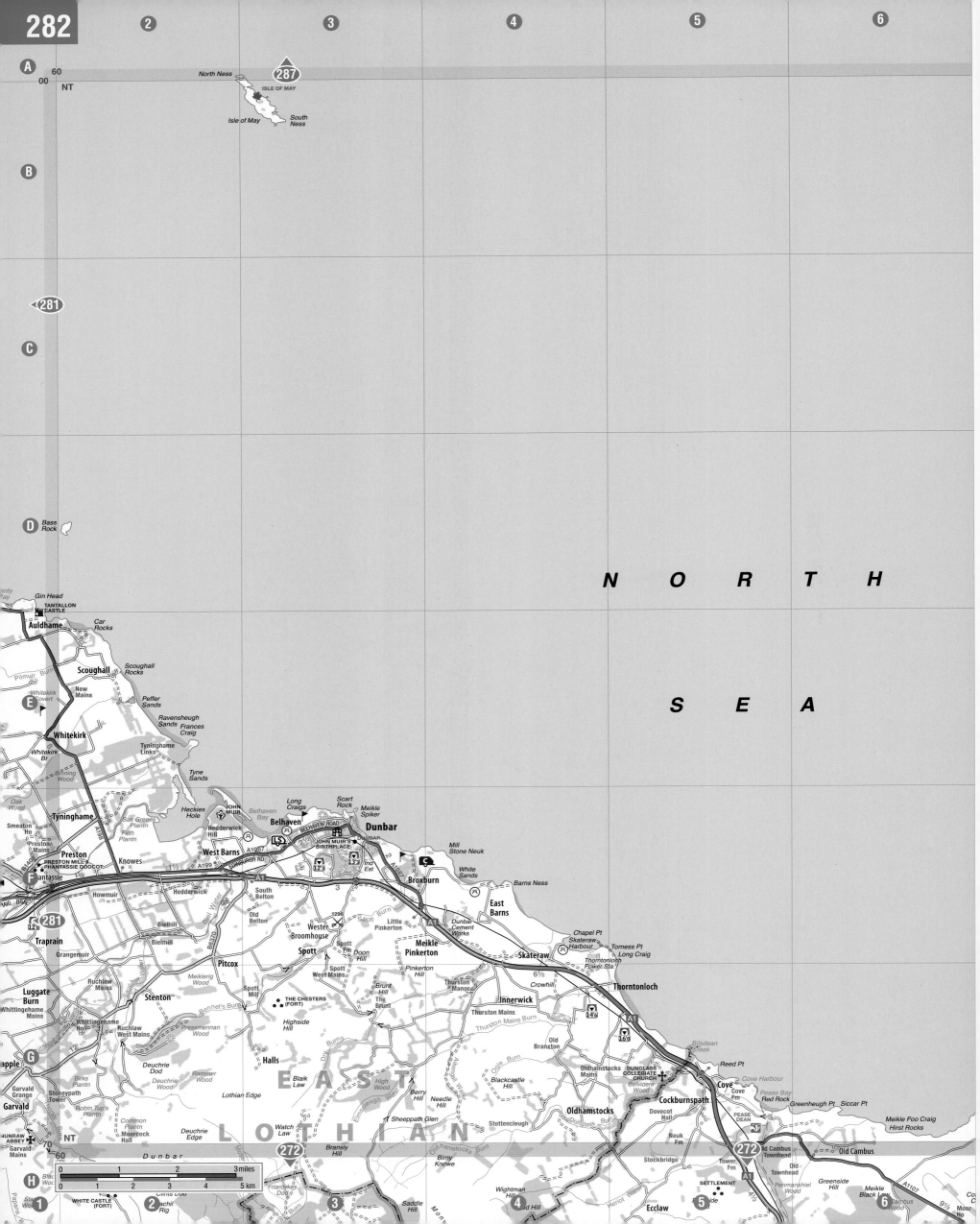

2 3 4 5 6

A 60
00
NT

North Ness
287
ISLE OF MAY
Isle of May
South Ness

B

281

C

D Bass
Rock

N O R T H

S E A

Gin Head
TANTALLON CASTLE
Auldhame
Car Rocks
Scoughall
Scoughall Rocks
Whitekirk Covert
New Mains
Peffer Sands
E Ravensheugh Sands
Frances Craig
Whitekirk
Whitekirk Br
Tyninghame Links
Pilmuir Burn
Binning Wood
Tyne Sands
Oak Wood
Heckies Hole
Long Craigs
Scart Rock
Meikle Spiker
JOHN MUIR
Belhaven Bay
Smeaton Ho
Tyninghame
Salt Greens Plantn
Filth Plantn
Hedderwick Hill
Belhaven
BELHAVEN ROAD
Dunbar
Preston Mains
Preston
Knowes
West Barns
A1087
JOHN MUIR'S BIRTHPLACE
Mill Stone Neuk
F **PRESTON MILL & PHANTASSIE DOOCOT**
A199
EDINBURGH RD
Ind Est
White Sands
Phantassie
1½
A1
Broxburn
Barns Ness
281
Howmuir
Hedderwick
South Belton
3
Dunbar Cement Works
East Barns
Traprain
Bielhill
Old Belton
1296
Wester Broomhouse
Little Pinkerton
Chapel Pt
Skateraw Harbour
Torness Pt
Long Craig
Grangemuir
Bielmill
B6370
Spott
Spott Fm
Doon Hill
Meikle Pinkerton
Thorntonloch Power Sta.
Pitcox
Spott West Mains
Pinkerton Hill
Thurston Manor
6½
Skateraw
Ruchlaw Mains
Meiklerig Wood
Spott Mill
Brunt Hill
Thurston Mains
Crowhill
Thorntonloch
Luggate Burn
Stenton
THE CHESTERS (FORT)
The Brunt
Innerwick
14'6
Whittingehame Mains
Bennet's Burn
Highside Hill
Thurston Mains Burn
Old Branxton
16'0
Whittingehame Ho
Ruchlaw West Mains
Pressmennan Wood
Bilsdean Creek
G Apple
Deuchrie Dod
Rammer Wood
Halls
Blaik Law
High Wood
Berry Hill
Blackcastle Hill
Oldhamstocks Mains
DUNGLASS COLLEGIATE CHURCH
Reed Pt
Cove Fm
Cove
Cove Harbour
Garvald Grange
Birks Plantn
E A S T
Lothian Edge
Needle Hill
Belvidere Wood
Pease Bay
Red Rock
Garvald
Stoneypath Tower
Common Plantn
Watch Law
L O T H I A N
Sheeppath Glen
Stottencleugh
Oldhamstocks
Dovecot Hall
PEASE DEAN
Greenheugh Pt
Siccar Pt
NUNRAW ABBEY
Garvald Mains
Robin Tup's Plantn
Deuchrie Edge
Moorcock Hall
70
NT
60
Dunbar
Branxly Hill
272
Birny Knowe
Neuk Fm
Old Townhead
Old Cambus
Stockbridge
Tower Fm
Meikle Poo Craig
Hirst Rocks

H 0   1   2   3 miles
0 1 2 3 4 5 km
WHITE CASTLE (FORT)
Friardykes
Wightman Hill
SETTLEMENT
Penmanshiel Wood
Greenside Hill
Saddle Hill
Ecclaw
A1107
Meikle Black Law

1 2 3 4 5 6

10
NT 00

Fast Castle Head
Wheat Stack
Telegraph Hill
FAST CASTLE

273
Oatlee Hill
Dowlaw Burn
St Abb's Head
Lumsdaine
273
ST ABB'S HEAD
Horsecastle Bay
Lumsdaine Moor
Coldingham Loch
SETTLEMENT
Mire Loch
Bell Hill
Starney Bay
dingham mmon
Cross Law

Lumsdaine Moor

A B C D E F G H

NT 70
10

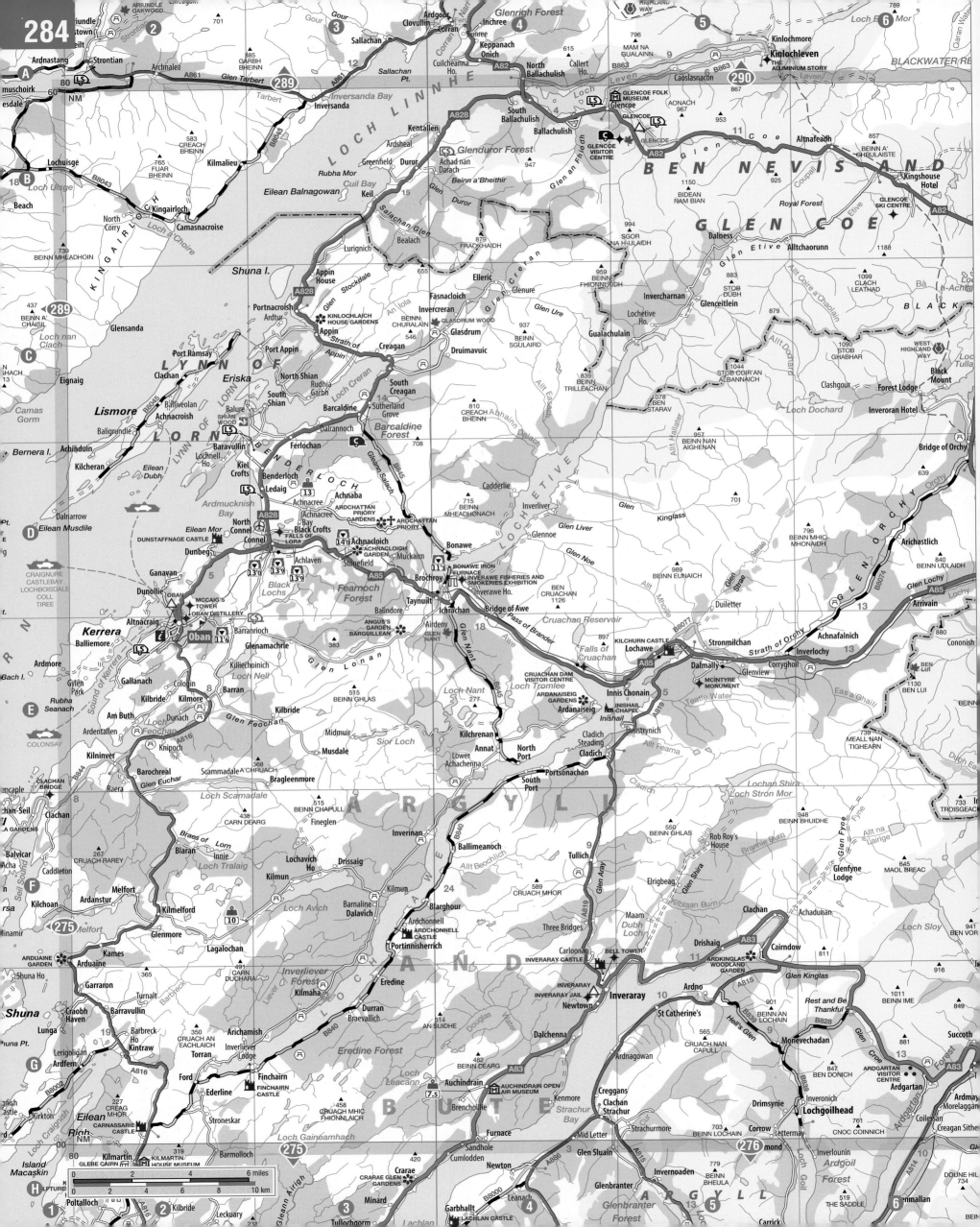

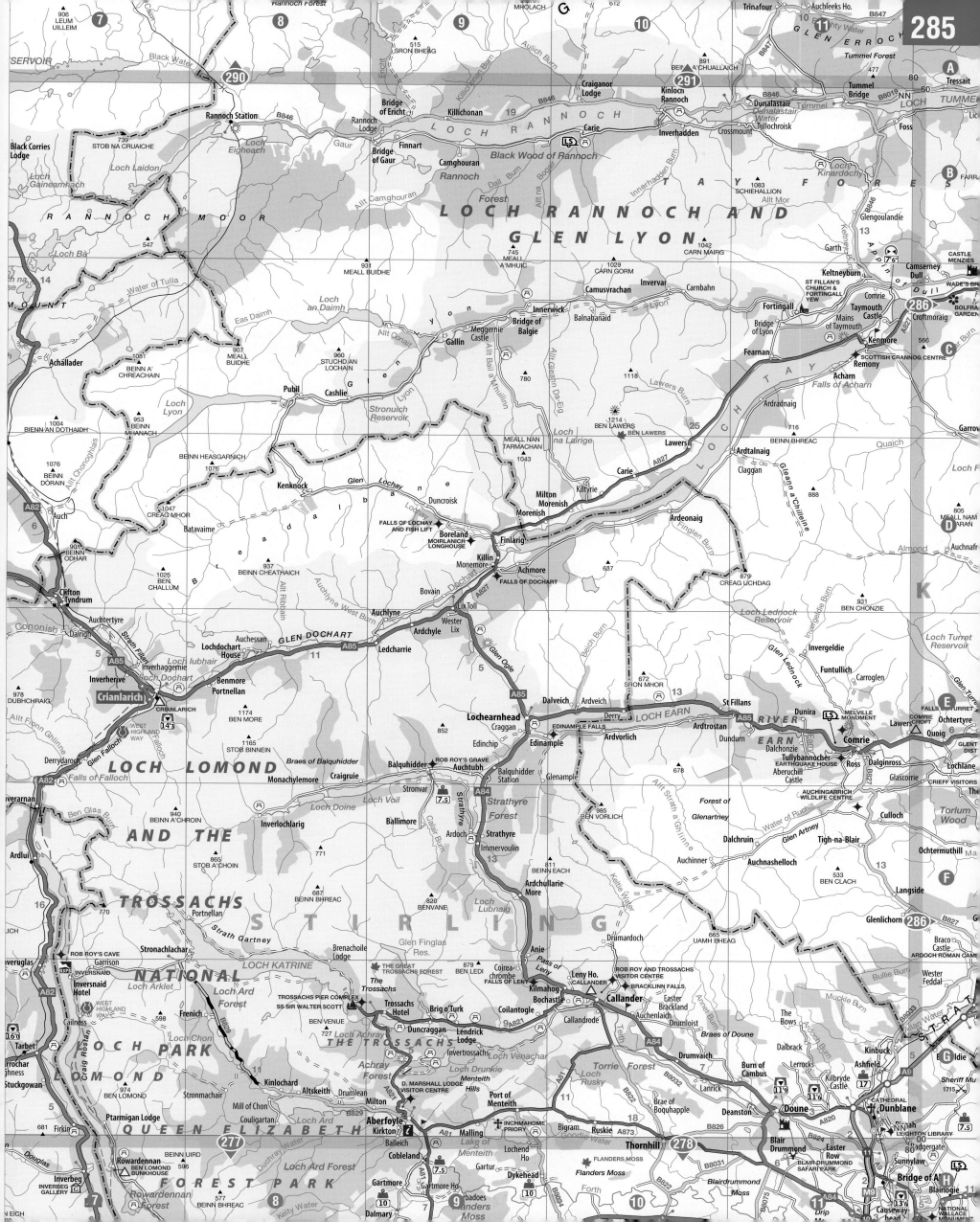

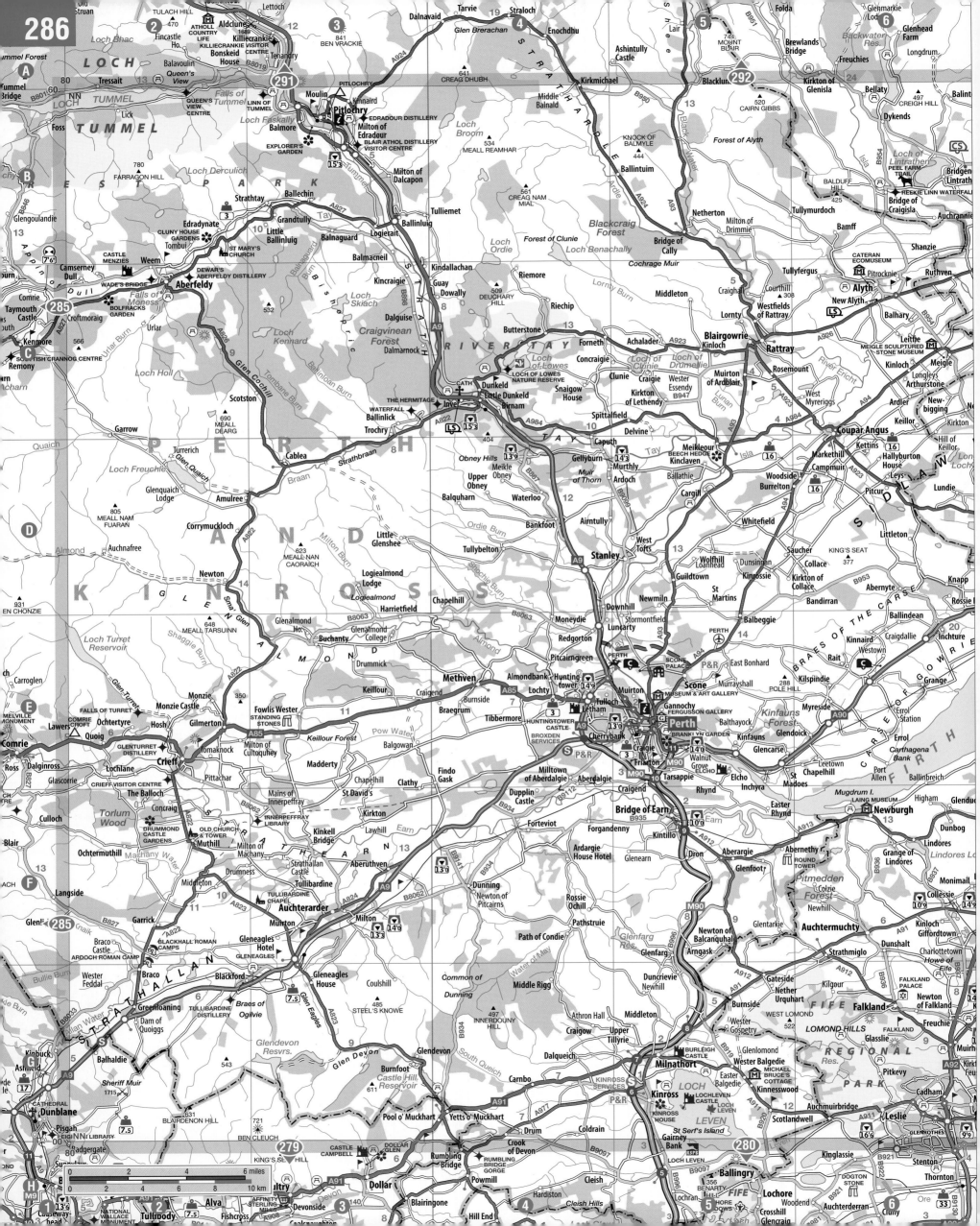

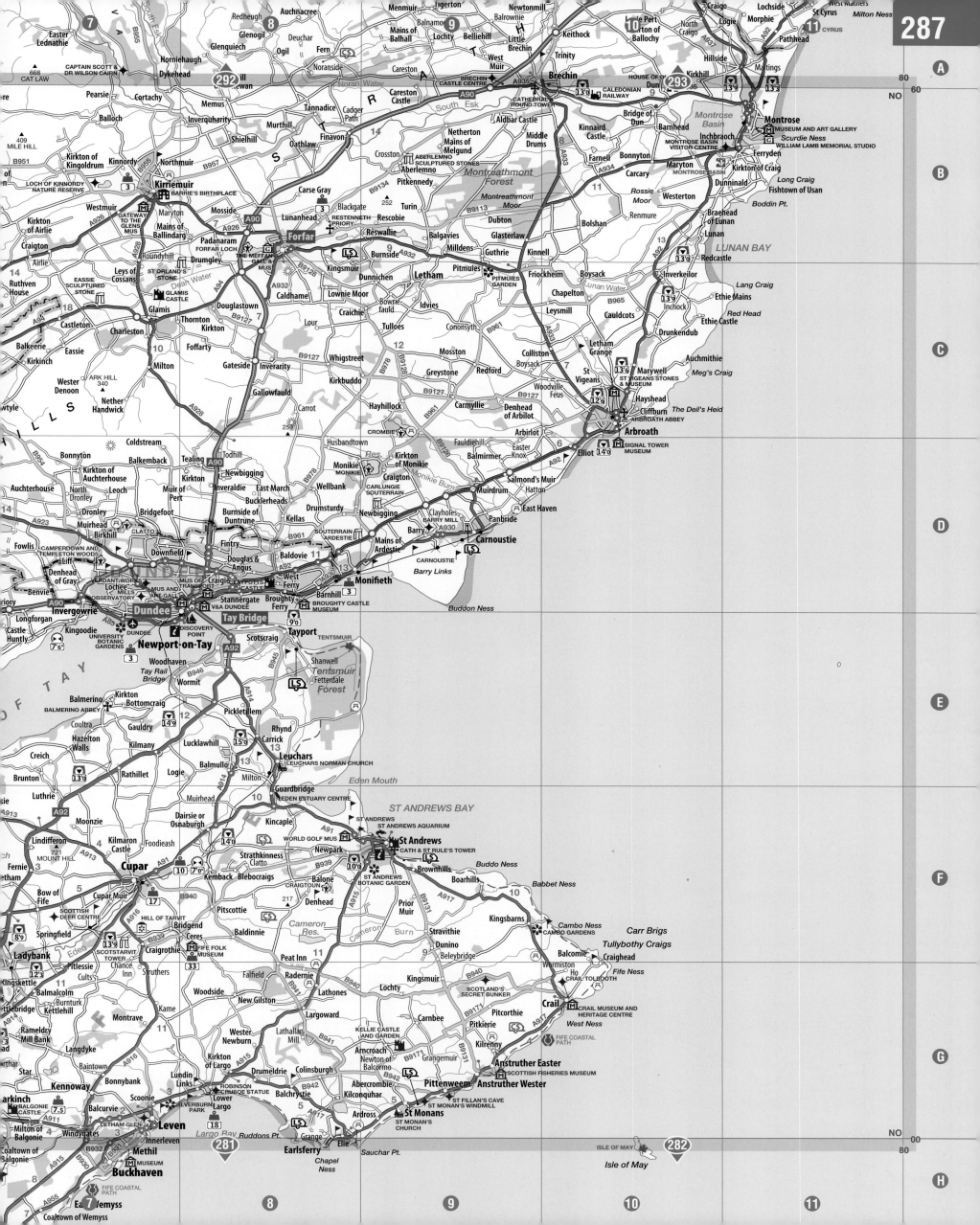

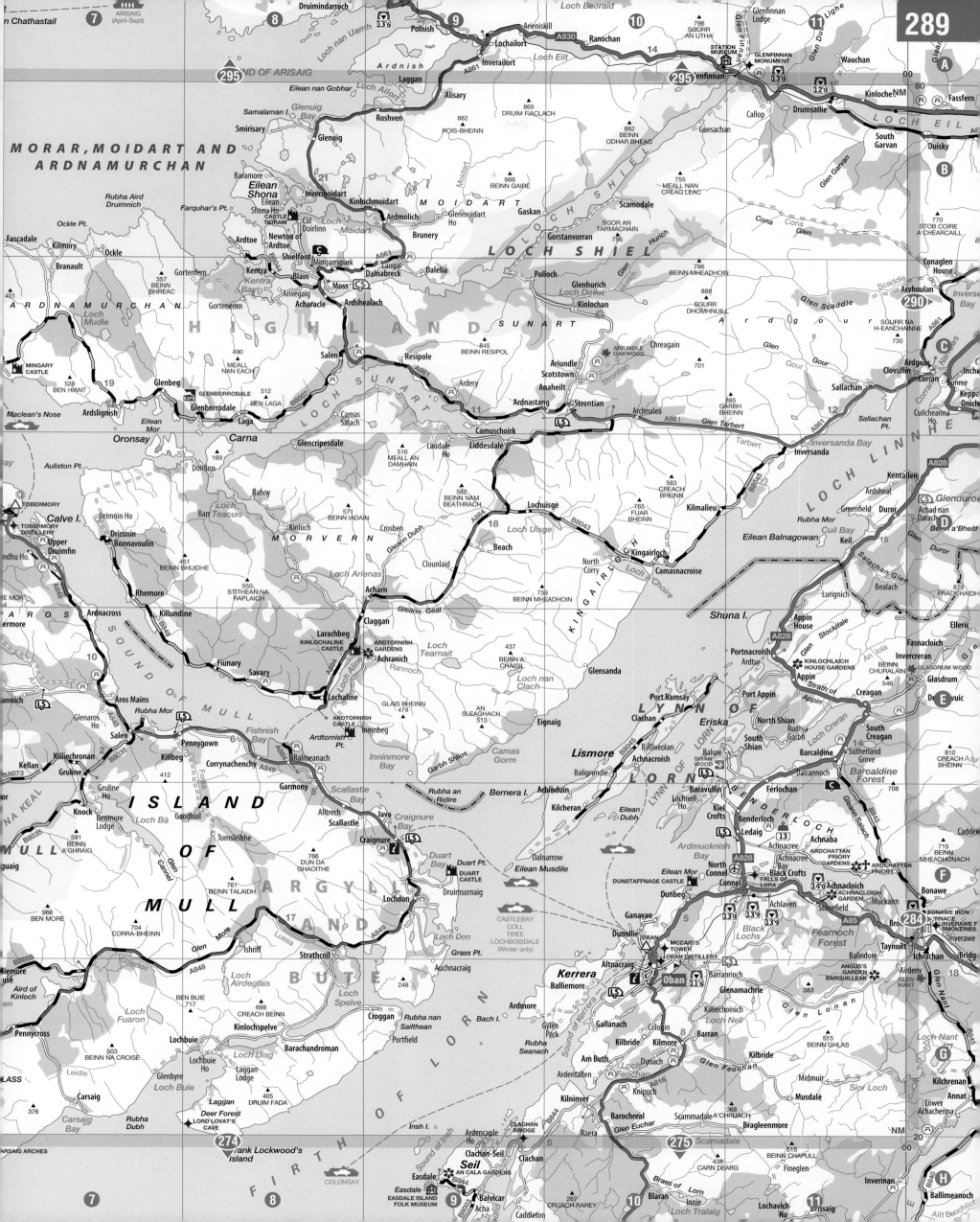

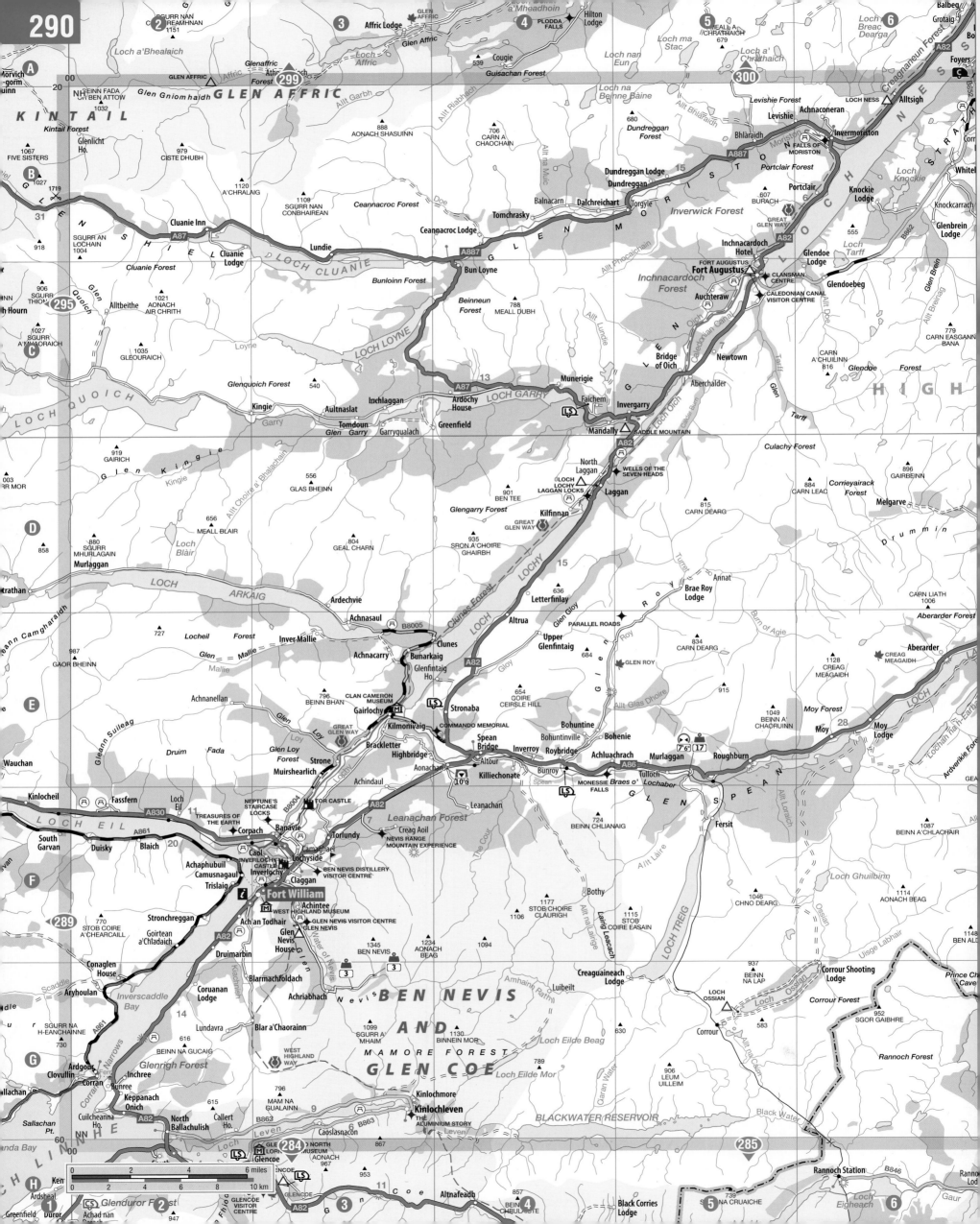

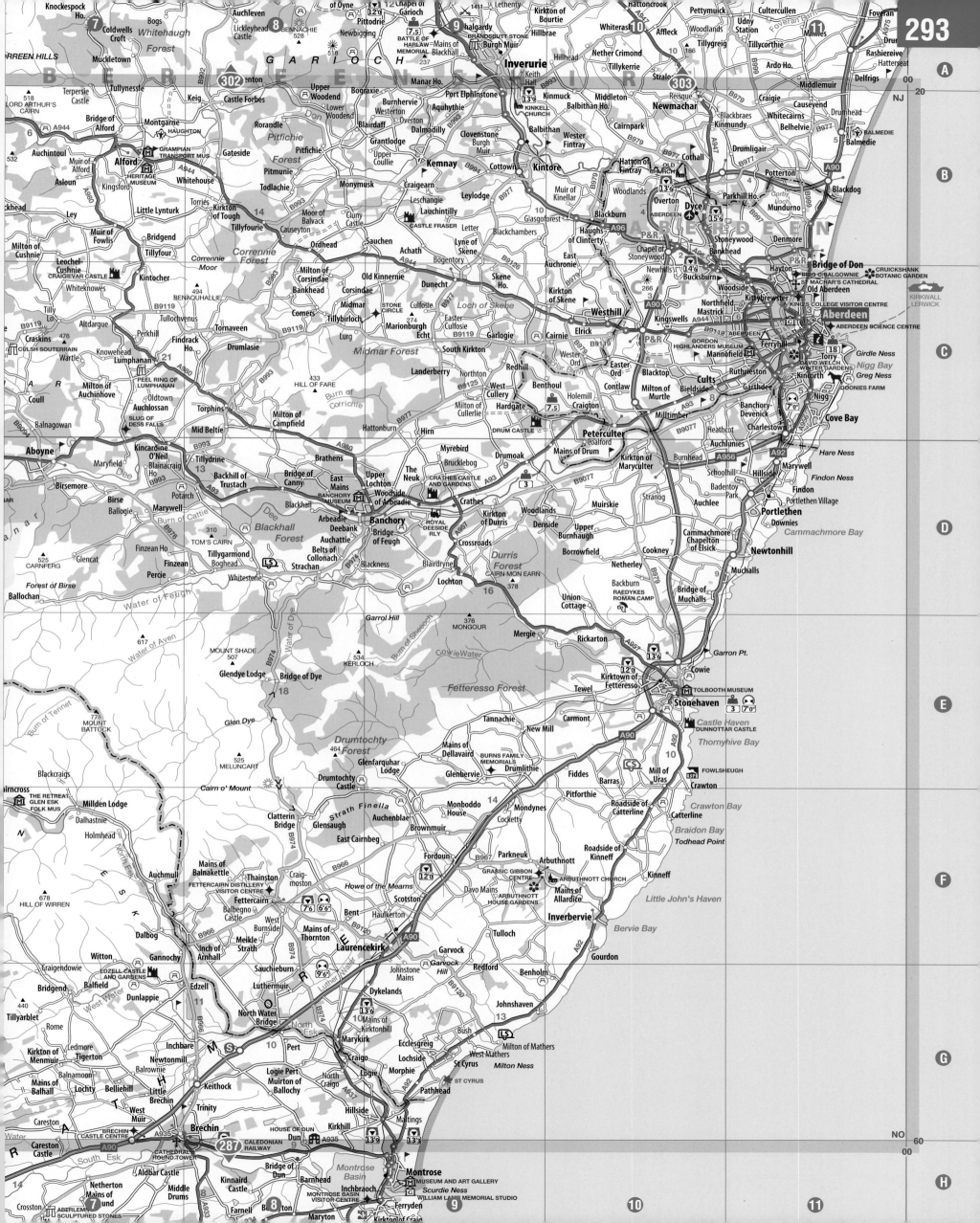

A

B

C

D

E

F

G

H

NG

00
40

297

NM
80
00

288

288

1 2 3 4 5 6

Ramasaig
Roag
Feorlig
Balmeanach
Sluggans
Torvaig
Vatten
Loch Connan
Shul
Termor
Portre
Hoe Rape
Orbost
Macleod's Tables
Greep
Harlosh
Aros Centre
Inver
488
HEALABHAL BHEAG
Balmore
Heatherfield
417
Penif
Hoe Point
Loch Varkasaig
Eabost West
Ose
A863
Glenmore
Peinmore
Geodha Mor
Harlosh I.
Eabost
Bracadale
Totardor
Loch Duagrich
Mugeary
A87
Tarner I.
Ullinish
Struan
Coillore
Conord
Loch Bracadale
Wiay
Portnalong
Gesto
Loch Harport
439
ROINEVAL
BA
BRAES
Oronsay
Ardtreck
Fernilea
B8009
Fiskavaig
Drynoch
A863
Crossal
Rubha nan Clach
ARNAVAL
369
TALISKER DISTILLERY
Carbost
Merkadale
Satran
Drynoch
MACLEOD'S MAIDENS
Idrigill Point
Gleann Oraid
Talisker Bay
Talisker
Sligachan Hotel

Eynort
445
BEINN BHREAC
Grula
459
Glen Brittle Forest
SGURR NAN GILLEAN 964
Loch Eynort
Glen Sligachan
Kraiknish
SGURR A'GHREADAIDH 973
THE CU
GLENBRITTLE
CUILLIN HILLS
Bualintur
Glenbrittle House
992 SGURR ALASDAIR
Loch Coruisk
Culnaneam
924 SGURR NAN EAG
Loch Brittle
Rubh an Dunain
Soay Sound
Soay
Mol-chlach
PRINCE CH

Canna
Garrisdale Pt.
A'Chill
Rubha Shamhnan Insir
Canna Harbour
Kilmory
Sanday
Sound of Canna
MALLAIG (Sun only)
Guirdil Bay
Kilmory Glen
388
Kinloch Glen
Rubha na Roinne
A'Bhrideanach
Loch Scresort
Oigh-sgeir
Kinloch
571 ORVAL
RÙM
RÙM
KINLOCH CASTLE
Rubha Port na Caranean
Schooner Pt.
Harris
Glen Harris
812 ASKIVAL
Rubha Sgorr an t-Snidhe
781 AINSHVAL
Rubha nam Meirleach
Bay of Laig
Cleadale
Rubha an Fhasaidh
Laig
Eigg
Sandavore
Kildor
Galmisda
393 AN SGURR
Eile
Eilean nan Each
SOUND OF EIGG
Gallanach
137
Port Mor
Muck

0   2   4   6 miles
0 2 4 6 8 10 km

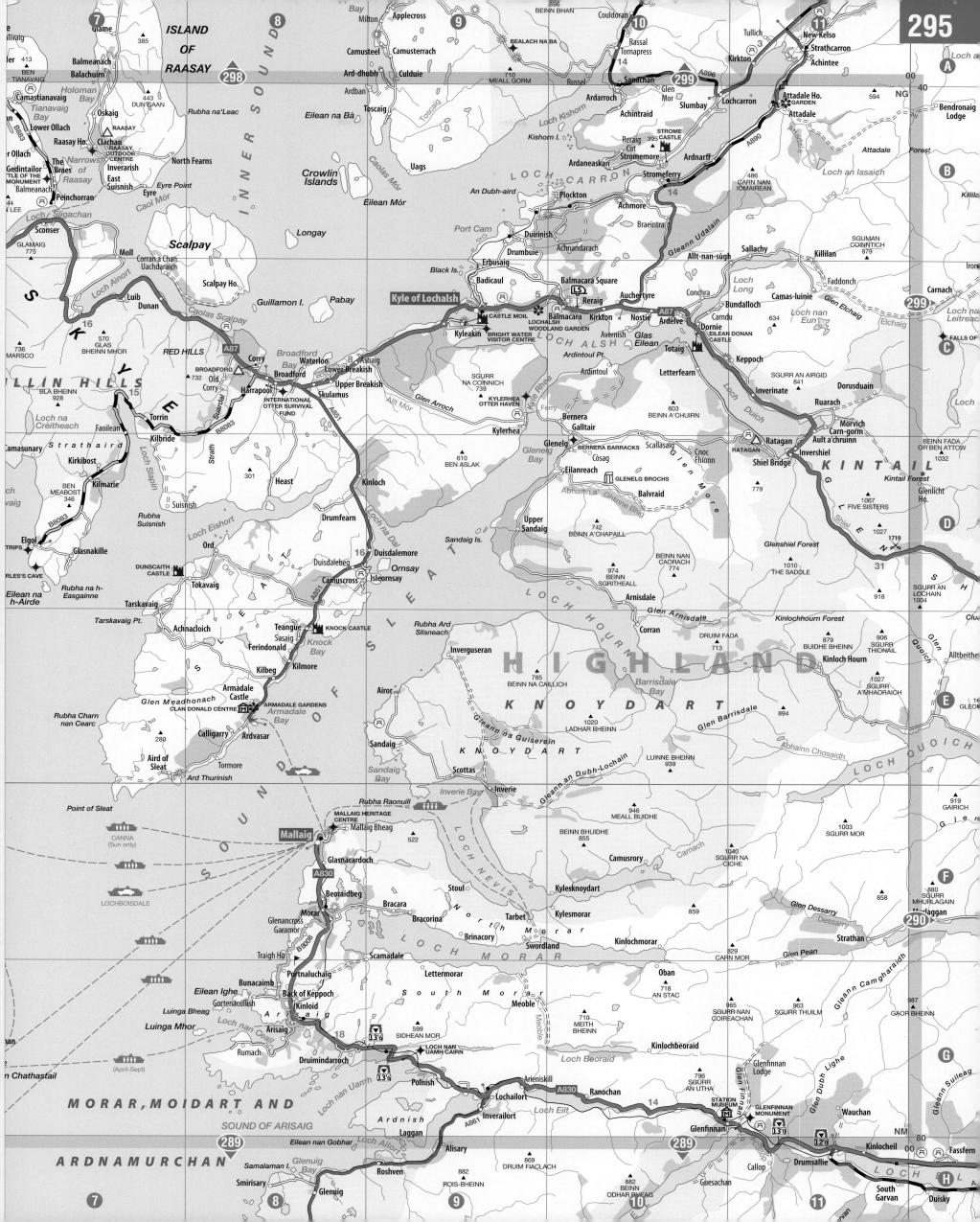

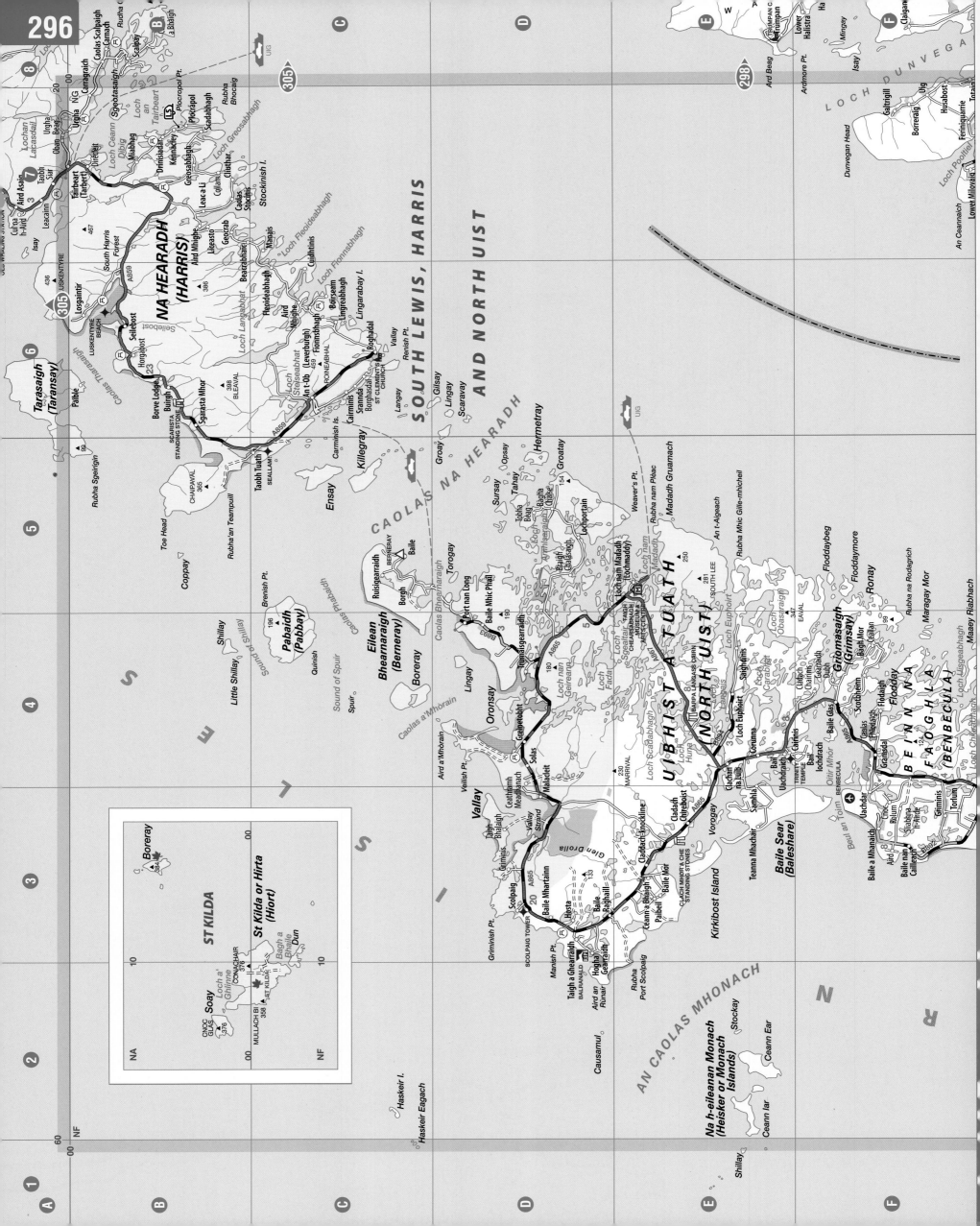

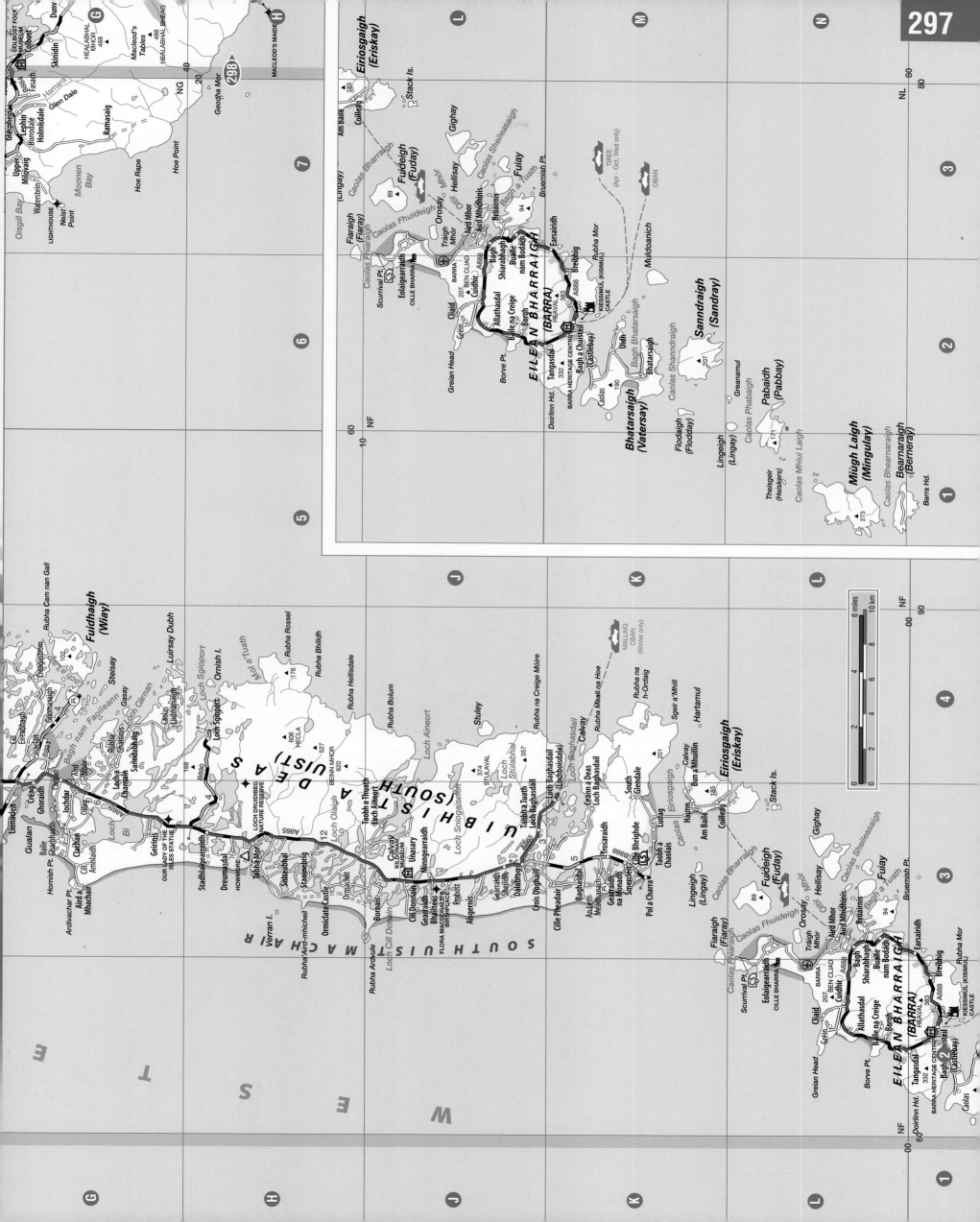

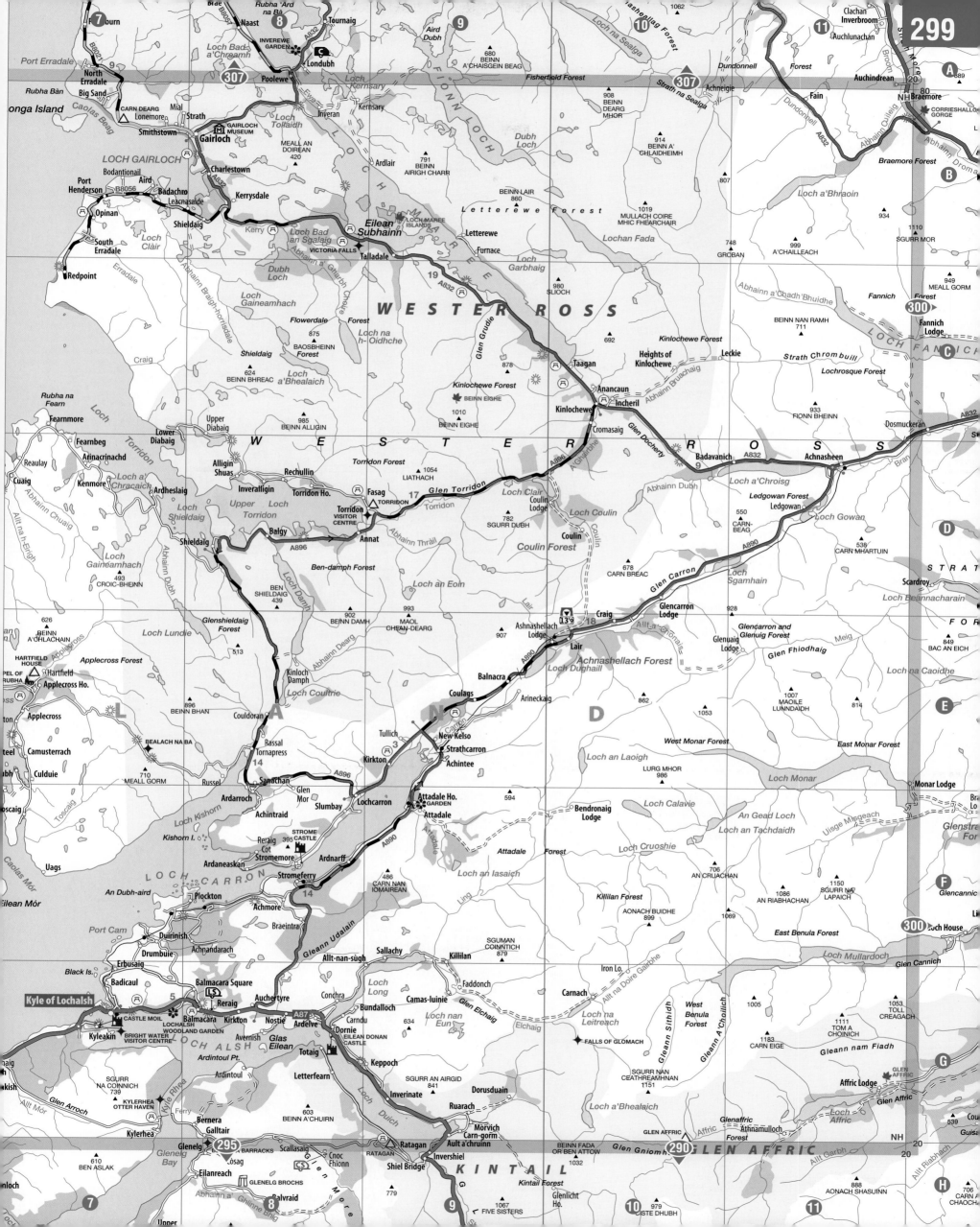

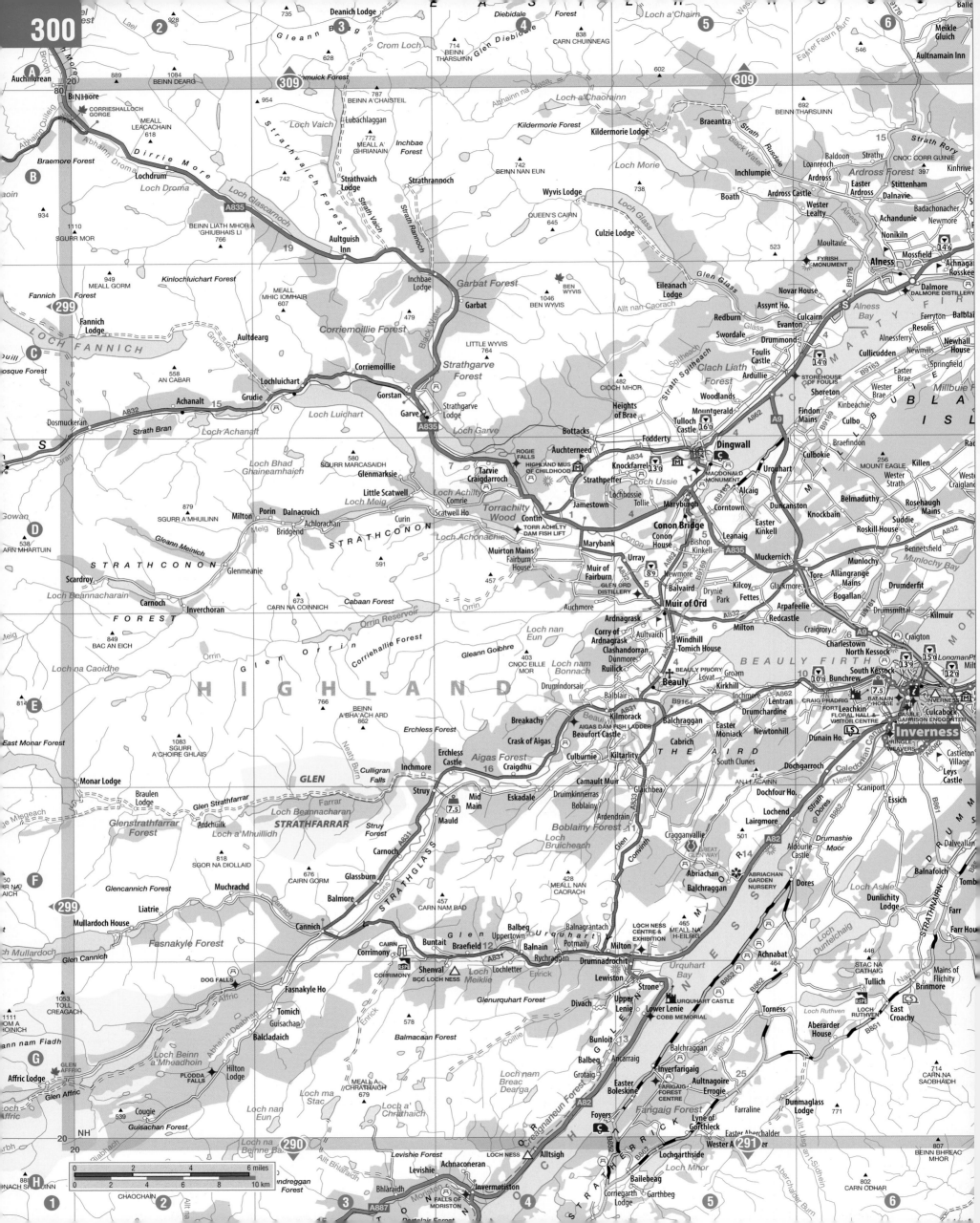

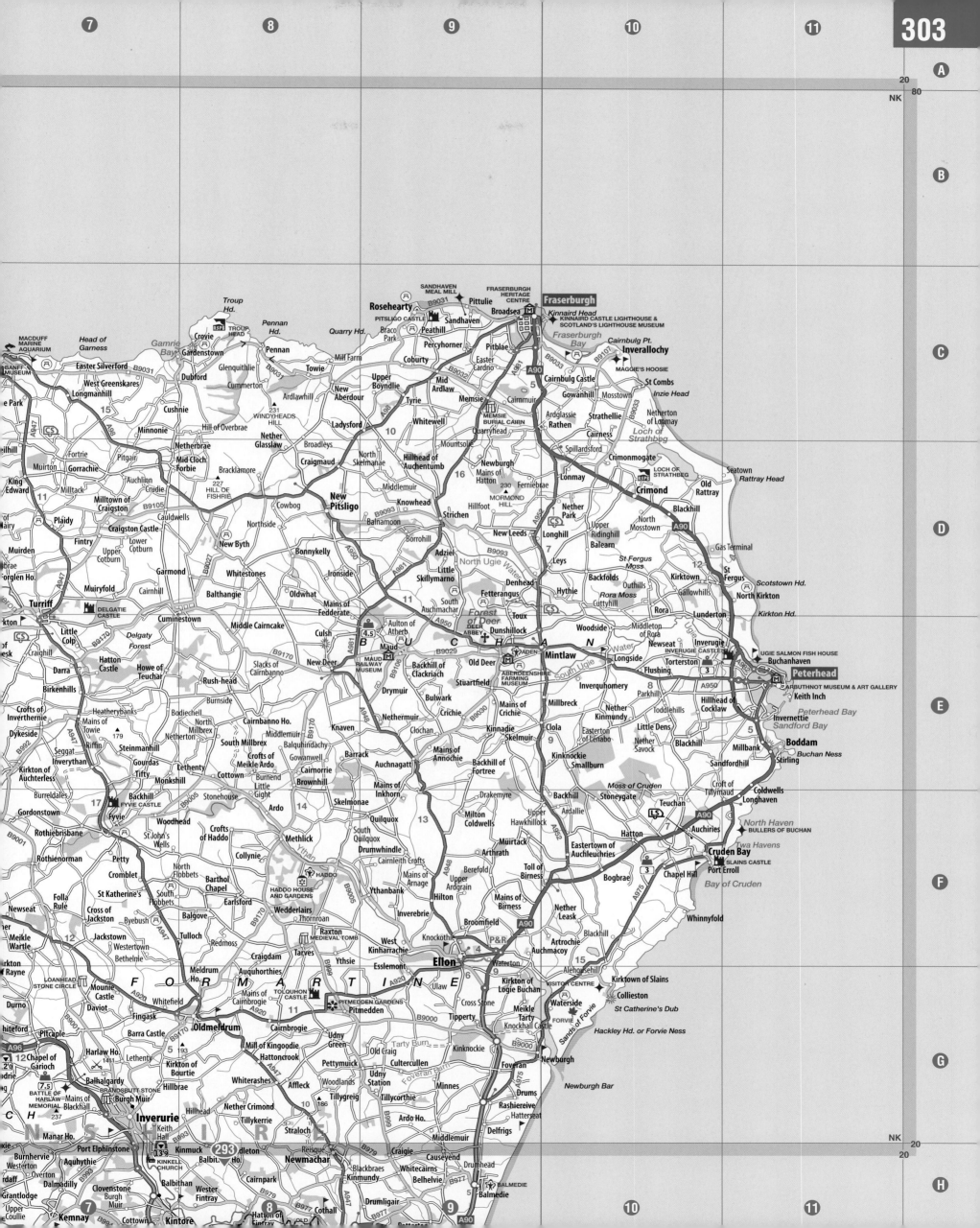

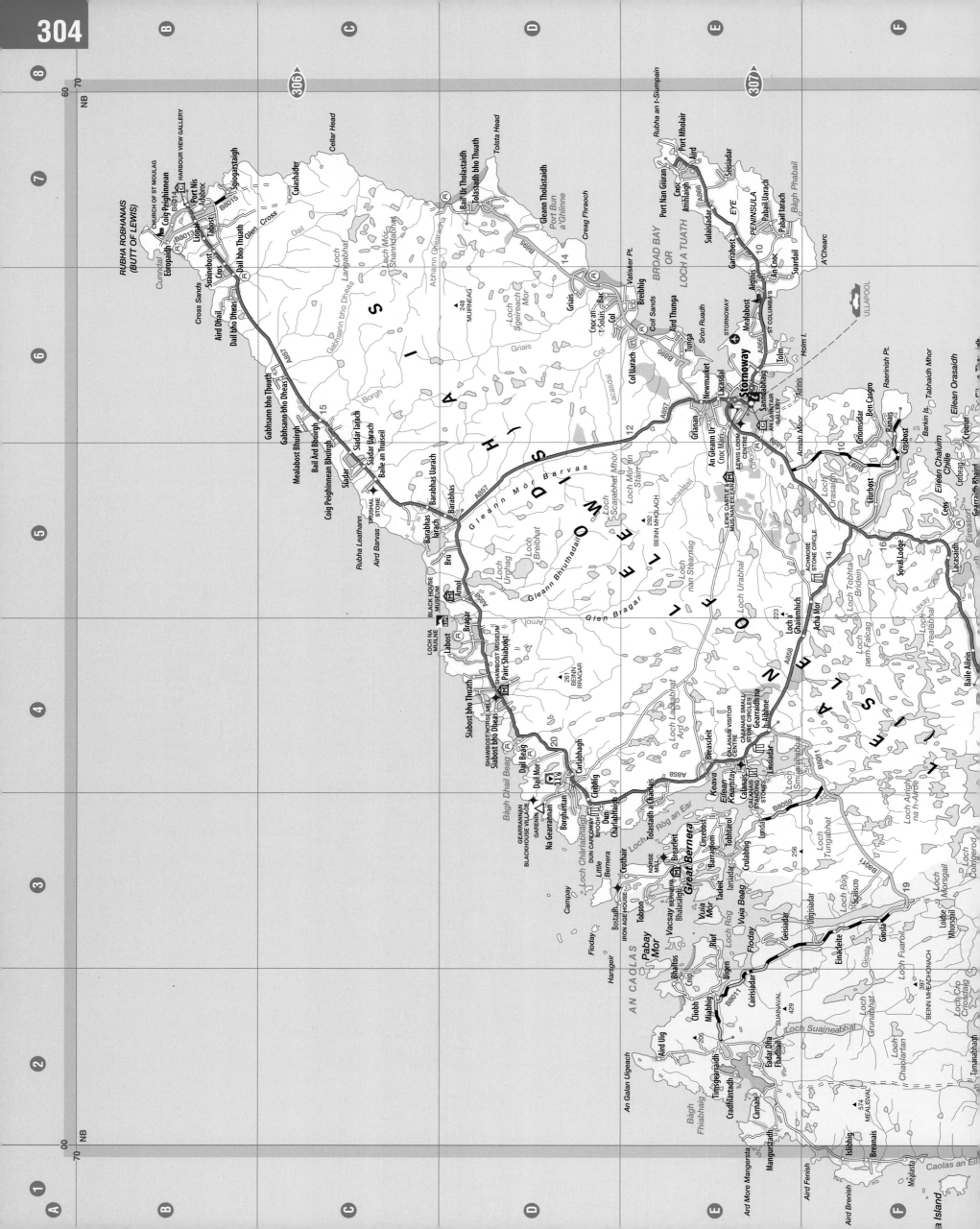

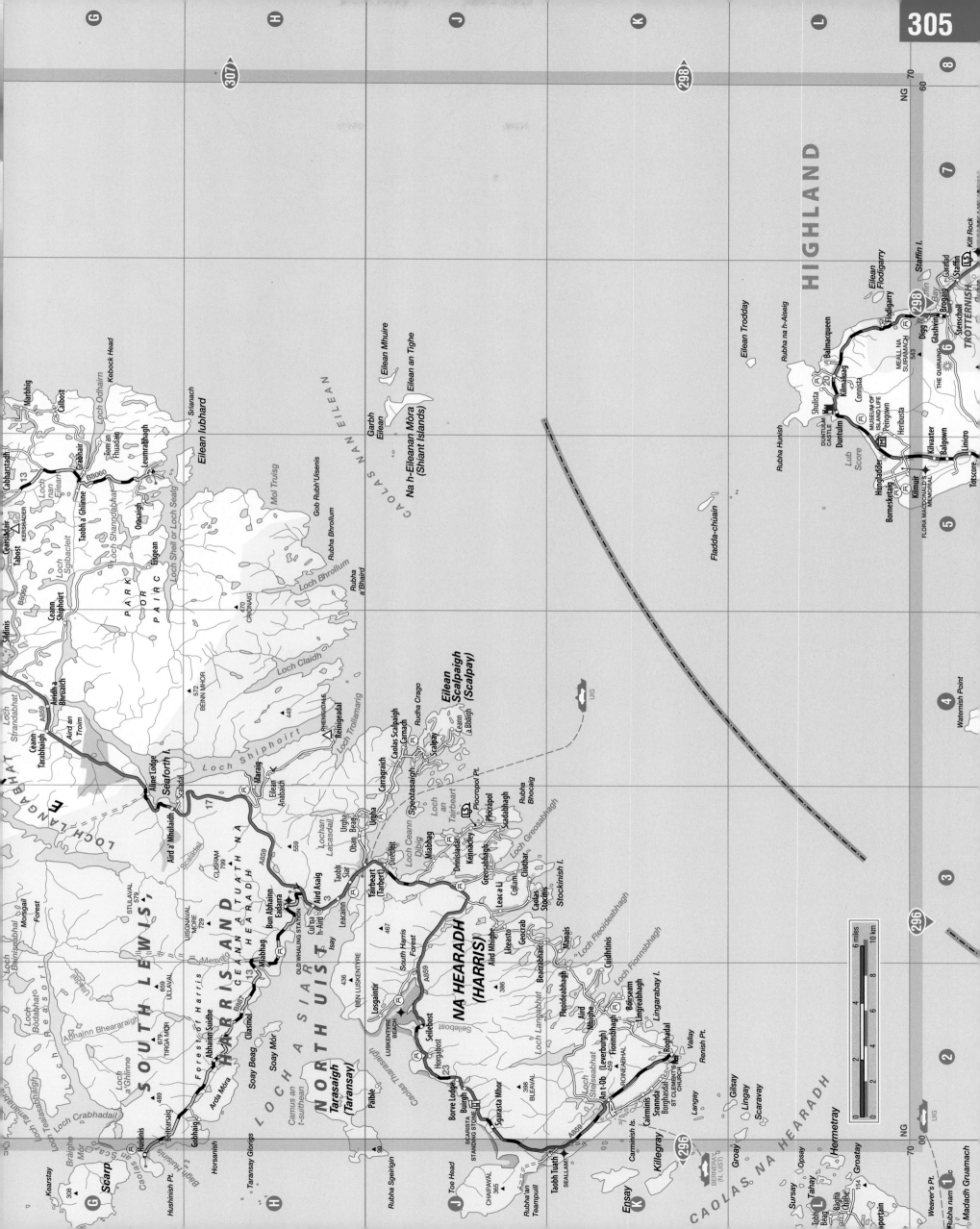

G   H   J   K   L

8

307

298

NG   60   70

7

HIGHLAND

Kilt Rock
Staffin I.
Garafad
Stenscholl
Staffin
298
Digg
Brogaig   Flodigarry
Glashvin
TROTTERNISH
6
Flodigarry
Eilean Trodday

Rubha na h-Aiseig
Eilean Flodigarry
Balmacqueen
MEALL NA
SUIRAMACH
543
THE QUIRAING
Peingown
Duntulm   MUSEUM OF
ISLAND LIFE
20
DUNTULM
CASTLE
Kilmaluag
Connista
Rubha Hunish
Shulista
Heribusta
Kilvaxter   Balgown
Kilmuir
FLORA MACDONALD'S
MEMORIAL
Hungladder
Bornesketaig
Lub
Score
Uig

5

Fladda-chuain

Eilean Troday

4

Waternish Point

296

3

UIG

NG   60   70

296

Weaver's Pt.
Rubha nam   1   c
Madadh Gruamach

2

1

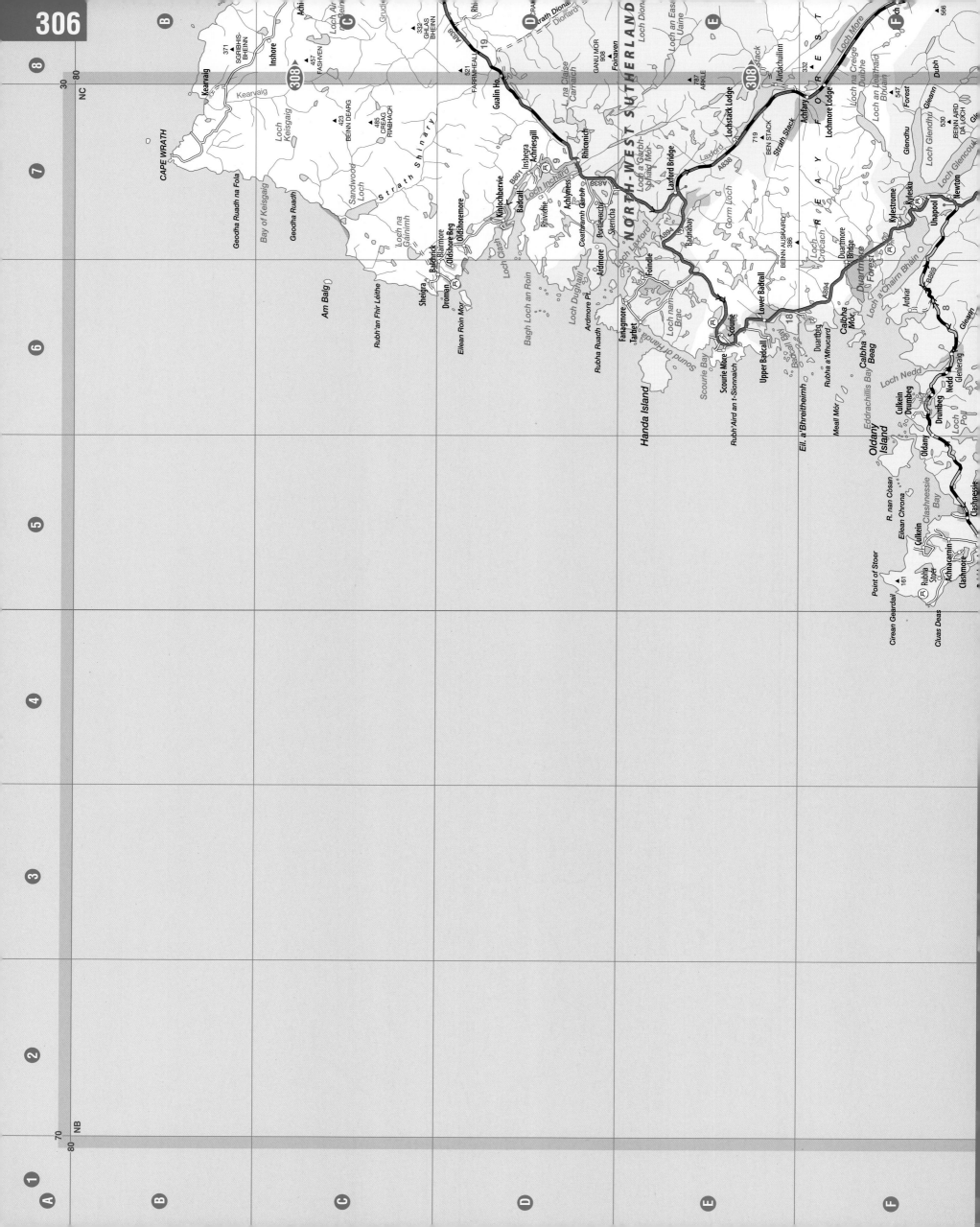

NORTH - WEST SUTHERLAND

CAPE WRATH

Kearvaig
Kearvaig

Inshore

SGRIBHS-
BHEINN
371

GHLAS
BHEINN
332

FASHVEN
457

Achī

Loch Aird

Grudie

DRA

Strath Dionar
Dionard

Rhi

Loch Dion

Loch an Easai
Uaine

Foinaven

GANU MOR
908

Ben

Loch More

Fch

566

BEINN DEARG
423

CREAG
RIABHACH
485

Loch
Keisgaig

Sandwood
Loch

Strath shinary

FARRMHEALL
521

Gualin Ho.

Loch na Claise
Carraich

ARKLE
787

Stack

Airdachuilinn

Lochstack Lodge

BEN STACK
719

Strath Stack

Achfary

Lodgmore Lodge

Loch na Creige
Dubhe

BEINN AIRD
DA LOCH
530

Glendhu
Forest

Loch Glendhu

Gl

Geodha Ruadh na Fola

Bay of Keisgaig

Geodha Ruadh

Loch na
Gáinimh

Am Balg

Rubh 'an Fhir Léithe

Sheigra

Baldnick
Blairmore
Oldshore-Beg
Oldshoremore

Droman

Oldshore Mor

Eilean Roin Mor

Rubh 'an Fhir Léithe

Loch Clash

Kinlochbervie

Badcall

Rhividhe

Achriesgill
Inshegra
B801

Rhiconich

Achlyness

Ceathramh Garbh

Loch Inchard

Loch Dughaill

Bagh Loch an Roin

Ardmore Pt

Ardmore

Portlevorchy

Skerricha

Rubha Ruadh

Loch nam
Brac

Handa Island

Sound of Handa

Fanagmore
Tarbet

Scourie Bay

Scourie More

Scourie

Upper Badcall

Lower Badcall

Duartbeg

Rubha a'Mhucard

Calbha
Mór

Duartmore
Bridge

Duartmore
Forest

Loch a'Chairn Bhain

Kylestrome

Kylesku

Loch
Glencoul

Newton

Ardvar

Eddrachillis Bay

Calbha
Beag

Meall Mór

Eil. a'Bhreitheimh

Rubh 'Aird an t-Sionnaich

Oldany
Island

Loch Nedd

Nedd

Drumbeg

Culkein
Drumbeg

Glenleraig

Oldany
Drumbeg

Clashnessie
Bay

Clashnessie

Point of Stoer

Cirean Geardail

R. nan Cosan

Eilean Chrona

Culkein

Rubha
Stoer

Cluas Deas

Adhnacarnin

Clashmore

Laxford Bridge

A838

A894

A894

Gorm Loch

Badnabay

BEINN AUSKAIRD
386

Loch Crocach

A838

18

Loch a' Garbh-
bhaid Mór

Loch a' Garbh

Loch Laxford

Loch Poll

Loch

Kylesku

Uapool

Loch Glencoul

9

19

308

308

8

30
80
NC
80
80
70
NB

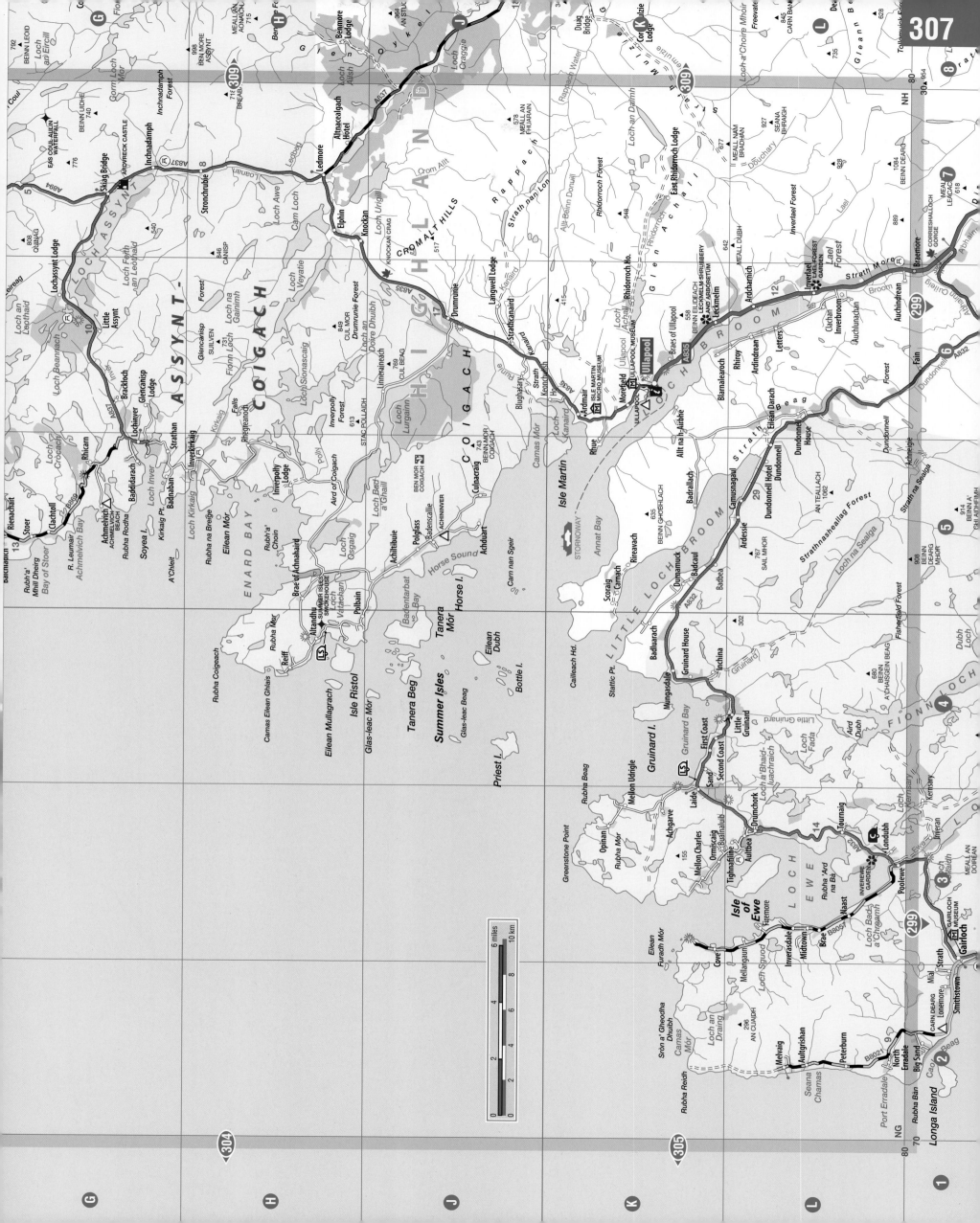

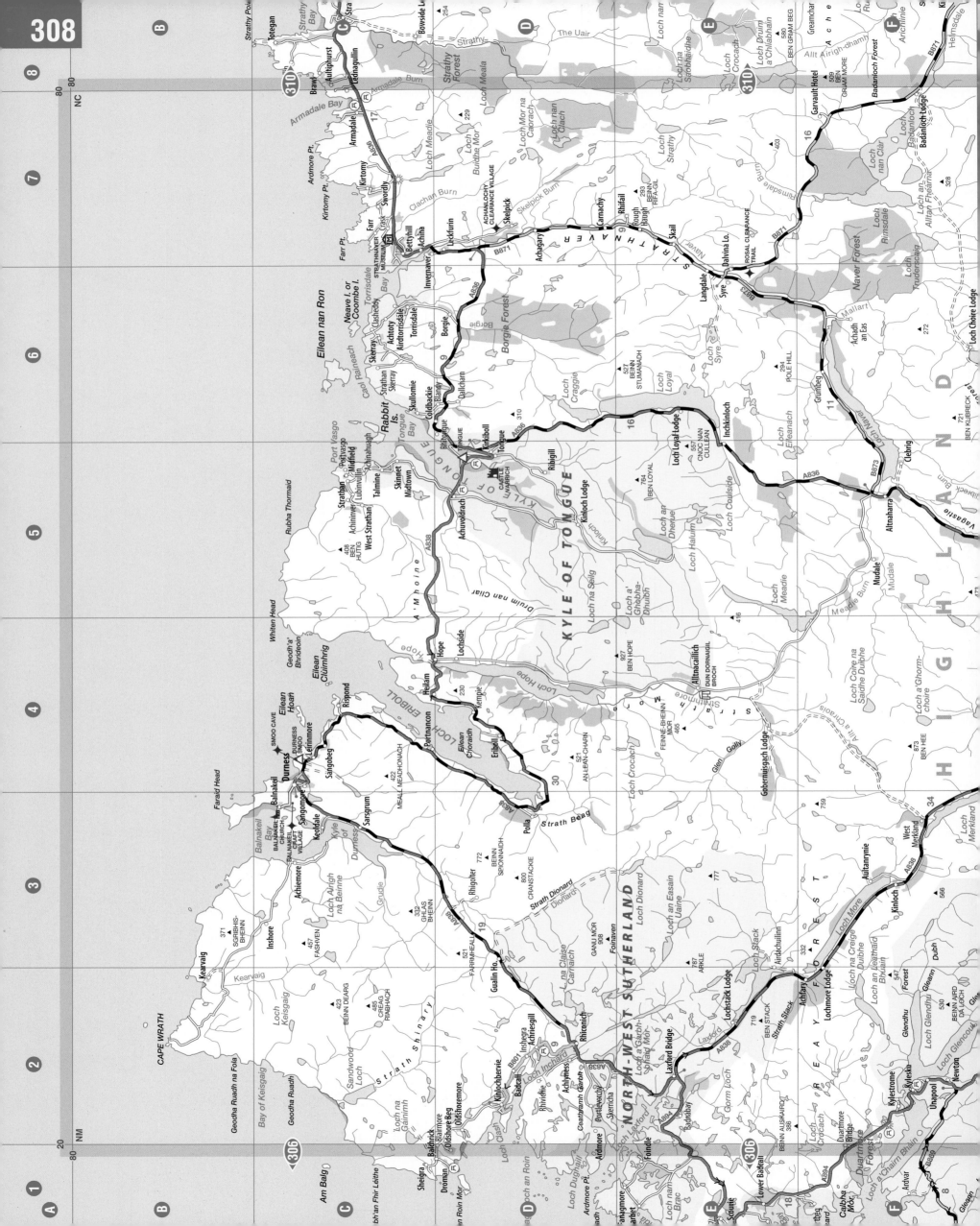

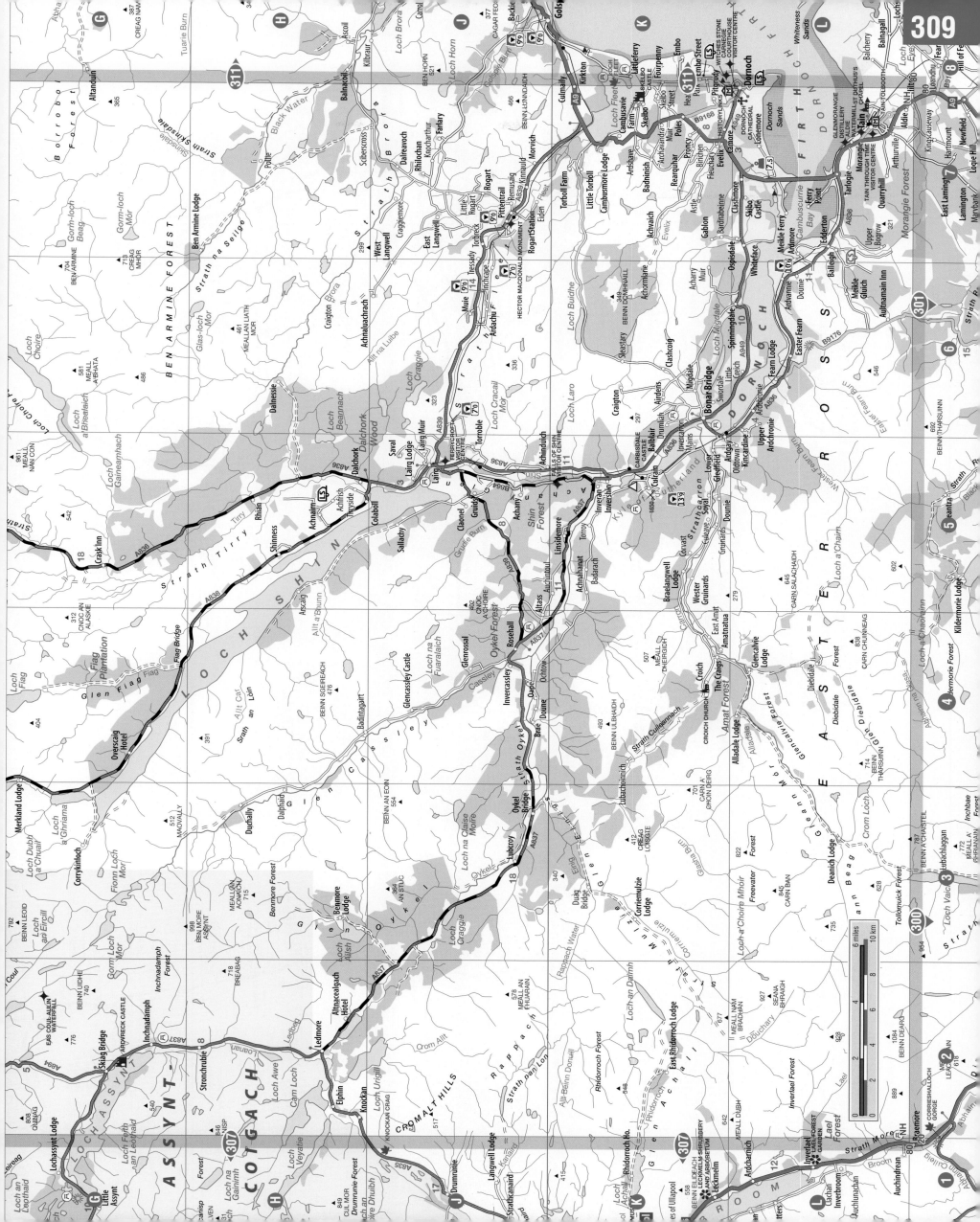

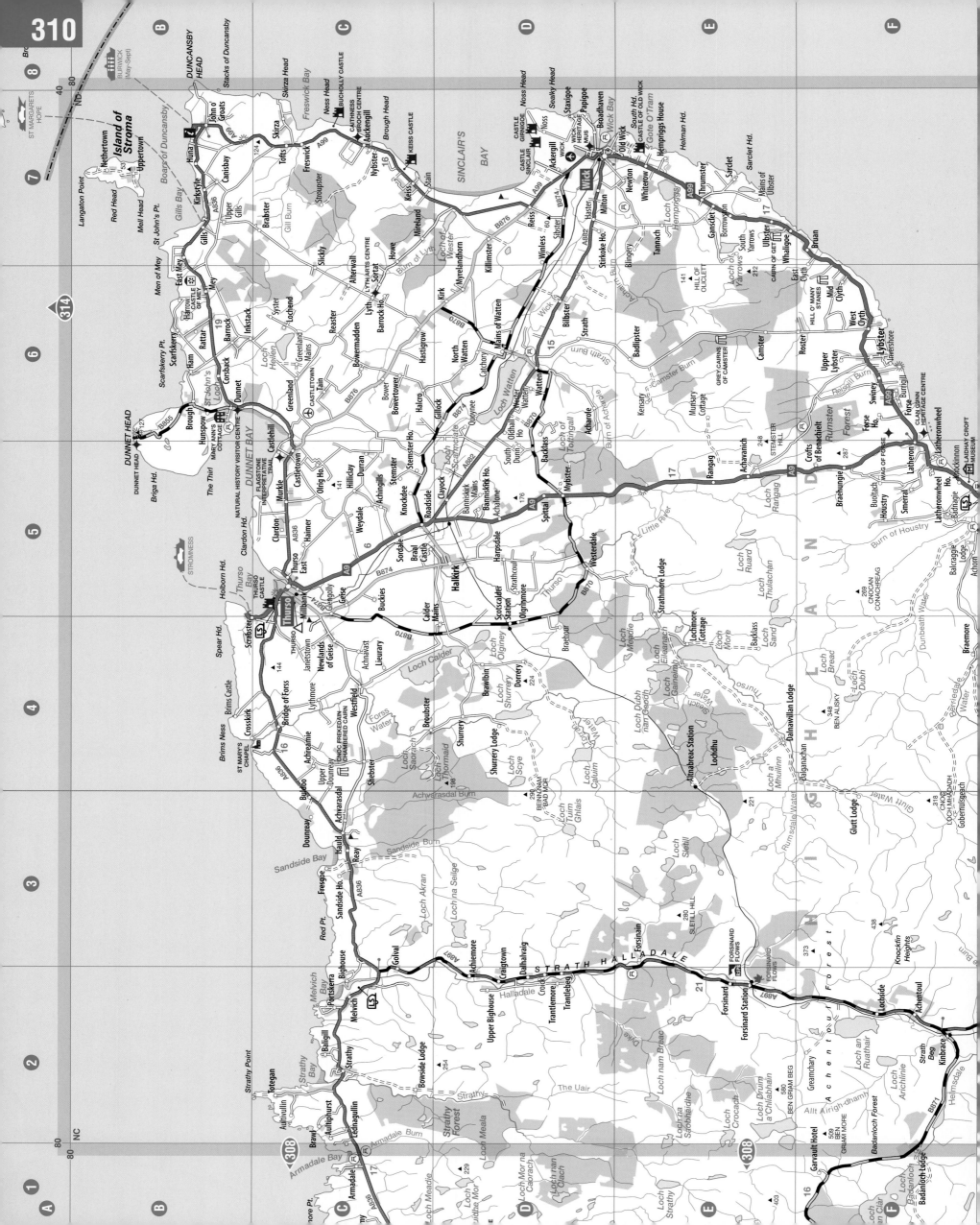

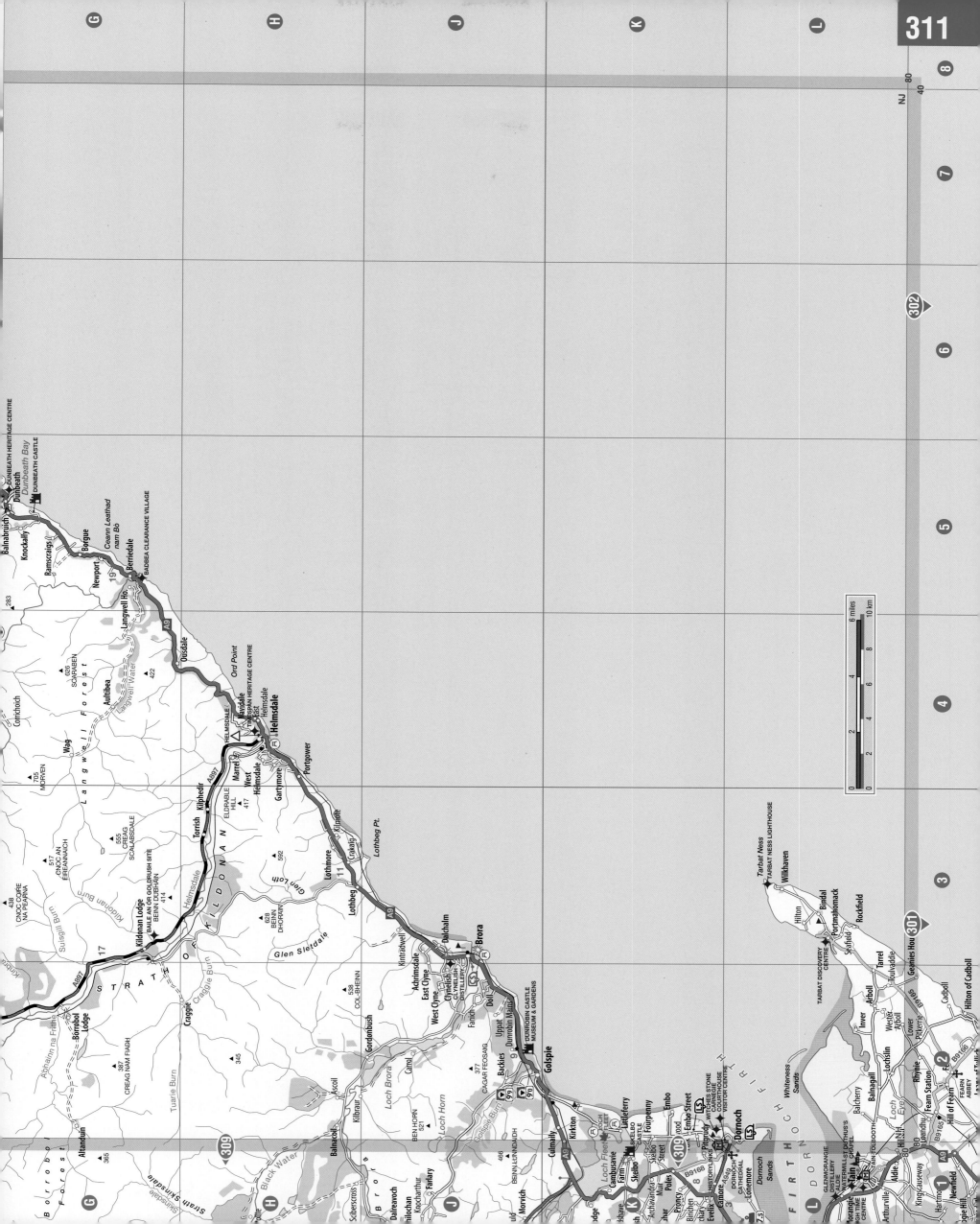

G   H   J   K   L

8
7
6
5
4
3
2
1

NJ   40   80

302

301

309

Dunbeath Heritage Centre
Dunbeath
Dunbeath Bay
Dunbeath Castle
Balnabruich
Knockally
Ramscraigs
Borgue
Newport
Ceann Leathad nam Bò
Berriedale
Badbea Clearance Village
19
283

Corrichoich
Scaraben
626
Aultibea
422
Ousdale
A9
Langwell Ho.
Langwell Water
Langwell Forest

Wag
705
Morven

517
Cnoc an Eireannaich
555
Creag Scalabsdale
Torrish
Kilphedir
A897
Eldrable Hill
417
Marrel
West Helmsdale
Gartymore
Portgower

Ord Point
Timespan Heritage Centre
Helmsdale
Navidale
Helmsdale
Kilbraur

438
Cnoc Coire na Pearna
Beinn Dubhain
414
Baile an or Goldrush Site
Kildonan Lodge
17

Suisgill Burn
Kildonan Burn
Helmsdale or Kildonan

592
628
Beinn Dhorain
Lothmore
11
Lothbeg
Crakaig
Kilmote
Lothbeg Pt.
Glen Loth

Borrobol Lodge
Altanduin
387
Creag nam Fiadh
365

Glen Sletdale
Kintradwell
Achrimsdale
East Clyne
West Clyne
Clynelish
Clynelish Distillery
A9
Brora

Craggie
Craggie Burn
538
Col-Bheinn
Gordonbush
Carrol
345
Ben Horn
521
Fanich
Uppat
Doll
Dalchalm
Dunrobin Mains
Dunrobin Castle Museum & Gardens
9

Tarbat Ness
Tarbat Ness Lighthouse
Wilkhaven
Hilton
Biddal
Portmahomack
Seafield
Rockfield
Geanies Hou
Tarbat Discovery Centre
Inver
Arboll
Lower Pitkerrie
West Arboll
Rhynie
Tarrel
Loulvaddie
Cadboll
Hilton of Cadboll
Balchery
Balnagall
B9165
Fearn Station
Fearn Abbey
Hill of Fearn
Loch Eye

Borrobol Forest
Abhainn na Frithe
Tuarie Burn
Strath Skinsdale
Skinsdale

309
Scibercross
Dalreavoch
Knockarthur
Farlary

Black Water
Loch Brora
Ben Horn
Loch Horn

Balnacoil
Kilbraur
Ascoil
Cnoc

Borrobol

Strath of Kildonan

Strath Brora

Backies
Golspie
A9
B9168
Cagar Feosaig
39
9b

Loch Brora
Balnacoil
Kilbraur
Farlary
Morvich
Beinn Lunndaidh
466
Culmaily
Kirkton
Loch Fleet
Littleferry
Embo
Embo Street
Fourpenny
Skelbo Castle
Skelbo
Skelbo Farm
Cambusavie
Archaelandra
Muir
Poles
A9
Proncy
Birichen
8
Evelix
Camore
7.5
Dornoch
Witches Stone
Carnegie Courthouse
Dornoch Cathedral
Historylinks
Whiteness Sands
Dornoch Sands
Firth of Dornoch

Glenmorangie Distillery
Watermill
St Duthus's High Chapel
St Duthus
Tain
Aldie
Kingcausway
Morangie
Hartmore
Arthurville
309
A9
NH
80
Loandhu
Loch Eye
Kingcausway
Newfield
Balintore

Scale
6 miles
10 km
8
6
4
2
4
2
0
0

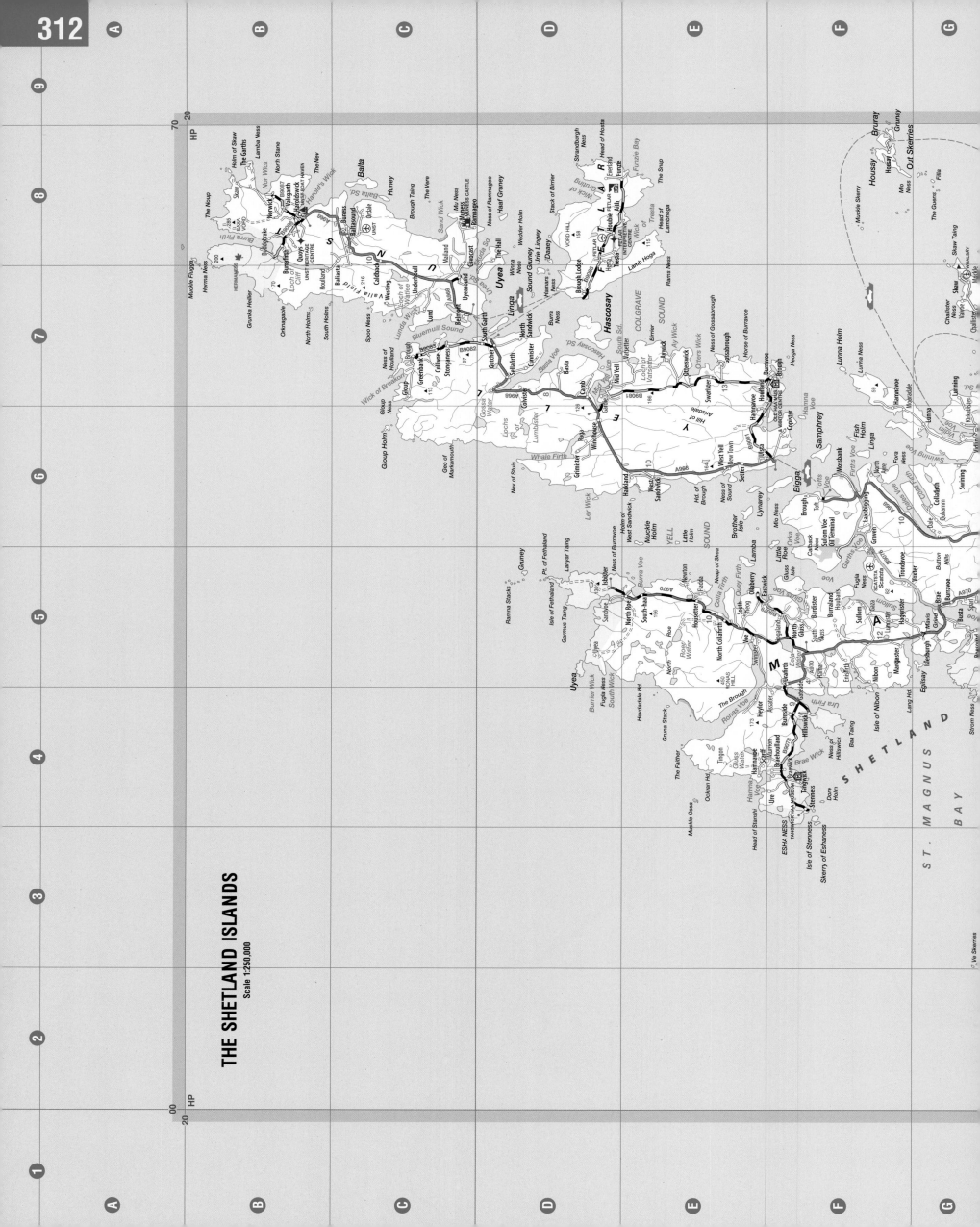

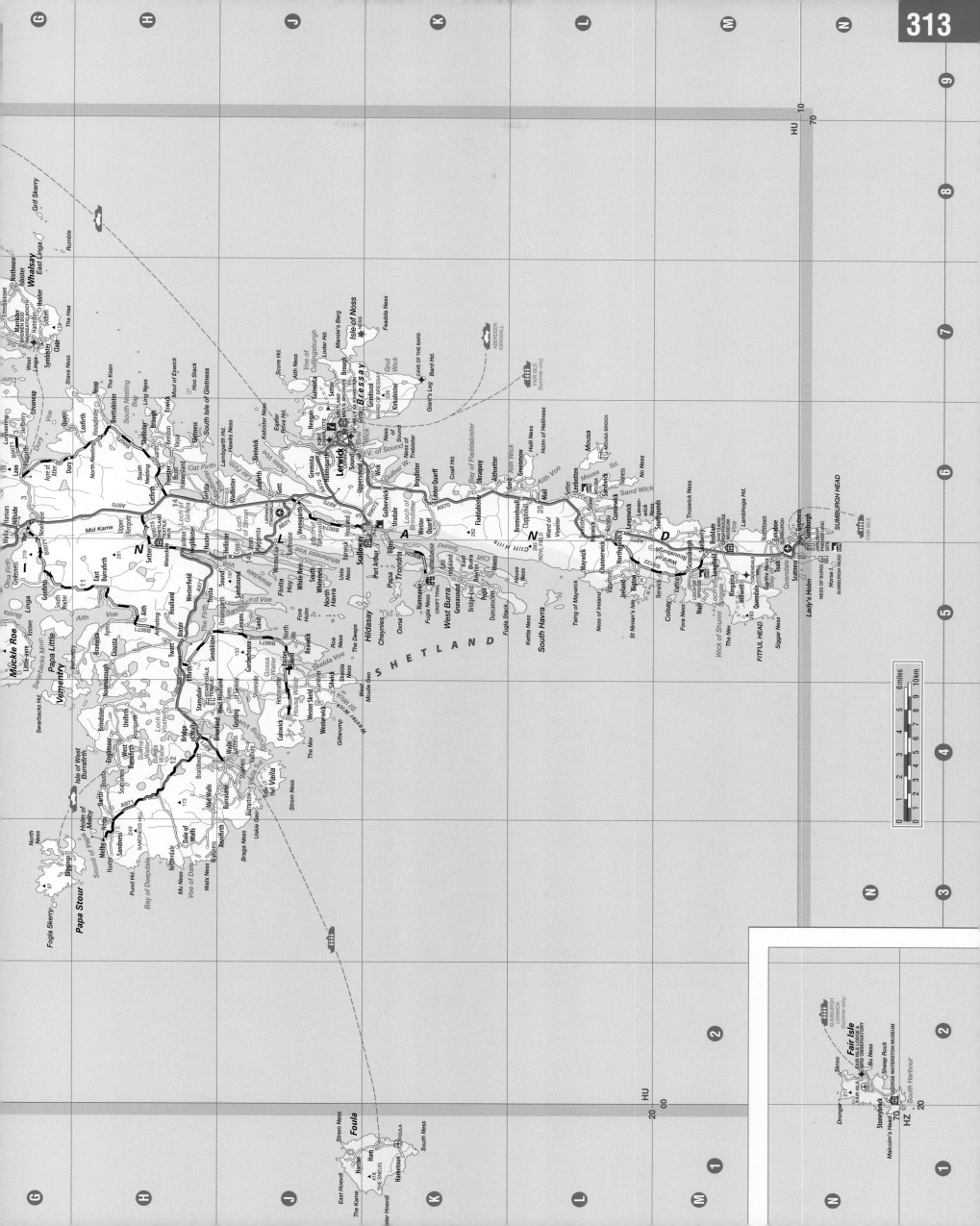

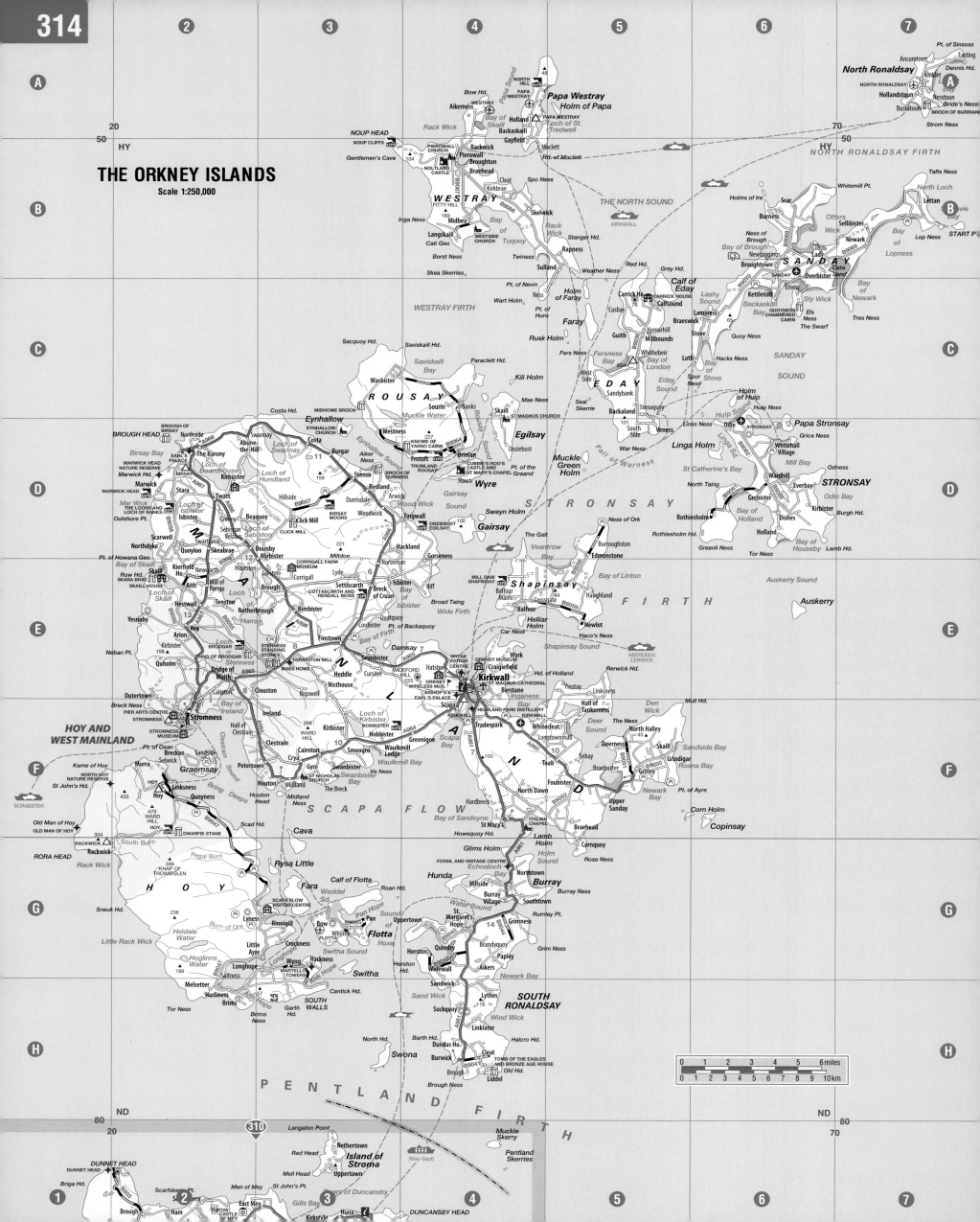

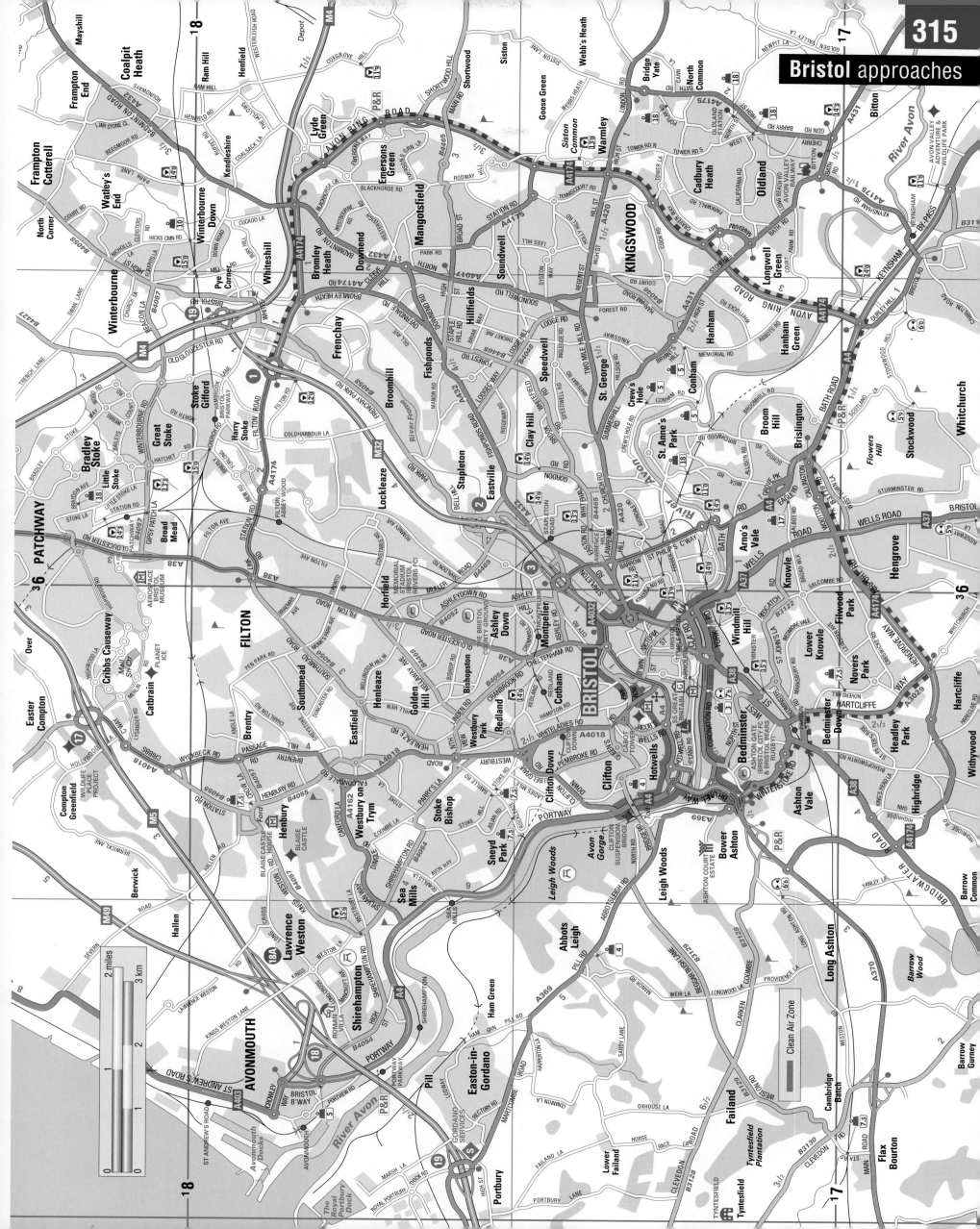

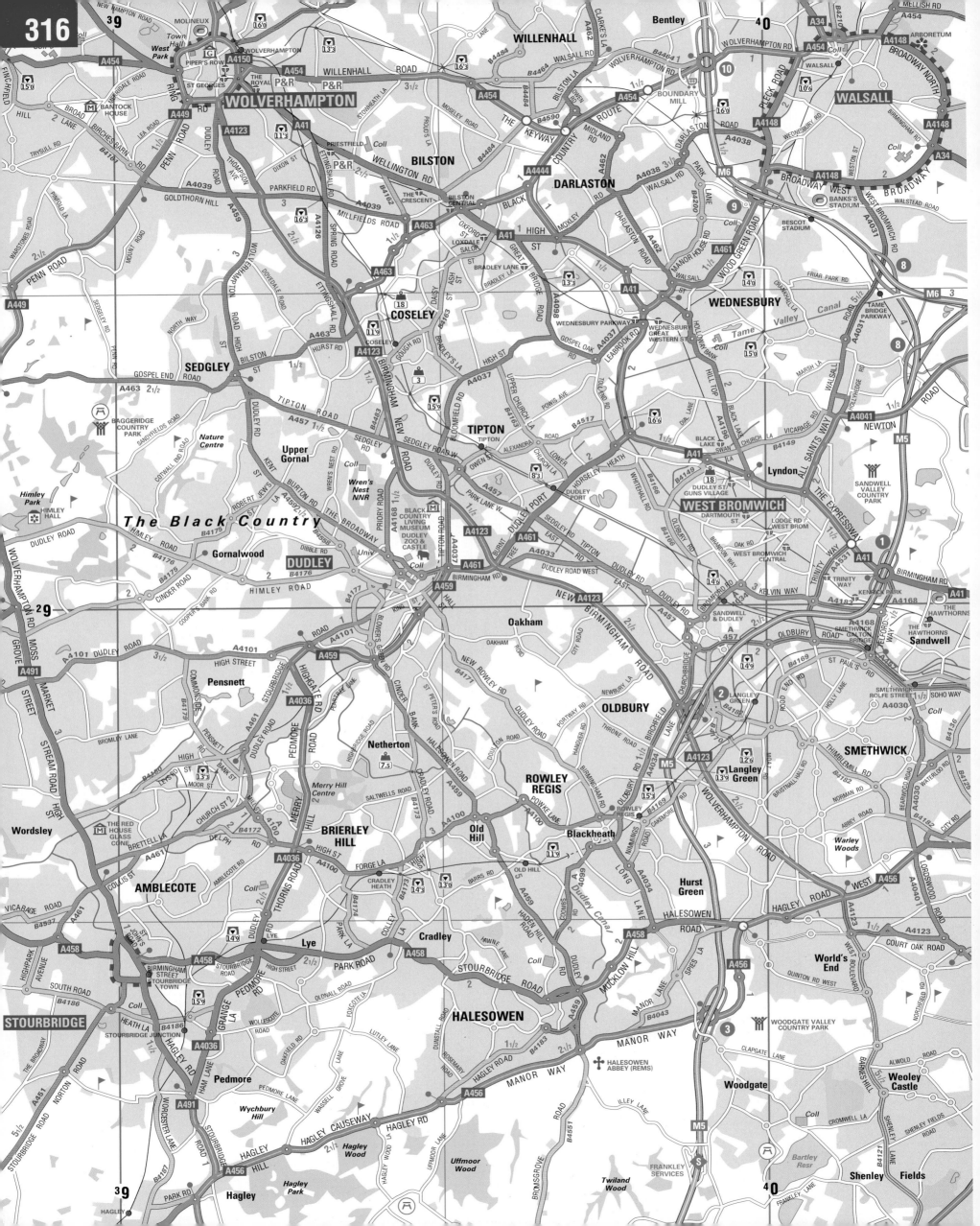

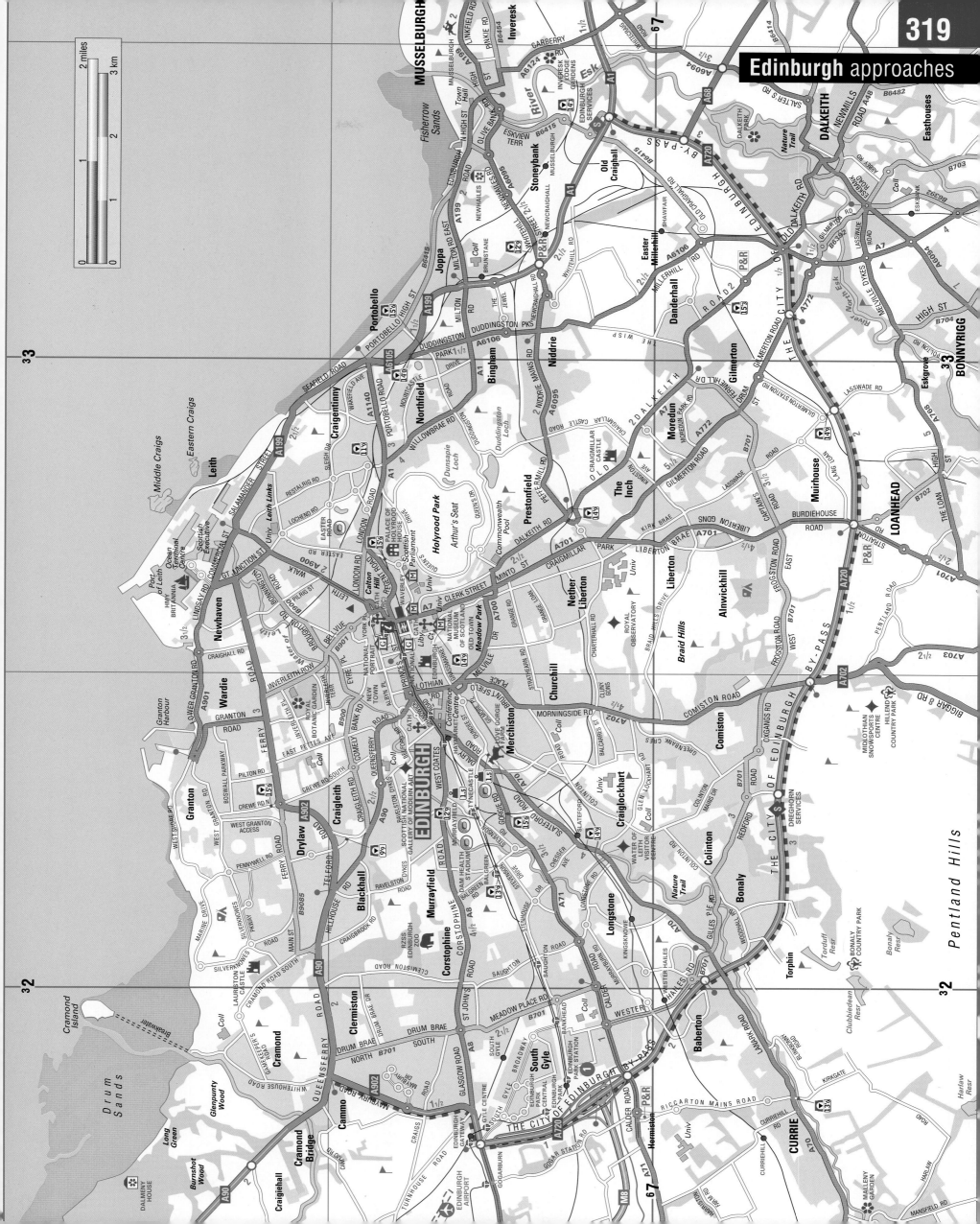

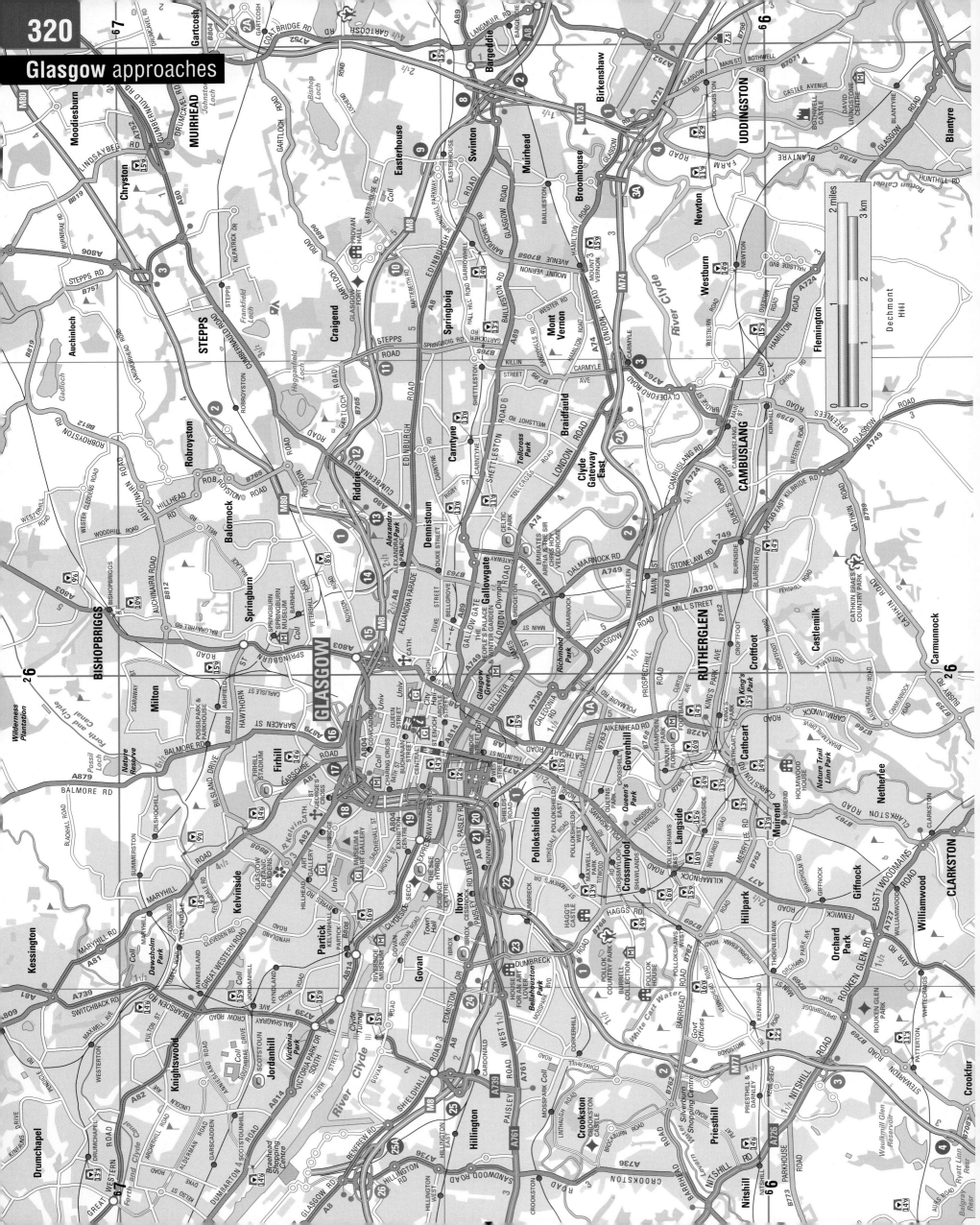

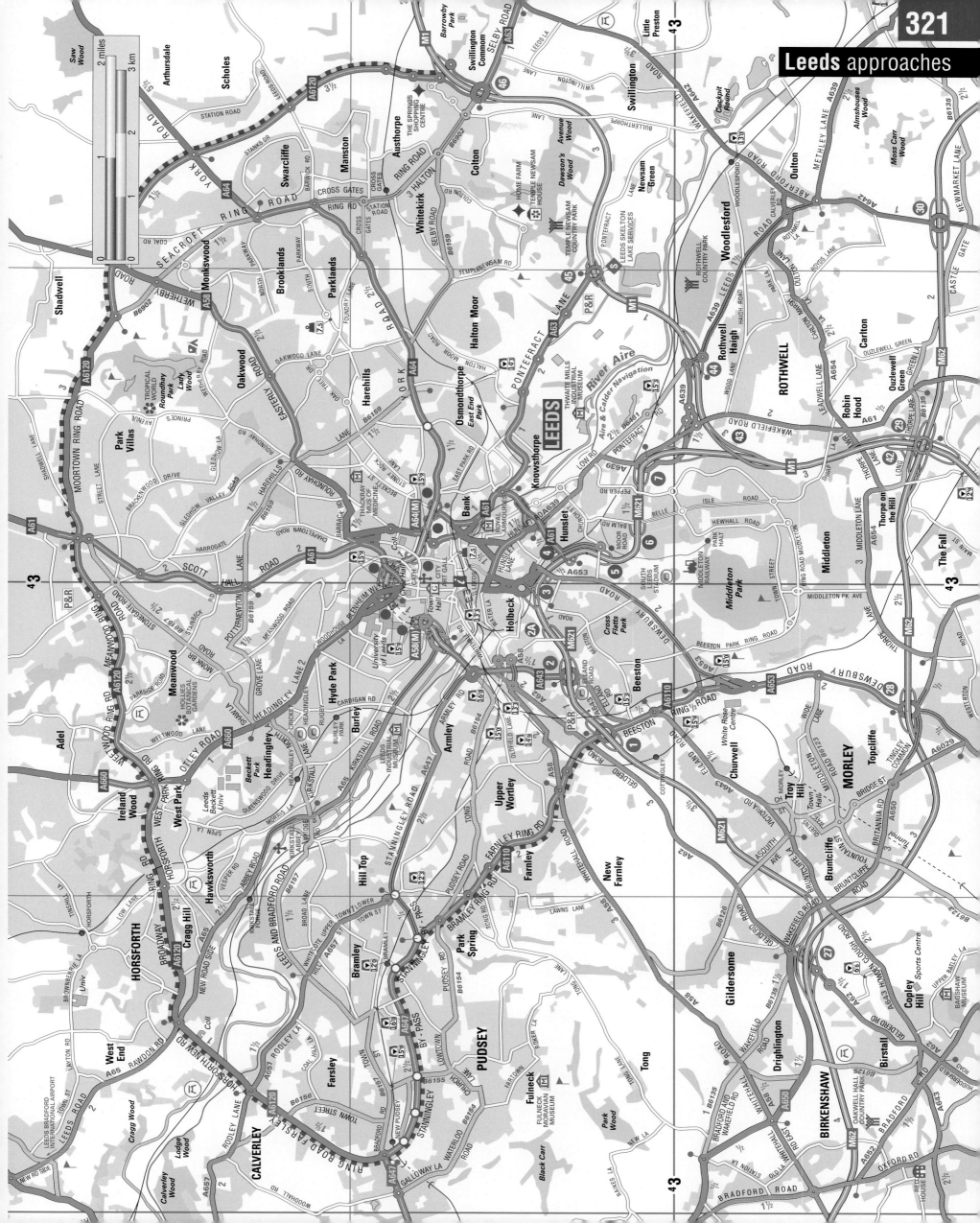

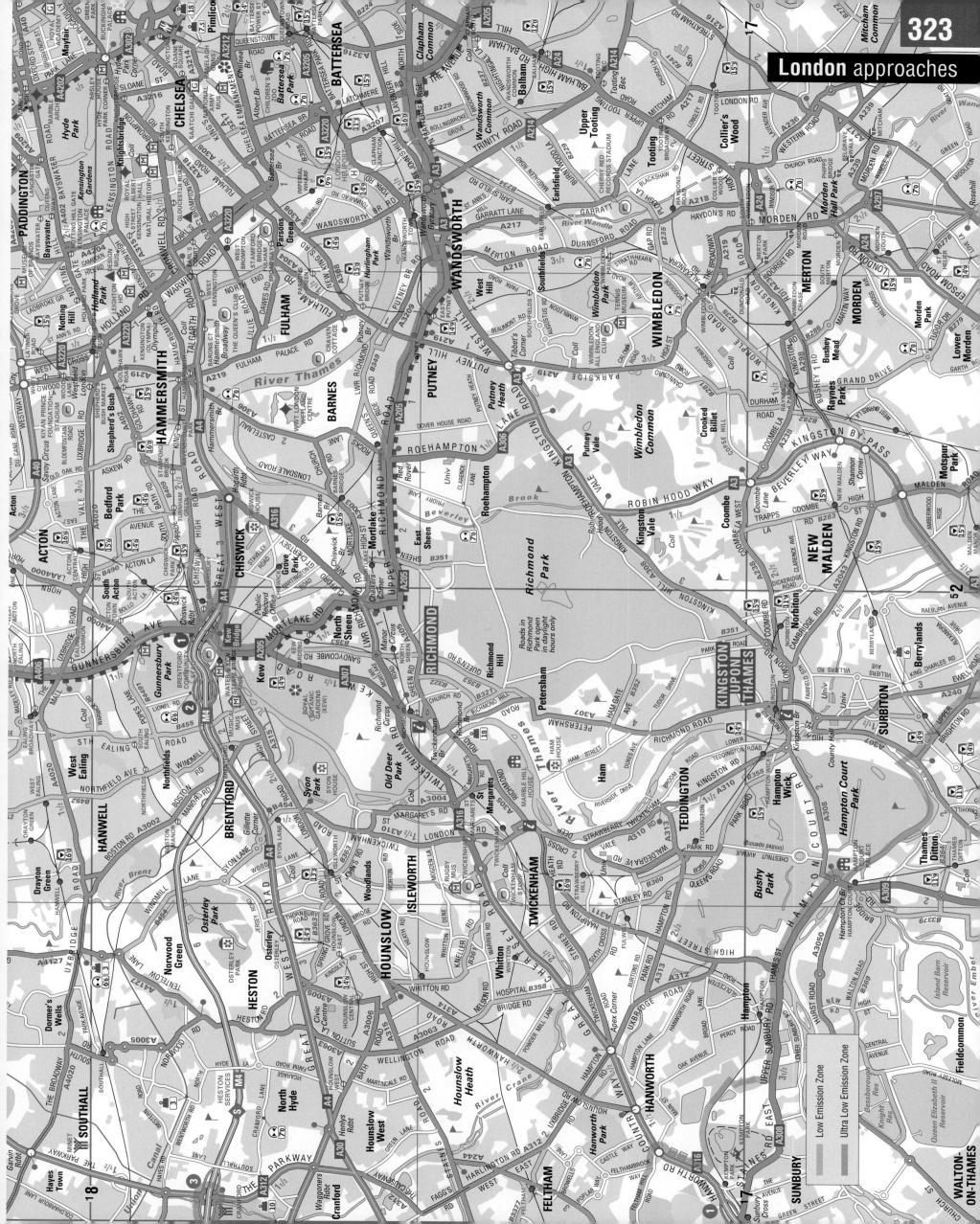

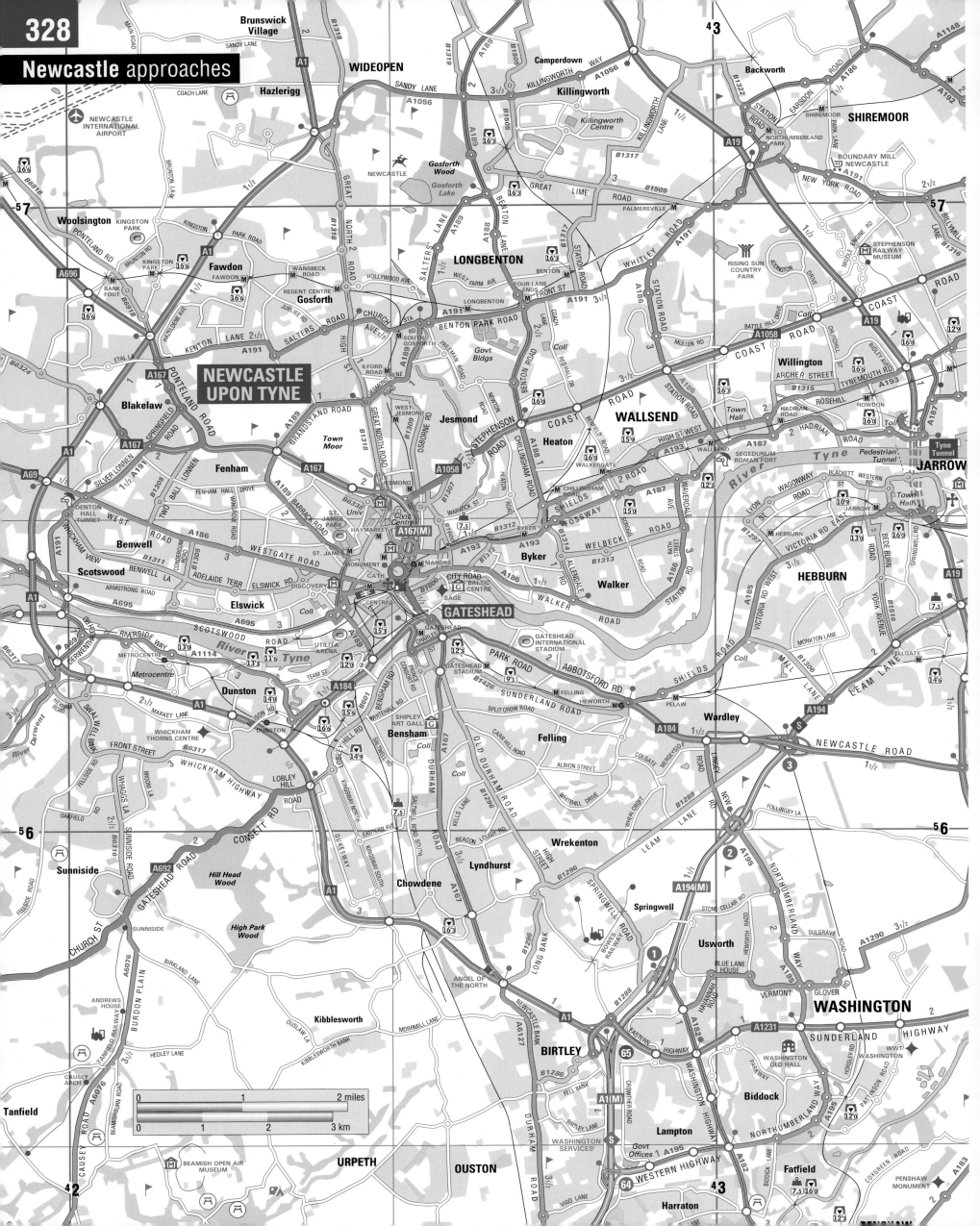

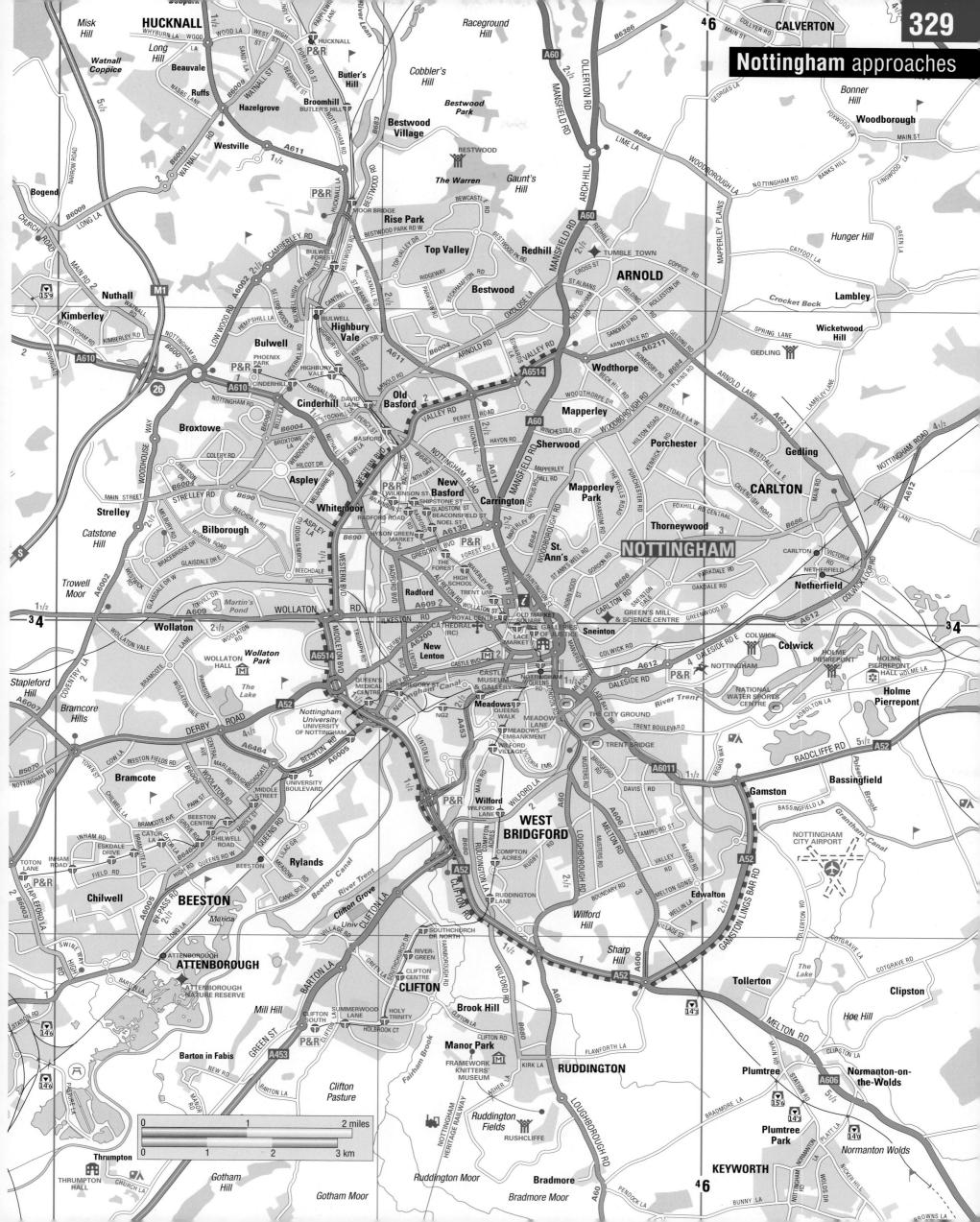

Aberdeen page 293 ● Aberystwyth page 128 ● Ashford page 54 ● Ayr page 257 ● Bangor page 179 ● Barrow-in-Furness page 210 ● Bath page 61 ● Berwick-upon-Tweed page 273

331

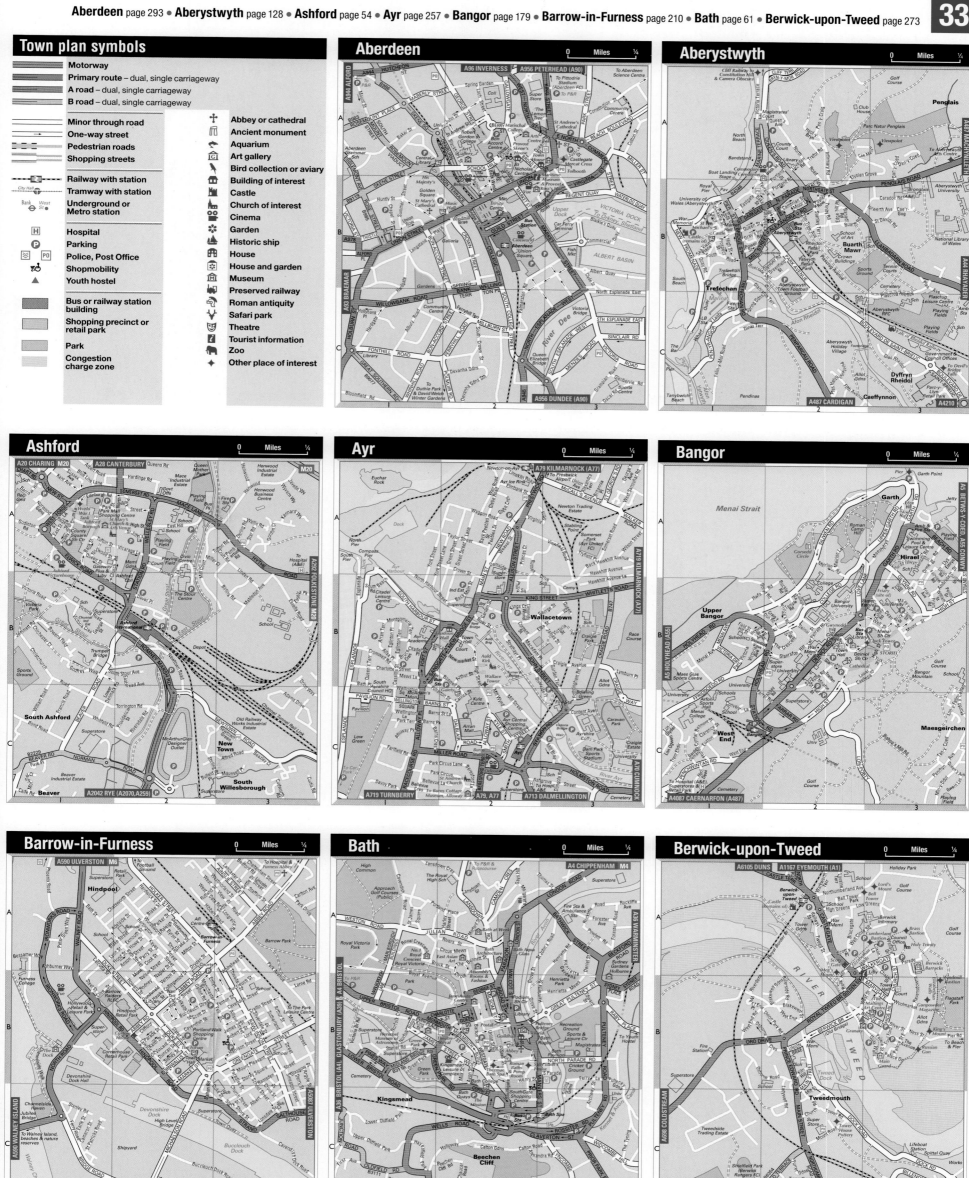

Birmingham

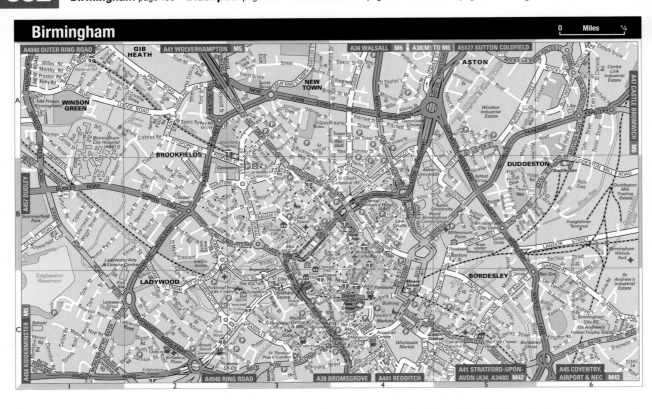

Blackpool

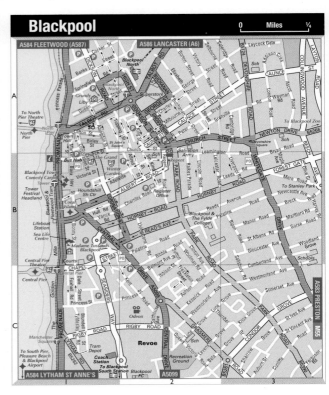

Bournemouth

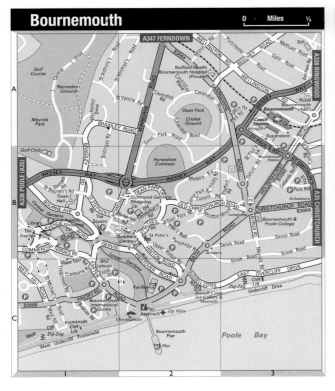

Bradford

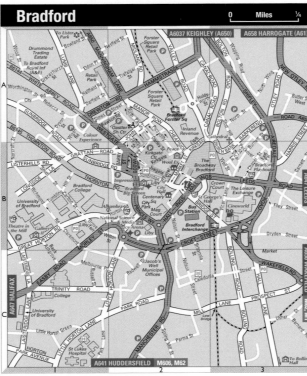

Brighton

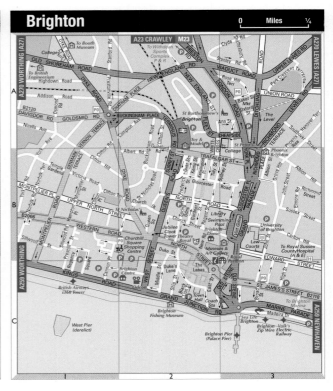

Bristol

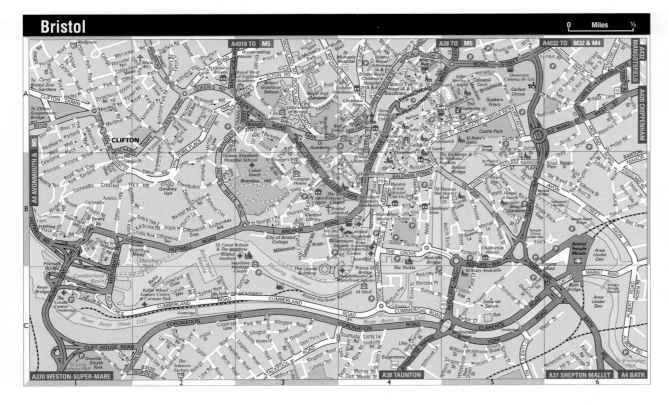

Bury St Edmunds

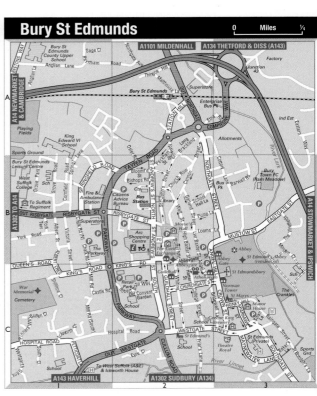

Cambridge page 123 ● **Canterbury** page 54 ● **Cardiff** page 59 ● **Carlisle** page 239 ● **Chelmsford** page 88 ● **Cheltenham** page 99 ● **Chester** page 166 ● **Chichester** page 22 ● **Colchester** page 107

333

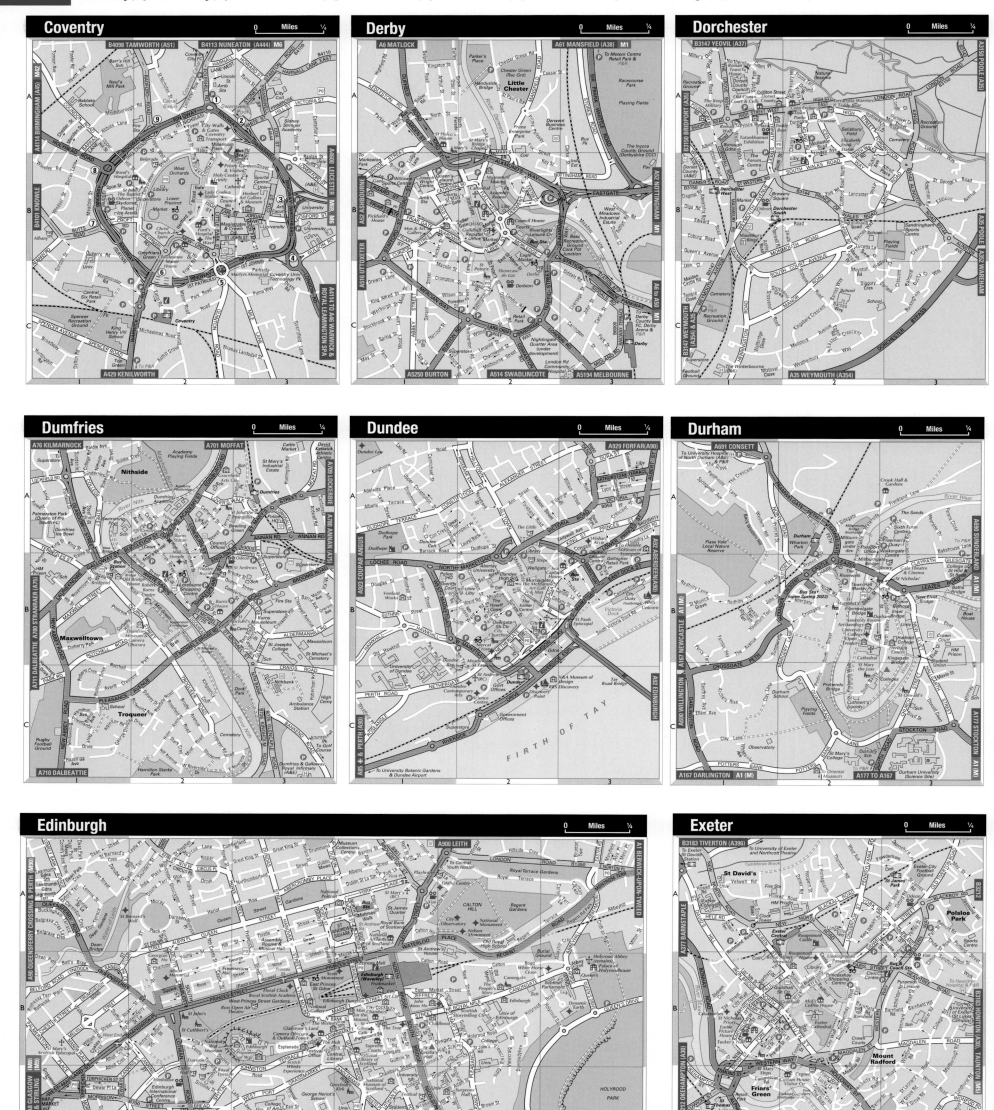

Fort William page 290 ● **Glasgow** page 267 ● **Gloucester** page 80 ● **Grimsby** page 201 ● **Hanley (Stoke-on-Trent)** page 168 ● **Harrogate** page 206 ● **Holyhead** page 178 ● **Hull** page 200

335

Fort William

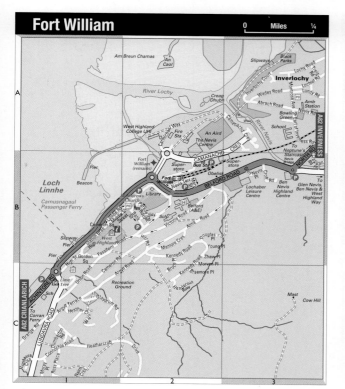

Glasgow

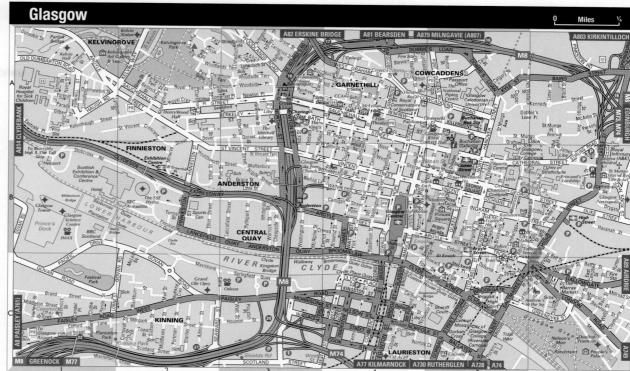

Gloucester

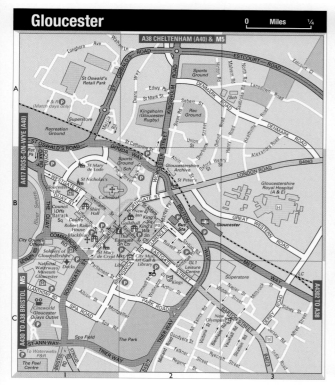

Grimsby

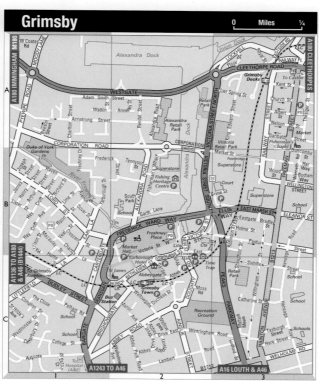

Hanley (Stoke-on-Trent)

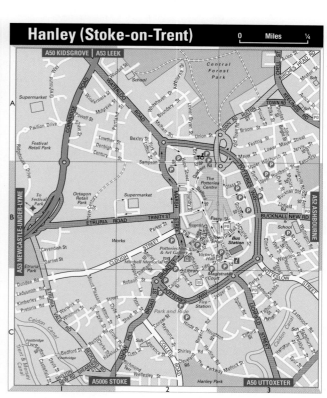

Harrogate

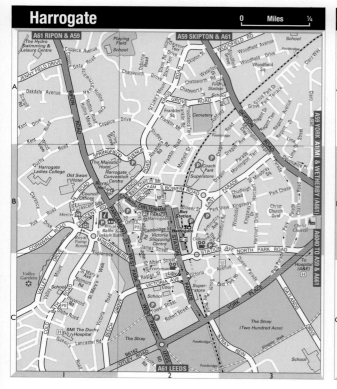

Holyhead / Caergybi

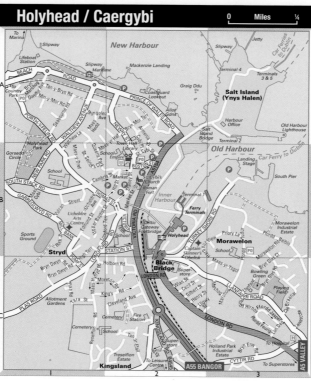

Hull

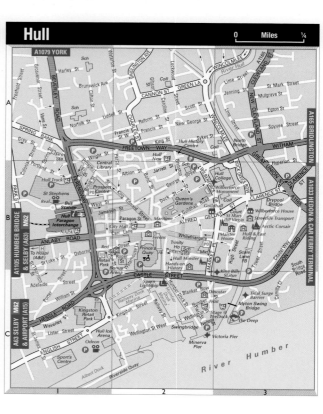

Inverness

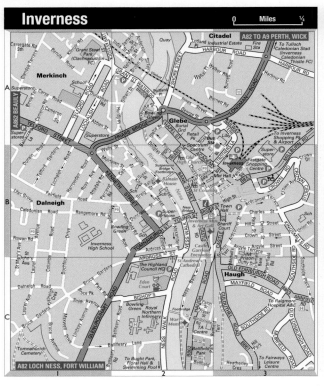

Ipswich

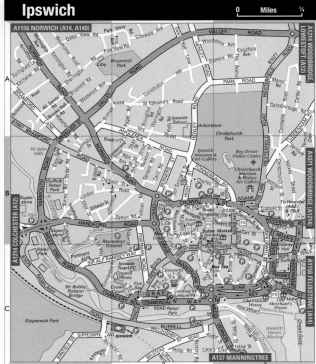

Kendal

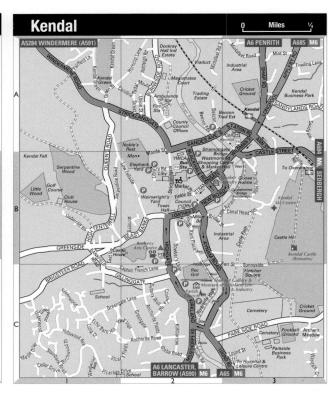

King's Lynn

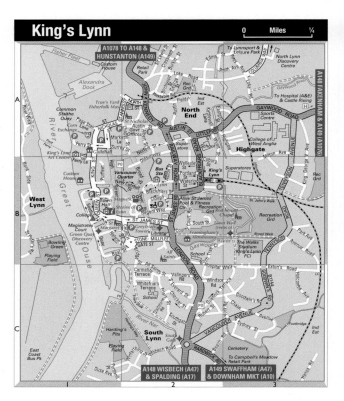

Leeds

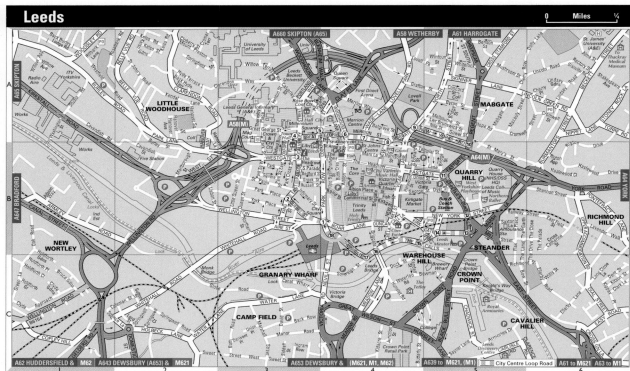

Lancaster

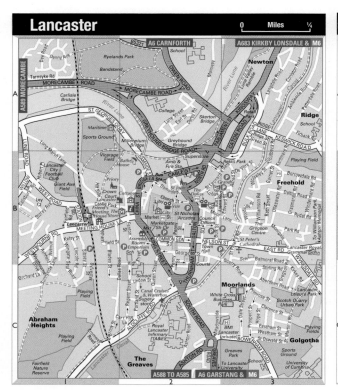

Leicester

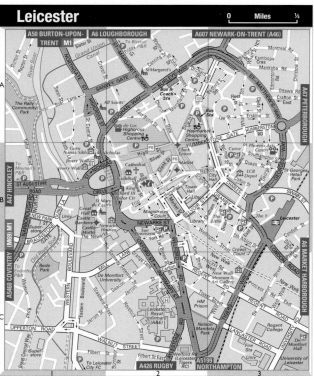

Lewes

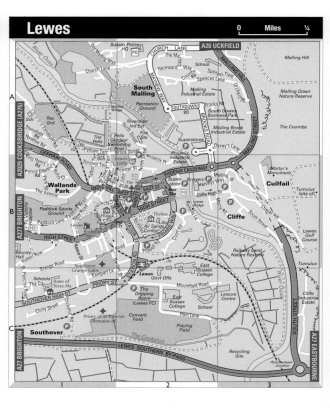

Lincoln page 189 ● Liverpool page 182 ● Llandudno page 180 ● Llanelli page 56 ● Luton page 103 ● Macclesfield page 184 ● Manchester page 184

337

Lincoln

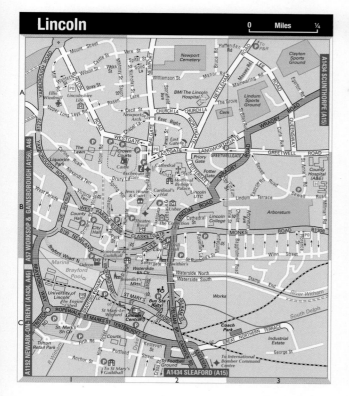

Liverpool

Llandudno

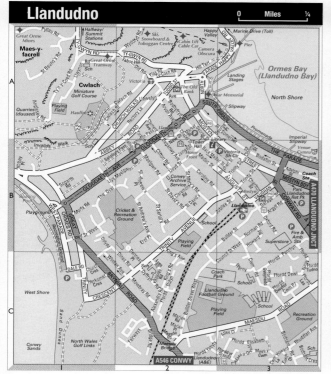

Llanelli

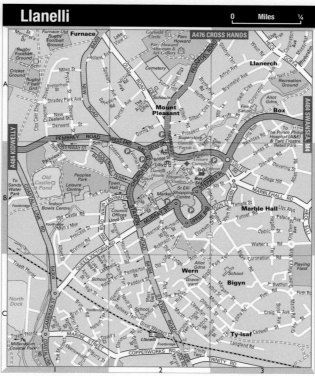

Luton

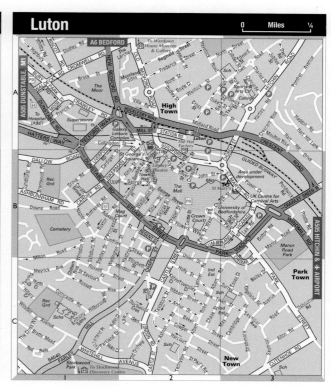

Macclesfield

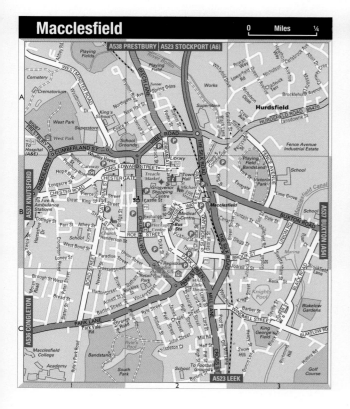

Manchester

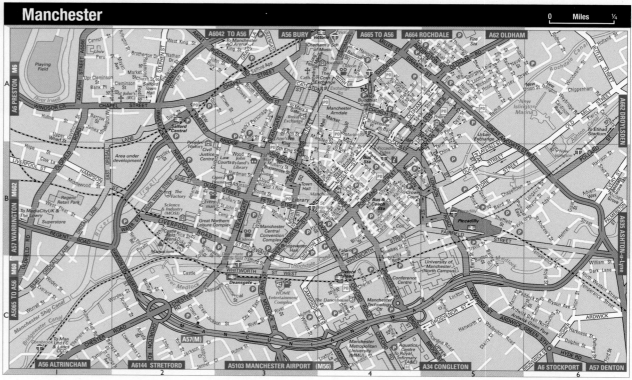

Maidstone

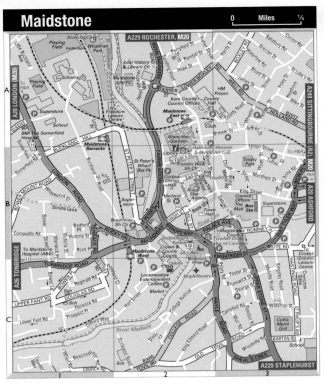

Merthyr Tydfil / Merthyr Tudful

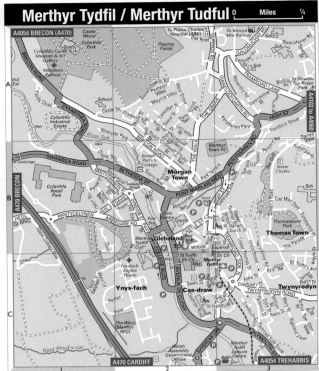

Middlesbrough

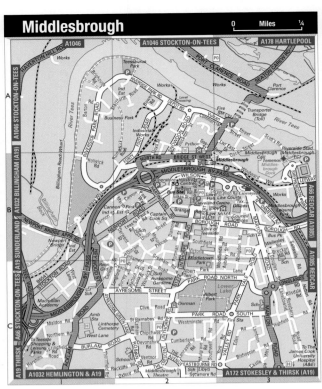

Milton Keynes

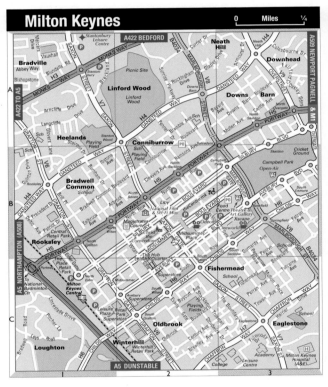

Newcastle upon Tyne

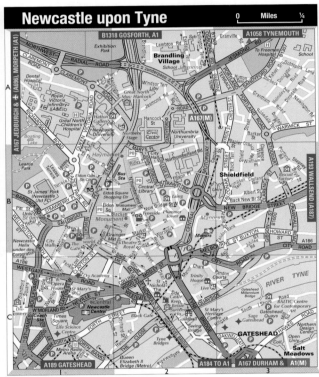

Newport / Casnewydd

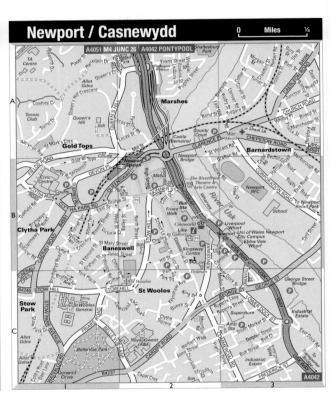

Newquay

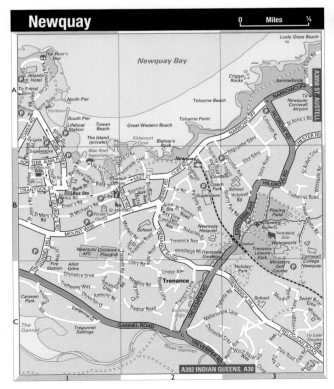

Newtown / Y Drenewydd

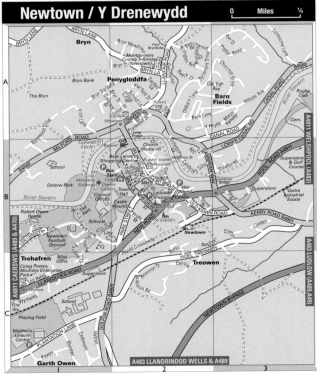

Northampton

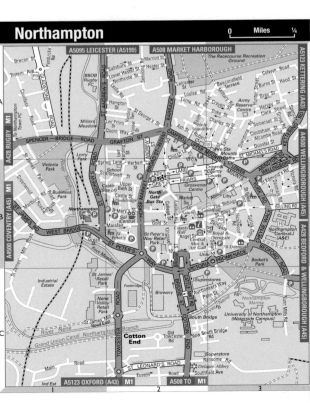

Norwich page 142 ● Nottingham page 153 ● Oban page 289 ● Oxford page 83 ● Perth page 286 ● Peterborough page 138 ● Plymouth page 7 ● Poole page 18 ● Portsmouth page 21

341

Norwich

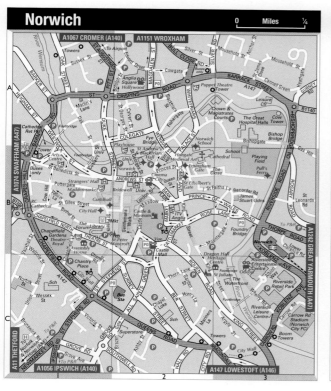

Nottingham

Oban

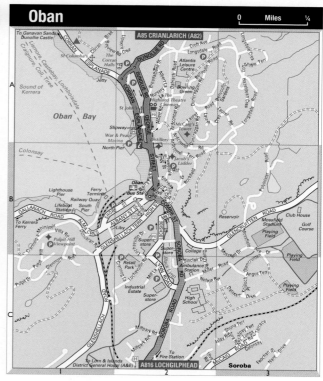

Oxford

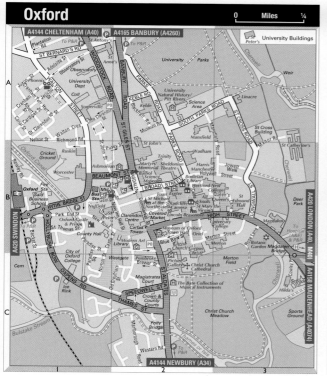

Perth

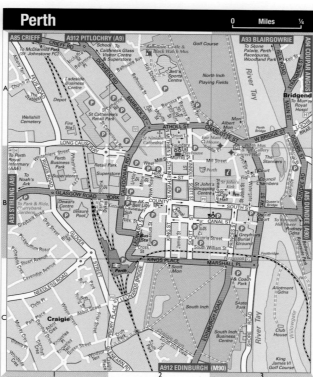

Peterborough

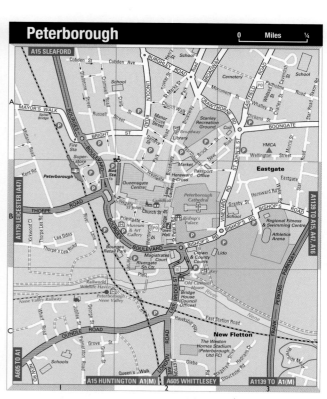

Plymouth

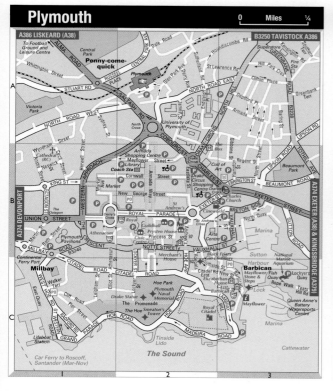

Poole

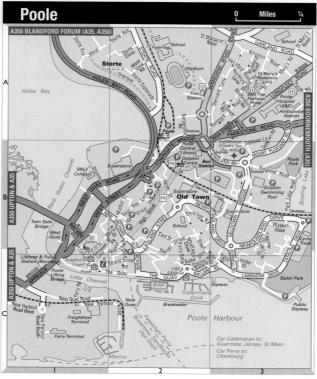

Portsmouth

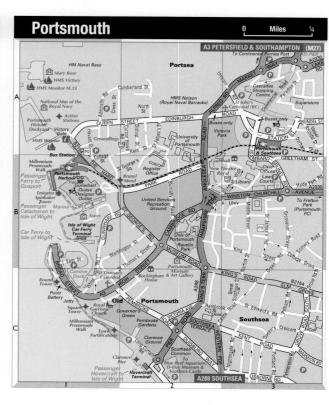

Preston
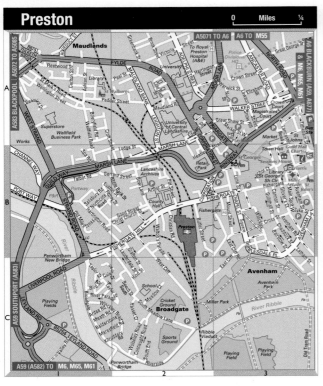

Reading
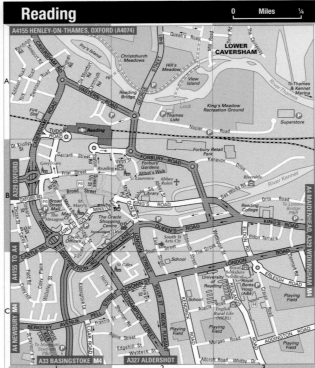

St Andrews
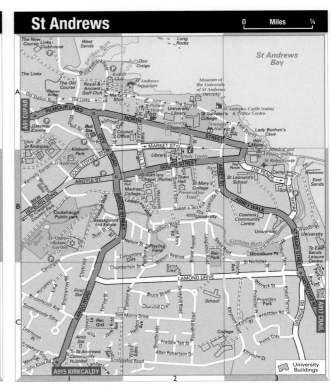

Salisbury
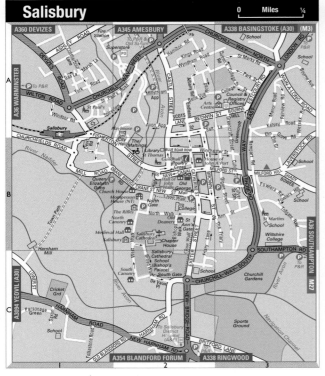

Scarborough
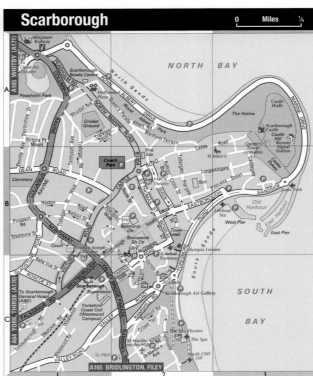

Shrewsbury
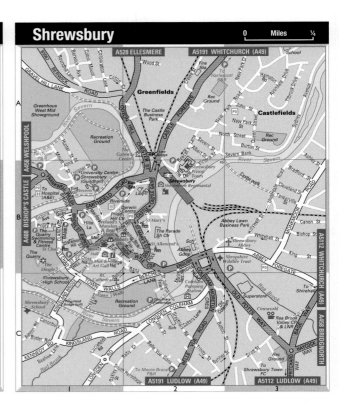

Sheffield
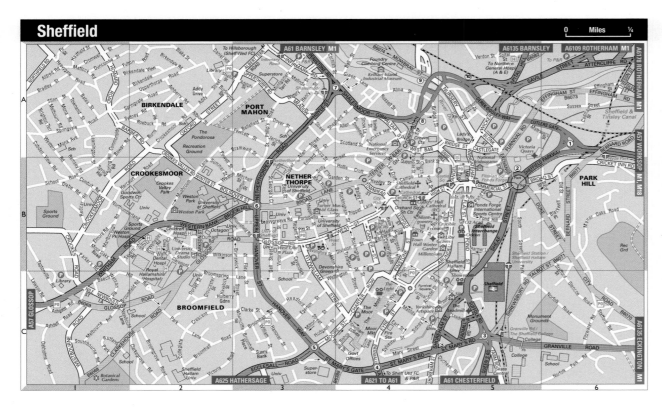

Southampton
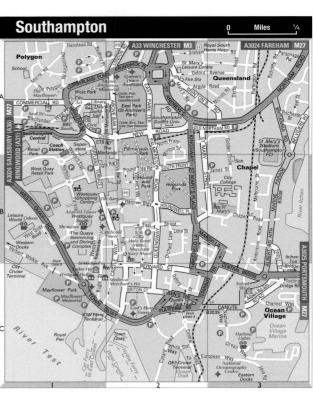

Southend page 69 ● Stirling page 278 ● Stoke page 168 ● Stratford-upon-Avon page 118 ● Sunderland page 243 ● Swansea page 56 ● Swindon page 63 ● Taunton page 28 ● Telford page 132

343

Southend-on-Sea

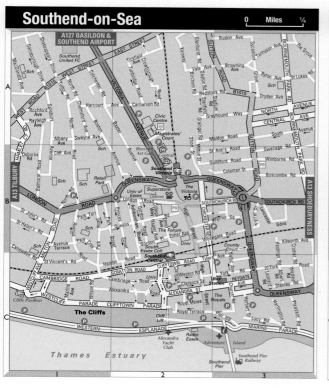

Stirling

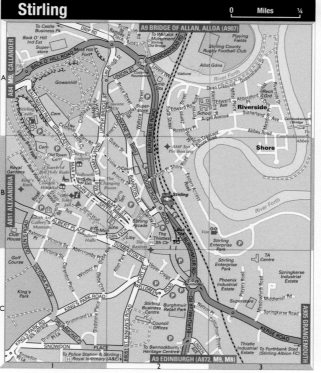

Stoke

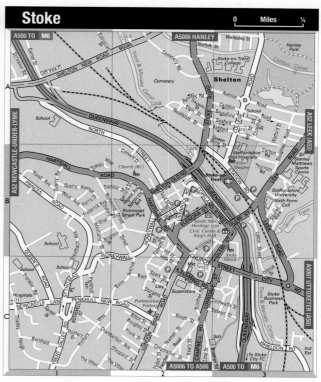

Stratford-upon-Avon

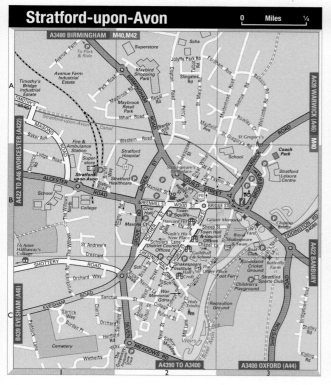

Sunderland

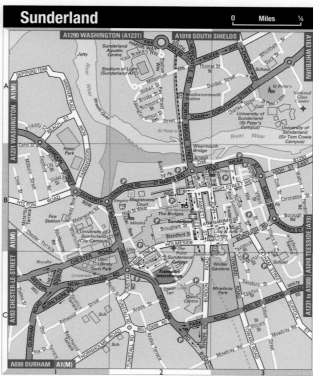

Swansea / Abertawe

Swindon

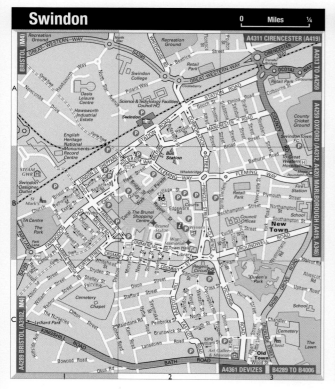

Taunton

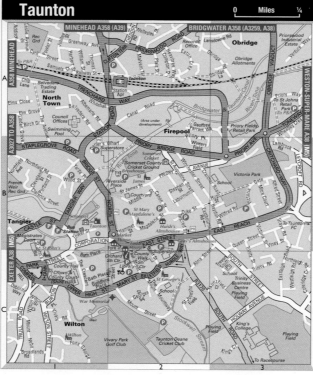

Telford

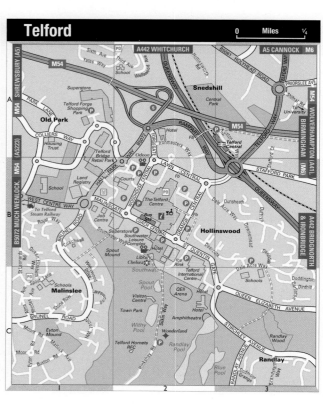

344

Torquay page 9 • Truro page 4 • Wick page 310 • Winchester page 33 • Windsor page 66 • Wolverhampton page 133 • Worcester page 117 • Wrexham page 166 • York page 207

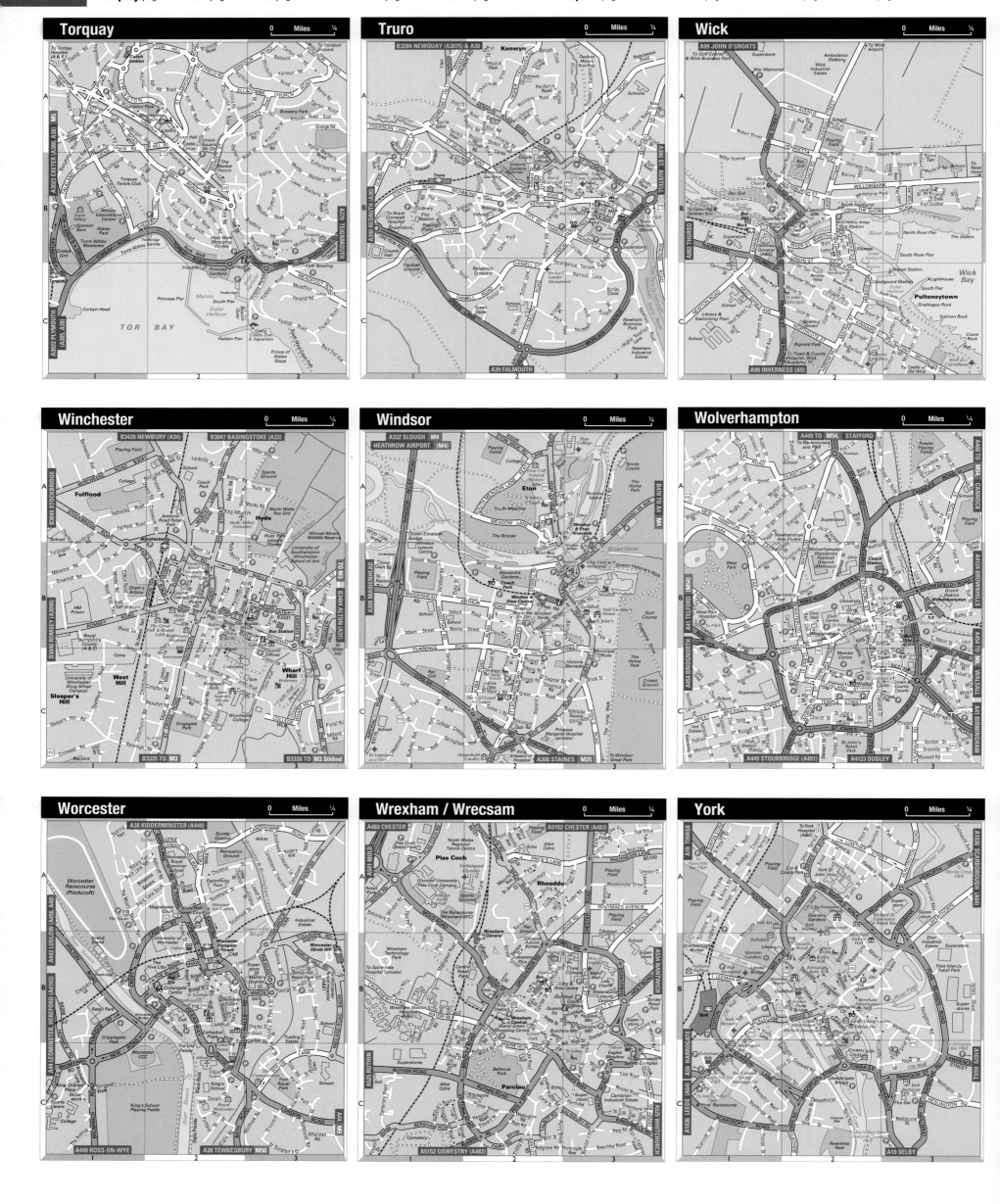

Town plan indexes

Aberdeen 331

Aberdeen ≋ B2
Aberdeen Grammar School A1
Academy, The B2
Albert Basin B3
Albert Quay B3
Albury Rd C1
Alford Place B1
Art Gallery 🏛 A2
Arts Centre 🏛 A2
Back Wynd A2
Baker St A1
Beach Boulevard A3
Belmont 🎦 B2
Belmont St B2
Berry St A2
Blackfriars St A2
Blaikie's Quay B3
Bloomfield Rd C1
Bon Accord Centre A2
Bon-Accord St B1/C1
Bridge St B2
Broad St A2
Bus Station B2
Car Ferry Terminal B3
Castlegate A3
Central Library A1
Chapel St B1
Cineworld 🎦 B2
Clyde St B3
College A2
College St B2
Commerce St A3
Commercial Quay B3
Community Centre A3/C1
Constitution St A3
Cotton St A3
Crown St B2
Denburn Rd A2
Devanha Gardens C2
Devanha Gdns South C2
East North St A3
Esslemont Avenue A1
Ferryhill Rd C2
Ferryhill Terrace C2
Fish Market B3
Fonthill Rd C1
Galleria B1
Gallowgate A2
George St A2
Glenbervie Rd C3
Golden Square B1
Grampian Rd C3
Great Southern Rd C1
Guild St B2
Hardgate B1/C1
His Majesty's Theatre 🎭 A1
Holburn St C1
Hollybank Place C1
Huntly St B1
Hutcheon St A1
Information Centre ℹ B2
John St A2
Justice St A3
King St A2
Langstane Place B1
Lemon Tree, The A2
Library C1
Loch St A2
Maberly St A1
Marischal College 🏛 A2
Maritime Mus & Provost Ross's House 🏛 B2
Market B2
Market St B2/B3
Menzies Rd C3
Mercat Cross ✦ A3
Millburn St C2
Miller St A3
Mount St A1
Music Hall 🎭 B1
North Esp East C3
North Esp West C2
Oscar Rd C3
Palmerston Rd C2
Park St A3
Police Station 🏢 A2
Polmuir Rd C2
Post Office 📮 A1/A2/A3/B1/C3
Provost Skene's Ho 🏛 A2
Queen Elizabeth Br C2
Queen St A2
Regent Quay B3
Regent Road B3
Robert Gordon's Coll. A2
Rose St B1
Rosemount Place A1
Rosemount Viaduct A1
St Andrew St A2
St Andrew's Cath ✝ A3
St Mary's Cathedral ✝ B1
St Nicholas Centre A2
St Nicholas St A2
School Hill A2
Sinclair Rd C3
Skene Square A1
Skene St B1
South College St C2
South Crown St C2
South Esp East C3
South Esp West C3
South Mount St A1
Sports Centre C3
Spring Garden A2
Springbank Terrace C2
Summer St B1
Superstore A2
Thistle St B1
Tolbooth 🏛 A3
Town House 🏛 A2
Trinity Centre B2
Union Row B1
Union Square B2
Union St B1/B2
University A2
Upper Dock B3
Upper Kirkgate A2
Victoria Bridge C3
Victoria Dock B3
Victoria Rd C3
Victoria St B2
Virginia St A3
Vue 🎦 B2
Waterloo Quay B3
Wellington Place B2
West North St A2
Whinhill Rd C1
Willowbank Rd C1
Windmill Brae B2

Aberystwyth 331

Aberystwyth Holiday Village C2
Aberystwyth Library and Ceredigion Archives . A2
Aberystwyth RFC C3
Aberystwyth Sta ≋ B2
Aberystwyth Town Football Ground B2
Aberystwyth Univ. B3
Alexandra Rd B2
Ambulance Station C3
Baker St B1
Banadl Rd B2
Bandstand A1
Bar, The C1
Bath St A2
Boat Landing Stage A1
Bvd de Saint-Brieuc C3
Bridge St B1
Bronglais Hospital Ⓗ B3
Bryn-y-Mor Rd A2
Buarth Rd B2
Bus Station B2
Cae Melyn A2
Cae'r-Gog B3
Cambrian St B2
Caradoc Rd B3
Caravan Site C2
Castle Theatre 🎭 B1
Castle (remains of) 🏰 B1
Castle St B1
Cemetery B3
Ceredigion Mus 🏛 A1
Chalybeate St B1
Cliff Terrace A2
Club House A2
Commodore 🎦 A1
County Court A2
Crown Buildings B2
Dan-y-Coed A3
Dinas Terrace C1
Eastgate B1
Edge-hill Rd B2
Elm Tree Avenue B2
Elysian Grove A2
Felin-y-Mor Rd C1
Fifth Avenue C2
Fire Station C1
Glanrafon Terrace B1
Glan Rheidol C3
Glyndwr Rd B2
Golf Course A3
Government & Council Offices C3
Gray's Inn Rd B1
Great Darkgate St B1
Greenfield St B2
Heol-y-Bryn A2
High St B1
Infirmary Rd A2
Iorwerth Avenue B3
King St B1
Lauraplace B1
Lifeboat Station C1
Llanbadarn Rd B3
Loveden Rd A2
Magistrates Court A1
Marina C1
Marine Terrace A1
Market Hall B1
Mill St B1
Moor Lane B2
National Liby of Wales . B3
New Promenade B1
New St B1
North Beach A1
North Parade B2
North Rd A2
Northgate St B2
Parc Natur Penglais A3
Parc-y-Llyn Retail Pk . C3
Park Avenue B2
Pavillion B1
Pen-y-Craig A2
Pen-yr-angor C1
Pendinas C1
Penglais Rd B3
Penrheidol C2
Pier St B1
Plas Avenue B3
Plas Helyg C2
Plascrug Avenue . . B2/C3
Plascrug Leisure Ctr . C3
Police Station 🏢 C2
Poplar Row B2
Portland Rd B2
Portland St A2
Post Office 📮 B1
Powell St B1
Prospect St B1
Quay Rd B1
Queen St B1
Queen's Avenue A2
Queen's Rd A2
Rheidol Retail Park B2
Riverside Terrace B1
St Davids Rd B3
St Michael's 🏰 B1
School of Art B2
Seaview Place B1
Shopmobility B2
South Beach B1
South Rd B1
Sports Ground B2
Spring Gardens C1
Stanley Terrace B2
Superstore B1/B2
Superstore B2/C3
Swimming Pool & Leisure Centre C3
Tanybwlch Beach C1
Tennis Courts B3
Terrace Rd B1
Trefechan Bridge B1
Trefechan Rd C2
Trefor Rd A2
Trinity Rd B2
University of Wales (Aberystwyth) B1
Vale of Rheidol Railway 🚂 C3
Vaynor St B2
Victoria Terrace A1
Viewpoint ✦ A2
Viewpoint ✦ A3
War Memorial B1
Wharf Quay C1
Y Lanfa C1
Ystwyth Retail Park . . . B2

Ashford 331

Adams Drive C3
Albert Rd A1
Alfred Rd C3
Apsley St A1
Ashford Borough Museum 🏛 A1
Ashford College B2
Ashford International Station ≋ B2
Ashford Picturehouse 🎦 A1
Bank St A1
Barrowhill Gardens A1
Beaver Industrial Est . C1
Beaver Rd C1
Beazley Court C3
Birling Rd B3
Blue Line Lane A1
Bond Rd C1
Bowens Field B1
Bulleid Place C2
Business Park A2
Cade Rd C1
Chart Rd A1
Chichester Close B1
Christchurch Rd B1
Chunnel Industrial Est . B1
Church Rd A1
Civic Centre A2
County Square Shopping Centre A1
Croft Rd A3
Cudworth Rd C3
Curtis Rd C3
Dering Rd A3
Dover Place B2
Drum Lane A1
East Hill A2
East St A1
Eastmead Avenue B2
Edinburgh Rd A1
Elwick Rd A1
Essella Park B3
Essella Rd B3
Fire Station A3
Forge Lane A1
Francis Rd C1
Gateway Plus and Liby . A1
George St B1
Godfrey Walk B1
Gordon Close A3
Government Offices A2
Hardinge Rd A2
Henwood A3
Henwood Bsns Centre . A3
Henwood Ind Est A3
High St A2
Hythe Rd A3
Javelin Way A3
Jemmett Rd B1
Kennard Way A3
Kent Avenue A1
Linden Rd B3
Lower Denmark Rd C1
Mabledon Avenue B3
Mace Industrial Est A2
Mace Lane A2
Maunsell Place C3
McArthurGlen Designer Outlet C2
Memorial Gardens A2
Mill Court A2
Miller Close A2
Mortimer Close C1
New St A1
Newtown Green C3
Newtown Rd B2/C3
Norman Rd C1
North St A2
Norwood Gardens A1
Norwood St A1
Old Railway Works Industrial Estate C3
Orion Way C3
Pk Mall Shopping Ctr . A1
Park Place A1
Park St A1/A2
Pemberton Rd A3
Police Station 🏢 A1
Post Office 📮 A1
Providence St C2
Queen St A1
Queens Rd A2
Regents Place A1
Riversdale Rd C2
Romney Marsh Rd B2
St John's Lane A2
St Mary's Church & Arts Venue 🏛 A1
Somerset Rd A2
South Stour Avenue B2
Star Rd A3
Station Rd B2
Stirling Rd C2
Stour Centre, The B2
Sussex Avenue A1
Tannery Lane A2
Torrington Rd C2
Trumper Bridge B1
Tufton Rd A3
Tufton St A1
Vicarage Lane A2
Victoria Crescent B1
Victoria Park B1
Victoria Rd B1
Wallis Rd A3
Wellesley Rd A2
West St A1
Whitfeld Rd C1
William Rd C1
World War I Tank ✦ . . . A1
Wyvern Way A3

Ayr 331

Ailsa Place B1
Alexandra Terrace A3
Allison St B2
Alloway Park C1
Alloway Place C1
Alloway St C2
Arran Mall C2
Arran Terrace B1
Arthur St B2
Ashgrove St C2
Auld Brig B2
Auld Kirk 🏰 B2
Ayr ≋ C2
Ayr Academy B1
Ayr Central Shopping Centre C2
Ayr Harbour A1
Ayr Ice Rink A2
Ayrshire College C3
Back Hawkhill Avenue . A3
Back Main St B2
Back Peebles St A2
Barns Crescent C1
Barns Park C1
Barns St C1
Barns Street Lane C1
Bath Place B1
Bellevue Crescent C1
Bellevue Lane C1
Beresford Lane C2
Beresford Terrace C2
Boswell Park B2
Britannia Place A3
Bruce Crescent B1
Burns Statue ✦ C2
Bus Station B1
Carrick St C2
Cassillis St B1
Cathcart St B1
Charlotte St B1
Citadel Leisure Ctr B1
Citadel Place B1
Compass Pier A1
Content Avenue C3
Content St B2
Craigie Avenue B3
Craigie Rd B3
Craigie Way B3
Cromwell Rd B1
Crown St A2
Dalblair Rd C2
Dam Park Sports Stadium C3
Damside A2
Dongola Rd C3
Eglinton Place B1
Eglinton Terrace B1
Elba St B2
Elmbank St A2
Esplanade B1
Euchar Rock A1
Farifield Rd C1
Fort St B1
Fothringham Rd C3
Fullarton St C1
Gaiety 🎭 C2
Garden St B2
George St B2
George's Avenue A3
Glebe Crescent A2
Glebe Rd A2
Gorden Terrace B3
Green St A2
Green Street Lane A2
Hawkhill Avenue A3
Hawkhill Avenue Lane . B3
High St B2
Holmston Rd C3
James St B3
John St B2
King St B2
Kings Court B2
Kyle Centre C2
Kyle St C2
Library B2
Limekiln Rd A2
Limonds Wynd B2
Loudoun Hall 🏛 B2
Lymburn Place B3
Macadam Place B2
Main St B2
Mcadam's Monument . C1
Mccall's Avenue A3
Mews Lane B1
Mill Brae C3
Mill St C2
Mill Wynd C2
Miller Rd C1
Montgomerie Terrace . B1
New Bridge B2
New Bridge St B2
New Rd A2
Newmarket St B2
Newton-on-Ayr Sta ≋ . A2
North Harbour St B1
North Pier A1
Odeon 🎦 C2
Park Circus C1
Park Circus Lane C1
Park Terrace C1
Pavilion Rd C1
Peebles St A2
Philip Square B2
Police Station 🏢 B2
Prestwick Rd B1
Princes Court A2
Queen St B3
Queen's Terrace B1
Racecourse Rd C1
River St B2
Riverside Place B2
Russell Drive A2
St Andrews Church 🏰 . C2
St George's Rd A3
Sandgate B1
Savoy Park C1
Smith St C2
Somerset Park (Ayr United FC) A3
Somerset Rd A3
South Beach Rd B1
South Harbour St B1
South Pier A1
Station Rd C2
Strathayr Place B2
Superstore A2/B2
Taylor St A2
Town Hall B2
Tryfield Place A3
Turner's Bridge B2
Union Avenue A3
Victoria Bridge C3
Victoria St B3
Viewfield Rd A3
Virginia Gardens A2
Waggon Rd A2
Walker Rd A3
Wallace Tower ✦ B2
Weaver St A2
Weir Rd A2
Wellington Lane C1
Wellington Square C1
West Sanouhar Rd A3
Whitletts Rd B3
Wilson St A3
York St A1
York Street Lane B1

Bangor 331

Abbey Rd C2
Albert St B1
Ambrose St A3
Ambulance Station A3
Arfon Sports Hall C1
Ashley Rd B3
Bangor Mountain B3
Bangor Station ≋ C1
Bangor University B2
Beach Rd A3
Belmont St C1
Bishop's Mill Rd C3
Brick St B3
Buckley Rd B2
Bus Station B3
Caellepa B2
Caernarfon Rd C1
Cathedral ✝ B2
Cemetery C1
Clarence St C1
Clock Tower ✦ B3
College B2
College Lane B2
College Rd B2
Convent Lane C1
Council Offices B2
Craig y Don Rd B2
Crescent, The B2
Dean St B3
Deiniol Rd B2
Deiniol Shopping Ctr . B2
Deiniol St B2
Edge Hill A3
Euston Rd C1
Fairview Rd A3
Farrar Rd C2
Ffordd Cynfal C1
Ffordd Islwyn A3
Ffordd y Castell C3
Ffriddoedd Rd B1
Field St B1
Fountain St A3
Friars Avenue B3
Friars Rd B3
Friary (Site of) ✦ B3
Gardd Deman C1
Garth Hill A3
Garth Point A3
Garth Rd A3
Glanrafon B2
Glanrafon Hill B2
Glynne Rd B3
Golf Course B3
Golf Course C2
Gorad Rd B1
Gorsedd Circle 🏛 A2
Gwern Las C3
Heol Dewi C1
High St B3/C2
Hill St B1
Holyhead Rd B1
Hwfa Rd B1
James St B3
Library B2
Llys Emrys A3
Lon Ogwen C1
Lon-Pobty C2
Lon-y-Felin C3
Lon-y-Glyder C1
Love Lane B2
Lower Penrallt Rd B2
Lower St B2
Maes Glas Sports Ctr . B1
Maes-y-Dref B3
Maeshyfryd A3
Meirion Lane A2
Meirion Rd A2
Menai Avenue B1
Menai College C1
Menai Shopping Ctr B3
Min-y-Ddol C3
Minafon B2
Mount St B3
Orme Rd A3
Parc Victoria B1
Penchwintan Rd C1
Penlon Grove B3
Penrhyn Avenue C3
Pier ✦ A3
Police Station 🏢 B2
Post Office 📮 . B2/B3/C3
Prince's Rd B2
Queen's Avenue C3
Sackville Rd B2
St Paul's St B2
Seion Rd A3
Seiriol Rd A3
Siliwen Rd A2
Snowdon View B1
Station Rd C1
STORIEL 🏛 B2
Strand St B3
Superstore B3/C2
Swimming Pool and Leisure Centre A3
Tan-y-Coed C3
Tegid Rd B3
Temple Rd B2
Theatr Gwynedd 🎭 B2
Totton Rd A3
Town Hall B2
Treflan B2
Trem Elidir C1
University B2
Upper Garth Rd A3
Victoria Avenue B1
Victoria Drive B1
Victoria St B1
Vron St B2
Well St B3
West End C1
William St B3
York Place B3

Barrow-in-Furness 331

Abbey Rd A3/B2
Adelaide St A2
Ainslie St A3
Albert St C3
Allison St B3
Anson St A2
AR Centre A2
Argyle St B3
Arthur St B3
Ashburner Way A1
Barrow Park A3
Barrow Raiders RLFC . B1
Barrow-in-Furness Station ≋ A2
Bath St A1/B2
Bedford Rd A3
Bessamer Way A1
Blake St A1/A2
Bridge Rd C1
Buccleuch Dock C3
Buccleuch Dock Rd C2/C3
Buccleuch St B2/B3
Byron St A2
Calcutta St A1
Cameron St C1
Carlton Avenue A3
Cavendish Dock Rd C3
Cavendish St B2/B3
Channelside Haven C1
Channelside Walk B1
Chatsworth St A2
Cheltenham St A3
Church St C3
Clifford St B2
Clive St B1
Collingwood St B2
Cook St A2
Cornerhouse Retail Pk B2
Cornwallis St B2
Courts A2
Crellin St B3
Cross St C3
Custom House ✦ B2
Dalkeith St B2
Dalton Rd B2/C2
Derby St B3
Devonshire Dock C2
Devonshire Dock Hall . B1
Dock Museum, The 🏛 . B1
Drake St A2
Dryden St A2
Duke St A1/B2/C3
Duncan St B2
Dundee St C2
Dundonald St B2
Earle St C1
Emlyn St B2
Exmouth St A2
Farm St C2
Fell St B3
Fenton St B3
Ferry Rd C1
Forum, The 🎭 B2
Furness College B1
Glasgow St B3
Goldsmith St A2
Greengate St B3
Hardwick St A2
Harrison St B3
Hartington St A2
Hawke St B2
Hibbert Rd A2
High Level Bridge C2
High St B2
Hindpool Rd B2
Hindpool Retail Park . B2
Holker St A2
Hollywood Retail & Leisure Park B1
Hood St A2
Howard St B2
Howe St A2
Ironworks Rd A1/B1
James St B3
Jubilee Bridge C1
Keith St B2
Keyes St A2
Lancaster St A3
Lawson St B2
Library B2
Lincoln St A3
Longreins Rd A3
Lonsdale St C3
Lord St B3
Lorne Rd B3
Lyon St A2
Manchester St B2
Market B2
Market St B2
Marsh St B3
Michaelson Rd C2
Milton St A2
Monk St B2
Mount Pleasant B3
Nan Tait Centre B2
Napier St B2
Nelson St B2
North Rd B1
Open Market B2
Parade St B2
Paradise St B3
Park Avenue A3
Park Drive A3
Parker St A2
Parry St A2
Peter Green Way A1
Phoenix Rd A1
Police Station 🏢 B2
Portland Walk Shopping Centre B2
Raleigh St A2
Ramsden St B3
Rawlinson St B3
Robert St B3
Rodney St B2
Rutland St A2
St Patricks Rd C1
St Vincent St B2
Salthouse Rd C3
School St B2
Scott St B2
Settle St A3
Shore St C3
Sidney St B2
Silverdale St B3
Slater St B2
Smeaton St B3
Stafford St A3
Stanley Rd C1
Stark St C3
Steel St B1
Storey Square B3
Strand C3
Superstore . . . A1/B1/C3
Sutherland St B3
Thwaite St B3
Town Hall B2
Town Quay C3
Vernon St B2
Vue Cinema 🎦 B2
Walney Rd A1
West Gate Rd A2
West View Rd A3
Westmorland St A3
Whitehead St A3
Wordsworth St A2

Bath 331

Alexandra Park C2
Alexandra Rd C2
Ambulance Station A3
Approach Golf Courses (Public) A1
Archway St C3
Assembly Rooms & Fashion Museum 🏛 . A2
Avon St B2
Barton St B2
Bath Abbey ✝ B2
Bath Aqua Glass 🏛 A2
Bath at Work Mus 🏛 A2
Bath College B2
Bath Rugby (The Rec) . B3
Bath Spa Station ≋ C3
Bathwick St A3
Beckford Road A3
Beechen Cliff Rd C2
Bennett St A2
Bloomfield Avenue C1
Broad Quay C2
Broad St B2
Brock St A1
Bus Station C2
Calton Gardens C2
Calton Rd C2
Camden Crescent A2
Cavendish Rd A1
Cemetery B1
Charlotte St B2
Chaucer Rd C2
Cheap St B2
Circus Mews A2
Claverton St C2
Corn St C2
Cricket Ground B3
Daniel St A3
East Asian Art Mus 🏛 . A2
Edward St B3
Ferry Lane B3
Fire Station A3
First Avenue C1
Forester Avenue A3
Forester Rd A3
Gays Hill A2
George St B2
Great Pulteney St B3
Green Park B1
Green Park Rd B2
Green Park Station ✦ . B1
Grove St B2
Guildhall 🏛 B2
Harley St A2
Hayesfield Park C1
Henrietta Gardens A3
Henrietta Mews B3
Henrietta Park B3
Henrietta Rd A3
Henrietta St B3
Henry St B2
Herschel Museum of Astronomy 🏛 B1
High Common A1
Holburne Museum 🏛 . B3
Holloway C2
James St West B1/B2
Jane Austen Centre 🏛 B2
Julian Rd A1
Junction Rd C1
Kingsmead Leisure Complex B2
Kipling Avenue C2
Lansdown Crescent A1
Lansdown Grove A2
Lansdown Rd A2
Library B2
London Rd A3
London St A2
Lower Bristol Rd B1
Lower Oldfield Park C1
Lyncombe Hill C3
Magistrates' Court B3
Manvers St B3
Maple Grove C1
Margaret's Hill A2
Marlborough Bldgs A1
Marlborough Lane B1
Midland Bridge Rd B1
Milk St B2
Milsom St B2
Mission The 🎭 B2
Monmouth St B2
Morford St A2
Museum of Bath Architecture, The 🏛 . A2
New King St B1
No 1 Royal Cres 🏛 A1
Norfolk Buildings B1
Norfolk Crescent B1
North Parade Rd B3
Oldfield Rd C1
Paragon A2
Pines Way B1
Podium Shopping Ctr . B2
Police Station 🏢 B3
Portland Place A2
Post Office 📮 B2/C2
Postal Museum 🏛 B2
Powlett Rd A3
Prior Park Rd C3
Pulteney Bridge ✦ B2
Pulteney Gardens B3
Pulteney Rd B3/C3
Queen Square B2
Raby Place B3
Recreation Ground B3
Rivers St A2
Rockliffe Avenue A3
Rockliffe Rd A3
Roman Baths & Pump Room 🏛 B2
Rossiter Rd C3
Royal Avenue A1
Royal Crescent A1
Royal High School, The A2
Royal Victoria Park A1
St James Square A1
St John's Rd A3
Sally Lunn's House ✦ . B2
Shakespeare Avenue . C2
Shopmobility B2
South Parade B3
SouthGate Shopping Centre C2
Sports & Leisure Ctr . B3
Spring Gardens C3
Stall St B2
Stanier Rd B1
Superstore A3/B1
Sydney Gardens A3
Sydney Place B3
Sydney Rd B3
Theatre Royal 🎭 B2
Thermae Bath Spa ✦ . B2
Thomas St A3
Tyning, The C3
Union St B2
University C3
Upper Bristol Rd B1
Upper Oldfield Park C1
Victoria Art Gallery 🏛 B2
Victoria Bridge Rd B1
Walcot St B2
Wells Rd C1
Westgate Buildings B2
Westgate St B2
Weston Rd A1
Widcombe Hill C3

Berwick-upon-Tweed 331

Avenue, The B3
Bank Hill B2
Bell Tower ✦ A3
Bell Tower Park A2
Berwick Barracks 🏛 A3
Berwick Br B2
Berwick Infirmary Ⓗ . . A3
Berwick-upon-Tweed ≋ A2
Billendean Rd C3
Blakewell Gardens B2
Blakewell St B2
Brass Bastion ✦ A3
Bridge St B3
Brucegate St A2
Castle (Remains of) 🏰 A2
Castle Terrace A2
Castlegate A2
Chapel St A3
Church Rd C2
Church St B3
Council Office A3
Court B3
Coxon's Lane A3
Cumberland Bastion ✦ A3
Dean Drive C2
Dock Rd C2/C3
Elizabethan Walls A2/B3
Fire Station B1
Flagstaff Park B3
Football Ground C3
Foul Ford B3
Golden Square B2
Golf Course A3
Granary ✦ B3
Greenwood C1
Gunpowder Magazine ✦ B3
Hide Hill B3
High Greens A2
Holy Trinity 🏰 A3
Information Centre ℹ . A2
Kiln Hill B2
King's Mount ✦ B3
Ladywell Rd C2
Library A3
Lifeboat Station C3
Lord's Mount ✦ A3
Lovaine Terrace A2
Low Greens A3
Main Guard 🏛 B3
Main St B2/C2
Maltings Art Centre, The ✦ B3
Marygate B3
Meg's Mount ✦ A2
Middle St C3
Mill St C2
Mount Rd C2
Museum 🏛 B3
Ness St B3
North Rd A2
Northumberland Ave . A2
Northumberland Rd . C2
Ord Drive B1
Osborne Crescent B2
Osborne Rd B1
Palace Grove B3
Palace St B3
Palace St East B3
Parade A3
Pier Rd B3
Playing Field C1
Police Station 🏢 B3
Post Office 📮 . B2/B3/C2
Prince Edward Rd B2
Prior Rd C2
Quay Walls C3
Railway St A2
Ravensdowne B3
Riverdene B1
Riverside Rd B2
Royal Border Br A2
Royal Tweed Br B2
Russian Gun ✦ B3
Scots Gate ✦ A2
Scott's Place A2
Shielfield Park (Berwick Rangers FC) C1
Shielfield Terrace C2
Silver St B3
Spittal Quay C3
Superstore . . . B1/C1/C2
Tower Gardens A2
Tower Ho Pottery ✦ . C2
Tower Rd C2
Town Hall B3
Turret Gardens C2
Tweedbank Retail Pk . C2
Tweed Dock B2
Tweed St A2
Tweedside Trading Est C1
Union Brae B2
Union Park Rd B2
Walkergate A3
Wallace Grove A3
War Memorial A2
War Memorial B2
Warkworth Terrace A2
Well Close Square A2
West End B2
West End Place B1
West End Rd B1
West St B3
West St C3
Windmill Bastion ✦ B3
Woolmarket B3
Works C3

Birmingham 332

Abbey St A2
Aberdeen St A1
Acorn Grove B2
Adams St A5
Adderley St C5
Albert St B4
Albion St B2
Alcester St C5
Aldgate Grove A3
All Saint's St A2
All Saints Rd A2
Allcock St C5
Allesley St A4
Allison St C4
Alma Crescent B6
Alston Rd C1
Arcadian Centre C4
Arthur St C6
Assay Office 🏛 B3
Ashted Circus B5
Aston Expressway A5
Aston St B4

Aston University B4/B5
Avenue Rd A5
Bacchus Rd A1
Bagot St B4
Banbury St B5
Barford Rd B1
Barford St C4
Barn St C5
Barnwell Rd C6
Barr St A3
Barrack St B5
Barwick St B4
Bath Row C3
Beaufort Rd C1
Belmont Row B5
Benson Rd A1
Berkley St C3
Bexhill Grove C3
Birchall St C5
Birmingham City FC C6
Birmingham City Hospital (A&E) A1
Birmingham City Univ B3
Birmingham Wheels Park ✦ B6
Bishopsgate St C3
Blews St A4
Bloomsbury St A6
Blucher St C3
Bordesley St C4
Bowyer St C5
Bradburne Way A5
Bradford St C5
Branston St A3
Brearley St A4
Brewery St A4
Bridge St C3
Bridge St West A4
Brindley Drive B3
Brindley Place C3
Broad St C3
Broad St Cineworld C2
Broadway Plaza ✦ C2
Bromley St C5
Bromsgrove St C4
Brookfield Rd A2
Browning St C2
Bryant St A1
BT Tower ✦ B3
Buckingham St A3
Bull St B4
Bull St B4
Bullring C4
Cambridge St C3
Camden Drive B3
Camden St B2
Cannon St C4
Cardigan St B5
Carlisle St A1
Carlyle Rd C1
Caroline St B3
Carver St B2
Cato St A6
Cattell Rd C6
Cattells Grove A6
Cawdor Crescent C1
Cecil St B4
Cemetery A2/B2
Cemetery Lane A2
Centenary Square C3
Ctr Link Industrial Est A6
Charlotte St B3
Cheapside C4
Chester St A5
Children's Hospital (A&E) B4
Church St B4
Claremont Rd A2
Clarendon Rd C1
Clark St C1
Clement St B3
Clissold St B2
Cliveland St B4
Coach Station C5
College St B2
Colmore Circus B4
Colmore Row B4
Commercial St C3
Constitution Hill B3
Convention Ctr, The C3
Cope St B2
Coplow St B1
Corporation St C4
Council House B3
County Court B4
Coveley Grove A2
Coventry Rd C6
Coventry St C5
Cox St B3
Crabtree Rd A2
Cregoe St C3
Crescent Avenue A2
Crescent Theatre C3
Crescent, The A2
Cromwell St A6
Cromwell St B3
Cube, The C3
Curzon Circle B5
Curzon St B5
Custard Factory ✦ C5
Cuthbert Rd B1
Dale End B4
Dart St C6
Dartmouth Circus A4
Dartmouth Middleway A5
Dental Hospital B4
Deritend C5
Devon St A6
Devonshire St A1
Digbeth High St C4
Dolman St B6
Dover St A1
Duchess Rd C2
Duddeston B6
Duddeston Manor Rd B5
Duddeston Mill Rd B6
Duddeston Mill Trading Estate B6
Dudley Rd B1
Edgbaston Village C2
Edmund St B3
Edward St B3
Elkington St A4
Ellen St B2
Ellis St C3
Erskine St B6
Essex St C4
Everyman C3
Eyre St B2
Farm Croft A3
Farm St A3
Fazeley St B4/C5
Felstead Way B5
Finstall Close B5
Five Ways C2
Five Ways C2
Fiveway Shopping Ctr C2
Fleet St B3
Floodgate St C5
Ford St A2
Fore St C4
Forster St B5
Francis Rd C2
Francis St B5
Frankfort St A4
Frederick St B3
Freeth St C1
Freightliner Terminal B6
Garrison Circus C5
Garrison Lane C6
Garrison St B6
Gas St C3
Geach St A4
George St B3
George St West B2
Gibb St C5
Gilby Rd C2
Gillott Rd B1
Glover St C5
Goode Avenue A2
Goodrick Way A6
Gordon St B6
Graham St B3
Grand Central Shopping Centre C4
Granville St C3
Gray St C6
Great Barr St C5
Great Charles St Queensway B3
Great Francis St B6
Great Hampton Row A3
Great Hampton St A3
Great King St A3
Great King St North A3
Great Lister St A5
Great Tindal St C2
Green Lane C6
Green St C5
Greenway St C6
Grosvenor St West C2
Guest Grove A3
Guild Close C2
Guildford Drive A4
Guthrie Close A3
Hagley Rd C1
Hall St B3
Hampton St A3
Handsworth New Rd A1
Hanley St B4
Harford St A3
Harmer Rd A2
Harold Rd C1
Hatchett St A4
Heath Mill Lane C5
Heath St B1
Heaton St A2
Heneage St B5
Henrietta St B4
Herbert Rd C6
High St C4
High St C5
Hilden Rd B5
Hill St C3/C4
Hindlow Close B6
Hingeston St B2
Hippodrome Theatre C4
HM Prison A1
Hockley Circus A2
Hockley Hill A3
Hockley St A3
Holliday St C3
Holloway Circus C4
Holloway Head C3
Holt St B5
Horse Fair C4
Hospital St A4
Howard St B3
Howe St B5
Hubert St A5
Hunters Rd A2
Hunters Vale A3
Huntly Rd C2
Hurst St C4
Icknield Port Rd B1
Icknield Square B2
Icknield St A2/B2
IKON C3
Inge St C4
Irving St C3
James Watt Queensway B4
Jennens Rd B5
Jewellery Quarter A3
Jewellery Quarter A3
Jewellery Quarter Museum B3
John Bright St C4
Keeley St C6
Kellett Rd B5
Kent St C4
Kenyon St B3
Key Hill A3
Key Hill Circus A2
Kilby Avenue C2
King Edwards Rd B2
King Edwards Rd C3
Kingston Rd C6
Kirby Rd A1
Ladywood Arts & Leisure Centre B1
Ladywood Circus C1
Ladywood Middleway C2/C3
Ladywood Rd C1
Lancaster St B4
Landor St B6
Law Courts B4
Lawley Middleway B5
Ledbury Close C2
Ledsam St B2
Lees St A1
Legge Lane B3
Lennox St A3
Library A6/C3
Library C3
Lighthorne Avenue B2
Link Rd B1
Lionel St B3
Lister St B5
Little Ann St C5
Little Hall Rd A6
Liverpool St C5
Livery St B3/B4
Lodge Rd A1
Lord St A5
Love Lane A5
Loveday St B4
Lower Dartmouth St C6
Lower Loveday St B4
Lower Tower St A4
Lower Trinity St C5
Lucus Circus A3
Ludgate Hill B3
Mailbox Centre & BBC C3
Margaret St B3
Markby Rd A1
Marroway St B1
Maxstoke St C6
Melvina Rd A6
Meriden St C4
Midland St B6
Milk St C5
Mill St A5
Millennium Point B5
Miller St A4
Milton St A4
Moat Lane C4
Montague Rd C1
Montague St C5
Monument Rd C1
Moor St Queensway C4
Moor Street C4
Moorsom St A4
Morville St C2
Mosborough Cres A3
Moseley St C4
Mott St B3
Mus & Art Gallery B3
Musgrave Rd A1
National Sea Life Centre C3
Navigation St C3
Nechell's Park Rd A6
Nechells Parkway B5
Nechells Place A6
New Alexandra C3
New Bartholomew St C4
New Canal St C5
New John St West A3
New Spring St B2
New St C4
New Street C4
New Summer St A4
New Town Row A4
Newhall Hill B3
Newhall St B3
Newton St B4
Newtown A4
Noel Rd C1
Norman St A1
Northbrook St B1
Northwood St B3
Norton St A2
Odeon C2
Old Crown House C5
Old Rep Theatre, The C4
Old Snow Hill B4
Oliver Rd C1
Oliver St A5
Osler St C1
Oxford St C5
Palmer St C5
Paradise Circus Queensway C3
Paradise St C3
Park Rd A2
Park St C4
Pavilions C4
Paxton Rd A2
Peel St A1
Pershore St C4
Phillips St A4
Pickford St C5
Pinfold St C4
Pitsford St A2
Plough & Harrow Rd C1
Police Station A4/B4/C2/C4
Pope St B2
Portland Rd C1
Post Office A5/B1/B3/B5/C3/C5
Preston Rd A1
Price St B4
Princip St B4
Printing House St B4
Priory Queensway B4
Pritchett St A4
Proctor St A5
Radnor St A2
Rea St C4
Regent Place B3
Register Office C3
Repertory Theatre C3
Reservoir Rd C1
Richard St A5
River St C5
Rocky Lane A5/A6
Rodney Close C2
Roseberry St B2
Rotton Park St B1
Royal Birmingham Conservatoire ✦ B5
Rupert St A5
Ruston St C2
Ryland St C2
St Andrew's Ind Est C6
St Andrew's Rd C6
St Andrew's St C6
St Bolton St C6
St Chads B4
St Chad's Cath (RC) B4
St Chads Queensway B4
St Clements Rd A6
St George's St A3
St James Place B5
St Marks Crescent B2
St Martin's C4
St Paul's B3
St Paul's B3
St Paul's Square B3
St Philip's B4
St Stephen's St A4
St Thomas' Peace Garden C3
St Vincent St C2
Saltley Rd A6
Sand Pits Parade B3
Severn St C3
Shadwell St B4
Sheepcote St C2
Shefford Rd A4
Sherborne St C2
Shylton's Croft C2
Skipton Rd C2
Smallbrook Queensway C4
Smith St A3
Snow Hill B4
Snow Hill Queensway B4
Soho, Benson Rd A1
South Rd A2
Spencer St B3
Spring Hill B2
Staniforth St B4
Station St C4
Steelhouse Lane B4
Stephenson St C4
Steward St B2
Stirling Rd C1
Stour St B2
Suffolk St Queensway C3
Summer Hill Rd B2
Summer Hill St B2
Summer Hill Terrace B2
Summer Lane A4
Summer Row B3
Summerfield Cres B1
Summerfield Park B1
Superstore B2
Sutton St C3
Swallow St C3
Sydney Rd C6
Symphony Hall C3
Talbot St A1
Temple Row C4
Temple St C4
Templefield St C6
Tenby St B3
Tenby St North B2
Tennant St C2/C3
Thimble Mill Lane A6
Thinktank (Science & Discovery) B5
Thomas St A4
Thorpe St C4
Tilton Rd C6
Tower St A4
Town Hall C3
Town Hall C3
Trent St C5
Turner's Buildings A1
Unett St A3
Union Terrace B5
Upper Trinity St C5
Utilita Arena ✦ C2
Uxbridge St A3
Vauxhall Grove B5
Vauxhall Rd B5
Vernon Rd C1
Vesey St B4
Viaduct St B5
Victoria Square C3
Villa St A3
Vittoria St B3
Vyse St B3
Walter St A6
Wardlow Rd A5
Warstone Lane B2
Washington St C3
Water St B3
Waterworks Rd C1
Watery Lane C5
Western Rd B1
Wharf St A2
Wheeler St A3
Whitehouse St A5
Whitmore St A2
Whittall St B4
Wholesale Market C4
Wiggin St B1
Willes Rd A1
Windsor Industrial Est A5
Windsor St A5
Windsor St B5
Winson Green Rd A1
Witton St C6
Wolseley St C6
Woodcock St B5

Blackpool 332

Abingdon St A1
Addison Crescent A3
Adelaide St B1
Albert Rd B2
Alfred St B2
Ascot Rd A3
Ashton Rd C2
Auburn Grove C3
Bank Hey St B1
Banks St A1
Beech Avenue A3
Bela Grove C2
Belmont Avenue B2
Birley St A1
Blackpool & Fleetwood Tram B1
Blackpool & the Fylde College B2
Blackpool FC C2
Blackpool North A2
Blackpool North A2
Blackpool Tower ✦ B1
Blundell St C1
Bonny St B1
Breck Rd B3
Bryan Rd A3
Buchanan St A2
Bus Hub B1
Cambridge Rd A3
Caunce St A2/A3
Central Drive B1/C2
Central Pier ✦ C1
Central Pier C1
Central Pier Theatre C1
Chapel St C1
Charles St A2
Charnley Rd B2
Church St A1/A2
Clinton Avenue B2
Coach Station A2/C1
Cocker St A1
Coleridge Rd A3
Collingwood Avenue A3
Comedy Carpet ✦ B1
Condor Grove C3
Cookson St A2
Coronation St B1
Corporation St A1
Courts B1
Cumberland Avenue B3
Cunliffe Rd C3
Dale St C1
Devonshire Rd A3
Devonshire Square A3
Dickson Rd A1
Elizabeth St A2
Ferguson Rd C3
Forest Gate B3
Foxhall Rd C1
Freckleton St C2
George St A2
Gloucester Avenue B3
Golden Mile, The C1
Gorse Rd B3
Gorton St A2
Grand Theatre, The B1
Granville Rd A2
Grasmere Rd C2
Grosvenor St A2
Grundy Art Gallery A1
Harvey Rd B3
Hornby Rd B2
Houndshill Shopping Centre B1
Hull Rd B1
Ibbison Court C2
Kent Rd C2
Keswick Rd C2
King St A2
Knox Grove C3
Laycock Gate A3
Layton Rd A3
Leamington Rd B2
Leeds Rd B3
Leicester Rd B2
Levens Grove C2
Library A1
Lifeboat Station B1
Lincoln Rd B2
Liverpool Rd B3
Livingstone Rd B2
London Rd A3
Lune Grove C2
Lytham Rd C1
Madame Tussaud's Blackpool B1
Manchester Square C1
Manor Rd B3
Maple Avenue B3
Market St A1
Marlboro Rd B3
Mere Rd B3
Milbourne St A2
Newcastle Avenue B3
Newton Drive A3
North Pier ✦ A1
North Pier A1
North Pier Theatre A1
Odeon C2
Olive Grove B3
Palatine Rd B2
Park Rd B2/C3
Peter St A2
Post Office B1/B2/B3
Princess Parade A1
Princess St C1/C2
Promenade A1/C1
Queen St A1
Queen Victoria Rd C2
Raikes Parade B2
Reads Avenue B2
Regent Cinema B2
Regent Rd B2
Register Office B2
Ribble Rd B2
Rigby Rd C1/C2
Ripon Rd B3
St Albans Rd B3
St Ives Avenue C3
St John's Square A1
St Vincent Avenue C3
Salisbury Rd B3
Salthouse Avenue C2
Salvation Army Ctr A2
Sands Way C2
Sea Life Centre B1
Seasiders Way C1
Selbourne Rd A2
Sharrow Grove C3
Somerset Avenue C3
South King St B2
Springfield Rd A1
Sutton Place B2
Talbot Rd A1/A2
Thornber Grove C2
Topping St A1
Tower B1
Town Hall A1
Tram Depot C1
Tyldesley Rd C1
Vance Rd B1
Victoria St B1
Victory Rd A2
Wayman Rd A3
Westmorland Ave. C2/C3
Whitegate Drive B3
Winter Gardens Theatre B1
Woodland Grove B3
Woolman Rd B2

Bournemouth 332

Ascham Rd A3
Avenue Rd B1
Ave Shopping Centre B1
Bath Rd C2
Beacon Rd C1
Beechey Rd A3
Bodorgan Rd B1
Bourne Avenue B1
Bournemouth A3
Bh2 Leisure C1
Bournemouth & Poole College B3
Bournemouth International Centre C1
Bournemouth Pier C2
Bournemouth Sta B3
Braidley Rd A1
Cavendish Place A2
Cavendish Rd A2
Central Drive A1
Central Gardens B1
Christchurch Rd B3
Cliff Lift C1/C3
Coach House Place A3
Coach Station A3
Commercial Rd B1
Cotlands Rd B3
Cranborne Rd C1
Cricket Ground A2
Cumnor Rd B2
Dean Park A2
Dean Park Crescent B2
Dean Park Rd A2
Durrant Rd B1
East Overcliff Drive C3
Exeter Crescent C1
Exeter Rd C1
Gervis Place B1
Gervis Rd B3
Glen Fern Rd B2
Golf Club B1
Grove Rd B3
Hinton Rd C2
Holdenhurst Rd B3
Horseshoe Common B2
Information Centre C2
Lansdowne B3
Lansdowne Rd A2
Lorne Park Rd B2
Lower Gardens B1/C2
Madeira Rd B2
Methuen Rd A3
Meyrick Park A1
Meyrick Rd B3
Milton Rd A2
Nuffield Health Bournemouth Hospital (private) A2
Oceanarium C2
Old Christchurch Rd B2
Ophir Rd A3
Oxford Rd B3
Park Rd A3
Parsonage Rd B2
Pavilion C2
Pier Approach C2
Pier Theatre C2
Police Station B3
Portchester Rd A3
Post Office B1/B3
Priory Rd C1
Quadrant, The B2
Recreation Ground A1
Richmond Gardens Shopping Centre B2
Richmond Hill Rd B1
Russell-Cotes Art Gallery & Museum C2
Russell Cotes Rd C2
St Anthony's Rd A1
St Michael's Rd C1
St Paul's A3
St Paul's Lane B3
St Paul's Rd A3
St Peter's B2
St Peter's B2
St Peter's Rd B2
St Stephen's Rd B1/B2
St Swithun's B3
St Swithun's Rd B3
St Swithun's Rd South B3
St Valerie Rd A2
St Winifred's Rd A2
Square, The B1
Stafford Rd B3
Terrace Rd B1
Town Hall B1
Tregonwell Rd C1
Triangle, The B1
Trinity Rd B2
Undercliff Drive C3
Upper Hinton Rd B2
Upper Terrace Rd C1
Wellington Rd A2/A3
Wessex Way A3/B1/B2
West Cliff Promenade C1
West Hill Rd C1
West Undercliff Prom C1
Westover Rd B2
Wimborne Rd A2
Wootton Mount B2
Wychwood Drive A1
Yelverton Rd B2
York Rd B3
Zig-Zag Walks C1/C3
Zip Wire ✦ C2

Bradford 332

Alhambra B2
Back Ashgrove B1
Barkerend Rd A3
Barnard Rd C3
Barry St B2
Bolling Rd C3
Bolton Rd A3
Bowland St A1
Bradford Big Screen ✦ B2
Bradford College B1
Bradford Forster Square A2
Bradford Interchange B3
Bradford Playhouse B3
Bridge St B2
Britannia St B2
Broadway Bradford, The B2
Burnett St B3
Bus Station B2
Butler St West A3
Caledonia St C2
Canal Rd A2
Carlton St B1
Cathedral A3
Centenary Square B2
Chapel St B3
Cheapside A2
Church Bank B3
Cineworld B3
City Hall B2
City Rd A1
Claremont B1
Colour Experience B1
Croft St B2
Crown Court B3
Darfield St A1
Darley St A2
Drewton Rd A1
Drummond Trading Estate A1
Dryden St B3
Dyson St A1
Easby Rd C1
East Parade B3
Eldon Place A1
Filey St B3
Forster Sq Retail Pk A2
Gallery II B1
Garnett St B3
Godwin St B2
Gracechurch St A1
Grattan Rd B1
Great Horton Rd B1/B2
Grove Terrace B1
Hall Ings B2
Hall Lane C3
Hallfield Rd A1
Hammstrasse A2
Harris St B3
Holdsworth St A2
Ice Arena ✦ B2
Impressions B2
Information Centre B2
Inland Revenue A2
Ivegate B2
Jacob's Well Municipal Offices B2
James St A2
John St A2
Kirkgate B2
Kirkgate Centre B2
Laisteridge Lane C1
Leeds Rd B3
Leisure Exchange, The B3
Library B1/B2
Listerhills Rd B1
Little Horton Green C1
Little Horton Lane C1
Longside Lane B1
Lower Kirkgate B2
Lumb Lane A1
Magistrates Court B2
Manchester Rd C2
Manningham Lane A1
Manor Row A2
Market C3
Market St B2
Melbourne Place C1
Midland Rd A2
Mill Lane C2
Morley St B1
National Science and Media Museum B2
Nelson St B2/C2
Nesfield St A2
New Otley Rd A3
Norcroft St B1
North Parade A2
North St A3
North Wing A3
Oastler Shopping Ctr A2
Otley Rd A3
Park Avenue C1
Park Lane C1
Park Rd C2
Parma St C2
Peace Museum B2
Peckover St B3
Piccadilly A2
Police Station C2
Post Office B1/B2/B3/C3
Princes Way B2
Prospect St C3
Radwell Drive C2
Rawson Rd A1
Rebecca St A1
Richmond Rd B1
Russell St C1
St George's Hall B2
St Lukes Hospital C1
Shipley Airedale Rd A3/B3
Shopmobility A2
Simes St A1
Smith St B1
Spring Mill St C2
Stott Hill A3
Sunbridge Rd A1/B1/B2
Theatre in the Mill B1
Thornton Rd A1/B1
Trafalgar St A2
Trinity Rd C1
Tumbling Hill St B1
Tyrrel St B2
Univ of Bradford B1/C1
Usher St C3
Valley Rd A2
Vicar Lane B3
Wakefield Rd C3
Wapping Rd A3
Well St B3
Westgate A1
White Abbey Rd A1
Wigan Rd A1
Wilton St B1
Wood St A1
Wool Exchange B2
Worthington St A1

Brighton 332

Addison Rd A1
Albert Rd B2
Albion Hill B3
Albion St B3
Ann St A3
Baker St A3
Black Lion St C2
Brighton A2
Brighton Centre C2
Brighton Fishing Museum C2
Brighton Pier (Palace Pier) ✦ C3
Brighton Zip Wire ✦ C3
British Airways i360 Tower ✦ C1
Broad St C3
Buckingham Place A2
Buckingham Rd B2
Cannon Place C1
Carlton Hill B3
Chatham Place A1
Cheapside A3
Church St B2
Churchill Square Shopping Centre B2
Clifton Hill B1
Clifton Place B1
Clifton Rd B1
Clifton St A2
Clifton Terrace B1
Clyde Rd A3
Coach Station C3
Compton Avenue A2
Davigdor Rd A1
Denmark Terrace B1
Ditchling Rd A3
Dome B2
Duke St B2
Duke's Lane C2
Dyke Rd A1/B2
East St C2
Edward St B3
Elmore Rd B3
Fleet St A2
Frederick St B2
Gardner St B2
Gloucester Place B3
Gloucester Rd B2
Goldsmid Rd A1
Grand Junction Rd C2
Grand Parade B3
Grove Hill B3
Guildford St A2
Hampton Place B1
Hanover Terrace A3
High St C3
Highdown Rd A1
Information Centre C2
John St B3
Jubilee Clock Tower B2
Kemp St B2
Kensington Place B2
Kings Rd C1
Lanes, The C2
Law Courts B3
Lewes Rd A3
Library B2
London Rd A3
Madeira Drive C3
Marine Parade C3
Middle St C2
Montpelier Place B1
Montpelier Rd B1
Montpelier St B1
Mus & Art Gallery B3
New England Rd A2
New England St A2
New Rd B2
Nizells Avenue A1
Norfolk Rd B1
Norfolk Terrace B1
North Rd B2
North St B2
Odeon C2
Old Shoreham Rd A1
Old Steine C3
Osmond Rd A1
Over St B2
Oxford St A3
Park Crescent Terrace A3
Phoenix Brighton B3
Phoenix Rise A3
Police Station B3
Post Office A1/A3/C3
Preston Rd A2
Preston St B1
Prestonville Rd A1
Queen's Rd B2
Queen Square B2
Regency Square C1
Regent St B2
Richmond Place B3
Richmond St B3
Richmond Terrace A3
Rose Hill Terrace A3
Royal Pavilion B2
St Bartholomew's A3
St James's St C3
St Nicholas Rd B2
St Nicholas' B2
St Peter's A3
Sea Life Brighton C3
Shaftesbury Rd A3
Ship St C2
Sillwood Rd B1
Sillwood St B1
Southover St A3
Spring Gardens B2
Stanford Rd A1
Stanley Rd A3
Surrey St B2
Sussex St B3
Swimming Pool B3
Sydney St B3
Temple Gardens B1
Terminus Rd A2
Theatre Royal B2
Tidy St B2
Town Hall C2
Toy & Model Mus A2
Trafalgar St B2
Union Rd A3
University of Brighton B3
Upper Lewes Rd A3
Upper North St B1
Viaduct Rd A3
Victoria Gardens B3
Victoria Rd B1
Volk's Electric Railway ✦ C3
West Pier (derelict) C1
West St C2
Western Rd B1
Whitecross St B2
YHA C3
York Place B3
York Rd B1

Bristol 332

Acramans Rd C4
Albert Rd C6
Alfred Hill A4
All Saint's St A4
All Saints' B4
Allington Rd C3
Alpha Rd C4
Ambra Vale B1
Ambra Vale East B2
Ambrose Rd B2
Amphitheatre & Waterfront Square ✦ C4
Anchor Rd B3
Anvil St B6
Arcade, The A5
Architecture Centre, The ✦ B4
Argyle Place B2
Arlington Villas A2
Arnolfini ✦ B4
Art Gallery A3
Ashton Gate Rd C2
Ashton Rd C1
Avon Bridge C1
Avon Crescent C1
Avon St B6
Baldwin St B4
Baltic Wharf C2
Baltic Wharf Leisure Ctr & Caravan Park ✦ C2
Baltic Wharf Marina C2
Barossa Place C4
Barton Manor B6
Barton Rd B6
Barton Vale B6
Bath Rd C6
Bathurst Basin C4
Bathurst Parade C4
Beauley Rd C3
Bedminster Bridge C5
Bedminster Parade C4
Bellevue B2
Bellevue Crescent B2
Bellevue Rd C6
Berkeley Place A2
Berkeley Square A3
Birch Rd C2
Blackfriars A4
Bond St A5
Braggs Lane A6
Brandon Hill B3
Brandon Steep B3
Bristol Aquarium B4
Bristol Beacon B4
Bristol Bridge B5
Bristol Cath (CE) B3
Bristol Eye Hospital (A&E) A4
Bristol Grammar School A3
Bristol Harbour Railway C3
Bristol Royal Children's Hospital A4
Bristol Royal Infirmary (A&E) A4
Bristol Temple Meads Station B6
Broad Plain B6
Broad Quay B4
Broad St A4
Broad Weir A5
Broadcasting House A3
Broadmead A5

Brunel Institute ✦ B3
Brunel Way C1
Brunswick Square A5
Burton Close C5
Bus Station A4
Butts Rd A3
Cabot Circus A5
Cabot Tower ✦ B3
Caledonia Place B1
Callowhill Court A5
Cambridge St C6
Camden Rd C3
Camp Rd A1
Canada Way C2
Cannon St A4
Canon's Way B3
Cantock's Close A3
Canynge Rd A1
Canynge Square A1
Castle Park A5
Castle St A5
Cathedral Walk B3
Catherine Meade St C4
Cattle Market Rd C6
Central Library B3
Charles Place B1
Charlotte St B3
Charlotte St South B3
Chatterton House B5
Chatterton Square C5
Chatterton St C5
Cheese Lane B5
Christchurch A4
Christchurch Rd A1
Christmas Steps ✦ A4
Church Lane B2/B5
Church St B5
City Museum A3
City of Bristol College B3
Civil and Family Justice Centre B5
Clare St B4
Clarence Rd C5
Cliff Rd C1
Clift House Rd C1
Clifton Cath (RC) ✝ A2
Clifton Down A1
Clifton Down Rd A1
Clifton Hill B2
Clifton Park A1/A2
Clifton Park Rd A1
Clifton Rd A2
Clifton Vale B1
Cliftonwood Crescent B2
Cliftonwood Rd B2
Cliftonwood Terrace B2
Cobblestone Mews A1
College Green B3
College Rd A1
College St B3
Colston Almshouses A4
Colston Avenue B4
Colston Parade C5
Colston St A4
Commercial Rd C4
Constitution Hill B2
Cooperage Lane C2
Corn St B4
Cornwallis Avenue B1
Cornwallis Crescent B1
Coronation Rd C2/C4
Council House B3
Counterslip B5
Create Centre, The ✦ C1
Crosby Row B2
Crown Court A4
Culver St B3
Cumberland Basin C1
Cumberland Close C2
Cumberland Rd C2/C3
Dean Lane C4
Deanery Rd B3
Denmark St B4
Dowry Square B1
Eaton Crescent A2
Elmdale Rd A3
Elton Rd A3
Eugene St A4/A6
Exchange and St Nicholas' Markets, The B4
Fairfax St A4
Fire Station B5
Floating Harbour C3
Fosseway, The A2
Foster Almshouses A4
Frayne Rd C1
Frederick Place A2
Freeland Place B1
Friary B5
Frogmore St B3
Fry's Hill B2
Galleries shopping centre, The A5
Gas Lane B6
Gasferry Rd C3
Georgian House B3
Glendale B1
Glentworth Rd B2
Gloucester St A1
Goldney Hall B2
Goldney Rd B1
Gordon Rd A2
Granby Hill B1
Grange Rd A1
Great Ann St A6
Great George Rd B3
Great George St A6/B3
Green St North B1
Green St South B1
Greenay Bush Lane C2
Greenbank Rd C2
Greville Smyth Park C1
Grove, The B4
Guildhall A4
Guinea St C4
Hamilton Rd C3
Hanbury Rd A2
Hanover Place C2
Harley Place A1
Haymarket A5
Hensman's Hill B1
High St B4
Highbury Villas A3
Hill St B3
Hill St C6
Hippodrome B4
Hopechapel Hill B1
Horfield Rd A4
Horsefair, The A5
Horton St B6
Host St A4
Hotwell Rd B1/B2
Houlton St A6
Howard Rd C3
IMAX Cinema B4
Islington Rd C3
Jacob St A5/A6
Jacob's Wells Rd B2
John Carr's Terrace B2
John Wesley's Chapel A5
Joy Hill B1
Jubilee St B6
Kensington Place A2
Kilkenny St B6
King St B4
Kingsland Rd B6
Kingston Rd C3
Lamb St A6
Lansdown Rd A2
Lawford St A6
Lawfords Gate A6
Leighton Rd C3
Lewins Mead A4
Lime Rd C2
Litfield Rd A1
Little Ann St A6
Little Caroline Place B1
Little George St A6
Little King St B4
Llandoger Trow B4
Lloyds' Building, The C3
Lodge St A4
Lord Mayor's Chapel, The B4
Lower Castle St A5
Lower Church Lane A4
Lower Clifton Hill B2
Lower Guinea St C4
Lower Lamb St B3
Lower Maudlin St A4
Lower Park Rd A4
Lower Sidney St C2
Lucky Lane C4
Lydstep Terrace C3
M Shed C4
Magistrates' Court A4
Manilla Rd A1
Mardyke Ferry Rd C2
Maritime Heritage Centre B3
Marlborough Hill A4
Marlborough St A4
Marsh St B4
Mead St C5
Merchant Dock B2
Merchant Seamen's Almshouses B4
Merchant St A5
Merchants Rd A1
Merchants Rd C1
Meridian Place A2
Meridian Vale A2
Merrywood Rd C3
Midland Rd A6
Milford St C3
Millennium Promenade B3
Millennium Square B3
Mitchell Lane B5
Mortimer Rd A1
Murray Rd C4
Myrtle Rd A3
Narrow Plain B5
Narrow Quay B4
Nelson St A4
New Charlotte St C4
New Kingsley Rd B6
New Queen St C5
New St A6
Newgate A5
Newton St A6
Norland Rd A1
North St C2
O2 Academy B3
Oakfield Grove A2
Oakfield Place A2
Oakfield Rd A2
Old Bread St B6
Old Market St A6
Old Park Hill A4
Oldfield Rd B1
Orchard Avenue B4
Orchard Lane B4
Orchard St B4
Osbourne Rd C3
Oxford St B6
Park Place A2
Park Rd C3
Park Row A3
Park St A3
Passage St B5
Pembroke Grove A2
Pembroke Rd A2
Pembroke Rd C3
Pembroke St A5
Penn St A5
Pennywell Rd A6
Percival Rd A1
Pero's Bridge B4
Perry Rd A4
Phipps St C2
Pip 'n' Jay B5
Plimsoll Bridge B1
Polygon Rd B1
Portland St A1
Portwall Lane B5
Post Office A1/A3/A5/ B1/B4/C4/C5
Prewett St C5
Prince St B4
Prince St Bridge C4
Princess St C5
Princess Victoria St B1
Priory Rd A3
Pump Lane C5
QEH Theatre A2
Quakers Friars A5
Quay St A4
Queen Charlotte St B4
Queen Elizabeth Hospital School B2
Queen Square B4
Queen St A5
Queen's Avenue A3
Queen's Parade B3
Queen's Rd A2/A3
Raleigh Rd C2
Randall Rd B2
Red Lodge A4
Redcliffe Backs B5
Redcliffe Bridge B4
Redcliffe Hill C5
Redcliffe Parade C4
Redcliffe St B5
Redcliffe Way B5
Redcross St A6
Redgrave Theatre A1
Regent St B1
Richmond Hill A2
Richmond Hill Avenue A2
Richmond Lane A2
Richmond Park Rd A2
Richmond St C6
Richmond Terrace A2
River St A6
Rownham Mead B2
Royal Fort Rd A3
Royal Park A2
Royal West of England Academy A3
Royal York Crescent B1
Royal York Villas B1
Rupert St A4
Russ St B6
St Andrew's Walk B2
St George's B3
St George's Rd B3
St James A4
St John's A4
St John's Rd C4
St Luke's Rd C5
St Mary Redcliffe C5
St Matthias Park A6
St Michael's Hill A3
St Michael's Hosp A3
St Michael's Park A3
St Nicholas St B4
St Paul St A5
St Paul's Rd A2
St Peter's (ruin) A5
St Philip's Bridge B5
St Philips Rd A6
St Stephen's B4
St Stephen's St B4
St Thomas St B5
St Thomas the Martyr B5
Sandford Rd B1
Sargent St C5
Saville Place B1
Ship Lane C5
Shopmobility A5
Showcase Cinema de Lux A5
Silver St A4
Sion Hill A1
Small St A4
Smeaton Rd C1
Somerset Square C5
Somerset St C5
Southernhay Avenue B2
Southville Rd C4
Spike Island Artspace C2
Spring St C5
Superstore C4
SS Great Britain and the Matthew B2
Stackpool Rd C3
Staight St B6
Stillhouse Lane C4
Sydney Row C2
Tankard's Close A3
Temple Back B5
Temple Back East B5
Temple Bridge B5
Temple Church B5
Temple Circus B5
Temple Gate C5
Temple St B5
Temple Way B5
Terrell St A4
Theatre Royal (Bristol Old Vic) B4
Thekla B4
Thomas Lane B5
Three Kings of Cologne A4
Three Queens Lane B5
Tobacco Factory, The C2
Tower Hill B5
Tower Lane A4
Trenchard St A4
Triangle South A3
Triangle West A3
Trinity Rd A6
Trinity St A6
Tyndall Avenue A3
Union St A5
Union St B6
Unity St A6
Unity St B3
University of Bristol A3
University Rd A3
Upper Byron Place A3
Upper Maudlin St A4
Upper Perry Hill C3
Upton Rd C2
Valentine Bridge B6
Victoria Grove C5
Victoria Rd C6
Victoria Rooms A2
Victoria Square A2
Victoria St B5
Vyvyan Rd A1
Vyvyan Terrace A1
Wade St A6
Walter St C2
Wapping Rd C4
Water Lane B5
Waterloo Rd A6
Waterloo St A1
Waterloo St A6
Watershed Media Centre ✦ B4
We the Curious ✦ B3
Welling Terrace B1
Welsh Back B4
West Mall A1
West St A6
Westfield Place A1
Wetherell Place A2
Whitehouse Place C5
Whitehouse St C5
Whiteladies Rd A2
Whitson St A4
William St C5
Willway St C5
Windsor Place B1
Wine St A4
Woodland Rd A3
Woodland Rise A3
Worcester Rd A1
Worcester Terrace A1
YHA B4
York Gardens B1
York Place A2
York Rd C5

Bury St Edmunds 332

Abbey Gardens B3
Abbey Gate B3
Abbeygate B2
Abbeygate St B2
Albert Crescent B1
Albert St B1
Angel Hill B2
Angel Lane B2
Anglian Lane A1
Arc Shopping Centre B2
Athenaeum C2
Baker's Lane C3
Barwell Rd B3
Beetons Way A1
Bishops Rd B2
Bloomfield St B2
Bridewell Lane C2
Bullen Close C1
Bury St Edmunds ≷ A2
Bury St Edmunds County Upper Sch A1
Bury St Edmunds Leisure Centre B1
Bury Town FC (Ram Meadow) B3
Bus Station B2
Business Park B3
Butter Market B2
Cannon St B2
Castle Rd C1
Cemetery C1
Chalk Rd (N) B1
Chalk Rd (S) B1
Church Row B2
Churchgate St C2
Citizens Advice Bureau B2
College St C2
Compiegne Way A3
Corn Exchange, The B2
Cornfield Rd B1
Cotton Lane B3
Courts B2
Covent Garden C2
Crown St C3
Cullum Rd C2
Eastern Way A3
Eastgate St B3
Enterprise Bsns Park A2
Etna Rd A2
Eyre Close C2
Fire & Ambulance Sta B1
Friar's Lane C2
Gage Close A1
Garland St B2
Greene King Brewery C3
Grove Park B1
Grove Rd B1
Guildhall C2
Guildhall St C2
Hatter St C2
High Baxter St B2
Honey Hill C2
Hospital Rd C1/C2
Ickworth Drive C1
Industrial Estate A3
Information Centre B2
Ipswich St A2
King Edward VI Sch A1
King's Rd C1/B2
Library B2
Long Brackland A2
Looms Lane B2
Lwr Baxter St B2
Malthouse Lane A2
Manor House C3
Maynewater Lane C3
Mill Rd C1
Mill Rd (South) C1
Minden Close B3
Moyse's Hall B2
Mustow St B3
Norman Tower C3
Northgate Avenue A2
Northgate St B2
Osier Rd A2
Out Northgate A2
Out Risbygate B1
Out Westgate C2
Parkway B1/C2
Parkway, The B1
Peckham St B2
Petticoat Lane C1
Phoenix Day Hosp C1
Pinners Way C1
Police Station C3
Post Office B2
Pump Lane B2
Queen's Rd B1
Raingate St C3
Raynham Rd A1
Retail Park C2
Risbygate St B1/B2
Robert Boby Way C2
St Andrew's St North B2
St Andrew's St South B2
St Botolph's Lane C3
St Edmund's C2
St Edmund's Abbey (Remains) ✦ B3
St Edmunds Hospital (Private) C3
St Edmundsbury ✝ C3
St John's St B2
St Marys C3
School Hall Lane B2
Shillitoe Close C1
South Close C1
Southgate St C3
Sparhawk St C3
Spring Lane B1
Springfield Rd B1
Station Hill A2
Swan Lane C3
Tayfen Rd B2
Theatre Royal C3
Thingoe Hill A2
Victoria St B1
Vinefields, The B3
War Memorial ✦ C1
Well St B2
West Suffolk College B1
Westgarth Gardens C1
Westgate St C2
Whiting St C2
York Rd B1
York Terrace B1

Cambridge 333

Abbey Rd A3
ADC A2
Anglia Ruskin Univ B3
Archaeology & Anthropology B2
Arts Picturehouse B2
Arts Theatre B1
Auckland Rd A3
Backs, The B1
Bateman St C2
Benet St B1
Bradmore St B3
Bridge St A1
Broad St B3
Brookside C2
Brunswick Terrace A3
Burleigh St B3
Bus Station B2
Butt Green A2
Cambridge Contemporary Art Gallery B1
Castle Mound ✦ A1
Castle St A1
Cemetery B3
Chesterton Lane A1
Christ's (College) B2
Christ's Lane B2
Christ's Pieces B2
City Rd B3
Clare Bridge B1
Clare (College) B1
Clarendon St B2
Coe Fen C2
Coronation St C2
Corpus Christi (Coll) B1
Court A3
Cross St C3
Crusoe Bridge C1
Darwin (College) C1
Devonshire Rd C3
Downing (College) C2
Downing St B2
Earl St B2
East Rd B3
Eden St B3
Elizabeth Way A3
Elm St B2
Emery St B3
Emmanuel (College) B2
Emmanuel Rd B2
Emmanuel St B2
Fair St A3
Fen Causeway, The C1
Fenner's Cricket Gd C3
Fire Station B3
Fitzroy St A3
Fitzwilliam Mus C2
Fitzwilliam St C2
Garrett Hostel Bridge B1
Glisson Rd C3
Gonville & Caius (Coll) B1
Gonville Place C2
Grafton Centre, The A3
Grand Arcade B2
Green St B1
Gresham Rd C3
Guest Rd B3
Guildhall B2
Harvey Rd C3
Hills Rd C3
Hobson St B2
Hughes Hall (College) B3
James St A3
Jesus (College) A2
Jesus Green A2
Jesus Lane A2
Jesus Terrace B3
John St B3
Kelsey Kerridge Sports Centre B3
Kettle's Yard A1
King's Bridge B1
King St A2
King's (College) B1
King's Coll Chapel B1
King's Parade B1
Lammas Land Rec Gd C1
Lensfield Rd C2
Library B2
Lion Yard B2
Little St Mary's Lane B1
Lyndewod Rd C3
Magdalene (College) A1
Magdalene St A1
Maid's Causeway A3
Malcolm St A2
Market St B1
Mathematical Bridge B1
Mawson Rd C3
Midsummer Common A3
Mill Lane B1
Mill Rd B3
Mill St C3
Mumford B3
Mus of Cambridge A1
Museum of Classical Archaeology C1
Napier St A3
New Square A2
Newmarket Rd A3
Newnham Rd C1
Norfolk St B3
Northampton St A1
Norwich St C2
Orchard St B2
Panton St C2
Paradise St B3
Park Parade A1
Park St A2
Park Terrace B2
Parker St B2
Parker's Piece B2
Parkside B3
Parkside Pools B3
Parsonage St A3
Pea's Hill B1
Pemberton Terrace C2
Pembroke (College) B2
Pembroke St B1
Perowne St B3
Peterhouse (College) C1
Petty Cury B2
Polar Museum, The C2
Police Station B3
Post Office A3/B2/C1/C2/C3
Queen's Lane B1
Queen's Rd B1
Queens' (College) B1
Regent St B2
Regent Terrace B2
Ridley Hall (College) C1
Riverside A3
Round Church, The A1
Russell St C2
St Andrew's St B2
St Benet's B1
St Catharine's (Coll) B1
St Eligius St C2
St John's (College) A1
St Mary's B1
St Paul's Rd C3
Saxon St C2
Sedgwick Museum B2
Sheep's Green C1
Shire Hall A1
Sidgwick Avenue C1
Sidney St A2
Sidney Sussex (Coll) A2
Silver St B1
Station Rd C3
Tenison Avenue C3
Tenison Rd C3
Tennis Court Rd B2
Thompson's Lane A1
Trinity (College) A1
Trinity Bridge B1
Trinity Hall (College) B1
Trinity St B1
Trumpington Rd C2
Trumpington St B1
Union Rd C2
University Botanic Gardens C2
Victoria Avenue A2
Victoria St B2
Warkworth St B3
Warkworth Terrace B3
Wesley House (Coll) A2
West Rd B1
Westcott House (Coll) A2
Westminster (Coll) A1
Whipple B2
Willis Rd B3
Willow Walk A2
YMCA C3
Zoology B2

Canterbury 333

Artillery St B2
Barton Mill Rd A3
Beaconsfield Rd A1
Beaney, The B2
Beverley Meadow A1
Beverley Rd A1
Bingley's Island B1
Black Griffin Lane B1
Broad Oak Rd A2
Broad St B2
Brymore Rd A3
Burgate B2
Bus Station C2
Canterbury Castle C1
Canterbury Christ Church University B3
Canterbury College C3
Canterbury East ≷ C1
Canterbury Tales, The ✦ B2
Canterbury West ≷ A1
Castle Row C1
Castle St C1
Cathedral ✝ B2
Causeway, The A2
Chaucer Rd A3
Christchurch Gate ✦ B2
City Council Offices A3
City Wall B2
Coach park A2
College Rd B3
Cossington Rd C2
Court B2
Craddock Rd A3
Crown & County Courts B3
Dane John Gardens C2
Dane John Mound ✦ C1
Deanery B2
Dover St C2
Duck Lane B2
Eastbridge Hosp B1
Edgar Rd B3
Ersham Rd C3
Ethelbert Rd C3
Fire Station C2
Forty Acres Rd A1
Friars, The B2
Gordon Rd C1
Greyfriars ✦ B1
Guildford Rd C1
Havelock St B2
Heaton Rd C1
High St B2
Information Ctr A2/B2
Ivy Lane B2
New St C1
King St B2
King's School B2/B3
King's School Recreation Ctr, The A2
Kingsmead Leisure Ctr A2
Kingsmead Rd A2
Kirby's Lane B1
Lansdown Rd C2
Lime Kiln Rd C1
Longport B3
Lower Chantry Lane C3
Mandeville Rd A1
Market Way A2
Marlowe Arcade B2
Marlowe Avenue C2
Marlowe Theatre B2
Martyrs Field Rd C1
Mead Way B1
Military Rd B2
Monastery St B2
Museum of Canterbury (Rupert Bear Mus) B1
New Dover Rd C3
New St C1
Norman Rd C2
North Holmes Rd B3
North Lane B1
Northgate A2
Nunnery Fields C2
Nunnery Rd C2
Oaten Hill C2
Odeon Cinema C2
Old Dover Rd C2
Old Palace B2
Old Ruttington Lane B2
Old Weavers B2
Orchard St B1
Oxford Rd C1
Palace St B2
Pilgrims Way C3
Pin Hill C1
Pine Tree Avenue A1
Police Station C2
Post Office B2, C1
Pound Lane B1
Puckle Lane C2
Raymond Avenue C2
Recreation Ground A2
Registry Office A2
Rheims Way B1
Rhodaus Close C2
Rhodaus Town C2
Roman Museum B2
Roper Gateway A1
Roper Rd A1
Rose Lane B2
Shopmobility B2
St Augustine's Abbey (remains) ✝ B3
St Augustine's Rd C3
St Dunstan's A1
St Dunstan's St A1
St George's Place C2
St George's St B2
St George's Tower ✦ B2
St Gregory's Rd B3
St John's Hospital A2
St Margaret's St B2
St Martin's B3
St Martin's Avenue B3
St Martin's Rd B3
St Michael's Rd A1
St Mildred's C1
St Peter's Grove B1
St Peter's Lane B2
St Peter's Place B1
St Peter's St B1
St Radigunds St B2
St Stephen's Court A1
St Stephen's Path A1
St Stephen's Rd A2
Salisbury Rd A1
Simmonds Rd C1
Spring Lane C3
Station Rd West B1
Stour St B1
Sturry Rd A3
Tourtel Rd A3
Tudor Rd C1
Union St B2
University for the Creative Arts C3
Vernon Place C2
Victoria Rd C1
Watling St B2
Westgate Gardens B1
Westgate Towers B1
Whitefriars B2
Whitehall Gardens B1
Whitehall Rd B1
Wincheap C1
York Rd C1
Zealand Rd C2

Cardiff Caerdydd 333

Adam St B3
Alexandra Gardens A2
Allerton St C1
Arran St A3
ATRiuM (University of Glamorgan) C3
Beauchamp St C1
Bedford St A3
Blackfriars Priory (rems) ✝ B1
Boulevard De Nantes B2
Brains Brewery C2
Brook St B1
Bute Park A1
Bute St C2
Bute Terrace C3
Callaghan Square C2/C3
Capitol Shopping Centre, The B3
Cardiff Arms Park (Cardiff Blues) B1
Cardiff Bridge B1
Cardiff Castle B2
Cardiff Central Sta ≷ C2
Cardiff Story, The B2
Cardiff Univ A1/A2/B3
Cardiff University Student's Union A2
Caroline St C2
Castle Green B2
Castle Mews A1
Castle St (Heol y Castell) B1
Cathays Station ≷ A2
Celerity Drive C3
Central Library C2
Charles St (Heol Siarl) B3
Churchill Way B3
City Hall A2
City Rd A3
Clare Rd C1
Clare St C1
Coburn St A3
Coldstream Terrace B1
College Rd A1
Colum Rd A1
Court C2
Court Rd C1
Craiglee Drive C3
Cranbrook St A3
Customhouse St C2
Cyfartha St A3
Despenser Place C1
Despenser St C1
Dinas St C1
Duke St (Heol y Dug) B2
Dumfries Place B3
East Grove A3
Ellen St C3
Fire Station B3
Fitzalan Place B3
Fitzhamon Emb C1
Fitzhamon Lane C1
Friary, The B2
g39 B2
Gloucester St C1
Glynrhondda St A2
Gordon Rd A3
Gorsedd Gardens B2
Green St B1
Greyfriars Rd B2
Hafod St C1
Hayes, The B2
Herbert St C3
High St B2
HM Prison B3
Industrial Estate C3
Information Centre B2
John St C3
Jubilee St C1
King Edward VII Ave A1
Kingsway (Ffordd y Brenin) B2
Knox Rd B3
Law Courts B2
Llanbleddian Gdns A2
Llantwit St A2
Lloyd George Avenue C3
Lower Cathedral Rd B1
Lowther Rd A3
Magistrates Court B3
Mansion House A3
Mardy St C1
Mark St B1
Market B2
Mary Ann St C3
Merches Gardens C1
Mill Lane C2
Millennium Bridge B1
Miskin St A2
Monmouth St C1
Motorpoint Arena Cardiff ✦ C3
Museum Avenue A2
Museum Place A2
National Museum Cardiff A2
National War Meml ✦ A2
Neville Place C1
New Theatre B2
Newport Rd B3
Northcote Lane A3
Northcote St A3
Parade, The A3
Park Grove A4
Park Place A2
Park St C2
Penarth Rd C2
Pendyris St C1
Plantaganet St C1
Post Office B2
Principality Stadium C1
Principality Stadium Tours (Gate 3) ✦ B2
Quay St B2
Queen's Arcade B2
Queen Anne Square A1
Queen St (Heol y Frenhines) B2
Queen St Station ≷ B3
Regimental Museums B2
Rhymney St A3
Richmond Rd A3
Royal Welsh College of Music and Drama A1
Russell St A3
Ruthin Gardens A2
St Andrews Place A2
St David's B2/C2
St David's ✝ B2
St David's Hall ✦ B2
St John the Baptist B2
St Mary St (Heol Eglwys Fair) B2
St Peter's St A3
Salisbury Rd A3
Sandon St B3
Schooner Way C3
Scott Rd C2
Scott St C2
Senghennydd Rd A2
Sherman Theatre A2
Sophia Gardens A1
Sophia Gardens Stadium ✦ A1
South Wales Baptist College A3
Sport Wales National Centre ✦ A1
Stafford Rd C1
Stadium Plaza C1
Station Terrace B3
Stuttgarter Strasse B2
Sussex St C1
Taffs Mead Embankment C1
Talworth St A3
Temple of Peace & Health ✦ A1
Treharris St A3
Trinity St B2
Tudor Lane C1
Tudor St C1
Tyndall St C3
Vue C1
Walk, The A3
Welsh Government A1
West Grove A3
Westgate St (Heol y Porth) B2
Windsor Place B3
Womanby St B2
Wood St C2
Working St B2
Wyeverne Rd A2

Carlisle 333

Abbey St A1
Aglionby St B3
Albion St C3
Alexander St C3
AMF Bowl ✦ C2
Annetwell St A1
Bank St B2
Bitts Park A1
Blackfriars St B2
Blencome St C1
Blunt St C1
Botchergate B2
Boustead's Grassing C2
Bowman St B3
Bridge St A1
Broad St B3
Brook St C3
Brunswick St B2
Bus Station B2
Caldew Bridge A1
Caldew St C1
Carlisle (Citadel) Station ≷ B2
Carlisle College A2
Castle A1
Castle St A1
Castle Way A1
Cathedral ✝ A1
Cecil St B2
Chapel St A2
Charles St B3
Charlotte St B1
Chatsworth Square A2
Chiswick St B2
Citadel, The ✦ B2
City Walls A1
Civic Centre A2
Clifton St C1
Close St B3
Collingwood St C1
Colville St C1
Colville Terrace C1
Council Offices B3
Court B2
Court St B2
Crosby St B2
Crown St C2
Currock Rd C2
Dacre Rd A1

Dale St C1
Denton St C1
Devonshire Walk A1
Duke's Rd A2
East Dale St C1
East Norfolk St C1
Eden Bridge A2
Edward St B3
Elm St B1
English St B2
Fire Station A2
Fisher St A1
Flower St B2
Freer St C1
Fusehill St A3
Georgian Way A2
Gloucester Rd C3
Golf Course A2
Graham St C1
Grey St B3
Guildhall Museum A2
Halfey's Lane B3
Hardwicke Circus A2
Hart St B3
Hewson St C2
Howard Place A3
Howe St B3
Information Centre A2
James St B2
Junction St B1
King St B2
Lancaster St B2
Lanes Shopping Centre, The B2
Laser Quest ✦ B2
Library A2
Lime St B1
Lindisfarne St C3
Linton St B3
Lismore Place A3
Lismore St B3
London Rd C3
Lonsdale Rd B2
Lord St C3
Lorne Crescent B1
Lorne St B1
Lowther St B2
Madford Retail Park B1
Magistrates' Court A2
Market Hall A2
Mary St B2
Memorial Bridge A3
Metcalfe St C1
Milbourne St B1
Myddleton St B3
Nelson St C1
Norfolk St C1
Old Fire Sta, The A2
Old Town Hall A2
Oswald St C3
Peter St A2
Petteril St B3
Pools B2
Portland Place B2
Portland Square B2
Post Office A2/B2/C1/C3
Princess St C2
Pugin St B1
Red Bank Terrace C2
Regent St C3
Richardson St C1
Rickerby Park A3
Rickergate A2
River St B3
Rome St C2
Rydal St B3
St Cuthbert's B2
St Cuthbert's Lane B2
St James' Park C1
St James' Rd C1
St Nicholas Gate Retail Park C3
St Nicholas St C3
Sands Centre, The A2
Scotch St A2
Shaddongate B1
Sheffield St B1
Shopmobility A2
South Henry St B3
South John St C2
South St B3
Spencer St B2
Station Retail Park B2
Strand Rd A2
Superstore B1
Sybil St B3
Tait St B2
Thomas St B1
Thomson St C3
Trafalgar St C1
Trinity Leisure Centre A2
Tullie Museum & Art Gallery A1
Tyne St C3
University of Cumbria B3
Viaduct Estate Rd B1
Victoria Place A2
Victoria Viaduct B2
Vue B2
Warwick Rd B2
Warwick Square B3
Water St B2
West Walls B1
Westmorland St C1

Chelmsford 333

Anchor St C1
Anglia Ruskin Univ A2
Arbour Lane B3
Baddow Rd B2/C3
Baker St C1
Barrack Square B2
Bellmead B2
Bishop Hall Lane A2
Bishop Rd A2
Bond St B2
Boswells Drive B3
Bouverie Rd C2
Bradford St C1
Braemar Avenue C1
Brook St A2
Broomfield Rd A1
Burgess Springs B1
Burns Crescent C2
Bus Station B1/B2
Cedar Avenue A1
Cedar Avenue West A1
Cemetery A1
Cemetery A2
Cemetery C1
Central Park B1
Chelmsford ✝ B2
Chelmsford A1
Chichester Drive A3
Chinery Close A3
City Council A1
Civic Centre A1
Civic Theatre B1
Cloudfm County Cricket Ground, The B2
College C1
Cottage Place A2
County Hall B2
Coval Avenue B1
Coval Lane B1
Coval Wells B1
Crown Court B2
Duke St B2
Elm Rd C1
Elms Drive A1
Essex Record Office, The B3
Fairfield Rd B1
Falcons Mead B1
George St C2
Glebe Rd A1
Godfrey's Mews C2
Goldlay Avenue C3
Goldlay Rd C2
Grove Rd C2
Hall St C2
Hamlet Rd C2
Hart St C1
Henry Rd A2
High Bridge Rd B2
High Chelmer Shopping Centre B2
High St B2
Hill Crescent B3
Hill Rd B3
Hill Rd Sth B3
Hillview Rd A3
HM Prison A3
Hoffmans Way A2
Hospital B2
Lady Lane C2
Langdale Gardens C3
Legg St B2
Library B2
Lionfield Terrace A3
Lower Anchor St C1
Lynmouth Avenue C2
Lynmouth Gardens C3
Magistrates Court B2
Maltese Rd A1
Manor Rd C2
Marconi Rd A2
Market B2
Market Rd B2
Marlborough Rd C1
Meadows Shopping Centre, The B2
Meadowside A3
Mews Court C2
Mildmay Rd C2
Moulsham Drive C2
Moulsham Mill ✦ C3
Moulsham St C1/C2
Navigation Rd B3
New London Rd B2/C1
New St A2/B2
New Writtle St C1
Nursery Rd C2
Orchard St C2
Odeon B2
Parker Rd C2
Parklands Drive A3
Parkway A1/B1/B2
Police Station A2
Post Office B2/C2
Primrose Hill A1
Prykes Drive B1
Queen St C1
Queen's Rd B3
Railway St A1
Rainsford Rd A1
Ransomes Way A2
Rectory Lane A2
Regina Rd A2
Riverside Ice & Leisure Centre B2
Riverside Retail Park A3
Rosebery Rd C2
Rothesay Avenue C1
St John's Rd C2
Sandringham Place B3
Seymour St B1
Shopmobility B2
Shrublands Close B3
Southborough Rd C1
Springfield Rd A3/B2/B3
Stapleford Close C1
Superstore B2/C3
Swiss Avenue A1
Telford Place A3
Tindal St B2
Townfield St A1
Trinity Rd B3
University B1
Upper Bridge Rd C1
Upper Roman Rd C2
Van Dieman's Rd C3
Viaduct Rd B1
Vicarage Rd C1
Victoria Rd A2
Victoria Rd South B2
Vincents Rd C2
Waterloo Lane B2
Weight Rd B3
Westfield Avenue A1
Wharf Rd B3
Writtle Rd C1
YMCA A2
York Rd C1

Cheltenham 333

Albert Rd A3
Albion St B3
All Saints Rd B3
Ambrose St B2
Andover Rd C1
Back Montpellier Terr C2
Bandstand ✦ C2
Bath Parade B2
Bath Rd C2
Bays Hill Rd C1
Bennington St B2
Berkeley St B3
Brewery Quarter, The A2
Brunswick St South A2
Bus Station B2
Carlton St B3
Central Cross Road A3
Cheltenham College C2
Cheltenham FC A3
Cheltenham General (A&E) C3
Cheltenham Ladies' College B2
Christchurch Rd B1
Cineworld A2
Clarence Rd A2
Clarence Square A2
Clarence St B2
Cleeveland St A1
College Baths Road C3
College Rd C2
Colletts Drive A2
Corpus St C3
Devonshire St A2
Douro Rd B1
Duke St B3
Dunalley Parade A2
Dunalley St A2
Everyman B2
Evesham Rd A3
Fairview Rd B3
Fairview St B3
Fire Station C3
Folly Lane A2
Gloucester Rd A1
Grosvenor St B3
Grove St A1
Hanover St A2
Hatherley St C1
Henrietta St A2
Hewlett Rd B3
High St B2/B3
Holst Birthplace Museum A3
Hudson St A2
Imperial Gardens C2
Imperial Lane B2
Imperial Square C2
Information Centre B2
Keynsham Rd C3
King St A2
Knapp Rd B2
Lansdown Crescent C1
Lansdown Rd C1
Leighton Rd B3
Library B2
London Rd C3
Lypiatt Rd C1
Magistrates' Court & Register Office B1
Malvern Rd B1
Manser St A2
Market St A1
Marle Hill Parade A2
Marle Hill Rd A2
Millbrook St A1
Milsom St A2
Montpellier Gardens C2
Montpellier Grove C2
Montpellier Parade C2
Montpellier Spa Rd C2
Montpellier St C1
Montpellier Terrace C2
Montpellier Walk C2
New St B2
North Place B2
Old Bath Rd C3
Oriel Rd B2
Overton Park Rd B1
Overton Rd B1
Oxford St C3
Parabola Rd B1
Park Place C1
Park St A1
Pittville Circus A3
Pittville Crescent A3
Pittville Lawn A3
Pittville Park A2
Playhouse B2
Portland St B3
Prestbury Rd A3
Prince's Rd C1
Priory St B3
Promenade B2
Queen St A1
Recreation Ground A2
Regent Arcade B2
Regent St B2
Rodney Rd B2
Royal Crescent B2
Royal Well Place B2
Royal Wells Rd B2
St George's Place B2
St Georges Rd B1
St Gregory's B2
St James St B3
St John's Avenue B3
St Luke's Rd C2
St Margarets Rd A2
St Mary's B2
St Matthew's B2
St Paul's Lane A2
St Paul's Rd A2
St Paul's St A2
St Stephen's Rd C1
Sandford Parks Lido C3
Sandford Mill Road C3
Sandford Park C3
Sandford Rd C2
Selkirk St A3
Sherborne Place B3
Sherborne St B3
Suffolk Parade C2
Suffolk Rd C1
Suffolk Square C1
Sun St A1
Swindon Rd B2
Sydenham Villas Rd C3
Tewkesbury Rd A1
The Courtyard B1
Thirlstaine Rd C2
Tivoli Rd C1
Tivoli St C1
Town Hall & Theatre B2
Townsend St A1
Trafalgar St C2
Union St B3
Univ of Gloucestershire (Francis Close Hall) A2
Univ of Gloucestershire (Hardwick) A1
Victoria Place B3
Victoria St A2
Vittoria Walk C2
Wellesley Rd A2
Wellington Rd A3
Wellington Square A3
Wellington St B2
West Drive A3
Western Rd B1
Wilson, The B2
Winchcombe St B3
Winston Churchill Memorial Gardens A1

Chester 333

Abbey Gateway A2
Appleyards Lane C3
Bars, The B3
Bedward Row B1
Beeston View C3
Bishop Lloyd's Palace B2
Black Diamond St A2
Bottoms Lane C3
Boughton B3
Bouverie St A1
Bus Interchange A2
Bridge St B2
Bridgegate C2
Brook St A3
Brown's Lane C2
Cambrian Rd A1
Canal St A2
Carrick Rd C1
Castle C2
Castle Drive C2
Cathedral ✝ B2
Catherine St A1
Cheshire Military Museum C2
Chester A3
Cheyney Rd A1
Chichester St A1
City Rd A3
City Walls B1/B2
City Walls Rd B1
Cornwall St A2
Cross Hey C3
Cross, The ✦ B2
Crown Court C2
Cuppin St B2
Curzon Park North C1
Curzon Park South C1
Dee Basin A1
Dee Lane B3
Delamere St A2
Deva Roman Discovery Centre B2
Dingle, The C1
Duke St B2
Eastgate B2
Eastgate St B2
Eaton Rd C2
Edinburgh Way C3
Elizabeth Crescent B3
Fire Station A2
Foregate St B2
Forum Studio B2
Forum, The B2
Frodsham St B2
Gamul House B2
Garden Lane A1
George St A2
Gladstone Avenue A1
God's Providence House B2
Gorse Stacks A2
Greenway St C2
Grosvenor Bridge C1
Grosvenor Museum B2
Grosvenor Park B3
Grosvenor Park Terrace C1
Grosvenor Shopping Centre B2
Grosvenor St B2
Groves Rd B3
Groves, The B3
Guildhall Museum B1
Handbridge C2
Hartington St C3
Hoole Way A2
Hunter St B2
Information Centre B2
King Charles' Tower ✦ A2
King St A2
Library B2
Lightfoot St A3
Little Roodee C2
Liverpool Rd A2
Love St B3
Lower Bridge St B2
Lower Park Rd B3
Lyon St A2
Magistrates Court B2
Meadows Lane C3
Meadows, The B3
Milton St A3
Minerva Roman Shrine ✦ C2
Miniature Railway ✦ B3
New Crane St B1
Nicholas St B2
Northgate A2
Northgate Arena A2
Northgate St A2
Nun's Rd B1
Old Dee Bridge ✦ C2
Overleigh Rd C2
Park St B2
Police Station B2
Post Office A2/A3
Princess St B2
Queen St B2
Queen's Park Rd C3
Queen's Rd A3
Race Course B1
Raymond St A1
River Lane C2
Roman Amphitheatre & Gardens B2
Roodee (Chester Racecourse), The B1
Russell St A3
St Anne St A2
St George's Crescent C3
St Martin's Gate A1
St Martin's Way B1
St Oswalds Way A2
Saughall Rd A1
Sealand Rd A1
South View Rd A1
Stanley Palace B1
Station Rd A3
Steven St A3
Storyhouse B2
Superstore B2
Tower Rd B1
Town Hall B2
Union St B3
University of Chester C2
Vicar's Lane B2
Victoria Crescent C3
Victoria Rd A2
Walpole St A1
Water Tower St A1
Water Tower, The ✦ B1
Watergate B1
Watergate St B2
Whipcord Lane A1
White Friars B2
York St B3

Chichester 333

Adelaide Rd A3
Alexandra Rd A3
Arts Centre B2
Ave de Chartres B1/B2
Barlow Rd A1
Basin Rd C2
Beech Avenue B1
Bishops Palace Gardens B2
Bishopsgate Walk A3
Bramber Rd C3
Broyle Rd A2
Bus Station B2
Caledonian Rd B3
Cambrai Avenue B3
Canal Place C2
Canal Wharf C2
Canon Lane B2
Cathedral ✝ B2
Cavendish St A1
Cawley Rd B2
Cedar Drive A1
Chapel St A2
Cherry Orchard Rd C3
Chichester B2
Chichester By-Pass C2/C3
Chichester College B1
Chichester Cinema B3
Chichester Festival A2
Chichester Gate Leisure Park C1
Churchside A2
Cineworld C1
City Walls B2
Cleveland Rd B3
College Lane A2
Cory Close C2
Council Offices B2
County Hall B2
District B2
Duncan Rd A1
Durnford Close A1
East Pallant B2
East Row B2
East St B2
East Walls B3
Eastland Rd C3
Ettrick Close B3
Ettrick Rd B3
Exton Rd C3
Fire Station A2
Football Ground A2
Franklin Place A2
Friary (Rems of) A2
Garland Close C3
Green Lane A3
Grove Rd C3
Guilden Rd B3
Guildhall A2
Hawthorn Close A1
Hay Rd C3
Henty Gardens B1
Herald Drive C3
Hornet, The B3
Information Centre B2
John's St B2
Joys Croft A3
Jubilee Park A3
Jubilee Rd A3
Juxon Close B2
Kent Rd A3
King George Gardens A2
King's Avenue C2
Kingsham Avenue C3
Kingsham Rd C2
Laburnum Grove B2
Leigh Rd C1
Lennox Rd A3
Lewis Rd A3
Library B2
Lion St B2
Litten Terrace A3
Litten, The A3
Little London B2
Lyndhurst Rd B3
Market B3
Market Avenue B2
Market Cross B2
Market Rd B3
Melbourne Rd A3
Minerva B2
Mount Lane B1
New Park Rd A3
Newlands Lane A1
North Pallant B2
North St A2
North Walls A2
Northgate A2
Novium, The B2
Oak Avenue A1
Oak Close A1
Oaklands Park A2
Oaklands Way A2
Orchard Avenue A1
Orchard St A1
Ormonde Avenue B3
Pallant House B2
Parchment St A1
Parklands Rd A1/B1
Peter Weston Place B3
Police Station C2
Post Office A1/B2/C3
Priory Lane A2
Priory Park A2
Priory Rd A2
Queen's Avenue C1
Riverside A3
Roman Amphitheatre B3
St Cyriacs A2
St Martins' St B2
St Pancras A3
St Paul's Rd A2
St Richard's Hospital (A&E) A3
Shamrock Close A3
Sherbourne Rd A1
Somerstown A2
South Bank C2
South Downs Planetarium ✦ C2
South Pallant B2
South St B2
Southgate B2
Spitalfield Lane A3
Stirling Rd B3
Stockbridge Rd C1/C2
Swanfield Drive A3
Terminus Ind Est C1
Tower St A2
Tozer Way A3
Turnbull Rd A3
Upton Rd C1
Velyn Avenue B3
Via Ravenna B1
Walnut Avenue A1
West St B2
Westgate B1
Westgate Fields B1
Westgate Leisure Ctr B1
Weston Avenue C1
Whyke Close C3
Whyke Lane B3
Whyke Rd C3
Winden Avenue B3

Colchester 333

Abbey Gateway ✝ C2
Albert St A1
Albion Grove C2
Alexandra Rd C1
Artillery St C3
Arts Centre B1
Balkerne Hill B1
Barrack St C3
Beaconsfield Rd C1
Beche Rd C3
Bergholt Rd A1
Bourne Rd C3
Brick Kiln Rd A1
Brigade Grove C2
Bristol Rd B2
Broadlands Way A3
Brook St B3
Bury Close B2
Bus Station C2
Butt Rd C1
Campion Rd C2
Cannon St C3
Canterbury Rd C2
Captain Gardens C2
Castle B2
Castle Park B2
Castle Rd B2
Catchpool Rd A1
Causton Rd B1
Chandlers Row C3
Circular Rd East C2
Circular Rd North C1
Circular Rd West C1
Clarendon Way A1
Claudius Rd C2
Colchester A1
Colchester Camp Abbey Field C1
Colchester Retail Park B1
Colchester Town C2
Colne Bank Avenue A1
Colne View Retail Park A2
Compton Rd A3
Cowdray Avenue A1/A2
Cowdray Centre, The A2
Crouch St B1
Crowhurst Rd B1
Culver Square Shopping Centre B1
Culver St East B2
Culver St West B1
Dilbridge Rd A3
East Hill B2
East St B3
East Stockwell St B1
Eld Lane B1
Essex Hall Rd A1
Exeter Drive B2
Fairfax Rd C2
Fire Station A2
Firstsite B2
Flagstaff Rd C1
Garrison Parade C2
George St B2
Gladstone Rd C2
Golden Noble Hill C2
Goring Rd A3
Granville Rd C3
Greenstead Rd B3
Guildford Rd B2
Harsnett Rd C3
Harwich Rd B3
Head St B1
High St B1/B2
High Woods Country Park A2
Hollytrees B2
Hyderabad Close C2
Hythe Hill C3
Information Centre B2
Jarmin Rd A2
Kendall Rd C2
Kimberley Rd C3
King Stephen Rd C3
Leisure World A2
Library B1
Lincoln Way B2
Lion Walk Shopping Centre B1
Lisle Rd C2
Lucas Rd C2
Magdalen Green C3
Magdalen St C2
Maidenburgh St B2
Maldon Rd C1
Manor Rd B1
Margaret Rd A1
Mason Rd A2
Mercers Way A1
Mercury B1
Mersea Rd C2
Meyrick Crescent C2
Mile End Rd A1
Military Rd C2
Mill St C2
Minories B2
Moorside B3
Morant Rd C3
Napier Rd C2
Natural History B2
New Town Rd C2
Norfolk Crescent A3
North Hill B1
North Station Rd A1
Northgate St B1
Nunns Rd B1
Odeon B1
Old Coach Rd B3
Old Heath Rd C3
Osborne St B2
Petrolea Close A1
Police Station C1
Popes Lane B1
Port Lane C3
Post Office B2/C1
Priory St B2
Queen St B2
Rawstorn Rd B1
Rebon St C3
Recreation Rd C3
Ripple Way A3
Roberts Rd C2
Roman Rd B2
Roman Wall B2
Romford Close A3
Rosebery Avenue B2
St Andrews Avenue B3
St Andrews Gardens B3
St Botolph St B2
St Botolphs B2
St John's Abbey (site of) ✝ C2
St John's St B1
St Johns Walk Shopping Centre B1
St Leonards Rd C3
St Marys Fields B1
St Peter's St B1
St Peters B1
Salisbury Avenue C1
Saw Mill Rd C3
Sergeant St C2
Serpentine Walk A1
Sheepen Place B1
Sheepen Rd B1
Sir Isaac's Walk B1
Smythies Avenue B2
South St C1
South Way C1
Sports Way A2
Suffolk Close A3
Superstore A1
Town Hall B1
Valentine Drive A3
Victor Rd C3
Wakefield Close B2
Wellesley Rd C1
Wells Rd B2/B3
West St C1
West Stockwell St B1
Weston Rd C3
Westway A1
Wickham Rd C1
Wimpole Rd C3
Winchester Rd C2
Winnock Rd C2
Worcester Rd B2

Coventry 334

Abbots Lane A1
Albany B1
Albany Rd B1
Alma St B3
Ambulance Station A2
Art Faculty B3
Asthill Grove C2
Bablake School A1
Barras Lane A1/B1
Barr's Hill School A1
Belgrade B2
Bishop St A2
Bond's Hospital B1
Broad Gate B2
Broadway C1
Burges, The B2
Bus Station A3
Butts Radial B1
Byron St A3
Canterbury St A3
Cathedral ✝ B3
Central Six Retail Park C1
Chester St A1
Cheylesmore Manor House B2
Christ Church Spire ✦ B2
City College A3
City Walls & Gates ✦ A2
Corporation St B2
Council House B2
Coundon Rd A1
Coventry Station C2
Coventry Transport Museum A2
Coventry University Technology Park C3
Cox St A3
Croft Rd B1
Dalton Rd C1
Deasy Rd C3
Earl St B2
Eaton Rd C2
Fairfax St B2
Fire Station A2
Foleshill Rd A2
Ford's Hospital B2
Fowler Rd A1
Friars Rd C2
Gordon St C1
Gosford St B3
Greyfriars Green B2
Greyfriars Rd B2
Gulson Rd B3
Hales St A2
Harnall Lane East A3
Harnall Lane West A2
Herbert Art Gallery & Museum B3
Hertford St B2
Hewitt Avenue A1
High St B2
Hill St B1
Holy Trinity B2
Holyhead Rd A1
Howard St A3
Huntingdon Rd C1
Information Centre B3
Jordan Well B3
King Henry VIII Sch C1
Lady Godiva Statue ✦ B2
Lamb St A2
Leicester Row A2
Library B2
Lincoln St A2
Little Park St B2
London Rd C3
Lower Ford St B3
Lower Precinct Shopping Centre B2
Magistrates & Crown Courts B2
Manor House Drive B2
Manor Rd C2
Market B2
Martyrs Memorial ✦ C2
Meadow St B1
Meriden St A1
Michaelmas Rd C2
Middleborough Rd A1
Mile Lane C3
Millennium Place A2
Much Park St B3
Naul's Mill Park A1
New Union B2
Odeon B1
Park Rd C2
Parkside C3
Planet Ice Arena B1
Post Office A3,B2
Primrose Hill St A3
Priory Gardens & Visitor Centre B2
Priory St B3
Puma Way C3
Quarryfield Lane C3
Queen's Rd B1
Quinton Rd C2
Radford Rd A2
Raglan St B3
Ringway (Hill Cross) A1
Ringway (Queens) B1
Ringway (Rudge) B1
Ringway (St Johns) B3
Ringway (St Nicholas) A2
Ringway (St Patricks) C2
Ringway (Swanswell) A2
Ringway (Whitefriars) B3
St John St B2
St John the Baptist B2
St Nicholas St A2
Sidney Stringer Acad. A3
Skydome B1
Spencer Avenue C1
Spencer Rec Gnd C1
Spencer Rd C1
Spon St B1
Sports Centre B3
Stoney Rd C2
Stoney Stanton Rd A3
Superstore B2
Swanswell Pool A3
Thomas Landsdail St C2
Tomson Avenue A1
Top Green C1
Tower St A2
Trinity St B2
University B3
University Sports Ctr. B3
Upper Hill St A1
Upper Well St A2
Victoria St A3
Vine St A3
Wave, The ✦ B2
Warwick Rd C2
Waveley Rd B1
West Orchards Shopping Centre B2
Westminster Rd C1
White St A3
Windsor St B1

Derby 334

Abbey St C1
Agard St B1
Albert St B2
Albion St B2
Ambulance Station B1
Arthur St A1
Ashlyn Rd B3
Assembly Rooms B2
Babington Lane C2
Bass Recreation Gd B3
Becket St B1
Belper Rd A1
Bold Lane B1
Bradshaw Way C2
Bradshaw Way Retail Park C2
Bridge St B1
Brook St B1
Burton Rd C1
Bus Station B2
Business Park A3
Caesar St A2
Canal St C3
Carrington St C3
Cathedral ✝ B2
Cathedral Rd B1
Charnwood St C2
Chester Green Rd A2
City Rd A2
Clarke St A3
Cock Pitt Junction B3
Council House B2
Courts B1
Cranmer Rd B3
Crompton St C1
Crown & County Courts B2
Curzon St B1
Darley Grove A1
Derbion C2
Derby C3
Derby C2
Derby Gaol B1
Derwent Bsns Centre A2
Derwent St B2
Drewry Lane C1
Duffield Rd A1
Duke St A2
Dunton Close B3
Eagle Market C2
East St B2
Eastgate B3
Exeter St B2
Farm St C1
Ford St B1
Forester St C1
Fox St A2
Friar Gate B1
Friary St B1
Full St B2
Garden St A1
Gerard St C1
Gower St C2
Green Lane C2
Grey St C1
Guildhall B2
Handyside Bridge A2
Harcourt St C1
Highfield Rd A1
Hill Lane C2
Incora County Ground (Derbyshire CCC), The B3
Information Centre B2
Iron Gate B2
John St C3
Joseph Wright Centre B1
Kedleston Rd A1
Key St B2
King Alfred St C1
King St A1
Kingston St A1
Lara Croft Way C2
Leopold St C2
Liversage St C3
Lodge Lane B1
London Rd C2
London Rd Community Hospital C2
Macklin St C1
Mansfield Rd A2
Market B2
Market Place B2
May St C1
Meadow Lane B3
Melbourne St C2
Mercian Way C1
Midland Rd C3
Monk St C1
Morledge B2
Mount St C1
Mus & Art Gallery B1

Museum of Making B2
North Parade A1
North St A1
Nottingham Rd B3
Osmaston Rd C2
Otter St A1
Park St C3
Parker St A1
Pickford's House B1
Police Station A2, B2
Post Office A1/A2/B1/C2/C3
Pride Parkway C3
Prime Enterprise Park A2
Prime Parkway A2
QUAD B2
Queens Leisure Ctr B1
Racecourse Park A3
Railway Terrace C3
Register Office B2
Riverlights Leisure Ctr B2
Sadler Gate B1
St Alkmund's Way B1/B2
St Helens House A1
St Mary's A1
St Mary's Bridge A2
St Mary's Bridge Chapel A2
St Mary's Gate B1
St Paul's Rd A2
St Peter's C2
St Peter's St C2
Showcase De Lux C2
Siddals Rd C3
Sir Frank Whittle Rd A3
Spa Lane C1
Spring St C1
Stafford St B1
Station Approach C3
Stockbrook St C1
Stores Rd A3
Traffic St C2
Wardwick B1
Werburgh St C1
West Avenue A1
West Meadows Ind Est B3
Wharf Rd A2
Wilmot St C2
Wilson St C1
Wood's Lane C1

Dorchester 334

Ackerman Rd B3
Acland Rd A2
Albert Rd A1
Alexandra Rd B1
Alfred Place B3
Alfred Rd B2
Alington Avenue B3
Alington Rd B3
Ashley Rd B1
Balmoral Crescent C3
Barnes Way B2/C2
Borough Gardens A1
Brewery Square B1
Bridport Rd A1
Buckingham Way C3
Caters Place A1
Cemetery A3/C1
Charles St A2
Coburg Rd B1
Colliton St A1
Cornwall Rd A1
Cromwell Rd B1
Culliford Rd B2
Culliford Rd North B2
Dagmar Rd B1
Damer's Rd B1
Diggory Crescent C2
Dinosaur Museum A2
Dorchester Bypass C2
Dorchester South Station B1
Dorchester West Station B1
Dorset County (A&E) B1
Dorset County Council Offices A1
Dorset County Mus A1
Duchy Close C3
Duke's Avenue B2
Durngate St A2
Durnover Court A3
Eddison Avenue B3
Edward Rd B1
Egdon Rd C2
Elizabeth Frink Statue B2
Farfrae Crescent B2
Forum Centre, The B1
Friary Hill A2
Friary Lane A2
Frome Terrace A2
Garland Crescent C3
Glyde Path Rd A1
Grosvenor Crescent C1
Grosvenor Rd C1
Grove, The A1
Gt Western Rd B1
Herrington Rd C1
High St East A2
High St Fordington A2
High Street West A1
Holloway Rd A2
Icen Way A2
Information Centre B2
Keep Military Museum, The A1
Kings Rd A3/B3
Kingsbere Crescent C2
Lancaster Rd B2
Library A1
Lime Close C1
Linden Avenue B2
London Close A3
London Rd A2/A3
Lubbecke Way A3
Lucetta Lane B2
Maiden Castle Rd C1
Manor Rd C2
Market B1
Marshwood Place B2
Maumbury Rd B1
Maumbury Rings B1
Mellstock Avenue C2
Mill St A3
Miller's Close A1
Mistover Close C1
Monmouth Rd B1/B2
Moynton Rd C2
Nature Reserve A2
North Square A2
Northernhay A1
Odeon B1
Old Crown Court & Cells A1
Olga Rd B1
Orchard St A2
Plaza B1
Police Station B1
Post Office A1
Pound Lane A2
Poundbury Rd A1
Prince of Wales Rd B2
Prince's St A1
Queen's Avenue B1
Roman Town House A1
Roman Wall A1
Rothesay Rd C2
St George's Rd B3
Salisbury Field A2
Sandringham Sports Centre B3
Shaston Crescent C2
Smokey Hole Lane B3
South Court Avenue C1
South St B1
South Walks Rd B2
Superstore C3
Teddy Bear Mus A1
Temple Close C1
Terracotta Warriors & Teddy Bear Mus A2
Town Hall A2
Town Pump A2
Trinity St A1
Tutankhamun Exhibition A1
Victoria Rd B1
Weatherbury Way C2
Wellbridge Close C1
West Mills Rd A1
West Walks Rd A1
Weymouth Avenue C1
Williams Avenue B1
Winterbourne (BMI) C1
Wollaston Rd A2
York Rd B2

Dumfries 334

Academy St A2
Aldermanhill Rd B3
Ambulance Station C3
Annan Rd A3
Ardwall Rd A3
Ashfield Drive A1
Atkinson Rd C1
Averill Crescent C1
Balliol Avenue C1
Bank St B2
Bankend Rd C3
Barn Slaps B3
Barrie Avenue B3
Beech Avenue A1
Bowling Green A3
Brewery St B2
Bridgend Theatre B1
Brodie Avenue C2
Brooke St B2
Broomlands Drive C1
Brooms Rd B3
Buccleuch St A2
Burns House B2
Burns Mausoleum B3
Burns St B2
Burns Statue A2
Bus Station B1
Cardoness St A3
Castle St A2
Catherine St A2
Cattle Market A3
Cemetery B3
Cemetery C2
Church Crescent A2
Church St B2
College Rd A1
College St A1
Corbelly Hill B1
Corberry Park B1
Cornwall Mt A3
Council Offices A2
Court A2
Craigs Rd C3
Cresswell Avenue B3
Cresswell Hill B3
Cumberland St B3
David Keswick Athletic Centre A3
David St B1
Dock Park C3
Dockhead B2
Dumfries A3
Dumfries Academy A2
Dumfries Ice Bowl A1
Dumfries Museum & Camera Obscura B2
Dumfries & Galloway Royal Infirmary (A&E) C3
East Riverside Drive C3
Edinburgh Rd A2
English St B2
Fire Station B3
Friar's Vennel A2
Galloway St B1
George Douglas Drive C1
George St A2
Gladstone Rd C2
Glasgow St A1
Glebe St B3
Glencaple Rd C3
Goldie Avenue A1
Goldie Crescent A1
Golf Course C3
Gracefield Arts Ctr A2
Greyfriars A2
Grierson Avenue B3
Hamilton Avenue C1
Hamilton Starke Park C2
Hazelrigg Avenue C1
Henry St B3
Hermitage Drive C1
High Cemetery C3
High St A2
Hill Avenue C2
Hill St B1
HM Prison B1
Holm Avenue C2
Hoods Loaning A3
Howgate St B1
Huntingdon Rd A3
Information Centre B2
Irish St B2
Irving St A2
King St A1
Kingholm Rd C3
Kirkpatrick Court C2
Laurieknowe B1
Leafield Rd B3
Library A2
Lochfield Rd A1
Loreburn Park A3
Loreburn St A2
Loreburn Shopping Centre B2
Lover's Walk A2
Martin Avenue B3
Mausoleum B3
Maxwell St B1
McKie Avenue B3
Mews Lane A2
Mid Steeple B2
Mill Green B2
Mill Rd B1
Moat Rd C2
Moffat Rd A3
Mountainhall Park C3
Nelson St B1
New Abbey Rd B1/C1
New Bridge B1
Newall Terrace A2
Nith Avenue A2
Nith Bank C3
Nithbank Hospital C3
Nithside Avenue A1
Odeon B2
Old Bridge B1
Old Bridge House B1
Palmerston Park (Queen of the South FC) A1
Park Rd C1
Pleasance Avenue C1
Police Headquarters A3
Police Station A2/A3
Portland Drive A1
Post Office B1/B2/B3
Priestlands Drive C1
Primrose St B1
Queen St B3
Queensberry St A2
Rae St A2
Richmond Avenue C2
Robert Burns Ctr B2
Roberts Crescent C1
Robertson Avenue C3
Robinson Drive C1
Rosefield Rd C2
Rosemount St B1
Rotchell Park C1
Rotchell Rd B1
Rugby Football Gd C1
Ryedale Rd C2
St Andrews B2
St John the Evangelist A2
St Josephs College B3
St Mary's Ind Est A3
St Mary's St A3
St Michael St B2
St Michael's B2
St Michael's Bridge B2
St Michael's Bridge Rd B2
St Michael's Cemetery B3
Shakespeare St B2
Solway Drive C2
Stakeford St A1
Stark Crescent C2
Station Rd A3
Steel Avenue A1
Sunderries Avenue A1
Sunderries Rd A1
Superstore B3
Suspension Brae B2
Swimming Pool A1
Terregles St B1
Theatre Royal B2
Troqueer Rd C2
Union St A1
Wallace St B3
Welldale B2
West Riverside Drive C2
White Sands B2

Dundee 334

Abertay University B2
Adelaide Place A1
Airlie Place C1
Albany Terrace A1
Albert St A3
Alexander St A2
Ann St A2
Arthurstone Terrace A3
Bank St B2
Barrack Rd A1
Barrack St B2
Bell St B2
Blinshall St B1
Broughty Ferry Rd A3
Brown St B1
Bus Station B3
Caird Hall B2
Camperdown St B3
Candle Lane B3
Carmichael St A1
City Churches B2
City Quay B3
City Square B2
Commercial St B2
Constable St A3
Constitution Crescent A1
Constitution Court A1
Constitution St A1/B2
Cotton Rd A3
Courthouse Square B1
Cowgate A3
Crescent St A3
Crichton St B2
Dens Brae A3
Dens Rd A3
Discovery Point C2
Douglas St B1
Drummond St A1
Dudhope Castle A1
Dudhope St A2
Dudhope Terrace A1
Dundee C2
Dundee Contemporary Arts C2
Dundee High School B2
Dundee Law A1
Dundee Rep C2
Dunhope Park A1
Dura St A3
East Dock St B3
East Marketgait B3
East Whale Lane B3
Erskine St A3
Euclid Crescent B2
Forebank Rd A2
Foundry Lane A3
Gallagher Retail Park B3
Gellatly St B3
Government Offices C2
Guthrie St B1
Hawkhill B1
Hilltown A2
HMS Unicorn B3
Howff Cemetery, The B2
Information Centre B2
Keiller Shopping Centre B2
Keiller Centre, The B2
King St A3
Kinghorne Rd A1
Ladywell Avenue A3
Laurel Bank A2
Law Rd A1
Law St A1
Library A2/A3
Library and Steps Theatre A2
Little Theatre, The A2
Lochee Rd B1
Lower Princes St A3
Lyon St A3
McManus Art Gallery & Museum, The B2
Meadow Side B2
Meadowside St Pauls B2
Mercat Cross B2
Murraygate B2
Nelson St A2
Nethergate B2/C1
North Lindsay St B2
North Marketgait B2
Old Hawkhill B1
Olympia Leisure Centre B3
Overgate Shopping Centre B2
Park Place B1
Perth Rd C1
Police Station B1
Post Office B2
Princes St A3
Prospect Place A2
Reform St B2
Riverside Drive C2
Riverside Esplanade C2
Roseangle C1
Rosebank St A2
RRS Discovery C2
St Andrew's C2
St Pauls Episcopal B3
Science Centre C2
Seagate B2
Sheriffs Court B1
Shopmobility B2
South George St A2
South Marketgait B3
South Tay St B2
South Victoria Dock Road B3
South Ward Rd B2
Tay Road Bridge C3
Thomson Avenue B2
Trades Lane B3
Union St B2
Union Terrace A1
University Library B2
University of Dundee B1
Upper Constitution Street A1
Verdant Works B1
V&A Museum of Design C2
Victoria Dock B3
Victoria Rd A2
Victoria St A3
Ward Rd B1
Wellgate B2
West Bell St B1
West Marketgait B1/B2
Westfield Place C1
William St A3
Wishart Arch A3

Durham 334

Alexander Crescent B2
Allergate B2
Archery Rise C1
Assembly Rooms B2
Avenue, The B1
Back Western Hill A1
Bakehouse Lane A3
Baths Bridge B3
Boat House B3
Boyd St C3
Bus Station B2
Castle Chare B2
Cathedral B2
Church St C3
Clay Lane C1
Claypath B3
College of St Hild & St Bede B3
County Hospital B1
Crescent, The A1
Crook Hall & Gardens A3
Crossgate B2
Crossgate Peth C1
Crown Court B3
Darlington Rd C1
Durham A2
Durham Castle B2
Durham School C2
Durham University (Science Site) C3
Ellam Avenue C1
Elvet Bridge B3
Elvet Court B3
Farnley Hey B1
Ferens Close A3
Fieldhouse Lane A1
Flass St B1
Flass Vale Local Nature Reserve A1
Framwelgate Bridge B2
Framwelgate A2
Framwelgate Peth A2
Framwelgate Waterside A2
Frankland Lane A3
Freeman's Place A3
Freeman's Quay Leisure Centre A3
Gala Theatre & Cinema B3
Geoffrey Avenue C1
Gilesgate B3
Grey College C3
Grove, The A1
Hallgarth St C3
Hatfield College B3
Hawthorn Terrace B1
Heritage Centre B3
HM Prison B3
John St B1
Kingsgate Bridge B3
Laburnum Terrace B1
Lawson Terrace B1
Leazes Rd B2/B3
Library B2
Margery Lane B2
Market B2
Mavin St C3
Millburngate B2
Millburngate Bridge B2
Millennium Bridge (foot/cycle) A2
Mountjoy Research Centre C3
Mus of Archaeology B2
New Elvet B3
New Elvet Bridge B3
North Bailey B3
North End A1
Observatory C1
Old Elvet B3
Open Treasure B2
Oriental Museum C2
Oswald Court C3
Passport Office A2
Percy Terrace B1
Pimlico C2
Police Station B3
Post Office A1/B2
Potters Bank C1/C2
Prebends Bridge C2
Prebends Walk C2
Prince Bishops Shopping Centre B3
Princes St A1
Providence Row A3
Quarryheads Lane C2
Redhills Lane B1
Redhills Terrace B1
Riverwalk, The B2
Saddler St B3
St Cuthbert's Society C2
St Margaret's B2
St Mary the Less C2
St Mary's College C2
St Monica Grove B1
St Nicholas' B3
St Oswald's C3
Sands, The A3
Shopmobility B3
Sidegate A2
Silver St B2
Sixth Form College A3
South Bailey C2
South Rd C3
South St B2
Springwell Avenue A1
Station Approach B2
Stockton Rd C3
Student Union B3
Summerville B1
Sutton St B2
Town Hall B2
University Arts Block B3
University College B2
Walkergate Centre A3
Wearside Drive A3
Western Hill A1
Wharton Park A2
Whinney Hill C3
Whitehouse Avenue C1
YHA C3

Edinburgh 334

Abbey Strand B6
Abbeyhill A6
Abbeyhill Crescent B6
Abbeymount A6
Abercromby Place A3
Adam St C5
Albany Lane A4
Albany St A4
Albert Memorial B2
Albyn Place A2
Alva Place A6
Alva St B1
Ann St A1
Appleton Tower C4
Archibald Place C3
Assembly Rooms & Musical Hall A3
Atholl Crescent B1
Atholl Crescent Lane C1
Bank St B4
Barony St A4
Beaumont Place C5
Belford Rd B1
Belgrave Crescent A1
Belgrave Cres Lane A1
Bell's Brae B1
Blackfriars St B4
Blair St B4
Bread St C2
Bristo Place C4
Bristo St C4
Brougham St C2
Broughton St A4
Brown St C5
Brunton Terrace A6
Buckingham Terrace A1
Burial Ground A6
Bus Station A4
Caledonian Crescent C1
Caledonian Rd C1
Calton Hill A4
Calton Hill A5
Calton Rd B4
Camera Obscura & Outlook Tower B3
Candlemaker Row C4
Canning St B2
Canongate B5
Canongate B5
Carlton St A1
Carlton Terrace A6
Carlton Terrace Lane A6
Castle St B2
Castle Terrace B2
Castlehill B3
Central Library B4
Chalmers Hospital C3
Chalmers St C3
Chambers St C4
Chapel St C4
Charles St C4
Charlotte Square B2
Chester St B1
Circus Lane A2
Circus Place A2
City Art Centre B4
City Chambers B4
City Observatory A5
Clarendon Crescent A1
Clerk St C5
Coates Crescent B1
Cockburn St B4
College of Art C3
Comely Bank Avenue A1
Comely Bank Row A1
Cornwall St C2
Cowans Close C5
Cowgate B4
Cranston St B5
Crichton St C4
Croft-An-Righ A6
Cumberland St A2
Dalry Place C1
Dalry Rd C1
Danube St A1
Darnawy St A2
David Hume Tower C4
Davie St C5
Dean Bridge A1
Dean Gardens A1
Dean Park Crescent A1
Dean Park Mews A1
Dean Park St A1
Dean Path B1
Dean St A1
Dean Terrace A1
Dewar Place C1
Dewar Place Lane C1
Doune Terrace A2
Drummond Place A3
Drummond St C5
Drumsheugh Gardens B1
Dublin Mews A3
Dublin St A4
Dublin St Lane South A4
Dumbiedykes Rd B5
Dundas St A3
Dynamic Earth B6
Earl Grey St C2
East Crosscauseway C5
East Market St B4
East Norton Place A6
East Princes St Gdns B3
Easter Rd A6
Edinburgh (Waverley) B4
Edinburgh Castle B3
Edinburgh Dungeon B4
Edinburgh International Conference Centre C2
Elder St A4
Esplanade B3
Eton Terrace A1
Eye Pavilion C3
Festival Office B3
Festival Theatre Edinburgh C4
Filmhouse C2
Fire Station C2
Floral Clock B3
Forres St A2
Forth St A4
Fountainbridge C2
Frederick St A3
Freemasons' Hall B3
Fruitmarket B4
Gardner's Crescent C2
George Heriot's School C3
George IV Bridge B4
George Square C4
George Square Lane C4
George St B3
Georgian House B2
Gladstone's Land B3
Glen St C3
Gloucester Lane A2
Gloucester Place A2
Gloucester St A2
Graham St C3
Grassmarket C3
Great King St A3
Great Stuart B1
Greenside Lane A5
Greenside Row A5
Greyfriars Kirk C4
Grindlay St C2
Grosvenor St C1
Grove St C1
Gullan's Close B5
Guthrie St B4
Hanover St A3
Hart St A4
Haymarket C1
Haymarket Station C1
Heriot Place C3
Heriot Row A2
High School Yard B5
High St B4
Hill Place C5
Hill St A2
Hillside Crescent A5
Holyrood Abbey (Remains) A6
Holyrood Gait B6
Holyrood Park C6
Holyrood Rd B5
Home St C2
Hope St B2
Horse Wynd B6
Howden St C5
Howe St A2
Hub, The B3
India Place A2
India St A2
Infirmary St B4
Information Centre B4
Jeffrey St B4
John Knox House B4
Johnston Terrace C3
Keir St C3
Kerr St A2
King's Stables Rd B2
Lady Lawson St C3
Lauriston Gardens C3
Lauriston Park C3
Lauriston Place C3
Lauriston St C3
Lawnmarket B3
Learmonth Gardens A1
Learmonth Terrace A1
Leith St A4
Lennox St A1
Lennox St Lane A1
Leslie Place A2
London Rd A5
Lothian Rd B2
Lothian St C4
Lower Menz Place A6
Lynedoch Place B1
Manor Place B1
Market St B4
Marshall St C4
Maryfield A6
McEwan Hall C4
Medical School C4
Melville St B1
Meuse Lane B4
Middle Meadow Walk C4
Milton St A6
Montrose Terrace A6
Moray Place A2
Morrison Link C1
Morrison St C1
Mound Place B3
Mound, The B3
Multrees Walk A4
Mus Collections Ctr A4
Mus of Childhood B5
Mus of Edinburgh B5
Museum of Fire C3
Mus on the Mound B4
National Archives of Scotland A4
National Museum of Scotland C4
National Gallery B3
National Library of Scotland B4
National Monument A5
National Portrait Gallery B4
National War Mus B3
Nelson Monument A5
Nelson St A3
New St B5
Nicolson Square C4
Nicolson St C4
Niddry St B4
North Bank St B3
North Bridge B4
North Charlotte St A2
North Meadow Walk C3
North St Andrew St A4
North St David St A3
North West Circus Pl A2
Northumberland St A3
Odeon C2
Old Royal High School A5
Old Tolbooth Wynd B5
OMNi Centre A4
Oxford Terrace A1
Palace of Holyroodhouse B6
Palmerston Place B1
Panmure Place C3
Parliament Square B4
People's Story, The B5
Playhouse Theatre A4
Pleasance C5
Police Station A4
Ponton St C2
Post Office A3/B4/B5/C1/C2/C4
Potterrow C4
Princes Mall B4
Princes St B3
Princes St B3
Prisoners of War B3
Queen's Gallery B6
Queen St A2
Queen Street Gardens A3
Queen's Drive B6/C6
Queensferry Rd A1
Queensferry St B1
Queensferry Street La B2
Radical Rd C6
Randolph Crescent B1
Regent Gardens A5
Regent Rd B5
Regent Rd Park A6
Regent Terrace A5
Richmond Lane C5
Richmond Place C5
Rose St B2
Ross Open Air Theatre B3
Rothesay Place B1
Rothesay Terrace B1
Roxburgh Place C5
Roxburgh St C5
Royal Bank of Scotland A4
Royal Circus A2
Royal Lyceum C2
Royal Mile, The B5
Royal Scottish Acad B3
Royal Terrace A5
Royal Terrace Gdns A5
Rutland Square B2
Rutland St B2
St Andrew Square A4
St Andrew Square A4
St Andrew's House A4
St Bernard's Cres A1
St Bernard's Well A1
St Cecilia's Hall B4
St Colme St A2
St Cuthbert's B2
St Giles' B4
St James Quarter Shopping Centre A4
St John St B5
St John's B2
St John's Hill B5
St Leonard's Hill C5
St Leonard's Lane C5
St Leonard's St C5
St Mary's A4
St Mary's Scottish Episcopal B1
St Mary's St B5
St Michael & All Saints C3
St Stephen St A2
Salisbury Crags C6
Saunders St A2
Scotch Whisky Experience B3
Scott Monument B4
Scottish Parliament B6
Scottish Storytelling Centre B5
Semple St C2
Shandwick Place B2
South Bridge B4
South Charlotte St B2
South College St C4
South Learmonth Gardens A1
South St Andrew St A4
South St David St A3
Spittal St C2
Stafford St B1
Student Centre C4
Surgeons' Hall C5
Supreme Courts B4
Teviot Place C4
Thistle St A3
Torphichen Place C1
Torphichen St C1
Traverse Theatre B2
Tron Square B4
Tron, The B4
Union St A4
University C4
University Library C4
Univ of Edinburgh B5
Upper Grove Place C1
Usher Hall C2
Vennel C3
Victoria St B3
Viewcraig Gardens B5
Viewcraig St B5
Vue A4
Walker St B1
Waterloo Place A4
Waverley Bridge B4
Wemyss Place A2
West Approach Rd C1
West Crosscauseway C5
West End B1
West Maitland St C1
West of Nicholson St C4
West Port C3
West Princes St Gdns B3
West Richmond St C5
West Tollcross C2
White Horse Close B6
William St B1
Windsor St A5
Writer's Mus, The B4
York Lane A4
York Place A4
York Place A4
Young St B2

Exeter 334

Alphington St C1
Athelstan Rd B3
Barnardo Rd C3
Barnfield Hill B3
Barnfield Rd B2/B3
Barnfield Theatre B2
Bartholomew St East B1
Bartholomew St West B1
Bear St B2
Beaufort Rd C1
Bedford St B2
Belgrave Rd A3
Belmont Rd A3
Blackall Rd A2
Blackboy Rd A3
Bonhay Rd B1
Bull Meadow Rd C2
Bus & Coach Station B3
Castle St B2
Catacombes B1
Cecil Rd C1
Cheeke St A3
Church Rd C1
Chute St A3
City Wall B1/B2
Civic Centre B2
Clifton Rd B3
Clifton St B3
Clock Tower A1
College Rd B3
Colleton Crescent C2
Commercial Rd C1
Coombe St B2
Cowick St C1
Crown Courts B2
Custom House Visitor Centre C2
Cygnet Theatre C2
Danes' Rd A2
Denmark Rd B3
Devon County Hall C3
Devonshire Place A3
Dinham Crescent B1
East Grove Rd C3
Edmund St C1
Elm Grove Rd A1
Exe St B1
Exeter Cathedral B2
Exeter Central Sta A1
Exeter City Football Ground A3
Exeter College A1
Exeter Picture Ho B1
Fire Station A1
Fore St B1
Friars Walk C2
Guildhall B2
Guildhall Shopping Ctr B2
Haven Rd C2
Heavitree Rd B3
Hele Rd A1
High St B2
HM Prison A2
Holloway St C2
Hoopern St A2
Horseguards A2
Howell Rd A1
Information Centre B3
Iron Bridge B1
Isca Rd C1
Jesmond Rd A3
King St B1
King William St A2
Larkbeare Rd C2
Leisure Centre C1
Library B2
Longbrook St A2
Longbrook Terrace A2
Lower North St B1
Lucky Lane C2
Lyndhurst Rd C3
Magdalen Rd B3
Magdalen St B2
Market B2
Market St B2
Marlborough Rd C3
Mary Arches St B1
Matford Avenue C3
Matford Lane C3
Matford Rd C3
May St A3
Mol's Coffee House B2
New Bridge St B1
New North Rd A1/A2
North St B1
Northernhay St B1
Norwood Avenue C3
Odeon A3
Okehampton St C1
Old Mill Close C2
Old Tiverton Rd A3
Oxford Rd A3
Paris St B2
Parr St A3
Paul St B1
Pennsylvania Rd A2
Portland Street A3
Post Office A3/B2/C1
Powderham Crescent A3
Preston St B1
Princesshay Shopping Centre B2
Pyramids Leisure Ctr B3
Quay, The C2
Queen St A1
Queen's Terrace A1
Queens Rd C1

Radford Rd C2
Richmond Rd A1
Roberts Rd C2
Rougemont Castle B2
Rougemont House ✦ B2
Royal Albert Memorial Museum B2
St David's Hill A1
St James' Pk Sta A3
St James' Rd A3
St Leonard's Rd C3
St Mary Steps C1
St Nicholas Priory B1
St Thomas Station C1
Sandford Walk B3
School Rd C1
Sidwell St A2
Smythen St B1
South St B2
Southernhay East B2
Southernhay West B2
Spicer Rd B3
Sports Centre A3
Summerland St A3
Sydney Rd C1
Tan Lane C2
Thornton Hill A2
Topsham Rd C3
Tucker's Hall B1
Tudor St B1
Underground Passages ✦ B2
University of Exeter (St Luke's Campus) B3
Velwell Rd A1
Verney St A3
Vue B3
Water Lane C1/C2
Weirfield Rd C2
Well St A3
West Avenue A2
West Grove Rd C3
Western Way A3/B1/B2
Willeys Avenue C1
Wonford Rd B3/C3
York Rd A2

Fort William 335

Abrach Rd A3
Achintore Rd C1
Alma Rd B2
Am Breun Chamas A2
Ambulance Station A3
An Aird A2
Argyll Rd C1
Argyll Terrace C1
Bank St B2
Belford Hospital B2
Ben Nevis Highland Centre B3
Black Parks A3
Braemore Place C2
Bruce Place C2
Bus Station B2
Camanachd Cres A3/B2
Cameron Rd C1
Cameron Square B1
Carmichael Way A2
Claggan Rd B3
Connochie Rd C1
Cow Hill C3
Creag Dhubh A2
Croft Rd B3
Douglas Place B2
Dudley Rd B2
Dumbarton Rd C1
Earl of Inverness Rd A3
Fassifern Rd B1
Fire Station A2
Fort William Station B2
Fort William (Remains) ✦ B2
Glasdrum Rd C1
Glen Nevis Place B3
Gordon Square B1
Grange Rd C1
Heathercroft Drive C1
Heather Croft Rd C1
Henderson Row C2
High St B1
Hill Rd B2
Information Centre A3
Inverlochy Court A3
Kennedy Rd B2/C2
Library B2
Lime Tree Gallery ✦ C1
Linnhe Rd B1
Lochaber Leisure Ctr B3
Lochiel Rd A3
Lochy Rd A3
Lundavra Crescent C1
Lundavra Rd C1
Lundy Rd A3
Mamore Crescent B2
Mary St B2
Middle St B1
Montrose Avenue A3
Moray Place C1
Morven Place C2
Nairn Crescent C1
Nevis Bridge B3
Nevis Centre, The A2
Nevis Rd A3
Nevis Terrace B2
North Rd B3
Obelisk B2
Parade Rd B2
Police Station C1
Post Office A3/B2
Ross Place C1
St Andrews B2
Shaw Place B2
Station Brae B1
Superstore B3
Treig Rd A3
Union Rd C1
Victoria Rd B2
Wades Rd A3
West Highland B1
West Highland College UHI A2
Young Place B2

Glasgow 335

Admiral St C2
Albert Bridge C5
Albion St B5
Anderston Station B3
Anderston Quay B3
Argyle Arcade B5
Argyle St A1/A2/B3/B4/B5
Argyle Street Station B5
Arlington St A3
Arts Centre B3
Ashley St A3
Bain St C6
Baird St A6
Baliol St A3
Ballater St C5
Barras (Market), The C6
Bath St A3
BBC Scotland B1
Bell St C6
Bell's Bridge B1
Bentinck St A2
Berkeley St A3
Bishop Lane B3
Black St A6
Blackburn St C2
Blackfriars St B6
Blantyre St A1
Blythswood Square A4
Blythswood St B4
Bothwell St B4
Brand St C1
Breadalbane St A2
Bridge St C4
Bridge St C4
Bridgegate C5
Briggait C5
Broomielaw B4
Broomielaw Quay Gardens B3
Brown St B4
Brunswick St B5
Buccleuch St A3
Buchanan Bus Station A5
Buchanan Galleries A5
Buchanan St B5
Buchanan St B5
Cadogan St B4
Caledonian University A5
Calgary St A5
Cambridge St A4
Canal St A5
Candleriggs B5
Carlton Place C4
Carnarvon St A3
Carrick St B4
Castle St B6
Cathedral Square B6
Cathedral St B5
Central Mosque C5
Ctr for Contemporary Arts A4
Centre St C4
Cessnock C1
Cessnock St C1
Charing Cross A3
Charlotte St C6
Cheapside St B3
Cineworld A5
Citizens' Theatre C5
City Chambers Complex B5
City Halls B5
City of Glasgow College (City Campus) B5
City of Glasgow College (Riverside Campus) C5
Clairmont Gardens A2
Claremont St A2
Claremont Terrace A2
Claythorne St C6
Cleveland St A3
Clifford Lane C1
Clifford St C1
Clifton Place A2
Clifton St A2
Clutha St C1
Clyde Arcade B2
Clyde Place C4
Clyde Place Quay C4
Clyde St C5
Clyde Walkway C3
Clydeside Expressway B2
Coburg St C4
Cochrane St B5
College St B6
Collins St B6
Commerce St C4
Cook St C4
Cornwall St C2
Couper St A5
Cowcaddens A4
Cowcaddens Rd A4
Crimea St B3
Custom Ho Quay Gdns C4
Dalhousie St A4
Dental Hospital A4
Derby St A2
Dobbie's Loan A4/A5
Dobbie's Loan Place A5
Dorset St A3
Douglas St B4
Doulton Fountain ✦ C6
Dover St A2
Drury St B4
Drygate B6
Duke St B6
Dunaskin St A1
Dunblane St A4
Dundas St B5
Dunlop St C5
East Campbell St C6
Eastvale Place A1
Eglinton St C4
Elderslie St A3
Elliot St B2
Elmbank St A3
Esmond St A1
Exhibition Centre Station B2
Festival Park C1
Film Theatre A4
Finnieston Quay B2
Finnieston St B2
Fire Station C6
Florence St C5
Fox St C5
Gallowgate C6
Garnet St A3
Garnethill St A4
Garscube Rd A4
George Square B5
George St B5
George V Bridge C4
Gilbert St A1
Glasgow Bridge C4
Glasgow Cathedral + B6
Glasgow Central Station B4
Glasgow City Free Church B4
Glasgow Green C6
Glasgow Necropolis ✦ B6
Glasgow Royal Concert Hall A5
Glasgow Science Centre ✦ B1
Glasgow Tower ✦ B1
Glassford St B5
Glebe St A6
Gorbals Cross C5
Gorbals St C5
Gordon St B4
Govan Rd B1/C1/C2
Grace St B3
Grafton Place A5
Grand Ole Opry ✦ C2
Grant St A3
Granville St A3
Gray St A2
Greendyke St C6
Grey Eagle St B7
Harley St C1
Harvie St C1
Haugh Rd A1
Havanah St B6
Heliport B1
Henry Wood Hall A2
High Court C5
High St B6
High Street Station B6
Hill St A3
Holland St A3
Holm St B4
Hope St A5
Houldsworth St B2
Houston Place C3
Houston St C3
Howard St C5
Hunter St C6
Hutcheson St B5
Hydepark St B3
Imax Cinema B1
India St A3
Information Centre B5
Ingram St B5
Jamaica St B4
James Watt St B4
John Knox St B6
John St B5
Kelvin Hall ✦ A1
Kelvin Statue ✦ A2
Kelvin Way A2
Kelvingrove Art Gallery & Museum A1
Kelvingrove Park A2
Kelvingrove St A2
Kelvinhaugh St A1
Kennedy St A6
Kent Rd A2
Killermont St A5
King St B5
King's, The A3
Kingston Bridge C3
Kingston St C4
Kinning Park C2
Kyle St A5
Lancefield Quay B2
Lancefield St B3
Langshot St C1
Lendel Place C1
Lighthouse, The ✦ B4
Lister St A6
Little St B3
London Rd C6
Lorne St C1
Lower Harbour B1
Lumsden St A1
Lymburn St A1
Lyndoch Crescent A3
Lynedoch Place A3
Lynedoch St A3
Maclellan St C1
Mair St C2
Maitland St A4
Mansell St C7
Mavisbank Gardens C2
Mcalpine St B3
Mcaslin St A6
McLean Square C2
McLellan Gallery A4
McPhater St A4
Merchants' House B5
Middlesex St C2
Middleton St C1
Midland St B4
Miller St B5
Millennium Bridge B1
Millroad St C6
Milnpark St C2
Milton St A4
Minerva St B2
Mitchell St West B4
Mitchell Liby, The ✦ A3
Modern Art Gallery B5
Moir St C6
Molendinar St C6
Moncur St C6
Montieth Row C6
Montrose St B5
Morrison St C3
Nairn St A1
National Piping Centre, The ✦ A5
Nelson Mandela Sq B5
Nelson St C4
Nelson's Monument C6
Newton Place A3
Newton St A3
Nicholson St C4
Nile St B5
Norfolk Court C4
Norfolk St C4
North Frederick St B5
North Hanover St B5
North Portland St B6
North St A3
North Wallace St A5
O2 ABC A4
O2 Academy ✦ C4
Odeon C3
Old Dumbarton Rd A1
Osborne St B5/C5
Oswald St B4
Overnewton St A1
Oxford St C4
Pacific Drive B1
Paisley Rd C3
Paisley Rd West C1
Park Circus A2
Park Gardens A2
Park St South A2
Park Terrace A2
Parkgrove Terrace A2
Parnie St C5
Parson St A6
Partick Bridge A1
Passport Office A5
Pavilion Theatre A4
Pembroke St A3
People's Palace C6
Pitt St A4/B4
Plantation Park C1
Plantation Quay B1
Police Museum B5
Police Station A4/A6
Port Dundas Rd A5
Port St B2
Portman St C2
Prince's Dock B1
Princes Square B5
Provand's Lordship B6
Queen St B5
Queen Street Station B5
Ramshorn B5
Renfrew St A3/A4
Renton St A5
Richmond St B5
Robertson St B4
Rose St A4
Rottenrow B5
Royal Concert Hall A5
Royal Conservatoire of Scotland A4
Royal Crescent A2
Royal Exchange Sq B5
Royal Highland Fusiliers Museum A3
West Glasgow Ambulatory Care A1
Royal Infirmary B6
Royal Terrace A2
Rutland Crescent C2
St Andrew's in the Square C6
St Andrew's (RC) + C5
St Andrew's St C5
St Enoch B5
St Enoch Shopping Ctr B5
St Enoch Square B4
St George's Rd A3
St James Rd B6
St Kent St C6
St Mungo Avenue A5/A6
St Mungo Museum of Religious Life & Art B6
St Mungo Place A6
St Vincent Crescent A2
St Vincent Place B5
St Vincent St B3/B4
St Vincent Terrace B3
Saltmarket C5
Sandyford Place A3
Sauchiehall St A2/A4
SEC Armadillo B2
School of Art A4
Sclater St B7
Scotland St C2
Scott St A4
Scottish Exhibition & Conference Centre B1
Seaward St C2
Shaftesbury St B3
Sheriff Court C5
Shields Rd C3
Shopmobility A5
Shuttle St B6
Somerset Place A2
South Portland St C4
Springburn Rd A6
Springfield Quay C3
SSE Hydro The B2
Stanley St C2
Stevenson St C6
Stewart St A4
Stirling Rd B6
Stobcross Quay B1
Stobcross Rd B1
Stock Exchange B5
Stockwell Place C5
Stockwell St B5
Stow College A4
Sussex St C2
Synagogue A3
Taylor Place A6
Tenement House A3
Teviot St A1
Theatre Royal A4
Tolbooth Steeple & Mercat Cross ✦ C6
Tower St C2
Trades House B5
Tradeston St C4
Transport Museum A1
Tron C5
Trongate B5
Tunnel St B2
Turnbull St C5
Union St B4
Univ of Strathclyde B6
Victoria Bridge C5
Virginia St B5
Wallace St C3
Walls St B6
Walmer Crescent C1
Warrock St B3
Washington St B3
Waterloo St B4
Watson St B6
Watt St C3
Wellington St B4
West Campbell St B4
West George St B4
West Graham St A4
West Greenhill Place B2
West Regent St A4
West Regent St B4
West St C4
West St C4
Whitehall St B3
Wilkes St C7
Wilson St B5
Woodlands Gate A3
Woodlands Rd A3
Woodlands Terrace A2
Woodside Place A3
Woodside Terrace A3
York St B4
Yorkhill Parade A1
Yorkhill St A1

Gloucester 335

Albion St C1
Alexandra Rd B3
Alfred St C3
All Saints Rd C2
Alvin St B2
Arthur St C2
Barrack Square B1
Barton St C2
Blackfriars + B1
Blenheim Rd C2
Bristol Rd C1
Brunswick Rd C2
Bruton Way B2
Bus Station B2
Cineworld C1
City Council Offices B1
City Museum, Art Gallery & Library B2
Clarence St B2
Commercial Rd B1
Council Offices B1
Courts B1
Cromwell St C2
Deans Way A2
Denmark Rd A3
Derby Rd C3
Docks ✦ C1
Eastgate St B2
Eastgate, The B1
Edwy Parade A2
Estcourt Close A3
Estcourt Rd A3
Falkner St C2
GL1 Leisure Centre C2
Gloucester Cath + B1
Gloucester Life B1
Gloucester Quays Outlet C1
Gloucester Station B2
Gloucestershire Archive B2
Gloucestershire Royal Hospital (A&E) B3
Goodyere St C2
Gouda Way A1
Great Western Rd B3
Guildhall B2
Heathville Rd A3
Henry Rd B3
Henry St B2
Hinton Rd A2
India Rd C3
Information Centre B1
Jersey Rd C3
King's C2
King's Walk Shopping Centre B2
Kingsholm (Gloucester Rugby) A2
Kingsholm Rd A2
Lansdown Rd A3
Library C2
Llanthony Rd C1
London Rd B3
Longhorn Avenue A1
Longsmith St B1
Malvern Rd A3
Market B2
Market Parade B2
Mercia Rd A1
Metz Way C3
Midland Rd C2
Millbrook St C3
Montpellier C1
Napier St C3
National Waterways Mus Gloucester C1
Nettleton Rd C2
New Inn B2
New Olympus C3
North Rd A3
Northgate St B2
Oxford Rd A2
Oxford St B2
Park & Ride Gloucester A1
Park Rd C2
Park St B2
Park, The C2
Parliament St C1
Peel Centre, The C1
Pitt St B1
Police Station C3
Post Office B2
Quay St B1
Quay, The B1
Recreation Ground A1/A2
Regent St C2
Robert Raikes Ho B1
Royal Oak Rd B1
Russell St B2
Ryecroft St C2
St Aldate St B2
St Ann Way C1
St Catherine St A2
St Mark St A2
St Mary de Crypt B1
St Mary de Lode B1
St Nicholas's B1
St Oswald's Rd A1
St Oswald's Retail Pk A1
St Peter's B2
Seabroke Rd A3
Sebert St A2
Severn Rd C1
Sherborne St B2
Shire Hall B1
Sidney St C3
Soldiers of Gloucestershire B1
Southgate St B1/C1
Spa Field C1
Spa Rd C1
Sports Ground A2/B2
Station Rd B2
Stratton Rd C3
Stroud Rd C1
Superstore A1
Swan Rd A2
Trier Way C1/C2
Union St A2
Vauxhall Rd C3
Victoria St C2
Walham Lane A1
Wellington St C2
Westgate Retail Park B1
Westgate St B1
Widden St C2
Worcester St B2

Grimsby 335

Abbey Drive East C2
Abbey Drive West C2
Abbey Park Rd C2
Abbey Rd C2
Abbey Walk C2
Abbeygate Shopping Centre C2
Abbotsway C2
Adam Smith St A1/A2
Ainslie St C2
Albert St A3
Alexandra Dock A2/B2
Alexandra Rd A2/B2
Alexandra Retail Park A2
Annesley St A2
Armstrong St A1
Arthur St B1
Augusta St C1
Bargate C1
Beeson St A1
Bethlehem St C2
Bodiam Way B3
Bradley St B3
Brighowgate C1/C2
Bus Station C2
Canterbury Drive C1
Cartergate B1/C1
Catherine St C3
Chantry Lane B1
Charlton St A1
Church Lane C2
Church St A3
Cleethorpe Rd A3
Close, The C1
College St C1
Compton Drive C1
Corporation Bridge A2
Corporation Rd A1
Court B2/B3
Crescent St B1
Deansgate C1
Doughty Rd C2
Dover St B1
Duchess St C2
Dudley St C1
Duke of York Gardens B1
Duncombe St B3
Earl Lane B1
East Marsh St B3
East St B2
Eastgate B3
Eastside Rd A3
Eaton Court C1
Eleanor St B3
Ellis Way B3
Fisherman's Chapel A3
Fisherman's Wharf B2
Fishing Heritage Centre B2
Flour Square A3
Frederick St B1
Frederick Ward Way B2
Freeman St A3/B3
Freshney Drive B1
Freshney Place B2
Garden St C2
Garibaldi St A3
Garth Lane B2
Grime St B3
Grimsby Docks Sta A3
Grimsby Town Sta C2
Hainton Avenue C3
Har Way B3
Hare St C3
Harrison St B1
Haven Avenue B1
Hay Croft Avenue B1
Hay Croft St B1
Heneage Rd B3/C3
Henry St B1
Holme St B3
Hume St C1
James St B1
Joseph St B1
Kent St A3
King Edward St A3
Lambert Rd C2
Library B2
Lime St B1
Lister St B1
Littlefield Lane C1
Lockhill A3
Lord St B1
Lower Spring St A3
Ludford St C3
Macaulay St B1
Mallard Mews C3
Manor Avenue C2
Market A3
Market Hall B2
Market St B3
Moody Lane A3
Moss Rd C2
Nelson St A3
New St B2
Osbourne St B2
Pasture St B3
Peaks Parkway C3
Pelham Rd C1
Police Station B3
Post Office B1/B2
Pyewipe Rd A1
Railway Place A3
Railway St A3
Recreation Ground C2
Rendel St A2
Retail Park A2/B3
Richard St B1
Ripon St B1
Robinson St East B3
Royal St A3
St Hilda's Avenue C1
St James C2
Sheepfold St B3/C3
Shopmobility B2
Sixhills St C3
South Park B2
Superstore B3/B2
Tasburgh St C3
Tennyson St B2
Thesiger St A3
Time Trap C2
Town Hall B2
Veal St B1
Victoria Retail Park A3
Victoria St North A2
Victoria St South B2
Victoria St West B2
Watkin St A1
Welholme Avenue C2
Welholme Rd C3
Wellington St B3
Wellowgate C2
Werneth Rd B3
West Coates Rd A1
Westgate A2
Westminster Drive C1
Willingham St C3
Wintringham Rd C2
Wood St B3
Yarborough Drive B1
Yarborough Hotel C2

Hanley 335

Acton St A3
Albion St B2
Argyle St C1
Ashbourne Grove A2
Avoca St A3
Baskerville Rd B3
Bedford Rd C1
Bedford St C1
Bethesda St B2
Bexley St A2
Birches Head Rd A3
Botteslow St C3
Boundary St A2
Broad St C2
Broom St A3
Bryan St A2
Bucknall New Rd B3
Bucknall Old Rd B3
Bus Station B3
Cannon St C2
Castlefield St C1
Cavendish St B1
Central Forest Park A2
Century Retail Park B1
Charles St B3
Cheapside B2
Chell St A3
Cinema A2
Clarke St C1
Cleveland Rd C2
Clifford St C3
Clough St B2
Clough St East B2
Clyde St C1
College Rd C2
Cooper St C2
Corbridge Rd A1
Cutts St C2
Davis St C1
Denbigh St A1
Derby St C3
Dilke St A3
Dudson Ctr, The A2
Dundas St A3
Dundee Rd C1
Dyke St B3
Eastwood Rd C3
Eaton St A3
Etruria Park B1
Etruria Rd B1
Etruria Vale Rd C1
Festing St A3
Festival Heights Retail Park A1
Festival Retail Park A1
Fire Station C2
Foundry St B2
Franklyn St C3
Garnet St B1
Garth St B3
George St A3
Gilman St B3
Glass St B3
Goodson St B3
Greyhound Way A1
Grove Place C1
Hampton St C3
Hanley Park C1
Hanley Park C2
Harding Rd C2
Hassall St B3
Havelock Place C1
Hazlehurst St C3
Hinde St C2
Hope St B2
Houghton St C2
Hulton St A3
Information Centre B2
Jasper St C2
Jervis St A3
John Bright St A3
John St B2
Keelings Rd A3
Kimberley Rd C1
Ladysmith Rd C1
Lawrence St C2
Leek Rd C3
Library C2
Lichfield St C3
Linfield Rd B3
Loftus St A2
Lower Bedford St C1
Lower Bryan St A2
Lower Mayer St A3
Lowther St A1
Magistrates Court C2
Malham St A2
Marsh St B2
Matlock St C3
Mayer St A3
Milton St C1
Mitchell Arts Centre B2
Moston St A3
Mount Pleasant C1
Mulgrave St A1
Mynors St B3
Nelson Place B3
New Century St B1
Octagon Retail Park B1
Ogden Rd C3
Old Hall St B3
Old Town Rd A3
Pall Mall B2
Palmerston St C3
Park and Ride C2
Parkway, The C2
Pavilion Drive A1
Pelham St C3
Percy St B2
Piccadilly B2
Picton St B3
Plough St A3
Police Station C2
Portland St A1
Post Office A3/B2
Potteries Centre, The B2
Potteries Museum & Art Gallery B2
Potteries Way B1
Powell St A1
Pretoria Rd C1
Quadrant Rd B2
Ranelagh St C2
Raymond St C2
Rectory Rd C1
Regent Rd C2
Regent Theatre B2
Richmond Terrace C2
Ridgehouse Drive A1
Robson St C2
St Ann St B3
St Luke St B3
Sampson St B2
Shaw St A1
Sheaf St C2
Shearer St C1
Shelton New Rd C1
Shirley Rd C2
Slippery Lane B2
Snow Hill C2
Spur St C3
Stafford St B2
Stubbs Lane C3
Sun St C1
Supermarket A1/B2
Superstore B2
Talbot St C3
Town Hall B2
Town Rd A3
Trinity St B2
Union St A2
Upper Hillchurch St A3
Upper Huntbach St B3
Victoria Hall B3
Warner St C2
Warwick St C1
Waterloo Rd A1
Waterloo St B3
Well St B3
Wellesley St C2
Wellington Rd B3
Wellington St B3
Whitehaven Drive A2
Whitmore St C1
Windermere St A1
Woodall St A1
Yates St C2
York St A2

Harrogate 335

Albert St C2
Alexandra Rd B2
Arthington Avenue B2
Ashfield Rd A2
Back Cheltenham Mount B2
Beech Grove C1
Belmont Rd C1
Bilton Drive A2
BMI The Duchy Hospital C1
Bower Rd B2
Bower St B2
Bus Station B2
Cambridge Rd B2
Cambridge St B2
Cemetery A2
Chatsworth Grove A2
Chatsworth Place A2
Chatsworth Rd A2
Chelmsford Rd B3
Cheltenham Cres B2
Cheltenham Mt B2
Cheltenham Parade B2
Christ Church B3
Christ Church Oval B3
Chudleigh Rd B3
Clarence Drive B1
Claro Rd A3
Claro Way A3
Coach Park B2
Coach Rd B3
Cold Bath Rd C1
Commercial St B2
Coppice Avenue A1
Coppice Drive A1
Coppice Gate A1
Cornwall Rd B1
Council Offices B1
Crescent Gardens B1
Crescent Rd B1
Dawson Terrace A2
Devonshire Place B3
Dixon Rd A2
Dixon Terrace A2
Dragon Avenue B3
Dragon Parade B2
Dragon Rd B2
Duchy Rd B1
East Parade B2
East Park Rd C3
Esplanade B1
Everyman C2
Fire Station A2
Franklin Mount A2
Franklin Rd B2
Franklin Square A2
Glebe Rd C1
Grove Park Court A3
Grove Park Terrace A3
Grove Rd A2
Hampsthwaite Rd A1
Harcourt Drive B3
Harcourt Rd B3
Harrogate Station B2
Harrogate Convention Centre B1
Harrogate Justice Centre (Magistrates' and County Courts) C2
Harrogate Ladies Coll B1
Harrogate Theatre B2
Heywood Rd C1
Hollins Crescent A1
Hollins Mews A1
Hollins Rd A1
Hydro Leisure Ctr, The A1
Information Centre B1
James St B2
Jenny Field Drive A1
John St B2
Kent Drive A1
Kent Rd A1
Kings Rd A2
Kingsway B3
Kingsway Drive B3
Lancaster Rd C1
Leeds Rd C2
Lime Grove B3
Lime St A3
Mayfield Grove B2
Mercer B1
Montpellier Hill B1
Mornington Crescent A3
Mornington Terrace B3
Mowbray Square B3
North Park Rd B3
Oakdale Avenue A1
Oatlands Drive C3
Odeon B2
Osborne Rd A2
Otley Rd C2
Oxford St B2
Parade, The B2
Park Chase B3
Park Parade B3
Park View B2
Parliament St B1
Police Station C3
Post Office B2/C1
Providence Terrace A2
Queen Parade C3
Queen's Rd C1
Raglan St C2
Regent Avenue A3
Regent Grove A3
Regent Parade A3
Regent St A3
Regent Terrace A3
Ripon Rd A1
Robert St C2
Royal Baths & Turkish Baths B1
Royal Pump Room B1
St Luke's Mount A2
St Mary's Avenue C1
St Mary's Walk C1
Scargill Rd A1
Skipton Rd A3

Skipton St A2
Slingsby Walk C3
South Park Rd C3
Spring Grove A1
Springfield Avenue B1
Station Avenue B2
Station Parade B2
Stray Rein C3
Stray, The C2/C3
Studley Rd A2
Superstore B2/C1
Swan Rd B1
Tower St C2
Trinity Rd C2
Union St B2
Valley Drive C1
Valley Gardens C1
Valley Mount C1
Victoria Avenue C2
Victoria Rd C1
Victoria Shopping Ctr B2
Waterloo St A2
West Park C2
West Park St C2
Wood View A1
Woodfield Avenue A3
Woodfield Drive A3
Woodfield Grove A3
Woodfield Rd A3
Woodfield Square A3
Woodside B3
York Place C3
York Rd B1

Holyhead Caergybi 335

Armenia St A2
Arthur St C2
Beach Rd A1
Boston St B2
Bowling Green C3
Bryn Erw Rd C3
Bryn Glas Close C3
Bryn Glas Rd C3
Bryn Gwyn Rd C1
Bryn Marchog A1
Bryn Mor Terrace A2
Bryngoleu Avenue A1
Cae Braenar C3
Cambria St B1
Captain Skinner's Obelisk B2
Cecil St C2
Celtic Gateway Footbridge B2
Cemetery C1/C2
Cleveland Avenue C2
Coastguard Lookout A2
Court B2
Cybi Place A2
Cyttir Rd C3
Edmund St B1
Empire B2
Ferry Terminals B2
Ffordd Beibio B3
Ffordd Feurig C3
Ffordd Hirnos C3
Ffordd Jasper C3
Ffordd Tudur B3
Fire Station C2
Garreglwyd Rd B1
Gilbert St C2
Gorsedd Circle B1
Gwelfor Avenue A1
Harbour Office A3
Harbour View B3
Henry St C2
High Terrace C1
Hill St B2
Holborn Rd C2
Holland Park Ind Est C3
Holyhead Park B1
Holyhead Station B2
King's Rd C2
Kingsland Rd C2
Lewascote C3
Library B2
Lifeboat Station A1
Llanfawr Close C3
Llanfawr Rd C3
Lligwy St C2
Lon Deg C3
London Rd C3
Longford Rd B1
Longford Terrace B1
Maes Cybi B1
Maes Hedd A1
Maes-Hyfryd Rd C1
Maes-y-Dref B1
Maes-yr-Haf A2/B1
Maes-yr-Ysgol C3
Marchog C3
Marina A1
Maritime Museum A1
Market B2
Market St B2
Mill Bank B1
Min-y-Mor Rd A1
Morawelon Ind Est B3
Morawelon Rd B3
Moreton Rd C1
New Park Rd B1
Newry St A2
Old Harbour Lighthouse A3
Plas Rd C1
Police Station B2
Porth-y-Felin Rd A1
Post Office A1/B2/B3
Prince of Wales Rd A2
Priory Lane B3
Pump St C1
Queens Park B1
Reseifion Rd C1
Rock St B1
Roman Fort B2
St Cybi St B2
St Cybi's Church B2
St Seiriol's Close B1
Salt Island Bridge A2
Seabourne Rd A1
South Stack Rd B1
Sports Ground B1
Stanley St B2
Station St B2
Superstore C2
Tan-y-Bryn Rd A1
Tan-yr-Efail C2
Tara St C1
Thomas St B1
Town Hall A2
Treseifion Estate C2
Turkey Shore Rd B2
Ucheldre Arts Ctr B1
Ucheldre Avenue B1
Upper Baptist St B1
Victoria Rd B2
Victoria Terrace B2
Vulcan St B1
Walthew Avenue A1
Walthew Lane A1
Wian St C2

Hull 335

Adelaide St C1
Albert Dock C1
Albion St B2
Alfred Gelder St B2
Anlaby Rd B1
Arctic Corsair B3
Beverley Rd A1
Blanket Row C2
Bond St B2
Bonus Arena B2
Bridlington Avenue A2
Brook St B1
Brunswick Avenue A1
Bus Station B1
Camilla Close C3
Cannon St A2
Caroline St A2
Carr Lane B2
Castle St C2
Central Library B1
Charles St A2
Citadel Way B3
Clarence St B3
Cleveland St A3
Clifton St A1
Colonial St B1
Court B2
Deep, The C3
Dinostar C2
Dock Office Row B3
Dock St B2
Drypool Bridge B3
Egton St A3
English St C1
Ferens Gallery B2
Ferensway B1
Fire Station A1
Francis St A2
Francis St West A2
Freehold St A1
Freetown Way A2
Früit Theatre C2
Garrison Rd B3
George St B2
Gibson St A2
Great Thornton St B1
Great Union St A3
Green Lane A2
Grey St A1
Grimston St B2
Grosvenor St A1
Guildhall B2
Guildhall Rd B2
Hands-on History B2
Harley St A1
Hessle Rd C1
High St B3
Hull Minster B2
Hull Paragon Interchange Sta B1
Hull & East Riding Museum B3
Hull Ice Arena C1
Hull City Hall B2
Hull College B3
Hull History Centre A2
Hull New Theatre A2
Hull Truck Theatre B1
Humber Dock Marina C2
Humber Dock St C2
Humber St C2
Hyperion St A3
Information Centre B1
Jameson St B1
Jarratt St B2
Jenning St A3
King Billy Statue C2
King Edward St B2
King St A2
Kingston Retail Park C1
Kingston St C2
Liddell St A1
Lime St A3
Lister St C1
Lockwood St A2
Maister House B3
Maritime Museum B2
Market B2
Market Place B2
Minerva Pier C2
Mulgrave St A3
Myton Swing Bridge C3
Myton St B1
NAPA (Northern Acad of Performing Arts) B1
Nelson St C2
New Cleveland St A3
New George St A2
Norfolk St A1
North Bridge A3
North St B1
Odeon C1
Old Harbour C3
Osborne St B1
Paragon St B2
Park St B1
Percy St A2
Pier St C2
Police Station B1
Porter St C1
Portland St B1
Post Office B1/B2
Posterngate B2
Prince's Quay B2
Prospect Centre B1
Prospect St B1
Queen's Gardens B2
Railway Dock Marina C2
Railway St C2
Real B1
Red Gallery B1
Reform St A2
Retail Park B1
Riverside Quay C2
Roper St B2
St James St C1
St Luke's St B1
St Mark St A3
St Mary the Virgin B3
St Stephens Shopping Centre B1
Scale Lane Footbridge B3
Scott St A2
South Bridge Rd B3
Sport's Centre C1
Spring Bank A1
Spring St B1
Spurn Lightship C2
Spyvee St A3
Stage @TheDock C3
Sykes St A2
Tidal Surge Barrier C3
Tower St B3
Trinity House B2
Vane St A1
Victoria Pier C2
Waterhouse Lane B2
Waterloo St A1
Waverley St C1
Wellington St C2
Wellington St West C2
West St B1
Whitefriargate B2
Wilberforce Drive B2
Wilberforce House B3
Wilberforce Monument B3
William St C1
Wincolmlee A3
Witham A3
Wright St A1

Inverness 336

Abban St A1
Academy St B2
Alexander Place B2
Anderson St A2
Annfield Rd C3
Ardconnel St B3
Ardconnel Terrace B3
Ardross Place B2
Ardross St B2
Argyle St B3
Argyle Terrace B3
Attadale Rd B1
Ballifeary Lane C2
Ballifeary Rd C1/C2
Balnacraig Lane A1
Balnain House B2
Balnain St B2
Bank St B2
Bellfield Park C2
Bellfield Terrace C3
Benula Rd A1
Birnie Terrace A1
Bishop's Rd C2
Bowling Green B2
Bridge St B2
Brown St A2
Bruce Avenue C1
Bruce Gardens C1
Bruce Park C1
Burial Ground A2
Burnett Rd A3
Bus Station B3
Caledonian Rd B1
Cameron Rd A1
Cameron Square A1
Carse Rd A1
Carsegate Rd Sth A1
Castle Garrison Encounter B2
Castle Rd B2
Castle St B3
Celt St B2
Chapel St A2
Charles St B3
Church St B2
Columba Rd B1/C1
Crown Avenue B3
Crown Circus B3
Crown Drive B3
Crown Rd B3
Crown St B3
Culduthel Rd C3
Dalneigh Crescent C1
Dalneigh Rd C1
Denny St B3
Dochfour Drive B1/C1
Douglas Row B2
Duffy Drive C3
Dunabban Rd A1
Dunain Rd B1
Duncraig St B2
Eastgate Shopping Ctr B3
Eden Court C2
Fairfield Rd B1
Falcon Square B3
Fire Station A3
Fraser St B2
Fraser St C2
Friars' Bridge A2
Friars' Lane B2
Friars' St A2
George St A2
Gilbert St A2
Glebe St A2
Glendoe Terrace A1
Glenurquhart Rd C1
Gordon Terrace B3
Gordonville Rd C2
Grant St A2
Grant Street Park (Clachnacuddin FC) A1
Greig St B2
Harbour Rd A3
Harrowden Rd B1
Haugh Rd C2
Heatherley Crescent C3
High St B3
Highland Council Headquarters, The C2
Hill Park C3
Hill St B3
HM Prison B3
Huntly Place A2
Huntly St B2
India St A2
Industrial Estate A3
Information Centre B2
Innes St A2
Inverness B3
Inverness High Sch B1
Inverness Museum & Art Gallery B2
Jamaica St A2
Kenneth St B2
Kilmuir Rd A1
King St B2
Kingsmills Rd B3
Laurel Avenue B1/C1
Library A3
Lilac Grove B1
Lindsay Avenue C1
Lochalsh Rd A1/B1
Longman Rd A3
Lotland Place A2
Lower Kessock St A1
Madras St A2
Maxwell Drive C1
Mayfield Rd C3
Millburn Rd B3
Mitchell's Lane C3
Montague Row B2
Muirfield Rd C3
Muirtown St B1
Nelson St A2
Ness Bank C2
Ness Bridge B2
Ness Walk B2/C2
Old Edinburgh Rd C3
Old High Church B2
Park Rd C1
Paton St C2
Perceval Rd B1
Planefield Rd B2
Police Station A3
Porterfield Bank C3
Porterfield Rd C3
Portland Place A2
Post Office A2/B1/B2
Queen St B2
Queensgate B2
Railway Terrace A3
Rangemore Rd B1
Reay St B3
Riverside St A2
Rose St A2
Ross Avenue B1
Rowan Rd B1
Royal Northern Infirmary C2
St Andrew's Cath C2
St Columba B2
St John's Avenue C1
St Mary's Avenue C1
Sheriff Court B3
Shore St A2
Smith Avenue C1
Southside Place C3
Southside Rd C3
Spectrum Centre B2
Strothers Lane B3
Superstore A1/B2
TA Centre C2
Telford Gardens B1
Telford Rd A1
Telford St A1
Tomnahurich Cemetery C1
Tomnahurich St B2
Town Hall B3
Union Rd B3
Union St B3
Victorian Market B3
Walker Place A2
Walker Rd A3
War Memorial C2
Waterloo Bridge A2
Wells St B1
Young St B2

Ipswich 336

Alderman Rd B2
All Saints' Rd A1
Alpe St B2
Ancaster Rd C1
Ancient House B3
Anglesea Rd B2
Ann St B2
Arboretum A2
Austin St C2
Avenue, The A3
Belstead Rd C2
Berners St B2
Bibb Way B1
Birkfield Drive C1
Black Horse Lane B2
Bolton Lane B3
Bond St C3
Bowthorpe Close B2
Bramford Lane A1
Bramford Rd A1
Bridge St C2
Brookfield Rd A1
Brooks Hall Rd A1
Broomhill Park A2
Broomhill Rd A1
Broughton Rd A2
Bulwer Rd B1
Burrell Rd C2
Bus Station B3
Butter Market B2
Buttermarket Shopping Centre, The B3
Cardinal Pk Leisure Pk C2
Carr St B3
Cecil Rd B2
Cecilia St C2
Chancery Rd C2
Charles St B2
Chevallier St A1
Christchurch Mansion & Wolsey Art Gallery B3
Christchurch Park A3
Christchurch St B3
Cineworld C2
Civic Centre B2
Civic Drive B2
Clarkson St B1
Cobbold St B3
Commercial Rd C2
Constable Rd A3
Constantine Rd C1
Constitution Hill A2
Corder Rd A3
Corn Exchange B2
Cotswold Avenue A2
Council Offices C2
County Hall B3
Crown Court C2
Crown St B2
Cullingham Rd B1
Cumberland St B2
Curriers Lane B2
Dale Hall Lane A2
Dales View Rd A1
Dalton Rd B2
Dillwyn St B1
Elliot St B1
Elm St B2
Elsmere Rd A3
Falcon St C2
Felaw St C3
Fire Station C2
Flint Wharf C3
Fonnereau Rd B2
Fore St C3
Foundation St C3
Franciscan Way C2
Friars St C2
Gainsborough Rd A3
Gatacre Rd B1
Geneva Rd B2
Gippeswyk Avenue C1
Gippeswyk Park C1
Grafton Way C2
Graham Rd A1
Great Whip St C3
Grimwade St C3
Handford Cut B1
Handford Rd B1
Henley Rd A2
Hervey St B3
High St B2
Holly Rd A2
Ipswich Haven Marina C3
Ipswich Museum & Art Gallery B2
Ipswich School A2
Ipswich Station C2
Ipswich Town FC (Portman Road) C2
Ivry St A2
Kensington Rd A1
Kesteven Rd C1
Key St C3
Kingsfield Avenue A3
Kitchener Rd A1
Library A1
Little's Crescent C2
London Rd B1
Low Brook St C3
Lower Orwell St C3
Luther Rd C2
Magistrates Court B2
Manor Rd A3
Mornington Avenue A1
Museum St B2
Neale St B3
New Cardinal St C2
New Cut East C3
New Wolsey B2
Newson St B2
Norwich Rd A1/B1
Oban St B2
Old Custom House C3
Old Foundry Rd B3
Old Merchant's Ho C3
Orford St B2
Paget Rd A2
Park Rd A3
Park View Rd A2
Peter's St C2
Philip Rd C2
Pine Avenue A2
Pine View Rd A2
Police Station B2
Portman Rd B2
Portmans Walk C1
Post Office B2
Princes St C2
Prospect St B1
Queen St B2
Ranelagh Rd C1
Recreation Ground B1
Rectory Rd C2
Regent Theatre B3
Reg Driver Visitor Centre B3
Retail Park C1
Retail Park C2
Richmond Rd A1
Rope Walk C3
Rose Lane C2
Russell Rd C2
St Edmund's Rd A2
St George's St B2
St Helen's St B3
Sherrington Rd A1
Shopmobility B2
Silent St C2
Sir Alf Ramsey Way C1
Sir Bobby Robson Bridge C1
Sirdar Rd B1
Sir John Mills Theatre B1
Soane St B3
Springfield Lane A1
Star Lane C3
Stevenson Rd B1
Stoke Quay C3
Suffolk College C3
Suffolk Retail Park B1
Superstore B1
Surrey Rd B1
Tacket St C3
Tavern St B3
Tower Ramparts B2
Tower Ramparts Shopping Centre B2
Tower St B3
Town Hall B2
Tuddenham Rd A3
University C3
Upper Brook St B3
Upper Orwell St B3
Valley Rd A2
Vermont Crescent B3
Vermont Rd B3
Vernon St C3
Warrington Rd A2
Waterloo Rd A1
Waterworks St C3
Wellington St B1
West End Rd B1
Westerfield Rd A3
Westgate St B2
Westholme Rd A1
Westwood Avenue A1
Willoughby Rd C2
Withipoll St B3
Woodbridge Rd B3
Woodstone Avenue A3
Yarmouth Rd B1

Kendal 336

Abbot Hall Art Gallery & Museum of Lakeland Life & Industry C2
Ambulance Station A2
Anchorite Fields C2
Anchorite Rd C2
Ann St A3
Appleby Rd A3
Archers Meadow C3
Ashleigh Rd A2
Aynam Rd B2
Bankfield Rd B1
Beast Banks B2
Beezon Fields A2
Beezon Rd A2
Beezon Trad Estate A3
Belmont B2
Birchwood Close C1
Blackhall Rd B2
Brewery Arts Ctr B2
Bridge St B2
Brigsteer Rd C1
Burneside Rd A2
Bus Station B2
Buttery Well Rd C2
Canal Head North B3
Captain French Lane C2
Caroline St A2
Castle Hill B3
Castle Howe B2
Castle Rd B3
Castle St A3/B3
Cedar Grove C1
Council Offices B2
County Council Offices A2
Cricket Ground A3
Cricket Ground C3
Cross Lane C2
Dockray Hall Ind Est A2
Dowker's Lane B2
East View B1
Echo Barn Hill C1
Elephant Yard B2
Fairfield Lane A1
Finkle St B2
Fire Station A2
Fletcher Square C3
Football Ground C3
Fowling Lane A3
Gillinggate C2
Glebe Rd C2
Golf Course B1
Goose Holme B3
Gooseholme Bridge B3
Green St A1
Greengate C2
Greengate Lane C1/C2
Greenside B1
Greenwood C1
Gulfs Rd B2
High Tenterfell B1
Highgate B2
Hillswood Avenue C1
Horncop Lane A2
Kendal A2
Kendal Business Park A3
Kendal Castle (Remains) B3
Kendal Fell B1
Kendal Green A1
Kendal Ski Centre B3
Kendal Station A3
Kent Place B2
Kirkbarrow C2
Kirkland C2
Library B2
Library Rd B2
Little Aynam B3
Little Wood B1
Long Close C1
Longpool A3
Lound Rd C3
Lound St C3
Low Fellside B2
Lowther St B2
Magistrates Court A2
Maple Drive C1
Market Place B2
Maude St B2
Miller Bridge B2
Milnthorpe Rd C2
Mint St A3
Mintsfeet Rd A3
Mintsfeet Rd South A2
New Rd B2
Noble's Rest B2
Parish Church C2
Park Side Rd C3
Parkside Bsns Park C3
Parr St B3
Police Station A2
Post Office A3/B2
Quaker Tapestry B2
Queen's Rd B1
Riverside Walk C2
Rydal Mount A2
Sandes Avenue A2
Sandgate A3
Sandylands Rd A3
Serpentine Rd B1
Serpentine Wood B1
Shap Rd A3
South Rd C2
Stainbank Rd C1
Station Rd A3
Stramongate B2
Stramongate Bridge B2
Stricklandgate A2/B2
Sunnyside C3
Thorny Hills B3
Town Hall B2
Undercliff Rd B1
Underwood C1
Union St A2
Vicar's Fields C2
Vicarage Drive C1/C2
Wainwright's Yard B2
Wasdale Close C3
Well Ings C2
Westmorland Shopping Centre & Market Hall B2
Westwood Avenue C1
Wildman St A3
Windermere Rd A1
YHA B2
YWCA B2

King's Lynn 336

Albert St A2
Albion St B2
Alive St James' Swimming Pool B2
All Saints B2
All Saints St B2
Austin Fields A2
Austin St A2
Avenue Rd B3
Bank Side B1
Beech Rd C2
Birch Tree Close B2
Birchwood St A2
Blackfriars Rd B2
Blackfriars St B2
Boal St B1
Bridge St B2
Broad St B2
Broad Walk B3
Burkitt St A2
Bus Station A2
Carmelite Terrace C2
Chapel St A2
Chase Avenue C3
Checker St C2
Church St B2
Clough Lane B2
Coburg St B2
College of West Anglia A3
Columbia Way A3
Common Staithe Quay A1
Corn Exchange A1
County Court Rd B2
Cresswell St A2
Custom House A1
East Coast Business Park C1
Eastgate St A2
Edma St A2
Exton's Rd C3
Ferry Lane B1
Ferry St A1
Framingham's Almshouses B2
Friars St C2
Friars Walk C2
Gaywood Rd A3
George St A2
Gladstone Rd C2
Goodwin's Rd C3
Green Quay Discovery Centre B1
Greyfriars' Tower B2
Guanock Terrace C2
Guildhall A1
Hansa Rd C3
Harding's Way C2
Hardwick Rd C2
Hextable Rd A2
High St B1
Holcombe Avenue C3
Hospital Walk C2
Information Centre B1
John Kennedy Rd A2
Kettlewell Lane A2
King George V Avenue B3
King St B1
King's Lynn Art Centre A1
King's Lynn Station B2
Library B2
Littleport St A2
Loke Rd A2
London Rd B2
Lynn Museum B2
Magistrates Court B1
Majestic B2
Market Lane A1
Millfleet B2
Milton Avenue A3
Nar Valley Walk C2
Nelson St B1
New Conduit St B2
Norfolk St A2
North Lynn Discovery Centre A3
North St A2
Oldsunway B2
Ouse Avenue C1
Page Stair Lane A1
Park Avenue B3
Police Station B2
Portland Place C1
Portland St B2
Purfleet B1
Queen St B1
Raby Avenue A3
Railway Rd A2
Red Mount Chapel B3
Regent Way B2
River Walk A1
Robert St C2
Shopmobility B2
St Ann's St A1
St James St B2
St James' Rd B2
St John's Walk B3
St Margaret's B1
St Nicholas A2
St Nicholas St A1
St Peter's Rd B1
Sir Lewis St A2
Smith Avenue A3
South Everard St C2
South Gate C2
South Quay B1
South St B2
Southgate St C2
Stonegate St B2
Stories of Lynn B1
Surrey St A1
Sydney St C3
Tennyson Avenue B3
Tennyson Rd B3
The Walks Stadium (King's Lynn FC) B3
Tower St B2
Town Hall B1
Town Wall (Remains) B3
True's Yard Fisherfolk Museum A2
Valingers Rd C2
Vancouver Avenue C2
Vancouver Quarter B2
Waterloo St B2
Wellesley St B2
Whitefriars Terrace C2
Windsor Rd C2
Winfarthing St C2
Wisbech Road C2
Wyatt St A2
York Rd C3

Lancaster 336

Aberdeen Rd C3
Aldcliffe Rd C2
Alfred St B3
Ambleside Rd A3
Ambulance & Fire Station B2
Ashfield Avenue B1
Ashton Rd C2
Assembly Rooms Emporium B2
Balmoral Rd B3
Bath House B2
Bath St B3
Blades St B1
BMI Lancaster (private) C3
Borrowdale Rd B3
Bowerham Rd C3
Brewery Lane B2
Bridge Lane B2
Brook St C1
Bulk Rd A3
Bulk St B2
Bus Station B2
Cable St B2
Canal Cruises & Waterbus C2
Carlisle Bridge A1
Carr House Lane C2
Castle B1
Castle Park B1
Caton Rd A3
China St B2
Church St B2
City Museum B2
Clarence St C3
Common Garden St B2
Coniston Rd A3
Cottage Museum B2
Council Offices B2
Courts B2
Cromwell Rd C2
Crown Court B1
Dale St C3
Dallas Rd B1/C1
Dalton Rd B3
Dalton Square B2
Damside St B2
De Vitre St B3
Dee Rd A1
Denny Avenue A1
Derby Rd A2
Dukes, The B2
Earl St A2
East Rd B3
Eastham St C3
Edward St B3
Fairfield Nature Reserve C1
Fairfield Rd B1
Fenton St B2
Firbank Rd A3
Friend's Meeting House B1
Garnet St B3
George St B2
Giant Axe Field B1
Grand B2
Grasmere Rd B3
Greaves Park C3
Greaves Rd C2
Green St A3
Gregson Centre, The B3
Gregson Rd C3
Greyhound Bridge A2
Greyhound Bridge Rd A2
High St B2
Hill Side B1
Hope St C3
Hubert Place B1
Information Centre B2
Kelsy St B1
Kentmere Rd B3
Keswick Road A3
King St B2
Kingsway A3
Kirkes Rd C3
Lancaster City Football Club B1
Lancaster Royal Grammar School B3
Lancaster Station B1
Langdale Rd A3
Ley Court B1
Library B2
Lincoln Rd B1
Lindow St C2
Lodge St B2
Long Marsh Lane B1
Lune Rd A1
Lune St A2
Lune Valley Ramble A3
Mainway A2
Maritime Museum A1
Marketgate Shopping Centre B2
Market St B2
Meadowside C2
Meeting House Lane B1
Millennium Bridge A2
Moor Lane B2
Moorgate B3
Morecambe Rd A1/A2
Nelson St B2
North Rd B2
Orchard Lane C1
Owen Rd A2
Park Rd B3
Parliament St A3
Patterdale Rd A3
Penny St B2
Police Station B2
Portland St C2
Post Office B2/B3
Primrose St C3
Priory B1
Prospect St C3
Quarry Rd B3
Queen St C2
Regent St C2
Ridge Lane A3
Ridge St A3
Royal Lancaster Infirmary (A&E) C2
Rydal Rd B3
Ryelands Park A1
St Georges Quay A1
St John's B2
St Leonard's Gate B2
St Martin's Rd C3
St Nicholas Arcades Shopping Centre B2
St Oswald St C3
St Peter's B3
St Peter's Rd B3
Salisbury Rd B1
Scotch Quarry Urban Park C3
Sibsey St B1
Skerton Bridge A2
South Rd C2
Station Rd B1
Stirling Rd C3
Storey Avenue B1
Storey, The B2
Sunnyside Lane C1
Sylvester St C1
Tarnsyke Rd A1
Thurnham St C2
Town Hall B2
Troutbeck Rd B3
Ulleswater Rd B3
University of Cumbria C3
Vicarage Field B1
Vue B2
West Rd B1
Westbourne Drive C1
Westbourne Rd B1
Westham St C3
Wheatfield St B1
White Cross Business Park C2
Williamson Rd B3
Willow Lane B1
Windermere Rd B3
Wingate-Saul Rd B1
Wolseley St B3
Woodville St B3
Wyresdale Rd C3

Leeds 336

Aire St B3
Albion Place B4
Albion St B4
Albion Way B1
Alma St A6
Ambulance Station B5
Arcades B4
Armley Rd B1
Armories Drive C5
Back Burley Lodge Rd A1
Back Hyde Terrace A2
Back Row C3
Bath Rd C3
Beckett St A6
Bedford St B3
Belgrave St A4
Belle Vue Rd A2
Benson St A5
Black Bull St C5
Blenheim Walk A3
Boar Lane B4
Bond St B4
Bow St C5
Bowman Lane C4
Brewery C4
Brewery Wharf C5
Bridge St A5/B5
Briggate B4
Bruce Gardens C1
Burley Rd A1
Burley St B1
Burmantofs St B6
Bus & Coach Station B5
Butterly St C4
Butts Crescent B4
Byron St A5
Call Lane B4
Calls, The B5
Calverley St A3/B3
Canal St B1
Canal Wharf C3
Carlisle Rd C5
Cavendish Rd A1
Cavendish St A2
Chadwick St C5
Cherry Place A6
Cherry Row A5
City Museum A4
City Varieties Music Hall B4
City Square B3
Civic Hall A3
Clarence Road C5
Clarendon Rd A2
Clarendon Way A3
Clark Lane C6
Clay Pit Lane A4
Cloberry St A2
Close, The B6
Clyde Approach C1
Clyde Gardens C1
Coleman St C2
Commercial St B4
Concord St A5
Cookridge St A4
Copley Hill C1
Core, The B4
Corn Exchange B4
Cromer Terrace A2
Cromwell St A5
Cross Catherine St B6
Cross Green Lane C6
Cross Stamford St A5
Crown & County Courts A3
Crown Point Bridge C5
Crown Point Rd C4
Crown Point Retail Pk C4
David St C3
Dent St C6
Derwent Place C3
Dial St C6
Dock St C4
Dolly Lane A6
Domestic St C2
Drive, The B6
Duke St B5
Duncan St B4
Dyer St B5
East Field St B6
East Parade B3
East St C5
Eastgate B5
Easy Rd C6
Edward St B4
Ellerby Lane C6
Ellerby Rd C6
Fenton St A3
Fire Station B2
First Direct Arena A4
Fish St B4
Flax Place B5
Garth, The B5
Gelderd Rd C1
George St B4
Globe Rd C2
Gower St A5
Grafton St A4
Grand Theatre B4
Granville Rd A6
Great George St A3
Great Wilson St C4
Greek St B3
Green Lane C1
Hanover Avenue A2
Hanover Lane A2
Hanover Square A2
Hanover Way A2
Harewood St B4
Harrison St B4
Haslewood Close B6
Haslewood Drive B6
Headrow, The B3/B4
High Court B5
Holbeck Lane C2
Holdforth Close C1
Holdforth Gardens B1
Holdforth Grove C1
Holdforth Place C1
Holy Trinity B4
Hope Rd A5
Hunslet Lane C4
Hunslet Rd C4
Hyde Terrace A2
Infirmary St B3
Information Centre B3
Ingram Row C3
ITV Yorkshire A1
Junction St C4
Kelso Gardens A2
Kelso Rd A2
Kelso St A2
Kendal Lane A2
Kendell St C4
Kidacre St C4
King Edward St B4
King St B3
Kippax Place C6
Kirkgate B4
Kirkgate Market B4
Kirkstall Rd A1
Kitson St C6
Knight's Way Bridge C5
Lady Lane B4
Lands Lane B4
Lane, The B5
Lavender Walk B6
Leeds Art Gallery B3
Leeds Beckett Univ A3
Leeds Bridge C4
Leeds Coll of Music B5
Leeds Discovery Ctr C5
Leeds General Infirmary (A&E) A3
Leeds Minster B5
Leeds Station B3
Library B3/B4
Light, The B4
Lincoln Green Rd A6
Lincoln Rd A6
Lindsey Gardens A6
Lindsey Rd A6
Lisbon St B3
Little Queen St B3
Long Close Lane C6
Lord St C2
Lovell Park A4
Lovell Park Hill A4
Lovell Park Rd A4
Lower Brunswick St A5
Mabgate A5
Macauly St A5
Magistrates Court A3
Manor Rd C3
Mark Lane B4
Marlborough St B2
Marsh Lane B5
Marshall St C3
Meadow Lane C4
Meadow Rd C4
Melbourne St A5
Merrion Centre A4
Merrion St A4
Merrion Way A4
Mill St B5
Millennium Square A3
Monk Bridge C2
Mount Preston St A2
Mushroom St A5
Neville St C4
New Briggate A4/B4
New Market St B4
New York Rd A5
New York St B5
Nile St A5
Nippet Lane A6
North St A4
Northern Ballet B5
Northern St B3
Oak Rd B1
Oxford Place B3
Oxford Row A3
Parade, The B6
Park Cross St B3
Park Lane A2
Park Place B3
Park Row B4
Park Square B3
Park Square East B3
Park Square West B3
Park St B3
Police Station B5
Pontefract Lane B6
Portland Crescent A3
Portland Way A3
Post Office B4/B5
Quarry House (NHS/DSS Headquarters) B5
Quebec St B3
Queen St B3
Radio Aire A1
Railway St B5
Rectory St A6
Regent St A5
Richmond St C5
Rigton Approach B6
Rigton Drive B6
Rillbank Lane A1
Rosebank Rd A1
Rose Bowl Conference Centre A3
Royal Armouries C5
Russell St B3
St Anne's Cath (RC) A4
St Anne's St B4
St James' Hospital A6
St John's Rd A2
St Johns Centre B4
St Mary's St B5
St Pauls St B3
Saxton Lane B5
Sayner Lane C5
Shakespeare Avenue A6
Shannon St B6
Sheepscar St South A5
Siddall St C3
Skinner Lane A5
South Parade B3
Sovereign St C4
Spence Lane C2
Springfield Mount A2
Springwell Court C2
Springwell Rd C2
Springwell St C2
Stoney Rock Lane A6
Studio Rd A1
Sutton St C2
Sweet St C3
Sweet St West C3
Swinegate B4
Templar St B5
Tetley, The C4
Thoresby Place A3
Torre Rd A6
Town Hall A3
Trinity Leeds B4
Union Place C3
Union St B5
University of Leeds A3
Upper Accommodation Rd B6
Upper Basinghall St B4
Vicar Lane B4
Victoria Bridge C4
Victoria Gate B4
Victoria Quarter B4
Victoria Rd C4
Vue B4
Wade Lane A4
Washington St A1
Water Lane C3
Waterloo Rd C4
Wellington Rd B2/C1
Wellington St B3
West St B2
West Yorkshire Playhouse B5
Westfield Rd A1
Westgate B3
Whitehall Rd B3/C2
Whitelock St A5
Willis St C6
Willow Approach A1
Willow Avenue A1
Willow Terrace Rd A3
Wintoun St A5
Woodhouse Lane A3/A4
Woodsley Rd A1
York Place B3
York Rd B6

Leicester 336

Abbey St A2
All Saints' A1
Aylestone Rd C2
Bath Lane A1
Bede Park C1
Bedford St A3
Bedford St South A3
Belgrave Gate A2
Belvoir St B2
Braunstone Gate B1
Burleys Way A2
Burnmoor St C2
Bus & Coach Station A2
Canning St A2
Carlton St C2
Castle Motte B1
Castle Gardens B1
Cathedral B2
Charles St B3
Chatham St B2
Christow St A3
Church Gate A2
City Hall B3
Clank St B2
Clock Tower B2
Clyde St A3
Colton St B3
Conduit St B3
Crafton St East A3
Craven St A1
Crown Courts B3
Curve B3
De Lux A2
De Montfort Hall C3
De Montfort St C3
De Montfort Univ C1
Deacon St C2
Dover St B3
Duns Lane B1
Dunton St A1
East St B3
East Bond Street A2
Eastern Boulevard C1
Edmonton Rd A3
Erskine St A3
Filbert St C1
Filbert St East C2
Fire Station C3
Fleet St A3
Friar Lane B2
Friday St A2
Gateway St C2
Gateway, The C2
Glebe St B3
Granby St B3
Grange Lane C2
Grasmere St C1
Great Central St A1
Great Hall B1
Guildhall B2
Guru Nanak Sikh Museum B1
Halford St B2
Havelock St C2
Haymarket Shopping Centre A2
High St A2
Highcross Shopping Centre A2
Highcross St A1
HM Prison C2
Horsefair St B2
Humberstone Gate B2
Humberstone Rd A3
Infirmary St C2
Information Centre B2
Jarrom St C2
Jewry Wall B1
Kamloops Crescent A3
King Richard III Visitor Centre B2
King St B2
Lancaster Rd C3
LCB Depot B3
Lee St A3
Leicester Royal Infirmary (A&E) C2
Leicester Station B3
Library B2
London Rd C3
Lower Brown St B2
Magistrates' Court B2
Manitoba Rd A3
Mansfield St A2
Market B2
Market St B2
Mill Lane C2
Montreal Rd A3
Narborough Rd North B1
Nelson Mandela Park C2
New Park St B1
New St B2
New Walk C3
New Walk Museum & Art Gallery C3
Newarke Houses B2
Newarke St B2
Newarke, The B1
Northgate St A1
Orchard St A2
Ottawa Rd A3
Oxford St C2
Phoenix Arts Centre B3
Police Station A3
Post Office B2
Prebend St C3
Princess Rd East C3
Princess Rd West C3
Queen St B3
Rally Community Park, The A2
Regent College C3
Regent Rd C2/C3
Repton St A1
Rutland St B3
St Augustine Rd B1
St Georges Retail Park B3
St George St B3
St Georges Way B3
St John St A2
St Margaret's A2
St Margaret's Way A2
St Martins B2
St Mary de Castro B1
St Matthew's Way A3
St Nicholas B1
St Nicholas Circle B1
Sanvey Gate A2
Silver St B2
Slater St A1
Soar Lane A1
South Albion St B3
Southampton St B3
Sue Townsend Theatre B2
Swain St B3
Swan St A1
Tigers Way C3
Tower St C3
Town Hall B2
Tudor Rd B1
University of Leicester C3
University Rd C3
Upperton Rd C1
Vaughan Way A2
Walnut St C2
Watling St A2
Welford Rd B2
Welford Rd (Leicester Tigers RC) C2
Wellington St B2
West St C3
West Walk C3
Western Boulevard C1
Western Rd C1
Wharf St North A3
Wharf St South A3
Y Theatre, The B3
Yeoman St B3
York Rd B2

Lewes 336

Abinger Place B1
All Saints Centre B2
Anne of Cleves Ho C1
Avenue, The B1
Barbican Ho Mus B1
Brewery B2
Brook St A2
Brooks Rd A2
Bus Station B2
Castle Ditch Lane B1
Castle Precincts B1
Chapel Hill B3
Church Lane A1/A2
Cliffe High St B2
Cliffe Industrial Est C3
Cluny St C1
Cockshut Rd C1
Convent Field C2
Coombe Rd A2
County Hall B1
Course, The B1
Court Rd B2
Crown Court B2
Cuilfail Tunnel B3
Davey's Lane A3
Dripping Room, The (Lewes FC) C2
East St B2
East Sussex College C2
Eastport Lane C1
Fire Station A2
Fisher St B2
Friars Walk B2
Garden St B1
Government Offices C2
Grange Rd B1
Ham Lane C2
Harveys Way B2
Hereward Way A2
High St B1/B2
Hop Gallery B2
Information Centre B2
Keere St B1
King Henry's Rd B1
Lancaster St B2
Landport Rd A1
Leisure Centre C3
Lewes Bridge B2
Lewes Castle B1
Lewes Golf Course B3
Lewes Southern By-Pass C2
Lewes Station B2
Library B2
Malling Brook Ind Est A3
Malling Down Nature Reserve A3
Malling Hill A3
Malling Industrial Est A2
Malling St A3/B3
Market St B2
Martlets, The A2
Martyr's Monument B3
Mayhew Way A2
Morris Rd B3
Mountfield Rd C2
Needlemakers, The B2
New Rd B1
Newton Rd A1
North St A2/B2
Offham Rd B1
Old Malling Way A1
Orchard Rd A3
Paddock Lane B1
Paddock Rd B1
Paddock Sports Gd B1
Park Rd B1
Pelham Terrace A1
Pells Outdoor Swimming Pool A1
Pells, The A1
Phoenix Causeway B2
Phoenix Industrial Est B2
Phoenix Place B2
Pinwell Rd B2
Police Station B1
Post Office B2
Prince Edward's Rd B1
Priory of St Pancras (remains of) C1
Priory St C1
Railway Lane B2
Railway Land Nature Reserve B3
Rotten Row B1
Riverside Ind Est A2
Rufus Close B1
St John St B2
St John's Terrace B1
St Nicholas Lane B2
St Pancras Rd C1
Sewage Works C3
South Downs Bsns Pk A3
South St B3/C3
Southdowns Rd A2
Southerham Junction C3
Southover Grange Gardens B1
Southover High St C1
Southover Rd B1
Spences Field A3
Spences Lane A2
Stansfield Rd A1
Station Rd B2
Station St B2
Sun St B1
Superstore A2/B2
Sussex Police HQ A2
Talbot Terrace B1
Thebes Gallery B2
Toronto Terrace B1
Town Hall B2
West St B2
White Hill B1
Willeys Bridge A1

Lincoln 337

Alexandra Terrace B1
Anchor St C1
Arboretum B3
Arboretum Avenue B3
Avenue, The B1
Baggholme Rd B3
Bailgate A2
Beaumont Fee B1
BMI The Lincoln Hospital A2
Brayford Way C1
Brayford Wharf East C1
Brayford Wharf North B1
Bruce Rd A2
Burton Rd A1
Bus Station (City) C2
Canwick Rd C2
Cardinal's Hat B2
Carline Rd B1
Castle B1
Castle St A1
Cathedral B2
Cathedral St B2
Cecil St A2
Chapel Lane A2
Cheviot St B3
Church Lane A2
City Hall B1
Clasketgate B2
Clayton Sports Gd A3
Coach Park C2
Collection, The B2
County Hospital (A&E) B3
County Hall B1
Courts C1
Cross St C2
Crown Courts B1
Curle Avenue A3
Danesgate B2
Drill Hall B2
Drury Lane B1
East Bight A2
East Gate A2
Eastcliff Rd B3
Eastgate B2
Egerton Rd A3
Ellis Windmill A1
Engine Shed, The C1
Exchequer Gate B2
Firth Rd C1
Flaxengate B2
Florence St B3
George St C3
Good Lane A2
Gray St A1
Great Northern Terrace C3
Greetwell Rd B3
Greetwellgate B3
Grove, The A3
Haffenden Rd A2
High St B2/C1
Hungate B2
James St A2
Jews House & Court B2
Kesteven St C2
Langworthgate A2
Lawn, The B1
Lee Rd A3
Library B2
Lincoln Central Station C2
Lincoln College B2
Lincolnshire Life A1
Lincoln University Technical Coll (UTC) B2
Lindum Rd B2
Lindum Sports Ground A3
Lindum Terrace B3
Liquorice Park B1
Mainwaring Rd A3
Manor Rd A2
Market C2
Massey Rd A3
Medieval Bishop's Palace B2
Mildmay St A1
Mill Rd A1
Millman Rd B3
Minster Yard B2
Monks Rd B3
Montague St B2
Mount St A1
Nettleham Rd A2
Newland B1
Newport A2
Newport Arch A2
Newport Cemetery A2
Northgate A2
Odeon C1
Orchard St B1
Oxford St C2
Park St B1
Pelham Bridge C2
Pelham St C2
Portland St C2
Post Office A1/B2/B3
Potter Gate B2
Priory Gate B2
Queensway A3
Rasen Lane A1
Ropewalk C1
Rosemary Lane B2
St Anne's Rd B3
St Benedict's C1
St Giles Avenue A3
St Mark's Shopping Centre C1
St Marks St C1
St Mary-le-Wigford C1
St Mary's St C2
St Nicholas St A2
St Rumbold's St B2
St Swithin's B2
Saltergate C1
Saxon St A1
Sewell Rd B3
Silver St B2
Sincil St C2
Spital St A2
Spring Hill B1
Stamp End C3
Steep Hill B2
Stonebow & Guildhall C2
Stonefield Avenue A2
Tentercroft St C1
Theatre Royal B2
Tritton Rd C1
Tritton Retail Park C1
Union Rd B1
University of Lincoln C1
Upper Lindum St B3
Upper Long Leys Rd A1
Usher B2
Vere St A2
Victoria St B1
Victoria Terrace B1
Vine St B3
Wake St A1
Waldeck St A1
Waterside North C2
Waterside Shopping Centre C2
Waterside South C2
West Parade B1
Westgate A2
Wigford Way C1
Williamson St A2
Wilson St A1
Winn St B3
Wragby Rd A3
Yarborough Rd A1

Liverpool 337

Abercromby Square C5
Addison St A3
Adelaide Rd B6
Ainsworth St B4
Albany Rd B6
Albert Edward Rd B6
Angela St C6
Anson St B4
Argyle St C3
Arrad St C4
Ashton St B5
Audley St A4
Back Leeds St A2
Basnett St B3
Bath St A1
Beacon, The B3
Beatles Story, The C2
Beckwith St C3
Bedford Close C5
Bedford St North C5
Bedford St South C5
Benson St C4
Berry St C4
Birkett St A4
Bixteth St B2
Blackburne Place C4
Bluecoat B3
Bold Place C4
Bold St C4
Bolton St B3
Bridport St B4
Bronte St B4
Brook St A1
Brownlow Hill B4/B5
Brownlow St B5
Brunswick Rd A5
Brunswick St B1
Bus Station C2
Butler Crescent A6
Byrom St A3
Caledonia St C4
Cambridge St C5
Camden St A4
Canada Boulevard B1
Canning Dock C2
Canterbury St A4
Cardwell St C6
Carver St A4
Cases St B3
Castle St B2
Catherine St C5
Cavern Club B3
Central Library A3
Chapel St B2
Charlotte St B3
Chatham Place C6
Chatham St C5
Cheapside B2
Chavasse Park C2
Chestnut St C5
Christian St A3
Church St B3
Clarence St B4
Clayton Square Shopping Centre B3
Coach Station A4
Cobden St A5
Cockspur St A2
College St C3
College St North A5
College St South A5
Colquitt St C4
Comus St A3
Concert St C3
Connaught Rd B6
Cook St B2
Copperas Hill B4
Cornwallis St C3
Covent Garden B2
Craven St A4
Cropper St B3
Crown St B5/C6
Cumberland St B2
Cunard Building B1
Dale St B2
Dansie St B4
Daulby St B5
Dawson St B3
Dental Hospital B5
Derby Square B2
Drury Lane B2
Duckinfield St B4
Duke St C3
Earle St A2
East St A2
Eaton St A2
Edgar St A3
Edge Lane B6
Edinburgh Rd A6
Edmund St B2
Elizabeth St B5
Elliot St B3
Empire Theatre B4
Empress Rd B6
Epstein Theatre B3
Epworth St A5
Erskine St A5
Everyman Theatre C5
Exchange St East B2
FACT C4
Falkland St A5
Falkner St C5/C6
Farnworth St A6
Fenwick St B2
Fielding St A6
Fire Station A4
Fleet St C3
Fraser St A4
Freemasons Row A2
Gardner Row A3
Gascoyne St A2
George St B2
Gibraltar Road A1
Gilbert St C3
Gildart St A4
Gill St B4
Goree B2
Gower St C2
Gradwell St C3
Great Crosshall St A3
Great George St C4
Great Howard St A1
Great Newton St B4
Greek St B4
Green Lane B4
Greenside A5
Greetham St C3
Gregson St A5
Grenville St C3
Grinfield St C6
Grove St C5
Guelph St A6
Hackins Hey B2
Haigh St A4
Hall Lane B6
Hanover St B3
Harbord St C6
Hardman St C4
Harker St A4
Hart St B4
Hatton Garden A2
Hawke St B4
Helsby St B6
Henry St C3
Highfield St A2
Highgate St B6
Hilbre St B4
Hope Place C4
Hope St C4
Hope University A5
Houghton St B3
Hunter St A3
Hutchinson St A6
Information Ctr B4/C2
Institute for the Performing Arts C4
International Slavery Museum C2
Irvine St B6
Irwell St B2
Islington A4
James St B2
James St Station B2
Jenkinson St A4
John Moores University A2/A3/A4/B4/C4
Johnson St A3
Jubilee Drive B6
Kempston St A4
Kensington A6
Kensington Gardens B6
Kensington St A6
Kent St C3
King Edward St A1
Kinglake St B6
Knight St C4
Lace St A3
Langsdale St A4
Law Courts C2
Leece St C4
Leeds St A2
Leopold Rd B6
Lime St B3
Lime St Station B4
Liver St C2
Liverpool Central Station B3
Liverpool Landing Stage B1
Liverpool Institute for Performing Arts (LIPA) C4
Liverpool ONE C2
Liverpool Wheel, The C2
London Rd A4/B4
Lord Nelson St B4
Lord St B2
Lovat St C6
Low Hill A5
Low Wood St A6
Lydia Ann St C3
M&S Bank Arena C2
Mansfield St A4
Marmaduke St B6
Marsden St A6
Martensen St B6
Marybone A3
Maryland St C4
Mason St B6
Mathew St B2
May St B4
Melville Place C6
Merseyside Maritime Museum C2
Metquarter B3
Metropolitan Cathedral (RC) B5
Midghall St A2
Molyneux Rd A6
Moor Place B4
Moorfields B2
Moorfields Station B2
Moss St A5
Mount Pleasant B4/B5
Mount St C4
Mount Vernon B6
Mulberry St C5
Municipal Buildings B2
Mus of Liverpool C2
Myrtle St C5
Naylor St A2
Nelson St C4
New Islington A4
New Quay B1
Newington St C3
North John St B2
North St A3
North View B6
Norton St A4
O2 Academy B4
Oakes St B5
Odeon B2
Old Hall St A1
Old Leeds St A2
Oldham Place C4
Oldham St C4
Olive St C6
Open Eye Gallery C3
Oriel St A2
Ormond St B2
Orphan St C6
Overbury St C6
Overton St B6
Oxford St C5
Paisley St A1
Pall Mall A2
Paradise St C3
Park Lane C3
Parker St B3
Parr St C3
Peach St B5
Pembroke Place B4
Pembroke St B5
Philharmonic Hall C5
Phythian Park A6
Pickop St A2
Pilgrim St C4
Pitt St C3
Playhouse Theatre B3
Pleasant St B4
Police HQ C2
Police Sta A4/A6/B4
Pomona St B4
Port of Liverpool Building B2
Post Office A2/A4/A5/B2/B3/B4/C4
Pownall St C2
Prescot St A5
Preston St B3
Princes Dock A1
Princes Gardens A2
Princes Jetty A1
Princes Parade B1
Princes St B2
Pythian St A6
Queen Square Bus Station B3
Queensland St C6
Queensway Tunnel (Docks exit) B1
Queensway Tunnel (Entrance) B3
Radio City B2
Ranelagh St B3
Redcross St B2
Renfrew St B6
Renshaw St B4
Richmond Row A4
Richmond St B3
Rigby St A2
Roberts St A1
Rock St B4
Rodney St C4
Rokeby St A4
Romily St A6
Roscoe Lane C4
Roscoe St C4
Rose Hill A3
Royal Albert Dock C2
Royal Court Theatre B3
Royal Liver Building B1
Royal Liverpool Hospital (A&E) B5
Royal Mail St B4
Rumford Place B2
Rumford St B2
Russell St B4
St Andrew St B4
St Anne St A4
St Georges Hall B3
St John's Centre B3
St John's Gardens B3
St John's Lane B3
St Joseph's Crescent A4
St Minishull St B5
St Nicholas Place B1
St Paul's Square A2
Salisbury St A4
Salthouse Dock C2
Salthouse Quay C2
Sandon St C5
Saxony Rd B6
Schomberg St A6
School Lane B2
Seel St C3
Seymour St B4
Shaw St A5
Shopmobility C2
Sidney Place C6
Sir Thomas St B3
Skelhorne St B4
Slater St C3
Smithdown Lane B6
Soho Square A4
Soho St A4
South John St B2
Springfield A4
Stafford St A4
Standish St A3
Stanley St B2
Strand St C2
Strand, The B2
Suffolk St C3
Sydney Jones Library C5
Tabley St C3
Tarleton St B3
Tate Liverpool Gallery C2
Teck St B6
Temple St B2
Titanic Memorial B1
Tithebarn St B2
Town Hall B2
Trowbridge St B4
Trueman St A3
Union St B2
Unity Theatre C4
University C5
University of Liverpool B5
Upper Baker St A6
Upper Duke St C4
Upper Frederick St C3
Vauxhall Rd A2
Vernon St B2
Victoria Gallery & Museum B5
Victoria St B2
Vine St C5
Wakefield St A4

Walker Art Gallery 🏛 A3
Walker St A6
Wapping C2
Water St B1/B2
Waterloo Rd A1
Wavertree Rd B6
West Derby Rd A6
West Derby St B5
Western Approaches War Museum 🏛 B2
Whitechapel B3
Whitley Gardens A5
William Brown St B3
William Henry St A4
Williamson Square B3
Williamson St B3
Williamson's Tunnels Heritage Centre ✦ C6
Women's Hospital Ⓗ C6
Wood St B3
World Museum, Liverpool 🏛 A3
York St C3

Llandudno 337

Abbey Place B1
Abbey Rd B1
Adelphi St B3
Alexandra Rd C2
Anglesey Rd A1
Argyll Rd B3
Arvon Avenue A2
Atlee Close C3
Augusta St B3
Back Madoc St B2
Bodafon St B3
Bodhyfryd Rd A2
Bodnant Crescent C3
Bodnant Rd C3
Bridge Rd C2
Bryniau Rd C1
Builder St B3
Builder St West C2
Cabin Lift Cable Car ✦ A2
Camera Obscura ✦ A3
Caroline Rd B2
Chapel St A2
Charlton St B3
Church Crescent C1
Church Walks A2
Claremont Rd B2
Clement Avenue A2
Clifton Rd B2
Clonmel St B3
Coach Station B3
Conway Rd B3
Conwy Archive Service B2
Council St West C3
Cricket and Rec Gd B2
Cwlach Rd A2
Cwlach St A1
Cwm Howard Lane C3
Cwm Place C3
Cwm Rd C3
Dale Rd C1
Deganwy Avenue B2
Denness Place C2
Dinas Rd C2
Dolydd B1
Erol Place B2
Ewloe Drive C3
Fairways C2
Ffordd Dewi C3
Ffordd Dulyn C2
Ffordd Dwyfor C3
Ffordd Elisabeth C3
Ffordd Gwynedd C3
Ffordd Las C3
Ffordd Morfa C3
Ffordd Penrhyn C3
Ffordd Tudno C3
Ffordd yr Orsedd C3
Ffordd Ysbyty C2
Fire & Ambulance Sta B3
Garage St B3
George St A2
Gloddaeth Avenue B1
Gloddaeth St B2
Gogarth Rd B1
Great Orme Mines ✦ A1
Great Ormes Rd B1
Great Orme Tramway ✦ A2
Happy Valley A2
Happy Valley Rd A3
Haulfre Gardens ✿ A1
Herkomer Crescent C1
Hill Terrace A2
Home Front Mus 🏛 B2
Hospice B1
Howard Rd B3
Information Centre ℹ B2
Invalids' Walk B1
James St B2
Jubilee St B3
King's Avenue C2
King's Rd C2
Knowles Rd C2
Lees Rd C2
Library B2
Llandudno 🏛 A2
Llandudno (A&E) Ⓗ C2
Llandudno Station ⇌ B3
Llandudno Football Gd C2
Llewelyn Avenue A2
Lloyd St B2
Lloyd St West B1
Llwynon Rd A1
Llys Maelgwn B1
Madoc St B2
Maelgwn Rd B2
Maes-y-Cwm C3
Maes-y-Orsedd C3
Maesdu Bridge C2
Maesdu Rd C2/C3
Marian Place C2
Marian Rd C2
Marine Drive (Toll) A3
Market St A2
Miniature Golf Course A1
Morfa Rd B1
Mostyn 🏛 B3
Mostyn Broadway B3
Mostyn St B3
Mowbray Rd C2
New St A2
Norman Rd B3
North Parade A2
North Wales Golf Links C1
Old Bank, The 🏛 A2
Old Rd A2
Oval, The B1
Oxford Rd B3
Parade, The B3
Parc Llandudno Retail Park B3
Pier ✦ A3
Plas Rd A2
Police Station 🚓 B3
Post Office ✉ A2/B3
Promenade A3
Pyllau Rd A1
Rectory Lane A2
Rhuddlan Avenue C3
St Andrew's Avenue B2
St Andrew's Place B2
St Beuno's Rd A1
St David's Place B2
St David's Rd B2
St George's Place A3
St Mary's Rd B2
St Seriol's Rd B2
Salisbury Pass B1
Salisbury Rd B2
Somerset St B3
South Parade A2
Stephen St B3
Tabor Hill A2
Town Hall B2
Trinity Avenue B1
Trinity Crescent C1
Trinity Square B3
Tudno St A2
Ty-Coch Rd A2
Ty-Gwyn Rd A1/A2
Ty'n-y-Coed Rd A1
Vaughan St B3
Victoria Shopping Centre B3
Victoria 🚋 A2
War Memorial ✦ A2
Werny Wylan C3
West Parade B1
Whiston Pass A2
Winllan Avenue C2
Wyddfyd Rd A2
York Rd A2

Llanelli 337

Alban Rd B3
Albert St B1
Als St B3
Amos St C1
Andrew St A3
Ann St C2
Annesley St B2
Arfryn Avenue A3
Avenue Cilfig, The A2
Belvedere Rd A1
Bigyn Park Terrace C3
Bigyn Rd C3
Bond Avenue C3
Brettenham St A1
Bridge St B2
Bryn Place C1
Bryn Rd C1
Bryn Terrace C1
Bryn-More Rd C1
Brynhyfryd Rd A2
Brynmelyn Avenue A3
Brynmor Rd B1
Burry St C1
Bus Station B2
Caersalem Terrace C2
Cambrian St C1
Caswell St C3
Cedric St B3
Cemetery A2
Chapman St A1
Charles Terrace C2
Church St B2
Clos Caer Elms A1
Clos Sant Paul C2
Coastal Link Rd B1/C1
Coldstream St B2
Coleshill Terrace B1
College Hill B3
College Square B3
Copperworks Rd C2
Coronation Rd C3
Corporation Avenue A3
Council Offices B2
Court B2
Cowell St B2
Cradock St C2
Craig Avenue C3
Cricket Ground A1
Derwent St A1
Dillwyn St C2
Druce St C1
Eastgate Leisure Complex ✦ B2
Elizabeth St B2
Emma St C2
Erw Rd B1
Felinfoel Rd A2
Fire Station A3
Firth Rd C3
Fron Terrace C3
Furnace United Rugby Football Ground A1
Gelli-On B2
George St C2
Gilbert Crescent A2
Gilbert Rd A2
Glanmor Rd C2
Glanmor Terrace C2
Glasfryn Terrace A3
Glenalla Rd B3
Glevering St B3
Goring Rd A2
Gorsedd Circle 🏛 A2
Grant St C3
Graveyard C2
Great Western Close C2
Greenway St B1
Hall St B2
Harries Avenue A2
Hedley Terrace A2
Heol Elli B3
Heol Goffa A3
Heol Nant-y-Felin A3
Heol Siloh B2
Hick St C2
High St C1
Indoor Bowls Centre B1
Inkerman St B2
Island Place B2
James St B3
John St B2
King George Avenue B3
Lake View Close A2
Lakefield Place C1
Lakefield Rd C1
Langland Rd C3
Leisure Centre B1
Library B2
Llanelli House 🏛 B2
Llanelli Parish Church ⛪ B2
Llanelli Station ⇌ C2
Llewellyn St C2
Lliedi Crescent A3
Lloyd St B2
Llys Alys B3
Llys Fran A3
Llysnewedd C1
Long Row A3
Maes Gors C2
Maesyrhaf A3
Mansel St C3
Marblehall Rd B3
Marborough Rd A3
Margam St C3
Marged St C2
Marine St C1
Mariners, The C1
Market B2
Market St B2
Marsh St C2
Martin Rd C3
Miles St A1
Mill Lane A3/B2
Mincing Lane B2
Murray St B2
Myn y Mor B1
Nathan St C1
Nelson Terrace C1
Nevill St C2
New Dock Rd C2
New Rd A1
New Zealand St A1
Odeon 🎦 B2
Old Lodge C2
Old Rd A2
Paddock St C2
Palace Avenue B3
Parc Howard A2
Parc Howard Museum & Art Gallery 🏛🏛 A2
Park Crescent B1
Park St B2
Parkview Terrace B1
Pemberton St C2
Pembrey Rd A1
Peoples Park B1
Police Station 🚓 B2
Post Office ✉ B2/C2
Pottery Place B3
Pottery St B3
Princess St B1
Prospect Place A2
Pryce St A1
Queen Mary's Walk C3
Queen Victoria Rd C1
Raby St B1
Railway Terrace C2
Ralph St B2
Ralph Terrace C1
Regalia Terrace B3
Rhydyrafon A3
Richard St B2
Robinson St B2
Roland Avenue A1
Russell St C3
St David's Close C1
St Elli Shopping Ctr B2
St Margaret's Drive A1
Spowart Avenue A1
Station Rd B2/C2
Stepney Place B2
Stepney St B2
Stewart St A1
Stradey Park Avenue A1
Sunny Hill A2
Superstore A2
Swansea Rd A3
Talbot St C3
Temple St B3
Thomas St A2
Tinopolos TV Studios ✦ B2
Toft Place A3
Town Hall B2
Traeth Ffordd C1
Trinity Rd C3
Trinity Terrace C2
Tunnel Rd B3
Tyisha Rd C3
Union Blgs A2
Upper Robinson St B2
Vauxhall Rd B2
Walter's Rd B3
Waun Lanyrafon B2
Waun Rd A3
Wern Rd B3
West End A2
Y Bwthyn C3
Zion Row B3

London 338

Abbey Orchard St E4
Abbey St E8
Abchurch Lane D7
Abingdon St E5
Achilles Way D3
Acton St B5
Addington St E5
Air St D4
Albany St B3
Albemarle St D4
Albert Embankment F5
Alberta St F6
Aldenham St A4
Alderney St F3
Aldersgate St C7
Aldford St D3
Aldgate ⊖ C8
Aldgate High St C8
Aldwych C5
Allsop Place B2
Alscot Rd E8
Amwell St B6
Angel ⊖ A6
Appold St C8
Argyle Square B5
Argyle St B5
Argyll St C4
Arnold Circus B8
Artillery Lane C8
Artillery Row E4
Ashbridge St B2
Association of Photographers Gallery 🏛 B7
Baker St ⊖ B2
Baker St B2
Balaclava Rd F8
Balcombe St B2
Baldwin's Gardens C6
Balfour St F7
Baltic St B7
Bank ⊖ C7
Bank Museum 🏛 C7
Bank of England C7
Bankside D7
Bankside Gallery 🏛 D6
Banner St B7
Barbican ⇌⊖ C7
Barbican Centre for Arts, The C7
Barbican Gallery 🏛 C7
Basil St E2
Bastwick St B7
Bateman's Row B8
Bath St B7
Bath Terrace E7
Bayley St C4
Baylis Rd E6
Bayswater Rd D2
Beak St D4
Beauchamp Place E2
Bedford Row C5
Bedford Square C4
Bedford St D5
Bedford Way B4
Beech St C7
Belgrave Place E3
Belgrave Rd F4
Belgrave Square E3
Bell Lane C8
Belvedere Rd E5
Berkeley Square D3
Berkeley St D3
Bermondsey St E8
Bernard St B5
Berners Place C4
Berners St C4
Berwick St C4
Bessborough St F4
Bethnal Green Rd B8
Bevenden St B7
Bevis Marks C8
BFI (British Film Institute) 🎦 D5
BFI London IMAX Cinema 🎦 D6
Bidborough St B5
Binney St C3
Birdcage Walk E4
Bishopsgate C8
Black Prince Rd F5
Blackfriars ⇌⊖ D6
Blackfriars Bridge D6
Blackfriars Rd E6
Blackfriars Passage D6
Blandford St C2
Blomfield St C7
Bloomsbury St C4
Bloomsbury Way C5
Bolton St D3
Bond St ⊖ C3
Borough ⊖ E7
Borough High St E7
Borough Rd E6
Boswell St C5
Bourne St F3
Bow St C5
Bowling Green Lane B6
Brad St D6
Brandon St F7
Bressenden Place E4
Brewer St D4
Brick St D3
Bridge St E5
Britannia Walk B7
British Film Institute (BFI) 🎦 D5
British Library 🏛 B4
British Museum 🏛 C5
Britton St B6
Broad Sanctuary E4
Broadley St C2
Broadway E4
Brompton Rd E2
Brompton Square E2
Brook Drive F6
Brook St D3
Brown St C2
Brunswick Place B7
Brunswick Shopping Centre, The B5
Brunswick Square B5
Brushfield St C8
Bruton St D3
Bryanston St C2
BT Centre C7
Buckingham Gate E4
Buckingham Palace 🏰 E4
Buckingham Palace Rd F3
Bunhill Row B7
Byward St D8
Cabinet War Rooms & Churchill Museum 🏛 E4
Cadogan Lane E3
Cadogan Place E2
Cadogan Square F2
Cadogan St F2
Cale St F2
Caledonian Rd A5
Calshot St A5
Calthorpe St B5
Calvert Avenue B8
Cambridge Circus C4
Cambridge Square C2
Cambridge St F3
Camomile St C8
Cannon St D7
Cannon St ⇌⊖ D7
Capel Manor College B3
Capland St B1
Carey St C5
Carlisle Lane E5
Carlisle Place E4
Carlton House Terrace D4
Carmelite St D6
Carnaby St C4
Carter Lane C6
Carthusian St C7
Cartwright Gardens B5
Castle Baynard St D6
Cavendish Place C3
Cavendish Square C3
Caxton Hall E4
Caxton St E4
Central St B7
Chalton St B4
Chancery Lane ⊖ C6
Chapel St C2
Chapel St E3
Charing Cross ⇌⊖ D5
Charing Cross Rd C4
Charles II St D4
Charles Dickens Museum, The 🏛 B5
Charles Square B7
Charles St D3
Charlotte Rd B8
Charlotte St C4
Chart St B7
Charterhouse Square C6
Charterhouse St C6
Chatham St F7
Cheapside C7
Chenies St C4
Chesham St E3
Chester Square F3
Chester Way F6
Chesterfield Hill D3
Cheval Place E2
Chiltern St C3
Chiswell St C7
Church St B2
City Garden Row A6
City Rd B7
City Thameslink ⇌ C6
City University, The B6
Claremont Square A6
Clarendon St F3
Clarges St D3
Clerkenwell Close B6
Clerkenwell Green B6
Clerkenwell Rd B6
Cleveland St C4
Clifford St D4
Clink Prison Mus 🏛 D7
Cliveden Place F3
Clock Museum 🏛 C7
Club Row B8
Cockspur St D4
Coleman St C7
Columbia Rd B8
Commercial Rd C9
Commercial St C8
Compton St B6
Conduit St D3
Congreve St F8
Connaught Square C2
Connaught St C2
Constitution Hill E3
Copperfield St E6
Coptic St C5
Cornhill C7
Cornwall Rd D6
Coronet St B8
County St E7
Courtauld Gallery 🏛 D5
Courtenay St F6
Covent Garden ⊖ D5
Covent Garden ✦ D5
Cowcross St C6
Cowper St B7
Crampton St F7
Cranbourn St D4
Craven St D5
Crawford Place C2
Crawford St C2
Creechurch Lane C8
Cricket Museum 🏛 B1
Cromer St B5
Cromwell Rd F1
Crosby Row E7
Crucifix Lane E8
Cumberland Gate D2
Cumberland St F3
Cumberland Terrace A3
Cuming Museum 🏛 F7
Curtain Rd B8
Curzon St D3
Cut, The E6
D'arblay St C4
Dante Rd F6
Davies St C3
Dean St C4
Deluxe Gallery 🏛 B8
Denbigh Place F4
Denmark St C4
Dering St C3
Devonshire St C3
Diana, Princess of Wales Memorial Fountain ✦ D1
Diana, Princess of Wales Memorial Walk E4
Dingley Rd B7
Dorset St C2
Doughty St B5
Douglas St F4
Dover St D3
Downing St E5
Draycott Avenue F2
Draycott Place F2
Druid St E8
Drummond St B4
Drury Lane C5
Drysdale St B8
Duchess St C3
Dufferin St B7
Duke of Wellington Pl E3
Duke St C3/D3
Duke St Hill D7
Duke's Place C8
Duncannon St D5
Dunton Rd F8
East Rd B7
East St F7
Eastcastle St C4
Eastcheap D8
Eastman Dental Hospital Ⓗ B5
Eaton Gate F3
Eaton Place E3
Eaton Square E3
Eaton Terrace F3
Ebury Bridge F3
Ebury Bridge Rd F3
Eccleston Bridge F3
Eccleston Square F3
Eccleston St E3
Edgware Rd C2
Edgware Rd ⊖ C2
Egerton Gardens E2
Eldon St C7
Elephant & Castle ⇌ F7
Elephant and Castle ⇌⊖ E6
Elephant Rd F7
Elizabeth Bridge F3
Elizabeth St F3
Elm Tree Rd B1
Elystan Place F2
Elystan St F2
Embankment ⊖ D5
Endell St C5
Endsleigh Place B4
Enid St E8
Ennismore Gardens E2
Erasmus St F4
Euston ⇌⊖ B4
Euston Rd B4
Euston Square ⊖ B4
Evelina Children's Hospital E5
Eversholt St A4
Exhibition Rd E1
Exmouth Market B6
Fair St E8
Falmouth Rd E7
Fann St B7
Farringdon ⇌⊖ C6
Farringdon Rd C6
Farringdon St C6
Featherstone St B7
Fenchurch St D8
Fenchurch St ⇌ D8
Fetter Lane C6
Finsbury Circus C7
Finsbury Pavement C7
Finsbury Square B7
Fitzalan St F6
Fitzmaurice Place D3
Fleet St C6
Fleming Lab. Mus 🏛 C1
Floral St D5
Florence Nightingale Museum 🏛 E5
Folgate St C8
Fore St C7
Foster Lane C7
Foundling Mus, The 🏛 B5
Francis St F4
Frazier St E6
Freemason's Hall C5
Friday St C7
Fulham Rd F1
Gainsford St E8
Garden Row E6
Gee St B7
Geological Museum 🏛 E1
George Row E9
George St C2
Gerrard St D4
Gibson Rd F5
Giltspur St C6
Glasshouse St D4
Glasshouse Walk F5
Gloucester Place C2
Gloucester Square C1
Gloucester St F4
Golden Hinde ⛴ D7
Golden Lane B7
Golden Square D4
Goodge St ⊖ C4
Goodge St C4
Gordon Hospital Ⓗ F4
Gordon Square B4
Goswell Rd B6
Gough St B5
Goulston St C8
Gower St B4
Gracechurch St D7
Grafton Way B4
Graham Terrace F3
Grange Rd E8
Grange Walk E8
Gray's Inn Rd B5
Great College St E5
Great Cumberland Pl C2
Great Dover St E7
Great Eastern St B8
Great Guildford St D7
Great Marlborough St C4
Great Ormond St B5
Great Ormond Street Children's Hosp Ⓗ B5
Great Percy St B5
Great Peter St E4
Great Portland St ⊖ B3
Great Portland St C3
Great Queen St C5
Great Russell St C4
Great Scotland Yard D5
Great Smith St E4
Great Suffolk St D6/E6
Great Titchfield St C4
Great Tower St D8
Great Windmill St D4
Greek St C4
Green Park ⊖ D4
Green St D3
Greencoat Place F4
Gresham St C7
Greville St B5/C6
Greycoat Hospital Sch E4
Greycoat Place E4
Grosvenor Crescent E3
Grosvenor Gardens E3
Grosvenor Place E3
Grosvenor Square D3
Grosvenor St D3
Grove End Rd B1
Guards Museum and Chapel 🏛 E4
Guildhall Art Gallery 🏛 C7
Guilford St B5
Guy's Hospital Ⓗ D7
Haberdasher St B7
Hackney Rd B8
Half Moon St D3
Halkin St E3
Hall PL B1
Hall St B6
Hallam St C3
Hamilton Close B1
Hampstead Rd B4
Hanover Square C3
Hans Crescent E2
Hans Rd E2
Hanway St C4
Hardwick St B6
Harewood Avenue B2
Harley St C3
Harper Rd E7
Harrington Rd F1
Harrison St B5
Harrowby St C2
Hasker St F2
Hastings St B5
Hatfields D6
Hay's Galleria D8
Hay's Mews D3
Hayles St F6
Haymarket D4
Hayward Gallery 🏛 D5
Helmet Row B7
Herbrand St B5
Hercules Rd E5
Hertford St D3
Heygate St F7
High Holborn C5
Hill St D3
HMS Belfast ⛴ D8
Hobart Place E3
Holborn ⊖ C5
Holborn C6
Holborn Viaduct C6
Holland St D6
Holmes Museum 🏛 B2
Holywell Lane B8
Horse Guards' Rd D4
Horseferry Rd F4
Houndsditch C8
Houses of Parliament 🏛 E5
Howland St C4
Hoxton Square B8
Hoxton St B8
Hugh St F3
Hunter St B5
Hunterian Museum 🏛 C5
Hyde Park D2
Hyde Park Corner ⊖ E3
Hyde Park Crescent C2
Hyde Park St C2
Imperial Coll London E1
Imperial College Rd E1
Imperial War Mus 🏛 E6
Information Centre ℹ D4, F3, C7
Inner Circle B3
Ironmonger Row B7
Jacob St E9
Jamaica Rd E8
James St C3
James St D5
Jermyn St D4
Jockey's Fields C5
John Carpenter St D6
John Fisher St D9
John Islip St F4
John St B5
Johnathan St F5
Judd St B5
Kennings Way F6
Kennington ⊖ F6
Kennington Lane F6
Kennington Park Rd F6
Kennington Rd E6/F6
Kensington Gardens D1
Kensington Gore E1
Kensington Rd E1
Keyworth St E6
King Charles St E5
King St D5
King William St C7
King's College London D5
King's Cross ⇌ A5
King's Cross Rd B5
King's Cross St Pancras ⊖ A5
King's Rd F2
Kingley St C4
Kingsland Rd B8
Kingsway C5
Kinnerton St E3
Kipling St E7
Knightsbridge ⊖ E2
Lamb St C8
Lamb's Conduit St C5
Lambeth Bridge F5
Lambeth High St F5
Lambeth North ⊖ E6
Lambeth Palace 🏰 E5
Lambeth Palace Rd E5
Lambeth Rd E6
Lambeth Walk F5
Lancaster Gate ⊖ D1
Lancaster Place D5
Lancaster St E6
Lancaster Terrace D1
Langham Place C3
Lant St E7
Leadenhall St C8
Leake St E5
Leather Lane C6
Leathermarket St E8
Leicester Square ⊖ D4
Leicester St D4
Leonard St B7
Leroy St E8
Lever St B7
Lexington St D4
Lidlington Place A4
Lime St D8
Lincoln's Inn Fields C5
Lindsey St C6
Lisle St D4
Lisson Grove B1
Lisson St C2
Liverpool St C8
Liverpool St ⇌⊖ C8
Lloyd Baker St B6
Lloyd Square B6
Lodge Rd B2
Lollard St F6
Lombard St C7
London Aquarium 🐟 E5
London Bridge ⇌⊖ D7
London Bridge Hospital Ⓗ D7
London City Hall 🏛 D8
London Dungeon 🏛 E5
London Guildhall Univ C7
London Rd E6
London St C1
London Transport Museum 🏛 D5
London Wall C7
London Eye ✦ E5
Long Acre D5
Long Lane C6
Long Lane E7
Longford St B3
Lord's Cricket Gd (MCC & Middlesex CCC) B1
Lower Belgrave St E3
Lower Grosvenor Pl E3
Lower Marsh E6
Lower Sloane St F3
Lower Thames St D7
Lowndes St E3
Ludgate Circus C6
Ludgate Hill C6
Lupus St F4
Luxborough St C3
Lyall St E3
Macclesfield Rd B7
Madame Tussaud's ✦ B3
Maddox St D3
Malet St C4
Mall, The E4
Maltby St E8
Manchester Square C3
Manchester St C3
Manciple St E7
Mandela Way F8
Mandeville Place C3
Mansell St D8
Mansion House 🏛 C7
Mansion House ⊖ D7
Maple St C4
Marble Arch ⊖ C2
Marble Arch D2
Marchmont St B5
Margaret St C4
Margery St B6
Mark Lane D8
Marlborough Rd D4
Marshall St C4
Marshalsea Rd E7
Marsham St E4
Marylebone ⇌⊖ B2
Marylebone High St C3
Marylebone Lane C3
Marylebone Rd B3/C2
Marylebone St C3
Mecklenburgh Square B5
Middle Temple Lane C6
Middlesex St (Petticoat Lane) C8
Midland Rd A4
Millbank F5
Milner St F2
Minories C8
Monck St E4
Monkton St F6
Monmouth St C5
Montagu Place C2
Montagu Square C2
Montagu St C5
Montague Place C4
Montpelier St E2
Montpelier Walk E2
Monument ⊖ D7
Monument St D7
Monument, The ✦ D7
Moor Lane C7
Moorfields C7
Moorfields Eye Hospital Ⓗ B7
Moorgate C7
Moorgate ⇌⊖ C7
Moreland St B6
Morley St E6
Mortimer St C4
Mossop St F2
Mount Pleasant B6
Mount St D3
Murray Grove A7
Mus of Gdn History 🏛 E5
Museum of London 🏛 C7
Museum St C5
Myddelton Square B6
Myddelton St B6
National Gallery 🏛 D4
National Hospital Ⓗ B5
National Portrait Gallery 🏛 D4
Natural History Museum 🏛 E1
Neal St C5
Nelson's Column ✦ D5
Neville St F1
New Bond St C3/D3
New Bridge St C6
New Cavendish St C3
New Change C7
New Fetter Lane C6
New Inn Yard B8
New Kent Rd F7
New North Rd A7
New Oxford St C4
New Scotland Yard E5
New Square C5
Newburn St F5
Newgate St C6
Newington Butts F6
Newington Causeway E7
Newton St C5
Nile St B7
Noble St C7
Noel St C4
Norfolk Crescent C2
Norfolk Square C1
North Audley St D3
North Carriage Drive D2
North Crescent C4
North Ride D2
North Row D3
North Wharf Rd C1
Northampton Square B6
Northington St B5
Northumberland Ave D5
Norton Folgate C8
Nottingham Place C3
Old Bailey C6
Old Broad St C7
Old Brompton Rd F1
Old Compton St C4
Old County Hall E5
Old Gloucester St C5
Old Jamaica Rd E9
Old Kent Rd F8
Old King Edward St C7
Old Marylebone Rd C2
Old Montague St C9
Old Nichol St B8
Old Paradise St F5
Old Spitalfields Mkt C8
Old St B7
Old St ⇌⊖ B7
Old Vic 🎭 E6
Onslow Gardens F1
Onslow Square F1
Ontario St E6
Open Air Theatre 🎭 B3
Operating Theatre Museum 🏛 D7
Orange St D4
Orchard St C3
Ossulston St A4
Outer Circle B2
Ovington Square E2
Oxford Circus ⊖ C4
Oxford St C3/C4
Paddington ⇌⊖ C1
Paddington St C3
Page's Walk E8
Palace St E4
Pall Mall D4
Pall Mall East D4
Pancras Rd A5
Panton St D4
Paris Garden D6
Park Crescent B3
Park Lane D3
Park Rd B2
Park St D3
Park St D7
Parker St C5
Parliament Square E5
Parliament St E5
Paternoster Square C6
Paul St B7
Pear Tree St B6
Pelham Crescent F2
Pelham St F1
Penfold St C2
Penton Place F6
Penton Rise B5
Penton St A6
Pentonville Rd A5/A6
Percival St B6
Petticoat Lane (Middlesex St) C8
Petty France E4
Phoenix Place B5
Phoenix Rd A4
Photo Gallery 🏛 D4
Piccadilly D3
Piccadilly Circus ⊖ D4
Pilgrimage St E7
Pimlico ⊖ F4
Pimlico Rd F3

Pitfield St B8
Pollock's Toy Mus C4
Polygon Rd A4
Pont St E2
Porchester Place C2
Portland Place C3
Portman Mews C3
Portman Square C3
Portman St C2
Portugal St C5
Postal Mus, The B5
Poultry C7
Praed St C1
Primrose St C8
Prince Consort Rd E1
Prince's Gardens E1
Princes St C7
Procter St C5
Provost St B7
Quaker St B8
Queen Anne St C3
Queen Elizabeth Hall D5
Queen Elizabeth St E8
Queen Square B5
Queen St D7
Queen Street Place D7
Queen Victoria St D6
Queens Gallery E4
Queensberry Place F1
Quilter St B9
Radnor St B7
Rathbone Place C4
Rawlings St F2
Rawstorne St B6
Red Lion Square C5
Red Lion St C5
Redchurch St B8
Redcross Way D7
Reedworth St F6
Regency St F4
Regent Square B5
Regent St C4
Regent's Park B3
Richmond Terrace E5
Ridgmount St C4
Riley Rd E8
Rivington St B8
Robert St B3
Rochester Row F4
Rockingham St E7
Rodney Rd F7
Rolls Rd F8
Ropemaker St C7
Rosebery Avenue B6
Rossmore Rd B2
Rothsay St E8
Rotten Row E2
Roupell St D6
Royal Acad of Arts D4
Royal Academy of Dramatic Art (RADA) B4
Royal Acad of Music B3
Royal Albert Hall E1
Royal Artillery Memorial E2
Royal Brompton Hospital F1/F2
Royal Coll of Nursing C3
Royal Coll of Surgeons C5
Royal Festival Hall D5
Royal London Hospital for Integrated Medicine C5
Royal Marsden Hosp F1
Royal National Theatre D6
Royal National Throat, Nose and Ear Hosp B5
Royal Opera House D5
Rushworth St E6
Russell Square B4
Russell Square B5
Rutland Gate E2
Saatchi Gall F2
Sackville St D4
Sadlers Wells B6
Saffron Hill C6
St Alban's St D4
St Andrew St C6
St Barnabas St F3
St Bartholomew's Hospital C6
St Botolph St C8
St Bride St C6
St George's Circus F6
St George's Drive F4
St George's Rd E6
St George's Square F4
St Giles High St C4
St James's Palace D4
St James's Park E4
St James's St D4
St John St B6
St John's Wood Rd B1
St Margaret St E5
St Mark's Hospital B6
St Martin's Lane D5
St Martin's Le Grand C7
St Mary Axe C8
St Mary's Hospital C1
St Pancras International A5
St Paul's C7
St Paul's Cathedral C7
St Paul's Churchyard C6
St Thomas St D7
St Thomas' Hospital E5
Sale Place C2
Sancroft St F5
Savile Row D4
Savoy Place D5
Savoy St D5
School of Hygiene & Tropical Medicine C4
Science Museum E1
Scrutton St B8
Sekforde St B6
Serpentine Gallery E1
Serpentine Rd D2
Seven Dials C5
Seward St B6
Seymour Place C2
Seymour St C2
Shad Thames D8/E8
Shaftesbury Avenue D4
Shakespeare's Globe Theatre D7
Shepherd Market D3
Sherwood St D4
Shoe Lane C6
Shoreditch High St B8
Shoreditch High St B8
Shorts Gardens C5
Shouldham St C2
Shrek's Adventure E5
Sidmouth St B5
Silk St C7
Sir John Soane's Museum C5
Skinner St B6
Sloane Avenue F2
Sloane Square F2
Sloane Square F3
Sloane St E2
Snow Hill C6
Soho Square C4
Somerset House D5
South Audley St D3
South Carriage Drive E2
South Eaton Place F3
South Kensington F1
South Molton St C3
South Parade F1
South Place C7
South St D3
South Terrace F2
South Wharf Rd C1
Southampton Row C5
Southampton St D5
Southwark D6
Southwark Bridge D7
Southwark Bridge Rd D7
Southwark Cath D7
Southwark Park Rd F8
Southwark St D7
Spa Rd E8
Speakers' Corner D2
Spencer St B6
Spital Square C8
Spring St C1
Stamford St D6
Stanhope St B4
Stanhope Terrace D1
Stephenson Way B4
Stock Exchange C6
Stoney St D7
Strand C6
Strathearn Place D2
Stratton St D3
Sumner St D6
Sussex Gardens C1
Sussex Place C1
Sussex Square D1
Sussex St F3
Sutton's Way B7
Swan St E7
Swanfield St B8
Swinton St B5
Sydney Place F1
Sydney St F2
Tabard St E7
Tabernacle St B7
Tachbrook St F4
Tanner St E8
Tate Britain F5
Tate Modern D7
Tavistock Place B5
Tavistock Square B4
Tea & Coffee Mus D7
Temple D6
Temple Avenue D6
Temple Place D5
Terminus Place E3
Thayer St C3
Theobald's Rd C5
Thorney St F5
Threadneedle St C7
Throgmorton St C7
Thurloe Place F1
Thurloe Square F2
Tonbridge St B5
Tooley St D8
Torrington Place B4
Tothill St E4
Tottenham Court Rd B4
Tottenham Ct Rd C4
Tottenham St C4
Tower Bridge D8
Tower Bridge App D8
Tower Bridge Rd E8
Tower Hill D8
Tower Hill D8
Tower of London, The D8
Toynbee St C8
Trafalgar Square D4
Trinity Square D8
Trinity St E7
Trocadero Centre D4
Tudor St D6
Turin St B9
Turnmill St C6
Tyers St F5
Ufford St E6
Union St D6
University Coll Hosp B4
University College London (UCL) B4
University of London C4
Univ of Westminster C3
University St B4
Upper Belgrave St E3
Upper Berkeley St C2
Upper Brook St D3
Upper Grosvenor St D3
Upper Ground D6
Upper Montague St C2
Upper St Martin's La D5
Upper Thames St D7
Upper Wimpole St C3
Upper Woburn Place B4
Vauxhall Bridge Rd F4
Vauxhall St F5
Vere St C3
Vernon Place C5
Vestry St B7
Victoria E3
Victoria and Albert Museum E1
Victoria Coach Station F3
Victoria Embankment D5
Victoria Place Shopping Centre F3
Victoria St E4
Villiers St D5
Vincent Square F4
Vinopolis City of Wine D7
Virginia Rd B8
Wakley St B6
Walbrook C7
Walcot Square F6
Wallace Collection C3
Walnut Tree Walk F6
Walton St F2
Walworth Rd F7
Wardour St C4/D4
Warner St B6
Warren St B4
Warren St B4
Warwick Square F4
Warwick Way F3
Waterloo E6
Waterloo Bridge D5
Waterloo East D6
Waterloo Rd E6
Watling St C7
Webber St E6
Welbeck St C3
Wellington Arch E3
Wellington Mus E3
Wellington Rd B2
Wellington Row B9
Wells St C4
Wenlock St A7
Wentworth St C8
West Carriage Drive D2
West Smithfield C6
West Square E6
Westbourne St D1
Westbourne Terrace C1
Westminster E5
Westminster Abbey E5
Westminster Bridge E5
Westminster Bridge Rd E6
Westminster Cathedral (RC) E4
Westminster City Hall E4
Westminster Hall E5
Weymouth St C3
Wharf Rd A7
Wharton St B5
Whitcomb St D4
White Cube B8
White Lion Hill D6
White Lion St A6
Whitechapel Rd C9
Whitecross St B7
Whitefriars St C6
Whitehall D5
Whitehall Place D5
Wigmore Hall C3
Wigmore St C3
William IV St D5
Willow Walk F8
Wilmington Square B6
Wilson St C7
Wilton Crescent E3
Wilton Rd F4
Wimpole St C3
Winchester St F3
Wincott St F6
Windmill Walk D6
Woburn Place B5
Woburn Square B4
Wood St C7
Woodbridge St B6
Wootton St D6
Wormwood St C8
Worship St B7
Wren St B5
Wynyatt St B6
Young Vic E6
York Rd E5
York St C2
York Terrace East B3
York Terrace West B3
York Way A5

Luton 337

Adelaide St B1
Albert Rd C2
Alma St B2
Alton Rd C3
Anthony Gardens C1
Arthur St C2
Ashburnham Rd B1
Ashton Rd C2
Back St A2
Bailey St C3
Baker St C2
Biscot Rd A1
Bolton Rd B3
Boyle Close A2
Brantwood Rd B1
Bretts Mead C1
Bridge St B2
Brook St A1
Brunswick St A3
Burr St A3
Bury Park Rd A1
Bute St B2
Buxton Rd B2
Cambridge St C3
Cardiff Grove B1
Cardiff Rd B1
Cardigan St A2
Castle St B2/C2
Chapel St C2
Charles St A3
Chase St C2
Cheapside B2
Chequer St C3
Chiltern Rise C1
Church St B2/B3
Cinema A2
Cobden St A3
College A3
Collingdon St A1
Concorde Avenue A3
Corncastle Rd C1
Cowper St C2
Crawley Green Rd B3
Crawley Rd A1
Crescent Rd A3
Crescent Rise A3
Cromwell Rd A1
Cross St A2
Cross Way, The C1
Crown Court B2
Cumberland St B2
Cutenhoe Rd C3
Dallow Rd B1
Downs Rd B1
Dudley St A2
Duke St A2
Dumfries St B1
Dunstable Place B2
Dunstable Rd A1/B1
Edward St A3
Elizabeth St C2
Essex Close C3
Farley Hill C1
Flowers Way B2
Francis St A1
Frederick St A2
Galaxy Leisure Complex A2
George St B2
George St West B2
Gordon St B2
Grove Rd B1
Guildford St A2
Haddon Rd A3
Harcourt St C2
Hart Hill Drive A3
Hart Hill Lane A3
Hartley Rd A3
Hastings St B2
Hat Factory, The B2
Hatters Way A1
Havelock Rd A2
Hibbert St C2
High Town Rd A3
Highbury Rd A1
Hightown Community Sports & Arts Centre A3
Hillary Crescent C1
Hillborough Rd C1
Hitchin Rd A3
Holly St C2
Holm C1
Hucklesby Way A2
Hunts Close C1
Inkerman St A2
John St B2
Jubilee St A3
Kelvin Close C2
King St B2
Kingsland Rd C3
Larches, The A2
Latimer Rd C2
Lawn Gardens C2
Lea Rd B3
Library B2
Library Rd B2
Library Theatre B2
Liverpool Rd B1
London Rd C2
Luton Station A2
Lyndhurst Rd B1
Magistrates Court B2
Mall, The B2
Manchester St B2
Manor Rd B3
Manor Road Park B3
May St C3
Meyrick Avenue C1
Midland Rd A2
Mill St A2
Milton Rd B1
Moor St A1
Moor, The A1
Moorland Gardens A2
Moulton Rise A3
Napier Rd B1
New Bedford Rd A1
New Town St C2
North St A3
Old Bedford Rd A2
Old Orchard C2
Osbourne Rd C3
Oxen Rd A3
Park Square B2
Park St B3/C3
Park St West B2
Park Viaduct B3
Parkland Drive C1
Police Station B1
Pomfret Avenue A3
Pondwicks Rd B3
Post Office A1/B2
Power Court B3
Princess St B1
Red Rails C1
Regent St B2
Reginald St A2
Rothesay Rd B1
Russell Rise C1
Russell St C1
Ruthin Close C1
St Ann's Rd B3
St George's Square B2
St Mary's B3
St Marys Rd B3
St Paul's Rd C2
St Saviour's Crescent C1
Salisbury Rd B1
Seymour Avenue C3
Seymour Rd C3
Silver St B2
South Rd C2
Stanley St B1
Station Rd A2
Stockwood Crescent C2
Stockwood Park C1
Strathmore Avenue C2
Stuart St B2
Studley Rd A1
Surrey St C3
Sutherland Place C1
Tavistock St C2
Taylor St A3
Telford Way A1
Tennyson Rd C2
Tenzing Grove C1
Thistle Rd B3
Town Hall B2
Townsley Close C2
UK Centre for Carnival Arts B3
Union St B2
Univ of Bedfordshire B3
Upper George St B2
Vicarage St B3
Villa Rd A2
Waldeck Rd A1
Wardown House Mus & Gallery A2
Wellington St B1/B2
Wenlock St A2
Whitby Rd A1
Whitehill Avenue C1
William St A2
Wilsden Avenue C1
Windmill Rd B3
Windsor St C2
Winsdon Rd B1
York St A3

Macclesfield 337

108 Steps B2
Abbey Rd A1
Alton Drive A3
Armett St C1
Athey St B1
Bank St C3
Barber St C3
Barton St C1
Beech Lane A2
Beswick St B1
Black Lane A2
Black Rd C3
Blakelow Gardens C3
Blakelow Rd C3
Bond St B1/C1
Bread St C1
Bridge St B1
Brock St A2
Brocklehurst Avenue A3
Brook St B3
Brookfield Lane B3
Brough St West C1
Brown St C1
Brynton Rd A2
Buckley St C2
Bus Station B2
Buxton Rd B3
Byrons St C2
Canal St B3
Carlsbrook Avenue A3
Castle St B2
Catherine St B1
Cemetery A1
Chadwick Terrace A3
Chapel St C2
Charlotte St B2
Chester Rd B1
Chestergate B1
Christ Church B1
Churchill Way B2
Coare St A1
Commercial Rd B2
Conway Crescent A3
Copper St C3
Cottage St B1
Crematorium A1
Crew Avenue A3
Crompton Rd B1/C1
Cross St C2
Crossall St C1
Cumberland St A1/B1
Dale St B3
Duke St B2
Eastgate B3
Exchange St B2
Fence Avenue B3
Fence Ave Ind Est A3
Flint St B3
Foden St A2
Fountain St B3
Garden St A3
Gas Rd B2
Gateway Gallery B1
George St B2
Glegg St B3
Golf Course C3
Goodall St B3
Grange Rd C1
Great King St B1
Green St B3
Grosvenor Shopping Centre B2
Gunco Lane C3
Half St C2
Hallefield Rd B3
Hatton St C1
Hawthorn Way A3
Heapy St C3
Henderson St B1
Heritage Centre B2
Hibel Rd A2
High St C2
Hobson St C2
Hollins Rd C3
Hope St West B1
Horseshoe Drive B1
Hurdsfield Rd A3
Information Centre B2
James St C2
Jodrell St B3
John St C2
Jordangate A2
King Edward St B2
King George's Field C3
King St B2
King's School A1
Knight Pool C3
Knight St C3
Lansdowne St A3
Library B2
Lime Grove B3
Loney St B1
Longacre St B1
Lord St C2
Lowe St C2
Lowerfield Rd A3
Lyon St B1
Macclesfield College C1
Macclesfield Sta B2
MADS Little Theatre C2
Marina B3
Market B2
Market Place B2
Masons Lane A3
Mill Lane C2
Mill Rd C2
Mill St B2
Moran Rd C1
New Hall St A2
Newton St C1
Nicholson Avenue A3
Nicholson Close A3
Northgate Avenue A2
Old Mill Lane C2
Paradise Mill C2
Paradise St B1
Park Green B2
Park Lane C1
Park Rd C1
Park St C2
Park Vale Rd C1
Parr St B1
Peel St C2
Percyvale St A3
Peter St C1
Pickford St B2
Pierce St B1
Pinfold St B1
Pitt St C2
Police Station B2
Pool St C2
Poplar Rd C2
Post Office B2
Pownall St A2
Prestbury Rd A1/B1
Queen Victoria St B2
Queen's Avenue A3
Registrar B2
Retail Park C2
Richmond Hill C3
Riseley St B1
Roan Court B3
Roe St B2
Rowan Way A3
Ryle St C2
Ryle's Park Rd C1
St George's St C2
St Michael's B2
Samuel St B2
Saville St C3
Shaw St B1
Silk Rd, The A2/B2
Slater St C1
Snow Hill C3
South Park C1
Spring Gardens A2
Statham St C2
Station St A2
Steeple St A3
Sunderland St B2
Superstore A1/A2/C2
Swettenham St B3
Thistleton Close C2
Thorp St B2
Town Hall B2
Townley St B2
Treacle Market B2
Turnock St C3
Union Rd B3
Union St B2
Victoria Park B3
Vincent St C2
Waters Green B2
Waterside C2
West Bond St B1
West Park A1
West Park Museum A1
Westbrook Drive A1
Westminster Rd A1
Whalley Hayes B1
Windmill St C3
Withyfold Drive A2
York St B3

Maidstone 340

Albion Place B3
All Saints B2
Allen St A3
Amphitheatre C2
Archbishop's Palace B2
Bank St B2
Barker Rd C2
Barton Rd C3
Beaconsfield Rd C1
Bedford Place B1
Bishops Way B2
Bluett St A3
BMI The Somerfield Hospital A1
Bower Lane C1
Bower Mount Rd B1
Bower Place C1
Bower St B1
Boxley Rd A3
Brenchley Gardens A2
Brewer St A3
Broadway B2
Broadway Shopping Centre B2
Brunswick St C3
Buckland Hill A1
Buckland Rd B1
Bus Station B3
Campbell Rd C3
Church Rd C1
Church St B3
Cinema C2
Clifford Way C1/C2
College Avenue C2
College Rd C2
Collis Memorial Gdn C3
Cornwallis Rd B1
Corpus Christi Hall B2
Council Offices B3
County Hall A2
County Rd A3
Crompton Gardens C3
Crown & County Courts B2
Curzon Rd A3
Dixon Close C2
Douglas Rd C1
Earl St B2
Eccleston Rd C2
Fairmeadow B2
Fisher St A2
Florence Rd C1
Foley St A3
Foster St C3
Freedom Leisure Centre A1/A2
Fremlin Walk Shopping Centre B2
Gabriel's Hill B3
George St C3
Grecian St A3
Hardy St A3
Hart St C2
Hastings Rd C3
Hayle Rd C3
Hazlitt B2
Heathorn St A3
Hedley St A3
High St B2
HM Prison A3
Holland Rd A3
Hope St A2
Information Centre B2
James St A3
James Whatman Way A2
Jeffrey St A3
Kent County Council Offices A2
Kent History & Liby Ctr A2
King Edward Rd C2
King St B3
Kingsley Rd C3
Knightrider St B3
Launder Way C1
Lesley Place A1
Library B2
Little Buckland Ave A1
Lockmeadow Leisure Complex C2
London Rd B1
Lower Boxley Rd A2
Lower Fant Rd C1
Magistrates Court B3
Maidstone Barracks Station A1
Maidstone East Sta A2
Maidstone Museum & Bentlif Art Gall B2
Maidstone Utd FC A2
Maidstone West Sta B2
Mall, The B3
Market C2
Market Buildings B2
Marsham St B3
Medway St B2
Melville Rd C3
Mill St B2
Millennium Bridge C2
Mote Rd B3
Muir Rd C3
Old Tovil Rd C2
Palace Avenue B3
Perryfield St A2
Police Station B3
Post Office B2/C3
Priory Rd C3
Prospect Place C1
Pudding Lane B2
Queen Anne Rd B3
Queens Rd A1
Randall St A2
Rawdon Rd C3
Reginald Rd C1
Riverstage A1
Rock Place B1
Rocky Hill B1
Romney Place B3
Rose Yard B2
Rowland Close C1
Royal Engineers' Rd A2
Royal Star Arcade B2
St Annes Court B1
St Faith's St B2
St Luke's Rd A3
St Peter St B2
St Peter's Bridge B2
St Peter's Wharf Retail Park B2
St Philip's Avenue C3
Salisbury Rd A3
Sandling Rd A2
Scott St A2
Scrubs Lane B1
Sheal's Crescent C3
Somerfield Lane B1
Somerfield Rd B1
Staceys St A2
Station Rd A2
Superstore A1/B2/B3
Terrace Rd B1
Tonbridge Rd C1
Tovil Rd C2
Town Hall B2
Trinity Park B3
Tufton St B3
Tyrwhitt-Drake Museum of Carriages B2
Union St B3
Upper Fant Rd C1
Upper Stone St C3
Victoria St B1
Warwick Place B1
Wat Tyler Way B3
Waterloo St C3
Waterlow Rd A3
Week St B2
Well Rd A3
Westree Rd C1
Wharf Rd C1
Whatman Park A1
Wheeler St A3
Whitchurch Close B1
Woodville Rd C3
Wyatt St B3
Wyke Manor Rd B3

Manchester 337

Adair St B6
Addington St A5
Adelphi St A1
Advent Way B6
Albert Square B3
Albion St C3
Ancoats Grove B6
Ancoats Grove North B6
Angela St C2
Aquatics Centre C4
Ardwick Green North C5
Ardwick Green Park C5
Ardwick Green South C5
Arlington St A2
Artillery St B3
Arundel St C2
Atherton St B2
Atkinson St B3
Aytoun St B4
Back Piccadilly A4
Baird St B5
Balloon St A4
Bank Place A1
Baring St B5
Barrack St C1
Barrow St A1
Bendix St A5
Bengal St A5
Berry St C5
Blackfriars Rd A3
Blackfriars St A3
Blantyre St C2
Bloom St B4
Blossom St A5
Boad St B5
Bombay St B4
Booth St A3
Booth St B4
Bootle St B3
Brazennose St B3
Brewer St A5
Bridge St A3
Bridgewater Hall B3
Bridgewater Place A4
Bridgewater St B2
Brook St C4
Brotherton Drive A2
Brown St A3
Brown St B4
Brunswick St C6
Brydon Avenue C6
Buddhist Centre A4
Bury St A2
Bus & Coach Station B4
Bus Station B4
Butler St A6
Buxton St C5
Byrom St B3
Cable St A5
Cambridge St C3/C4
Camp St B3
Canal St B4
Cannon St A1
Cardroom Rd A6
Carruthers St A6
Castle St C2
Castlefield Arena B2
Cateaton St A3
Cathedral A3
Cathedral St A3
Cavendish St C4
Chapel St A1/A3
Chapeltown St B5
Charles St C4
Charlotte St B4
Chatham St B4
Chepstow St B3
Chester Rd C1/C2
Chester St C4
Chetham's School of Music A3
China Lane B5
Chippenham Rd A6
Chorlton Rd C2
Chorlton St B4
Church St A2
Church St A4
City Park A4
City Rd East C3
Civil Justice Centre B2
Cleminson St A2
Clowes St A3
College Land A3
Collier St B2
Commercial St C3
Conference Centre C4
Cooper St B4
Copperas St A4
Corn Exchange, The A4
Cornbrook C1
Cornell St A5
Corporation St A4
Cotter St C6
Cotton St A5
Cow Lane B1
Cross St B3
Crown Court B4
Crown St C2
Dalberg St C6
Dale St A4/B5
Dancehouse, The C4
Dantzic St A4
Dark Lane C6
Dawson St C2
Dean St A5
Deansgate A3/B3/C2
Deansgate Castlefield C3
Deansgate Station C3
Dolphin St C6
Downing St C5
Ducie St B5
Duke Place B2
Duke St B2
Durling St C6
East Ordsall Lane A2/B1
Edge St A4
Egerton St C2
Ellesmere St C1
Everard St C1
Everyman B2
Every St B6
Exchange Square A4
Factory, The B2
Fairfield St B5
Faulkner St B4
Fennel St A3
Fire Station A5
Ford St A2
Ford St C6
Fountain St B4
Frederick St A2
Gartside St B2
Gaythorne St A1
George Leigh St A5
George St B4
Gore St A2
Goulden St A5
Granby Row B4
Gravel Lane A3
Great St B6
Great Ancoats St A5
Great Bridgewater St B3
Great George St A1
Great Jackson St C2
Great Marlborough St C4
Great Northern Leisure Complex B3
Greengate A3
Grosvenor St C5
Gun St A5
Hall St B3
Hampson St B1
Hanover St A4
Hanworth Close C5
Hardman St B3
Harkness St C6
Harrison St B6
Hart St B4
Helmet St B6
Henry St A5
Heyrod St B6
High St A4
Higher Ardwick C6
Hilton St A4/A5
Holland St A6
HOME Entertainment Complex C3
Hood St A5
Hope St B1
Hope St B4
Houldsworth St A5
Hoyle St C6
Hulme Hall Rd C1
Hulme St A1
Hulme St C3
Hyde Rd C6
Islington Way A1
Information Centre B4
Irwell St A2
Jackson Crescent C2
Jackson's Row B3
James St A1
Jenner Close C2
Jersey St A5
John Dalton St B3
John Ryland's Liby B3
John St A2
Kennedy St B3
Kincardine Rd C5
King St A3
King St West A3
Law Courts B3
Laystall St B5
Lever St A5
Library B3
Linby St C2
Little Lever St A4
Liverpool Rd B2
Liverpool St B1
Lloyd St B3
Lockton Close C5
London Rd B5
Long Millgate A3
Longacre St B6
Loom St A5
Lower Byrom St B2
Lower Mosley St B3
Lower Moss Lane C2
Lower Ormond St C4
Loxford Lane C4
Luna St A5
Major St B4
Mamucium B2
Manchester Arndale A4
Manchester Art Gallery B4
Manchester Central Convention Complex B3
Manchester Metropolitan University (MMU) B4/C4
Manchester Piccadilly Station B5
Manchester Technology Centre C4
Mancunian Way C3

Manor St C5
Marble St A4
Market St A2
Market St A4
Market St A4
Marsden St A3
Marshall St A5
Mayan Avenue A2
Medlock St C3
Middlewood St B1
Miller St A4
Minshull St B4
Mosley St A4
Mount St B3
Mulberry St B3
Murray St A5
Museum of Science & Industry (MOSI) 🏛 B2
Nathan Drive A2
National Football Museum 🏛 A4
Naval St A5
New Bailey St A2
New Elm Rd B2
New Islington A6
New Islington Sta B6
New Quay St B2
New Union St A6
Newton St A5
Nicholas St B4
North Western St C6
Oak St A4
Odeon A4/B3
Old Mill St A6
Oldfield Rd A1/C1
Oldham Rd A5
Oldham St A4
Opera House B3
Ordsall Lane C1
Oxford Rd C4
Oxford Rd ≥ C4
Oxford St B4
Paddock St C6
Palace Theatre B4
Pall Mall A3
Palmerston St B6
Parker St B4
Peak St B5
Penfield Close C5
Peoples' History Museum 🏛 B2
Peru St A1
Peter St B3
Piccadilly A4
Piccadilly B5
Piccadilly Gardens B4
Piercy St A6
Poland St A5
Police Museum 🏛 A5
Police Station B3/B5
Pollard St B6
Port St A5
Portland St B4
Portugal St East B5
Post Office . . A2/A4/A5/B3/B4/C4
Potato Wharf B2
Princess St B3/C4
Quay St A2
Quay St B2
Queen St B3
Radium St A5
Redhill St A5
Regent Retail Park B1
Regent Rd B1
Rice St B2
Richmond St B4
River St C3
Roby St B5
Rodney St A6
Rosamond St A2
Royal Exchange A3
Sackville St B4
St Andrew's St B6
St Ann St A3
St Ann's A3
St George's Avenue C1
St James St B4
St John St B3
St John's Cath (RC) ✝ . . A2
St Mary's B3
St Mary's Gate A3
St Mary's Parsonage A3
St Peter's Square B3
St Stephen St A2
Salford Approach A3
Salford Central ≥ A2
Sheffield St B5
Sherratt St A5
Shopmobility A4
Shudehill A4
Shudehill A4
Sidney St C4
Silk St A5
Silver St B4
Skerry Close C5
Snell St B6
South King St B3
Sparkle St B5
Spear St A4
Spring Gardens A4
Stanley St A2/B2
Store St B5
Superstore B1
Swan St A4
Tariff St B5
Tatton St C1
Temperance St B6/C6
Thirsk St C6
Thomas St A4
Thompson St A5
Tib Lane B3
Tib St A4
Town Hall (Manchester) B3
Town Hall (Salford) A2
Trafford St C3
Travis St B5
Trinity Way A2
Turner St A4
Union St C6
University of Manchester (North Campus) C5
University of Salford . . . A1
Upper Brook St C5
Upper Cleminson St A1
Upper Wharf St A1
Urban Exchange A5
Vesta St B6
Victoria A4
Victoria Station ≥ A4
Wadesdon Rd C5
Water St B2
Watson St B3
West Fleet St B1
West King St A2
West Mosley St B4
Weybridge Rd A6
Whitworth St B4
Whitworth St West C3
William St A2
William St C6
Wilmott St C3
Windmill St B3
Windsor Crescent A1
Withy Grove A4
Woden St C1
Wood St B3
Woodward St A6
Worrall St C1
Worsley St C2
York St B4
York St C2
York St C4

Merthyr Tydfil Merthyr Tudful 340

Aberdare Rd B2
Abermorlais Terrace B2
Alexandra Rd A3
Alma St C3
Arfryn Place C3
Argyle St C3
Avenue De Clichy C2
Beacons Place Shopping Centre C2
Bethesda St B2
Bishops Grove A3
Brecon Rd A1/B2
Briarmead A3
Bryn St C3
Bryntirion Rd B3/C3
Bus Station B2
Cae Mari Dwn B3
Caedraw Rd C2
Castle Square A1
Castle St B2
Chapel C2
Chapel Bank B1
Church St B3
Civic Centre B2
Clos Penderyn B1
Coedcae'r Court C3
College Boulevard C2
County and Crown Courts B2
Court St C3
Cromwell St B2
Cyfarthfa Castle, Mus and Art Gallery 🏛 . . . A1
Cyfarthfa Ind Est A1
Cyfarthfa Park A1
Cyfarthfa Retail Park . . . B1
Cyfarthfa Rd A1
Dane St A2
Dane Terrace A2
Danyparc B3
Darren View A3
Dixon St B2
Dyke St C3
Dynevor St B2
Elwyn Drive C3
Fire Station B2
Fothergill St B3
Galonuchaf Rd A3
Garth St B2
Georgetown B2
Grawen Terrace A2
Grove Park A2
Grove, The A2
Gurnos Rd A2
Gwaelodygarth Rd A2/A3
Gwaunfarren Grove A3
Gwaunfarren Rd A3
Gwendoline St A3
Hampton St C3
Hanover St A2
Heol S O Davies B1
Heol-Gerrig B1
High St A3/B2/B3/C2
Highland View C3
Howell Close B1
Jackson's Bridge B2
James St C3
John St B3
Joseph Parry's Cott 🏛 B2
Lancaster St A2
Library B2
Llewellyn St A2
Llwyfen St B2
Llwyn Berry B1
Llwyn Dic Penderyn B1
Llwyn-y-Gelynen C1
Lower Thomas St B3
Market C2
Mary St C3
Masonic St C2
Merthyr Tydfil College B2
Merthyr Town FC B3
Merthyr Tydfil Leisure Centre C3
Merthyr Tydfil Sta ≥ . . . C3
Meyrick Villas A2
Miniature Railway ✦ . . . A1
Mount St A2
Nantygwenith St B1
Norman Terrace B2
Oak Rd A2
Old Cemetery B3
Pandy Close A1
Pantycelynen B1
Parade, The B3
Park Terrace B2
Penlan View C2
Penry St B2
Pentwyn Villas A2
Penyard Rd B3
Penydarren Park A3
Penydarren Rd B3
Plymouth St C3
Police Station C2
Pont Marlais West B2
Post Office B2
Quarry Row B2
Queen's Rd B3
Rees St C3
Rhydycar Link C2
Riverside Park A1
St David's B3
St Tydfil's C2
St Tydfil's Avenue C3
St Tydfil's Square Shopping Centre C2
Saxon St A2
School of Nursing A2
Seward St A3
Shiloh Lane B3
Stone Circles B3
Stuart St A2
Summerhill Place B3
Superstore B3
Swan St C2
Swansea Rd B1
Taff Glen View C3
Taff Vale Court B3
Theatre Soar B2
Thomastown Park B3
Tramroad Lane A3
Tramroad Side B2
Tramroad Side North . . . B3
Tramroad Side South . . . C3
Trevithick Gardens C3
Trevithick St A3
Tudor Terrace B2
Twynyrodyn Rd C3
Union St B3
Upper Colliers Row B1
Upper Thomas St B3
Victoria St B2
Vue C2
Vulcan Rd B2
Walk, The B2
Warlow St C3
Well St A2
Welsh Assembly Government Offices . C2
Wern Lane C1
Wern, The (Merthyr RFC) C2
West Grove A2
William St C3
Yew St C3
Ynysfach Engine Ho ✦ C2
Ynysfach Rd C2

Middlesbrough 340

Abingdon Rd C3
Acklam Rd C1
Albert Park C2
Albert Rd B2
Albert Terrace C2
Ambulance Station C1
Aubrey St C3
Avenue, The C2
Ayresome Gardens C2
Ayresome Green Lane . C1
Ayresome St C2
Barton Rd A1
Bilsdale Rd C3
Bishopton Rd C3
Borough Rd B2/B3
Bowes Rd A2
Breckon Hill Rd B3
Bridge St West B2
Brighouse Rd A1
Burlam Rd C1
Bus Station B2
Cannon Park B1
Cannon Park Way B2
Cannon St B1
Captain Cook Square . . . B2
Carlow St C1
Castle Way C3
Chipchase Rd C2
Cineworld B3
Cleveland Centre B2
Clive Rd C2
Commercial St A2
Corporation Rd B2
Costa St C2
Council Offices B3
Crescent Rd C2
Crescent, The C2
Cumberland Rd C2
Depot Rd A2
Derwent St B2
Devonshire Rd C2
Diamond Rd B2
Dock St B3
Dorman Museum 🏛 C2
Douglas St B3
Eastbourne Rd C2
Eden Rd C3
Fire Station A3
Forty Foot Rd A2
Gilkes St B2
Gosford St A2
Grange Rd B2
Gresham Rd B2
Harehills Rd C1
Harford St C2
Hartington Rd B2
Haverton Hill Rd A1
Hey Wood St B1
Highfield Rd C3
Hillstreet Centre B2
Holwick Rd B1
Hutton Rd C3
Ironmasters Way B1
Lambton Rd C3
Lancaster Rd C2
Lansdowne Rd C3
Latham Rd C2
Law Courts B2/B3
Lees Rd B2
Leeway B3
Library B2/C2
Linthorpe Cemetery C1
Linthorpe Rd B2
Lloyd St B2
Longford St C2
Longlands Rd C3
Lower East St A3
Lower Lake C3
Macmillan Academy C1
Maldon Rd C1
Manor St B2
Marsh St B2
Marton Rd B3
Middlesbrough By-Pass B2/C1
Middlesbrough Coll B3
Middlesbrough Dock . . . B3
Middlesbrough Leisure Park B3
Middlesbrough Sta ≥ . . B2
Middletown Park C2
MIMA 🏛 B3
Mulgrave Rd C2
Newport Bridge B1
Newport Bridge Approach Rd B1
Newport Rd B2
North Ormesby Rd B3
North Rd B2
Northern Rd C1
Outram St B2
Oxford Rd C2
Park Lane C2
Park Rd North C2
Park Rd South C2
Park Vale Rd C3
Parliament Rd B1
Police Station A2
Port Clarence Rd A3
Portman St B2
Post Office B3/C1/C2
Princes Rd B2
Python 🏛 A2
Riverside Park Rd A1
Riverside Stadium (Middlesbrough FC) . B3
Rockliffe Rd C2
Romaldkirk Rd B1
Roman Rd C2
Roseberry Rd C3
St Barnabas' Rd C2
St Paul's Rd B2
Saltwells Rd B3
Scott's Rd A3
Seaton Carew Rd A3
Shepherdson Way B3
Shopmobility B2
Snowdon Rd A2
South West Ironmasters Park B1
Southfield Rd B2
Southwell Rd C2
Springfield Rd C1
Startforth Rd A2
Stockton Rd C1
Stockton St A2
Superstore B2
Surrey St C2
Sycamore Rd C2
Tax Offices B3
Tees Viaduct C1
Teessaurus Park A2
Teesside Tertiary Coll . C3
Temenos ✦ B3
Thornfield Rd C1
Town Hall B2
Transporter Bridge (Toll) A3
Union St B2
University of Teesside . B2
Upper Lake C2
Valley Rd C3
Ventnor Rd C2
Victoria Rd B2
Vulcan St A2
Warwick St C2
Wellesley Rd B3
West Lane C1
West Lane Hospital Ⓗ . . C1
Westminster Rd C2
Wilson St B2
Windward Way B3
Woodlands Rd B2
York Rd C3

Milton Keynes 340

Abbey Way A1
Arbrook Avenue B1
Armourer Drive A3
Arncliffe Drive A1
Avebury C2
Avebury Boulevard C2
Bankfield B3
Bayard Avenue A2
Belvedere A2
Bishopstone A1
Blundells Rd A1
Boundary, The C3
Boycott Avenue C2
Bradwell Common Bvd B1
Bradwell Rd C1
Bramble Avenue A2
Brearley Avenue C2
Breckland A1
Brill Place B1
Burnham Drive B1
Campbell Park B3
Cantle Avenue A3
Central Retail Park C1
Century Avenue C2
Chaffron Way C3
Childs Way C1
Christ the Cornerstone B2
Cineworld B2
Civic Offices B2
Cleavers Avenue B2
Colesbourne Drive A3
Conniburrow Bvd B2
Currier Drive A2
Dansteed Way . A2/A3/B1
Deltic Avenue B1
Downs Barn A2
Downs Barn Bvd A3
Eaglestone C3
Eelbrook Avenue B1
Elder Gate B1
Evans Gate C2
Fairford Crescent A3
Falcon Avenue B3
Fennel Drive A2
Fishermead Boulevard C3
Food Centre B3
Fulwoods Drive C3
Glazier Drive A2
Glovers Lane A1
Grafton Gate C1
Grafton St A1/C2
Gurnards Avenue B3
Harrier Drive C3
The Hub Leisure Quarter B2/C2
Ibstone Avenue B1
Langcliffe Drive A1
Leisure Centre C3
Leisure Plaza C1
Leys Rd C1
Library B2
Linceslade Grove C1
Linford Wood A2
Magistrates Court B2
Marlborough Gate B3
Marlborough St A2/B3
Mercers Drive A1
Midsummer C2
Midsummer Boulevard B2
Midsummer Place B2
Milton Keynes Central ≥ C1
Milton Keynes Hospital (A&E) Ⓗ C3
Monks Way A1
Mullen Avenue A3
Mullion Place C3
National Film & Sci-Fi Museum 🏛 B2
Neath Hill A3
North Elder C1
North Grafton B1
North Overgate A3
North Row B2
North Saxon B2
North Secklow B2
North Skeldon A3
North Witan B1
Oakley Gardens A3
Odeon B2
Oldbrook Boulevard C2
Open-Air Theatre B3
Overgate A3
Overstreet A3
Patriot Drive B1
Pencarrow Place B3
Penryn Avenue B3
Perran Avenue C3
Pitcher Lane C1
Place Retail Park, The . . C1
Police Station B2
Portway B2
Post Office A2/B2/B3
Precedent Drive B1
Quinton Drive B1
Ramsons Avenue B2
Retail Park C2
Rockingham Drive A2
Rooksley B1
Saxon Gate B2
Saxon St A1/C3
Secklow Gate B2
Shackleton Place C2
Shopmobility B2
Silbury Boulevard B2
Skeldon A3
South Enmore B3
South Grafton C2
South Row C2
South Saxon C2
South Secklow B3
South Witan C2
Springfield B3
Stainton Drive A1/B1
Stanton Wood A1
Stantonbury A1
Stantonbury Leisure Centre ✦ A1
Strudwick Drive C2
Sunrise Parkway A2
Superstore C1/C2
Theatre & Art Gallery B3
theCentre:mk B2
Tolcarne Avenue C3
Towan Avenue C3
Trueman Place C2
Vauxhall A1
Winterhill Retail Park . C2
Witan Gate B2
Xscape B3

Newcastle upon Tyne 340

Albert St B3
Argyle St B3
Back New Bridge St . . . B3
BALTIC Centre for Contemporary Art 🏛 C3
Barker St A3
Barrack Rd B1
Bath Lane B1
Bessie Surtees House ✦ C2
Bigg Market C2
Biscuit Factory 🏛 B3
Black Gate C2
Blackett St B2
Blandford Square C1
Boating Lake A1
Boyd St B3
Brandling Park A2
Bus Station B2
Buxton St B3
Byron St A3
Camden St B2
Castle Keep C2
Central Ⓜ C1
Central Library B2
Central Motorway B2
Chester St A3
Cineworld B1
City Hall B2
City Rd B3/C3
City Walls ✦ C1
Civic Centre A2
Claremont Rd A1
Clarence St B3
Clarence Walk B3
Clayton St C1/B1
Clayton St West C1
Close, The C2
Coach Station C1
College St B2
Collingwood St C2
Copland Terrace B3
Coppice Way B3
Corporation St B1
Courts C3
Crawhall Rd B3
Dean St C2
Dental Hospital A1
Dinsdale Place A3
Dinsdale Rd A3
Discovery 🏛 C1
Doncaster Rd A3
Durant Rd B2
Eldon Square B1
Eldon Square Shopping Centre B2
Ellison Place B2
Eskdale Terrace A2
Eslington Terrace A2
Exhibition Park A1
Falconar St B3
Fenkle St C1
Forth Banks C1
Forth St C1
Gallowgate B1
Gate, The ✦ B1
Gateshead Millennium Bridge C3
Gateshead Quays C3
Gibson St B3
Goldspink Lane A3
Grainger Market B2
Grainger St B2
Grantham Rd A3
Granville Rd A3
Great North Children's Hospital A1
Great North Museum: Hancock 🏛 A2
Grey St B2
Groat Market C2
Guildhall C2
Hancock St A2
Hanover St C2
Hatton Gallery 🏛 A1
Hawks Rd C3
Haymarket Ⓜ B2
Heber St B1
Helmsley Rd A3
High Bridge B2
High Level Bridge C2
Hillgate C3
Howard St B3
Hutton Terrace A3
Jesmond Ⓜ A2
Jesmond Rd A2/A3
John Dobson St B2
Jubilee Rd B3
Kelvin Grove A3
Kensington Terrace A2
Laing Gallery 🏛 B2
Lambton Rd A2
Leazes Crescent B1
Leazes Lane B1
Leazes Park B1
Leazes Park Rd B1
Leazes Terrace B1
Library A2
Life Science Centre ✦ C1
Live C2
Low Friar St C1
Manor Chare C2
Manors Ⓜ B2
Manors Station ≥ B2
Market St B2
Melbourne St B2
Mill Rd C3
Monument Ⓜ B2
Monument Mall Shopping Centre B2
Morpeth St A2
Mosley St C2
Napier St A3
New Bridge St West B2/B3
Newcastle Central Station ≥ C1
Newcastle University . . A1
Newgate St B1
Newington Rd A3
Northern Design Centre C3
Northern Stage Theatre A2
Northumberland Rd . . . B2
Northumberland St . . . B2
Northumbria University A2
Northwest Radial Rd . . A1
O2 Academy ✦ C1
Oakwellgate C3
Open University C3
Orchard St C2
Osborne Rd A2
Osborne Terrace A3
Pandon C3
Pandon Bank B3
Park Terrace A1
Percy St B1
Pilgrim St B2
Pipewellgate C2
Pitt St B1
Plummer Tower 🏛 A2
Police Station C1
Portland Rd A3/B3
Portland Terrace A3
Post Office B1/B2
Pottery Lane C1
Prudhoe Place B1
Prudhoe St B1
Quayside C2
Queen Elizabeth II Bridge C2
Queen Victoria Rd A1
Richardson Rd A1
Ridley Place B2
Rock Terrace B3
Rosedale Terrace A3
Royal Victoria Infirmary Ⓗ A1
Sage Gateshead ✦ C3
St Andrew's St B1
St James Ⓜ B1
St James' Boulevard . . . C1
St James' Park (Newcastle Utd FC) . . B1
St Mary's Heritage Centre ✦ C3
St Mary's (RC) ✝ C1
St Mary's Place B2
St Nicholas ✝ C2
St Nicholas St C2
St Thomas' St B1
Sandyford Rd A2/A3
Shield St B3
Shieldfield B3
Shopmobility B1
Side, The C2
Simpson Terrace B3
South Shore Rd C3
South St C1
Starbeck Avenue A3
Stepney Rd B3
Stoddart St B3
Stowell St B1
Strawberry Place B1
Swing Bridge C2
Temple St C1
Terrace Place B1
Theatre Royal B2
Times Square C1
Tower St B3
Trinity House C2
Tyne Bridge C2
Tyne Bridges ✦ C2
Tyne Theatre & Opera House C1
Tyneside B2
Victoria Square A2
Warwick St A3
Waterloo St C1
Wellington St B1
Westgate Rd C1/C2
Windsor Terrace A2
Worswick St B2
Wretham Place B3

Newport Casnewydd 340

Albert Terrace B1
Allt-yr-Yn Avenue A1
Alma St C2
Ambulance Station C3
Bailey St B2
Barrack Hill A2
Bath St A3
Bedford Rd B3
Belle Vue Lane C1
Belle Vue Park C1
Bishop St A3
Blewitt St B1
Bolt Close C3
Bolt St C3
Bond St A2
Bosworth Drive A1
Bridge St B1
Bristol St A3
Bryngwyn Rd B1
Brynhyfryd Avenue C1
Brynhyfryd Rd C1
Bus Station B2
Caerau Crescent C1
Caerau Rd B1
Caerleon Rd A3
Capel Crescent C2
Cardiff Rd C2
Caroline St B3
Castle (Remains) A2
Cedar Rd B3
Charles St B2
Charlotte Drive C2
Chepstow Rd A3
Church Rd A3
Cineworld B2
Civic Centre B1
Clarence Place A2
Clifton Place B1
Clifton Rd C1
Clyffard Crescent B1
Clytha Park Rd B1
Clytha Square C2
Coldra Rd C1
Collier St A3
Colne St B3
Comfrey Close A1
Commercial Rd C3
Commercial St B2
Corelli St A3
Corn St B2
Corporation Rd B3
Coulson Close C2
County Court A2
Courts A1, B1
Crawford St A3
Cyril St B3
Dean St A3
Devon Place B1
Dewsland Park Rd C2
Dolman B2
Dolphin St C3
East Dock Rd C3
East St B1
East Usk Rd A3
Ebbw Vale Wharf B3
Emlyn St B2
Enterprise Way C3
Eton Rd B3
Evans St A2
Factory Rd A2
Fields Rd B1
Francis Drive C2
Frederick St C3
Friars Rd C1
Friars Walk B2
Gaer Lane C1
George St C3
George Street Bridge . . . C3
Godfrey Rd B1
Gold Tops B1
Gore St A3
Gorsedd Circle C1
Grafton Rd A3
Graham St B1
Granville St C3
Harlequin Drive A1
Harrow Rd B3
Herbert Rd A3
Herbert Walk C2
Hereford St A3
High St B2
Hill St B2
Hoskins St A2
Information Centre B2
Ivor St B2
Jones St B1
Junction Rd A3
Keynshaw Avenue C2
King St C2
Kingsway B2
Kingsway Centre B2
Ledbury Drive A2
Library A3
Library, Museum & Art Gallery 🏛 B2
Liverpool Wharf B3
Llanthewy Rd B1
Llanvair Rd A3
Locke St A2
Lower Dock St C3
Lucas St A2
Manchester St A3
Market B2
Marlborough Rd B3
Mellon St C3
Mill St A2
Morgan St A3
Mountjoy Rd C2
Newport Bridge A2
Newport Centre B2
Newport RFC B3
Newport Station ≥ B2
North St B2
Oakfield Rd B1
Park Square C2
Police Station A3/C2
Post Office B2/C3
Power St A1
Prince St A3
Pugsley St A2
Queen St C2
Queen's Close A1
Queen's Hill A1
Queen's Hill Crescent . A1
Queensway B2
Railway St B2
Riverfront Theatre & Arts Centre, The . . . B2
Riverside A3
Rodney Rd B2
Royal Gwent (A&E) Ⓗ . C2
Rudry St A3
Rugby Rd B3
Ruperra Lane C3
Ruperra St C3
St Edmund St B1
St Mark's Crescent A1
St Mary St B1
St Vincent Rd A3
St Woolos ✝ C2
St Woolos General (no A&E) Ⓗ C1
St Woolos Rd B1
School Lane B2
Serpentine Rd B1
Shaftesbury Park A2
Sheaf Lane A3
Skinner St B2
Sorrel Drive A1
South Market St C3
Spencer Rd B1
Stow Hill B2/C1/C2
Stow Park Avenue C1
Stow Park Drive C1
TA Centre A1
Talbot St B2
Tennis Club A1
Tregare St A3
Trostrey St A3
Tunnel Terrace B1
Turner St A3
University of Wales Newport City Campus B3
Upper Dock St B2
Usk St A3
Usk Way B3/C3
Victoria Crescent B1
War Memorial A3
Waterloo Rd C1
West St B1
Wharves B2
Wheeler St A2
Whitby Place A3
Windsor Terrace B1
York Place C1

Newquay 340

Agar Rd B2
Alma Place B1
Ambulance Station B2
Anthony Rd C1
Atlantic Hotel A1
Bank St B1
Barrowfields A3
Bay View Terrace B2
Beach Rd B1
Beachfield Avenue B1
Beacon Rd A1
Belmont Place A1
Berry Rd B2
Blue Reef Aquarium B1
Boating Lake C2
Bus Station B1
Chapel Hill B1
Chester Rd A3
Cheviot Rd C1/C2
Chichester Crescent . . . C2
Chynance Drive C1
Chyverton Close C1
Cliff Rd B2
Coach Park B2
Colvreath Rd A3
Cornwall College Newquay B3
Council Offices B1
Crantock St B1
Crescent, The B1
Criggar Rocks A3
Dale Close C3
Dale Rd C3
Dane Rd A1
East St B2
Edgcumbe Avenue B3
Edgcumbe Gardens B3
Eliot Gardens B3
Elm Close C3
Ennor's Rd B1
Fernhill Rd B1
Fire Station B1
Fore St B1
Gannel Rd C2
Golf Driving Range B3
Gover Lane B1
Great Western Beach . A2
Grosvenor Avenue B2
Harbour A1
Hawkins Rd C2
Headleigh Rd B2
Hilgrove Rd A3/B3
Holywell Rd B3
Hope Terrace B1
Huer's Hut, The A1
Information Centre B1
Island Crescent B2
Jubilee St B1
Kew Close C3
Killacourt Cove A2
King Edward Crescent . A1
Lanhenvor Avenue B2
Library B1
Lifeboat Station A1
Lighthouse B1
Linden Avenue C2
Listry Rd C2
Lusty Glaze Beach A3
Lusty Glaze Rd A3
Manor Rd B1
Marcus Hill B2
Mayfield Rd B2
Meadowside C3
Mellanvrane Lane C2
Michell Avenue B2
Miniature Golf Course . C3
Miniature Railway ✦ . . B3
Mount Wise B1
Mowhay Close C3
Narrowcliff A3
Newquay ≥ A3
Newquay Hospital Ⓗ . . . B2
Newquay Town Football Ground B1
Newquay Zoo B3
North Pier A1
North Quay Hill A1
Oakleigh Terrace B2
Pargolla Rd B2
Pendragon Crescent . . . C3
Pengannel Close C1
Penina Avenue C3
Pirate's Quest 🏛 B1
Police Sta & Courts B2
Post Office B1/B2
Quarry Park Rd B3
Rawley Lane C2
Reeds Way B1
Robartes Rd B2
St Anne's Rd A3
St Aubyn Crescent B3
St George's Rd B1
St John's Rd B1
St Mary's Rd B1
St Michael's B1
St Michael's Rd B1
St Thomas' Rd B2
Seymour Avenue B2
South Pier A1
South Quay Hill A1
Superstore B2
Sweet Briar Crescent . C3
Sydney Rd A1
Tolcarne Beach A2
Tolcarne Point A2
Tolcarne Rd B2
Tor Rd B2
Towan Beach A1
Towan Blystra Rd B3
Tower Rd A1
Trebarwith Crescent . . . B2
Tredour Rd C2
Treforda Rd C3
Tregoss Rd B3
Tregunnel Hill B1/C1
Tregunnel Saltings C1
Trelawney Rd B2
Treloggan Lane C3

Treloggan Rd C3
Trembath Crescent C1
Trenance Avenue B2
Trenance Gardens B2
Trenance Lane C2
Trenance Leisure Park B3
Trenance Rd B2
Trenarth Rd B2
Treninnick Hill C3
Tretherras Rd B3
Trethewey Way C1
Trevemper Rd C2
Ulalia Rd B3
Vivian Close B2
Waterworld B3
Whitegate Rd B3
Wych Hazel Way C3

Newtown
Y Drenewydd 340

Ash Close A3
Back Lane B2
Baptist Chapel B2
Barn Lane A2
Bear Lanes
Shopping Centre B2
Beech Close A2
Beechwood Drive A2
Brimmon Close C2
Brimmon Rd C2
Broad St B2
Bryn Bank A1
Bryn Close A2
Bryn Gardens A1
Bryn Lane A1/A2
Bryn Meadows A2
Bryn St A2
Bryn, The A1
Brynglais Avenue A2
Brynglais Close A2
Bus Station B2
Byrnwood Drive A1
Cambrian Bridge B3
Cambrian Gardens B2
Cambrian Way B2
Canal Rd A3
Castle Mound B2
Cedewain C1
Ceiriog C2
Cemetery A3
Church (Remains of) B2
Churchill Drive A3
Cledan B3
Colwyn B3
Commercial St A2
Council Offices B1
Crescent St A1
Cwm Llanfair A2
Dinas B2
Dolafon Rd B3
Dolerw Park B1
Dolfor Rd C1
Fairfield Drive A2
Ffordd Croesawdy B2
Fire Station C1
Frankwell St A2
Frolic St B2
Fron Lane A1
Garden Lane A2
Gas St B2
Glyndwr C1
Golwgydre Lane B2
Gorsedd Circle B1
Hafren C1
Halfpenny Bridge B2
High St B2
Hillside Avenue A3
Hoel Treowen C2
Kerry Rd B3
Ladywell Shopping Ctr B2
Library B1
Llanfair Rd A2
Llanidloes Rd C1
Llys Ifor A2
Lon Cerddyn B1
Lon Helyg C1
Lonesome Lane A3
Long Bridge A2
Lower Canal Rd B3
Maldwyn Leisure Ctr C1
Market B2
Market St B2
Milford Rd B1
Mill Close B2
Miniature Railway B1
Montgomery County
Infirmary (Newtown)
A2
Mwyn Fynydd A3
New Church St B2
New Rd B2
Newtown Bypass C3
Newtown Football Gd B1
Newtown Station B2
Oak Tree Avenue A3
Old Kerry Rd B2
Oldbarn Lane A2
Oriel Davies Gallery B2
Park Close B1
Park Lane B1
Park St B2
Park, The B1
Parklands B1
Pavillion Court C1
Plantation Lane C1
Police Station B1
Pont Brynfedw A2
Pool Rd B3
Poplar Rd A3
Post Office B2
Powys C1
Powys Theatre A2
Regent B2
Robert Owen House B1
Robert Owen Mus B2
Rugby Club A3
St David's B2
School Lane A2
Sheaf St B3
Short Bridge St B2

Stone St B2
Superstore B3/C1
Sycamore Drive A2
Textile Museum A2
Town Hall B2
Union St A2
Vastre Industrial Est B3
War Memorial B2
WHSmith Museum B2
Wynfields C1
Y Ffrydd A3

Northampton 340

78 Derngate B3
Abington Square B3
Abington St B3
Alcombe St A3
All Saints' B2
Ambush St B1
Angel St B2
Army Reserve Centre A3
Arundel St A2
Ash St A2
Auctioneers Way C2
Bailiff St A2
Barrack Rd A2
BBOB Rugby FC A1
Beaconsfield
Terrace A3
Becket's Park C3
Bedford Rd B3
Billing Rd B3
Brecon St A1
Brewery C2
Bridge St C2
Broad St B2
Burns St A3
Bus Station B2
Campbell St A2
Castle (Site of) B2
Castle St B2
Cattle Market Rd C2
Central Museum &
Art Gallery B2
Charles St A3
Cheyne Walk B3
Church Lane A2
Clare St A3
Cloutsham St A3
College St B2
Colwyn Rd A3
Cotton End C2
Countess Rd A1
County Hall B2
Court A2
Craven St A3
Crown & County
Courts B3
Denmark Rd B3
Derngate B3
Doddridge Church B2
Drapery, The B2
Duke St A3
Dunster St A3
Earl St A3
Euston Rd C2
Fire Station A3
Foot Meadow B2
Gladstone Rd A1
Gold St B2
Grafton St A2
Gray St A3
Green St B1
Greenwood Rd B1
Greyfriars B2
Grosvenor Centre B2
Grove Rd A3
Guildhall B2
Hampton St A2
Harding Terrace A2
Hazelwood Rd B3
Herbert St B2
Hervey St A3
Hester St A2
Holy Sepulchre A2
Hood St A3
Horse Market B2
Hunter St A3
Information
Centre B2
Kettering Rd A3
Kingswell St B2
Lady's Lane B2
Leicester St A2
Leslie Rd A2
Library B3
Lorne Rd A2
Lorry Park A1
Louise Rd A2
Lower Harding St A2
Lower Hester St A2
Lower Mounts B3
Lower Priory St A2
Main Rd C1
Marefair B2
Market Square B2
Marlboro Rd B1
Marriott St A2
Millers Meadow A1
Military Rd A3
Mounts Baths Leisure
Centre A3
Nene Valley Retail Pk C1
New South Bridge Rd C2
Northampton General
Hospital (A&E) B3
Northampton Marina C3
Northampton Sta B1
Northcote St A2
Nunn Mills Rd C3
Old Towcester Rd C2
Overstone Rd A3
Pembroke Rd A1
Penn Court C2
Police Station B3
Post Office A1/B3
Quorn Way A2
Ransome Rd C3
Regent Square A2
Ridings, The B3

Robert St A2
Royal & Derngate
Theatres B3
St Andrew's Rd B1
St Andrew's St A2
St Edmund's Rd B3
St George's St A2
St Giles B3
St Giles St B3
St Giles' Terrace B3
St James Park Rd B1
St James Rd B1
St James Retail Park C1
St James' Mill Rd B1
St James' Mill Rd East C1
St Leonard's Rd C2
St Mary's St B2
St Michael's Rd A3
St Peter's B2
St Peter's Way
Shopping Precinct B2
St Peter's Way B2
Salisbury St A2
Scarletwell St B2
Semilong Rd A2
Sheep St B2
Sol Central
(Leisure Centre) B2
Somerset St A3
South Bridge C2
Southfield Avenue C2
Spencer Bridge Rd A1
Spencer Rd A3
Spring Gardens B3
Spring Lane B2
Superstore C2
Swan St B3
Tintern Avenue A1
Towcester Rd C2
Univ of Northampton
(Waterside Campus) C3
Upper Bath St B2
Upper Mounts A2
Victoria Park A1
Victoria Promenade B2
Victoria Rd B3
Victoria St A2
Wellingborough Rd B3
West Bridge B1
York Rd B3

Norwich 341

Albion Way C3
All Saints Green C2
Anchor St A3
Anglia Square A2
Argyle St C3
Arts Centre B1
Ashby St C2
Assembly House B1
Bank Plain B2
Barker St A1
Barn Rd A1
Barrack St A3
Ber St C2
Bethel St B1
Bishop Bridge A3
Bishopbridge Rd A3
Bishopgate A3
Blackfriars St A2
Botolph St A2
Bracondale C3
Brazen Gate C2
Bridewell Museum B2
Brunswick Rd C1
Bull Close Rd A2
Bus Station C2
Calvert St A2
Cannell Green A3
Carrow Rd C3
Castle &
Museum B2
Castle Mall B2
Castle Meadow B2
Cathedral B2
Cathedral (RC) B1
Cathedral Retail Park A1
Cattlemarket St B2
Chantry Place C1
Chantry Rd C1
Chapel Loke C2
Chapelfield East B1
Chapelfield Gardens B1
Chapelfield North B1
Chapelfield Rd B1
Cinema City B2
City Hall B1
City Rd C2
City Wall C1/C3
Close, The B2/B3
Colegate A2
Coslany St B1
Cow Hill B1
Cow Tower A3
Cowgate A2
Crown & Magistrates'
Courts A2
Dragon Hall Heritage
Centre C3
Duke St A1
Edward St A2
Elm Hill B2
Erpingham Gate B2
Fishergate A2
Forum, The B1
Foundry Bridge B3
Fye Bridge A2
Garden St C2
Gas Hill B3
Gentlemans Walk B2
Grapes Hill B1
Great Hospital Halls,
The A3
Grove Avenue C1
Grove Rd C1
Guildhall B1
Gurney Rd A3
Hall Rd C2
Heathgate A3
Heigham St A1

Hollywood A2
Horn's Lane C2
Hungate
Medieval Art B2
Ipswich Rd C1
ITV Anglia C3
James Stuart Gdns B3
King St B2
King St C3
Koblenz Avenue C3
Leisure Centre A3
Library B1
London St B2
Lower Clarence Rd B3
Maddermarket B1
Magdalen St A2
Mariners Lane C2
Market B2
Market Avenue B2
Mountergate B3
Mousehold St A3
Newmarket Rd C1
Norfolk St C1
Norwich City FC C3
Norwich Gallery B2
Norwich School B2
Norwich Station B3
Oak St A1
Odeon C3
Palace St A2
Pitt St A1
Playhouse B2
Police Station B1
Post Office
A2/B2/B3/C1
Pottergate B1
Prince of Wales Rd B2
Princes St B2
Pull's Ferry B3
Puppet Theatre A2
Queen St B2
Queens Rd C2
Recorder Rd B3
Riverside Entertainment
Centre C3
Riverside Leisure Ctr C3
Riverside Rd B3
Riverside Retail Park C3
Rosary Rd B3
Rose Lane B2
Rouen Rd C2
St Andrews St B2
St Augustines St A1
St Benedicts St B1
St Crispins Road A1
St Ethelbert's Gate B2
St Faiths Lane B3
St Georges St A2
St Giles St B1
St James Close A3
St Julians C2
St Leonards Rd B3
St Martin's Lane A1
St Peter Mancroft B2
St Peters St B1
St Stephens Rd C1
St Stephens St C1
Shopmobility C1
Silver Rd A2
Silver St A2
Southwell Rd C2
St. Andrew's &
Blackfriars' Hall B2
Strangers' Hall B1
Superstore C2
Surrey St C2
Sussex St A1
Theatre Royal B1
Theatre St B1
Thorn Lane C2
Thorpe Rd B3
Tombland B2
Union St C1
Vauxhall St B1
Victoria St C1
Vue B2
Walpole St B1
Waterfront, The C3
Wensum St A2
Wessex St C1
Westwick St A1
Wherry Rd C3
Whitefriars A2
Willow Lane B1

Nottingham 341

Abbotsford Drive A3
Addison St A1
Albert Hall B1
Alfred St Central A3
Alfreton Rd B1
All Saints St A1
Annesley Grove A2
Arboretum A1
Arboretum St A1
Arthur St A1
Arts Theatre B3
Ashforth St A3
Balmoral Rd A1
Barker Gate B3
Bath St B3
BBC Nottingham C3
Beacon Hill Rise B3
Belgrave Rooms B1
Bellar Gate B3
Belward St B3
Brewhouse Yard C2
Broad Marsh Bus Sta C2
Broad St B3
Brook St B3
Burns St A1
Burton St B2
Bus Station A2
Canal St C2
Carlton St B3
Carrington St C2
Castle C2
Castle Boulevard C1
Castle Gate C2
Castle Meadow Rd C1

Castle Meadow
Retail Pk C1
Castle Rd C2
Castle Wharf C2
Cavendish Rd East C1
Cemetery A1/B1
Chaucer St B1
Cheapside B2
Church Rd A3
City Link C3
City of Caves C2
Clarendon St B1
Cliff Rd C3
Clumber Rd East C1
Clumber St B2
College St B1
Collin St C2
Contemporary C3
Conway Close A2
Cornerhouse, The B2
Council House B2
Cranbrook St B3
Cranmer St A2
Cromwell St B1
Curzon St B3
Derby Rd B1
Dryden St A2
Exchange Centre, The B2
Fishpond Drive C1
Fletcher Gate B3
Forest Rd East A1
Forest Rd West A1
Friar Lane C2
Gedling Grove A1
Gedling St B3
George St B3
Gill St A2
Glasshouse St B2
Goldsmith St B2
Goose Gate B3
Great Freeman St A2
Guildhall B2
Hamilton Drive C1
Hampden St A1
Heathcote St B3
High Pavement C3
High School A1
HM Revenue &
Customs C2
Holles Crescent C1
Hope Drive C1
Hungerhill Rd A3
Huntingdon Drive C1
Huntingdon St A2
Information Centre B2
Instow Rise A3
International
Community Centre A2
Kent St B3
King St B2
Lace Market B3
Lace Mkt Theatre C3
Lamartine St B3
Leisure Centre C3
Lenton Rd C1
Lewis Close A3
Lincoln St B2
London Rd C3
Long Row B2
Low Pavement C2
Lower Parliament St B3
Magistrates' Court C2
Maid Marian Way B2
Mansfield Rd A2/B2
Middle Hill C2
Milton St B2
Mount St B2
National Ice Centre &
Motorpoint Arena C3
National Justice
Museum C3
Newcastle Drive B1
Newstead Grove A2
North Sherwood St A2
Nottingham Arena C3
Nottingham Cath B1
Nottingham College C3
Nottingham Station C3
Nottingham Trent
University A2/B2
Old Market Square B2
Oliver St A1
Park Drive C1
Park Row C1
Park Terrace B1
Park Valley C1
Park, The C1
Peas Hill Rd A3
Peel St A1
Pelham St B2
Peveril Drive C1
Plantagenet St A3
Playhouse Theatre B1
Plumptre St C3
Police Station B1/B2
Poplar St C3
Portland Rd B1
Post Office B2
Queen's Rd C3
Raleigh St A1
Regent St B1
Rick St B3
Robin Hood St B3
Robin Hood Statue C2
Ropewalk, The B1
Royal Centre B2
Royal Children Inn C2
Royal Concert Hall B2
St Ann's Hill Rd A2
St Ann's Way A2
St Ann's Well Rd A3
St James' St B2
St Mark's St B3
St Mary's Rest Garden B3
St Mary's Gate B3
St Nicholas C2
St Peter's C2
St Peter's Gate B2
Salutation Inn C2
Shakespeare St B2
Shelton St A2

Shopmobility A2
South Parade B2
South Rd C1
South Sherwood St B2
Station Street C3
Stoney St B3
Talbot St B1
Tattershall Drive C1
Tennis Drive B1
Tennyson St A1
Theatre Royal B2
Trent St C3
Trent University B2
Union Rd B3
Upper Parliament St B2
Victoria Centre B2
Victoria Leisure Ctr B3
Victoria Park B3
Victoria St B2
Walter St A1
Warser Gate B3
Watkin St A2
Waverley St A1
Wheeler Gate B2
Wilford Rd C2
Wilford St C2
Wollaton St B1
Woodborough Rd A2
Woolpack Lane B3
Ye Old Trip to
Jerusalem C2
York St A2

Oban 341

Aird's Crescent B2
Albany St B2
Albert Lane A2
Albert Rd A2
Alma Crescent B1
Ambulance Station C2
Angus Terrace C3
Ardconnel Rd A2
Ardconnel Terrace B2
Argyll Square B2
Argyll St B2
Atlantis Leisure Ctr A2
Bayview Rd A1
Benvoulin Rd A2
Bowling Green A2
Breadalbane St A2
Bus Station B2
Campbell St B2
College B2
Colonsay Terrace C3
Combie St B2
Corran Brae A1
Corran Esplanade A1/A2
Corran Halls, The A2
Court B2
Crannaig-a-
Mhinisteir B1
Crannog Lane C2
Croft Avenue A2
Dalintart Drive C3
Dalriach Rd A2
Distillery B2
Drummore Rd C2
Duncraggan Rd A2
Dunollie Rd A2
Dunuaran Rd B1
Feochan Grove C3
Ferry Terminal B1
Gallanach Rd B1
George St A2
Glencruitten Drive C3
Glencruitten Rd B3
Glenmore Rd C1
Glenshellach Rd C1
Glenshellach Terrace B2
Hazeldean Crescent A3
High St B2
Hill St B2
Industrial Estate C2
Information Centre B2
Islay Rd C3
Jacob's Ladder B2
Jura Rd C3
Knipoch Place C3
Laurel Crescent A2
Laurel Rd A2/A3
Library B1
Lifeboat Station B1
Lighthouse Pier B1
Lismore Crescent A2
Lochavullin Drive B2
Lochavullin Rd C2
Lochside St B2
Longsdale Crescent A3
Longsdale Rd A2/A3
Longsdale Terrace A3
Lunga Rd C3
Lynn Rd C2
Market St B2
McCaig Rd C3
McCaig's Tower A2
Mill Lane C2
Miller Rd C2
Millpark Avenue C2
Millpark Rd C2
Mossfield Avenue B3
Mossfield Drive B3
Mossfield Stadium B3
Nant Drive C3
Nelson Rd C2
North Pier B2
Nursery Lane A2
Oban B2
Oban Phoenix A2
Police Station B2
Polvinister Rd B3
Post Office A2/B2
Pulpit Drive C1
Pulpit Hill C1
Pulpit Hill Viewpoint
B1
Quarry Rd C2
Queen's Park Place B2
Railway Quay B1
Retail Park B2
Rockfield Rd B2

St Columba's A1
St John's A2
Scalpay Terrace C3
Shore St B1
Shuna Terrace C3
Sinclair Drive C2
Soroba Rd B2/C2
South Pier B1
Stevenson St B2
Tweedale St B2
Ulva Rd C2
Villa Rd B1
War & Peace A2

Oxford 341

Adelaide St A1
Albert St A1
All Souls (College) B2
Ashmolean Mus B2
Balliol (College) B2
Banbury Rd A2
Bate Collection of
Musical Instruments
C2
Beaumont St B1
Becket St B1
Blackhall Rd A2
Blue Boar St B2
Bodleian Library B2
Botanic Garden B3
Brasenose (College) B2
Brewer St C2
Broad St B2
Burton-Taylor
Theatre B2
Bus Station B1
Canal St A1
Cardigan St A1
Carfax Tower B2
Castle B1
Castle St B1
Catte St B2
Cemetery C1
Christ Church (Coll) B2
Christ Church Cath C2
Christ Church Mdw C2
City of Oxford College C1
Clarendon Centre B2
Cornmarket St B2
Corpus Christi (Coll) B2
County Hall B1
Covered Market B2
Cowley Place C3
Cranham St A1
Cranham Terrace A1
Cricket Ground B1
Crown & County
Courts C2
Deer Park B3
Exeter (College) B2
Fire Station B1
Folly Bridge C2
George St B1
Great Clarendon St A1
Harris Manchester
(College) B2
Hart St A1
Hertford (College) B2
High St B3
Hollybush Row B1
Holywell St B2
Hythe Bridge St B1
Ice Rink C1
Jericho St A1
Jesus (College) B2
Jowett Walk B3
Juxon St A1
Keble (College) A2
Keble Rd A2
Library B2
Linacre (College) A3
Lincoln (College) B2
Little Clarendon St A1
Longwall St B3
Magdalen (College) B3
Magdalen Bridge B2
Magdalen St B2
Magistrate's Court C2
Manor Rd B3
Mansfield (College) A2
Mansfield Rd A3
Market B1
Marlborough Rd C2
Martyrs' Memorial B2
Merton (College) B3
Merton Field B3
Merton St B2
Mus of Modern Art B2
Museum of Oxford B2
Museum Rd A2
New College (College) B3
New Inn Hall St B2
New Rd B1
New Theatre B2
Norfolk St C1
Nuffield (College) B1
Observatory A1
Observatory St A1
Odeon B1/B2
Old Fire Station B1
Old Greyfriars St C2
Oriel (College) B2
Oxford Castle &
Prison B1
Oxford Station B1
Oxford University
Research Centres A1
Oxpens Rd C1
Paradise Square C1
Paradise St B1
Park End St B1
Parks Rd A2/B2
Pembroke (College) C2
Phoenix A1
Picture Gallery C2
Plantation Rd A1
Playhouse B2
Police Station C2
Post Office A1/B2
Pusey St B1

Queen's (College) B3
Queen's Lane B3
Radcliffe Camera B2
Rewley Rd B1
Richmond Rd A1
Rose Lane B3
Ruskin (College) B1
Said Business School B1
St Aldates C2
St Anne's (College) A1
St Antony's (College) A1
St Bernard's Rd A1
St Catherine's (Coll) B3
St Cross Building A3
St Cross Rd A3
St Edmund Hall (Coll) B3
St Giles St A2
St Hilda's (College) C3
St John St B2
St John's (College) B2
St Mary the Virgin B2
St Michael at the
Northgate B2
St Peter's (College) B1
St Thomas St B1
Science Area A2
Science Museum B2
Sheldonian Theatre
B2
Somerville (College) A1
South Parks Rd A2
Speedwell St C2
Sports Ground C3
Thames St C2
Town Hall B2
Trinity (College) B2
Turl St B2
University Coll (Coll) B3
Univ Natural History Mus
& Pitt Rivers Mus A2
University Parks A2
Wadham (College) B2
Walton Crescent A1
Walton St A1
Western Rd C2
Westgate C2
Woodstock Rd A1
Worcester (College) B1

Perth 341

AK Bell Library B2
Abbot Crescent C1
Abbot St C1
Albany Terrace A1
Albert Monument A3
Alexandra St B2
Atholl St A2
Balhousie Avenue A2
Balhousie Castle & Black
Watch Museum A2
Balhousie St A2
Ballantine Place A1
Barossa Place A2
Barossa St A2
Barrack St A2
Bell's Sports Centre A2
Bellwood B3
Blair St B1
Burn Park C1
Bus Station B2
Caledonian Rd B2
Canal Crescent B2
Canal St B3
Cavendish Avenue C1
Charles St B2
Charlotte Place A2
Charlotte St A3
Church St A1
City Hall B3
Club House C3
Clyde Place C1
Coach Park C3
Commercial St A3
Concert Hall B3
Council Chambers B3
County Place B2
Court B3
Craigie Place C2
Crieff Rd A1
Croft Park C2
Cross St B2
Darnhall Crescent C1
Darnhall Drive C1
Dewars Centre B1
Dundee Rd B3
Dunkeld Rd A1
Earl's Dykes B1
Edinburgh Rd C3
Elibank St B1
Fair Maid's House B3
Fergusson B3
Feus Rd A1
Fire Station A1
Foundary Lane A2
Friar St C1
George St B3
Glamis Place C1
Glasgow Rd B1
Glenearn Rd C2
Glover St B1/C1
Golf Course A2
Gowrie St A3
Gray St B1
Graybank Rd B1
Greyfriars Burial Gd B3
Hay St A2
High St B2/B3
Inchaffray St A1
Industrial/Retail Park B1
Information Centre B2
Isla Rd A3
James St B2
Keir St A3
King Edward St B3
King James VI
Golf Course C3
King St B2
Kings Place C2
Kinnoull Causeway B2
Kinnoull St B2

Knowelea Place C1
Knowelea Terrace C1
Ladeside Bsns Centre A1
Leisure Pool B1
Leonard St B2
Lickley St B2
Lochie Brae A3
Long Causeway A1
Low St A2
Main St A3
Marshall Place C3
Melville St A2
Mill St B3
Milne St B2
Murray Crescent C1
Murray St B2
Needless Rd C1
New Rd B2
North Inch A3
North Methven St A2
Park Place C1
Perth B2
Perth Bridge A3
Perth Business Park B1
Perth Museum & Art
Gallery B3
Perth Station C2
Pickletulllum Rd B1
Pitheavlis Crescent C1
Playhouse B2
Police Station A2
Pomarium St B2
Post Office B2/C2
Princes St B3
Priory Place C2
Queen St C1
Queen's Bridge B3
Riggs Rd B1
Riverside B3
Riverside Park B3
Rodney Gardens B3
Rose Terrace A2
St Catherine's Rd A1/A2
St Catherine's
Retail Park A1
St John St B3
St John's Kirk B3
St John's Shopping Ctr B2
St Leonards Bridge C2
St Ninians Cathedral A2
Scott Monument C2
Scott St B2
Sheriff Court B3
Shore Rd C3
Skate Park C3
South Inch C2
South Inch Bsns Ctr C3
South Inch Park C2
South Inch View C2
South Methven St B2
South St B3
South William St B2
Stables, The A1
Stanners, The B3
Stormont St A2
Strathmore St A3
Stuart Avenue C1
Superstore B1/B2
Tay St B3
Union Lane A2
Victoria St B2
Watergate B3
Wellshill Cemetery A1
West Bridge St A3
West Mill St B2
Whitefriers Crescent B1
Whitefriers St B1
Wilson St C1
Windsor Terrace C1
Woodside Crescent C1
York Place B2
Young St C1

Peterborough 341

Athletics Arena B3
Bishop's Palace B2
Bishop's Rd B2/B3
Boongate A3
Bourges Boulevard A1
Bourges Retail Pk B1/B2
Bridge House
(Council Offices) C2
Bridge St B2
Bright St A1
Broadway A2
Broadway A2
Brook St A2
Burghley Rd A2
Bus Station B2
Cavendish St A3
Charles St A3
Church St B2
Church Walk A2
Cobden Avenue A1
Cobden St A1
Cowgate B2
Craig St A2
Crawthorne Rd A2
Cromwell Rd A1
Dickens St A3
Eastfield Rd A3
Eastgate B3
East Station Road C2
Fire Station A1
Fletton Avenue C2
Frank Perkins
Parkway C3
Geneva St A2
George St C1
Gladstone St A1
Glebe Rd C2
Gloucester Rd C3
Granby St B3
Grove St C1
Guildhall B2
Hadrians Court C3
Hawksbill Way C2
Henry St A2
Hereward Cross
(shopping) B2

Hereward Rd B3
Information Centre B2
Jubilee St C1
Kent Rd B1
Key Theatre C2
Kirkwood Close B1
Lea Gardens B1
Library A2
Lincoln Rd A2
London Rd C2
Long Causeway B2
Lower Bridge St C2
Magistrates Court B2
Manor House St A2
Mayor's Walk A1
Midland Rd A1
Monument St A2
Morris St A3
Mus & Art Gallery B2
Nene Valley Railway C1
New Rd A2
New Rd C1
Northminster A2
Old Customs House C2
Oundle Rd C1
Padholme Rd A3
Palmerston Rd C1
Park Rd A2
Passport Office B2
Peterborough Cath + B2
Peterborough Nene Valley C1
Peterborough Sta B1
Police Station B2
Post Office A3/B2
Priestgate B2
Queen's Walk C2
Queensgate Centre B2
Railworld Wildlife Haven C1
Regional Fitness & Swimming Centre B3
River Lane B1
Rivergate Shopping Centre B2
Riverside Mead C3
Russell St A1
St John's B2
St John's St A3
St Marks St A2
St Peter's Rd B2
Saxon Rd A3
Spital Bridge A1
Stagshaw Drive C3
Star Rd B3
Superstore B1
Thorpe Lea Rd B1
Thorpe Rd B1
Thorpe's Lea Rd B1
Tower St A2
Town Hall B2
Viersen Platz B2
Vineyard Rd B3
Wake Rd B3
Wellington St A3
Wentworth St B2
Westgate B2
Weston Homes Stadium (Peterborough United FC) The C2
Whalley St A3
Wharf Rd C1
Whitsed St A3
YMCA A3

Plymouth 341

Alma Rd A1
Anstis St B1
Armada Shopping Ctr B2
Armada St A3
Armada Way B2
Arts Centre B2
Athenaeum B1
Athenaeum St C1
Barbican C3
Barbican C3
Baring St A3
Bath St B1
Beaumont Park B3
Beaumont Rd B3
Black Friars Gin Distillery C2
Box, The B2
Breton Side B3
Coach Station B2
Castle St C3
Cathedral (RC) + B1
Cecil St B1
Central Park A1
Central Park Avenue A2
Charles Church B3
Charles Cross B3
Charles St B2
Cineworld B2
Citadel Rd C2
Citadel Rd East C2
Civic Centre B2
Cliff Rd C1
Clifton Place A3
Cobourg St A2
College of Art B2
Continental Ferry Port B1
Cornwall St B2
Crescent, The B1
Dale Rd A2
Deptford Place A3
Derry Avenue A2
Derry's Cross B1
Drake Circus B2
Drake Circus Shopping Centre B2
Drake Statue C2
Eastlake St B2
Ebrington St B3
Elizabethan House C3
Elliot St C1
Endsleigh Place A2
Exeter St B3
Fire Station A3
Fish Quay C3
Gibbons St A3
Glen Park Avenue A2
Grand Parade C1
Great Western Rd C1
Greenbank Rd A3
Greenbank Terrace A3
Guildhall B2
Hampton St B3
Harwell St B1
Hill Park Crescent A3
Hoe Approach B2
Hoe Rd C2
Hoe, The C2
Hoegate St C2
Houndiscombe Rd A2
Information Centre C3
James St A2
Kensington Rd A3
King St B1
Lambhay Hill C3
Leigham St C1
Library B2
Lipson Rd A3/B3
Lockyer St C2
Lockyers Quay C3
Madeira Rd C2
Marina B3
Market B1
Market Avenue B1
Martin St B1
Mayflower St B2
Mayflower Stone & Steps C3
Mayflower B3
Merchant's House B2
Millbay Rd B1
National Marine Aquarium C3
Neswick St B1
New George St B2
New St C3
North Cross A2
North Hill A3
North Quay B2
North Rd East A2
North Rd West A1
North St B3
Notte St B2
Octagon, The B1
Octagon St B1
Pennycomequick A1
Pier St C1
Plymouth Naval Memorial C2
Plymouth Pavilions B1
Plymouth Station A2
Police Station B3
Post Office B2,C1,C3
Princess St B2
Promenade, The C2
Prysten House B2
Queen Anne's Battery Watersports Centre C3
Radford Rd C1
Regent St B3
Rope Walk C3
Royal Citadel C2
Royal Parade B2
Royal Theatre B2
Russell Place A1
St Andrew's B2
St Andrew's Cross B2
St Andrew's St B2
St Lawrence Rd A2
Saltash Rd A2
Shopmobility B2
Smeaton's Tower C2
Southern Terrace A3
Southside St C2
Stuart Rd A1
Sutherland Rd A2
Sutton Rd B3
Sydney St A1
Teats Hill Rd C3
Tothill Avenue B3
Union St B1
Univ of Plymouth A2
Vauxhall St B2/3
Victoria Park A1
Walker Terrace C1
West Hoe Rd C1
Western Approach B1
Whittington St A1
Wyndham St B1

Poole 341

Ambulance Station A3
Baiater Gardens C2
Baiter Park C3
Ballard Close C2
Ballard Rd C2
Bay Hog Lane B1
BMI The Harbour Hospital A3
Bridge Approach C1
Bus Station B2
Castle St B2
Catalina Drive B3
Chapel Lane B2
Church St B1
Cinnamon Lane B1
Colborne Close B3
Dear Hay Lane B2
Denmark Lane A3
Denmark Rd A3
Dolphin Centre B2
East St B2
Elizabeth Rd A3
Emerson Rd B2
Ferry Rd C1
Ferry Terminal C1
Fire Station A2
Freightliner Terminal C1
Furnell Rd B3
Garland Rd A3
Green Rd B2
Heckford Lane A3
Heckford Rd A3
High St B2
High St North A3
Hill St B2
Holes Bay Rd A1
Hospital (A&E) A3
Information Centre C2
Kingland Rd B3
Kingston Rd A3
Labrador Drive C3
Lagland St B2
Lander Close C3
Lighthouse, Poole Centre for the Arts B3
Longfleet Rd A3
Maple Rd A3
Market Close B2
Market St B2
Mount Pleasant Rd B3
New Harbour Rd C1
New Harbour Rd South C1
New Harbour Rd West C1
New Orchard B1
New Quay Rd C1
New St B2
Newfoundland Drive B2
North St B2
Old Lifeboat C2
Old Orchard B2
Parish Rd A3
Park Lake Rd B3
Parkstone Rd A3
Perry Gardens B2
Pitwines Close B2
Police Station A2
Poole Central Library B2
Poole Lifting Bridge C1
Poole Park B2
Poole Station A2
Poole Museum C1
Post Office B2
Quay, The C2
RNLI College B1
St John's Rd A3
St Margaret's Rd A2
St Mary's Maternity Unit A3
St Mary's Rd A3
Seldown Bridge B3
Seldown Lane B3
Seldown Rd B3
Serpentine Rd A2
Scaplen's Court C1
Shaftesbury Rd A3
Skinner St B2
Slipway B1
Stanley Rd C2
Sterte Avenue A2
Sterte Avenue West A1
Sterte Close A2
Sterte Esplanade A2
Sterte Rd A2
Strand St C2
Superstore B3
Swimming Pool B3
Taverner Close B3
Thames St B1
Towngate Bridge B2
Twin Sails Bridge B1
Vallis Close C3
Waldren Close B3
West Quay B1
West Quay Rd B1
West St B1
West View Rd A2
Whatleigh Close B2
Wimborne Rd A3

Portsmouth 341

Action Stations C1
Admiralty Rd A1
Alfred Rd A2
Anglesea Rd B2
Arundel St B3
Aspex B1
Bishop St A2
Broad St C1
Buckingham House C2
Burnaby Rd B2
Bus Station B1
Camber Dock C1
Cambridge Rd B2
Car Ferry to Isle of Wight B1
Cascades Shopping Centre A3
Castle Rd C3
Civic Offices B3
Clarence Pier C2
College St B1
Commercial Rd A3
Cottage Grove B3
Cross St A1
Cumberland St A2
Duisburg Way C2
Durham St A3
East St B1
Edinburgh Rd A2
Elm Grove C3
Emirates Spinnaker Tower B1
Governor's Grn C1
Great Southsea St C3
Green Rd B3
Greetham St B3
Grosvenor St B3
Groundlings A2
Grove Rd North C3
Grove Rd South C3
Guildhall B3
Guildhall Walk B3
Gunwharf Quays Designer Outlet B1
Gunwharf Rd B1
Hambrook St C2
Hampshire Terrace B2
Hanover St A1
Hard, The B1
High St C2
HM Naval Base A1
HMS Nelson (Royal Naval Barracks) A2
HMS Monitor M.33 A1
HMS Victory A1
HMS Warrior A1
Hovercraft Terminal C2
Hyde Park Rd B3
Information Ctr A1/B3
Isambard Brunel Rd B3
Isle of Wight Car Ferry Terminal B1
Kent Rd C3
Kent St A2
King St B3
King's Rd C3
King's Terrace C2
Lake Rd A3
Law Courts B3
Library B3
Long Curtain Rd C2
Marina B1
Market Way A3
Marmion Rd C3
Mary Rose A1
Middle St B3
Millennium Promenade Walk B1/C1
Museum Rd B2
National Museum of the Royal Navy A1
Naval Recreation Gd C2
Nightingale Rd C3
Norfolk St B3
North St A2
Osborne Rd C3
Paradise St A3
Park Rd B2
Passenger Catamaran to Isle of Wight B1
Passenger Ferry to Gosport B1
Pelham Rd C3
Pembroke Gardens C2
Pier Rd C2
Point Battery C1
Police Station B3
Portsmouth & Southsea Station A3
Portsmouth Harbour Station B1
Portsmouth Historic Dockyard A1
Portsmouth Museum & Art Gallery B2
Post Office A1/A3/B3
Queen St A1
Queen's Crescent C3
Ravelin Park B2
Register Office B2
Round Tower C1
Royal Garrison Church C1
St Edward's Rd C3
St George's Rd B2
St George's Square B1
St George's Way B2
St James's Rd B3
St James's St A2
St John's Cath (RC) + A3
St Thomas's Cath + C1
St Thomas's St B2
Shopmobility A3/B1
Somers Rd B3
Southsea Common C2
Southsea Terrace C2
Square Tower C1
Station St A3
Town Fortifications C1
Unicorn Rd A2
United Services Recreation Ground B2
University of Portsmouth A2/B2
Univ of Portsmouth B3
Upper Arundel St A3
Victoria Avenue C2
Victoria Park A2
Victory Gate A1
Vue B1
Warblington St B1
Western Parade C2
White Hart Rd C1
Winston Churchill Ave B3

Preston 342

Adelphi St A2
Anchor Court B3
Aqueduct St A1
Ardee Rd C1
Arthur St B2
Ashton St A1
Avenham Lane B3
Avenham Park C3
Avenham Rd B3
Avenham St B3
Bairstow St B3
Balderstone Rd C1
Beamont Drive A1
Beech St South C2
Bird St C1
Bow Lane B2
Brieryfield Rd A1
Broadgate C1
Brook St A2
Bus Station A3
Butler St B2
Cannon St B3
Carlton St A1
Chaddock St B3
Channel Way B1
Chapel St B3
Christ Church St B2
Christian Rd B2
Cold Bath St A2
Coleman Court C1
Connaught Rd C2
Corporation St A2/B2
County Hall B2
Cricket Ground C2
Croft St A1
Cross St B3
Crown Court A3
Crown St A3
East Cliff C3
East Cliff Rd B3
Edward St A2
Elizabeth St A3
Euston St B1
Fishergate B2/B3
Fishergate Hill B2
Fishergate Shopping Centre B2
Fitzroy St B1
Fleetwood St A1
Friargate A3
Fylde Rd A1/A2
Gerrard St B2
Glover's Court B3
Good St B2
Grafton St B2
Great George St A3
Great Shaw St A3
Greenbank St A2
Guild Way B1
Guild Hall & Charter B3
Guildhall St B3
Harrington St A2
Harris Museum B3
Hartington Rd B1
Hasset Close C2
Heatley St B2
Hind St C2
Information Centre B3
Kilruddery Rd C1
Lancashire Archives B2
Lancaster Rd A3/B3
Latham St B3
Lauderdale St C2
Lawson St A3
Leighton St A2
Leyland Rd C1
Library A1
Library B3
Liverpool Rd C1
Lodge St B2
Lune St B3
Magistrate's Court A3
Main Sprit West B3
Maresfield Rd C1
Market St West A3
Marsh Lane B1/B2
Maudland Bank A2
Maudland Rd A2
Meadow Court C2
Meath Rd C1
Miller Arcade B3
Miller Park C3
Moor Lane A3
Mount St B3
North Rd A3
North St A3
Northcote Rd B1
Old Milestones B1
Old Tram Rd C3
Pedder St A1/A2
Peel St A2
Penwortham Bridge C2
Penwortham New Bridge C1
Pitt St B2
Playhouse A3
Police Station A3
Portway B1
Post Office B3
Preston Station B2
Retail Park B2
Ribble Bank St B2
Ribble Viaduct C2
Ribblesdale Place B3
Ringway B3
River Parade C1
Riverside C2
St George's Shopping Centre B3
St Georges B3
St John's Minster B3
St Johns Shopping Ctr A3
St Mark's Rd A1
St Walburges A1
Salisbury Rd B1
Sessions House B3
Snow Hill A3
South End C2
South Meadow Lane C2
Spa Rd B1
Sports Ground C2
Strand Rd B1
Syke St B3
Talbot Rd B1
Taylor St C1
Tithebarn St A3
Town Hall B3
Tulketh Brow A1
University of Central Lancashire A2
Valley Rd C1
Victoria St A2
Walker St A3
Walton's Parade B2
Warwick St A3
Wellfield Bsns Park A1
Wellfield Rd A1
Wellington St A1
West Cliff C2
West Strand A1
Winckley Rd C1
Winckley Square B3
Wolseley Rd C2

Reading 342

Abbey Ruins + B2
Abbey Square B2
Abbey St B2
Abbot's Walk B2
Acacia Rd C2
Addington Rd C3
Addison Rd A1
Allcroft Rd C3
Alpine St C2
Baker St B1
Berkeley Avenue C1
Bridge St B1
Brigham Rd A1
Broad St B1
Broad Street Mall B1
Carey St B1
Castle Hill C1
Castle St B1
Causeway, The A3
Caversham Rd A1
Christchurch Meadows A2
Civic Offices B1
Coley Hill C1
Coley Place C1
Craven Rd C3
Crown St C2
De Montfort Rd A1
Denmark Rd C3
Duke St B2
East St B2
Edgehill St C2
Eldon Rd B3
Eldon Terrace B3
Elgar Rd C1
Erleigh Rd C3
Field Rd C1
Fire Station A1
Fobney St B1
Forbury Gardens B2
Forbury Rd B2
Forbury Retail Park B2
Francis St C1
Friar St B1
Garrard St B1
Gas Works Rd B3
George St A2
Great Knollys St B1
Greyfriars B1
Grove, The B2
Gun St B1
Henry St C1
Hexagon Theatre, The B1
Hill's Meadow A2
Howard St B1
Inner Distribution Rd B1
Katesgrove Lane C1
Kenavon Drive B2
Kendrick Rd C2
King's Mdw Rec Gd A2
King's Rd B2
Library B2
London Rd C3
London St B2
Lynmouth Rd A1
Magistrate's Court B1
Market Place B2
Mill Lane B2
Mill Rd A2
Minster St B1
Morgan Rd C3
Mount Pleasant C2
Museum of English Rural Life (MERL) C3
Napier Rd A2
Newark St C2
Newport Rd A1
Oracle Shopping Centre, The B1
Orts Rd B3
Oxford Road B1
Pell St C1
Post Office B2
Queen Victoria St B1
Queen's Rd A2
Queen's Rd B2
Randolph Rd A1
Reading Bridge A2
Reading College B3
Reading Station A1
Redlands Rd C3
Riverside Museum B3
Rose Kiln Lane C1
Royal Berkshire Medical Museum C3
Royal Berks Hospital (A&E) C3
St Giles C2
St Laurence B2
St Mary's B1
St Mary's Butts B1
St Saviour's Rd C1
Send Rd A3
Sherman Rd C2
Sidmouth St B2
Silver St C2
South St B2
South St Arts Ctr B2
Southampton St C2
Station Rd B1
Superstore A3
Swansea Rd A1
Thames Lido A2
Tudor Road A1
University of Reading C3
Valpy St B2
Vastern Rd A1
Vue B2
Waldeck St C2
Watlington St B3
West St B1
Whitby Drive C3
Wolseley St C1
York Rd A1
Zinzan St B1

St Andrews 342

Abbey St B2
Abbey Walk B3
Abbotsford Crescent A1
Albany Park C3
Allan Robertson Drive C2
Ambulance Station C1
Anstruther Rd C3
Argyle St B1
Auld Burn Rd B2
Bassaguard Ind Est B1
Bell St B2
Blackfriars Chapel (Ruins) B2
Boase Avenue B2
Braid Crescent C3
Brewster Place C3
Bridge St B1
British Golf Mus A1
Broomfaulds Avenue C1
Bruce Embankment A1
Bruce St C2
Bus Station A1
Byre Theatre B2
Canongate C1
Cathedral and Priory (Ruins) + B3
Cemetery B3
Chamberlain St C1
Church St B2
Churchill Crescent C2
City Rd A1
Claybraes C1
Cockshaugh Public Park B1
Cosmos Community Centre B3
Council Office A2
Crawford Gardens C1
Doubledykes Rd B1
Drumcarrow Rd C1
East Sands B3
East Scores A3
Fire Station C1
Forrest St C1
Fraser Avenue C1
Freddie Tait St C2
Gateway Centre A1
Glebe Rd B2
Golf Place A1
Grange Rd C3
Greenside Place B2
Greyfriars Gardens A2
Hamilton Avenue C2
Hepburn Gardens B1
Holy Trinity B2
Horseleys Park C1
Information Centre B2
Irvine Crescent C3
James Robb Avenue C1
James St B1
John Knox Rd C1
Kennedy Gardens B1
Kilrymont Close C3
Kilrymont Place C3
Kilrymont Rd C3
Kinburn Park B1
Kinkell Terrace C3
Kinnesburn Rd B2
Ladebraes Walk B2
Lady Buchan's Cave A3
Lamberton Place C1
Lamond Drive C2
Langlands Rd B2
Largo Rd C1
Learmonth Place C1
Library B2
Links Clubhouse A1
Links, The A1
Livingstone Crescent B2
Long Rocks A2
Madras College B2
Market St A2
Martyr's Monument A1
Murray Park A2
Murray Place A2
Mus of the Univ of St Andrews (MUSA) A2
Nelson St B2
New Course, The A1
New Picture House A2
North Castle St A3
North St A2
Old Course, The A1
Old Station Rd A1
Pends, The B3
Pilmour Links A1
Pipeland Rd B2/C2
Police Station A2/C1
Post Office B2
Preservation Trust B2
Priestden Park C3
Priestden Place C3
Priestden Rd C3
Queen's Gardens B2
Queen's Terrace B2
Roundhill Rd C2
Royal & Ancient Golf Club A1
St Andrews B1
St Andrews Aquarium A2
St Andrews Botanic Garden B1
St Andrews Castle (Ruins) & Visitor Centre A2
St Leonard's School B3
St Mary St B3
St Mary's College B2
St Nicholas St C3
St Rules Tower B3
St Salvator's College A2
Sandyhill Crescent C2
Sandyhill Rd C2
Scooniehill Rd C2
Scores, The A2
Shields Avenue C3
Shoolbraids C2
Shore, The B3
Sloan St B1
South St B2
Spottiswoode Gdns C1
Station Rd A1
Swilcen Bridge A1
Tom Morris Drive C2
Tom Stewart Lane C1
Town Hall B2
Union St A2
University Chapel A2
University Library A2
University of St Andrews A1
Viaduct Walk B1
War Memorial B3
Wardlaw Gardens B1
Warrack St C3
Watson Avenue B2
West Port B2
West Sands A1
Westview B2
Windmill Rd A1
Winram Place C1
Wishart Gardens C2
Woodburn Park B3
Woodburn Place B3
Woodburn Terrace B3
Younger Hall A2

Salisbury 342

Albany Rd A2
Arts Centre A3
Ashley Rd A1
Avon Approach A2
Ayleswade Rd C2
Bedwin St A2
Belle Vue A2
Bishops Walk B2
Blue Boar Row B2
Bourne Avenue A3
Bourne Hill A3
Britford Lane C2
Broad Walk C2
Brown St B2
Castle St A2
Catherine St B2
Chapter House B2
Church House B2
Churchfields Rd B1
Churchill Gardens C3
Churchill Way East B3
Churchill Way North A3
Churchill Way South C2
Churchill Way West A1
City Hall B2
Close Wall B2
Coldharbour Lane A1
College St A3
Council and Registry Offices A1
Court A1
Crane Bridge Rd B2
Crane St B2
Cricket Ground C1
Culver St South B3
De Vaux Place C2
Devizes Rd A1
Dews Rd B1
Elm Grove B3
Elm Grove Rd A3
Endless St A2
Estcourt Rd A3
Exeter St C2
Fairview Rd A3
Fire Station A1
Fisherton St A1
Folkestone Rd C1
Fowlers Hill B3
Fowlers Rd B3
Friary Lane B2
Friary, The B3
Gas Lane A1
Gigant St B3
Greencroft B3
Greencroft St A3
Guildhall B2
Hall of John Halle B2
Hamilton Rd A2
Harnham Mill B1
Harnham Rd C1/C2
High St B2
Ho of John A'Port B2
Information Centre B2
Kelsey Rd A3
King's Rd A2
Laverstock Rd B3
Library B2
London Rd A3
Lower St C1
Maltings, The B2
Manor Rd A3
Marsh Lane A1
Medieval Hall B2
Milford Hill B3
Milford St B3
Mill Rd B1
Mill Stream Approach A2
Mompesson House B2
New Bridge Rd C2
New Canal B2
New Harnham Rd C2
New St B2
North Canonry B2
North Gate B2
North Walk B2
Old Blandford Rd C1
Old Deanery B2
Old George Hall B2
Park St A3
Parsonage Green C1
Playhouse Theatre A2
Police Station A3
Post Office A2/B2
Poultry Cross B2
Queen Elizabeth Gdns B1
Queen's Rd A3
Rampart Rd B3
Rifles, The B2
St Ann St B2
St Ann's Gate B2
St Marks Rd A3
St Martins B3
St Paul's A1
St Paul's Rd A1
St Thomas B2
Salisbury Cathedral + B2
Salisbury Cathedral Sch (Bishop's Palace) C2
Salisbury Mus, The B2
Salisbury Station A1
Salt Lane A3
Saxon Rd C1
Scots Lane A2
Shady Bower B3
Shopmobility B2
South Canonry C2
South Gate C2
Southampton Rd B2
Spire View A1
Sports Ground C3
Tollgate Rd B3
Town Path B1
Wain-a-Long Rd A3
Wessex Rd A3
West Walk C2
Wilton Rd A1
Wiltshire College B3
Winchester St B3
Windsor Rd A1
Wyndham Rd A2
YHA B3
York Rd A1

Scarborough 342

Aberdeen Walk B2
Albert Rd A2
Albion Rd C2
Auborough St B2
Balmoral Centre B2
Belle Vue St C1
Belmont Rd C2
Blenheim Terrace A2
Brunswick Shopping Centre B2
Castle Dykes B3
Castle Hill A3
Castle Rd B2
Castle Walls A3
Castlegate B3
Cemetery B1
Central Tramway B2
Coach Park B1
Columbus Ravine A1
Court B1
Crescent, The C2
Cricket Ground A1
Cross St B2
Crown Terrace C2
Dean Rd B1
Devonshire Drive A1
East Harbour B3
East Pier B3
Eastborough B2
Elmville Avenue B1
Esplanade C2
Falconers Rd B2
Falsgrave Rd C1
Fire Station B2
Foreshore Rd B2
Friargate B2
Gladstone Rd B1
Gladstone St B1
Hollywood Plaza A1
Holms, The A3
Hoxton Rd B1
King St B2
Library B2
Lifeboat Station B3
Londesborough Rd C1
Longwestgate B3
Marine Drive A3
Luna Park B3
Miniature Railway A1
Nelson St B1
Newborough B2
Nicolas St B2
North Marine Rd A1
North St B2
Northway B1
Old Harbour B3
Olympia Leisure B2
Peasholm Park A1
Peasholm Rd A1
Police Station B1
Post Office B2
Princess St B3
Prospect Rd B1
Queen St B2
Queen's Parade A2
Queen's Tower (Remains) A3
Ramshill Rd C2
Roman Signal Sta A3
Roscoe St C1
Rotunda Museum C2
Royal Albert Drive A2
Royal Albert Park A2
St Martin-on-the-Hill C2
St Martin's Avenue C2
St Mary's B3
St Thomas St B2
Sandside B3
Scarborough C1
Scarborough Art Gallery C2
Scarborough Bowls Centre A1
Scarborough Castle A3
Shopmobility C2
Somerset Terrace C2
South Cliff Lift C2
Spa Theatre, The C2
Spa, The C2
Stephen Joseph Theatre C1
Tennyson Avenue B1
Tollergate B2
Town Hall B2
Trafalgar Rd B1
Trafalgar Square A1
Trafalgar St West B1
Valley Bridge Parade C2
Valley Rd C1
Vernon Rd C2
Victoria Park Mount A1
Victoria Rd B1
West Pier B3
Westborough C1
Westover Rd C1
Westwood C1
Woodall Avenue A1
YMCA Theatre B2
York Place B2
Yorkshire Coast College (Westwood Campus) C1

Sheffield 342

Addy Drive A2
Addy St A2
Adelphi St A3
Albert Terrace Rd A3
Albion St A2
Aldred Rd A1
Allen St A4
Alma St A4
Angel St B5
Arundel Gate B5
Arundel St C4
Ashberry Rd A2
Ashdell Rd C1
Ashgate Rd C1
Athletics Centre B2
Attercliffe Rd A6
Bailey St B4
Ball St A4
Balm Green B4
Bank St B4
Barber Rd A2
Bard St B5
Barker's Pool B4
Bates St A1
Beech Hill Rd C1
Beet St B3
Bellefield St A3
Bernard Rd A6
Bernard St B6
Birkendale A2
Birkendale Rd A2
Birkendale View A1
Bishop St C4
Blackwell Place B6
Blake St A2
Blonk St A5
Bolsover St B2
Botanical Gardens ✿ C1
Bower Rd A1
Bradley St A1
Bramall Lane C4
Bramwell St A3
Bridge St A4/A5
Brighton Terrace Rd A1
Broad Lane B3
Broad St B6
Brocco St A3
Brook Hill B3
Broomfield Rd C1
Broomgrove Rd C2
Broomhall Place C3
Broomhall Rd C2
Broomhall St C3
Broomspring Lane C2
Brown St C5
Brunswick St B3
Burgess St B4
Burlington St A2
Burns Rd A2
Cadman St A6
Cambridge St B4
Campo Lane B4
Carver St B4
Castle Square 🚊 B5
Castlegate A5
Cathedral 🚊 B4
Cathedral (RC) ✝ B4
Cavendish St B3
Charles St C4
Charter Row C4
Children's Hospital Ⓗ B2
Church St B4
City Hall 🎭 B4
City Hall 🚊 B4
City Rd C6
Claremont Crescent B2
Claremont Place B2
Clarke St C3
Clarkegrove Rd C2
Clarkehouse Rd C1
Clarkson St B2
Cobden View Rd A1
Collegiate Crescent C2
Commercial St B5
Commonside A1
Conduit Rd B1
Cornish St A3
Corporation St A4
Cricket Inn Rd B6
Cromwell St A1
Crookes Rd B1
Crookes Valley Park B2
Crookes Valley Rd B2
Crookesmoor Rd A2
Crown Court A4
Crucible Theatre 🎭 B5
Cutlers' Hall 🏠 B4
Cutlers Gate A6
Daniel Hill A2
Dental Hospital Ⓗ B2
Derek Dooley Way A5
Devonshire Green B3
Devonshire St B3
Division St B4
Dorset St C2
Dover St A3
Duchess Rd C5
Duke St B5
Duncombe St A1
Durham Rd B2
Earl St C4
Earl Way C4
Ecclesall Rd C3
Edward St B3
Effingham Rd A6
Effingham St A6
Egerton St C3
Eldon St B3
Elmore Rd B1
Exchange St B5
Eyre St C4
Fargate B4
Farm Rd C5
Fawcett St A3
Filey St B3
Fir St A1
Fire Station C4
Fitzalan Square/ Ponds Forge 🚊 B5
Fitzwater Rd C6
Fitzwilliam Gate C4
Fitzwilliam St B3
Flat St B5
Foley St A6
Foundry Climbing Ctr A4
Fulton Rd A1
Furnace Hill A4
Furnival Rd A5
Furnival Square C4
Furnival St C4
Garden St B3
Gell St B3
Gibraltar St A4
Glebe Rd B1
Glencoe Rd C6
Glossop Rd B2/B3/C1
Gloucester St C2
Government Offices C4
Granville Rd C6
Granville Rd / The Sheffield College 🚊 C5
Graves Gallery 🏛 B5
Green Lane A4
Hadfield St A1
Hanover St C3
Hanover Way C3
Harcourt Rd B1
Harmer Lane B5
Havelock St C2
Hawley St B4
Haymarket B5
Headford St C3
Heavygate Rd A1
Henry St A3
High St B4
Hodgson St C3
Holberry Gardens C2
Hollis Croft B4
Holly St B4
Hounsfield Rd B3
Howard Rd A1
Hoyle St A3
Hyde Park 🚊 A6
Infirmary Rd A3
Infirmary Rd 🚊 A3
Jericho St A3
Johnson St A5
Kelham Island Industrial Museum 🏛 A4
Lawson Rd C1
Leadmill Rd C5
Leadmill St C5
Leadmill, The ✦ C5
Leamington St A1
Leavygreave Rd B3
Lee Croft B4
Leopold St B4
Leveson St A6
Library A2/B5/C1
Light, The 🎦 C4
Lyceum Theatre 🎭 B5
Malinda St A3
Maltravers St A5
Manor Oaks Rd B6
Mappin St B3
Marlborough Rd B1
Mary St C4
Matilda St C4
Matlock Rd A1
Meadow St A3
Melbourn Rd A1
Melbourne Avenue C1
Millennium Galleries 🏛 B5
Milton St C3
Mitchell St B3
Mona Avenue A1
Mona Rd A1
Montgomery Terr Rd A3
Montgomery Theatre 🎭 B4
Monument Grounds C6
Moor Oaks Rd B1
Moor, The C4
Moor Market C4
Moore St C3
Mowbray St A4
Mushroom Lane B2
National Emergency Service 🏛 A4
National Videogame 🏛 B5
Netherthorpe Rd B3
Netherthorpe Rd 🚊 B3
Newbould Lane C1
Nile St C1
Norfolk Park Rd C6
Norfolk Rd C6
Norfolk St B4
North Church St B4
Northfield Rd A1
Northumberland Rd B1
Nursery St A5
O2 Academy 🎭 B5
Oakholme Rd C1
Octagon B2
Odeon 🎦 B5
Old St B6
Orch Sq Shopping Ctr B4
Oxford St A2
Paradise St B4
Park Lane C2
Park Square B5
Parker's Rd B1
Pearson Building (University) C2
Penistone Rd A3
Pinstone St B4
Pitt St B3
Police Station 🚔 B5
Pond Hill B5
Pondorosa, The A2
Pond St B5
Ponds Forge International Sports Centre B5
Portobello St B3
Post Office ✉ A2/B3/B5/C1/C3/C4/C6
Powell St A2
Queen St B4
Queen's Rd C5
Ramsey Rd B1
Red Hill B3
Redcar Rd B1
Regent St B3
Rockingham St B4
Roebuck Rd A2
Royal Hallamshire Hospital Ⓗ C2
Russell St A4
Rutland Park C1
St George's Close B3
St Mary's Gate C3
St Mary's Rd C4/C5
St Philip's Rd A3
Savile St A5
School Rd B1
Scotland St A4
Severn Rd B1
Shalesmoor A4
Shalesmoor 🚊 A3
Sheaf St B5
Sheffield Cathedral ✝ B4
Sheffield Hallam Univ B5
Sheffield Ice Sports Ctr – Skate Central C5
Sheffield Institute of Arts 🏛 B5
Sheffield Interchange B5
Sheffield Parkway A6
Sheffield Station ⇌ C5
Sheffield Sta/ Sheffield Hallam Univ 🚊 B5
Sheffield University B2
Shepherd St A3
Shipton St A2
Shopmobility B3
Shoreham St C4
Showroom 🎦 C5
Shrewsbury Rd C5
Sidney St C4
Site Gallery 🏛 C5
Slinn St A1
Smithfield A4
Snig Hill A5
Snow Lane A4
Solly St B3
South Lane C4
South Street Park B5
Southbourne Rd C1
Spital Hill A5
Spital St A5
Spring Hill B1
Spring Hill Rd B1
Springvale Rd A1
Stafford Rd C6
Stafford St B6
Suffolk Rd C5
Summer St B2
Sunny Bank C3
Superstore A3/C3
Surrey St B4
Sussex St A6
Sutton St B3
Sydney Rd A2
Sylvester St C4
Talbot St B5
Taptonville Rd B1
Tenter St B4
Town Hall 🏠 B4
Townend St A1
Townhead St B4
Trafalgar St B4
Tree Root Walk B2
Trinity St A4
Trippet Lane B4
Turner Mus of Glass 🏛 B3
Union St B4
Univ Drama Studio 🎭 B2
Univ of Sheffield 🚊 B3
Upper Allen St A3
Upper Hanover St B3
Upperthorpe Rd A2/A3
Verdon St A5
Victoria Rd C2
Victoria St B3
Waingate B5
Watery St A3
Watson Rd C1
Wellesley Rd B2
Wellington St C3
West Bar A4
West Bar Green A4
West One Plaza B3
West St B3
West St 🚊 B4
Westbourne Rd C1
Western Bank B2
Western Rd A1
Weston Park B2
Weston Park Hosp Ⓗ B2
Weston Park Mus 🏛 B2
Weston St B2
Wharncliffe Rd C3
Whitham Rd B1
Wicker A5
Wilkinson St B2
William St C3
Winter Garden ✦ B4
Winter St B2
York St B4
Yorkshire Artspace C5
Young St C4

Shrewsbury 342

Abbey Foregate B3
Abbey Gardens B2
Abbey Lawn Bsns Park B3
Abbots House 🏠 B2
Albert St A2
Alma St B1
Ashley St A3
Ashton Rd C1
Avondale Drive A3
Bage Way C3
Barker St B1
Beacall's Lane A2
Beeches Lane C2
Beehive Lane C1
Belle Vue Gardens C2
Belle Vue Rd C2
Belmont Bank C1
Berwick Avenue A1
Berwick Rd A1
Betton St C2
Bishop St B3
Bradford St B3
Bridge St B1
Burton St A3
Bus Station B2
Butcher Row B2
Butler Rd C1
Bynner St C2
Canon St B3
Canonbury C1
Castle Bsns Park, The A2
Castle Foregate A2
Castle Gates B2
Castle Walk B3
Castle St B2
Cathedral (RC) ✝ C1
Chester St A2
Cineworld 🎦 C3
Claremont Bank B1
Claremont Hill B1
Cleveland St B3
Coleham Head B2
Coleham Pumping Station 🏛 C2
College Hill B1
Corporation Lane A1
Coton Crescent A1
Coton Hill A2
Coton Mount A1
Crescent Lane C1
Crewe St A2
Cross Hill B1
Dana, The B2
Darwin Centre B2
Dingle, The ✿ B1
Dogpole B2
English Bridge B2
Fish St B2
Frankwell B1
Gateway Ctr, The 🏛 A2
Gravel Hill Lane A1
Greenhous West Mid Showground A1
Greyfriars Rd C2
Hampton Rd A3
Haycock Way C3
High St B1
Hills Lane B1
Holywell St B3
Hunter St A1
Information Centre ℹ B1
Ireland's Mansion & Bear Steps 🏠 B1
John St A3
Kennedy Rd C1
King St B3
Kingsland Bridge C1
Kingsland Bridge (toll) C1
Kingsland Rd C1
Library B2
Lime St C2
Longden Coleham C2
Longden Rd C1
Longner St B1
Luciefelde Rd C1
Mardol B1
Marine Terrace C2
Market B1
Monkmoor Rd B3
Moreton Crescent C2
Mount St A1
New Park Close A3
New Park Rd A2
New Park St A3
North St A2
Oakley St C1
Old Coleham C2
Old Market Hall 🎦 B1
Old Potts Way C3
Par Shopping Ctr, The B2
Police Station 🚔 B1
Post Office ✉ B1/B2/B3
Pride Hill B1
Pride Hill Centre B1
Priory Rd B1
Pritchard Way C3
Quarry Swimming & Fitness Centre, The B1
Queen St A3
Raby Crescent C2
Rad Brook C1
Rea Brook C3
Rea Brook Valley Country Park & Local Nature Reserve C3
Riverside B1
Roundhill Lane A1
St Alkmund's ⛪ B2
St Chad's ⛪ B1
St Chad's Terrace B1
St John's Hill B1
St Julians Friars C2
St Mary's ⛪ B2
St Mary's St B2
Salters Lane C2
Scott St C3
Severn Theatre 🎭 B1
Severn Bank A3
Severn St A2
Shrewsbury ⇌ B2
Shrewsbury Abbey ⛪ B3
Shrewsbury High School C1
Shrewsbury Museum & Art Gall 🏛 B1
Shrewsbury Prison Tours ✦ B2
Shrewsbury School ✦ C1
Shropshire Regimental Museum 🏠 B2
Shropshire Wildlife Trust ✦ B3
Smithfield Rd B1
South Hermitage C1
Square, The B1
Superstore C3
Swan Hill B1
Sydney Avenue A3
Tankerville St B3
Tilbrook Drive A3
Town Walls C1
Trinity St C2
Underdale Rd B3
University Centre Shrewsbury (Guildhall) B1
Victoria Avenue B1
Victoria Quay B1
Victoria St B2
Welsh Bridge B1
Whitehall St B3
Wood St A2
Wyle Cop B2

Southampton 342

Above Bar St A2
Albert Rd North B3
Albert Rd South C3
Andersons Rd B3
Argyle Rd A2
Arundel Tower ✦ B1
Bargate, The ✦ B2
BBC South A1
Bedford Place A1
Belvidere Rd A3
Bernard St C2
Blechynden Terrace A1
Brinton's Rd A2
Britannia Rd A3
Briton St C2
Brunswick Place A2
Bugle St C1
Canute Rd C3
Castle Way C2
Catchcold Tower ✦ B1
Central Bridge C3
Central Rd C2
Channel Way C3
Chapel Rd B3
City Art Gallery 🏛 A1
City College B3
City Cruise Terminal C1
Civic Centre A1
Civic Centre Rd A1
Coach Station B1
Commercial Rd A1
Cumberland Place A1
Cunard Rd C2
Derby Rd A3
Devonshire Rd A1
Dock Gate 4 C2
Dock Gate 8 B1
East Park (Andrew's Park) A2
East Park Terrace A2
East St B2
Endle St B3
European Way C2
Fire Station A2
Floating Bridge Rd C3
God's House Tower ✦ C2
Golden Grove A3
Graham Rd A2
Guildhall A1
Hanover Buildings B2
Harbour Lights 🎦 C3
Harbour Parade B1
Hartington Rd A3
Havelock Rd A1
Henstead Rd A1
Herbert Walker Ave B1
High St B2
Hoglands Park B2
Holy Rood (Rems), Merchant Navy Memorial ⛪ B2
Houndwell Park B2
Houndwell Place B2
Hythe Ferry C2
Isle of Wight Ferry Terminal C1
James St B3
Kingsway A2
Leisure World B1
Library A1
Lime St B2
London Rd A2
Marine Parade B3
Marlands Shopping Centre, The A1
Marsh Lane B2
Mayflower Meml ✦ C1
Mayflower Park C1
Mayflower Theatre, The 🎭 A1
Medieval Merchant's House 🏠 C1
Melbourne St B3
Morris Rd A1
National Oceanography Centre ✦ C3
Neptune Way C3
New Rd A2
Nichols Rd A3
North Front A2
Northam Rd A3
Ocean Dock C2
Ocean Village Marina C3
Ocean Way C3
Odeon 🎦 B1
Ogle Rd B1
Old Northam Rd A2
Orchard Lane B2
Oxford Avenue A2
Oxford St C2
Palmerston Park A2
Palmerston Rd A2
Parsonage Rd A3
Peel St A3
Platform Rd C2
Polygon, The A1
Portland Terrace B1
Post Office ✉ B2
Pound Tree Rd B2
Quays Swimming & Diving Complex, The B1
Queen's Park C2
Queen's Peace Fountain ✦ A2
Queen's Terrace C2
Queensway B2
Radcliffe Rd A3
Rochester St A3
Royal Pier C1
Royal South Hants Hospital Ⓗ A2
St Andrew's Rd A2
St Mary's ⛪ B3
St Mary St A2
St Mary's Leisure Ctr A2
St Mary's Place B2
St Mary's Rd A2
St Mary's Stadium (Southampton FC) A3
St Michael's ⛪ C1
SeaCity Museum 🏛 A1
Showcase Cinema de Lux 🎦 B1
Solent Sky 🏛 C3
South Front B2
Southampton Central Station ⇌ A1
Southampton Solent University A2
Terminus Terrace C2
Threefield Lane B2
Titanic Engineers' Memorial ✦ A2
Town Quay C1
Town Walls B2
Tudor House 🏠 C1
Vincent's Walk B2
Westgate Hall 🏠 C1
West Marlands Rd A1
West Park A1
West Park Rd A1
West Quay Rd B1
West Quay Retail Park B1
Western Esplanade B1
Westquay Shopping Centre B1
Westquay South B1
White Star Way C2
Winton St A2

Southend-on-Sea 343

Adventure Island ✦ C3
Albany Avenue A1
Albert Rd C3
Alexandra Rd C2
Alexandra St C2
Alexandra Yacht Club ✦ C2
Ashburnham Rd B2
Avenue Rd B1
Avenue Terrace B1
Balmoral Rd B1
Baltic Avenue B3
Baxter Avenue A2/B2
Beecroft Art Gallery 🏛 B2
Bircham Rd A2
Boscombe Rd B3
Boston Avenue A1/B2
Bournemouth Park Rd A3
Browning Avenue A3
Bus Station C3
Byron Avenue A3
Cambridge Rd C1/C2
Canewdon Rd B1
Carnarvon Rd A2
Central Avenue A3
Central Museum 🏛 B2
Chelmsford Avenue A1
Chichester Rd B2
Church Rd C3
Civic Centre A2
Clarence Rd C2
Clarence St C2
Cliff Avenue B1
Cliffs Pavilion 🎭 C1
Clifftown Parade C2
Clifftown Rd C2
Colchester Rd A1
Coleman St B3
College Way B2
County Court B3
Cromer Rd B3
Crowborough Rd A2
Dryden Avenue A3
East St A2
Elmer Approach B2
Elmer Avenue B2
Forum, The B2
Gainsborough Drive A1
Gayton Rd A2
Glenhurst Rd A2
Gordon Place B2
Gordon Rd B2
Grainger Rd A2
Greyhound Way A3
Grove, The A3
Guildford Rd B3
Hamlet Court Rd B1
Hamlet Rd C1
Harcourt Avenue A1
Hartington Rd C3
Hastings Rd B3
Herbert Grove C3
Heygate Avenue C3
High St B2/C2
Information Centre ℹ C3
Kenway A2
Kilworth Avenue B3
Lancaster Gardens B3
London Rd B1
Lucy Rd C3
MacDonald Avenue A1
Magistrates' Court A2
Maldon Rd A2
Marine Avenue C1
Marine Parade C3
Marine Rd C1
Milton Rd B1
Milton St B2
Napier Avenue B2
North Avenue A3
North Rd A1/B1
Odeon 🎦 B2
Osborne Rd B1
Park Crescent B1
Park Rd B1
Park St B1
Park Terrace B1
Pier Hill C3
Pleasant Rd C3
Police Station 🚔 A2
Post Office ✉ B2/B3
Princes St B2
Queens Rd B2
Queensway B2/B3/C3
Radio Essex C2
Rayleigh Avenue A1
Redstock Rd A2
Rochford Avenue A1
Royal Mews C2
Royal Terrace C2
Royals Shopping Centre, The C3
Ruskin Avenue A3
St Ann's Rd B3
St Helen's Rd B1
St John's Rd B1
St Leonard's Rd C3
St Lukes Rd A3
St Vincent's Rd C1
Salisbury Avenue A1/B1
Scratton Rd C2
Shakespeare Drive A1
Shopmobility B2
Short St A2
South Avenue A3
Southchurch Rd B3
Southend Central ⇌ B2
Southend Pier Railway 🚂 C3
Southend United FC A1
Southend Victoria ⇌ B2
Stanfield Rd A2
Stanley Rd C3
Sutton Rd A3/B3
Swanage Rd B3
Sweyne Avenue A1
Sycamore Grove A3
Tennyson Avenue A3
Tickfield Avenue A2
Tudor Rd A1
Tunbridge Rd A2
Tylers Avenue B3
Tyrrel Drive B3
University of Essex B2/C2
Vale Avenue A2
Victoria Avenue A2
Victoria Shopping Centre, The B2
Warrior Square B3
Wesley Rd C3
West Rd A1
West St A1
Westcliff Avenue C1
Westcliff Parade C1
Western Esplanade C1
Weston Rd C2
Whitegate Rd B3
Wilson Rd C1
Wimborne Rd B3
York Rd C3

Stirling 343

Abbey Rd A3
Abbotsford Place A3
Abercromby Place C1
Albert Halls 🎭 B1
Albert Place B1
Alexandra Place A3
Allan Park C2
Ambulance Station A2
AMF Ten Pin Bowling ✦ B2
Argyll Avenue A3
Argyll's Lodging ✦ B1
Back O' Hill Ind Est A1
Back O' Hill Rd A1
Baker St B2
Ballengeich Pass A1
Balmoral Place B1
Barn Rd B1
Barnton St B2
Bastion, The ✦ C2
Bow St B1
Bruce St A2
Burghmuir Retail Park C2
Burghmuir Rd A2/B2/C2
Bus Station B2
Cambuskenneth Bridge A3
Castle Court B1
Causewayhead Rd A2
Cemetery A1
Changing Room, The 🏛 B1
Church of the Holy Rude ⛪ B1
Clarendon Place C1
Club House B1
Colquhoun St C3
Corn Exchange B2
Council Offices C2
Court B2
Cowane Centre 🎭 A2
Cowane St A2
Cowane's Hospital 🏠 B1
Crofthead Rd A1
Dean Crescent A3
Douglas St A2
Drip Rd A1
Drummond Lane C1
Drummond Place C1
Drummond Place Lane C1
Dumbarton Rd C2
Eastern Access Rd B2
Edward Avenue A3
Edward Rd A2
Forrest Rd A2
Fort A1
Forth Crescent B2
Forth St A2
Gladstone Place C1
Glebe Avenue C1
Glebe Crescent C1
Golf Course C1
Goosecroft Rd B2
Gowanhill A1
Greenwood Avenue B1
Harvey Wynd A1
Information Centre ℹ B1
Irvine Place B2
James St A2
John St B1
Kerse Rd C3
King's Knot ✦ B1
King's Park C1
King's Park Rd C1
Laurencecroft Rd A2
Leisure Pool B2
Library B2
Linden Avenue C2
Lovers Wk A2
Lower Back Walk B1
Lower Bridge St A2
Lower Castlehill A1
Mar Place B1
Meadow Place A3
Meadowforth Rd C3
Middlemuir Rd C3
Millar Place A3
Morris Terrace B2
Mote Hill A1
Murray Place B2
Nelson Place C2
Old Town Cemetery B1
Old Town Jail ✦ B1
Park Terrace C1
Phoenix Industrial Est C3
Players Rd C3
Port St C2
Post Office ✉ B2
Princes St B2
Queen St B2
Queen's Rd B1
Queenshaugh Drive A3
Ramsay Place A2
Riverside Drive A3
Ronald Place A1
Rosebery Place A2
Royal Gardens B1
Royal Gardens B1
St Mary's Wynd B1
St Ninian's Rd C2
Scott St A2
Seaforth Place B2
Shore Rd B2
Smith Art Gallery & Museum 🏛🏛 B1
Snowdon Place C1
Snowdon Place Lane C1
Spittal St B2
Springkerse Ind Est C3
Springkerse Rd C3
Stirling Arcade B2
Stirling Bsns Centre C2
Stirling Castle ♜ A1
Stirling County Rugby Football Club A3
Stirling Enterprise Pk B3
Stirling Old Bridge A2
Stirling Station ⇌ B2
Superstore A1/A2
Sutherland Avenue A3
TA Centre C3
Tannery Lane A2
Thistle Industrial Est C3
Thistles Shopping Centre, The B2
Tolbooth ✦ B1
Town Wall B1
Union St A2
Upper Back Walk B1
Upper Bridge St A1
Upper Castlehill B1
Upper Craigs C2
Victoria Place C1
Victoria Rd B1
Victoria Square B1/C1
Vue 🎦 B2
Wallace St A2
Waverley Crescent A3
Wellgreen Rd C2
Windsor Place C1
YHA ▲ B1

Stoke 343

Ashford St A3
Avenue Rd A3
Aynsley Rd A2
Barnfield C1
Bath St C2
Beresford St A3
Bilton St C2
Boon Avenue C2
Booth St C2
Boothen Rd C2/C3
Boughey St C2
Boughley Rd B3
Brighton St B1
Campbell Rd C2
Carlton Rd B3
Cauldon Rd A3
Cemetery A2
Cemetery Rd A2
Chamberlain Avenue C1
Church (RC) ⛪ B2
Church St C2
City Rd C3
Civic Centre & King's Hall 🏠 B3
Cliff Vale Place A1
College Rd A3
Convent Close B2
Copeland St B2
Cornwallis St C3
Corporation St C2
Crowther St A3
Dominic St B1
Elenora St B2
Elgin St B2
Epworth St A3
Etruscan St A1
Film Theatre 🎦 B3
Fleming Rd C2
Fletcher Rd C2
Floyd St B2
Foden St C2
Frank St C2
Franklin Rd C1
Frederick Avenue B1
Garden St C1
Garner St A1
Gerrard St B2
Glebe St B3
Greatbach Avenue B1
Hanley Park A3
Harris St B1
Hartshill Rd B1
Hayward St A2
Hide St B2
Higson Avenue B2
Hill St B2
Honeywall B2
Hunters Drive C1
Hunters Way C1
Keary St C2
Kingsway B2
Leek Rd B3
Library C2
Lime St C2
Liverpool Rd B2
London Rd C2
Lonsdale St C2
Lovatt St B2
Lytton St B3
Market C2
Newcastle Lane C1
Newlands St A2
Norfolk St A2
North St A1/B2
Northcote Avenue B2
Oldmill St C3
Oriel St B1
Oxford St B1
Penkhull New Rd C1
Penkhull St C1
Portmeirion Pottery ✦ C2
Post Office ✉ A3
Princes Rd B1
Pump St B2
Quarry Avenue B1
Quarry Rd B1
Queen Anne St A3
Queen's Rd C1
Queensway A1/B2/C3
Richmond St B1
Richmond St Park B1
Rothwell St C1
St Peter's ⛪ B3
St Thomas Place C1
Scrivenor Rd A1
Seaford St A3
Selwyn St C3
Shelton New Rd A1
Shelton Old Rd B2
Sheppard St C2
Sir Stanley Matthews Sports Centre B3
Spark St C2
Spencer Rd B3
Spode Museum Heritage Centre 🏛 B2
Spode St C2
Squires View B3
Staffordshire Univ B3
Station Rd B3
Stoke Business Park C3
Stoke Rd A2
Stoke-on-Trent Coll A3
Stoke-on-Trent Sta ⇌ B3
Sturgess St C2
Thistley Hough C1
Thornton Rd B3
Tolkien Way B1
Trent Valley Rd C1
Vale St B2
Villas, The C1
Watford St A3
Wellesley St A3
West Avenue B1
Westland St B1
Yeaman St C2
Yoxall Avenue B1

Stratford-upon-Avon 343

Albany Rd B1
Alcester Rd B1
Ambulance Station B1
Arden St B2
Avenue Farm A1
Ave Farm Ind Est A1
Avenue Rd A3
Baker Avenue A1
Bandstand C3
Benson Rd A3
Birmingham Rd A2
Boat Club B3
Borden Place C1
Bridge St B2
Bridgetown Rd C3
Bridgeway B3
Broad St C2
Broad Walk C2
Brookvale Rd C1
Brunel Way B1
Bull St C2
Butterfly Farm ✦ C3
Cemetery C1
Chapel Lane B2
Cherry Orchard C1
Chestnut Walk B2
Children's Playground C3
Church St C2
Civic Hall B2
Clarence Rd B1
Clopton Bridge ✦ B3

Clopton Rd A2
College B1
College Lane C2
College St C2
Community Sports Ctr B1
Council Offices (District) B2
Courtyard, The C2
Cox's Yard B3
Cricket Ground C3
Ely Gardens B2
Ely St B2
Evesham Rd C1
Fire Station B1
Foot Ferry C3
Fordham Avenue A2
Garrick Way C1
Gower Memorial B3
Great William St B2
Greenhill St B2
Greenway, The C2
Grove Rd B2
Guild St B2
Guildhall & School B2
Hall's Croft C2
Harvard House B2
Henley St B2
Hertford Rd C1
High St B2
Holton St C2
Holy Trinity C2
Information Centre B3
Jolyffe Park Rd A2
Kipling Rd C3
Library B2
Lodge Rd B1
Maidenhead Rd A3
Mansell St B2
Masons Court B2
Masons Rd A1
Maybird Shopping Pk A2
Maybrook Retail Park A2
Maybrook Rd A1
Mayfield Avenue A2
Meer St B2
Mill Lane C2
Moat House Hotel B3
Narrow Lane C2
Nash's Ho & New Pl B2
New St C2
Old Town C2
Orchard Way C1
Other Place, The C2
Paddock Lane C1
Park Rd A1
Payton St B2
Percy St A2
Police Station B2
Post Office B2
Recreation Ground C2
Regal Road A2
Rother St B2
Rowley Crescent A3
Royal Shakespeare Theatre B3
Ryland St C2
Saffron Meadow C2
St Andrew's Crescent B1
St Gregory's A3
St Gregory's Rd A3
St Mary's Rd A2
Sanctus Drive C2
Sanctus St C1
Sandfield Rd C2
Scholars Lane B2
Seven Meadows Rd C2
Shakespeare Institute C2
Shakespeare St B2
Shakespeare's Birthplace B2
Sheep St B2
Shelley Rd C3
Shipston Rd C3
Shottery Rd C1
Slingates Rd A2
Southern Lane C2
Station Rd B1
Stratford Healthcare B2
Stratford Hospital B2
Stratford Leisure Ctr B3
Stratford Sports Club B1
Stratford-upon-Avon Station B1
Swan Theatre B3
Swan's Nest Lane B3
Talbot Rd A2
Tiddington Rd B3
Timothy's Bridge Industrial Estate A1
Timothy's Bridge Rd A1
Town Hall & Council Offices B2
Town Square B2
Trinity Close C2
Tyler St B2
War Memorial Gdns B3
Warwick Rd B3
Waterside B3
Welcombe Rd A3
West St C2
Western Rd A2
Wharf Rd A2
Willows North, The B1
Willows, The B1
Wood St B2

Sunderland 343

Albion Place C2
Alliance Place B1
Argyle St C2
Ashwood St C1
Athenaeum St B2
Azalea Terrace C2
Beach St A1
Bedford St B2
Beechwood Terrace C1
Belvedere Rd C2
Blandford St B2
Borough Rd B3
Bridge Crescent B2
Bridge St B2
Bridges, The B2
Brooke St A2
Brougham St B2
Burdon Rd C2
Burn Park C1
Burn Park Rd C1
Burn Park Tech Park C1
Carol St B1
Charles St A3
Chester Rd C1
Chester Terrace B1
Church St A3
Civic Centre C2
Cork St B3
Coronation St B3
Cowan Terrace C2
Dame Dorothy St A2
Deptford Rd B1
Deptford Terrace A1
Derby St C2
Derwent St C2
Dock St A3
Dundas St A2
Durham Rd C1
Easington St A2
Egerton St C3
Empire B3
Empire Theatre B2
Farringdon Row B1
Fawcett St B2
Fire Station B1
Fox St C1
Foyle St B3
Frederick St B3
Hanover Place A1
Havelock Terrace C1
Hay St A2
Headworth Square B3
Hendon Rd B3
High St East B3
High St West B2/B3
Holmeside B2
Hylton Rd B1
John St B3
Kier Hardie Way A2
Lambton St B3
Laura St C3
Lawrence St B3
Library & Arts Centre B3
Lily St B1
Lime St B1
Livingstone Rd B2
Low Row B2
Magistrates' Court B3
Matamba Terrace B1
Millburn St B1
Millennium Way A2
Minster B2
Monkwearmouth Station Museum A2
Mowbray Park C3
Mowbray Rd C3
Murton St C3
National Glass Ctr A3
New Durham Rd C1
Newcastle Rd A2
Nile St B3
Norfolk St B3
North Bridge St A2
Northern Gallery for Contemporary Art (NGCA) B3
Otto Terrace C1
Park Lane C2
Park Lane Ⓜ C2
Park Rd C2
Paul's Rd B3
Peel St C3
Point, The B2
Police Station B2
Priestly Crescent A1
Queen St B2
Railway Row B1
Retail Park B1
Richmond St A2
Roker Avenue A2
Royalty Theatre C1
Royalty, The C1
Ryhope Rd C2
St Mary's Way B2
St Michael's Way B2
St Peter's A3
St Peter's Ⓜ A2
St Peter's Way A3
St Vincent St C3
Salem Rd C3
Salem St C3
Salisbury St C3
Sans St B3
Shopmobility B2
Silkworth Row B1
Southwick Rd A2
Stadium of Light (Sunderland AFC) A2
Stadium Way A2
Stobart St A2
Stockton Rd C2
Suffolk St C3
Sunderland Ⓜ B2
Sunderland Aquatic Centre A2
Sunderland College C2
Sunderland Mus B3
Sunderland St B3
Sunderland Station B2
Tatham St C3
Tavistock Place B3
Thelma St C1
Thomas St North A2
Thornholme Rd C1
Toward Rd C3
Transport Interchange C2
Trimdon St Way B1
Tunstall Rd C2
University Ⓜ C1
University Library C1
University of Sunderland (City Campus) B1
University of Sunderland (St Peter's Campus) A3
Univ of Sunderland (Sir Tom Cowie Campus) A3
Vaux Brewery Way A2
Villiers St B3
Villiers St South B3
Vine Place C2
Violet St B1
Walton Lane B3
Waterworks Rd B1
Wearmouth Bridge B2
West Sunniside B3
West Wear St B3
Westbourne Rd B1
Western Hill C1
Wharncliffe B1
Whickham St A3
White House Rd C3
Wilson St North A2
Winter Gardens C3
Wreath Quay A1

Swansea Abertawe 343

Adelaide St C3
Albert Row C3
Alexandra Rd B3
Argyle St C1
Baptist Well Place A2
Beach St C1
Belle Vue Way B3
Berw Rd A1
Berwick Terrace A2
Bond St C1
Brangwyn Concert Hall C1
Bridge St A3
Brooklands Terrace B1
Brunswick St C1
Bryn-Syfi Terrace A2
Bryn-y-Mor Rd C1
Bullins Lane B1
Burrows Rd C1
Bus Station C2
Bus/Rail link A3
Cadfan Rd A1
Cadrawd Rd A1
Caer St B3
Carig Crescent A1
Carlton Terrace B2
Carmarthen Rd A3
Castle Square B3
Castle St B3
Catherine St C1
Cinema C3
Civic Centre & Library C2
Clarence St C2
Colbourne Terrace A2
Constitution Hill B1
Court B3
Creidiol Rd A2
Cromwell St B2
Crown Courts C1
Duke St B1
Dunvant Place C2
Dyfatty Park A3
Dyfatty St A3
Dyfed Avenue A1
Dylan Thomas Ctr B3
Dylan Thomas Theatre C3
Eaton Crescent C1
Eigen Crescent A1
Elfed Rd A1
Emlyn Rd A1
Evans Terrace A3
Fairfield Terrace B1
Ffynone Drive B1
Ffynone Rd B1
Fire Station B3
Firm St A2
Fleet St C1
Francis St C1
Fullers Row B2
George St B2
Glamorgan St C2
Glynn Vivian Art Gallery B3
Gower Coll Swansea C1
Graig Terrace A3
Grand Theatre C2
Granogwen Rd A2
Guildhall C1
Guildhall Rd South C1
Gwent Rd A1
Gwynedd Avenue A1
Hafod St A3
Hanover St B1
Harcourt St B2
Harries St A2
Heathfield B2
Henrietta St B1
Hewson St B2
High St A3/B3
High View A2
Hill St A2
Historic Ships Berth C3
HM Prison C2
Islwyn Rd A1
King Edward's Rd C1
Kingsway, The B2
LC, The C3
Long Ridge A2
Madoc St C2
Mansel St B2
Maritime Quarter C3
Market B3
Mayhill Gardens B1
Mayhill Rd A1
Milton Terrace A2
Mission Gallery C3
Montpelier Terrace B1
Morfa Rd A3
Mount Pleasant B2
National Waterfront Museum C3
New Cut Rd A3
New St A3
Nicander Parade A2
Nicander Place A2
Nicholl St B2
Norfolk St B2
North Hill Rd A2
Northampton Lane B2
Observatory C3
Orchard St B3
Oxford St B2
Oystermouth Rd C1
Page St B2
Pant-y-Celyn Rd B1
Parc Tawe North B3
Parc Tawe Shopping & Leisure Centre B3
Patti Pavilion C1
Paxton St C2
Pen-y-Graig Rd A1
Penmaen Terrace B1
Phillips Parade C1
Picton Terrace B2
Plantasia B3
Plantasia B3
Police Station B2
Post Office A1/A2/C1/C2
Powys Avenue A1
Primrose St B2
Princess Way B3
Promenade B2
Pryder Gardens A1
Quadrant Shopping Centre C2
Quay Park B3
Rhianfa Lane B1
Rhondda St B2
Richardson St C2
Rodney St C1
Rose Hill B1
Rosehill Terrace B1
Russell St B1
St Helen's Avenue C1
St Helen's Crescent C1
St Helen's Rd C1
St James Gardens B1
St James's Crescent B1
St Mary's B3
Sea View Terrace A3
Singleton St C2
South Dock C3
Stanley Place B2
Strand B3
Swansea Castle B3
Swansea Metropolitan University B2
Swansea Museum C3
Swansea Station A3
Taliesyn Rd B1
Tan y Marian Rd A1
Tegid Rd A2
Teilo Crescent A1
Tenpin Bowling B3
Terrace Rd B1/B2
Tontine St A3
Townhill Rd A1
Tramshed, The C3
Trawler Rd C3
Union St B2
Upper Strand A3
Vernon St A3
Victoria Quay C3
Victoria Rd B3
Vincent St C1
Walter Rd B1
Watkin St A2
Waun-Wen Rd A2
Wellington St C2
Westbury St C1
Western St C1
Westway C2
William St C2
Wind St B3
Woodlands Terrace B1
YMCA B2
York St C3

Swindon 343

Albert St C3
Albion St C1
Alfred St A2
Alvescot Rd C3
Art Gallery & Mus C3
Ashford Rd C1
Aylesbury St A2
Bath Rd C2
Bathampton St B1
Bathurst Rd B3
Beatrice St A2
Beckhampton St B3
Bowood Rd C1
Bristol St B1
Broad St A3
Brunel Shopping Centre, The B2
Brunel Statue B2
Brunswick St C2
Bus Station B2
Cambria Bridge Rd B1
Cambria Place B1
Canal Walk B2
Carr St B1
Cemetery C1/C3
Chandler Close C3
Chapel C1
Chester St B1
Christ Church C3
Church Place B1
Cirencester Way A3
Clarence St B2
Clifton St C1
Cockleberry A2
Colbourne A3
Colbourne St A3
College St B2
Commercial Rd B2
Corporation St A2
Council Offices B3
County Cricket Gd A3
County Rd A3
Courts B2
Cricklade Street C3
Crombey St B1/C2
Cross St C2
Curtis St B1
Deacon St C1
Designer Outlet (Great Western) B1
Dixon St C2
Dover St C2
Dowling St C2
Drove Rd C3
Dryden St C1
Durham St C3
East St B1
Eastcott Hill C2
Eastcott Rd C2
Edgeware Rd B2
Edmund St C2
Elmina Rd A3
Emlyn Square B1
English Heritage National Monuments Record Centre B1
Euclid St B3
Exeter St B1
Fairview C1
Faringdon Rd B1
Farnsby St B1
Fire Station B3
Fleet St B2
Fleming Way B2/B3
Florence St A2
Gladstone St A3
Gooch St A2
Graham St A3
Great Western Way A1/A2
Groundwell Rd B3
Hawksworth Way A1
Haydon St A2
Henry St B2
Hillside Avenue C1
Holbrook Way B2
Hunt St C3
Hydro B1
Hythe Rd C2
Information Centre B2
Joseph St C1
Kent Rd C2
King William St C2
Kingshill Rd C1
Lansdown Rd C2
Lawn, The C3
Leicester St B3
Library B2
Lincoln St B3
Little London C3
London St B1
Magic B3
Maidstone Rd C2
Manchester Rd A3
Maxwell St B1
Milford St B2
Milton Rd B1
Morse St C2
Newcastle St B3
Newcombe Drive A1
Hawsworth Ind Est A1
Newhall St C2
North St C2
North Star A1
North Star Avenue A1
Northampton St B3
Nurseries, The C1
Oasis Leisure Centre A1
Ocotal Way A3
Okus Rd C1
Old Town C3
Oxford St B1
Parade, The B2
Park Lane B1
Park Lane B1
Park, The B1
Pembroke St C2
Plymouth St B3
Polaris Way A2
Police Station B2
Ponting St A2
Post Office B1/B2/C3
Poulton St A3
Princes St B2
Prospect Hill C2
Prospect Place C2
Queen St B2
Queen's Park C3
Radnor St C1
Read St C1
Reading St B1
Regent Circus C2
Regent St B2
Retail Park A2/A3/B3
Rosebery St A3
St Mark's B1
Salisbury St A3
Savernake St C2
Science & Technology Facilities Council HQ A2
Shelley St C1
Sheppard St B1
Shopmobility B2
South St C2
Southampton St B3
Spring Gardens B3
Stafford Street C2
Stanier St C2
Station Road A2
STEAM GWR B1
Swindon College A2
Swindon Rd C2
Swindon Station A2
Swindon Town Football Club A3
TA Centre B1
Tennyson St B1
Theobald St B1
Town Hall B2
Transfer Bridges A3
Union St C2
Upham Rd C3
Victoria Rd C3
Walcot Rd B3
War Memorial B2
Wells St B3
Western St C2
Westmorland Rd B3
Whalebridge B2
Whitehead St C1
Whitehouse Rd A2
William St C1
Wood St C3
Wyvern Theatre & Arts Centre B2
York Rd B3

Taunton 343

Addison Grove A1
Albemarle Rd A1
Alfred St B3
Alma St C2
Avenue, The A1
Bath Place C1
Belvedere Rd A1
Billet St B2
Billetfield C2
Birch Grove A1
Brewhouse Theatre B2
Bridge St B1
Bridgwater & Taunton Canal A2
Broadlands Rd C1
Burton Place C1
Bus Station B1
Canal Rd A2
Cann St C1
Canon St B2
Castle St B1
Cheddon Rd A2
Chip Lane A1
Clarence St B1
Cleveland St B1
Clifton Terrace A2
Coleridge Crescent C3
Compass Hill C1
Compton Close A2
Corporation St B1
Council Offices A1
County Walk Shopping Centre C2
Courtyard B2
Cranmer Rd B2
Crescent, The C1
Critchard Way B3
Cyril St A1
Deller's Wharf B1
Duke St B2
East Reach B3
East St B3
Eastbourne Rd B2
Eastleigh Rd C3
Eaton Crescent A2
Elm Grove A1
Elms Close A1
Fons George C1
Fore St B2
Fowler St A1
French Weir Rec Grd B1
Geoffrey Farrant Walk A2
Gray's Almshouses B2
Grays Rd B3
Greenway Avenue A1
Guildford Place C1
Hammet St B2
Haydon Rd B3
Heavitree Way A2
Herbert St A1
High St C2
Holway Avenue C3
Hugo St B3
Huish's Almshouses B2
Hurdle Way C2
Information Centre C2
Jubilee St A1
King's College C3
Kings Close C3
Laburnum St B2
Lambrook Rd B3
Lansdowne Rd A3
Leslie Avenue A1
Leycroft Rd B3
Library C2
Linden Grove A1
Magdalene St B2
Magistrates Court B1
Malvern Terrace A2
Market House B2
Mary St C2
Middle St B2
Mitre Court B3
Mount Nebo C1
Mount St C2
Mount, The C2
Mountway C2
Mus of Somerset B1
North St B2
Northfield Avenue B1
Northfield Rd B1
Northleigh Rd C3
Obridge Allotments A3
Obridge Lane A3
Obridge Rd A3
Obridge Viaduct A3
Orchard Shopping Ctr C2
Osborne Way C1
Park St C1
Paul St C2
Plais St A2
Playing Field C3
Police Station A1
Portland St B1
Post Office B1/B2
Priorswood Ind Est A3
Priorswood Rd A2
Priory Avenue B2
Priory Bridge Rd B2
Priory Fields Retail Pk A3
Priory Park A2
Priory Way A3
Queen St B3
Railway St A1
Records Office A2
Recreation Ground A1
Riverside Place B2
St Augustine St B2
St George's C2
St Georges Square C2
St James B2
St James St B2
St John's C1
St John's Rd B1
St Josephs Field C2
St Mary Magdalene's B2
Samuels Court A1
Shire Hall & Law Courts C1
Somerset County Cricket Ground B2
Somerset County Hall C1
Somerset Cricket B2
South Rd C3
South St C3
Staplegrove Rd B1
Station Approach A2
Station Rd A1
Stephen St B2
Superstore C2
Swimming Pool A1
Tancred St B2
Tangier Way B1
Tauntfield Close C3
Taunton Castle B1
Taunton Deane Cricket Club C2
Taunton Station A2
Thomas St A1
Toneway A3
Tower St B1
Trenchard Way A2
Trevor Smith Place C3
Trinity Bsns Centre C3
Trinity Rd C3
Trinity St B3
Trull Rd C1
Tudor House B2
Upper High St C1
Venture Way A3
Victoria Gate B3
Victoria Park B3
Victoria St B3
Viney St B3
Vivary Park Golf Club C2
Vivary Rd C1
War Memorial C1
Wellesley St A2
Wheatley Crescent A3
Whitehall A1
Wilfred Rd B3
William St A1
Wilton Church C1
Wilton Close C1
Wilton Grove C1
Wilton St C1
Winchester St B2
Winters Field B2
Wood St B1
Yarde Place B1

Telford 343

Alma Avenue C1
Amphitheatre C2
Bowling Alley B2
Brandsfarm Way C3
Brunel Rd B1
Bus Station B2
Buxton Rd C1
Central Park A2
Chelsea Gardens B2
Coach Central B2
Coachwell Close B1
Colliers Way A1
Courts B2
Dale Acre Way B3
Darliston C3
Deepdale B3
Deercote B2
Dinthill C3
Doddington C3
Dodmoor Grange C3
Downemead B3
Duffryn B3
Dunsheath B3
Euston Way A3
Eyton Mound C1
Eyton Rd C1
Forgegate A2
Grange Central B2
Hall Park Way B1
Hinkshay Rd C2
Hollinsworth Rd A2
Holyhead Rd A3
Housing Trust A1
Ice Rink B2
Information Centre B2
Ironmasters Way A2
Job Centre B1
Land Registry B1
Lawn Central B2
Lawnswood C1
Library B2
Malinsgate B1
Matlock Avenue C1
Moor Rd C1
Mount Rd C1
Odeon B2
Park Lane A1
Police Station B1
Post Office A2/B2/C1
Priorslee Avenue A3
Queen Elizabeth Ave C3
Queen Elizabeth Way B1
Queensway A2/B3
QEII Arena C2
Rampart Way A2
Randlay Avenue C3
Randlay Wood C3
Rhodes Avenue C1
Royal Way B1
St Leonards Rd B1
St Quentin Gate B2
Shifnal Rd A3
Silkin Way C2
Sixth Avenue A1
Southwater Leisure Complex B2
Southwater Way B1
Spout Lane C1
Spout Mound B1
Spout Way C1
Stafford Court B3
Stafford Park B3
Stirchley Avenue C3
Stone Row C1
Superstoore B1
Telford Bridge Retail Park A1
Telford Central Sta A3
Telford Centre, The B2
Telford Forge Shopping Park A1
Telford Hornets RFC C2
Telford International Centre C2
Telford Way A3
Third Avenue A2
Town Park C2
Town Park Visitor Ctr B2
Wellswood Avenue A2
West Centre Way B1
Withywood Drive C1
Wonderland C2
Woodhouse Central B2
Yates Way A1

Torquay 344

Abbey Rd B2
Alexandra Rd A2
Alpine Rd B3
AMF Bowling C3
Ash Hill Rd A2
Babbacombe Rd B3
Bampfylde Rd B1
Barton Rd A1
Beacon Quay C2
Belgrave Rd A1/B1
Belmont Rd A3
Berea Rd A3
Braddons Hill Rd East B3
Brewery Park A3
Bronshill Rd A2
Carlton Rd A3
Castle Circus A2
Castle Rd A2
Cavern Rd A3
Central B2
Chatsworth Rd A2
Chestnut Avenue B1
Church St A1
Coach Station A1
Corbyn Head C1
Croft Hill B1
Croft Rd B1
East St A1
Egerton Rd A3
Ellacombe Church Rd A3
Ellacombe Rd A2
Falkland Rd B1
Fleet St B2
Fleet Walk Shopping Centre B2
Grafton Rd B3
Grange Rd A3
Haldon Pier C2
Hatfield Rd A2
Highbury Rd A2
Higher Warberry Rd A3
Hillesdon Rd B3
Hoxton Rd A3
Hunsdon Rd B3
Information Centre B2
Inner Harbour C3
Kenwyn Rd A3
King's Drive, The B1
Laburnum St A1
Law Courts A2
Library A2
Lime Avenue B1
Living Coasts C3
Lower Warberry Rd B3
Lucius St B1
Lymington Rd A1
Magdalene Rd A1
Marina C2
Market Forum, The B2
Market St B2
Meadfoot Lane C3
Meadfoot Rd C3
Melville St B2
Middle Warberry Rd B3
Mill Lane A1
Montpellier Rd B3
Morgan Avenue A1
Museum Rd B3
Newton Rd A1
Oakhill Rd A1
Outer Harbour C2
Parkhill Rd C3
Pimlico B2
Police Station A1
Post Office A1/B2
Prince of Wales Steps C3
Princes Rd A3
Princes Rd East A3
Princes Rd West A3
Princess Gardens C2
Princess Pier C2
Princess Theatre C2
Rathmore Rd B1
Recreation Grd B1
Riviera International Centre B1
Rock End Avenue C3
Rock Rd B2
Rock Walk B2
Rosehill Rd A3
South West Coast Path C3
St Efride's Rd A1
St John's B3
St Luke's Rd B2
St Luke's Rd North B2
St Luke's Rd South B2
St Marychurch Rd A2
Scarborough Rd B1
Shedden Hill B2
South Pier C2
South St A1
Spanish Barn B1
Stitchill Rd B3
Strand B3
Sutherland Rd B3
Teignmouth Rd A1
Temperance St B2
Terrace, The B3
Thurlow Rd A1
Tor Bay B1
Tor Church Rd A1
Tor Hill Rd A1
Torbay Rd B2
Torquay Museum B3
Torquay Station C1
Torquay Tennis Club B1
Torre Abbey B1
Torre Abbey Meadows B1
Torre Abbey Sands B1
Torwood Gardens B3
Torwood St C3
Town Hall A2
Union Square Shopping Centre A2
Union St A1
Upton Hill A2
Upton Park A1
Upton Rd A1
Vanehill Rd C3
Vansittart Rd A1
Vaughan Parade C2
Victoria Parade C3
Victoria Rd A2
Warberry Rd West B2
Warren Rd B2
Windsor Rd A2/A3
Woodville Rd A3

Truro 344

Adelaide Ter B1
Agar Rd B3
Arch Hill C2
Arundell Place C2
Avenue, The A3
Avondale Rd B1
Back Quay B3
Barrack Lane C3
Barton Meadow A1
Benson Rd A2
Bishops Close A2
Bosvean Gardens B1
Bosvigo Gardens B1
Bosvigo Lane A1
Bosvigo Rd B2
Broad St A3
Burley Close C3
Bus Station B3
Calenick St B2
Campfield Hill B3
Carclew St B3
Carew Rd A2
Carey Park B2
Carlyon Rd A2
Carvoza Rd A3
Castle St B2
Cathedral View A2
Chainwalk Drive A2
Chapel Hill B1
Charles St B2
City Hall B3
City Rd B2
Coinage Hall B3
Comprigney Hill A1
Coosebean Lane A1
Copes Gardens A2
County Hall B1
Courtney Rd A2
Crescent Rd B1
Crescent Rise B1
Crescent, The B1
Daniell Court C2
Daniell Rd C2
Daniell St C2
Daubuz Close A2
Daubuz Moors Nature Reserve A3
Dobbs Lane B1
Edward St B2
Eliot Rd A2
Elm Court A3
Enys Close A1
Enys Rd A1
Fairmantle St B3
Falmouth Rd C2
Ferris Town B2
Fire Station B1
Frances St B2
George St B2
Green Close C2
Green Lane C1
Grenville Rd A2
Hall For Cornwall B3
Hendra Rd A2
Hendra Vean A1
High Cross B3
Higher Newham Lane C3
Higher Trehaverne A2
Hillcrest Avenue B1
Hospital B2
Hunkin Close A2
Hurland Rd C3
Infirmary Hill B2
James Place B3
Kenwyn Church Rd A1
Kenwyn Hill A1
Kenwyn Rd A2
Kenwyn St B2
Kerris Gardens A1
King St B3
Leats, The B2
Lemon Quay B3
Lemon St Gallery B3
Library B1/B3
Malpas Rd B3
Magistrates Court A3
Market B3
Merrifield Close B1
Mitchell Hill A3

Moresk Close A3
Moresk Rd A3
Morlaix Avenue C3
Nancemere Rd A3
Newham Bsns Park C3
Newham Industrial Est C3
Newham Rd C3
Northfield Drive C3
Oak Way A3
Palace's Terrace A3
Park View C2
Pendarves Rd A2
Plaza Cinema B3
Police Station A2/B3
Post Office B3
Prince's St B3
Pydar St A2
Quay St B3
Redannick Crescent C2
Redannick Lane B2
Richard Lander Monument C2
Richmond Hill B1
River St B2
Rosedale Rd A2
Royal Cornwall Mus B2
St Aubyn Rd C3
St Clement St B3
St George's Rd A1
Standing Cross B3
School Lane C2
Spires, The A2
Station Rd B1
Stokes Rd A2
Strangways Terrace C3
Tabernacle St B3
Trehaverne Lane A2
Tremayne Rd A2
Treseder's Gardens A3
Treworder Rd B1
Treyew Rd B1
Truro Cathedral B3
Truro Harbour Office B3
Truro Station B3
Union St B2
Upper School Lane C2
Victoria Gardens B2
Waterfall Gardens B2

Wick 344

Ackergill Crescent A2
Ackergill St A2
Albert St C2
Ambulance Station A2
Argyle Square C2
Assembly Rooms C2
Bank Row C2
Bankhead B1
Barons Well B2
Barrogill St C2
Bay View B3
Bexley Terrace C3
Bignold Park C2
Bowling Green C2
Breadalbane Terrace C2
Bridge of Wick B1
Bridge St B2
Brown Place C2
Burn St B2
Bus Station B1
Caithness General Hospital (A&E) B1
Cliff Rd B1
Coach Rd B2
Coastguard Station C3
Corner Crescent B3
Coronation St C1
Council Offices B2
Court B2
Crane Rock C3
Dempster St C2
Dunnet Avenue A2
Fire Station B2
Francis St C1
George St A1
Girnigoe St B2
Glamis Rd B2
Gowrie Place B1
Grant St C2
Green Rd B2
Gunns Terrace B3
Harbour Quay B2
Harbour Rd C3
Harbour Terrace C2
Harrow Hill C2
Henrietta St A2/B2
Heritage Museum C2
High St B2
Hill Avenue A2
Hillhead Rd B3
Hood St C1
Huddart St C2
Kenneth St C1
Kinnaird St C2
Kirk Hill B1
Langwell Crescent B3
Leishman Avenue B3
Leith Walk A2
Library B2
Liby & Swimming Pool C1
Lifeboat Station C3
Lighthouse C3
Lindsay Drive B3
Lindsay Place B3
Loch St C2
Louisburgh St B2
Lower Dunbar St C2
Macleay Lane B1
Macleod Rd B3
MacRae St C2
Martha Terrace B2
Miller Avenue B1
Miller Lane B1
Moray St C2
Mowat Place B3
Murchison St C3
Newton Avenue C1
Newton Rd C1
Nicolson St C3
North Highland Coll. B2
North River Pier B3
Northcote St C2
Owen Place A2
Police Station B1
Port Dunbar B3
Post Office B2/C2
Pulteney Distillery C2
River St B2
Robert St A1
Rutherford St C2
St John's Episcopal C2
Sandigoe Rd B3
Scalesburn B3
Seaforth Avenue C1
Shore Lane B2
Shore, The B2
Sinclair Drive B3
Sinclair Terrace C2
Smith Terrace C3
South Pier C3
South Quay C3
South Rd C1
South River Pier B3
Station Rd B1
Superstore A1/B1
Telford St B2
Thurso Rd B1
Thurso St B1
Town Hall B2
Union St B2
Upper Dunbar St C2
Vansittart St C3
Victoria Place B2
War Memorial A1
Well of Cairndhuna C3
Wellington Avenue C3
Wellington St C3
West Banks Avenue C1
West Banks Terrace C1
West Park C1
Whitehorse Park B2
Wick Harbour Bridge B2
Wick Industrial Estate A2
Wick Parish Church B1
Wick Station B1
Williamson St B2
Willowbank B2

Winchester 344

Andover Rd A2
Andover Rd Retail Pk A2
Archery Lane C2
Arthur Rd A2
Bar End Rd C3
Beaufort Rd C2
Beggar's Lane B3
Bereweeke Avenue A1
Bereweeke Rd A1
Boscobel Rd A2
Brassey Rd A2
Broadway B3
Brooks Shopping Centre, The B3
Bus Station B3
Butter Cross B2
Canon St C2
Castle Wall C2/C3
Cathedral C2
Cheriton Rd A1
Chesil St C3
Chesil Theatre C3
Christchurch Rd C1
City Mill B3
City Museum B2
City Rd B2
Clifton Rd B1
Clifton Terrace B2
Close Wall C2/C3
Coach Park A2
Colebrook St C3
College St C2
College Walk C3
Compton Rd C2
Council Offices C3
County Council Offices B2
Cranworth Rd A2
Cromwell Rd C1
Culver Rd C2
Discovery Centre B2
Domum Rd C3
Durngate Place B3
Eastgate St B3
East Hill C3
Edgar Rd C2
Egbert Rd A2
Elm Rd B1
Everyman C2
Fairfield Rd A1
Fire Station B3
Fordington Avenue B1
Fordington Rd A1
Friarsgate B3
Gordon Rd B3
Great Hall & Round Table, The B2
Greenhill Rd B1
Guildhall B3
Hatherley Rd A1
High St B2
Hillier Way A3
HM Prison B1
Hyde Abbey (Remains) A2
Hyde Abbey Rd B2
Hyde Close A2
Hyde St A2
Information Centre B3
Jane Austen's Ho C2
Jewry St B2
King Alfred Place A2
Kingsgate Arch C2
Kingsgate Park C2
Kingsgate Rd C2
Kingsgate St C2
Lankhills Rd A2
Law Courts B2
Library B2
Lower Brook St B3
Magdalen Hill B3
Market Lane B2
Mews Lane B1
Middle Brook St B3
Middle Rd B1
Military Museums B2
Milland Rd C3
Milverton Rd B1
Monks Rd A3
North Hill Close A2
North Walls B2
North Walls Rec Gnd A3
Nuns Rd A3
Oram's Arbour B1
Owens Rd A2
Parchment St B2
Park & Ride C3
Park Avenue B3
Playing Field A1
Police HQ B2
Portal Rd C3
Post Office B2/C1
Ranelagh Rd C1
Regimental Mus B2
River Park Leisure Ctr B3
Romans' Rd C2
Romsey Rd B1
Royal Hampshire County Hospital (A&E) B1
St Cross Rd C2
St George's St B2
St Giles Hill C3
St James Villas C2
St James' Lane B1
St James' Terrace B1
St John's B3
St John's St B3
St Michael's Rd C2
St Paul's Hill B1
St Peter St B2
St Swithun St C2
St Thomas St C2
Saxon Rd A2
School of Art B3
Sleepers Hill Rd C1
Southgate St B2
Sparkford Rd C1
Square, The B2
Staple Gardens B2
Station Rd B2
Step Terrace B1
Stockbridge Rd A1
Stuart Crescent C1
Sussex St B2
Swan Lane B2
Tanner St B3
Theatre Royal B2
Tower St B2
Union St B3
Univ of Southampton (Winchester School of Art) B3
Univ of Winchester (King Alfred Campus) C1
Upper Brook St B2
Wales St B3
Water Lane B3
Weirs, The C3
West End Terrace B1
Western Rd B1
Westgate B2
Wharf Hill C3
Winchester Station A2
Winnall Moors Wildlife Reserve A3
Wolvesey Castle C3
Worthy Lane A2
Worthy Rd A2

Windsor 344

Adelaide Square C3
Albany Rd C2
Albert St B1
Alexandra Gardens B2
Alexandra Rd C2
Alma Rd B2
Arthur Rd B2
Bachelors Acre B3
Barry Avenue B2
Beaumont Rd C2
Bexley St B1
Boat House B2
Brocas St B2
Brocas, The A2
Brook St C3
Bulkeley Avenue C1
Castle Hill B3
Charles St B2
Claremont Rd C2
Clarence Crescent B2
Clarence Rd B1
Clewer Court Rd B1
Coach Park B2
College Crescent C1
Cricket Ground C3
Dagmar Rd C2
Datchet Rd B3
Devereux Rd C2
Dorset Rd C2
Duke St B1
Elm Rd C1
Eton College A3
Eton College Natural History Museum A2
Eton Court A2
Eton Square A2
Eton Wick Rd A2
Farm Yard B3
Fire Station C2
Frances Rd C2
Frogmore Drive B3
Gloucester Place C3
Goslar Way C1
Goswell Hill B2
Goswell Rd B2
Green Lane C1
Grove Rd C2
Guildhall B3
Helena Rd C2
Helston Lane B1
High St A2/B3
Holy Trinity C2
Home Park, The A3/C3
Household Cavalry C2
Imperial Rd C1
Information Centre B2
Keats Lane A2
King Edward VII Ave A3
King Edward VII Hospital C2
King George V Memorial B3
King Stable St A2
King's Rd C3
Library A2/B2
Long Walk, The C3
Maidenhead Rd B1
Meadow Lane A2
Municipal Offices C3
Nell Gwynne's Ho B3
Osborne Rd C2
Oxford Rd B1
Park St B3
Peascod St B2
Police Station C2
Post Office A2/C1
Princess Margaret Hospital (private) C2
Old Court Art Space, The C2
Queen Elizabeth Bridge A1
Queen Victoria's Walk B3
Queen's Rd C2
River St B2
Romney Island A3
Romney Lock A3
Romney Lock Rd A3
Russell St C2
St George's Chapel B3
St John's B3
St John's Chapel A2
St Leonards Rd C2
St Mark's Rd C2
Sheet St C3
Shopmobility B2
South Meadow A2
South Meadow Lane A2
Springfield Rd C1
Stovell Rd B1
Sunbury Rd A2
Tangier Lane A2
Temple Rd C2
Thames St B3
Theatre Royal B3
Trinity Place C2
Vansittart Rd B1/C1
Victoria Barracks C2
Victoria St C2
Westmead C1
White Lilies Island A1
William St B2
Windsor & Eton Central B2
Windsor & Eton Riverside A3
Windsor Bridge B3
Windsor Castle B3
Windsor Leisure Ctr B1
Windsor Relief Rd A1
Windsor Royal Station Shopping Centre B2
Windsor Yards B2
York Avenue C1
York Rd C1

Wolverhampton 344

Albion St B3
Arena B2
Art Gallery B2
Ashland St C1
Austin St A1
Badger Drive A3
Bailey St A3
Bath Avenue B1
Bath Rd B1
Bell St C2
Berry St B3
Bilston Rd C3
Bilston St C3
Birmingham Canal A3
Bone Mill Lane A2
Brewery Rd B1
Bright St A1
Burton Crescent B3
Bus Station B3
Cambridge St A3
Camp St B2
Cannock Rd A3
Castle St C2
Chapel Ash C1
Cherry St C1
Chester St A1
Church Lane C2
Church St C2
Civic Centre B2
Civic Hall B2
Clarence Rd B2
Cleveland St C2
Clifton St C1
Coach Station B2
Compton Rd B1
Corn Hill B3
Coven St A3
Craddock St A1
Cross St North A2
Crown & County Courts C3
Crown St A2
Culwell St B3
Dale St C1
Darlington St C1
Devon Rd A1
Drummond St B2
Dudley Rd C2
Dudley St B2
Duke St C3
Dunkley St B1
Dunstall Avenue A2
Dunstall Hill A2
Dunstall Rd A1/A2
Evans St A1
Fawdry St A1
Field St B3
Fire Station C1
Fiveways A2
Fowler Playing Fields A3
Fox's Lane A2
Francis St A2
Fryer St B3
Gloucester St A1
Gordon St C3
Graiseley St C1
Grand B3
Granville St C3
Great Brickkiln St C1
Great Hampton St A1
Great Western St A2
Grimstone St B3
Harrow St A1
Hilton St A3
Hive Library The B2
Horseley Fields C3
Humber Rd C1
Jack Hayward Way A2
Jameson St A1
Jenner St C3
Kennedy Rd B3
Kimberley St C1
King St B2
Laburnum St C1
Lansdowne Rd B1
Leicester St A1
Lever St C3
Library C3
Lichfield St B2
Light House B3
Little's Lane B3
Lock St B3
Lord St C1
Lowe St A1
Maltings, The B2
Mander Centre C2
Mander St C2
Market C2
Market St B2
Maxwell Rd C3
Merridale St C1
Middlecross C3
Molineux St B2
Mostyn St A1
Newhampton Arts Centre B1
New Hampton Rd East A1
New Elms Lane A3
North Rd A2
Oaks Crescent C1
Oxley St A2
Paget St A1
Park Avenue B1
Park Road East A1
Park Road West B1
Paul St C2
Pelham St C1
Penn Rd C2
Piper's Row B3
Piper's Row C3
Pitt St C2
Police Station C3
Pool St C2
Poole St A3
Post Office A1/B2/B2/C2/C3
Powlett St C3
Queen St B2
Raby St C3
Railway Drive B3
Red Hill St A2
Red Lion St B2
Retreat St C1
Ring Rd B2
Royal, The C3
Rugby St A1
Russell St C1
St Andrew's B1
St David's B3
St George's C3
St George's Parade C2
St James St C3
St John's C2
St John's C2
St John's Retail Park C2
St John's Square C2
St Mark's C1
St Marks Rd C1
St Marks St C1
St Patrick's B2
St Peter's B2
St Peter's B2
Salisbury St C1
Salop St C2
School St C2
Sherwood St A2
Smestow St A3
Snow Hill C2
Springfield Rd A3
Stafford St A2/B2
Staveley Rd A1
Steelhouse Lane C3
Stephenson St C1
Stewart St C2
Sun St B3
Tempest St C2
Temple St C2
Tettenhall Rd B1
Thomas St C2
Thornley St B2
Tower St C2
University B2
Upper Zoar St C1
Vicarage Rd C3
Victoria St C2
Walpole St A1
Walsall St C3
Ward St C3
Warwick St C3
Water St A3
Waterloo Rd B2
Wednesfield Rd B3
West Park (not A&E) B1
West Park Swimming Pool B1
Wharf St C3
Whitmore Hill B2
Wolverhampton B3
Wolverhampton B3
Wolverhampton St George's C2
Wolverhampton Wanderers Football Gnd (Molineux) B2
Worcester St C2
Wulfrun Centre C2
Yarwell Close A3
York St C3
Zoar St C1

Worcester 344

Albany Terrace A1
Angel Place B2
Angel St B2
Ashcroft Rd A2
Athelstan Rd C3
Avenue, The C1
Back Lane North A1
Back Lane South A1
Barbourne Rd A2
Bath Rd C2
Battenhall Rd C3
Bridge St B2
Britannia Square A1
Broad St B2
Bromwich Lane C1
Bromwich Rd C1
Bromyard Rd C1
Bus Station B2
Butts, The B2
Carden St B3
Castle St A2
Cathedral C2
Cathedral Plaza B2
Charles St B3
Chequers Lane B1
Chestnut St A2
Chestnut Walk A2
Citizens' Advice Bureau B2
City Walls Rd B2
Cole Hill C3
College St C2
Commandery, The C3
Cripplegate Park B1
Croft Rd B1
Cromwell St B3
Cross, The B2
Crowngate Centre B2
Deansway B2
Diglis Parade C2
Diglis Rd C2
Edgar Tower C2
Farrier St A2
Foregate St B2
Fort Royal Hill C3
Fort Royal Park C3
Foundry St B3
Friar St C2
George St B3
Grand Stand Rd B1
Greenhill C3
Greyfriars B2
Guildhall B2
Henwick Rd B1
High St B2
Hill St B3
Hive, The B2
Huntingdon Hall B2
Hylton Rd B1
Information Centre B2
King Charles Place Shopping Centre C1
King's School C2
King's School Playing Field C2
Kleve Walk C2
Lansdowne Crescent A3
Lansdowne Rd A3
Lansdowne Walk A3
Laslett St A3
Little Chestnut St A2
Little London A2
London Rd C3
Lowell St A3
Lowesmoor B2
Lowesmoor Terrace A3
Lowesmoor Wharf A3
Magistrates Court A2
Midland Rd B3
Mill St C2
Moors Severn Terrace, The A1
Mus & Art Gallery A2
Museum of Royal Worcester C2
New Rd C1
New St B2
Northfield St A2
Odeon B2
Old Palace The C2
Padmore St B3
Park St C3
Pheasant St B3
Pitchcroft Racecourse A1
Police Station A2
Portland St C2
Post Office B2
Quay St B2
Queen St B2
Rainbow Hill A3
Recreation Ground A2
Reindeer Court B2
Rogers Hill A3
Sabrina Terrace A1
St Dunstan's Cre. C3
St John's C1
St Martin's Gate B3
St Martin's Quarter B3
St Oswald's Rd A2
St Paul's St B3
St Swithin's Church B2
St Wulstans Crescent C3
Sansome Walk A2
Severn St C2
Shambles, The B2
Shaw St B2
Shire Hall Crown Ct A2
Shrub Hill Rd B3
Shrub Hill Retail Park B3
Slingpool Walk C1
South Parade B2
Southfield St A2
Sports Centre A3
Stanley Rd B3
Swan, The A1
Swimming Pool A2
Tallow Hill B3
Tennis Walk A2
Tolladine Rd B3
Tudor House B2
Tybridge St B1
Tything, The A2
Univ of Worcester B2
Vincent Rd B3
Vue C2
Washington St A3
Woolhope Rd C3
Worcester Bridge B2
Worcester County Cricket Club C1
Worcester Foregate Street B2
Worcester Shrub Hill B3
Worcester Royal Grammar School A2
Wylds Lane C3

Wrexham Wrecsam 344

Abbot St B2
Acton Rd A3
Albert St C3
Alexandra Rd C1
Aran Rd A3
Barnfield C3
Bath Rd C2
Beeches, The A3
Beechley Rd C3
Belgrave Rd C2
Bellevue Park C2
Bellevue Rd C2
Belvedere Drive A1
Bennion's Rd C3
Berse Rd A1
Bersham Rd C1
Birch St C3
Bodhyfryd A3
Border Retail Park B3
Bradley Rd C2
Bright St B1
Bron-y-Nant B1
Brook St C2
Bryn-y-Cabanau Rd C3
Bury St C3
Bus Station B2
Butchers Market B3
Caia Rd C3
Cambrian Ind Est C3
Caxton Place B2
Cemetery C1
Centenary Rd C1
Central Retail Park B2
Chapel St C2
Charles St B3
Chester Rd A3
Chester St B3
Cilcen Grove A3
Citizens Advice Bureau B2
Cobden Rd B1
Council Offices B3
County B2
Crescent Rd B3
Crispin Lane A2
Croesnewyth Rd B1
Cross St A2
Cunliffe St A2
Derby Rd C3
Dolydd Rd B1
Duke St B2
Eagles Meadow C3
Earle St C2
East Avenue A2
Edward St C2
Egerton St B2
Empress Rd C1
Erddig Rd C2
Fairy Rd C2
Fire Station B2
Foster Rd A3
Foxwood Drive C1
Garden Rd A2
General Market B3
Gerald St B2
Gibson St C1
Glyndwr University Plas Coch Campus A1
Greenbank St C3
Greenfield A2
Grosvenor Rd B2
Grove Park B2
Grove Park Rd B3
Grove Rd A3
Guildhall B2
Haig Rd C3
Hampden Rd C2
Hazel Grove A3
Henblas St B3
High St B3
Hightown Rd C3
Hill St B2
Holt Rd B3
Holt St B3
Hope St B2
Huntroyde Avenue C3
Information Centre B3
Island Green Shopping Centre B2
Jobcentre Plus B2
Jubilee Rd B2
King St B2
Kingsmills Rd C3
Lambpit St B3
Law Courts B3
Lawson Close A3
Lawson Rd A3
Lea Rd C2
Library & Arts Centre B2
Lilac Way B1
Llys David Lord B1
Lorne St A2
Maesgwyn Rd B1
Maesydre Rd A3
Manley Rd B3
Market St B3
Mawddy Avenue A2
Mayville Avenue A2
Memorial Gallery B2
Memorial Hall B3
Mold Rd A1
Mount St C3
Neville Crescent A3
New Rd A2
North Wales Regional Tennis Centre A1
Oak Drive A3
Odeon C3
Park Avenue A3
Park St A2
Peel St C1
Pen y Bryn C2
Pentre Felin C2
Penymaes Avenue A3
Peoples Market B3
Percy St C2
Pines, The A3
Plas Coch Rd A1
Plas Coch Retail Park A1
Police Station B3
Post Office A2/B3/C3
Powell Rd B3
Poyser St C2
Price's Lane A2
Primose Way B1
Princess St C1
Queen St B3
Queens Square B2
Regent St B2
Rhosddu Rd A2/B2
Rhosnesni Lane A3
Rivulet Rd C3
Ruabon Rd C2
Ruthin Rd C1/C2
St Giles C3
St Giles Way C3
St James Court A2
St Mary's B2
Salisbury Rd C3
Salop Rd C3
Sontley Rd C2
Spring Rd A2
Stanley St C3
Stansty Rd A2
Station Approach B2
Studio B2
Superstore B3/C1
Talbot Rd C2
Techniquest Glyndwr A2
Town Hill C2
Trevor St C2
Trinity St B2
Tuttle St C3
Vale Park A1
Vernon St B2
Vicarage Hill B2
Victoria Rd C2
Walnut St A2
War Memorial B3
Waterworld Leisure Centre B3
Watery Rd B1/B2
Wellington Rd C2
Westminster Drive A3
William Aston Hall A1
Windsor Rd A1
Wrecsam
Wrexham AFC A1
Wrexham Central B2
Wrexham General B2
Wrexham Maelor Hospital (A&E) B1
Wrexham Technology Park B1
Wynn Avenue A2
Yale College B3
Yale Grove A3
Yorke St C3

York 344

Aldwark B2
Barbican Rd C3
Bar Convent Living Heritage Centre C1
Barley Hall B2
Bishopgate St C2
Bishopshill Senior C2
Bishopthorpe Rd C2
Blossom St C1
Bootham A1
Bootham Crescent A1
Bootham Terrace A1
Bridge St B2
Brook St A2
Brownlow St A2
Burton Stone Lane A1
Castle Museum C2
Castlegate B2
Cemetery Rd C3
Cherry St C2
City Screen B2
City Wall A2/B1/C3
Clarence St A2
Clementhorpe C2
Clifford St B2
Clifford's Tower B2
Clifton A1
Coach park A2
Coney St B2
Coppergate Centre B2
Cromwell Rd C2
Crown Court C2
Davygate B2
Deanery Gardens A2
DIG B2
Dodsworth Avenue A3
Eboracum Way A3
Ebor Industrial Estate B3
Eldon St A2
Everyman C1
Fairfax House B2
Fire Station C3
Fishergate C3
Foss Islands Rd B3
Foss Islands Retail Pk B3
Fossbank A3
Garden St A2
George St C3
Gillygate A2
Goodramgate B2
Grand Opera House B2
Grosvenor Terrace A1
Guildhall B2
Hallfield Rd A3
Heslington Rd C3
Heworth Green A3
Holy Trinity B2
Hope St C3
Huntington Rd A3
Information Centre B2
James St B3
Jorvik Viking Ctr B2
Kent St C3
Lawrence St C3
Layerthorpe A3
Leeman Rd B1
Lendal B2
Lendal Bridge B1
Library A2/B1
Longfield Terrace A1
Lord Mayor's Walk A2
Lowther St A2
Mansion House B2
Margaret St C3
Marygate A1
Melbourne St C3
Merchant Adventurers' Hall B2
Merchant Taylors' Hall B2
Micklegate B1
Micklegate Bar C1
Monkgate A2
Moss St C1
Museum Gdns B1
Museum St B1
National Railway Museum B1
Navigation Rd B3
Newton Terrace C2
North Parade A1
North St B2
Nunnery Lane C1
Nunthorpe Rd C1
Ouse Bridge B2
Paragon St C3
Park Grove A3
Park St C1
Parliament St B2
Peasholme Green B3
Penley's Grove St A2
Piccadilly B2
Police Station B2
Post Office B1/B2/C3
Priory St B1
Queen Anne's Rd A1
Regimental Mus B2
Richard III Experience at Monk Bar A2
Roman Bath B2
Rowntree Park C2
St Andrewgate B2
St Benedict Rd C1
St John St A2
St Olave's Rd A1
St Peter's Grove A1
St Saviourgate B2
Scarcroft Hill C1
Scarcroft Rd C1
Shambles, The B2
Shopmobility B1
Skeldergate C2
Skeldergate Bridge C2
Station Rd B1
Stonebow, The B2
Stonegate B2
Superstore A3
Sycamore Terrace A1
Terry Avenue C2
Theatre Royal B2
Thorpe St C1
Toft Green B1
Tower St C2
Townend St A2
Treasurer's House A2
Trinity Lane B1
Undercroft Mus A2
Union Terrace A2
Victor St C2
Vine St C2
Walmgate B3
War Memorial B1
Wellington St C3
York Art Gallery A1
York Barbican C3
York Brewery B1
York Dungeon, The B2
York Minster A2
York St John Univ. A2
York Station B1

361

Abbreviations used in the index

Aberdeen	Aberdeen City
Aberds	Aberdeenshire
Ald	Alderney
Anglesey	Isle of Anglesey
Angus	Angus
Argyll	Argyll and Bute
Bath	Bath and North East Somerset
BCP	Bournemouth, Christchurch and Poole
Bedford	Bedford
Blackburn	Blackburn with Darwen
Blackpool	Blackpool
Bl Gwent	Blaenau Gwent
Borders	Scottish Borders
Brack	Bracknell
Bridgend	Bridgend
Brighton	City of Brighton and Hove
Bristol	City and County of Bristol
Bucks	Buckinghamshire
Caerph	Caerphilly
Cambs	Cambridgeshire
Cardiff	Cardiff
Carms	Carmarthenshire
C Beds	Central Bedfordshire
Ceredig	Ceredigion
Ches E	Cheshire East
Ches W	Cheshire West and Chester
Clack	Clackmannanshire
Conwy	Conwy
Corn	Cornwall
Cumb	Cumbria
Darl	Darlington
Denb	Denbighshire
Derby	City of Derby
Derbys	Derbyshire
Devon	Devon
Dorset	Dorset
Dumfries	Dumfries and Galloway
Dundee	Dundee City
Durham	Durham
E Ayrs	East Ayrshire
Edin	City of Edinburgh
E Dunb	East Dunbartonshire
E Loth	East Lothian
E Renf	East Renfrewshire
Essex	Essex
E Sus	East Sussex
E Yorks	East Riding of Yorkshire
Falk	Falkirk
Fife	Fife
Flint	Flintshire
Glasgow	City of Glasgow
Glos	Gloucestershire
Gtr Man	Greater Manchester
Guern	Guernsey
Gwyn	Gwynedd
Halton	Halton
Hants	Hampshire
Hereford	Herefordshire
Herts	Hertfordshire
Highld	Highland
Hrtlpl	Hartlepool
Hull	Hull
Invclyd	Inverclyde
IoM	Isle of Man
IoW	Isle of Wight
Jersey	Jersey
Kent	Kent
Lancs	Lancashire
Leicester	City of Leicester
Leics	Leicestershire
Lincs	Lincolnshire
London	Greater London
Luton	Luton
Mbro	Middlesbrough
Medway	Medway
Mers	Merseyside
Midloth	Midlothian
M Keynes	Milton Keynes
Mon	Monmouthshire
Moray	Moray
M Tydf	Merthyr Tydfil
N Ayrs	North Ayrshire
Neath	Neath Port Talbot
NE Lincs	North East Lincolnshire
Newport	City and County of Newport
N Lanark	North Lanarkshire
N Lincs	North Lincolnshire
N Nhants	North Northamptonshire
Norf	Norfolk
Northumb	Northumberland
Nottingham	City of Nottingham
Notts	Nottinghamshire
N Som	North Somerset
N Yorks	North Yorkshire
Orkney	Orkney
Oxon	Oxfordshire
Pboro	Peterborough
Pembs	Pembrokeshire
Perth	Perth and Kinross
Plym	Plymouth
Powys	Powys
Ptsmth	Portsmouth
Reading	Reading
Redcar	Redcar and Cleveland
Renfs	Renfrewshire
Rhondda	Rhondda Cynon Taff
Rutland	Rutland
S Ayrs	South Ayrshire
Scilly	Scilly
S Glos	South Gloucestershire
Shetland	Shetland
Shrops	Shropshire
S Lanark	South Lanarkshire
Slough	Slough
Som	Somerset
Soton	Southampton
Southend	Southend-on-Sea
Staffs	Staffordshire
Stirling	Stirling
Stockton	Stockton-on-Tees
Stoke	Stoke-on-Trent
Suff	Suffolk
Sur	Surrey
Swansea	Swansea
Swindon	Swindon
S Yorks	South Yorkshire
T&W	Tyne and Wear
Telford	Telford and Wrekin
Thurrock	Thurrock
Torbay	Torbay
Torf	Torfaen
V Glam	The Vale of Glamorgan
Warks	Warwickshire
Warr	Warrington
W Berks	West Berkshire
W Dunb	West Dunbartonshire
Wilts	Wiltshire
Windsor	Windsor and Maidenhead
W Isles	Western Isles
W Loth	West Lothian
W Mid	West Midlands
W Nhants	West Northamptonshire
Wokingham	Wokingham
Worcs	Worcestershire
Wrex	Wrexham
W Sus	West Sussex
W Yorks	West Yorkshire
York	City of York

Index to road maps of Britain

How to use the index

Example **Witham Friary** Som **45** E8

- E8 — grid square
- 45 — page number
- Som — county or unitary authority

Aar–All

A

Aaron's Hill Sur 50 E3
Aaron's Town Cumb 240 E2
Abbas Combe Som 30 C2
Abberley Worcs 116 D5
Abberton Essex 89 B8
Worcs 117 G9
Abberwick Northumb 264 G4
Abbess End Essex 87 C9
Abbess Roding Essex 87 C9
Abbey Devon 27 E10
Abbeycwmhir Powys 113 C11
Abbey-cwm-hir Powys 113 C11
Abbeydale Glos 80 B5
S Yorks 186 E4
Abbeydale Park S Yorks 186 E4
Abbey Dore Hereford 97 E7
Abbey Field Essex 107 G9
Abbey Gate Kent 53 B9
Abbey Green Shrops 149 C10
Staffs 169 D7
Abbey Hey Gtr Man 184 B5
Abbeyhill Edin 280 G5
Abbey Hulton Stoke 168 F6
Abbey Mead Sur 66 F4
Abbey St Bathans Borders 272 C5
Abbeystead Lancs 203 C7
Abbey Town Cumb 238 G5
Abbey Village Lancs 194 C6
Abbey Wood London 68 D3
Abbots Bickington Devon 24 E5
Abbots Bromley Staffs 151 E11
Abbotsbury Dorset 17 D7
Abbotsford W Sus 36 C4
Abbotsham Devon 24 B6
Abbotskerswell Devon 9 B7
Abbots Langley Herts 85 E9
Abbotsleigh Devon 8 F6
Abbots Leigh N Som 60 E4
Abbotsley Cambs 122 F4
Abbot's Meads Ches W 166 B5
Abbots Morton Worcs 117 F10
Abbots Ripton Cambs 122 B4
Abbots Salford Warks 117 G11
Abbotstone Hants 48 G5
Abbotswood Hants 32 C5
Sur 50 C4
Abbots Worthy Hants 48 G3
Abbotts Ann Hants 47 E10
Abcott Shrops 115 B7
Abdon Shrops 131 F11
Abdy S Yorks 186 B6
Aber Ceredig 93 B9
Aberaeron Ceredig 111 E9
Aberaman Rhondda 77 E8
Aberangell Gwyn 146 G6
Aber-Arad Carms 92 D6
Aberarder Highld 290 E6
Aberarder House Highld 300 G6
Aberarder Lodge Highld 291 E7
Aberargie Perth 286 F5
Aberarth Ceredig 111 E9
Aberavon Neath 57 C8
Aber-banc Ceredig 93 C7
Aberbargoed Caerph 77 E11
Aberbechan Powys 130 E2
Aberbeeg Bl Gwent 78 E2
Aberbran Powys 95 F9
Abercanaid M Tydf 77 E9
Abercarn Caerph 78 G2
Abercastle Pembs 91 E7
Abercegir Powys 128 C6
Aberchalder Highld 290 C5
Aberchirder Aberds 302 D6
Abercorn W Loth 279 F11
Aber Cowarch Gwyn 147 F7
Abercraf Powys 76 C4
Abercregan Neath 57 B11
Abercrombie Fife 287 G9
Abercwmboi Rhondda 77 F8
Abercych Pembs 92 C4
Abercynafon Powys 77 B9
Abercynffig *=Aberkenfig*
Bridgend 57 E11
Abercynon Rhondda 77 F9
Aberdalgie Perth 286 E4
Aberdâr *=Aberdare*
Rhondda 77 E7
Aberdare *=Aberdâr*
Rhondda 77 E7
Aberdaron Gwyn 144 D3
Aberdeen Aberdeen 293 C11
Aberdesach Gwyn 162 E6
Aberdour Fife 280 D3
Aberdovey *=Aberdyfi*
Gwyn 128 D2
Aberdulais Neath 76 E3
Aberdyfi *=Aberdovey*
Gwyn 128 D2
Aberedw Powys 95 B11
Abereiddy Pembs 90 E5
Abererch Gwyn 145 B7
Aberfan M Tydf 77 E9
Aberfeldy Perth 286 C2
Aberffraw Anglesey 162 B5
Aberffrwd Ceredig 112 B3
Mon 78 D5
Aberford W Yorks 206 F4
Aberfoyle Stirlinging 285 G9
Abergarw Bridgend 58 C2
Abergarwed Neath 76 E4
Abergavenny Mon 78 C3
Abergele Conwy 180 F6
Aber-Giâr Carms 93 C10
Abergorlech Carms 93 E11
Abergwaun *=Fishguard*
Pembs 91 D9
Abergwesyn Powys 113 G7
Abergwili Carms 93 G8
Abergwynant Gwyn 146 F3
Abergwynfi Neath 57 B11
Aber-gwynfi Neath 57 B11
Abergwyngregyn Gwyn 179 G11
Abergynolwyn Gwyn 128 B3
Aber-Hirnant Gwyn 147 C9
Aberhosan Powys 128 D6
Aberkenfig *=Abercynffig*
Bridgend 57 E11
Aberlady E Loth 281 E9
Aberlemno Angus 287 B9
Aberlerry Ceredig 128 E2
Aberllefenni Gwyn 128 B5
Aberllydan *=Broad Haven*
Pembs 72 C5
Aberllynfi *=Three Cocks*
Powys 96 D3
Abermagwr Ceredig 112 C3
Abermaw *=Barmouth*
Gwyn 146 F2
Abermeurig Ceredig 111 F11
Aber miwl *=Abermule*
Powys 130 E3
Abermorddu Flint 166 D4
Abermule *=Aber-miwl*
Powys 130 E3
Abernaint Powys 148 E2
Abernant Carms 92 G6
Powys 130 D3
Aber-nant Rhondda 77 E8
Abernethy Perth 286 F5
Abernyte Perth 286 D6
Aber-oer Wrex 166 F3
Aberogwr *=Ogmore by Sea*
V Glam 57 F11
Aberpennar *=Mountain Ash*
Rhondda 77 F8
Aberporth Ceredig 110 G5
Aber-Rhiwlech Gwyn 147 E8
Aberriw *=Berriew*
Powys 130 C3
Abersoch Gwyn 144 D6
Abersychan Torf 78 E3
Abertawe *=Swansea*
Swansea 56 C6
Aberteifi *=Cardigan*
Ceredig 92 B3
Aberthin V Glam 58 D4
Abertillery Bl Gwent 78 E2
Abertridwr Caerph 58 B6
Powys 147 F10
Abertrinant Gwyn 128 B2
Abertysswg Caerph 77 D10
Aberuchill Castle
Perth 285 E11
Aberuthven Perth 286 F3
Aber-Village Powys 96 G2
Aberyscir Powys 95 F9
Aberystwyth Ceredig 111 A11
Abhainn Suidhe
W Isles 305 H2
Abingdon-on-Thames
Oxon 83 F7
Abinger Common Sur 50 D6
Abinger Hammer Sur 50 D5
Abington S Lanark 259 E10
W Nhants 120 E5
Abington Pigotts Cambs 104 C6
Abington Vale
W Nhants 120 E5
Abingworth W Sus 35 D10
Ab Kettleby Leics 154 E4
Ab Lench Worcs 117 G10
Ablington Glos 81 D10
Wilts 47 D7
Abney Derbys 185 F11
Aboyne Aberds 293 D7
Abraham Heights Lancs 211 G9
Abram Gtr Man 194 G6
Abriachan Highld 300 F5
Abridge Essex 87 F7
Abronhill N Lanark 278 F5
Abshot Hants 33 F8
Abson S Glos 61 E8
Abthorpe W Nhants 102 B2
Abune-the-Hill Orkney 314 D2
Aby Lincs 190 F6
Acaster Malbis York 207 D7
Acaster Selby N Yorks 207 E7
Accrington Lancs 195 B9
Acha Argyll 275 B8
Argyll 288 D3
Achabraid Argyll 275 E9
Achachork Highld 298 E4
Achadh an Eas Highld 308 F6
Achad nan Darach
Highld 284 B4
Achadunan Argyll 284 F5
Achafolla Argyll 275 B8
Achagary Highld 308 D7
Achaglass Argyll 255 C8
Achahoish Argyll 275 F8
Achalader Perth 286 C5
Achallader Argyll 285 C7
Achalone Highld 310 D5
Acha Mor W Isles 304 F5
Achanalt Highld 300 C2
Achanamara Argyll 275 E8
Achandunie Highld 300 B6
Achanelid Argyll 275 E11
Ach'an Todhair Highld 290 F2
Achany Highld 309 J5
Achaphubuil Highld 290 F2
Acharacle Highld 289 C8
Acharn Highld 289 D9
Perth 285 C11
Acharole Highld 310 D6
Acharossan Argyll 275 F10
Acharry Muir Highld 309 K6
Achath Aberds 293 B9
Achavanich Highld 310 E5
Achavelgin Highld 301 D9
Achavraat Highld 301 E9
Achddu Carms 74 E6
Achdregnie Moray 302 G2
Achduart Highld 307 J5
Achentoul Highld 310 F2
Achfary Highld 306 F7
Achfrish Highld 309 H5
Achgarve Highld 307 K3
Achiemore Highld 308 C3
Highld 310 D2
A'Chill Highld 294 E4
Achiltibuie Highld 307 J5
Achina Highld 308 C7
Achinahuagh Highld 308 C5
Achindaul Highld 290 E3
Achindown Highld 301 E8
Achinduich Highld 309 J5
Achinduin Argyll 289 F10
Achingills Highld 310 C5
Achininver Highld 308 C5
Achintee Highld 290 F3
Highld 299 E9
Achintraid Highld 295 B10
Achlaven Argyll 289 F11
Achlean Highld 291 D10
Achleck Argyll 288 E6
Achlorachan Highld 300 D3
Achluachrach Highld 290 E4
Achlyness Highld 306 D7
Achmelvich Highld 307 G5
Achmore Highld 295 B10
Stirlinging 285 D9
Achnaba Argyll 275 E10
Argyll 289 F11
Achnabat Highld 300 F5
Achnabreck Argyll 275 D9
Achnacarnin Highld 306 F5
Achnacarry Highld 290 E3
Achnacloich Argyll 289 F11
Highld 295 E7
Achnaconeran Highld 290 B6
Achnacraig Argyll 288 E6
Achnacree Argyll 289 F11
Achnacree Bay Argyll 289 F11
Achnacroish Argyll 289 E10
Achnadrish Argyll 288 D6
Achnafalnich Argyll 284 E6
Achnagarron Highld 300 C6
Achnaha Highld 288 C6
Achnahanat Highld 309 K5
Achnahannet Highld 301 G9
Achnahard Argyll 288 G5
Achnairn Highld 309 H5
Achnaluachrach Highld 309 J6
Achnandarach Highld 295 B10
Achnanellan Highld 290 E2
Achnasaul Highld 290 E3
Achnasheen Highld 299 D11
Achnashelloch Argyll 275 D9
Achnavast Highld 310 C4
Achneigie Highld 299 B10
Achormlarie Highld 309 K6
Achorn Highld 310 F5
Achosnich Highld 288 C6
Achranich Highld 289 E9
Achreamie Highld 310 C4
Achriabhach Highld 290 G3
Achriesgill Highld 306 D7
Achrimsdale Highld 311 J3
Achtoty Highld 308 C6
Achurch N Nhants 137 G10
Achuvoldrach Highld 308 D5
Achvaich Highld 309 K7
Achvarasdal Highld 310 C3
Ackenthwaite Cumb 211 C10
Ackergill Highld 310 D7
Acklam Mbro 225 B9
N Yorks 216 G5
Ackleton Shrops 132 D5
Acklington Northumb 252 C6
Ackton W Yorks 198 C2
Ackworth Moor Top
W Yorks 198 D2
Acle Norf 161 G8
Acock's Green W Mid 134 G2
Acol Kent 71 F10
Acomb Northumb 241 D10
York 207 C7
Acre Gtr Man 196 F2
Lancs 195 C9
Acrefair Wrex 166 G3
Acres Nook Staffs 168 E4
Acre Street W Sus 21 B11
Acton Ches E 167 E10
Dorset 18 F5
London 67 C8
Shrops 130 G6
Staffs 168 G4
Suff 107 C7
Worcs 116 D6
Wrex 166 E4
Acton Beauchamp
Hereford 116 G3
Acton Bridge Ches W 183 F9
Acton Burnell Shrops 131 C10
Acton Green Hereford 116 G3
London 67 D8
Acton Pigott Shrops 131 C10
Acton Place Suff 107 B7
Acton Reynald Shrops 149 E10
Acton Round Shrops 132 D2
Acton Scott Shrops 131 F9
Acton Trussell Staffs 151 F8
Acton Turville S Glos 61 C10
Adabroc W Isles 304 B7
Adambrae W Loth 269 A10
Adam's Green Dorset 29 F8
Adbaston Staffs 150 D5
Adber Dorset 29 C9
Adbolton Notts 154 B2
Adderbury Oxon 101 D9
Adderley Shrops 150 B3
Adderley Green Stoke 168 G6
Adderstone Northumb 264 C4
Addiewell W Loth 269 C9
Addingham W Yorks 205 D7
Addingham Moorside
W Yorks 205 D7
Addington Bucks 102 F4
Corn 6 B5
Kent 53 B7
London 67 G11
Addinston Borders 271 E10
Addiscombe London 67 F10
Addlestone Sur 66 G5
Addlestonemoor Sur 66 F4
Addlethorpe Lincs 175 B8
Adel W Yorks 205 F11
Adeney Telford 150 F4
Adeyfield Herts 85 D9
Adfa Powys 129 C11
Adforton Hereford 115 C8
Adgestone IoW 21 D7
Adisham Kent 55 C8
Adlestrop Glos 100 F4
Adlingfleet E Yorks 199 C10
Adlington Ches E 184 E6
Lancs 194 E6
Adlington Park Lancs 194 E5
Admaston Staffs 151 E10
Telford 150 G2
Admington Warks 100 B4
Adpar Ceredig 92 C6
Adsborough Som 28 B3
Adscombe Som 43 F7
Adstock Bucks 102 E4
Adstone W Nhants 119 G11
Adswood Gtr Man 184 D5
Adversane W Sus 35 C9
Advie Highld 301 F11
Adwalton W Yorks 197 B8
Adwell Oxon 83 F11
Adwick le Street
S Yorks 198 F4
Adwick upon Dearne
S Yorks 198 G3
Adziel Aberds 303 D9
Ae Dumfries 247 F11
Ae Village Dumfries 247 F11
Affetside Gtr Man 195 E9
Affleck Aberds 303 G8
Affpuddle Dorset 18 C2
Affric Lodge Highld 299 G11
Afon Eitha Wrex 166 F3
Afon-wen Flint 181 G10
Afon Wen Gwyn 145 B8
Afton IoW 20 D2
Agar Nook Leics 153 G9
Agbrigg W Yorks 197 D10
Aggborough Worcs 116 B6
Agglethorpe N Yorks 213 B11
Aglionby Cumb 239 F10
Agneash IoM 192 D5
Aifft Denb 165 B10
Aigburth Mers 182 D5
Aiginis W Isles 304 E6
Aike E Yorks 209 D7
Aikenway Moray 302 E2
Aikerness Orkney 314 A4
Aikers Orkney 314 G4
Aiketgate Cumb 230 B5
Aikton Cumb 239 G7
Ailby Lincs 190 F6
Ailey Hereford 96 B6
Ailstone Warks 118 G4
Ailsworth Pboro 138 D2
Aimes Green Essex 86 E5
Ainderby Quernhow
N Yorks 215 C7
Ainderby Steeple
N Yorks 224 G6
Aingers Green Essex 108 G2
Ainley Top W Yorks 196 D6
Ainsdale Mers 193 E10
Ainsdale-on-Sea Mers 193 E9
Ainstable Cumb 230 B6
Ainsworth Gtr Man 195 E9
Ainthorpe N Yorks 226 D4
Aintree Mers 182 B5
Aird Argyll 275 C8
Dumfries 236 C2
Highld 299 B7
W Isles 296 F3
W Isles 304 E7
Airdachuilinn Highld 306 E7
Aird a Mhachair
W Isles 297 G3
Aird a' Mhulaidh
W Isles 305 G3
Aird Asaig W Isles 305 H3
Aird Dhail W Isles 304 B6
Airdens Highld 309 K6
Airdeny Argyll 289 G11
Aird Mhidhinis W Isles 297 L3
Aird Mhighe W Isles 296 C6
W Isles 305 J3
Aird Mhòr W Isles 297 G4
Aird Mhor W Isles 297 L3
Aird of Sleat Highld 295 E7
Airdrie N Lanark 268 B5
Airds of Kells Dumfries 237 B8
Aird Thunga W Isles 304 E6
Airdtorrisdale Highld 308 C6
Aird Uig W Isles 304 E2
Airedale W Yorks 198 B3
Aire View N Yorks 204 D5
Airidh a Bhruaich
W Isles 305 G4
Airieland Dumfries 237 D9
Airinis W Isles 304 E6
Airlie Angus 287 B7
Airlies Dumfries 236 D5
Airmyn E Yorks 199 B8
Airntully Perth 286 D4
Airor Highld 295 E9
Airth Falk 279 D7
Airthrey Castle
Stirlinging 278 B6
Airton N Yorks 204 B4
Airyhassen Dumfries 236 E5
Airy Hill N Yorks 227 D7
Airyligg Dumfries 236 C4
Aisby Lincs 155 B10
Lincs 188 C5
Aisgernis W Isles 297 J3
Aish Devon 8 C3
Devon 8 D6
Aisholt Som 43 F7
Aiskew N Yorks 214 B5
Aislaby N Yorks 216 B5
N Yorks 227 D7
Stockton 225 C8
Aisthorpe Lincs 188 E6
Aith Orkney 314 E2
Shetland 312 D8
Shetland 313 H5
Aithnen Powys 148 E4
Aithsetter Shetland 313 K6
Aitkenhead S Ayrs 245 B8
Aitnoch Highld 301 F9
Akeld Northumb 263 D11
Akeley Bucks 102 D4
Akenham Suff 108 B2
Albany T&W 243 F7
Albaston Corn 12 G4
Alberbury Shrops 149 G7
Albert Town Pembs 72 B6
Albert Village Leics 152 F6
Albourne W Sus 36 D3
Albourne Green W Sus 36 D3
Albrighton Shrops 132 C6
Shrops 149 F9
Albro Castle Ceredig 92 B3
Alburgh Norf 142 F5
Albury Herts 105 G8
Sur 50 D5
Albury End Herts 105 G8
Albury Heath Sur 50 D5
Albyfield Cumb 240 G2
Alby Hill Norf 160 C3
Alcaig Highld 300 D5
Alcaston Shrops 131 F9
Alcester Dorset 30 C5
Warks 117 F11
Alcester Lane's End
W Mid 133 G11
Alciston E Sus 23 D8
Alcombe Som 42 D3
Wilts 61 F10
Alconbury Cambs 122 B3
Alconbury Weald
Cambs 122 B4
Alconbury Weston
Cambs 122 B3
Aldbar Castle Angus 287 B9
Aldborough Norf 160 C3
N Yorks 215 F8
Aldborough Hatch
London 68 B3
Aldbourne Wilts 63 D9
Aldbrough E Yorks 209 F10
Aldbrough St John
N Yorks 224 C4
Aldbury Herts 85 C7
Aldcliffe Lancs 211 G9
Aldclune Perth 291 G11
Aldeburgh Suff 127 F9
Aldeby Norf 143 E8
Aldenham Herts 85 F10
Alderbrook E Sus 37 B8
Alderbury Wilts 31 B11
Aldercar Derbys 170 F6
Alderford Norf 160 F2
Alder Forest Gtr Man 184 B3
Alderholt Dorset 31 E10
Alderley Glos 80 G3
Alderley Edge Ches E 184 F4
Alderman's Green
W Mid 135 G7
Aldermaston W Berks 64 F5
Aldermaston Soke
W Berks 64 G6
Aldermaston Wharf
W Berks 64 F6
Alderminster Warks 100 B4
Aldermoor Soton 32 D5
Alder Moor Staffs 152 D4
Alderney BCP 18 C6
Alder Row Som 45 E9
Aldersbrook London 68 B2
Alder's End Hereford 98 C2
Aldersey Green Ches W 167 D7
Aldershawe Staffs 134 B2
Aldershot Hants 49 C11
Alderton Glos 99 E10
Shrops 149 E9
Suff 108 C6
Wilts 61 C10
W Nhants 102 B4
Alderton Fields Glos 99 E10
Alderwasley Derbys 170 E4
Aldfield N Yorks 214 F5
Aldford Ches W 166 D6
Aldgate Rutland 137 C9
Aldham Essex 107 F8
Suff 107 B10
Aldie Highld 309 L7
Aldingbourne W Sus 22 B6
Aldingham Cumb 210 E5
Aldington Kent 54 F5
Worcs 99 C11
Aldington Frith Kent 54 F4
Aldivalloch Moray 302 G3
Aldochlay Argyll 277 C7
Aldon Shrops 115 B8
Aldoth Cumb 229 B8
Aldourie Castle Highld 300 F6
Aldreth Cambs 123 C8
Aldridge W Mid 133 C11
Aldringham Suff 127 E8
Aldrington Brighton 36 F3
Aldsworth Glos 81 C11
Aldunie Moray 302 G3
Aldwark Derbys 170 D2
N Yorks 215 G9
Aldwarke S Yorks 186 C6
Aldwick W Sus 22 D6
Aldwincle N Nhants 137 G10
Aldworth W Berks 64 D5
Alehouseburn Aberds 302 C6
Alehousehill Aberds 303 G10
Ale Oak Shrops 130 G4
Alexandria W Dunb 277 F7
Aley Som 43 F7
Aley Green C Beds 85 B9
Alfardisworthy Devon 24 E3
Alfington Devon 15 B8
Alfold Sur 50 G4
Alfold Bars W Sus 50 G4
Alfold Crossways Sur 50 F4
Alford Aberds 293 B7
Lincs 191 F7
Som 44 G6
Alfred's Well Worcs 117 C8
Alfreton Derbys 170 D6
Alfrick Worcs 116 G4
Alfrick Pound Worcs 116 G4
Alfriston E Sus 23 E8
Algakirk Lincs 156 B5
Algaltraig Argyll 275 F11
Algarkirk Lincs 156 B5
Alhampton Som 44 G6
Aline Lodge W Isles 305 G3
Alisary Highld 289 B9
Alkborough N Lincs 199 C11
Alkerton Glos 80 D3
Oxon 101 C7
Alkham Kent 55 E9
Alkington Shrops 149 B10
Alkmonton Derbys 152 B3
Alkrington Garden Village
Gtr Man 195 G11
Alladale Lodge Highld 309 L4
Allaleigh Devon 8 E6
Allanaquoich Aberds 292 D3
Allanbank Borders 271 F10
N Lanark 268 D6
Allangrange Mains
Highld 300 D6
Allanshaugh Borders 271 F8
Allanshaws Borders 271 G9
Allanton Borders 273 E7
N Lanark 269 D7
S Lanark 268 E4
Allaston Glos 79 E10
Allathasdal W Isles 297 L2
Allbrook Hants 33 C7
All Cannings Wilts 62 G5
Allendale Town
Northumb 241 F8
Allen End Warks 134 D3
Allenheads Northumb 232 B3
Allensford Durham 242 G3
Allens Green Herts 87 B7
Allensmore Hereford 97 D9
Allenton Derby 153 C7
Allenwood Cumb 239 F11
Aller Devon 9 B7
Devon 27 F9
Dorset 30 G3
Som 28 B6
Allerby Cumb 229 D7
Allerford Som 27 B11
Som 42 D2
Aller Park Devon 9 B7
Allerston N Yorks 217 C7
Allerthorpe E Yorks 207 D11
Allerton Mers 182 D6
W Yorks 205 G8
Allerton Bywater
W Yorks 198 B2
Allerton Mauleverer
N Yorks 206 B4
Allesley W Mid 134 G6
Allestree Derby 152 B6
Allet Corn 4 F5
Allexton Leics 136 C6
Allgreave Ches E 169 B7
Allhallows Medway 69 D10
Allhallows-on-Sea
Medway 69 D10
Alligin Shuas Highld 299 D8
Allimore Green Staffs 151 F7
Allington Kent 53 B8
Lincs 172 G5
Wilts 47 F8
Wilts 61 D11
Wilts 62 G5
Allington Bar Wilts 61 E11
Allithwaite Cumb 211 D7
Alloa Clack 279 C7
Allonby Cumb 229 C7
Allostock Ches W 184 G2
Alloway S Ayrs 257 F8
Allowenshay Som 28 E5
All Saints Devon 28 G4
All Saints South Elmham
Suff 142 G6
Allscot Shrops 132 D4
Allscott Telford 150 G2
All Stretton Shrops 131 D9
Allt Carms 75 E9
Alltami Flint 166 B3
Alltbeithe Highld 290 C2
Alltchaorunn Highld 284 B5
Alltforgan Powys 147 E9
Alltmawr Powys 95 B11
Alltnacaillich Highld 308 E4
Allt-na-giubhsaich
Aberds 292 E4
Allt na h-Airbhe Highld 307 K6
Allt-nan-sùgh Highld 295 C11
Alltrech Argyll 289 F8
Alltsigh Highld 290 B6
Alltwalis Carms 93 E8
Alltwen Neath 76 E2
Alltyblaca Ceredig 93 B10
Allt-yr-yn Newport 59 B9

Allwood Green Suff 125 C10
Alma Notts 171 E7
Almagill Dumfries 238 B3
Almeley Hereford 114 G6
Almeley Wooton
Hereford 114 G6
Almer Dorset 18 B4
Almholme S Yorks 198 F5
Almington Staffs 150 C4
Alminstone Cross Devon 24 C4
Almondbank Perth 286 E4
Almondbury W Yorks 197 D7
Almondsbury S Glos 60 C6
Almondvale W Loth 269 B11
Almshouse Green Essex 106 E5
Alne N Yorks 215 F9
Alne End Warks 118 F2
Alne Hills Warks 118 E2
Alness Highld 300 C6
Alnessferry Highld 300 C6
Alne Station N Yorks 215 F10
Alnham Northumb 263 G11
Alnmouth Northumb 264 G6
Alnwick Northumb 264 G5
Alperton London 67 C7
Alphamstone Essex 107 D7
Alpheton Suff 125 G7
Alphington Devon 14 C4
Alpington Norf 142 C5
Alport Derbys 170 C2
Powys 130 D5
Alpraham Ches E 167 D9
Alresford Essex 107 G11
Alrewas Staffs 152 F3
Alsager Ches E 168 D3
Alsagers Bank Staffs 168 F4
Alscot Bucks 84 E4
Alsop en le Dale
Derbys 169 D11
Alston Cumb 231 B10
Devon 28 G4
Alstone Glos 99 E9
Glos 99 G8
Som 43 D10
Alstonefield Staffs 169 D10
Alston Sutton Som 44 C2
Alswear Devon 26 C2
Alt Gtr Man 196 G2
Altandhu Highld 307 H4
Altanduin Highld 311 G2
Altarnun Corn 11 E10
Altass Highld 309 J4
Altbough Hereford 97 E10
Altdargue Aberds 293 C7
Alterwall Highld 310 C6
Altham Lancs 203 G11
Alt Hill Gtr Man 196 G2
Althorne Essex 88 F6
Althorpe N Lincs 199 F10
Alticane S Ayrs 244 F6
Alticry Dumfries 236 D4
Altmore Windsor 65 D11
Altnabreac Station
Highld 310 E4
Altnacealgach Hotel
Highld 307 H7
Altnacraig Argyll 289 G10
Altnafeadh Highld 284 B6
Altnaharra Highld 308 F5
Altofts W Yorks 197 C11
Alton Derbys 170 C5
Hants 49 F8
Staffs 169 G9
Wilts 47 D7
Alton Barnes Wilts 62 G6
Altonhill E Ayrs 257 B10
Alton Pancras Dorset 30 G2
Alton Priors Wilts 62 G6
Altonside Moray 302 D2
Altour Highld 290 E4
Altrincham Gtr Man 184 D3
Altrua Highld 290 E4
Altskeith Stirling 285 G8
Altyre Ho Moray 301 D10
Alum Rock W Mid 134 F2
Alva Clack 279 B7
Alvanley Ches W 183 G7
Alvaston Derby 153 C7
Alvechurch Worcs 117 C10
Alvecote Warks 134 C4
Alvediston Wilts 31 C7
Alveley Shrops 132 G5
Alverdiscott Devon 25 B8
Alverstoke Hants 21 B8
Alverstone IoW 21 D7
Alverthorpe W Yorks 197 C10
Alverton Notts 172 G3
Alves Moray 301 C11
Alvescot Oxon 82 E3
Alveston S Glos 60 B6
Warks 118 F4
Alveston Down S Glos 60 B6
Alveston Hill Warks 118 G4
Alvie Highld 291 C10
Alvingham Lincs 190 C5
Alvington Glos 79 E10
Som 29 D8
Alwalton Cambs 138 D2
Alway Newport 59 B10
Alweston Dorset 29 E11
Alwington Devon 24 C6
Alwinton Northumb 251 B10
Alwoodley W Yorks 205 E11
Alwoodley Gates
W Yorks 206 E2
Alwoodley Park
W Yorks 205 E11
Alyth Perth 286 C6
Amalebra Corn 1 B5
Amalveor Corn 1 B5
Amatnatua Highld 309 K4
Am Baile W Isles 297 K3
Ambaston Derbys 153 C8
Ambergate Derbys 170 E4
Amber Hill Lincs 174 F2
Amberley Glos 80 E5
Hereford 97 B10
W Sus 35 E8
Amble Northumb 253 C7
Amblecote W Mid 133 F7
Ambler Thorn W Yorks 196 B5
Ambleside Cumb 221 E7
Ambleston Pembs 91 F10
Ambrosden Oxon 83 B10
Am Buth Argyll 289 G10
Amcotts N Lincs 199 E11
Amen Corner Brack 65 F10
Amersham Bucks 85 F7
Amersham Common
Bucks 85 F7
Amersham Old Town
Bucks 85 F7
Amersham on the Hill
Bucks 85 F7
Amerton Staffs 151 D9
Amesbury Bath 45 B7
Wilts 47 E7
Ameysford Dorset 31 G9
Amington Staffs 134 C4
Amisfield Dumfries 247 G11
Amlwch Anglesey 178 C6
Amlwch Port Anglesey 179 C7
Ammanford = Rhydaman
Carms 75 C10
Ammerham Som 28 F5
Amod Argyll 255 D8
Amotherby N Yorks 216 E4
Ampfield Hants 32 C6
Ampleforth N Yorks 215 D11
Ampney Crucis Glos 81 E9
Ampney St Mary Glos 81 E9
Ampney St Peter Glos 81 E9
Amport Hants 47 E9
Ampthill C Beds 103 D10
Ampton Suff 125 C7
Amroth Pembs 73 D11
Amulree Perth 286 D2
Amwell Herts 85 C11
Anagach Highld 301 G10
Anaheilt Highld 289 C10
Anancaun Highld 299 C10
An Caol Highld 298 D6
Ancarraig Highld 300 G4
Ancaster Lincs 173 G7
Anchor Shrops 130 G3
Anchorage Park Ptsmth 33 G11
Anchor Corner Norf 141 D10
Anchorsholme Blackpool 202 E2
Anchor Street Norf 160 E6
An Cnoc W Isles 304 E6
Ancoats Gtr Man 184 B5
Ancroft Northumb 273 F9
Ancroft Northmoor
Northumb 273 F9
Ancrum Borders 262 E4
Ancton W Sus 35 G7
Ancumtoun Orkney 314 A7
Anderby Lincs 191 F8
Anderby Creek Lincs 191 F8
Andersea Som 43 G10
Andersfield Som 43 G8
Anderson Dorset 18 B3
Anderton Ches W 183 F10
Corn 7 E8
Lancs 194 E6
Andertons Mill Lancs 194 E4
Andover Hants 47 D11
Andover Down Hants 47 D11
Andoversford Glos 81 B8
Andreas IoM 192 C5
Andwell Hants 49 C7
Anelog Gwyn 144 D3
Anerley London 67 F10
Anfield Mers 182 C5
Angarrack Corn 2 B3
Angarrick Corn 3 B7
Angelbank Shrops 115 B11
Angersleigh Som 27 D11
Angerton Cumb 238 F6
Angle Pembs 72 E5
An Gleann Ur W Isles 304 E6
Angmering W Sus 35 G9
Angram N Yorks 206 D6
N Yorks 223 F7
Anick Northumb 241 D11
Anie Stirling 285 F9
Ankerdine Hill Worcs 116 F4
Ankerville Highld 301 B8
Anlaby E Yorks 200 B4
Anlaby Park Hull 200 B5
An Leth Meadhanach
W Isles 297 K3
Anmer Norf 158 D4
Anmore Hants 33 E11
Annan Dumfries 238 D5
Annaside Cumb 210 B1
Annat Argyll 284 E4
Highld 290 D5
Highld 299 D8
Anna Valley Hants 47 E10
Annbank S Ayrs 257 E10
Annesley Notts 171 E8
Annesley Woodhouse
Notts 171 E7
Annfield Plain Durham 242 G5
Anniesland Glasgow 267 B10
Annifirth Shetland 313 J3
Annishader Highld 298 D4
Annis Hill Suff 143 F7
Annitsford T&W 243 C7
Annscroft Shrops 131 B9
Ann's Hill Hants 33 G9
Annwell Place Derbys 152 F6
Ansdell Lancs 193 B10
Ansells End Herts 85 B11
Ansford Som 44 G6
Ansley Warks 134 E5
Ansley Common Warks 134 E6
Anslow Staffs 152 D4
Anslow Gate Staffs 152 D3
Anstead Brook Sur 50 G2
Anstey Herts 105 E8
Leics 135 B10
Anstruther Easter Fife 287 G9
Anstruther Wester Fife 287 G9
Ansty Hants 49 E8
Warks 135 G7
Wilts 31 B7
W Sus 36 C3
Ansty Coombe Wilts 31 B7
Ansty Cross Dorset 30 G3
Anthill Common Hants 33 E10
Anthony Corn 7 E7
Anthony's Cross Glos 98 G4
Anthorn Cumb 238 F5
Antingham Norf 160 C5
An t-Ob W Isles 296 C6
Anton's Gowt Lincs 174 F3
Antonshill Falk 279 E7
Antony Corn 7 E7
Antony Passage Corn 7 D8
Antrobus Ches W 183 F10
Anvil Green Kent 54 D6
Anvilles W Berks 63 F10
Anwick Lincs 173 E10
Anwoth Dumfries 237 D7
Aonachan Highld 290 E4
Aoradh Argyll 274 G3
Apedale Staffs 168 F4
Aperfield London 52 B2
Apes Dale Worcs 117 C9
Apes Hall Cambs 139 E11
Apethorpe N Nhants 137 D10
Apeton Staffs 151 F7
Apley Lincs 189 F10
Apley Forge Shrops 132 D4
Apperknowle Derbys 186 F5
Apperley Glos 99 F7
Apperley Bridge
W Yorks 205 F9
Apperley Dene
Northumb 242 F3
Appersett N Yorks 223 G7
Appin Argyll 289 E11
Appin House Argyll 289 E11
Appleby N Lincs 200 E3
Appleby-in-Westmorland
Cumb 231 G9
Appleby Magna Leics 134 B6
Appleby Parva Leics 134 B6
Applecross Highld 299 E7
Applecross Ho Highld 299 E7
Appledore Devon 27 E9
Devon 40 G3
Kent 39 B7
Appledore Heath Kent 54 G3
Appleford Oxon 83 G8
Applegarthtown
Dumfries 248 G4
Applehouse Hill Windsor 65 C10
Applemore Hants 32 F5
Appleshaw Hants 47 D10
Applethwaite Cumb 229 F11
Appleton Halton 183 D8
Oxon 82 E6
Appleton-le-Moors
N Yorks 216 B4
Appleton-le-Street
N Yorks 216 E4
Appleton Park Warr 183 E10
Appleton Roebuck
N Yorks 207 E7
Appleton Thorn Warr 183 E10
Appleton Wiske N Yorks 225 E7
Appletreehall Borders 262 F2
Appletreewick
N Yorks 213 G11
Appley IoW 21 C8
Som 27 C9
Appley Bridge Lancs 194 F4
Apse Heath IoW 21 E7
Apsey Green Suff 126 E5
Apsley Herts 85 D9
Apsley End C Beds 104 E2
Apuldram W Sus 22 C4
Aqueduct Telford 132 B3
Aquhythie Aberds 293 B9
Arabella Highld 301 B8
Arbeadie Aberds 293 D8
Arberth = Narberth
Pembs 73 C10
Arbirlot Angus 287 C10
Arboll Highld 311 L2
Arborfield Wokingham 65 F9
Arborfield Cross
Wokingham 65 F9
Arborfield Garrison
Wokingham 65 F9
Arbourthorne S Yorks 186 D5
Arbroath Angus 287 C10
Arbury Cambs 123 E8
Arbuthnott Aberds 293 F9
Archavandra Muir
Highld 309 K7
Archdeacon Newton
Darl 224 B5
Archenfield Hereford 96 C5
Archiestown Moray 302 E2
Archnalea Highld 289 C10
Arclid Ches E 168 C3
Arclid Green Ches E 168 C3
Ardachu Highld 309 J6
Ardailly Argyll 255 B7
Ardalanish Argyll 274 B4
Ardallie Aberds 303 F10
Ardalum Ho Argyll 288 F6
Ardamaleish Argyll 275 G11
Ardanaiseig Argyll 284 E4
Ardaneaskan Highld 295 B10
Ardanstur Argyll 275 B9
Ardargie House Hotel
Perth 286 F4
Ardarroch Highld 295 B10
Ardban Highld 295 B9
Ardbeg Argyll 254 C5
Argyll 276 E3
Ardcharnich Highld 307 L6
Ardchiavaig Argyll 274 B4
Ardchonnell Argyll 275 B10
Ardchronie Highld 309 L6
Ardchuilk Highld 300 F2
Ardchullarie More
Stirling 285 F9
Ardchyle Stirling 285 E9
Ardclach Highld 301 E9
Ard-dhubh Highld 299 E7
Arddleen Powys 148 F5
Ardechvie Highld 290 D3
Ardeley Herts 104 F6
Ardelve Highld 295 C10
Arden Argyll 277 E7
E Renf 267 D10
Ardencaple Ho Argyll 275 B8
Ardendrain Highld 300 F5
Arden Park Gtr Man 184 C6
Ardens Grafton Warks 118 G2
Ardentallen Argyll 289 G10
Ardentinny Argyll 276 D3
Ardentraive Argyll 275 F11
Ardeonaig Stirling 285 D10
Ardersier Highld 301 D7
Ardery Highld 289 C9
Ardessie Highld 307 L5
Ardfern Argyll 275 C9
Ardfernal Argyll 274 F6
Ardgartan Argyll 284 G6
Ardgay Highld 309 K5
Ardglassie Aberds 303 C10
Ardgour Highld 290 G2
Ardgye Moray 301 C11
Ardheslaig Highld 299 D7
Ardiecow Moray 302 C5
Ardinamir Argyll 275 B8
Ardindrean Highld 307 L6
Ardingly W Sus 36 B4
Ardington Oxon 64 B2
Ardington Wick Oxon 64 B2
Ardintoul Highld 295 C10
Ardlair Aberds 302 G5
Highld 299 B9
Ardlamey Argyll 255 C7
Ardlamont Ho Argyll 275 G10
Ardlawhill Aberds 303 C8
Ardleigh Essex 107 F11
Ardleigh Green London 68 B4
Ardleigh Heath Essex 107 E10
Ardler Perth 286 C6
Ardley Oxon 101 F10
Ardley End Essex 87 C8
Ardlui Argyll 285 F7
Ardlussa Argyll 275 E7
Ardmair Highld 307 K6
Ardmay Argyll 284 G6
Ardmenish Argyll 274 F6
Ardminish Argyll 255 C7
Ardmolich Highld 289 B9
Ardmore Argyll 289 G9
Highld 306 D7
Highld 309 L7
Ardnacross Argyll 289 E7
Ardnadam Argyll 276 F3
Ardnagowan Argyll 284 G4
Ardnagrask Highld 300 E5
Ardnarff Highld 295 B10
Ardnastang Highld 289 C10
Ardnave Argyll 274 F3
Ardneil N Ayrs 266 F3
Ardno Argyll 284 G5
Ardo Aberds 303 F8
Ardoch Argyll 277 F7
Perth 286 D4
Ardoch *continued*
Stirling 285 F9
Ardochy House Highld 290 C4
Ardo Ho Aberds 303 G9
Ardoyne Aberds 302 G6
Ardpatrick Argyll 275 G8
Ardpatrick Ho Argyll 255 B8
Ardpeaton Argyll 276 D4
Ardradnaig Perth 285 C11
Ardrishaig Argyll 275 E9
Ardross Fife 287 G9
Highld 300 B6
Ardrossan N Ayrs 266 G4
Ardross Castle Highld 300 B6
Ardshave Highld 309 K7
Ardsheal Highld 289 D11
Ardshealach Highld 289 C8
Ardskenish Argyll 274 D4
Ardsley S Yorks 197 F11
Ardslignish Highld 289 C7
Ardtalla Argyll 254 B5
Ardtalnaig Perth 285 D11
Ardtaraig Argyll 275 E11
Ardtoe Highld 289 B8
Ardtreck Highld 294 B5
Ardtrostan Perth 285 E10
Ardtur Argyll 289 E11
Arduaine Argyll 275 B8
Ardullie Highld 300 C5
Ardvannie Highld 309 L6
Ardvar Highld 306 F6
Ardvasar Highld 295 E8
Ardveich Stirling 285 E10
Ardverikie Highld 291 E7
Ardvorlich Perth 285 E10
Ardwell Dumfries 236 E3
Moray 302 F3
S Ayrs 244 E5
Ardwell Mains Dumfries 236 E3
Ardwick Gtr Man 184 B5
Areley Kings Worcs 116 C6
Arford Hants 49 F10
Argoed Caerph 77 F11
Powys 113 E9
Powys 130 E5
Shrops 130 G6
Shrops 148 E6
Argos Hill E Sus 37 B9
Arichamish Argyll 275 C10
Arichastlich Argyll 284 D6
Aridhglas Argyll 288 G5
Arieniskill Highld 295 G9
Arileod Argyll 288 D3
Arinacrinachd Highld 299 D7
Arinagour Argyll 288 D4
Arineckaig Highld 299 E9
Arion Orkney 314 E2
Arisaig Highld 295 G8
Ariundle Highld 289 C10
Arivegaig Highld 289 C8
Arivoichallum Argyll 254 C4
Arkendale N Yorks 215 G7
Arkesden Essex 105 E9
Arkholme Lancs 211 E11
Arkleby Cumb 229 D8
Arkleton Dumfries 249 E9
Arkle Town N Yorks 223 E10
Arkley London 86 F2
Arksey S Yorks 198 F5
Arkwright Town Derbys 186 G6
Arle Glos 99 G8
Arlebrook Glos 80 D4
Arlecdon Cumb 219 B10
Arlescote Warks 101 B7
Arlesey C Beds 104 D3
Arleston Telford 150 G3
Arley Ches E 183 E11
Arley Green Ches E 183 E11
Arlingham Glos 80 C2
Arlington Devon 40 E6
E Sus 23 D8
Glos 81 D10
Arlington Beccott Devon 40 E6
Armadale Highld 308 C7
W Loth 269 B8
Armadale Castle Highld 295 E8
Armathwaite Cumb 230 B6
Armigers Essex 105 F11
Arminghall Norf 142 C5
Armitage Staffs 151 F11
Armitage Bridge
W Yorks 196 E6
Armley W Yorks 205 G11
Armscote Warks 100 C4
Armsdale Staffs 150 C5
Armshead Staffs 168 F6
Armston N Nhants 137 F11
Armthorpe S Yorks 198 F6
Arnabost Argyll 288 D4
Arnaby Cumb 210 C3
Arncliffe N Yorks 213 E8
Arncroach Fife 287 G9
Arndilly Ho Moray 302 E2
Arne Dorset 18 D5
Arnesby Leics 136 E2
Arngask Perth 286 F5
Arnisdale Highld 295 D10
Arnish Highld 298 E5
Arniston Midloth 270 C6
Arnol W Isles 304 D5
Arnold E Yorks 209 E8
Notts 171 F9
Arno's Vale Bristol 60 E6
Arnprior Stirling 278 C2
Arnside Cumb 211 D9
Aros Mains Argyll 289 E7
Arowry Wrex 149 B9
Arpafeelie Highld 300 D6
Arpinge Kent 55 F7
Arrad Foot Cumb 210 C6
Arram E Yorks 208 E6
Arrathorne N Yorks 224 G4
Arreton IoW 20 D6
Arrington Cambs 122 G6
Arrivain Argyll 284 D6
Arrochar Argyll 284 G6
Arrow Warks 117 F11
Arrowe Hill Mers 182 D3
Arrowfield Top Worcs 117 C10
Arrow Green Hereford 115 F8
Arrunden W Yorks 196 F6
Arscaig Highld 309 H5
Arscott Shrops 131 B8
Arthill Ches E 184 D2
Arthington W Yorks 205 E11
Arthingworth W Nhants 136 G5
Arthog Gwyn 146 G2
Arthrath Aberds 303 F9
Arthursdale W Yorks 206 F3
Arthurstone Perth 286 C6
Arthurville Highld 309 L7
Artington Sur 50 D3
Artrochie Aberds 303 F10
Arundel W Sus 35 F8
Arwick Orkney 314 D3
Aryhoulan Highld 290 G2
Asby Cumb 229 G7
Ascog Argyll 266 C2
Ascoil Highld 311 H2
Ascot Windsor 66 F2
Ascott Warks 100 E6
Ascott d'Oyley Oxon 82 B4
Ascott Earl Oxon 82 B3
Ascott-under-Wychwood
Oxon 82 B4
Asenby N Yorks 215 D7
Asfordby Leics 154 F4
Asfordby Hill Leics 154 F4
Asgarby Lincs 173 F10
Lincs 174 B4
Ash Devon 8 F6
Dorset 30 E5
Kent 55 B9
Kent 68 G5
Som 28 C3
Som 29 C7
Sur 49 C11
Ashaig Highld 295 C8
Ashampstead W Berks 64 D5
Ashampstead Green
W Berks 64 D5
Ashansworth Hants 48 B2
Ashbank Kent 53 C10
Ash Bank Staffs 168 F6
Ashbeer Som 42 F5
Ashbocking Suff 126 G3
Ashbourne Derbys 169 F11
Ashbrittle Som 27 C9
Ashbrook Shrops 131 E9
Ash Bullayne Devon 26 G3
Ashburnham Forge
E Sus 23 B11
Ashburton Devon 8 B5
Ashbury Devon 12 B6
Oxon 63 C9
Ashby N Lincs 200 F2
Ashby by Partney Lincs 174 B6
Ashby cum Fenby
NE Lincs 201 G9
Ashby de la Launde
Lincs 173 D9
Ashby-de-la-Zouch
Leics 153 F7
Ashby Folville Leics 154 G4
Ashby Hill NE Lincs 201 G8
Ashby Magna Leics 135 E11
Ashby Parva Leics 135 F10
Ashby Puerorum Lincs 190 G4
Ashby St Ledgers
W Nhants 119 D11
Ashby St Mary Norf 142 C6
Ashchurch Glos 99 E8
Ashcombe Devon 14 F4
Ashcombe Park N Som 59 G10
Ashcott Som 44 F2
Ashcott Corner Som 44 F2
Ashculme Devon 27 E10
Ashdon Essex 105 C11
Ashe Hants 48 D4
Asheldham Essex 89 E7
Ashen Essex 106 C4
Ashendon Bucks 84 C2
Asheridge Bucks 84 E6
Ashey IoW 21 D7
Ashfield Argyll 275 E8
Carms 94 F3
Hants 32 D5
Hereford 97 G11
Shrops 148 D6
Stirling 285 G11
Suff 126 E4
Ashfield Cum Thorpe
Suff 126 E4
Ashfield Green Suff 124 F5
Suff 126 C5
Ashfields Shrops 150 D4
Ashfold Crossways
W Sus 36 B2
Ashfold Side N Yorks 214 F2
Ashford Devon 8 F3
Devon 40 F4
Hants 31 E10
Kent 54 E4
Sur 66 E5
Ashford Bowdler
Shrops 115 C10
Ashford Carbonell
Shrops 115 C10
Ashford Common Sur 66 E5
Ashford Hill Hants 64 G5
Ashford in the Water
Derbys 185 G11
Ashgate Derbys 186 G5
Ashgill S Lanark 268 F5
Ash Green Sur 50 D2
Warks 134 F6
Ashgrove Bath 45 B8
Ash Grove Wrex 166 G5
Ash Hill Devon 14 G4
Ashiestiel Borders 261 B10
Ashill Devon 27 E9
Norf 141 C7
Som 28 D4
Ashingdon Essex 88 G5
Ashington BCP 18 B6
Northumb 253 F7
Som 29 C9
W Sus 35 D10
Ashington End Lincs 175 B8
Ashintully Castle Perth 292 G3
Ashkirk Borders 261 E11
Ashlett Hants 33 G7
Ashleworth Glos 98 F6
Ashley Cambs 124 E3
Ches E 184 E3
Devon 25 E10
Dorset 31 G10
Glos 80 G6
Hants 19 B11
Hants 47 G11
Kent 55 D10
N Nhants 136 E5
Staffs 150 B5
Wilts 61 F10
Ashley Dale Staffs 150 B5
Ashley Down Bristol 60 D5
Ashley Green Bucks 85 D7
Ashleyhay Derbys 170 E3
Ashley Heath Ches E 184 D3
Dorset 31 G10
Staffs 150 B4
Ashley Moor Hereford 115 D9
Ashley Park Sur 66 F6
Ash Magna Shrops 149 B11
Ashmanhaugh Norf 160 E6
Ashmansworth Hants 48 B2
Ashmansworthy Devon 24 D4
Ashmead Green Glos 80 F3
Ashmill Devon 12 B3
Ash Mill Devon 26 C3
Ash Moor Devon 26 D3
Ashmore Dorset 30 D6
Ashmore Green W Berks 64 F4
Ashmore Lake W Mid 133 D9
Ashmore Park W Mid 133 C9
Ashnashellach Lodge
Highld 299 E10
Ashopton Derbys 185 D11
Ashorne Warks 118 F6
Ashover Derbys 170 C4
Ashover Hay Derbys 170 C5
Ashow Warks 118 C6
Ash Parva Shrops 149 B11
Ashperton Hereford 98 C2
Ashprington Devon 8 D6
Ash Priors Som 27 B11
Ashreigney Devon 25 E10
Ashridge Court Devon 25 G11
Ash Street Suff 107 B10
Ashtead Sur 51 B7
Ash Thomas Devon 27 E8
Ashton Corn 2 D4
Hants 33 D9
Hereford 115 E10
Invclyd 276 F4
N Nhants 137 F11
Pboro 138 B2
Som 44 D2
W Nhants 102 B5
Ashton Common Wilts 45 B11
Ashton Gate Bristol 60 E5
Ashton Green E Sus 23 C7
Ashton Hayes Ches W 167 B8
Ashton Heath Halton 183 F9
Ashton-in-Makerfield
Gtr Man 183 B9
Ashton Keynes Wilts 81 G8
Ashton under Hill Worcs 99 D9
Ashton-under-Lyne
Gtr Man 184 B6
Ashton upon Mersey
Gtr Man 184 C3
Ashton Vale Bristol 60 E5
Ashurst Hants 32 E4
Kent 52 F4
Lancs 194 F3
W Sus 35 D11
Ashurst Bridge Hants 32 E4
Ashurst Wood W Sus 52 F2
Ashvale Bl Gwent 77 C10
Ash Vale Sur 49 C11
Ashwater Devon 12 B3
Ashwell Devon 14 G3
Herts 104 D5
Rutland 155 G7
Som 28 D5
Ashwell End Herts 104 C5
Ashwellthorpe Norf 142 D2
Ashwick Som 44 D6
Ashwicken Norf 158 F4
Ashwood Staffs 133 F7
Ashybank Borders 262 F2
Askam in Furness Cumb 210 D4
Askern S Yorks 198 E5
Askerswell Dorset 16 C6
Askerton Hill Lincs 172 F4
Askett Bucks 84 D4
Askham Cumb 230 G6
Notts 188 G2
Askham Bryan York 207 D7
Askham Richard York 206 D6
Asknish Argyll 275 D10
Askrigg N Yorks 223 G8
Askwith N Yorks 205 D9
Aslackby Lincs 155 C11
Aslacton Norf 142 E3
Aslockton Notts 154 B4
Asloun Aberds 293 B7
Asney Som 44 F3
Aspall Suff 126 D3
Aspatria Cumb 229 C8
Aspenden Herts 105 F7
Asperton Lincs 156 B5
Aspley Nottingham 171 G8
Staffs 150 C6
Aspley Guise C Beds 103 D8
Aspley Heath C Beds 103 D8
Warks 117 C11
Aspull Gtr Man 194 F6
Aspull Common
Gtr Man 183 B10
Assater Shetland 312 F4
Asselby E Yorks 199 B8
Asserby Lincs 191 F7
Asserby Turn Lincs 191 F7
Assington Suff 107 D8
Assington Green Suff 124 G5
Assynt Ho Highld 300 C5
Astbury Ches E 168 C4
Astcote W Nhants 120 G3
Asterby Lincs 190 F3
Asterley Shrops 131 B7
Asterton Shrops 131 E7
Asthall Oxon 82 C3
Asthall Leigh Oxon 82 C4
Astle Ches E 184 G4
Highld 309 K7
Astley Gtr Man 195 G8
Shrops 149 F10
Warks 134 F6
Worcs 116 D5
Astley Abbotts Shrops 132 D4
Astley Bridge Gtr Man 195 E8
Astley Cross Worcs 116 D6
Astley Green Gtr Man 184 B2
Astmoor Halton 183 E8
Aston Ches E 167 F10
Ches W 183 F9
Derbys 152 C3
Derbys 185 E11
Flint 166 B4
Hereford 115 C9
Hereford 115 E9
Herts 104 G5
Oxon 82 E4
Powys 130 E5
Shrops 132 E6
Shrops 149 D10
Staffs 151 E7
Staffs 168 G3
S Yorks 187 D7
Telford 132 B2
W Mid 133 F11
Wokingham 65 C9
Aston Abbotts Bucks 102 G6
Aston Bank Worcs 116 C2
Aston Botterell Shrops 132 G2
Aston-by-Stone Staffs 151 C8
Aston Cantlow Warks 118 F2
Aston Clinton Bucks 84 C5
Aston Crews Hereford 98 G3
Aston Cross Glos 99 E8
Aston End Herts 104 G5
Aston Eyre Shrops 132 E3
Aston Fields Worcs 117 D9
Aston Flamville Leics 135 E9
Aston Ingham Hereford 98 G3
Aston juxta Mondrum
Ches E 167 D11
Aston le Walls
W Nhants 119 G9
Aston Magna Glos 100 D3
Aston Munslow Shrops 131 F10
Aston on Carrant Glos 99 E8
Aston on Clun Shrops 131 G7
Aston-on-Trent Derbys 153 D8
Aston Pigott Shrops 130 B6
Aston Rogers Shrops 130 B6
Aston Rowant Oxon 84 F2
Aston Sandford Bucks 84 D3
Aston Somerville Worcs 99 D10
Aston Square Shrops 148 D6
Aston Subedge Glos 100 C2
Aston Tirrold Oxon 64 B5
Aston Upthorpe Oxon 64 B5
Astrop W Nhants 101 D10
Astrope Herts 84 C5
Astwick C Beds 104 D4
Astwith Derbys 170 C6
Astwood M Keynes 103 B9
Worcs 117 D8
Worcs 117 F7
Astwood Bank Worcs 117 E10
Aswarby Lincs 173 G9
Aswardby Lincs 190 G5
Atcham Shrops 131 B10
Atch Lench Worcs 117 G10
Athelhampton Dorset 17 C11
Athelington Suff 126 C4
Athelney Som 28 B4
Athelstaneford E Loth 281 F10
Atherfield Green IoW 20 F5
Atherington Devon 25 C9
W Sus 35 G8
Athersley North
S Yorks 197 F11
Athersley South
S Yorks 197 F11
Atherstone Som 28 D5
Warks 134 D6
Atherstone on Stour
Warks 118 G4
Atherton Gtr Man 195 G7
Athnamulloch Highld 299 G11
Athron Hall Perth 286 G4
Atley Hill N Yorks 224 E5
Atlow Derbys 170 F2
Attadale Highld 295 B11
Attadale Ho Highld 295 B11
Attenborough Notts 153 B10
Atterbury M Keynes 103 D7
Atterby Lincs 189 C7
Attercliffe S Yorks 186 D5
Atterley Shrops 132 D2
Atterton Leics 135 D7
Attleborough Norf 141 D10
Warks 135 E7
Attlebridge Norf 160 F2
Attleton Green Suff 124 G4
Atwick E Yorks 209 C9
Atworth Wilts 61 F11
Auberrow Hereford 97 B9
Aubourn Lincs 172 C6
Auch Argyll 285 D7
Auchagallon N Ayrs 255 D9
Auchallater Aberds 292 E3
Auchareoch N Ayrs 255 E10
Aucharnie Aberds 302 E6
Auchattie Aberds 293 D8
Auchavan Angus 292 G3
Auchbreck Moray 302 G2
Auchenback E Renf 267 D10
Auchenbainzie Dumfries 247 D8
Auchenblae Aberds 293 F9
Auchenbrack Dumfries 247 D7
Auchenbreck Argyll 255 C8
Argyll 275 E11
Auchencairn Dumfries 237 D9
Dumfries 247 G11
N Ayrs 256 D2
Auchencairn Ho
Dumfries 237 D10
Auchencar N Ayrs 255 D9
Auchencarroch W Dunb 277 E8
Auchencrosh S Ayrs 236 B3
Auchencrow Borders 273 C7
Auchendinny Midloth 270 C5
Auchengray S Lanark 269 E9
Auchenhalrig Moray 302 C3
Auchenharvie N Ayrs 266 G5
Auchenheath S Lanark 268 G6
Auchenhew N Ayrs 256 E2
Auchenlaich Stirling 285 G10
Auchenleck Dumfries 237 D9
Auchenlochan Argyll 275 F10
Auchenmalg Dumfries 236 D4
Auchenreoch E Dunb 278 F3
Auchensoul S Ayrs 245 E7
Auchentibber S Lanark 268 E3
Auchentiber N Ayrs 267 F7
Auchertyre Highld 295 C10
Auchessan Stirling 285 E8
Auchgourish Highld 291 B11
Auchindrain Argyll 284 G4
Auchindrean Highld 307 L6
Auchininna Aberds 302 E6
Auchinleck Dumfries 236 B6
E Ayrs 258 E3
Auchinloch N Lanark 278 G3
Auchinner Perth 285 F10
Auchinraith S Lanark 268 D3
Auchinroath Moray 302 D2
Auchinstarry N Lanark 278 F4
Auchintoul Aberds 293 B7
Highld 309 K5
Auchiries Aberds 303 F10
Auchlee Aberds 293 D10
Auchleeks Ho Perth 291 G9
Auchleven Aberds 302 G6
Auchlinn Aberds 303 D7
Auchlochan S Lanark 259 B8
Auchlossan Aberds 293 C7
Auchlunachan Highld 307 L6
Auchlunies Aberds 293 D10
Auchlyne Stirling 285 E9
Auchmacoy Aberds 303 F9
Auchmair Moray 302 G3
Auchmantle Dumfries 236 C3
Auchmenzie Aberds 302 G5
Auchmillan E Ayrs 258 D2
Auchmithie Angus 287 C10
Auchmore Highld 300 D4
Auchmuirbridge Fife 286 G6
Auchmull Angus 293 F7
Auchnacraig Argyll 289 G9
Auchnacree Angus 292 G6
Auchnafree Perth 286 D2
Auchnagallin Highld 301 F10
Auchnagarron Argyll 275 E11
Auchnagatt Aberds 303 E9
Auchnaha Argyll 275 E10
Auchnahillin Highld 301 F7
Auchnarrow Moray 302 G2
Auchnashelloch Perth 285 F11
Auchnotteroch Dumfries 236 C1
Aucholzie Aberds 292 D5
Auchrannie Angus 286 B6
Auchroisk Highld 301 G10
Auchronie Angus 292 E6
Auchterarder Perth 286 F3
Auchteraw Highld 290 C5
Auchterderran Fife 280 B4
Auchterhouse Angus 287 D7
Auchtermuchty Fife 286 F6
Auchterneed Highld 300 D4
Auchtertool Fife 280 C4
Auchtertyre Moray 301 D11
Stirling 285 E7
Auchtubh Stirling 285 E9
Auckengill Highld 310 C7
Auckley S Yorks 199 G7
Audenshaw Gtr Man 184 B6
Audlem Ches E 167 G11
Audley Staffs 168 E3
Audley End Essex 105 D10
Essex 106 D6
Norf 142 G2
Suff 125 G7
Auds Aberds 302 C6
Aughertree Cumb 229 D11
Aughton E Yorks 207 F10
Lancs 193 F11
Lancs 211 F10
S Yorks 187 D7
Wilts 47 B8
Aughton Park Lancs 194 F2
Aukside Durham 232 F4
Auldearn Highld 301 D9
Aulden Hereford 115 G9
Auldgirth Dumfries 247 F10
Auldhame E Loth 281 E11
Auldhouse S Lanark 268 E2
Auldtown of Carnoustie
Aberds 302 E6
Ault a'chruinn Highld 295 C11
Aultanrynie Highld 308 F3
Aultbea Highld 307 L3
Aultdearg Highld 300 C2
Aultgrishan Highld 307 L2
Aultguish Inn Highld 300 B3
Ault Hucknall Derbys 171 B7
Aultibea Highld 311 G4
Aultiphurst Highld 310 C2
Aultivullin Highld 310 C2
Aultmore Highld 301 G10
Moray 302 D4
Aultnagoire Highld 300 G5
Aultnamain Inn Highld 309 L6
Aultnaslat Highld 290 C3
Aulton Aberds 302 G6
Aulton of Atherb Aberds 303 E9
Aultvaich Highld 300 E5
Aunby Lincs 155 G10
Aundorach Highld 291 B11
Aunk Devon 27 G8
Aunsby Lincs 155 B10
Auquhorthies Aberds 303 G8
Aust S Glos 60 B5
Austendike Lincs 156 E5
Austen Fen Lincs 190 C5
Austenwood Bucks 66 B3
Austerfield S Yorks 187 C11
Austerlands Gtr Man 196 F3
Austhorpe W Yorks 206 G3
Austrey Warks 134 B5
Austwick N Yorks 212 F5
Authorpe Lincs 190 E6
Authorpe Row Lincs 191 G8
Avebury Wilts 62 F6
Avebury Trusloe Wilts 62 F5
Aveley Thurrock 68 C5
Avening Glos 80 F5
Avening Green S Glos 80 G2
Averham Notts 172 E3
Avernish Highld 295 C10
Avery Hill London 68 E2
Aveton Gifford Devon 8 F3
Avielochan Highld 291 B11
Aviemore Highld 291 B10
Avington Hants 48 G4
W Berks 63 F11
Avoch Highld 301 D7
Avon Hants 19 B8
Wilts 62 D3
Avonbridge Falk 279 G8
Avoncliff Wilts 45 B10
Avon Dassett Warks 101 B8
Avonmouth Bristol 60 D4
Avonwick Devon 8 D4
Awbridge Hants 32 C4
Awhirk Dumfries 236 D2
Awkley S Glos 60 B5
Awliscombe Devon 27 G10
Awre Glos 80 D2
Awsworth Notts 171 G7
Axbridge Som 44 C2
Axford Hants 48 E6
Wilts 63 F8
Axmansford Hants 64 G5
Axminster Devon 15 B11
Axmouth Devon 15 C11
Axton Flint 181 E10
Axtown Devon 7 B10
Axwell Park T&W 242 E5
Aycliff Kent 55 E10
Aycliffe Durham 233 G11
Aydon Northumb 242 D2
Aykley Heads Durham 233 C11
Aylburton Glos 79 E10
Aylburton Common
Glos 79 E10
Ayle Northumb 231 B10
Aylesbeare Devon 14 C6
Aylesbury Bucks 84 C4
Aylesby NE Lincs 201 F8
Aylesford Kent 53 B8
Aylesham Kent 55 C8
Aylestone Leicester 135 C11
Aylestone Hill Hereford 97 C10
Aylestone Park
Leicester 135 C11
Aylmerton Norf 160 B3
Aylsham Norf 160 D3
Aylton Hereford 98 D3
Aylworth Glos 100 G2
Aymestrey Hereford 115 D8
Aynho W Nhants 101 E10
Ayot Green Herts 86 C2
Ayot St Lawrence Herts 85 B11
Ayot St Peter Herts 86 B2
Ayr S Ayrs 257 E8
Ayre of Atler Shetland 313 G6
Ayres Shetland 313 H5
Ayres End Herts 85 C11
Ayres of Selivoe
Shetland 313 J4
Ayres Quay T&W 243 F9
Aysgarth N Yorks 213 B10
Ayshford Devon 27 D8
Ayside Cumb 211 C7
Ayston Rutland 137 C7
Aythorpe Roding Essex 87 B9
Ayton Borders 273 C8
T&W 243 F7
Ayton Castle Borders 273 C8
Aywick Shetland 312 E7
Azerley N Yorks 214 E5

B

Babbacombe Torbay 9 B8
Babbington Notts 171 G7
Babbinswood Shrops 148 C6
Babbs Green Herts 86 B5
Babcary Som 29 B9
Babel Carms 94 D6
Babel Green Suff 106 B4
Babell Flint 181 G11
Babeny Devon 13 F9
Babingley Norf 158 D3
Babraham Cambs 123 G10
Babworth Notts 187 E11
Bac W Isles 304 D6

Bachau Anglesey 178 E6
Bache Shrops 131 G9
Bacheldre Powys 130 E4
Bachelor's Bump E Sus 38 E4
Bache Mill Shrops 131 F10
Bach-y-gwreiddyn
Swansea 75 E10
Backaland Orkney 314 C5
Backaskaill Orkney 314 A4
Backbarrow Cumb 211 C7
Backbower Gtr Man 185 C7
Backburn Aberds 293 D10
Backe Carms 74 B3
Backfolds Aberds 303 D10
Backford Ches W 182 G6
Backford Cross Ches W 182 G5
Backhill Aberds 303 F7
Aberds 303 F10
Backhill of Clackriach
Aberds 303 E9
Backhill of Fortree
Aberds 303 E9
Backhill of Trustach
Aberds 293 D8
Backies Highld 311 J2
Backlass Highld 310 D6
Highld 310 E4
Back Muir Fife 279 D11
Back of Keppoch Highld 295 G8
Back o' th' Brook Staffs 169 E9
Back Rogerton E Ayrs 258 E3
Back Street Suff 124 F4
Backwell N Som 60 F3
Backwell Common
N Som 60 F3
Backwell Green N Som 60 F3
Backworth T&W 243 C8
Bacon End Essex 87 B10
Baconend Green Essex 87 B10
Bacon's End W Mid 134 F3
Baconsthorpe Norf 160 B2
Bacton Hereford 97 E7
Norf 160 C6
Suff 125 D11
Bacton Green Norf 160 C6
Suff 125 D10
Bacup Lancs 195 C11
Badachonacher Highld 300 B6
Badachro Highld 299 B7
Badanloch Lodge Highld 308 F7
Badarach Highld 309 K5
Badavanich Highld 299 D11
Badbea Highld 307 K5
Badbury Swindon 63 C7
Badbury Wick Swindon 63 C7
Badby W Nhants 119 F11
Badcall Highld 306 D7
Badcaul Highld 307 K5
Baddeley Edge Stoke 168 E6
Baddeley Green Stoke 168 E6
Baddesley Clinton
Warks 118 C4
Baddesley Ensor Warks 134 D5
Baddidarach Highld 307 G5
Baddoch Aberds 292 E3
Baddock Highld 301 D7
Baddow Park Essex 88 E2
Badeach Moray 302 F2
Badenscallie Highld 307 J5
Badenscoth Aberds 303 F7
Badentoy Park Aberds 293 D11
Badenyon Aberds 292 B5
Badgall Corn 11 D10
Badgeney Cambs 139 D8
Badger Shrops 132 D5
Badgergate Stirling 278 B5
Badger's Hill Worcs 99 B10
Badger's Mount Kent 68 G3
Badger Street Som 28 D3
Badgeworth Glos 80 B6
Badgworth Som 43 C11
Badharlick Corn 11 D11
Badicaul Highld 295 C9
Badingham Suff 126 D6
Badintagairt Highld 309 H4
Badlesmere Kent 54 C4
Badlipster Highld 310 E6
Badluarach Highld 307 K4
Badminton S Glos 61 C10
Badnaban Highld 307 G5
Badnabay Highld 306 E7
Badnagie Highld 310 F5
Badninish Highld 309 K7
Badrallach Highld 307 K5
Badsey Worcs 99 C11
Badshalloch W Dunb 277 D9
Badshot Lea Sur 49 D11
Badsworth W Yorks 198 E3
Badwell Ash Suff 125 D9
Badwell Green Suff 125 D10
Badworthy Devon 8 C3
Bae Cinmel = Kinmel Bay
Conwy 181 E7
Bae Colwyn = Colwyn Bay
Conwy 180 F4
Bae Penrhyn = Penrhyn Bay
Conwy 180 E4
Baffins Ptsmth 33 G11
Bagber Dorset 30 E3
Bagby N Yorks 215 C9
Bagby Grange N Yorks 215 C9
Bag Enderby Lincs 190 G5
Bagendon Glos 81 D8
Bagginswood Shrops 132 G3
Baggrow Cumb 229 C9
Bàgha Chàise W Isles 296 D5
Bagh a Chaisteil
W Isles 297 M2
Bagham Kent 54 C5
Baghasdal W Isles 297 K3
Bagh Mor W Isles 296 F4
Bagh Shiarabhagh
W Isles 297 L3
Bagillt Flint 182 F2
Baginton Warks 118 C6
Baglan Neath 57 C8
Bagley Shrops 149 D8
Som 44 D3
W Yorks 205 F10
Bagley Green Som 27 D10
Bagley Marsh Shrops 149 D7
Bagmore Hants 49 E7
Bagnall Staffs 168 E6
Bagnor W Berks 64 F3
Bagpath Glos 80 E5
Glos 80 G4
Bagshaw Derbys 185 E9
Bagshot Sur 66 G2
Wilts 63 F10
Bagshot Heath Sur 66 G2
Bagslate Moor
Gtr Man 195 E11
Bagstone S Glos 61 B7
Bagthorpe Norf 158 C5
Notts 171 E7
Baguley Gtr Man 184 D4
Bagworth Leics 135 B8
Bagwyllydiart Hereford 97 F8
Bagwy Llydiart Hereford 97 F8
Bail Ard Bhuirgh
W Isles 304 C6
Bailbrook Bath 61 F9
Baildon W Yorks 205 F9
Baildon Green W Yorks 205 F8
Baile W Isles 296 C5
Baile Ailein W Isles 304 F4
Baile a Mhanaich
W Isles 296 F3
Baile an Truiseil
W Isles 304 C5
Bailebeag Highld 291 B7
Baile Boidheach Argyll 275 F8
Baile Gharbhaidh
W Isles 297 G3
Baile Glas W Isles 296 F4
Baile Mhartainn
W Isles 296 D3
Baile Mhic Phail
W Isles 296 D4
Baile Mor Argyll 288 G4
W Isles 296 E3
Baile na Creige W Isles 297 L2
Baile nan Cailleach
W Isles 296 F3
Baile Raghaill W Isles 296 D3
Bailey Green Hants 33 B11
Baileyhead Cumb 240 B2
Bailiesward Aberds 302 F4
Bailiff Bridge W Yorks 196 C6
Baillieston Glasgow 268 C3
Bail' Iochdrach W Isles 296 F4
Bailrigg Lancs 202 B5
Bail Uachdraich
W Isles 296 E4
Bail' Ur Tholastaidh
W Isles 304 D7
Bainbridge N Yorks 223 G8
Bainsford Falk 279 E7
Bainshole Aberds 302 F6
Bainton E Yorks 208 C5
Oxon 101 F11
Pboro 137 B11
Baintown Fife 287 G7
Bairnkine Borders 262 F5
Baker's Cross Kent 53 F9
Bakers End Herts 86 B5
Baker's Hill Glos 79 C9
Baker Street Thurrock 68 C6
Baker's Wood Bucks 66 B4
Bakesdown Corn 24 G2
Bakestone Moor Derbys 187 F8
Bakewell Derbys 170 B2
Bala = Y Bala Gwyn 147 B8
Balachroick Highld 291 C10
Balachuirn Highld 298 E5
Balance Hill Staffs 151 C11
Balavil Highld 291 C9
Balavoulin Perth 291 G10
Balbeg Highld 300 F4
Highld 300 G4
Balbeggie Perth 286 E5
Balbegno Castle Aberds 293 F8
Balbithan Aberds 293 B9
Balbithan Ho Aberds 293 B10
Balblair Highld 300 E5
Highld 301 C7
Highld 309 K5
Balby S Yorks 198 G5
Balcherry Highld 311 L2
Balchladich Highld 306 F5
Balchraggan Highld 300 E5
Highld 300 F5
Highld 300 G5
Balchrick Highld 306 D6
Balchrystie Fife 287 G8
Balcladaich Highld 300 G2
Balcombe W Sus 51 G10
Balcombe Lane W Sus 51 G10
Balcomie Fife 287 F10
Balcraggie Lodge Highld 310 F5
Balcurvie Fife 287 G7
Baldersby N Yorks 215 D7
Baldersby St James
N Yorks 215 D7
Balderstone Gtr Man 196 E2
Lancs 203 G8
Balderton Ches W 166 C5
Notts 172 E4
Baldhu Corn 4 G5
Baldingstone Gtr Man 195 E10
Baldinnie Fife 287 F8
Baldock Herts 104 E4
Baldon Row Oxon 83 E9
Baldoon Highld 300 B6
Baldovie Dundee 287 D8
Baldrine IoM 192 D5
Baldslow E Sus 38 E3
Baldwin IoM 192 D4
Baldwinholme Cumb 239 G8
Baldwin's Gate Staffs 168 G3
Baldwins Hill W Sus 51 F11
Bale Norf 159 B10
Balearn Aberds 303 D10
Balemartine Argyll 288 E1
Balephuil Argyll 288 E1
Balerno Edin 270 B3
Balerominhor Argyll 274 D4
Balevullin Argyll 288 E1
Balfield Angus 293 G7
Balfour Orkney 314 E4
Balfour Mains Orkney 314 E4
Balfron Stirling 277 D10
Balfron Station Stirling 277 D10
Balgaveny Aberds 302 E6
Balgavies Angus 287 B9
Balgonar Fife 279 C10
Balgove Aberds 303 F8
Balgowan Highld 291 D8
Perth 286 E3
Balgown Highld 298 C3
Balgrennie Aberds 292 C6
Balgrochan E Dunb 278 F2
Balgy Highld 299 D8
Balhaldie Stirling 286 G2
Balhalgardy Aberds 303 G7
Balham London 67 E9
Balhary Perth 286 C6
Baliasta Shetland 312 C8
Baligill Highld 310 C2
Baligortan Argyll 288 E5
Baligrundle Argyll 289 E10
Balindore Argyll 289 F11
Balinoe Argyll 288 E1
Balintore Angus 286 B6
Highld 301 B8
Balintraid Highld 301 B7
Balintuim Aberds 292 E3
Balk N Yorks 215 C9
Balkeerie Angus 287 C7
Balkemback Angus 287 D7
Balk Field Notts 188 E2
Balkholme E Yorks 199 B9
Balkissock S Ayrs 244 G4
Ball Corn 10 G6
Shrops 148 D6
Ballabeg IoM 192 E3
Ballacannel IoM 192 D5
Ballachraggan Moray 301 E11
Ballachrochin Highld 301 F8
Ballachulish Highld 284 B4
Balladen Lancs 195 C10
Ballajora IoM 192 C5
Ballaleigh IoM 192 D4
Ballamodha IoM 192 E3
Ballantrae S Ayrs 244 G3
Ballaquine IoM 192 D5
Ballard's Ash Wilts 62 C5
Ballards Gore Essex 88 G6
Ballard's Green Warks 134 E5
Ballasalla IoM 192 C4
IoM 192 E3
Ballater Aberds 292 D5
Ballathie Perth 286 D5
Ballaugh IoM 192 C4
Ballaveare IoM 192 E4
Ballcorach Moray 301 G11
Ballechin Perth 286 B3
Balleich Stirling 277 B10
Balleigh Highld 309 L7
Ballencrieff E Loth 281 F9
Ballencrieff Toll
W Loth 279 G9
Ballentoul Perth 291 G10
Ball Green Stoke 168 E5
Ball Haye Green Staffs 169 D7
Ballhill Devon 24 C3
Ball Hill Hants 64 G2
Ballidon Derbys 170 E2
Balliekine N Ayrs 255 D9
Balliemore Argyll 275 E11
Argyll 289 G10
Ballikinrain Stirling 277 D11
Ballimeanoch Argyll 284 F4
Ballimore Argyll 275 E10
Stirling 285 F9
Ballinaby Argyll 274 G3
Ballinbreich Fife 286 E6
Ballindean Perth 286 E6
Ballingdon Suff 107 C7
Ballingdon Bottom Herts 85 C8
Ballinger Bottom Bucks 84 E6
Ballinger Bottom (South)
Bucks 84 E6
Ballinger Common Bucks 84 E6
Ballingham Hereford 97 E11
Ballingham Hill Hereford 97 E11
Ballingry Fife 280 B3
Ballinlick Perth 286 C3
Ballinluig Perth 286 B3
Ballintean Highld 291 C10
Ballintuim Perth 286 B5
Balliveolan Argyll 289 E10
Balloch Angus 287 B7
Highld 301 E7
N Lanark 278 G4
W Dunb 277 E7
Ballochan Aberds 293 D7
Ballochearn Stirling 277 D11
Ballochford Moray 302 F3
Ballochmorrie S Ayrs 244 G6
Ball o'Ditton Halton 183 D7
Ballogie Aberds 293 D7
Balls Cross W Sus 35 B7
Balls Green Essex 107 G11
E Sus 52 F3
W Sus 35 C10
Ball's Green Glos 80 F5
Balls Hill W Mid 133 E9
Ballygown Argyll 288 E6
Ballygrant Argyll 274 G4
Ballygroggan Argyll 255 F7
Ballyhaugh Argyll 288 D3
Balmacara Highld 295 C10
Balmacara Square
Highld 295 C10
Balmaclellan Dumfries 237 B8
Balmacneil Perth 286 B3
Balmacqueen Highld 298 B4
Balmae Dumfries 237 E8
Balmaha Stirling 277 C8
Balmalcolm Fife 287 G7
Balmalloch N Lanark 278 F4
Balmeanach Argyll 288 F6
Argyll 289 E8
Highld 295 B7
Highld 298 E3
Highld 298 E5
Balmedie Aberds 293 B11
Balmer Shrops 149 C8
Balmer Heath Shrops 149 C8
Balmerino Fife 287 E7
Balmerlawn Hants 32 G4
Balmesh Dumfries 236 D3
Balmichael N Ayrs 255 D10
Balminnoch Dumfries 236 C4
Balmirmer Angus 287 D9
Balmoral Borders 261 B11
Balmore E Dunb 278 G2
Highld 298 E2
Highld 300 F3
Highld 301 E8
Perth 286 B3
Balmule Fife 280 D4
Balmullo Fife 287 E8
Balmungie Highld 301 D7
Balmurrie Dumfries 236 C4
Balnaboth Angus 292 G5
Balnabreich Moray 302 D3
Balnabruaich Highld 301 C7
Balnabruich Highld 311 G5
Balnacarn Highld 290 B4
Balnacoil Highld 311 H2
Balnacra Highld 299 E9
Balnacruie Highld 301 G9
Balnafoich Highld 300 F6
Balnagall Highld 311 L2
Balnagowan Aberds 293 C7
Balnagrantach Highld 300 F4
Balnaguard Perth 286 B3
Balnahanaid Perth 285 C10
Balnahard Argyll 274 D5
Argyll 288 F6
Balnain Highld 300 F4
Balnakeil Highld 308 C3
Balnakelly Aberds 293 B7
Balnaknock Highld 298 C4
Balnamoon Aberds 303 D9
Angus 293 G7
Balnapaling Highld 301 C7
Balne N Yorks 198 D5
Balnoon Corn 2 B2
Balochroy Argyll 255 B8
Balole Argyll 274 G4
Balone Fife 287 F8
Balornock Glasgow 268 B2
Balquharn Perth 286 D4
Balquhidder Stirling 285 E9
Balquhidder Station
Stirling 285 E9
Balquhindachy Aberds 303 E8
Balrownie Angus 293 G7
Balsall W Mid 118 B4
Balsall Common W Mid 118 B4
Balsall Heath W Mid 133 G11
Balsall Street W Mid 118 B4
Balsam Cambs 123 G11
Balscote Oxon 101 C7
Balscott Oxon 101 C7
Balsham Cambs 123 G11
Balsporran Cottages
Highld 291 F8
Balstonia Thurrock 69 C7
Baltasound Shetland 312 C8
Balterley Staffs 168 E3
Balterley Green Staffs 168 E3
Balterley Heath Staffs 168 E2
Baltersan Dumfries 236 C6
Balthangie Aberds 303 D8
Balthayock Perth 286 E5
Baltonsborough Som 44 G4
Balure Argyll 289 E11
Balvaird Highld 300 D5
Balvenie Moray 302 E3
Balvicar Argyll 275 B8
Balvraid Highld 295 D10
Highld 301 F8
Balwest Corn 2 C3
Bamber Bridge Lancs 194 B5
Bamber's Green Essex 105 G11
Bamburgh Northumb 264 C5
Bamff Perth 286 B6
Bamford Derbys 186 E2
Gtr Man 195 E11
Bamfurlong Glos 99 G8
Gtr Man 194 G5
Bampton Cumb 221 B10
Devon 27 C7
Oxon 82 E4
Bampton Grange Cumb 221 B10
Banavie Highld 290 F3
Banbury Oxon 101 C9
Bancffosfelen Carms 75 C7
Banchor Highld 301 E9
Banchory Aberds 293 D8
Banchory-Devenick
Aberds 293 C11
Bancycapel Carms 74 B6
Banc-y-Darren Ceredig 128 G3
Bancyfelin Carms 74 B4
Bancyffordd Carms 93 D8
Bandirran Perth 286 D6
Bandonhill London 67 G9
Bandrake Head Cumb 210 B6
Banff Aberds 302 C6
Bangor Gwyn 179 G9
Bangor is y coed = Bangor
on Dee Wrex 166 F5
Bangor on Dee = Bangor-is-
y-coed Wrex 166 F5
Bangors Corn 11 B10
Bangor Teifi Ceredig 93 C7
Banham Norf 141 F11
Bank Hants 32 F3
Bankend Dumfries 238 D2
Bank End Cumb 210 B3
Cumb 228 D6
Bank Fold Blackburn 195 C8
Bankfoot Perth 286 D4
Bankglen E Ayrs 258 G4
Bankhead Aberdeen 293 B10
Aberds 293 C8
Dumfries 236 C2
Falk 278 E6
S Lanark 269 G7
Bank Hey Blackburn 203 G9
Bank Houses Lancs 202 C4
Bankland Som 28 B4
Bank Lane Gtr Man 195 D9
Bank Newton N Yorks 204 C4
Banknock Falk 278 F5
Banks Cumb 240 E3
Lancs 193 C11
Orkney 314 C4
Bank's Green Worcs 117 D9
Bankshead Shrops 130 F6
Bankshill Dumfries 248 G5
Bankside Falk 279 E7
Bank Street Worcs 116 E2
Bank Top Gtr Man 195 E8
Lancs 194 F4
Stoke 168 E5
T&W 242 D4
W Yorks 196 C6
W Yorks 205 F9
Banners Gate W Mid 133 D11
Banningham Norf 160 D4
Banniskirk Ho Highld 310 D5
Banniskirk Mains Highld 310 D5
Bannister Green Essex 106 G3
Bannockburn Stirling 278 C5
Banns Corn 4 F4
Banstead Sur 51 B8
Bantam Grove W Yorks 197 B9
Bantaskin Falk 279 F7
Bantham Devon 8 G3
Banton N Lanark 278 F5
Banwell N Som 43 B11
Banyard's Green Suff 126 C5
Bapchild Kent 70 G2
Baptist End W Mid 133 F8
Bapton Wilts 46 F3
Barabhas W Isles 304 D5
Barabhas Iarach
W Isles 304 D5
Barabhas Uarach
W Isles 304 C5
Barachandroman Argyll 289 G8
Baramore Highld 289 B8
Barassie S Ayrs 257 C8
Baravullin Argyll 289 F10
Barbadoes Stirling 277 B11
Barbaraville Highld 301 B7
Barbauchlaw W Loth 269 B8
Barber Booth Derbys 185 E10
Barber Green Cumb 211 C7
Barber's Moor Lancs 194 D3
Barbican Plym 7 E9
Barbieston S Ayrs 257 F10
Barbon Cumb 212 C2
Barbourne Worcs 116 F6
Barbreck Ho Argyll 275 C9
Barbridge Ches E 167 D10
Barbrook Devon 41 D8
Barby W Nhants 119 C10
Barby Nortoft
W Nhants 119 C11
Barcaldine Argyll 289 E11
Barcelona Corn 6 E4
Barcheston Warks 100 D5
Barclose Cumb 239 E10
Barcombe E Sus 36 E6
Barcombe Cross E Sus 36 D6
Barcroft W Yorks 204 F6
Barden N Yorks 224 G2
Bardennoch Dumfries 246 E3
Barden Park Kent 52 D5
Barden Scale N Yorks 205 B7
Bardfield End Green
Essex 106 E2
Bardfield Saling Essex 106 F3
Bardister Shetland 312 F5
Bardnabeinne Highld 309 K7
Bardney Lincs 173 B10
Bardon Leics 153 G8
Bardon Mill Northumb 241 E7
Bardowie E Dunb 277 G11
Bardown E Sus 37 B11
Bardrainney Invclyd 276 G6
Bardrishaig Argyll 275 B8
Bardsea Cumb 210 E6
Bardsey W Yorks 206 E3
Bardsley Gtr Man 196 G2
Bardwell Suff 125 C8
Bare Lancs 211 G9
Bare Ash Som 43 F9
Bareless Northumb 263 B9
Bar End Hants 33 B7
Barepot Cumb 228 F6
Bareppa Corn 3 D7
Barfad Argyll 275 G9
Dumfries 236 C5
Barford Norf 142 B2
Sur 49 F11
Warks 118 E5
Barford St John Oxon 101 E8
Barford St Martin Wilts 46 G5
Barford St Michael
Oxon 101 E8
Barfrestone Kent 55 C9
Bargaly Dumfries 236 C6
Bargarran Renfs 277 G9
Bargate Derbys 170 F5
Bargeddie N Lanark 268 C4
Bargoed Caerph 77 F10
Bargrennan Dumfries 236 B5
Barham Cambs 122 B2
Kent 55 C8
Suff 126 G2
Barharrow Dumfries 237 D8
Barhill Dumfries 237 C10
Bar Hill Cambs 123 E7
Staffs 168 G3
Barholm Dumfries 237 D7
Lincs 155 G11
Barkby Leics 136 B2
Barkby Thorpe Leics 136 B2
Barkers Green Shrops 149 D10
Barkers Hill Wilts 30 B6
Barkestone-le-Vale
Leics 154 C5
Barkham Wokingham 65 F9
Barking London 68 C2
Suff 125 G11
Barking Riverside London 68 C3
Barkingside London 68 B2
Barking Tye Suff 125 G11
Barkisland W Yorks 196 D5
Barkla Shop Corn 4 E4
Barkston Lincs 172 G6
N Yorks 206 F5
Barkston Ash N Yorks 206 F5
Barkway Herts 105 D7
Barlake Som 45 D7
Barlanark Glasgow 268 C3
Barland Powys 114 E5
Barland Common
Swansea 56 D5
Barlaston Staffs 151 B7
Barlavington W Sus 35 D7
Barlborough Derbys 187 F7
Barlby N Yorks 207 G8
Barlestone Leics 135 B8
Barley Herts 105 D7
Lancs 204 E2
Barleycroft End Herts 105 F8
Barley End Bucks 85 C7
Barley Green Lancs 204 E2
Barley Mow T&W 243 G7
Barleythorpe Rutland 136 B6
Barling Essex 70 B2
Barlings Lincs 189 G9
Barlow Derbys 186 G4
N Yorks 198 B6
T&W 242 E5
Barlow Moor Gtr Man 184 C4
Barmby Moor E Yorks 207 D11
Barmby on the Marsh
E Yorks 199 B7
Barmer Norf 158 C6
Barming Heath Kent 53 B8
Barmolloch Argyll 275 D9
Bar Moor T&W 242 E4
Barmoor Castle
Northumb 263 B11
Barmoor Lane End
Northumb 264 B2
Barmouth = Abermaw
Gwyn 146 F2
Barmpton Darl 224 B6
Barmston E Yorks 209 B9
T&W 243 F8
Barmulloch Glasgow 268 B2
Barnaby Green Suff 127 B9
Barnacabber Argyll 276 D3
Barnack Pboro 137 B11
Barnacle Warks 135 G7
Barnaline Argyll 275 B10
Barnard Castle Durham 223 B11
Barnard Gate Oxon 82 C6
Barnardiston Suff 106 B4
Barnard's Green Worcs 98 B5
Barnardtown Newport 59 B10
Barnbarroch Dumfries 237 D10
Barnbow Carr W Yorks 206 F3
Barnburgh S Yorks 198 G3
Barnby Suff 143 F9
Barnby Dun S Yorks 198 F6
Barnby in the Willows
Notts 172 E5
Barnby Moor Notts 187 E11
Barncluith S Lanark 268 E4
Barndennoch Dumfries 247 F9
Barne Barton Plym 7 D8
Barnehurst London 68 D4
Barnes Cray London 68 D4
Barnes Hall S Yorks 186 B4
Barnes Street Kent 52 D6
Barnet London 86 F2
Barnetby le Wold
N Lincs 200 F5
Barnet Gate London 86 F2
Barnettbrook Worcs 117 B7
Barnett Brook Ches E 167 G10
Barney Norf 159 C9
Barnfield Kent 54 D2
Barnfields Hereford 97 C9
Staffs 169 D7
Barnham Suff 125 B7
W Sus 35 G7
Barnham Broom Norf 141 B11
Barnhead Angus 287 B10
Barnhill Ches W 167 E7
Dundee 287 D8
Moray 301 D11
Barnhills Dumfries 236 B1
Barningham Durham 223 C11
Suff 125 B9
Barningham Green Norf 160 C2
Barnmoor Green Warks 118 E3
Barnoldby le Beck
NE Lincs 201 G8
Barnoldswick Lancs 204 D3
N Yorks 212 E4
Barns Borders 260 B6
Barnsbury London 67 C10
Barnsdale Rutland 137 B8
Barns Green W Sus 35 B10
Barnside W Yorks 197 F7
Barnsley Glos 81 D9
Shrops 132 E5
S Yorks 197 F10
Barnsole Kent 55 B9
Barnstaple Devon 40 G5
Barnston Essex 87 B10
Mers 182 E3
Barnstone Notts 154 B4
Barnt Green Worcs 117 C10
Barnton Ches W 183 F10
Edin 280 F3
Barnwell N Nhants 137 G10
Barnwell All Saints
N Nhants 137 G10
Barnwell St Andrew
N Nhants 137 F10
Barnwood Glos 80 B5
Barochreal Argyll 289 G10
Barons Cross Hereford 115 F9
Barr Highld 289 D8
S Ayrs 245 E7
Som 27 C11
Barra Castle Aberds 303 G7
Barrachan Dumfries 236 E5
Barrachnie Glasgow 268 C3
Barrack Aberds 303 E8
Barrack Hill Newport 59 B10
Barraer Dumfries 236 C5
Barraglom W Isles 304 E3
Barrahormid Argyll 275 E8
Barran Argyll 289 G10
Barranrioch Argyll 289 G10
Barrapol Argyll 288 E1
Barras Aberds 293 E10
Cumb 222 C6
Barrasford Northumb 241 C10
Barravullin Argyll 275 C9
Barr Common W Mid 133 D11
Barregarrow IoM 192 D4
Barrets Green Ches E 167 D9
Barrhead E Renf 267 D9
Barrhill S Ayrs 244 G6
Barrington Cambs 105 B7
Som 28 D5
Barripper Corn 2 B4
Barrmill N Ayrs 267 E7
Barrock Highld 310 B6
Barrock Ho Highld 310 C6
Barrow Glos 99 G7
Lancs 203 F10
Rutland 155 F7
Shrops 132 C3
Som 44 E5
Suff 124 E5
S Yorks 186 B5
Barroway Drove Norf 139 C11
Barrow Bridge Gtr Man 195 E7
Barrowburn Northumb 263 G9
Barrow Burn Northumb 263 G9
Barrowby Lincs 155 B7
Barrowcliff N Yorks 217 B10
Barrow Common N Som 60 F4
Barrowden Rutland 137 C8
Barrowford Lancs 204 F3
Barrow Green Kent 70 G3
Barrow Gurney N Som 60 F4
Barrow Hann N Lincs 200 C5
Barrow Haven N Lincs 200 C5
Barrowhill Kent 54 F6
Barrow Hill Derbys 186 F6
Dorset 18 B5
Barrow-in-Furness
Cumb 210 F4
Barrow Island Cumb 210 F3
Barrowmore Estate
Ches W 167 B7
Barrow Nook Lancs 194 G2
Barrows Green Ches E 167 D11
Cumb 211 B10
Notts 171 E7
Barrow's Green Mers 183 D8
Barrow Street Wilts 45 G10
Barrow upon Humber
N Lincs 200 C5
Barrow upon Soar
Leics 153 F11
Barrow upon Trent
Derbys 153 D7
Barrow Vale Bath 60 G6
Barrow Wake Glos 80 B6
Barry Angus 287 D9
V Glam 58 F6
Barry Dock V Glam 58 F6
Barry Island V Glam 58 F6
Barsby Leics 154 G3
Barsham Suff 143 F7
Barshare E Ayrs 258 F3
Barstable Essex 69 B8
Barston W Mid 118 B4
Bartestree Hereford 97 C11
Barthol Chapel Aberds 303 F8
Bartholomew Green
Essex 106 G4
Barthomley Ches E 168 E3
Bartington Ches W 183 F10
Bartley Hants 32 E4
Bartley Green W Mid 133 G10
Bartlow Cambs 105 B11
Barton Cambs 123 F8
Ches W 166 E6
Glos 80 B4
Glos 99 F11
IoW 20 D6
Lancs 193 F11
Lancs 202 F6
N Som 43 B11
N Yorks 224 D4
Oxon 83 D9
Torbay 9 B8
Warks 118 G2
Barton Abbey Oxon 101 G9
Barton Bendish Norf 140 B4
Barton Court Hereford 98 C4
Barton End Glos 80 F4
Barton Gate Devon 41 E7
Staffs 152 F3
Barton Green Staffs 152 F3
Barton Hartshorn Bucks 102 E2
Barton Hill Bristol 60 E6
N Yorks 216 G4
Barton in Fabis Notts 153 C10
Barton in the Beans
Leics 135 B7
Barton-le-Clay C Beds 103 E11
Barton-le-Street
N Yorks 216 E4
Barton-le-Willows
N Yorks 216 G4
Barton Mills Suff 124 C4
Barton on Sea Hants 19 C10
Barton on the Heath
Warks 100 E5
Barton St David Som 44 G4
Barton Seagrave
N Nhants 121 B7
Bartonsham Hereford 97 D10
Barton Stacey Hants 48 E2
Barton Town Devon 41 E7
Barton Turf Norf 161 E7
Barton Turn Staffs 152 F4
Barton-under-Needwood
Staffs 152 F3
Barton-upon-Humber
N Lincs 200 C4
Barton Upon Irwell
Gtr Man 184 B3
Barton Waterside
N Lincs 200 C4
Barugh S Yorks 197 F10
Barugh Green S Yorks 197 F10
Barway Cambs 123 B10
Barwell Leics 135 D8
London 67 G7
Barwick Devon 25 F9
Herts 86 B5
Som 29 E9
Barwick in Elmet
W Yorks 206 F3
Baschurch Shrops 149 E8
Bascote Warks 119 E8
Bascote Heath Warks 119 E7
Base Green Suff 125 E10
Basford Shrops 131 F7
Staffs 168 F5
Basford Green Staffs 169 E7
Bashall Eaves Lancs 203 E9
Bashley Hants 19 B10
Bashley Park Hants 19 B10
Basildon Essex 69 B8
Basingstoke Hants 48 C6
Baslow Derbys 186 G3
Bason Bridge Som 43 D10
Bassaleg Newport 59 B9
Bassenthwaite Cumb 229 E10
Bassett Soton 32 D6
S Yorks 186 E3
Bassett Green Soton 32 D6
Bassingbourn Cambs 104 C6
Bassingfield Notts 154 B2
Bassingham Lincs 172 C6
Bassingthorpe Lincs 155 D9
Bassus Green Herts 104 F6
Basta Shetland 312 D7
Basted Kent 52 B6
Baston Lincs 156 G2
Bastonford Worcs 116 G6
Bastwick Norf 161 F8
Baswich Staffs 151 E8
Baswick Steer E Yorks 209 D7
Batavaime Stirling 285 D8
Batch Som 43 B10
Batchcott Shrops 115 C9
Batchfields Hereford 98 B3
Batchley Worcs 117 D10
Batchworth Herts 85 G9
Batchworth Heath Herts 85 G9
Batcombe Dorset 29 G10
Som 45 F7
Bate Heath Ches E 183 F11
Bateman's Green
Worcs 117 B11
Bateman's Hill Pembs 73 E8
Batemoor S Yorks 186 E5
Batford Herts 85 B10
Bath Bath 61 F8
Bathampton Bath 61 F9
Bathealton Som 27 C9
Batheaston Bath 61 F9
Bathford Bath 61 F9
Bathgate W Loth 269 B9
Bathley Notts 172 D3
Bathpool Corn 11 G11
Som 28 B3
Bath Side Essex 108 E5
Bath Vale Ches E 168 C5
Bathville W Loth 269 B8
Bathway Som 44 C5
Bathwick Bath 61 F9
Batlers Green Herts 85 F11
Batley W Yorks 197 C8
Batley Carr W Yorks 197 C8
Batsford Glos 100 E3
Batson Devon 9 G9
Batsworthy Devon 26 D4
Batten's Green Som 28 D3
Battenton Green Worcs 116 D6
Battersby N Yorks 225 D11
Battersea London 67 D9
Battisborough Cross
Devon 7 F11
Battisford Suff 125 G11
Battisford Tye Suff 125 G10
Battle E Sus 38 D2
Powys 95 E10
Battledown Glos 99 G9
Battledown Cross Devon 25 F7
Battlefield Shrops 149 F10
Battlesbridge Essex 88 G3
Battlescombe Glos 80 D6
Battlesden C Beds 103 F9
Battlesea Green Suff 126 B4
Battleton Som 26 B6
Battlies Green Suff 125 E7
Battram Leics 135 B8
Battramsley Hants 20 B2
Battramsley Cross Hants 20 B2
Batt's Corner Hants 49 E10
Battyeford W Yorks 197 C7
Batworthy Devon 13 D10
Bauds of Cullen Moray 302 C4
Baugh Argyll 288 E2
Baughton Worcs 99 C7
Baughurst Hants 48 B5
Baulking Oxon 82 G4
Baumber Lincs 190 G2
Baunton Glos 81 E8
Baverstock Wilts 46 G4
Bawburgh Norf 142 B3
Bawdeswell Norf 159 E10
Bawdrip Som 43 F10
Bawdsey Suff 108 C6
Bawsey Norf 158 F3
Bawtry S Yorks 187 C11
Baxenden Lancs 195 B9
Baxterley Warks 134 D5
Baxter's Green Suff 124 F5
Bay Dorset 30 B4
Highld 298 D2
Baybridge Hants 33 C8
Northumb 241 G11
Baycliff Cumb 210 E5
Baydon Wilts 63 D9
Bayford Herts 86 D4
Som 30 B2
Bay Gate Lancs 203 D11
Bay Horse Lancs 202 C5
Bayles Cumb 231 C10
Bayley's Hill Kent 52 C4
Baylham Suff 126 G2
Baylis Green Worcs 117 C11
Baynard's Green Oxon 101 F10
Baynhall Worcs 99 B7
Baysdale Abbey N Yorks 225 D11
Baysham Hereford 97 F11
Bayston Hill Shrops 131 B9
Bayswater London 67 C9
Baythorne End Essex 106 C4
Baythorpe Lincs 174 G2
Bayton Worcs 116 C3
Bayton Common Worcs 116 C4
Bay View Kent 70 E4
Bayworth Oxon 83 E8
Beach Highld 289 D9
S Glos 61 E8
Beachampton Bucks 102 D5
Beachamwell Norf 140 B5
Beachans Moray 301 E10
Beacharr Argyll 255 C7
Beachborough Kent 55 F7
Beach Hay Worcs 116 C4
Beachlands E Sus 23 E11
Beachley Glos 79 G9
Beacon Corn 2 B5
Devon 27 F11
Devon 28 F2
Beacon Down E Sus 37 C9
Beacon End Essex 107 G9
Beaconhill Northumb 243 B7
Beacon Hill Bath 61 F9
Bucks 84 G6
Cumb 210 E4
Dorset 18 C5
Essex 88 C5
Kent 53 G10
Notts 172 E4
Suff 108 B4
Sur 49 F11
Beacon Lough T&W 243 F7
Beacon's Bottom Bucks 84 F3
Beaconsfield Bucks 66 B2
Beaconside Staffs 151 E8
Beacrabhaic W Isles 305 J3
Beadlam N Yorks 216 C3
Beadlow C Beds 104 D2
Beadnell Northumb 264 D6
Beaford Devon 25 E9
Beal Northumb 273 G11
N Yorks 198 B4
Bealach Highld 289 D11
Bealach Maim Argyll 275 E10
Bealbury Corn 7 B7
Beal's Green Kent 53 G9
Bealsmill Corn 12 F3
Beambridge Shrops 131 F10
Beam Bridge Som 27 D10
Beam Hill Staffs 152 D4
Beamhurst Staffs 151 B11
Beamhurst Lane Staffs 151 B11
Beaminster Dorset 29 G7
Beamish Durham 242 G6
Beamond End Bucks 84 F6
Beamsley N Yorks 205 C7
Bean Kent 68 E5
Beanacre Wilts 62 F2
Beancross Falk 279 F8
Beanhill M Keynes 103 D7
Beanley Northumb 264 F3
Beansburn E Ayrs 257 B10
Beanthwaite Cumb 210 C4
Beaquoy Orkney 314 D3
Bear Cross BCP 19 B7
Beard Hill Som 44 E6
Beardly Batch Som 44 E6
Beardwood Blackburn 195 B7
Beare Devon 27 G7
Beare Green Sur 51 E7
Bearley Warks 118 E3
Bearley Cross Warks 118 E3
Bearnus Argyll 288 E5
Bearpark Durham 233 C10
Bearsbridge Northumb 241 F7
Bearsden E Dunb 277 G10
Bearsted Kent 53 B9
Bearstone Shrops 150 B4
Bearwood BCP 18 B6
Hereford 115 F7
W Mid 133 F10
Beasley Staffs 168 F4
Beattock Dumfries 248 C3
Beauchamp Roding
Essex 87 C9
Beauchief S Yorks 186 E4
Beauclerc Northumb 242 E2
Beaudesert Warks 118 D3
Beaufort Bl Gwent 77 C11
Beaufort Castle Highld 300 E5
Beaulieu Hants 32 G5
Beaulieu Park Essex 88 C2
Beaulieu Wood Dorset 30 F2
Beauly Highld 300 E5
Beaumaris Anglesey 179 F10
Beaumont Cumb 239 F8
Essex 108 G3
Windsor 66 E3
Beaumont Hill Darl 224 B5
Beaumont Leys
Leicester 135 B11
Beausale Warks 118 C4
Beauvale Notts 171 F8
Beauworth Hants 33 B9
Beavan's Hill Hereford 98 G3
Beaworthy Devon 12 B5
Beazley End Essex 106 F4
Bebington Mers 182 E4
Bebside Northumb 253 G7
Beccles Suff 143 E8
Becconsall Lancs 194 C2
Beck Bottom Cumb 210 C5
W Yorks 197 C10
Beckbury Shrops 132 C5
Beckces Cumb 230 F4
Beckenham London 67 F11
Beckermet Cumb 219 D10
Beckermonds N Yorks 213 C7
Beckery Som 44 F3
Beckett End Norf 140 D5
Beckfoot Cumb 220 E3
Cumb 229 B7
Beck Foot Cumb 222 F2
W Yorks 205 F8
Beckford Worcs 99 D9
Beckhampton Wilts 62 F5
Beck Head Cumb 211 C8
Beck Hole N Yorks 226 E6
Beck Houses Cumb 221 F11
Beckingham Lincs 172 E5
Notts 188 D3
Beckington Som 45 C10
Beckjay Shrops 115 B7
Beckley E Sus 38 C5
Hants 19 B10
Oxon 83 C9
Beckley Furnace E Sus 38 C4
Beck Row Suff 124 B3
Beckside Cumb 212 B2
Beck Side Cumb 210 C4
Cumb 211 C7
Beckton London 68 C2
Beckwith N Yorks 205 C11
Beckwithshaw N Yorks 205 C11
Becontree London 68 B3
Bedale N Yorks 214 B5
Bedburn Durham 233 E8
Bedchester Dorset 30 D5
Beddau Rhondda 58 B5
Beddgelert Gwyn 163 F9
Beddingham E Sus 36 F6
Beddington London 67 G10
Beddington Corner
London 67 F9
Bedfield Suff 126 D4
Bedford Bedford 121 G11
Gtr Man 183 B11
Bedford Park London 67 D8
Bedgebury Cross Kent 53 G8
Bedgrove Bucks 84 C4
Bedham W Sus 35 C8
Bedhampton Hants 22 B2

Bedingfield Suff 126 D3
Bedingham Green Norf 142 E5
Bedlam N Yorks 214 G5
Som 45 D9
Bedlam Street W Sus 36 D3
Bedlar's Green Essex 105 G10
Bedlington Northumb 253 G7
Bedlington Station
Northumb 253 G7
Bedlinog M Tydf 77 E9
Bedminster Bristol 60 E5
Bedminster Down Bristol 60 F5
Bedmond Herts 85 E9
Bednall Staffs 151 F9
Bednall Head Staffs 151 F9
Bedrule Borders 262 F4
Bedstone Shrops 115 B7
Bedwas Caerph 59 B7
Bedwell Herts 104 G4
Wrex 166 F5
Bedwellty Caerph 77 E11
Bedwellty Pits Bl Gwent 77 D11
Bedwlwyn Wrex 148 B4
Bedworth Warks 135 F7
Bedworth Heath Warks 134 F6
Bedworth Woodlands
Warks 134 F6
Bed-y-coedwr Gwyn 146 D4
Beeby Leics 136 B3
Beech Hants 49 F7
Staffs 151 B7
Beechcliff Staffs 151 B7
Beechcliffe W Yorks 205 E7
Beechen Cliff Bath 61 G9
Beech Hill Gtr Man 194 F5
W Berks 65 G7
Beechingstoke Wilts 46 B5
Beech Lanes W Mid 133 F10
Beechwood Halton 183 E8
Newport 59 B10
W Mid 118 B5
W Yorks 206 F2
Beecroft C Beds 103 G10
Beedon W Berks 64 D3
Beedon Hill W Berks 64 D3
Beeford E Yorks 209 C8
Beeley Derbys 170 B3
Beelsby NE Lincs 201 G8
Beenham W Berks 64 F5
Beenham's Heath
Windsor 65 D10
Beenham Stocks
W Berks 64 F5
Beeny Corn 11 C8
Beer Devon 15 D10
Som 44 G2
Beercrocombe Som 28 C4
Beer Hackett Dorset 29 E9
Beesands Devon 8 G6
Beesby Lincs 191 E7
Beeslack Midloth 270 C4
Beeson Devon 8 G6
Beeston C Beds 104 B3
Ches W 167 D8
Norf 159 F8
Notts 153 B10
W Yorks 205 G11
Beeston Hill W Yorks 205 G11
Beeston Park Side
W Yorks 197 B9
Beeston Regis Norf 177 E11
Beeston Royds
W Yorks 205 G11
Beeston St Lawrence
Norf 160 E6
Beeswing Dumfries 237 C10
Beetham Cumb 211 D9
Som 28 E3
Beetley Norf 159 F9
Beffcote Staffs 150 F6
Began Cardiff 59 C8
Begbroke Oxon 83 C7
Begdale Cambs 139 B9
Begelly Pembs 73 D10
Beggar Hill Essex 87 E10
Beggarington Hill
W Yorks 197 C9
Beggars Ash Hereford 98 D4
Beggars Bush W Sus 35 F11
Beggar's Bush Powys 114 E5
Beggars Pound V Glam 58 F4
Beggearn Huish Som 42 F4
Beguildy Powys 114 B3
Beighton Norf 143 B7
S Yorks 186 E6
Beighton Hill Derbys 170 E3
Beili-glas Mon 78 C4
Beitearsaig W Isles 305 G1
Beith N Ayrs 266 E6
Bekesbourne Kent 55 B7
Bekesbourne Hill Kent 55 B7
Belah Cumb 239 F9
Belan Powys 130 C4
Belaugh Norf 160 F5
Belbins Hants 32 C5
Belbroughton Worcs 117 B8
Belchalwell Dorset 30 F3
Belchalwell Street Dorset 30 F3
Belchamp Otten Essex 106 C6
Belchamp St Paul Essex 106 C5
Belchamp Walter Essex 106 C6
Belcher's Bar Leics 135 B8
Belchford Lincs 190 F3
Beleybridge Fife 287 F9
Belfield Gtr Man 196 E2
Belford Northumb 264 C4
Belgrano Conwy 181 F7
Belgrave Ches W 166 C5
Leicester 135 B11
Staffs 134 C4
Belgravia London 67 D9
Belhaven E Loth 282 F3
Belhelvie Aberds 293 B11
Belhinnie Aberds 302 G4
Bellabeg Aberds 292 B5
Bellamore S Ayrs 244 F6
Bellanoch Argyll 275 D8
Bellanrigg Borders 260 B6
Bellasize E Yorks 199 B10
Bellaty Angus 286 B6
Bell Bar Herts 86 D3
Bell Busk N Yorks 204 B4
Bell Common Essex 86 E6
Belleau Lincs 190 F6
Belle Eau Park Notts 171 D11
Belle Green S Yorks 197 F11
Bellehiglash Moray 301 F11
Belle Isle W Yorks 197 B10
Bell End Worcs 117 B8
Bellerby N Yorks 224 G2
Belle Vale Mers 182 D6
W Mid 133 G9
Bellever Devon 13 F9
Bellevue Worcs 117 C9
Belle Vue Cumb 229 E8
Cumb 239 F9
Gtr Man 184 B5
Shrops 149 G9
S Yorks 198 G5
Belle Vue *continued*
W Yorks 197 D10
Bellfield E Ayrs 257 B10
Bellfields Sur 50 C3
Bell Green London 67 E11
W Mid 135 G7
Bell Heath Worcs 117 B9
Bell Hill Hants 34 C2
Belliehill Angus 293 G7
Bellingdon Bucks 84 D6
Bellingham London 67 E11
Northumb 251 G8
Bellmount Norf 157 E10
Belloch Argyll 255 D7
Bellochantuy Argyll 255 D7
Bell o' th' Hill Ches W 167 F8
Bellsbank E Ayrs 245 C11
Bell's Close T&W 242 E5
Bell's Corner Suff 107 D9
Bellshill N Lanark 268 C4
Northumb 264 C4
Bellside N Lanark 268 D6
Bellsmyre W Dunb 277 F8
Bellspool Borders 260 B5
Bellsquarry W Loth 269 C10
Bells Yew Green E Sus 52 F6
Belluton Bath 60 G6
Bellyeoman Fife 280 D2
Belmaduthy Highld 300 D6
Belmesthorpe Rutland 155 G10
Belmont Blackburn 195 D7
Durham 234 C2
E Sus 38 E4
London 67 G9
London 85 G11
Oxon 63 B11
S Ayrs 257 E8
Shetland 312 C7
Belnacraig Aberds 292 B5
Belnagarrow Moray 302 E3
Belnie Lincs 156 C5
Belowda Corn 5 C9
Belper Derbys 170 F4
Belper Lane End Derbys 170 F4
Belph Derbys 187 F8
Belsay Northumb 242 B4
Belses Borders 262 D3
Belsford Devon 8 D5
Belsize Herts 85 E8
Belstead Suff 108 C2
Belston S Ayrs 257 E9
Belstone Devon 13 C8
Belstone Corner Devon 13 B8
Belthorn Blackburn 195 C8
Beltinge Kent 71 F7
Beltingham Northumb 241 E7
Beltoft N Lincs 199 F10
Belton Leics 153 E8
Lincs 155 B8
N Lincs 199 F9
Norf 143 C9
Belton in Rutland
Rutland 136 C6
Beltring Kent 53 D7
Belts of Collonach
Aberds 293 D8
Belvedere London 68 D3
W Loth 269 B9
Belvoir Leics 154 C6
Bembridge IoW 21 D8
Bemersyde Borders 262 C3
Bemerton Wilts 46 G6
Bemerton Heath Wilts 46 G6
Bempton E Yorks 218 E3
Benacre Suff 143 G10
Ben Alder Lodge Highld 291 F7
Ben Armine Lodge
Highld 309 H7
Benbuie Dumfries 246 D6
Ben Casgro W Isles 304 F6
Benchill Gtr Man 184 D4
Bencombe Glos 80 F3
Benderloch Argyll 289 F11
Bendish Herts 104 G3
Bendronaig Lodge
Highld 299 F10
Benenden Kent 53 G10
Benfield Dumfries 236 C5
Benfieldside Durham 242 G3
Bengal Pembs 91 E9
Bengate Norf 160 D6
Bengeo Herts 86 C4
Bengeworth Worcs 99 C10
Bengrove Glos 99 E9
Benhall Glos 99 G8
Benhall Green Suff 127 E7
Benhall Street Suff 127 E7
Benhilton London 67 F9
Benholm Aberds 293 G10
Beningbrough N Yorks 206 B6
Benington Herts 104 G5
Lincs 174 F5
Benington Sea End
Lincs 174 F6
Benllech Anglesey 179 E8
Benmore Argyll 276 E2
Stirling 285 E8
Benmore Lodge Argyll 289 F7
Highld 309 H3
Bennacott Corn 11 C11
Bennah Devon 14 E2
Bennan N Ayrs 255 E10
Bennane Lea S Ayrs 244 F3
Bennetland E Yorks 199 B10
Bennetsfield Highld 300 D6
Bennett End Bucks 84 F3
Bennetts End Herts 85 D9
Benniworth Lincs 190 E2
Benover Kent 53 D8
Ben Rhydding W Yorks 205 D8
Bensham T&W 242 E6
Benslie N Ayrs 266 G6
Benson Oxon 83 G10
Benston Shetland 313 H6
Bent Aberds 293 F8
Benter Som 44 D6
Bentfield Bury Essex 105 F9
Bentfield Green Essex 105 F10
Bentgate Gtr Man 196 E2
Bent Gate Lancs 195 C9
Benthall Northumb 264 D6
Shrops 132 C3
Bentham Glos 80 B6
Benthoul Aberdeen 293 C10
Bentilee Stoke 168 F6
Bentlass Pembs 73 E7
Bentlawnt Shrops 130 C6
Bentley Essex 87 F9
E Yorks 208 F6
Hants 49 E9
Suff 108 D2
S Yorks 198 F5
Warks 134 D5
W Mid 133 D9
Worcs 117 D9
Bentley Common Warks 134 D5
Bentley Heath Herts 86 F2
W Mid 118 B3
Bentley Rise S Yorks 198 G5
Benton Devon 41 F7
Benton Green W Mid 118 B5
Bentpath Dumfries 249 E8
Bents W Loth 269 C9
Bents Head W Yorks 205 F7
Bentwichen Devon 41 G8
Bentworth Hants 49 E7
Benvie Dundee 287 D7
Benville Dorset 29 G8
Benwell T&W 242 E6
Benwick Cambs 138 E6
Beobridge Shrops 132 E5
Beoley Worcs 117 D11
Beoraidbeg Highld 295 F8
Bepton W Sus 34 D5
Berden Essex 105 F9
Bere Alston Devon 7 B8
Berechurch Essex 107 G9
Bere Ferrers Devon 7 C9
Berefold Aberds 303 F9
Berepper Corn 2 E5
Bere Regis Dorset 18 C2
Bergh Apton Norf 142 C6
Berghers Hill Bucks 66 B2
Berhill Som 44 F2
Berinsfield Oxon 83 F9
Berkeley Glos 79 F11
Berkeley Heath Glos 79 F11
Berkeley Road Glos 80 E2
Berkeley Towers
Ches E 167 E11
Berkhamsted Herts 85 D7
Berkley Som 45 D10
Berkley Down Som 45 D9
Berkley Marsh Som 45 D10
Berkswell W Mid 118 B4
Bermondsey London 67 D10
Bermuda Warks 135 F7
Bernards Heath Herts 85 D11
Bernera Highld 295 C10
Berner's Cross Devon 25 F10
Berner's Hill E Sus 53 G8
Berners Roding Essex 87 D10
Bernice Argyll 276 C2
Bernisdale Highld 298 D4
Berrick Salome Oxon 83 G10
Berriedale Highld 311 G5
Berrier Cumb 230 F3
Berriew = *Aberriw*
Powys 130 C3
Berrington Northumb 273 G10
Shrops 131 B10
Worcs 115 D11
Berrington Green
Worcs 115 D11
Berriowbridge Corn 11 F11
Berrow Som 43 C10
Worcs 98 E5
Berrow Green Worcs 116 F4
Berry Swansea 56 D3
Berry Brow W Yorks 196 E6
Berry Cross Devon 25 E7
Berry Down Cross Devon 40 E5
Berryfield Wilts 61 G11
Berryfields Oxon 84 B3
Berrygate Hill E Yorks 201 C8
Berry Hill Glos 79 C9
Pembs 91 C11
Stoke 168 F6
Worcs 117 E7
Berryhillock Moray 302 C5
Berrylands London 67 F7
Berry Moor S Yorks 197 G9
Berrynarbor Devon 40 D5
Berry Pomeroy Devon 8 C6
Berrysbridge Devon 26 G6
Berry's Green London 52 B2
Bersham Wrex 166 F4
Berstane Orkney 314 E4
Berth-ddu Flint 166 B2
Berthengam Flint 181 F10
Berwick E Sus 23 D8
Kent 54 F6
S Glos 60 C5
Berwick Bassett Wilts 62 E5
Berwick Hill Northumb 242 B5
Berwick Hills Mbro 225 B10
Berwick St James Wilts 46 F5
Berwick St John Wilts 30 C6
Berwick St Leonard
Wilts 46 G2
Berwick-upon-Tweed
Northumb 273 E9
Berwick Wharf Shrops 149 G10
Berwyn Denb 165 G11
Bescaby Leics 154 D6
Bescar Lancs 193 E11
Bescot W Mid 133 D10
Besford Shrops 149 E11
Worcs 99 C8
Bessacarr S Yorks 198 G6
Bessels Green Kent 52 B4
Bessels Leigh Oxon 83 E7
Besses o' th' Barn
Gtr Man 195 F10
Bessingby E Yorks 218 F3
Bessingham Norf 160 B3
Best Beech Hill E Sus 52 G6
Besthorpe Norf 141 D11
Notts 172 C4
Bestwood Nottingham 171 G9
Bestwood Village Notts 171 F9
Beswick E Yorks 208 D6
Gtr Man 184 B5
Betchcott Shrops 131 D8
Betchton Heath Ches E 168 C3
Betchworth Sur 51 D8
Bethania Ceredig 111 E11
Gwyn 163 E10
Gwyn 164 F2
Bethany Corn 6 D6
Bethel Anglesey 178 G5
Corn 5 E10
Gwyn 147 B9
Gwyn 163 B8
Bethelnie Aberds 303 F7
Bethersden Kent 54 E2
Bethesda Gwyn 163 B10
Pembs 73 B9
Bethlehem Carms 94 F3
Bethnal Green London 67 C10
Betley Staffs 168 F3
Betley Common Staffs 168 F2
Betsham Kent 68 E6
Betteshanger Kent 55 C10
Bettiscombe Dorset 16 B3
Bettisfield Wrex 149 B9
Betton Shrops 130 C6
Shrops 150 B3
Betton Strange Shrops 131 B10
Bettws Bridgend 58 B2
Mon 78 B3
Newport 78 G3
Bettws Cedewain Powys 130 D2
Bettws Gwerfil Goch
Denb 165 F8
Bettws Ifan Ceredig 92 B6
Bettws Newydd Mon 78 D5
Bettws-y-crwyn Shrops 130 G4
Bettyhill Highld 308 C7
Betws Bridgend 57 D11
Carms 75 C10
Betws Bledrws Ceredig 111 G11
Betws-Garmon Gwyn 163 D8
Betws Ifan Ceredig 92 B6
Betws-y-Coed Conwy 164 D4
Betws-yn-Rhos Conwy 180 G6
Beulah Ceredig 92 B5
Powys 113 G8
Bevendean Brighton 36 F4
Bevercotes Notts 187 G11
Bevere Worcs 116 F6
Beverley E Yorks 208 F6
Beverston Glos 80 G5
Bevington Glos 79 F11
Bewaldeth Cumb 229 E10
Bewbush W Sus 51 F8
Bewcastle Cumb 240 C3
Bewdley Worcs 116 B5
Bewerley N Yorks 214 G3
Bewholme E Yorks 209 C9
Bewley Common Wilts 62 F2
Bewlie Borders 262 D3
Bewlie Mains Borders 262 D3
Bewsey Warr 183 D9
Bexfield Norf 159 D10
Bexhill E Sus 38 F2
Bexley London 68 E3
Bexleyheath London 68 D3
Bexleyhill W Sus 34 B6
Bexon Kent 53 B11
Bexwell Norf 140 C2
Beyton Suff 125 E8
Beyton Green Suff 125 E8
Bhalasaigh W Isles 304 E3
Bhaltos W Isles 304 E2
Bhatarsaigh W Isles 297 M2
Bhlàraidh Highld 290 B5
Bibstone S Glos 79 G11
Bibury Glos 81 D10
Bicester Oxon 101 G11
Bickenhall Som 28 D3
Bickenhill W Mid 134 G3
Bicker Lincs 156 B4
Bicker Bar Lincs 156 B4
Bicker Gauntlet Lincs 156 B4
Bickershaw Gtr Man 194 G6
Bickerstaffe Lancs 194 G2
Bickerton Ches E 167 E8
Devon 9 G11
N Yorks 206 C5
Bickford Staffs 151 G7
Bickham Som 42 E3
Bickingcott Devon 26 B3
Bickington Devon 13 G11
Devon 40 G4
Bickleigh Devon 7 C10
Devon 26 F6
Bickleton Devon 40 G4
Bickley Ches W 167 F8
London 68 F2
Worcs 116 C2
Bickley Moss Ches W 167 F8
Bickley Town Ches W 167 F8
Bickleywood Ches W 167 F8
Bickmarsh Warks 100 B2
Bicknacre Essex 88 E3
Bicknoller Som 42 F6
Bicknor Kent 53 B11
Bickton Hants 31 E11
Bicton Hereford 115 E9
Pembs 72 D4
Shrops 130 G5
Shrops 149 F8
Bicton Heath Shrops 149 G9
Bidborough Kent 52 E5
Bidden Hants 49 D8
Biddenden Kent 53 F11
Biddenden Green Kent 53 E11
Biddenham Bedford 103 B10
Biddestone Wilts 61 E11
Biddick T&W 243 F8
Biddick Hall T&W 243 E9
Biddisham Som 43 C11
Biddlesden Bucks 102 C2
Biddlestone Northumb 251 B11
Biddulph Staffs 168 D5
Biddulph Moor Staffs 168 D6
Bideford Devon 25 B7
Bidford-on-Avon Warks 118 G2
Bidlake Devon 12 D5
Bidston Mers 182 C3
Bidston Hill Mers 182 D3
Bidwell C Beds 103 G10
Bielby E Yorks 207 E11
Bieldside Aberdeen 293 C10
Bierley IoW 20 F6
W Yorks 205 G9
Bierton Bucks 84 B4
Bigbury Devon 8 F3
Bigbury-on-Sea Devon 8 G3
Bigby Lincs 200 F5
Bigfrith Windsor 65 C11
Biggar Cumb 210 F3
S Lanark 260 B2
Biggar Road N Lanark 268 C5
Biggin Derbys 169 D11
Derbys 170 F3
N Yorks 206 F6
Thurrock 69 D7
Biggings Shetland 313 G3
Biggin Hill London 52 B2
Biggleswade C Beds 104 C3
Bighouse Highld 310 C2
Bighton Hants 48 G6
Biglands Cumb 239 G7
Big Mancot Flint 166 B4
Bignall End Staffs 168 E4
Bignor W Sus 35 E7
Bigods Essex 106 G2
Bigram Stirling 285 G10
Bigrigg Cumb 219 C10
Big Sand Highld 299 B7
Bigswell Orkney 314 E3
Bigton Shetland 313 L5
Bilberry Corn 5 C10
Bilborough Nottingham 171 G8
Bilbrook Som 42 E4
Staffs 133 C7
Bilbrough N Yorks 206 D6
Bilbster Highld 310 D6
Bilby Notts 187 E10
Bildershaw Durham 233 G10
Bildeston Suff 107 B9
Billacombe Plym 7 E10
Billacott Corn 11 C11
Billericay Essex 87 G11
Billesdon Leics 136 C4
Billesley Warks 118 F2
W Mid 133 G11
Billesley Common
W Mid 133 G11
Billingborough Lincs 156 C2
Billinge Mers 194 G4
Billingford Norf 126 B3
Norf 159 E10
Billingham Stockton 234 G5
Billinghay Lincs 173 E11
Billingley S Yorks 198 G2
Billingshurst W Sus 35 B9
Billingsley Shrops 132 F4
Billington C Beds 103 G8
Lancs 203 F10
Staffs 151 E7
Billockby Norf 161 G8
Bill Quay T&W 243 E7
Billy Mill T&W 243 D8
Billy Row Durham 233 D9
Bilmarsh Shrops 149 D9
Bilsborrow Lancs 202 F6
Bilsby Lincs 191 F7
Bilsby Field Lincs 191 F7
Bilsdon Devon 14 C2
Bilsham W Sus 35 G7
Bilsington Kent 54 G4
Bilson Green Glos 79 C11
Bilsthorpe Notts 171 C10
Bilsthorpe Moor Notts 171 D11
Bilston Midloth 270 C5
W Mid 133 D9
Bilstone Leics 135 B7
Bilting Kent 54 D5
Bilton E Yorks 209 G9
Northumb 264 G6
N Yorks 206 B2
Warks 119 C9
Bilton Haggs N Yorks 206 D5
Bilton in Ainsty N Yorks 206 D5
Bimbister Orkney 314 E3
Binbrook Lincs 190 C2
Binchester Blocks
Durham 233 E10
Bincombe Dorset 17 E9
Som 43 F7
Bindal Highld 311 L3
Bindon Som 27 C10
Binegar Som 44 D6
Bines Green W Sus 35 D11
Binfield Brack 65 E10
Binfield Heath Oxon 65 D8
Bingfield Northumb 241 C11
Bingham Edin 280 G6
Notts 154 B4
Bingley W Yorks 205 F8
Bings Heath Shrops 149 F10
Binham Norf 159 B9
Binley Hants 48 C2
W Mid 119 B7
Binley Woods Warks 119 B7
Binnegar Dorset 18 D3
Binniehill Falk 279 G7
Binscombe Sur 50 D3
Binsey Oxon 83 D7
Binsoe N Yorks 214 D4
Binstead Hants 49 E9
IoW 21 C7
Binsted Hants 49 E9
W Sus 35 F7
Binton Warks 118 G2
Bintree Norf 159 E10
Binweston Shrops 130 C6
Birch Essex 88 B6
Gtr Man 195 F11
Birch Acre Worcs 117 C11
Birchall Hereford 98 D3
Staffs 169 E7
Bircham Newton Norf 158 C5
Bircham Tofts Norf 158 C5
Birchan Coppice Worcs 116 C6
Birchanger Essex 105 G10
Birch Berrow Worcs 116 E4
Birchburn N Ayrs 255 E10
Birch Cross Staffs 152 C2
Birchden E Sus 52 F4
Birchencliffe W Yorks 196 D6
Birchend Hereford 98 C3
Birchendale Staffs 151 B11
Bircher Hereford 115 D9
Birches Green W Mid 134 E2
Birches Head Stoke 168 F5
Birchett's Green E Sus 53 G7
Birchfield Highld 301 G9
W Mid 133 E11
Birch Green Essex 88 B6
Herts 86 C3
Lancs 194 F3
Worcs 99 B7
Birchgrove Cardiff 59 D7
E Sus 36 B6
Swansea 57 B8
Birchhall Corner Essex 107 E10
Birch Heath Ches W 167 C8
Birch Hill Brack 65 F11
Ches W 183 G8
Birchill Devon 28 G4
Birchills W Mid 133 D10
Birchington Kent 71 F9
Birchley Heath Warks 134 E5
Birchmoor Warks 134 C5
Birchmoor Green
C Beds 103 E8
Bircholt Forstal Kent 54 E5
Birchover Derbys 170 C2
Birch Vale Derbys 185 D8
Birchwood Herts 86 D2
Lincs 172 B6
Som 28 E2
Warr 183 C10
Birchy Hill Hants 19 B11
Bircotes Notts 187 C10
Birdbrook Essex 106 C4
Birdbush Wilts 30 C6
Birdfield Argyll 275 D10
Birdforth N Yorks 215 D9
Birdham W Sus 22 D4
Birdholme Derbys 170 B5
Birdingbury Warks 119 D8
Birdlip Glos 80 C6
Birdsall N Yorks 216 F6
Birds Edge W Yorks 197 F8
Birds End Suff 124 E5
Birdsgreen Shrops 132 F5
Birds Green Essex 87 D9
Birdsmoorgate Dorset 28 G5
Birdston E Dunb 278 F3
Bird Street Suff 125 G10
Birdwell S Yorks 197 G10
Birdwood Glos 80 B2
Birgham Borders 263 B7
Birichen Highld 309 K7
Birkacre Lancs 194 D5
Birkby Cumb 229 D7
N Yorks 224 E6
W Yorks 196 D6
Birkdale Mers 193 D10
Birkenbog Aberds 302 C5
Birkenhead Mers 182 D4
Birkenhills Aberds 303 E7
Birkenshaw N Lanark 268 C3
S Lanark 268 F5
W Yorks 197 B8
Birkenshaw Bottoms
W Yorks 197 B8
Birkenside Borders 271 G11
Birkett Mire Cumb 230 G2
Birkhall Aberds 292 D5
Birkhill Angus 287 D7
Borders 260 F6
Borders 271 G11
Birkholme Lincs 155 E9
Birkhouse W Yorks 197 C7
Birkin N Yorks 198 B4
Birks Cumb 222 G3
W Yorks 197 B9
Birkshaw Northumb 241 D7
Birley Hereford 115 G9
Birley Carr S Yorks 186 C4
Birley Edge S Yorks 186 C4
Birleyhay Derbys 186 E5
Birling Kent 69 G7
Northumb 252 B6
Birling Gap E Sus 23 F9
Birlingham Worcs 99 C8
Birmingham W Mid 133 F11
Birnam Perth 286 C4
Birniehill S Lanark 268 E2
Birse Aberds 293 D7
Birsemore Aberds 293 D7
Birstall Leics 135 B11
W Yorks 197 B8
Birstall Smithies
W Yorks 197 B8
Birstwith N Yorks 205 B10
Birthorpe Lincs 156 C2
Birtle Gtr Man 195 E10
Birtley Hereford 115 D7
Northumb 241 B9
Shrops 131 E9
T&W 243 F7
Birtley Green Sur 50 E4
Birtsmorton Worcs 98 D6
Birts Street Worcs 98 D5
Bisbrooke Rutland 137 D7
Biscathorpe Lincs 190 D2
Biscombe Som 27 E11
Biscot Luton 103 G11
Biscovey Corn 5 E11
Bisham Windsor 65 C10
Bishampton Worcs 117 G9
Bish Mill Devon 26 B2
Bishon Common Hereford 97 C8
Bishop Auckland
Durham 233 F10
Bishopbridge Lincs 189 C8
Bishopbriggs E Dunb 278 G2
Bishop Burton E Yorks 208 F5
Bishopdown Wilts 47 G7
Bishop Kinkell Highld 300 D5
Bishop Middleham
Durham 234 E2
Bishopmill Moray 302 C2
Bishop Monkton
N Yorks 214 F6
Bishop Norton Lincs 189 C7
Bishopsbourne Kent 55 C7
Bishops Cannings Wilts 62 G4
Bishop's Castle Shrops 130 F6
Bishop's Caundle Dorset 29 E11
Bishop's Cleeve Glos 99 F9
Bishop's Down Dorset 29 E11
Bishops Frome Hereford 98 B3
Bishopsgarth Stockton 234 G4
Bishopsgate Sur 66 E3
Bishops Green Essex 87 B5
Bishop's Green W Berks 64 G4
Bishop's Hull Som 28 C2
Bishop's Itchington
Warks 119 F7
Bishops Lydeard Som 27 B11
Bishop's Norton Glos 98 G6
Bishops Nympton Devon 26 C3
Bishop's Offley Staffs 150 D5
Bishop's Quay Corn 2 D6
Bishop's Stortford
Herts 105 G9
Bishop's Sutton Hants 48 G6
Bishop's Tachbrook
Warks 118 E6
Bishops Tawton Devon 40 G5
Bishopsteignton Devon 14 G4
Bishopstoke Hants 33 D7
Bishopston Bristol 60 D5
Swansea 56 D5
Bishopstone Bucks 84 C4
E Sus 23 E7
Hereford 97 C8
Kent 71 F8
Swindon 63 C8
Wilts 31 B9
Bishopstrow Wilts 45 E11
Bishop Sutton Bath 44 B5
Bishop's Waltham Hants 33 D9
Bishopswood Som 28 E3
Bishop's Wood Staffs 132 B6
Bishopsworth Bristol 60 F5
Bishop Thornton
N Yorks 214 G5
Bishopthorpe York 207 D7
Bishopton Darl 234 G3
Dumfries 236 E6
N Yorks 214 E6
Renfs 277 G8
Warks 118 F3
Bishopwearmouth T&W 243 F9
Bishop Wilton E Yorks 207 B11
Bishpool Newport 59 B10
Bishton Newport 59 B11
Staffs 151 E10
Bisley Glos 80 D6
Sur 50 B3
Bisley Camp Sur 50 B2
Bispham Blackpool 202 E2
Bispham Green Lancs 194 E3
Bissoe Corn 4 G5
Bissom Corn 3 C7
Bisterne Hants 31 G10
Bisterne Close Hants 32 G2
Bitchet Green Kent 52 C5
Bitchfield Lincs 155 D9
Bittadon Devon 40 E4
Bittaford Devon 8 D3
Bittering Norf 159 F8
Bitterley Shrops 115 B11
Bitterne Soton 33 E7
Bitterne Park Soton 32 E6
Bitterscote Staffs 134 C4
Bitteswell Leics 135 F10
Bittles Green Dorset 30 C5
Bitton S Glos 61 F7
Bix Oxon 65 B8
Bixter Shetland 313 H5
Blaby Leics 135 D11
Blackacre Dumfries 248 E2
Blackadder West
Borders 272 E6
Blackawton Devon 8 E6
Black Bank Cambs 139 F10
Warks 135 F7
Black Banks Darl 224 C5
Black Barn Lincs 157 D8
Blackbeck Cumb 219 D10
Blackbird Leys Oxon 83 E9
Blackborough Devon 27 F9
Norf 158 G3
Blackborough End Norf 158 G3
Black Bourton Oxon 82 E3
Blackboys E Sus 37 C8
Blackbraes Aberds 293 B10
Blackbrook Derbys 170 F4
Derbys 185 E9
Mers 183 B8
Staffs 150 B5
Sur 51 D7
Blackburn Aberds 293 B10
Aberds 302 F5
Blackburn 195 B7
Blackburn *continued*
S Yorks 186 C5
W Loth 269 B9
Black Callerton T&W 242 D5
Black Carr Norf 141 D11
Blackcastle Midloth 271 D8
Blackchambers Aberds 293 B9
Black Clauchrie S Ayrs 245 G7
Black Corner W Sus 51 F9
Black Corries Lodge
Highld 284 B6
Blackcraig Dumfries 246 G6
Blackcraigs Angus 293 E7
Black Crofts Argyll 289 F11
Black Cross Corn 5 C8
Black Dam Hants 48 C6
Blackden Heath Ches E 184 G3
Blackditch Oxon 82 D6
Blackdog Aberds 293 B11
Black Dog Devon 26 F4
Blackdown Dorset 28 G5
Hants 33 C8
Warks 118 D6
Blackdyke Cumb 238 G4
Blackdykes E Loth 281 E11
Blacker Hill S Yorks 197 G11
Blacketts Kent 70 F2
Blackfell T&W 243 F7
Blackfen London 68 E3
Blackfield Hants 32 G6
Blackford Cumb 239 E9
Dumfries 248 G4
Perth 286 G2
Shrops 131 G11
Som 29 B11
Som 42 D2
Som 44 D2
Blackford Bridge
Gtr Man 195 F10
Blackfordby Leics 152 F6
Blackfords Staffs 151 G9
Blackgang IoW 20 F5
Blackgate Angus 287 B8
Blackhall Aberds 293 D8
Edin 280 G4
Renfs 267 C9
Blackhall Colliery
Durham 234 D5
Blackhall Mill T&W 242 F4
Blackhall Rocks Durham 234 D5
Blackham E Sus 52 F3
Blackhaugh Borders 261 B10
Blackheath Essex 107 G10
London 67 D11
Suff 127 C8
Sur 50 D4
W Mid 133 F9
Blackheath Park London 68 D2
Black Heddon Northumb 242 B3
Blackhill Aberds 303 D10
Aberds 303 E10
Aberds 303 F10
Durham 242 G3
Hants 32 D4
Highld 298 D3
Black Hill W Yorks 204 E6
Blackhillock Moray 302 E4
Blackhills Highld 301 D9
Moray 302 D2
Swansea 56 C5
Blackhorse Devon 14 C5
S Glos 61 D7
Black Horse Drove
Cambs 139 E11
Blackjack Lincs 156 B5
Black Lake W Mid 133 E9
Blackland Wilts 62 F4
Blacklands E Sus 38 E4
Hereford 98 C2
Black Lane Gtr Man 195 F9
Blacklaw Aberds 302 D6
Blackleach Lancs 202 G5
Blackley Gtr Man 195 G11
W Yorks 196 D6
Blacklunans Perth 292 G3
Black Marsh Shrops 130 D6
Blackmarstone Hereford 97 D10
Blackmill Bridgend 58 B2
Blackminster Worcs 99 C11
Blackmoor Bath 60 G5
Gtr Man 195 G7
Hants 49 G9
N Som 60 G3
Som 27 D11
Black Moor Lancs 194 E3
W Yorks 205 F11
Blackmoorfoot W Yorks 196 E5
Blackmoor Gate Devon 41 E7
Blackmore Essex 87 E10
Shrops 130 B6
Blackmore End Essex 106 E4
Herts 85 B11
Worcs 98 C6
Black Mount Argyll 284 C6
Blackness Aberds 293 D8
E Sus 52 G4
Falk 279 F11
Blacknest Hants 49 E9
Windsor 66 F3
Blacknoll Dorset 18 D2
Black Notley Essex 106 G5
Blacko Lancs 204 E3
Blackoe Shrops 149 B10
Blackpark Dumfries 236 C5
Black Park Wrex 166 G4
Black Pill Swansea 56 C6
Blackpole Worcs 117 F7
Black Pole Lancs 202 F5
Blackpool Blackpool 202 F2
Devon 7 E11
Devon 9 F7
Devon 14 G2
Pembs 73 C9
Blackpool Gate Cumb 240 B2
Blackridge W Loth 269 B7
Blackrock Argyll 274 G4
Bath 60 F6
Mon 78 C2
Black Rock Brighton 36 G4
Corn 2 C5
Blackrod Gtr Man 194 E6
Blackshaw Dumfries 238 D2
Blackshaw Head
W Yorks 196 B3
Blackshaw Moor Staffs 169 D8
Blacksmith's Corner
Suff 108 C2
Blacksmith's Green Suff 126 D2
Blacksnape Blackburn 195 C8
Blackstone Worcs 116 C5
W Sus 36 D2
Black Street Suff 143 F10
Black Tar Pembs 73 D7
Blackthorn Oxon 83 B10
Blackthorpe Suff 125 E8
Blacktoft E Yorks 199 C10
Blacktop Aberdeen 293 C10
Black Torrington Devon 25 F7
Blacktown Newport 59 C9
Black Vein Caerph 78 G2
Blackwall Derbys 170 F3
Blackwall *continued*
London 67 C11
Blackwall Tunnel
London 67 C11
Blackwater BCP 19 B8
Corn 4 F4
Hants 49 B11
IoW 20 D6
Norf 159 E11
Som 28 D3
Blackwaterfoot N Ayrs 255 E9
Blackwater Lodge
Moray 302 G3
Blackweir Cardiff 59 D7
Blackwell Cumb 239 G10
Darl 224 C5
Derbys 170 D6
Derbys 185 G10
Devon 27 B8
Warks 100 C4
Worcs 117 C9
W Sus 51 F11
Blackwood Caerph 77 F11
S Lanark 268 G5
Warr 183 C10
Blackwood Hill Staffs 168 D6
Blacon Ches W 166 B5
Bladbean Kent 55 D7
Blades N Yorks 223 F9
Bladnoch Dumfries 236 D6
Bladon Oxon 82 C6
Blaenannerch Ceredig 92 B4
Blaenau Carms 75 C10
Flint 166 D2
Blaenau Dolwyddelan
Conwy 164 E2
Blaenau Ffestiniog
Gwyn 164 F2
Blaenau-Gwent Bl Gwent 78 E2
Blaenavon Torf 78 D3
Blaenbedw Fawr
Ceredig 111 G7
Blaencaerau Bridgend 57 C11
Blaencelyn Ceredig 111 G7
Blaen-Cil-Llech Ceredig 92 C6
Blaen Clydach Rhondda 77 G7
Blaencwm Rhondda 76 F6
Blaendulais = *Seven Sisters*
Neath 76 D4
Blaendyryn Powys 95 D8
Blaenffos Pembs 92 D3
Blaengarw Bridgend 76 G6
Blaengwrach Neath 76 D5
Blaengwynfi Neath 57 B11
Blaen-gwynfi Neath 57 B11
Blaenllechau Rhondda 77 F8
Blaen-pant Ceredig 92 C5
Blaenpennal Ceredig 112 E2
Blaenplwyf Ceredig 111 B11
Blaenporth Ceredig 92 B5
Blaenrhondda Rhondda 76 E6
Blaenwaun Carms 92 F4
Blaen-waun Carms 92 F4
Ceredig 111 G7
Blaen-y-coed Carms 92 F6
Blaenycwm Ceredig 112 B6
Blaen-y-cwm Bl Gwent 77 C10
Denb 147 C10
Gwyn 146 E4
Powys 147 E11
Blagdon N Som 44 B4
Torbay 9 C7
Blagdon Hill Som 28 D2
Blagill Cumb 231 B10
Blaguegate Lancs 194 F3
Blaich Highld 290 F2
Blain Highld 289 C8
Blaina Bl Gwent 78 D2
Blainacraig Ho Aberds 293 D7
Blair Fife 280 C6
Blair Atholl Perth 291 G10
Blairbeg N Ayrs 256 C2
Blairburn Fife 279 D9
Blairdaff Aberds 293 B8
Blair Drummond Stirling 278 B4
Blairdryne Aberds 293 D9
Blairglas Argyll 276 D6
Blairgorm Highld 301 G10
Blairgowrie Perth 286 C5
Blairhall Fife 279 D10
Blairhill N Lanark 268 B4
Blairingone Perth 279 B9
Blairland N Ayrs 266 F6
Blairlinn N Lanark 278 G5
Blairlogie Stirling 278 B6
Blairlomond Argyll 276 B3
Blairmore Argyll 276 E3
Highld 306 D6
Blairnamarrow Moray 292 B4
Blairquhosh Stirling 277 E10
Blair's Ferry Argyll 275 G10
Blairskaith E Dunb 277 F11
Blaisdon Glos 80 B2
Blaise Hamlet Bristol 60 D5
Blakebrook Worcs 116 B6
Blakedown Worcs 117 B7
Blake End Essex 106 G4
Blakelands M Keynes 103 C7
Blakelaw Borders 263 C7
T&W 242 D6
Blakeley Staffs 133 E7
Blakeley Lane Staffs 169 F7
Blakelow Ches E 167 E11
Blakemere Hereford 97 C7
Blakenall Heath
W Mid 133 C10
Blakeney Glos 79 D11
Norf 177 E8
Blakenhall Ches E 168 F2
W Mid 133 D8
Blakeshall Worcs 132 G6
Blakesley W Nhants 120 G2
Blanchland Northumb 241 G11
Blandford Camp Dorset 30 F6
Blandford Forum Dorset 30 F5
Blandford St Mary Dorset 30 F5
Bland Hill N Yorks 205 C10
Blandy Highld 308 D6
Blanefield Stirling 277 F11
Blanerne Borders 272 D6
Blank Bank Staffs 168 F4
Blankney Lincs 173 C9
Blantyre S Lanark 268 D3
Blar a'Chaorainn Highld 290 G3
Blaran Argyll 275 B9
Blarghour Argyll 275 B10
Blarmachfoldach Highld 290 G2
Blarnalearoch Highld 307 K6
Blasford Hill Essex 88 C2
Blashford Hants 31 F11
Blaston Leics 136 D6
Blatchbridge Som 45 D9
Blatherwycke N Nhants 137 D9
Blawith Cumb 210 B5
Blaxhall Suff 127 F7
Blaxton S Yorks 199 G7
Blaydon T&W 242 E5
Blaydon Burn T&W 242 E5
Blaydon Haughs T&W 242 E5
Bleach Green Cumb 219 B9
Suff 126 B4

Bleadney Som 44 D3
Bleadon N Som 43 B10
Bleak Acre Hereford . . 98 B2
Bleak Hall M Keynes . . 103 D7
Bleak Hey Nook
  Gtr Man 196 F4
Bleak Hill Hants 31 E10
Blean Kent 70 G6
Bleasby Lincs 189 E10
  Notts 172 F2
Bleasby Moor Lincs . . 189 E10
Bleasdale Lancs 203 D7
Bleatarn Cumb 222 C4
Blebocraigs Fife 287 F8
Bleddfa Powys 114 D4
Bledington Glos 100 G4
Bledlow Bucks 84 E3
Bledlow Ridge Bucks . . 84 F3
Bleet Wilts 45 B11
Blegbie E Loth 271 C9
Blegbury Devon 24 B2
Blencarn Cumb 231 E8
Blencogo Cumb 229 B9
Blendworth Hants 34 E2
Blenheim Oxon 83 D9
  Oxon 83 E9
Blenheim Park Norf . . 158 C6
Blenkinsopp Hall
  Northumb 240 E5
Blennerhasset Cumb . . 229 C9
Blervie Castle Moray . . 301 D10
Bletchingdon Oxon . . 83 B8
Bletchingley Sur 51 C10
Bletchley M Keynes . . 103 E7
  Shrops 150 C2
Bletherston Pembs 91 G11
Bletsoe Bedford 121 F10
Blewbury Oxon 64 B4
Blibby Kent 54 F4
Blickling Norf 160 D3
Blidworth Notts 171 D9
Blidworth Bottoms
  Notts 171 D9
Blidworth Dale Notts . . 171 E9
Blindburn Northumb . . 263 G6
Blindcrake Cumb 229 E8
Blindley Heath Sur . . 51 D11
Blindmoor Som 28 E3
Blingery Highld 310 E7
Blisland Corn 11 G6
Blissford Hants 31 E11
Bliss Gate Worcs 116 C4
Blisworth W Nhants . . 120 G4
Blitterlees Cumb 238 G4
Blockley Glos 100 D3
Blofield Norf 142 B6
Blofield Heath Norf . . 160 G6
Blo' Norton Norf 125 B10
Bloodman's Corner
  Suff 143 D10
Bloomfield Bath 45 B7
  Bath 61 G8
  Borders 262 E3
  W Mid 133 E9
Bloomsbury London . . 67 C10
Blore Staffs 150 C4
  Staffs 169 F10
Bloreheath Staffs 150 B4
Blossomfield W Mid . . 118 B2
Blount's Green Staffs . . 151 C11
Blowick Mers 193 D11
Blowinghouse Corn 4 E4
Bloxham Oxon 101 D8
Bloxholm Lincs 173 E9
Bloxwich W Mid 133 C9
Bloxworth Dorset 18 C3
Blubberhouses N Yorks . 205 B9
Blue Anchor Corn 5 D8
  Som 42 E4
  Swansea 56 B4
Bluebell Telford 149 G11
Blue Bell Hill Kent 69 G8
Bluecairn Borders 271 G10
Blue Hill Herts 104 G5
Blue Row Essex 89 C8
Bluetown Kent 54 B2
Blue Town Kent 70 D2
Blue Vein Wilts 61 F10
Bluewater Kent 68 E5
Blughasary Highld 307 J6
Blundellsands Mers . . 182 B4
Blundeston Suff 143 D10
Blundies Staffs 132 F6
Blunham C Beds 122 G3
Blunsdon St Andrew
  Swindon 62 B6
Bluntington Worcs 117 C7
Bluntisham Cambs 123 C7
Blunts Corn 6 C6
Blunt's Green Warks . . 118 D2
Blurton Stoke 168 G5
Blyborough Lincs 188 C6
Blyford Suff 127 B8
Blymhill Staffs 150 G6
Blymhill Lawns Staffs . . 150 G6
Blyth Borders 270 F2
  Northumb 253 G8
  Notts 187 D10
Blyth Bridge Borders . . 270 F2
Blythburgh Suff 127 B9
Blythe Borders 271 F11
Blythe Bridge Staffs . . 169 G2
Blythe Marsh Staffs . . 169 G2
Blyth End Warks 134 E4
Blythswood Renfs 267 B10
Blyton Lincs 188 C5
Boarhills Fife 287 F9
Boarhunt Hants 33 F10
Boarsgreave Lancs 195 C10
Boarshead E Sus 52 G4
Boars Hill Oxon 83 E7
Boarstall Bucks 83 C10
Boasley Cross Devon . . 12 C5
Boath Highld 300 B5
Boat of Garten Highld . . 291 B11
Bobbing Kent 69 F11
Bobbington Staffs 132 F6
Bobbingworth Essex . . 87 D8
Bobby Hill Suff 125 C10
Boblainy Highld 300 F4
Bocaddon Corn 6 D3
Bochastle Stirling 285 G10
Bockhanger Kent 54 E4
Bocking Essex 106 G5
Bocking Churchstreet
  Essex 106 F5
Bocking's Elm Essex . . 89 B11
Bockleton Worcs 115 E11
Bockmer End Bucks . . 65 B10
Bocombe Devon 24 C5
Bodantionail Highld . . 299 B7
Boddam Aberds 303 E11
  Shetland 313 M5
Bodden Som 44 E6
Boddington Glos 99 F7
Bodedern Anglesey . . 178 E4
Bodellick Corn 10 G5
Bodelva Corn 5 E11
Bodelwyddan Denb . . 181 F8
Bodenham Hereford . . 115 G10

Bodenham continued
  Wilts 31 B11
Bodenham Bank Hereford . 98 E2
Bodenham Moor
  Hereford 115 G10
Bodermid Gwyn 144 D3
Bodewryd Anglesey . . 178 C5
Bodfari Denb 181 G9
Bodffordd Anglesey . . 178 F6
Bodham Norf 177 E10
Bodiam E Sus 38 B3
Bodicote Oxon 101 D9
Bodieve Corn 10 G5
Bodiggo Corn 5 D10
Bodinnick Corn 6 E2
Bodle Street Green
  E Sus 23 C11
Bodley Devon 41 D7
Bodmin Corn 5 B11
Bodmiscombe Devon . . 27 F10
Bodney Norf 140 D6
Bodorgan Anglesey . . 162 B5
Bodsham Kent 54 E6
Boduan Gwyn 144 B6
Boduel Corn 6 C4
Bodwen Corn 5 C10
Bodymoor Heath Warks . 134 E3
Bofarnel Corn 6 C2
Bogallan Highld 300 D6
Bogbrae Aberds 303 F10
Bogend Borders 272 F5
  S Ayrs 257 C9
Bogentory Aberds 293 C9
Boghall Midloth 270 B4
  W Loth 269 B9
Boghead Aberds 293 D8
  S Ayrs 268 G5
Bogmoor Moray 302 C3
Bogniebrae Aberds . . 302 E5
  Aberds 302 E6
Bognor Regis W Sus . . 22 C6
Bograxie Aberds 293 B9
Bogs Aberds 302 G5
Bogs Bank Borders 270 E3
Bogside N Lanark 268 E6
Bogthorn W Yorks 204 F6
Bogton Aberds 302 D6
Bogtown Aberds 302 C5
Bogue Dumfries 246 G4
Bohemia E Sus 38 E4
  Wilts 32 D2
Bohenie Highld 290 E4
Bohetherick Corn 7 B8
Bohortha Corn 3 C9
Bohuntine Highld 290 E4
Bohuntinville Highld . . 290 E4
Boirseam W Isles 296 C6
Bojewyan Corn 1 C3
Bokiddick Corn 5 C11
Bolahaul Fm Carms . . 74 B6
Bolam Durham 233 G9
  Northumb 252 G5
Bolam West Houses
  Northumb 252 G5
Bolas Heath Telford . . 150 E3
Bolberry Devon 9 G8
Bold Heath Mers 183 D8
Boldmere W Mid 134 E2
Boldon T&W 243 E9
Boldon Colliery T&W . . 243 E8
Boldre Hants 20 B2
Boldron Durham 223 C10
Bole Notts 188 D3
Boleside Borders 261 C11
Boley Park Staffs 134 B2
Bolham Devon 27 E7
  Notts 188 E2
Bolham Water Devon . . 27 E11
Bolholt Gtr Man 195 E9
Bolingey Corn 4 D5
Bolitho Corn 2 C5
Bollihope Durham 232 E6
Bollington Ches E 184 F6
Bollington Cross Ches E . 184 F6
Bolney W Sus 36 C3
Bolnhurst Bedford 121 F11
Bolnore W Sus 36 C4
Bolshan Angus 287 B10
Bolsover Derbys 170 B6
Bolsterstone S Yorks . . 186 B3
Bolstone Hereford 97 E11
Boltby N Yorks 215 B9
Bolter End Bucks 84 G3
Bolton Corn 231 G8
  E Loth 281 G10
  E Yorks 207 C11
  Gtr Man 195 F8
  Northumb 264 G4
  W Yorks 205 F9
Bolton Abbey N Yorks . 205 C7
Bolton Bridge N Yorks . 205 C7
Bolton-by-Bowland
  Lancs 203 D11
Boltonfellend Cumb . . 239 D11
Boltongate Cumb 229 C10
Bolton Green Lancs . . 194 D5
Bolton Houses Lancs . . 202 G4
Bolton-le-Sands Lancs . 211 F9
Bolton Low Houses
  Cumb 229 C10
Bolton New Houses
  Cumb 229 C10
Bolton-on-Swale
  N Yorks 224 F5
Bolton Percy N Yorks . . 206 E6
Bolton Town End Lancs . 211 F9
Bolton upon Dearne
  S Yorks 198 G3
Bolton Wood Lane
  Cumb 229 C11
Bolton Woods W Yorks . 205 F9
Boltshope Park Durham . 232 B4
Bolventor Corn 11 F9
Bomarsund Northumb . . 253 G7
Bombie Dumfries 237 D9
Bomby Cumb 221 B10
Bomere Heath Shrops . . 149 F9
Bonaly Edin 270 B4
Bonar Bridge Highld . . 309 K6
Bonawe Argyll 284 D4
Bonby N Lincs 200 D4
Boncath Pembs 92 D4
Bonchester Bridge
  Borders 262 G3
Bonchurch IoW 21 F7
Bondend Glos 80 B5
Bond End Staffs 152 F3
Bondleigh Devon 25 G11
Bondman Hays Leics . . 135 B9
Bonds Lancs 202 E5
Bondstones Devon 25 F9
Bonehill Devon 13 F10

Bonehill continued
  Staffs 134 C3
Bo'ness Falk 279 E9
Bonhill W Dunb 277 F7
Boningale Shrops 132 C6
Bonjedward Borders . . 262 E5
Bonkle N Lanark 268 D6
Bonnavoulin Highld . . 289 D7
Bonning Gate Cumb . . 221 F9
Bonnington Borders . . 261 B7
  Edin 270 B2
  Kent 54 F5
Bonnybank Fife 287 G7
Bonnybridge Falk 278 E6
Bonnykelly Aberds 303 D8
Bonnyrigg and Lasswade
  Midloth 270 B6
Bonnyton Aberds 302 F6
  Angus 287 B10
  Angus 287 D7
  E Ayrs 257 B10
Bonsall Derbys 170 D3
Bonskeid House Perth . 291 G10
Bonson Som 43 E8
Bont Mon 78 B5
Bont Fawr Carms 94 F4
Bont goch = Elerch
  Ceredig 128 F3
Bonthorpe Lincs 191 G7
Bontnewydd Ceredig . . 112 D2
  Gwyn 163 D7
Bont-newydd Conwy . . 181 G8
Bont Newydd Gwyn . . 146 E5
  Gwyn 164 G2
Bontuchel Denb 165 D9
Bonvilston = Tresimwn
  V Glam 58 E5
Bon-y-maen Swansea . . 57 B7
Boode Devon 40 F4
Booker Bucks 84 G4
Bookham Dorset 30 G2
Booleybank Shrops . . 149 D11
Boon Borders 271 F11
Boon Hill Staffs 168 E4
Boorley Green Hants . . 33 E8
Boosbeck Redcar 226 B3
Boose's Green Essex . . 106 E6
Boot Cumb 220 E3
Booth W Yorks 196 B4
Booth Bank Ches E . . 184 D2
Boothby Graffoe Lincs . 173 D7
Boothby Pagnell Lincs . 155 C9
Boothen Stoke 168 G5
Boothferry E Yorks . . 199 B8
Boothgate Derbys 170 F5
Booth Green Ches E . . 184 E6
Boothroyd W Yorks . . 197 C8
Boothsdale Ches W . . 167 B8
Boothstown Gtr Man . . 195 G8
Boothtown W Yorks . . 196 B5
Boothville W Nhants . . 120 E5
Booth Wood W Yorks . . 196 D4
Bootle Cumb 210 B2
  Mers 182 B4
Booton Norf 160 E2
Boots Green Ches W . . 184 G3
Boot Street Suff 108 B4
Booze N Yorks 223 E10
Boquhan Stirling 277 D10
Boquio Corn 2 C5
Boraston Shrops 116 C2
Boraston Dale Shrops . 116 C2
Borden Kent 69 G11
  W Sus 34 C4
Border S Yorks 186 G3
Bordesley W Mid 133 F11
Bordesley Green W Mid . 134 F2
Bordlands Borders 270 F3
Bordley N Yorks 213 G8
Bordon Hants 49 F10
Bordon Camp Hants . . 49 F9
Boreham Essex 88 D3
  Wilts 45 E11
Boreham Street E Sus . 23 C11
Borehamwood Herts . . 85 F11
Boreland Dumfries 236 C5
  Dumfries 248 E5
  Fife 280 C6
  Stirling 285 D9
Boreland of Southwick
  Dumfries 237 C11
Boreley Worcs 116 D6
Borestone Stirling 278 C5
Borgh W Isles 296 F3
  W Isles 297 L2
  W Isles 296 C6
Borghastan W Isles . . 304 D3
Borgie Highld 308 D6
Borgue Dumfries 237 E8
  Highld 311 G5
Borley Essex 106 C6
Borley Green Essex . . 106 C6
  Suff 125 E9
Bornais W Isles 297 J3
Bornesketaig Highld . . 298 B3
Borness Dumfries 237 E8
Borough Scilly 1 G3
Boroughbridge N Yorks . 215 F7
Borough Green Kent . . 52 B6
Borough Marsh
  Wokingham 65 D9
Borough Park W Mid . . 134 B4
Borough Post Som 28 C4
Borras Wrex 166 E4
Borras Head Wrex 166 E5
Borreraig Highld 296 F7
Borrobol Lodge Highld . 311 G2
Borrodale Highld 295 B7
Borrohill Aberds 303 D9
Borrowash Derbys 153 C8
Borrowby N Yorks 215 B8
  N Yorks 226 B5
Borrowdale Cumb 220 C5
Borrowfield Aberds . . 293 D10
Borrowston Highld 310 E7
Borrowstoun Mains
  Falk 279 E9
Borstal Medway 69 F8
Borth = Y Borth Ceredig . 128 E2
Borth-y-Gest Gwyn . . 145 B11
Borve Highld 298 E4
Borve Lodge W Isles . . 305 J2
Borwick Lancs 211 E10
Borwick Rails Cumb . . 210 D3
Bosavern Corn 1 C3
Bosbury Hereford 98 C3
Boscadjack Corn 2 C5
Boscastle Corn 11 C2
Boscean Corn 1 C3
Boscombe Bmouth 19 C8
  Wilts 47 F8
Boscoppa Corn 5 E10

Boscreege Corn 2 C5
Bosham W Sus 22 C4
Bosham Hoe W Sus . . 22 C4
Bosherston Pembs 73 G7
Boskednan Corn 1 C4
Boskenna Corn 1 E4
Boslake Corn 4 G3
Bosley Ches E 168 B6
Boslowick Corn 3 C11
Boslymon Corn 5 C11
Bosoughan Corn 5 C7
Bosporthennis Corn . . 1 C4
Bossall N Yorks 216 G4
Bossiney Corn 11 D7
Bossingham Kent 54 E6
Bossington Hants 47 G10
  Som 55 B8
Bostadh W Isles 304 D3
Bostock Green Ches W . 167 B11
Boston Lincs 174 G4
Boston Long Hedges
  Lincs 174 F5
Boston Spa W Yorks . . 206 D4
Boston West Lincs 174 F3
Boswednack Corn 1 B4
Boswin Corn 2 C5
Boswinger Corn 5 G9
Boswyn Corn 2 C5
Botallack Corn 1 C3
Botany Bay London 86 F3
Botcherby Cumb 239 F10
Botcheston Leics 135 B9
Botesdale Suff 125 B10
Bothal Northumb 252 F6
Bothamsall Notts 187 G11
Bothel Cumb 229 D9
Bothampstead W Berks . 64 D4
Bothenhampton Dorset . 16 C5
Bothwell S Lanark 268 D4
Botley Bucks 85 D6
  Hants 33 E8
  Oxon 83 D7
Botloe's Green Glos . . 98 F4
Botolph Claydon Bucks . 102 G4
Botolphs W Sus 35 F11
Bottacks Highld 300 C4
Botternell Corn 11 G11
Bottesford Leics 154 B6
  N Lincs 199 F11
Bottisham Cambs 123 E10
Bottlesford Wilts 46 B6
Bottom Boat W Yorks . . 197 C11
Bottomcraig Fife 287 E7
Bottom House Staffs . . 169 E8
Bottomley W Yorks . . 196 D5
Bottom of Hutton Lancs . 194 B3
Bottom o' th' Moor
  Gtr Man 195 E7
Bottom Pond Kent 53 B11
Bottoms Corn 1 E3
Botton N Yorks 226 D4
Botton Head Lancs . . 212 F2
Bottreaux Mill Devon . . 26 B4
Bottrells Close Bucks . . 85 G7
Botts Green Warks 134 E4
Botusfleming Corn 7 C8
Botwnnog Gwyn 144 C5
Bough Beech Kent 52 D3
Boughrood Powys 96 D2
Boughrood Brest Powys . 96 D2
Boughspring Glos 79 G11
Boughton Ches W 166 B6
  Lincs 173 F10
  Norf 140 C3
  Notts 171 B11
  W Nhants 120 D5
Boughton Aluph Kent . . 54 D4
Boughton Corner Kent . 54 D4
Boughton Green Kent . 53 C9
Boughton Heath
  Ches W 166 B6
Boughton Lees Kent . . 54 D4
Boughton Malherbe
  Kent 53 D11
Boughton Monchelsea
  Kent 53 C9
Boughton Street Kent . 54 B5
Bougton End C Beds . . 103 D9
Boulby Redcar 226 B5
Boulder Clough
  W Yorks 196 C4
Bouldnor IoW 20 D3
Bouldon Shrops 131 F10
Boulmer Northumb 265 G2
Boulsdon Glos 98 G4
Boulston Pembs 72 C6
Boultenstone Aberds . . 292 B6
Boultham Lincs 173 B7
Boultham Moor Lincs . . 173 B7
Boulton Derbys 153 C7
Boundary Leics 152 F6
  Staffs 169 G7
Boundstone Sur 49 E10
Bounds Thorne Devon . 24 D5
Bountis Thorne Devon . 24 D5
Bourn Cambs 122 F6
Bournbrook W Mid 133 G10
Bourne Lincs 155 E11
  S Som 44 B3
Bourne End Bedford . . 121 E10
  C Beds 103 C9
  Herts 85 D8
Bournemouth BCP 19 C7
Bournes Green Glos . . 80 E6
  Southend 70 B2
Bournheath Worcs 117 C8
Bournmoor Durham . . 243 G8
Bournside Glos 99 G8
Bournstream Glos 80 G2
Bournville W Mid 133 G10
Bourton Bucks 102 E4
  Dorset 45 G9
  N Som 59 G11
  Oxon 63 B8
  Shrops 131 D11
  Wilts 46 F3
Bourton on Dunsmore
  Warks 119 C8
Bourton-on-the-Hill
  Glos 100 E3
Bourton-on-the-Water
  Glos 100 G3
Bousd Argyll 288 C4
Boustead Hill Cumb . . 239 F7
Bousta Shetland 313 H4
Bouth Cumb 210 B6
Bouthwaite N Yorks . . 214 E2
Bouts Worcs 117 F10
Bovain Stirling 285 D9
Boveney Bucks 66 D2
Boveridge Dorset 31 E9
Boverton V Glam 58 F3
Bovey Tracey Devon . . 14 F2

Bovingdon Herts 85 E8
  Herts 85 E8
Bovingdon Green Bucks . 65 B10
  Herts 87 D8
Boviner Essex 87 D8
Bovington Camp Dorset . 18 D2
Bow Borders 271 G9
  Devon 26 G2
  Orkney 314 G3
  Oxon 82 G4
Bowbank Durham 232 G4
Bowbeck Suff 125 B8
Bow Brickhill M Keynes . 103 E8
Bowbridge Glos 80 E5
Bowbrook Shrops 149 G9
Bow Broom S Yorks . . 187 B7
Bowburn Durham 234 D2
Bowcombe IoW 20 D5
Bow Common London . 67 C11
Bowd Devon 15 C8
Bowden Borders 262 C3
  Devon 8 G6
  Dorset 30 G3
Bowden Hill Wilts 62 F2
Bowdens Som 28 B6
Bowderdale Cumb 222 E3
Bowdon Gtr Man 184 D3
Bowen Hill Aberds 303 C9
Bower Northumb 251 G7
Bower Ashton Bristol . . 60 E5
Bowerchalke Wilts 31 C8
Bower Heath Herts 85 B9
Bower Hinton Som 29 D7
Bowerhope Borders . . 261 E7
Bower House Tye Suff . 107 C9
Bowermadden Highld . 310 C6
Bowers Staffs 150 B6
Bowers Gifford Essex . 69 B9
Bowershall Fife 279 C11
Bowertower Highld . . 310 C6
Bowes Durham 223 C9
Bowgreave Lancs 202 E5
Bowgreen Gtr Man 184 D3
Bowhill Borders 261 D10
  Fife 280 B4
Bowhouse Dumfries . . 238 D2
Bowhousebog or Liquo
  N Lanark 269 D7
Bowing Park Mers 182 D6
Bowithick Corn 11 E9
Bowker's Green Lancs . 194 G2
Bowland Bridge Cumb . 211 B8
Bowldown Wilts 62 B2
Bowlee Gtr Man 195 F10
Bowley Hereford 98 C3
Bowley Lane Hereford . 98 C3
Bowley Town Hereford . 115 G10
Bowlhead Green Sur . . 50 F2
Bowling W Dunb 277 G9
  W Yorks 205 G9
Bowling Alley Hants . . 49 D9
Bowling Bank Wrex . . 166 F5
Bowling Green Corn . . 5 D10
Bowmanstead Cumb . . 220 F6
Bowmore Argyll 274 B4
Bowness-on-Solway
  Cumb 238 E6
Bowness-on-Windermere
  Cumb 221 F8
Bow of Fife Fife 287 F7
Bowridge Hill Dorset . . 30 B4
Bowrie-fauld Angus . . 287 C9
Bowsden Northumb . . 273 G9
Bowshank Borders 271 F9
Bowsey Hill Windsor . . 65 C10
Bowside Lodge Highld . 310 C2
Bowston Cumb 221 F9
Bow Street Ceredig . . 128 G2
  Norf 141 D10
Bowthorpe Norf 142 B4
Bowyer's Common Hants . 34 B3
Box Glos 80 E4
  Wilts 61 F10
Boxbush Glos 80 C2
  Glos 98 G5
Box End Bedford 103 B10
Boxford Suff 107 C9
  W Berks 64 E2
Boxgrove W Sus 22 B6
Box Hill Sur 51 C7
  Wilts 61 F10
Boxley Kent 53 B9
Boxmoor Herts 85 D9
Box's Shop Corn 24 G2
Boxted Essex 107 E10
  Suff 124 G6
Boxted Cross Essex . . 107 E10
Boxted Heath Essex . . 107 E10
Box Trees W Mid 118 C2
Boxwell Glos 80 G4
Boxworth Cambs 122 E6
Boxworth End Cambs . 123 D7
Boyard Wood Hants . . 32 C6
Boyden End Suff 124 F4
Boyden Gate Kent 71 G7
Boylestone Derbys 152 B3
Boylestonfield Derbys . 152 B3
Boyndie Aberds 302 C6
Boynton E Yorks 218 F2
Boys Hill Dorset 29 E11
Boys Village V Glam . . 58 F4
Boythorpe Derbys 186 G5
Boyton Corn 12 C2
  Suff 108 C6
  Wilts 46 F3
Boyton Cross Essex . . 87 D10
Boyton End Suff 106 C3
  Suff 106 C3
Bozeat N Nhants 121 F8
Bozen Green Herts 105 F8
Braaid IoM 192 E4
Braal Castle Highld . . 310 C5
Brabling Green Suff . . 126 E5
Brabourne Kent 54 E5
Brabourne Lees Kent . . 54 E5
Brabster Highld 310 C7
Bracadale Highld 294 B5
Bracara Highld 295 F9
Braceborough Lincs . . 155 G11
Bracebridge Lincs 173 B7
Bracebridge Heath
  Lincs 173 B7
Bracebridge Low Fields
  Lincs 173 B7

Braceby Lincs 155 B10
Bracewell Lancs 204 D3
Bracken Bank W Yorks . 204 F6
Brackenber Cumb 222 B4
Brackenbottom N Yorks . 212 E6
Brackenfield Derbys . . 170 D5
Brackenhall W Yorks . . 197 D7
Bracken Hill W Yorks . . 197 C7
Brackenlands Cumb . . 229 B11
Bracken Park W Yorks . 206 E3
Brackenthwaite Cumb . 229 B11
  Cumb 229 G9
  N Yorks 205 C11
Brackla = Bragle
  Bridgend 58 D2
Bracklamore Aberds . . 303 D8
Bracklesham W Sus . . 22 D4
Brackletter Highld 290 E3
Brackley Argyll 255 D11
  W Nhants 101 D11
Brackloch Highld 307 G6
Bracknell Brack 65 F11
Braco Perth 286 G2
Bracobrae Moray 302 D5
Braco Castle Perth . . 286 F2
Bracon N Lincs 199 F9
Bracon Ash Norf 142 D3
Bracora Highld 295 F9
Bracorina Highld 295 F9
Bradaford Devon 12 B3
Bradbourne Derbys . . 170 E2
Bradbury Durham 234 F2
Bradda IoM 192 F2
Bradden W Nhants 102 B2
Braddocks Hay Staffs . 168 D5
Bradeley Stoke 168 E5
Bradeley Green Ches E . 167 G8
Bradenham Bucks 84 F4
  Norf 141 B8
Bradenstoke Wilts 62 D4
Brades Village W Mid . . 133 E9
Bradfield Devon 27 F9
  Essex 108 E2
  Norf 160 C5
  W Berks 64 E6
Bradfield Combust Suff . 125 F7
Bradfield Green
  Ches E 167 D11
Bradfield Heath Essex . 108 E2
Bradfield St Clare Suff . 125 F8
Bradfield St George
  Suff 125 E8
Bradford Corn 11 F8
  Derbys 170 C2
  Devon 24 F6
  Gtr Man 184 B5
  Northumb 264 C5
  W Yorks 205 G9
Bradford Abbas Dorset . 29 E9
Bradford Leigh Wilts . . 61 G10
Bradford-on-Avon
  Wilts 61 G10
Bradford-on-Tone Som . 27 C11
Bradford Peverell Dorset . 17 C9
Bradgate S Yorks 186 C5
Bradiford Devon 40 G5
Brading IoW 21 D8
Bradley Ches W 183 F8
  Derbys 170 F2
  Glos 80 G2
  Hants 48 E6
  NE Lincs 201 F8
  Staffs 151 F7
  W Mid 133 D8
  Wrex 166 E4
  W Yorks 205 F10
Bradley Cross Som . . 44 C3
Bradley Fold Gtr Man . 195 F9
Bradley Green Ches W . 167 F8
  Som 43 E8
  Som 43 F9
  Warks 134 C4
  Worcs 117 E9
Bradley in the Moors
  Staffs 169 G9
Bradley Mills W Yorks . 197 D7
Bradley Mount Ches E . 184 F6
Bradley Stoke S Glos . 60 C6
Bradlow Hereford 98 D4
Bradmore Notts 153 C11
  W Mid 133 D7
Bradney Shrops 132 D5
  Som 43 F10
Bradninch Devon 27 F8
Bradnock's Marsh
  W Mid 118 B4
Bradnop Staffs 169 D8
Bradnor Green Hereford . 114 F5
Bradpole Dorset 16 C5
Bradshaw Gtr Man . . 195 E8
  W Yorks 196 C5
  W Yorks 196 D6
Bradstone Devon 12 E3
Bradville M Keynes . . 102 C6
Bradwall Green Ches E . 168 C2
Bradway S Yorks 186 E4
Bradwell Derbys 185 E11
  Essex 89 D7
  Essex 106 G6
  M Keynes 102 D6
  Norf 143 B10
  Staffs 168 E4
Bradwell Common
  M Keynes 102 D6
Bradwell Grove Oxon . 82 D2
Bradwell Hills Derbys . 185 E11
Bradwell on Sea Essex . 89 D8
Bradwell Waterside
  Essex 89 D7
Bradworthy Devon 24 D4
Bradworthy Cross Devon . 24 D4
Brae Dumfries 237 B10
  Highld 307 L3
  Highld 309 J4
  Shetland 312 G5
Braeantra Highld 300 B5
Braedownie Angus 292 F4
Braeface Falk 278 E5
Braefield Highld 300 F4
Braefindon Highld 300 D6
Braegrum Perth 286 E4
Braehead Dumfries . . 236 D6
  Orkney 314 B4
  Orkney 314 D5
  S Lanark 257 C9
  S Lanark 269 F8
  Stirling 278 D6
Braehead of Lunan
  Angus 287 B10
Braehoulland Shetland . 312 F4
Braehungie Highld . . 310 F5
Braeintra Highld 295 B10
Braelangwell Lodge
  Highld 309 K5
Braemar Aberds 292 D3
Braemore Highld 299 B11

Braemore continued
  Highld 310 F4
Brae of Achnahaird
  Highld 307 H5
Brae of Boquhapple
  Stirling 285 G10
Braepark Edin 280 F3
Brae Roy Lodge Highld . 290 D5
Braeside Invclyd 276 F4
  N Yorks 205 C11
Braes of Enzie Moray . 302 D3
Braes of Ullapool Highld . 307 K6
Braeswick Orkney 314 C6
Braevallich Argyll 275 C10
Brafferton Darl 233 G11
  N Yorks 215 E8
Brafield-on-the-Green
  W Nhants 120 F6
Bragar W Isles 304 D4
Bragbury End Herts . . 104 G5
Bragenham Bucks 103 F8
Bragle = Brackla
  Bridgend 58 D2
Bragleenmore Argyll . . 289 G11
Braichmelyn Gwyn . . 163 B10
Braichyfedw Powys . . 129 E7
Braid Edin 280 G4
Braides Lancs 202 C4
Braidfauld Glasgow . . 268 C2
Braidley N Yorks 213 C10
Braidwood S Lanark . . 268 F6
Braigh Chalasaigh
  W Isles 296 D5
Braigo Argyll 274 G3
Brailsford Derbys 170 G3
Brailsford Green Derbys . 170 G3
Brain's Green Glos . . 79 D11
Brainshaugh Northumb . 252 C6
Braintree Essex 106 G5
Braiseworth Suff 126 C3
Braishfield Hants 32 B5
Braiswick Essex 107 F9
Braithwaite Cumb 229 G9
  S Yorks 198 E6
  S Yorks 204 E6
Braithwell S Yorks 187 C8
Brakefield Green Norf . 141 B10
Brakenhill W Yorks . . 198 D2
Bramber W Sus 35 E11
Brambridge Hants 33 B7
Bramcote Notts 153 B10
  Warks 135 F8
Bramcote Hills Notts . . 153 B10
Bramcote Mains Warks . 135 F8
Bramdean Hants 33 B10
Bramerton Norf 142 C5
Bramfield Herts 86 B3
  Suff 127 C7
Bramford Suff 108 B2
Bramhall Gtr Man 184 D5
Bramhall Moor Gtr Man . 184 D6
Bramham W Yorks 206 E4
Bramhope W Yorks . . 205 E11
Bramley Derbys 186 F6
  Hants 48 B6
  Sur 50 D4
  S Yorks 187 C7
  W Mid 133 E10
  W Yorks 205 F10
Bramley Corner Hants . 48 B6
Bramley Green Hants . 48 B6
Bramley Head N Yorks . 205 B9
Bramley Vale Derbys . . 171 B7
Bramling Kent 55 B8
Brampford Speke Devon . 14 B4
Brampton Cambs 122 C4
  Cumb 231 G9
  Cumb 240 E2
  Derbys 186 G5
  Hereford 97 D8
  Lincs 188 F4
  Norf 160 E4
  Suff 143 G8
  S Yorks 198 G2
Brampton Abbotts
  Hereford 98 G2
Brampton Ash N Nhants . 136 F5
Brampton Bryan
  Hereford 115 C7
Brampton en le Morthen
  S Yorks 187 D7
Brampton Park Cambs . 122 C4
Brampton Street Suff . 143 G8
Bramshall Staffs 151 C11
Bramshaw Hants 32 D3
Bramshill Hants 65 G8
Bramshott Hants 49 G10
Bramwell Som 28 B6
Branault Highld 289 C7
Brancaster Norf 176 E3
Brancaster Staithe Norf . 176 E3
Brancepeth Durham . . 233 D10
Branch End Northumb . 242 E3
Branchill Moray 301 D10
Brand End Lincs 174 F5
Brandelhow Cumb 229 G10
Branderburgh Moray . . 302 B2
Brandesburton E Yorks . 209 D8
Brandeston Suff 126 E4
Brand Green Glos 98 F4
Brandhill Shrops 115 B8
Brandis Corner Devon . 24 G6
Brandiston Norf 160 E2
Brandon Durham 233 D10
  Lincs 172 F6
  Northumb 264 F2
  Suff 140 F4
  Warks 119 B8
Brandon Bank Cambs . 140 F2
Brandon Creek Norf . . 140 D2
Brandon Parva Norf . . 141 B11
Brandsby N Yorks 215 E11
Brandwood Shrops . . 149 D9
Brandwood End
  W Mid 117 B11
Brandy Carr W Yorks . 197 C10
Brandy Hole Essex . . 88 F4
Brandyquoy Orkney . . 314 G4
Brandy Wharf Lincs . . 189 B8
Brane Corn 1 D4
Bran End Essex 106 F2
Branksome BCP 18 C6
Branksome Park BCP . 19 C7
Bransby Lincs 188 F5
Branscombe Devon . . 15 D10
Bransford Worcs 116 G6
Bransgore Hants 19 B9

Bransholme Hull 209 G8
Branson's Cross Worcs . 117 C11
Branston Leics 154 D6
  Lincs 173 B8
  Staffs 152 E4
Branston Booths Lincs . 173 B8
Branstone IoW 21 E7
Bransty Cumb 219 B9
Brant Broughton Lincs . 172 E6
Brantham Suff 108 E2
Branthwaite Cumb 229 D11
  Cumb 229 G8
Branthwaite Edge Cumb . 229 G7
Brantingham E Yorks . 200 B2
Branton Northumb 264 F2
  S Yorks 198 G6
Branton Green N Yorks . 215 G8
Branxholme Borders . . 261 G11
Branxholm Park
  Borders 261 G11
Branxton Northumb . . 263 B9
Brascote Leics 135 C8
Brassey Green Ches W . 167 C8
Brassington Derbys . . 170 E2
Brasted Kent 52 C3
Brasted Chart Kent . . 52 C3
Brathens Aberds 293 D8
Bratoft Lincs 175 B7
Brattle Kent 54 G2
Brattleby Lincs 188 E6
Bratton Som 42 D2
  Telford 150 G2
  Wilts 46 C2
Bratton Clovelly Devon . 12 C5
Bratton Fleming Devon . 40 F6
Bratton Seymour Som . 29 B11
Braughing Herts 105 F7
Braughing Friars Herts . 105 F7
Braulen Lodge Highld . 299 F10
Braunston W Nhants . . 119 D10
Braunstone Leics 135 C11
Braunstone Town
  Leicester 135 C11
Braunston-in-Rutland
  Rutland 136 B6
Braunton Devon 40 F3
Brawby N Yorks 216 D4
Brawith N Yorks 225 D10
Brawl Highld 310 C2
Brawlbin Highld 310 D4
Bray Windsor 66 D2
Braybrooke N Nhants . 136 G5
Braydon Side Wilts . . 62 B4
Brayford Devon 41 G7
Brayfordhill Devon . . 41 G7
Brays Grove Essex 87 D7
Bray Shop Corn 12 G2
Braystones Cumb 219 D10
Brayswick Worcs 98 B6
Braythorn N Yorks 205 D10
Brayton N Yorks 198 B6
Braytown Dorset 18 D2
Bray Wick Windsor . . 65 D11
Braywoodside Windsor . 65 D11
Brazacott Corn 11 C11
Brazenhill Staffs 151 E7
Brea Corn 4 G3
Breach Bath 60 G6
  Kent 69 F10
  W Sus 22 B3
Breachwood Green
  Herts 104 G2
Breaden Heath Shrops . 149 B8
Breadsall Derbys 153 B7
Breadsall Hilltop Derby . 153 B7
Breadstone Glos 80 E2
Bread Street Glos 80 D4
Breage Corn 2 D4
Breakachy Highld 300 E4
Brealeys Devon 25 D8
Bream Glos 79 E10
Breamore Hants 31 D11
Bream's Meend Glos . 79 E9
Brean Som 43 D9
Breanais W Isles 304 F1
Brearley W Yorks 196 B4
Brearton N Yorks 214 G6
Breascleit W Isles 304 E4
Breaston Derbys 153 C9
Brechfa Carms 93 G11
Brechin Angus 293 G8
Breckan Orkney 314 F2
Breckles Norf 141 E8
Breck of Cruan Orkney . 314 E3
Breckrey Highld 298 C5
Brecks S Yorks 187 C7
Brecon Powys 95 F10
Bredbury Gtr Man 184 C6
Bredbury Green
  Gtr Man 184 C6
Brede E Sus 38 D4
Bredenbury Hereford . 116 F2
Bredfield Suff 126 G5
Bredgar Kent 69 G11
Bredhurst Kent 69 G9
Bredicot Worcs 117 G8
Bredon Worcs 99 D8
Bredon's Hardwick
  Worcs 99 D8
Bredon's Norton Worcs . 99 D8
Bredwardine Hereford . 96 C6
Breedon on the Hill
  Leics 153 E8
Breeds Essex 87 C11
Breedy Butts Lancs . . 202 E2
Breibhig W Isles 297 M2
  W Isles 304 E6
Breich W Loth 269 C9
Breightmet Gtr Man . . 195 F8
Breighton E Yorks 207 G10
Breinton Hereford 97 D9
Breinton Common
  Hereford 97 C9
Breiwick Shetland 313 J6
Brelston Green Hereford . 97 G11
Bremhill Wilts 62 E3
Bremhill Wick Wilts . . 62 E3
Bremirehoull Shetland . 313 L6
Brenachoile Lodge
  Stirling 285 G8
Brenchley Kent 53 E7
Brenchoillie Argyll 284 G4
Brendon Devon 41 D8
  Devon 24 D4
  Devon 41 D9

Brentwood Essex 87 G9
Brenzett Kent 39 B8
Brenzett Green Kent 39 B8
Brereton Staffs 151 F11
Brereton Cross Staffs 151 F11
Brereton Green Ches E 168 C3
Brereton Heath Ches E 168 C4
Breretonhill Staffs 151 F11
Bressingham Norf 141 G11
Bressingham Common
Norf 141 G11
Bretby Derbys 152 E5
Bretford Warks 119 B8
Bretforton Worcs 99 C11
Bretherdale Head
Cumb 221 E11
Bretherton Lancs 194 C3
Brettabister Shetland 313 H6
Brettenham Norf 141 G8
Suff 125 G9
Bretton Derbys 186 F2
Flint 166 C5
Pboro 138 C3
Brewer's End Essex 105 G11
Brewers Green Norf 142 G2
Brewer Street Sur 51 C10
Brewlands Bridge
Angus 292 G3
Brewood Staffs 133 B7
Briach Moray 301 D10
Briants Puddle Dorset 18 C2
Briar Hill W Nhants 120 F4
Brick End Essex 105 F11
Brickendon Herts 86 D4
Bricket Wood Herts 85 E10
Brickfields Worcs 117 F7
Brickhill Bedford 121 G11
Brick Hill Sur 66 G3
Brick House End Essex 105 F9
Brickhouses Ches E 168 C3
Brick Houses S Yorks 186 E4
Brick-kiln End Notts 171 D9
Brickkiln Green Essex 106 E4
Bricklehampton Worcs 99 C9
Bride IoM 192 B5
Bridekirk Cumb 229 E8
Bridell Pembs 92 C3
Bridestowe Devon 12 D6
Brideswell Aberds 302 F5
Bridford Devon 14 D2
Bridfordmills Devon 14 D2
Bridge Corn 2 D6
Corn 4 G3
Kent 55 C7
Som 28 F5
Bridge Ball Devon 41 D8
Bridge End Bedford 121 G10
Cumb 230 B3
Devon 8 F3
Durham 232 D6
Essex 106 E3
Flint 166 D4
Hereford 98 B2
Lincs 156 B2
Northumb 241 D10
Northumb 241 E10
Oxon 83 G9
Bridge-End Shetland 313 K5
Bridge End Sur 50 B5
Warks 118 E5
Worcs 98 E6
Bridgefoot Aberds 292 C6
Angus 287 D7
Cumb 229 F7
Bridge Green Essex 105 D9
Norf 142 G2
Bridgehampton Som 29 C9
Bridge Hewick N Yorks 214 E6
Bridgehill Durham 242 G3
Bridge Ho Argyll 254 B4
Bridgeholm Green
Derbys 185 E8
Bridgehouse Gate
N Yorks 214 F3
Bridgelands Borders 261 C11
Bridgemary Hants 33 G9
Bridgemere Ches E 168 F2
Bridgemont Derbys 185 E8
Bridgend Aberds 293 B7
Aberds 302 F5
Angus 293 G7
Argyll 255 D8
Argyll 274 G4
Argyll 275 D9
Corn 6 D2
Cumb 221 C7
Devon 7 F11
Fife 287 F7
Glos 80 E4
Highld 300 D3
Invclyd 276 F5
Moray 302 F3
N Lanark 278 G3
Pembs 92 B3
W Loth 279 F10
Bridgend = *Pen-y-Bont ar-ogwr* Bridgend 58 C2
Bridgend of Lintrathen
Angus 286 B6
Bridgeness Falk 279 E10
Bridge of Alford Aberds 293 B7
Bridge of Allan Stirling 278 B5
Bridge of Avon Moray 301 F11
Moray 301 G11
Bridge of Awe Argyll 284 E4
Bridge of Balgie Perth 285 C9
Bridge of Cally Perth 286 B5
Bridge of Canny Aberds 293 D8
Bridge of Craigisla
Angus 286 B6
Bridge of Dee Dumfries 237 D9
Bridge of Don
Aberdeen 293 B11
Bridge of Dun Angus 287 B10
Bridge of Dye Aberds 293 E8
Bridge of Earn Perth 286 F5
Bridge of Ericht Perth 285 B9
Bridge of Feugh Aberds 293 D9
Bridge of Forss Highld 310 C4
Bridge of Gairn Aberds 292 D5
Bridge of Gaur Perth 285 B9
Bridge of Lyon Perth 285 C11
Bridge of Muchalls
Aberds 293 D10
Bridge of Muick Aberds 292 D5
Bridge of Oich Highld 290 C5
Bridge of Orchy Argyll 284 D6
Bridge of Waith Orkney 314 E2
Bridge of Walls
Shetland 313 H4
Bridge of Weir Renfs 267 B7
Bridge Reeve Devon 25 E11
Bridgerule Devon 24 G3
Bridges Corn 5 D10
Shrops 131 D7
Bridge Sollers Hereford 97 C8
Bridge Street Suff 107 B7
Bridgeton Glasgow 268 C2
Bridgetown Corn 12 D2
Bridgetown *continued*
Devon 8 C6
Som 42 G2
Staffs 133 B9
Bridge Town Warks 118 G4
Bridge Trafford Ches W 183 G7
Bridge Yate S Glos 61 E7
Bridgham Norf 141 F9
Bridgnorth Shrops 132 E4
Bridgtown Staffs 133 B9
Bridgwater Som 43 F10
Bridlington E Yorks 218 F3
Bridport Dorset 16 C5
Bridstow Hereford 97 G11
Brierfield Lancs 204 F2
Brierholme Carr
S Yorks 199 E7
Brierley Glos 79 B10
Hereford 115 F9
S Yorks 198 E2
Brierley Hill W Mid 133 F8
Brierton Hrtlpl 234 E5
Briery Cumb 229 G11
Briery Hill Bl Gwent 77 D11
Briestfield W Yorks 197 D8
Brigflatts Cumb 222 G2
Brigg N Lincs 200 F3
N Lincs 200 F4
Briggate Norf 160 D6
Briggswath N Yorks 227 D7
Brigham Cumb 229 E7
Cumb 229 G11
E Yorks 209 C7
Brighouse W Yorks 196 C6
Brighstone IoW 20 E4
Brightgate Derbys 170 D3
Brighthampton Oxon 82 E5
Brightholmlee S Yorks 186 B3
Brightley Devon 13 B7
Brightling E Sus 37 C11
Brightlingsea Essex 89 B9
Brighton Brighton 36 G4
Corn 5 E8
Brighton Hill Hants 48 D6
Brighton le Sands Mers 182 B4
Brightons Falk 279 F8
Brightside S Yorks 186 D5
Brightwalton W Berks 64 D2
Brightwalton Green
W Berks 64 D2
Brightwalton Holt
W Berks 64 D2
Brightwell Suff 108 C4
Brightwell Baldwin
Oxon 83 F11
Brightwell cum Sotwell
Oxon 83 G9
Brigmerston Wilts 47 D7
Brignall Durham 223 C11
Brig o'Turk Stirling 285 G9
Brigsley NE Lincs 201 G9
Brigsteer Cumb 211 B9
Brigstock N Nhants 137 F8
Brill Bucks 83 C11
Corn 2 D6
Brilley Hereford 96 B5
Brilley Mountain Powys 114 G5
Brimaston Pembs 91 G8
Brimfield Hereford 115 D10
Brimington Derbys 186 G6
Brimington Common
Derbys 186 G6
Brimley Devon 13 F11
Devon 28 G4
Brimpsfield Glos 80 C6
Brimps Hill Glos 79 B11
Brimpton W Berks 64 G5
Brimpton Common
W Berks 64 G5
Brims Orkney 314 H2
Brims Castle Highld 310 B4
Brimscombe Glos 80 E5
Brimsdown London 86 F5
Brimstage Mers 182 E4
Brinacory Highld 295 F9
Brincliffe S Yorks 186 D4
Brind E Yorks 207 G10
Brindham Som 44 E4
Brindister Shetland 313 H4
Shetland 313 K6
Brindle Lancs 194 C6
Brindle Heath Gtr Man 195 G10
Brindley Ches E 167 E9
Brindley Ford Stoke 168 E5
Brindwoodgate Derbys 186 F4
Brineton Staffs 150 G6
Bringewood Forge
Hereford 115 C9
Bringhurst Leics 136 E6
Bringsty Common
Hereford 116 F4
Brington Cambs 121 B11
Brinian Orkney 314 D4
Briningham Norf 159 C10
Brinkhill Lincs 190 G5
Brinkley Cambs 124 G2
Notts 172 E2
Brinkley Hill Hereford 97 E11
Brinklow M Keynes 103 D8
Warks 119 B8
Brinkworth Wilts 62 C4
Brinmore Highld 300 G6
Brinnington Gtr Man 184 C6
Brinscall Lancs 194 C6
Brinsea N Som 60 G2
Brinsford Staffs 133 B8
Brinsley Notts 171 F7
Brinsop Hereford 97 C8
Brinsop Common
Hereford 97 C8
Brinsworth S Yorks 186 D6
Brinsworthy Devon 41 G9
Brinton Norf 159 B10
Brisco Cumb 239 G10
Briscoe Cumb 219 C10
Briscoerigg N Yorks 205 C11
Brisley Norf 159 E8
Brislington Bristol 60 E6
Brissenden Green Kent 54 F2
Bristnall Fields W Mid 133 F9
Bristol Bristol 60 E5
Briston Norf 159 C11
Britain Bottom S Glos 61 B9
Britannia Lancs 195 C11
Britford Wilts 31 B11
Brithdir Caerph 77 E11
Ceredig 92 B6
Gwyn 146 F5
Brithem Bottom Devon 27 E8
British Torf 78 E3
Briton Ferry = *Llansawel*
Neath 57 C8
Britten's Bath 45 B7
Britwell Slough 66 C3
Britwell Salome Oxon 83 G11
Brixham Torbay 9 D8
Brixton Devon 7 E11
London 67 D10
Brixton Deverill Wilts 45 F11
Brixworth W Nhants 120 C4
Brize Norton Oxon 82 D4
Broad Alley Worcs 117 D7
Broad Blunsdon
Swindon 81 G11
Broadbottom Gtr Man 185 C7
Broadbridge W Sus 22 B4
Broadbridge Heath
W Sus 50 G6
Broadbury Devon 12 B5
Broadbush Swindon 81 G11
Broad Campden Glos 100 D3
Broad Carr W Yorks 196 D5
Broad Chalke Wilts 31 B8
Broad Clough Lancs 195 C11
Broadclyst Devon 14 B5
Broad Colney Herts 85 E11
Broad Common Worcs 117 D7
Broadfield Gtr Man 195 E10
Invclyd 276 G6
Lancs 194 C4
Lancs 195 B8
Pembs 73 E10
W Sus 51 G9
Broadford Highld 295 C8
Sur 50 D3
Broad Ford Kent 53 F8
Broadford Bridge W Sus 35 C9
Broadgate Hants 32 C6
Broadgrass Green Suff 125 E9
Broad Green Cambs 124 F3
C Beds 103 C9
Essex 105 D8
Essex 107 G7
London 67 F10
Mers 182 C6
Suff 124 F5
Suff 125 F11
Worcs 116 F5
Worcs 117 C9
Broadgreen Wood Herts 86 D4
Broadhalgh Gtr Man 195 E11
Broadham Green Sur 51 C11
Broadhaugh Borders 249 B10
Broadhaven Highld 310 D7
Broad Haven = *Aberllydan*
Pembs 72 C5
Broadheath Gtr Man 184 D3
Broad Heath Powys 114 E6
Staffs 151 D7
Worcs 116 D3
Broadhembury Devon 27 G10
Broadhempston Devon 8 B6
Broad Hill Cambs 123 B11
Broad Hinton Wilts 62 D6
Broadholm Derbys 170 F4
Broadholme Derbys 170 F5
Lincs 188 G5
Broad Ings E Yorks 208 C2
Broadland Row E Sus 38 D4
Broadlands Devon 14 G3
Broadlane Corn 2 C4
Broad Lane Corn 4 G3
Broad Lanes Shrops 132 F5
Broadlay Carms 74 D5
Broad Laying Hants 64 G2
Broad Layings Hants 64 G2
Broadley Lancs 195 D11
Moray 302 C3
Broadley Common Essex 86 D6
Broadleys Aberds 303 C8
Broad Marston Worcs 100 B2
Broadmayne Dorset 17 D10
Broad Meadow Staffs 168 F4
Broadmeadows
Borders 261 C10
Broadmere Hants 48 D6
Broadmoor Pembs 73 D9
Sur 50 D6
Broadmoor Common
Hereford 98 D2
Broadmore Green
Worcs 116 G6
Broadoak Dorset 16 B4
Glos 80 C2
Hants 33 E8
Shrops 149 F9
Wrex 166 D5
Broad Oak Carms 93 G11
Cumb 220 G2
Dorset 30 E3
E Sus 37 C10
E Sus 38 D4
Hants 49 C9
Hereford 97 G9
Kent 54 F4
Kent 71 G7
Mers 183 B8
Shrops 132 F5
Broadoak End Herts 86 C4
Broadoak Park Gtr Man 195 G9
Broad Parkham Devon 24 C5
Broadplat Oxon 65 C8
Broadrashes Moray 302 D4
Broadrock Glos 79 F8
Broadsands Torbay 9 D7
Broadsea Aberds 303 C9
Broad's Green Essex 87 C11
Wilts 62 F3
Broadshard Som 28 E6
Broadstairs Kent 71 F11
Broadstone BCP 18 B6
Kent 53 D11
Mon 79 E8
Shrops 131 F10
Broad Street E Sus 38 D5
Kent 53 B10
Kent 54 E6
Kent 55 E7
Medway 69 E9
Suff 107 C9
Wilts 46 B6
Broadstreet Common
Newport 59 C11
Broad Street Green
Essex 88 D5
Broad Tenterden Kent 53 G11
Broad Town Wilts 62 D5
Broadwas Worcs 116 F5
Broadwater Herts 104 G4
W Sus 35 G11
Broadwater Down Kent 52 F5
Broadwaters Worcs 116 B6
Broadwath Cumb 239 F11
Broadway Carms 74 D3
Carms 74 D5
Pembs 72 C5
Som 28 D4
Suff 127 B7
Worcs 99 D11
Broadway Lands
Hereford 97 E11
Broadwell Glos 79 C9
Glos 100 F4
Oxon 82 E3
Warks 119 D9
Broadwey Dorset 17 E9
Broadwindsor Dorset 28 G6
Broadwood Kelly Devon 25 F10
Broadwoodwidger Devon 12 D4
Brobury Hereford 96 C6
Brochel Highld 298 E5
Brochroy Argyll 284 D4
Brock Lancs 202 E6
Brockamin Worcs 116 G5
Brockbridge Hants 33 D10
Brockdish Norf 126 B4
Brockencote Worcs 117 C7
Brockenhurst Hants 32 G4
Brocketsbrae S Lanark 259 B8
Brockfield Devon 28 F4
Brockford Green Suff 126 D2
Brockford Street Suff 126 D2
Brockhall W Nhants 120 E2
Brockhall Village
Lancs 203 F10
Brockham Sur 51 D7
Brockham End Bath 61 F8
Brockham Park Sur 51 D8
Brockhampton Glos 99 F8
Glos 99 G10
Hants 22 B2
Hereford 97 E11
Brockhampton Green
Dorset 30 F2
Brockhill Borders 261 E9
Brock Hill Essex 88 F2
Brockholes W Yorks 197 E7
Brockhollands Glos 79 D10
Brockhurst Derbys 170 C4
Hants 33 G10
Warks 135 G9
Brocklebank Cumb 230 C2
Brocklehirst Dumfries 238 C3
Brocklesby Lincs 200 E6
Brockley London 67 E11
N Som 60 F3
Brockley Corner Suff 124 C6
Brockley Green Suff 106 B4
Suff 124 G6
Brockleymoor Cumb 230 D5
Brockloch Dumfries 246 D2
Brockmanton Hereford 115 F10
Brockmoor W Mid 133 F8
Brockscombe Devon 12 C5
Brock's Green Hants 64 G4
Brock's Watering Norf 142 E2
Brockton Shrops 130 C6
Shrops 130 F6
Shrops 131 E11
Shrops 132 C4
Staffs 150 C6
Telford 150 F4
Brockweir Glos 79 E8
Brockwell Som 42 E2
Brockwood Hants 33 B10
Brockworth Glos 80 B5
Brocton Corn 5 B10
Staffs 151 F9
Brodick N Ayrs 256 B2
Brodie Moray 301 D9
Brodiesord Aberds 302 C5
Brodsworth S Yorks 198 F4
Brogaig Highld 298 C4
Brogborough C Beds 103 D9
Broke Hall Suff 108 C3
Brokenborough Wilts 62 B2
Broken Cross Ches E 184 G5
Ches W 183 G11
Broken Green Herts 105 G8
Brokerswood Wilts 45 C10
Brokes N Yorks 224 F3
Brombil Neath 57 D9
Bromborough Mers 182 E4
Bromborough Pool
Mers 182 E4
Bromdon Shrops 132 G2
Brome Suff 126 B2
Bromesberrow Glos 98 E4
Bromesberrow Heath
Glos 98 E4
Brome Street Suff 126 B3
Bromeswell Suff 126 G6
Bromfield Cumb 229 B9
Shrops 115 B9
Bromford W Mid 134 E2
Bromham Bedford 121 G10
Wilts 62 F3
Bromley Herts 105 G8
London 67 C11
London 68 F2
Shrops 132 D4
Shrops 149 D8
S Yorks 186 B4
W Mid 133 F8
Bromley Common London 68 F2
Bromley Cross Essex 107 F11
Gtr Man 195 E8
Bromley Green Kent 54 F3
Bromley Hall Staffs 150 C5
Bromley Heath S Glos 61 D7
Bromley Park London 67 F11
Bromley Wood Staffs 152 E2
Bromlow Shrops 130 C6
Brompton London 67 D9
Medway 69 F9
N Yorks 217 C8
N Yorks 225 F7
Shrops 131 B10
Brompton-by-Sawdon
N Yorks 217 C8
Brompton-on-Swale
N Yorks 224 F4
Brompton Ralph Som 42 G5
Brompton Regis Som 42 G3
Bromsash Hereford 98 G2
Bromsberrow Heath Glos 98 E4
Bromsgrove Worcs 117 C9
Bromstead Common
Staffs 150 F6
Bromstead Heath Staffs 150 F6
Bromstone Kent 71 F11
Bromyard Hereford 116 G3
Bromyard Downs
Hereford 116 F3
Bronaber Gwyn 146 C4
Broncroft Shrops 131 F10
Brondesbury London 67 C8
Brondesbury Park London 67 C8
Broneirion Powys 129 F10
Brongest Ceredig 92 B6
Brongwyn Ceredig 92 C5
Bronington Wrex 149 B9
Bronllys Powys 96 D2
Bronnant Ceredig 112 D2
Bronwydd Ceredig 93 C7
Bronwydd Arms Carms 93 G8
Bronydd Powys 96 B4
Bronygarth Shrops 148 B5
Brook Carms 74 D3
Devon 12 G5
Devon 14 C2
Hants 32 B4
Hants 32 E3
IoW 20 E3
Kent 54 E5
Sur 50 D5
Sur 50 F2
Brook Bottom Gtr Man 185 D7
Gtr Man 196 G3
Lancs 202 E6
Brooke Norf 142 D5
Rutland 136 B6
Brookenby Lincs 190 B2
Brookend Glos 79 E11
Glos 79 F9
Oxon 100 G6
Brook End Bedford 121 E11
Cambs 121 C11
C Beds 104 B3
Herts 104 F6
M Keynes 103 C8
Wilts 61 C10
Worcs 99 B7
Brookfield Derbys 185 B8
Lancs 203 G7
Mbro 225 B9
Renfs 267 C8
Brookfoot W Yorks 196 C6
Brookgreen IoW 20 E3
Brook Green London 67 D8
Suff 125 F7
Brookhampton Oxon 83 F10
Shrops 131 E11
Som 29 B10
Brook Hill Hants 32 E3
Notts 153 C11
Brookhouse Blackburn 195 B7
Ches E 184 F6
Denb 165 B9
Lancs 211 G10
S Yorks 187 D8
W Yorks 196 B5
Brookhouse Green
Ches E 168 C4
Brookhouses Derbys 185 D8
Staffs 169 G7
Brookhurst Mers 182 E4
Brookland Kent 39 B7
Brooklands Dumfries 237 B10
Gtr Man 184 C3
Shrops 167 G8
Sur 66 G5
W Yorks 206 F2
Brookleigh Devon 14 B5
Brookmans Park Herts 86 E2
Brookpits W Sus 35 G8
Brook Place Sur 66 G3
Brookrow Shrops 116 C2
Brooks Corn 6 C3
Powys 130 D2
Brooksbottoms Gtr Man 195 D9
Brooksby Leics 154 F3
Brooks End Kent 71 F9
Brooks Green W Sus 35 C10
Brookside Brack 66 E2
Derbys 186 G5
Telford 132 B3
Brook Street Essex 87 G9
Kent 52 D5
Kent 54 G2
Suff 106 B6
W Sus 36 B4
Brookthorpe Glos 80 C4
Brookvale Halton 183 E8
Brookville Norf 140 D4
Brook Waters Wilts 30 C6
Brookwood Sur 50 B2
Broom C Beds 104 C3
Cumb 231 G9
Devon 28 G4
E Renf 267 D10
Pembs 73 D10
S Yorks 186 C5
Warks 117 G11
Broombank Worcs 116 C3
Broome Norf 143 E7
Shrops 131 D10
Shrops 131 G8
Worcs 117 B8
Broomedge Warr 184 D2
Broome Park Northumb 264 G4
Broomer's Corner
W Sus 35 C10
Broomershill W Sus 35 D9
Broomfield Aberds 303 F9
Cumb 230 B2
Essex 88 D2
Kent 53 C10
Kent 71 F7
Som 43 G8
Wilts 61 D11
Broomfields Shrops 149 F8
Broomfleet E Yorks 199 B11
Broom Green Norf 159 E9
Broomhall Ches E 167 F10
Windsor 66 F3
Broomhall Green
Ches E 167 F10
Broomham E Sus 23 C8
Broomhaugh Northumb 242 E2
Broomhill Borders 261 D11
Bristol 60 D6
Ches W 167 B7
Highld 301 G9
Kent 55 B8
Norf 140 C2
Northumb 252 C6
Notts 171 F8
S Yorks 198 G2
Broom Hill Bristol 60 E6
Dorset 31 G8
Durham 242 G4
London 68 F3
Suff 108 B5
Worcs 117 B8
Broomhill Bank Kent 52 E5
Broomholm Norf 160 C6
Broomhouse Glasgow 268 C3
Broomlands N Ayrs 257 B8
Broomley Northumb 242 E2
Broompark Durham 233 C10
Broomridge Stirling 278 C6
Broom's Barn Suff 124 D5
Broom's Green Glos 98 E4
Broomsgrove E Sus 38 E4
Broomsthorpe Norf 158 D6
Broom Street Kent 70 G4
Broomton Highld 301 B8
Broomy Hill Hereford 97 D9
Broomy Lodge Hants 32 E2
Broomyshaw Staffs 169 F9
Brora Highld 311 J3
Broseley Shrops 132 C3
Brotherhouse Bar Lincs 156 G5
Brotheridge Green
Worcs 98 C6
Brotherlee Durham 232 D4
Brotherstone Borders 262 B4
Brothertoft Lincs 174 F3
Brotherton N Yorks 198 B3
Brothybeck Cumb 230 C2
Brotton Redcar 226 B3
Broubster Highld 310 C4
Brough Cumb 222 C5
Derbys 185 E11
E Yorks 200 B2
Highld 310 B6
Notts 172 D4
Orkney 314 E3
Orkney 314 H4
Shetland 312 C7
Shetland 312 F6
Shetland 312 F7
Shetland 313 G7
Brough *continued*
Shetland 313 H6
Shetland 313 J7
Broughall Shrops 167 G9
Brough Lodge Shetland 312 D7
Brough Sowerby Cumb 222 C5
Broughton Borders 260 B4
Bucks 84 C4
Cambs 122 B5
Edin 280 F5
Flint 166 C4
Hants 47 G10
Lancs 202 F6
M Keynes 103 C7
N Lincs 200 F3
N Nhants 120 B6
N Yorks 204 C4
N Yorks 216 E5
Orkney 314 B4
Oxon 101 D8
Shrops 132 E6
Staffs 150 C5
V Glam 58 E2
Broughton Astley Leics 135 E10
Broughton Beck Cumb 210 C5
Broughton Common
N Lincs 200 E3
Wilts 61 G11
Broughton Cross Cumb 229 E7
Broughton Gifford Wilts 61 G11
Broughton Green Worcs 117 E9
Broughton Hackett
Worcs 117 G8
Broughton in Furness
Cumb 210 B4
Broughton Lodges Leics 154 E4
Broughton Mills Cumb 220 G4
Broughton Moor Cumb 228 E6
Broughton Park
Gtr Man 195 G10
Broughton Poggs Oxon 82 E2
Broughtown Orkney 314 B6
Broughty Ferry Dundee 287 D8
Brow Edge Cumb 211 C7
Browhouses Dumfries 239 D7
Browland Shetland 313 H4
Brown Bank N Yorks 205 C10
Brownber Cumb 222 D4
Brownbread Street
E Sus 23 B11
Brown Candover Hants 48 F5
Brownedge Ches E 168 C3
Brown Edge Lancs 193 E11
Mers 183 C8
Staffs 168 E6
Brownheath Devon 27 D10
Shrops 149 D9
Brown Heath Ches W 167 B7
Hants 33 D8
Brownheath Common
Worcs 117 E7
Brownhill Aberds 302 E6
Aberds 303 E8
Blackburn 203 G9
Shrops 149 E8
Brownhills Fife 287 F9
Shrops 150 B3
W Mid 133 B10
Brownieside Northumb 264 E5
Browninghill Green
Hants 48 B5
Brown Knowl Ches W 167 E7
Brown Lees Staffs 168 D5
Brownlow Ches E 168 C4
Mers 194 G4
Brownlow Fold Gtr Man 195 E8
Brownlow Heath
Ches E 168 C4
Brown Moor W Yorks 206 G3
Brownmuir Aberds 293 F9
Brown's Bank Ches E 167 G10
Brown's End Glos 98 E4
Brown's Green W Mid 133 E10
Brownshill Glos 80 E5
Brownshill Green
W Mid 134 G6
Brownside Lancs 204 G3
Brownsover Warks 119 B10
Brownston Devon 8 E3
Brown Street Suff 125 E11
Browns Wood M Keynes 103 D8
Browsburn N Lanark 268 C5
Browston Green Norf 143 C9
Browtop Cumb 229 G7
Broxa N Yorks 227 G8
Broxbourne Herts 86 D5
Broxburn E Loth 282 F3
W Loth 279 G11
Broxfield Northumb 264 F6
Broxholme Lincs 188 F6
Broxted Essex 105 F11
Broxton Ches W 167 E7
Broxtowe Nottingham 171 G8
Broxwood Hereford 115 G7
Broyle Side E Sus 23 C7
Brù W Isles 304 D5
Bruairnis W Isles 297 L3
Bruan Highld 310 F7
Bruar Lodge Perth 291 F10
Brucefield Fife 280 D2
Brucehill W Dunb 277 F7
Bruche Warr 183 D10
Brucklebog Aberds 293 D9
Bruera Ches W 166 C6
Bruern Abbey Oxon 100 G5
Bruichladdich Argyll 274 G3
Bruisyard Suff 126 D6
Brumby N Lincs 199 F11
Brunant Powys 130 B5
Brund Staffs 169 C10
Brundall Norf 142 B6
Brundish Norf 143 D7
Suff 126 D5
Brundish Street Suff 126 C5
Brundon Suff 107 C7
Brunery Highld 289 B9
Brunnion Corn 2 B2
Brunshaw Lancs 204 G3
Brunstane Edin 280 G6
Brunstock Cumb 239 F10
Brunswick Gtr Man 184 B4
Brunswick Park London 86 G3
Brunswick Village T&W 242 C6
Bruntcliffe W Yorks 197 B9
Brunt Hamersland
Shetland 313 H6
Brunthwaite W Yorks 205 D7
Bruntingthorpe Leics 136 F2
Brunton Fife 287 E7
Northumb 264 E6
Wilts 47 B8
Brushes Gtr Man 185 B7
Brushfield Derbys 185 G11
Brushford Devon 25 F11
Som 26 B6
Bruton Som 45 G7
Bryans Midloth 270 C6
Bryan's Green Worcs 117 D7
Bryanston Dorset 30 F5
Bryant's Bottom Bucks 84 F5
Brydekirk Dumfries 238 C5
Bryher Scilly 1 G3
Brymbo Conwy 180 G4
Wrex 166 E3
Brympton Som 29 D8
Brympton D'Evercy Som 29 D8
Bryn Caerph 77 F11
Carms 75 E8
Ches W 183 G10
Gtr Man 194 G5
Gwyn 179 G9
Neath 57 C10
Powys 130 C3
Rhondda 76 D6
Shrops 130 F5
Swansea 56 C4
Brynafan Ceredig 112 C4
Brynamman Carms 76 C2
Brynawel Caerph 77 G11
Brynberian Pembs 92 D2
Brynbryddan Neath 57 C9
Neath 57 C9
Bryn Bwbach Gwyn 146 B2
Bryncae Rhondda 58 C3
Rhondda 58 C3
Bryn Celyn Anglesey 179 F10
Flint 181 F11
Bryncethin Bridgend 58 C2
Bridgend 58 C2
Bryncir Gwyn 163 G7
Bryncoch Bridgend 58 C2
Bryn-coch Neath 57 B8
Bryn Common Flint 166 D3
Bryncroes Gwyn 144 C4
Bryncrug Gwyn 128 C2
Brynderwen Powys 130 D3
Bryndu Carms 75 D8
Bryn Du Anglesey 178 G4
Bryn Dulas Conwy 180 F6
Bryneglwys Denb 165 F10
Bryn Eglwys Gwyn 163 B10
Brynford Flint 181 G11
Bryn Gates Gtr Man 194 G5
Brynglas Newport 59 B10
Bryn-glas Conwy 164 B4
Brynglas Sta Gwyn 128 C2
Bryn Golau Rhondda 58 B3
Bryngwran Anglesey 178 F4
Bryngwyn Ceredig 92 B5
Mon 78 D5
Powys 96 B3
Brynhenllan Pembs 91 D10
Bryn-henllan Pembs 91 D10
Brynheulog Bridgend 57 C11
Brynhoffnant Ceredig 110 G6
Bryniau Denb 181 E9
Bryning Lancs 194 B2
Brynithel Bl Gwent 78 E2
Bryn-Iwan Carms 92 E6
Brynllywarch Powys 130 F3
Brynmawr Bl Gwent 77 C11
Bryn-mawr Gwyn 144 C4
Bryn Mawr Powys 148 F5
Brynmenyn Bridgend 58 B2
Brynmill Swansea 56 C6
Brynmorfudd Conwy 164 C4
Bryn Myrddin Carms 93 G8
Brynna Rhondda 58 C3
Bryn-nantllech Conwy 164 B6
Brynnau Gwynion
Rhondda 58 C3
Bryn-newydd Denb 165 G11
Bryn Offa Wrex 166 F4
Brynore Shrops 149 B7
Bryn-penarth Powys 130 C2
Bryn Pen-y-lan Wrex 166 G4
Bryn Pydew Conwy 180 F4
Brynrefail Anglesey 179 D7
Gwyn 163 C9
Bryn Rhyd-yr-Arian
Conwy 165 B7
Bryn-rhys Conwy 180 F4
Brynsadler Rhondda 58 C4
Bryn Saith Marchog
Denb 165 E9
Brynsiencyn Anglesey 163 B7
Bryn Sion Gwyn 147 F7
Brynsworthy Devon 40 G4
Bryn Tanat Powys 148 E4
Brynteg Anglesey 179 E7
Ceredig 93 C9
Wrex 166 E4
Bryntirion Bridgend 57 E11
Bryn-y-cochin Shrops 149 B7
Bryn-y-gwenin Mon 78 B4
Bryn-y-maen Conwy 180 F4
Bryn-yr-Eos Wrex 166 G3
Bryn-yr-eryr Gwyn 162 F5
Bryn-yr-ogof Denb 165 D11
Buaile nam Bodach
W Isles 297 L3
Bualintur Highld 294 C6
Bualnaluib Highld 307 K3
Buarthmeini Gwyn 146 C6
Bubbenhall Warks 119 C7
Bubblewell Glos 80 E5
Bubnell Derbys 186 G2
Bubwith E Yorks 207 F10
Buccleuch Borders 261 G8
Buchanan Smithy
Stirling 277 D9
Buchanhaven Aberds 303 E11
Buchan Hill W Sus 51 G9
Buchanty Perth 286 E3
Buchley E Dunb 277 G11
Buchlyvie Stirling 277 C11
Buckabank Cumb 230 B3
Buckbury Worcs 98 E6
Buckden Cambs 122 D3
N Yorks 213 D8
Buckenham Norf 143 B7
Buckerell Devon 27 G10
Bucket Corner Hants 32 C6
Buckfast Devon 8 B4
Buckfastleigh Devon 8 B4
Buckham Dorset 29 G7
Buckhaven Fife 281 B7
Buck Hill Wilts 62 E3
Buckholm Borders 261 B11
Buckholt Mon 79 B8
Buckhorn Devon 12 B3
Buckhorn Weston Dorset 30 C3
Buckhurst Kent 53 E10
Buckhurst Hill Essex 86 G6
Buckie Moray 302 C4
Buckies Highld 310 C5
Buckingham Bucks 102 E3
Buckland Bucks 84 C5
Devon 8 G3
Devon 14 G3
Glos 99 D11
Hants 20 B2
Herts 105 E7
Kent 55 E10
Oxon 82 F4
Sur 51 C8
Buckland Brewer Devon 24 C6
Buckland Common Bucks 84 D6
Buckland Dinham Som 45 C9
Buckland Down Som 45 C8
Buckland End W Mid 134 F2
Buckland Filleigh Devon 25 F7
Buckland in the Moor
Devon 13 G10
Buckland Marsh Oxon 82 F4
Buckland Monachorum
Devon 7 B9
Buckland Newton
Dorset 29 F11
Buckland Ripers Dorset 17 E8
Bucklands Borders 262 F2
Buckland St Mary Som 28 E3
Buckland Valley Kent 55 E10
Bucklandwharf Bucks 84 C5
Bucklebury W Berks 64 E5
Bucklebury Alley
W Berks 64 E4
Bucklegate Lincs 156 B6
Buckleigh Devon 24 B6
Bucklerheads Angus 287 D8
Bucklers Hard Hants 20 B4
Bucklesham Suff 108 C4
Buckley = *Bwcle* Flint 166 C3
Buckley Green Warks 118 D3
Buckley Hill Mers 182 B4
Bucklow Hill Ches E 184 E2
Buckminster Leics 155 E7
Buckmoorend Bucks 84 E4
Bucknall Lincs 173 B11
Stoke 168 F6
Bucknell Oxon 101 F11
Shrops 115 C7
Buckoak Ches W 183 G8
Buckover S Glos 79 G11
Buckpool Moray 302 C4
W Mid 133 F7
Buckridge Worcs 116 C4
Bucksburn Aberdeen 293 C10
Buck's Cross Devon 24 C4
Bucks Green W Sus 50 G5
Buckshaw Village Lancs 194 C5
Bucks Hill Herts 85 E9
Bucks Horn Oak Hants 49 E10
Buckskin Hants 48 C6
Buck's Mills Devon 24 C5
Buckton E Yorks 218 E3
Hereford 115 C7
Northumb 264 B3
Buckton Vale Gtr Man 196 G3
Buckworth Cambs 122 B2
Budbrooke Warks 118 D5
Budby Notts 171 B10
Buddgbrake Shetland 312 B8
Buddileigh Staffs 168 F3
Budd's Titson Corn 24 G2
Bude Corn 24 F2
Budge's Shop Corn 6 D6
Budlake Devon 14 B5
Budle Northumb 264 B5
Budleigh Som 27 D11
Budleigh Salterton Devon 15 E7
Budlett's Common E Sus 37 C7
Budock Water Corn 3 C7
Budworth Heath
Ches W 183 F11
Buersil Head Gtr Man 196 E2
Buerton Ches E 167 G11
Buffler's Holt Bucks 102 D3
Bufton Leics 135 B8
Bugbrooke W Nhants 120 F3
Bugford Devon 40 E6
Bughtlin Edin 280 G3
Buglawton Ches E 168 C5
Bugle Corn 5 D10
Bugle Gate Worcs 116 D6
Bugley Dorset 30 C3
Wilts 45 E11
Bugthorpe E Yorks 207 B11
Building End Essex 105 D8
Buildwas Shrops 132 C2
Builth Road Powys 113 G10
Builth Wells Powys 113 G10
Buirgh W Isles 305 J2
Bulbourne Herts 84 C6
Bulbridge Wilts 46 G5
Bulby Lincs 155 D11
Bulcote Notts 171 G11
Buldoo Highld 310 C3
Bulford Wilts 47 E7
Bulford Camp Wilts 47 E7
Bulkeley Ches E 167 E8
Bulkeley Hall Shrops 168 G2
Bulkington Warks 135 F7
Wilts 46 B2
Bulkworthy Devon 24 E5
Bullamoor N Yorks 225 G7
Bull Bay = *Porthllechog*
Anglesey 178 C6
Bullbridge Derbys 170 E5
Bullbrook Brack 65 F11
Bulleign Kent 53 G11
Bullenhill Wilts 45 B11
Bullen's Green Herts 86 D2
Bulley Glos 80 B3
Bullgill Cumb 229 D7
Bull Hill Hants 20 B2
Bullhurst Hill Derbys 170 G3
Bullinghope Hereford 97 D10
Bullington Hants 48 E3
Lincs 189 F9
Bullo Glos 79 D11
Bullock's Horn Wilts 81 G7
Bullockstone Kent 71 F7
Bulls Cross London 86 F4
Bulls Green Som 45 D8
Bull's Green Herts 86 B3
Norf 143 E8
Bull's Hill Hereford 97 G11
Bullwood Argyll 276 G3
Bullyhole Bottom Mon 79 F7
Bulmer Essex 106 C6
N Yorks 216 F3
Bulmer Tye Essex 106 D6
Bulphan Thurrock 68 B6
Bulstrode Herts 85 E8
Bulthy Shrops 148 G6
Bulverhythe E Sus 38 F3
Bulwark Aberds 303 E9
Mon 79 G8
Bulwell Nottingham 171 F8
Bulwell Forest
Nottingham 171 F8
Bulwick Leics 136 E3
N Nhants 137 E9
Bumble's Green Essex 86 D6
Bumwell Hill Norf 142 E2
Bun Abhainn Eadarra
W Isles 305 H3
Bunacaimb Highld 295 G8
Bun a'Mhuillin W Isles 297 K3
Bunarkaig Highld 290 E3
Bunbury Ches E 167 D9
Bunbury Heath Ches E 167 D9
Bunce Common Sur 51 D8
Bunchrew Highld 300 E6
Bundalloch Highld 295 C10
Buness Shetland 312 C8
Bunessan Argyll 288 G5
Bungay Suff 142 F6
Bunkers Hill Gtr Man 184 D6
Oxon 83 B7
Bunker's Hill Cambs 139 B8
Lincs 174 E3

Bunker's Hill *continued*
Lincs 189 G7
Norf 142 B3
Suff 143 C10
Bunloit Highld 300 G5
Bun Loyne Highld 290 C4
Bunnahabhain Argyll 274 F5
Bunny Notts 153 D11
Bunny Hill Notts 153 D11
Bunree Highld 290 G2
Bunroy Highld 290 E4
Bunsley Bank Ches E 167 G11
Bunstead Hants 32 C6
Buntait Highld 300 F3
Buntingford Herts 105 F7
Bunting's Green Essex 106 E6
Bunwell Norf 142 E2
Bunwell Bottom Norf 142 D2
Buoltach Highld 310 F5
Burbage Derbys 185 G8
Leics 135 E8
Wilts 63 G8
Burcher Hereford 114 E6
Burchett's Green
Windsor 65 C10
Burcombe Wilts 46 G5
Burcot Oxon 83 F9
Worcs 117 C9
Burcote Shrops 132 D4
Burcott Bucks 84 B4
Bucks 103 G7
Som 44 D4
Burdiehouse Edin 270 B5
Burdon T&W 243 G9
Burdonshill V Glam 58 E6
Burdrop Oxon 101 D7
Bures Suff 107 E8
Bures Green Suff 107 D8
Burford Ches E 167 E10
Devon 24 C4
Oxon 82 C3
Shrops 115 D11
Som 44 E5
Burg Argyll 288 E5
Argyll 288 G6
Burgar Orkney 314 D3
Burgate Hants 31 D11
Suff 125 B11
Burgates Hants 34 B3
Burgedin Powys 148 G4
Burge End Herts 104 E2
Burgess Hill W Sus 36 D4
Burgh Suff 126 G4
Burgh by Sands Cumb 239 F8
Burgh Castle Norf 143 B9
Burghclere Hants 64 G3
Burghclere Common
Hants 64 G3
Burgh Common Norf 141 E11
Burghead Moray 301 C11
Burghfield W Berks 65 F7
Burghfield Common
W Berks 64 F6
Burghfield Hill W Berks 65 F7
Burgh Heath Sur 51 B8
Burgh Hill E Sus 23 C8
E Sus 38 B2
Burghill Hereford 97 C9
Burgh le Marsh Lincs 175 B8
Burgh Muir Aberds 293 B9
Aberds 303 G7
Burgh next Aylsham
Norf 160 D4
Burgh on Bain Lincs 190 D2
Burgh St Margaret
= *Fleggburgh* Norf 161 G8
Burgh St Peter Norf 143 E9
Burgh Stubbs Norf 159 C10
Burghwallis S Yorks 198 E4
Burgois Corn 10 G4
Burham Kent 69 G8
Burham Court Kent 69 G8
Buriton Hants 34 C2
Burland Ches E 167 E10
Burlawn Corn 10 G5
Burleigh Brack 65 E11
Glos 80 E5
Burlescombe Devon 27 D9
Burleston Dorset 17 C11
Burlestone Devon 8 F6
Burley Hants 32 G2
Rutland 155 G7
Shrops 131 G9
W Yorks 205 G11
Burley Beacon Hants 32 G2
Burleydam Ches E 167 G10
Burley Gate Hereford 97 B11
Burley in Wharfedale
W Yorks 205 D9
Burley Lawn Hants 32 G2
Burley Lodge Hants 32 F2
Burley Street Hants 32 G2
Burley Woodhead
W Yorks 205 E9
Burlinch Som 28 B3
Burlingham Green Norf 161 G7
Burlingjobb Powys 114 F5
Burlish Park Worcs 116 C6
Burlorne Tregoose Corn 5 B10
Burlow E Sus 23 B9
Burlton Shrops 149 D9
Burmantofts W Yorks 206 G2
Burmarsh Hereford 97 B10
Kent 54 G5
Burmington Warks 100 D5
Burn N Yorks 198 B5
Burnage Gtr Man 184 C5
Burnard's Ho Devon 24 G4
Burnaston Derbys 152 C5
Burnbank S Lanark 268 D4
Burn Bridge N Yorks 206 C2
Burnby E Yorks 208 D2
Burncross S Yorks 186 B4
Burndell W Sus 35 G7
Burnden Gtr Man 195 F8
Burnedge Gtr Man 196 E2
Burnend Aberds 303 E8
Burneside Cumb 221 F10
Burness Orkney 314 B6
Burneston N Yorks 214 B6
Burnett Bath 61 F7
Burnfoot Borders 261 G10
Borders 262 F2
Dumfries 237 C9
Dumfries 247 E11
E Ayrs 245 B10
N Lanark 268 B5
Perth 286 G3
Burngreave S Yorks 186 D5
Burnham Bucks 66 C2
N Lincs 200 D5
Burnham Deepdale
Norf 176 E4
Burnham Green Herts 86 B3
Burnham Market Norf 176 E4
Burnham Norton Norf 176 E4
Burnham-on-Crouch
Essex 88 F6
Burnham-on-Sea Som 43 D10
Burnham Overy Staithe
Norf 176 E4
Burnham Overy Town
Norf 176 E4
Burnham Thorpe Norf 176 E5
Burnhead Aberds 293 D10
Borders 262 F2
Dumfries 247 D9
Dumfries 247 G10
S Ayrs 244 C6
Burnhervie Aberds 293 B9
Burnhill Green Staffs 132 C5
Burnhope Durham 233 B9
Burnhouse N Ayrs 267 E7
Burnhouse Mains
Borders 271 F8
Burniere Corn 10 G5
Burniestrype Moray 302 C3
Burniston N Yorks 227 G10
Burnlee W Yorks 196 F6
Burnley Lancs 204 G2
Burnley Lane Lancs 204 G2
Burnley Wood Lancs 204 G2
Burnmouth Borders 273 C9
Burn Naze Lancs 202 E2
Burn of Cambus
Stirling 285 G11
Burnopfield Durham 242 F5
Burnrigg Cumb 239 F11
Burnsall N Yorks 213 G10
Burn's Green Herts 104 G6
Burnside Aberds 303 E8
Angus 287 B9
E Ayrs 258 G3
Fife 286 G5
Perth 286 E4
Shetland 312 F4
S Lanark 268 C2
T&W 243 G8
W Loth 279 G11
Burnside of Duntrune
Angus 287 D8
Burnstone Devon 24 C4
Burnswark Dumfries 238 B5
Burnt Ash Glos 80 E5
Burntcommon Sur 50 C4
Burntheath Derbys 152 C4
Burnt Heath Derbys 186 F2
Essex 107 F11
Burnt Hill W Berks 64 E5
Burnthouse Corn 3 B7
Burnt Houses Durham 233 G8
Burntisland Fife 280 D4
Burnt Mills Essex 88 G2
Burnt Oak E Sus 37 B8
London 86 G2
Burnton E Ayrs 245 B11
Burnt Tree W Mid 133 E9
Burnturk Fife 287 G7
Burntwood Staffs 133 B11
Burntwood Green
Staffs 133 B11
Burntwood Pentre Flint 166 C3
Burnt Yates N Yorks 214 G5
Burnworthy Som 27 D11
Burnwynd Edin 270 B2
Burpham Sur 50 C4
W Sus 35 F8
Burradon Northumb 251 B11
T&W 243 C7
Burrafirth Shetland 312 B8
Burraland Shetland 312 F5
Shetland 313 J4
Burras Corn 2 C5
Burrastow Shetland 313 J4
Burraton Corn 7 D8
Burraton Coombe Corn 7 D8
Burravoe Shetland 312 F7
Shetland 312 G5
Burray Village Orkney 314 G4
Burreldales Aberds 303 F7
Burrells Cumb 222 B3
Burrelton Perth 286 D6
Burridge Devon 28 F4
Devon 40 F5
Hants 33 E8
Burrigill Highld 310 F6
Burrill N Yorks 214 B4
Burringham N Lincs 199 F10
Burrington Devon 25 D10
Hereford 115 C8
N Som 44 B3
Burrough End Cambs 124 F2
Burrough Green Cambs 124 F2
Burrough on the Hill
Leics 154 G5
Burroughs Grove Bucks 65 B11
Burroughston Orkney 314 D5
Burrow Devon 14 B5
Som 28 C6
Som 42 E2
Burrowbridge Som 43 G11
Burrow-bridge Som 28 B5
Burrowhill Sur 66 G3
Burrows Cross Sur 50 D5
Burrowsmoor Holt
Notts 172 G2
Burrsville Park Essex 89 B11
Burrswood Kent 52 F4
Burry Swansea 56 C3
Burry Green Swansea 56 C3
Burry Port = *Porth Tywyn*
Carms 74 E6
Burscott Devon 24 C4
Burscough Lancs 194 E2
Burscough Bridge Lancs 194 E2
Bursdon Devon 24 D3
Bursea E Yorks 208 G2
Burshill E Yorks 209 D7
Bursledon Hants 33 F7
Burslem Stoke 168 F5
Burstall Suff 107 C11
Burstallhill Suff 107 B11
Burstock Dorset 28 G6
Burston Devon 26 G2
Norf 142 G2
Staffs 151 C8
Burstow Sur 51 E10
Burstwick E Yorks 201 B8
Burtersett N Yorks 213 B7
Burtholme Cumb 240 E2
Burthorpe Suff 124 E5
Burthwaite Cumb 230 B4
Burtle Som 43 E11
Burtle Hill Som 43 E11
Burtoft Lincs 156 B5
Burton BCP 17 C9
BCP 19 C9
Ches W 167 C8
Ches W 182 G4
Lincs 189 G7
Northumb 264 C5
Pembs 73 D7
Som 29 E8
Som 43 E7
V Glam 58 F4
Wilts 45 G10
Wilts 61 D10
Wrex 166 D5
Burton Agnes E Yorks 218 G2
Burton Bradstock Dorset 16 D5
Burton Corner Lincs 174 F4
Burton Dassett Warks 119 G7
Burton End Cambs 106 B2
Essex 105 G10
Burton Ferry Pembs 73 D7
Burton Fleming
E Yorks 217 E11
Burton Green Essex 106 F6
W Mid 118 B5
Wrex 166 D4
Burton Hastings Warks 135 E8
Burton-in-Kendal
Cumb 211 D10
Burton in Lonsdale
N Yorks 212 E3
Burton Joyce Notts 171 G10
Burton Latimer
N Nhants 121 C8
Burton Lazars Leics 154 F5
Burton-le-Coggles
Lincs 155 D9
Burton Leonard
N Yorks 214 G6
Burton Manor Staffs 151 E8
Burton on the Wolds
Leics 153 E11
Burton Overy Leics 136 D3
Burton Pedwardine
Lincs 173 G10
Burton Pidsea E Yorks 209 G10
Burton Salmon N Yorks 198 B3
Burton Stather N Lincs 199 D11
Burton upon Stather
N Lincs 199 D11
Burton upon Trent
Staffs 152 E5
Burton Westwood
Shrops 132 D2
Burtonwood Warr 183 C9
Burwardsley Ches W 167 D8
Burwarton Shrops 132 F2
Burwash E Sus 37 C11
Burwash Common
E Sus 37 C10
Burwash Weald E Sus 37 C10
Burwell Cambs 123 D11
Lincs 190 F5
Burwen Anglesey 178 C6
Burwick Orkney 314 H4
Shetland 313 J5
Burwood Shrops 131 F9
Burwood Park Sur 66 G6
Bury Cambs 138 G5
Gtr Man 195 E10
Som 26 B6
W Sus 35 E8
Buryas Br Corn 1 D4
Burybank Staffs 151 B7
Bury End Bedford 121 G9
C Beds 104 E2
Worcs 99 D11
Bury Green Herts 86 E4
Herts 105 G8
Bury Hollow W Sus 35 E8
Bury Park Luton 103 G11
Bury St Edmunds Suff 125 E7
Bury's Bank W Berks 64 F3
Burythorpe N Yorks 216 G5
Busbiehill N Ayrs 257 B9
Busbridge Sur 50 E3
Busby E Renf 267 D11
Buscot Oxon 82 F2
Buscott Som 44 F2
Bush Aberds 293 G9
Corn 24 F2
Bush Bank Hereford 115 G9
Bushbury Sur 51 D7
W Mid 133 C8
Bushby Leics 136 C3
Bush Crathie Aberds 292 D4
Bush End Essex 87 B9
Bush Estate Norf 161 D8
Bushey Dorset 18 E5
Herts 85 G10
Bushey Ground Oxon 82 D4
Bushey Heath Herts 85 G11
Bushey Mead London 67 F8
Bushfield Cumb 249 G11
Bush Green Norf 141 D10
Norf 142 F4
Suff 125 F8
Bush Hill Park London 86 F4
Bushley Worcs 99 E7
Bushley Green Worcs 99 E7
Bushmead Bedford 122 E2
Bushmoor Shrops 131 F8
Bushton Wilts 62 D5
Bushy Common Norf 159 G9
Bushy Hill Sur 50 C4
Busk Cumb 231 C8
Gtr Man 196 F2
Buslingthorpe Lincs 189 D9
Bussage Glos 80 E5
Bussex Som 43 F11
Busta Shetland 312 G5
Bustard Green Essex 106 F2
Bustard's Green Norf 142 E3
Bustatoun Orkney 314 A7
Busveal Corn 4 G4
Butcher's Common Norf 160 E6
Butcher's Cross E Sus 37 B9
Butcombe N Som 60 G4
Butetown Cardiff 59 D7
Bute Town Caerph 77 D10
Butlane Head Shrops 149 G8
Butleigh Som 44 G4
Butleigh Wootton Som 44 G4
Butlersbank Shrops 149 E11
Butlers Cross Bucks 85 G7
Butler's Cross Bucks 84 D4
Butler's End Warks 134 G4
Butler's Hill Notts 171 F8
Butlers Marston Warks 118 G6
Butley Suff 127 G7
Butley High Corner Suff 109 B7
Butley Low Corner Suff 109 B7
Butley Town Ches E 184 F6
Butlocks Heath Hants 33 F7
Butter Bank Staffs 151 E7
Butterburn Cumb 240 C5
Buttercrambe N Yorks 207 B10
Butteriss Gate Corn 2 C6
Butterknowle Durham 233 F8
Butterleigh Devon 27 F7
Butterley Derbys 170 C4
Derbys 170 E6
Buttermere Cumb 220 B3
Wilts 63 G10
Butterrow Glos 80 E5
Butters Green Staffs 168 E4
Buttershaw W Yorks 196 B6
Butterstone Perth 286 C4
Butterton Staffs 168 G4
Staffs 169 D9
Butterwick Cumb 221 B10
Durham 234 F3
Lincs 174 G5
N Yorks 216 D4
N Yorks 217 E9
Butteryhaugh Northumb 250 E4
Butt Green Ches E 167 E11
Buttington Powys 130 B5
Butt Lane Staffs 168 E4
Buttonbridge Shrops 116 B4
Button Haugh Green
Suff 125 D9
Buttonoak Worcs 116 B5
Button's Green Suff 125 G8
Butts Devon 14 D2
Buttsash Hants 32 F6
Buttsbear Cross Corn 24 G3
Buttsbury Essex 87 F11
Butts Green Essex 105 E9
Butt's Green Essex 88 E3
Hants 32 B4
Buttsole Kent 55 C10
Butt Yeats Lancs 211 F11
Buxhall Suff 125 F10
Buxhall Fen Street
Suff 125 F10
Buxley Borders 272 E6
Buxted E Sus 37 C7
Buxton Derbys 185 G9
Norf 160 E4
Buxworth Derbys 185 E8
Bwcle = *Buckley* Flint 166 C3
Bwlch Flint 181 G11
Powys 96 G2
Bwlch-derwin Gwyn 163 F7
Bwlchgwyn Wrex 166 E3
Bwlch-Llan Ceredig 111 F11
Bwlchnewydd Carms 93 G7
Bwlch-newydd Carms 93 G7
Bwlchtocyn Gwyn 144 D6
Bwlch-y-cibau Powys 148 F3
Bwlch-y-cwm Cardiff 58 C6
Bwlchyddar Powys 148 E3
Bwlch-y-fadfa Ceredig 93 B8
Bwlch-y-ffridd Powys 129 D11
Bwlchygroes Pembs 92 D4
Bwlchyllyn Gwyn 163 D8
Bwlch-y-Plain Powys 114 B4
Bwlch-y-sarnau Powys 113 C10
Bybrook Kent 54 E4
Bycross Hereford 97 C7
Byeastwood Bridgend 58 C2
Byebush Aberds 303 F7
Bye Green Bucks 84 C5
Byerhope Northumb 232 B3
Byermoor T&W 242 F5
Byers Green Durham 233 E10
Byfield W Nhants 119 G10
Byfleet Sur 66 G5
Byford Hereford 97 C7
Byford Common Hereford 97 C7
Bygrave Herts 104 D5
Byker T&W 243 E7
Byland Abbey N Yorks 215 D10
Bylchau Conwy 165 C7
Byley Ches W 168 B2
Bynea Carms 56 B4
Byram N Yorks 198 B3
Byrness Northumb 251 C7
Bythorn Cambs 121 B11
Byton Hereford 115 E7
Byton Hand Hereford 115 E7
Bywell Northumb 242 E2
Byworth W Sus 35 C7

C

Cabbacott Devon 24 C6
Cabbage Hill Brack 65 E11
Cabharstadh W Isles 304 F5
Cabin Shrops 130 F6
Cablea Perth 286 D3
Cabourne Lincs 200 G6
Cabrach Argyll 274 G5
Moray 302 G3
Cabrich Highld 300 E5
Cabus Lancs 202 D5
Cackle Hill Lincs 157 D7
Cackleshaw W Yorks 204 F6
Cackle Street E Sus 23 B11
E Sus 37 B7
E Sus 38 D4
Cadboll Highld 301 B8
Cadbury Devon 26 G6
Cadbury Barton Devon 25 D11
Cadbury Heath S Glos 61 E7
Cadder E Dunb 278 G2
Cadderlie Argyll 284 D4
Caddington C Beds 85 B9
Caddleton Argyll 275 B8
Caddonfoot Borders 261 C10
Caddonlee Borders 261 B10
Cadeby Leics 135 C8
S Yorks 198 G4
Cadeleigh Devon 26 F6
Cademuir Borders 260 B6
Cader Denb 165 C8
Cade Street E Sus 37 C10
Cadger Path Angus 287 B8
Cad Green Som 28 D4
Cadgwith Corn 2 G6
Cadham Fife 286 G6
Cadishead Gtr Man 184 C2
Cadle Swansea 56 B6
Cadley Lancs 202 G6
Wilts 47 C8
Wilts 63 F8
Cadmore End Bucks 84 G3
Cadnam Hants 32 E3
Cadney N Lincs 200 G4
Cadney Bank Wrex 149 C9
Cadole Flint 166 C2
Cadoxton V Glam 58 F6
Cadoxton-Juxta-Neath
Neath 57 B9
Cadshaw Blackburn 195 D8
Cadwell Herts 104 E3
Cadzow S Lanark 268 E4
Caeathro Gwyn 163 C7
Cae Clyd Gwyn 164 G2
Cae-gors Carms 75 E9
Caehopkin Powys 76 C4
Caemorgan Ceredig 92 B3
Caenby Lincs 189 D8
Caenby Corner Lincs 189 D7
Caerau Bridgend 57 C11
Cardiff 58 D6
Caerau Park Newport 59 B9
Cae'r-bont Powys 76 C4
Cae'r-bryn Carms 75 C9
Caerdeon Gwyn 146 F2
Caer-Estyn Wrex 166 D4
Caerfarchell Pembs 90 F5
Caer-Farchell Pembs 90 F5
Caerffili = *Caerphilly*
Caerph 59 B7
Caerfyrddin = *Carmarthen*
Carms 93 G8
Caergeiliog Anglesey 178 F4
Caergwrle Flint 166 D4
Caergybi = *Holyhead*
Anglesey 178 E2
Caerhendy Neath 57 C9
Caerhun Gwyn 163 B9
Cae'r-Lan Powys 76 C4
Caerleon Newport 78 G4
Caer Llan Mon 79 D7
Caermead V Glam 58 F3
Caermeini Pembs 92 E2
Caernarfon Gwyn 163 C7
Caerphilly = *Caerffili*
Caerph 59 B7
Caersws Powys 129 E10
Caerwedros Ceredig 111 F7
Caerwent Mon 79 G7
Caerwent Brook Mon 60 B3
Caerwych Gwyn 146 B2
Caerwys Flint 181 G10
Caethle Gwyn 128 D2
Cage Green Kent 52 D5
Caggan Highld 291 B10
Caggle Street Mon 78 B5
Cailness Stirling 285 G7
Caim Anglesey 179 E10
Cainscross Glos 80 D4
Caio Carms 94 D3
Cairinis W Isles 296 E4
Cairisiadar W Isles 304 E2
Cairminis W Isles 296 C6
Cairnbaan Argyll 275 D9
Cairnbanno Ho Aberds 303 E8
Cairnborrow Aberds 302 E4
Cairnbrogie Aberds 303 G8
Cairnbulg Castle
Aberds 303 C10
Cairncross Angus 292 F6
Borders 273 C7
Cairnderry Dumfries 236 B5
Cairndow Argyll 284 F5
Cairness Aberds 303 C10
Cairneyhill Fife 279 D10
Cairnfield Ho Moray 302 C4
Cairngaan Dumfries 236 F3
Cairngarroch Dumfries 236 E2
Cairnhill Aberds 302 F6
Aberds 303 D7
N Lanark 268 C5
Cairnie Aberds 293 C10
Aberds 302 E4
Cairnlea S Ayrs 244 G6
Cairnleith Crofts Aberds 303 F9
Cairnmuir Aberds 303 C9
Cairnorrie Aberds 303 E8
Cairnpark Aberds 293 B10
Dumfries 247 D9
Cairnryan Dumfries 236 C2
Cairnton Orkney 314 F3
Cairston Orkney 314 E2
Caister-on-Sea Norf 161 G10
Caistor Lincs 200 G6
Caistor St Edmund Norf 142 C4
Caistron Northumb 251 C11
Caitha Bowland Borders 271 G9
Cakebole Worcs 117 C7
Calais Street Suff 107 D9
Calanais W Isles 304 E4
Calbost W Isles 305 G6
Calbourne IoW 20 D4
Calceby Lincs 190 F5
Calcoed Flint 181 G11
Calcot Glos 81 C9
W Berks 65 E7
Calcot Row W Berks 65 E7
Calcott Kent 71 G7
Shrops 149 G8
Calcott's Green Glos 80 B3
Calcutt N Yorks 206 B2
Wilts 81 G10
Caldback Shetland 312 C8
Caldbeck Cumb 230 D2
Caldbergh N Yorks 213 B11
Caldecote Cambs 122 F6
Cambs 138 F2
Herts 104 D4
Warks 135 E7
W Nhants 120 G3
Caldecote Hill Herts 85 G11
Caldecott N Nhants 121 D9
Oxon 83 F7
Rutland 137 E7
Caldecotte M Keynes 103 D7
Calder Cumb 219 E10
Calderbank N Lanark 268 C5
Calder Bridge Cumb 219 D10
Calderbrook Gtr Man 196 D2
Caldercruix N Lanark 268 B6
Calder Grove W Yorks 197 D10
Calder Hall Cumb 219 E10
Calder Mains Highld 310 D4
Caldermill S Lanark 268 G3
Caldermoor Gtr Man 196 D2
Calderstones Mers 182 D6
Calder Vale Lancs 202 D6
Calderwood S Lanark 268 D2
Caldhame Angus 287 C8
Caldicot = *Cil-y-coed*
Mon 60 B3
Caldmore W Mid 133 D10
Caldwell Derbys 152 F5
N Yorks 224 C3
Caldy Mers 182 D2
Caledrhydiau Ceredig 111 G9
Cale Green Gtr Man 184 D5
Calenick Corn 4 G6
Caleys Fields Worcs 100 C4
Calf Heath Staffs 133 B8
Calford Green Suff 106 B3
Calfsound Orkney 314 C5
Calgary Argyll 288 D5
Califer Moray 301 D10
California Cambs 139 G10
Falk 279 F8
Norf 161 G10
Suff 108 C3
W Mid 133 G10
Calke Derbys 153 E7
Callakille Highld 298 D6
Callaly Northumb 252 B3
Callander Stirling 285 G10
Callandrode Stirling 285 G10
Callands Warr 183 C9
Callaughton Shrops 132 D2
Callendar Park Falk 279 F7
Callert Ho Highld 290 G2
Callerton T&W 242 D5
Callerton Lane End
T&W 242 D5
Callestick Corn 4 E5
Calligarry Highld 295 E8
Callington Corn 7 B7
Callingwood Staffs 152 E3
Calloose Corn 2 B3
Callop Highld 289 B11
Callow Derbys 170 E3
Hereford 97 E9
Callow End Worcs 98 B6
Callow Hill Mon 79 B8
Som 44 E4
Wilts 62 C4
Worcs 116 C4
Callow Marsh Hereford 98 B3
Callows Grave Worcs 115 D11
Calmore Hants 32 E4
Calmsden Glos 81 D8
Calne Wilts 62 E4
Calne Marsh Wilts 62 E4
Calow Derbys 186 G6
Calow Green Derbys 170 B6
Calrofold Ches E 184 G6
Calshot Hants 33 G7
Calstock Corn 7 B8
Calstone Wellington
Wilts 62 F4
Calthorpe Norf 160 C3
Oxon 101 D9
Calthwaite Cumb 230 C5
Calton Glasgow 268 C2
N Yorks 204 B4
Staffs 169 E10
Calton Lees Derbys 170 B3
Calvadnack Corn 2 B5
Calveley Ches E 167 D9
Calver Derbys 186 G2
Calverhall Shrops 150 B2
Calver Hill Hereford 97 B7
Calverleigh Devon 26 E6
Calverley W Yorks 205 F10
Calver Sough Derbys 186 F2
Calvert Bucks 102 G3
Calverton M Keynes 102 D5
Notts 171 F10
Calvine Perth 291 G10
Calvo Cumb 238 G4
Cam Glos 80 F3
Camaghael Highld 290 F3
Camas an Staca Argyll 274 G5
Camas-luinie Highld 295 C11
Camasnacroise Highld 289 D10
Camas Salach Highld 289 C8
Camastianavaig Highld 295 B7
Camasunary Highld 295 D7
Camault Muir Highld 300 E5
Camb Shetland 312 D7
Camber E Sus 39 D7
Camberley Sur 65 G11
Camberwell London 67 D10
Camblesforth N Yorks 199 B7
Cambo Northumb 252 F2
Cambois Northumb 253 G8
Camborne Corn 4 G3
Cambourne Cambs 122 F6
Cambridge Borders 271 F11
Cambs 123 F9
Glos 80 E3
W Yorks 205 D10
Cambridge Batch N Som 60 F4
Cambridge Town
Southend 70 C2
Cambrose Corn 4 F3
Cambus Clack 279 C7
Cambusavie Farm
Highld 309 K7
Cambusbarron Stirling 278 C5
Cambusdrenny Stirling 278 C5
Cambuskenneth Stirling 278 C6
Cambuslang S Lanark 268 D2
Cambusmore Lodge
Highld 309 K7
Cambusnethan
N Lanark 268 D6
Camden London 67 C9
Camden Hill Kent 53 F9
Camden Park Kent 52 F5
Cameley Bath 44 B6
Camelford Corn 11 E8
Camel Green Dorset 31 E10
Camelon Falk 279 E7
Camelsdale Sur 49 G11
Camer Kent 69 F7
Cameron Fife 280 B6
Cameron Bridge Fife 280 B6
Camerory Highld 301 F10
Camer's Green Worcs 98 D5
Camerton Bath 45 B7
Cumb 228 E6
E Yorks 201 B8
Camghouran Perth 285 B9
Cammachmore Aberds 293 D11
Cammeringham Lincs 188 E6
Camnant Powys 113 F11
Camoquhill Stirling 277 D10
Camore Highld 309 K7
Camp Lincs 172 E5
Campbeltown Argyll 255 E8
Camp Corner Oxon 83 E10
Camperdown T&W 243 C7
Camphill Derbys 185 F11
Camp Hill N Yorks 214 C6
Pembs 73 C10
Warks 134 E6
W Yorks 196 D5
Campion Hills Warks 118 D6
Campions Essex 87 C7
Cample Dumfries 247 E9
Campmuir Perth 286 D6
Campsall S Yorks 198 E4
Campsea Ashe Suff 126 F6
Camps End Cambs 106 C2
Campsey Ash Suff 126 F6
Campsfield Oxon 83 B7
Camps Heath Suff 143 E10
Campton C Beds 104 D2
Camptoun E Loth 281 F10
Camptown Borders 262 G5
Camp Town W Yorks 206 F2
Camquhart Argyll 275 E10
Camrose Pembs 91 G8
Camserney Perth 286 C2
Camster Highld 310 E6
Camuschoirk Highld 289 C9
Camuscross Highld 295 D8
Camusnagaul Highld 290 F2
Highld 307 L5
Camusrory Highld 295 F10
Camusteel Highld 299 E7
Camusterrach Highld 299 E7
Camusvrachan Perth 285 C10
Canada Hants 32 D3
Lincs 200 G6
Canadia E Sus 38 D2
Canal Foot Cumb 210 D6
Canal Side S Yorks 199 E7
Canbus Clack 279 C7
Candacraig Ho Aberds 292 B5
Candlesby Lincs 175 B7
Candle Street Suff 125 C10
Candy Mill S Lanark 269 G11
Cane End Oxon 65 D7
Caneheath E Sus 23 D9
Canewdon Essex 88 G5
Canford Bottom Dorset 31 G8
Canford Cliffs BCP 19 D7
Canford Heath BCP 18 C6
Canford Magna BCP 18 B6
Cangate Norf 160 F6
Canham's Green Suff 125 D11
Canholes Derbys 185 G8
Canisbay Highld 310 B7
Canklow S Yorks 186 C6
Canley W Mid 118 B6
Cann Dorset 30 C5
Cannalidgey Corn 5 B8
Cannard's Grave Som 44 E6
Cann Common Dorset 30 C5
Cannich Highld 300 F3
Cannington Som 43 F9
Canning Town London 68 C2
Cannock Staffs 133 B9
Cannock Wood Staffs 151 G10
Cannon's Green Essex 87 D9
Cannop Glos 79 C10
Canonbie Dumfries 239 B9
Canon Bridge Hereford 97 C8
Canonbury London 67 C10
Canon Frome Hereford 98 C3
Canon Pyon Hereford 97 B9
Canons Ashby
W Nhants 119 G11
Canonsgrove Som 28 C2
Canons Park London 85 G11
Canon's Town Corn 2 B2
Canterbury Kent 54 B6
Cantley Norf 143 C7
S Yorks 198 G6
Cantlop Shrops 131 B10
Canton Cardiff 59 D7
Cantraybruich Highld 301 E7
Cantraydoune Highld 301 E7
Cantraywood Highld 301 E7
Cantsfield Lancs 212 E2
Canvey Island Essex 69 C9
Canwick Lincs 173 B7
Canworthy Water Corn 11 C10
Caol Highld 290 F3
Caolas Argyll 288 E2
W Isles 297 M2
Caolas Fhlodaigh
W Isles 296 F4
Caolas Liubharsaigh
W Isles 297 G4
Caolas Scalpaigh
W Isles 305 J4
Caolas Stocinis W Isles 305 J3
Caol Ila Argyll 274 F5
Caolasnacon Highld 290 G3
Capel Carms 75 E8
Kent 52 E6
Sur 51 E7
Capel Bangor Ceredig 128 G3
Capel Betws Lleucu
Ceredig 112 F2
Capel Carmel Gwyn 144 D3
Capel Coch Anglesey 179 E7
Capel Cross Kent 53 E8
Capel Curig Conwy 164 D2
Capel Cynon Ceredig 93 B7
Capel Dewi Carms 93 G9
Ceredig 93 C9
Ceredig 128 G2
Capel Garmon Conwy 164 D4
Capel Green Suff 109 B7
Capel-gwyn Anglesey 178 F4
Capel Gwyn Carms 93 G9
Capel Gwynfe Carms 94 G4
Capel Hendre Carms 75 C9
Capel Hermon Gwyn 146 D4
Capel Isaac Carms 93 F11
Capel Iwan Carms 92 D5
Capel-le-Ferne Kent 55 F8
Capel Llanilltern Cardiff 58 C5
Capel Mawr Anglesey 178 G6
Capel Newydd = *Newchapel*
Pembs 92 D4
Capel Parc Anglesey 178 D6
Capel St Andrew Suff 109 B7
Capel St Mary Suff 107 D11
Capel Seion Carms 75 C8
Ceredig 112 B2
Capel Siloam Conwy 164 E4
Capel Tygwydd Ceredig 92 C5
Capel Uchaf Gwyn 162 F6
Capelulo Conwy 180 F2
Capel-y-ffin Powys 96 E5
Capel-y-graig Gwyn 163 B8
Capenhurst Ches W 182 G5
Capernwray Lancs 211 E10
Capheaton Northumb 252 G2
Capland Som 28 D4
Cappercleuch Borders 260 E6
Capplegill Dumfries 248 B4
Capstone Medway 69 F9
Captain Fold Gtr Man 195 E11
Capton Devon 8 E6
Som 42 F5
Caputh Perth 286 D4
Caradon Town Corn 11 G11
Carbis Corn 5 D10
Carbis Bay Corn 2 B2
Carbost Highld 294 B5
Highld 298 E4
Carbrain N Lanark 278 G5
Carbrook S Yorks 186 D5
Carbrooke Norf 141 C9
Carburton Notts 187 G10
Carcant Borders 271 E7
Carcary Angus 287 B10
Carclaze Corn 5 E10
Carclew Corn 3 B7
Car Colston Notts 172 G2
Carcroft S Yorks 198 E4
Cardenden Fife 280 C4
Cardeston Shrops 149 G7
Cardew Cumb 230 B2
Cardewlees Cumb 239 G8
Cardiff Cardiff 59 D7
Cardigan = *Aberteifi*
Ceredig 92 B3
Cardinal's Green Cambs 106 B2
Cardington Bedford 103 B11
Shrops 131 D10
Cardinham Corn 6 B2
Cardonald Glasgow 267 C10
Cardow Moray 301 E11
Cardrona Borders 261 B8
Cardross Argyll 276 F6
Cardurnock Cumb 238 F5
Careby Lincs 155 F10
Careston Angus 293 G7
Careston Castle Angus 287 B9
Care Village Leics 136 D4
Carew Pembs 73 E8
Carew Cheriton Pembs 73 E8
Carew Newton Pembs 73 E8
Carey Hereford 97 E11
Carey Park Corn 6 E4
Carfin N Lanark 268 D5
Carfrae E Loth 271 B11
Carfury Corn 1 C4
Cargate Common Norf 142 E2
Cargenbridge Dumfries 237 B11
Cargill Perth 286 D5
Cargo Cumb 239 F9
Cargo Fleet Mbro 234 G6
Cargreen Corn 7 C8
Carham Northumb 263 B8
Carhampton Som 42 E4
Carharrack Corn 4 G4
Carie Perth 285 B10
Perth 285 D10
Carines Corn 4 D5
Carisbrooke IoW 20 D5
Cark Cumb 211 D7
Carkeel Corn 7 C8
Carlabhagh W Isles 304 D4
Carland Cross Corn 5 E7
Carlbury N Yorks 224 B4
Carlby Lincs 155 G11
Carlecotes S Yorks 197 G7
Carleen Corn 2 C4
Carlenrig Borders 249 C9
Carlesmoor N Yorks 214 E3
Carleton Cumb 219 D10
Cumb 230 F6
Cumb 239 G10
Lancs 202 F2
N Yorks 204 D5
W Yorks 198 C3
Carleton Forehoe Norf 141 B11
Carleton Hall Cumb 219 F11
Carleton-in-Craven
N Yorks 204 D5
Carleton Rode Norf 142 E2
Carleton St Peter Norf 142 C6
Carley Hill T&W 243 F9
Carlidnack Corn 3 D7
Carlincraig Aberds 302 E6
Carlingcott Bath 45 B7
Carlinghow W Yorks 197 C8
Carlingwark Devon 27 E11
Carlin How Redcar 226 B4
Carlisle Cumb 239 F10
Carloggas Corn 5 B7
Corn 5 E9
Carloonan Argyll 284 F4
Carlops Borders 270 D3
Carlton Bedford 121 F9
Cambs 124 G2
Leics 135 C7
Notts 171 G10
N Yorks 198 C6
N Yorks 213 C11
N Yorks 216 B2
N Yorks 224 C3
Stockton 234 G3
Suff 127 E7
S Yorks 197 E11
W Yorks 197 B10
Carlton Colville Suff 143 F10
Carlton Curlieu Leics 136 D3
Carlton Green Cambs 124 G2
Carlton Husthwaite
N Yorks 215 D9
Carlton in Cleveland
N Yorks 225 E10
Carlton in Lindrick
Notts 187 E9
Carlton le Moorland
Lincs 172 D6
Carlton Miniott N Yorks 215 C7
Carlton on Trent Notts 172 C3
Carlton Purlieus
N Nhants 136 F6
Carlton Scroop Lincs 172 G6
Carluddon Corn 5 D10
Carluke S Lanark 268 E6
Carlyon Bay Corn 5 E11
Carmarthen = *Caerfyrddin*
Carms 93 G8
Carmel Anglesey 178 E5
Carms 75 B9
Flint 181 F11
Gwyn 163 E7
Powys 113 D11
Carmichael S Lanark 259 B10
Carminow Cross Corn 5 B11
Carmont Aberds 293 E10
Carmunnock Glasgow 268 D2
Carmyle Glasgow 268 C2
Carmyllie Angus 287 C9
Carnaby E Yorks 218 F2
Carnach Highld 299 G10
Highld 307 K5
W Isles 305 J4
Carnachy Highld 308 D7
Càrnais W Isles 304 E2
Carnan W Isles 297 G3
Carn Arthen Corn 2 B5
Carnbahn Perth 285 C10
Carnbee Fife 287 G9
Carnbo Perth 286 G4
Carnbrea Corn 4 G3
Carn Brea Village Corn 4 G3
Carnbroe N Lanark 268 C4
Carndu Highld 295 C10
Carnduff S Lanark 268 F3
Carnduncan Argyll 274 G3
Carne Corn 3 B10
Corn 3 E7
Corn 5 D9
Carnebone Corn 2 C6
Carnedd Powys 129 E10
Carnetown Rhondda 77 G9
Carnforth Lancs 211 E9
Lancs 211 E10
Carnglas Swansea 56 C6
Carn-gorm Highld 295 C11
Carnhedryn Pembs 90 F6
Carnhedryn Uchaf Pembs 90 F5
Carnhell Green Corn 2 B4
Carnhot Corn 4 F4
Carnkie Corn 2 B5
Corn 2 C6
Carnkief Corn 4 E5
Carno Powys 129 D9
Carnoch Highld 300 D2
Highld 300 F3
Carnock Fife 279 D10
Carnon Downs Corn 4 G5
Carnousie Aberds 302 D6
Carnoustie Angus 287 D9
Carnsmerry Corn 5 D10
Carn Towan Corn 1 D3
Carntyne Glasgow 268 B2
Carnwadric E Renf 267 D10
Carnwath S Lanark 269 F9
Carnyorth Corn 1 C3
Caroe Corn 11 C9
Carol Green W Mid 118 B5
Carpalla Corn 5 E9
Carpenders Park Herts 85 G10
Carpenter's Hill Worcs 117 C11
Carperby N Yorks 213 B10
Carpley Green N Yorks 213 B8
Carr Gtr Man 195 D9
S Yorks 187 C8
Carradale Argyll 255 D9
Carragraich W Isles 305 J3
Carr Bank Cumb 211 D9
Carrbridge Highld 301 G9
Carrbrook Gtr Man 196 G3
Carr Cross Lancs 193 E11
Carreglefn Anglesey 178 D5
Carreg-wen Pembs 92 C4
Carreg y Garth Gwyn 163 B9
Carr Gate W Yorks 197 C10
Carr Green Gtr Man 184 D2
Carr Hill T&W 243 E7
Carrhouse Devon 26 F3
Carr Houses Mers 193 G10
Carrick Argyll 275 E10
Dumfries 237 D7
Fife 287 E8
Carrick Castle Argyll 276 C3
Carrick Ho Orkney 314 C5
Carriden Falk 279 E10
Carrington Gtr Man 184 C2
Lincs 174 E4
Midloth 270 C6
Nottingham 171 G9
Carroch Dumfries 246 E5

Carrog Conwy 164 F3
Denb 165 G10
Carroglen Perth 285 E11
Carrol Highld 311 J2
Carron Falk 279 E7
Moray 302 E2
Carronbridge Dumfries 247 D9
Carron Bridge Stirling 278 E4
Carronshore Falk 279 E7
Carrot Angus 287 C8
Carroway Head Staffs 134 D3
Carrow Hill Mon 78 G6
Carrshield Northumb 232 B2
Carrutherstown
Dumfries 238 C4
Carr Vale Derbys 171 B7
Carrville Durham 234 C2
Carry Argyll 275 G10
Carsaig Argyll 275 E8
Argyll 289 G7
Carscreugh Dumfries 236 D4
Carsegowan Dumfries 236 D6
Carse Gray Angus 287 B8
Carse Ho Argyll 275 G8
Carseriggan Dumfries 236 C5
Carsethorn Dumfries 237 D11
Carshalton London 67 G9
Carshalton Beeches
London 67 G9
Carshalton on the Hill
London 67 G9
Carsington Derbys 170 E3
Carskiey Argyll 255 G7
Carsluith Dumfries 236 D6
Carsphairn Dumfries 246 E3
Carstairs S Lanark 269 F8
Carstairs Junction
S Lanark 269 F9
Carswell Marsh Oxon 82 F4
Cartbridge Sur 50 B4
Carterhaugh Borders 261 D10
Carter Knowle S Yorks 186 E4
Carter's Clay Hants 32 C4
Carter's Green Essex 87 C8
Carter's Hill Wokingham 65 F9
Carterspiece Glos 79 C9
Carterton Oxon 82 D3
Carterway Heads
Northumb 242 G2
Carthamartha Corn 12 F3
Carthew Corn 2 B5
Corn 5 D10
Carthorpe N Yorks 214 C6
Cartington Northumb 252 C2
Cartland S Lanark 269 F7
Cartledge Derbys 186 F4
Cartmel Cumb 211 D7
Cartmel Fell Cumb 211 B8
Cartsdyke Invclyd 276 F5
Cartworth W Yorks 196 F6
Carty Port Dumfries 236 C6
Carway Carms 75 D7
Carwinley Cumb 239 C10
Carwynnen Corn 2 B5
Cary Fitzpaine Som 29 B9
Carzantic Corn 12 E3
Carzield Dumfries 247 G11
Carzise Corn 2 C3
Cascob Powys 114 D4
Cashes Green Glos 80 D4
Cashlie Perth 285 C8
Cashmoor Dorset 31 E7
Cas Mael = *Puncheston*
Pembs 91 F10
Cassey Compton Glos 81 C9
Cassington Oxon 83 C7
Cassop Durham 234 D2
Castallack Corn 1 D5
Castell Conwy 164 B3
Denb 165 B10
Castellau Rhondda 58 B5
Castell-Howell Ceredig 93 B8
Castell nedd = *Neath*
Neath 57 B8
Castell Newydd Emlyn
= *Newcastle Emlyn*
Carms 92 C6
Castell-y-bwch Torf 78 G3
Castell-y-rhingyll Carms 75 C9
Casterton Cumb 212 D2
Castle Corn 28 G4
Som 27 B9
Castle Acre Norf 158 F6
Castle Ashby W Nhants 121 F7
Castle Bolton N Yorks 223 G10
Castle Bromwich W Mid 134 F2
Castle Bytham Lincs 155 F9
Castlebythe Pembs 91 F10
Castle Caereinion
Powys 130 B3
Castle Camps Cambs 106 C2
Castle Carlton Lincs 190 E5
Castle Carrock Cumb 240 F2
Castlecary N Lanark 278 F5
Castle Cary Som 44 G6
Castle Combe Wilts 61 D10
Castlecraig Highld 301 C8
Castle Craig Borders 270 G2
Castlecroft Staffs 133 D7
Castle Donington Leics 153 D8
Castle Douglas Dumfries 237 C9
Castle Eaton Swindon 81 F10
Castle Eden Durham 234 D4
Castle End Pboro 138 B2
Castlefairn Dumfries 246 F6
Castlefields Halton 183 E8
Castle Fields Shrops 149 G10
Castle Forbes Aberds 293 B8
Castleford W Yorks 198 B2
Castle Frome Hereford 98 B3
Castle Gate Corn 1 C5
Castlegreen Shrops 130 F6
Castle Green London 68 C3
Sur 66 G3
S Yorks 197 G9
Castle Gresley Derbys 152 F5
Castlehead Renfs 267 C9
Castle Heaton Northumb 273 G8
Castle Hedingham
Essex 106 D5
Castlehill Argyll 254 B4
Borders 260 B6
Highld 310 C5
S Ayrs 257 E9
W Dunb 277 F7
Castle Hill E Sus 37 B9
Gtr Man 184 C6
Kent 53 E7
Suff 108 B3
Worcs 116 F5
Castle Huntly Perth 287 E7
Castle Kennedy
Dumfries 236 D3
Castlemaddy Dumfries 246 F3
Castlemartin Pembs 72 F6
Castlemilk Dumfries 238 B5
Glasgow 268 D2
Castlemorris Pembs 91 E8
Castlemorton Worcs 98 D5
Castle O'er Dumfries 248 E6
Castlerigg Cumb 229 G11
Castle Rising Norf 158 E3
Castleside Durham 233 B7
Castle Street W Yorks 196 C3
Castle Stuart Highld 301 E7
Castlethorpe M Keynes 102 C6
N Lincs 200 F3
Castleton Angus 287 C7
Argyll 275 E9
Derbys 185 E11
Gtr Man 195 E11
Moray 301 G11
Newport 59 C9
N Yorks 226 D3
Castleton Village Highld 300 E6
Castle Toward Argyll 266 B2
Castletown Ches W 166 E6
Cumb 230 E6
Dorset 17 G9
Highld 301 E7
Highld 310 C5
IoM 192 F3
Staffs 151 E8
T&W 243 F9
Castle Town W Sus 36 E2
Castletump Glos 98 F4
Castle-upon-Alun
V Glam 58 E2
Castle Vale W Mid 134 E2
Castleweary Borders 249 C10
Castlewigg Dumfries 236 E6
Castley N Yorks 205 D11
Castling's Heath Suff 107 C9
Caston Norf 141 D9
Castor Pboro 138 D2
Caswell Swansea 56 D5
Catacol N Ayrs 255 C10
Cat Bank Cumb 220 F6
Catbrain S Glos 60 C5
Catbrook Mon 79 E8
Catch Flint 182 G2
Catchall Corn 1 D4
Catchems Corner
W Mid 118 B4
Catchems End Worcs 116 B5
Catchgate Durham 242 G5
Catchory Highld 310 D6
Catcleugh Northumb 250 C6
Catcliffe S Yorks 186 D6
Catcomb Wilts 62 D4
Catcott Som 43 F11
Caterham Sur 51 B10
Catfield Norf 161 E7
Catfirth Shetland 313 H6
Catford London 67 E11
Catforth Lancs 202 F5
Cathays Cardiff 59 D7
Cathays Park Cardiff 59 D7
Cathcart Glasgow 267 C11
Cathedine Powys 96 F2
Catherine-de-Barnes
W Mid 134 G3
Catherine Slack
W Yorks 196 B5
Catherington Hants 33 E11
Catherton Shrops 116 B3
Cat Hill S Yorks 197 F8
Cathiron Warks 119 B9
Catholes Cumb 222 G3
Cathpair Borders 271 F9
Catisfield Hants 33 F8
Catley Lane Head
Gtr Man 195 D11
Catley Southfield
Hereford 98 C3
Catlodge Highld 291 D8
Catlowdy Cumb 239 B11
Catmere End Essex 105 D9
Catmore W Berks 64 C3
Caton Devon 13 G11
Lancs 211 G10
Caton Green Lancs 211 F10
Catrine E Ayrs 258 D2
Cat's Ash Newport 78 G5
Cat's Common Norf 160 E6
Cats Edge Staffs 169 E7
Catsfield E Sus 38 E2
Catsfield Stream E Sus 38 E2
Catsgore Som 29 B8
Catsham Som 44 G5
Catshaw S Yorks 197 G8
Catshill W Mid 133 B11
Worcs 117 C9
Cat's Hill Cross Staffs 150 C6
Catslackburn Borders 261 D8
Catslip Oxon 65 B8
Catstree Shrops 132 D4
Cattadale Argyll 274 G4
Cattal N Yorks 206 C4
Cattawade Suff 108 E2
Cattedown Plym 7 E9
Catterall Lancs 202 E5
Catterick N Yorks 224 F4
Catterick Bridge
N Yorks 224 F4
Catterick Garrison
N Yorks 224 F3
Catterlen Cumb 230 E5
Catterline Aberds 293 F10
Catterton N Yorks 206 D6
Catteshall Sur 50 E3
Catthorpe Leics 119 B11
Cattistock Dorset 17 B7
Cattle End W Nhants 102 C3
Catton Northumb 241 F8
N Yorks 215 D7
Catwick E Yorks 209 D8
Catworth Cambs 121 C11
Caudle Green Glos 80 C6
Caudlesprings Norf 141 C8
Caulcott C Beds 103 C9
Oxon 101 G10
Cauld Borders 261 G11
Cauldcoats Holdings
Falk 279 F10
Cauldcots Angus 287 C10
Cauldhame Stirling 278 C2
Cauldmill Borders 262 G2
Cauldon Staffs 169 F9
Cauldon Lowe Staffs 169 F9
Cauldwells Aberds 303 D7
Caulkerbush Dumfries 237 D11
Caulside Dumfries 249 G10
Caundle Marsh Dorset 29 E11
Caunsall Worcs 132 G6
Caunton Notts 172 D2
Causeway Hants 33 C11
Hants 34 C2
Mon 60 B2
Causewayend S Lanark 260 B2
Causeway End Cumb 210 C6
Cumb 211 B9
Dumfries 236 C6
Essex 87 B11
Wilts 62 C4
Causeway Foot W Yorks 197 E7
W Yorks 205 G7
Causeway Green W Mid 133 F9
Causewayhead Cumb 238 G4
Stirling 278 B6
Causewaywood Shrops 131 D10
Causey Durham 242 F6
Causeyend Aberds 293 B11
Causey Park Bridge
Northumb 252 E5
Causeyton Aberds 293 B8
Caute Devon 24 E6
Cautley Cumb 222 G3
Cavendish Suff 106 B6
Cavendish Bridge Leics 153 D8
Cavenham Suff 124 D5
Cavers Carre Borders 262 D3
Caversfield Oxon 101 F11
Caversham Reading 65 E8
Caversham Heights
Reading 65 D8
Caverswall Staffs 169 G7
Cavil E Yorks 207 G11
Cawdor Highld 301 D8
Cawkeld E Yorks 208 C5
Cawkwell Lincs 190 F3
Cawood N Yorks 207 F7
Cawsand Corn 7 E8
Cawston Norf 160 E2
Warks 119 C9
Cawthorne N Yorks 216 B5
S Yorks 197 F9
Cawthorpe Lincs 155 E11
Cawton N Yorks 216 D2
Caxton Cambs 122 F6
Caynham Shrops 115 C11
Caythorpe Lincs 172 F6
Notts 171 F11
Cayton N Yorks 217 C11
Ceallan W Isles 296 F4
Ceann a Bhaigh W Isles 296 E3
Ceann a Bhàigh
W Isles 305 J4
Ceannacroc Lodge
Highld 290 B4
Ceann a Deas Loch
Baghasdail W Isles 297 K3
Ceann Shiphoirt
W Isles 305 G4
Ceann Tarabhaigh
W Isles 305 G4
Cearsiadair W Isles 304 F5
Ceathramh Meadhanach
W Isles 296 D4
Cefn Newport 59 B9
Powys 148 G5
Cefn Berain Conwy 165 B7
Cefn-brith Conwy 164 E6
Cefn-bryn-brain Carms 76 C2
Cefn-bychan Swansea 56 B4
Wrex 166 G3
Cefncaeau Carms 56 B4
Cefn Canol Powys 148 C4
Cefn-coch Conwy 164 B5
Cefn Coch Powys 129 C10
Powys 148 D2
Cefn-coed-y-cymmer
M Tydf 77 D8
Cefn Cribbwr Bridgend 57 E11
Cefn Cross Bridgend 57 E11
Cefn-ddwysarn Gwyn 147 B9
Cefn Einion Shrops 130 F5
Cefneithin Carms 75 C9
Cefn-eurgain Flint 166 B2
Cefn Fforest Caerph 77 F11
Cefn Glas Bridgend 57 E11
Cefn Golau Bl Gwent 77 D10
Cefn-gorwydd Powys 95 B8
Cefn Hengoed Caerph 77 F10
Cefn-hengoed Swansea 57 B7
Cefn Llwyd Ceredig 128 G2
Cefn-mawr Wrex 166 G3
Cefnpennar Rhondda 77 E8
Cefn Rhigos Rhondda 76 D6
Cefn-y-bedd Flint 166 D4
Cefn-y-Crib Torf 78 F2
Cefn-y-Garth Swansea 76 E2
Cefn-y-pant Carms 92 F3
Cegidfa = *Guilsfield*
Powys 148 G4
Cei-bach Ceredig 111 F8
Ceinewydd = *New Quay*
Ceredig 111 F7
Ceint Anglesey 179 F7
Ceinws Powys 128 B5
Cellan Ceredig 94 B2
Cellarhead Staffs 169 F7
Cellarhill Kent 70 G3
Celyn-Mali Flint 165 B11
Cemaes Anglesey 178 C5
Cemmaes Powys 128 B6
Cemmaes Road
= *Glantwymyn* Powys 128 C6
Cenarth Carms 92 C5
Cenin Gwyn 163 F7
Central Invclyd 276 F5
Central Milton Keynes
M Keynes 102 D6
Ceos W Isles 304 F5
Ceres Fife 287 F8
Ceri = *Kerry* Powys 130 F2
Cerne Abbas Dorset 29 G11
Cerney Wick Glos 81 F9
Cerrigceinwen Anglesey 178 G6
Cerrig Llwydion Neath 57 C9
Cerrig-mân Anglesey 179 C7
Cerrigydrudion Conwy 165 F7
Cess Norf 161 F8
Cessford Borders 262 E6
Ceunant Gwyn 163 C8
Chaceley Glos 99 E7
Chaceley Hole Glos 98 E6
Chaceley Stock Glos 99 F7
Chacewater Corn 4 G4
Chackmore Bucks 102 D3
Chacombe W Nhants 101 C9
Chadbury Worcs 99 B10
Chadderton Gtr Man 196 F2
Chadderton Fold
Gtr Man 195 F11
Chaddesden Derby 153 B7
Chaddesley Corbett
Worcs 117 C7
Chaddlehanger Devon 12 F5
Chaddlewood Plym 7 D11
Chaddleworth W Berks 64 D2
Chadkirk Gtr Man 184 D6
Chadlington Oxon 100 G6
Chadshunt Warks 118 G6
Chadsmoor Staffs 151 G9
Chadstone W Nhants 121 F7
Chad Valley W Mid 133 F10
Chadwell Leics 154 E5
Shrops 150 G5
Chadwell End Bedford 121 D11
Chadwell Heath London 68 B3
Chadwell St Mary
Thurrock 68 D6
Chadwick Worcs 116 D6
Chadwick End W Mid 118 C4
Chadwick Green Mers 183 B8
Chaffcombe Som 28 E5
Chafford Hundred
Thurrock 68 D5
Chagford Devon 13 D10
Chailey E Sus 36 D5
Chainbridge Cambs 139 C8
Chain Bridge Lincs 174 G4
Chainhurst Kent 53 D8
Chalbury Dorset 31 F8
Chalbury Common Dorset 31 F8
Chaldon Sur 51 B10
Chaldon Herring or East
Chaldon Dorset 17 E11
Chale IoW 20 F5
Chale Green IoW 20 F5
Chalfont Common Bucks 85 G8
Chalfont Grove Bucks 85 G7
Chalfont St Giles Bucks 85 G7
Chalfont St Peter Bucks 85 G8
Chalford Glos 80 E5
Oxon 84 E2
Wilts 45 C11
Chalford Hill Glos 80 E5
Chalgrave C Beds 103 F10
Chalgrove Oxon 83 F10
Chalk Kent 69 E7
Chalk End Essex 87 C10
Chalkfoot Cumb 230 B2
Chalkhill Norf 141 C7
Chalkhouse Green Oxon 65 D8
Chalkshire Bucks 84 D4
Chalksole Kent 55 E9
Chalkway Som 28 F5
Chalkwell Kent 69 G11
Southend 69 B11
Challaborough Devon 8 G3
Challacombe Devon 41 E7
Challister Shetland 312 G7
Challoch Dumfries 236 C5
Challock Kent 54 C4
Chalmington Dorset 29 G9
Chalton C Beds 103 F10
Hants 34 D2
Chalvedon Essex 69 B8
Chalvey Slough 66 D3
Chalvington E Sus 23 D8
Chambercombe Devon 40 D4
Chamber's Green Kent 54 E2
Champson Devon 26 B4
Chance Inn Fife 287 F7
Chancery = *Rhydgaled*
Ceredig 111 B11
Chance's Pitch Hereford 98 C4
Chandler's Cross Herts 85 F9
Worcs 98 D5
Chandler's Ford Hants 32 C6
Chandlers Green Hants 49 B8
Channel's End Bedford 122 F2
Channel Tunnel Kent 55 F7
Channerwick Shetland 313 L6
Chantry Devon 25 C9
Som 45 D8
Suff 108 C2
Chapel Corn 4 C6
Cumb 229 E10
Fife 280 C5
Chapel Allerton Som 44 C2
W Yorks 206 F2
Chapel Amble Corn 10 F5
Chapel Brampton
W Nhants 120 D4
Chapel Chorlton Staffs 150 B6
Chapel Cleeve Som 42 E4
Chapel Cross E Sus 37 C10
Chapel End Bedford 103 B11
Bedford 122 F2
Cambs 138 G2
C Beds 103 C11
Ches E 167 G11
Essex 105 G11
N Nhants 138 F2
Warks 134 E6
Chapel-en-le-Frith
Derbys 185 E9
Chapel Field Gtr Man 195 F9
Norf 161 E7
Chapel Fields W Mid 118 B6
York 207 C7
Chapelgate Lincs 157 E8
Chapel Green Herts 104 D6
Warks 119 E9
Warks 134 F5
Chapel Haddlesey
N Yorks 198 B5
Chapelhall N Lanark 268 C5
Chapel Head Cambs 138 G6
Chapelhill Dumfries 248 E3
Highld 301 B8
N Ayrs 266 G4
Perth 286 D4
Perth 286 E3
Perth 286 E6
Chapel Hill Aberds 303 F10
Glos 79 E10
Lincs 174 E2
Mon 79 F8
N Yorks 206 D2
Chapel House Lancs 194 F3
Chapel Knapp Wilts 61 F11
Chapelknowe Dumfries 239 C8
Chapel Lawn Shrops 114 B6
Chapel-le-Dale
N Yorks 212 D4
Chapel Leigh Som 27 B10
Chapel Mains Borders 271 G11
Chapel Milton Derbys 185 E9
Chapel of Garioch
Aberds 303 G7
Chapel of Stoneywood
Aberdeen 293 B10
Chapel on Leader
Borders 271 G11
Chapel Outon Dumfries 236 E6
Chapel Plaister Wilts 61 F10
Chapel Row Essex 88 E3
E Sus 23 C10
W Berks 64 F5
Chapels Blackburn 195 C7
Cumb 210 C4
Chapel St Leonards
Lincs 191 G9
Chapel Stile Cumb 220 D6
Chapelthorpe W Yorks 197 D10
Chapelton Angus 287 C10
Devon 25 B9
Highld 291 B11
S Lanark 268 F3
Chapelton Row Dumfries 237 E8
Chapeltown Blackburn 195 D8
Moray 302 G2
S Yorks 186 B5
W Yorks 206 F2
Chapel Town Corn 5 D7
Chapman's Hill Worcs 117 B9
Chapmanslade Wilts 45 D10
Chapman's Town E Sus 23 B10
Chapmans Well Devon 12 C3
Chapmore End Herts 86 B4
Chappel Essex 107 F7
Charaton Cross Corn 6 B6
Charcott Kent 52 D4
Chard Som 28 F4
Chard Junction Dorset 28 G4
Chardleigh Green Som 28 E4
Chardstock Devon 28 G4
Charfield S Glos 80 G2
Charfield Green S Glos 80 G2
Charfield Hill S Glos 80 G2
Charford Worcs 117 D9
Chargrove Glos 80 B6
Charing Kent 54 D3
Charing Cross Dorset 31 E10
Charing Heath Kent 54 D2
Charing Hill Kent 54 C3
Charingworth Glos 100 D4
Charlbury Oxon 82 B5
Charlcombe Bath 61 F8
Charlcutt Wilts 62 D3
Charlecote Warks 118 F5
Charlemont W Mid 133 E10
Charles Devon 41 G7
Charles Bottom Devon 41 G7
Charlesfield Borders 262 D3
Dumfries 238 D5
Charleshill Sur 49 E11
Charleston Angus 287 C7
Renfs 267 C9
Charlestown Aberdeen 293 C11
Corn 5 E10
Derbys 185 C8
Dorset 17 F9
Fife 279 E11
Gtr Man 195 G10
Gtr Man 195 G11
Highld 299 B8
Highld 300 E6
W Yorks 196 B3
W Yorks 205 F9
Charlestown of Aberlour
Moray 302 E2
Charles Tye Suff 125 G10
Charlesworth Derbys 185 C8
Charleton Devon 8 G5
Charlinch Som 43 F8
Charlottetown Fife 286 F6
Charlton Hants 47 D11
Herts 104 F3
London 68 D2
Northumb 251 F8
Oxon 64 B2
Redcar 226 B2
Som 28 B3
Som 44 E6
Som 45 C7
Sur 66 F5
Telford 149 G11
Wilts 30 C6
Wilts 46 B6
Wilts 62 B3
W Nhants 101 D10
Worcs 99 B10
Worcs 116 C6
W Sus 34 E5
Charlton Abbots Glos 99 G10
Charlton Adam Som 29 B8
Charlton-All-Saints
Wilts 31 C11
Charltonbrook S Yorks 186 B4
Charlton Down Dorset 17 C9
Charlton Horethorne
Som 29 C11
Charlton Kings Glos 99 G9
Charlton Mackrell Som 29 B8
Charlton Marshall Dorset 30 G5
Charlton Musgrove Som 30 B2
Charlton on Otmoor
Oxon 83 B9
Charlton on the Hill
Dorset 30 G5
Charlton Park Glos 99 G9
Charlton St Peter Wilts 46 B6
Charlwood E Sus 51 G11
Hants 49 G7
Sur 51 E8
Charlynch Som 43 F8
Charminster BCP 19 C8
Dorset 17 C9
Charmouth Dorset 16 C3
Charnage Wilts 45 G10
Charndon Bucks 102 G3
Charnes Staffs 150 C5
Charney Bassett Oxon 82 G5
Charnock Green Lancs 194 D5
Charnock Hall S Yorks 186 E5
Charnock Richard
Lancs 194 D5
Charsfield Suff 126 F5
Chart Corner Kent 53 C9
Charter Alley Hants 48 B5
Charterhouse Som 44 B3
Chartershall Stirling 278 C6
Charterville Allotments
Oxon 82 C4
Chartham Kent 54 C6
Chartham Hatch Kent 54 B6
Chart Hill Kent 53 D9
Chartridge Bucks 84 E6
Chart Sutton Kent 53 D10
Charvil Wokingham 65 D9
Charwelton W Nhants 119 F10
Chase Cross London 87 G8
Chase End Street Worcs 98 D5
Chase Hill S Glos 61 B8
Chase Terrace Staffs 133 B10
Chasetown Staffs 133 B10
Chastleton Oxon 100 F4
Chasty Devon 24 G4
Chatburn Lancs 203 E11
Chatcull Staffs 150 C5
Chatford Shrops 131 B9
Chatham Caerph 59 B8
Medway 69 F9
Chatham Green Essex 88 B2
Chathill Northumb 264 D5
Chat Hill W Yorks 205 G8
Chatley Worcs 117 E7
Chattenden Medway 69 E9
Chatter End Essex 105 F9
Chatteris Cambs 139 F7
Chatterley Staffs 168 E4
Chattern Hill Sur 66 E5
Chatterton Lancs 195 D9
Chattisham Suff 107 C11
Chattle Hill Warks 134 E3
Chatto Borders 263 F7
Chatton Northumb 264 D3
Chaulden Herts 85 D8
Chaul End C Beds 103 G11
Chavel Shrops 149 G8
Chavenage Green Glos 80 F5
Chavey Down Brack 65 F11
Chawleigh Devon 26 E2
Chawley Oxon 83 E7
Chawson Worcs 117 E7
Chawston Bedford 122 F3
Chawton Hants 49 F8
Chaxhill Glos 80 C2
Chazey Heath Oxon 65 D7
Cheadle Gtr Man 184 D5
Staffs 169 G8
Cheadle Heath Gtr Man 184 D5
Cheadle Hulme Gtr Man 184 D5
Cheadle Park Staffs 169 G8
Cheam London 67 G8
Cheapside Herts 105 E8
Sur 50 B4
Windsor 66 F2
Chearsley Bucks 84 C2
Chebsey Staffs 151 D7
Checkendon Oxon 65 C7
Checkley Ches E 168 F2
Hereford 97 D11
Staffs 151 B10
Checkley Green Ches E 168 F2
Chedburgh Suff 124 F5
Cheddar Som 44 C3
Cheddington Bucks 84 B6
Cheddleton Staffs 169 E7
Cheddleton Heath
Staffs 169 E7
Cheddon Fitzpaine Som 28 B2
Chedglow Wilts 80 G6
Chedgrave Norf 143 D7
Chedington Dorset 29 F7
Chediston Suff 127 B7
Chediston Green Suff 127 B7
Chedworth Glos 81 C9
Chedworth Laines Glos 81 C8
Chedzoy Som 43 F10
Cheeklaw Borders 272 E5
Cheeseman's Green Kent 54 F4
Cheetam Hill Gtr Man 195 G10
Cheglinch Devon 40 E4
Chegworth Kent 53 C10
Cheldon Devon 26 E2
Chelfham Devon 40 F6
Chelford Ches E 184 G4
Chellaston Derby 153 C7
Chell Heath Stoke 168 E5
Chellington Bedford 121 F9
Chells Herts 104 F5
Chelmarsh Shrops 132 F4
Chelmer Village Essex 88 D2
Chelmick Shrops 131 E9
Chelmondiston Suff 108 D4
Chelmorton Derbys 169 B10
Chelmsford Essex 88 D2
Chelmsine Som 27 D11
Chelmsley Wood W Mid 134 F3
Chelsea London 67 D9
Chelsfield London 68 G3
Chelsham Sur 51 B11
Chelston Som 27 C11
Torbay 9 C7
Chelston Heathfield
Som 27 C11
Chelsworth Suff 107 B9
Chelsworth Common
Suff 107 B9
Cheltenham Glos 99 G8
Chelveston N Nhants 121 D9
Chelvey N Som 60 F3
Chelvey Batch N Som 60 F3
Chelwood Bath 60 G6
Chelwood Common
E Sus 36 B6
Chelwood Gate E Sus 36 B6
Chelworth Wilts 81 G7
Chelworth Lower Green
Wilts 81 G9
Chelworth Upper Green
Wilts 81 G9
Chelynch Som 45 E7
Chemistry Shrops 167 G8
Cheney Longville
Shrops 131 G8
Chenhalls Corn 2 B3
Chenies Bucks 85 F8
Cheny Longville Shrops 131 G8
Chepstow Mon 79 G8
Chequerbent Gtr Man 195 F7
Chequerfield W Yorks 198 C3
Chequers Corner Norf 139 B9
Chequertree Kent 54 F4
Cherhill Wilts 62 E4
Cherington Glos 80 F6
Warks 100 D5
Cheriston Devon 24 B3
Cheriton Devon 41 D8
Hants 33 B9
Kent 55 F7
Swansea 56 C3
Cheriton Bishop Devon 13 C11
Cheriton Cross Devon 13 C11
Cheriton Fitzpaine Devon 26 F5
Cheriton or Stackpole Elidor
Pembs 73 F7
Cherrington Telford 150 E3
Cherrybank Perth 286 E5
Cherry Burton E Yorks 208 E5
Cherry Green Essex 105 F11
Herts 105 F7
Cherry Hinton Cambs 123 F9
Cherry Orchard Shrops 149 G9
Worcs 117 G7
Cherry Tree Blackburn 195 B7
Gtr Man 185 C7
Cherrytree Hill Derby 153 B7
Cherry Willingham
Lincs 189 G8
Chertsey Sur 66 F4
Chertsey Meads Sur 66 F5
Cheselbourne Dorset 17 B11
Chesham Bucks 85 E7
Gtr Man 195 E10
Chesham Bois Bucks 85 F7
Cheshunt Herts 86 E5
Chesley Kent 69 G11
Cheslyn Hay Staffs 133 B9
Chessetts Wood Warks 118 C3
Chessington London 67 G7
Chessmount Bucks 85 E7
Chestall Staffs 151 G11
Chester Ches W 166 B6
Chesterblade Som 45 E7
Chesterfield Derbys 186 G5
Staffs 134 B2
Chesterhill Midloth 271 B7
Chesterhope Northumb 251 F9
Chesterknowes Borders 262 D2
Chester-le-Street
Durham 243 G7
Chester Moor Durham 233 B11
Chesters Borders 262 E4
Borders 262 G4
Chesterton Cambs 123 E9
Cambs 138 D2
Glos 81 E8
Oxon 101 G11
Shrops 132 D5
Staffs 168 F4
Warks 118 F6
Chesterton Green
Warks 118 F6
Chesterwood Northumb 241 D8
Chestfield Kent 70 F6
Chestnut Hill Cumb 229 G11
Chestnut Street Kent 69 G11
Cheston Devon 8 D3
Cheswardine Shrops 150 D4
Cheswell Telford 150 F4
Cheswick Northumb 273 F10
Cheswick Buildings
Northumb 273 F10
Cheswick Green W Mid 118 B2
Chetnole Dorset 29 F10
Chettiscombe Devon 27 E7
Chettisham Cambs 139 G10
Chettle Dorset 31 E7
Chetton Shrops 132 E3
Chetwode Bucks 102 F2
Chetwynd Aston Telford 150 F5
Cheveley Cambs 124 E3
Chevening Kent 52 B3
Cheverell's Green Herts 85 B9
Chevin End W Yorks 205 E9
Chevington Suff 124 F5
Chevithorne Devon 27 D7
Chew Magna Bath 60 G5
Chew Moor Gtr Man 195 F7
Chew Stoke Bath 60 G5
Chewton Keynsham Bath 61 F7
Chewton Mendip Som 44 C5
Cheylesmore W Mid 118 B6
Chichacott Devon 13 B8
Chicheley M Keynes 103 B8
Chichester W Sus 22 C5
Chickenley W Yorks 197 C9
Chickerell Dorset 17 E8
Chicklade Wilts 46 G2
Chickney Essex 105 F11
Chicksands C Beds 104 D2
Chicksgrove Wilts 46 G3
Chickward Hereford 114 G5
Chidden Hants 33 D11
Chiddingfold Sur 50 F3
Chiddingly E Sus 23 C8
Chiddingstone Kent 52 D3
Chiddingstone Causeway
Kent 52 D4
Chiddingstone Hoath
Kent 52 E3
Chideock Dorset 16 C4
Chidgley Som 42 F4
Chidham W Sus 22 C3
Chidswell W Yorks 197 C9
Chieveley W Berks 64 E3
Chignall St James
Essex 87 D11
Chignall Smealy Essex 87 C11
Chigwell Essex 86 G6
Chigwell Row Essex 87 G7
Chilbolton Hants 47 F11
Chilbolton Down Hants 48 F2
Chilbridge Dorset 31 G7
Chilcomb Hants 33 B8
Chilcombe Dorset 16 C6
Som 42 F6
Chilcompton Som 44 C6
Chilcote Leics 152 G5
Childerditch Essex 68 B6
Childerley Gate Cambs 123 F7
Childer Thornton
Ches W 182 F5
Child Okeford Dorset 30 E4
Childrey Oxon 63 B11
Childsbridge Kent 52 B5
Child's Ercall Shrops 150 E3
Child's Hill London 67 B8
Childswickham Worcs 99 D11
Childwall Mers 182 D6
Childwick Bury Herts 85 C10
Childwick Green Herts 85 C10
Chilfrome Dorset 17 B7
Chilgrove W Sus 34 E4
Chilham Kent 54 C5
Chilhampton Wilts 46 G5
Chilla Devon 24 G6
Chillaton Devon 12 E4
Chillenden Kent 55 C9
Chillerton IoW 20 E5
Chillesford Suff 127 G7
Chillingham Northumb 264 D3
Chillington Devon 8 G5
Som 28 E5
Chillmill Kent 53 E7
Chilmark Wilts 46 G3
Chilmington Green Kent 54 E3
Chilsham E Sus 23 C10
Chilson Oxon 82 B4
Som 28 G4
Chilson Common Som 28 G4
Chilsworthy Corn 12 G4
Devon 24 F4
Chiltern Green C Beds 85 B10
Chilthorne Domer Som 29 D8
Chiltington E Sus 36 D5
Chilton Bucks 83 C11
Durham 233 F11
Kent 71 G11
Oxon 64 B3
Suff 107 C7
Chilton Candover Hants 48 E5
Chilton Cantelo Som 29 C9
Chilton Foliat Wilts 63 E10
Chilton Lane Durham 234 E2
Chilton Moor T&W 234 B2
Chilton Polden Som 43 F11
Chilton Street Suff 106 B5
Chilton Trinity Som 43 F9
Chilvers Coton Warks 135 E7
Chilwell Notts 153 B10
Chilworth Hants 32 D6
Sur 50 D4
Chilworth Old Village
Hants 32 D6
Chimney Oxon 82 E5
Chimney-end Oxon 82 B4
Chimney Street Suff 106 B4
Chineham Hants 49 C7
Chingford London 86 G5
Chingford Green London 86 G5
Chingford Hatch London 86 G5
Chinley Derbys 185 E8
Chinley Head Derbys 185 E9
Chinnor Oxon 84 E3
Chipley Som 27 C10
Chipmans Platt Glos 80 D3
Chipnall Shrops 150 C4
Chippenhall Green Suff 126 B5
Chippenham Cambs 124 D3
Wilts 62 E2
Chipperfield Herts 85 E8
Chipping Herts 105 E7
Lancs 203 E8
Chipping Barnet London 86 F2
Chipping Campden
Glos 100 D3
Chipping Hill Essex 88 B4
Chipping Norton Oxon 100 F6
Chipping Ongar Essex 87 E8
Chipping Sodbury S Glos 61 C8
Chipping Warden
W Nhants 101 B9
Chipstable Som 27 B8
Chipstead Kent 52 B3
Sur 51 B9
Chirbury Shrops 130 D5
Chirk = *Y Waun* Wrex 148 B5
Chirk Bank Shrops 148 B5
Chirk Green Wrex 148 B5
Chirmorrie S Ayrs 236 B4
Chirnside Borders 273 D7
Chirnsidebridge
Borders 273 D7
Chirton T&W 243 D8
Wilts 46 B5
Chisbridge Cross Bucks 65 B10
Chisbury Wilts 63 F9
Chiselborough Som 29 E7
Chiseldon Swindon 63 D7
Chiserley W Yorks 196 B4
Chislehampton Oxon 83 F9
Chislehurst London 68 E2
Chislehurst West London 68 E2
Chislet Kent 71 G8
Chislet Forstal Kent 71 G8
Chiswell Dorset 17 G9
Chiswell Green Herts 85 E10
Chiswick London 67 D8
Chiswick End Cambs 105 B7
Chisworth Derbys 185 C7
Chitcombe E Sus 38 C4
Chithurst W Sus 34 C4
Chittering Cambs 123 C9
Chitterley Devon 26 G6
Chitterne Wilts 46 E3
Chittlehamholt Devon 25 C11
Chittlehampton Devon 25 B10
Chittoe Wilts 62 F3
Chitts Hills Essex 107 F9
Chitty Kent 71 G8
Chivelstone Devon 9 G10
Chivenor Devon 40 G4
Chivery Bucks 84 D6
Chobham Sur 66 G3
Choicelee Borders 272 E4
Cholderton Wilts 47 E8
Cholesbury Bucks 84 D6
Chollerford Northumb 241 C10
Chollerton Northumb 241 C10
Cholmondeston
Ches E 167 C10
Cholsey Oxon 64 B5
Cholstrey Hereford 115 F9
Cholwell Bath 44 B6
Chop Gate N Yorks 225 F11
Choppington Northumb 253 G7
Chopwell T&W 242 F4
Chorley Ches E 167 E9
Lancs 194 D5
Shrops 132 G3
Staffs 151 G11
Chorley Common W Sus 34 B4
Chorleywood Herts 85 F8
Chorleywood Bottom
Herts 85 F8
Chorleywood West Herts 85 F8
Chorlton Ches E 168 E2
Chorlton-cum-Hardy
Gtr Man 184 C4
Chorlton Lane Ches W 167 F7
Choulton Shrops 131 F7
Chowdene T&W 243 F7
Chowley Ches W 167 D7
Chownes Mead W Sus 36 C4
Chreagain Highld 289 C10
Chrishall Essex 105 D8
Christchurch BCP 19 C9
Cambs 139 D9
Glos 79 C9
Newport 59 B10
Christian Malford Wilts 62 D3
Christleton Ches W 166 B6
Christmas Common Oxon 84 G2
Christon N Som 43 B11
Christon Bank Northumb 264 E6
Christow Devon 14 D2
Chryston N Lanark 278 G3
Chub Tor Devon 7 B10
Chuck Hatch E Sus 52 G3
Chudleigh Devon 14 F3
Chudleigh Knighton
Devon 14 F2
Chulmleigh Devon 25 E11
Chunal Derbys 185 C8
Church Lancs 195 B8
Churcham Glos 80 B3
Church Aston Telford 150 F4
Churchbank Shrops 114 B6
Church Brampton
W Nhants 120 D4
Churchbridge Corn 6 D4
Staffs 133 B9
Church Brough Cumb 222 C5
Church Broughton
Derbys 152 C4
Church Charwelton
W Nhants 119 F10
Church Clough Lancs 204 F3
Church Common Hants 34 B2
Church Coombe Corn 4 G3
Church Cove Corn 2 G6
Church Crookham
Hants 49 C10
Churchdown Glos 80 B5
Church Eaton Staffs 150 F6
Churchend Essex 89 G8
Essex 106 G2
Glos 80 D3
Reading 65 E7
S Glos 80 G2
Church End Bedford 122 F2
Bucks 84 B6
Bucks 84 D2
Cambs 121 C11
Cambs 123 C7
Cambs 123 D7
Cambs 138 G4
Cambs 139 B7
C Beds 85 B8
C Beds 103 E9
C Beds 103 G9
C Beds 104 D3
C Beds 122 G3
Essex 88 B2
Essex 105 C11
Essex 105 F11
Essex 106 F4
E Yorks 209 C7
Glos 80 D2
Glos 99 D7
Hants 49 B7
Herts 85 C10
Herts 85 F8
Herts 104 E5
Herts 105 G8
Lincs 156 C4
Lincs 190 B6
London 67 C8
London 86 G2
Norf 157 F10
Oxon 82 D5
Oxon 100 E6
Suff 108 D4
Sur 50 B5
Warks 134 E4
Warks 134 E5
W Mid 119 B7
Worcs 98 C6
Church Enstone Oxon 101 G7
Churches Green E Sus 23 B10
Church Fenton N Yorks 206 F6
Churchfield Hereford 98 B4
W Mid 133 E10
Churchfields Wilts 31 B10
Churchgate Herts 86 E4
Churchgate Street Essex 87 C7
Church Green Devon 15 B9

Church Green *continued*
Norf 141 E11
Church Gresley Derbys 152 F5
Church Hanborough
Oxon 82 C6
Church Hill Ches W 167 C10
Pembs 73 C7
Staffs 151 G10
W Mid 133 D9
Worcs 117 D11
Church Hougham Kent 55 E9
Church Houses N Yorks 226 F3
Churchill Devon 28 G4
Devon 40 E5
N Som 44 B2
Oxon 100 G5
Worcs 117 B7
Worcs 117 G8
Churchill Green N Som 60 G2
Churchinford Som 28 E2
Church Knowle Dorset 18 E4
Church Laneham Notts 188 F4
Church Langton Leics 136 E4
Church Lawford Warks 119 B8
Church Lawton Ches E 168 D4
Church Leigh Staffs 151 B10
Church Lench Worcs 117 G10
Church Mayfield Staffs 169 G11
Church Minshull
Ches E 167 C11
Churchmoor Rough
Shrops 131 F8
Church Norton W Sus 22 D5
Church Oakley Hants 48 C5
Churchover Warks 135 G10
Church Preen Shrops 131 D10
Church Pulverbatch
Shrops 131 C8
Churchstanton Som 27 E11
Churchstoke Powys 130 E5
Churchstow Devon 8 F4
Church Stowe W Nhants 120 F2
Church Street Essex 106 C5
Kent 69 E8
Church Stretton Shrops 131 E9
Churchton Pembs 73 D10
Churchtown Corn 11 F7
Cumb 230 C3
Derbys 170 C3
Devon 24 G3
Devon 41 E7
IoM 192 C5
Lancs 202 E5
Mers 193 D11
Shrops 130 F5
Som 42 F3
Church Town Corn 4 G3
Leics 153 F7
N Lincs 199 F9
Sur 51 C11
Church Village Rhondda 58 B5
Church Warsop Notts 171 B9
Church Westcote Glos 100 G4
Church Whitfield Kent 55 D10
Church Wilne Derbys 153 C8
Churchwood W Sus 35 D8
Churnet Grange Staffs 169 E7
Churnsike Lodge
Northumb 240 B5
Churscombe Torbay 9 C7
Churston Ferrers Torbay 9 D8
Churt Sur 49 F11
Churton Ches W 166 D6
Churwell W Yorks 197 B9
Chute Cadley Wilts 47 C10
Chute Standen Wilts 47 C10
Chwefforddd Conwy 180 G4
Chwilog Gwyn 145 B8
Chwitffordd = *Whitford*
Flint 181 F10
Chyandour Corn 1 C5
Chyanvounder Corn 2 E5
Chycoose Corn 3 B8
Chynhale Corn 2 C4
Chynoweth Corn 2 C2
Chyvarloe Corn 2 E5
Cicelyford Mon 79 E8
Cilan Uchaf Gwyn 144 E5
Cilau Pembs 91 D8
Cilcain Flint 165 B11
Cilcennin Ceredig 111 E10
Cilcewydd Powys 130 C4
Cilfor Gwyn 146 B2
Cilfrew Neath 76 E3
Cilfynydd Rhondda 77 G9
Cilgerran Pembs 92 C3
Cilgwyn Carms 94 F4
Ceredig 92 C6
Gwyn 163 E7
Pembs 91 D11
Ciliau Aeron Ceredig 111 F9
Cill Amhlaidh W Isles 297 G3
Cill Donnain W Isles 297 J3
Cille Bhrighde W Isles 297 K3
Cill Eireabhagh W Isles 297 G4
Cille Pheadair W Isles 297 K3
Cilmaengwyn Neath 76 D2
Cilmery Powys 113 G10
Cilsan Carms 93 G11
Ciltalgarth Gwyn 164 G5
Ciltwrch Powys 96 C3
Cilybebyll Neath 76 E2
Cil y coed = *Caldicot*
Mon 60 B3
Cilycwm Carms 94 D5
Cimla Neath 57 B9
Cinderford Glos 79 C11
Cinderhill Derbys 170 F5
Nottingham 171 G8
Cinder Hill Gtr Man 195 F9
Kent 52 D4
W Mid 133 E8
W Sus 36 B5
Cinnamon Brow Warr 183 C10
Cippenham Slough 66 C2
Cippyn Pembs 92 B2
Circebost W Isles 304 E3
Cirencester Glos 81 E8
Ciribhig W Isles 304 D3
City London 67 C10
Powys 130 F4
V Glam 58 D3
City Dulas Anglesey 179 D7
Clabhach Argyll 288 D3
Clachaig Argyll 276 E2
Highld 292 B2
N Ayrs 255 E10
Clachan Argyll 255 B8
Argyll 275 B8
Argyll 284 F5
Argyll 289 E10
Highld 295 B7
Highld 298 C4
Highld 307 L6
W Isles 297 G3
Clachaneasy Dumfries 236 B5
Clachanmore Dumfries 236 E2
Clachan na Luib
W Isles 296 E4
Clachan of Campsie
E Dunb 278 F2
Clachan of Glendaruel
Argyll 275 E10
Clachan-Seil Argyll 275 B8
Clachan Strachur Argyll 284 G4
Clachbreck Argyll 275 F8
Clachnabrain Angus 292 G5
Clachtoll Highld 307 G5
Clackmannan Clack 279 C8
Clackmarras Moray 302 D2
Clacton-on-Sea Essex 89 B11
Cladach N Ayrs 256 B2
Cladach Chairinis
W Isles 296 F4
Cladach Chireboist
W Isles 296 E3
Claddach Argyll 254 B2
Claddach-knockline
W Isles 296 E3
Cladich Argyll 284 E4
Cladich Steading Argyll 284 E4
Cladswell Worcs 117 F10
Claggan Highld 289 E8
Highld 290 F3
Perth 285 D11
Claigan Highld 298 D2
Claines Worcs 117 F7
Clandown Bath 45 B7
Clanfield Hants 33 D11
Oxon 82 E3
Clanking Bucks 84 D4
Clanville Hants 47 D10
Som 44 G6
Wilts 62 D2
Claonaig Argyll 255 B9
Claonel Highld 309 J5
Clapgate Dorset 31 G8
Herts 105 G8
Clapham Bedford 121 G10
Devon 14 D3
London 67 D9
N Yorks 212 F4
W Sus 35 F9
Clapham Green
Bedford 121 G10
N Yorks 205 B10
Clapham Hill Kent 70 G6
Clapham Park London 67 E9
Clap Hill Kent 54 F5
Clapper Corn 10 G6
Clapper Hill Kent 53 F10
Clappers Borders 273 D8
Clappersgate Cumb 221 E7
Clapphoull Shetland 313 L6
Clapton Som 28 F6
Som 44 C6
W Berks 63 E11
Clapton in Gordano
N Som 60 E3
Clapton-on-the-Hill
Glos 81 B11
Clapton Park London 67 B11
Clapworthy Devon 25 C11
Clarach Ceredig 128 G2
Clarack Aberds 292 D6
Clara Vale T&W 242 E4
Clarbeston Pembs 91 G10
Clarbeston Road Pembs 91 G10
Clarborough Notts 188 E2
Clardon Highld 310 C5
Clare Oxon 83 F11
Suff 106 B5
Clarebrand Dumfries 237 C9
Claregate W Mid 133 C7
Claremont Park Sur 66 G6
Claremount W Yorks 196 B5
Clarencefield Dumfries 238 D3
Clarence Park N Som 59 G10
Clarendon Park
Leicester 135 C11
Clareston Pembs 73 C7
Clarilaw Borders 262 D3
Borders 262 F2
Clarken Green Hants 48 C5
Clark Green Ches E 184 F6
Clarksfield Gtr Man 196 G2
Clark's Green Sur 51 F7
Clark's Hill Lincs 157 E7
Clarkston E Renf 267 D11
N Lanark 268 B5
Clase Swansea 57 B7
Clashandorran Highld 300 E5
Clashcoig Highld 309 K6
Clasheddy Highld 308 C6
Clashgour Argyll 284 C6
Clashindarroch Aberds 302 F4
Clashmore Highld 306 F5
Highld 309 L7
Clashnessie Highld 306 F5
Clashnoir Moray 302 G2
Clate Shetland 313 G7
Clatford Wilts 63 F7
Clatford Oakcuts Hants 47 F10
Clathy Perth 286 F3
Clatt Aberds 302 G5
Clatter Powys 129 E9
Clatterford IoW 20 D5
Clatterford End Essex 87 C10
Essex 87 D9
Essex 87 E8
Clatterin Bridge Aberds 293 F8
Clatto Fife 287 F8
Clatworthy Som 42 G5
Clauchlands N Ayrs 256 C2
Claughton Lancs 202 E6
Lancs 211 F11
Mers 182 D4
Clavelshay Som 43 G9
Claverdon Warks 118 E3
Claverham N Som 60 F2
Claverhambury Essex 86 E6
Clavering Essex 105 E9
Claverley Shrops 132 E5
Claverton Bath 61 G9
Claverton Down Bath 61 G9
Clawdd-côch V Glam 58 D5
Clawdd-newydd Denb 165 E9
Clawdd Poncen Denb 165 G9
Clawthorpe Cumb 211 D10
Clawton Devon 12 B3
Claxby Lincs 189 C10
Lincs 191 G7
Claxby St Andrew Lincs 191 G7
Claxton Norf 142 C6
N Yorks 216 G3
Claybokie Aberds 292 D2
Claybrooke Magna Leics 135 F9
Claybrooke Parva Leics 135 F9
Clay Common Suff 143 G9
Clay Coton W Nhants 119 B11
Clay Cross Derbys 170 C5
Claydon Glos 99 E8
Oxon 119 G9
Suff 126 G2
Clay End Herts 104 F6
Claygate Dumfries 239 B9
Kent 52 C6
Kent 53 E8
Sur 67 G7
Claygate Cross Kent 52 B6
Clayhall Hants 21 B8
London 86 G6
Clayhanger Devon 27 C8
Som 28 E4
W Mid 133 C10
Clayhidon Devon 27 D11
Clayhill E Sus 38 C4
Hants 32 F4
Clay Hill Bristol 60 E6
London 86 F4
W Berks 64 E5
Clayhithe Cambs 123 E10
Clayholes Angus 287 D9
Clay Lake Lincs 156 E5
Clayland Stirling 277 D11
Clay Mills Derbys 152 D5
Clayock Highld 310 D5
Claypit Hill Cambs 123 G7
Claypits Devon 27 B7
Glos 80 D3
Kent 55 B9
Suff 140 G4
Claypole Lincs 172 F5
Clays End Bath 61 G8
Claythorpe Lincs 190 F6
Clayton Gtr Man 184 B5
Staffs 168 G5
S Yorks 198 F3
W Sus 36 E3
W Yorks 205 G8
Clayton Brook Lancs 194 C5
Clayton Green Lancs 194 C5
Clayton Heights
W Yorks 205 G8
Clayton-le-Dale Lancs 203 G9
Clayton-le-Moors
Lancs 203 G10
Clayton-le-Woods
Lancs 194 C5
Clayton West W Yorks 197 E9
Clayworth Notts 188 D2
Cleadale Highld 294 G6
Cleadon T&W 243 E9
Cleadon Park T&W 243 E9
Clearbrook Devon 7 B10
Clearwell Glos 79 D9
Newport 59 B9
Clearwood Wilts 45 D10
Cleasby N Yorks 224 C5
Cleat Orkney 314 B4
Orkney 314 H4
Cleatlam Durham 224 B2
Cleator Cumb 219 C10
Cleator Moor Cumb 219 B10
Cleave Devon 28 G2
Clebrig Highld 308 F5
Cleckheaton W Yorks 197 B7
Cleddon Mon 79 E8
Cleedownton Shrops 131 G11
Cleehill Shrops 115 B11
Cleekhimin N Lanark 268 D5
Cleemarsh Shrops 131 G11
Clee St Margaret
Shrops 131 G11
Cleestanton Shrops 115 B11
Cleethorpes NE Lincs 201 F10
Cleeton St Mary Shrops 116 B2
Cleeve Glos 80 C2
N Som 60 F3
Oxon 64 C6
Cleeve Hill Glos 99 F9
Cleeve Prior Worcs 99 B11
Cleghorn S Lanark 269 F8
Clegyrnant Powys 129 B8
Clehonger Hereford 97 D9
Cleirwy = *Clyro* Powys 96 C4
Cleish Perth 279 B11
Cleland N Lanark 268 D5
Clements End Glos 79 D9
Clement's End C Beds 85 B8
Clement Street Kent 68 E4
Clench Wilts 63 G7
Clench Common Wilts 63 F7
Clencher's Mill Hereford 98 D4
Clenchwarton Norf 157 E11
Clennell Northumb 251 B10
Clent Worcs 117 B8
Cleobury Mortimer
Shrops 116 B3
Cleobury North Shrops 132 F2
Cleongart Argyll 255 D7
Clephanton Highld 301 D8
Clerkenwater Corn 5 B11
Clerkenwell London 67 C10
Clerk Green W Yorks 197 C8
Clerklands Borders 262 E2
Clermiston Edin 280 G3
Clestrain Orkney 314 F3
Cleuch Head Borders 262 G3
Cleughbrae Dumfries 238 C3
Clevancy Wilts 62 D5
Clevans Renfs 267 B7
Clevedon N Som 60 E2
Cleveley Oxon 101 G7
Cleveleys Lancs 202 E2
Cleverton Wilts 62 B3
Clevis Bridgend 57 F10
Clewer Som 44 C2
Clewer Green Windsor 66 D2
Clewer New Town
Windsor 66 D3
Clewer Village Windsor 66 D3
Cley next the Sea Norf 177 E8
Cliaid W Isles 297 L2
Cliasmol W Isles 305 H2
Cliburn Cumb 231 G7
Click Mill Orkney 314 D3
Cliddesden Hants 48 D6
Cliff Derbys 185 D8
Warks 134 D4
Cliffburn Angus 287 C10
Cliffe Lancs 203 G10
Medway 69 D8
N Yorks 207 G9
N Yorks 224 B4
Cliff End E Sus 38 E5
W Yorks 196 D6
Cliffe Woods Medway 69 E8
Clifford Devon 24 C4
Hereford 96 B4
W Yorks 206 E4
Clifford Chambers
Warks 118 G3
Clifford's Mesne Glos 98 G4
Cliffs End Kent 71 G10
Clifftown Southend 69 B11
Clifton Bristol 60 E5
C Beds 104 D3
Ches W 183 F8
Cumb 230 F6
Derbys 169 G11
Devon 40 E5
Gtr Man 195 G9
Lancs 202 G5
Northumb 252 G6
Nottingham 153 C11
N Yorks 205 D9
Oxon 101 E9
Stirling 285 D7
S Yorks 186 C6
S Yorks 187 B8
Worcs 98 B6
W Yorks 197 C7
Clifton *continued*
York 207 C7
Clifton Campville Staffs 152 G5
Cliftoncote Borders 263 E8
Clifton Green Gtr Man 195 G9
Clifton Hampden Oxon 83 F8
Clifton Junction
Gtr Man 195 G9
Clifton Manor C Beds 104 D3
Clifton Maybank Dorset 29 E9
Clifton Moor York 207 B7
Clifton Reynes
M Keynes 121 G8
Clifton upon Dunsmore
Warks 119 B10
Clifton upon Teme
Worcs 116 E4
Cliftonville Kent 71 E11
N Lanark 268 B4
Norf 160 B6
Climping W Sus 35 G8
Climpy S Lanark 269 D8
Clink Som 45 D9
Clinkham Wood Mers 183 B8
Clint N Yorks 205 B11
Clint Green Norf 159 G10
Clintmains Borders 262 C4
Clints N Yorks 224 E2
Cliobh W Isles 304 E2
Clipiau Gwyn 146 G6
Clippesby Norf 161 G8
Clippings Green Norf 159 G10
Clipsham Rutland 155 F9
Clipston Notts 154 C2
W Nhants 136 G4
Clipstone C Beds 103 F8
Clitheroe Lancs 203 E10
Cliuthar W Isles 305 J3
Clive Ches W 167 B11
Shrops 149 E10
Clive Green Ches W 167 C11
Clive Vale E Sus 38 E4
Clivocast Shetland 312 C8
Clixby Lincs 200 G6
Cloatley Wilts 81 G7
Cloatley End Wilts 81 G7
Clocaenog Denb 165 E9
Clochan Aberds 303 E9
Moray 302 C4
Clock Face Mers 183 C8
Clock House London 67 G9
Clockmill Borders 272 E5
Clock Mills Hereford 96 B5
Cloddiau Powys 130 B4
Cloddymoss Moray 301 D9
Clodock Hereford 96 F6
Cloford Som 45 E8
Cloford Common Som 45 E8
Cloigyn Carms 74 C6
Clola Aberds 303 E10
Clophill C Beds 103 D11
Clopton N Nhants 137 G11
Suff 126 G4
Clopton Corner Suff 126 G4
Clopton Green Suff 124 G5
Suff 125 E9
Closeburn Dumfries 247 E9
Close Clark IoM 192 E3
Close House Durham 233 F10
Closworth Som 29 E9
Clothall Herts 104 E5
Clothall Common Herts 104 E5
Clotton Ches W 167 C8
Clotton Common
Ches W 167 C8
Cloudesley Bush Warks 135 F9
Clouds Hereford 97 D11
Cloud Side Staffs 168 C6
Clough Gtr Man 196 D2
Gtr Man 196 F2
W Yorks 196 E5
Clough Dene Durham 242 F5
Cloughfold Lancs 195 C10
Clough Foot W Yorks 196 C2
Clough Hall Staffs 168 E4
Clough Head W Yorks 196 C5
Cloughton N Yorks 227 G10
Cloughton Newlands
N Yorks 227 F10
Clounlaid Highld 289 D9
Clousta Shetland 313 H5
Clouston Orkney 314 E2
Clova Aberds 302 G4
Angus 292 F5
Clovelly Devon 24 C4
Clove Lodge Durham 223 B8
Clovenfords Borders 261 B10
Clovenstone Aberds 293 B9
Cloves Moray 301 C11
Clovullin Highld 290 G2
Clowance Wood Corn 2 C4
Clow Bridge Lancs 195 B10
Clowne Derbys 187 F7
Clows Top Worcs 116 C4
Cloy Wrex 166 G5
Cluanie Inn Highld 290 B2
Cluanie Lodge Highld 290 B2
Clubmoor Mers 182 C5
Clubworthy Corn 11 C11
Cluddley Telford 150 G2
Clun Shrops 130 G6
Clunbury Shrops 131 G7
Clunderwen Carms 73 B10
Clune Highld 301 D9
Highld 301 G7
Clunes Highld 290 E4
Clungunford Shrops 115 B7
Clunie Aberds 302 D6
Perth 286 C5
Clunton Shrops 130 G6
Cluny Fife 280 B4
Cluny Castle Aberds 293 B8
Highld 291 D8
Clutton Bath 44 B6
Ches W 167 E7
Clutton Hill Bath 44 B6
Clwt-grugoer Conwy 165 C7
Clwt-y-bont Gwyn 163 C9
Clwydyfagwyr M Tydf 77 D8
Clydach Mon 78 C2
Swansea 75 E11
Clydach Terrace Powys 77 C11
Clydach Vale Rhondda 77 G7
Clydebank W Dunb 277 G9
Clyffe Pypard Wilts 62 D5
Clynder Argyll 276 E4
Clyne Neath 76 E4
Clynelish Highld 311 J2
Clynnog-fawr Gwyn 162 F6
Clyro = *Cleirwy* Powys 96 C4
Clyst Honiton Devon 14 C5
Clyst Hydon Devon 27 G8
Clyst St George Devon 14 D5
Clyst St Lawrence Devon 27 G8
Clyst St Mary Devon 14 C5
Cnìp W Isles 304 E2
Cnoc Amhlaigh W Isles 304 E7
Cnoc an t-Solais
W Isles 304 D6
Cnocbreac Argyll 274 F5
Cnoc Fhionn Highld 295 D10
Cnoc Màiri W Isles 304 E6
Cnoc Rolum W Isles 296 F3
Cnwch-coch Ceredig 112 B3
Coachford Aberds 302 E4
Coad's Green Corn 11 F11
Coal Aston Derbys 186 F5
Coal Bank Darl 234 G3
Coalbrookdale Telford 132 C3
Coalbrookvale Bl Gwent 77 D11
Coalburn S Lanark 259 C8
Coalburns T&W 242 E4
Coalcleugh Northumb 232 B2
Coaley Glos 80 E3
Coaley Peak Glos 80 E3
Coalford Aberds 293 D10
Coalhall E Ayrs 257 F10
Coalhill Essex 88 F3
Coalmoor Telford 132 B3
Coalpit Field Warks 135 F7
Coalpit Heath S Glos 61 C7
Coalpit Hill Staffs 168 E4
Coal Pool W Mid 133 C10
Coalport Telford 132 C3
Coalsnaughton Clack 279 B8
Coaltown of Balgonie
Fife 280 B5
Coaltown of Wemyss
Fife 280 B6
Coalville Leics 153 G8
Coalway Glos 79 C9
Coanwood Northumb 240 F5
Coarsewell Devon 8 E4
Coat Som 29 C7
Coatbridge N Lanark 268 C4
Coatdyke N Lanark 268 C5
Coate Swindon 63 C7
Wilts 62 G4
Coates Cambs 138 D6
Glos 81 E7
Lancs 204 D3
Lincs 188 E6
Midloth 270 C4
Notts 188 E4
W Sus 35 D7
Coatham Redcar 235 F7
Coatham Mundeville
Darl 233 G11
Coatsgate Dumfries 248 B3
Cobairdy Aberds 302 E5
Cobbaton Devon 25 B10
Cobbler's Corner Worcs 116 F5
Cobbler's Green Norf 142 E5
Cobbler's Plain Mon 79 E7
Cobbs Warr 183 D10
Cobb's Cross Glos 98 E5
Cobbs Fenn Essex 106 E5
Cobby Syke N Yorks 205 B9
Coberley Glos 81 B7
Cobhall Common
Hereford 97 D9
Cobham Kent 69 F7
Sur 66 G6
Cobleland Stirling 277 B10
Cobler's Green Essex 87 B11
Cobley Dorset 31 C8
Cobley Hill Worcs 117 C10
Cobnash Hereford 115 E9
Cobridge Stoke 168 F5
Cobscot Shrops 150 B3
Coburty Aberds 303 C9
Cockadilly Glos 80 E4
Cock Alley Derbys 186 G6
Cock and End Suff 124 G4
Cockayne N Yorks 226 F2
Cockayne Hatley
C Beds 104 B5
Cock Bank Wrex 166 F5
Cock Bevington Warks 117 G11
Cock Bridge Aberds 292 C4
Cockburnspath Borders 282 G5
Cock Clarks Essex 88 E4
Cockden Lancs 204 G3
Cockenzie and Port Seton
E Loth 281 F8
Cocker Bar Lancs 194 C4
Cockerham Lancs 202 C5
Cockermouth Cumb 229 E8
Cockernhoe Herts 104 G2
Cockernhoe Green
Herts 104 G2
Cockersdale W Yorks 197 B8
Cockerton Darl 224 B5
Cockett Swansea 56 C6
Cocketty Aberds 293 F9
Cockfield Durham 233 G8
Suff 125 G8
Cockfosters London 86 F3
Cock Gate Hereford 115 D9
Cock Green Essex 87 B11
Cockhill Som 44 G6
Cock Hill N Yorks 206 B6
Cocking W Sus 34 D5
Cocking Causeway
W Sus 34 D5
Cockington Torbay 9 C7
Cocklake Som 44 D2
Cocklaw Northumb 241 C10
Cockleford Glos 81 C7
Cockley Beck Cumb 220 E4
Cockley Cley Norf 140 C5
Cockley Hill W Yorks 197 D7
Cock Marling E Sus 38 D5
Cocknowle Dorset 18 E4
Cockpole Green
Wokingham 65 C9
Cocks Corn 4 E5
Cocks Green Suff 125 F7
Cockshead Ceredig 112 F2
Cockshoot Hereford 97 D11
Cockshutford Shrops 131 F11
Cockshutt Shrops 132 G4
Shrops 149 D8
Cock Street Kent 53 C9
Suff 107 D9
Cockthorpe Norf 177 E7
Cockwells Corn 2 C2
Cockwood Devon 14 E5
Som 43 E8
Cockyard Derbys 185 F8
Hereford 97 E8
Codda Corn 11 F9
Coddenham Suff 126 G2
Coddenham Green Suff 126 F2
Coddington Ches W 167 D7
Hereford 98 C4
Notts 172 E4
Codford St Mary Wilts 46 F3
Codford St Peter Wilts 46 F3
Codicote Herts 86 B2
Codicote Bottom Herts 86 B2
Codmore Bucks 85 E7
Codmore Hill W Sus 35 C9
Codnor Derbys 170 F6
Codnor Breach Derbys 170 F6
Codnor Gate Derbys 170 E6
Codnor Park Derbys 170 E6
Codrington S Glos 61 D8
Codsall Staffs 133 C7
Codsall Wood Staffs 132 B6
Codsend Som 41 F11
Coedcae Bl Gwent 77 D11
Coedcae *continued*
Torf 78 D3
Coed Cwnwr Mon 78 F6
Coed Darcy Neath 76 F2
Coedely Rhondda 58 B4
Coed Eva Torf 78 G3
Coedkernew Newport 59 C9
Coed Llai = *Leeswood*
Flint 166 D3
Coed Mawr Gwyn 179 G9
Coed Morgan Mon 78 C5
Coedpoeth Wrex 166 E3
Coed-Talon Flint 166 D3
Coedway Powys 148 G6
Coed-y-bryn Ceredig 93 C7
Coed-y-caerau Newport 78 G5
Coed-y-fedw Mon 78 D6
Coed y Garth Ceredig 128 E3
Coed y go Shrops 148 D5
Coed-y-paen Mon 78 F4
Coed-y-parc Gwyn 163 B10
Coed-yr-ynys Powys 96 G3
Coed Ystumgwern
Gwyn 145 E11
Coed-y-wlad Powys 130 B4
Coelbren Powys 76 C4
Coffee Hall M Keynes 103 D7
Coffinswell Devon 9 B7
Cofton Devon 14 E5
Cofton Common
W Mid 117 B10
Cofton Hackett Worcs 117 B10
Cog V Glam 59 F7
Cogan V Glam 59 E7
Cogenhoe W Nhants 120 E6
Cogges Oxon 82 D5
Coggeshall Essex 106 G6
Coggeshall Hamlet
Essex 107 G7
Coggins Mill E Sus 37 B9
Coignafearn Lodge
Highld 291 B8
Coignascallan Highld 291 B9
Coig Peighinnean
W Isles 304 B7
Coig Peighinnean Bhuirgh
W Isles 304 C6
Coilacriech Aberds 292 D5
Coilantogle Stirling 285 G9
Coilessan Argyll 284 G6
Coilleag W Isles 297 K3
Coillemore Highld 300 B6
Coillore Highld 294 B5
Coirea-chrombe Stirling 285 G9
Coisley Hill S Yorks 186 E6
Coity Bridgend 58 C2
Cokenach Herts 105 D7
Cokhay Green Derbys 152 D5
Col W Isles 304 D6
Colaboll Highld 309 H5
Colan Corn 5 C7
Colaton Raleigh Devon 15 D7
Colbost Highld 298 E2
Colburn N Yorks 224 F3
Colby Cumb 231 G9
IoM 192 E3
Norf 160 C4
Colchester Essex 107 F10
Colchester Green Suff 125 F8
Colcot V Glam 58 F6
Cold Ash W Berks 64 F4
Cold Ashby W Nhants 120 B3
Cold Ash Hill Hants 49 G10
Cold Ashton S Glos 61 E9
Cold Aston Glos 81 B10
Coldbackie Highld 308 D6
Coldbeck Cumb 222 E4
Coldblow London 68 E4
Cold Blow Pembs 73 C10
Cold Brayfield
M Keynes 121 G8
Coldbrook Powys 96 D3
Cold Christmas Herts 86 B5
Cold Cotes N Yorks 212 E4
Coldean Brighton 36 F4
Coldeast Devon 14 G2
Coldeaton Derbys 169 D10
Cold Elm Glos 98 E6
Colden W Yorks 196 B3
Colden Common Hants 33 C7
Coldfair Green Suff 127 E8
Coldham Cambs 139 C8
Staffs 133 B7
Coldham's Common
Cambs 123 F9
Cold Hanworth Lincs 189 E8
Coldharbour Corn 4 F5
Devon 27 E9
Dorset 17 E9
Glos 79 E9
Kent 52 C5
London 68 D4
Sur 50 E6
Cold Harbour Dorset 18 D4
Herts 85 B10
Kent 69 G11
Lincs 155 C9
Oxon 64 D6
Wilts 45 B11
Wilts 45 D11
Windsor 65 D10
Cold Hatton Telford 150 E2
Cold Hatton Heath
Telford 150 E2
Cold Hesledon Durham 234 B4
Cold Hiendley W Yorks 197 E11
Cold Higham W Nhants 120 G3
Coldingham Borders 273 B8
Cold Inn Pembs 73 D10
Cold Kirby N Yorks 215 C10
Coldmeece Staffs 151 C7
Cold Moss Heath
Ches E 168 C3
Cold Newton Leics 136 B4
Cold Northcott Corn 11 D10
Cold Norton Essex 88 E4
Coldoch Stirling 278 B3
Cold Overton Leics 154 G6
Coldra Newport 59 B11
Coldrain Perth 286 G4
Coldred Kent 55 D9
Coldridge Devon 25 F11
Cold Row Lancs 202 E3
Coldstream Angus 287 D7
Borders 263 B8
Coldvreath Corn 5 D9
Coldwaltham W Sus 35 D8
Cold Well Staffs 151 G11
Coldwells Aberds 303 E11
Coldwells Croft Aberds 302 G5
Cole Som 45 G7
Colebatch Shrops 130 F6
Colebrook Devon 27 F8
Colebrooke Devon 13 B11
Coleburn Moray 302 D2
Coleby Lincs 173 C7
N Lincs 199 D11
Cole End Essex 105 D11
Warks 134 F3
Coleford Devon 26 G3
Glos 79 C9
Coleford *continued*
Som 45 D7
Coleford Water Som 42 G6
Colegate End Norf 142 F3
Cole Green Herts 86 C3
Herts 105 E8
Colehall W Mid 134 F2
Cole Henley Hants 48 C3
Colehill Dorset 31 G8
Coleman Green Herts 85 C11
Coleman's Hatch E Sus 52 G3
Colemere Shrops 149 C8
Colemore Hants 49 G8
Colemore Green Shrops 132 D4
Coleorton Leics 153 F8
Coleorton Moor Leics 153 F8
Cole Park London 67 E7
Colerne Wilts 61 E10
Colesbourne Glos 81 C7
Colesbrook Dorset 30 B4
Cole's Cross Dorset 28 G5
Colesden Bedford 122 F2
Coles Green Suff 107 C11
Worcs 116 G5
Cole's Green Suff 126 E5
Coleshill Bucks 85 F7
Oxon 82 G2
Warks 134 F4
Coles Meads Sur 51 C9
Colestocks Devon 27 G9
Colethrop Glos 80 C4
Coley Bath 44 B5
Reading 65 E8
W Yorks 196 B6
Colfin Dumfries 236 D2
Colgate W Sus 51 G8
Colgrain Argyll 276 E6
Colham Green London 66 C5
Colindale London 67 B8
Colinsburgh Fife 287 G8
Colinton Edin 270 B4
Colintraive Argyll 275 F11
Colkirk Norf 159 D8
Collace Perth 286 D6
Collafield Glos 79 C11
Collafirth Shetland 312 G6
Collam W Isles 305 J3
Collamoor Head Corn 11 C9
Collaton Devon 9 G9
Collaton St Mary Torbay 9 D7
College Milton S Lanark 268 D2
College of Roseisle
Moray 301 C11
College Park London 67 C8
College Town Brack 65 G11
Collennan S Ayrs 257 C8
Collessie Fife 286 F6
Colleton Mills Devon 25 D11
Collett's Br Norf 139 B9
Collett's Green Worcs 116 G6
Collier Row London 87 G8
Collier's End Herts 105 G7
Collier's Green E Sus 38 C3
Kent 53 F9
Colliers Hatch Essex 87 E8
Collier Street Kent 53 D8
Collier's Wood London 67 E9
Colliery Row T&W 234 B2
Collieston Aberds 303 G10
Collin Dumfries 238 B2
Collingbourne Ducis
Wilts 47 C8
Collingbourne Kingston
Wilts 47 B8
Collingham Notts 172 C4
W Yorks 206 D3
Collington Hereford 116 E2
Collingtree W Nhants 120 F5
Collingwood Northumb 243 B7
Collins End Oxon 65 D7
Collins Green Warr 183 C9
Worcs 116 F4
Collipriest Devon 27 E7
Colliston Angus 287 C10
Colliton Devon 27 G9
Collycroft Warks 135 F7
Collyhurst Gtr Man 195 G11
Collynie Aberds 303 F8
Collyweston N Nhants 137 C9
Colmonell S Ayrs 244 F4
Colmslie Borders 262 B2
Colmsliehill Borders 271 G10
Colmworth Bedford 122 F2
Colnabaichin Aberds 292 C4
Colnbrook Slough 66 D4
Colne Cambs 123 B7
Lancs 204 E3
Colne Bridge W Yorks 197 C7
Colne Edge Lancs 204 E3
Colne Engaine Essex 107 E7
Colnefields Cambs 123 B7
Colney Norf 142 B3
Colney Hatch London 86 G3
Colney Heath Herts 86 D2
Colney Street Herts 85 E11
Coln Rogers Glos 81 D9
Coln St Aldwyns Glos 81 D10
Coln St Dennis Glos 81 C9
Cologin Argyll 289 G10
Colpitts Grange
Northumb 241 F11
Colpy Aberds 302 F6
Colquhar Borders 270 G6
Colscott Devon 24 E5
Colshaw Staffs 169 B8
Colsterdale N Yorks 214 C2
Colsterworth Lincs 155 E8
Colston E Dunb 268 B2
Pembs 91 F9
Colston Bassett Notts 154 C3
Colstrope Bucks 65 B9
Coltfield Moray 301 C11
Colt Hill Hants 49 C8
Colthouse Cumb 221 F7
Colthrop W Berks 64 F4
Coltishall Norf 160 F5
Coltness N Lanark 268 D6
Colton
Cumb 210 B6
Norf 142 B2
N Yorks 206 E6
Staffs 151 E11
Suff 125 D7
W Yorks 206 G3
Colton Hills Staffs 133 D8
Colt Park Cumb 210 E5
Colt's Green S Glos 61 C8
Colt's Hill Kent 52 E6
Col Uarach W Isles 304 E6
Columbia T&W 243 F8
Columbjohn Devon 14 B5
Colva Powys 114 G4
Colvend Dumfries 237 D10
Colvister Shetland 312 D7
Colwall Hereford 98 C4
Colwall Green Hereford 98 C4
Colwall Stone Hereford 98 C5
Colwell IoW 20 D2
Northumb 241 B11
Colwich Staffs 151 E10
Colwick Notts 171 G10
Colwinston = *Tregolwyn*
V Glam 58 D2
Colworth W Sus 22 C6
Colwyn Bay = *Bae Colwyn*
Conwy 180 F4
Colychurch Bridgend 58 D2
Colyford Devon 15 C10
Colyton Devon 15 C10
Colzie Fife 286 F6
Combe Devon 7 E10
Devon 8 B4
Devon 9 G9
E Sus 37 B10
Hereford 114 E6
Oxon 82 B6
Som 28 B6
W Berks 63 G11
Combe Almer Dorset 18 B5
Combebow Devon 12 D5
Combe Common Sur 50 F3
Combe Down Bath 61 G9
Combe Fishacre Devon 8 C6
Combe Florey Som 43 G7
Combe Hay Bath 45 B8
Combeinteignhead
Devon 14 G4
Combe Martin Devon 40 D5
Combe Moor Hereford 115 E7
Combe Pafford Torbay 9 B8
Combe Raleigh Devon 27 G11
Comberbach Ches W 183 F10
Comberford Staffs 134 B3
Comberton Cambs 123 F7
Hereford 115 D9
Combe St Nicholas Som 28 E4
Combe Throop Som 30 C2
Combpyne Devon 15 C11
Combrew Devon 40 G4
Combridge Staffs 151 B11
Combrook Warks 118 G6
Combs Derbys 185 F8
Suff 125 F10
W Yorks 197 D8
Combs Ford Suff 125 F11
Combwich Som 43 E9
Comers Aberds 293 C8
Come-to-Good Corn 4 G6
Comeytrowe Som 28 C2
Comford Corn 2 B6
Comfort Corn 2 D6
Comhampton Worcs 116 D6
Comins Coch Ceredig 128 G2
Comiston Edin 270 B4
Comley Shrops 131 D9
Commercial End
Cambs 123 E11
Commins Denb 165 C10
Commins Capel Betws
Ceredig 112 F2
Commins Coch Powys 128 C6
Common Cefn-llwyn
Mon 78 G4
Commondale N Yorks 226 C3
Common Edge Blackpool 202 G2
Common End Cumb 228 G6
Derbys 170 C6
Common Hill Hereford 97 E11
Commonmoor Corn 6 B4
Common Moor Corn 6 B4
Common Platt Wilts 62 B6
Commonside Ches W 183 G8
Derbys 170 G2
Notts 171 D7
Common Side Ches W 167 B9
Derbys 170 F6
Derbys 186 F4
Commonwood Herts 85 E8
Shrops 149 D9
Wrex 166 E5
Common-y-coed Mon 60 B2
Comp Kent 52 B6
Compass Som 43 G9
Compstall Gtr Man 185 C7
Compton Derbys 169 F11
Devon 9 C7
Hants 32 B4
Hants 33 B7
Plym 7 D9
Staffs 132 G6
Sur 49 D11
Sur 50 D3
W Berks 64 D4
Wilts 46 C6
W Mid 133 D7
W Sus 34 E3
W Yorks 206 E3
Compton Abbas Dorset 30 D5
Compton Abdale Glos 81 B9
Compton Bassett Wilts 62 E4
Compton Beauchamp
Oxon 63 B9
Compton Bishop Som 43 B11
Compton Chamberlayne
Wilts 31 B8
Compton Common Bath 60 G6
Compton Dando Bath 60 G6
Compton Dundon Som 44 G3
Compton Durville Som 28 D6
Compton End Hants 33 B7
Compton Green Glos 98 F4
Compton Greenfield
S Glos 60 C5
Compton Martin Bath 44 B4
Compton Pauncefoot
Som 29 B10
Compton Valence Dorset 17 C7
Comrie Fife 279 D10
Highld 300 D4
Perth 285 C11
Perth 285 E11
Comrue Dumfries 248 F3
Conaglen House Highld 290 G2
Conanby S Yorks 187 B7
Conchra Argyll 275 E11
Highld 295 C10
Concord T&W 243 F8
Concraig Perth 286 F2
Concraigie Perth 286 C5
Conder Green Lancs 202 B5
Conderton Worcs 99 D9
Condicote Glos 100 F3
Condorrat N Lanark 278 G4
Condover Shrops 131 B9
Coney Hall London 67 G11
Coney Hill Glos 80 B5
Coneyhurst W Sus 35 C10
Coneysthorpe N Yorks 216 E4
Coneythorpe N Yorks 206 B3
Coney Weston Suff 125 B9
Conford Hants 49 G10
Congash Highld 301 G10
Congdon's Shop Corn 11 F11
Congeith Dumfries 237 C10
Congelow Kent 53 D7
Congerstone Leics 135 B7
Congham Norf 158 E4
Congleton Ches E 168 C5
Congleton Edge Ches E 168 C5
Congl-y-wal Gwyn 164 G2

Congresbury N Som. 60 G2
Congreve Staffs 151 G8
Conham Bristol 60 E6
Conicavel Moray 301 D9
Coningsby Lincs 174 D2
Conington Cambs 122 D6
Cambs 138 F3
Conisbrough S Yorks 187 B8
Conisby Argyll 274 G3
Conisholme Lincs 190 B6
Coniston Cumb 220 F6
E Yorks 209 F9
Coniston Cold N Yorks 204 B4
Conistone N Yorks 213 F9
Conkwell Wilts 61 G9
Connage Moray 302 C4
Connah's Quay Flint 166 B3
Connel Argyll 289 F11
Connel Park E Ayrs 258 G4
Conniburrow M Keynes 103 D7
Connista Highld 298 B4
Connon Corn 6 C3
Connor Downs Corn 2 B3
Conock Wilts 46 B5
Conon Bridge Highld 300 D5
Conon House Highld 300 D5
Cononish Stirling 285 E7
Cononley N Yorks 204 D5
Cononley Woodside
N Yorks 204 D5
Cononsyth Angus 287 C9
Conordan Highld 295 B7
Conquermoor Heath
Telford 150 F3
Consall Staffs 169 F7
Consett Durham 242 G4
Constable Burton
N Yorks 224 G3
Constable Lee Lancs 195 C10
Constantine Corn 2 D6
Constantine Bay Corn 10 G3
Contin Highld 300 D4
Contlaw Aberdeen 293 C10
Conwy Conwy 180 F3
Conyer Kent 70 G3
Conyers Green Suff 125 D7
Cooden E Sus 38 F2
Cooil IoM 192 E4
Cookbury Devon 24 F6
Cookbury Wick Devon 24 F5
Cookham Windsor 65 B11
Cookham Dean Windsor 65 C11
Cookham Rise Windsor 65 C11
Cookhill Worcs 117 F11
Cookley Suff 126 B6
Worcs 132 G6
Cookley Green Oxon 83 G11
Cookney Aberds 293 D10
Cookridge W Yorks 205 E11
Cooksbridge E Sus 36 E6
Cooksey Corner Worcs 117 D8
Cooksey Green Worcs 117 D8
Cook's Green Essex 89 B11
Suff 125 G9
Cookshill Staffs 168 G6
Cooksland Corn 5 B11
Cooksmill Green Essex 87 D10
Cooksongreen Ches W 183 G9
Coolham W Sus 35 C10
Cooling Medway 69 D9
Coolinge Kent 55 F8
Cooling Street Medway 69 E8
Coombe Bucks 84 D4
Corn 4 G2
Corn 4 G5
Corn 4 G6
Corn 5 E9
Corn 6 C4
Corn 24 E2
Devon 14 G4
Devon 27 D8
Glos 80 G3
Hants 33 C11
Kent 55 B9
London 67 E8
Som 28 B3
Som 28 F6
Wilts 30 C5
Wilts 47 C7
Coombe Bissett Wilts 31 B10
Coombe Dingle Bristol 60 D5
Coombe Hill Glos 99 F7
Coombe Keynes Dorset 18 E2
Coombes W Sus 35 F11
Coombesdale Staffs 150 B6
Coombeswood W Mid 133 F9
Coomb Hill Kent 69 G7
Coombs End S Glos 61 C9
Coombses Som 28 F4
Coopersale Common
Essex 87 E7
Coopersale Street Essex 87 E7
Cooper's Corner Kent 52 D3
Cooper's Green E Sus 37 C7
Herts 85 D11
Cooper's Hill C Beds 103 D10
Sur 66 E3
Cooper Street Kent 55 B10
Cooper Turning
Gtr Man 194 F6
Cootham W Sus 35 E9
Copcut Worcs 117 E7
Copdock Suff 108 C2
Coped Hall Wilts 62 C5
Copenhagen Denb 165 B8
Copford Essex 107 G8
Copford Green Essex 107 G8
Copgrove N Yorks 214 G6
Copister Shetland 312 F6
Cople Bedford 104 B2
Copley Durham 233 F7
Gtr Man 185 B7
W Yorks 196 C5
Copley Hill W Yorks 197 B8
Coplow Dale Derbys 185 F11
Copmanthorpe York 207 D7
Copmere End Staffs 150 D6
Copnor Ptsmth 33 G11
Copp Lancs 202 F4
Coppathorne Corn 24 G2
Coppenhall Ches E 168 D2
Staffs 151 F8
Coppenhall Moss
Ches E 168 D2
Copperhouse Corn 2 B3
Coppice Gtr Man 196 G2
Coppicegate Shrops 132 G4
Coppingford Cambs 138 G3
Coppins Corner Kent 54 D2
Coppleham Som 42 G2
Copplestone Devon 26 G3
Coppull Lancs 194 E5
Coppull Moor Lancs 194 E5
Copsale W Sus 35 C11
Copse Hill London 67 E8
Copster Green Lancs 203 G9
Copster Hill Gtr Man 196 G2
Copston Magna Warks 135 F9
Cop Street Kent 55 B9
Copt Green Warks 118 D3
Copthall Green Essex 86 E6
Copt Heath W Mid 118 B3
Copt Hewick N Yorks 214 E6
Copthill Durham 232 C3
Copthorne Ches E 167 G11
Corn 11 C11
Shrops 149 G9
Sur 51 F10
Coptiviney Shrops 149 B8
Copt Oak Leics 153 G9
Copton Kent 54 B4
Copy's Green Norf 159 B8
Copythorne Hants 32 E4
Corbets Tey London 68 B5
Corbridge Northumb 241 E11
Corbriggs Derbys 170 B6
Corby N Nhants 137 F7
Corby Glen Lincs 155 E9
Corby Hill Cumb 239 F11
Cordon N Ayrs 256 C2
Cordwell Norf 142 E2
Coreley Shrops 116 C2
Cores End Bucks 66 B2
Corfe Som 28 D2
Corfe Castle Dorset 18 E5
Corfe Mullen Dorset 18 B5
Corfton Shrops 131 F9
Corfton Bache Shrops 131 F9
Corgarff Aberds 292 C4
Corgee Corn 5 C10
Corhampton Hants 33 C10
Corlae Dumfries 246 D5
Corlannau Neath 57 C9
Corley Warks 134 F6
Corley Ash Warks 134 F5
Corley Moor Warks 134 F5
Cornaa IoM 192 D5
Cornabus Argyll 254 C4
Cornaigbeg Argyll 288 E1
Cornaigmore Argyll 288 C4
Argyll 288 E1
Cornard Tye Suff 107 C8
Cornbank Midloth 270 C4
Cornbrook Shrops 116 B2
Corncatterach Aberds 302 F5
Cornel Conwy 164 C2
Corner Row Lancs 202 F4
Cornett Hereford 97 B11
Corney Cumb 220 G2
Cornforth Durham 234 E2
Cornharrow Dumfries 246 E5
Cornhill Aberds 302 D5
Powys 96 C2
Stoke 168 E5
Cornhill-on-Tweed
Northumb 263 B9
Cornholme W Yorks 196 B2
Cornish Hall End Essex 106 D3
Cornquoy Orkney 314 G5
Cornriggs Durham 232 C2
Cornsay Durham 233 C8
Cornsay Colliery
Durham 233 C9
Cornton Stirling 278 B5
Corntown Highld 300 D5
V Glam 58 D2
Cornwell Oxon 100 F5
Cornwood Devon 8 D2
Cornworthy Devon 8 D6
Corpach Highld 290 F2
Corpusty Norf 160 C2
Corran Highld 290 G2
Highld 295 E10
Corran a Chan Uachdaraich
Highld 295 C7
Corranbuie Argyll 275 G9
Corrany IoM 192 D5
Corrichoich Highld 311 G4
Corrie N Ayrs 255 C11
Corrie Common
Dumfries 248 F6
Corriecravie N Ayrs 255 E10
Corriecravie Moor
N Ayrs 255 E10
Corriedoo Dumfries 246 G5
Corriegarth Lodge
Highld 291 B7
Corriemoillie Highld 300 C3
Corriemulzie Lodge
Highld 309 K3
Corrievarkie Lodge
Perth 291 F7
Corrievorrie Highld 301 G7
Corrigall Orkney 314 E3
Corrimony Highld 300 F3
Corringham Lincs 188 C5
Thurrock 69 C8
Corris Gwyn 128 B5
Corris Uchaf Gwyn 128 B4
Corrour Highld 290 G5
Corrour Shooting Lodge
Highld 290 G6
Corrow Argyll 284 G5
Corry Highld 295 C8
Corrybrough Highld 301 G8
Corrydon Perth 292 G3
Corryghoil Argyll 284 E5
Corrykinloch Highld 309 G3
Corrylach Argyll 255 D8
Corrymuckloch Perth 286 D2
Corrynachenchy Argyll 289 E8
Corry of Ardnagrask
Highld 300 E5
Corsback Highld 310 B6
Corscombe Dorset 29 F8
Corse Aberds 302 E6
Glos 98 F5
Corse Lawn Worcs 98 E6
Corse of Kinnoir Aberds 302 E5
Corsewall Dumfries 236 C2
Corsham Wilts 61 E11
Corsindae Aberds 293 C8
Corsley Wilts 45 D10
Corsley Heath Wilts 45 D10
Corsock Dumfries 237 B9
Corston Bath 61 F7
Orkney 314 E3
Wilts 62 C2
Corstorphine Edin 280 G3
Cors-y-Gedol Gwyn 145 E11
Cortachy Angus 287 B7
Corton Suff 143 D10
Wilts 46 E2
Corton Denham Som 29 C10
Cortworth S Yorks 186 B6
Coruanan Lodge Highld 290 G2
Corunna W Isles 296 E4
Corvast Highld 309 K5
Corwen Denb 165 G9
Cory Devon 24 D5
Coryates Dorset 17 D8
Coryton Cardiff 58 C6
Devon 12 E5
Thurrock 69 C8
Còsag Highld 295 D10
Cosby Leics 135 E10
Coscote Oxon 64 B4
Coseley W Mid 133 E8
Cosford Warks 119 B9
Cosgrove W Nhants 102 C5
Cosham Ptsmth 33 F11
Cosheston Pembs 73 E8
Cosmeston V Glam 59 F7
Cosmore Dorset 29 F11
Cossall Notts 171 G7
Cossall Marsh Notts 171 G7
Cosses S Ayrs 244 G4
Cossington Leics 154 G2
Som 43 E11
Costa Orkney 314 D3
Costessey Norf 160 G3
Costessey Park Norf 160 G3
Costhorpe Notts 187 D9
Costislost Corn 10 G6
Costock Notts 153 D11
Coston Leics 154 E6
Norf 141 B11
Coswinsawsin Corn 2 B4
Cote Oxon 82 E4
Som 43 E10
W Sus 35 F10
Cotebrook Ches W 167 B9
Cotehill Cumb 239 G11
Cotes Cumb 211 B9
Leics 153 E11
Staffs 150 C6
Cotesbach Leics 135 G10
Cotes Heath Staffs 150 C6
Cotes Park Derbys 170 E6
Cotford St Lukes Som 27 B11
Cotgrave Notts 154 B2
Cothall Aberds 293 B10
Cotham Bristol 60 E5
Notts 172 F3
Cothelstone Som 43 G7
Cotheridge Worcs 116 G5
Cotherstone Durham 223 B10
Cothill Oxon 83 F7
Cotland Mon 79 E8
Cotleigh Devon 28 G2
Cotmanhay Derbys 171 G7
Cotmarsh Wilts 62 D5
Cotmaton Devon 15 D8
Coton Cambs 123 F8
Shrops 149 C10
Staffs 134 B3
Staffs 150 E6
Staffs 151 C9
W Nhants 120 C3
Coton Clanford Staffs 151 E7
Coton Hayes Staffs 151 C9
Coton Hill Shrops 149 G9
Staffs 151 C9
Coton in the Clay Staffs 152 D3
Coton in the Elms
Derbys 152 F4
Coton Park Derbys 152 F5
Cotonwood Shrops 149 B10
Staffs 150 E6
Cotswold Community
Wilts 81 F8
Cott Devon 8 C5
Cottam E Yorks 217 F9
Lancs 202 G6
Notts 188 F4
Cottartown Highld 301 F10
Cottenham Cambs 123 D8
Cottenham Park London 67 F8
Cotterdale N Yorks 222 G6
Cottered Herts 104 F6
Cotterhill Woods
S Yorks 187 E9
Cotteridge W Mid 117 B10
Cotterstock N Nhants 137 E10
Cottesbrooke W Nhants 120 C4
Cottesmore Rutland 155 G8
Cotteylands Devon 26 E6
Cottingham E Yorks 208 G6
N Nhants 136 E6
Cottingley W Yorks 205 F8
Cottisford Oxon 101 E11
Cotton Staffs 169 F9
Suff 125 D11
Cotton End Bedford 103 B11
W Nhants 120 F5
Cotton Stones W Yorks 196 C4
Cotton Tree Lancs 204 F4
Cottonworth Hants 47 F11
Cottown Aberds 293 B9
Aberds 302 G5
Aberds 303 E8
Cotts Devon 7 B8
Cottwood Devon 25 E10
Cotwall Telford 150 F2
Cotwalton Staffs 151 B8
Coubister Orkney 314 E3
Couch Green Hants 48 G4
Couch's Mill Corn 6 D2
Coughton Hereford 97 G11
Warks 117 E11
Coughton Fields Warks 117 F11
Cougie Highld 300 G2
Coulaghailtro Argyll 275 G8
Coulags Highld 299 E9
Coulby Newham Mbro 225 B10
Coulderton Cumb 219 D9
Couldoran Highld 299 E8
Couligartan Stirling 285 G8
Coulin Highld 299 D10
Coulin Lodge Highld 299 D10
Coull Aberds 293 C7
Argyll 274 G3
Coulmony Ho Highld 301 E9
Coulport Argyll 276 D4
Coulsdon London 51 B9
Coulshill Perth 286 G3
Coulston Wilts 46 C3
Coulter S Lanark 260 C2
Coultings Som 43 E8
Coulton N Yorks 216 E2
Coultra Fife 287 E7
Cound Shrops 131 C11
Coundlane Shrops 131 B11
Coundmoor Shrops 131 C11
Coundon Durham 233 F10
W Mid 134 G6
Coundongate Durham 233 F10
Coundon Grange
Durham 233 F10
Countersett N Yorks 213 B8
Countess Wilts 47 E7
Countess Cross Essex 107 E7
Countess Wear Devon 14 D4
Countesthorpe Leics 135 D11
Countisbury Devon 41 D8
County Oak W Sus 51 F9
Coupar Angus Perth 286 C6
Coup Green Lancs 194 B5
Coupland Cumb 222 B4
Northumb 263 C10
Cour Argyll 255 C9
Courance Dumfries 248 E3
Coursley Som 42 G6
Court-at-Street Kent 54 F5
Court Barton Devon 14 D2
Court Colman Bridgend 57 E11
Court Corner Hants 48 B6
Courteenhall W Nhants 120 G5
Court Henry Carms 93 G11
Courthill Perth 286 C5
Court House Green
W Mid 135 G7
Courtsend Essex 89 G8
Courtway Som 43 G8
Cousland Midloth 271 B7
Cousley Wood E Sus 53 G7
Couston Argyll 275 F11
Cova Shetland 313 J5
Cove Argyll 276 E4
Borders 282 G5
Devon 27 D7
Hants 49 B11
Highld 307 K3
Cove Bay Aberdeen 293 C11
Cove Bottom Suff 127 B9
Covehithe Suff 143 G10
Coven Staffs 133 B8
Covender Hereford 98 C2
Coveney Cambs 139 G9
Covenham St Bartholomew
Lincs 190 C4
Covenham St Mary
Lincs 190 C4
Coven Heath Staffs 133 C8
Coven Lawn Staffs 133 B8
Coventry W Mid 118 B6
Coverack Corn 3 F7
Coverack Bridges Corn 2 C5
Coverham N Yorks 214 B2
Covesea Moray 301 B11
Covingham Swindon 63 B7
Covington Cambs 121 C11
S Lanark 259 B11
Cowan Bridge Lancs 212 D2
Cow Ark Lancs 203 D9
Cowbar Redcar 226 B5
Cowbeech E Sus 23 C10
Cowbeech Hill E Sus 23 C10
Cowbit Lincs 156 F5
Cowbog Aberds 303 D8
Cowbridge Lincs 174 F4
Som 42 E3
Cowbridge = Y Bont-Faen
V Glam 58 E3
Cowcliffe W Yorks 196 D6
Cowdale Derbys 185 G9
Cowden Kent 52 E3
Cowdenbeath Fife 280 C3
Cowdenburn Borders 270 E4
Cowen Head Cumb 221 F9
Cowers Lane Derbys 170 F4
Cowes IoW 20 B5
Cowesby N Yorks 215 B9
Cowesfield Green Wilts 32 C3
Cowfold W Sus 36 C2
Cowgill Cumb 212 B5
Cow Green Suff 125 D11
Cowgrove Dorset 18 B5
Cowhill Derbys 170 F5
S Glos 79 G10
Cow Hill Lancs 203 G7
Cowhorn Hill S Glos 61 E7
Cowie Aberds 293 E10
Stirling 278 D6
Cowlands Corn 4 G6
Cowleaze Corner Oxon 82 E4
Cowley Derbys 186 F4
Devon 14 B4
Glos 81 C7
London 66 C5
Oxon 83 E8
Cowleymoor Devon 27 E7
Cowley Peachy London 66 C5
Cowling Lancs 194 D5
N Yorks 204 E5
N Yorks 214 B4
Cowlinge Suff 124 G4
Cowlow Derbys 185 G9
Cowmes W Yorks 197 D7
Cowpe Lancs 195 C10
Cowpen Northumb 253 G7
Cowpen Bewley
Stockton 234 G5
Cowplain Hants 33 E11
Cow Roast Herts 85 C7
Cowshill Durham 232 C3
Cowslip Green N Som 60 G3
Cowstrandburn Fife 279 C10
Cowthorpe N Yorks 206 C4
Coxall Hereford 115 C7
Coxbank Ches E 167 G11
Coxbench Derbys 170 G5
Coxbridge Som 44 F4
Cox Common Suff 143 G8
Coxford Corn 11 B9
Norf 158 D6
Soton 32 D5
Coxgreen Staffs 132 F6
Cox Green Gtr Man 195 E8
Sur 50 G5
Windsor 65 D11
Coxheath Kent 53 C8
Coxhill Kent 55 D8
Cox Hill Corn 4 G4
Coxhoe Durham 234 D2
Coxley Som 44 E4
W Yorks 197 D9
Coxley Wick Som 44 E4
Coxlodge T&W 242 D6
Cox Moor Notts 171 D8
Coxpark Corn 12 G4
Coxtie Green Essex 87 F9
Coxwold N Yorks 215 D10
Coychurch Bridgend 58 D2
Coylton S Ayrs 257 E10
Coylumbridge Highld 291 B11
Coynach Aberds 292 C6
Coynachie Aberds 302 F4
Coytrahen Bridgend 57 D11
CoytrahÛn Bridgend 57 D11
Crabadon Devon 8 E5
Crabbet Park W Sus 51 F10
Crabble Kent 55 E9
Crabbs Cross Worcs 117 E10
Crabbs Green Herts 105 F9
Crabgate Norf 159 D11
Crab Orchard Dorset 31 F9
Crabtree Plym 7 D10
W Sus 36 B2
Crabtree Green Wrex 166 G4
Crackaig Argyll 274 G6
Crackenedge W Yorks 197 C8
Crackenthorpe Cumb 231 G9
Crackington Haven Corn 11 B8
Crackley Staffs 168 E4
Warks 118 C5
Crackleybank Shrops 150 G5
Crackpot N Yorks 223 F9
Crackthorn Corner
Suff 125 B10
Cracoe N Yorks 213 G9
Cracow Moss Ches E 168 F2
Staffs 168 F3
Craddock Devon 27 E9
Cradhlastadh W Isles 304 E2
Cradle Edge W Yorks 205 F7
Cradle End Herts 105 G9
Cradley Hereford 98 B4
W Mid 133 G8
Cradley Heath W Mid 133 F8
Cradoc Powys 95 E10
Crafthole Corn 7 E7
Crafton Bucks 84 B5
Crag Bank Lancs 211 E9
Crag Foot Lancs 211 E9
Craggan Highld 301 G10
Moray 301 F11
Stirling 285 E9
Cragganvallie Highld 300 F5
Craggenmore Moray 301 F11
Cragg Hill W Yorks 205 F10
Craggie Highld 301 F7
Highld 311 H2
Craggiemore Highld 309 J7
Cragg Vale W Yorks 196 C4
Craghead Durham 242 G6
Crahan Corn 2 C5
Crai Powys 95 G7
Craibstone Moray 302 D4
Craichie Angus 287 C9
Craig Dumfries 237 B8
Dumfries 237 C8
Highld 299 E10
Craiganor Lodge Perth 285 B10
Craig Berthlwyd M Tydf 77 F9
Craig Castle Aberds 302 G4
Craig-cefn-parc
Swansea 75 E11
Craigdallie Perth 286 E6
Craigdam Aberds 303 F8
Craigdarroch Dumfries 246 E6
Highld 300 D4
Craigdhu Highld 300 E4
Craig Douglas Borders 261 E7
Craigearn Aberds 293 B9
Craigellachie Moray 302 E2
Craigencallie Ho
Dumfries 237 B7
Craigencross Dumfries 236 C2
Craigend Borders 271 F9
Glasgow 268 B3
Perth 286 E3
Perth 286 E5
Stirling 278 D5
Craigendive Argyll 275 E11
Craigendoran Argyll 276 E6
Craigendowie Angus 293 G7
Craigends Renfs 267 B8
Craigens Argyll 274 G3
E Ayrs 258 F3
Craigentinny Edin 280 G5
Craigerne Borders 261 B7
Craighall Perth 286 C5
Craighat Stirling 277 E9
Craighead Fife 287 G10
Highld 301 C7
Craighill Aberds 303 E7
Craighlaw Mains
Dumfries 236 C5
Craighouse Argyll 274 G6
Craigie Aberds 293 B11
Dundee 287 D8
Perth 286 C5
Perth 286 E5
S Ayrs 257 C10
S Ayrs 257 E8
Craigiefield Orkney 314 E4
Craigiehall Edin 280 F3
Craigielaw E Loth 281 F9
Craigierig Borders 260 E6
Craigleith Edin 280 G4
Craig Llangiwg Neath 76 D2
Craig-llwyn Shrops 148 D4
Craiglockhart Edin 280 G4
Craig Lodge Argyll 275 G10
Craigmalloch E Ayrs 245 E11
Craigmaud Aberds 303 D8
Craigmill Stirling 278 B6
Craigmillar Edin 280 G5
Craigmore Argyll 266 B2
Craig-moston Aberds 293 F8
Craignant Shrops 148 B5
Craignell Dumfries 237 B7
Craigneuk N Lanark 268 C5
N Lanark 268 D5
Craignish Castle Argyll 275 C8
Craignure Argyll 289 F9
Craigo Angus 293 G8
Craigow Perth 286 G4
Craig Penllyn V Glam 58 D3
Craigrory Highld 300 E6
Craigrothie Fife 287 F7
Craigroy Moray 301 D11
Craigruie Stirling 285 E8
Craig's End Essex 106 D4
Craigsford Mains
Borders 262 B3
Craigshall Dumfries 237 D10
Craigshill W Loth 269 B11
Craigside Durham 233 D8
Craigston Castle Aberds 303 D7
Craigton Aberdeen 293 C10
Angus 287 B7
Angus 287 D9
Glasgow 267 C10
Highld 300 E6
Highld 309 H6
Highld 309 K6
Craigtown Highld 310 D2
Craig-y-don Conwy 180 E3
Craig-y-Duke Swansea 76 E2
Craig-y-nos Powys 76 B4
Craig-y-penrhyn
Ceredig 128 E3
Craig-y-Rhacca Caerph 59 B7
Craik Borders 249 B8
Crail Fife 287 G10
Crailing Borders 262 E5
Crailinghall Borders 262 E5
Crakaig Highld 311 H3
Crakehill N Yorks 215 E8
Crakemarsh Staffs 151 B11
Crambe N Yorks 216 G4
Crambeck N Yorks 216 F4
Cramhurst Sur 50 E2
Cramlington Northumb 243 B7
Cramond Edin 280 F3
Cramond Bridge Edin 280 F3
Crampmoor Hants 32 C5
Cranage Ches E 168 B3
Cranberry Staffs 150 B6
Cranborne Dorset 31 E9
Cranbourne Brack 66 E2
Hants 48 C6
Cranbrook Devon 14 B6
Kent 53 F9
London 68 B2
Cranbrook Common Kent 53 F9
Crane Moor S Yorks 197 G10
Crane's Corner Norf 159 G8
Cranfield C Beds 103 C9
Cranford Devon 24 C4
London 66 D6
Cranford St Andrew
N Nhants 121 B8
Cranford St John
N Nhants 121 B8
Cranham Glos 80 C5
London 68 B5
Cranhill Glasgow 268 B2
Warks 118 G2
Crank Mers 183 B8
Crank Wood Gtr Man 194 G6
Cranleigh Sur 50 F5
Cranley Suff 126 C3
Cranley Gardens London 67 B9
Cranmer Green Suff 125 C10
Cranmore IoW 20 D3
Som 45 E7
Cranna Aberds 302 D6
Crannich Argyll 289 E7
Crannoch Moray 302 D4
Cranoe Leics 136 D5
Cransford Suff 126 E6
Cranshaws Borders 272 C3
Cranstal IoM 192 B5
Cranswick E Yorks 208 C6
Crantock Corn 4 C5
Cranwell Lincs 173 F8
Cranwich Norf 140 E5
Cranworth Norf 141 C9
Craobh Haven Argyll 275 C8
Crapstone Devon 7 B10
Crarae Argyll 275 D10
Crask Highld 308 C7
Crask Inn Highld 309 G5
Craskins Aberds 293 C7
Crask of Aigas Highld 300 E4
Craster Northumb 265 F7
Craswall Hereford 96 D5
Crateford Shrops 132 F4
Staffs 133 B8
Cratfield Suff 126 B6
Crathes Aberds 293 D9
Crathie Aberds 292 D4
Highld 291 D7
Crathorne N Yorks 225 D8
Craven Arms Shrops 131 G8
Crawcrook T&W 242 E4
Crawford Lancs 194 G3
S Lanark 259 E11
Crawfordsyke S Lanark 269 F7
Crawfordjohn S Lanark 259 E9
Crawick Dumfries 259 G7
Crawley Devon 28 F3
Hants 48 G2
Oxon 82 C4
W Sus 51 F9
Crawley Down W Sus 51 F10
Crawley End Essex 105 C8
Crawley Hill Sur 65 G11
Crawleyside Durham 232 C5
Crawshaw W Yorks 197 E8
Crawshawbooth Lancs 195 B10
Crawton Aberds 293 F10
Cray N Yorks 213 D8
Perth 292 G3
Crayford London 68 E4
Crayke N Yorks 215 E11
Craymere Beck Norf 159 C11
Crays Hill Essex 88 G2
Cray's Pond Oxon 64 C6
Crazies Hill Wokingham 65 C9
Creacombe Devon 26 D4
Creagan Argyll 289 E11
Creagan Sithe Argyll 284 G6
Creag Aoil Highld 290 F3
Creagastrom W Isles 297 G4
Creag Ghoraidh
W Isles 297 G3
Creaguaineach Lodge
Highld 290 G5
Creaksea Essex 88 F6
Creamore Bank Shrops 149 C10
Crean Corn 1 E3
Creaton W Nhants 120 C4
Creca Dumfries 238 C6
Credenhill Hereford 97 C9
Crediton Devon 26 G4
Creebridge Dumfries 236 C6
Creech Dorset 18 E4
Creech Bottom Dorset 18 E4
Creech Heathfield Som 28 B3
Creech St Michael Som 28 B3
Creed Corn 5 F8
Creediknowe Shetland 312 G7
Creegbrawse Corn 4 G4
Creekmoor BCP 18 C6
Creekmouth London 68 C3
Creeksea Essex 88 F6
Creeting Bottoms Suff 126 F2
Creeting St Mary Suff 125 F11
Creeton Lincs 155 E10
Creetown Dumfries 236 D6
Creggans Argyll 284 G4
Cregneash IoM 192 F2
Creg-ny-Baa IoM 192 D4
Cregrina Powys 114 G2
Creich Fife 287 E7
Creigau Mon 79 F7
Creighton Staffs 151 B11
Creigiau Cardiff 58 C5
Crelly Corn 2 C5
Cremyll Corn 7 E9
Crendell Dorset 31 E9
Crepkill Highld 298 E4
Creslow Bucks 102 G6
Cressage Shrops 131 C11
Cressbrook Derbys 185 G11
Cresselly Pembs 73 D9
Cressex Bucks 84 G4
Cress Green Glos 80 E3
Cressing Essex 106 G5
Cresswell Northumb 253 E7
Staffs 151 B9
Cresswell Quay Pembs 73 D9
Creswell Derbys 187 G8
Staffs 151 D7
Staffs 151 D8
Creswell Green Staffs 151 G11
Cretingham Suff 126 E4
Cretshengan Argyll 275 G8
Creunant = Crynant
Neath 76 E3
Crewe Ches E 168 D2
Ches W 166 E6
Crewe-by-Farndon
Ches W 166 E6
Crewgarth Cumb 231 E8
Crewgreen Powys 148 F6
Crewkerne Som 28 F6
Crews Hill London 86 F4
Crew's Hole Bristol 60 E6
Crewton Derby 153 C7
Crianlarich Stirling 285 E7
Cribbs Causeway S Glos 60 C5
Cribden Side Lancs 195 C9
Cribyn Ceredig 111 G10
Criccieth Gwyn 145 B9
Crich Derbys 170 E5
Crich Carr Derbys 170 E4
Crichie Aberds 303 E9
Crichton Midloth 271 C7
Crick Mon 79 G7
W Nhants 119 C11
Crickadarn Powys 95 C11
Cricket Hill Hants 65 G10
Cricket Malherbie Som 28 E5
Cricket St Thomas Som 28 F5
Crickham Som 44 D2
Crickheath Shrops 148 E5
Crickheath Wharf
Shrops 148 E5
Crickhowell Powys 78 B2
Cricklade Wilts 81 G10
Cricklewood London 67 B8
Crickmery Shrops 150 D3
Crick's Green Hereford 116 G2
Criddlestyle Hants 31 E11
Cridling Stubbs N Yorks 198 C4
Cridmore IoW 20 E5
Crieff Perth 286 E2
Criggan Corn 5 C10
Criggion Powys 148 F5
Crigglestone W Yorks 197 D10
Crimble Gtr Man 195 E11
Crimchard Som 28 F4
Crimdon Park Durham 234 D5
Crimond Aberds 303 D10
Crimonmogate Aberds 303 D10
Crimp Corn 24 D3
Crimplesham Norf 140 C3
Crimscote Warks 100 B4
Crinan Argyll 275 D8
Crinan Ferry Argyll 275 D8
Crindau Newport 59 B10
Crindledyke N Lanark 268 D6
Cringleford Norf 142 B3
Cringles W Yorks 204 D6
Cringletie Borders 270 G4
Crinow Pembs 73 C10
Cripple Corner Essex 107 E7
Cripplesease Corn 2 B2
Cripplestyle Dorset 31 E9
Cripp's Corner E Sus 38 C3
Crispie Argyll 275 F10
Crist Derbys 185 E8
Critchell's Green Hants 32 B3
Critchill Som 45 D9
Critchmere Sur 49 G11
Crit Hall Kent 53 G9
Crizeley Hereford 97 E8
Croanford Corn 10 G6
Croasdale Cumb 219 B11
Crobeag W Isles 304 F5
Crockenhill Kent 68 F4
Crocker End Oxon 65 B8
Crockerhill Hants 33 F9
W Sus 22 B6
Crockernwell Devon 13 C11
Crockers Devon 40 F5
Crocker's Ash Hereford 79 B8
Crockerton Wilts 45 E11
Crockerton Green Wilts 45 E11
Crocketford or Ninemile Bar
Dumfries 237 B10
Crockey Hill York 207 D8
Crockham Heath
W Berks 64 G2
Crockham Hill Kent 52 C2
Crockhurst Street Kent 52 E6
Crockleford Heath
Essex 107 F10
Crockleford Hill Essex 107 F10
Crockness Orkney 314 G3
Crock Street Som 28 E4
Croesau Bach Shrops 148 D4
Croeserw Neath 57 B11
Croes-goch Pembs 87 E11
Croes-Hywel Mon 78 C4
Croes-lan Ceredig 93 C7
Croes Llanfair Mon 78 D4
Croesor Gwyn 163 G10
Croespenmaen Caerph 77 F11
Croes-wian Flint 181 G10
Croesyceiliog Carms 74 B6
Torf 78 F4
Croes-y-mwyalch Torf 78 G4
Croes y pant Mon 78 E4
Croesywaun Gwyn 163 D8
Croft Hereford 115 D9
Leics 135 D10
Lincs 175 C8
Pembs 92 C3
Warr 183 C10
Croftamie Stirling 277 D9
Croftfoot S Lanark 268 C2
Croftlands Cumb 210 D5
Croftmalloch W Loth 269 C8
Croft Mitchell Corn 2 B5
Croftmoraig Perth 285 C11
Croft of Tillymaud
Aberds 303 F11
Crofton Cumb 239 G8
London 68 F2
Wilts 63 G9
W Yorks 197 D11
Croft-on-Tees N Yorks 224 D5
Crofts Dumfries 237 B9
Crofts Bank Gtr Man 184 B3
Crofts of Benachielt
Highld 310 F5
Crofts of Haddo Aberds 303 F8
Crofts of Inverthernie
Aberds 303 E7
Crofts of Meikle Ardo
Aberds 303 E8
Crofty Swansea 56 B4
Croggan Argyll 289 G9
Croglin Cumb 231 B7
Croich Highld 309 K4
Croick Highld 310 D2
Croig Argyll 288 D5
Crois Dughaill W Isles 297 J3
Cromarty Highld 301 C7
Cromasaig Highld 299 C10
Crombie Fife 279 D10
Crombie Castle Aberds 302 D5
Cromblet Aberds 303 F7
Cromdale Highld 301 G10
Cromer Herts 104 F5
Norf 160 A4
Cromer-Hyde Herts 86 C2
Cromford Derbys 170 D3
Cromhall S Glos 79 G11
Cromhall Common
S Glos 61 B7
Cromor W Isles 304 F6
Crompton Fold Gtr Man 196 F2
Cromra Highld 291 D7
Cromwell Notts 172 C3
Cromwell Bottom
W Yorks 196 C6
Cronberry E Ayrs 258 E4
Crondall Hants 49 D9
Cronk-y-Voddy IoM 192 D4
Cronton Mers 183 D7
Crook Cumb 221 G9
Devon 27 G11
Durham 233 D9
Crookdake Cumb 229 C9
Crooke Gtr Man 194 F5
Crooked Billet London 67 E8
Crookedholm E Ayrs 257 B11
Crooked Soley Wilts 63 E10
Crooked Withies Dorset 31 F9
Crookes S Yorks 186 D4
Crookesmoor S Yorks 186 D4
Crookfur E Renf 267 D10
Crookgate Bank Durham 242 F5
Crookhall Durham 242 G4
Crookham Northumb 263 B10
W Berks 64 G4
Crookham Village Hants 49 C9
Crookhaugh Borders 260 D4
Crookhill T&W 242 E5
Crookhouse Borders 263 C7
Crooklands Cumb 211 C10
Crook of Devon Perth 286 G4
Crookston Glasgow 267 C10
Cropredy Oxon 101 B9
Cropston Leics 153 G11
Cropthorne Worcs 99 C9
Cropton N Yorks 216 B5
Cropwell Bishop Notts 154 B3
Cropwell Butler Notts 154 B3
Cros W Isles 304 B7
Crosben Highld 289 D9
Crosbost W Isles 304 F5
Crosby Cumb 229 D7
IoM 192 E4
Mers 182 B4
N Lincs 199 E11
Crosby Court N Yorks 225 G7
Crosby Garrett Cumb 222 D4
Crosby-on-Eden Cumb 239 F11
Crosby Ravensworth
Cumb 222 C2
Crosby Villa Cumb 229 D7
Croscombe Som 44 E5
Crosemere Shrops 149 D8
Crosland Edge W Yorks 196 E6
Crosland Hill W Yorks 196 E6
Crosland Moor W Yorks 196 D6
Croslands Park Cumb 210 E4
Cross Devon 40 F3
Devon 40 G6
Shrops 149 B7
Som 44 C2
Crossaig Argyll 255 B9
Crossal Highld 294 B6
Crossapol Argyll 288 E1
Cross Ash Mon 78 B6
Cross-at-Hand Kent 53 D9
Cross Bank Worcs 116 C4
Crossbrae Aberds 302 D6
Crossburn Falk 279 G7
Crossbush W Sus 35 F8
Crosscanonby Cumb 229 D7
Cross Coombe Corn 4 E4
Crosscrake Cumb 211 B10
Crossdale Street Norf 160 B4
Cross End Bedford 121 F11
Essex 107 E7
M Keynes 103 D8
Crossens Mers 193 D11
Crossflatts W Yorks 205 E8
Crossford Fife 279 D11
S Lanark 268 F6
Crossgate Lincs 156 D4
Orkney 314 E4
Staffs 151 B8
Cross Gate W Sus 35 E8
Crossgatehall E Loth 271 B7
Crossgates Cumb 229 G7
Fife 280 D2
N Yorks 217 C10
Powys 113 E11
Cross Gates W Yorks 205 F7
W Yorks 206 G3
Crossgill Cumb 231 C10
Lancs 211 G11
Crossgreen Shrops 149 F9
Cross Green Devon 12 D3
Staffs 133 B8
Suff 124 G6
Suff 125 F7
Suff 125 G9
Telford 150 G2
Warks 119 F7
W Yorks 206 G2
Crosshands Carms 92 G3
Cross Hands Carms 75 C9
Cross-hands Carms 92 G3
Cross Hands Pembs 73 C9
Cross Heath Staffs 168 F4
Crosshill E Ayrs 257 E11
Fife 280 B3
S Ayrs 245 B8
Cross Hill Corn 10 G6
Derbys 170 F6
Glos 79 F9
Cross Hills N Yorks 204 E6
Cross Holme N Yorks 225 F11
Crosshouse E Ayrs 257 B9
Cross Houses Shrops 131 B10
Shrops 132 E3
Crossings Cumb 240 B2
Cross in Hand E Sus 37 C9
Leics 135 G10
Cross Inn Carms 74 C3
Ceredig 111 E10
Ceredig 111 F7
Rhondda 58 C5
Crosskeys Caerph 78 G2
Cross Keys Kent 52 C4
Wilts 61 E11
Crosskirk Highld 310 B4
Crosslands Cumb 210 B6
Cross Lane Ches E 167 C11
Cross Lane Head Shrops 132 D4
Crosslanes Shrops 148 F6
Cross Lanes Corn 2 E5
Dorset 30 G3
N Yorks 215 F10
Oxon 65 D7
Wrex 166 F5
Crosslee Borders 261 F8
Renfs 267 B8
Crossley Hall W Yorks 205 G8
Cross Llyde Hereford 97 F8
Crossmichael Dumfries 237 C9
Crossmill E Renf 267 D10
Crossmoor Lancs 202 F4
Crossmount Perth 285 B11
Cross Oak Powys 96 G2
Cross of Jackston
Aberds 303 F7
Cross o' th' hands
Derbys 170 F3
Cross o' th' Hill Ches W 167 F7
Crosspost W Sus 36 C3
Crossroads Aberds 293 D9
E Ayrs 257 C11
Fife 281 B7
Cross Roads Devon 12 D5
W Yorks 204 F6
Cross Stone Aberds 303 G9
Cross Street Suff 126 B3
Crosston Angus 287 B9
Crosstown Corn 24 D2
V Glam 58 F4
Cross Town Ches E 184 F3
Crosswater Sur 49 F11
Crossway Hereford 98 E2
Mon 78 B6
Powys 113 F11
Crossway Green Mon 79 G8
Worcs 116 D6
Crossways Dorset 17 D11
Kent 68 D5
Mon 96 G6
S Glos 79 G11
Sur 49 F11

Crosswell =Ffynnongroes
Pembs 92 D2
Crosswood Ceredig 112 C3
Crosthwaite Cumb 221 G8
Croston Lancs 194 D3
Crostwick Norf 160 F5
Crostwight Norf 160 D6
Crothair W Isles 304 E3
Crouch Kent 52 B6
Kent 54 B5
Crouch End London 67 B9
Crouchers W Sus 22 C4
Croucheston Wilts 31 B9
Crouch Hill Dorset 30 E2
Crouch House Green
Kent 52 D2
Croughly Moray 301 G11
Croughton W Nhants 101 E10
Crovie Aberds 303 C8
Crow Hants 31 G11
Crowan Corn 2 C4
Crowborough E Sus 52 G4
Staffs 168 D6
Crowborough Warren
E Sus 52 G4
Crowcombe Som 42 F6
Crowcroft Worcs 116 G5
Crowden Derbys 185 B9
Devon 12 B5
Crowder Park Devon 8 D4
Crowdhill Hants 33 C7
Crowdicote Derbys 169 B10
Crowdleham Kent 52 B5
Crowdon N Yorks 227 F9
Crow Edge S Yorks 197 G7
Crowell Oxon 84 F2
Crowell Hill Oxon 84 F3
Crowfield Suff 126 F2
W Nhants 102 C2
Crowgate Street Norf 160 E6
Crowgreaves Shrops 132 D4
Crow Green Essex 87 F9
Crowhill Gtr Man 184 B6
M Keynes 102 D6
Crow Hill Hereford 98 F2
Crowhole Derbys 186 F4
Crowhurst E Sus 38 E3
Sur 51 D11
Crowhurst Lane End
Sur 51 D11
Crowland Lincs 156 G4
Crowlas Corn 2 C2
Crowle N Lincs 199 E9
Worcs 117 F8
Crowle Green Worcs 117 F8
Crowle Hill N Lincs 199 E9
Crowle Park N Lincs 199 E9
Crowmarsh Gifford Oxon 64 B6
Crown Corner Suff 126 C5
Crown East Worcs 116 G6
Crown Nest W Yorks 205 F8
Crownfield Bucks 84 F4
Crownhill Plym 7 D9
Crown Hills Leicester 136 C2
Crownland Suff 125 D10
Crownpits Sur 50 E3
Crownthorpe Norf 141 C11
Crowntown Corn 2 C4
Crown Wood Brack 65 F11
Crows-an-wra Corn 1 D3
Crow's Green Essex 106 F3
Crowshill Norf 141 B8
Crowsley Oxon 65 D8
Crowsnest Shrops 131 C7
Crow's Nest Corn 6 B5
Crowther's Pool Powys 96 B4
Crowthorne Brack 65 G10
Crowton Ches W 183 G9
Crow Wood Halton 183 D8
Croxall Staffs 152 G3
Croxby Lincs 189 B11
Croxby Top Lincs 189 B11
Croxdale Durham 233 D11
Croxden Staffs 151 B11
Croxley Green Herts 85 F9
Croxteth Mers 182 B6
Croxton Cambs 122 E4
N Lincs 200 E5
Norf 141 F7
Norf 159 C9
Staffs 150 C5
Croxtonbank Staffs 150 C5
Croxton Green Ches E 167 E8
Croxton Kerrial Leics 154 D6
Croy Highld 301 E7
N Lanark 278 F4
Croyde Devon 40 F2
Croyde Bay Devon 40 F2
Croydon Cambs 104 B6
London 67 F10
Crozen Hereford 97 B11
Crubenbeg Highld 291 D8
Crubenmore Lodge
Highld 291 D8
Cruckmeole Shrops 131 B8
Cruckton Shrops 149 G8
Cruden Bay Aberds 303 F10
Crudgington Telford 150 F2
Crudie Aberds 303 D7
Crudwell Wilts 81 G7
Crug Powys 114 C3
Crugmeer Corn 10 F4
Crugybar Carms 94 D3
Cruise Hill Worcs 117 E10
Crulabhig W Isles 304 E3
Crumlin Caerph 78 F2
Crumplehorn Corn 6 E4
Crumpsall Gtr Man 195 G10
Crumpsbrook Shrops 116 B2
Crumpton Hill Worcs 98 B5
Crundale Kent 54 D5
Pembs 73 B7
Cruwys Morchard Devon 26 E5
Crux Easton Hants 48 B2
Cruxton Dorset 17 B8
Crwbin Carms 75 C7
Crya Orkney 314 F3
Cryers Hill Bucks 84 F5
Crymlyn Gwyn 179 G10
Crymych Pembs 92 E3
Crynant =Creunant
Neath 76 E3
Crynfryn Ceredig 111 E11
Cuaich Highld 291 E8
Cuaig Highld 299 D7
Cuan Argyll 275 B8
Cubbington Warks 118 D6
Cubeck N Yorks 213 B9
Cubert Corn 4 D5
Cubitt Town London 67 D11
Cubley S Yorks 197 G8
Cubley Common Derbys 152 B3
Cublington Bucks 102 G6
Hereford 97 D8
Cuckfield W Sus 36 B4
Cucklington Som 30 B3
Cuckney Notts 187 G9
Cuckold's Green Suff 143 G9
Wilts 46 B3
Cuckoo Green Suff 143 D10
Cuckoo Hill Notts 188 C2
Cuckoo's Corner Hants 49 E8
Wilts 46 B4
Cuckoo's Knob Wilts 63 G7
Cuckoo Tye Suff 107 C7
Cuckron Shetland 313 H6
Cucumber Corner Norf 143 B7
Cuddesdon Oxon 83 E10
Cuddington Bucks 84 C2
Ches W 183 G10
Cuddington Heath
Ches W 167 F7
Cuddy Hill Lancs 202 F5
Cudham London 52 B2
Cudlipptown Devon 12 F6
Cudliptown Devon 12 F6
Cudworth Som 28 E5
Sur 51 E8
S Yorks 197 F11
Cudworth Common
S Yorks 197 F11
Cuerden Green Lancs 194 C5
Cuerdley Cross Warr 183 D8
Cufaude Hants 48 B6
Cuffern Pembs 91 G7
Cuffley Herts 86 E4
Cuiashader W Isles 304 C7
Cuidhir W Isles 297 L2
Cuidhtinis W Isles 296 C6
Cuiken Midloth 270 C4
Cuilcheanna Ho Highld 290 G2
Cuin Argyll 288 D6
Culbo Highld 300 C6
Culbokie Highld 300 D6
Culburnie Highld 300 E4
Culcabock Highld 300 E6
Culcairn Highld 300 C6
Culcharry Highld 301 D8
Culcheth Warr 183 B11
Culcronchie Dumfries 237 C7
Cùl Doirlinn Highld 289 B8
Culdrain Aberds 302 F5
Culduie Highld 299 E7
Culeave Highld 309 K5
Culford Suff 124 D6
Culfordheath Suff 125 C7
Culfosie Aberds 293 C9
Culgaith Cumb 231 F8
Culham Oxon 83 F8
Culkein Highld 306 F5
Culkein Drumbeg Highld 306 F6
Culkerton Glos 80 F6
Cullachie Highld 301 G9
Cullen Moray 302 C5
Cullercoats T&W 243 C9
Cullicudden Highld 300 C6
Cullingworth W Yorks 205 F7
Cullipool Argyll 275 B8
Cullivoe Shetland 312 C7
Culloch Perth 285 F11
Culloden Highld 301 E7
Cullompton Devon 27 F8
Culmaily Highld 311 K2
Culmazie Dumfries 236 D5
Culm Davy Devon 27 D10
Culmer Sur 50 F2
Culmers Kent 70 G5
Culmington Shrops 131 G9
Culmore Stirling 278 B3
Culmstock Devon 27 E10
Culnacraig Highld 307 J5
Cul na h-Aird W Isles 305 H3
Culnaightrie Dumfries 237 D9
Culnaknock Highld 298 C5
Culnaneam Highld 294 C6
Culpho Suff 108 B4
Culrain Highld 309 K5
Culra Lodge Highld 291 F7
Culross Fife 279 D9
Culroy S Ayrs 257 G8
Culscadden Dumfries 236 E6
Culsh Aberds 292 D5
Aberds 303 E8
Culshabbin Dumfries 236 D5
Culswick Shetland 313 J4
Cultercullen Aberds 303 G9
Cults Aberdeen 293 C10
Aberds 302 F5
Dumfries 236 E6
Fife 287 G7
Culverlane Devon 8 C4
Culverstone Green Kent 68 G6
Culverthorpe Lincs 173 G8
Culworth W Nhants 101 B10
Culzie Lodge Highld 300 B5
Cumberlow Green Herts 104 E6
Cumbernauld N Lanark 278 G5
Cumbernauld Village
N Lanark 278 F5
Cumber's Bank Wrex 149 B8
Cumberworth Lincs 191 G8
Cumdivock Cumb 230 B2
Cumeragh Village Lancs 203 F7
Cuminestown Aberds 303 D8
Cumledge Borders 272 D5
Cumlewick Shetland 313 L6
Cumlodden Argyll 275 D11
Cumloden Dumfries 236 C6
Cummersdale Cumb 239 G9
Cummerton Aberds 303 C8
Cummertrees Dumfries 238 D4
Cummingston Moray 301 C11
Cumnock E Ayrs 258 E3
Cumnor Oxon 83 E7
Cumnor Hill Oxon 83 D7
Cumrew Cumb 240 G2
Cumwhinton Cumb 239 G10
Cumwhitton Cumb 240 G2
Cundall N Yorks 215 E8
Cundy Cross S Yorks 197 F11
Cundy Hos S Yorks 186 B4
Cunninghamhead
N Ayrs 267 G7
Cunnister Shetland 312 D7
Cupar Fife 287 F7
Cupar Muir Fife 287 F7
Cupernham Hants 32 C5
Cupid Green Herts 85 D9
Cupid's Hill Mon 97 F8
Curbar Derbys 186 G3
Curborough Staffs 152 G2
Curbridge Hants 33 E8
Oxon 82 D4
Curdridge Hants 33 E8
Curdworth Warks 134 E3
Curgurrell Corn 3 B9
Curin Highld 300 D3
Curland Som 28 D3
Curland Common Som 28 D3
Curlew Green Suff 127 D7
Curling Tye Green Essex 88 D4
Curload Som 28 B4
Currarie S Ayrs 244 E5
Currian Vale Corn 5 D9
Curridge W Berks 64 E3
Currie Edin 270 B3
Currock Cumb 239 G10
Curry Lane Corn 11 C11
Curry Mallet Som 28 C4
Curry Rivel Som 28 B5
Cursiter Orkney 314 E3
Curteis' Corner Kent 53 F11
Curtisden Green Kent 53 E8
Curtisknowle Devon 8 E4
Curtismill Green Essex 87 F8
Cury Corn 2 E5
Cusbay Orkney 314 C5
Cusgarne Corn 4 G5
Cushnie Aberds 303 C7
Cushuish Som 43 G7
Cusop Hereford 96 C4
Custards Hants 32 F3
Custom House London 68 C2
Cusveorth Coombe Corn 4 G5
Cusworth S Yorks 198 G4
Cutcloy Dumfries 236 F6
Cutcombe Som 42 F2
Cutgate Gtr Man 195 E11
Cuthill E Loth 281 G7
Cutiau Gwyn 146 F2
Cutlers Green Essex 105 E11
Cutler's Green Som 44 C5
Cutmadoc Corn 5 C11
Cutmere Corn 6 C6
Cutnall Green Worcs 117 D7
Cutsdean Glos 99 E11
Cutsyke W Yorks 198 C2
Cutteslowe Oxon 83 C8
Cutthorpe Derbys 186 G4
Cuttiford's Door Som 28 E4
Cutts Shetland 313 K6
Cuttybridge Pembs 72 B6
Cuttyhill Aberds 303 D10
Cuxham Oxon 83 F11
Cuxton Medway 69 F8
Cuxwold Lincs 201 G7
Cwm Bl Gwent 77 D11
Denb 181 F9
Neath 57 C10
Powys 129 D11
Powys 130 E5
Shrops 114 B6
Swansea 57 B7
Cwmafan Neath 57 C9
Cwmaman Rhondda 77 F8
Cwmann Carms 93 B11
Cwmavon Torf 78 D3
Cwmbach Carms 75 E7
Carms 92 F5
Powys 96 D3
Rhondda 77 E8
Cwmbâch Rhondda 77 E8
Cwmbach Llechrhyd
Powys 113 G10
Cwmbelan Powys 129 G8
Cwmbran Torf 78 G3
Cwmbrwyno Ceredig 128 G4
Cwm-byr Carms 94 E2
Cwm Capel Carms 75 E7
Cwmcarn Caerph 78 G2
Cwmcarvan Mon 79 D7
Cwm-celyn Bl Gwent 78 D2
Cwm-Cewydd Gwyn 147 G7
Cwmcoednerth Ceredig 92 B6
Cwm-cou Ceredig 92 C5
Cwmcrawnon Powys 77 B10
Cwmcych Carms 92 D5
Cwmdare Rhondda 77 E7
Cwm Dows Caerph 78 F2
Cwmdu Carms 94 E2
Powys 96 G3
Swansea 56 C6
Cwmduad Carms 93 E7
Cwm-Dulais Swansea 75 E10
Cwmdwr Carms 94 E4
Cwmerfyn Ceredig 128 G3
Cwmfelin Bridgend 57 D11
M Tydf 77 E9
Cwmfelin Boeth Carms 73 B11
Cwm felin fach Caerph 77 G11
Cwmfelin Mynach Carms 92 G4
Cwmffrwd Carms 74 B6
Cwm Ffrwd-oer Torf 78 E3
Cwm-Fields Torf 78 E3
Cwm Gelli Caerph 77 F11
Cwmgiedd Powys 76 C3
Cwmgors Neath 76 C2
Cwmgwili Carms 75 C9
Cwmgwrach Neath 76 E5
Cwm Gwyn Swansea 56 C6
Cwm Head Shrops 131 F8
Cwm-hesgen Gwyn 146 D5
Cwmhiraeth Carms 92 D6
Cwm-hwnt Rhondda 76 D6
Cwmifor Carms 94 F3
Cwm Irfon Powys 95 B7
Cwmisfael Carms 75 B7
Cwm-Llinau Powys 128 B6
Cwmllynfell Neath 76 C2
Cwm-mawr Carms 75 C8
Cwm-miles Carms 92 G3
Cwm Nant-gam
Bl Gwent 78 C2
Cwmnantyrodyn
Caerph 77 F11
Cwmorgan Pembs 92 E5
Cwmparc Rhondda 77 F7
Cwm-parc Rhondda 77 F7
Cwmpengraig Carms 92 D6
Cwm Penmachno
Conwy 164 F3
Cwmpennar Rhondda 77 E8
Cwm Plysgog Ceredig 92 C3
Cwmrhos Powys 96 G3
Cwmrhydyceirw
Swansea 57 B7
Cwmsychpant Ceredig 93 B9
Cwmsyfiog Caerph 77 E11
Cwmsymlog Ceredig 128 G3
Cwmtillery Bl Gwent 78 D2
Cwm-twrch Isaf Powys 76 C3
Cwm-twrch Uchaf
Powys 76 C3
Cwmwdig Water Pembs 90 E6
Cwmwysg Powys 95 F7
Cwm-y-glo Carms 75 C9
Gwyn 163 C8
Cwmynyscoy Torf 78 F3
Cwmyoy Mon 96 G5
Cwmystwyth Ceredig 112 C5
Cwrt Gwyn 128 C3
Cwrt-newydd Ceredig 93 B9
Cwrt-y-cadno Carms 94 C3
Cwrt-y-gollen Powys 78 B2
Cydweli =Kidwelly
Carms 74 D6
Cyffordd Llandudno
=Llandudno Junction
Conwy 180 F3
Cyffylliog Denb 165 D9
Cyfronydd Powys 130 B2
Cymau Flint 166 D3
Cymdda Bridgend 58 C2
Cymer Neath 57 B11
Cymmer Rhondda 77 G8
Cyncoed Cardiff 59 C7
Cynghordy Carms 94 C6
Cynheidre Carms 75 D7
Cynonville Neath 57 B10
Cyntwell Cardiff 58 D6
Cynwyd Denb 165 G9
Cynwyl Elfed Carms 93 F7
Cywarch Gwyn 147 F7

D

Daccombe Devon 9 B8
Dacre Cumb 230 F5
N Yorks 214 G3
Dacre Banks N Yorks 214 G3
Daddry Shield Durham 232 D3
Dadford Bucks 102 D3
Dadlington Leics 135 D8
Dafarn Faig Gwyn 163 F7
Dafen Carms 75 E8
Daffy Green Norf 141 B9
Dagdale Staffs 151 C11
Dagenham London 68 C3
Daggons Dorset 31 E10
Daglingworth Glos 81 D7
Dagnall Bucks 85 B7
Dagtail End Worcs 117 E10
Dagworth Suff 125 E10
Dail Beag W Isles 304 D4
Dail bho Dheas W Isles 304 B6
Dail bho Thuath
W Isles 304 B6
Daill Argyll 274 G4
Dailly S Ayrs 245 C7
Dail Mor W Isles 304 D4
Dainton Devon 9 B7
Dairsie or Osnaburgh
Fife 287 F8
Daisy Green Suff 125 D10
Suff 125 D11
Daisy Hill Gtr Man 195 G7
W Yorks 197 B9
W Yorks 205 G8
Daisy Nook Gtr Man 196 G2
Dalabrog W Isles 297 J3
Dalavich Argyll 275 B10
Dalbeattie Dumfries 237 C10
Dalbeg Highld 291 B8
Dalblair E Ayrs 258 F4
Dalbog Angus 293 F7
Dalbrack Stirling 285 G11
Dalbury Derbys 152 C5
Dalby IoM 192 E3
Lincs 190 G6
N Yorks 216 E2
Dalchalloch Perth 291 G9
Dalchalm Highld 311 J3
Dalchenna Argyll 284 G4
Dalchirach Moray 301 F11
Dalchonzie Perth 285 E11
Dalchork Highld 309 H5
Dalchreichart Highld 290 B4
Dalchruin Perth 285 F11
Dalderby Lincs 174 B2
Dale Cumb 230 C6
Gtr Man 196 F3
Pembs 72 D4
Shetland 312 G6
Dale Abbey Derbys 153 B8
Dalebank Derbys 170 C5
Dale Bottom Cumb 229 G11
Dale Brow Ches E 184 F6
Dale End Derbys 170 C2
N Yorks 204 D5
Dale Head Cumb 221 B8
Dale Hill E Sus 53 G7
E Sus 53 G8
Dalelia Highld 289 C9
Dale Moor Derbys 153 B8
Dale of Walls Shetland 313 H3
Dales Brow Gtr Man 195 G9
Dales Green Staffs 168 D5
Daless Highld 301 F8
Dalestie Moray 292 B3
Dalestorth Notts 171 C8
Dalfaber Highld 291 B11
Dalfoil Stirling 277 D11
Dalganachan Highld 310 E4
Dalgarven N Ayrs 266 F5
Dalgety Bay Fife 280 E3
Dalginross Perth 285 E11
Dalguise Perth 286 C3
Dalhalvaig Highld 310 D2
Dalham Suff 124 E4
Dalhastnie Angus 293 F7
Dalhenzean Perth 292 G3
Dalinlongart Argyll 276 E2
Dalkeith Midloth 270 B6
Dallam Warr 183 C9
Dallas Moray 301 D11
Dallas Lodge Moray 301 D11
Dallcharn Highld 308 D6
Dalleagles E Ayrs 258 G3
Dallicott Shrops 132 E5
Dallimores IoW 20 C6
Dallinghoo Suff 126 G5
Dallington E Sus 23 B11
W Nhants 120 E4
Dallow N Yorks 214 E3
Dalmadilly Aberds 293 B9
Dalmally Argyll 284 E5
Dalmarnock Glasgow 268 C2
Perth 286 C3
Dalmary Stirling 277 B10
Dalmellington E Ayrs 245 B11
Dalmeny Edin 280 F2
Dalmigavie Highld 291 B9
Dalmigavie Lodge
Highld 301 G7
Dalmilling S Ayrs 257 E9
Dalmore Highld 300 C6
Dalmuir W Dunb 277 G9
Dalnabreck Highld 289 C8
Dalnacardoch Lodge
Perth 291 F9
Dalnacroich Highld 300 D3
Dalnaglar Castle Perth 292 G3
Dalnahaitnach Highld 301 G8
Dalnamein Lodge Perth 291 G9
Dalnarrow Argyll 289 F9
Dalnaspidal Lodge
Perth 291 F8
Dalnavaid Perth 292 G2
Dalnavie Highld 300 B6
Dalnaw Dumfries 236 B5
Dalnawillan Lodge
Highld 310 E4
Dalness Highld 284 B5
Dalnessie Highld 309 H6
Dalphaid Highld 309 H3
Dalqueich Perth 286 G4
Dalrannoch Argyll 289 E11
Dalreavoch Highld 309 J7
Dalriach Highld 301 F10
Dalrigh Stirling 285 E7
Dalry Edin 280 G4
N Ayrs 266 F5
Dalrymple E Ayrs 257 G9
Dalscote W Nhants 120 G3
Dalserf S Lanark 268 E6
Dalshannon N Lanark 278 G4
Dalston Cumb 239 G9
London 67 C10
Dalswinton Dumfries 247 F10
Dalton Cumb 211 D10
Dumfries 238 C4
Lancs 194 F3
Northumb 241 F10
Northumb 242 C4
Dalton *continued*
N Yorks 215 D8
N Yorks 224 D2
S Lanark 268 D3
S Yorks 187 C7
W Yorks 197 D7
Dalton-in-Furness
Cumb 210 E4
Dalton-le-Dale Durham 234 B4
Dalton Magna S Yorks 187 C7
Dalton-on-Tees
N Yorks 224 D5
Dalton Parva S Yorks 187 C7
Dalton Piercy Hrtlpl 234 E5
Dalveallan Highld 300 F6
Dalveich Stirling 285 E10
Dalvina Lo Highld 308 E6
Dalwey Telford 132 B3
Dalwhinnie Highld 291 E8
Dalwood Devon 28 G3
Dalwyne S Ayrs 245 D8
Damask Green Herts 104 F5
Damems W Yorks 204 F6
Damerham Hants 31 D10
Damery Glos 80 G2
Damgate Norf 143 B8
Norf 161 F9
Dam Green Norf 141 F11
Damhead Moray 301 D10
Dam Head W Yorks 196 B6
Damhead Holdings
Midloth 270 B5
Dam Mill Staffs 133 C7
Damnaglaur Dumfries 236 F3
Dam of Quoiggs Perth 286 G2
Damside Borders 270 F3
Dam Side Lancs 202 D4
Danaway Kent 69 G11
Danbury Essex 88 E3
Danbury Common Essex 88 E3
Danby N Yorks 226 D4
Danby Wiske N Yorks 224 F6
Dan Caerlan Rhondda 58 C5
Dancers Hill Herts 86 F2
Dancing Green Hereford 98 G2
Dandaleith Moray 302 E2
Danderhall Midloth 270 B6
Dandy Corner Suff 125 D11
Danebank Ches E 185 E7
Dane Bank Gtr Man 184 B6
Danebridge Ches E 169 B7
Dane End Herts 104 G6
Danegate E Sus 52 G5
Danehill E Sus 36 B6
Dane in Shaw Ches E 168 C5
Danemoor Green Norf 141 B11
Danesbury Herts 86 B2
Danesfield Bucks 65 C10
Danesford Shrops 132 E4
Daneshill Hants 49 C7
Danesmoor Derbys 170 C6
Danes Moss Ches E 184 G6
Dane Street Kent 54 C5
Daneway Glos 80 E6
Dangerous Corner
Gtr Man 195 G7
Lancs 194 E4
Daniel's Water Kent 54 E3
Danna na Cloiche Argyll 275 F7
Dannonchapel Corn 10 E6
Danskine E Loth 271 B11
Danthorpe E Yorks 209 G10
Danygraig Caerph 78 G2
Danzey Green Warks 118 D2
Dapple Heath Staffs 151 D10
Darby End W Mid 133 F8
Darby Green Hants 65 G10
Darbys Green Worcs 116 F4
Darby's Hill W Mid 133 F9
Darcy Lever Gtr Man 195 F8
Dardy Powys 78 B2
Darenth Kent 68 E5
Daresbury Halton 183 E9
Daresbury Delph Halton 183 E9
Darfield S Yorks 198 G2
Darfoulds Notts 187 F9
Dargate Kent 70 G5
Dargate Common Kent 70 G5
Dargavel Village Renfs 277 G8
Darite Corn 6 B5
Darkland Moray 302 C2
Darland Wrex 166 D5
Darlaston W Mid 133 D9
Darlaston Green W Mid 133 D9
Darley N Yorks 205 B10
Shrops 132 D3
Darley Abbey Derby 153 B7
Darley Bridge Derbys 170 C3
Darley Dale Derbys 170 C3
Darleyford Corn 11 G11
Darley Green Warks 118 C3
Darleyhall Herts 104 G2
Darley Head N Yorks 205 B9
Darley Hillside Derbys 170 C3
Darlingscott Warks 100 C4
Darlington Darl 224 C5
Darliston Shrops 149 C11
Darlton Notts 188 G3
Darmsden Suff 125 G11
Darnall S Yorks 186 D5
Darnaway Castle Moray 301 D9
Darnford Staffs 134 B2
Darnhall Ches W 167 C10
Darnhall Mains Borders 270 F4
Darn Hill Gtr Man 195 E10
Darnick Borders 262 C2
Darowen Powys 128 C6
Darra Aberds 303 E7
Darracott Devon 24 D2
Devon 40 F3
Darras Hall Northumb 242 C5
Darrington W Yorks 198 D3
Darrow Green Norf 142 F5
Darsham Suff 127 D8
Darshill Som 44 E6
Dartford Kent 68 E4
Dartford Crossing Kent 68 D5
Dartington Devon 8 C5
Dartmeet Devon 13 G9
Dartmouth Devon 9 E7
Dartmouth Park London 67 B9
Darton S Yorks 197 F10
Darvel E Ayrs 258 B3
Darvillshill Bucks 84 F4
Darwell Hole E Sus 23 B11
Darwen Blackburn 195 C7
Dassels Herts 105 F7
Datchet Windsor 66 D3
Datchet Common
Windsor 66 D3
Datchworth Herts 86 B3
Datchworth Green Herts 86 B3
Daubhill Gtr Man 195 F8
Daugh of Kinermony
Moray 302 E2
Dauntsey Wilts 62 C3
Dauntsey Lock Wilts 62 C3
Dava Moray 301 F10
Davenham Ches W 183 G11
Davenport Ches E 168 B4
Gtr Man 184 D5
Davenport Green
Ches E 184 F4
Gtr Man 184 D4
Daventry W Nhants 119 E11
Davidson's Mains Edin 280 F4
Davidston Highld 301 C7
Davidstow Corn 11 D9
David Street Kent 68 G6
David's Well Powys 113 B11
Davington Dumfries 248 C6
Kent 70 G4
Daviot Aberds 303 G7
Highld 301 F7
Davis's Town E Sus 23 B8
Davoch of Grange
Moray 302 D4
Davo Mains Aberds 293 F9
Davyhulme Gtr Man 184 B3
Daw Cross N Yorks 205 C11
Dawdon Durham 234 B4
Daw End W Mid 133 C10
Dawesgreen Sur 51 D8
Dawker Hill N Yorks 207 F7
Dawley Telford 132 B3
Dawley Bank Telford 132 B3
Dawlish Devon 14 F5
Dawlish Warren Devon 14 F5
Dawn Conwy 180 G5
Daw's Cross Essex 107 E7
Daw's Green Som 27 C11
Daws Heath Essex 69 B10
Dawshill Worcs 116 G6
Daw's House Corn 12 E2
Dawsmere Lincs 157 C8
Daybrook Notts 171 F9
Day Green Ches E 168 D3
Dayhills Staffs 151 C9
Dayhouse Bank Worcs 117 B9
Daylesford Glos 100 F4
Daywall Shrops 148 C5
Ddol Flint 181 G10
Ddôl Cownwy Powys 147 F10
Ddrydwy Anglesey 178 G5
Deacons Hill Herts 85 F11
Deadman's Cross
C Beds 104 C2
Deadman's Green
Staffs 151 B10
Deadwater Hants 49 F10
Northumb 250 D4
Deaf Hill Durham 234 D3
Deal Hall Essex 89 F8
Kent 55 C11
Dean Cumb 229 F7
Devon 8 C4
Devon 40 D6
Devon 40 E4
Devon 41 D8
Dorset 31 D7
Edin 280 G4
Hants 33 D9
Hants 48 G2
Lancs 195 B11
Oxon 100 G6
Som 45 E7
Dean Bank Durham 233 E11
Deanburnhaugh
Borders 261 G9
Dean Court Oxon 83 D7
Dean Cross Devon 40 E4
Deane Gtr Man 195 F7
Hants 48 C4
Deanend Dorset 31 D7
Dean Head S Yorks 197 G9
Deanich Lodge Highld 309 L3
Deanland Dorset 31 D7
Deanlane End W Sus 34 E2
Dean Lane Head
W Yorks 205 G7
Dean Park Renfs 267 B10
Dean Prior Devon 8 C4
Dean Row Ches E 184 E5
Deans W Loth 269 B10
Deans Bottom Kent 69 G11
Deanscales Cumb 229 F7
Deansgreen Ches E 183 D11
Dean's Green Warks 118 D2
Deanshanger W Nhants 102 D5
Deans Hill Kent 69 G11
Deanston Stirling 285 G11
Dean Street Kent 53 C8
Dearham Cumb 229 D7
Dearnley Gtr Man 196 D2
Debach Suff 126 G4
Debdale Gtr Man 184 B5
Debden Essex 86 F6
Essex 105 E11
Debden Cross Essex 105 E11
Debden Green Essex 86 F6
Essex 105 E11
De Beauvoir Town
London 67 C10
Debenham Suff 126 E3
Deblin's Green Worcs 98 B6
Dechmont W Loth 279 G10
Deckham T&W 243 E7
Deddington Oxon 101 E9
Dedham Essex 107 E11
Dedham Heath Essex 107 E11
Dedridge W Loth 269 B11
Dedworth Windsor 66 D2
Deebank Aberds 293 D8
Deecastle Aberds 292 D6
Deene N Nhants 137 E8
Deenethorpe N Nhants 137 E9
Deepcar S Yorks 186 B3
Deepclough Derbys 185 B8
Deepcut Sur 50 B2
Deepdale C Beds 104 B4
Cumb 212 C4
N Yorks 213 D7
Deepdene Sur 51 D7
Deepfields W Mid 133 E8
Deeping Gate Lincs 138 B2
Deeping St James Lincs 138 B3
Deeping St Nicholas
Lincs 156 F4
Deepthwaite Cumb 211 C10
Deepweir Mon 60 B3
Deerhill Moray 302 D4
Deerhurst Glos 99 F7
Deerhurst Walton Glos 99 F7
Deerland Pembs 73 C7
Deerness Orkney 314 F5
Deer's Green Essex 105 E9
Deerstones N Yorks 205 C7
Deerton Street Kent 70 G3
Defford Worcs 99 C8
Defynnog Powys 95 F8
Deganwy Conwy 180 F3
Degar V Glam 58 D4
Degibna Corn 2 D5
Deighton N Yorks 225 E7
W Yorks 197 D7
York 207 E8
Deiniolen Gwyn 163 C9
Deishar Highld 291 B11
Delabole Corn 11 E7
Delamere Ches W 167 B9
Delfour Highld 291 C10
Delfrigs Aberds 303 G9
Delliefure Highld 301 F10
Dell Lodge Highld 292 B2
Dell Quay W Sus 22 C4
Delly End Oxon 82 C5
Delnabo Moray 292 B3
Delnadamph Aberds 292 C4
Delnamer Angus 292 G3
Delph Gtr Man 196 F3
Delves Durham 233 B8
Delvine Perth 286 C5
Delvin End Essex 106 D5
Dembleby Lincs 155 B10
Demelza Corn 5 C9
Denaby Main S Yorks 187 B7
Denbeath Fife 281 B7
Denbigh Denb 165 B9
Denbury Devon 8 B6
Denby Derbys 170 F5
Denby Bottles Derbys 170 F5
Denby Common Derbys 170 F6
Denby Dale W Yorks 197 F8
Denchworth Oxon 82 G5
Dendron Cumb 210 E4
Denel End C Beds 103 D10
Denend Aberds 302 F6
Dene Park Kent 52 C5
Deneside Durham 234 B4
Denford N Nhants 121 B9
Staffs 169 E7
Dengie Essex 89 E7
Denham Bucks 66 B4
Bucks 102 G5
Suff 124 E5
Suff 126 C3
Denham Corner Suff 126 C3
Denham End Suff 124 E5
Denham Green Bucks 66 B4
Denham Street Suff 126 C3
Denhead Aberds 303 D9
Fife 287 F8
Denhead of Arbilot
Angus 287 C9
Denhead of Gray
Dundee 287 D7
Denholm Borders 262 F3
Denholme W Yorks 205 G7
Denholme Clough
W Yorks 205 G7
Denholme Edge
W Yorks 205 G7
Denholme Gate
W Yorks 205 G7
Denholmhill Borders 262 F3
Denio Gwyn 145 B7
Denmead Hants 33 E11
Denmore Aberdeen 293 B11
Denmoss Aberds 302 E6
Dennington Suff 126 D5
Dennington Corner Suff 126 D5
Dennington Hall Suff 126 D5
Denny Falk 278 E6
Denny Bottom Kent 52 F5
Denny End Cambs 123 D9
Dennyloanhead Falk 278 E6
Denny Lodge Hants 32 F4
Dennystown W Dunb 277 F7
Denshaw Gtr Man 196 E3
Denside Aberds 293 D10
Densole Kent 55 E8
Denston Suff 124 G5
Denstone Staffs 169 G9
Denstroude Kent 70 G6
Dent Cumb 212 B4
Dent Bank Durham 232 F4
Denton Cambs 138 F2
Darl 224 B4
E Sus 23 E7
Gtr Man 184 B6
Kent 55 D8
Kent 69 E7
Lincs 155 C7
Norf 142 F5
N Yorks 205 D8
Oxon 83 E9
W Nhants 120 F6
Denton Burn T&W 242 D5
Denton Holme Cumb 239 G10
Denton's Green Mers 183 B7
Denver Norf 140 C2
Denvilles Hants 22 B2
Denwick Northumb 264 G6
Deopham Norf 141 C11
Deopham Green Norf 141 D10
Deopham Stalland
Norf 141 D10
Depden Suff 124 F5
Depden Green Suff 124 F5
Deppers Bridge Warks 119 F7
Deptford London 67 D11
T&W 243 F9
Wilts 46 F4
Derby Derbys 153 B7
Devon 40 G5
Derbyhaven IoM 192 F3
Derbyshire Hill Mers 183 C8
Dereham Norf 159 G9
Dergoals Dumfries 236 D4
Deri Caerph 77 E10
Derriford Plym 7 D9
Derril Devon 24 G4
Derringstone Kent 55 D8
Derrington Shrops 132 E2
Staffs 151 E7
Derriton Devon 24 G4
Derry Stirling 285 E10
Derrydaroch Stirling 285 E7
Derry Downs London 68 F3
Derry Fields Wilts 81 G8
Derryguaig Argyll 288 F6
Derry Hill Wilts 62 E3
Derry Lodge Aberds 292 D2
Derrythorpe N Lincs 199 F10
Dersingham Norf 158 C3
Dertfords Wilts 45 D10
Dervaig Argyll 288 D6
Derwen Bridgend 58 C2
Denb 165 E9
Derwenlas Powys 128 D4
Derwydd Carms 75 B10
Desborough N Nhants 136 G6
Desford Leics 135 C9
Deskryshiel Aberds 292 B6
Detchant Northumb 264 B3
Detling Kent 53 B9
Deuchar Angus 292 G6
Deuddwr Powys 148 F4
Deuxhill Shrops 132 F3
Devauden Mon 79 F7
Deveral Corn 2 B3
Devil's Bridge
=Pontarfynach
Ceredig 112 B4
Devitts Green Warks 134 E5
Devizes Wilts 62 G4
Devol Invclyd 276 G6
Devonport Plym 7 E9
Devonside Clack 279 B8
Devon Village Clack 279 B8
Devoran Corn 3 B7
Dewar Borders 270 F6
Dewartown Midloth 271 C7
Dewes Green Essex 105 E9
Dewlands Common
Dorset 31 F9
Dewlish Dorset 17 B11
Dewsbury W Yorks 197 C8
Dewsbury Moor
W Yorks 197 C8
Dewshall Court Hereford 97 E9
Dhoon IoM 192 D5
Dhoor IoM 192 C5
Dhowin IoM 192 B5
Dhustone Shrops 115 B11
Dial Green W Sus 34 B6
Dial Post W Sus 35 D11
Dibberford Dorset 29 G7
Dibden Hants 32 F6
Dibden Purlieu Hants 32 F6
Dickens Heath W Mid 118 B2
Dickleburgh Norf 142 G3
Dickleburgh Moor Norf 142 G3
Dickon Hills Lincs 174 D6
Didbrook Glos 99 E11
Didcot Oxon 64 B4
Diddington Cambs 122 D3
Diddlebury Shrops 131 F10
Diddywell Devon 25 B7
Didley Hereford 97 E9
Didling W Sus 34 D4
Didlington Norf 140 D5
Didmarton Glos 61 B10
Didsbury Gtr Man 184 C4
Didworthy Devon 8 C3
Diebidale Highld 309 L4
Digbeth W Mid 133 F11
Digby Lincs 173 E9
Digg Highld 298 C4
Diggle Gtr Man 196 F4
Diglis Worcs 116 G6
Digmoor Lancs 194 F3
Digswell Herts 86 B3
Digswell Park Herts 86 C2
Digswell Water Herts 86 C3
Dihewyd Ceredig 111 F9
Dilham Norf 160 D6
Dilhorne Staffs 169 G7
Dillarburn S Lanark 268 G6
Dill Hall Lancs 195 B8
Dillington Cambs 122 D2
Som 28 D5
Dilston Northumb 241 E11
Dilton Marsh Wilts 45 D11
Dilwyn Hereford 115 G8
Dimlands V Glam 58 F3
Dimmer Som 44 G6
Dimple Derbys 170 C3
Gtr Man 195 D8
Dimsdale Staffs 168 F4
Dimson Corn 12 G4
Dinas Carms 92 E5
Corn 10 G4
Gwyn 144 B5
Gwyn 163 D7
Dinas Cross Pembs 91 D10
Dinas Dinlle Gwyn 162 D6
Dinas-Mawddwy Gwyn 147 G7
Dinas Mawr Conwy 164 E4
Dinas Powys V Glam 59 E7
Dinbych y Pysgod =Tenby
Pembs 73 E10
Dinckley Lancs 203 F9
Dinder Som 44 E5
Dinedor Hereford 97 D10
Dinedor Cross Hereford 97 D10
Dines Green Worcs 116 F6
Dingestow Mon 79 C7
Dinghurst N Som 44 B2
Dingle Mers 182 D5
Dingleden Kent 53 G10
Dingleton Borders 262 C2
Dingley N Nhants 136 F5
Dingwall Highld 300 D5
Dinlabyre Borders 250 E2
Dinmael Conwy 165 G8
Dinnet Aberds 292 D6
Dinnington Som 28 E6
S Yorks 187 D8
T&W 242 C6
Dinorwic Gwyn 163 C9
Dinton Bucks 84 C3
Wilts 46 G4
Dinwoodie Mains
Dumfries 248 E4
Dinworthy Devon 24 D4
Dipford Som 28 C2
Dipley Hants 49 B8
Dippenhall Sur 49 D10
Dippertown Devon 12 E4
Dippin N Ayrs 256 E2
Dipple Devon 24 D4
Moray 302 D3
S Ayrs 244 C6
Diptford Devon 8 D4
Dipton Durham 242 G5
Diptonmill Northumb 241 E10
Dirdhu Highld 301 G10
Direcleit W Isles 305 J3
Dirleton E Loth 281 E10
Dirt Pot Northumb 232 B3
Discoed Powys 114 E5
Discove Som 45 G7
Diseworth Leics 153 E9
Dishes Orkney 314 D6
Dishforth N Yorks 215 E7
Dishley Leics 153 E10
Disley Ches E 185 E7
Diss Norf 126 B2
Disserth Powys 113 F10
Distington Cumb 228 G6
Ditchampton Wilts 46 G5
Ditcheat Som 44 F6
Ditchfield Bucks 84 G4
Ditchford Hill Worcs 100 D4
Ditchingham Norf 142 E6
Ditchling E Sus 36 D4
Ditherington Shrops 149 G10
Ditteridge Wilts 61 F10
Dittisham Devon 9 E7
Ditton Halton 183 D7
Kent 53 B8
Ditton Green Cambs 124 F3
Ditton Priors Shrops 132 F2
Dittons E Sus 23 E10
Divach Highld 300 G4
Divlyn Carms 94 D5
Dixton Glos 99 E9
Mon 79 C8
Dizzard Corn 11 B9
Dobcross Gtr Man 196 F3
Dobs Hill Flint 166 C4
Dobson's Bridge Shrops 149 C9
Dobwalls Corn 6 C4
Doccombe Devon 13 D11
Dochfour Ho Highld 300 F6
Dochgarroch Highld 300 E6
Dockeney Norf 143 E7
Dockenfield Sur 49 E10
Docker Lancs 211 E11
Docking Norf 158 B5
Docklow Hereford 115 F11

Dockray Cumb 230 G3
Dockroyd W Yorks 204 F6
Doc Penfro = Pembroke Dock Pembs 73 E7
Docton Devon 24 C2
Dodbrooke Devon 8 G4
Dodburn Borders 249 B11
Doddenham Worcs 116 F5
Doddinghurst Essex 87 F9
Doddington Cambs 139 E7
Kent 54 B2
Lincs 188 G6
Northumb 263 C11
Shrops 116 B2
Doddiscombsleigh Devon 14 D3
Doddshill Norf 158 C3
Doddycross Corn 6 C6
Dodford W Nhants 120 E2
Worcs 117 C8
Dodington S Glos 61 C9
Som 43 E7
Dodleston Ches W 166 C5
Dodmarsh Hereford 97 C11
Dodscott Devon 25 D8
Dods Leigh Staffs 151 C10
Dodworth S Yorks 197 F10
Dodworth Bottom S Yorks 197 G10
Dodworth Green S Yorks 197 G10
Doe Bank W Mid 134 D2
Doe Green Warr 183 D9
Doehole Derbys 170 D5
Doe Lea Derbys 171 B7
Doffcocker Gtr Man 195 E7
Dogdyke Lincs 174 D2
Dog & Gun Mers 182 B5
Dog Hill Gtr Man 196 F3
Dogingtree Estate Staffs 151 G9
Dogley Lane W Yorks 197 E7
Dogmersfield Hants 49 C9
Dogridge Wilts 62 B5
Dogsthorpe Pboro 138 C3
Dog Village Devon 14 B5
Doirlinn Highld 289 D8
Dolanog Powys 147 G11
Dolau Powys 114 D2
Rhondda 58 C3
Dolbenmaen Gwyn 163 G8
Dole Ceredig 128 F2
Dolemeads Bath 61 G9
Doley Staffs 150 D4
Dolfach Powys 129 C8
Dol-ffanog Gwyn 146 G4
Dolfor Powys 130 F2
Dol-fôr Powys 128 B6
Dolgarrog Conwy 164 B3
Dolgellau Gwyn 146 F4
Dolgerdd Ceredig 111 G8
Dolgoch Gwyn 128 C3
Dolgran Carms 93 E8
Dolhelfa Powys 113 C8
Dolhendre Gwyn 147 C7
Doll Highld 311 J2
Dollar Clack 279 B9
Dolley Green Powys 114 D5
Dollis Hill London 67 B8
Dollwen Ceredig 128 G3
Dolphin Flint 181 G11
Dolphingstone E Loth 281 G7
Dolphinholme Lancs 202 C6
Dolphinston Borders 262 F5
Dolphinton S Lanark 270 F2
Dolton Devon 25 E9
Dolwen Conwy 180 G5
Powys 129 B9
Dolwyd Conwy 180 F4
Dolwyddelan Conwy 164 E2
Dôl-y-Bont Ceredig 128 F2
Dol-y-cannau Powys 96 B3
Dolydd Gwyn 163 D7
Dolyhir Powys 114 F4
Dolymelinau Powys 129 D11
Dolywern Wrex 148 B4
Domewood Sur 51 E10
Domgay Powys 148 F5
Dommett Som 28 E3
Doncaster S Yorks 198 G5
Doncaster Common S Yorks 198 G6
Dones Green Ches W 183 F10
Donhead St Andrew Wilts 30 C6
Donhead St Mary Wilts 30 C6
Donibristle Fife 280 D3
Doniford Som 42 E5
Donington Lincs 156 B4
Shrops 132 C6
Donington Eaudike Lincs 156 B4
Donington le Heath Leics 153 G8
Donington on Bain Lincs 190 E2
Donington South Ing Lincs 156 C4
Donisthorpe Leics 152 G6
Don Johns Essex 106 F6
Donkey Street Kent 54 G6
Donkey Town Sur 66 G2
Donna Nook Lincs 190 B6
Donnington Glos 100 F3
Hereford 98 E4
Shrops 131 B11
Telford 150 G4
W Berks 64 F3
W Sus 22 C5
Donnington Wood Telford 150 G4
Donwell T&W 243 F7
Donyatt Som 28 E4
Doomsday Green W Sus 35 B11
Doonfoot S Ayrs 257 F8
Dora's Green Hants 49 D10
Dorback Lodge Highld 292 B2
Dorcan Swindon 63 C7
Dorchester Dorset 17 C9
Oxon 83 G9
Dordale Worcs 117 C8
Dordon Warks 134 C5
Dore S Yorks 186 E4
Dores Highld 300 F5
Dorking Sur 51 D7
Dorking Tye Suff 107 D8
Dorley's Corner Suff 127 D7
Dormansland Sur 52 E2
Dormans Park Sur 51 E11
Dormanstown Redcar 235 G7
Dormer's Wells London 66 C6
Dormington Hereford 97 C11
Dormston Worcs 117 F9
Dorn Glos 100 E4
Dornal S Ayrs 236 B4
Dorney Bucks 66 D2
Dorney Reach Bucks 66 D2
Dorn Hill Worcs 100 E3
Dornie Highld 295 C10
Dornoch Highld 309 L7
Dornock Dumfries 238 D6
Dorrery Highld 310 D4
Dorridge W Mid 118 B3
Dorrington Lincs 173 E9
Shrops 131 C9
Dorsington Warks 100 B2
Dorstone Hereford 96 C6
Dorton Bucks 83 C11
Dorusduain Highld 295 C11
Doseley Telford 132 B3
Dosmuckeran Highld 300 C2
Dosthill Staffs 134 C4
Staffs 134 D4
Dothan Anglesey 178 G5
Dothill Telford 150 G2
Dottery Dorset 16 B5
Doublebois Corn 6 C3
Double Hill Bath 45 B8
Dougarie N Ayrs 255 D9
Doughton Glos 80 G5
Norf 159 D7
Douglas IoM 192 E4
S Lanark 259 C8
Douglas & Angus Dundee 287 D8
Douglastown Angus 287 C8
Douglas Water S Lanark 259 B9
Douglas West S Lanark 259 C8
Doulting Som 44 E6
Dounby Orkney 314 D2
Doune Highld 291 C10
Highld 309 J4
Stirling 285 G11
Doune Park Aberds 303 C7
Douneside Aberds 292 C6
Dounie Argyll 275 D8
Highld 309 K5
Highld 309 L6
Dounreay Highld 310 C3
Doura N Ayrs 266 G6
Dousland Devon 7 B10
Dovaston Shrops 149 E7
Dovecot Mers 182 C6
Dovecothall Glasgow 267 D10
Dove Green Notts 171 E7
Dove Holes Derbys 185 F9
Dovenby Cumb 229 E7
Dovendale Lincs 190 E4
Dove Point Mers 182 C2
Dover Gtr Man 194 G6
Kent 55 E10
Dovercourt Essex 108 E5
Doverdale Worcs 117 D7
Doverhay Som 41 D11
Doveridge Derbys 152 C2
Doversgreen Sur 51 D9
Dowally Perth 286 C4
Dowanhill Glasgow 267 B11
Dowbridge Lancs 202 G4
Dowdeswell Glos 81 B7
Dowe Hill Norf 161 F10
Dowlais M Tydf 77 D10
Dowlais Top M Tydf 77 D9
Dowland Devon 25 E9
Dowles Worcs 116 B5
Dowlesgreen Wokingham 65 F10
Dowlish Ford Som 28 E5
Dowlish Wake Som 28 E5
Downall Green Gtr Man 194 G5
Down Ampney Glos 81 F10
Downan Moray 301 F11
S Ayrs 244 G3
Downcraig Ferry N Ayrs 266 D3
Downderry Corn 6 E6
Downe London 68 G2
Downend Glos 80 F4
IoW 20 D6
S Glos 60 D6
W Berks 64 D3
Down End Som 43 E10
Downfield Dundee 287 D7
Down Field Cambs 124 C2
Downgate Corn 11 G11
Corn 12 G3
Down Hall Cumb 239 G7
Downham Essex 88 F2
Lancs 203 E11
London 67 E11
Northumb 263 C9
Downham Market Norf 140 C2
Down Hatherley Glos 99 G7
Downhead Som 29 B9
Som 45 D7
Downhead Park M Keynes 103 C7
Downhill Corn 5 B7
Perth 286 D4
T&W 243 F9
Downholland Cross Lancs 193 F11
Downholme N Yorks 224 F2
Downicary Devon 12 C3
Downies Aberds 293 D11
Downinney Corn 11 C10
Downley Bucks 84 G4
Down Park W Sus 51 F10
Downs V Glam 58 E6
Down St Mary Devon 26 G2
Downside C Beds 103 G10
E Sus 23 E9
N Som 60 F3
Som 44 D6
Sur 50 B6
Sur 51 B7
Down Street E Sus 36 C6
Down Thomas Devon 7 E10
Downton Hants 19 C11
Powys 114 E4
Shrops 149 G10
Wilts 31 C11
Downton on the Rock Hereford 115 C8
Dowsby Lincs 156 D2
Dowsdale Lincs 156 G5
Dowslands Som 28 C2
Dowthwaitehead Cumb 230 G3
Doxey Staffs 151 E8
Doxford Park T&W 243 G9
Doynton S Glos 61 E8
Drabblegate Norf 160 D4
Draethen Newport 59 B8
Draffan S Lanark 268 F5
Dragley Beck Cumb 210 D5
Dragonby N Lincs 200 E2
Dragons Green W Sus 35 C10
Drakehouse S Yorks 186 E6
Drakeland Corner Devon 7 D11
Drakelow Worcs 132 G6
Drakemyre Aberds 303 F9
N Ayrs 266 E5
Drake's Broughton Worcs 99 B8
Drakes Cross Worcs 117 B11
Drakestone Green Suff 107 B9
Drakewalls Corn 12 G4
Draughton N Yorks 204 C6
W Nhants 120 B5
Drawbridge Corn 6 B3
Drax N Yorks 199 B7
Draycot Oxon 83 D10
Draycot Cerne Wilts 62 D2
Draycote Warks 119 C8
Draycot Fitz Payne Wilts 62 G6
Draycot Foliat Swindon 63 D7
Draycott Derbys 153 C8
Glos 80 E2
Glos 100 D3
Shrops 132 E6
Som 29 C8
Som 44 C3
Worcs 99 B7
Draycott in the Clay Staffs 152 D3
Draycott in the Moors Staffs 169 G7
Drayford Devon 26 E3
Drayton Leics 136 E6
Lincs 156 B4
Norf 160 G3
Oxon 83 G7
Oxon 101 C8
Ptsmth 33 F11
Som 28 C6
Som 29 D7
Warks 118 F3
W Nhants 119 E11
Worcs 117 B8
Drayton Bassett Staffs 134 C3
Drayton Beauchamp Bucks 84 C6
Drayton Parslow Bucks 102 F6
Drayton St Leonard Oxon 83 F10
Drebley N Yorks 205 B7
Dreemskerry IoM 192 C5
Dreenhill Pembs 72 C6
Drefach Carms 75 C8
Carms 92 G5
Carms 93 D7
Dre-fach Carms 75 B11
Ceredig 93 B10
Drefelin Carms 93 D7
Dreggie Highld 301 G10
Dreghorn Edin 270 B4
N Ayrs 257 B9
Dre-gôch Denb 165 B10
Drellingore Kent 55 E8
Drem E Loth 281 F10
Dresden Stoke 168 G6
Dreumasdal W Isles 297 H3
Drewsteignton Devon 13 C10
Driby Lincs 190 G5
Driffield E Yorks 208 B6
Glos 81 F9
Drift Corn 1 D4
Drigg Cumb 219 F11
Drighlington W Yorks 197 B8
Drimnin Highld 289 D7
Drimnin Ho Highld 289 D7
Drimpton Dorset 28 F6
Drimsynie Argyll 284 G5
Dringhoe E Yorks 209 C9
Dringhouses York 207 D7
Drinisiadar W Isles 305 J3
Drinkstone Suff 125 E9
Drinkstone Green Suff 125 E9
Drishaig Argyll 284 F5
Drissaig Argyll 275 B10
Drive End Dorset 29 F9
Driver's End Herts 86 B2
Drochedlie Aberds 302 C5
Drochil Borders 270 G3
Drointon Staffs 151 D10
Droitwich Spa Worcs 117 E7
Droman Highld 306 D6
Dromore Dumfries 237 C7
Dron Perth 286 F5
Dronfield Derbys 186 F5
Dronfield Woodhouse Derbys 186 F4
Drongan E Ayrs 257 F10
Dronley Angus 287 D7
Droop Dorset 30 F3
Drope Cardiff 58 D6
Dropping Well S Yorks 186 C5
Droughduil Dumfries 236 D3
Droxford Hants 33 D10
Droylsden Gtr Man 184 B6
Drub W Yorks 197 B7
Druggers End Worcs 98 D5
Druid Denb 165 G8
Druidston Pembs 72 B5
Druim Highld 301 D9
Druimarbin Highld 290 F2
Druimavuic Argyll 284 C4
Druimdrishaig Argyll 275 F8
Druimindarroch Highld 295 G8
Druimkinnerras Highld 300 F4
Druimnacroish Argyll 288 E6
Druimsornaig Argyll 289 F9
Druimyeon More Argyll 255 B7
Drum Argyll 275 F10
Edin 270 B6
Perth 286 G4
Drumardoch Stirling 285 F10
Drumbeg Highld 306 F6
Drumblade Aberds 302 E5
Drumblair Aberds 302 E6
Drumbuie Dumfries 246 G3
Highld 295 B9
Drumburgh Cumb 239 F7
Drumburn Dumfries 237 C11
Drumchapel Glasgow 277 G10
Drumchardine Highld 300 E5
Drumchork Highld 307 L3
Drumclog S Lanark 258 B4
Drumdelgie Aberds 302 E4
Drumderfit Highld 300 D6
Drumdollo Aberds 302 F6
Drumeldrie Fife 287 G8
Drumelzier Borders 260 C4
Drumfearn Highld 295 D8
Drumgask Highld 291 D8
Drumgelloch N Lanark 268 B5
Drumgley Angus 287 B8
Drumgreen Angus 292 F6
Drumguish Highld 291 D9
Drumhead Aberds 293 B11
Drumin Moray 301 F11
Drumindorsair Highld 300 E4
Drumlasie Aberds 293 C8
Drumlean Stirling 285 G8
Drumlemble Argyll 255 F7
Drumliah Highld 309 K6
Drumligair Aberds 293 B11
Drumlithie Aberds 293 E9
Drumloist Stirling 285 G10
Drummersdale Lancs 193 E11
Drummick Perth 286 E3
Drummoddie Dumfries 236 E5
Drummond Highld 300 C6
Drummore Dumfries 236 F3
Drummuir Moray 302 E3
Drummuir Castle Moray 302 E3
Drumnadrochit Highld 300 G5
Drumnagorrach Moray 302 D5
Drumness Perth 286 F2
Drumoak Aberds 293 D9
Drumore Argyll 255 E8
Drumpark Dumfries 247 G9
Drumpellier N Lanark 268 B4
Drumphail Dumfries 236 C4
Drumrash Dumfries 237 B8
Drumrunie Highld 307 J6
Drumry W Dunb 277 G10
Drums Aberds 303 G9
Drumsallie Highld 289 B11
Drumsmittal Highld 300 E6
Drumstinchall Dumfries 237 D10
Drumsturdy Angus 287 D8
Drumtochty Castle Aberds 293 F8
Drumtroddan Dumfries 236 E5
Drumuie Highld 298 E4
Drumuillie Highld 301 G9
Drumvaich Stirling 285 G10
Drumwalt Dumfries 236 D5
Drumwhindle Aberds 303 F9
Drunkendub Angus 287 C10
Drury Flint 166 C3
Drurylane Norf 141 C8
Drury Lane Wrex 167 G7
Drury Square Norf 159 F8
Drybeck Cumb 222 B3
Drybridge Moray 302 C4
N Ayrs 257 B9
Drybrook Glos 79 B10
Dryburgh Borders 262 C3
Dryden Borders 261 E11
Dry Doddington Lincs 172 F4
Dry Drayton Cambs 123 E7
Dryhill Kent 52 B3
Dry Hill Hants 49 F7
Dryhope Borders 261 E7
Drylaw Edin 280 F4
Drym Corn 2 C4
Drymen Stirling 277 D9
Drymere Norf 140 B5
Drymuir Aberds 303 E9
Drynachan Lodge Highld 301 F8
Drynain Argyll 276 D3
Drynham Wilts 45 B11
Drynie Park Highld 300 D5
Drynoch Highld 294 B6
Dry Sandford Oxon 83 E7
Dryslwyn Carms 93 G11
Dry Street Essex 69 B7
Dryton Shrops 131 B11
Drywells Aberds 302 D6
Duag Bridge Highld 309 K3
Duartbeg Highld 306 F6
Duartmore Bridge Highld 306 F6
Dubbs Cross Devon 12 C3
Dubford Aberds 303 C8
Dubhchladach Argyll 275 G9
Dublin Suff 126 D3
Dubton Angus 287 B9
Dubwath Cumb 229 E9
Duchally Highld 309 H3
Duchlage Argyll 276 D6
Duchrae Dumfries 246 G5
Duck Corner Suff 109 C7
Duck End Bedford 103 C11
Bedford 121 G9
Bucks 102 F5
Cambs 122 E4
Essex 105 G10
Essex 106 E3
Essex 106 F3
Duckend Green Essex 106 G4
Duckhole S Glos 79 G10
Ducklington Ches W 167 E7
Ducklington Oxon 82 D5
Duckmanton Derbys 186 G6
Duck's Cross Bedford 122 F2
Ducks Island London 86 F2
Duckswich Worcs 98 D6
Dudbridge Glos 80 E4
Dudden Hill London 67 B8
Duddenhoe End Essex 105 D9
Duddingston Edin 280 G5
Duddington N Nhants 137 C9
Duddlestone Som 28 C2
Duddleswell E Sus 37 B7
Duddlewick Shrops 132 G3
Duddo Northumb 273 G8
Duddon Ches W 167 C8
Duddon Bridge Cumb 210 B3
Duddon Common Ches W 167 B8
Dudleston Shrops 148 B6
Dudleston Grove Shrops 149 B7
Dudleston Heath (Criftins) Shrops 149 B7
Dudley T&W 243 C7
W Mid 133 E8
Dudley Hill W Yorks 205 G9
Dudley Port W Mid 133 E9
Dudley's Fields W Mid 133 C9
Dudley Wood W Mid 133 F8
Dudlows Green Warr 183 E10
Dudsbury Dorset 19 B7
Dudswell Herts 85 D7
Dudwells Pembs 91 G8
Duerdon Devon 24 D4
Duffield Derbys 170 G4
Duffieldbank Derbys 170 G5
Duffryn Neath 57 B10
Newport 59 B9
Shrops 130 G4
Dufftown Moray 302 F3
Duffus Moray 301 C11
Dufton Cumb 231 F9
Duggleby N Yorks 217 F7
Duich Argyll 254 B4
Duilletter Argyll 284 D5
Duinish Perth 291 G8
Duirinish Highld 295 B9
Duisdalebeg Highld 295 D8
Duisdalemore Highld 295 D9
Duisky Highld 290 F2
Duke End Warks 134 F4
Dukesfield Northumb 241 F10
Dukestown Bl Gwent 77 C10
Dukinfield Gtr Man 184 B6
Dulas Anglesey 179 D7
Dulcote Som 44 E5
Dulford Devon 27 F9
Dull Perth 286 C2
Dullatur N Lanark 278 F4
Dullingham Cambs 124 F2
Dullingham Ley Cambs 124 F2
Dulnain Bridge Highld 301 G9
Duloch Fife 280 D2
Duloe Bedford 122 E3
Corn 6 D4
Dulsie Highld 301 E9
Dulverton Som 26 B6
Dulwich London 67 E10
Dulwich Village London 67 E10
Dumbarton W Dunb 277 F7
Dumbleton Glos 99 D10
Dumcrieff Dumfries 248 C4
Dumfries Dumfries 237 B11
Dumgoyne Stirling 277 E10
Dummer Hants 48 D5
Dumpford W Sus 34 C4
Dumpinghill Devon 24 F6
Dumpling Green Norf 159 G10
Dumplington Gtr Man 184 B3
Dumpton Kent 71 F11
Dun Angus 287 B10
Dunach Argyll 289 G10
Dunadd Argyll 275 D9
Dunain Ho Highld 300 E6
Dunalastair Perth 285 B11
Dunan Highld 295 C7
Dunans Argyll 275 D9
Argyll 275 D11
Dunball Som 43 E10
Dunbar E Loth 282 F3
Dunbeath Highld 311 G5
Dunbeg Argyll 289 F10
Dunblane Stirling 285 G11
Dunbog Fife 286 F6
Dunbridge Hants 32 B4
Duncansclett Shetland 313 K5
Duncanston Highld 300 D5
Duncanstone Aberds 302 G5
Dun Charlabhaigh W Isles 304 D3
Dunchideock Devon 14 D3
Dunchurch Warks 119 C9
Duncombe Lancs 202 F6
Duncote W Nhants 120 G3
Duncow Dumfries 247 G11
Duncraggan Stirling 285 G9
Duncrievie Perth 286 G5
Duncroisk Stirling 285 D9
Duncton W Sus 35 D7
Dundas Ho Orkney 314 H4
Dundee Dundee 287 D8
Dundeugh Dumfries 246 F3
Dundon Som 44 G3
Dundonald Fife 280 C4
S Ayrs 257 C9
Dundon Hayes Som 44 G3
Dundonnell Highld 307 L5
Dundonnell Hotel Highld 307 L5
Dundonnell House Highld 307 L6
Dundraw Cumb 229 B10
Dundreggan Highld 290 B6
Dundreggan Lodge Highld 290 B5
Dundrennan Dumfries 237 E9
Dundridge Hants 33 D9
Dundry N Som 60 F5
Dundurn Perth 285 E11
Dundyvan N Lanark 268 C4
Dunecht Aberds 293 C9
Dunfermline Fife 279 D11
Dunfield Glos 81 F10
Dunford Bridge S Yorks 197 G7
Dungate Kent 54 B2
Dunge Wilts 45 C11
Dungeness Kent 39 D9
Dungworth S Yorks 186 D3
Dunham Notts 188 G4
Dunham-on-the-Hill Ches W 183 G7
Dunham on Trent Notts 188 G4
Dunhampstead Worcs 117 E8
Dunhampton Worcs 116 D6
Dunham Town Gtr Man 184 D2
Dunham Woodhouses Gtr Man 184 D2
Dunholme Lincs 189 F8
Dunino Fife 287 F9
Dunipace Falk 278 E6
Dunira Perth 285 E11
Dunkeld Perth 286 C4
Dunkerton Bath 45 B8
Dunkeswell Devon 27 F10
Dunkeswick N Yorks 206 D2
Dunkirk Cambs 139 F10
Ches W 182 G5
Kent 54 B5
Norf 160 D4
Nottingham 153 B11
S Glos 61 B9
Staffs 168 E4
Wilts 62 G3
Dunk's Green Kent 52 C6
Dunlappie Angus 293 G7
Dunley Hants 48 C3
Worcs 116 D5
Dunlichity Lodge Highld 300 F6
Dunlop E Ayrs 267 F8
Dunmaglass Lodge Highld 300 G5
Dunmere Corn 5 B10
Dunmore Argyll 275 G8
Falk 279 D7
Highld 300 E5
Dunnerholme Cumb 210 D4
Dunnet Highld 310 B6
Dunnichen Angus 287 C9
Dunnikier Fife 280 C5
Dunninald Angus 287 B11
Dunning Perth 286 F4
Dunnington E Yorks 209 C9
Warks 117 G11
York 207 C9
Dunningwell Cumb 210 C3
Dunnockshaw Lancs 195 B10
Dunnose IoW 21 F7
Dunnsheath Shrops 149 F9
Dunn Street Kent 54 D3
Kent 69 G9
Dunollie Argyll 289 F10
Dunoon Argyll 276 F3
Dunragit Dumfries 236 D3
Dunrobin Mains Highld 311 J2
Dunrostan Argyll 275 E8
Duns Borders 272 E5
Dunsa Derbys 186 G2
Dunsby Lincs 156 D2
Dunscar Gtr Man 195 E8
Dunscore Dumfries 247 G9
Dunscroft S Yorks 199 F7
Dunsdale Redcar 226 B2
Dunsden Green Oxon 65 D8
Dunsfold Sur 50 F4
Dunsfold Common Sur 50 F4
Dunsfold Green Sur 50 F4
Dunsford Devon 14 D2
Sur 50 F4
Dunshalt Fife 286 F6
Dunshillock Aberds 303 E9
Dunsill Notts 171 C7
Dunsinnan Perth 286 D5
Dunskey Ho Dumfries 236 D2
Dunslea Corn 11 G11
Dunsley N Yorks 227 C7
Staffs 133 G7
Dunsmore Bucks 84 D5
Warks 119 B10
Dunsop Bridge Lancs 203 C9
Dunstable C Beds 103 G10
Dunstal Staffs 151 D11
Dunstall Staffs 152 E3
Dunstall Common Worcs 99 C7
Dunstall Green Suff 124 E4
Dunstall Hill W Mid 133 C8
Dunstan Northumb 265 F7
Dunstan Steads Northumb 264 E6
Dunster Som 42 E3
Duns Tew Oxon 101 F9
Dunston Derbys 186 G5
Dunston *continued*
Lincs 173 C9
Norf 142 C4
Staffs 151 F8
T&W 242 E6
Dunstone Devon 7 E11
Devon 8 G5
Dunston Heath Staffs 151 F8
Dunston Hill T&W 242 E6
Dunsville S Yorks 198 F6
Dunswell E Yorks 209 F7
Dunsyre S Lanark 269 F11
Dunterton Devon 12 F3
Dunthrop Oxon 101 F7
Duntisbourne Abbots Glos 81 D7
Duntisbourne Leer Glos 81 D7
Duntisbourne Rouse Glos 81 D7
Duntish Dorset 29 F11
Duntocher W Dunb 277 G9
Dunton Bucks 102 G6
C Beds 104 C4
Norf 159 C7
Dunton Bassett Leics 135 E10
Dunton Green Kent 52 B4
Dunton Patch Norf 159 C7
Dunton Wayletts Essex 87 G11
Duntrune Castle Argyll 275 D8
Duntulm Highld 298 B4
Dunure S Ayrs 257 F7
Dunvant = Dynfant Swansea 56 C5
Dunvegan Highld 298 E2
Dunveth Corn 10 G5
Dunwear Som 43 F10
Dunwich Suff 127 C9
Dunwood Staffs 168 D6
Dupplin Castle Perth 286 F4
Durdar Cumb 239 G10
Durgan Corn 3 D7
Durgates E Sus 52 G6
Durham Durham 233 C11
Durisdeer Dumfries 247 C9
Durisdeermill Dumfries 247 C9
Durkar W Yorks 197 D10
Durleigh Som 43 F9
Durleighmarsh W Sus 34 C3
Durley Hants 33 D8
Wilts 63 G8
Durley Street Hants 33 D8
Durlock Kent 55 B9
Durlow Common Hereford 98 D2
Durn Gtr Man 196 D2
Durnamuck Highld 307 K5
Durness Highld 308 C4
Durnfield Som 29 C7
Durno Aberds 303 G7
Durns Town Hants 19 B11
Duror Highld 289 D11
Durran Argyll 275 C10
Highld 310 C5
Durrant Green Kent 53 F11
Durrants Hants 22 B2
Durrington Wilts 47 E7
W Sus 35 F10
Durrisdale Orkney 314 D3
Dursley Glos 80 F3
Wilts 45 C11
Dursley Cross Glos 98 G3
Durston Som 28 B3
Durweston Dorset 30 F5
Dury Shetland 313 G6
Duryard Devon 14 C4
Duston W Nhants 120 E4
Dutch Village Essex 69 C9
Duthil Highld 301 G9
Dutlas Powys 114 B4
Duton Hill Essex 106 F2
Dutson Corn 12 D2
Dutton Ches W 183 F9
Duxford Cambs 105 B9
Oxon 82 F5
Duxmoor Shrops 115 B8
Dwygyfylchi Conwy 180 F2
Dwyran Anglesey 162 B6
Dyce Aberdeen 293 B10
Dyche Som 43 E7
Dye House Northumb 241 F10
Dyer's Common S Glos 60 C5
Dyer's Green Cambs 105 B7
Dyffryn Bridgend 57 C11
Carms 92 G6
Ceredig 110 G5
Pembs 91 D8
Dyffryn Ardudwy Gwyn 145 E11
Dyffryn-bern Ceredig 110 G5
Dyffryn Castell Ceredig 128 G5
Dyffryn Ceidrych Carms 94 F4
Dyffryn Cellwen Neath 76 D5
Dyke Lincs 156 E2
Moray 301 D9
Dykehead Angus 292 G5
N Lanark 269 D7
Stirling 277 B11
Dykelands Aberds 293 G9
Dykends Angus 286 B6
Dykeside Aberds 303 E7
Dykesmains N Ayrs 266 G5
Dylife Powys 129 E7
Dymchurch Kent 39 B9
Dymock Glos 98 E4
Dynfant = Dunvant Swansea 56 C5
Dyrham S Glos 61 D8
Dysart Fife 280 C6
Dyserth Denb 181 F9

E

Eabost Highld 294 B5
Eabost West Highld 298 E3
Each End Kent 55 B10
Eachway Worcs 117 B9
Eachwick Northumb 242 C4
Eadar Dha Fhadhail W Isles 304 E2
Eagland Hill Lancs 202 D4
Eagle Lincs 172 B5
Eagle Barnsdale Lincs 172 B5
Eagle Moor Lincs 172 B5
Eaglesfield Cumb 229 F7
Dumfries 238 C6
Eaglesham E Renf 267 E11
Eaglestone M Keynes 103 D7
Eaglethorpe N Nhants 137 E11
Eagle Tor Derbys 170 C2
Eagley Gtr Man 195 E8
Eairy IoM 192 E3
Eakley Lanes M Keynes 120 G6
Eakring Notts 171 C11
Ealand N Lincs 199 E9
Ealing London 67 C7
Eals Northumb 240 F5
Eamont Bridge Cumb 230 F6
Earby Lancs 204 D3
Earcroft Blackburn 195 C7
Eardington Shrops 132 E4
Eardisland Hereford 115 F8
Eardisley Hereford 96 B6
Eardiston Shrops 149 D7
Worcs 116 D3
Earith Cambs 123 C7
Earle Northumb 263 D11
Earlestown Mers 183 B9
Earley Wokingham 65 E9
Earlham Norf 142 B4
Earlish Highld 298 C3
Earls Barton N Nhants 121 E7
Earls Colne Essex 107 F7
Earl's Common Worcs 117 F9
Earl's Court London 67 D9
Earl's Croome Worcs 99 C7
Earlsdon W Mid 118 B6
Earl's Down E Sus 23 B10
Earlsferry Fife 281 B9
Earlsfield Lincs 155 B8
London 67 E9
Earlsford Aberds 303 F8
Earl's Green Suff 125 D10
Earlsheaton W Yorks 197 C9
Earl Shilton Leics 135 D9
Earlsmill Moray 301 D9
Earl Soham Suff 126 E4
Earl Sterndale Derbys 169 B9
Earlston Borders 262 B3
E Ayrs 257 B10
Earlstone Common Hants 64 G3
Earl Stoneham Suff 126 F2
Earl Stonham Suff 126 F2
Earlstoun Dumfries 246 G4
Earlswood Mon 79 F7
Sur 51 D9
Warks 118 C2
Earnley W Sus 22 D4
Earnock S Lanark 268 E3
Earnshaw Bridge Lancs 194 C4
Earsairidh W Isles 297 M3
Earsdon T&W 243 C8
Earsham Norf 142 F6
Earsham Street Suff 126 B4
Earswick York 207 B8
Eartham W Sus 22 B6
Earthcott Green S Glos 61 B7
Easby N Yorks 224 E3
N Yorks 225 D11
Easdale Argyll 275 B8
Easebourne W Sus 34 C5
Easenhall Warks 119 B9
Eashing Sur 50 E2
Easington Bucks 83 C11
Durham 234 C4
E Yorks 201 D11
Lancs 203 C10
Northumb 264 C4
Oxon 83 F11
Oxon 101 D9
Redcar 226 B4
Easington Colliery Durham 234 C4
Easington Lane T&W 234 B3
Easingwold N Yorks 215 F10
Easole Street Kent 55 C9
Eason's Green E Sus 23 B8
Eassie Angus 287 C7
East Aberthaw V Glam 58 F4
Eastacombe Devon 25 B8
Devon 25 C9
Eastacott Devon 25 C10
East Acton London 67 C8
East Adderbury Oxon 101 D9
East Allington Devon 8 F5
East Amat Highld 309 K4
East Anstey Devon 26 B5
East Anton Hants 47 D11
East Appleton N Yorks 224 F4
East Ardsley W Yorks 197 B10
East Ashling W Sus 22 B4
East Aston Hants 48 D2
East Auchronie Aberds 293 C10
East Ayton N Yorks 217 B9
East Bank Bl Gwent 78 D2
East Barkwith Lincs 189 E11
East Barming Kent 53 C8
East Barnby N Yorks 226 C6
East Barnet London 86 F3
East Barns E Loth 282 F4
East Barsham Norf 159 C8
East Barton Suff 125 D8
East Beach W Sus 22 E5
East Beckham Norf 177 E11
East Bedfont London 66 E5
East Bergholt Suff 107 D11
East Bierley W Yorks 197 B7
East Bilney Norf 159 F9
East Blackdene Durham 232 D3
East Blatchington E Sus 23 E7
East Bloxworth Dorset 18 C3
East Boldon T&W 243 E9
East Boldre Hants 32 G5
East Bonhard Perth 286 E5
Eastbourne Darl 224 C6
E Sus 23 F10
East Bower Som 43 F10
East Brent Som 43 C11
Eastbridge Suff 127 D9
East Bridgford Notts 171 G11
East Briscoe Durham 223 B9
Eastbrook Som 28 C2
V Glam 59 E7
East Buckland Devon 41 G7
East Budleigh Devon 15 E7
Eastburn E Yorks 208 B5
W Yorks 204 E6
Eastburn Br W Yorks 204 E6
East Burnham Bucks 66 C3
East Burrafirth Shetland 313 H5
East Burton Dorset 18 D2
Eastbury London 85 G9
W Berks 63 D10
East Butsfield Durham 233 B8
East Butterleigh Devon 27 F7
East Butterwick N Lincs 199 F10
Eastby N Yorks 204 C6
East Cairnbeg Aberds 293 F9
East Calder W Loth 269 B11
East Carleton Norf 142 C3
East Carlton N Nhants 136 F6
W Yorks 205 E10
East Chaldon or Chaldon Herring Dorset 17 E11
East Challow Oxon 63 B11
East Charleton Devon 8 G5
East Chelborough Dorset 29 F9
East Chiltington E Sus 36 D5
East Chinnock Som 29 E7
East Chisenbury Wilts 46 C6
East Cholderton Hants 47 D9
Eastchurch Kent 70 E3
East Clandon Sur 50 C5
East Claydon Bucks 102 F4
East Clevedon N Som 60 E2
East Clyne Highld 311 J3
East Clyth Highld 310 F7
East Coker Som 29 E8
Eastcombe Glos 80 E5
East Combe Som 43 G7
East Common N Yorks 207 G8
East Compton Dorset 30 D5
Som 44 E6
East Cornworthy Devon 8 D6
Eastcote London 66 B6
W Mid 118 B3
W Nhants 120 G3
Eastcote Village London 66 B6
Eastcott Corn 24 D3
Wilts 46 B4
East Cottingwith E Yorks 207 E10
Eastcotts Bedford 103 B11
Eastcourt Wilts 63 G8
Wilts 81 G7
East Cowes IoW 20 B6
East Cowick E Yorks 199 C7
East Cowton N Yorks 224 E6
East Cramlington Northumb 243 B7
East Cranmore Som 45 E7
East Creech Dorset 18 E4
East Croachy Highld 300 G6
East Croftmore Highld 291 B11
East Curthwaite Cumb 230 B2
East Dean E Sus 23 F9
Glos 98 G3
Hants 32 B3
W Sus 34 E6
East Dene S Yorks 186 C6
East Denton T&W 242 D5
East Didsbury Gtr Man 184 C5
Eastdon Devon 14 F5
Eastdown Devon 8 F6
East Down Devon 40 E6
East Drayton Notts 188 F3
East Dulwich London 67 E10
East Dundry N Som 60 F5
East Ella Hull 200 B5
Eastend Essex 86 C6
Oxon 100 G6
East End Bedford 122 F2
Bucks 84 B4
C Beds 103 C9
Dorset 18 B5
Essex 89 D8
E Yorks 201 B9
E Yorks 209 B9
E Yorks 209 G9
Glos 81 E11
Hants 20 B3
Hants 33 C11
Hants 64 G2
Herts 105 F9
Kent 53 E11
Kent 53 F10
Kent 70 E3
M Keynes 103 C8
N Som 60 E3
Oxon 82 C5
Oxon 101 D9
Oxon 101 E7
S Glos 61 E9
Som 29 B10
Som 44 C5
Som 45 D7
Suff 108 E2
Suff 126 F3
East End Green Herts 86 C3
Easter Aberchalder Highld 291 B7
Easter Ardross Highld 300 B6
Easter Balgedie Perth 286 G5
Easter Balmoral Aberds 292 D4
Easter Boleskine Highld 300 G5
Easter Brackland Stirling 285 G10
Easter Brae Highld 300 C6
Easter Cardno Aberds 303 C9
Easter Compton S Glos 60 C5
Easter Cringate Stirling 278 D4
Easter Culfosie Aberds 293 C9
Easter Davoch Aberds 292 C6
Easter Earshaig Dumfries 248 C2
Easter Ellister Argyll 254 B3
Easter Fearn Highld 309 L6
Easter Galcantray Highld 301 E8
Eastergate W Sus 22 B6
Easterhouse Glasgow 268 B3
Easter Housebyres Borders 262 B2
Easter Howgate Midloth 270 C4
Easter Howlaws Borders 272 G4
Easter Kinkell Highld 300 D5
Easter Knox Angus 287 D9
Easter Langlee Borders 262 B2
Easter Lednathie Angus 292 G5
Easter Milton Highld 301 D9
Easter Moniack Highld 300 E5
Eastern Green W Mid 134 G5
Easter Ord Aberdeen 293 C10
Easter Quarff Shetland 313 K6
Easter Rhynd Perth 286 F5
Easter Row Stirling 278 B5
Easterside Mbro 225 B10
Easter Silverford Aberds 303 C7
Easter Skeld Shetland 313 J5
Easter Softlaw Borders 263 C7
Easterton Wilts 46 C4
Easterton of Lenabo Aberds 303 E10
Easterton Sands Wilts 46 B4
Eastertown Som 43 C10
Eastertown of Auchleuchries Aberds 303 F10
Easter Tulloch Highld 291 B11
Easter Whyntie Aberds 302 C6
East Everleigh Wilts 47 C8
East Ewell Sur 67 G8
East Farleigh Kent 53 C8
East Farndon W Nhants 136 F4
East Fen Common Cambs 124 C2
East Ferry Lincs 188 B4
Eastfield Borders 262 D2
Bristol 60 D5
N Lanark 269 C7
N Lanark 278 G4
Northumb 243 B7
N Yorks 217 C10
Pboro 138 D4
S Lanark 268 C2
S Yorks 197 G9
Eastfield Hall Northumb 252 B6
East Fields W Berks 64 F3
East Finchley London 67 B9
East Finglassie Fife 280 B5
East Firsby Lincs 189 D8
East Fleet Dorset 17 E8
East Fortune E Loth 281 F10
East Garforth W Yorks 206 G4
East Garston W Berks 63 D11
Eastgate Durham 232 D5
Norf 160 E2
Pboro 138 D4
East Gateshead T&W 243 E7
East Ginge Oxon 64 B2
East Gores Essex 107 G7
East Goscote Leics 154 G2

East Grafton Wilts 63 G9
East Grange Moray 301 C10
East Green Hants 49 E9
Suff 124 G3
Suff 127 D8
East Grimstead Wilts 32 B2
East Grinstead W Sus 51 F11
East Guldeford E Sus 38 C6
East Haddon W Nhants 120 D3
East Hagbourne Oxon 64 B4
Easthall Herts 104 G3
East Halton N Lincs 200 D6
Eastham Mers 182 E5
Worcs 116 D3
East Ham London 68 C2
Eastham Ferry Mers 182 E5
East Hampnett W Sus 22 B6
Easthampstead Brack 65 F11
Easthampton Hereford 115 E8
East Hanney Oxon 82 G6
East Hanningfield Essex 88 E3
East Hardwick W Yorks 198 D3
East Harling Norf 141 F9
East Harlsey N Yorks 225 F8
East Harnham Wilts 31 B10
East Harptree Bath 44 B5
East Hartford Northumb 243 B7
East Harting W Sus 34 D3
East Hatch Wilts 30 B6
East Hatley Cambs 122 G5
Easthaugh Norf 159 F11
East Hauxwell N Yorks 224 G3
East Haven Angus 287 D9
Eastheath Wokingham 65 F10
East Heckington Lincs 173 G11
East Hedleyhope
Durham 233 C9
East Helmsdale Highld 311 H4
East Hendred Oxon 64 B3
East Herringthorpe
S Yorks 187 C7
East Herrington T&W 243 G9
East Heslerton N Yorks 217 D8
East Hewish N Som 59 G11
East Hill Kent 68 G5
East Hoathly E Sus 23 B8
East Hogaland Shetland 313 K5
East Holme Dorset 18 D3
East Holton Dorset 18 C5
East Holywell Northumb 243 C8
Easthope Shrops 131 D11
Easthopewood Shrops 131 D11
East Horndon Essex 68 B6
Easthorpe Essex 107 G8
Leics 154 B6
Notts 172 E2
East Horrington Som 44 D5
East Horsley Sur 50 C5
East Horton Northumb 264 C2
Easthouse Shetland 313 J5
Easthouses Midloth 270 B6
East Howdon T&W 243 D8
East Howe BCP 19 B7
East Huntspill Som 43 E10
East Hyde C Beds 85 B10
East Ilkerton Devon 41 D8
East Ilsley W Berks 64 C3
Easting Orkney 314 A7
Eastington Devon 26 F2
Glos 80 D3
Glos 81 C10
East Keal Lincs 174 C5
East Kennett Wilts 62 F6
East Keswick W Yorks 206 E3
East Kilbride S Lanark 268 E2
East Kimber Devon 12 B5
East Kingston W Sus 35 G9
East Kirkby Lincs 174 C4
East Knapton N Yorks 217 D7
East Knighton Dorset 18 D2
East Knowstone Devon 26 C4
East Knoyle Wilts 45 G11
East Kyloe Northumb 264 B3
East Kyo Durham 242 G5
East Lambrook Som 28 D6
East Lamington Highld 301 B7
Eastland Gate Hants 33 E11
East Langdon Kent 55 D10
East Langton Leics 136 E4
East Langwell Highld 309 J7
East Lavant W Sus 22 B5
East Lavington W Sus 34 D6
East Law Northumb 242 G3
East Layton N Yorks 224 D3
Eastleach Martin Glos 82 D2
Eastleach Turville Glos 81 D11
East Leake Notts 153 D11
East Learmouth
Northumb 263 B9
Eastleigh Devon 25 B7
Hants 32 D6
East Leigh Devon 8 E3
Devon 25 F11
East Lexham Norf 159 F7
East Lilburn Northumb 264 E2
Eastling Kent 54 B3
East Linton E Loth 281 F11
East Liss Hants 34 B3
East Lockinge Oxon 64 B2
East Loftus Redcar 226 B4
East Looe Corn 6 E5
East Lound N Lincs 188 B3
East Lulworth Dorset 18 E3
East Lutton N Yorks 217 F8
East Lydeard Som 27 B11
East Lydford Som 44 G5
East Lyng Som 28 B4
East Mains Aberds 293 D8
Borders 271 F11
S Lanark 268 E2
East Malling Kent 53 B8
East Malling Heath Kent 53 B7
East March Angus 287 D8
East Marden W Sus 34 E4
East Markham Notts 188 G2
East Marsh NE Lincs 201 E9
East Martin Hants 31 D9
East Marton N Yorks 204 C4
East Melbury Dorset 30 C5
East Meon Hants 33 C11
East Mere Devon 27 D7
East Mersea Essex 89 C9
East Mey Highld 310 B7
East Molesey Sur 67 F7
Eastmoor Derbys 186 G4
Norf 140 C4
East Moor W Yorks 197 C10
East Moors Cardiff 59 D8
East Morden Dorset 18 B4
East Morton W Yorks 205 E7
East Moulsecoomb
Brighton 36 F4
East Ness N Yorks 216 D3
East Newton E Yorks 209 F11
N Yorks 216 D2
Eastney Ptsmth 21 B9
Eastnor Hereford 98 D4
East Norton Leics 136 C5
East Nynehead Som 27 C11
East Oakley Hants 48 C5
Eastoft N Lincs 199 D10
East Ogwell Devon 14 G2
Eastoke Hants 21 B10
Easton Bristol 60 E6
Cambs 122 C2
Cumb 239 C10
Cumb 239 F7
Devon 8 F3
Devon 13 D10
Dorset 17 G9
Hants 48 G4
IoW 20 D2
Lincs 155 D8
Norf 160 G2
Som 44 D4
Suff 126 F5
W Berks 64 E2
Wilts 61 E11
Easton Grey Wilts 61 B11
Easton in Gordano
N Som 60 D4
Easton Maudit N Nhants 121 F7
Easton on the Hill
N Nhants 137 C10
Easton Royal Wilts 63 G8
Easton Town Som 44 G5
Wilts 61 B11
East Orchard Dorset 30 D4
East Ord Northumb 273 E9
Eastover Som 43 F10
East Panson Devon 12 C3
Eastpark Dumfries 238 D2
East Parley BCP 19 B8
East Peckham Kent 53 D7
East Pennard Som 44 F5
East Perry Cambs 122 D3
East Portholland Corn 5 G9
East Portlemouth Devon 9 G9
East Prawle Devon 9 G10
East Preston W Sus 35 G9
East Pulham Dorset 30 F2
East Putford Devon 24 D5
East Quantoxhead Som 42 E6
East Rainton T&W 234 B2
East Ravendale NE Lincs 190 B2
East Raynham Norf 159 D7
Eastrea Cambs 138 D5
East Rhidorroch Lodge
Highld 307 K7
Eastriggs Dumfries 238 D6
East Rigton W Yorks 206 E3
Eastrington E Yorks 199 B9
Eastrip Wilts 61 E10
East Rolstone N Som 59 G11
East Rounton N Yorks 225 E8
East Row N Yorks 227 C7
East Rudham Norf 158 D6
East Runton Norf 177 E11
East Ruston Norf 160 D6
Eastry Kent 55 C10
East Saltoun E Loth 271 B9
East Sheen London 67 D8
East Sherford Devon 7 E11
East Skelston Dumfries 247 F8
East Sleekburn
Northumb 253 G7
East Somerton Norf 161 F9
East Stanley Durham 242 G6
East Stockwith Lincs 188 C3
East Stoke Dorset 18 D3
Notts 172 F3
Som 29 D7
East Stour Dorset 30 C4
East Stour Common
Dorset 30 C4
East Stourmouth Kent 71 G9
East Stowford Devon 25 B10
East Stratton Hants 48 F4
East Street Kent 55 B10
Som 44 F4
East Studdal Kent 55 D10
East Suisnish Highld 295 B7
East Taphouse Corn 6 C3
East-the-Water Devon 25 B7
East Third Borders 262 B4
East Thirston Northumb 252 D5
East Tilbury Thurrock 69 D7
East Tisted Hants 49 G8
East Torrington Lincs 189 E10
East Town Som 42 G6
Som 44 E6
Wilts 45 B11
East Trewent Pembs 73 F8
East Tuddenham Norf 159 G11
East Tuelmenna Corn 6 B4
East Tytherley Hants 32 B3
East Tytherton Wilts 62 E3
East Village Devon 26 F4
V Glam 58 E3
Eastville Bristol 60 E6
Lincs 174 D6
East Wall Shrops 131 E10
East Walton Norf 158 F4
East Water Som 44 C4
East Week Devon 13 C9
Eastwell Leics 154 D5
East Wellow Hants 32 C4
East Wemyss Fife 280 B6
East Whitburn W Loth 269 B9
Eastwick Herts 86 C6
Shetland 312 F5
East Wickham London 68 D3
East Williamston Pembs 73 E9
East Winch Norf 158 F3
East Winterslow Wilts 47 G8
East Wittering W Sus 21 B11
East Witton N Yorks 214 B2
Eastwood Hereford 98 C2
Notts 171 F7
Southend 69 B10
S Yorks 186 C6
W Yorks 196 B3
East Woodburn
Northumb 251 F10
Eastwood End Cambs 139 E8
Eastwood Hall Notts 171 F7
East Woodhay Hants 64 G2
East Woodlands Som 45 E9
East Worldham Hants 49 F8
East Worlington Devon 26 E3
East Worthing W Sus 35 G11
East Wretham Norf 141 E8
East Youlstone Devon 24 D3
Eathorpe Warks 119 D7
Eaton Ches E 168 B5
Ches W 167 C9
Hereford 115 F10
Leics 154 D5
Norf 142 B4
Notts 188 F2
Oxon 82 E6
Shrops 131 F7
Shrops 131 F10
Eaton Bishop Hereford 97 D8
Eaton Bray C Beds 103 G9
Eaton Constantine
Shrops 131 B11
Eaton Ford Cambs 122 E3
Eaton Green C Beds 103 G9
Eaton Hastings Oxon 82 F3
Eaton Mascott Shrops 131 B10
Eaton on Tern Shrops 150 E3
Eaton Socon Cambs 122 F3
Eaton upon Tern Shrops 150 E3
Eau Brink Norf 157 F11
Eau Withington
Hereford 97 C10
Eaves Green W Mid 134 G5
Eavestone N Yorks 214 F4
Ebberly Hill Devon 25 D9
Ebberston N Yorks 217 C7
Ebbesbourne Wake Wilts 31 C7
Ebblake Hants 31 F10
Ebbw Vale Bl Gwent 77 D11
Ebchester Durham 242 F4
Ebdon N Som 59 G11
Ebernoe W Sus 35 B7
Ebford Devon 14 D5
Ebley Glos 80 D4
Ebnal Ches W 167 F7
Ebnall Hereford 115 F9
Ebreywood Shrops 149 F10
Ebrington Glos 100 C3
Ecchinswell Hants 48 B4
Ecclaw Borders 272 B5
Ecclefechan Dumfries 238 C5
Eccle Riggs Cumb 210 B4
Eccles Borders 272 G5
Gtr Man 184 B3
Kent 69 G8
Ecclesall S Yorks 186 E4
Ecclesfield S Yorks 186 C5
Ecclesgreig Aberds 293 G9
Eccleshall Staffs 150 D6
Eccleshill W Yorks 205 F9
Ecclesmachan W Loth 279 G11
Eccles on Sea Norf 161 D8
Eccles Road Norf 141 E10
Eccleston Ches W 166 C6
Lancs 194 D4
Mers 183 B7
Eccleston Park Mers 183 C7
Eccliffe Dorset 30 B3
Eccup W Yorks 205 E11
Echt Aberds 293 C9
Eckford Borders 262 D6
Eckfordmoss Borders 262 D6
Eckington Derbys 186 F6
Worcs 99 C8
Eckington Corner E Sus 23 D8
Ecklands S Yorks 197 G8
Eckworthy Devon 24 D6
Ecton N Nhants 120 E6
Staffs 169 D9
Ecton Brook W Nhants 120 E6
Edale Derbys 185 D10
Edale End Derbys 185 D11
Edbrook Som 43 E8
Edburton W Sus 36 E2
Edderside Cumb 229 B7
Edderton Highld 309 L7
Eddington Kent 71 F7
W Berks 63 F10
Eddistone Devon 24 C3
Eddleston Borders 270 F4
Eddlewood S Lanark 268 E4
Edenbridge Kent 52 D2
Edenfield Lancs 195 D9
Edenhall Cumb 231 E7
Edenham Lincs 155 E11
Eden Mount Cumb 211 D8
Eden Park London 67 F11
Edensor Derbys 170 B2
Edentaggart Argyll 276 C6
Edenthorpe S Yorks 198 F6
Edentown Cumb 239 F9
Eden Vale Durham 234 D4
Wilts 45 C11
Ederline Argyll 275 C9
Edern Gwyn 144 B5
Edford Som 45 D7
Edgarley Som 44 F4
Edgbaston W Mid 133 G11
Edgcote W Nhants 101 B10
Edgcott Bucks 102 G3
Som 41 F10
Edgcumbe Corn 2 C6
Edge Glos 80 D4
Shrops 131 B7
Edgebolton Shrops 149 E11
Edge End Glos 79 C9
Lancs 203 G10
Edgefield Norf 159 C11
Edgefield Street Norf 159 C11
Edge Fold Blackburn 195 D8
Gtr Man 195 F8
Edge Green Ches W 167 E7
Gtr Man 183 B9
Norf 141 F10
Edgehill Warks 101 B7
Edge Hill Mers 182 C5
Warks 134 D4
Edgeley Gtr Man 184 D5
Edge Mount S Yorks 186 C3
Edgerley Shrops 148 F6
Edgerston Borders 262 G5
Edgerton W Yorks 196 D6
Edgeside Lancs 195 C10
Edgeworth Glos 80 D6
Edginswell Devon 9 B7
Edgiock Worcs 117 E10
Edgmond Telford 150 F4
Edgmond Marsh Telford 150 E4
Edgton Shrops 131 F7
Edgware London 85 G11
Edgwick W Mid 134 G6
Edgworth Blackburn 195 D8
Edham Borders 262 B6
Edial Staffs 133 B11
Edinample Stirling 285 E9
Edinbane Highld 298 D3
Edinburgh Edin 280 G5
Edinchip Stirling 285 E9
Edingale Staffs 152 G4
Edingight Ho Moray 302 D5
Edinglassie Ho Aberds 292 B5
Edingley Notts 171 D11
Edingthorpe Norf 160 C6
Edingthorpe Green Norf 160 C6
Edington Som 43 E11
Wilts 46 C2
Edingworth Som 43 C11
Edintore Moray 302 E4
Edistone Devon 24 C2
Edithmead Som 43 D10
Edith Weston Rutland 137 B8
Edlaston Derbys 169 G11
Edlesborough Bucks 85 B7
Edlingham Northumb 252 B4
Edlington Lincs 190 G2
Edmondsham Dorset 31 E9
Edmondsley Durham 233 B10
Edmondstown Rhondda 77 G8
Edmondthorpe Leics 155 F7
Edmonston S Lanark 269 G11
Edmonstone Orkney 314 D5
Edmonton Corn 10 G5
London 86 G4
Edmundbyers Durham 242 G2
Ednam Borders 262 B6
Ednaston Derbys 170 G2
Edney Common Essex 87 E11
Edradynate Perth 286 B2
Edrom Borders 272 D6
Edstaston Shrops 149 C10
Edstone Warks 118 E3
Edvin Loach Hereford 116 F3
Edwalton Notts 153 B11
Edwardstone Suff 107 C8
Edwardsville M Tydf 77 F9
Edwinsford Carms 94 E2
Edwinstowe Notts 171 B10
Edworth C Beds 104 C4
Edwyn Ralph Hereford 116 F2
Edzell Angus 293 G7
Efail-fôch Neath 57 B9
Efail Isaf Rhondda 58 C5
Efailnewydd Gwyn 145 B7
Efailwen Carms 92 F2
Efenechtyd Denb 165 D10
Effingham Sur 50 C6
Effirth Shetland 313 H5
Effledge Borders 262 F3
Efflinch Staffs 152 F3
Efford Devon 26 G5
Plym 7 D10
Egbury Hants 48 C2
Egdon Worcs 117 G8
Egerton Gtr Man 195 E8
Kent 54 D2
Egerton Forstal Kent 53 D11
Egerton Green Ches E 167 E8
Egford Som 45 D9
Eggbeare Corn 12 D2
Eggborough N Yorks 198 C5
Eggbuckland Plym 7 D10
Eggesford Station
Devon 25 E11
Eggington C Beds 103 F9
Egginton Derbys 152 D5
Egginton Common
Derbys 152 D5
Egglesburn Durham 232 G5
Egglescliffe Stockton 225 C8
Eggleston Durham 232 G5
Egham Sur 66 E4
Egham Hythe Sur 66 E4
Egham Wick Sur 66 E3
Egleton Rutland 137 B7
Eglingham Northumb 264 F4
Egloshayle Corn 10 G5
Egloskerry Corn 11 D11
Eglwysbach Conwy 180 G4
Eglwys-Brewis V Glam 58 F4
Eglwys Cross Wrex 167 G7
Eglwys Fach Ceredig 128 D3
Eglwyswen Pembs 92 D3
Eglwyswrw Pembs 92 D2
Egmanton Notts 172 B2
Egmere Norf 159 B8
Egremont Cumb 219 C10
Mers 182 C4
Egton N Yorks 226 D6
Egton Bridge N Yorks 226 D6
Egypt Bucks 66 B3
Hants 48 E3
W Berks 64 D2
W Yorks 205 G7
Eiden Highld 309 J7
Eight Ash Green Essex 107 F8
Eighton Banks T&W 243 F7
Eignaig Highld 289 E9
Eign Hill Hereford 97 D10
Eil Highld 291 B10
Eilanreach Highld 295 D10
Eildon Borders 262 C3
Eileanach Lodge Highld 300 C5
Eilean Anabaich
W Isles 305 H4
Eilean Darach Highld 307 L6
Eilean Shona Ho Highld 289 B8
Einacleite W Isles 304 F3
Einsiob = Evenjobb
Powys 114 E5
Eisgean W Isles 305 G5
Eisingrug Gwyn 146 C2
Elan Village Powys 113 D8
Elberton S Glos 60 B6
Elborough N Som 43 B11
Elbridge Shrops 149 E7
W Sus 22 C6
Elburton Plym 7 E10
Elcho Perth 286 E5
Elcock's Brook Worcs 117 E10
Elcombe Glos 80 F3
Swindon 62 C6
Elcot W Berks 63 F11
Eldene Swindon 63 C7
Eldernell Cambs 138 D6
Eldersfield Worcs 98 E6
Elderslie Renfs 267 C8
Elder Street Essex 105 E11
Eldon Durham 233 F10
Eldon Lane Durham 233 F10
Eldrick S Ayrs 245 G7
Eldroth N Yorks 212 F5
Eldwick W Yorks 205 E8
Elemore Vale T&W 234 B3
Elerch = Bont-goch
Ceredig 128 F3
Elfhowe Cumb 221 F9
Elford Northumb 264 C5
Staffs 152 G3
Elford Closes Cambs 123 C10
Elgin Moray 302 C2
Elgol Highld 295 D7
Elham Kent 55 E7
Eliburn W Loth 269 B10
Elie Fife 287 G8
Elim Anglesey 178 D5
Eling Hants 32 E5
W Berks 64 D4
Elishader Highld 298 C5
Elishaw Northumb 251 D9
Elizafield Dumfries 238 C2
Elkesley Notts 187 F11
Elkington W Nhants 120 B2
Elkins Green Essex 87 E10
Elkstone Glos 81 C7
Ellacombe Torbay 9 C8
Ellan Highld 301 G8
Elland W Yorks 196 C6
Elland Lower Edge
W Yorks 196 C6
Elland Upper Edge
W Yorks 196 C6
Ellary Argyll 275 F8
Ellastone Staffs 169 G10
Ellel Lancs 202 B5
Ellemford Borders 272 C4
Ellenborough Cumb 228 D6
Ellenbrook Herts 86 D2
IoM 192 E4
Ellenglaze Corn 4 D5
Ellenhall Staffs 150 D6
Ellen's Green Sur 50 F5
Ellerbeck N Yorks 225 F8
Ellerburn N Yorks 216 C6
Ellerby N Yorks 226 C5
Ellerdine Telford 150 E2
Ellerdine Heath Telford 150 E2
Ellerhayes Devon 27 G7
Elleric Argyll 284 C4
Ellerker E Yorks 200 B2
Ellerton E Yorks 207 F10
N Yorks 224 F5
Shrops 150 D4
Ellesborough Bucks 84 D4
Ellesmere Shrops 149 C8
Ellesmere Park Gtr Man 184 B3
Ellesmere Port Ches W 182 F6
Ellicombe Som 42 E3
Ellingham Hants 31 F10
Norf 143 E7
Northumb 264 D5
Ellingstring N Yorks 214 C3
Ellington Cambs 122 C3
Northumb 253 E7
Ellington Thorpe Cambs 122 C3
Elliot Angus 287 D10
Elliots Green Som 45 D9
Elliot's Town Caerph 77 E10
Ellisfield Hants 48 D6
Elliston Borders 262 D3
Ellistown Leics 153 G8
Ellon Aberds 303 F9
Ellonby Cumb 230 D4
Ellough Suff 143 F8
Elloughton E Yorks 200 B2
Ellwood Glos 79 D9
Elm Cambs 139 B9
Elmbridge Glos 80 B5
Worcs 117 D8
Elm Corner Sur 50 B5
Elm Cross Wilts 62 D6
Elmdon Essex 105 D9
W Mid 134 G3
Elmdon Heath W Mid 134 G3
Elmer W Sus 35 G7
Elmers End London 67 F11
Elmers Green Lancs 194 F3
Elmers Marsh W Sus 34 B5
Elmesthorpe Leics 135 D9
Elmfield IoW 21 C8
Elm Hill Dorset 30 B4
Elmhurst Bucks 84 B4
Staffs 152 G2
Elmley Castle Worcs 99 C9
Elmley Lovett Worcs 117 D7
Elmore Glos 80 B3
Elmore Back Glos 80 B3
Elm Park London 68 B4
Elmscott Devon 24 C2
Elmsett Suff 107 B11
Elms Green Hereford 115 F10
Worcs 116 D4
Elmslack Lancs 211 D9
Elmstead Essex 107 F11
London 68 E2
Elmstead Heath Essex 107 G11
Elmstead Market
Essex 107 G11
Elmsted Kent 54 E6
Elmsthorpe Leics 135 D9
Elmstone Kent 71 G9
Elmstone Hardwicke
Glos 99 F8
Elmswell E Yorks 208 B5
Suff 125 E9
Elmton Derbys 187 G8
Elness Orkney 314 C6
Elphin Highld 307 H7
Elphinstone E Loth 281 G7
Elrick Aberds 293 C10
Elrig Dumfries 236 E5
Elrigbeag Argyll 284 F5
Elrington Northumb 241 E9
Elscar S Yorks 197 G11
Elsdon Hereford 114 G6
Northumb 251 E10
Elsecar S Yorks 186 B5
S Yorks 197 G11
Elsenham Essex 105 F10
Elsenham Sta Essex 105 F10
Elsfield Oxon 83 C8
Elsham N Lincs 200 E4
Elsing Norf 159 F11
Elslack N Yorks 204 D4
Elson Hants 33 G10
Shrops 149 B7
Elsrickle S Lanark 269 G11
Elstead Sur 50 E2
Elsted W Sus 34 D4
Elsthorpe Lincs 155 E11
Elstob Durham 234 G2
Elston Devon 26 G3
Notts 172 F3
Wilts 46 E5
Elstone Devon 25 D11
Elstow Bedford 103 B11
Elstree Herts 85 F11
Elstronwick E Yorks 209 G10
Elswick Lancs 202 F4
T&W 242 E6
Elswick Leys Lancs 202 F4
Elsworth Cambs 122 E6
Elterwater Cumb 220 E6
Eltham London 68 E2
Eltisley Cambs 122 F5
Elton Cambs 137 E11
Ches W 183 F7
Derbys 170 C2
Glos 80 C2
Gtr Man 195 E9
Hereford 115 C9
Notts 154 B5
Stockton 225 B8
Elton Green Ches W 183 G7
Elton's Marsh Hereford 97 C9
Eltringham Northumb 242 E3
Elvanfoot S Lanark 259 F11
Elvaston Derbys 153 C8
Elveden Suff 124 B6
Elvet Hill Durham 233 C11
Elvingston E Loth 281 G9
Elvington Kent 55 C9
York 207 D9
Elwell Devon 41 G7
Dorset 17 E9
Elwick Hrtlpl 234 E5
Northumb 264 B4
Elworth Ches E 168 C2
Elworthy Som 42 G5
Ely Cambs 139 G10
Cardiff 58 D6
Emberton M Keynes 103 B7
Embleton Cumb 229 E9
Durham 234 F4
Northumb 264 E6
Embo Highld 311 K2
Emborough Som 44 C6
Embo Street Highld 311 K2
Embsay N Yorks 204 C6
Emerson Park London 68 B4
Emerson's Green S Glos 61 D7
Emerson Valley
M Keynes 102 E6
Emery Down Hants 32 F3
Emley W Yorks 197 E8
Emmbrook Wokingham 65 F9
Emmer Green Reading 65 D8
Emmett Carr Derbys 187 F7
Emmington Oxon 84 E2
Emneth Norf 139 B9
Emneth Hungate Norf 139 B10
Emorsgate Norf 157 E10
Empingham Rutland 137 B8
Empshott Hants 49 G9
Empshott Green Hants 49 G8
Emscote Warks 118 D5
Emstrey Shrops 149 G10
Emsworth Hants 22 B2
Enborne W Berks 64 F2
Enborne Row W Berks 64 G2
Enchmarsh Shrops 131 D10
Enderby Leics 135 D10
Endmoor Cumb 211 C10
Endon Staffs 168 E6
Endon Bank Staffs 168 E6
Energlyn Caerph 58 B6
Enfield London 86 F4
Worcs 117 D10
Enfield Highway London 86 F5
Enfield Lock London 86 F5
Enfield Town London 86 F4
Enfield Wash London 86 F5
Enford Wilts 46 C6
Engamoor Shetland 313 H4
Engedi Anglesey 178 F5
Engine Common S Glos 61 C7
Englefield W Berks 64 E6
Englefield Green Sur 66 E3
Englesea-brook Ches E 168 E3
English Bicknor Glos 79 B9
Englishcombe Bath 61 G8
English Frankton
Shrops 149 D9
Engollan Corn 10 G3
Enham Alamein Hants 47 D11
Enis Devon 25 B9
Enisfirth Shetland 312 F5
Enmore Som 43 G8
Enmore Field Hereford 115 E9
Enmore Green Dorset 30 C5
Ennerdale Bridge
Cumb 219 B11
Enniscaven Corn 5 D9
Enoch Dumfries 247 C9
Enochdhu Perth 292 G2
Ensay Argyll 288 E5
Ensbury BCP 19 B7
Ensbury Park BCP 19 C7
Ensdon Shrops 149 F8
Ensis Devon 25 B9
Enslow Oxon 83 B7
Enstone Oxon 101 G7
Enterkinfoot Dumfries 247 C9
Enterpen N Yorks 225 D9
Enton Green Sur 50 E3
Enville Staffs 132 F6
Eolaigearraidh W Isles 297 L3
Eorabus Argyll 288 G5
Eòropaidh W Isles 304 B7
Epney Glos 80 C3
Epperstone Notts 171 F11
Epping Essex 87 E7
Epping Green Essex 86 D6
Herts 86 D3
Epping Upland Essex 86 E6
Eppleby N Yorks 224 C3
Eppleworth E Yorks 208 G6
Epsom Sur 67 G8
Epwell Oxon 101 C7
Epworth N Lincs 199 G9
Epworth Turbary
N Lincs 199 G9
Erbistock Wrex 166 G5
Erbusaig Highld 295 C9
Erchless Castle Highld 300 E4
Erdington W Mid 134 E2
Eredine Argyll 275 C10
Eriboll Highld 308 D4
Ericstane Dumfries 260 G3
Eridge Green E Sus 52 F5
Erines Argyll 275 F9
Eriswell Suff 124 B4
Erith London 68 D4
Erlestoke Wilts 46 C3
Ermine Lincs 189 G7
Ermington Devon 8 E2
Ernesettle Plym 7 D8
Erpingham Norf 160 C3
Erriottwood Kent 54 B2
Errogie Highld 300 G5
Errol Perth 286 E6
Errol Station Perth 286 E6
Erskine Renfs 277 G9
Erskine Bridge Renfs 277 G9
Ervie Dumfries 236 C2
Erwarton Suff 108 E4
Erwood Powys 95 C11
Eryholme N Yorks 224 D6
Eryrys Denb 166 D2
Escomb Durham 233 E9
Escott Som 42 F5
Escrick N Yorks 207 E8
Esgairdawe Carms 94 C2
Esgairgeiliog Powys 128 B5
Esgyryn Conwy 180 F4
Esh Durham 233 C9
Esher Sur 66 G6
Eshiels Borders 261 B7
Esholt W Yorks 205 E9
Eshott Northumb 252 D6
Eshton N Yorks 204 B4
Esh Winning Durham 233 C9
Eskadale Highld 300 F4
Eskbank Midloth 270 B6
Eskdale Green Cumb 220 E2
Eskdalemuir Dumfries 249 D7
Eske E Yorks 209 E7
Eskham Lincs 190 B5
Eskholme S Yorks 198 D6
Esknish Argyll 274 G4
Esk Valley N Yorks 226 E6
Eslington Park
Northumb 264 G2
Esperley Lane Ends
Durham 233 G8
Esprick Lancs 202 F4
Essendine Rutland 155 G10
Essendon Herts 86 D3
Essich Highld 300 F6
Essington Staffs 133 C9
Esslemont Aberds 303 G9
Eston Redcar 225 B11
Estover Plym 7 D10
Eswick Shetland 313 H6
Etal Northumb 263 B10
Etchilhampton Wilts 62 G4
Etchingham E Sus 38 B2
Etchinghill Kent 55 F7
Staffs 151 F10
Etchingwood E Sus 37 C8
Etherley Dene Durham 233 F9
Ethie Castle Angus 287 C10
Ethie Mains Angus 287 C10
Etling Green Norf 159 G10
Etloe Glos 79 D11
Eton Windsor 66 D3
Eton Wick Windsor 66 D2
Etruria Stoke 168 F5
Etsell Shrops 131 C7
Etterby Cumb 239 F9
Etteridge Highld 291 D8
Ettersgill Durham 232 F3
Ettiley Heath Ches E 168 C2
Ettingshall W Mid 133 D8
Ettingshall Park W Mid 133 D8
Ettington Warks 100 B5
Etton E Yorks 208 E5
Pboro 138 B2
Ettrick Borders 261 G7
Ettrickbridge Borders 261 E9
Ettrickdale Argyll 275 G11
Ettrickhill Borders 261 G7
Etwall Derbys 152 C5
Etwall Common Derbys 152 C5
Eudon Burnell Shrops 132 F3
Eudon George Shrops 132 F3
Euston Suff 125 B7
Euximoor Drove Cambs 139 D9
Euxton Lancs 194 D5
Evanstown Bridgend 58 B3
Evanton Highld 300 C6
Evedon Lincs 173 F9
Eve Hill W Mid 133 E8
Evelix Highld 309 K7
Evendine Hereford 98 C5
Evenjobb = Einsiob
Powys 114 E5
Evenley W Nhants 101 E11
Evenlode Glos 100 F4
Even Pits Hereford 97 D11
Even Swindon Swindon 62 B6
Evenwood Durham 233 G9
Evenwood Gate Durham 233 G9
Everbay Orkney 314 D6
Evercreech Som 44 F6
Everdon W Nhants 119 F11
Everingham E Yorks 208 E2
Everland Shetland 312 D8
Everleigh Wilts 47 C8
Everley N Yorks 217 B9
Eversholt C Beds 103 E9
Evershot Dorset 29 G9
Eversley Essex 69 B8
Hants 65 G9
Eversley Centre Hants 65 G9
Eversley Cross Hants 65 G9
Everthorpe E Yorks 208 G4
Everton C Beds 122 G4
Hants 19 C11
Mers 182 C5
Notts 187 C11
Evertown Dumfries 239 B9
Evesbatch Hereford 98 B3
Evesham Worcs 99 C10
Evington Kent 54 D6
Leicester 136 C2
Ewanrigg Cumb 228 D6
Ewden Village S Yorks 186 B3
Ewell Sur 67 G8
Ewell Minnis Kent 55 E9
Ewelme Oxon 83 G10
Ewen Glos 81 F8
Ewenny V Glam 58 D2
Ewerby Lincs 173 F10
Ewerby Thorpe Lincs 173 F10
Ewes Dumfries 249 E9
Ewesley Northumb 252 E3
Ewhurst Sur 50 E5
Ewhurst Green E Sus 38 C3
Sur 50 F5
Ewloe Flint 166 B4
Ewloe Green Flint 166 B3
Ewood Blackburn 195 B7
Ewood Bridge Lancs 195 C9
Eworthy Devon 12 C5
Ewshot Hants 49 D10
Ewyas Harold Hereford 97 F7
Exbourne Devon 25 G10
Exbury Hants 20 B4
Exceat E Sus 23 F8
Exebridge Devon 26 C6
Exelby N Yorks 214 B5
Exeter Devon 14 C4
Exford Som 41 F11
Exfords Green Shrops 131 B9
Exhall Warks 118 F2
Warks 135 F7
Exlade Street Oxon 65 C7
Exley W Yorks 196 C5
Exley Head W Yorks 204 F6
Exminster Devon 14 D4
Exmouth Devon 14 E6
Exnaboe Shetland 313 M5
Exning Suff 124 D2
Exted Kent 55 E7
Exton Devon 14 D5
Hants 33 C10
Rutland 155 G8
Som 42 G2
Exwick Devon 14 C4
Eyam Derbys 186 F2
Eydon W Nhants 119 G10
Eye Hereford 115 E9
Pboro 138 C4
Suff 126 C2
Eye Green Pboro 138 C4
Eyemouth Borders 273 C8
Eyeworth C Beds 104 B4
Eyhorne Street Kent 53 C10
Eyke Suff 126 G6
Eynesbury Cambs 122 F3
Eynort Highld 294 C5
Eynsford Kent 68 F4
Eynsham Oxon 82 D6
Eype Dorset 16 C5
Eyre Highld 295 B7
Highld 298 D4
Eyres Monsell
Leicester 135 D11
Eythorne Kent 55 D9
Eyton Hereford 115 E9
Shrops 131 F7
Shrops 149 G7
Wrex 166 G4
Eyton on Severn
Shrops 131 B11
Eyton upon the Weald
Moors Telford 150 G3

F

Faberstown Wilts 47 C9
Faccombe Hants 47 B11
Faceby N Yorks 225 E9
Fachell Gwyn 163 B8
Fachwen Gwyn 163 C9
Facit Lancs 195 D11
Fackley Notts 171 C7
Faddiley Ches E 167 E9
Faddonch Highld 295 C11
Fadmoor N Yorks 216 B3
Faerdre Swansea 75 E11
Fagley W Yorks 205 G9
Fagwyr Swansea 75 E11
Faichem Highld 290 C4
Faifley W Dunb 277 G10
Failand N Som 60 E4
Failford S Ayrs 257 D11
Failsworth Gtr Man 195 G11
Fain Highld 299 B11
Faindouran Lodge
Moray 292 C2
Fairbourne Gwyn 146 G2
Fairbourne Heath Kent 53 C11
Fairburn N Yorks 198 B3
Fairburn House Highld 300 D4
Fair Cross London 68 B3
Fairfield Clack 279 C7
Derbys 185 G9
Gtr Man 184 B6
Gtr Man 195 E10
Kent 39 B7
Mers 182 C5
Stockton 225 B8
Worcs 99 C10
Worcs 117 B8
Fairfield Park Bath 61 F9
Fairfields Glos 98 E4
Fairford Glos 81 E11
Fair Green Norf 158 F3
Fairhaven Lancs 193 B10
N Ayrs 255 C10
Fairhill S Lanark 268 E4
Fair Hill Cumb 230 E6
Fairlands Sur 50 C3
Fairlee IoW 20 C6
Fairlie N Ayrs 266 D4
Fairlight E Sus 38 E5
Fairlight Cove E Sus 38 E5
Fairlop London 87 G7
Fairmile BCP 19 C9
Devon 15 B7
Sur 66 G6
Fairmilehead Edin 270 B4
Fair Moor Northumb 252 F5
Fairoak Caerph 77 F11
Staffs 150 C5
Fair Oak Hants 33 D7
Hants 64 G5
Lancs 203 D8
Fair Oak Green Hants 65 G7
Fairseat Kent 68 G6
Fairstead Essex 88 B3
Norf 158 F2
Fairview Glos 99 G9
Fairwarp E Sus 37 B7
Fairwater Cardiff 58 D6
Torf 78 G3
Fairwood Wilts 45 C10
Fairy Cottage IoM 192 D5
Fairy Cross Devon 24 C6
Fakenham Norf 159 D8
Fakenham Magna Suff 125 B8
Fala Midloth 271 C8
Fala Dam Midloth 271 C8
Falahill Borders 271 D7
Falcon Hereford 98 E2
Falcon Lodge W Mid 134 D2
Falconwood London 68 D3
Falcutt W Nhants 101 C11
Faldingworth Lincs 189 E9
Faldonside Borders 262 C2
Falfield Fife 287 G8
S Glos 79 G11
Falkenham Suff 108 D5
Falkenham Sink Suff 108 D5
Falkirk Falk 279 F7
Falkland Fife 286 G6
Falla Borders 262 G6
Fallgate Derbys 170 C5
Fallin Stirling 278 C6
Fallinge Derbys 170 B3
Fallings Heath W Mid 133 D9
Fallowfield Gtr Man 184 C5
Fallside N Lanark 268 C4
Falmer E Sus 36 F5
Falmouth Corn 3 C8
Falnash Borders 249 B9
Falsgrave N Yorks 217 B10
Falside W Loth 269 B9
Falsidehill Borders 272 G3
Falstone Northumb 250 F6
Fanagmore Highld 306 E6
Fancott C Beds 103 F10
Fangdale Beck
N Yorks 225 G11
Fangfoss E Yorks 207 C11
Fanich Highld 311 J2
Fankerton Falk 278 E5
Fanmore Argyll 288 E6
Fanner's Green Essex 87 C11
Fannich Lodge Highld 300 C2
Fans Borders 272 G2
Fanshowe Ches E 184 G5
Fant Kent 53 B8
Faoilean Highld 295 C7
Far Arnside Cumb 211 D8
Far Bank S Yorks 198 E6
Far Banks Lancs 194 C2
Far Bletchley M Keynes 103 E7
Farcet Cambs 138 E4
Far Coton Leics 135 C7
Far Cotton W Nhants 120 F4
Farden Shrops 115 B11
Fareham Hants 33 F9
Far End Cumb 220 F6
Farewell Staffs 151 G11
Far Forest Worcs 116 C4
Farforth Lincs 190 F4
Far Green Glos 80 E3
Farhill Derbys 170 C5
Far Hoarcross Staffs 152 E2
Faringdon Oxon 82 F3
Farington Lancs 194 B4
Farington Moss Lancs 194 C4
Farlam Cumb 240 F3
Farlands Booth Derbys 185 D9
Farlary Highld 309 J7
Far Laund Derbys 170 F5
Farleigh N Som 60 F3
Sur 67 G11
Farleigh Court Sur 67 G11
Farleigh Green Kent 53 C8
Farleigh Hungerford
Som 45 B10
Farleigh Wallop Hants 48 D6
Farleigh Wick Wilts 61 G10
Farlesthorpe Lincs 191 G7
Farleton Cumb 211 C10
Lancs 211 F11
Farley Bristol 60 E2
Derbys 170 C3
Shrops 131 B7
Shrops 132 C2
Staffs 169 G9
Wilts 32 B2
Far Ley Staffs 132 D5
Farley Green Suff 124 G4
Sur 50 D5
Farley Hill Luton 103 G11
Wokingham 65 G8
Farleys End Glos 80 B3
Farlington N Yorks 216 F2
Ptsmth 33 F11
Farlow Shrops 132 G2
Farmborough Bath 61 G7
Farmbridge End Essex 87 C10
Farmcote Glos 99 F11

Farmcote *continued*
Shrops 132 E5
Farmington Glos 81 B10
Farmoor Oxon 82 D6
Far Moor Gtr Man 194 G4
Farms Common Corn 2 C5
Farmtown Moray 302 D5
Farm Town Leics 153 F7
Farnah Green Derbys 170 F4
Farnborough Hants 49 C11
London 68 G2
Warks 101 B8
W Berks 64 C2
Farnborough Green
Hants 49 B11
Farnborough Park
Hants 49 B11
Farnborough Street
Hants 49 B11
Farncombe Sur 50 E3
Farndish Bedford 121 E8
Farndon Ches W 166 E6
Notts 172 E3
Farnell Angus 287 B10
Farnham Dorset 31 D7
Essex 105 G9
N Yorks 215 G7
Suff 127 E7
Sur 49 D10
Farnham Common Bucks 66 C3
Farnham Green Essex 105 F9
Farnham Park Bucks 66 C3
Farnham Royal Bucks 66 C3
Farnhill N Yorks 204 D6
Farningham Kent 68 F4
Farnley N Yorks 205 D10
W Yorks 205 G11
Farnley Bank W Yorks 197 E7
Farnley Tyas W Yorks 197 E7
Farnsfield Notts 171 D10
Farnworth Gtr Man 195 F8
Halton 183 D8
Far Oakridge Glos 80 E6
Farr Highld 291 C10
Highld 300 F6
Highld 308 C7
Farraline Highld 300 G5
Farr House Highld 300 F6
Farringdon Devon 14 C6
T&W 243 G9
Farrington Dorset 30 D4
Farrington Gurney Bath 44 B6
Far Royds W Yorks 205 G11
Far Sawrey Cumb 221 F7
Farsley W Yorks 205 F10
Farsley Beck Bottom
W Yorks 205 F10
Farther Howegreen
Essex 88 E4
Farthing Corner
Medway 69 G10
Farthing Green Kent 53 D10
Farthinghoe W Nhants 101 D10
Farthingloe Kent 55 E9
Farthingstone W Nhants 120 F2
Far Thrupp Glos 80 E5
Fartown W Yorks 196 D6
Farway Devon 15 B9
Farway Marsh Devon 28 G4
Fasach Highld 297 G7
Fasag Highld 299 D8
Fascadale Highld 289 B7
Faslane Port Argyll 276 D4
Fasnacloich Argyll 284 C4
Fasnakyle Ho Highld 300 G3
Fassfern Highld 290 F2
Fatfield T&W 243 G8
Fattahead Aberds 302 D6
Faucheldean W Loth 279 G11
Faugh Cumb 240 G2
Faughill Borders 262 C2
Fauld Staffs 152 D3
Fauldhouse W Loth 269 C8
Fauldiehill Angus 287 D9
Fauldshope Borders 261 D10
Faulkbourne Essex 88 B3
Faulkland Som 45 C8
Fauls Shrops 149 C11
Faverdale Darl 224 B5
Faversham Kent 70 G4
Favillar Moray 302 F2
Fawdington N Yorks 215 E8
Fawdon Northumb 264 F2
T&W 242 D6
Fawfieldhead Staffs 169 C9
Fawkham Green Kent 68 F5
Fawler Oxon 63 B10
Oxon 82 B5
Fawley Bucks 65 B9
Hants 33 G7
W Berks 63 C11
Fawley Bottom Bucks 65 B8
Fawley Chapel Hereford 97 F11
Faxfleet E Yorks 199 C11
Faygate W Sus 51 G8
Fazakerley Mers 182 B5
Fazeley Staffs 134 C4
Feagour Highld 291 D7
Fearby N Yorks 214 C3
Fearn Highld 301 B8
Fearnan Perth 285 C11
Fearnbeg Highld 299 D7
Fearnhead Warr 183 C10
Fearn Lodge Highld 309 L6
Fearnmore Highld 299 C7
Fearn Station Highld 301 B8
Fearnville W Yorks 206 F2
Featherstone Staffs 133 B8
W Yorks 198 C2
Featherwood Northumb 251 C8
Feckenham Worcs 117 E10
Fedw Fawr Anglesey 179 E10
Feering Essex 107 G7
Feetham N Yorks 223 F9
Fegg Hayes Stoke 168 E5
Fèith Mhor Highld 301 G8
Feizor N Yorks 212 F5
Felbridge Sur 51 F11
Felbrigg Norf 160 B4
Felcourt Sur 51 E11
Felden Herts 85 E8
Felderland Kent 55 B10
Feldy Ches E 183 F11
Felhampton Shrops 131 F8
Felin-Crai Powys 95 G7
Felindre Carms 75 C7
Carms 93 D7
Carms 93 G11
Carms 94 E3
Carms 94 F4
Ceredig 111 F10
Powys 96 D3
Powys 96 G3
Powys 130 C3
Powys 130 G3
Rhondda 58 C3
Swansea 75 E10
Felindre Farchog Pembs 92 D2
Felinfach Ceredig 111 F10
Felinfach *continued*
Powys 95 E11
Felinfoel Carms 75 E8
Felingwmisaf Carms 93 G10
Felingwmuchaf Carms 93 G10
Felin Newydd Carms 94 D3
Felin-newydd Powys 96 D2
Felin Newydd = *New Mills*
Powys 129 C11
Felin Puleston Wrex 166 F4
Felin-Wnda Ceredig 92 B6
Felinwynt Ceredig 110 G4
Felixkirk N Yorks 215 C9
Felixstowe Suff 108 E5
Felixstowe Ferry Suff 108 D6
Felkington Northumb 273 G8
Felkirk W Yorks 197 E11
Felldyke Cumb 219 B11
Fell End Cumb 222 F4
Fellgate T&W 243 E8
Felling T&W 243 E7
Felling Shore T&W 243 E7
Fell Lane W Yorks 204 E6
Fellside T&W 242 E5
Fell Side Cumb 230 D2
Felmersham Bedford 121 F9
Felmingham Norf 160 D5
Felmore Essex 69 B8
Felpham W Sus 35 H7
Felsham Suff 125 F8
Felsted Essex 106 G3
Feltham London 66 E6
Som 28 D2
Felthamhill London 66 E5
Felthorpe Norf 160 F3
Felton Hereford 97 B11
Northumb 252 C5
N Som 60 F4
Felton Butler Shrops 149 F7
Feltwell Norf 140 E4
Fenay Bridge W Yorks 197 D7
Fence Lancs 204 F2
Fence Houses T&W 243 G8
Fencott Oxon 83 B9
Fen Ditton Cambs 123 E9
Fen Drayton Cambs 122 D6
Fen End Lincs 156 E4
W Mid 118 B4
Fengate Norf 160 E3
Pboro 138 D4
Fenham Northumb 273 G11
T&W 242 D6
Fenhouses Lincs 174 G3
Feniscliffe Blackburn 195 B7
Feniscowles Blackburn 194 B6
Feniton Devon 15 B8
Fenlake Bedford 103 B11
Fenn Green Shrops 132 G5
Fennington Som 27 B11
Fenn's Bank Wrex 149 B10
Fenn Street Medway 69 D9
Fenny Bentley Derbys 169 E11
Fenny Bridges Devon 15 B8
Fenny Castle Som 44 E4
Fenny Compton Warks 119 G8
Fenny Drayton Leics 134 D6
Fenny Stratford
M Keynes 103 E7
Fenrother Northumb 252 E5
Fen Side Lincs 174 D4
Fenstanton Cambs 122 D6
Fenstead End Suff 124 G6
Fen Street Norf 141 G11
Suff 125 B9
Suff 125 B11
Fenton Cambs 122 B6
Cumb 240 F2
Lincs 172 E5
Lincs 188 F4
Northumb 263 C11
Stoke 168 G5
Fentonadle Corn 11 F7
Fenton Barns E Loth 281 E10
Fenton Low Stoke 168 F5
Fenton Pits Corn 5 C11
Fenton Town Northumb 263 C11
Fenwick E Ayrs 267 G9
Northumb 242 C3
Northumb 273 G11
S Yorks 198 D5
Feochaig Argyll 255 F8
Feock Corn 3 B8
Feolin Ferry Argyll 274 G5
Ferguslie Park Renfs 267 C9
Ferindonald Highld 295 E8
Feriniquarrie Highld 296 F7
Ferlochan Argyll 289 E11
Fern Angus 292 G6
Bucks 65 B11
Fern Bank Gtr Man 185 B7
Ferndale Kent 52 E5
Rhondda 77 F7
Ferndown Dorset 31 G9
Ferne Wilts 30 C6
Ferness Highld 301 E9
Ferney Green Cumb 221 F8
Fernham Oxon 82 G3
Fernhill Gtr Man 195 E10
Rhondda 77 F8
W Sus 51 E10
Fern Hill Suff 106 B6
Fernhill Gate Gtr Man 195 F7
Fernhill Heath Worcs 117 F7
Fernhurst W Sus 34 B5
Fernie Fife 287 F7
Ferniebrae Aberds 303 D9
Ferniegair S Lanark 268 E4
Ferniehirst Borders 271 G8
Fernilea Highld 294 B5
Fernilee Derbys 185 F8
Fernsplatt Corn 4 G5
Ferrensby N Yorks 215 G7
Ferring W Sus 35 G9
Ferrybridge W Yorks 198 C3
Ferryden Angus 287 B11
Ferryhill Aberdeen 293 C11
Durham 233 E11
Ferry Hill Cambs 139 G7
Ferryhill Station
Durham 234 E2
Ferry Point Highld 309 L7
Ferryside = *Glan-y-Fferi*
Carms 74 C5
Ferryton Highld 300 C6
Fersfield Norf 141 G11
Fersit Highld 290 F5
Feshiebridge Highld 291 C10
Fetcham Sur 50 B6
Fetterangus Aberds 303 D9
Fettercairn Aberds 293 F8
Fetterdale Fife 287 E8
Fettes Highld 300 D5
Fewcott Oxon 101 F10
Fewston N Yorks 205 C9
Fewston Bents N Yorks 205 C9
Ffairfach Carms 94 G2
Ffair-Rhos Ceredig 112 D4
Ffaldybrenin Carms 94 C2
Ffarmers Carms 94 C3
Ffawyddog Powys 78 B2
Ffodun = *Forden* Powys 130 C4
Ffont y gari = *Font y gary*
V Glam 58 F5
Fforddlas Powys 96 D4
Ffordd-las Denb 165 C10
Ffordd-y-Gyfraith
Bridgend 57 E11
Fforest Carms 75 E9
Fforest-fach Swansea 56 B6
Fforest Gôch Neath 76 E2
Ffostrasol Ceredig 93 B7
Ffos-y-ffin Ceredig 111 E8
Ffos-y-go Wrex 166 E4
Ffridd Powys 130 D3
Ffrith Wrex 166 D3
Ffrwd Gwyn 163 D7
Ffwl y mwn = *Fonmon*
V Glam 58 F4
Ffynnon Carms 74 B5
Ffynnon ddrain Carms 93 G8
Ffynnongroes = *Crosswell*
Pembs 92 D2
Ffynnon Gron Pembs 91 F8
Ffynnongroyw Flint 181 E10
Ffynnon Gynydd Powys 96 C3
Ffynnon-oer Ceredig 111 G10
Fickleshole Sur 67 G11
Fidden Argyll 288 G5
Fiddes Aberds 293 E10
Fiddington Glos 99 E8
Som 43 E8
Fiddington Sands Wilts 46 C4
Fiddleford Dorset 30 E4
Fiddler' Green Norf 141 D10
Fiddler's Ferry Mers 193 C11
Warr 183 D9
Fiddler's Green Glos 99 G8
Hereford 97 D11
Fiddlers Hamlet Essex 87 E7
Field Hereford 114 G6
Som 44 E6
Staffs 151 C10
Field Assarts Oxon 82 C4
Field Broughton Cumb 211 C7
Field Common Sur 66 F6
Field Dalling Norf 159 B10
Field Green Kent 38 B3
Field Head Leics 135 B9
Fields End Herts 85 D8
Field's Place Hereford 115 G8
Fifehead Magdalen
Dorset 30 C3
Fifehead Neville Dorset 30 E3
Fifehead St Quintin
Dorset 30 E3
Fife Keith Moray 302 D4
Fifield Oxon 82 B2
Wilts 46 C6
Windsor 66 D2
Fifield Bavant Wilts 31 B8
Figheldean Wilts 47 D7
Filands Wilts 62 B2
Filby Norf 161 G9
Filby Heath Norf 161 G9
Filchampstead Oxon 83 D7
Filey N Yorks 218 C2
Filgrave M Keynes 103 B7
Filham Devon 8 D2
Filkins Oxon 82 E2
Filleigh Devon 25 B11
Devon 26 E2
Fillingham Lincs 188 D6
Fillongley Warks 134 F5
Filmore Hill Hants 33 B11
Filton S Glos 60 D6
Filwood Park Bristol 60 F5
Fimber E Yorks 217 G7
Finavon Angus 287 B8
Finberry Kent 54 F4
Fincastle Ho Perth 291 G10
Finchairn Argyll 275 C10
Fincham Mers 182 C6
Norf 140 B3
Finchampstead
Wokingham 65 G9
Finchdean Hants 34 E2
Finchingfield Essex 106 E3
Finchley London 86 G3
Findern Derbys 152 C6
Findhorn Moray 301 C10
Findhorn Bridge Highld 301 G8
Findochty Moray 302 C4
Findo Gask Perth 286 E4
Findon Aberds 293 D11
W Sus 35 F10
Findon Mains Highld 300 C6
Findon Valley W Sus 35 F10
Findrack Ho Aberds 293 C8
Finedon N Nhants 121 C8
Fineglen Argyll 275 B10
Fine Street Hereford 96 D6
Fingal Street Suff 126 D4
Fingask Aberds 303 G7
Fingerpost Worcs 116 C4
Fingest Bucks 84 G3
Finghall N Yorks 214 B3
Fingland Cumb 239 F7
Dumfries 259 F7
Finglesham Kent 55 C10
Fingringhoe Essex 107 G10
Finham W Mid 118 B6
Finkle Street S Yorks 186 B4
Finlarig Stirling 285 D9
Finmere Oxon 102 E2
Finnart Perth 285 B9
Finney Green Ches E 184 E5
Staffs 168 F3
Finningham Suff 125 D11
Finningley S Yorks 187 B11
Finnygaud Aberds 302 D5
Finsbury London 67 C10
Finsbury Park London 67 B10
Finstall Worcs 117 D9
Finsthwaite Cumb 211 B7
Finstock Oxon 82 B5
Finstown Orkney 314 E3
Fintry Aberds 303 D7
Dundee 287 D8
Stirling 278 D2
Finwood Warks 118 D3
Finzean Aberds 293 D8
Finzean Ho Aberds 293 D7
Fionnphort Argyll 288 G5
Fionnsbhagh W Isles 296 C6
Firbank Cumb 222 G2
Firbeck S Yorks 187 D9
Firby N Yorks 214 B5
N Yorks 216 F4
Firemore Highld 307 L3
Firgrove Gtr Man 196 E2
Firkin Argyll 285 G7
Firle E Sus 23 D7
Firsby Lincs 175 C7
Firsdown Wilts 47 G8
Firs Lane Gtr Man 194 G6
First Coast Highld 307 K4
Firswood Gtr Man 184 B4
Firth Borders 262 E2
Firth Moor Darl 224 C6
Firth Park S Yorks 186 C5
Fir Toll Kent 54 E2
Fir Tree Durham 233 E8
Fir Vale S Yorks 186 C5
Firwood Fold Gtr Man 195 E8
Fishbourne IoW 21 C7
W Sus 22 C4
Fishburn Durham 234 E3
Fishcross Clack 279 B7
Fisherford Aberds 302 F6
Fishermead M Keynes 103 D7
Fisher Place Cumb 220 B6
Fisherrow E Loth 280 G6
Fishersgate Brighton 36 F3
Fishers Green Herts 104 F4
Fisher's Pond Hants 33 C7
Fisherstreet W Sus 50 G3
Fisherton Highld 301 D7
S Ayrs 257 F7
Fisherton de la Mere
Wilts 46 F4
Fisherwick Staffs 134 B3
Fishery Windsor 65 C11
Fishguard = *Abergwaun*
Pembs 91 D9
Fishlake S Yorks 199 E7
Fishleigh Devon 25 F8
Fishleigh Barton Devon 25 C9
Fishleigh Castle Devon 25 F8
Fishley Norf 161 G8
W Mid 133 C10
Fishmere End Lincs 156 B5
Fishponds Bristol 60 D6
Fishpool Glos 98 F3
Gtr Man 195 F10
N Yorks 205 D10
Fishpools Powys 114 D3
Fishtoft Lincs 174 G5
Fishtoft Drove Lincs 174 F4
Fishtown of Usan
Angus 287 B11
Fishwick Borders 273 E8
Lancs 194 B5
Fiskavaig Highld 294 B5
Fiskerton Lincs 189 G8
Notts 172 E2
Fitling E Yorks 209 G11
Fittleton Wilts 46 D6
Fittleworth W Sus 35 D8
Fitton End Cambs 157 G8
Fitton Hill Gtr Man 196 G2
Fitz Shrops 149 F8
Fitzhead Som 27 B10
Fitzwilliam W Yorks 198 D2
Fiunary Highld 289 E8
Five Acres Glos 79 C9
Five Ash Down E Sus 37 C7
Five Ashes E Sus 37 C9
Five Bells Som 42 E5
Five Bridges Hereford 98 B3
Fivecrosses Ches W 183 F8
Fivehead Som 28 C5
Five Houses IoW 20 D4
Five Lane Ends Lancs 202 C6
Fivelanes Corn 11 E10
Five Lanes Mon 78 G6
Five Oak Green Kent 52 D6
Five Oaks W Sus 35 B9
Five Roads Carms 75 D7
Five Ways Warks 118 D4
Five Wents Kent 53 C10
Fixby W Yorks 196 C6
Flackley Ash E Sus 38 C5
Flack's Green Essex 88 B3
Flackwell Heath Bucks 65 B11
Fladbury Worcs 99 B9
Fladbury Cross Worcs 99 B9
Fladda Shetland 312 E5
Fladdabister Shetland 313 K6
Flagg Derbys 169 B10
Flaggoners Green
Hereford 116 G2
Flamborough E Yorks 218 E4
Flamstead Herts 85 C9
Flamstead End Herts 86 E4
Flansham W Sus 35 G7
Flanshaw W Yorks 197 C10
Flappit Spring W Yorks 205 F7
Flasby N Yorks 204 B4
Flash Staffs 169 B8
Flashader Highld 298 D3
Flask Inn N Yorks 227 E8
Flathurst W Sus 35 C7
Flaunden Herts 85 E8
Flawborough Notts 172 G3
Flawith N Yorks 215 F9
Flax Bourton N Som 60 F4
Flaxby N Yorks 206 B3
Flaxholme Derbys 170 G4
Flaxlands Norf 142 E2
Flaxley Glos 79 B11
Flax Moss Lancs 195 C9
Flaxpool Som 42 F6
Flaxton N Yorks 216 G3
Fleckney Leics 136 E2
Flecknoe Warks 119 E10
Fledborough Notts 188 G4
Fleet Dorset 17 E8
Hants 22 C2
Hants 49 C10
Lincs 157 E7
Fleet Downs Kent 68 E5
Fleetend Hants 33 F8
Fleet Hargate Lincs 157 E7
Fleetlands Hants 33 G9
Fleets N Yorks 213 G9
Fleetville Herts 85 D11
Fleetwood Lancs 202 D2
Fleggburgh =
Burgh St Margaret Norf 161 G8
Fleming Field Durham 234 C3
Flemings Kent 55 B9
Flemington V Glam 58 E4
Flemington S Lanark 268 D3
S Lanark 268 G4
Flempton Suff 124 D6
Fleoideabhagh W Isles 296 C6
Fletchersbridge Corn 6 B2
Fletcher's Green Kent 52 C4
Fletchertown Cumb 229 C10
Fletching E Sus 36 C6
Fletching Common
E Sus 36 C6
Fleuchary Highld 309 K7
Fleuchlang Dumfries 237 D8
Fleur-de-lis Caerph 77 F11
Flexbury Corn 24 F2
Flexford Hants 32 C6
Sur 50 D2
Flimby Cumb 228 E6
Flimwell E Sus 53 G8
Flint Flint 182 G2
Flint Cross Cambs 105 C8
Flintham Notts 172 F2
Flint Hill Durham 242 G5
Flint Mountain = *Mynydd Fflint* Flint 182 G2
Flinton E Yorks 209 F10
Flint's Green W Mid 134 G5
Flintsham Hereford 114 F6
Flishinghurst Kent 53 F9
Flitcham Norf 158 D4
Flitholme Cumb 222 B5
Flitton C Beds 103 D11
Flitwick C Beds 103 D10
Flixborough N Lincs 199 D11
Flixborough Stather
N Lincs 199 E11
Flixton Gtr Man 184 C2
N Yorks 217 D10
Suff 142 F6
Flockton W Yorks 197 E8
Flockton Green
W Yorks 197 D8
Flockton Moor W Yorks 197 E8
Flodaigh W Isles 296 F4
Flodden Northumb 263 B10
Flodigarry Highld 298 B4
Floodgates Hereford 114 F5
Flood's Ferry Cambs 139 E7
Flood Street Hants 31 D10
Flookburgh Cumb 211 D7
Flordon Norf 142 D3
Flore W Nhants 120 E2
Florence Stoke 168 G6
Flotterton Northumb 251 C11
Flowers Bottom Bucks 84 F4
Flowers Green E Sus 23 C10
Flowery Field Gtr Man 184 B6
Flowton Suff 107 B11
Fluchter E Dunb 277 G11
Flugarth Shetland 313 G6
Flushdyke W Yorks 197 C9
Flush House W Yorks 196 F6
Flushing Aberds 303 E10
Corn 3 C8
Corn 3 D7
Flyford Flavell Worcs 117 G9
Foals Green Suff 126 C5
Fobbing Thurrock 69 C8
Fochabers Moray 302 D3
Fochriw Caerph 77 D10
Fockerby N Lincs 199 D10
Fodderletter Moray 301 G11
Fodderstone Gap Norf 140 B3
Fodderty Highld 300 D5
Foddington Som 29 B9
Foel Powys 147 G9
Foel-gastell Carms 75 C8
Foffarty Angus 287 C8
Foggathorpe E Yorks 207 F11
Foggbrook Gtr Man 184 D6
Fogo Borders 272 F5
Fogorig Borders 272 F5
Fogrigarth Shetland 313 H4
Fogwatt Moray 302 D2
Foindle Highld 306 E6
Folda Angus 292 G3
Fold Head Lancs 195 D11
Fold Hill Lincs 175 E7
Foldrings S Yorks 186 C3
Fole Staffs 151 B10
Foleshill W Mid 135 G7
Foley Park Worcs 116 B6
Folke Dorset 29 E11
Folkestone Kent 55 F8
Folkingham Lincs 155 C11
Folkington E Sus 23 E9
Folksworth Cambs 138 F2
Folkton N Yorks 217 D11
Folla Rule Aberds 303 F7
Folley Shrops 132 D5
Follifoot N Yorks 206 C2
Follingsby T&W 243 E8
Folly Dorset 30 G2
Pembs 91 G8
Folly Cross Devon 25 F7
Folly Gate Devon 13 B7
Folly Green Essex 106 F6
Fonmon = *Ffwl-y-mwn*
V Glam 58 F4
Fonston Corn 11 C10
Fonthill Bishop Wilts 46 G2
Fonthill Gifford Wilts 46 G2
Fontmell Magna Dorset 30 D5
Fontmell Parva Dorset 30 E4
Fontwell W Sus 35 F7
Font-y-gary = *Ffont-y-gari*
V Glam 58 F5
Foodieash Fife 287 F7
Foolow Derbys 185 F11
Footbridge Glos 99 F10
Footherley Staffs 134 C2
Footrid Worcs 116 C3
Foots Cray London 68 E3
Forbestown Aberds 292 B5
Force Forge Cumb 220 G6
Force Green Kent 52 B2
Force Mills Cumb 220 G6
Forcett N Yorks 224 C3
Ford Argyll 275 C9
Bucks 84 D3
Derbys 186 E6
Devon 8 E2
Devon 8 G5
Devon 24 C6
Devon 28 G2
Glos 99 F11
Hereford 115 F10
Kent 71 F8
Mers 182 B4
Northumb 263 B10
Pembs 91 F9
Plym 7 D9
Shrops 149 G8
Som 27 B9
Som 44 C5
Staffs 169 E9
Wilts 47 G7
Wilts 61 E10
W Sus 35 G7
Forda Devon 12 C6
Devon 40 F3
Fordbridge W Mid 134 F3
Fordcombe Kent 52 E4
Fordell Fife 280 D3
Forden = *Ffodun* Powys 130 C4
Ford End Essex 87 B11
Essex 105 E9
Forder Corn 7 D8
Forder Green Devon 8 B5
Ford Forge Northumb 263 B10
Fordgate Som 43 G10
Ford Green Lancs 202 D5
Stoke 168 E5
Fordham Cambs 124 C2
Essex 107 F8
Norf 140 D2
Fordham Heath Essex 107 F8
Ford Heath Shrops 149 G8
Ford Hill Northumb 263 B11
Fordhouses W Mid 133 C8
Fordingbridge Hants 31 E10
Fordington Lincs 190 G6
Fordley T&W 243 C7
Fordon E Yorks 217 D10
Fordoun Aberds 293 F9
Ford's Green E Sus 36 B6
Suff 125 D11
Fordstreet Essex 107 F8
Ford Street Som 27 D11
Fordton Devon 14 B2
Fordwater Devon 28 G4
Fordwells Oxon 82 C4
Fordwich Kent 55 B7
Fordyce Aberds 302 C5
Forebridge Staffs 151 E8
Foredale N Yorks 212 F6
Forehill S Ayrs 257 E8
Foreland Fields IoW 21 D9
Foreland Ho Argyll 274 G3
Foremark Derbys 152 D6
Forest Becks Lancs 203 C11
Forestburn Gate
Northumb 252 D3
Forest Coal Pit Mon 96 G5
Forestdale London 67 G11
Foresterseat Moray 301 D11
Forest Gate Hants 33 E10
London 68 C2
Forest Green Glos 80 E4
Sur 50 E6
Forest Hall Cumb 221 E10
T&W 243 D7
Forest Head Cumb 240 F3
Forest Hill London 67 E11
Oxon 83 D9
Wilts 63 F8
Forest Holme Lancs 195 B10
Forest-in-Teesdale
Durham 232 F3
Forest Lane Head
N Yorks 206 B2
Forest Lodge Argyll 284 C6
Highld 292 B2
Perth 291 F11
Forest Mill Clack 279 C9
Forest Moor N Yorks 206 B2
Forestreet Devon 24 E5
Forest Row E Sus 52 G2
Forestside W Sus 34 E3
Forest Side IoW 20 D5
Forest Town Notts 171 C9
Forewoods Common
Wilts 61 G10
Forfar Angus 287 B8
Forgandenny Perth 286 F4
Forge Corn 4 F3
Powys 128 D5
Forge Hammer Torf 78 F3
Forge Side Torf 78 D2
Forgewood N Lanark 268 D4
Forgie Moray 302 D3
Forglen Ho Aberds 302 D6
Forgue Aberds 302 E6
Forhill Worcs 117 B11
Formby Mers 193 F10
Forncett End Norf 142 E2
Forncett St Mary Norf 142 E3
Forncett St Peter Norf 142 E3
Forneth Perth 286 C4
Fornham All Saints Suff 124 D6
Fornham St Genevieve
Suff 124 D6
Fornham St Martin Suff 125 D7
Fornighty Highld 301 D9
Forrabury Corn 11 C7
Forres Moray 301 D10
Forrestfield N Lanark 269 B7
Forrest Lodge Dumfries 246 F3
Forry's Green Essex 106 E5
Forsbrook Staffs 169 G7
Forse Highld 310 F6
Forse Ho Highld 310 F6
Forshaw Heath Warks 117 C11
Forsinain Highld 310 E3
Forsinard Highld 310 E2
Forsinard Station Highld 310 E2
Forstal Kent 53 B8
Forston Dorset 17 B9
Fort Augustus Highld 290 C5
Forteviot Perth 286 F4
Fort George Highld 301 D7
Forth S Lanark 269 E8
Forthampton Glos 99 E7
Forthay Glos 80 F2
Forth Road Bridge Edin 280 F2
Fortingall Perth 285 C11
Fortis Green London 67 B9
Fort Matilda Invclyd 276 F5
Forton Hants 33 G10
Hants 48 E2
Lancs 202 C5
Shrops 149 F8
Som 28 F4
Staffs 150 E5
Forton Heath Shrops 149 F8
Fortrie Aberds 302 E6
Aberds 303 D7
Fortrose Highld 301 D7
Fortuneswell Dorset 17 G9
Fort William Highld 290 F3
Forty Green Bucks 84 E3
Bucks 84 G6
Forty Hill London 86 F4
Forward Green Suff 125 F11
Forwood Glos 80 E5
Fosbury Wilts 47 B10
Foscot Oxon 100 G4
Foscote Bucks 102 D4
Wilts 61 D11
W Nhants 102 B3
Fosdyke Lincs 156 C6
Fosdyke Bridge Lincs 156 C6
Foss Perth 285 B11
Foss Cross Glos 81 D9
Fossebridge Glos 81 C9
Fostall Kent 70 G5
Fosten Green Kent 53 F10
Fosterhouses S Yorks 199 E7
Foster's Booth
W Nhants 120 G3
Foster's Green Worcs 117 D9
Foster Street Essex 87 D7
Foston Derbys 152 C3
Leics 136 D2
Lincs 172 G5
N Yorks 216 F3
Foston on the Wolds
E Yorks 209 B8
Fotherby Lincs 190 C4
Fothergill Cumb 228 E6
Fotheringhay N Nhants 137 E11
Foubister Orkney 314 F5
Foul Anchor Cambs 157 F9
Foulbridge Cumb 230 B4
Foulby W Yorks 197 D11
Foulden Borders 273 D8
Norf 140 D5
Foul End Warks 134 E4
Foulford Hants 31 F11
Foulis Castle Highld 300 C5
Foul Mile E Sus 23 B10
Foulride Green E Sus 23 E9
Foulridge Lancs 204 E3
Foulsham Norf 159 E10
Foundry Corn 2 B3
Foundry Hill Norf 159 D11
Fountain Bridgend 57 E11
Fountainhall Borders 271 F8
Four Ashes Bucks 84 F5
Staffs 132 F6
Staffs 133 B8
Suff 125 C10
W Mid 118 B3
Four Crosses Powys 129 B11
Four Crosses *continued*
Powys 148 F5
Staffs 133 B9
Wrex 166 E3
Four Elms Devon 28 F3
Kent 52 D3
Four Foot Som 44 G5
Four Forks Som 43 F8
Four Gates Gtr Man 194 F6
Four Gotes Cambs 157 F9
Four Houses Corner
W Berks 64 F6
Four Lane End S Yorks 197 G9
Fourlane Ends Derbys 170 D5
Four Lane Ends
Blackburn 195 B7
Ches W 167 C9
Gtr Man 195 E9
W Yorks 205 G8
Four Lanes Corn 2 B5
Fourlanes End Ches E 168 D4
Four Marks Hants 49 G7
Four Mile Bridge
Anglesey 178 F3
Four Mile Elm Glos 80 C4
Four Oaks E Sus 38 C5
Glos 98 F3
Kent 70 G3
W Mid 134 D2
W Mid 134 G4
Four Oaks Park W Mid 134 D2
Fourpenny Highld 311 K2
Four Points W Berks 64 D5
Four Pools Worcs 99 C10
Four Roads Carms 74 D6
IoM 192 F3
Fourstones Northumb 241 D9
Four Throws Kent 38 B3
Four Wantz Essex 87 C10
Four Wents Kent 53 F9
Fovant Wilts 31 B8
Foveran Aberds 303 G9
Fowey Corn 6 E2
Fowler's Plot Som 43 F10
Fowley Common Warr 183 B11
Fowlis Angus 287 D7
Fowlis Wester Perth 286 E3
Fowlmere Cambs 105 B8
Fownhope Hereford 97 E11
Foxash Estate Essex 107 E11
Foxbar Renfs 267 C9
Foxbury London 68 E2
Foxcombe Hill Oxon 83 E7
Fox Corner C Beds 103 F8
Sur 50 C3
Foxcote Glos 81 B8
Som 45 B8
Foxcotte Hants 47 D10
Foxdale IoM 192 E3
Foxdown Hants 48 C4
Foxearth Essex 106 C6
Foxendown Kent 69 F7
Foxfield Cumb 210 B4
Foxford W Mid 135 G7
Foxham Wilts 62 D3
Fox Hatch Essex 87 F9
Fox Hill Bath 61 G9
Hereford 98 B3
Foxhills Hants 32 E4
Foxhole Corn 5 E9
Norf 142 D4
Swansea 57 C7
Fox Hole Swansea 56 D5
Foxholes N Yorks 217 E10
Fox Holes Wilts 45 E11
Foxhunt Green E Sus 23 B8
Fox Lane Hants 49 B11
Foxley Hereford 97 B8
Norf 159 E10
Staffs 168 E3
Wilts 61 B11
Foxlydiate Worcs 117 D10
Fox Royd W Yorks 197 D8
Fox Street Essex 107 F10
Foxt Staffs 169 F8
Foxton Cambs 105 B8
Durham 234 F3
Leics 136 E4
N Yorks 225 F8
Foxup N Yorks 213 D7
Foxwist Green Ches W 167 B10
Foxwood Shrops 116 B2
Foy Hereford 97 F11
Foyers Highld 300 G4
Foynesfield Highld 301 D8
Fraddam Corn 2 C3
Fraddon Corn 5 D8
Fradley Staffs 152 G3
Fradley Junction Staffs 152 G2
Fradswell Staffs 151 C9
Fraisthorpe E Yorks 218 G3
Framfield E Sus 37 C7
Framingham Earl Norf 142 C5
Framingham Pigot Norf 142 C5
Framlingham Suff 126 E5
Frampton Dorset 17 B8
Lincs 156 B6
Frampton Cotterell
S Glos 61 C7
Frampton Court Glos 99 E10
Frampton End S Glos 61 C7
Frampton Mansell Glos 80 E6
Frampton on Severn
Glos 80 D2
Frampton West End
Lincs 174 G3
Framsden Suff 126 F3
Framwellgate Moor
Durham 233 C11
France Lynch Glos 80 E6
Franche Worcs 116 B6
Frandley Ches W 183 F10
Frankby Mers 182 D2
Frankfort Norf 160 E6
Franklands Gate
Hereford 97 B10
Frankley Worcs 133 G9
Frankley Green Worcs 133 G9
Frankley Hill Worcs 117 B9
Frank's Bridge Powys 114 F2
Frankton Warks 119 C8
Frankwell Shrops 149 G9
Frans Green Norf 160 G2
Frant E Sus 52 F5
Fraserburgh Aberds 303 C9
Frating Essex 107 G11
Frating Green Essex 107 G11
Fratton Ptsmth 21 B9
Freasley Warks 134 D4
Freathy Corn 7 E8
Frecheville S Yorks 186 E5
Freckenham Suff 124 C3
Freckleton Lancs 194 B2
Fredley Sur 51 C7
Freebirch Derbys 186 G4
Freeby Leics 154 E6
Freefolk Hants 48 D3
Freehay Staffs 169 G8
Freeland Oxon 82 C6
Renfs 267 B9
Freeland Corner Norf 160 F3
Freemantle Soton 32 E6
Freester Shetland 313 H6
Freethorpe Norf 143 B8
Free Town Gtr Man 195 E10
Freezy Water London 86 F5
Freiston Lincs 174 G5
Freiston Shore Lincs 174 G5
Fremington Devon 40 G4
N Yorks 223 F10
Frenchay S Glos 60 D6
Frenchbeer Devon 13 D9
Frenches Green Essex 106 G4
Frenchmoor Hants 32 B3
French Street Kent 52 C3
Frenchwood Lancs 194 B4
Frenich Stirling 285 G8
Frensham Sur 49 E10
Frenze Norf 142 G2
Fresgoe Highld 310 C3
Freshbrook Swindon 62 C6
Freshfield Mers 193 F9
Freshford Bath 61 G9
Freshwater IoW 20 D2
Freshwater Bay IoW 20 D2
Freshwater East Pembs 73 F8
Fressingfield Suff 126 B5
Freston Suff 108 D3
Freswick Highld 310 C7
Fretherne Glos 80 D2
Frettenham Norf 160 F4
Freuchie Fife 286 G6
Freuchies Angus 292 G4
Freystrop Pembs 73 C7
Friarn Som 43 F7
Friar Park W Mid 133 E10
Friars Cliff BCP 19 C9
Friar's Gate E Sus 52 G3
Friar's Hill E Sus 38 E5
Friarton Perth 286 E5
Friday Bridge Cambs 139 C9
Friday Hill London 86 G5
Friday Street E Sus 23 E10
Suff 126 G6
Suff 127 E7
Sur 50 D6
Fridaythorpe E Yorks 208 B3
Friendly W Yorks 196 C5
Friern Barnet London 86 G3
Friesland Argyll 288 D3
Friesthorpe Lincs 189 E9
Frieston Lincs 172 F6
Frieth Bucks 84 G3
Frieze Hill Som 28 B2
Friezeland Notts 171 E7
Frilford Oxon 82 F6
Frilford Heath Oxon 82 F6
Frilsham W Berks 64 E4
Frimley Sur 49 B11
Frimley Green Sur 49 B11
Frimley Ridge Sur 49 B11
Frindsbury Medway 69 E8
Fring Norf 158 C4
Fringford Oxon 102 F2
Friningham Kent 53 B10
Frinkle Green Essex 106 C4
Frinsted Kent 53 B11
Frinton-on-Sea Essex 108 G4
Friockheim Angus 287 C9
Friog Gwyn 146 G2
Frisby Leics 136 C4
Frisby on the Wreake
Leics 154 F3
Friskney Lincs 175 D7
Friskney Eaudyke Lincs 175 D7
Friskney Tofts Lincs 175 E7
Friston E Sus 23 F8
Suff 127 E8
Fritchley Derbys 170 E5
Frith Kent 54 B2
Fritham Hants 32 E2
Frith Bank Lincs 174 F4
Frith Common Worcs 116 D3
Frithelstock Devon 25 D7
Frithelstock Stone Devon 25 D7
Frithend Hants 49 F10
Frith-hill Bucks 84 E6
Frith Hill Sur 50 E3
Frithsden Herts 85 D8
Frithville Lincs 174 E4
Frittenden Kent 53 E10
Frittiscombe Devon 8 G6
Fritton Norf 142 E4
Norf 143 C9
Norf 161 F8
Fritwell Oxon 101 F10
Frizinghall W Yorks 205 F8
Frizington Cumb 219 B10
Frizzeler's Green Suff 124 E5
Frobost W Isles 297 J3
Frocester Glos 80 E3
Frochas Powys 148 G5
Frodesley Shrops 131 C10
Frodingham N Lincs 199 E11
Frodsham Ches W 183 F8
Frogden Borders 263 D7
Frog End Cambs 123 F10
Cambs 123 G8
Froggatt Derbys 186 F2
Froghall Staffs 169 F8
Frogham Hants 31 E11
Kent 55 C9
Froghole Kent 52 C2
Frogholt Kent 55 F7
Frogland Cross S Glos 60 C6
Frog Moor Swansea 56 C3
Frogmore Devon 8 G5
Hants 33 C11
Hants 49 B10
Herts 85 E11
Frognal S Ayrs 257 D8
Frognall Lincs 156 G3
Frogpool Corn 4 G5
Frogs' Green Essex 105 D11
Frogshall Norf 160 B5
Frogwell Corn 6 B6
Frolesworth Leics 135 E10
Frome Som 45 D9
Fromebridge Glos 80 D3
Fromefield Som 45 D9
Frome St Quintin Dorset 29 G9
Fromes Hill Hereford 98 B3
Fromington Hereford 97 B10
Fron Denb 165 B9
Gwyn 145 B7
Gwyn 163 D8
Powys 113 D11
Powys 129 C8
Powys 130 C4
Powys 130 D3
Shrops 148 B5
Fron-Bache Denb 166 G2
Froncysyllte Wrex 166 G3
Fron-dêg Wrex 166 F3
Frongoch Gwyn 147 B8
Fron Isaf Wrex 166 G3
Frost Devon 26 F3
Frostenden Suff 143 G9
Frostenden Corner Suff 143 G9
Frosterley Durham 232 D6
Frost Hill N Som 60 G2

Frostlane Hants 32 F6
Frost Row Norf 141 C10
Frotoft Orkney 314 D4
Froxfield C Beds 103 E9
Wilts 63 F9
Froxfield Green Hants 34 B2
Froyle Hants 49 E9
Fryern Hill Hants 32 C6
Fryerning Essex 87 E10
Fryerns Essex 69 B8
Fryton N Yorks 216 E3
Fugglestone St Peter
Wilts 46 G6
Fulbeck Lincs 172 E6
Northumb 252 F5
Fulbourn Cambs 123 F10
Fulbrook Oxon 82 C3
Fulflood Hants 33 B7
Fulford Som 28 B2
Staffs 151 B9
York 207 D8
Fulham London 67 D8
Fulking W Sus 36 E2
Fullabrook Devon 40 E4
Fullarton Glasgow 268 C2
N Ayrs 257 B8
Fuller's End Essex 105 F10
Fuller's Moor Ches W 167 E7
Fuller Street Essex 88 B2
Fullerton Hants 47 F11
Fulletby Lincs 190 G3
Fullshaw S Yorks 197 G8
Full Sutton E Yorks 207 B10
Fullwell Cross London 86 G6
Fullwood E Ayrs 267 E8
Gtr Man 196 F2
Fulmer Bucks 66 B3
Fulmodestone Norf 159 C9
Fulneck W Yorks 205 G10
Fulnetby Lincs 189 F9
Fulney Lincs 156 E5
Fulready Warks 100 B5
Fulshaw Park Ches E 184 E4
Fulstone W Yorks 197 F7
Fulstow Lincs 190 B4
Fulthorpe Stockton 234 G4
Fulwell Oxon 101 G7
T&W 243 F9
Fulwood Lancs 202 G6
Som 28 C2
S Yorks 186 D4
Fundenhall Norf 142 D3
Fundenhall Street Norf 142 D2
Funtington W Sus 22 B3
Funtley Hants 33 F9
Funtullich Perth 285 E11
Funzie Shetland 312 D8
Furley Devon 28 G3
Furnace Argyll 284 G4
Carms 74 E6
Carms 75 E8
Ceredig 128 D3
Highld 299 B9
Furnace End Warks 134 E4
Furnace Green W Sus 51 F9
Furnace Wood W Sus 51 F11
Furneaux Pelham Herts 105 F8
Furner's Green E Sus 36 B6
Furness Vale Derbys 185 E8
Furneux Pelham Herts 105 F8
Furnham Som 28 F4
Further Ford End Essex 105 E9
Further Quarter Kent 53 F11
Furtho W Nhants 102 C5
Furze Devon 25 B10
Furzebrook Dorset 18 E4
Furzedown Hants 32 B5
London 67 E9
Furzehill Devon 41 D8
Dorset 31 G8
Furze Hill Hants 31 E11
Furzeley Corner Hants 33 E11
Furze Platt Windsor 65 C11
Furzey Lodge Hants 32 G5
Furzley Hants 32 D3
Furzton M Keynes 102 D6
Fyfett Som 28 E2
Fyfield Essex 87 D9
Glos 82 E2
Hants 47 D9
Oxon 82 F6
Wilts 63 F7
Wilts 63 G7
Fylingthorpe N Yorks 227 D8
Fyning W Sus 34 C4
Fyvie Aberds 303 F7

G

Gabalfa Cardiff 59 D7
Gabhsann bho Dheas
W Isles 304 C6
Gabhsann bho Thuath
W Isles 304 C6
Gable Head Hants 21 B10
Gablon Highld 309 K7
Gabroc Hill E Ayrs 267 E9
Gadbrook Sur 51 D8
Gaddesby Leics 154 G3
Gadebridge Herts 85 D8
Gadfa Anglesey 179 D7
Gadfield Elm Worcs 98 E5
Gadlas Shrops 149 B7
Gadlys Rhondda 77 E7
Gadshill Kent 69 E8
Gaer Newport 59 B9
Powys 96 G3
Gaer-fawr Mon 78 F6
Gaerllwyd Mon 78 F6
Gaerwen Anglesey 179 G7
Gagingwell Oxon 101 F8
Gaick Lodge Highld 291 E9
Gailey Staffs 151 G8
Gailey Wharf Staffs 151 G8
Gainfield Oxon 82 F4
Gainford Durham 224 B3
Gain Hill Kent 53 D8
Gainsborough Lincs 188 C4
Suff 108 C3
Gainsford End Essex 106 D4
Gairletter Argyll 276 E3
Gairloch Highld 299 B8
Gairlochy Highld 290 E3
Gairney Bank Perth 280 B2
Gairnshiel Lodge
Aberds 292 C4
Gaisgill Cumb 222 D2
Gaitsgill Cumb 230 B3
Galadean Borders 271 G11
Galashiels Borders 261 B11
Galdlys Flint 182 G2
Gale Gtr Man 196 D2
Galgate Lancs 202 B5
Galhampton Som 29 B10
Gallaberry Dumfries 247 G11
Gallachoille Argyll 275 E8
Gallanach Argyll 288 C4
Argyll 289 G10
Highld 294 G6
Gallantry Bank Ches E 167 E8
Gallatown Fife 280 C5
Galley Common Warks 134 E6
Galleyend Essex 88 E2
Galley Hill Cambs 122 D6
Lincs 190 F6
Galleywood Essex 88 E2
Galligill Cumb 231 B11
Gallin Perth 285 C9
Gallovie Highld 291 E7
Gallowfauld Angus 287 C8
Gallowhill Glasgow 267 D11
Renfs 267 B9
Gallowhills Aberds 303 D10
Gallows Corner London 87 G8
Gallowsgreen Torf 78 D3
Gallows Green Essex 106 F2
Essex 107 F8
Staffs 169 G9
Worcs 117 E8
Gallows Inn Derbys 171 G7
Gallowstree Common
Oxon 65 C7
Galltair Highld 295 C10
Galltegfa Denb 165 D10
Gallt Melyd = *Meliden*
Denb 181 E9
Gallt-y-foel Gwyn 163 C9
Gallypot Street E Sus 52 F3
Galmington Som 28 C2
Galmisdale Highld 294 G6
Galmpton Devon 8 G3
Torbay 9 D7
Galon Uchaf M Tydf 77 D9
Galphay N Yorks 214 E5
Galston E Ayrs 258 B2
Galtrigill Highld 296 F7
Gam Corn 11 F7
Gamble Hill W Yorks 205 G11
Gamblesby Cumb 231 D8
Gamble's Green Essex 88 C3
Gamelsby Cumb 239 G7
Gamesley Derbys 185 C8
Gamlingay Cambs 122 G4
Gamlingay Cinques
Cambs 122 G4
Gamlingay Great Heath
Cambs 122 G4
Gammaton Devon 25 B7
Gammaton Moor Devon 25 C7
Gammersgill N Yorks 213 C11
Gamston Notts 154 B2
Notts 188 F2
Ganarew Hereford 79 B8
Ganavan Argyll 289 F10
Ganders Green Glos 98 G4
Gang Corn 6 B6
Ganllwyd Gwyn 146 E4
Gannetts Dorset 30 D3
Gannochy Angus 293 F7
Perth 286 E5
Gansclet Highld 310 E7
Ganstead E Yorks 209 G9
Ganthorpe N Yorks 216 E3
Ganton N Yorks 217 D9
Gants Hill London 68 B2
Ganwick Corner Herts 86 F3
Gaodhail Argyll 289 F8
Gappah Devon 14 F3
Garafad Highld 298 C4
Garamor Highld 295 F8
Garbat Highld 300 C4
Garbhallt Argyll 275 D11
Garboldisham Norf 141 G10
Garbole Highld 301 G7
Garden City Bl Gwent 77 D11
Flint 166 B4
Gardeners Green
Wokingham 65 F10
Gardenstown Aberds 303 C7
Garden Village Swansea 56 B5
S Yorks 186 B3
Wrex 166 E4
W Yorks 206 G4
Garderhouse Shetland 313 J5
Gardham E Yorks 208 E5
Gardie Shetland 312 D7
Gardin Shetland 312 G6
Gare Hill Som 45 E9
Garelochhead Argyll 276 C4
Garford Oxon 82 F6
Garforth W Yorks 206 G4
Gargrave N Yorks 204 C4
Gargunnock Stirling 278 C4
Garizim Conwy 179 F11
Garker Corn 5 E10
Garlandhayes Devon 27 D11
Garlands Cumb 239 G10
Garleffin S Ayrs 244 G3
Garlic Street Norf 142 G4
Garlieston Dumfries 236 E6
Garliford Devon 26 B3
Garlinge Kent 71 F10
Garlinge Green Kent 54 C6
Garlogie Aberds 293 C9
Garmelow Staffs 150 D5
Garmond Aberds 303 D8
Garmondsway Durham 234 E2
Garmony Argyll 289 E8
Garmouth Moray 302 C3
Garmston Shrops 132 B2
Garn Powys 130 G2
Garnant Carms 75 C11
Garndiffaith Torf 78 E3
Garndolbenmaen Gwyn 163 G7
Garnedd Conwy 164 E2
Garnett Bridge Cumb 221 F10
Garnetts Essex 87 B10
Garnfadryn Gwyn 144 C5
Garnkirk N Lanark 268 B3
Garnlydan Bl Gwent 77 C11
Garnsgate Lincs 157 E8
Garnswllt Swansea 75 D10
Garn-swllt Swansea 75 D10
Garn-yr-erw Torf 78 C2
Garrabost W Isles 304 E7
Garrachra Argyll 275 E11
Garra Eallabus Argyll 274 F3
Garralburn Moray 302 D4
Garraron Argyll 275 C9
Garras Corn 2 E6
Garreg Flint 181 F10
Gwyn 163 G10
Garrets Green W Mid 134 F2
Garrick Perth 286 F2
Garrigill Cumb 231 C10
Garrison Stirling 285 G7
Garriston N Yorks 224 G3
Garroch Dumfries 246 G3
Garrogie Lodge Highld 291 B7
Garros Highld 298 C4
Garrow Perth 286 C2
Garrowhill Glasgow 268 C3
Garrygualach Highld 290 C3
Garryhorn Dumfries 246 E2
Garsdale Cumb 212 B4
Garsdale Head Cumb 222 G5
Garsdon Wilts 62 B3
Garshall Green Staffs 151 C9
Garsington Oxon 83 E9
Garstang Lancs 202 D5
Garston Herts 85 F10
Garston *continued*
Mers 182 E6
Garswood Mers 183 B9
Gartachoil Stirling 277 C10
Gartbreck Argyll 254 B3
Gartcosh N Lanark 268 B3
Garth Bridgend 57 C11
Ceredig 128 G2
Flint 181 E10
Gwyn 179 G9
Newport 59 B9
Newport 78 G4
Perth 285 B11
Powys 95 B9
Powys 114 C5
Shetland 313 H4
Shetland 313 H6
Wrex 166 G3
Garthamlock Glasgow 268 B3
Garthbeg Highld 291 B7
Garthbrengy Powys 95 E10
Garthdee Aberdeen 293 C11
Gartheli Ceredig 111 F11
Garthmyl Powys 130 D3
Garthorpe Leics 154 E6
N Lincs 199 D11
Garth Owen Powys 130 E2
Garth Row Cumb 221 F10
Garth Trevor Wrex 166 G3
Gartlea N Lanark 268 C5
Gartloch Glasgow 268 B3
Gartly Aberds 302 F5
Gartmore Stirling 277 B10
Gartmore Ho Stirling 277 B10
Gartnagrenach Argyll 255 B8
Gartness N Lanark 268 C5
Stirling 277 D10
Gartocharn W Dunb 277 D8
Garton E Yorks 209 F11
Garton-on-the-Wolds
E Yorks 208 B5
Gartsherrie N Lanark 268 B4
Gartur Stirling 277 B11
Gartymore Highld 311 H4
Garvald E Loth 281 G11
Garvamore Highld 291 D7
Garvard Argyll 274 D4
Garvault Hotel Highld 308 F7
Garve Highld 300 C3
Garvestone Norf 141 B10
Garvock Aberds 293 F9
Invclyd 276 G5
Garvock Hill Fife 280 D2
Garway Hereford 97 G9
Garway Hill Hereford 97 F8
Gaskan Highld 289 B9
Gasper Wilts 45 G9
Gastard Wilts 61 F11
Gasthorpe Norf 141 G9
Gaston Green Essex 87 B7
Gatacre Park Shrops 132 F5
Gatcombe IoW 20 D5
Gateacre Mers 182 D6
Gatebeck Cumb 211 B10
Gate Burton Lincs 188 E4
Gateford Notts 187 E9
Gateford Common
Notts 187 E9
Gateforth N Yorks 198 B5
Gatehead E Ayrs 257 B9
Gate Helmsley N Yorks 207 B9
Gatehouse Northumb 251 F7
Gatehouse of Fleet
Dumfries 237 D8
Gatelawbridge
Dumfries 247 D10
Gateley Norf 159 E9
Gatenby N Yorks 214 B6
Gatesgarth Cumb 220 B3
Gateshead T&W 243 E7
Gatesheath Ches W 167 C7
Gateside Aberds 293 B8
Angus 287 C8
Dumfries 248 E4
E Renf 267 D9
Fife 286 G5
N Ayrs 267 E7
Shetland 312 F4
Gatewen Wrex 166 E4
Gatherley Devon 12 E3
Gathurst Gtr Man 194 F4
Gatlas Newport 78 G4
Gatley End Cambs 104 C5
Gtr Man 184 D4
Gatton Sur 51 C9
Gattonside Borders 262 B2
Gatwick Glos 80 C2
Gatwick Airport W Sus 51 E9
Gaufron Powys 113 D9
Gaulby Leics 136 C3
Gauldry Fife 287 E7
Gauntons Bank Ches E 167 F9
Gaunt's Common Dorset 31 F8
Gaunt's Earthcott S Glos 60 C6
Gaunt's End Essex 105 F10
Gautby Lincs 189 G11
Gavinton Borders 272 E5
Gawber S Yorks 197 F10
Gawcott Bucks 102 E3
Gawsworth Ches E 168 B5
Gawthorpe W Yorks 197 C9
W Yorks 197 D7
Gawthrop Cumb 212 B3
Gawthwaite Cumb 210 C5
Gay Bowers Essex 88 E3
Gaydon Warks 119 G7
Gayfield Orkney 314 A4
Gayhurst M Keynes 103 B7
Gayle N Yorks 213 B7
Gayles N Yorks 224 D2
Gay Street W Sus 35 C9
Gayton Mers 182 E3
Norf 158 F4
Staffs 151 D9
W Nhants 120 G4
Gayton Engine Lincs 191 D7
Gayton le Marsh Lincs 190 E6
Gayton le Wold Lincs 190 D2
Gayton Thorpe Norf 158 F4
Gaywood Norf 158 E2
Gaza Shetland 312 F5
Gazeley Suff 124 E4
Geanies House Highld 301 B8
Gearraidh Bhailteas
W Isles 297 J3
Gearraidh Bhaird
W Isles 304 F5
Gearraidh Dubh W Isles 296 F4
Gearraidh na h-Aibhne
W Isles 304 E4
Gearraidh na Monadh
W Isles 297 K3
Geàrraidh Sheilidh
W Isles 297 J3
Geary Highld 298 C2
Geat Wolford Warks 100 E4
Geddes House Highld 301 D8
Gedding Suff 125 F9
Geddington N Nhants 137 G7
Gedgrave Hall Suff 109 B8
Gedintailor Highld 295 B7
Gedling Notts 171 G10
Gedney Lincs 157 E8
Gedney Broadgate Lincs 157 E8
Gedney Drove End
Lincs 157 D9
Gedney Dyke Lincs 157 D8
Gedney Hill Lincs 156 G6
Gee Cross Gtr Man 185 C7
Geeston Rutland 137 C9
Gegin Wrex 166 E3
Geilston Argyll 276 F6
Geinas Denb 165 B9
Geirinis W Isles 297 G3
Geise Highld 310 C5
Geisiadar W Isles 304 E3
Geldeston Norf 143 E7
Gell Conwy 164 B5
Gelli Pembs 73 B9
Rhondda 77 G7
Gellideg M Tydf 77 D8
Gellifor Denb 165 C10
Gelligaer Caerph 77 F10
Gelli-gaer Neath 57 C9
Gelligroes Caerph 77 G11
Gelli-hôf Caerph 77 F11
Gellilydan Gwyn 146 B3
Gellinud Neath 76 E2
Gellinudd Neath 76 E2
Gellyburn Perth 286 D4
Gellygron Neath 76 E2
Gellywen Carms 92 G5
Gelsmoor Leics 153 F8
Gelston Dumfries 237 D9
Lincs 172 G6
Gembling E Yorks 209 B8
Gemini Warr 183 C9
Gendros Swansea 56 B6
Genesis Green Suff 124 F4
Gentleshaw Staffs 151 G11
Geocrab W Isles 305 J3
Georgefield Dumfries 249 E7
George Green Bucks 66 C4
Georgeham Devon 40 F3
George Nympton Devon 26 C2
Georgetown Bl Gwent 77 D10
Georgia Corn 1 B5
Gergask Highld 291 D8
Gerlan Gwyn 163 B10
Germansweek Devon 12 C4
Germiston Glasgow 268 B2
Germoe Corn 2 D3
Gernon Bushes Essex 87 E7
Gerrans Corn 3 B9
Gerrard's Bromley
Staffs 150 C5
Gerrards Cross Bucks 66 B4
Gerrick Redcar 226 C4
Geseilfa Powys 129 E8
Gestingthorpe Essex 106 D6
Gesto Ho Highld 294 B5
Geuffordd Powys 148 G4
Geufron Denb 166 G2
Gibbet Hill Warks 135 G10
W Mid 118 C6
Gibb Hill Ches W 183 F10
Gibbshill Dumfries 237 B9
Gib Heath W Mid 133 F11
Gibraltar Bedford 103 B10
Bucks 84 C3
Kent 55 F8
Gibshill Invclyd 276 G6
Gibsmere Notts 172 F2
Giddeahall Wilts 61 E11
Giddy Green Dorset 18 D2
Gidea Park London 68 B4
Gidleigh Devon 13 D9
Giffard Park M Keynes 103 C7
Giffnock E Renf 267 D11
Gifford E Loth 271 B10
Giffordland N Ayrs 266 F5
Giffordtown Fife 286 F6
Gigg Gtr Man 195 F10
Giggetty Staffs 133 E7
Giggleswick N Yorks 212 G6
Gignog Pembs 91 G7
Gilberdyke E Yorks 199 B10
Gilbert's Coombe Corn 4 G3
Gilbert's End Worcs 98 C6
Gilbert's Green Warks 118 C2
Gilbertstone W Mid 134 G2
Gilbert Street Hants 49 G7
Gilchriston E Loth 271 B9
Gilcrux Cumb 229 D8
Gildersome W Yorks 197 B8
Gildersome Street
W Yorks 197 B8
Gildingwells S Yorks 187 D9
Gilesgate Durham 233 C11
Gilesgate Moor
Durham 233 C11
Gileston V Glam 58 F4
Gilfach Caerph 77 F11
Hereford 96 E6
Gilfach Goch Rhondda 58 B3
Gilfachrheda Ceredig 111 F8
Gilgarran Cumb 228 G6
Gill N Yorks 204 E5
Gillamoor N Yorks 216 B3
Gillan Corn 3 E7
Gillar's Green Mers 183 B7
Gillbank Cumb 221 F7
Gillbent Gtr Man 184 E5
Gillen Highld 298 D2
Gillesbie Dumfries 248 E5
Gilling East N Yorks 216 D2
Gillingham Dorset 30 B4
Medway 69 F9
Norf 143 E8
Gilling West N Yorks 224 D3
Gillmoss Mers 182 B6
Gillock Highld 310 D6
Gillow Heath Staffs 168 D5
Gills Highld 310 B7
Gill's Green Kent 53 G9
Gillway Staffs 134 C4
Gilmanscleuch Borders 261 E8
Gilmerton Edin 270 B5
Perth 286 E2
Gilmonby Durham 223 C9
Gilmorton Leics 135 F11
Gilmourton S Lanark 268 G3
Gilnow Gtr Man 195 F8
Gilroyd S Yorks 197 G10
Gilsland Northumb 240 D4
Gilsland Spa Cumb 240 D4
Gilson Warks 134 E3
Gilstead W Yorks 205 F8
Gilston Borders 271 D8
Herts 86 C6
Gilston Park Herts 86 C6
Giltbrook Notts 171 F7
Gilver's Lane Worcs 98 C6
Gilwell Park Essex 86 F5
Gilwern Mon 78 C2
Gimingham Norf 160 B5
Ginclough Ches E 185 F7
Ginger's Green E Sus 23 C10
Giosla W Isles 304 F3
Gipping Suff 125 E11
Gipsey Bridge Lincs 174 F3
Gipsy Row Suff 107 D11
Gipsyville Hull 200 B5
Gipton W Yorks 206 F2
Gipton Wood W Yorks 206 F2
Girdle Toll N Ayrs 266 G6
Girlington W Yorks 205 G8
Girlsta Shetland 313 H6
Girsby Lincs 190 D2
N Yorks 225 D7
Girt Som 29 C10
Girtford C Beds 104 B3
C Beds 122 G3
Girthon Dumfries 237 D8
Girton Cambs 123 E8
Notts 172 B4
Girvan S Ayrs 244 D5
Gisburn Lancs 204 D2
Gisleham Suff 143 F10
Gislingham Suff 125 C11
Gissing Norf 142 F2
Gittisham Devon 15 B8
Givons Grove Sur 51 C7
Glachavoil Argyll 275 F11
Glackmore Highld 300 D6
Glack of Midthird Moray 302 E3
Gladestry Powys 114 F4
Gladsmuir E Loth 281 G9
Glaichbea Highld 300 F5
Glais Swansea 76 E2
Glaisdale N Yorks 226 D5
Glame Highld 298 E5
Glamis Angus 287 C7
Glan Adda Gwyn 179 G9
Glanafon Pembs 73 B7
Glanaman Carms 75 C11
Glan-Conwy Conwy 164 E4
Glandford Norf 177 E8
Glan-Duar Carms 93 C10
Glandwr Caerph 78 E2
Pembs 92 F3
Glan-Dwyfach Gwyn 163 G7
Glandy Cross Carms 92 F2
Glandyfi Ceredig 128 D3
Glan Gors Anglesey 179 F7
Glangrwyney Powys 78 B2
Glanhanog Powys 129 D8
Glanmule Powys 130 E3
Glanrafon Ceredig 128 G2
Glanrhyd Gwyn 144 B5
Pembs 92 C2
Glan-rhyd Gwyn 163 D7
Powys 76 D3
Glantlees Northumb 252 B4
Glanton Northumb 264 G3
Glanton Pike Northumb 264 G3
Glan-traeth Anglesey 178 F3
Glantwymyn = *Cemmaes Road* Powys 128 C6
Glanvilles Wootton
Dorset 29 F11
Glanwern Ceredig 128 F2
Glanwydden Conwy 180 E4
Glan-y-don Flint 181 F11
Glan y Ffer = *Ferryside*
Carms 74 C5
Glan-y-llyn Rhondda 58 C6
Glan-y-môr Carms 74 C4
Glan-y-nant Caerph 77 F10
Powys 129 G8
Glan-yr-afon Anglesey 179 E10
Flint 181 E10
Gwyn 164 G6
Gwyn 165 G8
Shrops 148 E4
Glan-y-wern Gwyn 146 C2
Glapthorn N Nhants 137 E10
Glapwell Derbys 171 B7
Glas-allt Shiel Aberds 292 E4
Glasbury Powys 96 D3
Glaschoil Highld 301 F10
Glascoed Denb 181 G7
Mon 78 E4
Powys 129 F11
Powys 148 G2
Glascote Staffs 134 C4
Glascwm Powys 114 G3
Glasdir Flint 181 E10
Glasdrum Argyll 284 C4
Glasfryn Conwy 164 E6
Glasgoed Ceredig 92 B6
Glasgoforest Aberds 293 B10
Glasgow Glasgow 267 B11
Glashvin Highld 298 C4
Glasinfryn Gwyn 163 B9
Glasnacardoch Highld 295 F8
Glasnakille Highld 295 D7
Glasphein Highld 297 G7
Glaspwll Powys 128 D4
Glassburn Highld 300 F3
Glassenbury Kent 53 F8
Glasserton Dumfries 236 F6
Glassford S Lanark 268 F4
Glassgreen Moray 302 C2
Glasshoughton W Yorks 198 C2
Glasshouse Glos 98 G4
Glasshouse Hill Glos 98 G4
Glasshouses N Yorks 214 G3
Glasslie Fife 286 G6
Glasson Cumb 228 D6
Cumb 239 E7
Lancs 202 B4
Glassonby Cumb 231 D7
Glasterlaw Angus 287 B9
Glaston Rutland 137 C7
Glastonbury Som 44 F4
Glatton Cambs 138 F3
Glazebrook Warr 183 C11
Glazebury Warr 183 B11
Glazeley Shrops 132 F4
Gleadless S Yorks 186 E5
Gleadless Valley
S Yorks 186 E5
Gleadmoss Ches E 168 B4
Gleadsmoss Ches E 168 B4
Gleanhead Dumfries 245 G10
Gleann Tholàstaidh
W Isles 304 D7
Gleaston Cumb 210 E5
Glebe Hants 33 D9
Shetland 313 J6
T&W 243 F8
Glecknabae Argyll 275 G11
Gledhow W Yorks 206 F2
Gledrid Shrops 148 B5
Gleiniant Powys 129 E9
Glemsford Suff 106 B6
Glen Dumfries 237 B10
Dumfries 237 D7
Glenallachie Moray 302 E2
Glenalmond College
Perth 286 E3
Glenalmond Ho Perth 286 E3
Glenamachrie Argyll 289 G11
Glenample Stirling 285 E9
Glenancross Highld 295 F8
Glenapp Castle S Ayrs 244 G3
Glenaros Ho Argyll 289 E7
Glen Auldyn IoM 192 C5
Glenbarr Argyll 255 D7
Glenbeg Highld 289 C7
Highld 301 G10
Glen Bernisdale Highld 298 E4
Glenbervie Aberds 293 E9
Glenboig N Lanark 268 B4
Glenborrodale Highld 289 C8
Glenbranter Argyll 276 B2
Glenbreck Borders 260 E3
Glenbrein Lodge Highld 290 B6
Glenbrittle House
Highld 294 C6
Glenbrook Edin 270 B2
Glenbuchat Castle
Aberds 292 B5
Glenbuchat Lodge
Aberds 292 B5
Glenbuck E Ayrs 259 D7
Glenburn Renfs 267 C9
Glenbyre Argyll 289 G7
Glencalvie Lodge Highld 309 L4
Glencanisp Lodge
Highld 307 G6
Glencaple Dumfries 237 C11
Glencarron Lodge
Highld 299 D10
Glencarse Perth 286 E5
Glencassley Castle
Highld 309 J4
Glencat Aberds 293 D7
Glenceitlein Highld 284 C5
Glencoe Highld 284 B4
Glencraig Fife 280 B3
Glencripesdale Highld 289 D8
Glencrosh Dumfries 247 F7
Glendavan Ho Aberds 292 C6
Glendearg Borders 262 B2
Glendevon Perth 286 G3
Glendoebeg Highld 290 C6
Glendoe Lodge Highld 290 C6
Glendoick Perth 286 E6
Glendoll Lodge Angus 292 F4
Glendoune S Ayrs 244 D5
Glenduckie Fife 286 F6
Glendye Lodge Aberds 293 E8
Gleneagles Hotel Perth 286 F3
Gleneagles House Perth 286 G3
Glenearn Perth 286 F5
Glenegedale Argyll 254 B4
Glenelg Highld 295 D10
Glenernie Moray 301 E10
Glenfarg Perth 286 F5
Glenfarquhar Lodge
Aberds 293 E9
Glenferness House
Highld 301 E9
Glenfeshie Lodge
Highld 291 D10
Glenfiddich Lodge
Moray 302 F3
Glenfield Leics 135 B10
Glenfinnan Highld 295 G10
Glenfinnan Lodge
Highld 295 G11
Glenfintaig Ho Highld 290 E4
Glenfoot Perth 286 F5
Glenfyne Lodge Argyll 284 F6
Glengap Dumfries 237 D8
Glengarnock N Ayrs 266 E6
Glengolly Highld 310 C5
Glengorm Castle Argyll 288 D6
Glengoulandie Perth 285 B11
Glengrasco Highld 298 E4
Glenhead Farm Angus 292 G4
Glen Ho Borders 261 C7
Glenholt Plym 7 C10
Glenhoul Dumfries 246 F4
Glenhurich Highld 289 C10
Glenkerry Borders 261 G7
Glenkiln Dumfries 237 B10
Glenkindie Aberds 292 B6
Glenlair Dumfries 237 B9
Glenlatterach Moray 301 D11
Glenlee Dumfries 246 G4
Glenleigh Park E Sus 38 F2
Glenleraig Highld 306 F6
Glenlichorn Perth 285 F11
Glenlicht Ho Highld 290 B2
Glenlivet Moray 301 G11
Glenlochar Dumfries 237 C9
Glenlochsie Perth 292 F2
Glenlocksie Lodge
Perth 292 F2
Glenloig N Ayrs 255 D10
Glenlomond Perth 286 G5
Glenluce Dumfries 236 D4
Glenlussa Ho Argyll 255 E8
Glenmallan Argyll 276 B5
Glenmark Angus 292 E6
Glenmarkie Lodge
Angus 292 G4
Glenmarksie Highld 300 D3
Glenmavis N Lanark 268 B4
W Loth 269 B9
Glenmaye IoM 192 E3
Glenmayne Borders 261 C11
Glenmeanie Highld 300 D2
Glenmidge Dumfries 247 F9
Glenmoidart Ho Highld 289 B9
Glen Mona IoM 192 D5
Glen Mor Highld 295 B10
Glenmore Argyll 275 G11
Argyll 289 G8
Highld 298 E4
Glenmore Lodge
Highld 291 C11
Glenmoy Angus 292 G6
Glen Nevis House Highld 290 F3
Glennoe Argyll 284 D4
Glen of Newmill Moray 302 D4
Glenogil Angus 292 G6
Glenowen Pembs 73 D7
Glen Parva Leics 135 D11
Glenprosen Lodge
Angus 292 G4
Glenprosen Village
Angus 292 G5
Glenquaich Lodge
Perth 286 D2
Glenquiech Angus 292 G6
Glenquithlie Aberds 303 C8
Glenrath Borders 260 C6
Glenrazie Dumfries 236 C5
Glenreasdell Mains
Argyll 255 B9
Glenree N Ayrs 255 E10
Glenridding Cumb 221 B7
Glenrosa N Ayrs 256 B2
Glenrossal Highld 309 J4
Glenrothes Fife 286 G6
Glensanda Highld 289 E10
Glensaugh Aberds 293 F8
Glensburgh Falk 279 E8
Glenshero Lodge Highld 291 D7
Glenshoe Lodge Perth 292 G3
Glen Sluain Argyll 275 D11
Glenstockadale
Dumfries 236 C2
Glenstriven Argyll 275 F11
Glentaggart S Lanark 259 D8
Glen Tanar House
Aberds 292 D6
Glentarkie Perth 286 F5
Glenternie Borders 260 B6
Glentham Lincs 189 C8
Glentirranmuir Stirling 278 C3
Glenton Aberds 302 G6
Glentress Borders 261 B7
Glentromie Lodge
Highld 291 D9
Glen Trool Lodge
Dumfries 245 G10
Glentrool Village
Dumfries 236 B5
Glentruan IoM 192 B5
Glentruim House Highld 291 D8
Glentworth Lincs 188 D6
Glenuaig Lodge Highld 299 E11
Glenuig Highld 289 B8
Glenure Argyll 284 C4
Glenurquhart Highld 301 C7
Glen Vic Askil Highld 298 E3
Glenview Argyll 284 E5
Glen Village Falk 279 F7
Glen Vine IoM 192 E4
Glespin S Lanark 259 D8
Gletness Shetland 313 H6
Glewstone Hereford 97 G11
Glinton Pboro 138 B3
Globe Town London 67 C11
Glodwick Gtr Man 196 G2
Glogue Pembs 92 E4
Glooston Leics 136 D4
Glororum Northumb 264 C5
Glossop Derbys 185 C8
Gloster Hill Northumb 253 C7
Gloucester Glos 80 B4
Gloup Shetland 312 C7
Gloweth Corn 4 G5
Glusburn N Yorks 204 E6
Glutt Lodge Highld 310 F3
Glutton Bridge Staffs 169 B9
Gluvian Corn 5 C8
Glympton Oxon 101 G8
Glyn Mon 79 F7
Powys 129 F8
Glynarthen Ceredig 92 B6
Glynbrochan Powys 129 G8
Glyn Castle Neath 76 E4
Glyn-Ceiriog Wrex 148 B4
Glyncoch Rhondda 77 G9
Glyncoed Bl Gwent 77 C11
Glyncorrwg Neath 57 B11
Glyn-Cywarch Gwyn 146 C2
Glynde E Sus 23 D7
Glyndebourne E Sus 23 C7
Glyndyfrdwy Denb 165 G10
Glynedd = *Glyn neath*
Neath 76 D5
Glyne Gap E Sus 38 F3
Glyn Etwy Bl Gwent 77 D11
Glynhafren Powys 129 G7
Glynllan Bridgend 58 B2
Glynmorlas Shrops 148 B6
Glyn-neath = *Glynedd*
Neath 76 D5
Glynogwr Bridgend 58 B3
Glyntaff Rhondda 58 B5
Glyntawe Powys 76 B4
Gnosall Staffs 150 E6
Gnosall Heath Staffs 150 E6
Goadby Leics 136 D4
Goadby Marwood Leics 154 D5
Goatacre Wilts 62 D4
Goatham Green E Sus 38 C4
Goathill Dorset 29 D11
Goathland N Yorks 226 E6
Goathurst Som 43 G9
Goathurst Common Kent 52 C3
Goat Lees Kent 54 D4
Gobernuisgach Lodge
Highld 308 E4
Gobernuisgeach Highld 310 F3
Gobhaig W Isles 305 H2
Gobley Hole Hants 48 D6
Gobowen Shrops 148 C6
Godalming Sur 50 E3
Goddards Bucks 84 G3
Goddard's Corner Suff 126 D5
Goddard's Green Kent 53 G10
W Berks 65 F7
Goddards' Green W Sus 36 C3
Godden Green Kent 52 B5
Goddington London 68 F3
Godley Gtr Man 185 B7
Godleybrook Staffs 169 G7
Godley Hill Gtr Man 185 C7
Godleys Green E Sus 36 D5
Godmanchester Cambs 122 C4
Godmanstone Dorset 17 B9
Godmersham Kent 54 C5
Godney Som 44 E3
Godolphin Cross Corn 2 C4
Godre'r-graig Neath 76 D3
God's Blessing Green
Dorset 31 G8
Godshill Hants 31 E11
IoW 20 E6
Godstone Sur 51 C10
Godswinscroft Hants 19 B9
Godwell Devon 8 D3
Godwick Norf 159 E8
Godwinscroft Hants 19 B9
Goetre Mon 78 D4
Goferydd Anglesey 178 E2
Goff's Oak Herts 86 E4
Gogar Edin 280 G3
Goginan Ceredig 128 G3
Goirtean a'Chladaich
Highld 290 F2
Golan Gwyn 163 G8
Golant Corn 6 E2
Golberdon Corn 12 G2
Golborne Gtr Man 183 B10
Golcar W Yorks 196 D6
Golch Flint 181 F11
Goldcliff Newport 59 C11
Golden Balls Oxon 83 F9
Golden Cross E Sus 23 C8
E Sus 23 C10
Golden Green Kent 52 D6
Golden Grove Carms 75 B9
Goldenhill Stoke 168 E5
Golden Hill Bristol 60 D5
Hants 19 B11
Pembs 73 E7
Pembs 91 G9
Golden Park Devon 24 C2
Golden Pot Hants 49 E8
Golden Valley Derbys 170 E6
Glos 99 G8
Hereford 98 B3
Golder Field Hereford 115 E11
Golders Green London 67 B9
Goldfinch Bottom
W Berks 64 G4
Goldhanger Essex 88 D6
Gold Hill Dorset 30 E4
Norf 139 E10
Golding Shrops 131 C10
Goldington Bedford 121 G11
Goldsborough N Yorks 206 B3
N Yorks 226 C6
Gold's Cross Bath 60 G5
Golds Green W Mid 133 E9
Goldsithney Corn 2 C2
Goldstone Shrops 150 D4
Goldthorn Park W Mid 133 D8
Goldthorpe S Yorks 198 G3
Goldworthy Devon 24 C5
Golford Kent 53 F9
Golftyn Flint 182 G3
Golgotha Kent 55 D9
Gollanfield Highld 301 D8
Gollawater Corn 4 E5
Gollinglith Foot
N Yorks 214 C3
Golly Wrex 166 D4
Golsoncott Som 42 F4
Golspie Highld 311 J2
Golval Highld 310 C2
Golynos Torf 78 E3
Gomeldon Wilts 47 F7
Gomersal W Yorks 197 B8
Gometra Ho Argyll 288 E5
Gomshall Sur 50 D5
Gonalston Notts 171 F11
Gonamena Corn 11 G11
Gonerby Hill Foot Lincs 155 B8
Gonfirth Shetland 313 G5
Good Easter Essex 87 C10
Gooderstone Norf 140 C5
Goodleigh Devon 40 G6
Goodley Stock Kent 52 C2
Goodmanham E Yorks 208 E3
Goodmayes London 68 B3
Goodnestone Kent 55 C9
Kent 70 G4
Goodrich Hereford 79 B9
Goodrington Torbay 9 D7
Good's Green Worcs 132 G5
Goodshaw Lancs 195 B10
Goodshaw Chapel
Lancs 195 B10
Goodshaw Fold Lancs 195 B10
Goodstone Devon 13 G11
Goodwick = *Wdig* Pembs 91 D8
Goodworth Clatford
Hants 47 E11
Goodyers End Warks 134 F6
Goodyhills Cumb 229 B8
Goole E Yorks 199 C8
Goom's Hill Worcs 117 G10
Goonabarn Corn 5 E9
Goonbell Corn 4 F4
Goon Gumpas Corn 4 G4
Goonhavern Corn 4 E5
Goonhusband Corn 2 D5
Goonlaze Corn 2 B6
Goonown Corn 4 E4
Goonpiper Corn 3 B8
Goonvrea Corn 4 F4
Gooseberry Green Essex 87 F11
Goose Eye W Yorks 204 E6
Gooseford Devon 13 C9
Goose Green Cumb 211 C10
Essex 108 F2
Gtr Man 194 G5
Hants 32 F4
Herts 86 D5
Kent 52 C6
Kent 53 F10
Lancs 194 C3
Norf 142 F2
S Glos 61 C8
W Sus 34 C3
W Sus 35 D10
Gooseham Mill Devon 24 D2
Goosehill W Yorks 197 C11
Goose Hill Hants 64 G4
Goosehill Green Worcs 117 E8
Goosemoor Staffs 150 F6
Goosemoor Green
Staffs 151 G11
Goosenford Som 28 B2
Goose Pool Hereford 97 D9
Goosewell Devon 40 D5
Goosey Oxon 82 G5
Goosnargh Lancs 203 F7
Goostrey Ches E 184 G3
Gorbals Glasgow 267 C11
Gorcott Hill Warks 117 D11
Gord Shetland 313 L6
Gorddinog Conwy 179 G11
Gordon Borders 272 G2
Gordonbush Highld 311 J2
Gordonsburgh Moray 302 C4
Gordonstoun Moray 301 C11
Gordonstown Aberds 302 D5
Aberds 303 F7
Gore Dorset 29 D9
Kent 55 B10
Gorebridge Midloth 270 C6
Gore Cross Wilts 46 C4
Gore End Hants 64 G2
Gorefield Cambs 157 G8
Gorehill W Sus 35 C7
Gore Pit Essex 88 B5
Gore Street Kent 71 F9
Gorgie Edin 280 G4
Gorhambury Herts 85 D10
Goring Oxon 64 C6
Goring-by-Sea W Sus 35 G10
Goring Heath Oxon 65 D7
Gorleston-on-Sea
Norf 143 C10
Gornalwood W Mid 133 E8
Gorrachie Aberds 303 D7
Gorran Churchtown Corn 5 G9
Gorran Haven Corn 5 G10
Gorran High Lanes Corn 5 G9
Gorrenberry Borders 249 D11
Gorrig Ceredig 93 C8
Gorse Covert Warr 183 C11
Gorsedd Flint 181 F11
Gorse Hill Gtr Man 184 B4
Swindon 63 B7
Gorseinon Swansea 56 B5
Gorseness Orkney 314 E4
Gorsethorpe Notts 171 B9
Gorseybank Derbys 170 E3
Gorsgoch Ceredig 111 G9
Gorslas Carms 75 C9
Gorsley Glos 98 F3
Gorsley Common
Hereford 98 F3
Gorsley Ley Staffs 133 B11
Gorstage Ches W 183 G10
Gorstan Highld 300 C3
Gorstanvorran Highld 289 B10
Gorstella Ches W 166 C5
Gorsteyhill Ches E 168 E2
Gorst Hill Worcs 116 C4
Gorstyhill Staffs 168 E2
Gorsty Hill Staffs 151 D11
Gortan Argyll 274 G3
Gortenacullish Highld 295 G8
Gorteneorn Highld 289 C8

Gortenfern Highld 289 C8
Gortinanane Argyll 255 C8
Gorton Gtr Man 184 B5
Gortonallister N Ayrs 256 D2
Gosbeck Suff 126 F3
Gosberton Lincs 156 C4
Gosberton Cheal Lincs 156 D4
Gosberton Clough Lincs 156 D3
Goscote W Mid 133 C10
Goseley Dale Derbys 152 E6
Gosfield Essex 106 F5
Gosford Hereford 115 D10
Oxon 83 C7
Gosford Green W Mid 118 B6
Gosforth Cumb 219 E11
T&W 242 D6
Gosforth Valley Derbys 186 F4
Gosland Green Suff 124 G5
Gosling Green Suff 107 C9
Gosmere Kent 54 B4
Gosmore Herts 104 F3
Gospel Ash Staffs 132 E6
Gospel End Village
Staffs 133 E7
Gospel Green W Sus 50 G2
Gospel Oak London 67 B9
Gosport Hants 21 B8
Hants 32 C5
Gossabrough Shetland 312 E7
Gossard's Green C Beds 103 C9
Gossington Glos 80 E2
Gossops Green W Sus 51 F9
Goswick Northumb 273 F11
Gotham Dorset 31 E9
E Sus 38 F2
Notts 153 C10
Gothelney Green Som 43 F9
Gotherington Glos 99 F9
Gothers Corn 5 D9
Gott Argyll 288 E2
Shetland 313 J6
Gotton Som 28 B2
Goudhurst Kent 53 F8
Goukstone Moray 302 D4
Goulceby Lincs 190 F3
Goulton N Yorks 225 E9
Gourdas Aberds 303 E7
Gourdon Aberds 293 F10
Gourock Invclyd 276 F4
Govan Glasgow 267 B11
Govanhill Glasgow 267 C11
Gover Hill Kent 52 C6
Goverton Notts 172 E2
Goveton Devon 8 F5
Govilon Mon 78 C3
Gowanhill Aberds 303 C10
Gowanwell Aberds 303 E8
Gowdall E Yorks 198 C6
Gowerton = *Tre-Gwyr*
Swansea 56 B5
Gowhole Derbys 185 E8
Gowkhall Fife 279 D11
Gowkthrapple N Lanark 268 E5
Gowthorpe E Yorks 207 C11
Goxhill E Yorks 209 E9
N Lincs 200 C6
Goxhill Haven N Lincs 200 B6
Goybre Neath 57 D9
Goytre Neath 57 D9
Gozzard's Ford Oxon 83 F7
Grabhair W Isles 305 G5
Graby Lincs 155 D11
Gracca Corn 5 D10
Gracemount Edin 270 B5
Grade Corn 2 G6
Graffham W Sus 34 D6
Grafham Cambs 122 D3
Sur 50 E4
Grafton Hereford 97 D9
N Yorks 215 G8
Oxon 82 E3
Shrops 149 F8
Worcs 99 D9
Worcs 115 E11
Grafton Flyford Worcs 117 F9
Grafton Regis W Nhants 102 B5
Grafton Underwood
N Nhants 137 G8
Grafty Green Kent 53 D11
Grahamston Falk 279 E7
Graianrhyd Denb 166 D2
Graig Carms 74 E6
Conwy 180 G4
Denb 181 G9
Rhondda 58 B5
Wrex 148 B4
Graig-Fawr Swansea 75 E10
Graig-fechan Denb 165 E10
Graig Felen Swansea 75 E11
Graig Penllyn V Glam 58 D3
Graig Trewyddfa Swansea 57 B7
Grain Medway 69 D11
Grains Bar Gtr Man 196 F3
Grainsby Lincs 190 B3
Grainthorpe Lincs 190 B5
Grainthorpe Fen Lincs 190 B5
Graiselound N Lincs 188 B3
Grampound Corn 5 F8
Grampound Road Corn 5 E8
Gramsdal W Isles 296 F4
Granborough Bucks 102 F5
Granby Notts 154 B5
Grandborough Warks 119 D9
Grandpont Oxon 83 D8
Grandtully Perth 286 B3
Grange Cumb 220 B5
Dorset 31 G8
E Ayrs 257 B10
Fife 287 G8
Halton 183 E8
Lancs 203 G7
Medway 69 F9
Mers 182 D2
NE Lincs 201 F9
N Yorks 223 G8
Perth 286 E6
Warr 183 C10
Grange Crossroads
Moray 302 D4
Grange Estate Dorset 31 G10
Grange Hall Moray 301 C10
Grange Hill Durham 233 F10
Essex 86 G6
Grangemill Derbys 170 D2
Grange Moor W Yorks 197 D8
Grangemouth Falk 279 E8
Grangemuir Fife 287 G9
Grange of Cree
Dumfries 236 D6
Grange of Lindores Fife 286 F6
Grange-over-Sands
Cumb 211 D8
Grangepans Falk 279 E10
Grange Park London 86 F4
Mers 183 C7
Swindon 62 C6
W Nhants 120 F5
Grangetown Cardiff 59 E7
Redcar 235 G7
Grangetown *continued*
T&W 243 G10
Grange Villa Durham 242 G6
Grange Village Glos 79 C11
Granish Highld 291 B11
Gransmoor E Yorks 209 B8
Gransmore Green
Essex 106 G3
Granston = *Treopert*
Pembs 91 E7
Grantchester Cambs 123 F8
Grantham Lincs 155 B8
Grantley N Yorks 214 F4
Grantley Hall N Yorks 214 F4
Grantlodge Aberds 293 B9
Granton Dumfries 248 B3
Edin 280 F4
Grantown Aberds 302 D5
Grantown-on-Spey
Highld 301 G10
Grantsfield Hereford 115 E10
Grantshouse Borders 272 B6
Grant Thorold NE Lincs 201 F9
Graplin Dumfries 237 E8
Grappenhall Warr 183 D10
Grasby Lincs 200 G5
Grasmere Cumb 220 D6
Grasscroft Gtr Man 196 G3
Grassendale Mers 182 D5
Grassgarth Cumb 221 F8
Cumb 230 C2
Grass Green Essex 106 D4
Grassholme Durham 232 G4
Grassington N Yorks 213 G10
Grassmoor Derbys 170 B6
Grassthorpe Notts 172 B3
Grasswell T&W 243 G8
Grateley Hants 47 E9
Gratton Devon 24 E5
Gratwich Staffs 151 C10
Gravel Ches W 167 B11
Gravel Castle Kent 55 D8
Graveley Cambs 122 E4
Herts 104 F4
Gravelhill Shrops 149 G9
Gravel Hill Bucks 85 G8
Gravel Hole Gtr Man 196 F2
Shrops 149 B7
Gravelly Hill W Mid 134 E2
Gravels Shrops 130 D6
Gravelsbank Shrops 130 C6
Graven Shetland 312 F6
Graveney Kent 70 G5
Graven Hill Oxon 101 G11
Gravenhunger Moss
Shrops 168 G2
Gravesend Herts 105 F8
Kent 68 E6
Grayingham Lincs 188 B6
Grayrigg Cumb 221 F11
Grays Thurrock 68 D6
Grayshott Hants 49 F11
Grayson Green Cumb 228 F5
Grayswood Sur 50 G2
Graythorp Hrtlpl 234 F6
Grazeley Wokingham 65 F7
Grazeley Green W Berks 65 F7
Greagdhubh Lodge
Highld 291 D8
Greamchary Highld 310 F2
Greasbrough S Yorks 186 B6
Greasby Mers 182 D3
Greasley Notts 171 F7
Great Abington Cambs 105 B10
Great Addington
N Nhants 121 B9
Great Alne Warks 118 F2
Great Altcar Lancs 193 F10
Great Amwell Herts 86 C5
Great Asby Cumb 222 C3
Great Ashfield Suff 125 D9
Great Ashley Wilts 61 G10
Great Ayton N Yorks 225 C11
Great Baddow Essex 88 E2
Great Bardfield Essex 106 E3
Great Barford Bedford 122 G2
Great Barrington Glos 82 C2
Great Barrow Ches W 167 B7
Great Barton Suff 125 D7
Great Barugh N Yorks 216 D4
Great Bavington
Northumb 251 G11
Great Bealings Suff 108 B4
Great Bedwyn Wilts 63 G9
Great Bentley Essex 108 G2
Great Berry Essex 69 B7
Great Billing W Nhants 120 E6
Great Bircham Norf 158 C5
Great Blakenham Suff 126 G2
Great Blencow Cumb 230 E5
Great Bolas Telford 150 E2
Great Bookham Sur 50 C6
Great Bosullow Corn 1 C4
Great Bourton Oxon 101 B9
Great Bowden Leics 136 F4
Great Bower Kent 54 C4
Great Bradley Suff 124 G3
Great Braxted Essex 88 C5
Great Bricett Suff 125 G10
Great Brickhill Bucks 103 E8
Great Bridge W Mid 133 E9
Great Bridgeford Staffs 151 D7
Great Brington
W Nhants 120 D3
Great Bromley Essex 107 F11
Great Broughton Cumb 229 E7
N Yorks 225 D10
Great Buckland Kent 69 G7
Great Budworth
Ches W 183 F11
Great Burdon Darl 224 B6
Great Burgh Sur 51 B8
Great Burstead Essex 87 G11
Great Busby N Yorks 225 D10
Great Canfield Essex 87 B9
Great Carlton Lincs 190 D6
Great Casterton Rutland 137 B9
Rutland 137 B10
Great Cellws Powys 113 E11
Great Chalfield Wilts 61 G11
Great Chart Kent 54 E3
Great Chatwell Staffs 150 G5
Great Chell Stoke 168 E5
Great Chesterford
Essex 105 C10
Great Cheveney Kent 53 E8
Great Cheverell Wilts 46 C3
Great Chilton Durham 233 E11
Great Chishill Cambs 105 D8
Great Clacton Essex 89 B11
Great Claydons Essex 88 E3
Great Cliff W Yorks 197 D10
Great Clifton Cumb 228 F6
Great Coates NE Lincs 201 F8
Great Comberton Worcs 99 C9
Great Common Suff 143 F7
W Sus 35 B8
Great Corby Cumb 239 G11
Great Cornard Suff 107 C7
Great Cowden E Yorks 209 E10
Great Coxwell Oxon 82 G3
Great Crakehall
N Yorks 224 G4
Great Cransley
N Nhants 120 B6
Great Cressingham
Norf 141 C7
Great Crosby Mers 182 B4
Great Crosthwaite
Cumb 229 G11
Great Cubley Derbys 152 B3
Great Dalby Leics 154 G4
Great Denham Bedford 103 B10
Great Doddington
N Nhants 121 E7
Great Doward Hereford 79 B9
Great Dunham Norf 159 G7
Great Dunmow Essex 106 G2
Great Durnford Wilts 46 F6
Great Easton Essex 106 F2
Leics 136 E6
Great Eccleston Lancs 202 E4
Great Edstone N Yorks 216 C4
Great Ellingham Norf 141 D10
Great Elm Som 45 D8
Great Eppleton T&W 234 B3
Greater Doward Hereford 79 B9
Great Eversden Cambs 123 G7
Great Fencote N Yorks 224 G5
Greatfield Wilts 62 B5
Great Finborough Suff 125 F10
Greatford Lincs 155 G11
Great Fransham Norf 159 G7
Great Gaddesden Herts 85 C8
Greatgap Bucks 84 B6
Greatgate Staffs 169 G9
Great Gate Staffs 169 G9
Great Gidding Cambs 138 G2
Great Givendale
E Yorks 208 C2
Great Glemham Suff 126 E6
Great Glen Leics 136 D3
Great Gonerby Lincs 155 B7
Great Gransden Cambs 122 F5
Great Green Cambs 104 C5
Norf 142 F5
Suff 125 B11
Suff 125 F8
Suff 126 B2
Great Habton N Yorks 216 D5
Great Hale Lincs 173 G10
Great Hallingbury Essex 87 B8
Greatham Hants 49 G9
Hrtlpl 234 F5
W Sus 35 D8
Great Hampden Bucks 84 E4
Great Harrowden
N Nhants 121 C7
Great Harwood Lancs 203 G10
Great Haseley Oxon 83 E10
Great Hatfield E Yorks 209 E9
Great Haywood Staffs 151 E9
Staffs 151 E10
Great Heath W Mid 134 G6
Great Heck N Yorks 198 C5
Great Henny Essex 107 D7
Great Hinton Wilts 46 B2
Great Hivings Bucks 85 E7
Great Hockham Norf 141 E9
Great Holcombe Oxon 83 F10
Great Holland Essex 89 B12
Great Hollands Brack 65 F11
Great Holm M Keynes 102 D6
Great Honeyborough
Pembs 73 D7
Great Horkesley Essex 107 E9
Great Hormead Herts 105 F7
Great Horton W Yorks 205 G8
Great Horwood Bucks 102 E5
Great Houghton
S Yorks 198 F2
W Nhants 120 F5
Great Howarth Gtr Man 196 D2
Great Hucklow Derbys 185 F11
Great Job's Cross Kent 38 B4
Great Kelk E Yorks 209 B8
Great Kendale E Yorks 217 G10
Great Kimble Bucks 84 D4
Great Kingshill Bucks 84 F5
Great Langton N Yorks 224 F5
Great Lea Common
Reading 65 F8
Great Leighs Essex 88 B2
Great Lever Gtr Man 195 F8
Great Limber Lincs 200 F6
Great Linford M Keynes 103 C7
Great Livermere Suff 125 C7
Great Longstone Derbys 186 G2
Great Lumley Durham 233 B11
Great Lyth Shrops 131 B9
Great Malgraves Thurrock 69 C7
Great Malvern Worcs 98 B5
Great Maplestead Essex 106 E6
Great Marton Blackpool 202 F2
Great Marton Moss
Blackpool 202 G2
Great Massingham Norf 158 E5
Great Melton Norf 142 B2
Great Milton Oxon 83 E10
Great Missenden Bucks 84 E5
Great Mitton Lancs 203 F10
Great Mongeham Kent 55 C10
Greatmoor Bucks 102 G4
Great Moor Gtr Man 184 D6
Staffs 132 D6
Great Moulton Norf 142 E3
Great Munden Herts 105 G7
Great Musgrave Cumb 222 C5
Greatness Kent 52 B4
Great Ness Shrops 149 F7
Great Notley Essex 106 G4
Great Oak Mon 78 D5
Great Oakley Essex 108 F3
N Nhants 137 F7
Great Offley Herts 104 F2
Great Ormside Cumb 222 B4
Great Orton Cumb 239 G8
Great Ouseburn
N Yorks 215 G8
Great Oxendon
W Nhants 136 G4
Great Oxney Green
Essex 87 D11
Great Palgrave Norf 158 G6
Great Parndon Essex 86 D6
Great Pattenden Kent 53 E8
Great Paxton Cambs 122 E4
Great Plumpton Lancs 202 G3
Great Plumstead Norf 160 G6
Great Ponton Lincs 155 C8
Great Preston W Yorks 198 B2
Great Purston
W Nhants 101 D10
Great Raveley Cambs 138 G5
Great Rissington Glos 81 B11
Great Rollright Oxon 100 E6
Great Ryburgh Norf 159 D9
Great Ryle Northumb 264 G2
Great Ryton Shrops 131 C9
Great Saling Essex 106 F4
Great Salkeld Cumb 231 D7
Great Sampford Essex 106 D2
Great Sankey Warr 183 D9
Great Saredon Staffs 133 B9
Great Saxham Suff 124 E5
Great Shefford W Berks 63 E11
Great Shelford Cambs 123 G9
Great Shoddesden Hants 47 D9
Great Smeaton N Yorks 224 E6
Great Snoring Norf 159 C8
Great Somerford Wilts 62 C3
Great Stainton Darl 234 G2
Great Stambridge Essex 88 G5
Great Staughton Cambs 122 E2
Great Steeping Lincs 174 C6
Great Stoke S Glos 60 C6
Great Stonar Kent 55 B10
Greatstone-on-Sea Kent 39 C9
Great Stretton Leics 136 C3
Great Strickland Cumb 231 G7
Great Stukeley Cambs 122 C4
Great Sturton Lincs 190 F2
Great Sutton Ches W 182 F5
Shrops 131 G10
Great Swinburne
Northumb 241 B10
Great Tew Oxon 101 F7
Great Tey Essex 107 F7
Great Thirkleby N Yorks 215 D9
Great Thurlow Suff 124 G3
Great Torrington Devon 25 D7
Great Tosson Northumb 252 C2
Great Totham Essex 88 C5
Great Tows Lincs 190 C2
Great Tree Corn 6 D5
Great Urswick Cumb 210 E5
Great Wakering Essex 70 B2
Great Waldingfield Suff 107 C8
Great Walsingham Norf 159 B8
Great Waltham Essex 87 C11
Great Warley Essex 87 G9
Great Washbourne Glos 99 E9
Great Weeke Devon 13 D10
Great Weldon N Nhants 137 F8
Great Welnetham Suff 125 F7
Great Wenham Suff 107 D11
Great Whittington
Northumb 242 C2
Great Wigborough Essex 89 C7
Great Wilbraham
Cambs 123 F10
Great Wilne Derbys 153 C8
Great Wishford Wilts 46 F5
Great Witchingham
Norf 160 E2
Great Witcombe Glos 80 C6
Great Witley Worcs 116 D5
Great Wolford Warks 100 E4
Greatworth W Nhants 101 C11
Great Wratting Suff 106 B3
Great Wymondley Herts 104 F4
Great Wyrley Staffs 133 B9
Great Wytheford
Shrops 149 F11
Great Yarmouth Norf 143 B10
Great Yeldham Essex 106 D5
Greave Gtr Man 184 C6
Lancs 195 C11
Grebby Lincs 174 B6
Greeba IoM 192 D4
Green Denb 165 B9
Pembs 73 E7
Powys 130 E5
Greenacres Gtr Man 196 F2
Greenan Argyll 275 G11
Greenbank Ches W 183 G10
Falk 279 F7
Shetland 312 C7
Green Bank Cumb 211 C7
Green Bottom Corn 4 F5
Glos 79 B11
Greenburn W Loth 269 C8
Green Close N Yorks 212 F4
Green Clough W Yorks 205 G7
Green Crize Hereford 97 D10
Greencroft Durham 242 G5
Green Cross Sur 49 F11
Greendale Ches E 184 F5
Greendikes Northumb 264 D3
Greendown Som 44 C5
Green Down Devon 28 G3
Greendykes Northumb 264 D3
Greenend N Lanark 268 C4
Oxon 100 G6
Green End Bedford 103 B10
Bedford 121 E11
Bedford 122 E2
Bedford 122 G2
Bucks 84 F4
Bucks 103 E8
Cambs 122 C4
Cambs 123 F7
C Beds 103 D11
Herts 85 D8
Herts 104 E5
Herts 104 E6
Herts 104 G6
Herts 105 F7
Lancs 204 D4
N Yorks 226 E6
Warks 134 F5
Greenfaulds N Lanark 278 G5
Greenfield C Beds 103 E11
Glasgow 268 C2
Gtr Man 196 G3
Highld 289 D11
Highld 290 C4
Oxon 84 G2
Greenfield = *Maes-Glas*
Flint 181 F11
Greenfoot N Lanark 268 B4
Greenford London 66 C6
Greengairs N Lanark 278 G5
Greengarth Hall Cumb 219 E11
Greengate Gtr Man 196 D2
Norf 159 F10
Green Gate Devon 27 D8
Greengates W Yorks 205 F9
Greengill Cumb 229 D8
Green Hailey Bucks 84 E4
Greenhalgh Lancs 202 F4
Greenhall S Lanark 268 D3
Greenham Dorset 28 G6
Som 27 C9
W Berks 64 F3
Green Hammerton
N Yorks 206 B5
Greenhaugh Northumb 251 F7
Green Haworth Lancs 195 B9
Greenhead Borders 261 D11
Dumfries 247 D9
N Lanark 268 E6
Northumb 240 D5
Staffs 169 F7
Green Head Cumb 230 B3
Green Heath Staffs 151 G9
Greenheys Gtr Man 195 G8
Greenhill Dumfries 238 B4
Durham 234 B3
Falk 278 F6
Hereford 98 B4
Kent 71 F7
Leics 153 G8
Greenhill *continued*
London 67 B7
S Yorks 186 E4
Worcs 99 B10
Worcs 116 B6
Green Hill Kent 53 C9
Lincs 155 B8
Wilts 62 B5
W Yorks 206 F4
Greenhill Bank Shrops 149 B7
Greenhillocks Derbys 170 F6
Greenhills N Ayrs 267 E7
S Lanark 268 E2
Greenhithe Kent 68 E5
Greenholm E Ayrs 258 B2
Greenholme Cumb 221 D11
Greenhouse Borders 262 E3
Greenhow N Yorks 214 G2
Greenhow Hill N Yorks 214 G2
Greenigoe Orkney 314 F4
Greenland Highld 310 C6
S Yorks 186 D5
Greenland Mains Highld 310 C6
Greenlands Bucks 65 B9
Worcs 117 D11
Green Lane Devon 13 F11
Hereford 98 B2
Powys 130 D3
Warks 117 E11
Warks 118 B6
Greenlaw Aberds 302 D6
Borders 272 F4
Greenlaw Mains Midloth 270 C4
Greenlea Dumfries 238 B2
Greenley M Keynes 102 C6
Greenloaning Perth 286 G2
Greenlooms Ches W 167 C7
Greenman's Lane Wilts 62 C3
Greenmeadow Swindon 62 B6
Torf 78 F3
Green Moor S Yorks 186 B3
Greenmount Gtr Man 195 E9
Greenmow Shetland 313 L6
Greenoak E Yorks 199 B10
Greenock Invclyd 276 F5
Greenock West Invclyd 276 F5
Greenodd Cumb 210 C6
Green Ore Som 44 C5
Green Parlour Bath 45 C8
Green Quarter Cumb 221 E9
Greenrigg W Loth 269 C8
Greenrow Cumb 238 G4
Greens Borders 249 F11
Green St Green London 68 G3
Greensforge Staffs 133 F7
Greensgate Norf 160 F2
Greenside Cumb 222 E4
Derbys 186 F5
Gtr Man 184 B6
T&W 242 E4
W Yorks 197 D7
Green Side W Yorks 197 E7
W Yorks 205 G11
Greensidehill Northumb 263 F11
Greens Norton
W Nhants 102 B3
Greensplat Corn 5 D9
Greenstead Essex 107 F10
Greenstead Green Essex 106 F6
Greensted Essex 87 E8
Greensted Green Essex 87 E8
Green Street Essex 87 F10
E Sus 38 E3
Glos 80 B5
Glos 80 E3
Herts 85 F11
Herts 105 G9
Worcs 99 B7
Worcs 99 C7
W Sus 35 C10
Greenstreet Green
Suff 107 B10
Green Street Green Kent 68 E5
London 68 G3
Green Tye Herts 86 B6
Greenway Hereford 98 E4
Pembs 91 E11
Som 27 B11
V Glam 58 E5
Greenwell Cumb 240 F2
Greenwells Borders 262 C3
Greenwich London 67 D11
Suff 108 C3
Wilts 46 G2
Greenwith Common Corn 4 G5
Greenwoods Essex 87 F11
Greeny Orkney 314 D2
Greep Highld 298 E2
Greet Glos 99 E10
Kent 54 B2
Greete Shrops 115 C11
Greetham Lincs 190 G4
Rutland 155 G8
Greetland W Yorks 196 C5
Greetland Wall Nook
W Yorks 196 C5
Greetwell N Lincs 200 G2
Gregg Hall Cumb 221 G9
Gregson Lane Lancs 194 B5
Gregynog Powys 129 D11
Grèin W Isles 297 L2
Greinetobht W Isles 296 D4
Greinton Som 44 F2
Gremista Shetland 313 J6
Grenaby IoM 192 E3
Grendon N Nhants 121 E7
Warks 134 C5
Grendon Bishop
Hereford 115 F11
Grendon Common
Warks 134 D5
Grendon Green
Hereford 115 F11
Grendon Underwood
Bucks 102 G3
Grenofen Devon 12 G5
Grenoside S Yorks 186 C4
Greosabhagh W Isles 305 J3
Gresford Wrex 166 E5
Gresham Norf 160 B3
Greshornish Highld 298 D3
Gressenhall Norf 159 F9
Gressingham Lancs 211 F11
Gresty Green Ches E 168 E2
Greta Bridge Durham 223 C11
Gretna Dumfries 239 D8
Gretna Green Dumfries 239 D8
Gretton Glos 99 E10
N Nhants 137 E7
Shrops 131 D10
Gretton Fields Glos 99 E10
Grewelthorpe N Yorks 214 D4
Greyfield Bath 44 B6
Greygarth N Yorks 214 E3
Grey Green N Lincs 199 F9
Greylake Som 43 G11
Greylake Fosse Som 44 F2
Greynor Carms 75 D9
Greynor-isaf Carms 75 D9
Greyrigg Dumfries 248 F3
Greys Green Oxon 65 C8
Greysouthen Cumb 229 F7
Greystead Northumb 251 F7
Greystoke Cumb 230 E4
Greystoke Gill Cumb 230 F4
Greystone Aberds 292 D6
Aberds 302 F6
Angus 287 C9
Cumb 211 D10
Dumfries 237 B11
Greystonegill N Yorks 212 F3
Greystones S Yorks 186 D4
Warks 99 B11
Greytree Hereford 97 F11
Greywell Hants 49 C8
Griais W Isles 304 D6
Grianan W Isles 304 E6
Gribb Dorset 28 G5
Gribthorpe E Yorks 207 F11
Gridley Corner Devon 12 C3
Griff Warks 135 F7
Griffins Hill W Mid 133 G10
Griffithstown Torf 78 F3
Griffydam Leics 153 F8
Grigg Kent 53 E11
Griggs Green Hants 49 G10
Grillis Corn 2 B5
Grilstone Devon 26 C2
Grimbister Orkney 314 E3
Grimblethorpe Lincs 190 D2
Grimeford Village Lancs 194 E6
Grimes Hill Worcs 117 B11
Grimesthorpe S Yorks 186 C5
Grimethorpe S Yorks 198 F2
Griminis W Isles 296 D3
W Isles 296 F3
Grimister Shetland 312 D6
Grimley Worcs 116 E6
Grimness Orkney 314 G4
Grimoldby Lincs 190 D5
Grimpo Shrops 149 D7
Grimsargh Lancs 203 G7
Grimsbury Oxon 101 C9
Grimsby NE Lincs 201 E9
Grimscote W Nhants 120 G3
Grimscott Corn 24 F3
Grimshaw Blackburn 195 C8
Grimshaw Green Lancs 194 E3
Grimsthorpe Lincs 155 E10
Grimston E Yorks 209 F11
Leics 154 E3
Norf 158 E4
York 207 C8
Grimstone Dorset 17 C8
Grimstone End Suff 125 D8
Grinacombe Moor Devon 12 C4
Grindale E Yorks 218 E2
Grindigar Orkney 314 F5
Grindiscol Shetland 313 K6
Grindle Shrops 132 C5
Grindleford Derbys 186 F2
Grindleton Lancs 203 D11
Grindley Staffs 151 D10
Grindley Brook Shrops 167 G8
Grindlow Derbys 185 F11
Grindon Northumb 273 G8
Staffs 169 E9
Stockton 234 F3
T&W 243 G9
Grindonmoor Gate
Staffs 169 E9
Grindsbrook Booth
Derbys 185 D10
Gringley on the Hill
Notts 188 C2
Grinsdale Cumb 239 F9
Grinshill Shrops 149 E10
Grinstead Hill Suff 125 G11
Grinton N Yorks 223 F10
Griomasaigh W Isles 297 G4
Griomsidar W Isles 304 F5
Grisdale Cumb 222 G5
Grishipoll Argyll 288 D3
Grisling Common E Sus 36 C6
Gristhorpe N Yorks 217 C11
Griston Norf 141 D8
Gritley Orkney 314 F5
Grittenham Wilts 62 C4
Grittlesend Hereford 98 B4
Grittleton Wilts 61 C11
Grizebeck Cumb 210 C4
Grizedale Cumb 220 G6
Groam Highld 300 E5
Grobister Orkney 314 D6
Grobsness Shetland 313 G5
Groby Leics 135 B10
Groes Conwy 165 C8
Neath 57 D9
Groes Efa Denb 165 B10
Groes-faen Rhondda 58 C5
Groes-fawr Denb 165 B10
Groesffordd Gwyn 144 B5
Powys 95 F11
Groesffordd Marli Denb 181 G8
Groeslon Gwyn 163 C8
Gwyn 163 D7
Groes-lwyd Mon 96 G6
Powys 148 G4
Groespluan Powys 130 B4
Groes-wen Caerph 58 B6
Grogport Argyll 255 C9
Gromford Suff 127 F7
Gronant Flint 181 E9
Gronwen Shrops 148 D5
Groombridge E Sus 52 F4
Grosmont Mon 97 G8
N Yorks 226 D6
Gross Green Warks 119 F7
Grotaig Highld 300 G4
Groton Suff 107 C9
Grotton Gtr Man 196 G3
Grougfoot Falk 279 F10
Grove Bucks 103 G8
Dorset 17 G10
Hereford 98 C2
Kent 71 G8
Notts 188 F2
Oxon 82 G6
Pembs 73 E7
Grove End Kent 69 G11
Warks 100 D6
Warks 134 D3
Grove Green Kent 53 B9
Grovehill E Yorks 208 F6
Herts 85 D9
Grove Hill E Sus 23 C10
Kent 71 G8
Grove Park London 67 D8
London 68 E2
Groves Kent 55 B9
Grovesend Swansea 75 E9
Grove Town W Yorks 198 C3
Grove Vale W Mid 133 E10
Grubb Street Kent 68 F5
Grub Street Staffs 150 D5
Grudie Highld 300 C3
Gruids Highld 309 J5
Gruinard House Highld 307 K4
Gruinards Highld 309 K5
Grula Highld 294 C5
Gruline Argyll 289 E7
Gruline Ho Argyll 289 F7
Grumbeg Highld 308 F6
Grumbla Corn 1 D4
Grunasound Shetland 313 K5
Grundisburgh Suff 126 G4
Grunsagill Lancs 203 C11
Gruting Shetland 313 J4
Grutness Shetland 313 N6
Gryn Goch Gwyn 162 F6
Gualachulain Highld 284 C5
Gualin Ho Highld 308 D3
Guardbridge Fife 287 F8
Guard House W Yorks 204 E6
Guarlford Worcs 98 B6
Guay Perth 286 C4
Gubbion's Green Essex 88 B2
Gubblecote Herts 84 C6
Guesachan Highld 289 B10
Guestling Green E Sus 38 E5
Guestling Thorn E Sus 38 D4
Guestwick Norf 159 D11
Guestwick Green Norf 159 D11
Guide Blackburn 195 B8
Guide Bridge Gtr Man 184 B6
Guide Post Northumb 253 F7
Guilden Morden Cambs 104 C5
Guilden Sutton Ches W 166 B6
Guildford Sur 50 D3
Guildford Park Sur 50 D3
Guildiehaugh W Loth 269 B9
Guildtown Perth 286 D5
Guilford Pembs 73 D7
Guilsborough W Nhants 120 C3
Guilsfield = *Cegidfa*
Powys 148 G4
Guilthwaite S Yorks 187 D7
Guilton Kent 55 B9
Guineaford Devon 40 F5
Guisachan Highld 300 G3
Guisborough Redcar 226 B2
Guiseley W Yorks 205 E9
Guist Norf 159 D9
Guith Orkney 314 C5
Guiting Power Glos 99 G11
Gulberwick Shetland 313 K6
Gullane E Loth 281 E9
Guller's End Worcs 99 D7
Gulling Green Suff 124 F6
Gullom Holme Cumb 231 F9
Gulval Corn 1 C5
Gulworthy Devon 12 G4
Gumfreston Pembs 73 E10
Gumley Leics 136 E3
Gummow's Shop Corn 5 D7
Gunby E Yorks 207 F10
Lincs 155 E8
Lincs 175 B7
Gundenham Som 27 C10
Gundleton Hants 48 G6
Gun Green Kent 53 G9
Gun Hill E Sus 23 C9
Gunn Devon 40 G6
Gunnersbury London 67 D7
Gunnerside N Yorks 223 F9
Gunnerton Northumb 241 C10
Gunness N Lincs 199 E10
Gunnislake Corn 12 G4
Gunnista Shetland 313 J7
Gunstone Staffs 133 C7
Guns Village W Mid 133 E9
Gunter's Bridge W Sus 35 C7
Gunthorpe Lincs 188 B4
Norf 159 C10
Notts 171 G11
Pboro 138 C3
Rutland 137 B7
Gunton Suff 143 D10
Gunville IoW 20 D5
Gunwalloe Corn 2 E5
Gunwalloe Fishing Cove
Corn 2 E5
Gupworthy Som 42 F3
Gurnard IoW 20 B5
Gurnett Ches E 184 G6
Gurney Slade Som 44 D6
Gurnos M Tydf 77 D8
Powys 76 D3
Gushmere Kent 54 B4
Gussage All Saints Dorset 31 E8
Gussage St Andrew
Dorset 31 E7
Gussage St Michael
Dorset 31 E7
Gustard Wood Herts 85 B11
Guston Kent 55 E10
Gutcher Shetland 312 D7
Guthram Gowt Lincs 156 E3
Guthrie Angus 287 B9
Guyhirn Cambs 139 C7
Guyhirn Gull Cambs 139 C7
Guy's Cliffe Warks 118 D5
Guy's Head Lincs 157 D9
Guy's Marsh Dorset 30 C4
Guyzance Northumb 252 C6
Gwaelod-y-garth Cardiff 58 C6
Gwaenysgor Flint 181 E9
Gwalchmai Anglesey 178 F5
Gwalchmai Uchaf
Anglesey 178 F5
Gwallon Corn 2 C2
Gwastad Pembs 91 G10
Gwastadgoed Gwyn 145 G11
Gwastadnant Gwyn 163 D10
Gwaun-Cae-Gurwen
Neath 76 C2
Gwaun-Leision Neath 76 C2
Gwavas Corn 2 D5
Corn 2 E5
Gwbert Ceredig 92 B3
Gweda Corn 2 C4
Gwedna Corn 2 C4
Gweek Corn 2 D6
Gwehelog Mon 78 E5
Gwenddwr Powys 95 C11
Gwennap Corn 2 B6
Gwenter Corn 2 F6
Gwernaffield-y-Waun
Flint 166 C2
Gwernafon Powys 129 E8
Gwerneirin Powys 129 F10
Powys 130 G3
Gwernesney Mon 78 E6
Gwernogle Carms 93 E10
Gwernol Denb 166 E2
Gwern y brenin Shrops 148 D6
Gwernydd Powys 129 C11
Gwernymynydd Flint 166 C2
Gwern-y-Steeple V Glam 58 D5
Gwersyllt Wrex 166 E4
Gwespyr Flint 181 E10
Gwills Corn 4 D6
Gwinear Corn 2 B3
Gwinear Downs Corn 2 C4
Gwithian Corn 2 A3
Gwredog Anglesey 178 D6
Gwrhay Caerph 77 F11
Gwyddelwern Denb 165 F9
Gwyddgrug Carms 93 D9
Gwynfryn Wrex 166 E3
Gwystre Powys 113 D11
Gwytherin Conwy 164 C5
Gyfelia Wrex 166 F4
Gyffin Conwy 180 F3
Gylen Park Argyll 289 G10
Gyre Orkney 314 F3
Gyrn Denb 165 D11
Gyrn-goch Gwyn 162 F6

H

Habberley Shrops 131 C7
Worcs 116 B6
Habergham Lancs 204 G2
Habertoft Lincs 175 B8
Habin W Sus 34 C4
Habrough NE Lincs 200 E6
Haccombe Devon 14 G3
Haceby Lincs 155 B10
Hacheston Suff 126 F6
Hackbridge London 67 F9
Hackenthorpe S Yorks 186 E6
Hackford Norf 141 C11
Hackforth N Yorks 224 G4
Hack Green Ches E 167 F10
Hackland Orkney 314 D3
Hackleton W Nhants 120 F6
Hacklinge Kent 55 C10
Hackman's Gate Worcs 117 B7
Hackness N Yorks 227 G9
Orkney 314 G3
Som 43 D10
Hackney London 67 C10
Hackney Wick London 67 C11
Hackthorn Lincs 189 E7
Wilts 47 D7
Hackthorpe Cumb 230 G6
Haclait W Isles 297 G4
Haconby Lincs 156 D2
Hacton London 68 B4
Haddacott Devon 25 C8
Hadden Borders 263 B7
Haddenham Bucks 84 D2
Cambs 123 B9
Haddenham End Field
Cambs 123 B9
Haddington E Loth 281 G10
Lincs 172 C6
Haddiscoe Norf 143 D8
Haddoch Aberds 302 E5
Haddon Cambs 138 E2
Ches E 169 B7
Hade Edge W Yorks 196 F6
Hademore Staffs 134 B3
Haden Cross W Mid 133 F9
Hadfield Derbys 185 B8
Hadham Cross Herts 86 B6
Hadham Ford Herts 105 G8
Hadleigh Essex 69 B10
Suff 107 C10
Hadleigh Heath Suff 107 C9
Hadley London 86 F2
Telford 150 G3
Worcs 117 E7
Hadley Castle Telford 150 G3
Hadley End Staffs 152 E2
Hadley Wood London 86 F3
Hadlow Kent 52 D6
Hadlow Down E Sus 37 C8
Hadlow Stair Kent 52 D6
Hadnall Shrops 149 F10
Hadspen Som 45 G7
Hadstock Essex 105 C11
Hadston Northumb 253 D7
Hady Derbys 186 G5
Hadzor Worcs 117 E8
Haffenden Quarter Kent 53 E11
Hafod Swansea 57 C7
Hafod-Dinbych Conwy 164 E5
Hafod Grove Pembs 92 C2
Hafodiwan Ceredig 111 G7
Hafod-lom Conwy 180 G5
Hafod-y-Green Denb 181 G8
Hafodyrynys Bl Gwent 78 F2
Hag Fold Gtr Man 195 G7
Haggate Gtr Man 196 F2
Lancs 204 F3
Haggbeck Cumb 239 C11
Haggersta Shetland 313 J5
Haggerston London 67 C10
Northumb 273 G10
Hagginton Hill Devon 40 D5
Haggrister Shetland 312 F5
Haggs Falk 278 F5
Haghill Glasgow 268 B2
Hagley Hereford 97 C11
Worcs 133 G8
Hagloe Glos 79 D11
Hagmore Green Suff 107 D9
Hagnaby Lincs 174 C4
Lincs 191 F7
Hagnaby Lock Lincs 174 D4
Hague Bar Derbys 185 D7
Hagworthingham Lincs 174 B4
Haigh Gtr Man 196 F6
S Yorks 197 E9
Haigh Moor W Yorks 197 C9
Haighton Green Lancs 203 G7
Haighton Top Lancs 203 G7
Haile Cumb 219 D10
Hailes Glos 99 E10
Hailey Herts 86 C5
Oxon 64 B6
Oxon 82 C5
Hailsham E Sus 23 D9
Hailstone Hill Wilts 81 G9
Hail Weston Cambs 122 E3
Haimer Highld 310 C5
Haimwood Powys 148 F6
Hainault London 87 G7
Haine Kent 71 F11
Hainford Norf 160 F4
Hains Dorset 30 D3
Hainton Lincs 189 E11
Hainworth W Yorks 205 F7
Hainworth Shaw
W Yorks 205 F7
Hairmyres S Lanark 268 E2
Haisthorpe E Yorks 218 G2
Hakeford Devon 40 F6
Hakin Pembs 72 D5
Halabezack Corn 2 C6
Halam Notts 171 E11
Halamanning Corn 2 C3
Halbeath Fife 280 D2
Halberton Devon 27 E8
Halcon Som 28 B2
Halcro Highld 310 C6
Haldens Herts 86 C2
Hale Cumb 211 D10
Gtr Man 184 D3
Halton 183 E7
Hants 31 D11
Kent 71 F9
Medway 69 F9
Som 30 B3
Sur 49 D10
Hale Bank Halton 183 E7
Hale Barns Gtr Man 184 D3
Halecommon W Sus 34 C4
Hale Coombe N Som 44 B2
Hale End London 86 G5
Hale Green E Sus 23 C9

Hale Mills Corn 4 G5
Hale Nook Lancs 202 E3
Hales Norf 143 D7
Staffs 150 C4
Hales Bank Hereford 116 G2
Halesfield Telford 132 C4
Halesgate Lincs 156 D6
Hales Green Derbys 169 G11
Norf 143 D7
Halesowen W Mid 133 G9
Hales Park Worcs 116 B5
Hales Place Kent 54 B6
Hales Street Norf 142 F3
Hale Street Kent 53 D7
Hales Wood Hereford 98 E2
Halesworth Suff 127 B7
Halewood Mers 183 D7
Half Moon Village Devon 14 B3
Halford Shrops 131 G8
Warks 100 B5
Halfpenny Cumb 211 B10
Halfpenny Furze Carms 74 C3
Halfpenny Green Staffs 132 E6
Halfway Carms 75 E8
Carms 94 E2
Carms 94 E6
S Yorks 186 E6
W Berks 64 F2
Wilts 45 D11
Halfway Bridge W Sus 34 C6
Halfway House Shrops 148 G6
Halfway Houses
Gtr Man 195 F9
Kent 70 E2
Halfway Street Kent 55 D9
Halgabron Corn 11 D7
Halifax W Yorks 196 B5
Halkburn Borders 271 G9
Halket E Ayrs 267 E8
Halkirk Highld 310 D5
Halkyn = *Helygain* Flint 182 G2
Halkyn Mountain Flint 182 G2
Hallam Fields Derbys 153 B9
Halland E Sus 23 B8
Hallaton Leics 136 D5
Hallatrow Bath 44 B6
Hallbankgate Cumb 240 F3
Hall Bower W Yorks 196 E6
Hall Broom S Yorks 186 D3
Hall Cross Lancs 202 G4
Hall Dunnerdale Cumb 220 F4
Halleaths Dumfries 248 G3
Hallen S Glos 60 C5
Hallend Warks 118 D2
Hall End Bedford 103 B10
C Beds 103 D11
Lincs 174 E6
S Glos 61 B8
Warks 134 C5
Hallew Corn 5 D10
Hallfield Gate Derbys 170 D5
Hall Flat Worcs 117 C9
Hallgarth Durham 234 C2
Hall Garth York 207 C9
Hallglen Falk 279 F7
Hall Green Ches E 168 D4
Essex 106 D5
Lancs 194 C3
Lancs 194 F4
W Mid 133 E10
W Mid 134 G2
W Mid 135 G7
Wrex 167 G7
W Yorks 197 D10
Hall Grove Herts 89 C8
Halliburton Borders 261 B11
Borders 272 F3
Hallin Highld 298 D2
Halling Medway 69 G8
Hallingbury Street
Essex 87 B8
Hallington Lincs 190 D4
Northumb 241 B11
Hall i' th' Wood Gtr Man 195 E8
Halliwell Gtr Man 195 E8
Hall of Clestrain Orkney 314 F2
Hall of Tankerness
Orkney 314 F5
Hall of the Forest
Shrops 130 G4
Hallon Shrops 132 D5
Hallonsford Shrops 132 D5
Halloughton Notts 171 E11
Hallow Worcs 116 F6
Hallowes Derbys 186 F5
Hallow Heath Worcs 116 F6
Hallowsgate Ches W 167 B8
Hallrule Borders 262 G3
Halls E Loth 282 G3
Hallsands Devon 9 G11
Hall Santon Cumb 220 E2
Hall's Cross E Sus 23 D11
Hallsford Bridge Essex 87 E9
Halls Green Essex 86 D6
Hall's Green Herts 104 F5
Kent 52 D4
Hallspill Devon 25 C7
Hallthwaites Cumb 210 B3
Hall Waberthwaite
Cumb 220 F2
Hallwood Green Glos 98 E3
Hallworthy Corn 11 D9
Hallyards Borders 260 B6
Hallyburton House
Perth 286 D6
Hallyne Borders 270 G3
Halmer End Staffs 168 F3
Halmond's Frome
Hereford 98 B3
Halmore Glos 79 E11
Halmyre Mains Borders 270 F3
Halnaker W Sus 22 B6
Halsall Lancs 193 E11
Halse Som 27 B10
W Nhants 101 C11
Halsetown Corn 2 B2
Halsfordwood Devon 14 C3
Halsham E Yorks 201 B9
Halsinger Devon 40 F4
Halstead Essex 106 E6
Kent 68 G3
Leics 136 B4
Halstock Dorset 29 F8
Halsway Som 42 F6
Haltcliff Bridge Cumb 230 D3
Halterworth Hants 32 C5
Haltham Lincs 174 C2
Haltoft End Lincs 174 F5
Halton Bucks 84 C5
Halton 183 E8
Lancs 211 G10
Northumb 241 D11
Wrex 148 B6
W Yorks 206 G2
Halton Barton Corn 7 B8
Halton Brook Halton 183 E8
Halton East N Yorks 204 C6
Halton Fenside Lincs 174 C6
Halton Gill N Yorks 213 D7
Halton Green Lancs 211 F10
Halton Holegate Lincs 174 B6
Halton Lea Gate
Northumb 240 F5
Halton Moor W Yorks 206 G2
Halton Shields
Northumb 242 D2
Halton View Halton 183 D8
Halton West N Yorks 204 C2
Haltwhistle Northumb 240 E6
Halvergate Norf 143 B8
Halvosso Corn 2 C6
Halwell Devon 8 E5
Halwill Devon 12 B4
Halwill Junction Devon 24 G6
Halwin Corn 2 C5
Ham Devon 28 G2
Glos 79 F11
Glos 99 G9
Highld 310 B6
Kent 55 C10
London 67 E7
Plym 7 D9
Shetland 313 K1
Som 27 C11
Som 28 B3
Som 28 E3
Som 45 D7
Wilts 63 G10
Hamar Shetland 312 F5
Hamarhill Orkney 314 C5
Hamars Shetland 313 G6
Hambleden Bucks 65 B9
Hambledon Hants 33 E10
Sur 50 F3
Hamble-le-Rice Hants 33 F7
Hambleton Lancs 202 E3
N Yorks 205 C7
N Yorks 207 G7
Hambleton Moss Side
Lancs 202 E3
Hambridge Som 28 C5
Hambrook S Glos 60 D6
W Sus 22 B3
Ham Common Dorset 30 B4
Hameringham Lincs 174 B4
Hamerton Cambs 122 B2
Hametoun Shetland 313 K1
Ham Green Bucks 83 B11
Hants 48 G2
Hereford 98 C4
Kent 38 B5
Kent 69 F10
N Som 60 D4
Wilts 61 G11
Worcs 117 E10
Ham Hill Kent 69 G8
Hamilton S Lanark 268 D3
Hamister Shetland 313 G7
Hamlet Dorset 29 F9
Hammer W Sus 49 G11
Hammer Bottom Hants 49 G11
Hammerfield Herts 85 D8
Hammerpot W Sus 35 F9
Hammersmith Derbys 170 E5
London 67 D8
Hammerwich Staffs 133 B11
Hammerwood E Sus 52 F2
Hammill Kent 55 B9
Hammond Street Herts 86 E4
Hammoon Dorset 30 E4
Ham Moor Sur 66 G5
Hamnavoe Shetland 312 E4
Shetland 312 E6
Shetland 312 F6
Shetland 313 K5
Hamnish Clifford
Hereford 115 F10
Hamp Som 43 F10
Hampden Park E Sus 23 E10
Hampen Glos 81 B9
Hamperden End Essex 105 E11
Hamperley Shrops 131 F8
Hampers Green W Sus 35 C7
Hampeth Northumb 252 B5
Hampnett Glos 81 B10
Hampole S Yorks 198 E4
Hampreston Dorset 19 B7
Hampsfield Cumb 211 C8
Hampson Green Lancs 202 C5
Hampstead London 67 B9
Hampstead Garden Suburb
London 67 B9
Hampstead Norreys
W Berks 64 D4
Hampsthwaite N Yorks 205 B11
Hampton Kent 71 F7
London 66 F6
Shrops 132 F4
Swindon 81 G11
Worcs 99 C10
Hampton Bank Shrops 149 C9
Hampton Beech Shrops 130 B6
Hampton Bishop
Hereford 97 D11
Hampton Fields Glos 80 F5
Hampton Gay Oxon 83 B7
Hampton Green Ches W 167 F8
Glos 80 E5
Hampton Hargate Pboro 138 E3
Hampton Heath Ches W 167 F7
Hampton Hill London 66 E6
Hampton in Arden
W Mid 134 G4
Hampton Loade Shrops 132 F5
Hampton Lovett Worcs 117 D7
Hampton Lucy Warks 118 F5
Hampton Magna Warks 118 D5
Hampton on the Hill
Warks 118 E5
Hampton Park Hereford 97 D10
Soton 32 D6
Hampton Poyle Oxon 83 B8
Hamptons Kent 52 C6
Hampton Vale Pboro 138 E3
Hampton Wick London 67 F7
Hamptworth Wilts 32 D2
Hamrow Norf 159 E8
Hamsey E Sus 36 E6
Hamsey Green London 51 B10
Hamshill Glos 80 E3
Hamstall Ridware Staffs 152 F2
Hamstead IoW 20 C4
W Mid 133 E10
Hamstead Marshall
W Berks 64 F2
Hamsterley Durham 233 E8
Durham 242 F4
Hamstreet Kent 54 G4
Ham Street Som 44 G5
Hamworthy BCP 18 C5
Hanbury Staffs 152 D3
Worcs 117 E9
Hanbury Woodend
Staffs 152 D3
Hanby Lincs 155 C10
Hanchett Village Suff 106 B3
Hanchurch Staffs 168 G4
Handbridge Ches W 166 B6
Handcross W Sus 36 B3
Handforth Ches E 184 E5
Hand Green Ches W 167 C8
Handless Shrops 131 E7
Handley Ches W 167 D7
Derbys 170 C5
Handley Green Essex 87 E11
Handsacre Staffs 151 F11
Handside Herts 86 C2
Handsworth S Yorks 186 D6
W Mid 133 E10
Handsworth Wood
W Mid 133 E11
Handy Cross Bucks 84 G5
Devon 24 B6
Som 42 G6
Hanford Dorset 30 E4
Stoke 168 G5
Hangersley Hants 31 F11
Hanging Bank Kent 52 C3
Hanging Heaton
W Yorks 197 C9
Hanging Houghton
W Nhants 120 C5
Hanging Langford Wilts 46 F4
Hangingshaw Borders 261 C9
Dumfries 248 F4
Hangleton Brighton 36 F3
W Sus 35 G9
Hangsman Hill S Yorks 199 E7
Hanham S Glos 60 E6
Hanham Green S Glos 60 E6
Hankelow Ches E 167 F11
Hankerton Wilts 81 G7
Hankham E Sus 23 D10
Hanley Stoke 168 F5
Hanley Castle Worcs 98 C6
Hanley Child Worcs 116 E3
Hanley Swan Worcs 98 C6
Hanley William Worcs 116 D3
Hanlith N Yorks 213 G8
Hanmer Wrex 149 B9
Hannaford Devon 25 B10
Hannafore Corn 6 E5
Hannah Lincs 191 F8
Hanningfields Green
Suff 125 G7
Hannington Hants 48 B4
Swindon 81 G11
W Nhants 120 C6
Hannington Wick
Swindon 81 F11
Hanscombe End C Beds 104 E2
Hansel Devon 8 F6
Hansel Village S Ayrs 257 C9
Hansley Cross Staffs 169 G9
Hanslope M Keynes 102 B6
Hanthorpe Lincs 155 E11
Hanwell London 67 C7
Oxon 101 C8
Hanwood Shrops 131 B8
Hanwood Bank Shrops 149 G8
Hanworth Brack 65 F11
London 66 E6
Norf 160 B3
Happendon S Lanark 259 C9
Happisburgh Norf 161 C7
Happisburgh Common
Norf 161 D7
Hapsford Ches W 183 G7
Som 45 D9
Hapton Lancs 203 G11
Norf 142 D3
Hararden = *Penarlâg*
Flint 166 B4
Harberton Devon 8 D5
Harbertonford Devon 8 D5
Harbledown Kent 54 B6
Harborne W Mid 133 G10
Harborough Magna
Warks 119 B9
Harborough Parva
Warks 119 B9
Harbottle Northumb 251 C10
Harbour Heights E Sus 36 G6
Harbourland Kent 53 B9
Harbourneford Devon 8 C4
Harbours Hill Worcs 117 D9
Harbour Village Pembs 91 D8
Harbridge Hants 31 E10
Harbridge Green Hants 31 E10
Harburn W Loth 269 C10
Harbury Warks 119 F7
Harby Leics 154 C4
Notts 188 G5
Harcombe Devon 14 E3
Devon 15 C9
Harcombe Bottom Devon 16 B2
Harcourt Hill Oxon 83 E7
Hardbreck Orkney 314 F4
Hardeicke Glos 80 C4
Harden S Yorks 197 G7
W Mid 133 C10
W Yorks 205 F7
Hardendale Cumb 221 C11
Hardenhuish Wilts 62 E2
Harden Park Ches E 184 F4
Hardgate Aberds 293 C9
Dumfries 237 C10
N Yorks 214 G5
W Dunb 277 G10
Hardham W Sus 35 D8
Hardhorn Lancs 202 F3
Hardingham Norf 141 C10
Hardings Booth Staffs 169 C9
Hardingstone W Nhants 120 F5
Hardings Wood Staffs 168 E4
Hardington Som 45 C8
Hardington Mandeville
Som 29 E8
Hardington Marsh Som 29 F8
Hardington Moor Som 29 E8
Hardiston Perth 279 B11
Hardisworthy Devon 24 C2
Hardley Hants 32 G6
Hardley Street Norf 143 C7
Hardmead M Keynes 103 B8
Hardrow N Yorks 223 G7
Hardstoft Derbys 170 C6
Hardstoft Common
Derbys 170 C6
Hardway Hants 33 G10
Som 45 G8
Hardwick Bucks 84 B4
Cambs 122 D3
Cambs 123 F7
N Nhants 121 D7
Norf 142 F4
Norf 158 F2
Oxon 82 D5
Oxon 101 C8
Oxon 101 F11
Shrops 131 E7
Stockton 234 G4
S Yorks 187 D7
W Mid 133 D11
Hardwicke Glos 80 C3
Glos 99 F8
Hereford 96 C5
Hardwick Green Worcs 98 E6
Hardwick Village Notts 187 F10
Hardy's Green Essex 107 G8
Hare Som 28 D3
Hare Appletree Lancs 202 B6
Hareby Lincs 174 B4
Harecroft W Yorks 205 F7
Hareden Lancs 203 C8
Hare Edge Derbys 186 G4
Harefield London 85 G9
Soton 33 E7
Harefield Grove London 85 G9
Haregate Staffs 169 D7
Hare Green Essex 107 G11
Hare Hatch Wokingham 65 D10
Harehill Derbys 152 B3
Harehills W Yorks 206 G2
Harehope Borders 270 G4
Northumb 264 E3
Harelaw Durham 242 G5
Hareleeshill S Lanark 268 E5
Hareplain Kent 53 F10
Haresceugh Cumb 231 C8
Harescombe Glos 80 C4
Haresfield Glos 80 C4
Swindon 82 G2
Haresfinch Mers 183 B8
Hareshaw N Lanark 268 C6
Hareshaw Head
Northumb 251 F9
Harestanes E Dunb 278 G3
Harestock Hants 48 G3
Hare Street Essex 86 D6
Herts 104 F6
Herts 105 F7
Harewood W Yorks 206 D2
Harewood End Hereford 97 F10
Harewood Hill W Yorks 204 F6
Harford Carms 94 C2
Devon 8 D2
Devon 40 G6
Hargate Norf 142 E2
Hargate Hill Derbys 185 C8
Hargatewall Derbys 185 F10
Hargrave Ches W 167 C7
N Nhants 121 C10
Suff 124 F5
Harker Cumb 239 E9
Harker Marsh Cumb 229 E7
Harkland Shetland 312 E6
Harknett's Gate Essex 86 D6
Harkstead Suff 108 E3
Harlaston Staffs 152 G4
Harlaw Ho Aberds 303 G7
Harlaxton Lincs 155 C7
Harlech Gwyn 145 C11
Harlequin Notts 154 B3
Harlescott Shrops 149 F10
Harlesden London 67 C8
Harlesthorpe Derbys 187 F7
Harleston Devon 8 F5
Norf 142 G4
Suff 125 F10
Harlestone W Nhants 120 E4
Harle Syke Lancs 204 F3
Harley Shrops 131 C11
S Yorks 186 B5
Harleyholm S Lanark 259 B10
Harley Shute E Sus 38 F3
Harleywood Glos 80 F4
Harling Road Norf 141 F9
Harlington C Beds 103 E10
London 66 D5
S Yorks 198 G3
Harlosh Highld 298 E2
Harlow Essex 86 C6
Harlow Carr N Yorks 205 C11
Harlow Green T&W 243 F7
Harlow Hill Northumb 242 D3
N Yorks 205 C11
Harlthorpe E Yorks 207 F10
Harlton Cambs 123 G7
Harlyn Corn 10 F3
Harman's Corner Kent 69 G11
Harman's Cross Dorset 18 E5
Harmans Water Brack 65 F11
Harmby N Yorks 214 B2
Harmer Green Herts 86 B3
Harmer Hill Shrops 149 E9
Harmondsworth London 66 D5
Harmston Lincs 173 C7
Harnage Shrops 131 C11
Harnham Northumb 242 B3
Wilts 31 B10
Wilts 31 B11
Harnhill Glos 81 E9
Harold Hill London 87 G8
Harold Park London 87 G9
Haroldston West Pembs 72 B5
Haroldswick Shetland 312 B8
Harold Wood London 87 G8
Harome N Yorks 216 C2
Harpenden Herts 85 C10
Harpenden Common
Herts 85 C10
Harper Green Gtr Man 195 F8
Harperley Durham 242 G5
Harper's Gate Staffs 169 D7
Harper's Green Norf 159 E8
Harpford Devon 15 C7
Harpham E Yorks 217 G11
Harpley Norf 158 D5
Worcs 116 E3
Harpole W Nhants 120 E3
Harpsdale Highld 310 D5
Harpsden Oxon 65 C9
Harpsden Bottom Oxon 65 C9
Harpswell Lincs 188 D6
Harpton Powys 114 F4
Harpurhey Gtr Man 195 G11
Harpur Hill Derbys 185 G9
Harraby Cumb 239 G10
Harracott Devon 25 B9
Harrapool Highld 295 C8
Harras Cumb 219 B9
Harraton T&W 243 G7
Harrier Shetland 313 J1
Harrietfield Perth 286 E3
Harrietsham Kent 53 C11
Harringay London 67 B10
Harrington Cumb 228 F5
Lincs 190 G5
N Nhants 136 G5
Harringworth N Nhants 137 D8
Harris Highld 294 F5
Harriseahead Staffs 168 D5
Harriston Cumb 229 C9
Harrogate N Yorks 206 C2
Harrold Bedford 121 F8
Harrop Dale Gtr Man 196 F4
Harrow Highld 310 B6
London 67 B7
Harrowbarrow Corn 7 B7
Harrowbeer Devon 7 B10
Harrowby Lincs 155 B8
Harrowden Bedford 103 B11
Harrowgate Hill Darl 224 B5
Harrowgate Village
Darl 224 B5
Harrow Green Suff 125 G7
Harrow Hill Glos 79 B10
Harrow on the Hill
London 67 B7
Harrow Street Suff 107 D9
Harrow Weald London 85 G11
Harry Stoke S Glos 60 D6
Harston Cambs 123 G8
Harston *continued*
Leics 154 C6
Harswell E Yorks 208 E2
Hart Hrtlpl 234 E5
Hartbarrow Cumb 221 G8
Hartburn Northumb 252 F3
Stockton 225 B8
Hartcliffe Bristol 60 F5
Hart Common Gtr Man 194 F6
Hartest Suff 124 G6
Hartest Hill Suff 124 G6
Hartfield E Sus 52 F3
Highld 299 E7
Hartford Cambs 122 C5
Ches W 183 G10
Som 27 B7
Hartfordbeach
Ches W 183 G10
Hartfordbridge Hants 49 B9
Hartford End Essex 87 B11
Hartforth N Yorks 224 D3
Hartgrove Dorset 30 D4
Harthill Ches W 167 D8
N Lanark 269 C8
S Yorks 187 E7
Hart Hill Luton 104 G2
Hartington Derbys 169 C10
Hartland Devon 24 C3
Hartle Worcs 117 B8
Hartlebury Shrops 132 D4
Worcs 116 C6
Hartlebury Common
Worcs 116 C6
Hartlepool Hrtlpl 234 E6
Hartley Cumb 222 D5
Kent 53 G9
Kent 68 F6
Northumb 243 B8
Plym 7 D9
Hartley Green Kent 68 F6
Staffs 151 D9
Hartley Mauditt Hants 49 F8
Hartley Westpall Hants 49 B7
Hartley Wintney Hants 49 B9
Hartlington N Yorks 213 G10
Hartlip Kent 69 G10
Hartmoor Dorset 30 C3
Hartmount Highld 301 B7
Hartoft End N Yorks 226 G5
Harton N Yorks 216 G4
Shrops 131 F9
T&W 243 E9
Hartpury Glos 98 F5
Hartsgreen Shrops 132 G5
Hart's Green Suff 125 F7
Hartshead W Yorks 197 C7
Hartshead Green
Gtr Man 196 G3
Hartshead Moor Side
W Yorks 197 C7
Hartshead Moor Top
W Yorks 197 B7
Hartshead Pike
Gtr Man 196 G3
Hartshill Stoke 168 F5
Warks 134 E6
Hart's Hill W Mid 133 F8
Hartshill Green Warks 134 E6
Hartshorne Derbys 152 E6
Hartsop Cumb 221 C8
Hart Station Hrtlpl 234 D5
Hartswell Som 27 B9
Hartwell Staffs 151 B8
W Nhants 120 G5
Hartwith N Yorks 214 G4
Hartwood Lancs 194 D5
N Lanark 268 D6
Hartwoodburn Borders 261 D11
Harvel Kent 68 G6
Harvest Hill W Mid 134 G5
Harvieston Stirling 277 D11
Harvills Hawthorn
W Mid 133 E9
Harvington Worcs 99 B11
Worcs 117 C7
Harvington Cross Worcs 99 B11
Harvington Hill Worcs 99 B10
Harwell Notts 187 C11
Oxon 64 B3
Harwich Essex 108 E5
Harwood Durham 232 E2
Gtr Man 195 E8
Harwood Dale N Yorks 227 F9
Harwood Lee Gtr Man 195 E8
Harwood on Teviot
Borders 249 B10
Harworth Notts 187 C10
Hasbury W Mid 133 G9
Hascombe Sur 50 E3
Haselbech W Nhants 120 B4
Haselbury Plucknett Som 29 E7
Haseley Warks 118 D4
Haseley Green Warks 118 D4
Haseley Knob Warks 118 C4
Haselor Warks 118 F2
Hasfield Glos 98 F6
Hasguard Pembs 72 D5
Haskayne Lancs 193 F11
Hasketon Suff 126 G4
Hasland Derbys 170 B5
Haslemere Sur 50 G2
Haslingbourne W Sus 35 C7
Haslingden Lancs 195 C9
Haslingfield Cambs 123 G8
Haslington Ches E 168 D2
Hasluck's Green W Mid 118 B2
Hassall Ches E 168 D3
Hassall Green Ches E 168 D3
Hassell Street Kent 54 D5
Hassendean Borders 262 E2
Hassingham Norf 143 B7
Hassocks W Sus 36 D3
Hassop Derbys 186 G2
Haster Highld 310 D7
Hasthorpe Lincs 175 B7
Hastigrow Highld 310 C6
Hasting Hill T&W 243 G9
Hastingleigh Kent 54 E5
Hastings E Sus 38 F4
Som 28 D4
Hastingwood Essex 87 D7
Hastoe Herts 84 D6
Haston Shrops 149 E10
Haswell Durham 234 C3
Haswell Moor Durham 234 C3
Haswell Plough Durham 234 C3
Haswellsykes Borders 260 B6
Hatch C Beds 104 B3
Devon 8 F4
Hants 49 C7
Wilts 30 B6
Hatch Beauchamp Som 28 C4
Hatch Bottom Hants 33 E7
Hatch End Bedford 121 E11
London 85 G10
Hatchet Gate Hants 32 G5
Hatchet Green Hants 31 D11
Hatch Farm Hill W Sus 34 B6
Hatch Green Som 28 D4
Hatching Green Herts 85 C10
Hatchmere Ches W 183 G9
Hatch Warren Hants 48 D6
Hatcliffe NE Lincs 201 G8
Hateley Heath W Mid 133 E10
Hatfield Hereford 115 F11
Herts 86 D2
S Yorks 199 F7
Worcs 117 G7
Hatfield Broad Oak Essex 87 B8
Hatfield Chase S Yorks 199 E8
Hatfield Garden Village
Herts 86 D2
Hatfield Heath Essex 87 B8
Hatfield Hyde Herts 86 C2
Hatfield Peverel Essex 88 C3
Hatfield Woodhouse
S Yorks 199 F7
Hatford Oxon 82 G4
Hatherden Hants 47 C10
Hatherleigh Devon 25 G8
Hatherley Glos 99 G8
Hathern Leics 153 E9
Hatherop Glos 81 D11
Hathersage Derbys 186 E2
Hathersage Booths
Derbys 186 E2
Hathershaw Gtr Man 196 G2
Hatherton Ches E 167 F11
Staffs 151 G9
Hatley St George Cambs 122 G5
Hatston Orkney 314 E4
Hatt Corn 7 C7
Hatterseat Aberds 303 G9
Hattersley Gtr Man 185 C7
Hatt Hill Hants 32 B4
Hattingley Hants 48 F6
Hatton Aberds 303 F10
Angus 287 D9
Derbys 152 D4
Lincs 189 F11
London 66 D5
Moray 301 D11
Shrops 131 E9
Warks 118 D4
Warr 183 E9
Hattonburn Aberds 293 C9
Hatton Castle Aberds 303 E7
Hattoncrook Aberds 303 G8
Hatton Grange Shrops 132 C5
Hatton Heath Ches W 167 C7
Hatton Hill Sur 66 G2
Hattonknowe Borders 270 F4
Hatton of Fintray
Aberds 293 B10
Hatton Park N Nhants 121 D7
Haugh E Ayrs 257 D11
Gtr Man 196 E2
Lincs 190 F6
Haugham Lincs 190 E4
Haugh-head Borders 261 B8
Haugh Head Northumb 264 D2
Haughland Orkney 314 E5
Haughley Suff 125 E10
Haughley Green Suff 125 E10
Haughley New Street
Suff 125 E10
Haugh of Glass Moray 302 F4
Haugh of Kilnmaichlie
Moray 301 F11
Haugh of Urr Dumfries 237 C10
Haughs of Clinterty
Aberdeen 293 B10
Haughton Ches E 167 D9
Notts 187 G11
Powys 148 F6
Shrops 132 B4
Shrops 132 D3
Shrops 149 D7
Shrops 149 F11
Staffs 151 E7
Haughton Castle
Northumb 241 C10
Haughton Green
Gtr Man 184 C6
Haughton Le Skerne
Darl 224 B6
Haughurst Hill W Berks 64 G5
Haulkerton Aberds 293 F9
Haultwick Herts 104 G6
Haunn Argyll 288 E5
W Isles 297 K3
Haunton Staffs 152 G4
Hauxton Cambs 123 G8
Havannah Ches E 168 C5
Havant Hants 22 B2
Haven Hereford 97 B11
Hereford 115 G8
Haven Bank Lincs 174 E2
Haven Side E Yorks 201 B7
Havenstreet IoW 21 C7
Havercroft W Yorks 197 E11
Haverfordwest = *Hwlffordd*
Pembs 73 B7
Haverhill Suff 106 B3
Haverigg Cumb 210 D3
Havering-atte-Bower
London 87 G8
Haveringland Norf 160 E3
Haversham M Keynes 102 C6
Haverthwaite Cumb 210 C6
Haverton Hill Stockton 234 G5
Haviker Street Kent 53 D8
Havyatt Som 44 F4
Havyatt Green N Som 60 G3
Hawarden = *Penarlâg*
Flint 166 B4
Hawbridge Worcs 99 B8
Hawbush Green Essex 106 G5
Hawcoat Cumb 210 E4
Hawcross Glos 98 E5
Hawddamor Gwyn 146 F3
Hawen Ceredig 92 B6
Hawes N Yorks 213 B7
Hawes' Green Norf 142 D4
Hawes Side Blackpool 202 G2
Hawford Worcs 116 E6
Hawgreen Shrops 150 D2
Hawick Borders 262 F2
Hawkchurch Devon 28 G4
Hawkcombe Som 41 D11
Hawkedon Suff 124 G5
Hawkenbury Kent 52 F5
Kent 53 E10
Hawkeridge Wilts 45 C11
Hawkerland Devon 15 D7
Hawkersland Cross
Hereford 97 B10
Hawkesbury S Glos 61 B9
Warks 135 G7
Hawkesbury Upton
S Glos 61 B9
Hawkes End W Mid 134 G6
Hawkesley W Mid 117 B10
Hawk Green Gtr Man 185 D7
Hawkhill Northumb 264 G6
Hawk Hill Cumb 228 F6
Hawkhope Northumb 250 F6
Hawkhurst Kent 53 G9
Hawkhurst Common
E Sus 23 B8
Hawkinge Kent 55 F8
Hawkin's Hill Essex 106 E3
Hawkley Gtr Man 194 G5
Hants 34 B2
Hawkridge Som 41 G11
Hawksdale Cumb 230 B3
Hawks Green Staffs 151 G9
Hawkshaw Blackburn 195 D9
Hawkshead Cumb 221 F7
Hawkshead Hill Cumb 220 F6
Hawks Hill Bucks 66 B2
Hawk's Hill Sur 51 B7
Hawksland S Lanark 259 B8
Hawkspur Green
Essex 106 E3
Hawks Stones W Yorks 196 B2
Hawkswick N Yorks 213 E9
Hawksworth Notts 172 G3
W Yorks 205 E9
W Yorks 205 F11
Hawkwell Essex 88 G4
Hawley Hants 49 B11
Kent 68 E4
Hawley Bottom Devon 28 G2
Hawley Lane Hants 49 B11
Hawling Glos 99 G11
Hawn Orkney 314 D4
Hawnby N Yorks 215 B10
Hawne W Mid 133 G9
Haworth W Yorks 204 F6
Haws Bank Cumb 220 F6
Hawstead Suff 125 F7
Hawstead Green Suff 125 F7
Hawthorn Durham 234 B4
Hants 49 G7
Rhondda 58 B6
Wilts 61 F11
Hawthorn Corner Kent 71 F8
Hawthorn Hill Brack 65 E11
Lincs 174 D2
Hawthorns Staffs 168 F4
Hawthorpe Lincs 155 D10
Hawton Notts 172 E3
Haxby York 207 B8
Haxey N Lincs 188 B3
N Lincs 199 G9
Haxey Carr N Lincs 199 G9
Haxted Sur 52 D2
Haxton Wilts 46 D6
Hay Corn 10 G5
Haybridge Shrops 116 C2
Som 44 D4
Telford 150 G3
Haydock Mers 183 B9
Haydon Bath 45 C7
Dorset 29 D11
Som 28 C3
Som 44 D5
Swindon 62 B6
Haydon Bridge
Northumb 241 E8
Haydon Wick Swindon 62 B6
Haye Corn 7 B7
Haye Fm Corn 6 B6
Hayes London 66 C6
London 68 F2
Staffs 169 C9
Hayes End London 66 C5
Hayes Knoll Wilts 81 G10
Hayes Town London 66 C6
Hayfield Derbys 185 D8
Fife 280 C5
Hay Field S Yorks 187 B10
Hayfield Green
S Yorks 187 B11
Haygate Telford 150 G2
Haygrass Som 28 C2
Hay Green Essex 87 E10
Herts 104 D6
Norf 157 F10
Hayhill E Ayrs 257 F11
Hayhillock Angus 287 C9
Haylands IoW 21 C7
Hayle Corn 2 B3
Hayley Green W Mid 133 G8
Hay Mills W Mid 134 G2
Haymoor End Som 28 B4
Haymoor Green
Ches E 167 E11
Hayne Devon 26 F5
Haynes C Beds 103 C11
Haynes Church End
C Beds 103 C11
Haynes West End
C Beds 103 C11
Hay-on-Wye Powys 96 C4
Hayscastle Pembs 91 F7
Hayscastle Cross Pembs 91 G8
Haysford Pembs 91 G8
Hayshead Angus 287 C10
Hayston E Dunb 278 G2
Haystoun Borders 261 B7
Hay Street Herts 105 F7
Haythorne Dorset 31 F8
Hayton Aberdeen 293 C11
Cumb 229 C8
Cumb 240 F2
E Yorks 208 D2
Notts 188 E2
Hayton's Bent Shrops 131 G10
Haytor Vale Devon 13 F11
Haytown Devon 24 E5
Haywards Heath W Sus 36 C4
Haywood S Lanark 269 E9
S Yorks 198 E5
Haywood Oaks Notts 171 D10
Hazard's Green E Sus 23 C11
Hazelbank S Lanark 268 F6
Hazelbeach Pembs 72 E6
Hazelbury Bryan Dorset 30 F2
Hazeleigh Essex 88 E4
Hazel End Essex 105 G9
Hazeley Hants 49 B8
Hazeley Bottom Hants 49 B9
Hazeley Heath Hants 49 B9
Hazeley Lea Hants 49 B8
Hazelgrove Notts 171 F8
Hazel Grove Gtr Man 184 D6
Hazelhurst Gtr Man 195 D9
Gtr Man 195 G9
Gtr Man 196 G3
Hazelslack Cumb 211 D9
Hazelslade Staffs 151 G10
Hazel Street Kent 53 B11
Kent 53 F7
Hazel Stub Suff 106 C3
Hazelton Glos 81 B9
Hazelton Walls Fife 287 E7
Hazelwood Derbys 170 F4
Devon 8 E4
London 68 G2
Hazlehead S Yorks 197 G7
Hazlemere Bucks 84 F5
Hazler Shrops 131 E9
Hazlerigg T&W 242 C6
Hazles Staffs 169 F8
Hazlescross Staffs 169 F8
Hazleton Glos 81 B9
Hazlewood N Yorks 205 C7
Hazon Northumb 252 C5
Heacham Norf 158 B3
Headbourne Worthy
Hants 48 G3
Headbrook Hereford 114 F6
Headcorn Kent 53 E10
Headingley W Yorks 205 F11
Headington Oxon 83 D8
Headington Hill Oxon 83 D8
Headlam Durham 224 B3
Headless Cross Cumb 211 D7
Worcs 117 D10
Headley Hants 49 F10
Hants 64 G4
Sur 51 C8
Headley Down Hants 49 F10
Headley Heath Worcs 117 B11
Headley Park Bristol 60 F5
Head of Muir Falk 278 E6
Headon Devon 24 G5
Notts 188 F2
Heads S Lanark 268 F4
Headshaw Borders 261 E11
Heads Nook Cumb 239 F11
Headstone London 66 B6
Headwell Fife 279 D11
Heady Hill Gtr Man 195 E10
Heage Derbys 170 E5
Healaugh N Yorks 206 D5
N Yorks 223 F10
Heald Green Gtr Man 184 D4
Healds Green Gtr Man 195 F11
Heale Devon 40 D6
Som 28 B5
Som 28 D2
Som 45 E7
Healey Gtr Man 195 D11
Northumb 242 F2
N Yorks 214 C3
W Yorks 197 C8
W Yorks 197 D9
Healey Cote Northumb 252 C4
Healeyfield Durham 233 B7
Healey Hall Northumb 242 F2
Healing NE Lincs 201 E8
Heamoor Corn 1 C5
Heaning Cumb 221 F8
Heanish Argyll 288 E2
Heanor Derbys 170 F6
Heanor Gate Derbys 170 F6
Heanton Punchardon
Devon 40 F4
Heap Bridge Gtr Man 195 E10
Heapham Lincs 188 D5
Hearn Hants 49 F10
Hearnden Green Kent 53 D10
Hearthstane Borders 260 D4
Hearthstone Derbys 170 D4
Hearts Delight Kent 69 G11
Heasley Mill Devon 41 G8
Heast Highld 295 D8
Heath Cardiff 59 D7
Derbys 170 B6
Halton 183 E8
Heath and Reach
C Beds 103 F8
Heath Charnock Lancs 194 E5
Heath Common W Sus 35 E10
W Yorks 197 D11
Heathcot Aberds 293 C10
Heathcote Derbys 169 C10
Shrops 150 D3
Warks 118 E6
Heath Cross Devon 13 B10
Devon 14 C2
Heath End Bucks 84 F5
Bucks 85 D7
Derbys 153 E7
Hants 64 G2
Hants 64 G5
S Glos 61 B7
Sur 49 D10
Warks 118 E4
W Mid 133 C10
W Sus 35 D7
Heather Leics 153 G7
Heathercombe Devon 13 E10
Heatherfield Highld 298 E4
Heather Row Hants 49 C8
Heatherside Sur 50 B2
Heatherwood Park
Highld 311 K2
Heatherybanks Aberds 303 E7
Heathfield Cambs 105 B9
Devon 14 F2
E Sus 37 C9
Glos 80 F2
Hants 33 F9
Lincs 189 C10
N Yorks 214 F2
S Ayrs 257 E9
Som 27 B11
Som 43 G7
Heathfield Village Oxon 83 B8
Heath Green Hants 48 F6
Worcs 117 C11
Heathhall Dumfries 237 B11
Heath Hayes Staffs 151 G10
Heath Hill Shrops 150 G5
Heath House Som 44 D2
Heathlands Wokingham 65 F10
Heath Lanes Telford 150 E2
Heath Park London 68 B4
Heathrow Airport London 66 D5
Heath Side Kent 68 E4
Heathstock Devon 28 G2
Heathton Shrops 132 E6
Heathtop Derbys 152 C4
Heath Town W Mid 133 D8
Heathwaite Cumb 221 F8
N Yorks 225 E9
Heatley Staffs 151 D11
Warr 184 D2
Heaton Gtr Man 195 F7
Lancs 211 G8
Staffs 169 C7
T&W 243 D7
W Yorks 205 G8
Heaton Chapel Gtr Man 184 C5
Heaton Mersey Gtr Man 184 C5
Heaton Moor Gtr Man 184 C5
Heaton Norris Gtr Man 184 C5
Heaton Royds W Yorks 205 F8
Heaton's Bridge Lancs 194 E2
Heaton Shay W Yorks 205 F8
Heaven's Door Som 29 C10
Heaverham Kent 52 B5
Heaviley Gtr Man 184 D6
Heavitree Devon 14 C4
Hebburn T&W 243 E8
Hebburn Colliery T&W 243 D8
Hebburn New Town
T&W 243 E8
Hebden N Yorks 213 G10
Hebden Bridge W Yorks 196 B3
Hebden Green Ches W 167 B10
Hebing End Herts 104 G6
Hebron Anglesey 179 E7
Carms 92 F3
Northumb 252 F5
Heck Dumfries 248 G3

Heckdyke N Lincs 188 B3
Heckfield Hants 65 G8
Heckfield Green Suff 126 B3
Heckfordbridge Essex 107 G8
Heckingham Norf 143 D7
Heckington Lincs 173 G10
Heckmondwike
W Yorks 197 C8
Heddington Wilts 62 F3
Heddington Wick Wilts 62 F3
Heddle Orkney 314 E3
Heddon Devon 25 B11
Heddon-on-the-Wall
Northumb 242 D4
Hedenham Norf 142 E6
Hedge End Dorset 30 F4
Hants 33 E7
Hedgehog Bridge Lincs 174 F3
Hedgerley Bucks 66 B3
Hedgerley Green Bucks 66 B3
Hedgerley Hill Bucks 66 B3
Hedging Som 28 B4
Hedley Hill Durham 233 C9
Hedley on the Hill
Northumb 242 F3
Hednesford Staffs 151 G9
Hedon E Yorks 201 B7
Hedsor Bucks 66 B2
Hedworth T&W 243 E8
Heelands M Keynes 102 D6
Heeley S Yorks 186 E5
Hegdon Hill Hereford 115 G11
Heggerscales Cumb 222 C6
Heggle Lane Cumb 230 D3
Heglibister Shetland 313 H5
Heighington Darl 233 G11
Lincs 173 B8
Heighley Staffs 168 F3
Height End Lancs 195 C9
Heightington Worcs 116 C5
Heights Gtr Man 196 F3
Heights of Brae Highld 300 C5
Heights of Kinlochewe
Highld 299 C10
Heilam Highld 308 C4
Heiton Borders 262 C6
Helbeck Cumb 222 B5
Hele Devon 12 C2
Devon 13 G10
Devon 27 G7
Devon 40 D4
Som 27 C11
Torbay 9 B8
Helebridge Corn 24 G2
Helensburgh Argyll 276 E5
Helford Corn 3 D7
Helford Passage Corn 3 D7
Helham Green Herts 86 B5
Helhoughton Norf 159 D7
Helions Bumpstead
Essex 106 C3
Hellaby S Yorks 187 C8
Helland Corn 11 G7
Som 28 C4
Hellandbridge Corn 11 G7
Hell Corner W Berks 63 G11
Hellesdon Norf 160 G4
Hellesveor Corn 2 A2
Hellidon W Nhants 119 F10
Hellifield N Yorks 204 B3
Hellifield Green
N Yorks 204 B3
Hellingly E Sus 23 C9
Hellington Norf 142 C6
Hellister Shetland 313 J5
Hellman's Cross Essex 87 B9
Helm Northumb 252 D5
N Yorks 223 G8
Helmburn Borders 261 E9
Helmdon W Nhants 101 C11
Helme W Yorks 196 E5
Helmingham Suff 126 F3
Helmington Row
Durham 233 D9
Helmsdale Highld 311 H4
Helmshore Lancs 195 C9
Helmside Cumb 212 B3
Helmsley N Yorks 216 C2
Helperby N Yorks 215 F8
Helperthorpe N Yorks 217 E9
Helpringham Lincs 173 G10
Helpston Pboro 138 B2
Helsby Ches W 183 F7
Helscott Corn 24 G2
Helsey Lincs 191 G8
Helston Corn 2 D5
Helstone Corn 11 E7
Helston Water Corn 4 G5
Helton Cumb 230 G6
Helwith N Yorks 223 E11
Helwith Bridge N Yorks 212 F6
Helygain = *Halkyn* Flint 182 G2
Hemblington Norf 160 G6
Hemblington Corner
Norf 160 G6
Hembridge Som 44 F5
Hemel Hempstead Herts 85 D9
Hemerdon Devon 7 D11
Hemford Shrops 130 C6
Hem Heath Stoke 168 G5
Hemingbrough N Yorks 207 G9
Hemingby Lincs 190 G2
Hemingfield S Yorks 197 G11
Hemingford Abbots
Cambs 122 C5
Hemingford Grey
Cambs 122 C5
Hemingstone Suff 126 G3
Hemington Leics 153 D9
N Nhants 137 F11
Som 45 C8
Hemley Suff 108 C5
Hemlington Mbro 225 C10
Hemp Green Suff 127 D7
Hempholme E Yorks 209 C7
Hempnall Norf 142 E4
Hempnall Green Norf 142 E4
Hempriggs House
Highld 310 E7
Hemp's Green Essex 107 F8
Hempshill Vale Notts 171 G8
Hempstead Essex 106 D2
Medway 69 G9
Norf 160 B2
Norf 161 D8
Hempsted Glos 80 B4
Hempton Norf 159 D8
Oxon 101 E8
Hempton Wainhill Oxon 84 E3
Hemsby Norf 161 F9
Hemsted Kent 54 E6
Hemswell Lincs 188 C6
Hemswell Cliff Lincs 188 D6
Hemsworth Dorset 31 F7
S Yorks 186 E5
W Yorks 198 E2
Hemyock Devon 27 E10
Henaford Devon 24 D2
Hen Bentref Llandegfan
Anglesey 179 G9
Henbrook Worcs 117 D8
Henbury Bristol 60 D5
Ches E 184 G5
Dorset 18 B5
Hendomen Powys 130 D4
Hendon London 67 B8
T&W 243 F10
Hendra Corn 2 B6
Corn 2 C5
Corn 2 D3
Corn 2 F6
Corn 5 C9
Corn 5 D9
Corn 11 E7
Hendrabridge Corn 6 B5
Hendraburnick Corn 11 D8
Hendra Croft Corn 4 D5
Hendre Flint 165 B11
Gwyn 110 B2
Powys 129 D9
Hendre-ddu Conwy 164 B5
Hendredenny Park
Caerph 58 B6
Hendreforgan Rhondda 58 B3
Hendrerwydd Denb 165 C10
Hendrewen Swansea 75 D10
Hendy Carms 75 E9
Hendy-Gwyn Carms 74 B2
Hendy Gwyn = *Whitland*
Carms 73 B11
Hên-efail Denb 165 C9
Heneglwys Anglesey 178 F6
Hen-feddau fawr Pembs 92 E4
Henfield S Glos 61 D7
W Sus 36 D2
Henford Devon 12 C3
Henfords Marsh Wilts 45 E11
Henghurst Kent 54 F3
Hengoed Caerph 77 F10
Denb 165 D9
Powys 114 G4
Shrops 148 C5
Hengrave Norf 160 F2
Suff 124 D6
Hengrove Bristol 60 F6
Hengrove Park Bristol 60 F5
Henham Essex 105 F10
Heniarth Powys 130 B2
Henlade Som 28 C3
Henleaze Bristol 60 D5
Henley Dorset 29 G11
Glos 80 B6
Shrops 115 B10
Shrops 131 F9
Som 44 G2
Suff 126 G3
Wilts 47 B10
Wilts 61 F10
W Sus 34 B5
Henley Common W Sus 34 B5
Henley Green W Mid 135 G7
Henley-in-Arden Warks 118 D3
Henley-on-Thames Oxon 65 C9
Henley's Down E Sus 38 E2
Henley Street Kent 69 F7
Henllan Ceredig 93 C7
Denb 165 B8
Henllan Amgoed Carms 92 G3
Henlle Shrops 148 C6
Henllys Torf 78 G3
Henllys Vale Torf 78 G3
Henlow C Beds 104 D3
Hennock Devon 14 E2
Henny Street Essex 107 D7
Henryd Conwy 180 G3
Henry's Moat Pembs 91 F10
Hensall N Yorks 198 C5
Henshaw Northumb 241 E7
W Yorks 205 E10
Hensingham Cumb 219 B9
Hensington Oxon 83 B7
Henstead Suff 143 F9
Hensting Hants 33 C7
Henstridge Devon 40 E5
Som 30 D2
Henstridge Ash Som 30 C2
Henstridge Bowden
Som 29 C11
Henstridge Marsh Som 30 C2
Henton Oxon 84 E3
Som 44 D3
Henwood Corn 11 G11
Oxon 83 E7
Henwood Green Kent 52 E6
Heogan Shetland 313 J6
Heol-ddu Carms 75 E7
Swansea 56 B6
Heolgerrig M Tydf 77 D8
Heol-laethog Bridgend 58 C2
Heol-las Bridgend 58 C2
Swansea 57 B7
Heol Senni Powys 95 G8
Heol-y-gaer Powys 96 D3
Heol-y-mynydd V Glam 57 G11
Hepburn Northumb 264 E3
Hepple Northumb 251 C11
Hepscott Northumb 252 G6
Hepthorne Lane Derbys 170 C6
Heptonstall W Yorks 196 B3
Hepworth Suff 125 C9
W Yorks 197 F7
Herbrandston Pembs 72 D5
Hereford Hereford 97 C10
Heribusta Highld 298 B4
Heriot Borders 271 E7
Hermiston Edin 280 G3
Hermitage Borders 250 D2
Dorset 29 F10
W Berks 64 E4
W Sus 22 B3
Hermitage Green Mers 183 C10
Hermit Hill S Yorks 197 G10
Hermit Hole W Yorks 205 F7
Hermon Anglesey 162 B5
Carms 93 E7
Carms 94 F3
Pembs 92 E4
Herne Kent 71 F7
Herne Bay Kent 71 F7
Herne Common Kent 71 F7
Herne Hill London 67 E10
Herne Pound Kent 53 C7
Herner Devon 25 B9
Hernhill Kent 70 G5
Herniss Corn 2 C6
Herodsfoot Corn 6 C4
Heron Cross Stoke 168 G5
Heronden Kent 55 C9
Herongate Essex 87 G10
Heronsford S Ayrs 244 G4
Heronsgate Herts 85 G8
Heron's Ghyll E Sus 37 B7
Herons Green Bath 44 B5
Heronston Bridgend 58 D2
Herra Shetland 312 D8
Herriard Hants 49 D7
Herringfleet Suff 143 D9
Herring's Green
Bedford 103 C11
Herringswell Suff 124 C4
Herringthorpe S Yorks 186 C6
Hersden Kent 71 G8
Hersham Corn 24 F3
Sur 66 G6
Herstmonceux E Sus 23 C10
Herston Dorset 18 F6
Orkney 314 G4
Hertford Herts 86 C4
Hertford Heath Herts 86 C4
Hertingfordbury Herts 86 C4
Hesketh Bank Lancs 194 C2
Hesketh Lane Lancs 203 E8
Hesketh Moss Lancs 194 C2
Hesket Newmarket
Cumb 230 D2
Heskin Green Lancs 194 D4
Hesleden Durham 234 D4
Hesleyside Northumb 251 G8
Heslington York 207 C8
Hessay York 206 C6
Hessenford Corn 6 D6
Hessett Suff 125 E8
Hessle E Yorks 200 B4
W Yorks 198 D2
Hest Bank Lancs 211 F9
Hester's Way Glos 99 G8
Hestinsetter Shetland 313 J4
Heston London 66 D6
Hestwall Orkney 314 E2
Heswall Mers 182 E3
Hethe Oxon 101 F11
Hethel Norf 142 C3
Hethelpit Cross Glos 98 F5
Hethersett Norf 142 C3
Hethersgill Cumb 239 D11
Hetherside Cumb 239 D10
Hetherson Green
Ches W 167 F8
Hethpool Northumb 263 D9
Hett Durham 233 D11
Hetton N Yorks 204 B5
Hetton Downs T&W 234 B3
Hetton-le-Hill T&W 234 B3
Hetton-le-Hole T&W 234 B3
Hetton Steads Northumb 264 B2
Heugh Northumb 242 C3
Heugh-head Aberds 292 B5
Heveningham Suff 126 C6
Hever Kent 52 E3
Heversham Cumb 211 C9
Hevingham Norf 160 E3
Hewas Water Corn 5 F9
Hewelsfield Glos 79 E9
Hewelsfield Common
Glos 79 E8
Hewer Hill Cumb 230 D3
Hew Green N Yorks 205 B10
Hewish N Som 60 G2
Som 28 F6
Hewood Dorset 28 G5
Heworth T&W 243 E7
York 207 C8
Hexham Northumb 241 E10
Hextable Kent 68 E4
Hexthorpe S Yorks 198 G5
Hexton Herts 104 E2
Hexworthy Devon 13 G9
Hey Lancs 204 E3
Heybridge Essex 87 F10
Essex 88 D5
Heybridge Basin Essex 88 D5
Heybrook Bay Devon 7 F10
Heydon Cambs 105 C8
Norf 160 D2
Heydour Lincs 155 B10
Heyford Park Oxon 101 F10
Hey Green W Yorks 196 E4
Heyheads Gtr Man 196 G3
Hey Houses Lancs 193 B10
Heylipol Argyll 288 E1
Heylor Shetland 312 E4
Heyope Powys 114 C4
Heyrod Gtr Man 185 B7
Heysham Lancs 211 G8
Heyshaw N Yorks 214 G3
Heyshott W Sus 34 D5
Heyshott Green W Sus 34 D5
Heyside Gtr Man 196 F2
Heytesbury Wilts 46 E2
Heythrop Oxon 101 F7
Heywood Gtr Man 195 E11
Wilts 45 C11
Hibaldstow N Lincs 200 G3
Hibb's Green Suff 125 G7
Hickford Hill Essex 106 C5
Hickleton S Yorks 198 F3
Hickling Norf 161 E8
Notts 154 D3
Hickling Green Norf 161 E8
Hickling Heath Norf 161 E8
Hickling Pastures Notts 154 D3
Hickmans Green Kent 54 B5
Hicks Forstal Kent 71 G7
Hicks Gate Bath 60 F6
Hick's Mill Corn 4 G5
Hickstead W Sus 36 C3
Hidcote Bartrim Glos 100 C3
Hidcote Boyce Glos 100 C3
Hifnal Shrops 132 D4
Higginshaw Gtr Man 196 F2
High Ackworth W Yorks 198 D2
Higham Derbys 170 D5
Fife 286 F6
Kent 69 E8
Lancs 204 F2
Suff 107 D10
Suff 124 E4
S Yorks 197 F10
Higham Common
S Yorks 197 F10
Higham Dykes
Northumb 242 B4
Higham Ferrers
N Nhants 121 D9
Higham Gobion C Beds 104 E2
Higham Hill London 86 G5
Higham on the Hill
Leics 135 D7
Highampton Devon 25 G7
Highams Park London 86 G5
Higham Wood Kent 52 D5
High Angerton Northumb 252 F3
High Bankhill Cumb 231 C7
High Banton N Lanark 278 E4
High Barn Lincs 174 C5
High Barnes T&W 243 F9
High Barnet London 86 F2
High Beach Essex 86 F6
High Bentham N Yorks 212 F3
High Bickington Devon 25 C10
High Biggins Cumb 212 D2
High Birkwith N Yorks 212 D5
High Birstwith N Yorks 205 B10
High Blantyre S Lanark 268 D3
High Bonnybridge Falk 278 F6
High Bradfield S Yorks 186 C3
High Bradley N Yorks 204 D6
High Bray Devon 41 G7
Highbridge Cumb 230 C3
Hants 33 C7
Highld 290 E3
Som 43 D10
Highbridge *continued*
W Mid 133 C10
Highbrook W Sus 51 G11
High Brooms Kent 52 E5
High Brotheridge Glos 80 C5
High Bullen Devon 25 C8
Highburton W Yorks 197 E7
Highbury London 67 B10
Ptsmth 33 G11
Som 45 D7
Highbury Vale
Nottingham 171 G8
High Buston Northumb 252 B6
High Callerton
Northumb 242 C5
High Cark Cumb 211 C7
High Casterton Cumb 212 D2
High Catton E Yorks 207 C10
High Church Northumb 252 F5
Highclere Hants 64 G2
Highcliffe BCP 19 C10
Derbys 186 F2
High Cogges Oxon 82 D5
High Common Norf 141 B9
High Coniscliffe Darl 224 B4
High Crompton Gtr Man 196 F2
High Cross Cambs 123 F8
Corn 2 D6
E Sus 37 B9
Hants 34 B2
Herts 85 F10
Herts 86 B5
Newport 59 B9
Warks 118 D3
W Sus 36 D2
High Crosshill S Lanark 268 C2
High Cunsey Cumb 221 G7
High Dubmire T&W 234 B2
High Dyke Durham 232 F5
High Easter Essex 87 C10
High Eggborough
N Yorks 198 C5
High Eldrig Dumfries 236 C4
High Ellington N Yorks 214 C3
Higher Alham Som 45 E7
Higher Ansty Dorset 30 G3
Higher Ashton Devon 14 E3
Higher Audley Blackburn 195 B7
Higher Bal Corn 4 E4
Higher Ballam Lancs 202 G3
Higher Bartle Lancs 202 G6
Higher Bebington Mers 182 D4
Higher Berry End
C Beds 103 E9
Higher Blackley
Gtr Man 195 G10
Higher Boarshaw
Gtr Man 195 F11
Higher Bockhampton
Dorset 17 C10
Higher Bojewyan Corn 1 C3
Higher Boscaswell Corn 1 C3
Higher Brixham Torbay 9 D8
Higher Broughton
Gtr Man 195 G10
Higher Burrow Som 28 C6
Higher Burwardsley
Ches W 167 D8
Higher Ercall Telford 149 F11
Higher Chalmington
Dorset 29 G9
Higher Cheriton Devon 27 G10
Higher Chillington Som 28 E5
Higher Chisworth
Derbys 185 C7
Highercliff Corn 6 D4
Higher Clovelly Devon 24 C4
Higher Condurrow Corn 2 B5
Higher Crackington Corn 11 B9
Higher Cransworth Corn 5 B9
Higher Croft Blackburn 195 B7
Higher Denham Bucks 66 B4
Higher Dinting Derbys 185 C8
Higher Disley Ches E 185 E7
Higher Downs Corn 2 C3
Higher Durston Som 28 B3
Higher End Gtr Man 194 G4
Higher Folds Gtr Man 195 G7
Higherford Lancs 204 E3
Higher Gabwell Torbay 9 B8
Higher Green Gtr Man 195 G8
Higher Halstock Leigh
Dorset 29 F8
Higher Heysham Lancs 211 G8
Higher Hogshead
Lancs 195 C11
Higher Holton Som 29 B11
Higher Hurdsfield
Ches E 184 G6
Higher Kingcombe
Dorset 16 B6
Higher Kinnerton Flint 166 C4
Higher Land Corn 12 G3
Higher Marsh Som 30 C2
Higher Melcombe Dorset 30 G2
Higher Menadew Corn 5 D10
Higher Molland Devon 41 G8
Higher Muddiford Devon 40 F5
Higher Nyland Dorset 30 C2
Higher Penwortham
Lancs 194 B4
Higher Pertwood Wilts 45 F11
Higher Porthpean Corn 5 E10
Higher Poynton Ches E 184 E6
Higher Prestacott Devon 12 B3
Higher Rads End
C Beds 103 E9
Higher Ridge Shrops 149 C7
Higher Rocombe Barton
Devon 9 B8
Higher Row Dorset 31 G8
Higher Runcorn Halton 183 E8
Higher Sandford
Dorset 29 C10
Higher Shotton Flint 166 B4
Higher Shurlach
Ches W 183 G11
Higher Slade Devon 40 D4
Higher Street Som 42 E6
Higher Tale Devon 27 G9
Higher Tolcarne Corn 5 B7
Higher Totnell Dorset 29 F10
Highertown Corn 4 G6
Corn 11 E8
Higher Town Corn 5 C10
Scilly 1 F4
Som 42 D3
Higher Tremarcoombe
Corn 6 B5
Higher Vexford Som 42 F6
Higher Walreddon Devon 12 G5
Higher Walton Lancs 194 B5
Warr 183 D9
Higher Wambrook Som 28 F3
Higher Warcombe Devon 40 D3
Higher Weaver Devon 27 G9
Higher Whatcombe
Dorset 30 G4
Higher Wheelton Lancs 194 C6
Higher Whitley
Ches W 183 E10
Higher Wincham
Ches W 183 F11
Higher Woodsford
Dorset 17 D11
Higher Wraxall Dorset 29 G9
Higher Wych Ches W 167 G7
High Etherley Durham 233 F9
High Ferry Lincs 174 F5
Highfield E Yorks 207 F10
Glos 79 E10
Gtr Man 194 G5
Gtr Man 195 F8
Herts 85 D9
N Ayrs 266 E6
Oxon 101 G11
Soton 32 E6
S Yorks 186 D5
T&W 242 F4
High Field Lancs 203 C10
Highfields Cambs 123 F7
Derbys 170 B6
Essex 88 B5
Glos 80 F3
Leicester 136 C2
Northumb 273 E9
Staffs 151 E8
S Yorks 198 F4
High Flatts W Yorks 197 F8
High Forge Durham 242 G6
High Friarside Durham 242 F5
High Gallowhill E Dunb 278 G2
High Garrett Essex 106 F5
Highgate E Sus 52 G2
Kent 53 G9
London 67 B9
Powys 130 D2
S Yorks 198 G3
W Mid 133 F11
High Grange Durham 233 E9
High Grantley N Yorks 214 F4
High Green Cumb 221 E8
Norf 141 B8
Norf 142 B2
Norf 159 G8
Shrops 132 G4
Suff 125 E7
S Yorks 186 B4
Worcs 99 B7
W Yorks 197 E7
High Halden Kent 53 F11
High Halstow Medway 69 D9
High Ham Som 44 G2
High Handenhold
Durham 242 G6
High Harrington Cumb 228 F6
High Harrogate N Yorks 206 B2
High Haswell Durham 234 C3
High Hatton Shrops 150 E2
High Hauxley Northumb 253 C7
High Hawsker N Yorks 227 D8
High Heath Shrops 150 D3
W Mid 133 C10
High Hesket Cumb 230 C5
High Hesleden Durham 234 D5
High Hill Cumb 229 G11
High Houses Essex 87 C11
High Hoyland S Yorks 197 E9
High Hunsley E Yorks 208 F4
High Hurstwood E Sus 37 B7
High Hutton N Yorks 216 F5
High Ireby Cumb 229 D10
High Kelling Norf 177 E10
High Kilburn N Yorks 215 D10
High Lands Durham 233 F8
Highlane Ches E 168 B5
Derbys 186 E6
High Lane Gtr Man 185 D7
Worcs 116 E3
Highlanes Corn 10 G4
Staffs 150 C5
High Lanes Corn 2 B3
High Laver Essex 87 D8
Highlaws Cumb 229 B8
Highleadon Glos 98 G5
High Legh Ches E 184 E2
Highleigh W Sus 22 D4
High Leven Stockton 225 C8
Highley Shrops 132 G4
High Littleton Bath 44 B6
High Longthwaite
Cumb 229 B11
High Lorton Cumb 229 F9
High Marishes N Yorks 216 D6
High Marnham Notts 188 G4
High Melton S Yorks 198 G4
High Mickley Northumb 242 E3
High Mindork Dumfries 236 D5
Highmoor Cumb 229 B11
Oxon 65 B8
High Moor Derbys 187 E7
Lancs 194 E4
Highmoor Cross Oxon 65 C8
Highmoor Hill Mon 60 B3
High Moorsley T&W 234 B2
Highnam Glos 80 B3
Highnam Green Glos 98 G5
High Nash Glos 79 C9
High Newton Cumb 211 C8
High Newton-by-the-Sea
Northumb 264 D6
High Nibthwaite Cumb 210 B5
Highoak Norf 141 C11
High Oaks Cumb 222 G2
High Offley Staffs 150 D5
High Ongar Essex 87 E9
High Onn Staffs 150 F6
High Onn Wharf Staffs 150 F6
High Park Cumb 221 G10
Mers 193 D11
Highridge Bristol 60 F5
High Risby N Lincs 200 E2
Highroad Well Moor
W Yorks 196 B5
High Roding Essex 87 B10
High Rougham Suff 125 E8
High Row Cumb 230 D3
Cumb 230 G3
High Salvington W Sus 35 F10
High Scales Cumb 229 B9
High Sellafield Cumb 219 E10
High Shaw N Yorks 223 G7
High Shields T&W 243 D9
High Shincliffe Durham 233 C11
High Side Cumb 229 E10
High Southwick T&W 243 F9
High Spen T&W 242 F4
High Stakesby N Yorks 227 C7
Highstead Kent 71 F8
Highsted Kent 70 G2
High Stoop Durham 233 C8
Highstreet Kent 70 G5
High Street Corn 5 E9
Kent 53 G8
Pembs 73 B11
Suff 107 B7
Suff 127 C8
Suff 127 F8
Suff 143 G7
Highstreet Green Essex 106 E5
Sur 50 F3
High Street Green Suff 125 F10
High Sunderland
Borders 261 C11
Hightae Dumfries 238 B3
Highter's Heath W Mid 117 B11
High Throston Hrtlpl 234 E5
High Tirfergus Argyll 255 F7
Hightown Ches E 168 C5
Hants 31 G11
Mers 193 G10
Soton 33 E7
Wrex 166 F4
W Yorks 197 C7
High Town Luton 103 G11
Shrops 132 E4
Staffs 151 G9
Hightown Green Suff 125 F9
Hightown Heights
W Yorks 197 C7
High Toynton Lincs 174 B3
High Trewhitt Northumb 252 B2
High Urpeth Durham 242 G6
High Valleyfield Fife 279 D10
High Walton Cumb 219 C9
High Warden Northumb 241 D10
High Water Head Cumb 220 F6
Highway Corn 4 G4
Hereford 97 B9
Som 29 C7
Wilts 62 E4
Windsor 65 C11
Highweek Devon 14 G2
High Westwood Durham 242 F4
High Whinnow Cumb 239 G8
Highwood Devon 27 F10
Dorset 18 D3
Essex 87 E10
Hants 31 F11
Worcs 116 D3
Highwood Hill London 86 G2
High Woolaston Glos 79 F9
High Worsall N Yorks 225 D7
Highworth Swindon 82 G2
Highworthy Devon 24 F6
High Wray Cumb 221 F7
High Wych Herts 87 C7
High Wycombe Bucks 84 G5
Hilborough Norf 140 C6
Hilborough Ho Norf 140 C6
Hilcot Glos 81 B7
Hilcote Derbys 171 D7
Hilcot End Glos 81 E9
Hilcott Wilts 46 B6
Hildenborough Kent 52 D5
Hilden Park Kent 52 D5
Hildersham Cambs 105 B10
Hildersley Hereford 98 G2
Hilderstone Staffs 151 C8
Hilderthorpe E Yorks 218 F3
Hilfield Dorset 29 F10
Hilgay Norf 140 D2
Hill S Glos 79 G10
Warks 119 D9
W Mid 134 D2
Hillam N Yorks 198 B4
Hillbeck Cumb 222 B5
Hillblock Pembs 73 B8
Hillborough Kent 71 F8
Hill Bottom Oxon 64 D6
Hillbourne BCP 18 C6
Hillbrae Aberds 302 E6
Aberds 303 G7
Hill Brow W Sus 34 B3
Hillbutts Dorset 31 G7
Hill Chorlton Staffs 150 B5
Hillcliffe Warr 183 D10
Hillcliffane Derbys 170 F3
Hillcommon Som 27 B11
Hill Common Norf 161 E8
Hill Corner Som 45 D10
Hill Croome Worcs 99 C7
Hillcross Derbys 152 C6
Hill Dale Lancs 194 E3
Hill Deverill Wilts 45 E11
Hilldyke Lincs 174 F4
Hill Dyke Lincs 174 F4
Hillend Fife 280 E2
N Lanark 268 B6
N Som 43 B11
Shrops 132 E6
Swansea 56 C2
Hill End Durham 232 D6
Fife 279 B10
Glos 99 D8
London 85 G8
N Yorks 205 C7
Som 29 E8
Worcs 117 E8
Hillend Green Glos 98 F4
Hillersland Glos 79 C9
Hillerton Devon 13 B10
Hillesden Bucks 102 F3
Hillesden Hamlet Bucks 102 E3
Hillesley Glos 61 B9
Hillfarance Som 27 C11
Hillfarrance Som 27 C11
Hillfield Devon 8 E6
W Mid 118 B2
Hillfields S Glos 60 D6
W Mid 118 B6
Hillfoot Aberds 303 D9
W Yorks 205 G10
Hillfoot End C Beds 104 E2
Hill Furze Worcs 99 B9
Hill Gate Hereford 97 F9
Hillgreen W Berks 64 D3
Hill Green Essex 105 E9
Kent 69 G10
Hillgrove W Sus 34 B6
Hillhampton Hereford 97 B11
Hillhead Aberds 302 F5
Aberds 303 G8
Corn 5 C11
Devon 9 E8
E Ayrs 257 B10
S Ayrs 257 F10
Hill Head Hants 33 G8
Northumb 241 D10
Hillhead of Auchentumb
Aberds 303 D9
Hillhead of Blairy
Aberds 302 D6
Hillhead of Cocklaw
Aberds 303 E10
Hill Hoath Kent 52 E3
Hill Hook W Mid 134 C2
Hillhouse Borders 271 D10
Hill Houses Shrops 116 B2
Hilliard's Cross Staffs 152 G3
Hilliclay Highld 310 C5
Hillingdon London 66 C5
Hillingdon Heath London 66 C5
Hillington Glasgow 267 C10
Norf 158 D4
Hillis Corner IoW 20 C5
Hillmoor Devon 27 E10
Hillmorton Warks 119 C10
Hill Mountain Pembs 73 D7
Hillockhead Aberds 292 B6
Aberds 292 C5
Hillock Vale Lancs 195 B9
Hill of Beath Fife 280 C3
Hill of Drip Stirling 278 B5
Hill of Fearn Highld 301 B8
Hill of Keillor Angus 286 C6
Hill of Mountblairy
Aberds 302 D6
Hill of Overbrae Aberds 303 C8
Hill Park Hants 33 F9
Kent 52 B2
Hillpool Worcs 117 B7
Hillpound Hants 33 D9
Hill Ridware Staffs 151 F11
Hillsborough S Yorks 186 C4
Hillside Aberds 293 D11
Angus 293 G9
Devon 8 C4
Devon 27 F11
Hants 49 C9
Mers 193 E10
Orkney 314 D3
Orkney 314 G4
Shetland 313 G6
Shrops 131 F11
Wilts 81 G9
Hill Side Hants 34 B3
S Yorks 197 G8
Worcs 116 E5
W Yorks 197 D7
Hill Somersal Derbys 152 C2
Hills Town Derbys 171 B7
Hillstreet Hants 32 D4
Hill Street Kent 54 D6
Hillswick Shetland 312 F4
Hilltop Bl Gwent 77 D11
Bucks 85 E7
Derbys 170 C4
Hill Top Derbys 186 F5
Durham 232 G5
Durham 233 C10
Durham 242 G5
Gtr Man 195 G8
Hants 32 G6
Notts 171 F7
N Yorks 214 G3
N Yorks 214 G5
Staffs 133 B7
S Yorks 186 C5
S Yorks 186 D3
S Yorks 187 B7
S Yorks 197 F9
Warks 134 E5
Warks 135 E7
W Mid 133 E9
W Sus 34 C5
W Yorks 196 E5
W Yorks 197 D10
W Yorks 205 G7
W Yorks 205 G11
Hillview T&W 243 G9
Hill View Dorset 18 B5
Hillway IoW 21 D8
Hillwell Shetland 313 M5
Hill Wood W Mid 134 C2
Hill Wootton Warks 118 D6
Hillyfields Hants 32 D5
Hilmarton Wilts 62 D4
Hilperton Wilts 45 B11
Hilperton Marsh Wilts 45 B11
Hilsea Ptsmth 33 G11
Hilston E Yorks 209 G11
Hiltingbury Hants 32 C6
Hilton Aberds 303 F9
Borders 273 E7
Cambs 122 D5
Cumb 231 G10
Derbys 152 C4
Dorset 30 G3
Durham 233 G9
Highld 309 L7
Highld 311 L3
Shrops 132 D5
Staffs 133 B11
Stockton 225 C9
Hilton House Gtr Man 194 F6
Hilton Lodge Highld 300 G2
Hilton of Cadboll Highld 301 B8
Hilton Park Gtr Man 195 G10
Himbleton Worcs 117 F8
Himley Staffs 133 E7
Hincaster Cumb 211 C10
Hinchley Wood Sur 67 F7
Hinchliffe Mill W Yorks 196 F6
Hinchwick Glos 100 E2
Hinckley Leics 135 E8
Hinderclay Suff 125 B10
Hinderton Ches W 182 F4
Hinderwell N Yorks 226 B5
Hindford Shrops 148 C6
Hindhead Sur 49 F11
Hindle Fold Lancs 203 G10
Hindley Gtr Man 194 G6
Northumb 242 F2
Hindley Green Gtr Man 194 G6
Hindlip Worcs 117 F7
Hindolveston Norf 159 D10
Hindon Wilts 46 G2
Hindpool Cumb 210 F3
Hindringham Norf 159 B9
Hindsford Gtr Man 195 G7
Hingham Norf 141 C10
Hinstock Shrops 150 D3
Hintlesham Suff 107 C11
Hinton Glos 79 E11
Hants 19 B10
Hereford 96 D6
S Glos 61 D8
Shrops 131 B8
Som 29 C10
W Nhants 119 G10
Hinton Ampner Hants 33 B9
Hinton Blewett Bath 44 B5
Hinton Charterhouse
Bath 45 B9
Hinton Cross Worcs 99 C10
Hinton-in-the-Hedges
W Nhants 101 D11
Hinton Martell Dorset 31 F8
Hinton on the Green
Worcs 99 C10
Hinton Parva Dorset 31 G7
Swindon 63 C8
Hinton St George Som 28 E6
Hinton St Mary Dorset 30 D3
Hinton Waldrist Oxon 82 F5
Hints Shrops 116 C2
Staffs 134 C3
Hinwick Bedford 121 E8
Hinwood Shrops 131 B7
Hinxhill Kent 54 E5
Hinxton Cambs 105 B9
Hinxworth Herts 104 C4
Hipperholme W Yorks 196 B6
Hipplecote Worcs 116 F4
Hipswell N Yorks 224 F3
Hirael Gwyn 179 G9
Hiraeth Carms 92 G3
Hirn Aberds 293 C9
Hirnant Powys 147 E11
Hirst N Lanark 269 B7
Northumb 253 F7
Hirst Courtney N Yorks 198 C6
Hirwaen Denb 165 C10
Hirwaun Rhondda 77 D7
Hirwaun Common
Bridgend 58 C2
Hiscott Devon 25 B8
Hislop Borders 249 C9
Hisomley Wilts 45 D11
Histon Cambs 123 E8
Hitcham Suff 125 G9
Hitchill Dumfries 238 D4
Hitchin Herts 104 F3
Hitchin Hill Herts 104 F3
Hitcombe Bottom Wilts 45 E10
Hither Green London 67 E11
Hittisleigh Devon 13 C10
Hittisleigh Barton Devon 13 B10
Hive E Yorks 208 G2
Hixon Staffs 151 D10
Hoaden Kent 55 B9
Hoar Cross Staffs 152 E2
Hoarwithy Hereford 97 F10
Hoath Kent 71 G8
Hoath Corner Kent 52 E3
Hobarris Shrops 114 B6
Hobbister Orkney 314 F3
Hobble End Staffs 133 B10
Hobbles Green Suff 124 G4
Hobbs Cross Essex 87 C7
Essex 87 F7
Hobbs Wall Bath 61 G7
Hob Hill Ches W 167 E7
Hobkirk Borders 262 G3
Hobroyd Derbys 185 C8
Hobson Durham 242 F5
Hoby Leics 154 F3
Hoccombe Som 27 B10
Hockenden London 68 F3
Hockerill Herts 105 G9
Hockering Norf 159 G11
Hockering Heath Norf 159 G11
Hockerton Notts 172 D2
Hockholler Som 27 C11
Hockholler Green Som 27 C11
Hockley Ches E 184 E6
Essex 88 G4
Kent 54 B3
Staffs 134 C4
W Mid 118 B5
Hockley Heath W Mid 118 C3
Hockliffe C Beds 103 F9
Hockwold cum Wilton
Norf 140 F4
Hockworthy Devon 27 D8
Hocombe Hants 32 C6
Hoddesdon Herts 86 D5
Hoddlesden Blackburn 195 C8
Hoddomcross Dumfries 238 C5
Hoddom Mains Dumfries 238 C5
Hoden Worcs 99 B11
Hodgefield Staffs 168 E6
Hodgehill Ches E 168 B4
W Mid 134 F2
Hodgeston Pembs 73 F8
Hodley Powys 130 E3
Hodnet Shrops 150 D2
Hodnetheath Shrops 150 D2
Hodsock Notts 187 D10
Hodsoll Street Kent 68 G6
Hodson Swindon 63 C7
Hodthorpe Derbys 187 F8
Hoe Hants 33 D9
Norf 159 F9
Sur 50 D5
Hoe Benham W Berks 64 F2
Hoe Gate Hants 33 E10
Hoff Cumb 222 B3
Hoffleet Stow Lincs 156 B4
Hogaland Shetland 312 F5
Hogben's Hill Kent 54 B4
Hogganfield Glasgow 268 B2
Hoggard's Green Suff 125 F7
Hoggeston Bucks 102 G6
Hoggington Wilts 45 B10
Hoggrill's End Warks 134 E4
Hogha Gearraidh
W Isles 296 D3
Hog Hatch Sur 49 D10
Hoghton Lancs 194 B6
Hoghton Bottoms Lancs 194 B6
Hogley Green W Yorks 196 F6
Hognaston Derbys 170 E2
Hogpits Bottom Herts 85 E8
Hogsthorpe Lincs 191 G8
Hogstock Dorset 31 F7
Holbeach Lincs 157 E7
Holbeach Bank Lincs 157 D7
Holbeach Clough Lincs 156 D6
Holbeach Drove Lincs 156 G6
Holbeache Worcs 116 B5
Holbeach Hurn Lincs 157 D7
Holbeach St Johns
Lincs 156 F6
Holbeach St Marks
Lincs 157 C7
Holbeach St Matthew
Lincs 157 C8
Holbeck Notts 187 G8
W Yorks 205 G11
Holbeck Woodhouse
Notts 187 G8
Holberrow Green
Worcs 117 F10
Holbeton Devon 8 E2
Holborn London 67 C10
Holborough Kent 69 G8
Holbrook Derbys 170 G5
Suff 108 D3
S Yorks 186 E6
Holbrook Common
S Glos 61 E7
Holbrook Moor Derbys 170 F5
Holbrooks W Mid 134 G6
Holburn Northumb 264 B2
Holbury Hants 32 G6
Holcombe Devon 14 G5
Gtr Man 195 D9
Som 45 D7
Holcombe Brook
Gtr Man 195 E9
Holcombe Rogus Devon 27 D9
Holcot W Nhants 120 D5
Holdbrook London 86 F5
Holden Lancs 203 D11
Holdenby W Nhants 120 D3
Holden Fold Gtr Man 196 F2
Holdenhurst BCP 19 B8
Holder's Green Essex 106 F2
Holders Hill London 86 G2
Holdfast Worcs 99 D7
Holdgate Shrops 131 F11
Holdingham Lincs 173 F9
Holditch Dorset 28 G4
Holdsworth W Yorks 196 B5
Holdworth S Yorks 186 C3
Hole Devon 24 D4
W Yorks 204 F6
Hole Bottom W Yorks 196 C2
Holefield Borders 263 C8
Holehills N Lanark 268 B5
Holehouse Derbys 185 C8
Holehouses Ches E 184 F2

Hole-in-the-Wall
Hereford 98 F2
Holemill Aberdeen 293 C10
Holemoor Devon 24 F6
Hole's Hole Devon 7 B8
Holestane Dumfries 247 D9
Holestone Derbys 170 C4
Hole Street W Sus 35 E10
Holewater Devon 41 F8
Holford Som 43 E7
Holgate York 207 C7
Holker Cumb 211 D7
Holkham Norf 176 E5
Hollacombe Devon 24 G5
Devon 26 G4
Hollacombe Hill Devon 7 E10
Holland Orkney 314 A4
Orkney 314 D6
Sur 52 C2
Holland Fen Lincs 174 F2
Holland Lees Lancs 194 F4
Holland-on-Sea Essex 89 B12
Hollands Som 29 D9
Hollandstoun Orkney 314 A7
Hollee Dumfries 239 D7
Hollesley Suff 109 C7
Hollicombe Torbay 9 C7
Hollies Common Staffs 150 E6
Hollinfare Warr 183 C11
Hollingbourne Kent 53 B10
Hollingbury Brighton 36 F4
Hollingdean Brighton 36 F4
Hollingdon Bucks 103 F7
Hollingrove E Sus 37 C11
Hollingthorpe W Yorks 197 D10
Hollington Derbys 152 B4
E Sus 38 E3
Hants 48 B2
Staffs 151 B11
Hollington Cross Hants 48 B2
Hollington Grove
Derbys 152 B4
Hollingwood Derbys 186 G6
Hollingworth Gtr Man 185 B8
Hollin Hall Lancs 204 F4
Hollin Park W Yorks 206 F2
Hollins Cumb 222 G3
Derbys 186 G4
Gtr Man 195 F8
Gtr Man 195 F10
Gtr Man 195 F11
Staffs 168 D6
Staffs 168 E4
Staffs 169 F7
Hollinsclough Staffs 169 B9
Hollins End S Yorks 186 E5
Hollinsgreen Ches E 168 C2
Hollins Green Warr 183 C11
Hollins Lane Lancs 202 C5
Shrops 149 B10
Hollinswood Telford 132 B4
Hollinthorpe W Yorks 206 G3
Hollinwood Gtr Man 196 G2
Shrops 149 B10
Hollis Green Devon 27 F9
Hollis Head Devon 27 G7
Hollocombe Devon 25 E10
Hollocombe Town
Devon 25 E10
Holloway Derbys 170 D4
Wilts 45 G11
Windsor 65 C10
Holloway Hill Sur 50 E3
Hollow Brook Bath 60 G5
Hollowell W Nhants 120 C3
Hollow Meadows
S Yorks 186 D2
Hollowmoor Heath
Ches W 167 B7
Hollow Oak Dorset 18 C2
Hollows Dumfries 239 B9
Hollow Street Kent 71 G8
Holly Bank W Mid 133 C11
Hollyberry End W Mid 134 G5
Holly Brook Som 44 D4
Hollybush Caerph 77 E11
E Ayrs 257 G9
Stoke 168 G5
Torf 78 G3
Worcs 98 D5
Holly Bush Wrex 166 G6
Hollybush Corner Bucks 66 B3
Suff 125 F8
Hollybushes Kent 54 B2
Hollybush Hill Bucks 66 C3
Essex 89 B10
Hollycroft Leics 135 E8
Holly Cross Windsor 65 C10
Holly End Norf 139 B9
Holly Green Bucks 84 E3
Worcs 99 C7
Holly Hill N Yorks 224 E3
Hollyhurst Shrops 131 D9
Warks 135 F7
Hollym E Yorks 201 B10
Hollywaste Shrops 116 B2
Hollywater Hants 49 G10
Hollywood Worcs 117 B11
Holmacott Devon 25 B8
Holman Clavel Som 28 D2
Holmbridge W Yorks 196 F6
Holmbury St Mary Sur 50 E6
Holmbush Corn 5 E10
Dorset 28 G5
Holmcroft Staffs 151 D8
Holme Cambs 138 F3
C Beds 104 C3
Cumb 211 D10
N Lincs 200 F2
Notts 172 D4
N Yorks 215 C7
W Yorks 196 F6
W Yorks 205 G9
Holmebridge Dorset 18 D3
Holme Chapel Lancs 195 B11
Holme Green C Beds 104 C3
N Yorks 207 E7
Wokingham 65 F10
Holme Hale Norf 141 B7
Holme Hill NE Lincs 201 F9
Holme Lacy Hereford 97 D11
Holme Lane Notts 154 B2
Holme Marsh Hereford 114 G6
Holme Mills Cumb 211 D10
Holme next the Sea
Norf 176 E2
Holme-on-Spalding-Moor
E Yorks 208 F2
Holme on the Wolds
E Yorks 208 D5
Holme Pierrepont Notts 154 B2
Holmer Hereford 97 C10
Holmer Green Bucks 84 F6
Holmes Lancs 194 D2
Holme St Cuthbert
Cumb 229 B8
Holmes Chapel Ches E 168 B3
Holmesdale Derbys 186 F5
Holmesfield Derbys 186 F4
Holme Slack Lancs 203 G7
Holmes's Hill E Sus 23 C8
Holmeswood Lancs 194 D2
Holmethorpe Sur 51 C9
Holmewood Derbys 170 B6
Holme Wood W Yorks 205 G9
Holmfield W Yorks 196 B5
Holmfirth W Yorks 196 F6
Holmhead Angus 293 F7
Dumfries 246 F6
E Ayrs 258 E3
Holmhill Dumfries 247 D9
Holmisdale Highld 297 G7
Holmley Common
Derbys 186 F5
Holmpton E Yorks 201 C11
Holmrook Cumb 219 F11
Holmsgarth Shetland 313 J6
Holmside Durham 233 B10
Holmsleigh Green Devon 28 G2
Holmston S Ayrs 257 E9
Holmwood Corner Sur 51 E7
Holmwrangle Cumb 230 B6
Holne Devon 8 B4
Holnest Dorset 29 E11
Holnicote Som 42 D2
Holsworthy Devon 24 G4
Holsworthy Beacon
Devon 24 F5
Holt Dorset 31 G8
Hants 49 C8
Mers 183 C7
Norf 159 B11
Wilts 61 G11
Worcs 116 E6
Wrex 166 E6
Holtby York 207 C9
Holt End Hants 49 F7
Worcs 117 D11
Holt Fleet Worcs 116 E6
Holt Green Lancs 193 G11
Holt Head W Yorks 196 E5
Holt Heath Dorset 31 G9
Worcs 116 E6
Holt Hill Kent 53 B8
Staffs 152 D2
Holton Oxon 83 D10
Som 29 B11
Suff 127 B7
Holton cum Beckering
Lincs 189 E10
Holton Heath Dorset 18 C4
Holton le Clay Lincs 201 G9
Holton le Moor Lincs 189 B9
Holton St Mary Suff 107 D11
Holt Park W Yorks 205 E11
Holt Pound Hants 49 E10
Holts Gtr Man 196 G3
Holtspur Bucks 84 G6
Holt Wood Dorset 31 F8
Holtye E Sus 52 F3
Holway Dorset 28 G5
Dorset 29 C10
Flint 181 F11
Som 28 C2
Holwell Dorset 30 E2
Herts 104 E3
Leics 154 E4
Oxon 82 D2
Som 45 D8
Holwellbury C Beds 104 E3
Holwick Durham 232 F4
Holworth Dorset 17 E11
Holybourne Hants 49 E8
Holy City Devon 28 G3
Holy Cross T&W 243 D8
Worcs 117 B8
Holyfield Essex 86 E5
Holyhead = *Caergybi*
Anglesey 178 E2
Holy Island Northumb 273 B11
Holylee Borders 261 B9
Holymoorside Derbys 170 B4
Holyport Windsor 65 D11
Holystone Northumb 251 C11
Holytown N Lanark 268 C5
Holy Vale Scilly 1 G4
Holywell Cambs 122 C6
C Beds 85 B8
Corn 4 D5
Dorset 29 G9
E Sus 23 F9
Glos 80 G3
Hereford 97 C7
Herts 85 F9
Northumb 243 C8
Som 29 E8
Warks 118 D3
Holywell = *Treffynnon*
Flint 181 F11
Holywell Green
W Yorks 196 D5
Holywell Lake Som 27 C10
Holywell Row Suff 124 B4
Holywood Dumfries 247 G10
Homedowns Glos 99 E8
Homer Shrops 132 C2
Homer Green Mers 193 G10
Homersfield Suff 142 F5
Homerton London 67 B11
Hom Green Hereford 97 G11
Homington Wilts 31 B10
Honeybourne Worcs 100 C2
Honeychurch Devon 25 G10
Honeydon Bedford 122 F2
Honey Hall N Som 60 G2
Honeyhill Wokingham 65 F10
Honey Hill Kent 70 G6
Honeystreet Wilts 62 G6
Honey Street Wilts 62 G6
Honey Tye Suff 107 D9
Honeywick C Beds 103 G9
Honicknowle Plym 7 D9
Honiley Warks 118 C4
Honing Norf 160 D6
Honingham Norf 160 G2
Honington Lincs 172 G6
Suff 125 C8
Warks 100 C5
Honiton Devon 27 G11
Honkley Wrex 166 D4
Honley W Yorks 196 E6
Honley Moor W Yorks 196 E6
Honnington Telford 150 F4
Honor Oak London 67 E11
Honor Oak Park London 67 E11
Honresfeld Gtr Man 196 D2
Hoo Kent 71 G9
Hoober S Yorks 186 B6
Hoobrook Worcs 116 C6
Hood Green S Yorks 197 G10
Hood Hill S Yorks 186 B5
Hood Manor Warr 183 D9
Hooe E Sus 23 D11
Plym 7 E10
Hooe Common E Sus 23 C11
Hoo End Herts 85 B11
Hoofield Ches W 167 C8
Hoo Green Ches E 184 E2
Hoohill Blackpool 202 F2
Hoo Hole W Yorks 196 B4
Hook Cambs 139 E8
Devon 28 F4
Hook *continued*
E Yorks 199 B9
Hants 33 F8
Hants 49 C8
London 67 G7
Pembs 73 C7
Wilts 62 C5
Hook-a-gate Shrops 131 B9
Hook Bank Worcs 98 C6
Hooke Dorset 16 B6
Hook End Essex 87 F9
Oxon 65 C7
W Mid 134 G4
Hooker Gate T&W 242 F4
Hookgate Staffs 150 B4
Hook Green Kent 53 F7
Kent 68 F6
Hook Heath Sur 50 B3
Hook Norton Oxon 101 E7
Hook Park Hants 33 G7
Hook's Cross Herts 104 G5
Hook Street Glos 79 F11
Wilts 62 C5
Hookway Devon 14 B3
Hookwood Sur 51 E9
Hoole Ches W 166 B6
Hoole Bank Ches W 166 B6
Hooley Sur 51 B9
Hooley Bridge Gtr Man 195 E11
Hooley Brow Gtr Man 195 E11
Hooley Hill Gtr Man 184 B6
Hoo Meavy Devon 7 B10
Hoop Mon 79 D8
Hoopers Pool Wilts 45 C10
Hoops Devon 24 C5
Hoo St Werburgh
Medway 69 E9
Hooton Ches W 182 F5
Hooton Levitt S Yorks 187 C8
Hooton Pagnell S Yorks 198 F3
Hooton Roberts S Yorks 187 B7
Hopcroft's Holt Oxon 101 F9
Hope Derbys 185 E11
Devon 9 G8
Highld 308 D4
Powys 130 B5
Shrops 130 C6
Staffs 169 D10
Hope = *Yr Hôb* Flint 166 D4
Hope Bagot Shrops 115 C11
Hopebeck Cumb 229 G9
Hope Bowdler Shrops 131 E9
Hopedale Staffs 169 D10
Hope End Green Essex 105 G11
Hope Green Ches E 184 E6
Hopeman Moray 301 C11
Hope Mansell Hereford 79 B10
Hope Park Shrops 130 C6
Hopesay Shrops 131 G7
Hopesgate Shrops 130 C6
Hope's Green Essex 69 B9
Hope's Rough Hereford 98 B2
Hopetown W Yorks 197 C11
Hope under Dinmore
Hereford 115 G10
Hopgoods Green
W Berks 64 F4
Hopkinstown Rhondda 77 G9
Hopley's Green Hereford 114 G6
Hopperton N Yorks 206 B4
Hop Pole Lincs 156 G3
Hopsford Warks 135 G8
Hopstone Shrops 132 E5
Hopton Derbys 170 E3
Shrops 149 D11
Shrops 149 E7
Staffs 151 D8
Suff 125 B9
Hoptonbank Shrops 116 B2
Hopton Cangeford
Shrops 131 G10
Hopton Castle Shrops 115 B7
Hoptongate Shrops 131 G10
Hoptonheath Shrops 115 B7
Hopton Heath Staffs 151 D9
Hopton on Sea Norf 143 D10
Hopton Wafers Shrops 116 B2
Hopwas Staffs 134 B3
Hopwood Gtr Man 195 F11
Worcs 117 B10
Hopworthy Devon 24 G4
Horam E Sus 23 B9
Horbling Lincs 156 B2
Horbury W Yorks 197 D9
Horbury Bridge
W Yorks 197 D9
Horbury Junction
W Yorks 197 D10
Horcott Glos 81 E11
Horden Durham 234 C4
Horderley Shrops 131 F8
Hordle Hants 19 B11
Hordley Shrops 149 C7
Horeb Carms 75 D7
Carms 93 F10
Ceredig 93 C7
Flint 166 D3
Horfield Bristol 60 D6
Horgabost W Isles 305 J2
Horham Suff 126 C4
Horkesley Heath Essex 107 F9
Horkstow N Lincs 200 D3
Horkstow Wolds
N Lincs 200 D3
Horley Oxon 101 C8
Sur 51 E9
Horn Ash Dorset 28 G5
Hornblotton Som 44 G5
Hornblotton Green Som 44 G5
Hornby Lancs 211 F11
N Yorks 224 G4
N Yorks 225 D7
Horncastle Lincs 174 B3
Reading 65 E7
Hornchurch London 68 B4
Horncliffe Northumb 273 F8
Horndean Borders 273 F7
Hants 34 E2
Horndon Devon 12 F6
Horndon on the Hill
Thurrock 69 C7
Horne Sur 51 E10
Horner Som 41 D11
Horne Row Essex 88 E3
Horner's Green Suff 107 C9
Hornestreet Essex 107 E10
Horney Common E Sus 37 B7
Horn Hill Som 43 E8
Hornick Corn 5 E9
Horniehaugh Angus 292 G6
Horning Norf 160 F6
Horninghold Leics 136 D6
Horninglow Staffs 152 D4
Horningsea Cambs 123 E9
Horningsham Wilts 45 E10
Horningtoft Norf 159 E8
Horningtops Corn 6 C5
Hornsbury Som 28 E4
Hornsby Cumb 240 G2
Horns Corner Kent 38 B2
Horns Cross Devon 24 C5
E Sus 38 C4
Hornsea E Yorks 209 D10
Hornsea Bridge
E Yorks 209 D10
Hornsea Burton
E Yorks 209 D10
Hornsey London 67 B10
Hornsey Vale London 67 B10
Horns Green Kent 52 B3
Horn Street Kent 55 F7
Kent 69 G7
Hornton Oxon 101 B7
Horpit Swindon 63 C8
Horrabridge Devon 7 B10
Horringer Suff 124 E6
Horringford IoW 20 D6
Horrocks Fold Gtr Man 195 E8
Horrocksford Lancs 203 E10
Horsalls Kent 53 C11
Horsebridge Devon 12 G4
Hants 47 G10
Shrops 131 B7
Horse Bridge Staffs 169 E7
Horsebrook Devon 8 D4
Staffs 151 G7
Horsecastle N Som 60 F2
Horsedown Wilts 61 D10
Horsedowns Corn 2 C4
Horsehay Telford 132 B3
Horseheath Cambs 106 B2
Horseholm Dumfries 238 C2
Horsehouse N Yorks 213 C10
Horseley Heath W Mid 133 E9
Horsell Sur 50 B3
Horsell Birch Sur 50 B3
Horseman's Green
Wrex 166 G6
Horseman Side Essex 87 F8
Horsemere Green W Sus 35 G7
Horsenden Bucks 84 E3
Horsepools Glos 80 C4
Horseway Cambs 139 F8
Horseway Head
Hereford 114 E6
Horsey Norf 161 E9
Som 43 F10
Horsey Corner Norf 161 E9
Horsey Down Wilts 81 G9
Horsford Norf 160 F3
Horsforth W Yorks 205 F10
Horsforth Woodside
W Yorks 205 F10
Horsham W Sus 51 G7
Worcs 116 F4
Horsham St Faith Norf 160 F4
Horshoe Green Kent 52 E3
Horsington Lincs 173 B11
Som 30 C2
Horsley Derbys 170 G5
Glos 80 F4
Northumb 242 D3
Northumb 251 D8
Horsley Cross Essex 108 F2
Horsleycross Street
Essex 108 F2
Horsleyhill Borders 262 F2
Horsley Hill T&W 243 D9
Horsleyhope Durham 233 B7
Horsleys Green Bucks 84 F3
Horsley Woodhouse
Derbys 170 G5
Horsmonden Kent 53 E7
Horspath Oxon 83 E9
Horstead Norf 160 F5
Horsted Green E Sus 23 B7
Horsted Keynes W Sus 36 B5
Horton Bucks 84 B6
Dorset 31 F8
Kent 54 B6
Lancs 204 C3
S Glos 61 C9
Shrops 149 D9
Som 28 E4
Staffs 168 D6
Swansea 56 D3
Telford 150 G3
Wilts 62 G5
Windsor 66 D4
W Nhants 120 G6
Horton Common Dorset 31 F9
Horton Cross Som 28 D4
Horton-cum-Studley
Oxon 83 C9
Horton Green Ches W 167 F7
Horton Heath Dorset 31 F9
Hants 33 D7
Horton in Ribblesdale
N Yorks 212 E6
Horton Kirby Kent 68 F5
Hortonlane Shrops 149 G8
Horton Wharf Bucks 84 B6
Hortonwood Telford 150 G3
Horwich Gtr Man 194 E6
Horwich End Derbys 185 E8
Horwood Devon 25 B8
Horwood Riding S Glos 61 B8
Hoscar Lancs 194 E3
Hose Leics 154 D4
Hoselaw Borders 263 C8
Hoses Cumb 220 G4
Hosey Hill Kent 52 C3
Hosh Perth 286 E2
Hosta W Isles 296 D3
Hoswick Shetland 313 L6
Hotham E Yorks 208 G3
Hothfield Kent 54 D3
Hotley Bottom Bucks 84 E5
Hoton Leics 153 E11
Hotwells Bristol 60 E5
Houbans Shetland 312 F5
Houbie Shetland 312 D8
Houdston S Ayrs 244 D5
Hough Argyll 288 E1
Ches E 168 E2
Ches E 184 F5
Hougham Lincs 172 G5
Hough Green Halton 183 D7
Hough-on-the-Hill
Lincs 172 F6
Hough Side W Yorks 205 G10
Houghton Cambs 122 C5
Cumb 239 F10
Hants 47 G10
Northumb 242 D4
Pembs 73 D7
W Sus 35 E8
Houghton Bank Darl 233 G10
Houghton Conquest
C Beds 103 C10
Houghton Green E Sus 38 C6
Warr 183 C10
Houghton-le-Side
Darl 233 G10
Houghton-le-Spring
T&W 234 B2
Houghton on the Hill
Leics 136 C3
Houghton Regis
C Beds 103 G10
Houghton St Giles Norf 159 B8
Houghwood Mers 194 G4
Houlland Shetland 312 B7
Shetland 312 F7
Shetland 313 H5
Shetland 313 J6
Houlsyke N Yorks 226 D4
Houlton Warks 119 C11
Hound Hants 33 F7
Hound Green Hants 49 B8
Hound Hill Dorset 31 G7
Houndmills Hants 48 C6
Houndscroft Glos 80 E5
Houndslow Borders 272 F2
Houndsmoor Som 27 B10
Houndstone Som 29 D8
Houndwood Borders 272 C6
Hounsdown Hants 32 E5
Hounsley Batch N Som 60 G4
Hounslow London 66 D6
Hounslow Green Essex 87 B11
Hounslow West London 66 D6
Hourston Orkney 314 E2
Housabister Shetland 313 H6
Housay Shetland 312 F8
Househill Highld 301 D8
House of Daviot Highld 301 E7
House of Glenmuick
Aberds 292 D5
Houses Hill W Yorks 197 D7
Housetter Shetland 312 E5
Housham Tye Essex 87 C8
Houss Shetland 313 K5
Houston Renfs 267 B8
Houstry Highld 310 F5
Houton Orkney 314 F3
Hove Brighton 36 G3
Hove Edge W Yorks 196 C6
Hoveringham Notts 171 F11
Hoveton Norf 160 F6
Hovingham N Yorks 216 D3
How Cumb 240 F2
Howbeck Bank Ches E 167 F11
Howbrook S Yorks 186 B4
How Caple Hereford 98 E2
Howden Borders 262 E5
E Yorks 199 B8
W Loth 269 B11
Howden Clough
W Yorks 197 B8
Howden-le-Wear
Durham 233 E9
Howdon T&W 243 D8
Howdon Pans T&W 243 D8
Howe Highld 310 C7
Norf 142 C5
N Yorks 214 C6
Howe Bridge Gtr Man 195 G7
Howegreen Essex 88 E4
Howe Green Essex 87 B8
Essex 88 E2
Warks 134 F6
Howell Lincs 173 F10
How End C Beds 103 C10
Howe of Teuchar
Aberds 303 E7
Howe Street Essex 87 C11
Essex 106 E3
Howey Powys 113 F11
Howford Borders 261 B8
Borders 261 E9
Howgate Cumb 228 G5
Midloth 270 D4
Howgill Cumb 222 F2
Lancs 204 D2
N Yorks 205 B7
How Green Kent 52 D3
How Hill Norf 161 F7
Howick Mon 79 F8
Northumb 265 F7
Howick Cross Lancs 194 B4
Howle Durham 233 F7
Telford 150 E3
Howleigh Som 28 D2
Howlett End Essex 105 E11
Howley Glos 80 G2
Som 28 F3
Warr 183 D10
Hownam Borders 263 F7
Hownam Mains Borders 263 E7
Howpasley Borders 249 B8
Howsen Worcs 116 G5
Howsham N Lincs 200 G4
N Yorks 216 G4
Howslack Dumfries 248 B3
Howtel Northumb 263 C9
Howt Green Kent 69 F11
Howton Hereford 97 F8
Howtown Cumb 221 B8
Howwood Renfs 267 C7
How Wood Herts 85 E10
Hoxne Suff 126 B3
Hoxton London 67 C10
Hoy Orkney 314 F2
Hoylake Mers 182 D2
Hoyland S Yorks 197 G11
Hoyland Common
S Yorks 197 G11
Hoylandswaine S Yorks 197 G9
Hoyle W Sus 34 D6
Hoyle Mill S Yorks 197 F11
Hubbard's Hill Kent 52 C4
Hubberholme N Yorks 213 D8
Hubberston Pembs 72 D5
Hubbersty Head Cumb 221 G8
Hubberton Green
W Yorks 196 C4
Hubbert's Bridge Lincs 174 G3
Huby N Yorks 205 D11
N Yorks 215 F11
Hucclecote Glos 80 B5
Hucking Kent 53 B10
Hucknall Notts 171 F8
Huddersfield W Yorks 196 D6
Huddington Worcs 117 F8
Huddisford Devon 24 D4
Huddlesford Staffs 134 B3
Hud Hey Lancs 195 C9
Hudnall Herts 85 C8
Hudnalls Glos 79 E8
Hudswell N Yorks 224 E3
Wilts 61 F11
Huggate E Yorks 208 B3
Hugglepit Devon 24 C4
Hugglescote Leics 153 G8
Hughenden Valley Bucks 84 F5
Hughley Shrops 131 D11
Hugh Mill Lancs 195 C10
Hugh Town Scilly 1 G4
Hugus Corn 4 G5
Huish Devon 25 B7
Devon 25 E8
Wilts 62 G6
Huish Champflower Som 27 B9
Huish Episcopi Som 28 B6
Huisinis W Isles 305 G1
Hulcote C Beds 103 D8
W Nhants 102 B4
Hulcott Bucks 84 B5
Hulland Derbys 170 F2
Hulland Moss Derbys 170 F3
Hulland Ward Derbys 170 F3
Hullavington Wilts 61 C11
Hullbridge Essex 88 G4
Hull End Derbys 185 E9
Hulme Gtr Man 184 B4
Staffs 168 F6
Warr 183 C10
Hulme End Staffs 169 D10
Hulme Walfield Ches E 168 B4
Hulseheath Ches E 184 E2
Hulverstone IoW 20 E3
Hulver Street Suff 143 F9
Humber Devon 14 G3
Hereford 115 F10
Humber Bridge N Lincs 200 C4
Humberston NE Lincs 201 F10
Humberstone Leicester 136 B2
Humberston Fitties
NE Lincs 201 F10
Humbie E Loth 271 C9
Humbledon T&W 243 F9
Humble Green Suff 107 B8
Humbleton E Yorks 209 G10
Northumb 263 D11
Humby Lincs 155 C10
Hume Borders 272 G4
Hummersknott Darl 224 C5
Humshaugh Northumb 241 C10
Huna Highld 310 B7
Huncoat Lancs 203 G11
Huncote Leics 135 D10
Hundalee Borders 262 F4
Hundall Derbys 186 F5
Hunderthwaite Durham 232 G5
Hunderton Hereford 97 D9
Hundleby Lincs 174 B5
Hundle Houses Lincs 174 E3
Hundleshope Borders 260 B6
Hundleton Pembs 73 E7
Hundon Suff 106 B4
Hundred Acres Hants 33 E9
Hundred End Lancs 194 C2
Hundred House Powys 114 G2
Hungarton Leics 136 B3
Hungate W Yorks 197 B11
Hungerford Hants 31 E11
Shrops 131 F10
Som 42 E4
W Berks 63 F10
Windsor 65 E10
Hungerford Green
W Berks 64 D5
Hungerford Newtown
W Berks 63 E11
Hunger Hill Gtr Man 195 F7
Lancs 194 E4
Hungershall Park Kent 52 F5
Hungerstone Hereford 97 D8
Hungerton Lincs 155 D7
Hungladder Highld 298 B3
Hungreyhatton Shrops 150 D3
Hunmanby N Yorks 217 D11
Hunmanby Moor
N Yorks 218 D2
Hunningham Warks 119 D7
Hunningham Hill Warks 119 D7
Hunnington Worcs 133 G9
Hunny Hill IoW 20 D5
Hunsdon Herts 86 C6
Hunsdonbury Herts 86 C6
Hunsingore N Yorks 206 C4
Hunslet W Yorks 206 G2
Hunslet Carr W Yorks 206 G2
Hunsonby Cumb 231 D7
Hunspow Highld 310 B6
Hunstanton Norf 175 G11
Hunstanworth Durham 232 B5
Hunsterson Ches E 167 F11
Hunston Suff 125 D9
W Sus 22 C5
Hunston Green Suff 125 D9
Hunstrete Bath 60 G6
Hunsworth W Yorks 197 B7
Hunt End Worcs 117 E10
Huntenhull Green Wilts 45 D10
Huntercombe End Oxon 65 B7
Hunters Forstal Kent 71 F7
Hunter's Quay Argyll 276 F3
Huntham Som 28 B4
Hunthill Lodge Angus 292 F6
Huntingdon Cambs 122 C4
Huntingfield Suff 126 C6
Huntingford Dorset 45 G10
S Glos 80 G2
Huntington Ches W 166 C6
E Loth 281 F9
Hereford 97 C9
Hereford 114 G5
Staffs 151 G9
Telford 132 B3
York 207 B8
Hunting-tower Perth 286 E4
Huntley Glos 80 B2
Staffs 169 G8
Huntly Aberds 302 F5
Huntlywood Borders 272 G2
Hunton Hants 48 F3
Kent 53 D8
N Yorks 224 G3
Hunton Bridge Herts 85 E9
Hunt's Corner Norf 141 F11
Huntscott Som 42 E2
Hunt's Cross Mers 182 D6
Hunts Green Warks 134 D3
Hunt's Green Bucks 84 E5
W Berks 64 E2
Huntsham Devon 27 C8
Huntshaw Devon 25 C8
Huntshaw Water Devon 25 C8
Hunt's Hill Bucks 84 F4
Hunt's Lane Leics 135 C9
Huntspill Som 43 D10
Huntstile Som 43 G9
Huntworth Som 43 G10
Hunwick Durham 233 E9
Hunworth Norf 159 B11
Hurcott Som 28 D5
Som 29 B8
Worcs 117 B7
Hurdcott Wilts 47 G7
Hurdley Powys 130 E5
Hurdsfield Ches E 184 G6
Hurgill N Yorks 224 E3
Hurlet Glasgow 267 C10
Hurley Warks 134 D4
Windsor 65 C10
Hurley Bottom Windsor 65 C10
Hurley Common Warks 134 D4
Hurlford E Ayrs 257 B11
Hurliness Orkney 314 H2
Hurlston Lancs 194 E2
Hurlston Green Lancs 193 E11
Hurn BCP 19 B8
E Yorks 208 E6
Hurn's End Lincs 174 F6
Hursey Dorset 28 G6
Hursley Hants 32 B6
Hurst Cumb 230 C4
Dorset 17 C11
Gtr Man 196 G2
N Yorks 223 E10
Som 29 D7
Hurst *continued*
Wokingham 65 E9
Hurstbourne Priors
Hants 48 D2
Hurstbourne Tarrant
Hants 47 C11
Hurstead Gtr Man 196 D2
Hurst Green Essex 89 B9
E Sus 38 B2
Lancs 203 F9
Sur 51 C11
W Mid 133 F9
Hurst Hill W Mid 133 E8
Hurstley Hereford 97 B7
Hurst Park Sur 66 F6
Hurstpierpoint W Sus 36 D3
Hurst Wickham W Sus 36 D3
Hurstwood Lancs 204 G3
Hurtmore Sur 50 D3
Hurworth-on-Tees Darl 224 C6
Hurworth Place Darl 224 D5
Hury Durham 223 B9
Husabost Highld 298 D2
Husbands Bosworth
Leics 136 G2
Husbandtown Angus 287 D8
Husborne Crawley
C Beds 103 D9
Husthwaite N Yorks 215 D10
Hutcherleigh Devon 8 E5
Hutchesontown
Glasgow 267 C11
Hutchwns Bridgend 57 F10
Hut Green N Yorks 198 C5
Huthwaite Notts 171 D7
Hutlerburn Borders 261 E10
Huttock Top Lancs 195 C11
Huttoft Lincs 191 F8
Hutton Borders 273 E9
Cumb 230 F4
Essex 87 F10
E Yorks 208 C6
Lancs 194 B3
N Som 43 B11
Hutton Bonville N Yorks 224 E6
Hutton Buscel N Yorks 217 C9
Hutton Conyers N Yorks 214 E6
Hutton Cranswick
E Yorks 208 C6
Hutton End Cumb 230 D4
Hutton Gate Redcar 225 B11
Hutton Hang N Yorks 214 B3
Hutton Henry Durham 234 D4
Hutton-le-Hole
N Yorks 226 G4
Hutton Magna Durham 224 C2
Hutton Mount Essex 87 G10
Hutton Roof Cumb 211 D11
Cumb 230 E3
Hutton Rudby N Yorks 225 D9
Huttons Ambo N Yorks 216 F5
Hutton Sessay N Yorks 215 D9
Hutton Village Redcar 225 C11
Hutton Wandesley
N Yorks 206 C6
Huxham Devon 14 B4
Huxham Green Som 44 F5
Huxley Ches W 167 C8
Huxter Shetland 313 G7
Shetland 313 H3
Shetland 313 H5
Huxton Borders 273 B7
Huyton Mers 182 C6
Huyton Park Mers 182 C6
Huyton Quarry Mers 183 C7
Hwlffordd = *Haverfordwest*
Pembs 73 B7
Hycemoor Cumb 210 B1
Hyde Glos 80 E5
Glos 99 F11
Gtr Man 184 B6
Hants 31 E11
Hants 48 G3
Hereford 115 F9
Hyde Chase Essex 88 E4
Hyde End W Berks 64 G5
Hyde Heath Bucks 84 E6
Hyde Lea Staffs 151 E8
Hyde Park S Yorks 198 G5
Hydestile Sur 50 E3
Hylton Castle T&W 243 F9
Hylton Red House T&W 243 F9
Hyltons Crossways Norf 160 D4
Hyndburn Bridge
Lancs 203 G10
Hyndford Bridge
S Lanark 269 G8
Hyndhope Borders 261 E9
Hynish Argyll 288 F1
Hyssington Powys 130 E6
Hystfield Glos 79 F11
Hythe Hants 32 F6
Kent 55 G7
Som 44 C2
Sur 66 E4
Hythe End Windsor 66 E4
Hythie Aberds 303 D10
Hyton Cumb 210 B1

I

Iarsiadar W Isles 304 E3
Ibberton Dorset 30 F3
Ible Derbys 170 D2
Ibsley Hants 31 F11
Ibstock Leics 153 G8
Ibstone Bucks 84 G3
Ibthorpe Hants 47 C11
Ibworth Hants 48 C5
Icelton N Som 59 F11
Ichrachan Argyll 284 D4
Ickburgh Norf 140 E6
Ickenham London 66 B5
Ickenthwaite Cumb 210 B6
Ickford Bucks 83 D11
Ickham Kent 55 B8
Ickleford Herts 104 E3
Icklesham E Sus 38 D5
Ickleton Cambs 105 C9
Icklingham Suff 124 C5
Ickornshaw N Yorks 204 E5
Ickwell C Beds 104 B3
Ickwell Green C Beds 104 B3
Icomb Glos 100 G4
Icy Park Devon 8 F3
Idbury Oxon 82 B2
Iddesleigh Devon 25 F9
Ide Devon 14 C3
Ideford Devon 14 F3
Ide Hill Kent 52 C3
Iden E Sus 38 C6
Iden Green Kent 53 F8
Kent 53 G10
Idle W Yorks 205 F9
Idle Moor W Yorks 205 F9
Idless Corn 4 F6
Idlicote Warks 100 C5
Idmiston Wilts 47 F7
Idole Carms 74 B6
Idridgehay Derbys 170 F3
Idridgehay Green
Derbys 170 F3
Idrigill Highld 298 C3
Idstone Oxon 63 C9
Idvies Angus 287 C9
Iet-y-bwlch Carms 92 F3
Iffley Oxon 83 E8
Ifield W Sus 51 F8
Ifield Green W Sus 51 F9
Ifieldwood W Sus 51 F8
Ifold W Sus 50 G4
Iford BCP 19 C8
E Sus 36 F6
Ifton Heath Shrops 148 B6
Ightfield Shrops 149 B11
Ightfield Heath Shrops 149 B11
Ightham Kent 52 B5
Igtham Common Kent 52 B5
Iken Suff 127 F8
Ilam Staffs 169 E10
Ilchester Som 29 C8
Ilchester Mead Som 29 C8
Ilderton Northumb 264 E2
Ileden Kent 55 C8
Ilford London 68 B2
Som 28 D5
Ilfracombe Devon 40 D4
Ilkeston Derbys 171 G7
Ilketshall St Andrew
Suff 143 F7
Ilketshall St Lawrence
Suff 143 G7
Ilketshall St Margaret
Suff 142 F6
Ilkley W Yorks 205 D8
Illand Corn 11 F11
Illey W Mid 133 G9
Illidge Green Ches E 168 C3
Illington Norf 141 F8
Illingworth W Yorks 196 B5
Illogan Corn 4 G3
Illogan Highway Corn 4 G3
Illshaw Heath W Mid 118 C2
Illston on the Hill Leics 136 D4
Ilmer Bucks 84 D3
Ilmington Warks 100 C4
Ilminster Som 28 E5
Ilsington Devon 13 F11
Ilston Swansea 56 C5
Ilton N Yorks 214 D3
Som 28 D5
Imachar N Ayrs 255 C9
Imber Wilts 46 D3
Imeraval Argyll 254 C4
Immervoulin Stirling 285 F9
Immingham NE Lincs 201 E7
Impington Cambs 123 E8
Ince Ches W 183 F7
Ince Blundell Mers 193 G10
Ince in Makerfield
Gtr Man 194 G5
Inchbae Lodge Highld 300 C4
Inchbare Angus 293 G8
Inchberry Moray 302 D3
Inchbraoch Angus 287 B11
Inchbrook Glos 80 E4
Inchcape Highld 309 J6
Incheril Highld 299 C10
Inchgrundle Angus 292 F6
Inchina Highld 307 K4
Inchinnan Renfs 267 B9
Inchkinloch Highld 308 E5
Inchlaggan Highld 290 C3
Inchlumpie Highld 300 B5
Inchmore Highld 300 E3
Highld 300 E5
Inchnacardoch Hotel
Highld 290 B5
Inchnadamph Highld 307 G7
Inchock Angus 287 C10
Inch of Arnhall Aberds 293 F8
Inchree Highld 290 G2
Inchrory Moray 292 C3
Inchs Corn 5 C9
Inchture Perth 286 E6
Inchyra Perth 286 E5
Indian Queens Corn 5 D8
Inerval Argyll 254 C4
Ingatestone Essex 87 F11
Ingbirchworth S Yorks 197 F8
Ingerthorpe N Yorks 214 F5
Ingestre Staffs 151 E9
Ingham Lincs 188 E6
Norf 161 D7
Suff 125 C7
Ingham Corner Norf 161 D7
Ingleborough Norf 157 F9
Ingleby Derbys 152 D6
Lincs 188 F5
Ingleby Arncliffe
N Yorks 225 E8
Ingleby Barwick
Stockton 225 C9
Ingleby Cross N Yorks 225 E9
Ingleby Greenhow
N Yorks 225 D11
Ingleigh Green Devon 25 F10
Inglemire Hull 209 G7
Inglesbatch Bath 61 G8
Inglesham Swindon 82 F2
Ingleton Durham 233 G9
N Yorks 212 E3
Inglewhite Lancs 202 E6
Ingmanthorpe N Yorks 206 C4
Ingoe Northumb 242 C2
Ingol Lancs 202 G6
Ingoldisthorpe Norf 158 C3
Ingoldmells Lincs 175 B9
Ingoldsby Lincs 155 C10
Ingon Warks 118 F4
Ingram Northumb 264 F2
Ingrams Green W Sus 34 C4
Ingrave Essex 87 G10
Ingrow W Yorks 205 F7
Ings Cumb 221 F8
Ingst S Glos 60 B5
Ingthorpe Rutland 137 B9
Ingworth Norf 160 D3
Inham's End Cambs 138 D5
Inhurst Hants 64 G5
Inkberrow Worcs 117 F10
Inkerman Durham 233 D8
Inkersall Derbys 186 G6
Inkersall Green Derbys 186 G6
Inkford Worcs 117 C11
Inkpen W Berks 63 G11
Inkpen Common
W Berks 63 G11
Inkstack Highld 310 B6
Inlands W Sus 34 G3
Inmarsh Wilts 62 G2
Inn Cumb 221 D8
Innellan Argyll 276 G3
Inner Hope Devon 9 G8
Innerleithen Borders 261 B8
Innerleven Fife 287 G7
Innermessan Dumfries 236 C2
Innerwick E Loth 282 G4
Perth 285 C9

Innie Argyll 275 B9
Inninbeg Highld 289 E8
Innis Chonain Argyll 284 E5
Innistrynich Argyll 284 E5
Innox Hill Som 45 D9
Innsworth Glos 99 G7
Insch Aberds 302 G6
Insh Highld 291 C10
Inshegra Highld 306 D7
Inshore Highld 308 C3
Inskip Lancs 202 F5
Inskip Moss Side Lancs 202 F5
Instoneville S Yorks 198 E5
Instow Devon 40 G3
Insworke Corn 7 E8
Intack Blackburn 195 B8
Intake S Yorks 186 E5
S Yorks 198 G5
W Yorks 205 F10
Interfield Worcs 98 B5
Intwood Norf 142 C3
Inver Aberds 292 D4
Highld 311 L2
Perth 286 C4
Inveralort Highld 295 G9
Inveraldie Angus 287 D8
Inveralivaig Highld 298 E4
Inveralligin Highld 299 D8
Inverallochy Aberds 303 C10
Inveran Highld 299 B8
Highld 309 K5
Inveraray Argyll 284 G4
Inverarish Highld 295 B7
Inverarity Angus 287 C8
Inverarnan Stirling 285 F7
Inverasdale Highld 307 L3
Inverawe Ho Argyll 284 D4
Inverbeg Argyll 276 B6
Inverbervie Aberds 293 F10
Inverboyndie Aberds 302 C6
Inverbroom Highld 307 L6
Invercarron Mains
Highld 309 K5
Invercassley Highld 309 J4
Invercauld House
Aberds 292 D3
Inverchaolain Argyll 275 F11
Invercharnan Highld 284 C5
Inverchoran Highld 300 D2
Invercreran Argyll 284 C4
Inverdruie Highld 291 B11
Inverebrie Aberds 303 F9
Invereck Argyll 276 E2
Inverernan Ho Aberds 292 B5
Invereshie House
Highld 291 C10
Inveresk E Loth 280 G6
Inverey Aberds 292 E2
Inverfarigaig Highld 300 G5
Invergarry Highld 290 C5
Invergelder Aberds 292 D4
Invergeldie Perth 285 E11
Invergordon Highld 301 C7
Invergowrie Perth 287 D7
Inverguseran Highld 295 E9
Inverhadden Perth 285 B10
Inverhaggernie Stirling 285 E7
Inverharroch Moray 302 F3
Inverherive Stirling 285 E7
Inverie Highld 295 F9
Inverinan Argyll 275 B10
Inverinate Highld 295 C11
Inverkeilor Angus 287 C10
Inverkeithing Fife 280 E2
Inverkeithny Aberds 302 E6
Inverkip Invclyd 276 G4
Inverkirkaig Highld 307 H5
Inverlael Highld 307 L6
Inverleith Edin 280 F4
Inverliever Lodge Argyll 275 C9
Inverliver Argyll 284 D4
Inverlochlarig Stirling 285 F8
Inverlochy Argyll 284 E5
Highld 290 F3
Moray 301 G11
Inverlounin Argyll 276 B4
Inverlussa Argyll 275 E7
Inver Mallie Highld 290 E3
Invermark Lodge Angus 292 E6
Invermoidart Highld 289 B8
Invermoriston Highld 290 B6
Invernaver Highld 308 C7
Inverneill Argyll 275 E9
Inverness Highld 300 E6
Invernettie Aberds 303 E11
Invernoaden Argyll 276 B2
Inveronich Argyll 284 G6
Inveroran Hotel Argyll 284 C6
Inverpolly Lodge Highld 307 H5
Inverquharity Angus 287 B8
Inverquhomery Aberds 303 E10
Inverroy Highld 290 E4
Inversanda Highld 289 D11
Invershiel Highld 295 D11
Invershin Highld 309 K5
Invershore Highld 310 F6
Inversnaid Hotel Stirling 285 G7
Invertrossachs Stirling 285 G9
Inverugie Aberds 303 E11
Inveruglas Argyll 285 G7
Inveruglass Highld 291 C10
Inverurie Aberds 303 G7
Inverurar Perth 285 C10
Inverythan Aberds 303 E7
Inwardleigh Devon 13 B7
Inwood Shrops 131 D9
Inworth Essex 88 B5
Iochdar W Isles 297 G3
Iping W Sus 34 C5
Ipplepen Devon 8 B6
Ipsden Oxon 64 B6
Ipsley Worcs 117 D11
Ipstones Staffs 169 F8
Ipswich Suff 108 C3
Irby Mers 182 E3
Irby in the Marsh Lincs 175 C7
Irby upon Humber
NE Lincs 201 G7
Irchester N Nhants 121 D8
Ireby Cumb 229 D10
Lancs 212 D3
Ireland C Beds 104 C2
Orkney 314 F3
Shetland 313 L5
Wilts 45 C10
Ireland's Cross Shrops 168 G2
Ireland Wood W Yorks 205 F11
Ireleth Cumb 210 D4
Ireshopeburn Durham 232 D3
Ireton Wood Derbys 170 F3
Irlam Gtr Man 184 C2
Irlams o' th' Height
Gtr Man 195 G9
Irnham Lincs 155 D10
Iron Acton S Glos 61 C7
Ironbridge Telford 132 C3
Iron Bridge Cambs 139 D9
Iron Cross Warks 117 G11
Irongray Dumfries 237 B11
Iron Lo Highld 299 G10
Ironmacannie Dumfries 237 B8
Irons Bottom Sur 51 D9
Ironside Aberds 303 D8
Ironville Derbys 170 E6
Irstead Norf 161 E7
Irstead Street Norf 161 F7
Irthington Cumb 239 E11
Irthlingborough
N Nhants 121 C8
Irton N Yorks 217 C10
Irvine N Ayrs 257 B8
Irwell Vale Lancs 195 C9
Isabella Pit Northumb 253 G8
Isallt Bach Anglesey 178 F3
Isauld Highld 310 C3
Isbister Orkney 314 D2
Orkney 314 E3
Shetland 312 D5
Shetland 313 G7
Isel Cumb 229 E9
Isfield E Sus 36 D6
Isham N Nhants 121 C7
Ishriff Argyll 289 F8
Isington Hants 49 E9
Island Carr N Lincs 200 F3
Islands Common Cambs 122 E3
Islay Ho Argyll 274 G4
Isle Abbotts Som 28 C5
Isle Brewers Som 28 C5
Isleham Cambs 124 C2
Isle of Axholme N Lincs 199 F9
Isle of Dogs London 67 D11
Isle of Man Dumfries 238 B2
Isle of Whithorn
Dumfries 236 F6
Isleornsay Highld 295 D9
Islesburgh Shetland 312 G5
Islesteps Dumfries 237 B11
Isleworth London 67 D7
Isley Walton Leics 153 D8
Islibhig W Isles 304 F1
Islington London 67 C10
Telford 150 E4
Islip N Nhants 121 B9
Oxon 83 C8
Isombridge Telford 150 G2
Istead Rise Kent 68 F6
Isycoed Wrex 166 E6
Itchen Soton 32 E6
Itchen Abbas Hants 48 G4
Itchen Stoke Hants 48 G5
Itchingfield W Sus 35 B10
Itchington S Glos 61 B7
Itteringham Norf 160 C2
Itteringham Common
Norf 160 D3
Itton Devon 13 B9
Mon 79 F7
Itton Common Mon 79 F7
Ivegill Cumb 230 C4
Ivelet N Yorks 223 F8
Iver Bucks 66 C4
Iver Heath Bucks 66 C4
Iveston Durham 242 G4
Ivinghoe Bucks 84 B6
Ivinghoe Aston Bucks 85 B7
Ivington Hereford 115 F9
Ivington Green Hereford 115 F9
Ivybridge Devon 8 D2
Ivy Chimneys Essex 86 E6
Ivychurch Kent 39 B8
Ivy Cross Dorset 30 C5
Ivy Hatch Kent 52 C5
Ivy Todd Norf 141 B7
Iwade Kent 69 F11
Iwerne Courtney or Shroton
Dorset 30 E5
Iwerne Minster Dorset 30 E5
Iwood N Som 60 G3
Ixworth Suff 125 C8
Ixworth Thorpe Suff 125 C8

J

Jackfield Telford 132 C3
Jack Green Lancs 194 B5
Jack Hayes Staffs 168 F6
Jack Hill N Yorks 205 C10
Jack in the Green Devon 14 B6
Jacksdale Notts 170 E6
Jack's Green Essex 105 G11
Glos 80 D5
Jack's Hatch Essex 86 D6
Jackson Bridge
W Yorks 197 F7
Jackstown Aberds 303 F7
Jacobstow Corn 11 B9
Jacobstowe Devon 25 G9
Jacobs Well Sur 50 C3
Jagger Green W Yorks 196 D5
Jameston Pembs 73 F9
Jamestown Dumfries 249 D8
Highld 300 D4
W Dunb 277 E7
Jamphlars Fife 280 B4
Janetstown Highld 310 C4
Janke's Green Essex 107 F8
Jarrow T&W 243 D8
Jarvis Brook E Sus 37 B8
Jasper's Green Essex 106 F4
Java Argyll 289 F9
Jawcraig Falk 278 F6
Jaw Hill W Yorks 197 C9
Jaywick Essex 89 C11
Jealott's Hill Brack 65 E11
Jeaniefield Borders 271 G10
Jedburgh Borders 262 E5
Jedurgh Borders 262 F5
Jeffreyston Pembs 73 D9
Jellyhill E Dunb 278 G2
Jemimaville Highld 301 C7
Jennetts Hill W Berks 64 E5
Jennyfield N Yorks 205 B11
Jericho Gtr Man 195 E10
Jersey Farm Herts 85 D11
Jersey Marine Neath 57 C8
Jerviswood S Lanark 269 F7
Jesmond T&W 243 D7
Jevington E Sus 23 E9
Jewell's Cross Corn 24 G3
Jingle Street Mon 79 C7
Jockey End Herts 85 C8
Jodrell Bank Ches E 184 G3
Johnby Cumb 230 E4
John O'Gaunt Leics 136 B4
John O'Gaunts
W Yorks 197 B11
John o'Groats Highld 310 B7
John's Cross E Sus 38 C2
Johnshaven Aberds 293 G9
Johnson Fold Gtr Man 195 E7
Johnson's Hillock
Lancs 194 C5
Johnson Street Norf 161 F7
Johnston Pembs 72 C6
Johnstone Renfs 267 C8
Johnstonebridge
Dumfries 248 E3
Johnstone Mains
Aberds 293 F9
Johnstown Carms 74 B6
Wrex 166 F4
Jolly's Bottom Corn 4 F5
Joppa Corn 2 B3
Edin 280 G6
S Ayrs 257 F10
Jordan Green Norf 159 E11
Jordanhill Glasgow 267 B10
Jordans Bucks 85 G7
Jordanston Pembs 91 E8
Jordanthorpe S Yorks 186 E5
Jordon S Yorks 186 C6
Joyford Glos 79 C9
Joy's Green Glos 79 B10
Jubilee Gtr Man 196 E2
Notts 170 E6
Jugbank Staffs 150 B5
Jump S Yorks 197 G11
Jumpers Common BCP 19 C8
Jumpers Green BCP 19 C8
Jumper's Town E Sus 52 G3
Junction N Yorks 204 D6
Juniper Northumb 241 F10
Juniper Green Edin 270 B3
Jurby East IoM 192 C4
Jurby West IoM 192 C4
Jurston Devon 13 E9
Jury's Gap E Sus 39 D7

K

Kaber Cumb 222 C5
Kaimend S Lanark 269 F9
Kaimes Edin 270 B5
Kaimrig End Borders 269 G11
Kalemouth Borders 262 D6
Kame Fife 287 G7
Kames Argyll 275 B9
Argyll 275 F10
E Ayrs 258 D5
Kates Hill W Mid 133 E9
Kea Corn 4 G6
Keadby N Lincs 199 E10
Keal Cotes Lincs 174 C5
Kearby Town End
N Yorks 206 D2
Kearnsey Kent 55 E9
Kearsley Gtr Man 195 F9
Kearstwick Cumb 212 C2
Kearton N Yorks 223 F9
Kearvaig Highld 306 B7
Keasden N Yorks 212 F4
Kebroyd W Yorks 196 C4
Keckwick Halton 183 E9
Keddington Lincs 190 D4
Keddington Corner
Lincs 190 D5
Kedington Suff 106 B4
Kedleston Derbys 170 G4
Kedslie Borders 271 G11
Keekle Cumb 219 B10
Keelars Tye Essex 107 G11
Keelby Lincs 201 E7
Keele Staffs 168 F4
Keeley Green Bedford 103 B10
Keelham W Yorks 205 G7
Keenley Northumb 241 F7
Keenthorne Som 43 F8
Keeres Green Essex 87 C9
Keeston Pembs 72 B6
Keevil Wilts 46 B2
Kegworth Leics 153 D9
Kehelland Corn 4 G2
Keig Aberds 293 B8
Keighley W Yorks 205 E7
Keil Highld 289 D11
Keilarsbrae Clack 279 C7
Keilhill Aberds 303 D7
Keillmore Argyll 275 E7
Keillor Perth 286 C6
Keillour Perth 286 E3
Keills Argyll 274 G5
Keils Argyll 274 G6
Keinton Mandeville Som 44 G4
Keir Mill Dumfries 247 E9
Keisby Lincs 155 D10
Keiss Highld 310 C7
Keistle Highld 298 D4
Keith Moray 302 D4
Keith Hall Aberds 303 G7
Keith Inch Aberds 303 E11
Keithock Angus 293 G8
Kelbrook Lancs 204 E4
Kelby Lincs 173 G8
Kelcliffe W Yorks 205 E9
Keld Cumb 221 C11
N Yorks 223 E7
Keldholme N Yorks 216 B4
Keld Houses N Yorks 214 G2
Kelfield N Lincs 199 G10
N Yorks 207 F7
Kelham Notts 172 D3
Kelhurn Argyll 276 F6
Kellacott Devon 12 D4
Kellamergh Lancs 194 B2
Kellan Argyll 289 E7
Kellas Angus 287 D8
Moray 301 D11
Kellaton Devon 9 G11
Kellaways Wilts 62 D3
Kelleth Cumb 222 D3
Kelleythorpe E Yorks 208 B5
E Yorks 208 B6
Kelling Norf 177 E9
Kellingley N Yorks 198 C4
Kellington N Yorks 198 C5
Kelloe Durham 234 D2
Kelloholm Dumfries 258 G6
Kells Cumb 219 B9
Kelly Corn 10 G6
Devon 12 E3
Kelly Bray Corn 12 G3
Kelmarsh W Nhants 120 B4
Kelmscott Oxon 82 F3
Kelsale Suff 127 D7
Kelsall Ches W 167 B8
Kelsall Hill Ches W 167 B8
Kelsay Argyll 254 B2
Kelshall Herts 104 D6
Kelsick Cumb 238 G5
Kelso Borders 262 C6
Kelstedge Derbys 170 C4
Kelstern Lincs 190 C3
Kelsterton Flint 182 G3
Kelston Bath 61 F8
Keltneyburn Perth 285 C11
Kelton Dumfries 237 B11
Durham 232 G4
Kelty Fife 280 B2
Keltybridge Fife 280 B2
Kelvedon Essex 88 B5
Kelvedon Hatch Essex 87 F9
Kelvin S Lanark 268 E2
Kelvindale Glasgow 267 B11
Kelvinside Glasgow 267 B11
Kelynack Corn 1 D3
Kemacott Devon 41 D7
Kemback Fife 287 F8
Kemberton Shrops 132 C4
Kemble Glos 81 F7
Kemble Wick Glos 81 F7
Kemerton Worcs 99 D8
Kemeys Commander
Mon 78 E4
Kemincham Ches E 168 B4
Kemnay Aberds 293 B9
Kempe's Corner Kent 54 D4
Kempie Highld 308 D4
Kempley Glos 98 F3
Kempley Green Glos 98 F3
Kempsey Worcs 99 B7
Kempsford Glos 81 F11
Kemps Green Warks 118 C2
Kempshott Hants 48 C6
Kempston Bedford 103 B10
Kempston Church End
Bedford 103 B10
Kempston Hardwick
Bedford 103 B10
Kempston West End
Bedford 103 B9
Kempton Shrops 131 G7
Kemp Town Brighton 36 G4
Kemsing Kent 52 B4
Kemsley Kent 70 F2
Kemsley Street Kent 69 G10
Kenardington Kent 54 G3
Kenchester Hereford 97 C8
Kencot Oxon 82 E3
Kendal Cumb 221 G10
Kendal End Worcs 117 C10
Kendleshire S Glos 61 D7
Kendon Caerph 77 F11
Kendoon Dumfries 246 F4
Kendray S Yorks 197 F11
Kenfig Bridgend 57 E10
Kenfig Hill Bridgend 57 E10
Kengharair Argyll 288 E6
Kenilworth Warks 118 C5
Kenknock Stirling 285 D8
Kenley London 51 B10
Shrops 131 C11
Kenmore Argyll 284 G4
Highld 299 D7
Perth 285 C11
Kenmure Dumfries 237 B8
Kenn Devon 14 D4
N Som 60 F2
Kennacley W Isles 305 J3
Kennacraig Argyll 275 G9
Kennards House Corn 11 E11
Kenneggy Corn 2 D3
Kenneggy Downs Corn 2 D3
Kennerleigh Devon 26 F4
Kennet Clack 279 C8
Kennet End Suff 124 D4
Kennethmont Aberds 302 G5
Kennett Cambs 124 D3
Kennford Devon 14 D4
Kenninghall Norf 141 F10
Kenninghall Heath
Norf 141 G10
Kennington Kent 54 E4
London 67 D10
Oxon 83 E8
Kenn Moor Gate N Som 60 F2
Kennoway Fife 287 G7
Kenny Som 28 D4
Kenny Hill Suff 124 B3
Kennythorpe N Yorks 216 F5
Kenovay Argyll 288 E1
Kensaleyre Highld 298 D4
Kensal Green London 67 C8
Kensal Rise London 67 C8
Kensal Town London 67 C8
Kensary Highld 310 E6
Kensington London 67 D9
Kensworth C Beds 85 B8
Kentallen Highld 284 B4
Kentchurch Hereford 97 F8
Kentford Suff 124 D4
Kentisbeare Devon 27 F9
Kentisbury Devon 40 E6
Kentisbury Ford Devon 40 E6
Kentish Town London 67 C9
Kentmere Cumb 221 E9
Kenton Devon 14 E5
London 67 B7
Suff 126 D3
T&W 242 D6
Kenton Bankfoot T&W 242 D6
Kenton Bar T&W 242 D6
Kenton Corner Suff 126 D4
Kenton Green Glos 80 C3
Kentra Highld 289 C8
Kentrigg Cumb 221 G10
Kents Corn 11 B9
Kents Bank Cumb 211 D7
Kent's Green Glos 98 G4
Kents Hill M Keynes 103 D7
Kent's Oak Hants 32 C4
Kent Street E Sus 38 D3
Kent 53 C7
W Sus 36 C2
Kenwick Shrops 149 C8
Kenwick Park Shrops 149 D8
Kenwyn Corn 4 F6
Kenyon Warr 183 B10
Keoldale Highld 308 C3
Keonchulish Ho Highld 307 K6
Kepdowrie Stirling 277 C11
Kepnal Wilts 63 G7
Keppanach Highld 290 G2
Keppoch Highld 295 C11
Keprigan Argyll 255 F7
Kepwick N Yorks 225 G9
Kerchesters Borders 263 B7
Kerdiston Norf 159 E11
Keresforth Hill S Yorks 197 F10
Keresley W Mid 134 G6
Keresley Newlands
Warks 134 G6
Kerfield Borders 270 G5
Kerley Downs Corn 4 G5
Kernborough Devon 8 G5
Kerne Bridge Hereford 79 B9
Kernsary Highld 299 B8
Kerridge Ches E 184 F6
Kerridge-end Ches E 184 F6
Kerris Corn 1 D4
Kerry = Ceri Powys 130 F2
Kerrycroy Argyll 266 C2
Kerry Hill Staffs 168 F6
Kerrysdale Highld 299 B8
Kerry's Gate Hereford 97 E7
Kersal Gtr Man 195 G10
Kersall Notts 172 C2
Kersbrook Cross Corn 12 F2
Kerscott Devon 25 B10
Kersey Suff 107 C10
Kersey Tye Suff 107 C9
Kersey Upland Suff 107 C9
Kershopefoot Cumb 249 G11
Kersoe Worcs 99 C9
Kerswell Devon 27 F9
Kerswell Green Worcs 99 B7
Kerthen Wood Corn 2 C3
Kesgrave Suff 108 B4
Kessingland Suff 143 F10
Kessingland Beach
Suff 143 F10
Kessington E Dunb 277 G11
Kestle Corn 5 F9
Kestle Mill Corn 5 D7
Keston London 68 G2
Keston Mark London 68 F2
Keswick Cumb 229 G11
Norf 142 C4
Norf 161 C7
Kete Pembs 72 E4
Ketford Glos 98 E4
Ketley Telford 150 G3
Ketley Bank Telford 150 G3
Ketsby Lincs 190 F5
Kettering N Nhants 121 B7
Ketteringham Norf 142 C3
Kettins Perth 286 D6
Kettlebaston Suff 125 G9
Kettlebridge Fife 287 G7
Kettlebrook Staffs 134 C4
Kettleburgh Suff 126 E5
Kettle Corner Kent 53 C8
Kettle Green Herts 86 B6
Kettlehill Fife 287 G7
Kettleholm Dumfries 238 B4
Kettleness N Yorks 226 B6
Kettleshulme Ches E 185 F7
Kettleshume Ches E 185 F7
Kettlesing N Yorks 205 B10
Kettlesing Bottom
N Yorks 205 B10
Kettlesing Head
N Yorks 205 B10
Kettlestone Norf 159 C9
Kettlethorpe Lincs 188 F4
W Yorks 197 D10
Kettletoft Orkney 314 C6
Kettlewell N Yorks 213 E9
Ketton Rutland 137 C9
Kevingtown London 68 F3
Kew London 67 D7
Keward Som 44 E4
Kew Bridge London 67 D7
Kewstoke N Som 59 G10
Kexbrough S Yorks 197 F9
Kexby Lincs 188 D5
York 207 C10
Keybridge Corn 11 G7
Keycol Kent 69 G11
Keyford Som 45 D9
Key Green Ches E 168 C5
N Yorks 226 E6
Keyham Leics 136 B3
Keyhaven Hants 20 C2
Keyingham E Yorks 201 B8
Keymer W Sus 36 D4
Keynsham Bath 61 F7
Keysers Estate Essex 86 D5
Key's Green Kent 53 F7
Keysoe Bedford 121 E11
Keysoe Row Bedford 121 E11
Keyston Cambs 121 B10
Key Street Kent 69 G11
Keyworth Notts 154 C2
Khantore Aberds 292 D4
Kibbear Som 28 C2
Kibblesworth T&W 242 F6
Kibworth Beauchamp
Leics 136 E3
Kibworth Harcourt
Leics 136 E3
Kidbrooke London 68 D2
Kidburngill Cumb 229 G7
Kiddal Lane End
W Yorks 206 F4
Kiddemore Green Staffs 133 B7
Kidderminster Worcs 116 B6
Kiddington Oxon 101 G8
Kidd's Moor Norf 142 C2
Kidlington Oxon 83 C7
Kidmore End Oxon 65 D7
Kidnal Ches W 167 F7
Kidsdale Dumfries 236 F6
Kidsgrove Staffs 168 E4
Kidstones N Yorks 213 C9
Kidwelly = Cydweli
Carms 74 D6
Kiel Crofts Argyll 289 F11
Kielder Northumb 250 E4
Kierfiold Ho Orkney 314 E2
Kiff Green W Berks 64 F5
Kilbagie Fife 279 D8
Kilbarchan Renfs 267 C8
Kilbeg Highld 295 E8
Kilberry Argyll 275 G8
Kilbirnie N Ayrs 266 E6
Kilbowie W Dunb 277 G10
Kilbraur Highld 311 H2
Kilbride Argyll 254 C4
Argyll 275 D9
Argyll 289 G10
Argyll 289 G11
Highld 295 C7
Kilbridemore Argyll 275 D11
Kilbryde Castle Stirling 285 G11
Kilburn Angus 292 G5
Derbys 170 F5
London 67 C9
N Yorks 215 D10
Kilby Leics 136 D2
Kilby Bridge Leics 136 D2
Kilchamaig Argyll 275 G9
Kilchattan Argyll 255 E11
Kilchattan Bay Argyll 266 E2
Kilchenzie Argyll 255 E7
Kilcheran Argyll 289 F10
Kilchiaran Argyll 274 G3
Kilchoan Argyll 275 B8
Highld 288 C6
Kilchoman Argyll 274 G3
Kilchrenan Argyll 284 E4
Kilconquhar Fife 287 G8
Kilcot Glos 98 F3
Kilcoy Highld 300 D5
Kilcreggan Argyll 276 E4
Kildale N Yorks 226 D2
Kildalloig Argyll 255 F8
Kildary Highld 301 B7
Kildaton Ho Argyll 254 C5
Kildavanan Argyll 275 G11
Kildermorie Lodge
Highld 300 B5
Kildonan Dumfries 236 D2
Highld 298 D3
N Ayrs 256 E2
Kildonan Lodge Highld 311 G3
Kildonnan Highld 294 G6
Kildrum N Lanark 278 F5
Kildrummy Aberds 292 B6
Kildwick N Yorks 204 D6
Kilfinan Argyll 275 F10
Kilfinnan Highld 290 D4
Kilgetty Pembs 73 D10
Kilgour Fife 286 G6
Kilgrammie S Ayrs 245 C7
Kilgwrrwg Common Mon 79 F7
Kilhallon Corn 5 E11
Kilham E Yorks 217 G11
Northumb 263 C9
Kilkeddan Argyll 255 E8
Kilkenneth Argyll 288 E1
Kilkenny Glos 81 B8
Kilkerran Argyll 255 F8
Kilkhampton Corn 24 E3
Killamarsh Derbys 187 E7
Killaworgey Corn 5 C8
Killay Swansea 56 C6
Killbeg Argyll 289 E8
Killean Argyll 255 C7
Killearn Stirling 277 D10
Killegruer Argyll 255 D7
Killen Highld 300 D6
Killerby Darl 224 B3
Killichonan Perth 285 B9
Killiechoinich Argyll 289 G10
Killiechonate Highld 290 E4
Killiechronan Argyll 289 E7
Killiecrankie Perth 291 G11
Killiemor Argyll 288 F6
Killiemore House Argyll 288 G6
Killilan Highld 295 B11
Killimster Highld 310 D7
Killin Stirling 285 D9
Killinallan Argyll 274 F4
Killingbeck W Yorks 206 G2
Killinghall N Yorks 205 B11
Killington Cumb 212 B2
Devon 41 D7
Killingworth T&W 243 C7
Killingworth Moor T&W 243 C7
Killingworth Village
T&W 243 C7
Killin Lodge Highld 291 C7
Killivose Corn 2 B4
Killmahumaig Argyll 275 D8
Killochyett Borders 271 F9
Killocraw Argyll 255 D7
Killundine Highld 289 E7
Killylung Dumfries 247 G11
Kilmacolm Invclyd 267 B7
Kilmaha Argyll 275 C10
Kilmahog Stirling 285 G10
Kilmalieu Highld 289 D10
Kilmaluag Highld 298 B4
Kilmany Fife 287 E7
Kilmarie Highld 295 D7
Kilmarnock E Ayrs 257 B10
Kilmaron Castle Fife 287 F7
Kilmartin Argyll 275 D9
Kilmaurs E Ayrs 267 G8
Kilmelford Argyll 275 B9
Kilmeny Argyll 274 G4
Kilmersdon Som 45 C7
Kilmeston Hants 33 B9
Kilmichael Argyll 255 E7
Argyll 275 F10
Kilmichael Glassary
Argyll 275 D9
Kilmichael of Inverlussa
Argyll 275 E8
Kilmington Devon 15 B11
Wilts 45 F9
Kilmington Common
Wilts 45 F9
Kilmoluaig Argyll 288 E1
Kilmonivaig Highld 290 E3
Kilmorack Highld 300 E4
Kilmore Argyll 289 G10
Highld 295 E8
Kilmory Argyll 275 F8
Highld 289 B7
Highld 294 E5
N Ayrs 255 E10
Kilmory Lodge Argyll 275 C8
Kilmote Highld 311 H3
Kilmuir Highld 298 B3
Highld 298 E2
Highld 300 E6
Highld 301 B7
Kilmun Argyll 275 B10
Argyll 276 E3
Kilnave Argyll 274 F3
Kilncadzow S Lanark 269 F7
Kilndown Kent 53 G8
Kiln Green Hereford 79 B10
Wokingham 65 D10
Kilnhill Cumb 229 E10
Kilnhurst S Yorks 187 B7
Kilninian Argyll 288 E5
Kilninver Argyll 289 G10
Kiln Pit Hill Northumb 242 G2
Kilnsea E Yorks 201 D12
Kilnsey N Yorks 213 F9
Kilnwick E Yorks 208 D5
Kilnwick Percy E Yorks 208 C2
Kilnwood Vale W Sus 51 G8
Kiloran Argyll 274 D4
Kilpatrick N Ayrs 255 E10
Kilpeck Hereford 97 E8
Kilphedir Highld 311 H3
Kilpin E Yorks 199 B9
Kilpin Pike E Yorks 199 B9
Kilrenny Fife 287 G9
Kilsby W Nhants 119 C11
Kilspindie Perth 286 E6
Kilsyth N Lanark 278 F4
Kiltarlity Highld 300 E5
Kilton Notts 187 F9
Redcar 226 B4
Som 43 E7
Kilton Thorpe Redcar 226 B3
Kiltyrie Perth 285 D10
Kilvaxter Highld 298 C3
Kilve Som 43 E7
Kilvington Notts 172 G3
Kilwinning N Ayrs 266 G6
Kimberley Norf 141 C11
Notts 171 G8
Kimberworth S Yorks 186 C6
Kimberworth Park
S Yorks 186 C6
Kimblesworth Durham 233 B11
Kimble Wick Bucks 84 D4
Kimbolton Cambs 121 D11
Hereford 115 E10
Kimbridge Hants 32 B4
Kimcote Leics 135 F11
Kimmeridge Dorset 18 F4
Kimmerston Northumb 263 B11
Kimpton Hants 47 D9
Herts 85 B11
Kimworthy Devon 24 E4
Kinabus Argyll 254 C3
Kinbeachie Highld 300 C6
Kinbrace Highld 310 F2
Kinbuck Stirling 285 G11
Kincaidston S Ayrs 257 F9
Kincaple Fife 287 F8
Kincardine Fife 279 D8
Highld 309 L6
Kincardine Bridge Falk 279 D8
Kincardine O'Neil
Aberds 293 D7
Kinclaven Perth 286 D5
Kincorth Aberdeen 293 C11
Kincorth Ho Moray 301 C10
Kincraig Highld 291 C10
Kincraigie Perth 286 C3
Kindallachan Perth 286 C3
Kine Moor S Yorks 197 G9
Kineton Glos 99 F11
Warks 118 G6
Kineton Green W Mid 134 G2
Kinfauns Perth 286 E5
Kingairloch Highld 289 D10
Kingarth Argyll 255 B11
Kingates IoW 20 F6
Kingbeare Corn 11 G11
Kingcoed Mon 78 D6
Kingdown N Som 60 G4
King Edward Aberds 303 D7
Kingerby Lincs 189 C9
Kingfield Sur 50 B4
Kingford Devon 24 F3
Devon 25 D10
Kingham Oxon 100 G5
Kinghay Wilts 30 B5
Kingholm Quay
Dumfries 237 B11
Kinghorn Fife 280 D5
Kingie Highld 290 C3
Kinglassie Fife 280 B4
Kingledores Borders 260 D4
Kingoodie Perth 287 E7
King's Acre Hereford 97 C9
Kingsand Corn 7 E8
Kingsash Bucks 84 D5
Kingsbarns Fife 287 F9
Kingsbridge Devon 8 G4
Som 42 F3
King's Bromley Staffs 152 F2
Kingsbrook Oxfordshire 84 C4
Kingsburgh Highld 298 D3
Kingsbury London 67 B8
Warks 134 D4
Kingsbury Episcopi Som 28 C6
Kingsbury Regis Som 29 D11
King's Caple Hereford 97 F11
Kingscauseway Highld 301 B7
Kingscavil W Loth 279 F10
Kingsclere Hants 48 B4
Kingsclere Woodlands
Hants 64 G4
King's Cliffe N Nhants 137 D10
Kings Clipstone Notts 171 C10
Kingscote Glos 80 F4
Kingscott Devon 25 D8
King's Coughton Warks 117 F11
Kingscourt Glos 80 E4
Kingscross N Ayrs 256 D2
Kingsditch Glos 99 G8
Kingsdon Som 29 B8
Kingsdown Kent 54 B2
Kent 55 D11
Swindon 63 B7
Wilts 61 F10
King's Dyke Cambs 138 D4
Kingseat Fife 280 C2
Kingseathill Fife 280 D2
King's End Worcs 116 G6
Kingsett Devon 12 E6
Kingsey Bucks 84 D2
Kingsfield Hereford 97 B10
Kingsfold Lancs 194 B4
W Sus 51 F7
Kingsford Aberds 293 B7
E Ayrs 267 F8
Worcs 132 G6
Kingsforth N Lincs 200 D4
King's Furlong Hants 48 C6
Kingsgate Kent 71 E11
King's Green Glos 98 E5
Worcs 116 E5
Kingshall Green Suff 125 E8
Kingshall Street Suff 125 E8
Kingsheanton Devon 40 F5
King's Heath W Mid 133 G11
W Nhants 120 E4
Kings Hedges Cambs 123 E9
Kingshill Glos 80 F3
Swindon 62 C6
Kings Hill Glos 81 E8
King's Hill Kent 53 C7
W Mid 133 D9
Kingsholm Glos 80 B4
Kingshouse Hotel
Highld 284 B6
Kingshurst W Mid 134 F3
Kingside Hill Cumb 238 G5
Kingskerswell Devon 9 B7
Kingskettle Fife 287 G7
Kingsknowe Edin 280 G4
Kingsland Anglesey 178 E2
Hereford 115 E8
London 67 C10
Shrops 149 G9
Kings Langley Herts 85 E9
Kingsley Ches W 183 G9
Hants 49 F9
Staffs 169 F8
Kingsley Green W Sus 49 G11
Kingsley Holt Staffs 169 F8
Kingsley Moor Staffs 169 F7
Kingsley Park W Nhants 120 E5
Kingslow Shrops 132 D5
King's Lynn Norf 158 E2
King's Meaburn Cumb 231 G8
Kingsmead Hants 33 E9
Kingsmere Oxon 101 G11
King's Mills Derbys 153 D8
Wrex 166 F4
Kingsmoor Essex 86 D6
Kings Moss Mers 194 G4
Kingsmuir Angus 287 C8
Fife 287 G9
Kings Muir Borders 261 B7
King's Newnham Warks 119 B9
King's Newton Derbys 153 D7
Kingsnordley Shrops 132 F5
Kingsnorth Kent 54 F4
King's Norton Leics 136 C3
W Mid 117 B11
King's Nympton Devon 25 D11
King's Pyon Hereford 115 G8
Kings Ripton Cambs 122 B5
King's Somborne Hants 47 G11
King's Stag Dorset 30 E2
King's Stanley Glos 80 E4
King's Sutton W Nhants 101 D9
King's Tamerton Plym 7 D9
Kingstanding W Mid 133 E11
Kingsteignton Devon 14 G3
Kingsteps Highld 301 D9
King Sterndale Derbys 185 G9
King's Thorn Hereford 97 E10
Kingsthorpe W Nhants 120 E5
Kingsthorpe Hollow
W Nhants 120 E5
Kingston Cambs 122 F6
Devon 8 F2
Devon 9 E8
Dorset 18 F5
Dorset 30 F3
E Loth 281 E10
Gtr Man 184 B6
Hants 31 G11
IoW 20 E5
Kent 55 C7
M Keynes 103 D8
Moray 302 C3
Ptsmth 33 G11
Kingston *continued*
Suff 108 B5
Kingston Bagpuize Oxon 82 F6
Kingston Blount Oxon 84 F2
Kingston by Sea W Sus 36 G2
Kingston Deverill Wilts 45 F10
Kingstone Hereford 97 D8
Hereford 98 G2
Som 28 E5
Staffs 151 D11
S Yorks 197 F10
Kingstone Winslow Oxon 63 B9
Kingston Gorse W Sus 35 G9
Kingston Lisle Oxon 63 B10
Kingston Maurward
Dorset 17 C10
Kingston near Lewes
E Sus 36 F5
Kingston on Soar
Notts 153 D10
Kingston Park T&W 242 D6
Kingston Russell Dorset 17 C7
Kingston St Mary Som 28 B2
Kingston Seymour
N Som 60 F2
Kingston Stert Oxon 84 E2
Kingston upon Hull Hull 200 B5
Kingston upon Thames
London 67 F7
Kingston Vale London 67 E8
Kingstown Cumb 239 F9
King Street Essex 87 E9
King's Walden Herts 104 G3
Kingsway Bath 61 G8
Halton 183 D8
Kingswear Devon 9 E7
Kingswells Aberdeen 293 C10
Kingswinford W Mid 133 F7
Kingswood Bucks 83 B11
Essex 69 B8
Glos 80 G2
Hereford 114 G5
Herts 85 E10
Kent 53 C10
Powys 130 C4
S Glos 60 E6
Som 42 F6
Sur 51 B8
Warks 118 C3
Warr 183 C9
Kingswood Brook
Warks 118 C3
Kingswood Common
Staffs 132 C6
Worcs 116 D4
King's Worthy Hants 48 G3
Kingthorpe Lincs 189 F10
Kington Hereford 114 F5
S Glos 79 G10
Worcs 117 F9
Kington Langley Wilts 62 D2
Kington Magna Dorset 30 C3
Kington St Michael Wilts 62 D2
Kingussie Highld 291 C9
Kingweston Som 44 G4
Kinhrive Highld 301 B7
Kininvie Ho Moray 302 E3
Kinkell Bridge Perth 286 F3
Kinknockie Aberds 303 E10
Aberds 303 G9
Kinkry Hill Cumb 240 B2
Kinlet Shrops 132 G4
Kinloch Fife 286 F6
Highld 289 D8
Highld 294 F5
Highld 295 D8
Highld 308 F3
Perth 286 C5
Perth 286 C6
Kinlochan Highld 289 C10
Kinlochard Stirling 285 G8
Kinlochbeoraid Highld 295 G10
Kinlochbervie Highld 306 D7
Kinloch Damph Highld 299 E8
Kinlocheil Highld 289 B11
Kinlochewe Highld 299 C10
Kinloch Hourn Highld 295 E11
Kinloch Laggan Highld 291 E7
Kinlochleven Highld 290 G3
Kinloch Lodge Highld 308 D5
Kinlochmoidart Highld 289 B9
Kinlochmorar Highld 295 F10
Kinlochmore Highld 290 G3
Kinloch Rannoch Perth 285 B10
Kinlochspelve Argyll 289 G8
Kinloid Highld 295 G8
Kinloss Moray 301 C10
Kinmel Bay = Bae Cinmel
Conwy 181 E7
Kinmuck Aberds 293 B10
Kinmundy Aberds 293 B10
Kinnadie Aberds 303 E9
Kinnaird Perth 286 B3
Perth 286 E6
Kinnaird Castle Angus 287 B10
Kinnauld Highld 309 J7
Kinneff Aberds 293 F10
Kinneil Falk 279 E9
Kinnelhead Dumfries 248 C2
Kinnell Angus 287 B10
Kinnerley Shrops 148 E6
Kinnersley Hereford 96 B6
Worcs 99 C7
Kinnerton Powys 114 E4
Kinnerton Green Flint 166 C4
Kinninvie Durham 233 G7
Kinnordy Angus 287 B7
Kinoulton Notts 154 C3
Kinross Perth 286 G5
Kinrossie Perth 286 D5
Kinsbourne Green Herts 85 B10
Kinsey Heath Ches E 167 G11
Kinsham Hereford 115 E7
Worcs 99 D8
Kinsley W Yorks 198 E2
Kinson BCP 19 B7
Kintallan Argyll 275 E8
Kintbury W Berks 63 F11
Kintessack Moray 301 C9
Kintillo Perth 286 F5
Kintocher Aberds 293 C7
Kinton Hereford 115 C8
Shrops 149 F7
Kintore Aberds 293 B9
Kintour Argyll 254 B5
Kintra Argyll 254 C4
Argyll 288 G5
Kintradwell Highld 311 J3
Kintraw Argyll 275 C9
Kinuachdrachd Argyll 275 D8
Kinveachy Highld 291 B11
Kinver Staffs 132 G6
Kinwalsey Warks 134 F4
Kip Hill Durham 242 G6
Kiplin N Yorks 224 F5
Kippax W Yorks 206 G4
Kippen Stirling 278 C3
Kippford or Scaur
Dumfries 237 D10
Kippilaw Borders 262 D2

Kippilaw Mains Borders 262 D2
Kipping's Cross Kent 52 F6
Kippington Kent 52 C4
Kirbister Orkney 314 D6
Orkney 314 E2
Orkney 314 F3
Kirbuster Orkney 314 D2
Kirby Bedon Norf 142 B5
Kirby Bellars Leics 154 F4
Kirby Cane Norf 143 E7
Kirby Corner W Mid 118 B5
Kirby Cross Essex 108 G4
Kirby Fields Leics 135 C10
Kirby Green Norf 143 E7
Kirby Grindalythe
N Yorks 217 F8
Kirby Hill N Yorks 215 F7
N Yorks 224 D2
Kirby Knowle N Yorks 215 B9
Kirby-le-Soken Essex 108 G4
Kirby Misperton
N Yorks 216 D5
Kirby Moor Cumb 240 E2
Kirby Muxloe Leics 135 C10
Kirby Row Norf 143 E7
Kirby Sigston N Yorks 225 G8
Kirby Underdale
E Yorks 208 B2
Kirby Wiske N Yorks 215 C7
Kirdford W Sus 35 B8
Kirk Highld 310 D6
Kirkabister Shetland 312 G6
Shetland 313 K6
Kirkandrews Dumfries 237 E8
Kirkandrews-on-Eden
Cumb 239 F9
Kirkapol Argyll 288 E2
Kirkbampton Cumb 239 F8
Kirkbean Dumfries 237 D11
Kirkborough Cumb 229 D7
Kirkbrae Orkney 314 B4
Kirk Bramwith S Yorks 198 E6
Kirkbride Cumb 238 F6
Kirkbridge N Yorks 224 G5
Kirkbuddo Angus 287 C9
Kirkburn Borders 261 B7
E Yorks 208 B5
Kirkburton W Yorks 197 E7
Kirkby Lincs 189 C9
Mers 182 B6
N Yorks 225 D10
Kirkby Fenside Lincs 174 C4
Kirkby Fleetham
N Yorks 224 G5
Kirkby Green Lincs 173 D9
Kirkby Hill N Yorks 215 F7
Kirkby in Ashfield
Notts 171 D8
Kirkby-in-Furness
Cumb 210 C4
Kirkby la Thorpe Lincs 173 F10
Kirkby Lonsdale Cumb 212 D2
Kirkby Malham N Yorks 213 G7
Kirkby Mallory Leics 135 C9
Kirkby Malzeard
N Yorks 214 E4
Kirkby Mills N Yorks 216 B4
Kirkbymoorside
N Yorks 216 B3
Kirkby on Bain Lincs 174 C2
Kirkby Overblow
N Yorks 206 D2
Kirkby Stephen Cumb 222 D5
Kirkby Thore Cumb 231 F8
Kirkby Underwood
Lincs 155 D11
Kirkby Wharfe N Yorks 206 E6
Kirkby Woodhouse
Notts 171 E7
Kirkcaldy Fife 280 C5
Kirkcambeck Cumb 240 D2
Kirkcarswell Dumfries 237 E9
Kirkcolm Dumfries 236 C2
Kirkconnel Dumfries 258 G6
Kirkconnell Dumfries 237 C11
Kirkcowan Dumfries 236 C5
Kirkcudbright Dumfries 237 D8
Kirkdale Mers 182 C4
Kirk Deighton N Yorks 206 C3
Kirk Ella E Yorks 200 B4
Kirkfieldbank S Lanark 269 G7
Kirkforthar Feus Fife 286 G6
Kirkgunzeon Dumfries 237 C10
Kirk Hallam Derbys 171 G7
Kirkham Lancs 202 G4
N Yorks 216 F4
Kirkhamgate W Yorks 197 C9
Kirk Hammerton
N Yorks 206 B5
Kirkhams Gtr Man 195 F10
Kirkharle Northumb 252 G2
Kirkheaton Northumb 242 B2
W Yorks 197 D7
Kirkhill Angus 293 G8
E Renf 267 D11
Highld 300 E5
Midloth 270 C4
Moray 302 F2
W Loth 279 G11
Kirkholt Gtr Man 195 E11
Kirkhope Borders 261 E9
Kirkhouse Borders 261 C8
Cumb 240 F3
Kirkiboll Highld 308 D5
Kirkibost Highld 295 D7
Kirkinch Angus 287 C7
Kirkinner Dumfries 236 D6
Kirkintilloch E Dunb 278 G3
Kirk Ireton Derbys 170 E3
Kirkland Cumb 219 B11
Cumb 229 B11
Cumb 231 E8
Dumfries 247 E8
Dumfries 258 G6
S Ayrs 244 E6
Kirkland Guards Cumb 229 C9
Kirk Langley Derbys 152 B5
Kirkleatham Redcar 235 G7
Kirklees Gtr Man 195 E9
Kirklevington Stockton 225 D8
Kirkley Suff 143 E10
Kirklington Notts 171 D11
N Yorks 214 C6
Kirklinton Cumb 239 D10
Kirkliston Edin 280 G2
Kirkmaiden Dumfries 236 F3
Kirk Merrington
Durham 233 E11
Kirkmichael Perth 286 B4
S Ayrs 245 B8
Kirk Michael IoM 192 C4
Kirkmichael Mains
Dumfries 248 F2
Kirkmuirhill S Lanark 268 G5
Kirknewton Northumb 263 C10
W Loth 270 B2
Kirkney Aberds 302 F5
Kirk of Shotts N Lanark 268 C6
Kirkoswald Cumb 231 C7
S Ayrs 244 B6
Kirkpatrick Dumfries 247 E10
Kirkpatrick Durham
Dumfries 237 B9
Kirkpatrick-Fleming
Dumfries 239 C7
Kirk Sandall S Yorks 198 F6
Kirksanton Cumb 210 C2
Kirkshaw N Lanark 268 C4
Kirk Smeaton N Yorks 198 D4
Kirkstall W Yorks 205 F11
Kirkstead Borders 261 E7
Lincs 173 C11
Kirkstile Aberds 302 F5
Kirkstyle Highld 310 B7
Kirkthorpe W Yorks 197 C11
Kirkton Aberds 302 E6
Aberds 302 G6
Angus 286 C6
Angus 287 C8
Angus 287 D8
Argyll 275 C8
Borders 262 G2
Dumfries 247 G11
Fife 280 D4
Fife 287 E7
Highld 295 C10
Highld 299 E9
Highld 301 D7
Highld 309 K7
Perth 286 F3
S Lanark 259 E10
Stirling 285 G9
W Loth 269 B10
Kirktonhill Borders 271 E9
W Dunb 277 G7
Kirkton Manor Borders 260 B6
Kirkton of Airlie Angus 287 B7
Kirkton of Auchterhouse
Angus 287 D7
Kirkton of Auchterless
Aberds 303 E7
Kirkton of Barevan
Highld 301 E8
Kirkton of Bourtie
Aberds 303 G8
Kirkton of Collace
Perth 286 D5
Kirkton of Craig Angus 287 B11
Kirkton of Culsalmond
Aberds 302 F6
Kirkton of Durris
Aberds 293 D9
Kirkton of Glenbuchat
Aberds 292 B5
Kirkton of Glenisla
Angus 292 G4
Kirkton of Kingoldrum
Angus 287 B7
Kirkton of Largo Fife 287 G8
Kirkton of Lethendy
Perth 286 C5
Kirkton of Logie Buchan
Aberds 303 G9
Kirkton of Maryculter
Aberds 293 D10
Kirkton of Menmuir
Angus 293 G7
Kirkton of Monikie
Angus 287 D9
Kirkton of Oyne Aberds 302 G6
Kirkton of Rayne
Aberds 302 G6
Kirkton of Skene
Aberds 293 C10
Kirkton of Tough
Aberds 293 B8
Kirktoun E Ayrs 267 G8
Kirktown Aberds 303 D10
Kirktown of Alvah
Aberds 302 C6
Kirktown of Deskford
Moray 302 C5
Kirktown of Fetteresso
Aberds 293 E10
Kirktown of Mortlach
Moray 302 F3
Kirktown of Slains
Aberds 303 G10
Kirkurd Borders 270 G2
Kirkwall Orkney 314 E4
Kirkwhelpington
Northumb 251 G11
Kirkwood Dumfries 238 B4
N Lanark 268 C4
Kirk Yetholm Borders 263 D8
Kirmington N Lincs 200 E6
Kirmond le Mire Lincs 189 C11
Kirn Argyll 276 F3
Kirriemuir Angus 287 B7
Kirstead Green Norf 142 D5
Kirtlebridge Dumfries 238 C6
Kirtleton Dumfries 249 G7
Kirtling Cambs 124 F3
Kirtling Green Cambs 124 F3
Kirtlington Oxon 83 B7
Kirtomy Highld 308 C7
Kirton Lincs 156 B6
Notts 171 B11
Suff 108 D5
Kirton Campus W Loth 269 B10
Kirton End Lincs 174 G3
Kirton Holme Lincs 174 G3
Kirton in Lindsey
N Lincs 188 B6
Kiskin Cumb 210 B1
Kislingbury W Nhants 120 F3
Kitbridge Devon 28 G4
Kitchenroyd W Yorks 197 F8
Kitebrook Warks 100 E4
Kite Green Warks 118 D3
Kite Hill IoW 21 C7
Kites Hardwick Warks 119 D9
Kit Hill Dorset 30 D4
Kitlye Glos 80 E5
Kit's Coty Kent 69 G8
Kitt Green Gtr Man 194 F5
Kittisford Som 27 C9
Kittle Swansea 56 D5
Kitts End Herts 86 F2
Kitt's Green W Mid 134 F3
Kitt's Moss Gtr Man 184 E5
Kittwhistle Dorset 28 G5
Kittybrewster Aberdeen 293 C11
Kitwell W Mid 133 G9
Kitwood Hants 49 G7
Kivernoll Hereford 97 E9
Kiveton Park S Yorks 187 E7
Knaith Lincs 188 E4
Knaith Park Lincs 188 D4
Knaphill Sur 50 B3
Knapp Hants 32 C6
Perth 286 D6
Som 28 B4
Wilts 31 B8
Knapp Hill Wilts 30 B5
Knapthorpe Notts 172 D2
Knaptoft Leics 136 F2
Knapton Norf 160 C6
York 207 C7
Knapton Green Hereford 115 G8
Knapwell Cambs 122 E6
Knaresborough N Yorks 206 B3
Knarsdale Northumb 240 G5
Knatts Valley Kent 68 G5
Knauchland Moray 302 D5
Knaven Aberds 303 E8
Knave's Ash Kent 71 G7
Knaves Green Suff 126 D2
Knavesmire York 207 D7
Knayton N Yorks 215 B8
Knebworth Herts 104 G5
Knedlington E Yorks 199 B8
Kneesall Notts 172 C2
Kneesworth Cambs 104 C6
Kneeton Notts 172 F2
Knelston Swansea 56 D3
Knenhall Staffs 151 B8
Knettishall Suff 141 G9
Knightacott Devon 41 F7
Knightcote Warks 119 G7
Knightcott N Som 43 B11
Knightley Staffs 150 D6
Knightley Dale Staffs 150 E6
Knighton BCP 18 B6
Devon 7 F10
Dorset 29 E10
Leicester 135 C11
Oxon 63 B9
Som 43 E7
Staffs 150 D4
Staffs 168 G2
Wilts 63 E9
Worcs 117 F10
Knighton = Tref-y-Clawdd
Powys 114 C5
Knighton Fields
Leicester 135 C11
Knighton on Teme
Worcs 116 C2
Knightor Corn 5 D10
Knightsbridge Glos 99 F7
London 67 D9
Knight's End Cambs 139 E8
Knights Enham Hants 47 D11
Knight's Hill London 67 E10
Knightsmill Corn 11 E7
Knightsridge W Loth 269 B10
Knightswood Glasgow 267 B10
Knightwick Worcs 116 F4
Knill Hereford 114 E5
Knipe Fold Cumb 220 F6
Knipoch Argyll 289 G10
Knipton Leics 154 C6
Knitsley Durham 233 B8
Kniveton Derbys 170 E2
Knocharthur Highld 309 J7
Knock Argyll 289 F7
Cumb 231 F9
Moray 302 D5
Knockally Highld 311 G5
Knockan Highld 307 H7
Knockandhu Moray 302 G2
Knockando Moray 301 E11
Knockando Ho Moray 302 E2
Knockandoo Highld 301 G7
Knockbain Highld 300 D6
Knockbreck Highld 298 C2
Knockbrex Dumfries 237 E7
Knockcarrach Highld 290 B6
Knockdee Highld 310 C5
Knockdolian S Ayrs 244 F4
Knockdow Argyll 276 G2
Knockdown Glos 61 B10
Knockenbaird Aberds 302 G6
Knockenkelly N Ayrs 256 D2
Knockentiber E Ayrs 257 B9
Knockerdown Derbys 170 E2
Knockespock Ho Aberds 302 G5
Knockfarrel Highld 300 D5
Knockglass Dumfries 236 D2
Knockhall Kent 68 E5
Knockhall Castle
Aberds 303 G9
Knockholt Kent 52 B3
Knockholt Pound Kent 52 B3
Knockie Lodge Highld 290 B6
Knockin Shrops 148 E6
Knockinlaw E Ayrs 257 B10
Knockinnon Highld 310 F5
Knocklaw Northumb 252 C3
Knocklearn Dumfries 237 B9
Knocklearoch Argyll 274 G4
Knockmill Kent 68 G5
Knocknaha Argyll 255 F7
Knocknain Dumfries 236 C1
Knockothie Aberds 303 F9
Knockrome Argyll 274 F6
Knocksharry IoM 192 D3
Knockstapplemore
Argyll 255 F7
Knockvologan Argyll 274 B4
Knodishall Suff 127 E8
Knokan Argyll 288 G6
Knole Som 29 B7
Knollbury Mon 60 B2
Knoll Green Som 43 F8
Knolls Green Ches E 184 F4
Knoll Top N Yorks 214 F3
Knolton Wrex 149 B7
Knolton Bryn Wrex 149 B7
Knook Wilts 46 E2
Knossington Leics 136 B6
Knotbury Staffs 169 B8
Knott End-on-Sea
Lancs 202 D3
Knotting Bedford 121 E10
Knotting Green
Bedford 121 E10
Knottingley W Yorks 198 C4
Knott Lanes Gtr Man 196 G2
Knott Oak Som 28 E5
Knotts Cumb 230 G4
Lancs 203 C11
Knotty Ash Mers 182 C6
Knotty Corner Devon 24 B6
Knotty Green Bucks 84 G6
Knowbury Shrops 115 C11
Knowe Dumfries 236 B5
Shetland 313 G5
Knowefield Cumb 239 F10
Knowehead Aberds 293 C7
Aberds 302 D5
Dumfries 246 E4
Knowes E Loth 282 F2
Knowesgate Northumb 251 F11
Knowes of Elrick
Aberds 302 D6
Knoweton N Lanark 268 D5
Knowetop N Lanark 268 D5
Knowhead Aberds 303 D9
Knowl Bank Staffs 168 F3
Knowle Bristol 60 E6
Devon 15 E7
Devon 26 G3
Devon 27 F8
Devon 40 F3
Hants 33 F9
Shrops 115 C11
Som 43 F10
Wilts 63 G7
W Mid 118 B3
Knowle Fields Worcs 117 F10
Knowlegate Shrops 115 C11
Knowle Green Lancs 203 F8
Sur 66 E4
Knowle Grove W Mid 118 B3
Knowle Hill Sur 66 F3
Knowle Park W Yorks 205 E7
Knowle St Giles Som 28 E4
Knowlesands Shrops 132 E4
Knowles Hill Devon 14 G3
Knowl Green Essex 106 C5
Knowl Hill Windsor 65 D10
Knowlton Dorset 31 E8
Kent 55 C9
Knowl Wall Staffs 151 B7
Knowl Wood W Yorks 196 C2
Knowsley Mers 182 B6
Knowsthorpe W Yorks 206 G2
Knowstone Devon 26 C4
Knox Bridge Kent 53 E9
Knucklas Powys 114 C5
Knuston N Nhants 121 D8
Knutsford Ches E 184 F3
Knutton Staffs 168 F4
Knuzden Brook Lancs 195 B8
Knypersley Staffs 168 D5
Kraiknish Highld 294 C5
Krumlin W Yorks 196 D5
Kuggar Corn 2 F6
Kyleakin Highld 295 C9
Kyle of Lochalsh Highld 295 C9
Kylepark N Lanark 268 C3
Kylerhea Highld 295 C9
Kylesknoydart Highld 295 F10
Kylesku Highld 306 F7
Kylesmorar Highld 295 F10
Kylestrome Highld 306 F7
Kyllachy House Highld 301 G7
Kymin Hereford 97 B11
Mon 79 C8
Kynaston Hereford 97 E10
Shrops 149 E7
Kynnersley Telford 150 F3
Kyre Worcs 116 E2
Kyre Green Worcs 116 E2
Kyre Magna Worcs 116 E2
Kyre Park Worcs 116 E2
Kyrewood Worcs 116 D2

L

Labost W Isles 304 D4
Lacasaidh W Isles 304 F5
Lacasdal W Isles 304 E6
Laceby NE Lincs 201 F8
Laceby Acres NE Lincs 201 F8
Lacey Green Bucks 84 F4
Ches E 184 E4
Lach Dennis Ches W 184 G2
Lache Ches W 166 C5
Lackenby Redcar 225 B11
Lackford Suff 124 C5
Lacock Wilts 62 F2
Ladbroke Warks 119 F8
Laddenvean Corn 3 E7
Laddingford Kent 53 D7
Lade Kent 39 C9
Lade Bank Lincs 174 E5
Ladies Riggs N Yorks 214 F2
Ladmanlow Derbys 185 G8
Ladock Corn 5 E7
Ladwell Hants 32 C6
Lady Orkney 314 B6
Ladybank Fife 287 F7
Ladybrook Notts 171 C8
Ladyburn Invclyd 276 F6
Ladycross Corn 12 D2
Ladyes Hill Warks 118 C5
Lady Green Mers 193 G10
Lady Hall Cumb 210 B3
Lady Halton Shrops 115 B9
Lady House Gtr Man 196 E2
Ladykirk Borders 273 F7
Ladyoak Shrops 131 C7
Lady Park T&W 242 F6
Ladyridge Hereford 97 E11
Ladysford Aberds 303 C9
Lady's Green Suff 124 F5
Ladywell London 67 E11
Shrops 149 C9
W Loth 269 B10
Ladywood Telford 132 C3
W Mid 133 F11
Worcs 117 E7
Lady Wood W Yorks 206 F2
Laffak Mers 183 B8
Laga Highld 289 C8
Lagafater Lodge
Dumfries 236 B3
Lagalochan Argyll 275 B9
Lagavulin Argyll 254 C5
Lagg Argyll 274 F6
N Ayrs 255 E10
Laggan Argyll 254 B3
Highld 289 B9
Highld 290 D4
Highld 291 D8
S Ayrs 245 G7
Lagganlia Highld 291 C10
Laggan Lodge Argyll 289 G8
Lagganmullan Dumfries 237 D7
Lagganulva Argyll 288 E6
Lagness W Sus 22 C5
Laide Highld 307 K3
Laig Highld 294 G6
Laigh Carnduff S Lanark 268 F3
Laigh Fenwick E Ayrs 267 G9
Laigh Glengall S Ayrs 257 F8
Laighmuir E Ayrs 267 F9
Laighstonehall S Lanark 268 E4
Laindon Essex 69 B7
Lair Highld 299 E10
Perth 292 G3
Laira Plym 7 D10
Lairg Highld 309 J5
Lairg Lodge Highld 309 J5
Lairgmore Highld 300 F5
Lairg Muir Highld 309 J5
Laisterdyke W Yorks 205 G9
Laithes Cumb 230 E5
Laithkirk Durham 232 G5
Laity Moor Corn 4 F3
Lake BCP 18 C6
Devon 12 D6
Devon 24 F6
Devon 40 G5
IoW 21 E7
Wilts 46 F6
Lake End Bucks 66 D2
Lakenham Norf 142 B4
Lakenheath Suff 140 G4
Laker's Green Sur 50 F4
Lakesend Norf 139 D10
Lakeside Cumb 211 B7
Thurrock 68 D5
Worcs 117 D11
Laleham Sur 66 F5
Laleston = Trelales
Bridgend 57 F11
Lamanva Corn 3 C7
Lamarsh Essex 107 D7
Lamas Norf 160 E4
Lamb Corner Essex 107 E10
Lambden Borders 272 G4
Lamberden Kent 38 B4
Lamberhead Green
Gtr Man 194 G4
Lamberhurst Kent 53 F7
Lamberhurst Quarter
Kent 53 F7
Lamberton Borders 273 D9
Lambert's End W Mid 133 E9
Lambeth London 67 D10
Lambfair Green Suff 124 G4
Lambfoot Cumb 229 E9
Lambhill Glasgow 267 B11
Lambley Northumb 240 F5
Notts 171 F10
Lambourn W Berks 63 D10
Lambourne Corn 4 E5
Essex 87 F7
Lambourne End Essex 87 G7
Lambourn Woodlands
W Berks 63 D10
Lambridge Bath 61 F9
Lamb's Cross Kent 53 D9
Lambs Green W Sus 51 F8
Lambs' Green Dorset 18 B5
Lambston Pembs 72 B6
Lambton T&W 243 G7
Lamellion Corn 6 C4
Lamerton Devon 12 F5
Lamesley T&W 243 F7
Laminess Orkney 314 C6
Lamington Highld 301 B7
S Lanark 259 C11
Lamlash N Ayrs 256 C2
Lamledra Corn 5 G10
Lamloch Dumfries 246 D2
Lammack Blackburn 195 B7
Lamonby Cumb 230 D4
Lamorick Corn 5 C10
Lamorna Corn 1 E4
Lamorran Corn 5 G7
Lampardbrook Suff 126 E5
Lampeter = Llanbedr Pont
Steffan Ceredig 93 B11
Lampeter Velfrey Pembs 73 C11
Lamphey Pembs 73 E8
Lamplugh Cumb 229 G7
Lamport W Nhants 120 C5
Lampton London 66 D6
Lamyatt Som 45 F7
Lana Devon 12 B2
Devon 24 F4
Lanark S Lanark 269 G7
Lancaster Lancs 211 G9
Lanchester Durham 233 B9
Lancing W Sus 35 G11
Landbeach Cambs 123 D9
Landcross Devon 25 C7
Landerberry Aberds 293 C9
Landewednack Corn 2 G6
Landford Wilts 32 D3
Landford Manor Wilts 32 C3
Landfordwood Wilts 32 C3
Land Gate Gtr Man 194 G5
Landguard Manor IoW 21 E7
Landhill Devon 12 B4
Landican Mers 182 D3
Landimore Swansea 56 C3
Landkey Devon 40 G5
Landkey Newland Devon 40 G5
Landore Swansea 57 B7
Landport E Sus 36 E6
Ptsmth 33 G10
Landrake Corn 7 C7
Landscove Devon 8 B5
Landshipping Pembs 73 C8
Landshipping Quay
Pembs 73 C8
Landslow Green
Gtr Man 185 B7
Landulph Corn 7 C8
Landwade Suff 124 D2
Landywood Staffs 133 B9
Lane Corn 4 C6
Laneast Corn 11 E10
Lane Bottom Lancs 204 F3
W Yorks 205 F7
Lane End Bucks 84 G4
Lane-end Corn 5 B10
Lane End Cumb 220 G2
Derbys 170 C6
Devon 24 G6
Dorset 18 C3
Flint 166 C3
Glos 79 B10
Hants 33 B9
Hants 33 B11
IoW 21 D9
Kent 68 E5
Lancs 204 D3
Sur 49 E10
S Yorks 186 B5
Wilts 45 D10
W Yorks 204 F6
Lane Ends Ches E 168 D2
Ches E 185 E7
Cumb 210 C6
Derbys 152 C4
Gtr Man 185 C7
Lancs 194 D6
Lancs 203 C11
Lancs 203 G11
N Yorks 204 E5
Stoke 168 E5
W Yorks 205 F10
Lane Green Staffs 133 C7
Laneham Notts 188 F4
Lanehead Durham 232 C2
Northumb 251 F7
Lane Head Derbys 185 F11
Durham 224 C2
Gtr Man 183 B10
Pembs 73 E8
W Mid 133 C9
W Yorks 197 F7
Lane Heads Lancs 202 F4
Lanehouse Dorset 17 F9
Lanercost Cumb 240 E3
Lanescot Corn 5 D11
Lanesend Pembs 73 D9
Lanes End Bucks 84 D6
Lane's End Shrops 132 G2
Lanesfield W Mid 133 D8
Laneshaw Bridge Lancs 204 E4
Lane Side Lancs 195 C9
Laney Green Staffs 133 B9
Lanfach Caerph 78 F2
Langaford Devon 12 B4
Langage Devon 7 E11
Langal Highld 289 C9
Langaller Som 28 B3
Langar Notts 154 C4
Langbank Renfs 277 G7
Langbar N Yorks 205 C7
Langbaurgh N Yorks 225 C11
Langburnshiels Borders 250 C2
Langcliffe N Yorks 212 G6
Langdale Highld 308 E6
Langdale End N Yorks 227 G8
Langdon Corn 12 D2
Langdon Beck Durham 232 E3
Langdon Hills Essex 69 B7
Langdown Hants 32 F6
Langdyke Dumfries 238 C3
Fife 287 G7
Langenhoe Essex 89 B8
Langford C Beds 104 C3
Devon 14 B4
Devon 27 G8
Essex 88 D4
Notts 172 D4
Oxon 82 E2
Som 28 B2
Langford Budville Som 27 C10
Langford Green Devon 27 G8
N Som 44 B3
Langham Dorset 30 B3
Essex 107 E10
Norf 177 E8
Rutland 154 G6
Som 28 E4
Suff 125 C9
Langhaugh Borders 260 C6
Langho Lancs 203 G10
Langholm Dumfries 249 G9
Langholme N Lincs 188 B3
Langhope Borders 261 E10
Langland Swansea 56 D6
Langlee Borders 262 B2
Langleeford Northumb 263 E10
Langlee Mains Borders 262 B2
Langlees Falk 279 E7
Langley Ches E 184 G6
Derbys 170 F6
Essex 105 D8
Glos 99 F10
Gtr Man 195 F11
Hants 32 G6
Herts 104 G4
Kent 53 C10
Northumb 241 E8
Oxon 82 B4
Slough 66 D4
Som 27 B9
Warks 118 E3
W Mid 133 F9
W Sus 34 B4
Langley Burrell Wilts 62 D2
Langleybury Herts 85 E9
Langley Common
Derbys 152 B5
Wokingham 65 F9
Langley Corner Bucks 66 C4
Langley Green Derbys 152 B5
Essex 107 G7
Warks 118 E3
W Mid 133 F9
W Sus 51 F9
Langley Heath Kent 53 C10
Langley Marsh Som 27 B9
Langley Mill Derbys 170 F6
Langley Moor Durham 233 C11
Langley Park Durham 233 C10
Langley Street Norf 143 C7
Langley Vale Sur 51 B8
Langloan N Lanark 268 C4
Langney E Sus 23 E10
Langold Notts 187 D9
Langore Corn 12 D2
Langport Som 28 B6
Langrick Lincs 174 F3
Langrick Bridge Lincs 174 F3
Langridge Bath 61 F8
Langridge Ford Devon 25 C9
Langrigg Cumb 222 C5
Cumb 229 B9
Langrish Hants 34 C2
Langsett S Yorks 197 G8
Langshaw Borders 262 B2
Langside Glasgow 267 C11
Perth 285 F11
Langskaill Orkney 314 B4
Langstone Devon 13 E10
Hants 22 C2
Newport 78 G5
Langthorne N Yorks 224 G5
Langthorpe N Yorks 215 F7
Langthwaite N Yorks 223 E10
Langtoft E Yorks 217 F10
Lincs 156 G2
Langton Durham 224 B3
Lincs 174 B2
Lincs 190 G5
N Yorks 216 F5
Langton by Wragby
Lincs 189 F11
Langton Green Kent 52 F4
Suff 126 C2
Langton Herring Dorset 17 E8
Langton Long Blandford
Dorset 30 F5
Langton Matravers
Dorset 18 F6
Langtree Devon 25 D7
Langtree Week Devon 25 D7
Langwathby Cumb 231 E7
Langwell Ho Highld 311 G5
Langwell Lodge Highld 307 J6
Langwith Derbys 171 B8
Langwith Junction
Derbys 171 B8
Langworth Lincs 189 F9
Lanham Green Essex 106 G5
Lanivet Corn 5 C10
Lanjeth Corn 5 E9
Lanjew Corn 5 C9
Lank Corn 11 F7
Lanlivery Corn 5 D11
Lanner Corn 4 G4
Lanreath Corn 6 D3
Lanrick Stirling 285 G10
Lansallos Corn 6 E3
Lansbury Park Caerph 59 B7
Lansdown Bath 61 F8
Glos 99 G8
Lanstephan Corn 12 D2
Lanteglos Corn 11 E7
Lanteglos Highway Corn 6 E3
Lanton Borders 262 E4
Northumb 263 C10
Lantuel Corn 5 B9
Lantyan Corn 6 D2
Lapal W Mid 133 G9
Lapford Devon 26 F2
Lapford Cross Devon 26 F2
Laphroaig Argyll 254 C4
Lapley Staffs 151 G7
Lapworth Warks 118 C3
Larachbeg Highld 289 E8
Larbert Falk 279 E7
Larbreck Lancs 202 E4
Larches Lancs 202 G6
Larden Green Ches E 167 E9
Larg Highld 292 B2
Largie Aberds 302 F6
Largiebaan Argyll 255 F7
Largiemore Argyll 275 E10
Largoward Fife 287 G8
Largs N Ayrs 266 D4
Largue Aberds 302 E6
Largybeg N Ayrs 256 E3
Largymeanoch N Ayrs 256 E2
Largymore N Ayrs 256 E2
Larkfield Invclyd 276 F4
Kent 53 B8
W Yorks 205 F10
Larkhall Bath 61 F9
S Lanark 268 E5
Larkhill Wilts 46 E6
Lark Hill Gtr Man 195 G7
Larklands Derbys 171 G7
Larks' Hill Suff 108 B3
Larling Norf 141 F9
Larport Hereford 97 D11
Larrick Corn 12 F2
Larriston Borders 250 E2
Lartington Durham 223 B10
Lary Aberds 292 C5
Lasborough Glos 80 G4
Lasham Hants 49 E7
Lashenden Kent 53 E10
Lask Edge Staffs 168 D6
Lassington Glos 98 G5
Lassodie Fife 280 C2
Lastingham N Yorks 226 G4
Latcham Som 44 D2
Latchbrook Corn 7 D8
Latchford Herts 105 G7
Oxon 83 E11
Warr 183 D10
Latchingdon Essex 88 E5
Latchley Corn 12 G4
Latchmere Green Hants 64 G6
Latchmore Bank Essex 87 B7
Lately Common Warr 183 B11
Lathallan Mill Fife 287 G8
Lathbury M Keynes 103 B7
Latheron Highld 310 F5
Latheronwheel Highld 310 F5
Latheronwheel Ho
Highld 310 F5
Lathom Lancs 194 E3
Lathones Fife 287 G8
Latimer Bucks 85 F8
Latteridge S Glos 61 C7
Lattiford Som 29 B11
Lattinford Hill Suff 107 D11
Latton Wilts 81 F9
Latton Bush Essex 87 D7
Lauchintilly Aberds 293 B9
Laudale Ho Highld 289 D9
Lauder Borders 271 F10
Lauder Barns Borders 271 F10
Laugharne = Talacharn
Carms 74 C4
Laughern Hill Worcs 116 F5
Laughterton Lincs 188 F4
Laughton E Sus 23 C8
Leics 136 F3
Lincs 155 C11
Lincs 188 B4
Laughton Common
S Yorks 187 D8
Laughton en le Morthen
S Yorks 187 D8
Launcells Corn 24 F2
Launcells Cross Corn 24 F3
Launceston Corn 12 D2
Launcherley Som 44 E4
Laund Lancs 195 C10
Launton Oxon 102 G2
Laurencekirk Aberds 293 F9
Laurieston Dumfries 237 C8
Falk 279 F8
Lavendon M Keynes 121 G8
Lavenham Suff 107 B8
Laverackloch Moray 301 C11
Laverhay Dumfries 248 D4
Laverlaw Borders 261 B7
Laverley Som 44 F5
Lavernock V Glam 59 F7
Laversdale Cumb 239 E11
Laverstock Wilts 47 G7
Laverstoke Hants 48 D3
Laverton Glos 99 D11
N Yorks 214 E4
Som 45 C9
Lavington Sands Wilts 46 B4
Lavister Wrex 166 D5
Lavrean Corn 5 D10
Law S Lanark 268 E6
Lawers Perth 285 D10
Perth 285 E11
Lawford Essex 107 E11
Som 42 F6
Lawford Heath Warks 119 C9
Lawhill Perth 286 F3
Law Hill S Lanark 268 E6
Lawhitton Corn 12 E3
Lawkland N Yorks 212 F5
Lawkland Green
N Yorks 212 F5
Lawley Telford 132 B3
Lawn Swindon 63 C7
Lawnhead Staffs 150 E6
Lawns W Yorks 197 C10
Lawnswood W Yorks 205 F11
Lawnt Denb 165 B8
Lawrence Hill Newport 59 B10
Lawrence Weston
Bristol 60 D4
Lawrenny Pembs 73 D8
Lawrenny Quay Pembs 73 D8
Lawshall Suff 125 G7
Lawshall Green Suff 125 G7
Lawton Hereford 115 F8
Shrops 131 G10
Lawton-gate Ches E 168 D4
Lawton Heath End
Ches E 168 D3
Laxey IoM 192 D5
Laxfield Suff 126 C5
Laxfirth Shetland 313 H6
Shetland 313 J6
Laxford Bridge Highld 306 E7
Laxo Shetland 313 G6
Laxobigging Shetland 312 F6
Laxton E Yorks 199 B9
N Nhants 137 D8
Notts 172 B2
Laycock W Yorks 204 E6
Layer Breton Essex 88 B6
Layer de la Haye Essex 89 B7
Layer Marney Essex 88 B6
Layerthorpe York 207 C8
Layham Suff 107 C10
Laymore Dorset 28 G5
Layters Green Bucks 85 G7
Laytham E Yorks 207 F10
Layton Blackpool 202 F2
Lazenby Redcar 225 B11
Lazonby Cumb 230 D6
Lea Derbys 170 D4
Hereford 98 G3
Lancs 202 G5
Lincs 188 D4
Shrops 131 B8
Shrops 131 F7
Wilts 62 B3
Lea Bridge London 67 B11
Leabrooks Derbys 170 E6
Lea by Backford
Ches W 182 G5
Leacainn W Isles 305 H3
Leac a Li W Isles 305 J3
Leachkin Highld 300 E6
Leacnasaide Highld 299 B7
Leadburn Midloth 270 D4
Leadendale Staffs 151 B8
Leadenham Lincs 173 E7
Leaden Roding Essex 87 C9
Leadgate Cumb 231 C10
Durham 242 G4
T&W 242 F4
Leadhills S Lanark 259 G9
Leadingcross Green
Kent 53 C11
Leadmill Derbys 186 E2
Flint 166 C2
Lea End Worcs 117 B10
Leafield Oxon 82 B4
Wilts 61 F11
Lea Forge Ches E 168 F2
Leagrave Luton 103 G10
Leagreen Hants 19 C11
Lea Green Mers 183 C8
Lea Hall W Mid 134 F2
Lea Heath Staffs 151 D10
Leake Lincs 174 F6
N Yorks 225 G8
Leake Commonside
Lincs 174 E5
Leake Fold Hill Lincs 174 E6
Lealholm N Yorks 226 D5
Lealholm Side N Yorks 226 D5
Lea Line Hereford 98 G3
Lealt Argyll 275 D7
Highld 298 C5
Leam Derbys 186 F2
Lea Marston Warks 134 E4
Leamington Hastings
Warks 119 D8
Leamoor Common
Shrops 131 F8
Leamore W Mid 133 C9
Leamside Durham 234 B2
Leanach Argyll 275 D11
Leanachan Highld 290 F4
Leanaig Highld 300 D5
Leapgate Worcs 116 C6
Leargybreck Argyll 274 F6
Lease Rigg N Yorks 226 E6
Leasey Bridge Herts 85 C11
Leasgill Cumb 211 C9
Leasingham Lincs 173 F9
Leasingthorne Durham 233 F11
Leason Swansea 56 C3
Leasowe Mers 182 C3
Leatherhead Sur 51 B7
Leatherhead Common
Sur 51 B7
Leathern Bottle Glos 80 E2
Leathley N Yorks 205 D10
Leaths Dumfries 237 C9
Leaton Shrops 149 F9
Telford 150 G2
Leaton Heath Shrops 149 F9
Lea Town Lancs 202 G5
Lea Valley Herts 85 B11
Leaveland Kent 54 C4
Leavenheath Suff 107 D9
Leavening N Yorks 216 G5
Leavesden Green Herts 85 E9
Leaves Green London 68 G2
Lea Yeat Cumb 212 B5
Leazes Durham 242 F5
Lebberston N Yorks 217 C11
Leburnick Corn 12 E3
Lechlade-on-Thames
Glos 82 F2
Leck Lancs 212 D2
Leckford Hants 47 F11
Leckfurin Highld 308 D7
Leckgruinart Argyll 274 G3
Leckhampstead Bucks 102 D4
W Berks 64 D2
Leckhampstead Thicket
W Berks 64 D2
Leckhampton Glos 80 B6
Leckie Highld 299 C10
Leckmelm Highld 307 K6
Leckuary Argyll 275 D9
Leckwith V Glam 59 E7
Leconfield E Yorks 208 E6
Ledaig Argyll 289 F11
Ledburn Bucks 103 G8
Ledbury Hereford 98 D4
Ledcharrie Stirling 285 E9
Leddington Glos 98 E3
Ledgemoor Hereford 115 G8
Ledgowan Highld 299 D11
Ledicot Hereford 115 E8
Ledmore Angus 293 G7
Highld 307 H7
Lednagullin Highld 308 C7
Ledsham Ches W 182 G5
W Yorks 198 B3
Ledston W Yorks 198 B2
Ledstone Devon 8 F4
Ledston Luck W Yorks 206 G4
Ledwell Oxon 101 F8
Lee Argyll 288 G6
Devon 40 D3
Devon 40 E5
Hants 32 D5
Lancs 203 B7
London 67 E11
Northumb 241 F10
Shrops 149 C8
Leeans Shetland 313 J5
Lee Bank W Mid 133 F11
Leebotten Shetland 313 L6
Leebotwood Shrops 131 D9
Lee Brockhurst Shrops 149 D10
Leece Cumb 210 F4
Lee Chapel Essex 69 B7
Leechpool Mon 60 B4
Lee Clump Bucks 84 E6
Lee Common Bucks 84 E6
Leeds Kent 53 C10
W Yorks 205 G11
Leedstown Corn 2 C4
Leeford Devon 41 D9
Lee Gate Bucks 84 D5
Leegomery Telford 150 G3
Lee Ground Hants 33 F8
Lee Head Derbys 185 C8
Leeholme Durham 233 E10
Leek Staffs 169 D7
Leekbrook Staffs 169 E7
Leek Wootton Warks 118 D5
Lee Mill Devon 8 D2
Leeming N Yorks 214 B5
W Yorks 204 G6
Leeming Bar N Yorks 224 G5
Leemings Lancs 203 D10
Lee Moor Devon 7 C11
W Yorks 197 B10
Lee-on-the-Solent
Hants 33 G9

Lee-over-Sands Essex 89 C10
Lees Derbys 152 B5
Gtr Man 196 G3
W Yorks 204 F6
Leesthorpe Leics 154 G5
Leeswood = Coed-Llai
Flint 166 D3
Leetown Perth 286 E6
Leftwich Ches W 183 G11
Legar Powys 78 B2
Legbourne Lincs 190 E5
Legburthwaite Cumb 220 B6
Legerwood Borders 271 G11
Leggatt Hill W Sus 34 C6
Legsby Lincs 189 D10
Leicester Leicester 135 C11
Leicester Forest East
Leics 135 C10
Leicester Grange Warks 135 E8
Leigh Devon 26 E2
Dorset 18 B6
Dorset 29 F10
Dorset 30 F3
Glos 99 F7
Gtr Man 195 G7
Kent 52 D4
Shrops 130 C6
Sur 51 D8
Wilts 81 G9
Worcs 116 G5
Leigham Plym 7 D10
Leigh Beck Essex 69 C10
Leigh Common Som 30 B2
Leigh Delamere Wilts 61 D11
Leigh Green Kent 54 G2
Leighland Chapel Som 42 F4
Leigh-on-Sea Southend 69 B10
Leigh Park Hants 22 B2
Leigh Sinton Worcs 116 G5
Leighswood W Mid 133 C11
Leighterton Glos 80 G4
Leighton N Yorks 214 D3
Shrops 132 B2
Som 45 E8
Leighton = Tre'r llai
Powys 130 B4
Leighton Bromswold
Cambs 122 B2
Leighton Buzzard
C Beds 103 F8
Leigh upon Mendip Som 45 D7
Leigh Woods N Som 60 E5
Leinthall Earls Hereford 115 D8
Leinthall Starkes
Hereford 115 D8
Leintwardine Hereford 115 C8
Leire Leics 135 E10
Leirinmore Highld 308 C4
Leiston Suff 127 E8
Leitfie Perth 286 C6
Leith Edin 280 F5
Leithenhall Dumfries 248 D4
Leitholm Borders 272 G5
Lelant Corn 2 B2
Lelant Downs Corn 2 B2
Lelley E Yorks 209 G10
Lem Hill Worcs 116 C4
Lemington T&W 242 E5
Lemmington Hall
Northumb 264 G4
Lempitlaw Borders 263 C7
Lemsford Herts 86 C2
Lenacre Cumb 212 B3
Lenborough Bucks 102 E3
Lenchwick Worcs 99 B10
Lendalfoot S Ayrs 244 F4
Lendrick Lodge Stirling 285 G9
Lenham Kent 53 C11
Lenham Forstal Kent 54 C2
Lenham Heath Kent 54 D2
Lennel Borders 273 G7
Lennoxtown E Dunb 278 F2
Lent Bucks 66 C2
Lenten Pool Denb 165 B8
Lenton Lincs 155 C10
Nottingham 153 B11
Lenton Abbey
Nottingham 153 B10
Lentran Highld 300 E5
Lent Rise Bucks 66 C2
Lenwade Norf 159 F11
Leny Ho Stirling 285 G10
Lenzie E Dunb 278 G3
Lenziemill N Lanark 278 G5
Leoch Angus 287 D7
Leochel-Cushnie
Aberds 293 B7
Leominster Hereford 115 F9
Leomonsley Staffs 134 B2
Leonard Stanley Glos 80 E4
Leonardston Pembs 72 D6
Leorin Argyll 254 C4
Lepe Hants 20 B5
Lephin Highld 297 G7
Lephinchapel Argyll 275 D10
Lephinmore Argyll 275 D10
Leppington N Yorks 216 G5
Lepton W Yorks 197 D8
Lepton Edge W Yorks 197 D8
Lerigoligan Argyll 275 C9
Lerrocks Stirling 285 G11
Lerryn Corn 6 D2
Lerwick Shetland 313 J6
Lesbury Northumb 264 G6
Leschangie Aberds 293 B9
Le Skerne Haughton
Darl 224 B6
Leslie Aberds 302 G5
Fife 286 G6
Lesmahagow S Lanark 259 B8
Lesnewth Corn 11 C8
Lessendrum Aberds 302 E5
Lessingham Norf 161 D7
Lessness Heath London 68 D3
Lessonhall Cumb 238 G6
Leswalt Dumfries 236 C2
Letchmore Heath Herts 85 F11
Letchworth Garden City
Herts 104 E4
Letcombe Bassett Oxon 63 B11
Letcombe Regis Oxon 63 B11
Letham Angus 287 C9
Falk 279 D7
Fife 287 F7
Perth 286 E4
Letham Grange Angus 287 C10
Lethem Borders 250 B5
Lethen Ho Highld 301 D9
Lethenty Aberds 303 E8
Aberds 303 G7
Letheringham Suff 126 F5
Letheringsett Norf 159 B11
Lettaford Devon 13 E10
Lettan Orkney 314 B7
Letter Aberds 293 B9
Letterewe Highld 299 B9
Letterfearn Highld 295 C10
Letterfinlay Highld 290 D4
Lettermay Argyll 284 G5
Lettermorar Highld 295 G9
Lettermore Argyll 288 E6
Letters Highld 307 L6
Letterston = Treletert
Pembs 91 F8
Lettoch Highld 292 B2
Highld 301 F10
Moray 302 F3
Perth 291 G11
Letton Hereford 96 B6
Hereford 115 C7
Letton Green Norf 141 B9
Lett's Green Kent 52 B3
Letty Brongu Bridgend 57 D11
Letty Green Herts 86 C3
Letwell S Yorks 187 D9
Leuchars Fife 287 E8
Leuchars Ho Moray 302 C2
Leumrabhagh W Isles 305 G5
Levalsa Meor Corn 5 F10
Levan Invclyd 276 F4
Levaneap Shetland 313 G6
Levedale Staffs 151 F7
Level of Mendalgief
Newport 59 B10
Level's Green Essex 105 G9
Leven E Yorks 209 D8
Fife 287 G7
Levencorroch N Ayrs 256 E2
Levenhall E Loth 281 G7
Levens Cumb 211 B9
Leven Seat W Loth 269 D8
Levens Green Herts 105 G7
Levenshulme Gtr Man 184 C5
Leventhorpe W Yorks 205 G8
Levenwick Shetland 313 L6
Lever-Edge Gtr Man 195 F8
Leverington Cambs 157 G8
Leverington Common
Cambs 157 G8
Leverstock Green Herts 85 D9
Leverton Lincs 174 F6
W Berks 63 E10
Leverton Highgate Lincs 174 F6
Leverton Lucasgate
Lincs 174 F6
Leverton Outgate Lincs 174 F6
Levington Suff 108 D4
Levisham N Yorks 226 G6
Levishie Highld 290 B6
Lew Oxon 82 D4
Lewannick Corn 11 E11
Lewcombe Dorset 29 F9
Lewdown Devon 12 D4
Lewes E Sus 36 E6
Leweston Pembs 91 G8
Lewisham London 67 D11
Lewiston Highld 300 G5
Lewistown Bridgend 58 B2
Lewknor Oxon 84 F2
Leworthy Devon 24 G4
Devon 41 F7
Lewson Street Kent 70 G3
Lewth Lancs 202 F5
Lewthorn Cross Devon 13 F11
Lewtrenchard Devon 12 D5
Lexden Essex 107 G9
Ley Aberds 293 B7
Corn 6 B3
Som 41 F10
Leybourne Kent 53 B7
Leyburn N Yorks 224 G2
Leycett Staffs 168 F3
Leyfields Staffs 134 B4
Ley Green Herts 104 G3
Ley Hey Park Gtr Man 185 D7
Leyhill Bucks 85 E7
S Glos 79 G11
Ley Hill W Mid 134 D2
Leyland Lancs 194 C4
Leylodge Aberds 293 B9
Leymoor W Yorks 196 D6
Leys Aberds 292 C6
Aberds 303 D10
Cumb 219 B11
Perth 286 D6
Staffs 169 F8
Leys Castle Highld 300 E6
Leysdown-on-Sea Kent 70 E4
Leys Hill Hereford 79 B9
Leysmill Angus 287 C10
Leys of Cossans Angus 287 C7
Leysters Hereford 115 E11
Leysters Pole Hereford 115 E11
Leyton London 67 B11
Leytonstone London 67 B11
Lezant Corn 12 F2
Lezerea Corn 2 C5
Leziate Norf 158 F3
Lhanbryde Moray 302 C2
Liatrie Highld 300 F2
Libanus Powys 95 F9
Libberton S Lanark 269 G9
Libbery Worcs 117 F9
Liberton Edin 270 B5
Liceasto W Isles 305 J3
Lichfield Staffs 134 B2
Lick Perth 286 B2
Lickey Worcs 117 B9
Lickey End Worcs 117 C9
Lickfold W Sus 34 B6
Lickhill Worcs 116 C6
Lickleyhead Castle
Aberds 302 G6
Liddaton Devon 12 E5
Liddel Orkney 314 H4
Liddesdale Highld 289 D9
Liddeston Pembs 72 D5
Liddington Swindon 63 C8
Liden Swindon 63 C7
Lidgate Suff 124 F4
Lidget S Yorks 199 G7
Lidget Green W Yorks 205 G8
Lidgett Notts 171 B10
Lidgett Park W Yorks 206 F2
Lidham Hill E Sus 38 D4
Lidlington C Beds 103 D9
Lidsey W Sus 22 C6
Lidsing Kent 69 G9
Lidstone Oxon 101 G7
Lieurary Highld 310 C4
Liff Angus 287 D7
Lifford W Mid 117 B11
Lifton Devon 12 D3
Liftondown Devon 12 D3
Lightcliffe W Yorks 196 B6
Lighteach Shrops 149 C10
Lightfoot Green Lancs 202 G6
Lighthorne Warks 118 F6
Lighthorne Heath Warks 119 F7
Lighthorne Rough
Warks 118 F6
Lightmoor Telford 132 B3
Light Oaks Staffs 168 E6
Lightpill Glos 80 E4
Lightwater Sur 66 G2
Lightwood Shrops 132 E2
Shrops 150 D3
Staffs 169 G8
Stoke 168 G6
S Yorks 186 E5
Lightwood Green
Ches E 167 G10
Wrex 166 G5
Liglartrie S Ayrs 244 F6
Lilbourne W Nhants 119 B11
Lilburn Tower Northumb 264 E2
Lilford Gtr Man 195 G7
Lillesdon Som 28 C4
Lilleshall Telford 150 F4
Lilley Herts 104 F2
W Berks 64 D2
Lilliesleaf Borders 262 E2
Lillingstone Dayrell
Bucks 102 D4
Lillingstone Lovell
Bucks 102 C4
Lillington Dorset 29 E10
Warks 118 D6
Lilliput BCP 18 C6
Lilstock Som 43 E7
Lilybank Invclyd 276 G6
Lilyhurst Shrops 150 G4
Lilyvale Kent 54 F5
Limbrick Lancs 194 D6
Limbury Luton 103 G11
Limebrook Hereford 115 D7
Limefield Gtr Man 195 E10
Limehouse London 67 C11
Limehurst Gtr Man 196 G2
Limekilnburn S Lanark 268 E4
Limekiln Field Derbys 187 G7
Limekilns Fife 279 E11
Limerigg Falk 279 G7
Limerstone IoW 20 E4
Lime Side Gtr Man 196 G2
Limestone Brae
Northumb 231 B11
Lime Street Worcs 98 E6
Lime Tree Park W Mid 118 B5
Limington Som 29 C8
Limpenhoe Norf 143 C7
Limpenhoe Hill Norf 143 C8
Limpers Hill Wilts 45 G10
Limpley Stoke Wilts 61 G9
Limpsfield Sur 52 C2
Limpsfield Chart Sur 52 C2
Limpsfield Common Sur 52 C2
Linbriggs Northumb 251 B9
Linburn W Loth 270 B2
Linby Notts 171 E8
Linchmere W Sus 49 G11
Lincluden Dumfries 237 B11
Lincoln Lincs 189 G7
Lincomb Worcs 116 D6
Lincombe Devon 8 D4
Devon 40 D3
Lindale Cumb 211 C8
Lindal in Furness Cumb 210 D5
Lindean Borders 261 C11
Linden Glos 80 B4
Lindfield W Sus 36 B4
Lindford Hants 49 F10
Lindifferon Fife 287 F7
Lindley N Yorks 205 D10
W Yorks 196 D6
Lindley Green N Yorks 205 D10
Lindores Fife 286 F6
Lindow End Ches E 184 F4
Lindrick Dale S Yorks 187 E8
Lindridge Worcs 116 D3
Lindsell Essex 106 F2
Lindsey Suff 107 C9
Lindsey Tye Suff 107 B9
Lindwell W Yorks 196 C5
Lineholt Worcs 116 D6
Lineholt Common
Worcs 116 D6
Liney Som 43 F11
Linfitts Gtr Man 196 F3
Linford Hants 31 F11
Thurrock 69 D7
Lingague IoM 192 E3
Lingards Wood W Yorks 196 E5
Lingbob W Yorks 205 F7
Lingdale Redcar 226 B3
Lingen Hereford 115 D7
Lingfield Darl 224 C6
Sur 51 E11
Lingfield Common Sur 51 E11
Lingley Green Warr 183 D9
Lingley Mere Warr 183 D10
Lingreabhagh W Isles 296 C6
Lingwood Norf 143 B7
Linhope Borders 249 C10
Northumb 263 F11
Linicro Highld 298 C3
Link N Som 44 B3
Linkend Worcs 98 E6
Linkenholt Hants 47 B11
Linkhill Kent 38 B4
Linkinhorne Corn 12 G2
Linklater Orkney 314 H4
Linklet Orkney 314 A7
Linksness Orkney 314 E5
Orkney 314 F2
Linktown Fife 280 C5
Linley Shrops 131 E7
Shrops 132 D3
Linley Brook Shrops 132 D3
Linleygreen Shrops 132 D3
Linley Green Hereford 116 G3
Linlithgow W Loth 279 F10
Linlithgow Bridge
W Loth 279 F9
Linndhu Ho Argyll 289 D7
Linneraineach Highld 307 J6
Linns Angus 292 F3
Linnyshaw Gtr Man 195 G8
Linshiels Northumb 251 B9
Linsiadar W Isles 304 E4
Linsidemore Highld 309 K5
Linslade C Beds 103 F8
Linstead Parva Suff 126 B6
Linstock Cumb 239 F10
Linthorpe Mbro 225 B9
Linthurst Worcs 117 C9
Linthwaite W Yorks 196 E6
Lintlaw Borders 272 D6
Lintmill Moray 302 C5
Linton Borders 263 D7
Cambs 105 B11
Derbys 152 F5
Hereford 98 F3
Kent 53 D9
Northumb 253 E7
N Yorks 213 G9
W Yorks 206 D3
Linton Heath Derbys 152 F5
Linton Hill Hereford 98 G3
Linton-on-Ouse
N Yorks 215 G9
Lintridge Glos 98 E4
Lintz Durham 242 F5
Lintzford T&W 242 F4
Lintzgarth Durham 232 C4
Linwood Hants 31 F11
Lincs 189 D10
Renfs 267 C8
Lionacleit W Isles 297 G3
Lional W Isles 304 B7
Lions Green E Sus 23 B9
Liphook Hants 49 G10
Lipley Shrops 150 C4
Lippitts Hill Essex 86 F5
Liquo or Bowhousebog
N Lanark 269 D7
Liscard Mers 182 C4
Liscombe Som 41 G11
Liskeard Corn 6 C5
Liss Hants 34 B3
Lissett E Yorks 209 B8
Liss Forest Hants 34 B3
Lissington Lincs 189 E10
Lisson Grove London 67 C9
Listerdale S Yorks 187 C7
Listock Som 28 C4
Listoft Lincs 191 G8
Liston Essex 107 C7
Liston Garden Essex 106 B6
Lisvane Cardiff 59 C7
Liswerry Newport 59 B10
Litcham Norf 159 F7
Litchard Bridgend 58 C2
Litchborough W Nhants 120 G2
Litchfield Hants 48 C3
Litchurch Derbys 153 B7
Litherland Mers 182 B4
Litlington Cambs 104 C6
E Sus 23 E8
Litmarsh Hereford 97 B10
Little Abington Cambs 105 B10
Little Addington
N Nhants 121 C9
Little Airmyn E Yorks 199 B8
Little Almshoe Herts 104 F3
Little Alne Warks 118 E2
Little Altcar Mers 193 F10
Little Ann Hants 47 E10
Little Arowry Wrex 167 G7
Little Asby Cumb 222 D3
Little Ashley Wilts 61 G10
Little Assynt Highld 307 G6
Little Aston Staffs 133 C11
Little Atherfield IoW 20 E5
Little Ayre Orkney 314 G3
Little-ayre Shetland 313 G5
Little Ayton N Yorks 225 C11
Little Baddow Essex 88 D3
Little Badminton S Glos 61 C10
Little Ballinluig Perth 286 B3
Little Bampton Cumb 239 F7
Little Bardfield Essex 106 E3
Little Barford Bedford 122 F3
Little Barningham Norf 160 C2
Little Barrington Glos 82 C2
Little Barrow Ches W 183 G7
Little Barugh N Yorks 216 D5
Little Bavington
Northumb 241 B11
Little Bayham E Sus 52 F6
Little Bealings Suff 108 B4
Littlebeck N Yorks 227 D7
Little Beckford Glos 99 E9
Little Bedwyn Wilts 63 F9
Little Bentley Essex 108 F2
Little Berkhamsted Herts 86 D3
Little Billing W Nhants 120 E6
Little Billington C Beds 103 G8
Little Birch Hereford 97 E10
Little Bispham Blackpool 202 E2
Little Blakenham Suff 108 B2
Little Blencow Cumb 230 E5
Little Bloxwich W Mid 133 C10
Little Bognor W Sus 35 C8
Little Bolehill Derbys 170 E3
Little Bollington Ches E 184 D2
Little Bolton Gtr Man 184 B3
Little Bookham Sur 50 C6
Littleborough Devon 26 E4
Gtr Man 196 D2
Notts 188 E4
Little Bosullow Corn 1 C4
Littlebourne Kent 55 B8
Little Bourton Oxon 101 C9
Little Bowden Leics 136 F4
Little Boys Heath Bucks 84 F6
Little Bradley Suff 124 G3
Little Braithwaite
Cumb 229 G10
Little Brampton Shrops 131 G7
Little Braxted Essex 88 C4
Little Bray Devon 41 F7
Little Brechin Angus 293 G7
Littlebredy Dorset 17 D7
Little Brickhill
M Keynes 103 E8
Little Bridgeford Staffs 151 D7
Little Brington
W Nhants 120 E3
Little Bristol S Glos 80 G2
Little Britain Warks 118 G2
Little Bromley Essex 107 F11
Little Bromwich W Mid 134 F2
Little Broughton Cumb 229 E7
Little Budworth Ches W 167 B9
Little Burstead Essex 87 G11
Littlebury Essex 105 D10
Littlebury Green Essex 105 D9
Little Bytham Lincs 155 F10
Little Cambridge Essex 106 F2
Little Canfield Essex 105 G11
Little Canford BCP 18 B6
Little Carleton Lancs 202 F2
Little Carlton Lincs 190 D5
Notts 172 D3
Little Casterton
Rutland 137 B10
Little Catwick E Yorks 209 E8
Little Catworth Cambs 122 C2
Little Cawthorpe Lincs 190 E5
Little Chalfield Wilts 61 G11
Little Chalfont Bucks 85 F7
Little Chart Kent 54 D2
Little Chart Forstal Kent 54 D3
Little Chell Stoke 168 E5
Little Chester Derby 153 B7
Little Chesterford
Essex 105 C10
Little Chesterton Oxon 101 G11
Little Cheverell Wilts 46 C3
Little Chishill Cambs 105 D8
Little Clacton Essex 89 B11
Little Clanfield Oxon 82 E3
Little Clegg Gtr Man 196 E2
Little Clifton Cumb 229 F7
Little Coates NE Lincs 201 F8
Little Colp Aberds 303 E7
Little Comberton Worcs 99 C9
Little Comfort Corn 12 E2
Little Common E Sus 38 F2
Lincs 156 D6
Shrops 115 B7
W Sus 34 C6
Little Compton Warks 100 E5
Little Corby Cumb 239 F11
Little Cornard Suff 107 D7
Littlecote Bucks 102 G6
Littlecott Wilts 46 C6
Little Cowarne Hereford 116 G2
Little Coxwell Oxon 82 G3
Little Crakehall N Yorks 224 G4
Little Cransley N Nhants 120 B6
Little Crawley M Keynes 103 B8
Little Creaton W Nhants 120 C4
Little Creich Highld 309 L6
Little Cressingham Norf 141 D7
Little Crosby Mers 193 G10
Little Cubley Derbys 152 B3
Little Dalby Leics 154 G5
Little Dawley Telford 132 B3
Littledean Glos 79 C11
Littledean Hill Glos 79 C11
Little Dens Aberds 303 E10
Little Dewchurch
Hereford 97 E10
Little Ditton Cambs 124 F3
Little Doward Hereford 79 B8
Littledown BCP 19 C8
Hants 47 B10
Little Downham Cambs 139 G10
Little Drayton Shrops 150 C3
Little Driffield E Yorks 208 B6
Little Drybrook Glos 79 D9
Little Dunham Norf 159 G7
Little Dunkeld Perth 286 C4
Little Dunmow Essex 106 G3
Little Durnford Wilts 46 G6
Little Eastbury Worcs 116 F6
Little Easton Essex 106 G2
Little Eaton Derbys 170 G5
Little Eccleston Lancs 202 E4
Little Ellingham Norf 141 D10
Little End Cambs 122 F3
Essex 87 E8
E Yorks 208 F2
Little Everdon
W Nhants 119 F11
Little Eversden Cambs 123 G7
Little Faringdon Oxon 82 E2
Little Fencote N Yorks 224 G5
Little Fenton N Yorks 206 F6
Littleferry Highld 311 K2
Littlefield NE Lincs 201 F9
Littlefield Common Sur 50 C3
Littlefield Green
Windsor 65 D11
Little Finborough Suff 125 G10
Little Fransham Norf 159 G8
Little Frith Kent 54 B2
Little Gaddesden Herts 85 C7
Littlegain Shrops 132 D5
Little Gidding Cambs 138 G2
Little Gight Aberds 303 F8
Little Glemham Suff 126 F6
Little Glenshee Perth 286 D3
Little Gorsley Glos 98 F3
Little Gransden Cambs 122 F5
Little Green Cambs 104 B5
Notts 172 G2
Som 45 D8
Suff 125 C11
Wrex 167 G7
Little Grimsby Lincs 190 C4
Little Gringley Notts 188 E2
Little Gruinard Highld 307 L4
Little Habton N Yorks 216 D4
Little Hadham Herts 105 G8
Little Hale Lincs 173 G10
Norf 141 B8
Little Hallam Derbys 171 G7
Little Hallingbury Essex 87 B7
Littleham Devon 14 E6
Devon 24 C6
Little Hampden Bucks 84 E5
Littlehampton W Sus 35 G8
Little Haresfield Glos 80 D4
Little Harrowden
N Nhants 121 C7
Little Harwood
Blackburn 195 B7
Little Haseley Oxon 83 E10
Little Hatfield E Yorks 209 E9
Little Hautbois Norf 160 E5
Little Haven Pembs 72 C5
W Sus 51 G7
Little Hay Staffs 134 C2
Little Hayfield Derbys 185 D8
Little Haywood Staffs 151 E10
Little Heath Ches E 167 G11
Ches W 166 B6
Herts 85 D8
Herts 86 E3
London 68 B3
Staffs 151 F8
Sur 66 G6
W Berks 65 E7
W Mid 134 G6
Little Heck N Yorks 198 C5
Littlehempston Devon 8 C6
Little Henham Essex 105 E10
Little Henny Essex 107 D7
Little Herbert's Glos 81 B7
Little Hereford
Hereford 115 D11
Little Hill Hereford 97 F9
Som 28 E3
Little Holbury Hants 32 G6
Little Honeyborough
Pembs 73 D7
Little Hoole Moss Houses
Lancs 194 C3
Little Horkesley Essex 107 E9
Little Hormead Herts 105 F8
Little Horsted E Sus 23 B7
Little Horton Wilts 62 G4
W Yorks 205 G9
Little Horwood Bucks 102 E5
Littlehoughton
Northumb 264 F6
Little Houghton
S Yorks 198 G2
W Nhants 120 F6
Little Hucklow Derbys 185 F11
Little Hulton Gtr Man 195 G8
Little Humber E Yorks 201 C8
Little Hungerford
W Berks 64 E4
Little Ilford London 68 B2
Little Ingestre Staffs 151 E9
Little Inkberrow Worcs 117 F10
Little Irchester
N Nhants 121 D8
Little Keyford Som 45 D9
Little Kimble Bucks 84 D4
Little Kineton Warks 118 G6
Little Kingshill Bucks 84 F5
Little Knowles Green
Suff 124 F5
Little Langdale Cumb 220 E6
Little Langford Wilts 46 F4
Little Laver Essex 87 D8
Little Lawford Warks 119 B9
Little Layton Blackpool 202 F2
Little Leigh Ches W 183 F10
Little Leighs Essex 88 B2
Little Lepton W Yorks 197 E8
Little Leven E Yorks 209 D8
Little Lever Gtr Man 195 F9
Little Limber Lincs 200 E6
Little Linford M Keynes 102 C6
Little Load Som 29 C7
Little London Bucks 83 C10
Bucks 84 D5
Little London continued
Cambs 139 D8
Essex 105 F9
Essex 106 D3
E Sus 23 B9
Glos 80 B2
Hants 47 D11
Hants 48 B6
Lincs 156 E4
Lincs 157 E8
Lincs 189 D10
Lincs 190 F4
Norf 140 D5
Norf 160 C2
Norf 160 C5
Norf 160 E3
Oxon 83 E8
Powys 129 F10
Shrops 131 F10
Som 44 D6
Suff 125 F10
Worcs 116 C2
W Yorks 205 F10
Little Longstone
Derbys 185 G11
Little Lynturk Aberds 293 B7
Little Lyth Shrops 131 B9
Little Madeley Staffs 168 F3
Little Malvern Worcs 98 C5
Little Mancot Flint 166 B4
Little Maplestead Essex 106 E6
Little Marcle Hereford 98 D3
Little Marlow Bucks 65 B11
Little Marsden Lancs 204 F3
Little Marsh Bucks 102 G3
Norf 159 B10
Wilts 45 B11
Little Marton Blackpool 202 G2
Little Mascalls Essex 88 E2
Little Massingham Norf 158 E5
Little Melton Norf 142 B3
Little Merthyr Hereford 96 B5
Little Milford Pembs 73 C7
Littlemill Aberds 292 D5
E Ayrs 257 F11
Highld 301 D9
Northumb 264 F6
Little Mill Kent 53 D7
Mon 78 E4
Little Milton Newport 59 B11
Oxon 83 E10
Little Minster Oxon 82 C4
Little Missenden Bucks 84 F6
Little Mongeham Kent 55 C10
Littlemoor Derbys 170 C5
Dorset 17 E9
Little Moor Gtr Man 184 D6
Lancs 203 E10
Little Moor End Lancs 195 B8
Littlemore Oxon 83 E8
Little Morrell Warks 118 F6
Littlemoss Gtr Man 184 B6
Little Mountain Flint 166 C3
Little Musgrave Cumb 222 C5
Little Ness Shrops 149 F8
Little Neston Ches W 182 F3
Little Newcastle Pembs 91 F9
Little Newsham Durham 224 B2
Little Norlington E Sus 23 C7
Little Norton Som 29 D7
Little Oakley Essex 108 F4
N Nhants 137 F7
Little Odell Bedford 121 F9
Little Offley Herts 104 F2
Little Onn Staffs 150 F6
Little Ormside Cumb 222 B4
Little Orton Cumb 239 F9
Leics 134 B6
Little Ouse Norf 140 F2
Little Ouseburn N Yorks 215 G8
Littleover Derby 152 C6
Little Overton Wrex 166 G5
Little Oxney Green
Essex 87 D11
Little Packington Warks 134 G4
Little Parndon Essex 86 C6
Little Paxton Cambs 122 E3
Little Petherick Corn 10 G4
Little Pitlurg Moray 302 E4
Little Plumpton Lancs 202 G3
Little Plumstead Norf 160 G6
Little Ponton Lincs 155 C8
Littleport Cambs 139 F11
Little Posbrook Hants 33 G8
Little Poulton Lancs 202 F3
Little Preston Kent 53 B8
W Yorks 206 G3
Littler Ches W 167 B10
Little Raveley Cambs 122 B5
Little Reedness
E Yorks 199 C10
Little Reynoldston
Swansea 56 D3
Little Ribston N Yorks 206 C3
Little Rissington Glos 81 B11
Little Rogart Highld 309 J7
Little Rollright Oxon 100 E5
Little Ryburgh Norf 159 D9
Little Ryle Northumb 264 G2
Little Ryton Shrops 131 C9
Little Salisbury Wilts 63 G7
Little Salkeld Cumb 231 D7
Little Sampford Essex 106 E3
Little Sandhurst Brack 65 G10
Little Saredon Staffs 133 B8
Little Saxham Suff 124 E5
Little Scatwell Highld 300 D3
Little Scotland Gtr Man 194 E6
Little Sessay N Yorks 215 E9
Little Shelford Cambs 123 G9
Little Shoddesden Hants 47 D9
Little Shrewley Warks 118 D4
Little Shurdington Glos 80 B6
Little Silver Devon 26 F6
Devon 40 E4
Little Singleton Lancs 202 F3
Little Skillymarno
Aberds 303 D9
Little Skipwith N Yorks 207 F9
Little Smeaton N Yorks 198 D4
N Yorks 224 E6
Little Snoring Norf 159 C9
Little Sodbury S Glos 61 C9
Little Sodbury End
S Glos 61 C8
Little Somborne Hants 47 G11
Little Somerford Wilts 62 C3
Little Soudley Shrops 150 D4
Little Stainforth
N Yorks 212 F6
Little Stainton Darl 234 G2
Little Stanmore London 85 G11
Little Stanney Ches W 182 G6
Little Staughton Bedford 122 E2
Littlestead Green Oxon 65 D8
Little Steeping Lincs 174 C6
Little Stoke S Glos 60 C6
Staffs 151 C8
Littlestone-on-Sea Kent 39 C9
Little Stonham Suff 126 E2
Little Stretton Leics 136 C3
Little Stretton continued
Shrops 131 E8
Little Strickland Cumb 221 B11
Little Studley N Yorks 214 E6
Little Stukeley Cambs 122 B4
Little Sugnall Staffs 150 C6
Little Sutton Ches W 182 F5
Lincs 157 E9
Shrops 131 G10
Little Swinburne
Northumb 241 B10
Little Tarrington Hereford 98 C2
Little Tew Oxon 101 F7
Little Tey Essex 107 G7
Little Thetford Cambs 123 B10
Little Thirkleby N Yorks 215 D9
Little Thornage Norf 159 B11
Little Thornton Lancs 202 E3
Littlethorpe Leics 135 D10
N Yorks 214 F6
Little Thorpe Durham 234 C4
W Yorks 197 C7
Little Thurlow Suff 124 G3
Little Thurlow Green
Suff 124 G3
Little Thurrock Thurrock 68 D6
Littleton Bath 60 G5
Ches W 166 B6
Dorset 30 G5
Hants 48 G3
Perth 286 D6
Som 44 G3
Sur 50 D3
Sur 66 F5
Wilts 62 G2
Littleton Common Sur 66 E5
Littleton Drew Wilts 61 C10
Littleton-on-Severn
S Glos 60 B5
Littleton Panell Wilts 46 C4
Littleton-upon-Severn
S Glos 79 G9
Little Torboll Highld 309 K7
Little Torrington Devon 25 D7
Little Totham Essex 88 C5
Little Toux Aberds 302 D5
Littletown Durham 234 C2
IoW 20 C6
W Yorks 197 C8
Little Town Cumb 220 B4
Lancs 203 F9
Warr 183 C10
Little Tring Herts 84 C6
Little Twycross Leics 134 B6
Little Urswick Cumb 210 E5
Little Vantage W Loth 270 C2
Little Wakering Essex 70 B2
Little Walden Essex 105 C10
Little Waldingfield Suff 107 B8
Little Walsingham Norf 159 B8
Little Waltham Essex 88 C2
Little Walton Warks 135 G9
Little Warley Essex 87 G10
Little Warton Warks 134 C5
Little Washbourne Glos 99 E9
Little Weighton E Yorks 208 G5
Little Weldon N Nhants 137 F8
Little Welland Worcs 98 D6
Little Welnetham Suff 125 E7
Little Welton Lincs 190 D4
Little Wenham Suff 107 D11
Little Wenlock Telford 132 B2
Little Weston Som 29 B10
Little Whitehouse IoW 20 C5
Little Whittingham Green
Suff 126 B5
Littlewick Green
Windsor 65 D10
Little Wigborough Essex 89 B7
Little Wilbraham
Cambs 123 F10
Littlewindsor Dorset 28 G6
Little Wisbeach Lincs 156 C2
Little Wishford Wilts 46 F5
Little Witcombe Glos 80 B6
Little Witley Worcs 116 E5
Little Wittenham Oxon 83 G9
Little Wolford Warks 100 D5
Littlewood Staffs 133 B9
Little Wood Corner Bucks 84 E6
Little Woodcote London 67 G9
Littlewood Green
Warks 117 E11
Little Woolgarston
Dorset 18 E5
Littleworth Bedford 103 C11
Glos 80 E4
Glos 100 D2
Oxon 82 F4
Oxon 83 D9
Oxon 83 G10
Staffs 151 E8
Staffs 151 G10
S Yorks 187 B10
Warks 118 E4
Wilts 63 G7
Worcs 117 E9
Worcs 117 G7
W Sus 35 C11
Littleworth Common
Bucks 66 B2
Little Worthen Shrops 130 B6
Littleworth End Warks 134 D3
Little Wratting Suff 106 B3
Little Wymington
Bedford 121 D9
Little Wymondley Herts 104 F4
Little Wyrley Staffs 133 B10
Little Wytheford
Shrops 149 F11
Little Yeldham Essex 106 D5
Littley Green Essex 87 B11
Litton Derbys 185 F11
N Yorks 213 E8
Som 44 C5
Litton Cheney Dorset 17 C7
Litton Mill Derbys 185 G11
Liurbost W Isles 304 F5
Livermead Torbay 9 C8
Liverpool Mers 182 C4
Liverpool Airport Mers 182 E6
Liversedge W Yorks 197 C8
Liverton Devon 14 F2
Redcar 226 B4
Liverton Mines Redcar 226 B4
Liverton Street Kent 53 C11
Livesey Street Kent 53 C8
Livingshayes Devon 27 G7
Livingston W Loth 269 B11
Livingston Village
W Loth 269 B10
Lix Toll Stirling 285 D9
Lixwm Flint 181 G11
Lizard Corn 2 G6
Llaingoch Anglesey 178 E2
Llaithddu Powys 129 G11
Llampha V Glam 58 D2
Llan Powys 129 C7
Llanaber Gwyn 146 F2
Llanaelhaearn Gwyn 162 G5
Llanafan Ceredig 112 C3
Llanafan-fawr Powys 113 F9
Llanallgo Anglesey 179 D7
Llananno Powys 113 C11
Llanarmon Gwyn 145 B8
Llanarmon Dyffryn Ceiriog
Wrex 148 C3
Llanarmon Mynydd-mawr
Powys 148 D2
Llanarmon-yn-Ial
Denb 165 D11
Llanarth Ceredig 111 F8
Mon 78 C5
Llanarthne Carms 93 G10
Llanasa Flint 181 E10
Llanbabo Anglesey 178 D5
Llanbad Rhondda 58 C3
Llanbadarn Fawr
Ceredig 128 G2
Llanbadarn Fynydd
Powys 114 B2
Llanbadarn-y-Garreg
Powys 96 B2
Llanbadoc Mon 78 E5
Llanbadrig Anglesey 178 C5
Llanbeder Newport 78 G5
Llanbedr Gwyn 145 D11
Powys 96 B2
Powys 96 G4
Llanbedr-Dyffryn-Clwyd
Denb 165 D10
Llanbedrgoch Anglesey 179 E8
Llanbedrog Gwyn 144 C6
Llanbedr Pont Steffan
= Lampeter Ceredig 93 B11
Llanbedr-y-cennin
Conwy 164 B3
Llanberis Gwyn 163 C9
Llanbethery V Glam 58 F4
Llanbister Powys 114 C2
Llanblethian = Llanfleiddan
V Glam 58 E3
Llanboidy Carms 92 G4
Llanbradach Caerph 77 G10
Llanbrynmair Powys 129 C7
Llancadle = Llancatal
V Glam 58 F4
Llancaiach Caerph 77 F10
Llancarfan V Glam 58 E5
Llancatal = Llancadle
V Glam 58 F4
Llancayo Mon 78 E5
Llancloudy Hereford 97 G9
Llancowrid Powys 130 E3
Llancynfelyn Ceredig 128 E2
Llan-dafal Bl Gwent 77 E11
Llandaff Cardiff 59 D7
Llandaff North Cardiff 59 D7
Llandanwg Gwyn 145 D11
Llandarcy Neath 57 B8
Llandawke Carms 74 C3
Llanddaniel Fab
Anglesey 179 G7
Llanddarog Carms 75 B8
Llanddeiniol Ceredig 111 C11
Llanddeiniolen Gwyn 163 B8
Llandderfel Gwyn 147 B9
Llanddeusant Anglesey 178 D4
Carms 94 G5
Llanddew Powys 95 E11
Llanddewi Swansea 56 D3
Llanddewi-Brefi Ceredig 112 F3
Llanddewi Fach Mon 78 F4
Llanddewi'r Cwm Powys 95 B10
Llanddewi Rhydderch
Mon 78 C5
Llanddewi Skirrid Mon 78 B4
Llanddewi Velfrey
Pembs 73 B10
Llanddewi Ystradenni
Powys 114 D2
Llanddoged Conwy 164 C4
Llanddona Anglesey 179 F9
Llanddowror Carms 74 C3
Llanddulas Conwy 180 F6
Llanddwywe Gwyn 145 E11
Llanddyfynan Anglesey 179 F8
Llandecwyn Gwyn 146 B2
Llandefaelog Powys 95 E10
Llandefaelog Fach
Powys 95 E10
Llandefaelog-tre'r-graig
Powys 96 F2
Llandefalle Powys 96 D2
Llandegai Gwyn 179 G9
Llandegfan Anglesey 179 G9
Llandegla Denb 165 E11
Llandegley Powys 114 E2
Llandegveth Mon 78 F4
Llandegwning Gwyn 144 C5
Llandeilo Carms 94 G2
Llandeilo Graban Powys 95 C11
Llandeilo'r Fan Powys 95 E7
Llandeloy Pembs 91 F7
Llandenny Mon 78 E6
Llandenny Walks Mon 78 E5
Llandevaud Newport 78 G6
Llandevenny Mon 60 B2
Llandewi Ystradenny
Powys 114 D2
Llandilo Pembs 92 F2
Llandilo-yr-ynys Carms 93 G9
Llandinabo Hereford 97 F10
Llandinam Powys 129 F10
Llandissilio Pembs 92 G2
Llandogo Mon 79 E8
Llandough V Glam 58 E3
V Glam 59 E7
Llandovery = Llanymddyfri
Carms 94 E5
Llandow = Llandw
V Glam 58 E2
Llandre Carms 94 C3
Ceredig 128 F2
Llandrillo Denb 147 B10
Llandrillo-yn-Rhôs
Conwy 180 E4
Llandrindod Wells
Powys 113 E11
Llandrinio Powys 148 F5
Llandruidion Pembs 90 G5
Llandudno Conwy 180 E3
Llandudno Junction
= Cyffordd Llandudno
Conwy 180 F3
Llandudoch = St Dogmaels
Pembs 92 B3
Llandw = Llandow
V Glam 58 E2
Llandwrog Gwyn 163 D7
Llandybie Carms 75 B10
Llandyfaelog Carms 74 C6
Llandyfan Carms 75 B10
Llandyfriog Ceredig 92 C6
Llandyfrydog Anglesey 178 D6
Llandygwydd Ceredig 92 C4
Llandynan Denb 165 F11
Llandyrnog Denb 165 B10
Llandysilio Powys 148 F5
Llandyssil Powys 130 D3
Llandysul Ceredig 93 C8
Llanedeyrn Cardiff 59 C8

Llanedi Carms 75 D9
Llanedwen Anglesey 163 B8
Llaneglwys Powys 95 D11
Llanegryn Gwyn 110 B2
Llanegwad Carms 93 G10
Llaneilian Anglesey 179 C7
Llanelian yn-Rhôs
Conwy 180 F5
Llanelidan Denb 165 E10
Llanelieu Powys 96 E3
Llanellen Mon 78 C4
Llanelli Carms 56 B4
Llanelltyd Gwyn 146 F4
Llanelly Mon 78 C2
Llanelly Hill Mon 78 C2
Llanelwedd Powys 113 G10
Llanelwy = *St Asaph*
Denb 181 G8
Llanenddwyn Gwyn 145 E11
Llanengan Gwyn 144 D5
Llanerch Powys 130 E6
Llanerch Emrys Powys 148 E4
Llanerchymedd
Anglesey 178 E6
Llanerfyl Powys 129 B10
Llaneuddog Anglesey 179 D7
Llan eurgain = *Northop*
Flint 166 B2
Llanfabon Caerph 77 G10
Llanfachraeth Anglesey 178 E4
Llanfachreth Gwyn 146 E5
Llanfaelog Anglesey 178 G4
Llanfaelrhys Gwyn 144 D4
Llanfaenor Mon 78 B6
Llanfaes Anglesey 179 F10
Powys 95 F10
Llanfaethlu Anglesey 178 D4
Llanfaglan Gwyn 163 C7
Llanfair Gwyn 145 D11
Llanfair Caereinion
Powys 130 B2
Llanfair Clydogau
Ceredig 112 G2
Llanfair-Dyffryn-Clwyd
Denb 165 D10
Llanfairfechan Conwy 179 F11
Llanfair Kilgeddin Mon 78 D4
Llanfair Kilgheddin Mon 78 D4
Llanfair-Nant-Gwyn
Pembs 92 D3
Llanfairpwll-gwyngyll
Anglesey 179 G8
Llanfair Talhaiarn
Conwy 180 G6
Llanfair Waterdine
Shrops 114 B4
Llanfairyneubwll
Anglesey 178 F3
Llanfairynghornwy
Anglesey 178 C4
Llanfallteg Carms 73 B11
Llanfallteg West Carms 73 B10
Llanfaredd Powys 113 G11
Llanfarian Ceredig 111 B11
Llanfechain Powys 148 E3
Llanfechan Powys 113 G9
Llanfechell Anglesey 178 C5
Llanferres Denb 165 C11
Llan Ffestiniog Gwyn 164 G2
Llanfflewyn Anglesey 178 D5
Llanfigael Anglesey 178 E4
Llanfihangel-ar-arth
Carms 93 D9
Llanfihangel-Crucorney
Mon 96 G6
Llanfihangel Glyn Myfyr
Conwy 165 F7
Llanfihangel-helygen
Powys 113 E10
Llanfihangel Nant Bran
Powys 95 E8
Llanfihangel-nant-Melan
Powys 114 F3
Llanfihangel Rhydithon
Powys 114 D3
Llanfihangel Rogiet Mon 60 B2
Llanfihangel Tal-y-llyn
Powys 96 F2
Llanfihangel Tor y Mynydd
Mon 79 E7
Llanfihangel-uwch-Gwili
Carms 93 G9
Llanfihangel-y-Creuddyn
Ceredig 112 B3
Llanfihangel-yng-Ngwynfa
Powys 147 F11
Llanfihangel yn Nhowyn
Anglesey 178 F4
Llanfihangel-y-pennant
Gwyn 128 B3
Gwyn 163 F8
Llanfilo Powys 96 E2
Llanfleiddan = *Llanblethian*
V Glam 58 E3
Llanfoist Mon 78 C3
Llanfor Gwyn 147 B8
Llanfrechfa Torf 78 G4
Llanfrothen Gwyn 163 G10
Llanfrynach Powys 95 F11
Llanfwrog Anglesey 178 E4
Denb 165 D10
Llanfyllin Powys 148 F2
Llanfynydd Carms 93 F11
Flint 166 D3
Llanfyrnach Pembs 92 E4
Llangadfan Powys 147 G10
Llangadog Carms 74 D6
Carms 94 F4
Llangadwaladr Anglesey 162 B5
Powys 148 C3
Llangaffo Anglesey 162 B6
Llangain Carms 74 B5
Llangammarch Wells
Powys 95 B8
Llangan V Glam 58 D3
Llangarron Hereford 97 G10
Llangasty Talyllyn Powys 96 F2
Llangathen Carms 93 G11
Llangattock Powys 78 B2
Llangattock Lingoed
Mon 97 G7
Llangattock nigh Usk
Mon 78 D4
Llangattock-Vibon-Avel
Mon 79 B7
Llangedwyn Powys 148 E3
Llangefni Anglesey 179 F7
Llangeinor Bridgend 58 B2
Llangeitho Ceredig 112 F2
Llangeler Carms 93 D7
Llangendeirne Carms 75 C7
Llangennech Carms 75 E9
Llangennith Swansea 56 C2
Llangenny Powys 78 B2
Llangernyw Conwy 164 B5
Llangeview Mon 78 E5
Llangewydd Court
Bridgend 57 E11
Llangian Gwyn 144 D5
Llangloffan Pembs 91 E8
Llanglydwen Carms 92 F3
Llangoed Anglesey 179 F10
Llangoedmor Ceredig 92 B3
Llangollen Denb 166 G2
Llangolman Pembs 92 F2
Llangors Powys 96 F2
Llangorwen Ceredig 128 G2
Llangovan Mon 79 D7
Llangower Gwyn 147 C8
Llangrannog Ceredig 110 G6
Llangristiolus Anglesey 178 G6
Llangrove Hereford 79 B8
Llangua Mon 97 F7
Llangunllo Powys 114 C4
Llangunnor Carms 74 B6
Llangurig Powys 113 B8
Llangwm Conwy 165 G7
Mon 78 E6
Pembs 73 D7
Llangwnnadl Gwyn 144 C4
Llangwyfan Denb 165 B10
Llangwyfan-isaf
Anglesey 162 B4
Llangwyllog Anglesey 178 F6
Llangwyryfon Ceredig 111 C11
Llangybi Ceredig 112 G2
Gwyn 162 G6
Mon 78 F5
Llangyfelach Swansea 56 B6
Llangyndeyrn Carms 75 C7
Llangynhafal Denb 165 C10
Llangynidr Powys 77 B11
Llangyniew Powys 130 B2
Llangynin Carms 74 B2
Llangynog Carms 74 B4
Powys 147 D11
Llangynwyd Bridgend 57 D11
Llanhamlach Powys 95 F11
Llanharan Rhondda 58 C4
Llanharry Rhondda 58 C4
Llanhennock Mon 78 G5
Llanhilleth Bl Gwent 78 E2
Llanhowel Pembs 90 F6
Llanidloes Powys 129 G9
Llaniestyn Gwyn 144 C5
Llanifyny Powys 129 G7
Llanigon Powys 96 D4
Llanilar Ceredig 112 C2
Llanilid Rhondda 58 C3
Llanilltud Fawr = *Llantwit Major* V Glam 58 F3
Llanio Ceredig 112 F2
Llanion Pembs 73 E7
Llanishen Cardiff 59 C7
Mon 79 E7
Llanllawddog Carms 93 F9
Llanllechid Gwyn 163 B10
Llanllowell Mon 78 F5
Llanllugan Powys 129 C11
Llanllwch Carms 74 B5
Llanllwchaiarn Powys 130 E2
Llanllwni Carms 93 D9
Llanllwyd Shrops 130 G3
Llanllyfni Gwyn 163 E7
Llanmadoc Swansea 56 C2
Llanmaes Cardiff 58 D6
V Glam 58 F3
Llanmartin Newport 59 B11
Llanmerwig Powys 130 E3
Llanmihangel V Glam 58 E3
Llan-mill Pembs 73 C10
Llanmiloe Carms 74 D3
Llanmorlais Swansea 56 C4
Llannefydd Conwy 181 G7
Llannerch-y-môr Flint 181 F11
Llannon Carms 75 D8
Llan-non = *Llanon*
Ceredig 111 D10
Llannor Gwyn 145 B7
Llanon Pembs 90 E6
Llanon = *Llan-non*
Ceredig 111 D10
Llanover Mon 78 D4
Llanpumsaint Carms 93 F8
Llanreath Pembs 73 E7
Llanreithan Pembs 91 F7
Llanrhaeadr Denb 165 C9
Llanrhaeadr-ym-Mochnant
Powys 148 D2
Llanrhian Pembs 90 E6
Llanrhidian Swansea 56 C3
Llanrhos Conwy 180 E3
Llanrhyddlad Anglesey 178 D4
Llanrhystud Ceredig 111 D10
Llanrosser Hereford 96 D5
Llanrothal Hereford 79 B7
Llanrug Gwyn 163 C8
Llanrumney Cardiff 59 C8
Llanrwst Conwy 164 C4
Llansadurnen Carms 74 C3
Llansadwrn Anglesey 179 F9
Carms 94 E3
Llansaint Carms 74 D5
Llansamlet Swansea 57 B7
Llansanffraid Glan Conwy
Conwy 180 F4
Llansannan Conwy 164 B6
Llansannor V Glam 58 D3
Llansantffraed Ceredig 111 D10
Powys 96 G2
Llansantffraed Cwmdeuddwr
Powys 113 D9
Llansantffraed-in-Elwel
Powys 113 G11
Llansantffraid-ym-Mechain
Powys 148 E4
Llansawel Carms 94 D2
Llansawel = *Briton Ferry*
Neath 57 C8
Llansilin Powys 148 D4
Llansoy Mon 78 E6
Llanspyddid Powys 95 F10
Llanstadwell Pembs 72 D6
Llansteffan Carms 74 C5
Llanstephan Powys 96 C2
Llantarnam Torf 78 G4
Llanteems Mon 96 G6
Llanteg Pembs 73 C11
Llanthony Mon 96 F5
Llantilio Crossenny Mon 78 C5
Llantilio Pertholey Mon 78 B4
Llantood Pembs 92 C3
Llantrisant Anglesey 178 E5
Mon 78 F5
Rhondda 58 C4
Llantrithyd V Glam 58 E4
Llantwit Neath 57 B9
Llantwit Fardre Rhondda 58 B5
Llantwit Major = *Llanilltud Fawr* V Glam 58 F3
Llanussyllt = *Saundersfoot*
Pembs 73 E10
Llanuwchllyn Gwyn 147 C7
Llanvaches Newport 78 G6
Llanvair Discoed Mon 78 G6
Llanvapley Mon 78 C5
Llanvetherine Mon 78 B5
Llanveynoe Hereford 96 E6
Llanvihangel Crucorney
Mon 96 G6
Llanvihangel Gobion
Mon 78 D4
Llanvihangel-Ystern-Llewern Mon 78 C6
Llanwarne Hereford 97 F10
Llanwddyn Powys 147 F10
Llanwenarth Mon 78 C3
Llanwenog Ceredig 93 B9
Llanwern Newport 59 B11
Llanwinio Carms 92 F5
Llanwnda Gwyn 163 D7
Pembs 91 D8
Llanwnnen Ceredig 93 B10
Llanwnog Powys 129 E10
Llanwrda Carms 94 E4
Llanwrin Powys 128 C5
Llanwrthwl Powys 113 E9
Llanwrtud = *Llanwrtyd Wells*
Powys 95 B7
Llanwrtyd Wells = *Llanwrtud*
Powys 95 B7
Llanwyddelan Powys 129 C11
Llanyblodwel Shrops 148 E4
Llanybri Carms 74 C4
Llanybydder Carms 93 C10
Llanycefn Pembs 91 G11
Llanychaer Pembs 91 D9
Llanycil Gwyn 147 C8
Llanycrwys Carms 94 B2
Llanymawddwy Gwyn 147 F8
Llanymddyfri = *Llandovery*
Carms 94 E5
Llanymynech Powys 148 E5
Llanynghenedl Anglesey 178 E4
Llanynys Denb 165 C10
Llan-y-pwll Wrex 166 E5
Llanyrafon Torf 78 G4
Llanyre Powys 113 E10
Llanystumdwy Gwyn 145 B9
Llanywern Powys 96 F2
Llawhaden Pembs 73 B9
Llawnt Shrops 148 C5
Llawrdref Bellaf Gwyn 144 D5
Llawr-y-glyn Powys 129 E8
Llay Wrex 166 D4
Llechcynfarwy Anglesey 178 E5
Llecheiddior Gwyn 163 G7
Llechfaen Powys 95 F11
Llechfraith Gwyn 146 F3
Llechryd Caerph 77 D10
Ceredig 92 C4
Llechrydau Powys 148 C4
Llechwedd Conwy 180 F3
Lledrod Ceredig 112 C2
Llenmerewig Powys 130 E3
Llethrid Swansea 56 C4
Llettyrychen Carms 75 E7
Llidiad Nenog Carms 93 D10
Llidiardau Gwyn 147 B7
Llidiart-y-parc Denb 165 G10
Llithfaen Gwyn 162 G5
Lloc Flint 181 F10
Llong Flint 166 C3
Llowes Powys 96 C3
Lloyney Powys 114 B4
Llugwy Powys 128 D4
Llundain-fach Ceredig 111 F11
Llwydarth Bridgend 57 C11
Llwydcoed Rhondda 77 E7
Llwyn Denb 165 C9
Shrops 130 G5
Llwyncelyn Ceredig 111 F8
Llwyndafydd Ceredig 111 F7
Llwynderw Powys 130 C4
Llwyn-derw Powys 129 G8
Llwyndrain Pembs 95 E5
Llwyn-du Mon 78 B3
Llwynduris Ceredig 92 C4
Llwyndyrys Gwyn 162 G5
Llwyneinion Wrex 166 F3
Llwyngwril Gwyn 110 B2
Llwynhendy Carms 56 B4
Llwyn-hendy Carms 56 B4
Llwynmawr Wrex 148 B4
Llwyn-on Village M Tydf 77 C8
Llwyn-Têg Carms 75 D9
Llwyn-y-brain Carms 73 C11
Llwyn-y-go Shrops 148 E6
Llwynygog Powys 129 E7
Llwyn-y-groes Ceredig 111 F11
Llwynypia Rhondda 77 G7
Llwyn-yr-hwrdd Pembs 92 E4
Llynclys Shrops 148 E5
Llynfaes Anglesey 178 F6
Llysfaen Conwy 180 F5
Llyswen Powys 96 D2
Llysworney V Glam 58 E3
Llys-y-frôn Pembs 91 G10
Llywel Powys 95 E7
Llywernog Ceredig 128 G4
Load Brook S Yorks 186 D3
Loan Falk 279 F9
Loandhu Highld 301 B8
Loanend Northumb 273 E8
Loanhead Aberds 302 D6
Midloth 270 B5
Perth 286 D5
Loanreoch Highld 300 B6
Loans S Ayrs 257 C8
Loansdean Northumb 252 G5
Loans of Tullich Highld 301 B8
Lobb Devon 40 F3
Lobhillcross Devon 12 D5
Lobley Hill T&W 242 E6
Lobthorpe Lincs 155 E9
Loch a Charnain
W Isles 297 G4
Loch a' Ghainmhich
W Isles 304 F4
Lochailort Highld 295 G9
Lochaline Highld 289 E8
Lochanhully Highld 301 G9
Lochans Dumfries 236 D2
Locharbriggs Dumfries 247 G11
Lochassynt Lodge
Highld 307 G6
Lochavich Ho Argyll 275 B10
Lochawe Argyll 284 E5
Loch Baghasdail
W Isles 297 K3
Lochbuie Argyll 289 G8
Lochbuie Ho Argyll 289 G8
Lochcallater Lodge
Aberds 292 E3
Lochcarron Highld 295 B10
Loch Choire Lodge
Highld 308 F6
Lochdhu Highld 310 E4
Lochdochart House
Stirling 285 E8
Lochdon Argyll 289 F9
Lochdrum Highld 300 B2
Lochead Argyll 275 E11
Argyll 275 F8
Lochearnhead Stirling 285 E9
Lochee Dundee 287 D7
Loch Eil Highld 290 F2
Lochend Edin 280 G5
Highld 300 F5
Highld 310 C6
Lochend Ho Stirling 277 B11
Locherben Dumfries 247 D11
Lochetive Ho Highld 284 C5
Loch Euphoirt W Isles 296 E4
Lochfoot Dumfries 237 B10
Lochgair Argyll 275 D10
Lochgarthside Highld 291 B7
Lochgelly Fife 280 C3
Lochgilphead Argyll 275 E9
Lochgoilhead Argyll 284 G6
Loch Head Dumfries 236 E5
Dumfries 245 E11
Lochhill Moray 302 C2
Lochhussie Highld 300 D4
Lochinch Castle
Dumfries 236 C3
Lochindorb Lodge
Highld 301 F9
Lochinver Highld 307 G5
Lochlane Perth 286 E2
Lochletter Highld 300 G4
Loch Loyal Lodge Highld 308 E6
Lochluichart Highld 300 C3
Lochmaben Dumfries 248 G3
Lochmore Cottage
Highld 310 E4
Lochmore Lodge Highld 306 F7
Loch nam Madadh
W Isles 296 E5
Lochnell Ho Argyll 289 F10
Lochore Fife 280 B3
Lochorodale Argyll 255 F7
Lochportain W Isles 296 D5
Lochran Perth 280 B2
Lochranza N Ayrs 255 B10
Lochs Crofts Moray 302 C3
Loch Sgioport W Isles 297 H4
Lochside Aberds 293 G9
Highld 301 D8
Highld 308 D4
Highld 310 F2
S Ayrs 257 E8
Lochslin Highld 311 L2
Lochstack Lodge Highld 306 E7
Lochton Aberds 293 D9
Lochty Angus 293 G7
Fife 287 G9
Perth 286 E4
Lochuisge Highld 289 D9
Lochurr Dumfries 247 F7
Lochwinnoch Renfs 267 D7
Lochwood Dumfries 248 D3
Glasgow 268 B3
Lochyside Highld 290 F3
Lockengate Corn 5 C10
Lockerbie Dumfries 248 G4
Lockeridge Wilts 62 F6
Lockeridge Dene Wilts 62 F6
Lockerley Hants 32 B3
Lockhills Cumb 230 B6
Locking N Som 43 B11
Lockinge Oxon 64 B2
Locking Stumps Warr 183 C10
Lockington E Yorks 208 D5
Leics 153 D9
Lockleaze Bristol 60 D6
Lockleywood Shrops 150 D3
Locksbottom London 68 F2
Locksbrook Bath 61 G8
Locksgreen IoW 20 C4
Locks Heath Hants 33 F8
Lockton N Yorks 226 G6
Lockwood W Yorks 196 D6
Loddington Leics 136 C5
N Nhants 120 B6
Loddiswell Devon 8 F4
Loddon Norf 143 D7
Loddon Ingloss Norf 142 D6
Lode Cambs 123 E10
Lode Heath W Mid 134 G3
Loders Dorset 16 C5
Lodgebank Shrops 149 D11
Lodge Green N Yorks 223 F9
W Mid 134 G5
Lodge Hill Corn 6 C4
W Mid 133 G10
W Yorks 197 C9
Lodge Lees Kent 55 D8
Lodge Moor S Yorks 186 D3
Lodge Park Worcs 117 D10
Lodsworth W Sus 34 C6
Lodsworth Common
W Sus 34 C6
Lodway Bristol 60 D4
Lofthouse N Yorks 214 E2
W Yorks 197 B10
Lofthouse Gate
W Yorks 197 C10
Loftus Redcar 226 B4
Logan E Ayrs 258 E3
Loganlea W Loth 269 C9
Logan Mains Dumfries 236 E2
Loggerheads Denb 165 C11
Staffs 150 B4
Logie Angus 293 G8
Fife 287 E8
Moray 301 D10
Logiealmond Lodge
Perth 286 D3
Logie Coldstone Aberds 292 C6
Logie Hill Highld 301 B7
Logie Newton Aberds 302 F6
Logie Pert Angus 293 G8
Logierait Perth 286 B3
Login Carms 92 G3
Logmore Green Sur 50 D6
Loidse Mhorsgail
W Isles 304 F3
Lolworth Cambs 123 E7
Lomeshaye Lancs 204 F2
Lôn Gwyn 147 C7
Lonbain Highld 298 D6
Londesborough E Yorks 208 D3
London Apprentice Corn 5 E10
London Beach Kent 53 F11
London Colney Herts 85 E11
Londonderry N Yorks 214 B6
W Mid 133 F10
London End Cambs 121 D11
London Fields W Mid 133 E8
London Minstead Hants 32 E3
Londonthorpe Lincs 155 B9
Londubh Highld 307 L3
Lonemore Highld 299 B7
Highld 309 L7
Long Ashton N Som 60 E5
Long Bank Worcs 116 C5
Longbar N Ayrs 266 E6
Longbarn Warr 183 C10
Long Bennington Lincs 172 G4
Longbenton T&W 243 D7
Longborough Glos 100 F3
Long Bredy Dorset 17 C7
Longbridge Plym 7 D10
Warks 118 E5
W Mid 117 B10
Longbridge Deverill
Wilts 45 E11
Longbridge Hayes Stoke 168 E5
Longbridgemuir
Dumfries 238 D3
Long Buckby W Nhants 120 D2
Long Buckby Wharf
W Nhants 120 D2
Longburgh Cumb 239 F8
Longburton Dorset 29 E11
Longcause Devon 8 C5
Long Clawson Leics 154 D4
Longcliffe Derbys 170 D2
Long Common Hants 33 E8
Long Compton Staffs 151 E7
Warks 100 E5
Longcot Oxon 82 G3
Long Crendon Bucks 83 D11
Long Crichel Dorset 31 E7
Longcroft Cumb 238 F6
Falk 278 F5
Longcross Devon 12 F4
Sur 66 F3
Long Cross Wilts 45 G9
Longdale Cumb 222 D2
Longdales Cumb 230 C6
Long Dean Wilts 61 D11
Longden Shrops 131 B8
Longden Common
Shrops 131 C8
Long Ditton Sur 67 F7
Longdon Staffs 151 G11
Worcs 98 D6
Longdon Green Staffs 151 G11
Longdon Heath Worcs 98 D6
Longdon Hill End Worcs 98 D6
Longdon on Tern
Telford 150 F2
Longdown Devon 14 C3
Longdowns Corn 2 C6
Long Drax N Yorks 199 B7
Longdrum Angus 292 G4
Long Duckmanton
Derbys 186 G6
Long Eaton Derbys 153 C9
Longfield Kent 68 F6
Shetland 313 M5
Wilts 45 B11
Longfield Hill Kent 68 F6
Longfleet BCP 18 C6
Longford Derbys 152 B4
Glos 98 G6
Kent 52 B4
London 66 D4
Shrops 150 C2
Telford 150 F4
Warr 183 C10
W Mid 135 G7
Longfordlane Derbys 152 B4
Longforgan Perth 287 E7
Longformacus Borders 272 D3
Longframlington
Northumb 252 C4
Long Gardens Essex 106 D6
Long Green Ches W 183 G7
Suff 125 B11
Worcs 98 E6
Longham Dorset 19 B7
Norf 159 F8
Long Hanborough Oxon 82 C6
Longhaven Aberds 303 F11
Longhedge Wilts 45 E10
Longhill Aberds 303 D9
Longhirst Northumb 252 F6
Longhope Glos 79 B11
Orkney 314 G3
Longhorsley Northumb 252 E4
Longhoughton
Northumb 264 G6
Longhouse Bath 61 G8
Long Itchington Warks 119 D8
Long John's Hill Norf 142 B4
Longlands Cumb 229 D11
London 68 E2
Longlane Derbys 152 B5
W Berks 64 E3
Long Lane Telford 150 F2
Long Lawford Warks 119 B9
Long Lee W Yorks 205 E7
Longlevens Glos 99 G7
Longley W Yorks 196 C5
W Yorks 196 F6
Longley Estate S Yorks 186 C5
Longley Green Worcs 116 G4
Longleys Perth 286 C6
Long Load Som 29 C7
Longmanhill Aberds 303 C7
Long Marston Herts 84 B5
N Yorks 206 C6
Warks 100 B3
Long Marton Cumb 231 G9
Long Meadow Cambs 123 E10
Long Meadowend
Shrops 131 G8
Long Melford Suff 107 B7
Longmoor Camp Hants 49 G9
Longmorn Moray 302 D2
Longmoss Ches E 184 G5
Long Newnton Glos 80 G6
Longnewton Borders 262 D3
Stockton 225 B7
Long Newton E Loth 271 C10
Longney Glos 80 C3
Longniddry E Loth 281 F8
Longnor Shrops 131 C9
Staffs 151 G7
Staffs 169 C9
Longnor Park Shrops 131 C9
Long Oak Shrops 149 E7
Longparish Hants 48 E2
Longpark Cumb 239 E10
E Ayrs 257 B10
Long Park Hants 48 G2
Longport Stoke 168 F5
Long Preston N Yorks 204 B2
Longridge Glos 80 D5
Lancs 203 F8
Staffs 151 F8
W Loth 269 C9
Longridge End Glos 98 G6
Longrigg N Lanark 278 G6
Longriggend N Lanark 278 G6
Long Riston E Yorks 209 E8
Longrock Corn 1 C5
Long Sandall S Yorks 198 F6
Longscales N Yorks 205 B10
Longsdon Staffs 169 E7
Longshaw Gtr Man 194 G4
Staffs 169 F9
Longside Aberds 303 E10
Longsight Gtr Man 184 B5
Long Sight Gtr Man 196 F2
Longslow Shrops 150 B3
Longsowerby Cumb 239 G9
Longstanton Cambs 123 D7
Longstock Hants 47 F11
Longstone Corn 2 B2
Corn 11 G7
Edin 280 G4
Pembs 73 D10
Som 28 B5
Longstowe Cambs 122 G6
Long Stratton Norf 142 E3
Longstreet Wilts 46 C6
Long Street M Keynes 102 B5
Long Sutton Hants 49 D8
Lincs 157 E8
Som 29 B7
Longthorpe Pboro 138 D3
Long Thurlow Suff 125 D10
Longthwaite Cumb 230 G4
Longton Lancs 194 B3
Stoke 168 G6
Longtown Cumb 239 D9
Hereford 96 F6
Longtownmail Orkney 314 F4
Longview Mers 182 C6
Longville in the Dale
Shrops 131 E10
Longway Bank Derbys 170 E4
Longwell Green S Glos 61 E7
Long Whatton Leics 153 E9
Longwick Bucks 84 D3
Long Wittenham Oxon 83 G8
Longwitton Northumb 252 F3
Longwood Shrops 132 B2
W Yorks 196 D6
Longwood Edge
W Yorks 196 D6
Longworth Oxon 82 F5
Longyester E Loth 271 B10
Lon-las Swansea 57 B8
Lonmay Aberds 303 D10
Lonmore Highld 298 E2
Looe Corn 6 E5
Looe Mills Corn 6 C4
Loose Kent 53 C9
Loosegate Lincs 156 D6
Loose Hill Kent 53 C9
Loosley Row Bucks 84 E4
Lopcombe Corner Wilts 47 F9
Lopen Som 28 E6
Lopen Head Som 28 E6
Loppergarth Cumb 210 D5
Loppington Shrops 149 D9
Lopwell Devon 7 C9
Lorbottle Northumb 252 B2
Lorbottle Hall Northumb 252 B2
Lordsbridge Norf 157 G11
Lord's Hill Soton 32 D5
Lordshill Common Sur 50 E4
Lordswood Soton 32 D6
Lords Wood Medway 69 G9
Lornty Perth 286 C5
Loscoe Derbys 170 F6
W Yorks 198 C2
Loscombe Dorset 16 B6
Losgaintir W Isles 305 J2
Lossiemouth Moray 302 B2
Lossit Argyll 254 B2
Lossit Lodge Argyll 274 G5
Lostford Shrops 150 C2
Lostock Gtr Man 195 F7
Lostock Gralam
Ches W 183 F11
Lostock Green Ches W 183 G11
Lostock Hall Lancs 194 B4
Lostock Junction
Gtr Man 195 F7
Lostwithiel Corn 6 D2
Loth Orkney 314 C6
Lothbeg Highld 311 H3
Lothersdale N Yorks 204 D5
Lothianbridge Midloth 270 C6
Lothmore Highld 311 H3
Lottisham Som 44 G5
Loudwater Bucks 84 G6
Herts 85 F9
Loughborough Leics 153 F10
Loughor Swansea 56 B5
Loughton Essex 86 F6
M Keynes 102 D6
Shrops 132 G2
Lound Lincs 155 F11
Notts 187 D11
Suff 143 D10
Loundsley Green
Derbys 186 G5
Lount Leics 153 F7
Lour Angus 287 C8
Louth Lincs 190 D4
Lovat Highld 300 E5
Lovaton Devon 7 B10
Love Clough Lancs 195 B10
Lovedean Hants 33 E11
Love Green Bucks 66 C4
Lover Wilts 32 C2
Loversall S Yorks 187 B9
Loves Green Essex 87 E10
Lovesome Hill N Yorks 225 F7
Loveston Pembs 73 D9
Lovington Som 44 G5
Low Ackworth W Yorks 198 D3
Low Alwinton
Northumb 251 B10
Low Angerton Northumb 252 G3
Lowbands Glos 98 E5
Low Barlings Lincs 189 G9
Low Barugh S Yorks 197 F10
Low Bentham N Yorks 212 F2
Low Biggins Cumb 212 D2
Low Blantyre S Lanark 268 D3
Low Borrowbridge
Cumb 222 E2
Low Bradfield S Yorks 186 C3
Low Bradley N Yorks 204 D6
Low Braithwaite Cumb 230 C4
Low Bridge Wilts 62 E3
Lowbridge House
Cumb 221 E10
Low Brunton Northumb 241 C10
Low Burnham N Lincs 199 G9
Low Burton N Yorks 214 C4
Low Buston Northumb 252 B6
Lowca Cumb 228 G5
Low Catton E Yorks 207 C10
Low Clanyard Dumfries 236 F3
Low Common Norf 142 E2
Low Compton Gtr Man 196 F2
Low Coniscliffe Darl 224 C5
Low Cotehill Cumb 239 G11
Low Coylton S Ayrs 257 F10
Low Crosby Cumb 239 F10
Lowcross Hill Ches W 167 E7
Low Dalby N Yorks 217 B7
Lowdham Notts 171 F11
Low Dinsdale Darl 224 C6
Lowe Shrops 149 C10
Lowedges S Yorks 186 E4
Lowe Hill Staffs 169 D7
Low Eighton T&W 243 F7
Low Ellington N Yorks 214 C4
Lower Achachenna
Argyll 284 E4
Lower Aisholt Som 43 F8
Lower Allscot Shrops 132 D4
Lower Altofts W Yorks 197 C11
Lower Amble Corn 10 G5
Lower Ansty Dorset 30 G3
Lower Ardtun Argyll 288 G5
Lower Arncott Oxon 83 B10
Lower Ashtead Sur 51 B7
Lower Ashton Devon 14 E2
Lower Assendon Oxon 65 C8
Lower Badcall Highld 306 E6
Lower Ballam Lancs 202 G3
Lower Bartle Lancs 202 G5
Lower Basildon W Berks 64 D6
Lower Bassingthorpe
Lincs 155 D9
Lower Bearwood
Hereford 115 F7
Lower Bebington Mers 182 E4
Lower Beeding W Sus 36 B2
Lower Benefield
N Nhants 137 F9
Lower Bentley Worcs 117 D9
Lower Beobridge
Shrops 132 E5
Lower Berry Hill Glos 79 C9
Lower Binton Warks 118 G2
Lower Birchwood
Derbys 170 E6
Lower Bitchet Kent 52 C5
Lower Blandford St Mary
Dorset 30 F5
Lower Blunsdon
Swindon 81 G10
Lower Bobbingworth Green
Essex 87 D8
Lower Bockhampton
Dorset 17 C10
Lower Boddington
W Nhants 119 G9
Lower Bodham Norf 160 B2
Lower Bodinnar Corn 1 C4
Lower Bois Bucks 85 E7
Lower Bordean Hants 33 C11
Lower Boscaswell Corn 1 C3
Lower Bourne Sur 49 E10
Lower Bradley W Mid 133 D9
Lower Brailes Warks 100 D6
Lower Breakish Highld 295 C8
Lower Bredbury
Gtr Man 184 C6
Lower Breinton Hereford 97 D9
Lower Broadheath
Worcs 116 F6
Lower Brook Hants 32 B4
Lower Broughton
Gtr Man 184 B4
Lower Brynamman Neath 76 C2
Lower Brynn Corn 5 C9
Lower Buckenhill
Hereford 98 E2
Lower Buckland Hants 20 B2
Lower Bullingham
Hereford 97 D10
Lower Bullington Hants 48 E3
Lower Bunbury Ches E 167 D9
Lower Burgate Hants 31 D11
Lower Burrow Som 28 C6
Lower Burton Hereford 115 F8
Lower Bush Medway 69 F7
Lower Cadsden Bucks 84 E4
Lower Caldecote
C Beds 104 B3
Lower Cam Glos 80 E2
Lower Canada N Som 43 B11
Lower Carden Ches W 167 E7
Lower Catesby
W Nhants 119 F10
Lower Cator Devon 13 F9
Lower Caversham
Reading 65 E8
Lower Chapel Powys 95 D10
Lower Chedworth Glos 81 C9
Lower Cheriton Devon 27 G10
Lower Chicksgrove Wilts 46 G3
Lower Chute Wilts 47 C10
Lower Clapton London 67 B11
Lower Clent Worcs 117 B8
Lower Clicker Corn 6 C5
Lower Clopton Warks 118 F3
Lower Common Hants 48 E6
Hants 65 G9
Mon 78 B2
Mon 78 E4
Shrops 131 B9
Lower Copthurst Lancs 194 C5
Lower Cotburn Aberds 303 D7
Lower Cousley Wood
E Sus 53 G7
Lower Cox Street Kent 69 G10
Lower Cragabus Argyll 254 C4
Lower Creedy Devon 26 G4
Lower Croan Corn 10 G6
Lower Crossings Derbys 185 E8
Lower Cumberworth
W Yorks 197 F8
Lower Daggons Hants 31 E9
Lower Darwen Blackburn 195 B7
Lower Dean Bedford 121 D11
Devon 8 C4
Lower Dell Highld 292 B2
Lower Denby W Yorks 197 F8
Lower Denzell Corn 5 B7
Lower Deuchries
Aberds 302 D6
Lower Diabaig Highld 299 C7
Lower Dicker E Sus 23 C9
Lower Dinchope Shrops 131 G9
Lower Dowdeswell Glos 81 B8
Lower Down Shrops 130 G6
Lower Drift Corn 1 D4
Lower Dunsforth
N Yorks 215 G8
Lower Durston Som 28 B3
Lower Earley Wokingham 65 E9
Lower East Carleton
Norf 142 C3
Lower Eastern Green
W Mid 118 B5
Lower Edmonton London 86 G4
Lower Egleton Hereford 98 B2
Lower Elkstone Staffs 169 D9
Lower Ellastone Staffs 169 G10
Lower End Bucks 83 D11
Bucks 102 E4
C Beds 103 D8
C Beds 103 G9
Glos 81 E7
N Nhants 121 E7
Oxon 82 B4
W Nhants 120 F6
W Nhants 120 G5
Lower Everleigh Wilts 47 C7
Lower Eythorne Kent 55 D9
Lower Failand N Som 60 E4
Lower Faintree Shrops 132 F3
Lower Falkenham Suff 108 D5
Lower Farringdon Hants 49 F8
Lower Feltham London 66 E5
Lower Fittleworth W Sus 35 D8
Lowerford Lancs 204 F3
Lower Forge Shrops 132 F4
Lower Foxdale IoM 192 E3
Lower Frankton Shrops 149 C7
Lower Freystrop Pembs 73 C7
Lower Froyle Hants 49 E9
Lower Gabwell Devon 9 B8
Lower Gledfield Highld 309 K5
Lower Godney Som 44 E3
Lower Goldstone Kent 71 G9
Lower Gornal W Mid 133 E8
Lower Grange W Yorks 205 G8
Lower Gravenhurst
C Beds 104 D2
Lower Green Essex 88 E2
Essex 105 E8
Essex 106 E4
Lower Green *continued*
Gtr Man 184 B2
Herts 104 E3
Kent 52 E5
Kent 52 E6
Norf 159 B9
Staffs 133 B8
Suff 124 D4
Sur 66 F6
Warks 119 D10
W Berks 63 G11
Lower Grove Common
Hereford 97 F11
Lower Hacheston Suff 126 F6
Lower Halistra Highld 298 D2
Lower Halliford Sur 66 F5
Lower Halstock Leigh
Dorset 29 F8
Lower Halstow Kent 69 F11
Lower Hamswell S Glos 61 E8
Lower Hamworthy BCP 18 C6
Lower Hardres Kent 55 C7
Lower Hardwick
Hereford 115 F8
Lower Harpton Powys 114 E5
Lower Hartlip Kent 69 G10
Lower Hartshay Derbys 170 E5
Lower Hartwell Bucks 84 C3
Lower Hatton Staffs 150 B6
Lower Hawthwaite
Cumb 210 B4
Lower Haysden Kent 52 D5
Lower Hayton Shrops 131 G10
Lower Hazel S Glos 60 B6
Lower Heath Ches E 168 C5
Lower Hempriggs
Moray 301 C11
Lower Heppington Kent 54 C6
Lower Hergest Hereford 114 F5
Lower Herne Kent 71 F7
Lower Heyford Oxon 101 G9
Lower Heysham Lancs 211 G8
Lower Higham Kent 69 E8
Lower Highmoor Oxon 65 B8
Lower Holbrook Suff 108 E3
Lower Holditch Dorset 28 G4
Lower Holloway London 67 B10
Lower Holwell Dorset 31 E9
Lower Hook Worcs 98 C6
Lower Hookner Devon 13 E10
Lower Hopton Shrops 149 E7
W Yorks 197 D7
Lower Hordley Shrops 149 D7
Lower Horncroft W Sus 35 D8
Lower Horsebridge
E Sus 23 C9
Lowerhouse Ches E 184 F6
Lancs 204 G2
Lower House Halton 183 D8
Lower Houses W Yorks 197 D7
Lower Howsell Worcs 98 B5
Lower Illey Worcs 133 G9
Lower Island Kent 70 F6
Lower Kersal Gtr Man 195 G10
Lower Kilburn Derbys 170 F5
Lower Kilcott Glos 61 B9
Lower Killeyan Argyll 254 C3
Lower Kingcombe Dorset 17 B7
Lower Kingswood Sur 51 C8
Lower Kinnerton
Ches W 166 C4
Lower Kinsham
Hereford 115 E7
Lower Knapp Som 28 B4
Lower Knightley Staffs 150 E6
Lower Knowle Bristol 60 E5
Lower Langford N Som 60 G3
Lower Largo Fife 287 G8
Lower Layham Suff 107 C10
Lower Ledwyche
Shrops 115 C10
Lower Leigh Staffs 151 B10
Lower Lemington Glos 100 E4
Lower Lenie Highld 300 G5
Lower Lode Glos 99 E7
Lower Lovacott Devon 25 B8
Lower Loxhore Devon 40 F6
Lower Lydbrook Glos 79 B9
Lower Lye Hereford 115 D8
Lower Machen Newport 59 B8
Lower Maes-coed
Hereford 96 E6
Lower Mains Clack 279 B9
Lower Mannington
Dorset 31 F9
Lower Marsh Som 30 C2
Lower Marston Som 45 E9
Lower Meend Glos 79 E9
Lower Menadue Corn 5 D10
Lower Merridge Som 43 G8
Lower Mickletown
W Yorks 198 B2
Lower Middleton Cheney
W Nhants 101 C10
Lower Midway Derbys 152 E6
Lower Mill Corn 3 B10
Lower Milovaig Highld 296 F7
Lower Milton Som 44 D4
Lower Moor Wilts 81 G8
Worcs 99 B9
Lower Morton S Glos 79 G10
Lower Mountain Flint 166 D4
Lower Nazeing Essex 86 D5
Lower Netchwood
Shrops 132 E2
Lower Netherton Devon 14 G3
Lower New Inn Torf 78 F4
Lower Ninnes Corn 1 C5
Lower Nobut Staffs 151 C10
Lower North Dean Bucks 84 F5
Lower Norton Warks 118 E4
Lower Nyland Dorset 30 C2
Lower Ochrwyth Caerph 59 B8
Lower Odcombe Som 29 D8
Lower Oddington Glos 100 F4
Lower Ollach Highld 295 B7
Lower Padworth W Berks 64 F6
Lower Penarth V Glam 59 F7
Lower Penn Staffs 133 D7
Lower Pennington Hants 20 C2
Lower Penwortham
Lancs 194 B4
Lower Peover Ches W 184 G2
Lower Pexhill Ches E 184 G5
Lower Pilsley Derbys 170 C6
Lower Pitkerrie Highld 311 L2
Lower Place Gtr Man 196 E2
London 67 C8
Lower Pollicot Bucks 84 C2
Lower Porthkerry V Glam 58 F5
Lower Porthpean Corn 5 E10
Lower Quinton Warks 100 B3
Lower Rabber Hereford 114 G5
Lower Race Torf 78 E3
Lower Radley Oxon 83 F8
Lower Rainham Medway 69 F10
Lower Ratley Hants 32 C4
Lower Raydon Suff 107 D10
Lower Rea Glos 80 B4

Lower Ridge Devon 28 G2
Shrops 148 C6
Lower Roadwater Som 42 F4
Lower Rochford Worcs 116 D2
Lower Rose Corn 4 E5
Lower Row Dorset 31 G8
Lower Sapey Worcs 116 E3
Lower Seagry Wilts 62 C3
Lower Sheering Essex 87 C7
Lower Shelton C Beds 103 C9
Lower Shiplake Oxon 65 D9
Lower Shuckburgh Warks 119 E9
Lower Sketty Swansea 56 C6
Lower Slackstead Hants 32 B5
Lower Slade Devon 40 D4
Lower Slaughter Glos 100 G3
Lower Solva Pembs 87 G11
Lower Soothill W Yorks 197 C9
Lower Soudley Glos 79 D11
Lower Southfield Hereford 98 C3
Lower Stanton St Quintin Wilts 62 C2
Lower Stoke Medway 69 D10
W Mid 119 B7
Lower Stondon C Beds 104 D3
Lower Stone Glos 79 G11
Lower Stonnall Staffs 133 C11
Lower Stow Bedon Norf 141 E9
Lower Stratton Som 28 D6
Swindon 63 B7
Lower Street E Sus 38 E2
Norf 160 B5
Norf 160 C3
Norf 160 F6
Suff 108 E3
Suff 124 G5
Lower Strensham Worcs 99 C8
Lower Stretton Warr 183 E10
Lower Studley Wilts 45 B11
Lower Sundon C Beds 103 F10
Lower Swainswick Bath 61 F9
Lower Swanwick Hants 33 F7
Lower Swell Glos 100 F3
Lower Sydenham London 67 E11
Lower Tadmarton Oxon 101 D8
Lower Tale Devon 27 G9
Lower Tasburgh Norf 142 D3
Lower Tean Staffs 151 B10
Lower Thorpe W Nhants 101 B10
Lower Threapwood Wrex 166 G6
Lower Thurlton Norf 143 D8
Lower Thurnham Lancs 202 C5
Lower Thurvaston Derbys 152 B4
Lower Todding Hereford 115 B8
Lower Tote Highld 298 C5
Lowertown Corn 2 D5
Corn 5 C11
Devon 12 E5
Lower Town Devon 27 E8
Hereford 98 C2
Pembs 91 D9
Worcs 117 F7
W Yorks 204 G6
Lower Trebullett Corn 12 F2
Lower Tregunnon Corn 11 E10
Lower Treworrick Corn 6 B4
Lower Tuffley Glos 80 C4
Lower Turmer Hants 31 F10
Lower Twitchen Devon 24 D5
Lower Twydall Medway 69 F10
Lower Tysoe Warks 100 B6
Lower Upham Hants 33 D8
Lower Upnor Medway 69 E9
Lower Vexford Som 42 F6
Lower Wainhill Oxon 84 E3
Lower Walton Warr 183 D10
Lower Wanborough Swindon 63 C8
Lower Weacombe Som 42 E6
Lower Weald M Keynes 102 D5
Lower Wear Devon 14 D4
Lower Weare Som 44 C2
Lower Weedon W Nhants 120 F2
Lower Welson Hereford 114 G5
Lower Westholme Som 44 E5
Lower Westhouse N Yorks 212 E3
Lower Westmancote Worcs 99 D8
Lower Weston Bath 61 F8
Lower Whatcombe Dorset 30 G4
Lower Whatley Som 45 D8
Lower Whitley Ches W 183 F10
Lower Wick Glos 80 F2
Worcs 116 G6
Lower Wield Hants 48 E6
Lower Willingdon E Sus 23 E9
Lower Winchendon or Nether Winchendon Bucks 84 C2
Lower Withington Ches E 168 B4
Lower Wolverton Worcs 117 G8
Lower Woodend Aberds 293 B8
Bucks 65 B10
Lower Woodford Wilts 46 G6
Lower Woodley Corn 5 B10
Lower Woodside Herts 86 D2
Lower Woolston Som 29 B11
Lower Woon Corn 5 C10
Lower Wraxall Dorset 29 G9
Som 44 F6
Wilts 61 G10
Lower Wych Ches W 167 G7
Lower Wyche Worcs 98 C5
Lower Wyke W Yorks 197 B7
Lower Yelland Devon 40 G3
Lower Zeals Wilts 45 G9
Lowes Barn Durham 233 C11
Lowesby Leics 136 B4
Lowestoft Suff 143 E10
Loweswater Cumb 229 G8
Low Etherley Durham 233 F9
Low Fell T&W 243 F7
Lowfield S Yorks 186 D5
Lowfield Heath W Sus 51 E9
Low Fold W Yorks 205 F10
Lowford Hants 33 E7
Low Fulney Lincs 156 E5
Low Garth N Yorks 226 D4
Low Gate Northumb 241 E10
N Yorks 214 F5
Low Geltbridge Cumb 240 F2
Lowgill Cumb 222 F2
Lancs 212 G3
Low Grantley N Yorks 214 E4
Low Green N Yorks 205 B10
Suff 125 E7
W Yorks 205 F10
Low Greenside T&W 242 E4
Low Habberley Worcs 116 B6
Low Ham Som 28 B6
Low Hauxley Northumb 253 C7
Low Hawsker N Yorks 227 D8
Low Hesket Cumb 230 B5
Low Hesleyhurst Northumb 252 D3
Low Hill W Mid 133 C8
Low Hutton N Yorks 216 F5
Lowick Cumb 210 B5
N Nhants 137 G9
Northumb 264 B2
Lowick Bridge Cumb 210 B5
Lowick Green Cumb 210 B5
Low Knipe Cumb 230 G6
Low Laithe N Yorks 214 G3
Low Laithes S Yorks 197 G11
Lowlands Torf 78 F3
Low Leighton Derbys 185 D8
Low Lorton Cumb 229 F9
Low Marishes N Yorks 216 D6
Low Marnham Notts 172 B4
Low Mill N Yorks 226 F3
Low Moor Lancs 203 E10
W Yorks 197 B7
Lowmoor Row Cumb 231 F8
Low Moorsley T&W 234 B2
Low Moresby Cumb 228 G5
Lowna N Yorks 226 G3
Low Newton Cumb 211 C8
Low Newton-by-the-Sea Northumb 264 E6
Lownie Moor Angus 287 C8
Lowood Borders 262 B2
Low Prudhoe Northumb 242 E4
Low Risby N Lincs 200 E2
Low Row Cumb 229 C9
Cumb 240 E3
N Yorks 223 F9
Low Salchrie Dumfries 236 C2
Low Smerby Argyll 255 E8
Low Snaygill N Yorks 204 D5
Lowsonford Warks 118 D3
Low Street Norf 141 B10
Thurrock 69 D7
Low Tharston Norf 142 D3
Lowther Cumb 230 G6
Lowthertown Dumfries 238 D6
Lowtherville IoW 21 F7
Low Thornley T&W 242 E5
Lowthorpe E Yorks 217 G11
Lowton Gtr Man 183 B10
Som 27 D11
Lowton Common Gtr Man 183 B10
Lowton Heath Gtr Man 183 B10
Lowton St Mary's Gtr Man 183 B10
Low Torry Fife 279 D10
Low Town Shrops 132 E4
Low Toynton Lincs 190 G3
Low Valley S Yorks 198 G2
Low Valleyfield Fife 279 D10
Low Walton Cumb 219 C9
Low Waters S Lanark 268 E4
Low Westwood Durham 242 F4
Low Whinnow Cumb 239 G8
Low Whita N Yorks 223 F10
Low Wood Cumb 210 C6
Low Worsall N Yorks 225 C7
Low Wray Cumb 221 E7
Loxbeare Devon 26 D6
Loxford London 68 B2
Loxhill Sur 50 F4
Loxhore Devon 40 F6
Loxhore Cott Devon 40 F6
Loxley S Yorks 186 D4
Warks 118 G5
Loxley Green Staffs 151 C11
Loxter Hereford 98 C4
Loxton N Som 43 B11
Loxwood W Sus 50 G4
Loyter's Green Essex 87 C8
Loyterton Kent 70 G3
Lozells W Mid 133 F11
Lubachlaggan Highld 300 B3
Lubachoinnich Highld 309 K4
Lubberland Shrops 116 B2
Lubcroy Highld 309 J3
Lubenham Leics 136 F4
Lubinvullin Highld 308 C5
Lucas End Herts 86 E4
Lucas Green Lancs 194 C5
Sur 50 B2
Luccombe Som 42 E2
Luccombe Village IoW 21 F7
Lucker Northumb 264 C5
Luckett Corn 12 G3
Lucking Street Essex 106 E6
Luckington Wilts 61 C10
Lucklawhill Fife 287 E8
Luckwell Bridge Som 42 F2
Lucton Hereford 115 E8
Ludag W Isles 297 K3
Ludborough Lincs 190 B3
Ludbrook Devon 8 E3
Ludchurch Pembs 73 C10
Luddenden W Yorks 196 B4
Luddenden Foot W Yorks 196 C4
Ludderburn Cumb 221 G8
Luddesdown Kent 69 F7
Luddington N Lincs 199 D10
Warks 118 G3
Luddington in the Brook N Nhants 138 G2
Lude House Perth 291 G10
Ludford Lincs 190 D2
Shrops 115 C10
Ludgershall Bucks 83 B11
Wilts 47 C9
Ludgvan Corn 2 C2
Ludham Norf 161 F7
Ludlow Shrops 115 C10
Ludney Lincs 190 B5
Som 28 E5
Ludstock Hereford 98 D3
Ludstone Shrops 132 E6
Ludwell Wilts 30 C6
Ludworth Durham 234 C3
Luffenhall Herts 104 F5
Luffincott Devon 12 C2
Lufton Som 29 D8
Lugar E Ayrs 258 E3
Lugate Borders 271 G8
Luggate Burn E Loth 282 G2
Lugg Green Hereford 115 E9
Luggiebank N Lanark 278 G5
Lugsdale Halton 183 D8
Lugton E Ayrs 267 E8
Lugwardine Hereford 97 C11
Luib Highld 295 C7
Luibeilt Highld 290 G4
Lulham Hereford 97 C8
Lullenden Sur 52 E2
Lullington Derbys 152 G5
Som 45 C9
Lulsgate Bottom N Som 60 F4
Lulsley Worcs 116 F4
Lulworth Camp Dorset 18 E2
Lumb Lancs 195 C10
Lancs 195 D9
Lumb *continued*
W Yorks 196 C4
W Yorks 197 E7
Lumb Foot W Yorks 204 F6
Lumburn Devon 12 G5
Lumbutts W Yorks 196 C3
Lumby N Yorks 206 G5
Lumley W Sus 22 B3
Lumley Thicks Durham 243 G8
Lumloch E Dunb 268 B2
Lumphanan Aberds 293 C7
Lumphinnans Fife 280 C3
Lumsdaine Borders 273 B7
Lumsden Aberds 302 G4
Lunan Angus 287 B10
Lunanhead Angus 287 B8
Luncarty Perth 286 E4
Lund E Yorks 208 D5
N Yorks 207 G9
Shetland 312 C7
Lundal W Isles 304 E3
Lundavra Highld 290 G2
Lunderton Aberds 303 E11
Lundie Angus 286 D6
Highld 290 B3
Lundin Links Fife 287 G8
Lundwood S Yorks 197 F11
Lundy Green Norf 142 E4
Lunga Argyll 275 C8
Lunna Shetland 312 G6
Lunning Shetland 312 G7
Lunnister Shetland 312 F5
Lunnon Swansea 56 D4
Lunsford Kent 53 B7
Lunsford's Cross E Sus 38 E2
Lunt Mers 193 G10
Luntley Hereford 115 F7
Lunts Heath Halton 183 D8
Lupin Staffs 152 F2
Luppitt Devon 27 F11
Lupridge Devon 8 E4
Lupset W Yorks 197 D10
Lupton Cumb 211 C11
Lurg Aberds 293 C8
Lurgashall W Sus 34 B6
Lurignich Argyll 289 D11
Lurley Devon 26 E6
Lusby Lincs 174 B4
Lushcott Shrops 131 D11
Luson Devon 8 F2
Luss Argyll 277 C7
Lussagiven Argyll 275 E7
Lusta Highld 298 D2
Lustleigh Devon 13 E11
Lustleigh Cleave Devon 13 E11
Luston Hereford 115 E9
Lusty Som 45 G7
Luthermuir Aberds 293 G8
Luthrie Fife 287 F7
Lutley W Mid 133 G8
Luton Devon 14 F4
Devon 27 G9
Luton 103 G11
Medway 69 F9
Lutsford Devon 24 D3
Lutterworth Leics 135 G10
Lutton Devon 7 D11
Devon 8 C3
Lincs 157 D8
N Nhants 138 F2
Lutton Gowts Lincs 157 E8
Lutworthy Devon 26 D3
Luxborough Som 42 F3
Luxley Glos 98 G3
Luxted London 68 G2
Luxton Devon 28 E2
Luxulyan Corn 5 D11
Luzley Gtr Man 196 G3
Luzley Brook Gtr Man 196 F2
Lyatts Som 29 E8
Lybster Highld 310 F6
Lydbury North Shrops 131 F7
Lydcott Devon 41 F7
Lydd Kent 39 C8
Lydden Kent 55 D9
Kent 71 F11
Lyddington Rutland 137 D7
Lydd on Sea Kent 39 C9
Lyde Orkney 314 E3
Shrops 130 C6
Lydeard St Lawrence Som 42 G6
Lyde Cross Hereford 97 C10
Lyde Green Hants 49 B8
S Glos 61 D7
Lydford Devon 12 E6
Lydford Fair Place Som 44 G5
Lydford-on-Fosse Som 44 G5
Lydgate Derbys 186 F4
Gtr Man 196 G3
W Yorks 196 B2
Lydham Shrops 130 E6
Lydiard Green Wilts 62 B5
Lydiard Millicent Wilts 62 B5
Lydiard Plain Wilts 62 B5
Lydiard Tregoze Swindon 62 C6
Lydiate Mers 193 G11
Lydiate Ash Worcs 117 B9
Lydlinch Dorset 30 E2
Lydmarsh Som 28 F5
Lydney Glos 79 E10
Lydstep Pembs 73 F9
Lye W Mid 133 G8
Lye Cross N Som 60 G3
Lye Green Bucks 85 E7
E Sus 52 G4
Warks 118 D3
Wilts 45 B10
Lye Head Worcs 116 C5
Lye Hole N Som 60 G4
Lyewood Common E Sus 52 F4
Lyford Oxon 82 G5
Lymbridge Green Kent 54 E6
Lyme Green Ches E 184 G6
Lyme Regis Dorset 16 C2
Lymiecleuch Borders 249 C9
Lyminge Kent 55 E7
Lymington Hants 20 B2
Lyminster W Sus 35 G8
Lymm Warr 183 D11
Lymore Hants 19 C11
Lympne Kent 54 F6
Lympsham Som 43 C10
Lympstone Devon 14 E5
Lynbridge Devon 41 D8
Lynch Hants 48 D4
Som 42 D2
Lynchat Highld 291 C9
Lynchgate Shrops 131 F7
Lynch Hill Hants 48 D3
Slough 66 C2
Lyndale Ho Highld 298 D3
Lyndhurst Hants 32 F4
Lyndon Rutland 137 C8
Lyndon Green W Mid 134 F2
Lyne Borders 270 G4
Sur 66 F4
Lyneal Shrops 149 C8
Lyneal Mill Shrops 149 C9
Lyneal Wood Shrops 149 C9
Lyne Down Hereford 98 E2
Lyneham Oxon 100 G5
Wilts 62 D4
Lynemore Highld 301 G10
Lynemouth Northumb 253 E7
Lyne of Gorthleck Highld 300 G5
Lyne of Skene Aberds 293 B9
Lyness Orkney 314 G3
Lyne Station Borders 260 B6
Lynford Norf 140 E6
Lyng Norf 159 F11
Som 28 B4
Lyngate Norf 160 C5
Lyngford Som 28 B2
Lynmore Highld 301 F10
Lynmouth Devon 41 D8
Lynn Staffs 133 C11
Telford 150 F5
Lynnwood Borders 261 G11
Lynsore Bottom Kent 55 D7
Lynsted Kent 70 G2
Lynstone Corn 24 F2
Lynton Devon 41 D8
Lynwilg Highld 291 B10
Lynworth Glos 99 G9
Lyons T&W 234 B3
Lyon's Gate Dorset 29 F11
Lyon's Green Norf 159 G8
Lyonshall Hereford 114 F6
Lyons Hall Essex 88 B2
Lypiatt Glos 80 D6
Lyrabus Argyll 274 G3
Lytchett Matravers Dorset 18 B4
Lytchett Minster Dorset 18 C5
Lyth Highld 310 C6
Lytham Lancs 193 B11
Lytham St Anne's Lancs 193 B10
Lythbank Shrops 131 B9
Lythe N Yorks 226 C6
Lythes Orkney 314 H4
Lythmore Highld 310 C4

M

Maam Argyll 284 F5
Mabe Burnthouse Corn 3 C7
Mabie Dumfries 237 B11
Mabledon Kent 52 E5
Mablethorpe Lincs 191 D8
Macclesfield Ches E 184 G6
Macclesfield Forest Ches E 185 G7
Macduff Aberds 303 C7
Mace Green Suff 108 C2
Machan S Lanark 268 E5
Macharioch Argyll 255 G8
Machen Caerph 59 B8
Machrie N Ayrs 255 D9
Machrie Hotel Argyll 254 C4
Machrihanish Argyll 255 E7
Machroes Gwyn 144 D6
Machynlleth Powys 128 C4
Machynys Carms 56 B4
Mackerel's Common W Sus 35 B8
Mackerye End Herts 85 B11
Mackham Devon 27 F11
Mackney Oxon 64 B5
Mackside Borders 262 G4
Mackworth Derbys 152 B6
Macmerry E Loth 281 G8
Madderty Perth 286 E3
Maddington Wilts 46 E5
Maddiston Falk 279 F8
Maddox Moor Pembs 73 C7
Madehurst W Sus 35 E7
Madeley Staffs 168 G3
Telford 132 C3
Madeley Heath Staffs 168 F3
Worcs 117 B9
Madeley Park Staffs 168 G3
Madeleywood Telford 132 C3
Maders Corn 12 G2
Madford Devon 27 E10
Madingley Cambs 123 E7
Madjeston Dorset 30 B4
Madley Hereford 97 D8
Madresfield Worcs 98 B6
Madron Corn 1 C5
Maenaddwyn Anglesey 179 E7
Maenclochog Pembs 91 F11
Maendy V Glam 58 D4
Maenporth Corn 3 D7
Maentwrog Gwyn 163 G11
Maen-y-groes Ceredig 111 F7
Maer Corn 24 F2
Staffs 150 B5
Maerdy Carms 94 G2
Conwy 165 G8
Rhondda 77 F7
Maes-bangor Ceredig 128 G3
Maesbrook Shrops 148 E5
Maesbury Shrops 148 D6
Maesbury Marsh Shrops 148 D6
Maesgeirchen Gwyn 179 G9
Maes-glas Newport 59 B9
Maes Glas = *Greenfield* Flint 181 F11
Maesgwyn-Isaf Powys 148 G3
Maeshafn Denb 166 C2
Maesllyn Ceredig 93 C7
Maes llyn Ceredig 93 C7
Maesmynis Powys 95 B10
Maes Pennant Flint 181 F11
Maesteg Bridgend 57 C10
Maes-Treylow Powys 114 D5
Maesybont Carms 75 B9
Maesycoed Rhondda 58 B5
Maesycrugiau Carms 93 C9
Maesycwmmer Caerph 77 G11
Maes-y-dre Flint 166 C2
Maesygwartha Mon 78 C2
Maesymeillion Ceredig 93 B8
Maesypandy Powys 129 D9
Maesyrhandir Powys 129 E11
Magdalen Laver Essex 87 D8
Maggieknockater Moray 302 E3
Maggots End Essex 105 F9
Magham Down E Sus 23 C10
Maghull Mers 193 G11
Magor Mon 60 B2
Magpie Green Suff 125 B11
Mahaar Dumfries 236 B2
Maida Vale London 67 C9
Maidenbower W Sus 51 F9
Maiden Bradley Wilts 45 F10
Maidencombe Torbay 9 B8
Maidenhall Suff 108 C3
Maidenhead Windsor 65 C11
Maiden Head N Som 60 F5
Maidenhead Court Windsor 66 C2
Maiden Law Durham 233 B9
Maiden Newton Dorset 17 B7
Maidenpark Falk 279 E9
Maidens S Ayrs 244 B6
Maidensgrave Suff 108 B5
Maiden's Green Brack 65 E11
Maidensgrove Oxon 65 B8
Maiden's Hall Northumb 252 D6
Maidenwell Corn 11 G8
Lincs 190 F4
Maiden Wells Pembs 73 F7
Maidford W Nhants 120 G2
Maids Moreton Bucks 102 D4
Maidstone Kent 53 B9
Maidwell W Nhants 120 B4
Mail Shetland 313 L6
Mailand Shetland 312 C8
Mailingsland Borders 270 G4
Main Powys 148 F3
Maindee Newport 59 B10
Maindy Cardiff 59 D7
Mainholm S Ayrs 257 E9
Mains Cumb 229 G7
Mainsforth Durham 234 E2
Mains of Airies Dumfries 236 C1
Mains of Allardice Aberds 293 F10
Mains of Annochie Aberds 303 E9
Mains of Ardestie Angus 287 D9
Mains of Arnage Aberds 303 F9
Mains of Auchoynanie Moray 302 E4
Mains of Baldoon Dumfries 236 D6
Mains of Balhall Angus 293 G7
Mains of Ballindarg Angus 287 B8
Mains of Balnakettle Aberds 293 F8
Mains of Birness Aberds 303 F9
Mains of Blackhall Aberds 303 G7
Mains of Burgie Moray 301 D10
Mains of Cairnbrogie Aberds 303 G8
Mains of Cairnty Moray 302 D3
Mains of Clunas Highld 301 E8
Mains of Crichie Aberds 303 E9
Mains of Daltulich Highld 301 E7
Mains of Dalvey Highld 301 F11
Mains of Dellavaird Aberds 293 E9
Mains of Drum Aberds 293 D10
Mains of Edingight Moray 302 D5
Mains of Fedderate Aberds 303 E8
Mains of Flichity Highld 300 G6
Mains of Hatton Aberds 303 D9
Aberds 303 E7
Mains of Inkhorn Aberds 303 F9
Mains of Innerpeffray Perth 286 F3
Mains of Kirktonhill Aberds 293 G8
Mains of Laithers Aberds 302 E6
Mains of Mayen Moray 302 E5
Mains of Melgund Angus 287 B9
Mains of Taymouth Perth 285 C11
Mains of Thornton Aberds 293 F8
Mains of Towie Aberds 303 E7
Mains of Ulbster Highld 310 E7
Mains of Watten Highld 310 D6
Mainsriddle Dumfries 237 D11
Mainstone Shrops 130 F5
Maisemore Glos 98 G6
Maitland Park London 67 C9
Major's Green W Mid 118 B2
Makeney Derbys 170 G5
Malacleit W Isles 296 D3
Malborough Devon 9 G9
Malcoff Derbys 185 E9
Malden Rushett London 67 G7
Maldon Essex 88 D4
Malehurst Shrops 131 B7
Malham N Yorks 213 G8
Maligar Highld 298 C4
Malinbridge S Yorks 186 D4
Malinslee Telford 132 B3
Malkin's Bank Ches E 168 D3
Mallaig Highld 295 F8
Mallaig Bheag Highld 295 F8
Malleny Mills Edin 270 B3
Malling Stirling 285 G9
Mallows Green Essex 105 F9
Malltraeth Anglesey 162 B6
Mallwyd Gwyn 147 G7
Malmesbury Wilts 62 B2
Malmsmead Devon 41 D9
Malpas Ches W 167 F7
Corn 4 G6
Newport 78 G4
W Berks 64 E6
Malswick Glos 98 F4
Maltby Lincs 190 E4
Stockton 225 C9
S Yorks 187 C8
Maltby le Marsh Lincs 191 E7
Malting End Suff 124 G4
Malting Green Essex 107 G9
Maltings Angus 293 G9
Maltman's Hill Kent 54 E2
Malton N Yorks 216 E5
Malvern Common Worcs 98 C5
Malvern Link Worcs 98 B5
Malvern Wells Worcs 98 C5
Mambeg Argyll 276 D4
Mamble Worcs 116 C3
Mamhilad Mon 78 E4
Manaccan Corn 3 E7
Manadon Plym 7 D9
Manafon Powys 130 C2
Manais W Isles 296 C7
Manar Ho Aberds 303 G7
Manaton Devon 13 E11
Manby Lincs 190 D5
Mancetter Warks 134 D6
Manchester Gtr Man 184 B4
Manchester Airport Gtr Man 184 D4
Mancot Flint 166 B4
Mancot Royal Flint 166 B4
Mandally Highld 290 C4
Manea Cambs 139 F9
Maney W Mid 134 D2
Manfield N Yorks 224 C4
Mangaster Shetland 312 F5
Mangotsfield S Glos 61 D7
Mangrove Green Herts 104 G2
Mangurstadh W Isles 304 E2
Manhay Corn 2 C5
Manian-fawr Pembs 92 B3
Mankinholes W Yorks 196 C3
Manley Ches W 183 G8
Devon 27 E7
Manley Common Ches W 183 G8
Manmoel Caerph 77 E11
Man-moel Caerph 77 E11
Mannal Argyll 288 E1
Mannamead Plym 7 D9
Mannerston W Loth 279 F10
Manningford Abbots Wilts 46 B6
Manningford Bohune Wilts 46 B6
Manningford Bruce Wilts 46 B6
Manningham W Yorks 205 G9
Mannings Heath W Sus 36 B2
Mannington Dorset 31 F9
Manningtree Essex 107 E11
Mannofield Aberdeen 293 C11
Manor London 68 B2
Manorbier Pembs 73 F9
Manorbier Newton Pembs 73 F8
Manor Bourne Devon 7 F9
Manordeilo Carms 94 F3
Manor Estate S Yorks 186 D5
Manorhill Borders 262 C5
Manor Hill Corner Lincs 157 F8
Manor House W Mid 135 G7
Manorowen Pembs 91 D8
Manor Park Bucks 84 C4
Ches W 167 B11
E Sus 37 C7
London 68 B2
Notts 153 C11
Slough 66 C3
S Yorks 186 D5
W Yorks 205 D9
Manor Parsley Corn 4 F4
Manor Royal W Sus 51 F9
Man's Cross Essex 106 D5
Mansegate Dumfries 247 G9
Manselfield Swansea 56 D5
Mansel Lacy Hereford 97 B8
Mansell Gamage Hereford 97 C7
Manselton Swansea 57 B7
Mansergh Cumb 212 C2
Mansewood Glasgow 267 C11
Mansfield E Ayrs 258 G4
Notts 171 C8
Mansfield Woodhouse Notts 171 C8
Manson Green Norf 141 C10
Mansriggs Cumb 210 C5
Manston Dorset 30 D4
Kent 71 F10
W Yorks 206 F3
Manswood Dorset 31 F7
Manthorpe Lincs 155 B8
Lincs 155 F11
Mantles Green Bucks 85 F7
Manton N Lincs 200 G2
Notts 187 F9
Rutland 137 C7
Wilts 63 F7
Manton Warren N Lincs 200 F2
Manuden Essex 105 F9
Manwood Green Essex 87 C8
Manywells Height W Yorks 205 F7
Maperton Som 29 B11
Maplebeck Notts 172 C2
Maple Cross Herts 85 G8
Mapledurham Oxon 65 D7
Mapledurwell Hants 49 C7
Maple End Essex 105 D11
Maplehurst W Sus 35 C11
Maplescombe Kent 68 G5
Mapleton Derbys 169 F11
Mapperley Derbys 170 G6
Nottingham 171 G9
Mapperley Park Nottingham 171 G9
Mapperton Dorset 16 B6
Dorset 18 B4
Mappleborough Green Warks 117 D11
Mappleton E Yorks 209 E10
Mapplewell S Yorks 197 F10
Mappowder Dorset 30 F2
Maraig W Isles 305 H3
Marazanvose Corn 4 E6
Marazion Corn 2 C2
Marbhig W Isles 305 G6
Marbrack Dumfries 246 E3
Marbury Ches E 167 F9
March Cambs 139 D8
S Lanark 259 G11
Marcham Oxon 83 F7
Marchamley Shrops 149 D11
Marchamley Wood Shrops 149 C11
Marchington Staffs 152 C2
Marchington Woodlands Staffs 152 D2
Marchroes Gwyn 144 D6
Marchwiel Wrex 166 F5
Marchwood Hants 32 E5
Marcross V Glam 58 F2
Marden Hereford 97 B10
Kent 53 E8
T&W 243 C9
Wilts 46 B5
Marden Ash Essex 87 E9
Marden Beech Kent 53 E8
Marden's Hill E Sus 52 G3
Marden Thorn Kent 53 E9
Mardleybury Herts 86 B3
Mardu Shrops 130 G5
Mardy Mon 78 B4
Shrops 148 C5
Marefield Leics 136 B4
Mareham le Fen Lincs 174 C3
Mareham on the Hill Lincs 174 B3
Marehay Derbys 170 F5
Marehill W Sus 35 D9
Maresfield E Sus 37 C7
Maresfield Park E Sus 37 C7
Marfleet Hull 200 B6
Marford Wrex 166 D5
Margam Neath 57 D9
Margaret Marsh Dorset 30 D4
Margaret Roding Essex 87 C9
Margaretting Essex 87 E11
Margaretting Tye Essex 87 E11
Margate Kent 71 E11
Margery Sur 51 C9
Margnaheglish N Ayrs 256 C2
Margreig Dumfries 237 B10
Margrove Park Redcar 226 B3
Marham Norf 158 G4
Marhamchurch Corn 24 G2
Marholm Pboro 138 C2
Marian Flint 181 F9
Marian Cwm Denb 181 F9
Mariandyrys Anglesey 179 E10
Marianglas Anglesey 179 E8
Marian-glas Anglesey 179 E8
Mariansleigh Devon 26 C2
Marian y de = *South Beach* Gwyn 145 C7
Marian y mor = *West End* Gwyn 145 C7
Marine Town Kent 70 E2
Marionburgh Aberds 293 C9
Marishader Highld 298 C4
Marjoriebanks Dumfries 248 G3
Mark Dumfries 236 D3
Dumfries 237 C7
S Ayrs 236 B2
Som 43 D11
Markbeech Kent 52 E3
Markby Lincs 191 F7
Mark Causeway Som 43 D11
Mark Cross E Sus 23 C7
E Sus 52 G5
Markeaton Derbys 152 B6
Market Bosworth Leics 135 C8
Market Deeping Lincs 138 B2
Market Drayton Shrops 150 C3
Market Harborough Leics 136 F4
Markethill Perth 286 D6
Market Lavington Wilts 46 C4
Market Overton Rutland 155 F7
Market Rasen Lincs 189 D10
Market Stainton Lincs 190 F2
Market Warsop Notts 171 B9
Market Weighton E Yorks 208 E3
Market Weston Suff 125 B9
Markfield Leics 153 G9
Mark Hall North Essex 87 C7
Mark Hall South Essex 87 C7
Markham Caerph 77 E11
Markham Moor Notts 188 G2
Markinch Fife 286 G6
Markington N Yorks 214 F5
Markland Hill Gtr Man 195 F7
Markle E Loth 281 F11
Marksbury Bath 61 G7
Mark's Corner IoW 20 C5
Marks Gate London 87 G7
Marks Tey Essex 107 G8
Markyate Herts 85 B9
Marland Gtr Man 195 E11
Marlas Hereford 97 F8
Marl Bank Worcs 98 C5
Marlborough Wilts 63 F7
Marlbrook Hereford 115 G10
Worcs 117 C9
Marlcliff Warks 117 G11
Marldon Devon 9 C7
Marle Green E Sus 23 B9
Marle Hill Glos 99 G9
Marlesford Suff 126 F6
Marley Kent 55 C7
Kent 55 C10
Marley Green Ches E 167 F9
Marley Heights W Sus 49 G11
Marley Hill T&W 242 F6
Marley Pots T&W 243 F9
Marlingford Norf 142 B2
Mar Lodge Aberds 292 D2
Marloes Pembs 72 D3
Marlow Bucks 65 B10
Hereford 115 B8
Marlow Bottom Bucks 65 B11
Marlow Common Bucks 65 B10
Marlpit Hill Kent 52 D2
Marlpits E Sus 38 E2
Marlpool Derbys 170 F6
Marnhull Dorset 30 D3
Marnoch Aberds 302 D5
Marnock N Lanark 268 B4
Marple Gtr Man 185 D7
Marple Bridge Gtr Man 185 D7
Marpleridge Gtr Man 185 D7
Marr S Yorks 198 F4
Marrel Highld 311 H4
Marr Green Wilts 63 G8
Marrick N Yorks 223 F11
Marrister Shetland 313 G7
Marros Carms 74 D2
Marsden T&W 243 E9
W Yorks 196 E4
Marsden Height Lancs 204 F3
Marsett N Yorks 213 B8
Marsh Bucks 84 D4
Devon 28 E3
W Yorks 196 D6
W Yorks 204 F6
Marshall Meadows Northumb 273 D9
Marshall's Cross Mers 183 C8
Marshall's Elm Som 44 G3
Marshall's Heath Herts 85 B11
Marshalsea Dorset 28 G5
Marshalswick Herts 85 D11
Marsham Norf 160 E3
Marshaw Lancs 203 C7
Marsh Baldon Oxon 83 F9
Marsh Benham W Berks 64 F2
Marshborough Kent 55 B10
Marshbrook Shrops 131 F8
Marshchapel Lincs 190 B5
Marsh Common S Glos 60 C5
Marsh End Worcs 98 D6
Marshfield Newport 59 C9
S Glos 61 E9
Marshfield Bank Ches E 167 D11
Marshgate Corn 11 C9
Marsh Gate W Berks 63 F10
Marsh Gibbon Bucks 102 G2
Marsh Green Ches W 183 F8
Devon 14 C6
Gtr Man 194 F5
Kent 52 E2
Staffs 168 D5
Telford 150 G2
Marsh Houses Lancs 202 C5
Marshland St James Norf 139 B10
Marsh Lane Derbys 186 F6
Glos 79 D9
Marsh Mills Som 43 F7
Marshmoor Herts 86 D2
Marshside Kent 71 F8
Mers 193 D11
Marsh Side Norf 176 E3
Marsh Street Som 42 E3
Marshwood Dorset 16 B3
Marske N Yorks 224 E2
Marske-by-the-Sea Redcar 235 G8
Marston Ches W 183 F11
Hereford 115 F7
Lincs 172 G5
Oxon 83 D8
Staffs 150 G6
Staffs 151 D8
Warks 119 B8
Warks 134 E4
Wilts 46 B3
Marston Bigot Som 45 E9
Marston Doles Warks 119 F9
Marston Gate Som 45 D9
Marston Green W Mid 134 F3
Marston Hill Glos 81 F10
Marston Jabbett Warks 135 F7
Marston Magna Som 29 C9
Marston Meysey Wilts 81 F10
Marston Montgomery Derbys 152 B2
Marston Moretaine C Beds 103 C9
Marston on Dove Derbys 152 D4
Marston St Lawrence W Nhants 101 C10
Marston Stannett Hereford 115 F11
Marston Trussell W Nhants 136 F3
Marstow Hereford 79 B9
Marsworth Bucks 84 C6
Marten Wilts 47 B9
Marthall Ches E 184 F4
Martham Norf 161 F9
Marthwaite Cumb 222 G2
Martin Hants 31 D9
Kent 55 D10
Lincs 173 D10
Lincs 174 B2
Martindale Cumb 221 B8
Martin Dales Lincs 173 C11
Martin Drove End Hants 31 C9
Martinhoe Devon 41 D7
Martinhoe Cross Devon 41 D7
Martin Hussingtree Worcs 117 E7
Martin Mill Kent 55 D10
Martin Moor Lincs 174 C2
Martinscroft Warr 183 D11
Martin's Moss Ches E 168 C4
Martinstown Dorset 17 D8
Martinstown or Winterbourne St Martin Dorset 17 D8
Martlesham Suff 108 B4
Martlesham Heath Suff 108 B4
Martletwy Pembs 73 C8
Martley Worcs 116 E5
Martock Som 29 D7
Marton Ches E 168 B5
Ches W 167 B10
Cumb 210 D4
E Yorks 209 F9
Lincs 188 E4
Mbro 225 B10
N Yorks 215 G8
N Yorks 216 C4
Shrops 130 C5
Shrops 149 E8
Warks 119 D8
Marton Green Ches W 167 B10
Marton Grove Mbro 225 B9
Marton-in-the-Forest N Yorks 215 F11
Marton-le-Moor N Yorks 215 E7
Marton Moor Warks 119 D8
Marton Moss Side Blackpool 202 G2
Martyr's Green Sur 50 B5
Martyr Worthy Hants 48 G4
Marwick Orkney 314 D2
Marwood Devon 40 F4
Marybank Highld 300 D4
Highld 301 B7
Maryburgh Highld 300 D5
Maryfield Aberds 293 D7
Corn 7 D8
Maryhill Glasgow 267 B11
Marykirk Aberds 293 G8
Maryland Mon 79 D8
Marylebone Gtr Man 194 F5
Marypark Moray 301 F11
Maryport Cumb 228 D6
Dumfries 236 F3
Mary Tavy Devon 12 F6
Maryton Angus 287 B7
Angus 287 B10
Marywell Aberds 293 D7
Aberds 293 D11
Angus 287 C10
Masbrough S Yorks 186 C6
Mascle Bridge Pembs 73 D7
Masham N Yorks 214 C4
Mashbury Essex 87 C11
Masongill N Yorks 212 D3
Masonhill S Ayrs 257 E9
Mastin Moor Derbys 187 F7
Mastrick Aberdeen 293 C10
Matchborough Worcs 117 D11
Matching Essex 87 C8
Matching Green Essex 87 C8
Matching Tye Essex 87 C8
Matfen Northumb 242 C2
Matfield Kent 53 E7
Mathern Mon 79 G8
Mathon Hereford 98 B4
Mathry Pembs 91 E7
Matlaske Norf 160 C3
Matley Gtr Man 185 B7
Matlock Derbys 170 C3
Matlock Bank Derbys 170 C3
Matlock Bath Derbys 170 D3
Matlock Bridge Derbys 170 D3
Matlock Cliff Derbys 170 D4
Matlock Dale Derbys 170 D3
Matshead Lancs 202 E6
Matson Glos 80 B4
Matterdale End Cumb 230 G3
Mattersey Notts 187 D11
Mattersey Thorpe Notts 187 D11
Matthewsgreen Wokingham 65 F10
Mattingley Hants 49 B8
Mattishall Norf 159 G11
Mattishall Burgh Norf 159 G11
Mauchline E Ayrs 257 D11
Maud Aberds 303 E9
Maudlin Corn 5 C11
Dorset 28 F5
W Sus 22 B5
Maudlin Cross Dorset 28 F5
Maugersbury Glos 100 F4
Maughold IoM 192 C5
Mauld Highld 300 F4
Maulden C Beds 103 D11
Maulds Meaburn Cumb 222 B2
Maunby N Yorks 215 B7
Maund Bryan Hereford 115 G11
Maundown Som 27 B9
Mauricewood Midloth 270 C4
Mautby Norf 161 G9
Mavesyn Ridware Staffs 151 F11
Mavis Enderby Lincs 174 B5
Maviston Highld 301 D9
Mawbray Cumb 229 B7
Mawdesley Lancs 194 E3
Mawdlam Bridgend 57 E10
Mawgan Corn 2 D6
Mawgan Porth Corn 5 B7
Maw Green Ches E 168 D2
Mawla Corn 4 F4
Mawnan Corn 3 D7
Mawnan Smith Corn 3 D7
Mawsley N Nhants 120 B6
Mawson Green S Yorks 198 D6
Mawthorpe Lincs 191 G7
Maxey Pboro 138 B2
Maxstoke Warks 134 F4
Maxted Street Kent 54 E6

Maxton Borders 262 C4
Kent 55 E10
Maxwellheugh Borders 262 C6
Maxwelltown Dumfries 237 B11
Maxworthy Corn 11 C11
Mayals Swansea 56 C6
May Bank Staffs 168 F5
Maybole S Ayrs 257 G8
Maybury Sur 50 B4
Maybush Soton 32 E5
Mayer's Green W Mid 133 E10
Mayes Green Sur 50 F6
Mayeston Pembs 73 E8
Mayfair London 67 C9
Mayfield E Sus 37 B9
Midloth 271 C7
Northumb 243 B7
Staffs 169 F11
W Loth 269 B8
Mayford Sur 50 B3
Mayhill Swansea 56 C6
May Hill Mon 79 C8
May Hill Village Glos 98 G4
Mayland Essex 88 E6
Maylandsea Essex 88 E6
Maynard's Green E Sus 23 B9
Mayne Ho Moray 302 C2
Mayon Corn 1 D3
Maypole Kent 68 E4
Kent 71 G7
London 68 G3
Mon 79 B7
Scilly 1 G4
Maypole Green Essex 107 G9
Norf 143 D8
Suff 125 F8
Suff 126 D5
Mays Green Oxon 65 C8
May's Green N Som 59 G11
Sur 50 B5
Mayshill S Glos 61 C7
Maythorn S Yorks 197 F7
Maythorne Notts 171 D11
Maywick Shetland 313 L5
Mead Devon 13 G11
Devon 24 D2
Mead End Hants 19 B11
Hants 33 E11
Wilts 31 C8
Meadgate Bath 45 B7
Meadle Bucks 84 D4
Meadowbank Ches W 167 B11
Edin 280 G5
Meadowend Essex 106 C4
Meadowfield Durham 233 D10
Meadowfoot N Ayrs 266 F4
Meadow Green Hereford 116 F4
Meadow Hall S Yorks 186 C5
Meadow Head S Yorks 186 E4
Meadowley Shrops 132 E3
Meadowmill E Loth 281 G8
Meadows Nottingham 153 B11
Meadowtown Shrops 130 C6
Meads E Sus 23 F10
Meadside Oxon 83 G9
Mead Vale Sur 51 D9
Meadwell Devon 12 E4
Meaford Staffs 151 B7
Meagill N Yorks 205 B9
Mealabost W Isles 304 E6
Mealabost Bhuirgh
W Isles 304 C6
Mealasta W Isles 304 F1
Meal Bank Cumb 221 F10
Meal Hill W Yorks 197 F7
Mealrigg Cumb 229 B8
Mealsgate Cumb 229 C10
Meanwood W Yorks 205 F11
Mearbeck N Yorks 212 G6
Meare Som 44 E3
Meare Green Som 28 B4
Som 28 C3
Mearns Bath 45 B7
E Renf 267 D10
Mears Ashby N Nhants 120 D6
Measborough Dike
S Yorks 197 F11
Measham Leics 152 G6
Meath Green Sur 51 E9
Meathop Cumb 211 C8
Meaux E Yorks 209 F7
Meaver Corn 2 F5
Meavy Devon 7 B10
Medbourne Leics 136 E5
M Keynes 102 D6
Medburn Northumb 242 C4
Meddon Devon 24 D3
Meden Vale Notts 171 B9
Medhurst Row Kent 52 D3
Medlam Lincs 174 D4
Medlar Lancs 202 F4
Medlicott Shrops 131 E8
Medlyn Corn 2 C6
Medmenham Bucks 65 C10
Medomsley Durham 242 G4
Medstead Hants 49 F7
Meerbrook Staffs 169 C7
Meer Common Hereford 115 G7
Meer End W Mid 118 C4
Meerhay Dorset 29 G7
Meers Bridge Lincs 191 D7
Meersbrook S Yorks 186 E5
Meesden Herts 105 E8
Meeson Telford 150 E3
Meeson Heath Telford 150 E3
Meeth Devon 25 F8
Meethe Devon 25 C11
Meeting Green Suff 124 F4
Meeting House Hill
Norf 160 D6
Meggernie Castle Perth 285 C9
Meggethead Borders 260 E5
Meidrim Carms 92 G5
Meifod Denb 165 D8
Powys 148 G3
Meigle N Ayrs 266 B3
Perth 286 C6
Meikle Earnock
S Lanark 268 E4
Meikle Ferry Highld 309 L7
Meikle Forter Angus 292 G3
Meikle Gluich Highld 309 L6
Meikle Obney Perth 286 D4
Meikleour Perth 286 D5
Meikle Pinkerton
E Loth 282 F4
Meikle Strath Aberds 293 F8
Meikle Tarty Aberds 303 G9
Meikle Wartle Aberds 303 F7
Meinciau Carms 75 C7
Meir Stoke 168 G6
Meir Heath Staffs 168 G6
Melbourn Cambs 105 C7
Melbourne Derbys 153 D7
E Yorks 207 E11
S Lanark 269 G11
Melbury Abbas Dorset 30 D5
Melbury Bubb Dorset 29 F9
Melbury Osmond Dorset 29 F9
Melbury Sampford
Dorset 29 F9
Melby Shetland 313 H3
Melchbourne Bedford 121 D10
Melcombe Som 43 G9
Melcombe Bingham
Dorset 30 G3
Melcombe Regis Dorset 17 E9
Meldon Devon 13 C7
Northumb 252 G4
Meldreth Cambs 105 B7
Meldrum Ho Aberds 303 G8
Melfort Argyll 275 B9
Melgarve Highld 290 D6
Meliden *= Gallt Melyd*
Denb 181 E9
Melinbyrhedyn Powys 128 D6
Melin Caiach Caerph 77 F10
Melincourt Neath 76 E4
Melincryddan Neath 57 B8
Melinsey Corn 3 B10
Melin-y-coed Conwy 164 C4
Melin-y-ddôl Powys 129 B11
Melin-y-grug Powys 129 B11
Melin-y-Wig Denb 165 F8
Melkington Northumb 273 G7
Melkinthorpe Cumb 231 F7
Melkridge Northumb 240 E6
Melksham Wilts 62 G2
Melksham Forest Wilts 62 G2
Mellangaun Highld 307 L3
Mellangoose Corn 2 D5
Melldalloch Argyll 275 F10
Mell Green W Berks 64 D3
Mellguards Cumb 230 B4
Melling Lancs 211 E11
Mers 193 G11
Mellingey Corn 10 G4
Melling Mount Mers 194 G2
Mellis Suff 126 C2
Mellis Green Suff 125 C11
Mellon Charles Highld 307 K3
Mellon Udrigle Highld 307 K3
Mellor Gtr Man 185 D7
Lancs 203 G9
Mellor Brook Lancs 203 G8
Mells Som 45 D8
Suff 127 B8
Mells Green Som 45 D8
Melmerby Cumb 231 D8
N Yorks 213 B11
N Yorks 214 D6
Melon Green Suff 124 F6
Melplash Dorset 16 B5
Melrose Borders 262 C2
Melsetter Orkney 314 H2
Melsonby N Yorks 224 D3
Meltham W Yorks 196 E6
Meltham Mills W Yorks 196 E6
Melton E Yorks 200 B3
Suff 126 G5
Meltonby E Yorks 207 C11
Melton Constable Norf 159 C10
Melton Mowbray Leics 154 F5
Melton Ross N Lincs 200 E5
Melvaig Highld 307 L2
Melverley Shrops 148 F6
Melverley Green Shrops 148 F6
Melvich Highld 310 C2
Membland Devon 7 F11
Membury Devon 28 G3
Memsie Aberds 303 C9
Memus Angus 287 B8
Mena Corn 5 C10
Menabilly Corn 5 E11
Menadarva Corn 4 G2
Menagissey Corn 4 F4
Menai Bridge *= Porthaethwy*
Anglesey 179 G9
Mendham Suff 142 G5
Mendlesham Suff 126 D2
Mendlesham Green
Suff 125 E11
Menethorpe N Yorks 216 F5
Mengham Hants 21 B10
Menheniot Corn 6 C5
Menherion Corn 2 B6
Menithwood Worcs 116 D4
Menna Corn 5 E8
Mennock Dumfries 247 B8
Menston W Yorks 205 E9
Menstrie Clack 278 B6
Mentmore Bucks 84 B6
Menzion Borders 260 E3
Meoble Highld 295 G9
Meole Brace Shrops 149 G9
Meols Mers 182 C2
Meon Hants 33 G8
Meonstoke Hants 33 D10
Meopham Kent 68 F6
Meopham Green Kent 68 F6
Meopham Station Kent 68 F6
Mepal Cambs 139 G8
Meppershall C Beds 104 D2
Merbach Hereford 96 B6
Mercaton Derbys 170 G3
Merchant Fields
W Yorks 197 B7
Merchiston Edin 280 G4
Mere Ches E 184 E2
Wilts 45 G10
Mere Brow Lancs 194 D2
Mereclough Lancs 204 G3
Mere Green W Mid 134 D2
Worcs 117 E9
Merehead Wrex 149 B9
Mere Heath Ches W 183 G11
Meresborough Medway 69 G10
Mereside Blackpool 202 G2
Meretown Staffs 150 E5
Mereworth Kent 53 C7
Mergie Aberds 293 E9
Meriden Herts 85 F10
W Mid 134 G4
Merkadale Highld 294 B5
Merkland Dumfries 237 B9
N Ayrs 256 B2
S Ayrs 244 E6
Merkland Lodge Highld 309 G4
Merle Common Sur 52 D2
Merley BCP 18 B6
Merlin's Bridge Pembs 72 C6
Merlin's Cross Pembs 73 E7
Merridale W Mid 133 D7
Merridge Som 43 G8
Merrie Gardens IoW 21 E7
Merrifield Devon 8 F6
Devon 24 G3
Merrington Shrops 149 E9
Merrion Pembs 72 F6
Merriott Dorset 16 B6
Som 28 E6
Merriottsford Som 28 E6
Merritown BCP 19 B8
Merrivale Devon 12 F6
Hereford 98 G2
Merrow Sur 50 C4
Merrybent Darl 224 C4
Merry Field Hill Dorset 31 G8
Merry Hill Herts 85 G10
W Mid 133 D7
Merryhill Green
Wokingham 65 E9
Merrylee E Renf 267 D11
Merry Lees Leics 135 B9
Merrymeet Corn 6 B5
Merry Meeting Corn 11 G7
Merry Oak Soton 32 E6
Mersham Kent 54 F5
Merstham Sur 51 C9
Merston W Sus 22 C5
Merstone IoW 20 E6
Merther Corn 5 G7
Merther Lane Corn 5 G7
Merthyr Carms 93 G7
Merthyr Cynog Powys 95 D9
Merthyr-Dyfan V Glam 58 F6
Merthyr Mawr Bridgend 57 F11
Merthyr Tydfil M Tydf 77 D8
Merthyr Vale M Tydf 77 F9
Merton Devon 25 E8
London 67 E9
Norf 141 D8
Oxon 83 B9
Merton Park London 67 F9
Mervinslaw Borders 262 G5
Meshaw Devon 26 D3
Messing Essex 88 B5
Messingham N Lincs 199 G11
Mesty Croft W Mid 133 E9
Mesur-y-dorth Pembs 87 E11
Metal Bridge Durham 233 E11
Metfield Suff 142 G5
Metherell Corn 7 B8
Metheringham Lincs 173 C9
Methersgate Suff 108 B5
Methil Fife 281 B7
Methilhill Fife 281 B7
Methlem Gwyn 144 C3
Methley W Yorks 197 B11
Methley Junction
W Yorks 197 B11
Methley Lanes
W Yorks 197 B11
Methlick Aberds 303 F8
Methven Perth 286 E4
Methwold Norf 140 E4
Methwold Hythe Norf 140 E4
Mettingham Suff 143 F7
Metton Norf 160 B3
Mevagissey Corn 5 G10
Mewith Head N Yorks 212 F4
Mexborough S Yorks 187 B7
Mey Highld 310 B6
Meyrick Park BCP 19 C7
Meysey Hampton Glos 81 F10
Miabhag W Isles 305 H2
W Isles 305 J3
Miabhig W Isles 304 E2
Mial Highld 299 B7
Michaelchurch Hereford 97 F10
Michaelchurch Escley
Hereford 96 E6
Michaelchurch on Arrow
Powys 114 G4
Michaelston-le-Pit
V Glam 59 E7
Michaelston-y-Fedw
Newport 59 C8
Michaelstow Corn 11 F7
Michealston-super-Ely
Cardiff 58 D6
Michelcombe Devon 8 B3
Micheldever Hants 48 F4
Michelmersh Hants 32 B4
Mickfield Suff 126 E2
Micklebring S Yorks 187 C8
Mickleby N Yorks 226 C6
Micklefield Bucks 84 G5
W Yorks 206 G4
Micklefield Green Herts 85 F8
Mickleham Sur 51 C7
Micklehurst Gtr Man 196 G3
Mickleover Derby 152 C6
Micklethwaite Cumb 239 G7
W Yorks 205 E8
Mickleton Durham 232 G5
Glos 100 C3
Mickletown W Yorks 197 B11
Mickle Trafford Ches W 166 B6
Mickley Derbys 186 F4
N Yorks 214 D5
Shrops 150 C2
Mickley Green Suff 124 F6
Mickley Square
Northumb 242 E3
Midanbury Hants 33 E7
Mid Ardlaw Aberds 303 C9
Mid Auchinleck Invclyd 276 G6
Midbea Orkney 314 B4
Mid Beltie Aberds 293 C8
Mid Calder W Loth 269 B11
Mid Cloch Forbie
Aberds 303 D7
Mid Clyth Highld 310 F6
Middle Assendon Oxon 65 B8
Middle Aston Oxon 101 F9
Middle Balnald Perth 286 B4
Middle Barton Oxon 101 F8
Middle Bickenhill
W Mid 134 G4
Middlebie Dumfries 238 B6
Middle Bockhampton
BCP 19 B9
Middle Bourne Sur 49 E10
Middle Bridge N Som 60 D3
Middle Burnham Som 43 D10
Middle Cairncake
Aberds 303 E8
Middlecave N Yorks 216 E5
Middle Chinnock Som 29 E7
Middle Claydon Bucks 102 F4
Middle Cliff Staffs 169 E8
Middlecliffe S Yorks 198 F2
Middlecott Devon 13 D10
Devon 24 F6
Devon 26 F3
Middle Crackington Corn 11 B9
Middlecroft Derbys 186 G6
Middle Drums Angus 287 B9
Middle Duntisbourne
Glos 81 D7
Middlefield Falk 279 E7
Middleforth Green
Lancs 194 B4
Middle Green Bucks 66 C4
Som 27 D10
Suff 124 D4
Middleham N Yorks 214 B2
Middle Handley Derbys 186 F6
Middle Harling Norf 141 F9
Middle Herrington T&W 243 G9
Middlehill Corn 6 B5
Wilts 61 F10
Middle Hill Pembs 73 C7
Staffs 133 B9
Middlehope Shrops 131 F9
Middle Kames Argyll 275 E10
Middle Littleton Worcs 99 B11
Middle Luxton Devon 28 E2
Middle Madeley Staffs 168 F3
Middle Maes-coed
Hereford 96 E6
Middlemarsh Dorset 29 F11
Middle Marwood Devon 40 F4
Middle Mayfield Staffs 169 G10
Middle Mill Pembs 87 F11
Middlemoor Devon 12 G5
Middlemuir Aberds 303 D9
Aberds 303 E8
Aberds 303 G9
Middleport Stoke 168 F5
Middle Quarter Kent 53 F11
Middle Rainton T&W 234 B2
Middle Rasen Lincs 189 D9
Middlerig Falk 279 F8
Middle Rigg Perth 286 G4
Middle Rocombe Devon 9 B8
Middlesbrough Mbro 234 G5
Middlesceugh Cumb 230 C4
Middleshaw Cumb 211 B11
Middle Side Durham 232 F4
Middlesmoor N Yorks 213 E11
Middle Stoford Som 27 C11
Middle Stoke Devon 13 G9
Medway 69 D10
W Mid 119 B7
Middlestone Durham 233 E11
Middlestone Moor
Durham 233 E10
Middle Stoughton Som 44 D2
Middlestown W Yorks 197 D9
Middle Strath W Loth 279 G8
Middle Street Glos 80 E3
Middle Taphouse Corn 6 C3
Middlethird Borders 272 G3
Middlethorpe York 207 D7
Middleton Aberds 293 B10
Argyll 288 E1
Cumb 212 B2
Derbys 169 C11
Derbys 170 D3
Essex 107 D7
Gtr Man 195 F11
Hants 48 E2
Hereford 115 D10
Hrtlpl 234 E6
IoW 20 D2
Lancs 202 B4
Midloth 271 D7
N Nhants 136 F6
Norf 158 F3
Northumb 252 F3
Northumb 264 B4
N Yorks 205 D8
N Yorks 216 B5
Perth 286 C5
Perth 286 F2
Perth 286 G5
Shrops 115 B10
Shrops 130 D5
Shrops 148 D6
Suff 127 D8
Swansea 56 D2
Warks 134 D3
W Yorks 197 B10
Middleton Baggot
Shrops 132 E2
Middleton Cheney
W Nhants 101 C9
Middleton Green Staffs 151 B9
Middleton Hall
Northumb 263 D11
Middleton-in-Teesdale
Durham 232 F4
Middleton Junction
Gtr Man 195 G11
Middleton Moor Suff 127 D8
Middleton of Rora
Aberds 303 E10
Middleton One Row
Darl 225 C7
Middleton-on-Leven
N Yorks 225 D9
Middleton-on-Sea
W Sus 35 G7
Middleton on the Hill
Hereford 115 E10
Middleton-on-the-Wolds
E Yorks 208 D4
Middleton Place Cumb 219 G11
Middleton Priors
Shrops 132 E2
Middleton Quernhow
N Yorks 214 D6
Middleton St George
Darl 224 C6
Middleton Scriven
Shrops 132 F3
Middleton Stoney
Oxon 101 G10
Middleton Tyas N Yorks 224 D4
Middletown Cumb 219 D9
N Som 60 E3
Powys 148 G6
Warks 117 E11
Middle Town Scilly 1 F4
Middle Tysoe Warks 100 C6
Middle Wallop Hants 47 F9
Middle Weald M Keynes 102 D5
Middlewich Ches E 167 B11
Middlewick Wilts 61 E11
Middle Wick Glos 80 F2
Middle Winterslow Wilts 47 G8
Middlewood Ches E 184 E6
Corn 11 F11
S Yorks 186 C4
Middle Woodford Wilts 46 F6
Middlewood Green
Suff 125 E11
Middleyard Glos 80 E4
Middlezoy Som 43 G11
Middridge Durham 233 F11
Midelney Som 28 C6
Midfield Highld 308 C5
Midford Bath 61 G9
Midgard Borders 262 F3
Midge Hall Lancs 194 C4
Midgehole W Yorks 196 B3
Midgeholme Cumb 240 F4
Midgham W Berks 64 F5
Midgham Green W Berks 64 F5
Midgley W Yorks 196 B4
W Yorks 197 E9
Mid Holmwood Sur 51 D7
Midhopestones S Yorks 186 B2
Midhurst W Sus 34 C5
Mid Lambrook Som 28 D6
Midland Orkney 314 F3
Mid Lavant W Sus 22 B5
Midlem Borders 262 D2
Mid Letter Argyll 284 G4
Midlock S Lanark 259 E11
Mid Main Highld 300 F4
Midmar Aberds 293 C8
Midmuir Argyll 289 G11
Mid Murthat Dumfries 248 D3
Midpark Argyll 255 B11
Midplaugh Aberds 302 E5
Midsomer Norton Bath 45 C7
Midton Invclyd 276 F4
Midtown Highld 307 L3
Highld 308 C5
Midtown of Buchromb
Moray 302 E3
Midtown of Glass
Aberds 302 E4
Mid Urchany Highld 301 E8
Midville Lincs 174 D5
Mid Walls Shetland 313 H4
Midway Ches E 184 E6
Som 45 D7
Mid Yell Shetland 312 D7
Miekle Toux Aberds 302 D5
Migdale Highld 309 K6
Migvie Aberds 292 C6
Milarrochy Stirling 277 C8
Milber Devon 14 G3
Milborne Port Som 29 D11
Milborne St Andrew
Dorset 18 B2
Milborne Wick Som 29 C11
Milbourne Northumb 242 B4
Wilts 62 B2
Milburn Aberds 302 E5
Aberds 302 F6
Cumb 231 F9
Milbury Heath S Glos 79 G11
Milby N Yorks 215 F8
Milch Hill Essex 106 G4
Milcombe Corn 6 D4
Oxon 101 E8
Milden Suff 107 B9
Mildenhall Suff 124 C4
Wilts 63 F8
Milebrook Powys 114 C6
Milebush Kent 53 D9
Mile Cross Norf 160 G4
Mile Elm Wilts 62 F3
Mile End Cambs 140 G2
Devon 14 G2
Essex 107 F9
Glos 79 C9
London 67 C11
Suff 124 G6
Mileham Norf 159 F8
Mile Oak Brighton 36 F2
Kent 53 E7
Shrops 148 D6
Staffs 134 C3
Miles Green Staffs 168 F4
Sur 50 B3
Miles Hill W Yorks 205 F11
Milesmark Fife 279 D11
Miles Platting Gtr Man 184 B5
Miles's Green W Berks 64 F4
Mile Town Kent 70 E2
Milfield Northumb 263 C10
Milford Derbys 170 F5
Devon 24 C2
Powys 129 E11
Shrops 149 E8
Staffs 151 E9
Sur 50 E2
Wilts 31 B11
Milford Haven Pembs 72 D6
Milford on Sea Hants 19 C11
Milkhouse Water Wilts 63 G7
Milkieston Borders 270 F4
Milkwall Glos 79 D9
Milkwell Wilts 30 C6
Milland W Sus 34 B4
Millarston Renfs 267 C9
Millbank Aberds 303 E11
Highld 310 C5
Kent 71 F8
Mill Bank W Yorks 196 C4
Millbeck Cumb 229 F11
Millbounds Orkney 314 C5
Millbreck Aberds 303 E10
Millbridge Sur 49 E10
Millbrook C Beds 103 D10
Corn 7 E8
Devon 41 G9
Gtr Man 185 B7
Soton 32 E5
Mill Brow Gtr Man 185 D7
Millburn S Ayrs 257 D10
Millcombe Devon 8 F6
Mill Common Norf 142 C6
Suff 143 G8
Mill Corner E Sus 38 C4
Milldale Staffs 169 E10
Mill Dam N Yorks 212 F3
Millden Lodge Angus 293 F7
Milldens Angus 287 B9
Millend Glos 80 D3
Glos 80 F3
Mill End Bucks 65 C9
Cambs 124 F3
Glos 81 C10
Herts 85 G8
Herts 104 E6
Mill End Green Essex 106 F2
Millendreath Corn 6 E5
Millerhill Midloth 270 B6
Miller's Dale Derbys 185 G10
Miller's Green Derbys 170 E3
Essex 87 D9
Millersneuk E Dunb 278 G3
Millerston Glasgow 268 B2
Mill Farm Aberds 303 C8
Millfield Pboro 138 C3
T&W 243 F9
Millgate Lancs 195 D11
Norf 160 D3
Millgillhead Cumb 229 G7
Mill Green Cambs 106 B2
Essex 87 E10
Hants 64 G4
Herts 86 D2
Norf 142 G2
Shrops 150 D3
Suff 107 C9
Suff 125 F9
Suff 126 E2
W Mid 133 C11
Millhalf Hereford 96 B5
Millhall Kent 53 B8
Mill Hall Dumfries 237 E8
Millhayes Devon 27 E10
Devon 28 G2
Millhead Lancs 211 E9
Millheugh S Lanark 268 E5
Millhill Devon 12 G5
Mill Hill Blackburn 195 B7
Essex 88 G4
E Sus 23 D10
Glos 79 D10
Gtr Man 195 F8
Kent 55 C11
Lincs 175 B8
London 86 G2
Suff 125 G7
Mill Hills Suff 108 B5
Mill Hirst N Yorks 214 G3
Millholme Cumb 221 G11
Millhouse Argyll 275 F10
Cumb 230 D3
Millhousebridge
Dumfries 248 F4
Millhouse Green
S Yorks 197 G8
Millhouses S Yorks 186 E4
Millhouses *continued*
S Yorks 198 G2
Millikenpark Renfs 267 C8
Millin Cross Pembs 73 C7
Millington E Yorks 208 C2
Millington Green
Derbys 170 F3
Mill Lane Hants 49 C9
Mill Meads London 67 C11
Millmeece Staffs 150 C6
Millmoor Devon 27 E10
Millness Cumb 211 C10
Mill of Brydock Aberds 302 D6
Mill of Chon Stirling 285 G8
Mill of Haldane W Dunb 277 E8
Mill of Kingoodie
Aberds 303 G8
Mill of Lynebain Aberds 302 F4
Mill of Muiresk Aberds 302 E6
Mill of Rango Orkney 314 E2
Mill of Sterin Aberds 292 D5
Mill of Uras Aberds 293 E10
Millom Cumb 210 C3
Millook Corn 11 B9
Millow C Beds 104 C4
Mill Park Argyll 255 G8
Mill Place N Lincs 200 F3
Millpool Corn 2 C3
Corn 11 G8
Millport N Ayrs 266 E3
Millquarter Dumfries 246 G4
Mill Shaw W Yorks 205 G11
Mill Side Cumb 211 C8
Mill Street Kent 53 B7
Norf 159 F11
Suff 107 D9
Milltack Aberds 303 D7
Millthorpe Derbys 186 F4
Lincs 156 C2
Mill Throop BCP 19 B8
Millthrop Cumb 222 G3
Milltimber Aberdeen 293 C10
Milltown Aberds 292 C4
Corn 6 B2
Corn 6 D2
Derbys 170 C5
Devon 40 F5
Highld 301 E9
Milltown of Aberdalgie
Perth 286 E4
Milltown of Auchindoun
Moray 302 E3
Milltown of Craigston
Aberds 303 D7
Milltown of Edinvillie
Moray 302 E2
Milltown of Kildrummy
Aberds 292 B6
Milltown of Rothiemay
Moray 302 E5
Milltown of Towie
Aberds 292 B6
Millwall London 67 D11
Milnathort Perth 286 G5
Milner's Heath Ches W 167 C7
Milngavie E Dunb 277 G11
Milnquarter Falk 278 F6
Milnrow Gtr Man 196 E2
Milnsbridge W Yorks 196 D6
Milnshaw Lancs 195 B9
Milnthorpe Cumb 211 C9
W Yorks 197 D10
Milnwood N Lanark 268 D4
Milo Carms 75 B9
Milson Shrops 116 C2
Milstead Kent 54 B2
Milston Wilts 47 D7
Milthorpe W Nhants 101 B11
Milton Angus 287 C7
Angus 292 E6
Cambs 123 E9
Cumb 211 C10
Cumb 240 E3
Derbys 152 D6
Dumfries 236 D4
Dumfries 237 B10
Dumfries 247 G8
Fife 287 E8
Glasgow 267 B11
Highld 299 E7
Highld 300 D3
Highld 300 E5
Highld 300 F4
Highld 301 B7
Highld 301 E7
Highld 310 D7
Kent 69 E7
Moray 292 B3
Moray 302 C5
Notts 188 G2
N Som 59 G10
Oxon 83 G7
Oxon 101 E8
Pembs 73 E8
Perth 286 F3
Powys 114 G4
Ptsmth 21 B9
Som 29 C7
Stirling 285 G9
Stoke 168 E6
S Yorks 197 G11
W Dunb 277 G8
Wilts 45 G11
Milton Abbas Dorset 30 G4
Milton Bridge Midloth 270 C4
Milton Bryan C Beds 103 E9
Milton Clevedon Som 45 F7
Milton Coldwells Aberds 303 F9
Milton Combe Devon 7 B9
Milton Common Oxon 83 E11
Milton Coombe Devon 7 B9
Milton Damerel Devon 24 E5
Miltonduff Moray 301 C11
Milton End Glos 80 C2
Glos 81 E10
Milton Ernest Bedford 121 F10
Milton Green Ches W 167 D7
Devon 12 F4
Milton Heights Oxon 83 G7
Miltonhill Moray 301 C10
Milton Hill Devon 14 F4
Oxon 83 G7
Miltonise Dumfries 236 B3
Milton Keynes
M Keynes 103 D7
Milton Keynes Village
M Keynes 103 D7
Milton Lilbourne Wilts 63 G7
Milton Malsor W Nhants 120 F4
Milton Morenish Perth 285 D10
Milton of Auchinhove
Aberds 293 C7
Milton of Balgonie Fife 287 G7
Milton of Buchanan
Stirling 277 C8
Milton of Campfield
Aberds 293 C8
Milton of Campsie
E Dunb 278 F3
Milton of Corsindae
Aberds 293 C8
Milton of Cullerlie
Aberds 293 C9
Milton of Cultoquhey
Perth 286 E2
Milton of Cushnie
Aberds 293 B7
Milton of Dalcapon
Perth 286 B3
Milton of Drimmie
Perth 286 B5
Milton of Edradour
Perth 286 B3
Milton of Gollanfield
Highld 301 D7
Milton of Lesmore
Aberds 302 G4
Milton of Logie Aberds 292 C6
Milton of Machany
Perth 286 F3
Milton of Mathers
Aberds 293 G9
Milton of Murtle
Aberdeen 293 C10
Milton of Noth Aberds 302 G5
Milton of Tullich Aberds 292 D5
Milton on Stour Dorset 30 B3
Milton Regis Kent 70 F2
Milton Street E Sus 23 E8
Milton under Wychwood
Oxon 82 B3
Milverton Som 27 B10
Warks 118 D6
Milwich Staffs 151 C9
Milwr Flint 181 G11
Mimbridge Sur 66 G3
Minard Argyll 275 D10
Minard Castle Argyll 275 D10
Minchington Dorset 31 E7
Minchinhampton Glos 80 E5
Mindrum Northumb 263 C8
Minehead Som 42 D3
Minera Wrex 166 E3
Mineshope Corn 11 B9
Minety Wilts 81 G8
Minffordd Gwyn 145 B11
Gwyn 146 G4
Gwyn 179 G9
Mingarrypark Highld 289 C8
Mingoose Corn 4 F4
Miningsby Lincs 174 C4
Minions Corn 11 G11
Minishant S Ayrs 257 G8
Minllyn Gwyn 147 G7
Minnes Aberds 303 G9
Minngearraidh W Isles 297 J3
Minnigaff Dumfries 236 C6
Minnonie Aberds 303 C7
Minnow End Essex 88 C2
Minnygap Dumfries 248 D2
Minshull Vernon
Ches E 167 C11
Minskip N Yorks 215 G7
Minstead Hants 32 E3
Minsted W Sus 34 C5
Minster Kent 70 E3
Kent 71 G10
Minsterley Shrops 131 C7
Minster Lovell Oxon 82 C4
Minsterworth Glos 80 B3
Minterne Magna Dorset 29 G11
Minterne Parva Dorset 29 G11
Minting Lincs 189 G11
Mintlaw Aberds 303 E10
Minto Borders 262 E3
Minto Kames Borders 262 E3
Minton Shrops 131 E8
Mintsfeet Cumb 221 G10
Minwear Pembs 73 C8
Minworth W Mid 134 E3
Mirbister Orkney 314 E2
Mirehouse Cumb 219 B9
Mireland Highld 310 C7
Mirfield W Yorks 197 D8
Miserden Glos 80 D6
Misery Corner Norf 142 F5
Miskin Rhondda 58 C4
Rhondda 77 F8
Misselfore Wilts 31 C8
Misson Notts 187 C11
Misterton Leics 135 G11
Notts 188 C3
Som 29 F7
Misterton Soss Notts 188 B3
Mistley Essex 108 E2
Mistley Heath Essex 108 E2
Mitcham London 67 F9
Mitcheldean Glos 79 B11
Mitchell Corn 5 E7
Mitchell Hill Borders 260 C3
Mitchellslacks
Dumfries 247 D11
Mitchelston Borders 271 F9
Mitchel Troy Mon 79 C7
Mitcheltroy Common
Mon 79 D7
Mite Houses Cumb 219 F11
Mitford Northumb 252 F5
Mithian Corn 4 E4
Mithian Downs Corn 4 F4
Mitton Staffs 151 F7
Worcs 99 E8
Mixbury Oxon 102 E2
Mixenden W Yorks 196 B5
Mixtow Corn 6 E2
Moat Cumb 239 C10
Moats Tye Suff 125 F10
Mobberley Ches E 184 F3
Staffs 169 G8
Moblake Ches E 167 G11
Mobwell Bucks 84 E5
Moccas Hereford 97 C7
Mochdre Conwy 180 F4
Powys 129 F11
Mochrum Dumfries 236 E5
Mockbeggar Hants 31 F11
Kent 54 E6
Medway 69 E8
Mockerkin Cumb 229 G7
Moclett Orkney 314 B4
Modbury Devon 8 E3
Moddershall Staffs 151 B8
Model Village Derbys 187 G8
Warks 119 E8
Modest Corner Kent 52 E5
Moelfre Anglesey 179 D8
Conwy 181 G7
Powys 148 D3
Moel Tryfan Gwyn 163 D8
Moel-y-crio Flint 165 B11
Moffat Dumfries 248 B3
Moffat Mills N Lanark 268 C5
Mogador Sur 51 C8
Moggerhanger C Beds 104 B2
Mogworthy Devon 26 D5
Moira Leics 152 F6
Moity Powys 96 C3
Molash Kent 54 C4
Mol-chlach Highld 294 D6
Mold Flint 166 C2
Moldgreen W Yorks 197 D7
Molehill Green Essex 105 G11
Molehill Green *continued*
Essex 106 G4
Molescroft E Yorks 208 E6
Molesden Northumb 252 G4
Molesworth Cambs 121 B11
Molinnis Corn 5 D10
Moll Highld 295 B7
Molland Devon 26 B4
Mollington Ches W 182 G5
Oxon 101 B8
Mollinsburn N Lanark 278 G4
Monachty Ceredig 111 E10
Monachylemore Stirling 285 F8
Monar Lodge Highld 300 E2
Monaughty Powys 114 D4
Monboddo House
Aberds 293 F9
Mondaytown Shrops 130 B6
Mondynes Aberds 293 F9
Monemore Stirling 285 D9
Monevechadan Argyll 284 G5
Monewden Suff 126 F4
Moneyacres E Ayrs 267 E8
Moneydie Perth 286 E4
Moneyhill Herts 85 G8
Money Hill Leics 153 F7
Moneyrow Green
Windsor 65 D11
Moneystone Staffs 169 F9
Mongleath Corn 3 C7
Moniaive Dumfries 247 E7
Monifieth Angus 287 D8
Monikie Angus 287 D8
Monimail Fife 286 F6
Monington Pembs 92 C2
Monk Bretton S Yorks 197 F11
Monk End N Yorks 224 D5
Monken Hadley London 86 F3
Monkerton Devon 14 C5
Monk Fryston N Yorks 198 B4
Monk Hesleden Durham 234 D5
Monkhide Hereford 98 C2
Monkhill Cumb 239 F8
W Yorks 198 C3
Monkhopton Shrops 132 E2
Monkland Hereford 115 F9
Monkleigh Devon 25 C7
Monkmoor Shrops 149 G10
Monknash V Glam 58 E2
Monkokehampton Devon 25 F9
Monkscross Corn 12 G3
Monkseaton T&W 243 C8
Monks Eleigh Suff 107 B9
Monk's Gate W Sus 36 B2
Monks Heath Ches E 184 G4
Monk Sherborne Hants 48 B6
Monkshill Aberds 303 E7
Monks Hill Kent 53 E11
Monksilver Som 42 F5
Monks Kirby Warks 135 G9
Monk Soham Suff 126 D4
Monks Orchard London 67 F11
Monk's Park Wilts 61 F11
Monkspath W Mid 118 B2
Monks Risborough Bucks 84 E4
Monksthorpe Lincs 174 B6
Monkston Park
M Keynes 103 D7
Monk Street Essex 106 F2
Monkswood Midloth 270 C6
Mon 78 E4
W Yorks 206 F2
Monkton Devon 27 G11
Kent 71 G9
Pembs 73 E7
S Ayrs 257 D9
T&W 243 E8
V Glam 58 E2
Monkton Combe Bath 61 G9
Monkton Deverill Wilts 45 F11
Monkton Farleigh Wilts 61 F10
Monktonhall E Loth 280 G6
Monkton Heathfield Som 28 B3
Monkton Up Wimborne
Dorset 31 E8
Monkwearmouth T&W 243 F9
Monkwood Hants 49 G7
Monkwood Green
Worcs 116 E6
Monmarsh Hereford 97 B10
Monmore Green W Mid 133 D8
Monmouth *= Trefynwy*
Mon 79 C8
Monmouth Cap Mon 97 F7
Monnington on Wye
Hereford 97 C7
Monreith Dumfries 236 E5
Monreith Mains
Dumfries 236 E5
Montacute Som 29 D7
Montcliffe Gtr Man 195 E7
Montcoffer Ho Aberds 302 C6
Montford Argyll 266 C2
Shrops 149 G8
Montford Bridge Shrops 149 F8
Montgarrie Aberds 293 B7
Montgomery Powys 130 D4
Montgomery Lines
Hants 49 C11
Monton Gtr Man 184 B3
Montpelier Bristol 60 E5
Montrave Fife 287 G7
Montrose Angus 287 B11
Montsale Essex 89 F8
Monwode Lea Warks 134 E5
Monxton Hants 47 E10
Monyash Derbys 169 B11
Monymusk Aberds 293 B8
Monzie Perth 286 E2
Monzie Castle Perth 286 E2
Moodiesburn N Lanark 278 G3
Moolham Som 28 E5
Moon's Green Kent 38 B5
Moon's Moat Worcs 117 D11
Moonzie Fife 287 F7
Moor Som 28 D6
Mooradale Shetland 312 F6
Moor Allerton W Yorks 205 F11
Mooray Wilts 46 G3
Moorby Lincs 174 C3
Moorclose Cumb 228 F5
Gtr Man 195 F11
Moor Common Bucks 84 G4
Moorcot Hereford 115 F7
Moor Crichel Dorset 31 F7
Moor Cross Devon 8 D2
Moordown BCP 19 C7
Moore Halton 183 E9
Moor Edge W Yorks 205 F7
Moorend Cumb 239 G8
Derbys 170 F2
Dumfries 239 C7
Glos 80 C5
Glos 80 E2
Gtr Man 185 D7
S Glos 61 D7
Moor End Bucks 84 G4
Cambs 105 B7
C Beds 103 G9

Moor End *continued*
Durham 234 C2
E Yorks 208 F2
Glos 99 G9
Lancs 202 E3
N Yorks 207 F7
N Yorks 215 G7
S Yorks 197 G9
Worcs 117 F8
W Yorks 196 B5
W Yorks 206 D4
York 207 B9
Moorend Cross Hereford 98 B4
Moor End Field N Yorks 215 F8
Moorends S Yorks 199 D7
Moorfield Derbys 185 C8
Moorgate Norf 160 C3
S Yorks 186 C6
Moorgreen Hants 33 D7
Notts 171 F7
Moor Green Herts 104 F6
Staffs 169 G7
Wilts 61 F11
W Mid 133 G11
Moorhaigh Notts 171 C8
Moorhall Derbys 186 G4
Moor Hall W Mid 134 D2
Moorhampton Hereford 97 B7
Moorhaven Village Devon 8 D3
Moorhayne Devon 28 F2
Moorhead W Yorks 205 F8
Moor Head W Yorks 197 B8
W Yorks 197 E8
Moorhey Gtr Man 196 G2
Moorhole S Yorks 186 E6
Moorhouse Cumb 239 F8
Cumb 239 G7
Notts 172 B3
S Yorks 198 E3
Moorhouse Bank Sur 52 C2
Moorhouses Lincs 174 D3
Moorland or Northmoor Green Som 43 G10
Moorledge Bath 60 G5
Moorlinch Som 43 F11
Moor Monkton N Yorks 206 B6
Moor Monkton Moor N Yorks 206 B6
Moor of Balvack Aberds 293 B8
Moor of Granary Moray 301 D10
Moor of Ravenstone Dumfries 236 E5
Moor Park Cumb 229 D7
Hereford 97 C9
Herts 85 G9
Sur 49 D11
Moor Row Cumb 219 C10
Cumb 229 B10
Moorsholm Redcar 226 C3
Moorside Ches W 182 F3
Dorset 30 D3
Durham 233 B7
Gtr Man 195 G9
Gtr Man 196 F3
W Yorks 197 B8
W Yorks 205 F10
Moor Side Lancs 202 F5
Lancs 202 G4
Lincs 174 D2
W Yorks 197 B7
W Yorks 204 F6
Moorstock Kent 54 F6
Moor Street Kent 69 F10
Moorswater Corn 6 C4
Moorthorpe W Yorks 198 E3
Moor Top W Yorks 197 C7
Moortown Devon 12 B2
Devon 12 G6
Devon 25 C8
Hants 31 G11
IoW 20 E4
Lincs 189 B9
Telford 150 F2
W Yorks 206 F2
Morangie Highld 309 L7
Morar Highld 295 F8
Moravian Settlement Derbys 153 B8
Môrawelon Anglesey 178 E3
Morayhill Highld 301 E7
Morborne Cambs 138 E2
Morchard Bishop Devon 26 F3
Morchard Road Devon 26 G3
Morcombelake Dorset 16 C4
Morcott Rutland 137 C8
Morda Shrops 148 D5
Morden Dorset 18 B4
London 67 F9
Morden Green Cambs 104 C5
Morden Park London 67 F8
Mordiford Hereford 97 D11
Mordington Holdings Borders 273 D8
Mordon Durham 234 F2
More Shrops 130 E6
Morebath Devon 27 C7
Morebattle Borders 263 E7
Morecambe Lancs 211 G8
More Crichel Dorset 31 F7
Moredon Swindon 62 B6
Moredun Edin 270 B5
Morefield Highld 307 K6
Morehall Kent 55 F8
Moreleggan Argyll 284 G6
Moreleigh Devon 8 E5
Morenish Perth 285 D9
Moresby Cumb 228 G5
Moresby Parks Cumb 219 B9
Morestead Hants 33 B8
Moreton Dorset 18 D2
Essex 87 D8
Hereford 115 E10
Mers 182 C3
Oxon 82 E6
Oxon 83 E11
Staffs 150 F5
Staffs 152 D2
Moreton Corbet Shrops 149 E11
Moretonhampstead Devon 13 D11
Moreton-in-Marsh Glos 100 E4
Moreton Jeffries Hereford 98 B2
Moreton Morrell Warks 118 F6
Moreton on Lugg Hereford 97 B10
Moreton Paddox Warks 118 G6
Moreton Pinkney W Nhants 101 B11
Moreton Say Shrops 150 C2
Moreton Valence Glos 80 D3
Moretonwood Shrops 150 C2
Morfa Carms 56 B4
Carms 75 C9
Ceredig 110 G6
Gwyn 144 C3
Morfa Bach Carms 74 C5
Morfa Bychan Gwyn 145 B10
Morfa Dinlle Gwyn 162 D6
Morfa Glas Neath 76 D5
Morfa Nefyn Gwyn 162 G3
Morfydd Denb 165 F10
Morganstown Cardiff 58 C6
Morgan's Vale Wilts 31 C11
Moriah Ceredig 112 B2
Mork Glos 79 D9
Morland Cumb 231 G7
Morley Ches E 184 E4
Derbys 170 G5
Durham 233 F8
W Yorks 197 B9
Morley Green Ches E 184 E4
Morleymoor Derbys 170 G5
Morley Park Derbys 170 F5
Morley St Botolph Norf 141 D11
Morley Smithy Derbys 170 G5
Mornick Corn 12 G2
Morningside Edin 280 G3
N Lanark 268 D6
Morningthorpe Norf 142 E4
Morpeth Northumb 252 F6
Morphie Aberds 293 G9
Morrey Staffs 152 F2
Morridge Side Staffs 169 E8
Morrilow Heath Staffs 151 B9
Morris Green Essex 106 E4
Morriston = *Treforys* Swansea 57 B7
Morristown V Glam 59 E7
Morston Norf 177 E8
Mortehoe Devon 40 D3
Morthen S Yorks 187 D7
Mortimer W Berks 65 G7
Mortimer's Cross Hereford 115 E8
Mortimer West End Hants 64 G6
Mortlake London 67 D8
Mortomley S Yorks 186 B4
Morton Cumb 230 D4
Cumb 239 G9
Derbys 170 C6
IoW 21 D8
Lincs 155 E11
Lincs 172 C5
Lincs 188 C4
Norf 160 F2
Notts 172 E2
S Glos 79 G10
Shrops 148 E5
Morton Bagot Warks 118 E2
Morton Common Shrops 148 E5
Morton Mains Dumfries 247 D9
Morton Mill Shrops 149 E11
Morton-on-Swale N Yorks 224 G6
Morton Spirt Warks 117 G10
Morton Tinmouth Durham 233 G9
Morton Underhill Worcs 117 F10
Morvah Corn 1 B4
Morval Corn 6 D5
Morven Lodge Aberds 292 C5
Morvich Highld 295 C11
Highld 309 J7
Morville Shrops 132 E3
Morville Heath Shrops 132 E3
Morwellham Quay Devon 7 B8
Morwenstow Corn 24 E2
Mosborough S Yorks 186 E6
Moscow E Ayrs 267 G9
Mose Shrops 132 E5
Mosedale Cumb 230 E3
Moseley W Mid 133 D8
W Mid 133 G11
Worcs 116 F6
Moses Gate Gtr Man 195 F8
Mosley Common Gtr Man 195 G8
Moss Argyll 288 E1
Highld 289 C8
S Yorks 198 E5
Wrex 166 E4
Mossat Aberds 292 B6
Mossbank Shetland 312 F6
Moss Bank Halton 183 D8
Mers 183 B8
Mossbay Cumb 228 F5
Mossblown S Ayrs 257 E10
Mossbrow Gtr Man 184 D2
Mossburnford Borders 262 F5
Mossdale Dumfries 237 B8
Mossedge Cumb 239 D11
Moss Edge Lancs 202 D4
Lancs 202 E4
Mossend N Lanark 268 C4
Moss End Brack 65 E11
Ches E 183 F11
Mosser Mains Cumb 229 F8
Mossfield Highld 300 B6
Mossgate Staffs 151 B8
Mossgiel E Ayrs 257 D11
Mosshouses Borders 262 B2
Moss Houses Ches E 184 G5
Mosside Angus 287 B8
Moss Lane Ches E 184 G6
Mossley Ches E 168 C5
Gtr Man 196 G3
Mossley Brow Gtr Man 196 G3
Mossley Hill Mers 182 D5
Moss Nook Gtr Man 184 D4
Mers 183 C8
Moss of Barmuckity Moray 302 C2
Moss of Meft Moray 302 C2
Mosspark Glasgow 267 C10
Moss Pit Staffs 151 E8
Moss Side Cumb 238 G5
Gtr Man 184 B4
Moss-side Highld 301 D8
Moss Side Lancs 193 G11
Lancs 194 C4
Lancs 202 G3
Mers 182 B6
Moss-side Moray 302 D5
Mosstodloch Moray 302 D3
Mosston Angus 287 C9
Mosstown Aberds 303 C10
Mossy Lea Lancs 194 E4
Mosterton Dorset 29 F7
Moston Ches E 168 C2
Ches W 182 G6
Gtr Man 195 G11
Shrops 149 D11
Moston Green Ches E 168 C2
Mostyn Flint 181 E11
Mostyn Quay Flint 181 E11
Motcombe Dorset 30 B5
Mothecombe Devon 8 F2
Motherby Cumb 230 F4
Motherwell N Lanark 268 D5
Motspur Park London 67 F8
Mottingham London 68 E2
Mottisfont Hants 32 B4
Mottistone IoW 20 E4
Mottram in Longdendale Gtr Man 185 B7
Mottram Rise Gtr Man 185 B7
Mottram St Andrew Ches E 184 F5
Mott's Green Essex 87 B8
Mott's Mill E Sus 52 F4
Mouldsworth Ches W 183 G8
Moulin Perth 286 B3
Moulsecoomb Brighton 36 F4
Moulsford Oxon 64 C5
Moulsham Essex 88 D2
Moulsoe M Keynes 103 C8
Moultavie Highld 300 B6
Moulton Ches W 167 B11
Lincs 156 E6
N Yorks 224 E4
Suff 124 E3
V Glam 58 E5
W Nhants 120 D5
Moulton Chapel Lincs 156 F5
Moulton Eaugate Lincs 156 F6
Moulton Park W Nhants 120 E5
Moulton St Mary Norf 143 B7
Moulton Seas End Lincs 156 D6
Moulzie Angus 292 F4
Mounie Castle Aberds 303 G7
Mount Corn 4 D5
Corn 6 B2
Highld 301 E9
W Yorks 196 D5
Mountain Anglesey 178 E2
W Yorks 205 G7
Mountain Air Bl Gwent 77 D11
Mountain Ash = *Aberpennar* Rhondda 77 F8
Mountain Bower Wilts 61 D10
Mountain Cross Borders 270 F2
Mountain Street Kent 54 C5
Mountain Water Pembs 91 G8
Mount Ambrose Corn 4 G4
Mount Ballan Mon 60 B3
Mount Batten Plym 7 E9
Mountbenger Borders 261 D8
Mountbengerburn Borders 261 D8
Mountblow W Dunb 277 G9
Mount Bovers Essex 88 G4
Mount Bures Essex 107 E8
Mount Canisp Highld 301 B7
Mount Charles Corn 5 B10
Corn 5 E10
Mount Cowdown Wilts 47 C9
Mount End Essex 87 E7
Mount Ephraim E Sus 23 B7
Mounters Dorset 30 D3
Mountfield E Sus 38 C2
Mountgerald Highld 300 C5
Mount Gould Plym 7 D9
Mount Hawke Corn 4 F4
Mount Hermon Corn 2 F6
Sur 50 B4
Mount Hill S Glos 61 E7
Mountjoy Corn 5 C7
Mount Lane Devon 12 B3
Mountnessing Essex 87 F10
Mounton Mon 79 G8
Mount Pleasant Bucks 102 E3
Ches E 168 D4
Corn 5 C10
Derbys 152 D6
Derbys 152 F5
Derbys 170 F4
Devon 27 G11
Durham 233 E11
E Sus 23 B7
E Sus 36 D6
Flint 182 G2
Hants 19 B11
Kent 71 F10
London 85 G8
M Tydf 77 F9
Neath 57 B9
Norf 141 E9
Pembs 73 D8
Shrops 149 G9
Stockton 234 G4
Stoke 168 G5
Suff 106 B4
T&W 243 E7
Warks 135 F7
Worcs 99 D10
Worcs 117 E10
W Yorks 197 C8
Mount Sion Wrex 166 E3
Mount Skippett Oxon 82 B5
Mountsolie Aberds 303 D9
Mountsorrel Leics 153 F11
Mount Sorrel Wilts 31 C8
Mount Tabor W Yorks 196 B5
Mount Vernon Glasgow 268 C3
Mount Wise Corn 7 E9
Mousehill Sur 50 E2
Mousehole Corn 1 D5
Mousen Northumb 264 C4
Mousley End Warks 118 D4
Mouswald Dumfries 238 C3
Mouth Mill Devon 24 B3
Mowbreck Lancs 202 G4
Mow Cop Ches E 168 D5
Mowden Darl 224 B5
Essex 88 C3
Mowhaugh Borders 263 E8
Mowmacre Hill Leicester 135 B11
Mowshurst Kent 52 D3
Mowsley Leics 136 F2
Moxby N Yorks 215 F11
Moxley W Mid 133 D9
Moy Argyll 255 E8
Highld 290 E6
Highld 301 F7
Moy Hall Highld 301 F7
Moy Ho Moray 301 C10
Moyles Court Hants 31 F11
Moylgrove = *Trewyddel* Pembs 92 C2
Moy Lodge Highld 290 E6
Muasdale Argyll 255 C7
Muchalls Aberds 293 D11
Much Birch Hereford 97 E10
Much Cowardne Hereford 98 B2
Much Cowarne Hereford 98 B2
Much Dewchurch Hereford 97 E9
Muchelney Som 28 C6
Muchelney Ham Som 28 C6
Much Hadham Herts 86 B5
Much Hoole Lancs 194 C3
Much Hoole Moss Houses Lancs 194 C3
Much Hoole Town Lancs 194 C3
Muchlarnick Corn 6 D4
Much Marcle Hereford 98 E3
Muchrachd Highld 300 F2
Much Wenlock Shrops 132 C2
Muckairn Argyll 289 F11
Muckernich Highld 300 D5
Mucking Thurrock 69 C7
Muckle Breck Shetland 312 G7
Muckleford Dorset 17 C8
Mucklestone Staffs 150 B4
Muckleton Norf 158 B6
Shrops 149 E11
Muckletown Aberds 302 G5
Muckley Shrops 132 D2
Muckley Corner Staffs 133 B11
Muckley Cross Shrops 132 D2
Muckton Lincs 190 E5
Muckton Bottom Lincs 190 E5
Mudale Highld 308 F5
Mudd Gtr Man 185 C7
Muddiford Devon 40 F5
Muddlebridge Devon 40 G4
Muddles Green E Sus 23 C8
Mudeford BCP 19 C9
Mudford Som 29 D9
Mudford Sock Som 29 D9
Mudgley Som 44 D2
Mugdock Stirling 277 F11
Mugeary Highld 294 B6
Mugginton Derbys 170 G3
Muggintonlane End Derbys 170 G3
Muggleswick Durham 232 B6
Mugswell Sur 51 C9
Muie Highld 309 J6
Muir Aberds 292 E2
Muircleugh Borders 271 F10
Muirden Aberds 303 D7
Muirdrum Angus 287 D9
Muiredge Fife 281 B7
Muirend Glasgow 267 C11
Muirhead Angus 287 D7
Fife 286 G6
Fife 287 B8
N Lanark 268 B3
S Ayrs 257 C8
Muirhouse Edin 280 F4
N Lanark 268 D5
Muirhouselaw Borders 262 D4
Muirhouses Falk 279 E10
Muirkirk E Ayrs 258 D5
Muirmill Stirling 278 E4
Muir of Alford Aberds 293 B7
Muir of Fairburn Highld 300 D4
Muir of Fowlis Aberds 293 B7
Muir of Kinellar Aberds 293 B10
Muir of Miltonduff Moray 301 D11
Muir of Ord Highld 300 D5
Muir of Pert Angus 287 D8
Muirshearlich Highld 290 E3
Muirskie Aberds 293 D10
Muirtack Aberds 303 F9
Muirton Aberds 303 D7
Highld 301 C7
Perth 286 E5
Perth 286 F3
Muirton Mains Highld 300 D4
Muirton of Ardblair Perth 286 C5
Muirton of Ballochy Angus 293 G8
Muiryfold Aberds 303 D7
Muker N Yorks 223 F8
Mulbarton Norf 142 C3
Mulben Moray 302 D3
Mulberry Corn 5 B10
Mulfra Corn 1 C5
Mulindry Argyll 254 B4
Mulla Shetland 313 G6
Mullardoch House Highld 300 F2
Mullenspond Hants 47 D9
Mullion Corn 2 F5
Mullion Cove Corn 2 F5
Mumbles Hill Swansea 56 D6
Mumby Lincs 191 G8
Mumps Gtr Man 196 F2
Mundale Moray 301 D10
Munderfield Row Hereford 116 G2
Munderfield Stocks Hereford 116 G2
Mundesley Norf 160 B6
Mundford Norf 140 E6
Mundham Norf 142 D6
Mundon Essex 88 E5
Mundurno Aberdeen 293 B11
Mundy Bois Kent 54 D2
Munerigie Highld 290 C4
Muness Shetland 312 C8
Mungasdale Highld 307 K4
Mungrisdale Cumb 230 E3
Munlochy Highld 300 D6
Munsary Cottage Highld 310 E6
Munsley Hereford 98 C3
Munslow Shrops 131 F10
Munstone Hereford 97 C10
Murch V Glam 59 E7
Murchington Devon 13 D9
Murcot Worcs 99 C11
Murcott Oxon 83 B9
Wilts 81 G7
Murdieston Stirling 278 B3
Murdishaw Halton 183 E9
Murieston W Loth 269 C11
Murkle Highld 310 C5
Murlaggan Highld 290 D2
Highld 290 E5
Murra Orkney 314 F2
Murrayfield Edin 280 G4
Murrayshall Perth 286 E5
Murraythwaite Dumfries 238 C4
Murrell Green Hants 49 B8
Murrell's End Glos 98 E4
Glos 98 G5
Murrion Shetland 312 F4
Murrow Cambs 139 B7
Mursley Bucks 102 F6
Murston Kent 70 G2
Murthill Angus 287 B8
Murthly Perth 286 D4
Murton Cumb 231 G10
Durham 234 B3
Northumb 273 F9
Swansea 56 D5
T&W 243 C8
York 207 C8
Murton Grange N Yorks 215 B10
Murtwell Devon 8 D5
Musbury Devon 15 C11
Muscliff BCP 19 B7
Muscoates N Yorks 216 C3
Muscott W Nhants 120 E2
Musdale Argyll 289 G11
Mushroom Green W Mid 133 F8
Musselburgh E Loth 280 G6
Musselwick Pembs 72 D4
Mustard Hyrn Norf 161 F8
Muston Leics 154 B6
N Yorks 217 D11
Mustow Green Worcs 117 C7
Muswell Hill London 86 G3
Mutehill Dumfries 237 E8
Mutford Suff 143 F9
Muthill Perth 286 F2
Mutley Plym 7 D9
Mutterton Devon 27 G8
Mutton Hall E Sus 37 C9
Muxton Telford 150 G4
Mwdwl-eithin Flint 181 F11
Mwynbwll Flint 165 B11
Mybster Highld 310 D5
Myddfai Carms 94 F5
Myddle Shrops 149 E9
Myddlewood Shrops 149 E9
Myddyn-fych Carms 75 C10
Mydroilyn Ceredig 111 F9
Myerscough Lancs 202 F5
Myerscough Smithy Lancs 203 G8
Mylor Bridge Corn 3 B8
Mylor Churchtown Corn 3 B8
Mynachdy Cardiff 59 D7
Rhondda 77 F8
Mynachlog-ddu Pembs 92 E2
Mynd Shrops 115 C7
Myndd Llandegai Gwyn 163 B10
Myndtown Shrops 131 F7
Mynydd Bach Ceredig 112 B4
Mynydd-bach Mon 79 G7
Swansea 57 B7
Mynydd-bach-y-glo Swansea 56 B6
Mynydd Bodafon Anglesey 179 D7
Mynydd Fflint = *Flint Mountain* Flint 182 G2
Mynydd Gilan Gwyn 144 E5
Mynydd-isa Flint 166 C3
Mynyddislwyn Caerph 77 G11
Mynydd-llan Flint 181 G11
Mynydd Marian Conwy 180 F5
Mynydd Mechell Anglesey 178 D5
Mynyddygarreg Carms 74 D6
Mynytho Gwyn 144 C6
Myrebird Aberds 293 D9
Myrelandhorn Highld 310 D6
Myreside Perth 286 E6
Myrtle Hill Carms 94 E5
Mytchett Sur 49 B11
Mytchett Place Sur 49 C11
Mytholm W Yorks 196 B3
Mytholmes W Yorks 204 F6
Mytholmroyd W Yorks 196 B4
Mythop Lancs 202 G3
Mytice Aberds 302 F4
Myton Warks 118 E6
Myton Hall N Yorks 215 F8
Myton-on-Swale N Yorks 215 F8
Mytton Shrops 149 F8

N

Naast Highld 307 L3
Nab Hill W Yorks 197 D7
Nab's Head Lancs 194 B6
Naburn York 207 D7
Nab Wood W Yorks 205 F8
Naccolt Kent 54 E4
Nackington Kent 55 C7
Nacton Suff 108 C4
Nadderwater Devon 14 C3
Nafferton E Yorks 209 B7
Na Gearrannan W Isles 304 D3
Nag's Head Glos 80 F5
Naid-y-march Flint 181 G11
Nailbridge Glos 79 B10
Nailsbourne Som 28 B2
Nailsea N Som 60 D3
Nailstone Leics 135 B8
Nailsworth Glos 80 F5
Nailwell Bath 61 G8
Nairn Highld 301 D8
Nalderswood Sur 51 D8
Nance Corn 4 G3
Nanceddan Corn 2 C2
Nancegollan Corn 2 C4
Nancemellin Corn 4 G2
Nancenoy Corn 2 D6
Nancledra Corn 1 B5
Nangreaves Lancs 195 D10
Nanhoron Gwyn 144 C5
Nanhyfer = *Nevern* Pembs 91 D11
Nannau Gwyn 146 E4
Nannerch Flint 165 B11
Nanpantan Leics 153 F10
Nanpean Corn 5 D9
Nanquidno Corn 1 D3
Nanstallon Corn 5 B10
Nant Carms 74 B6
Denb 165 D11
Nant Alyn Flint 165 B11
Nant-ddu Powys 77 B8
Nanternis Ceredig 111 F7
Nantgaredig Carms 93 G9
Nantgarw Rhondda 58 B6
Nant-glas Powys 113 E9
Nantglyn Denb 165 C8
Nantgwyn Powys 113 B9
Nantithet Corn 2 E5
Nantlle Gwyn 163 E8
Nantmawr Shrops 148 E5
Nant Mawr Flint 166 C3
Nantmel Powys 113 D10
Nantmor Gwyn 163 F10
Nant Peris = *Old Llanberis* Gwyn 163 D10
Nantserth Powys 113 C9
Nant Uchaf Denb 165 D8
Nantwich Ches E 167 E11
Nant-y-Bai Carms 94 C5
Nant-y-Bwch Bl Gwent 77 C10
Nant-y-cafn Neath 76 D4
Nantycaws Carms 75 B7
Nant y Caws Shrops 148 D5
Nant-y-ceisiad Caerph 59 B8
Nant-y-derry Mon 78 D4
Nant-y-felin Conwy 179 G11
Nant-y-ffin Carms 93 E11
Nantyffyllon Bridgend 57 C11
Nantyglo Bl Gwent 77 C11
Nant-y-gollen Shrops 148 D4
Nant-y-moel Bridgend 76 G6
Nant-y-pandy Conwy 179 G11
Nant-y-Rhiw Conwy 164 D4
Nantyronen Station Ceredig 112 B3
Napchester Kent 55 D10
Naphill Bucks 84 F4
Napleton Worcs 99 B7
Napley Staffs 150 B4
Napley Heath Staffs 150 B4
Nappa N Yorks 204 C3
Nappa Scar N Yorks 223 G9
Napton on the Hill Warks 119 E9
Narberth = *Arberth* Pembs 73 C10
Narberth Bridge Pembs 73 C10
Narborough Leics 135 D10
Norf 158 G4
Narfords Som 28 F3
Narkurs Corn 6 D6
Narracott Devon 24 D5
Narrowgate Corner Norf 161 F8
Nasareth Gwyn 163 E7
Naseby W Nhants 120 B3
Nash Bucks 102 E5
Hereford 114 E6
Kent 55 B9
London 68 G2
Newport 59 C10
Shrops 116 C2
Som 29 E8
Nashend Glos 80 D5
Nash End Worcs 132 G5
Nashes Green Hants 49 D7
Nash Lee Bucks 84 D4
Nash Mills Herts 85 E9
Nash Street E Sus 23 C8
Kent 68 F6
Nassington N Nhants 137 D11
Nastend Glos 80 D3
Nast Hyde Herts 86 D2
Nasty Herts 105 G7
Natcott Devon 24 C3
Nateby Cumb 222 D5
Lancs 202 E5
Nately Scures Hants 49 C8
Natland Cumb 211 B10
Natton Glos 99 E8
Naughton Suff 107 B10
Naunton Glos 100 G2
Worcs 99 D7
Naunton Beauchamp Worcs 117 G9
Navant Hill W Sus 34 B6
Navenby Lincs 173 D7
Navestock Heath Essex 87 F8
Navestock Side Essex 87 F9
Navidale Highld 311 H4
Navity Highld 301 C7
Nawton N Yorks 216 C3
Nayland Suff 107 E9
Nazeing Essex 86 D6
Nazeing Gate Essex 86 D6
Nazeing Long Green Essex 86 E6
Nazeing Mead Essex 86 D5
Neacroft Hants 19 B9
Nealhouse Cumb 239 G8
Neal's Green Warks 134 G6
Neames Forstal Kent 54 B5
Neap Shetland 313 H7
Near Hardcastle N Yorks 214 F2
Near Sawrey Cumb 221 F7
Nearton End Bucks 102 F6
Neasden London 67 B8
Neasham Darl 224 C6
Neat Enstone Oxon 101 G7
Neath = *Castell-nedd* Neath 57 B8
Neath Abbey Neath 57 B8
Neatham Hants 49 E8
Neath Hill M Keynes 103 C7
Neatishead Norf 160 E6
Neat Marsh E Yorks 209 G9
Neaton Norf 141 C8
Nebo Anglesey 179 C7
Ceredig 111 D10
Conwy 164 D4
Gwyn 163 E7
Nebsworth Warks 100 C3
Nechells W Mid 133 F11
Necton Norf 141 B7
Nedd Highld 306 F6
Nedderton Northumb 252 G6
Nedge Hill Som 44 C5
Telford 132 B4
Nedging Suff 107 B9
Nedging Tye Suff 107 B10
Needham Norf 142 G4
Needham Green Essex 87 B9
Needham Market Suff 125 G11
Needham Street Suff 124 D4
Needingworth Cambs 122 C6
Needwood Staffs 152 E3
Neen Savage Shrops 116 B3
Neen Sollars Shrops 116 C3
Neenton Shrops 132 F2
Nefod Shrops 148 B6
Nefyn Gwyn 162 G4
Neighbourne Som 44 D6
Neight Hill Worcs 117 F8
Neilston E Renf 267 D9
Neinthirion Powys 129 B9
Neithrop Oxon 101 C8
Nelly Andrews Green Powys 130 B5
Nelson Caerph 77 F10
Lancs 204 F3
Nelson Village Northumb 243 B7
Nemphlar S Lanark 269 G7
Nempnett Thrubwell Bath 60 G4
Nene Terrace Lincs 138 B5
Nenthall Cumb 231 B11
Nenthead Cumb 231 C11
Nenthorn Borders 262 B5
Neopardy Devon 13 B11
Nepcote W Sus 35 F10
Nepgill Cumb 229 F7
Nep Town W Sus 36 D2
Nerabus Argyll 254 B3
Nercwys Flint 166 C2
Nerston S Lanark 268 D2
Nesbit Northumb 263 C11
Ness Ches W 182 F4
Orkney 314 C4
Nesscliffe Shrops 149 F7
Nessholt Ches W 182 F4
Nesstoun Orkney 314 A7
Neston Ches W 182 F3
Wilts 61 F11
Netchells Green W Mid 133 F11
Netham Bristol 60 E6
Nethanfoot S Lanark 268 F6
Nether Alderley Ches E 184 F4
Netheravon Wilts 46 D6
Nether Blainslie Borders 271 G10
Nether Booth Derbys 185 D10
Netherbrae Aberds 303 D7
Netherbrough Orkney 314 E3
Nether Broughton Leics 154 D3
Netherburn S Lanark 268 F6
Nether Burrow Lancs 212 D2
Nether Burrows Derbys 152 B5
Netherbury Dorset 16 B5
Netherby Cumb 239 C9
N Yorks 206 D2
Nether Cassock Dumfries 248 C6
Nether Cerne Dorset 17 B9
Nether Chanderhill Derbys 186 G4
Netherclay Som 28 C3
Nether Compton Dorset 29 D9
Nethercote Oxon 101 C9
Warks 119 E10
Nethercott Devon 12 B3
Devon 40 F3
Oxon 101 G9
Som 42 G6
Nether Crimond Aberds 303 G8
Netherdale Shetland 313 H3
Nether Dalgliesh Borders 249 B7
Nether Dallachy Moray 302 C3
Nether Edge S Yorks 186 E4
Netherend Glos 79 E9
Nether End Derbys 186 G3
Leics 154 G4
W Yorks 197 F8
Nether Exe Devon 26 G6
Netherfield E Sus 38 D2
M Keynes 103 D7
Notts 171 G10
Nethergate Norf 159 D11
Nether Glasslaw Aberds 303 D8
Nether Hall Leicester 136 B2
Netherhampton Wilts 31 B10
Nether Handley Derbys 186 F6
Nether Handwick Angus 287 C7
Nether Haugh S Yorks 186 B6
Nether Headon Notts 188 F2
Nether Heage Derbys 170 E5
Nether Heyford W Nhants 120 F3
Nether Hindhope Borders 263 G7
Nether Horsburgh Borders 261 B8
Nether Howecleuch S Lanark 260 G2
Nether Kellet Lancs 211 F10
Nether Kidston Borders 270 G4
Nether Kinmundy Aberds 303 E10
Nether Kirton E Renf 267 D9
Netherland Green Staffs 152 C2
Nether Langwith Notts 187 G8
Netherlaw Dumfries 237 E9
Netherlay Dorset 28 F6
Nether Leask Aberds 303 F10
Netherlee E Renf 267 D11
Nether Lenshie Aberds 302 E6
Netherley Aberds 293 D10
Mers 182 D6
W Yorks 196 E4
Nether Loads Derbys 170 B4
Nethermill Dumfries 248 F2
Nethermills Moray 302 D5
Nether Monynut Borders 272 C4
Nether Moor Derbys 170 B5
Nethermuir Aberds 303 E9
Netherne on-the-Hill Sur 51 B9
Netheroyd Hill W Yorks 196 D6
Nether Padley Derbys 186 F3
Nether Park Aberds 303 D10
Netherplace E Renf 267 D10
Nether Poppleton York 207 B7
Netherraw Borders 262 E3
Nether Row Cumb 230 D2
Nether Savock Aberds 303 E10
Netherseal Derbys 152 G5
Nether Shiels Borders 271 F8
Nether Silton N Yorks 225 G9
Nether Skyborry Shrops 114 C5
Nether Street Suff 125 E8
Netherstoke Dorset 29 F8
Nether Stowey Som 43 F7
Nether Street Essex 87 C9
Herts 86 B6
Netherthird E Ayrs 258 F3
Netherthong W Yorks 196 F6
Netherthorpe Derbys 186 G6
S Yorks 187 E8
Netherton Aberds 303 E8
Angus 287 B9
Ches W 183 F8
Corn 11 G11
Cumb 228 D6
Devon 14 G3
Glos 81 E11
Hants 47 B11
Hereford 97 F10
Mers 193 G11
N Lanark 268 E5
Northumb 251 B11
Oxon 82 F6
Perth 286 B5
Shrops 132 G4
Stirling 277 F11
W Mid 133 F8
Worcs 99 C9
W Yorks 196 E6
W Yorks 197 D9
Netherton of Lonmay Aberds 303 C10
Nethertown Cumb 219 D9
Highld 310 B7
Lancs 203 F10
Staffs 152 F2
Nether Urquhart Fife 286 G5
Nether Wallop Hants 47 F10
Nether Warden Northumb 241 D10
Nether Wasdale Cumb 220 E2
Nether Welton Cumb 230 B3
Nether Westcote Glos 100 G4
Nether Whitacre Warks 134 E4
Nether Winchendon or Lower Winchendon Bucks 84 C2
Netherwitton Northumb 252 E4
Netherwood E Ayrs 258 D5
Nether Worton Oxon 101 E8
Nether Yeadon W Yorks 205 E10
Nethy Bridge Highld 301 G10
Netley Hants 33 F7
Netley Hill Soton 33 E7
Netley Marsh Hants 32 E4
Nettacott Devon 14 B4
Netteswell Essex 87 C7
Nettlebed Oxon 65 B8
Nettlebridge Som 44 D6
Nettlecombe Dorset 16 B6
IoW 20 F6
Som 42 F4
Nettleden Herts 85 C8
Nettleham Lincs 189 F8
Nettlestead Kent 53 C7
Suff 107 B11
Nettlestead Green Kent 53 C7
Nettlestone IoW 21 C8
Nettlesworth Durham 233 B11
Nettleton Glos 80 C6
Lincs 200 G6
Wilts 61 D10
Nettleton Green Wilts 61 D10
Nettleton Hill W Yorks 196 D5
Nettleton Shrub Wilts 61 D10
Nettleton Top Lincs 189 B10
Netton Wilts 46 F6
Neuadd Carms 94 G3
Nevendon Essex 88 G2
Nevern = *Nanhyfer* Pembs 91 D11
Nevilles Cross Durham 233 C11
New Abbey Dumfries 237 C11
New Aberdour Aberds 303 C8
New Addington London 67 G11
Newall W Yorks 205 D10
Newall Green Gtr Man 184 D4
New Alresford Hants 48 G5
New Alyth Perth 286 C6
Newark Orkney 314 B7
Pboro 138 C4
Newark-on-Trent Notts 172 E3
New Arley Warks 134 F5
New Arram E Yorks 208 E6
Newarthill N Lanark 268 D5
New Ash Green Kent 68 F6
New Balderton Notts 172 E4
Newball Lincs 189 F9
Newbarn Kent 55 F7
New Barn Kent 68 F6
New Barnet London 86 F3
New Barnetby N Lincs 200 E5
Newbarns Cumb 210 E4
New Barton N Nhants 121 E7
New Basford Nottingham 171 G9
Newbattle Midloth 270 B6
New Beaupre V Glam 58 E4
New Beckenham London 67 E11
New Bewick Northumb 264 E3
Newbie Dumfries 238 D5
Newbiggin Cumb 210 F5
Cumb 211 D11
Cumb 219 G11
Cumb 230 F5
Cumb 231 B7
Cumb 231 F8
Durham 232 B5
Durham 232 F4
Durham 233 B8
N Yorks 213 B9
N Yorks 223 G9
Newbiggin-by-the-Sea Northumb 253 F8
Newbigging Aberds 303 G7
Angus 287 D8
Borders 262 F6
Edin 280 F2
S Lanark 269 F10
New-bigging Angus 286 C6
Newbiggings Orkney 314 B6
Newbiggin Hall Estate T&W 242 D6
Newbiggin-on-Lune Cumb 222 D4
New Bilton Warks 119 B9
Newbold Derbys 186 G5
Gtr Man 196 E2
Leics 136 B5
Leics 153 F8
Newbold Heath Leics 135 B8
Newbold on Avon Warks 119 B9
Newbold on Stour Warks 100 B4
Newbold Pacey Warks 118 F5
Newbolds W Mid 133 C8
Newbold Verdon Leics 135 C8
New Bolingbroke Lincs 174 D4
New Bolsover Derbys 187 G7
Newborough Pboro 138 B4
Staffs 152 D2
New Boston Mers 183 B9
New Botley Oxon 83 D7
Newbottle T&W 243 G8
W Nhants 101 D10
New Boultham Lincs 189 G7
Newbourne Suff 108 C5
New Bradwell M Keynes 102 C6
New Brancepeth Durham 233 C10
Newbridge Bath 61 F8
Caerph 78 F2
Ceredig 111 F10
Corn 1 C4
Corn 4 G5
Corn 7 B7
Dumfries 237 B11
Edin 280 G2
E Sus 52 G3
Hants 32 D3
IoW 20 D4
Lancs 204 F3
N Yorks 216 B6
Oxon 82 E6
Pembs 91 E8
Shrops 148 D6
W Mid 133 D7
Wrex 166 G3
New Bridge Wrex 166 G3
Newbridge Green Worcs 98 D6
Newbridge-on-Usk Mon 78 G5
Newbridge-on-Wye Powys 113 F10
New Brighton Flint 166 B3
Mers 182 C4
Wrex 166 E3
W Sus 22 B3
W Yorks 197 B9
W Yorks 205 F8
New Brimington Derbys 186 G6
New Brinsley Notts 171 E7
New Brotton Redcar 235 G9
Newbrough Northumb 241 D9
New Broughton Wrex 166 E4
New Buckenham Norf 141 E11
Newbuildings Devon 26 G3
New Buildings Bath 45 B7
Dorset 18 E5
Newburgh Aberds 303 D9
Aberds 303 G9
Borders 261 F8
Fife 286 F6
Lancs 194 E3
Newburn T&W 242 D5
Newbury Kent 54 B2
W Berks 64 F3
Wilts 45 E10
New Bury Gtr Man 195 F8
Newbury Park London 68 B2
Newby Cumb 231 G7
Lancs 204 D2
N Yorks 205 D11
N Yorks 212 E4
N Yorks 215 F7
N Yorks 225 C10
N Yorks 227 G10
Newby Bridge Cumb 211 B7
Newby Cote N Yorks 212 E4
Newby East Cumb 239 F11
Newby Head Cumb 231 G7
New Byth Aberds 303 D8
Newby West Cumb 239 G9
Newby Wiske N Yorks 215 B7
Newcastle Bridgend 58 D2
Mon 78 B6
Shrops 130 G4
Newcastle Emlyn = *Castell Newydd Emlyn* Carms 92 C6
Newcastleton or Copshaw Holm Borders 249 F11

Newcastle-under-Lyme
Staffs 168 F4
Newcastle upon Tyne
T&W 242 E6
New Catton Norf 160 G4
Newchapel Powys 129 G9
Staffs 168 E5
Sur 51 E11
Newchapel = *Capel Newydd*
Pembs 92 D4
New Charlton London 68 D2
New Cheltenham S Glos 61 E7
New Cheriton Hants 33 B9
Newchurch Bl Gwent 77 C11
Carms 93 G7
Hereford 115 G7
IoW 21 D7
Kent 54 G5
Lancs 195 C10
Mon 79 F7
Powys 114 G4
Staffs 152 E2
Newchurch in Pendle
Lancs 204 F2
New Clipstone Notts 171 C9
New Costessey Norf 160 G3
Newcott Devon 28 F2
New Coundon Durham 233 E10
New Cowper Cumb 229 B8
Newcraighall Edin 280 G6
New Crofton W Yorks 197 D11
New Cross Ceredig 112 B2
London 67 D11
Oxon 65 D9
Som 28 D6
New Cross Gate London 67 D11
New Cumnock E Ayrs 258 G4
New Deer Aberds 303 E8
New Delaval Northumb 243 B7
New Delph Gtr Man 196 F3
New Denham Bucks 66 C4
Newdigate Sur 51 E7
New Downs Corn 1 C3
Corn 4 E4
New Duston W Nhants 120 E4
New Earswick York 207 B8
New Eastwood Notts 171 F7
New Edlington S Yorks 187 B8
New Elgin Moray 302 C2
New Ellerby E Yorks 209 F9
Newell Green Brack 65 E11
New Eltham London 68 E2
New End Lincs 190 G2
Warks 118 E2
Worcs 117 F11
Newenden Kent 38 B4
New England Essex 106 C4
Lincs 175 D8
Pboro 138 C3
Som 28 E4
Newent Glos 98 F4
Newerne Glos 79 E10
New Farnley W Yorks 205 G10
New Ferry Mers 182 D4
Newfield Durham 233 E10
Durham 242 G6
Highld 301 B7
Stoke 168 E6
New Fletton Pboro 138 D3
Newford Scilly 1 G4
Newfound Hants 48 C5
New Fryston W Yorks 198 B3
Newgale Pembs 90 G6
New Galloway Dumfries 237 B8
Newgarth Orkney 314 E2
Newgate Lancs 194 F4
Norf 177 E9
Newgate Corner Norf 161 G8
Newgate Street Herts 86 D4
New Gilston Fife 287 G8
New Greens Herts 85 D10
New Grimsby Scilly 1 F3
New Ground Herts 85 C7
Newgrounds Hants 31 E11
Newhailes Edin 280 G6
New Hainford Norf 160 F4
Newhall Ches E 167 F10
Derbys 152 E5
Newhall Green Warks 134 F5
New Hall Hey Lancs 195 C10
Newhall House Highld 300 C6
Newhall Point Highld 301 C7
Newham Lincs 174 E3
Northumb 264 D5
New Hartley Northumb 243 B8
Newhaven Derbys 169 C11
Devon 24 C5
Edin 280 F5
E Sus 36 G6
New Haw Sur 66 G5
Newhay N Yorks 207 G9
New Headington Oxon 83 D9
New Heaton Northumb 273 G7
New Hedges Pembs 73 E10
New Herrington T&W 243 G8
Newhey Gtr Man 196 E2
Newhill Fife 286 F6
Perth 286 G5
S Yorks 186 B6
Newhills Aberdeen 293 C10
New Hinksey Oxon 83 E8
New Ho Durham 232 D3
New Holkham Norf 159 B7
New Holland N Lincs 200 C5
W Yorks 205 F7
Newholm N Yorks 227 C7
New Horwich Derbys 185 E8
New Houghton Derbys 171 B7
Norf 158 D5
Newhouse Borders 262 E2
N Lanark 268 C5
Shetland 313 G6
New House Kent 68 E6
Newhouses Borders 271 G10
New Houses Gtr Man 194 G5
N Yorks 212 E6
New Humberstone
Leicester 136 B2
New Hunwick Durham 233 E9
New Hutton Cumb 221 G11
New Hythe Kent 53 B8
Newick E Sus 36 C6
Newingreen Kent 54 F6
Newington Edin 280 G5
Kent 55 F7
Kent 69 G11
Kent 71 F11
London 67 D10
Notts 187 C11
Oxon 83 F10
Shrops 131 G8
Newington Bagpath Glos 80 G4
New Inn Carms 93 D9
Devon 24 F6
Mon 79 E7
Pembs 91 E11
Torf 78 F4
New Invention Shrops 114 B5
W Mid 133 C9
New Kelso Highld 299 E9
New Kingston Notts 153 D10
New Kyo Durham 242 G5
New Ladykirk Borders 273 F7
New Lanark S Lanark 269 G7
Newland Cumb 210 D6
E Yorks 199 B10
Glos 79 D9
Hull 209 G7
N Yorks 199 C7
Oxon 82 C5
Worcs 98 B5
Newland Bottom Cumb 210 C5
Newland Common
Worcs 117 E8
Newland Green Kent 54 D2
Newlandrig Midloth 271 C7
Newlands Borders 250 E2
Borders 262 E2
Cumb 229 G10
Cumb 230 D2
Derbys 170 F6
Dumfries 247 F11
Glasgow 267 C11
Highld 301 E7
Moray 302 D3
Northumb 242 F3
Notts 171 C9
Staffs 151 E11
Newlands Corner Sur 50 D4
Newlandsmuir S Lanark 268 E2
Newlands of Geise
Highld 310 C4
Newlands of Tynet
Moray 302 C3
Newlands Park Anglesey 178 E3
New Lane Lancs 194 E2
New Lane End Warr 183 B10
New Langholm Dumfries 249 G9
New Leake Lincs 174 D6
New Leeds Aberds 303 D9
Newliston Edin 280 G2
Fife 280 C5
New Lodge S Yorks 197 F10
New Longton Lancs 194 B4
Newlot Orkney 314 E5
New Lubbesthorpe
Leics 135 C10
New Luce Dumfries 236 C3
Newlyn Corn 1 D5
Newmachar Aberds 293 B10
Newmains N Lanark 268 D6
New Malden London 67 F8
Newman's End Essex 87 C8
Newman's Green Suff 107 C7
Newman's Place Hereford 96 B5
Newmarket Glos 80 F4
Suff 124 E2
W Isles 304 E6
New Marske Redcar 235 G8
New Marston Oxon 83 D8
New Marton Shrops 148 C6
New Micklefield
W Yorks 206 G4
Newmill Borders 261 G11
Corn 1 C5
Moray 302 D4
New Mill Aberds 293 E9
Borders 262 G2
Corn 1 C5
Corn 4 F6
Cumb 219 E11
Herts 84 C6
Wilts 63 G7
W Yorks 197 F7
Newmillerdam
W Yorks 197 D10
Newmill of Inshewan
Angus 292 G6
Newmills Corn 11 D11
Fife 279 D10
Highld 300 C6
New Mills Borders 271 F10
Ches E 184 E3
Corn 5 E7
Derbys 185 D7
Glos 79 E10
Hereford 98 D4
New Mills = *Felin Newydd*
Powys 129 C11
Newmills of Boyne
Aberds 302 D5
Newmiln Perth 286 D5
Newmilns E Ayrs 258 B2
New Milton Hants 19 B10
New Mistley Essex 108 E2
New Moat Pembs 91 F11
Newmore Highld 300 B6
Highld 300 D5
New Moston Gtr Man 195 G11
Newnes Shrops 149 C7
Newney Green Essex 87 D11
Newnham Cambs 123 F8
Glos 79 C11
Hants 49 C8
Herts 104 D4
Kent 54 B3
Warks 118 E3
W Nhants 119 F11
Newnham Bridge Worcs 116 D2
New Ollerton Notts 171 B11
New Oscott W Mid 133 E11
New Pale Ches W 183 G8
Newpark Fife 287 F8
New Park N Yorks 205 B11
New Parks Leicester 135 B11
New Passage S Glos 60 B4
New Pitsligo Aberds 303 D8
New Polzeath Corn 10 F4
Newpool Staffs 168 D5
Newport Corn 12 D2
Devon 40 G5
Dorset 18 C3
Essex 105 E10
E Yorks 208 G3
Glos 79 F11
Highld 311 G5
IoW 20 D6
Newport 59 B10
Norf 161 F10
Som 28 C4
Telford 150 F4
Newport = *Trefdraeth*
Pembs 91 D11
Newport-on-Tay Fife 287 E8
Newport Pagnell
M Keynes 103 C7
Newpound Common
W Sus 35 B9
Newquay Corn 4 C6
New Quay = *Ceinewydd*
Ceredig 111 F7
New Rackheath Norf 160 G5
New Radnor Powys 114 E4
New Rent Cumb 230 D5
New Ridley Northumb 242 F3
New Road Side N Yorks 204 E5
W Yorks 197 B7
New Romney Kent 39 C9
New Rossington
S Yorks 187 B10
New Row Ceredig 112 C4
Lancs 203 F8
New Row *continued*
N Yorks 226 C2
Newsam Green
W Yorks 206 G3
New Sarum Wilts 46 G6
New Sawley Derbys 153 C9
Newsbank Ches E 168 B4
New Scarbro W Yorks 205 G10
Newseat Aberds 303 E10
Aberds 303 F7
Newsells Herts 105 D7
Newsham Lancs 202 F6
Northumb 243 B8
N Yorks 215 C7
N Yorks 224 C2
New Sharlston
W Yorks 197 C11
Newsholme E Yorks 199 B8
Lancs 204 C2
W Yorks 204 F6
New Silksworth T&W 243 G9
New Skelton Redcar 226 B3
New Smithy Derbys 185 E9
Newsome W Yorks 196 E6
New Southgate London 86 G3
New Springs Gtr Man 194 F6
New Sprowston Norf 160 G4
New Stanton Derbys 153 B9
Newstead Borders 262 C3
Northumb 264 D5
Notts 171 E8
Staffs 168 G5
W Yorks 197 E11
New Stevenston
N Lanark 268 D5
New Street Kent 68 G6
Staffs 169 E9
Newstreet Lane Shrops 150 B2
New Swanage Dorset 18 E6
New Swannington Leics 153 F8
Newtake Devon 14 G3
New Thirsk N Yorks 215 C8
Newthorpe Notts 171 F7
N Yorks 206 G5
Newthorpe Common
Notts 171 F7
New Thundersley Essex 69 B9
Newtoft Lincs 189 D8
Newton Argyll 275 D11
Borders 262 E3
Borders 262 F2
Bridgend 57 F10
Cambs 105 B8
Cambs 157 G8
Cardiff 59 D8
C Beds 104 C4
Ches W 166 B6
Ches W 167 D8
Ches W 183 F8
Corn 5 C11
Cumb 210 E4
Derbys 170 D6
Dorset 30 E3
Dumfries 239 C7
Dumfries 248 E4
Gtr Man 185 B7
Hereford 96 C5
Hereford 96 E6
Hereford 115 D7
Hereford 115 G10
Highld 301 C7
Highld 301 E7
Highld 306 F7
Highld 310 E7
Lancs 202 F2
Lancs 202 G4
Lancs 203 C9
Lancs 211 E11
Lincs 155 B10
Mers 182 D2
Moray 301 C11
N Nhants 137 G7
Norf 158 F6
Northumb 242 E2
Notts 171 G11
Perth 286 D2
S Glos 79 G10
Shetland 312 E5
Shetland 313 K5
Shrops 132 D4
Shrops 149 C8
S Lanark 259 C10
S Lanark 268 C3
Som 42 F6
Staffs 151 D10
Suff 107 C8
Swansea 56 D6
S Yorks 198 G5
Warks 119 B10
Wilts 32 C2
W Loth 279 F11
W Mid 133 E10
Newton Abbot Devon 14 G3
Newtonairds Dumfries 247 G9
Newton Arlosh Cumb 238 F5
Newton Aycliffe
Durham 233 G11
Newton Bewley Hrtlpl 234 F5
Newton Blossomville
M Keynes 121 G8
Newton Bromswold
N Nhants 121 D9
Newton Burgoland
Leics 135 B7
Newton by Toft Lincs 189 D9
Newton Cross Pembs 91 F7
Newton Ferrers Devon 7 F10
Newton Flotman Norf 142 D4
Newtongrange Midloth 270 C6
Newton Green Mon 79 G8
Newton Hall Durham 233 B11
Northumb 242 D2
Newton Harcourt Leics 136 D2
Newton Heath
Gtr Man 195 G11
Newtonhill Aberds 293 D11
Highld 300 E5
Newton Hill W Yorks 197 C10
Newton Ho Aberds 302 G6
Newton Hurst Staffs 151 D11
Newtonia Ches E 167 B11
Newton Ketton Darl 234 G2
Newton Kyme N Yorks 206 E5
Newton-le-Willows
Mers 183 B9
N Yorks 214 B4
Newton Leyes Milton
Keynes 103 E7
Newton Longville
Bucks 102 E6
Newton Mearns
E Renf 267 D10
Newtonmill Angus 293 G8
Newtonmore Highld 291 D9
Newton Morrell
N Yorks 224 D4
Oxon 102 F2
Newton Mulgrave
N Yorks 226 B5
Newton of Ardtoe
Highld 289 B8
Newton of Balcanquhal
Perth 286 F5
Newton of Balcormo
Fife 287 G9
Newton of Falkland
Fife 286 G6
Newton of Mountblairy
Aberds 302 D6
Newton of Pitcairns
Perth 286 F4
Newton on Ayr S Ayrs 257 E8
Newton on Ouse
N Yorks 206 B6
Newton-on-Rawcliffe
N Yorks 226 G6
Newton on the Hill
Shrops 149 E9
Newton on the Moor
Northumb 252 B5
Newton on Trent Lincs 188 G4
Newton Park Argyll 266 B2
Mers 183 C9
Newton Peveril Dorset 18 B4
Newton Poppleford
Devon 15 D7
Newton Purcell Oxon 102 E2
Newton Regis Warks 134 B5
Newton Reigny Cumb 230 E5
Newton Rigg Cumb 230 E5
Newton St Boswells
Borders 262 C3
Newton St Cyres Devon 14 B3
Newton St Faith Norf 160 F4
Newton St Loe Bath 61 G8
Newton St Petrock Devon 24 E6
Newton Solney Derbys 152 D5
Newton Stacey Hants 48 E2
Newton Stewart
Dumfries 236 C6
Newton Tony Wilts 47 E8
Newton Tracey Devon 25 B8
Newton under Roseberry
Redcar 225 C11
Newton Underwood
Northumb 252 F4
Newton upon Derwent
E Yorks 207 D10
Newton Valence Hants 49 G8
Newton with Scales
Lancs 202 G4
Newton Wood Gtr Man 184 B6
New Totley S Yorks 186 F4
Newtown Argyll 284 G4
BCP 18 C6
Bl Gwent 77 C11
Bucks 85 E7
Caerph 78 G2
Cambs 121 D11
Ches E 184 E6
Ches W 183 F8
Corn 2 D3
Corn 11 F11
Cumb 229 B7
Cumb 239 F9
Cumb 240 E2
Derbys 185 E7
Devon 26 B3
Dorset 29 G7
Falk 279 E9
Glos 79 E11
Glos 80 D3
Glos 99 E8
Gtr Man 194 F5
Gtr Man 195 G9
Hants 21 B8
Hants 32 C4
Hants 32 E3
Hants 33 D8
Hants 33 E10
Hants 33 F7
Hants 49 G10
Hants 64 G3
Hereford 97 E10
Hereford 98 C2
Hereford 98 D3
Highld 290 C5
IoM 192 E4
IoW 20 C4
Mers 183 B7
Norf 143 B10
Northumb 252 C2
Northumb 263 C11
Northumb 264 D2
Oxon 65 C9
Powys 130 E2
Rhondda 77 F9
Shrops 132 C2
Shrops 149 C9
Shrops 149 E8
Som 28 E3
Som 43 F9
Staffs 133 C9
Staffs 168 C6
Staffs 169 C9
Wilts 30 B6
Wilts 63 G10
W Mid 133 F11
Worcs 116 F5
Worcs 117 E7
New Town Bath 45 B9
Bath 60 G5
Dorset 30 C3
Dorset 30 D6
Dorset 31 D7
Dorset 31 F7
Edin 280 G4
Edin 280 G5
E Loth 281 G8
E Sus 37 C7
Glos 99 E10
Kent 53 B7
Kent 68 E4
Lancs 203 F8
Luton 103 G11
Medway 69 G8
Oxon 100 F5
Reading 65 E8
Shetland 312 E6
Som 29 D9
Som 29 D11
Som 44 D3
Soton 33 E7
Swindon 63 C7
T&W 234 B2
T&W 243 E8
W Berks 64 D6
Wilts 46 C6
Wilts 63 E9
W Mid 133 B11
W Mid 133 E9
W Sus 35 B11
W Yorks 198 C3
Newtown-in-St Martin
Corn 2 E6
Newtown Linford Leics 135 B10
Newtown St Boswells
Borders 262 C3
Newtown Unthank Leics 135 C9
New Tredegar Caerph 77 E10
New Trows S Lanark 259 B8
Newtyle Angus 286 C6
New Ulva Argyll 275 E8
New Village E Yorks 209 G7
S Yorks 198 F5
New Walsoken Cambs 139 B9
New Waltham NE Lincs 201 G9
New Well Powys 113 B11
New Wells Powys 130 D3
New Whittington Derbys 186 F5
New Wimpole Cambs 104 B6
New Winton E Loth 281 G8
New Woodhouses
Shrops 167 G9
New Works Telford 132 B3
New Wortley W Yorks 205 G11
New Yatt Oxon 82 C5
Newyears Green London 66 B5
New York Lincs 174 D2
N Yorks 214 G3
T&W 243 C8
New Zealand Wilts 62 D4
Nextend Hereford 114 F6
Neyland Pembs 73 D7
Niarbyl IoM 192 E3
Nib Heath Shrops 149 F8
Nibley Glos 79 D11
S Glos 61 C7
Nibley Green Glos 80 F2
Nibon Shetland 312 F5
Nicholashayne Devon 27 D10
Nicholaston Swansea 56 D4
Nidd N Yorks 214 G6
Niddrie Edin 280 G5
Nigg Aberdeen 293 C11
Highld 301 B8
Nigg Ferry Highld 301 C7
Nightcott Som 26 B5
Nilig Denb 165 D8
Nimble Nook Gtr Man 196 G2
Nimlet S Glos 61 E8
Nimmer Som 28 E4
Nine Ashes Essex 87 E9
Ninebanks Northumb 241 G7
Nine Elms London 67 D9
Swindon 62 B6
Nine Maidens Downs Corn 2 B5
Nine Mile Burn Midloth 270 D3
Nineveh Worcs 116 C3
Worcs 116 E2
Ninewells Glos 79 C9
Nine Wells Pembs 90 G5
Ninfield E Sus 38 E2
Ningwood IoW 20 D3
Ningwood Common IoW 20 D3
Ninnes Bridge Corn 2 B2
Nisbet Borders 262 D5
Nisthouse Orkney 314 E3
Shetland 313 G7
Nithbank Dumfries 247 D9
Niton IoW 20 F6
Nitshill Glasgow 267 C10
Noah's Arks Kent 52 B5
Noah's Green Worcs 117 E10
Noak Bridge Essex 87 G11
Noak Hill Essex 87 G11
London 87 G8
Nob End Gtr Man 195 F9
Nobland Green Herts 86 B5
Noblethorpe S Yorks 197 F9
Nobold Shrops 149 G9
Nobottle W Nhants 120 E3
Nob's Crook Hants 33 C7
Nocton Lincs 173 C9
Noctorum Mers 182 D3
Nodmore W Berks 64 D2
Noel Park London 86 G4
Nogdam End Norf 143 C7
Nog Tow Lancs 202 G6
Noke Oxon 83 C8
Noke Street Medway 69 E8
Nolton Pembs 72 B5
Nolton Haven Pembs 72 B5
No Man's Heath Ches W 167 F8
Warks 134 B5
Nomansland Devon 26 E4
Herts 85 C11
Wilts 32 D3
No Man's Land Corn 6 D5
Hants 33 B8
Noneley Shrops 149 D9
Noness Shetland 313 L6
Nonikiln Highld 300 B6
Nonington Kent 55 C9
Nook Cumb 211 C10
Noon Nick W Yorks 205 F8
Noonsbrough Shetland 313 H4
Noonsun Ches E 184 F4
Noonvares Corn 2 C3
Noranside Angus 292 G6
Norbiton London 67 F7
Norbreck Blackpool 202 E2
Norbridge Hereford 98 C4
Norbury Ches E 167 F9
Derbys 169 G10
London 67 F10
Shrops 131 E7
Staffs 150 E5
Norbury Common
Ches E 167 F9
Norbury Junction Staffs 150 E5
Norbury Moor Gtr Man 184 D6
Norby N Yorks 215 C8
Shetland 313 H3
Norchard Worcs 116 D6
Norcote Glos 81 E8
Norcott Brook Ches W 183 E10
Norcross Blackpool 202 E2
Nordelph Norf 139 C11
Nordelph Corner Norf 141 C10
Norden Dorset 18 E4
Gtr Man 195 E11
Norden Heath Dorset 18 E4
Nordley Shrops 132 D3
Norham Northumb 273 F8
Norham West Mains
Northumb 273 F8
Nork Sur 51 B8
Norland Town W Yorks 196 C5
Norleaze Wilts 45 C11
Norley Ches W 183 G9
Devon 25 G8
Norley Common Sur 50 E4
Norleywood Hants 20 B3
Norlington E Sus 36 E6
Normacot Stoke 168 G6
Normanby N Lincs 199 D11
N Yorks 216 C4
Redcar 225 B10
Normanby-by-Spital
Lincs 189 D7
Normanby by Stow
Lincs 188 E5
Normanby le Wold
Lincs 189 B10
Norman Cross Cambs 138 E3
Normandy Sur 50 C2
Norman Hill Glos 80 F3
Norman's Bay E Sus 23 D11
Norman's Green Devon 27 G9
Normanston Suff 143 E10
Normanton Derby 152 C6
Leics 172 G4
Normanton *continued*
Lincs 172 F6
Notts 172 E2
Rutland 137 B8
Wilts 46 E6
W Yorks 197 C11
Normanton le Heath
Leics 153 G7
Normanton on Soar
Notts 153 E10
Normanton-on-the-Wolds
Notts 154 C2
Normanton on Trent
Notts 172 B3
Normanton Spring
S Yorks 186 E6
Normanton Turville
Leics 135 D9
Normoss Lancs 202 F2
Norney Sur 50 E2
Norr W Yorks 205 F7
Norrington Common
Wilts 61 G11
Norris Green Corn 7 B8
Mers 182 C5
Norris Hill Leics 152 F6
Norristhorpe W Yorks 197 C8
Norseman Orkney 314 E3
Northacre Norf 141 D9
North Acton London 67 C8
Northall Bucks 103 G9
Northallerton N Yorks 225 G7
Northall Green Norf 159 G9
Northam Devon 24 B6
Soton 32 E6
Northampton W Nhants 120 E5
North Anston S Yorks 187 E8
North Ascot Brack 66 F2
North Aston Oxon 101 F9
Northaw Herts 86 E3
Northay Devon 28 G5
Som 28 E3
North Ayre Shetland 312 F6
North Baddesley Hants 32 D5
North Ballachulish
Highld 290 G2
North Barrow Som 29 B10
North Barsham Norf 159 C8
North Batsom Som 41 G10
Northbeck Lincs 173 G9
North Beer Corn 12 C2
North Benfleet Essex 69 B9
North Bersted W Sus 22 C6
North Berwick E Loth 281 D11
North Bitchburn Durham 233 E9
North Blyth Northumb 253 G8
North Boarhunt Hants 33 E10
North Bockhampton BCP 19 B9
Northborough Pboro 138 B3
Northbourne BCP 19 B7
Kent 55 C10
North Bovey Devon 13 E10
North Bradley Wilts 45 C11
North Brentor Devon 12 E5
North Brewham Som 45 F8
Northbridge Street
E Sus 38 C2
Northbrook Dorset 17 C11
Hants 33 D9
Hants 48 F4
Oxon 101 G9
Wilts 46 C4
North Brook End Cambs 104 C5
North Broomage Falk 279 E7
North Buckland Devon 40 E3
North Burlingham Norf 161 G7
North Cadbury Som 29 B10
North Cairn Dumfries 236 B1
North Camp Hants 49 C11
North Carlton Lincs 188 F6
Notts 187 E9
North Carrine Argyll 255 G7
North Cave E Yorks 208 G3
North Cerney Glos 81 D8
North Chailey E Sus 36 C5
Northchapel W Sus 35 B7
North Charford Wilts 31 D11
North Charlton
Northumb 264 E5
North Cheam London 67 F8
North Cheriton Som 29 B11
Northchurch Herts 85 D7
North Cliff E Yorks 209 D10
North Cliffe E Yorks 208 F3
North Clifton Notts 188 G4
North Close Durham 233 E11
North Cockerington
Lincs 190 C5
North Coker Som 29 E8
North Collafirth
Shetland 312 E5
North Common S Glos 61 E7
Suff 125 B9
North Connel Argyll 289 F11
North Cornelly Bridgend 57 E10
North Corner Corn 3 F7
S Glos 61 C7
North Corriegills
N Ayrs 256 C2
North Corry Highld 289 D10
Northcote Devon 27 G11
North Cotes Lincs 201 G11
Northcott Corn 24 F2
Devon 12 C2
Devon 27 E9
Devon 27 F10
North Country Corn 4 G3
Northcourt Oxon 83 F8
North Court Som 41 F11
North Cove Suff 143 F9
North Cowton N Yorks 224 E5
North Craigo Angus 293 G8
North Crawley
M Keynes 103 C8
North Cray London 68 E3
North Creake Norf 159 B7
North Curry Som 28 B4
North Dalton E Yorks 208 C4
North Darley Corn 11 G11
North Dawn Orkney 314 F4
North Deighton N Yorks 206 C3
North Denes Norf 161 G10
Northdown Kent 71 E11
North Dronley Angus 287 D7
North Drumachter Lodge
Highld 291 F8
North Duffield N Yorks 207 F9
Northdyke Orkney 314 D2
North Dykes Cumb 230 D6
North Eastling Kent 54 B3
Northedge Derbys 170 B5
North Elham Kent 55 E7
North Elkington Lincs 190 C3
North Elmham Norf 159 E9
North Elmsall W Yorks 198 E3
North Elmshall W Yorks 198 E3
North Elphinestone
E Loth 281 G7
Northend Bath 61 F9
Bucks 84 G2
Essex 89 E7
Northend *continued*
Essex 105 D10
Warks 119 G7
North End Bath 60 G6
Bedford 103 B9
Bedford 121 F10
Bucks 102 F4
Bucks 102 F6
Cumb 239 F8
Devon 27 D10
Dorset 30 B4
Durham 233 C11
Essex 87 B11
Essex 106 D5
E Yorks 209 C9
E Yorks 209 E9
E Yorks 209 G11
Hants 31 D10
Hants 33 B9
Hants 64 G2
Leics 153 F11
Lincs 174 G2
Lincs 189 B8
Lincs 190 C5
Lincs 190 D6
Lincs 191 D7
Lincs 201 G10
London 67 B9
London 68 D4
N Lincs 200 C6
Norf 141 E10
Northumb 252 C4
N Som 60 F2
Ptsmth 33 G11
Som 28 B3
Wilts 81 G8
W Sus 35 F10
W Sus 35 G7
W Sus 51 F11
Northenden Gtr Man 184 C4
Northern Moor Gtr Man 184 C4
North Erradale Highld 307 L2
North Evington
Leicester 136 C2
North Ewster N Lincs 199 G10
North Fambridge Essex 88 F5
North Fearns Highld 295 B7
North Featherstone
W Yorks 198 C2
North Feltham London 66 E6
North Feorline N Ayrs 255 E10
North Ferriby E Yorks 200 B3
Northfield Aberdeen 293 C11
Borders 262 D3
Borders 273 B8
Edin 280 G5
E Yorks 200 B4
Highld 301 B7
M Keynes 103 C7
N Nhants 137 E7
Som 43 F9
W Mid 117 B10
Northfields Hants 33 B7
Lincs 137 B10
North Finchley London 86 G3
Northfleet Kent 68 E6
Northfleet Green Kent 68 E6
North Flobbets Aberds 303 F7
North Frodingham
E Yorks 209 C8
Northgate Lincs 156 D3
Som 27 B9
W Sus 51 F9
North Gluss Shetland 312 F5
North Gorley Hants 31 E11
North Green Norf 141 B10
Norf 142 F4
Suff 126 B6
Suff 126 E6
Suff 127 D7
North Greetwell Lincs 189 G8
North Grimston N Yorks 216 F6
North Halley Orkney 314 F5
North Halling Medway 69 F8
North Harrow London 66 B6
North Hayling Hants 22 C2
North Hazelrigg
Northumb 264 C3
North Heasley Devon 41 G8
North Heath W Berks 64 E3
W Sus 35 C9
North Hill Corn 11 F11
North Hillingdon London 66 C5
North Hinksey Oxon 83 D7
North Hinksey Village
Oxon 83 D7
North Ho Shetland 313 J5
North Holmwood Sur 51 D7
North Houghton Hants 47 G10
Northhouse Borders 249 B10
North Howden E Yorks 207 G11
North Huish Devon 8 D4
North Hyde London 66 D6
North Hykeham Lincs 172 B6
North Hylton T&W 243 F8
Northiam E Sus 38 B4
Northill C Beds 104 B2
Northington Glos 80 D2
Hants 48 F5
North Kelsey Lincs 200 G4
North Kelsey Moor
Lincs 200 G5
North Kensington London 67 C8
North Kessock Highld 300 E6
North Killingholme
N Lincs 200 D6
North Kilvington
N Yorks 215 B8
North Kilworth Leics 136 G2
North Kingston Hants 31 G11
North Kirkton Aberds 303 D11
North Kiscadale N Ayrs 256 D2
North Kyme Lincs 173 E11
North Laggan Highld 290 D4
North Lancing W Sus 35 F11
North Landing E Yorks 218 E4
Northlands Lincs 174 E4
Northlea Durham 243 G10
Northleach Glos 81 C10
North Lee Bucks 84 D4
North Lees N Yorks 214 E6
Northleigh Devon 15 B9
Devon 40 G6
North Leigh Kent 54 D6
Oxon 82 C5
North Leverton with
Habblesthorpe Notts 188 E3
Northlew Devon 12 B6
North Littleton Worcs 99 B11
North Looe Sur 67 G8
North Lopham Norf 141 G10
North Luffenham
Rutland 137 C8
North Marden W Sus 34 D4
North Marston Bucks 102 G5
North Middleton
Midloth 271 D7
Northumb 264 E2
North Millbrex Aberds 303 E8
North Molton Devon 26 B2
Northmoor Devon 24 D4
Northmoor *continued*
Oxon 82 E6
Northmoor Corner Som 43 G10
Northmoor Green or
Moorland Som 43 G10
North Moreton Oxon 64 B5
North Mosstown
Aberds 303 D10
North Motherwell
N Lanark 268 D4
North Moulsecoomb
Brighton 36 F4
Northmuir Angus 287 B7
North Mundham W Sus 22 C5
North Muskham Notts 172 D3
North Newbald E Yorks 208 F4
North Newington Oxon 101 D8
North Newnton Wilts 46 B6
North Newton Som 43 G9
Northney Hants 22 C2
North Nibley Glos 80 F2
North Oakley Hants 48 C4
North Ockendon London 68 C5
Northolt London 66 C6
Northop = *Llan-eurgain*
Flint 166 B2
Northop Hall Flint 166 B3
North Ormesby Mbro 234 G6
North Ormsby Lincs 190 C3
Northorpe Lincs 155 F11
Lincs 156 B4
Lincs 188 B5
W Yorks 197 C8
North Otterington
N Yorks 215 B7
Northover Som 29 C8
Som 44 F3
North Owersby Lincs 189 C9
Northowram W Yorks 196 B6
Northpark Argyll 275 G11
North Perrott Som 29 F7
North Petherton Som 43 G9
North Petherwin Corn 11 D11
North Pickenham Norf 141 B7
North Piddle Worcs 117 G9
North Poorton Dorset 16 B6
Northport Dorset 18 D4
North Port Argyll 284 E4
North Poulner Hants 31 F11
Northpunds Shetland 313 L6
North Queensferry Fife 280 E2
North Radworthy Devon 41 G9
North Rauceby Lincs 173 F8
North Reddish Gtr Man 184 C5
Northrepps Norf 160 B4
North Reston Lincs 190 E5
North Rigton N Yorks 205 D11
North Ripley Hants 19 B9
North Rode Ches E 168 B5
North Roe Shetland 312 E5
North Row Cumb 229 E10
North Runcton Norf 158 F2
North Sandwick
Shetland 312 D7
North Scale Cumb 210 F3
North Scarle Lincs 172 B5
North Seaton Northumb 253 F7
North Seaton Colliery
Northumb 253 F7
North Sheen London 67 D7
North Shian Argyll 289 E11
North Shields T&W 243 D9
North Shoebury Southend 70 B2
North Shore Blackpool 202 F2
Northside Aberds 303 D8
Orkney 314 D2
North Side Cumb 228 F6
Pboro 138 D5
North Skelmanae
Aberds 303 D9
North Skelton Redcar 226 B3
North Somercotes Lincs 190 B6
North Stainley N Yorks 214 D5
North Stainmore Cumb 222 B6
North Stifford Thurrock 68 C6
North Stoke Bath 61 F8
Oxon 64 B6
W Sus 35 E8
North Stoneham Hants 32 D6
Northstowe Cambs 123 D8
North Street Hants 31 D11
Hants 48 G6
Kent 54 B4
Medway 69 E10
W Berks 64 E6
North Sunderland
Northumb 264 C6
North Synton Borders 261 E11
North Tamerton Corn 12 B2
North Tawton Devon 25 G11
North Thoresby Lincs 190 B3
North Tidworth Wilts 47 D8
North Togston Northumb 252 C6
Northton Aberds 293 C9
Northtown Orkney 314 G4
Shetland 313 M5
North Town Devon 25 F8
Hants 49 C11
Som 29 B10
Som 44 E5
Windsor 65 C11
North Tuddenham
Norf 159 G10
Northumberland Heath
London 68 D4
Northville Torf 78 F3
North Walbottle T&W 242 D5
North Walney Cumb 210 F3
North Walsham Norf 160 C5
North Waltham Hants 48 D5
North Warnborough
Hants 49 C8
North Water Bridge
Angus 293 G8
North Waterhayne Devon 28 F3
North Watford Herts 85 F10
North Watten Highld 310 D6
Northway Devon 24 C5
Glos 99 E8
Som 27 B10
Swansea 56 D5
North Weald Bassett
Essex 87 E7
North Weirs Hants 32 G3
North Wembley London 67 B7
North Weston N Som 60 D3
Oxon 83 D11
North Wheatley Notts 188 D3
North Whilborough Devon 9 B7
North Whiteley Moray 302 E4
Northwich Ches W 183 G11
Northwick S Glos 60 B5
Som 43 D11
Worcs 116 F6
North Wick Bath 60 F5
North Widcombe Bath 44 B5
North Willingham
Lincs 189 D11
North Wingfield Derbys 170 B6

North Witham Lincs 155 E8
Northwold Norf 140 D5
Northwood Derbys 170 C3
IoW 20 C5
Kent 71 F11
London 85 G9
Mers 182 B6
Shrops 149 C9
Staffs 168 G5
Stoke 168 F5
Northwood Green Glos 80 B2
Northwood Hills London 85 G9
North Woolwich London 68 D2
North Wootton Dorset 29 E11
Norf 158 E2
Som 44 E5
North Wraxall Wilts 61 D10
North Wroughton
Swindon 63 C7
Norton Devon 9 E7
Devon 24 B3
E Sus 23 E7
Glos 99 G7
Halton 183 E9
Herts 104 E4
IoW 20 D2
Mon 78 B6
Notts 187 G9
N Som 59 G10
Powys 114 D6
Shrops 131 B11
Shrops 131 G9
Shrops 132 C4
Stockton 234 G4
Suff 125 D9
Swansea 56 D3
Swansea 56 D6
S Yorks 186 E5
S Yorks 198 D4
Wilts 61 C11
W Mid 133 G7
W Nhants 120 E2
Worcs 99 B10
Worcs 117 G7
W Sus 22 B6
W Sus 22 D5
Norton Ash Kent 70 G3
Norton Bavant Wilts 46 E2
Norton Bridge Staffs 151 C7
Norton Canes Staffs 133 B10
Norton Canon Hereford 97 B7
Norton Corner Norf 159 D11
Norton Disney Lincs 172 D5
Norton East Staffs 133 B10
Norton Ferris Wilts 45 F9
Norton Fitzwarren Som 27 B11
Norton Green Herts 104 G4
IoW 20 D2
Staffs 168 E6
W Mid 118 C3
Norton Hawkfield Bath 60 G5
Norton Heath Essex 87 E10
Norton in Hales Shrops 150 B4
Norton-in-the-Moors
Stoke 168 E5
Norton-Juxta-Twycross
Leics 134 B6
Norton-le-Clay N Yorks 215 E8
Norton Lindsey Warks 118 E4
Norton Little Green
Suff 125 D9
Norton Malreward Bath 60 F6
Norton Mandeville Essex 87 E9
Norton-on-Derwent
N Yorks 216 E5
Norton St Philip Som 45 B9
Norton Subcourse Norf 143 D8
Norton sub Hamdon Som 29 D7
Norton's Wood N Som 60 E2
Norton Woodseats
S Yorks 186 E5
Norwell Notts 172 C3
Norwell Woodhouse
Notts 172 C2
Norwich Norf 142 B4
Norwick Shetland 312 B8
Norwood Derbys 187 E7
Dorset 29 F8
Norwood End Essex 87 D9
Norwood Green London 66 D6
W Yorks 196 B6
Norwood Hill Sur 51 E8
Norwood New Town
London 67 E10
Norwoodside Cambs 139 D8
Noseley Leics 136 D4
Noss Highld 310 D7
Shetland 313 M5
Noss Mayo Devon 7 F11
Nosterfield N Yorks 214 C5
Nosterfield End Cambs 106 C2
Nostie Highld 295 C10
Notgrove Glos 100 G2
Nottage Bridgend 57 F10
Notter Corn 7 C7
Nottingham Nottingham 153 B11
Notting Hill London 67 C8
Nottington Dorset 17 E9
Notton Wilts 62 F2
W Yorks 197 E10
Nounsley Essex 88 C3
Noutard's Green Worcs 116 D5
Novar House Highld 300 C6
Nova Scotia Ches W 167 B10
Novers Park Bristol 60 F5
Noverton Glos 99 G9
Nowton Suff 125 E7
Nox Shrops 149 G8
Noyadd Trefawr Ceredig 92 B5
Noyadd Wilym Ceredig 92 C4
Nuffield Oxon 65 B7
Nun Appleton N Yorks 207 F7
Nunburnholme E Yorks 208 D2
Nuncargate Notts 171 E8
Nunclose Cumb 230 B5
Nuneaton Warks 135 E7
Nuneham Courtenay
Oxon 83 F9
Nuney Green Oxon 65 D7
Nunhead London 67 D11
Nun Hills Lancs 195 C11
Nun Monkton N Yorks 206 B6
Nunney Som 45 D8
Nunney Catch Som 45 E8
Nunnington N Yorks 216 D3
Nunnykirk Northumb 252 E3
Nunsthorpe NE Lincs 201 F9
Nunthorpe Mbro 225 C10
York 207 C8
Nunton Wilts 31 B11
Nunwick N Yorks 214 E6
Nupdown S Glos 79 F10
Nupend Glos 80 D3
Glos 80 F4
Nup End Bucks 84 B5
Herts 86 B2
Nuper's Hatch Essex 87 G8
Nuppend Glos 79 E10
Nuptown Brack 65 E11
Nursling Hants 32 D5
Nursted Hants 34 C3
Nursteed Wilts 62 G4
Nurston V Glam 58 F5
Nurton Staffs 132 D6
Nurton Hill Staffs 132 D6
Nutbourne W Sus 22 B3
W Sus 35 D9
Nutbourne Common
W Sus 35 D9
Nutburn Hants 32 C5
Nutcombe Sur 49 G11
Nutfield Sur 51 C10
Nut Grove Mers 183 C7
Nuthall Notts 171 G8
Nuthampstead Herts 105 E8
Nuthurst Warks 118 C3
W Sus 35 B11
Nutley E Sus 36 B6
Hants 48 E6
Nuttall Gtr Man 195 D9
Nutwell S Yorks 198 G6
Nybster Highld 310 C7
Nye N Som 60 G2
Nyetimber W Sus 22 D5
Nyewood W Sus 34 C4
Nyland Som 44 C3
Nymet Rowland Devon 26 F2
Nymet Tracey Devon 26 G2
Nympsfield Glos 80 E4
Nynehead Som 27 C10
Nythe Som 44 G2
Swindon 63 B7
Nyton W Sus 22 B6

O

Oadby Leics 136 C2
Oad Street Kent 69 G11
Oakall Green Worcs 116 E6
Oakamoor Staffs 169 G9
Oakbank W Loth 269 B11
Oak Bank Gtr Man 195 F10
Oak Cross Devon 12 B6
Oakdale BCP 18 C6
Caerph 77 F11
N Yorks 205 B11
Oake Som 27 B11
Oake Green Som 27 B11
Oaken Staffs 133 C7
Oakenclough Lancs 202 D6
Oakengates Telford 150 G4
Oakenholt Flint 182 G3
Oakenshaw Durham 233 D10
Lancs 203 G10
W Yorks 197 B7
Oakerthorpe Derbys 170 E5
Oakes W Yorks 196 D6
Oakfield Herts 104 F3
IoW 21 C7
Torf 78 G4
Oakford Ceredig 111 F9
Devon 26 C6
Oakfordbridge Devon 26 C6
Oakgrove Ches E 168 B6
M Keynes 103 D7
Oakham Rutland 137 B7
W Mid 133 F9
Oakhanger Ches E 168 E3
Hants 49 F9
Oakhill Som 44 D6
W Sus 51 G7
Oak Hill Stoke 168 G5
Suff 109 B7
Oakhurst Kent 52 C4
Oakington Cambs 123 E8
Oaklands Carms 74 B6
Herts 86 B2
Powys 113 G10
Oakleigh Park London 86 G3
Oakle Street Glos 80 B3
Oakley BCP 18 B6
Bedford 121 G10
Bucks 83 C10
Fife 279 D10
Glos 99 G9
Hants 48 C5
Oxon 84 E3
Staffs 150 B4
Suff 126 B3
Oakley Court Oxon 64 B6
Oakley Green Windsor 66 D2
Oakley Park Powys 129 F9
Suff 126 B3
Oakley Wood Oxon 64 B6
Oakmere Ches W 167 B9
Oakridge Glos 80 E6
Hants 48 C6
Oakridge Lynch Glos 80 E6
Oaks Shrops 131 C8
Oaksey Wilts 81 G7
Oaks Green Derbys 152 C3
Oakshaw Ford Cumb 240 B2
Oakshott Hants 34 B2
Oaks in Charnwood
Leics 153 F9
Oakthorpe Leics 152 G6
Oak Tree Darl 225 C7
Oakwell W Yorks 197 B8
Oakwood Derby 153 B7
London 86 F3
Northumb 241 D10
Warr 183 C11
W Yorks 206 F2
Oakwoodhill Sur 50 F6
Oakworth W Yorks 204 F6
Oape Highld 309 J4
Oare Kent 70 G4
Som 41 D10
W Berks 64 E4
Wilts 63 G7
Oareford Som 41 D10
Oasby Lincs 155 B10
Oath Som 28 B5
Oathill Dorset 28 F6
Oathlaw Angus 287 B8
Oatlands Glasgow 267 C11
N Yorks 205 C11
Oatlands Park Sur 66 G5
Oban Argyll 289 G10
Highld 295 G10
W Isles 305 H3
Obley Shrops 114 B6
Oborne Dorset 29 D11
Obthorpe Lincs 155 F11
Obthorpe Lodge Lincs 156 F2
Occlestone Green
Ches W 167 C11
Occold Suff 126 C3
Ocean Village Soton 32 E6
Ochiltree E Ayrs 258 E2
Ochr-y-foel Denb 181 F9
Ochtermuthill Perth 286 F2
Ochtertyre Perth 286 E2
Ochtow Highld 309 J4
Ockbrook Derbys 153 B8
Ocker Hill W Mid 133 E9
Ockeridge Worcs 116 E5
Ockford Ridge Sur 50 E3
Ockham Sur 50 B5
Ockle Highld 289 B7
Ockley Sur 50 F6
Ocle Pychard Hereford 97 B11
Octon E Yorks 217 F10
Octon Cross Roads
E Yorks 217 F10
Odam Barton Devon 26 D2
Odcombe Som 29 D8
Odd Down Bath 61 G8
Oddendale Cumb 221 C11
Odder Lincs 188 G6
Oddingley Worcs 117 F8
Oddington Glos 100 F4
Oxon 83 C9
Odell Bedford 121 F9
Odham Devon 25 G7
Odie Orkney 314 D6
Odiham Hants 49 C8
Odsal W Yorks 197 B7
Odsey Cambs 104 D5
Odstock Wilts 31 B10
Odstone Leics 135 B7
Offchurch Warks 119 D7
Offenham Worcs 99 B11
Offenham Cross Worcs 99 B11
Offerton Gtr Man 184 D6
T&W 243 F8
Offerton Green Gtr Man 184 D6
Offham E Sus 36 E5
Kent 53 B7
W Sus 35 F8
Offleyhay Staffs 150 D5
Offleymarsh Staffs 150 D5
Offleyrock Staffs 150 D5
Offord Cluny Cambs 122 D4
Offord D'Arcy Cambs 122 D4
Offton Suff 107 B11
Offwell Devon 15 B9
Ogbourne Maizey Wilts 63 E7
Ogbourne St Andrew
Wilts 63 E7
Ogbourne St George
Wilts 63 E8
Ogden W Yorks 205 G7
Ogdens Hants 31 E11
Ogil Angus 292 G6
Ogle Northumb 242 B4
Ogmore V Glam 57 F11
Ogmore-by-Sea = Aberogwr
V Glam 57 F11
Ogmore Vale Bridgend 76 G6
Okeford Fitzpaine Dorset 30 E4
Okehampton Devon 13 B7
Okehampton Camp
Devon 13 C7
Oker Derbys 170 C3
Okewood Hill Sur 50 F6
Okle Green Glos 98 F5
Okraquoy Shetland 313 K6
Okus Swindon 62 C6
Olchard Devon 14 F3
Old W Nhants 120 C5
Old Aberdeen
Aberdeen 293 C11
Old Alresford Hants 48 G5
Oldany Highld 306 F6
Old Arley Warks 134 E5
Old Balornock Glasgow 268 B2
Old Basford Nottingham 171 G8
Old Basing Hants 49 C7
Old Belses Borders 262 E3
Oldberrow Warks 118 D2
Old Bewick Northumb 264 E3
Old Bexley London 68 E3
Old Blair Perth 291 G10
Old Bolingbroke Lincs 174 B4
Oldborough Devon 26 F3
Old Boston Mers 183 B9
Old Bramhope
W Yorks 205 E10
Old Brampton Derbys 186 G4
Old Bridge of Tilt
Perth 291 G10
Old Bridge of Urr
Dumfries 237 C9
Oldbrook M Keynes 103 D7
Old Buckenham Norf 141 E11
Old Burdon T&W 243 G9
Old Burghclere Hants 48 B3
Oldbury Kent 52 B5
Shrops 132 E4
Warks 134 E6
W Mid 133 F9
Oldbury Naite S Glos 79 G10
Oldbury-on-Severn
S Glos 79 G10
Oldbury on the Hill Glos 61 B10
Old Byland N Yorks 215 B11
Old Cambus Borders 272 B6
Old Cardinham Castle
Corn 6 B2
Old Carlisle Cumb 229 B11
Old Cassop Durham 234 D2
Oldcastle Mon 96 G6
Oldcastle Heath Ches W 167 F7
Old Castleton Borders 250 E2
Old Catton Norf 160 G4
Old Chalford Oxon 100 F6
Old Church Stoke
Powys 130 E5
Old Clee NE Lincs 201 F9
Old Cleeve Som 42 E4
Old Colwyn Conwy 180 F5
Old Coppice Shrops 131 B9
Old Corry Highld 295 C8
Oldcotes Notts 187 D9
Old Coulsdon London 51 B10
Old Country Hereford 98 C4
Old Craig Aberds 303 G9
Angus 292 G4
Oldcroft Glos 79 D10
Old Crombie Aberds 302 D5
Old Cryals Kent 53 E7
Old Cullen Moray 302 C5
Old Dailly S Ayrs 244 D6
Old Dalby Leics 154 E3
Old Dam Derbys 185 F10
Old Deer Aberds 303 E9
Old Denaby S Yorks 187 B7
Old Ditch Som 44 D4
Old Dolphin W Yorks 205 G8
Old Down S Glos 60 B6
Old Duffus Moray 301 C11
Old Edlington S Yorks 187 B8
Old Eldon Durham 233 F10
Old Ellerby E Yorks 209 F9
Oldend Glos 80 D3
Old Fallings W Mid 133 C8
Oldfallow Staffs 151 G9
Old Farm Park
M Keynes 103 D8
Old Felixstowe Suff 108 D6
Oldfield Cumb 229 F7
Shrops 132 F3
Worcs 116 E6
W Yorks 196 E6
W Yorks 204 F6
Old Field Shrops 115 B9
Oldfield Brow Gtr Man 184 D3
Oldfield Park Bath 61 G8
Old Fletton Pboro 138 D3
Old Fold T&W 243 E7
Oldford Som 45 C9
Old Ford London 67 C11
Old Forge Hereford 79 B9
Oldfurnace Staffs 169 G8
Old Furnace Torf 78 E3
Old Gate Lincs 157 E8
Old Glossop Derbys 185 C8
Old Goginan Ceredig 128 G3
Old Goole E Yorks 199 C8
Old Gore Hereford 98 F2
Old Graitney Dumfries 239 D8
Old Grimsby Scilly 1 F3
Oldhall Renfs 267 C10
Old Hall Powys 129 G8
Oldhall Green Suff 125 F7
Old Hall Green Herts 105 G7
Oldhall Ho Highld 310 D6
Old Hall Street Norf 160 C6
Oldham Gtr Man 196 F2
Oldham Edge Gtr Man 196 F2
Oldhamstocks E Loth 282 G4
Old Harlow Essex 87 C7
Old Hatfield Herts 86 D2
Old Heath Essex 107 G10
Old Heathfield E Sus 37 C9
Old Hill W Mid 133 F9
Old Hills Worcs 98 B6
Old Hunstanton Norf 175 G11
Oldhurst Cambs 122 B6
Old Hurst Cambs 122 B5
Old Hutton Cumb 211 B11
Oldington Shrops 132 D4
Old Johnstone Dumfries 248 D6
Old Kea Corn 4 G6
Old Kilpatrick W Dunb 277 G9
Old Kinnernie Aberds 293 C9
Old Knebworth Herts 104 G4
Oldland S Glos 61 E7
Oldland Common S Glos 61 E7
Old Langho Lancs 203 F10
Old Laxey IoM 192 D5
Old Leake Lincs 174 E6
Old Leckie Stirling 278 C3
Old Lindley W Yorks 196 D5
Old Linslade C Beds 103 F8
Old Llanberis = Nant Peris
Gwyn 163 D10
Old Malden London 67 F8
Old Malton N Yorks 216 E5
Old Marton Shrops 148 C6
Old Mead Essex 105 F10
Oldmeldrum Aberds 303 G8
Old Micklefield
W Yorks 206 G4
Old Mill Corn 12 G3
Old Milton Hants 19 C10
Old Milverton Warks 118 D5
Oldmixon N Som 43 B10
Old Monkland N Lanark 268 C4
Old Nenthorn Borders 262 B5
Old Netley Hants 33 F7
Old Neuadd Powys 129 F11
Old Newton Suff 125 E11
Old Oak Common London 67 C8
Old Park Corn 6 B4
Telford 132 B3
Old Passage S Glos 60 B5
Old Perton Staffs 133 D7
Old Philpstoun W Loth 279 F11
Old Polmont Falk 279 F8
Old Portsmouth Ptsmth 21 B8
Old Quarrington
Durham 234 D2
Old Radnor Powys 114 F5
Old Rattray Aberds 303 D10
Old Rayne Aberds 302 G6
Old Romney Kent 39 B8
Old Shirley Soton 32 E5
Oldshore Beg Highld 306 D6
Old Shoreham W Sus 36 F2
Oldshoremore Highld 306 D7
Old Snydale W Yorks 198 C2
Old Sodbury S Glos 61 C9
Old Somerby Lincs 155 C9
Oldstead N Yorks 215 C10
Old Stillington Stockton 234 G3
Old Storridge Common
Worcs 116 G4
Old Stratford W Nhants 102 C5
Old Struan Perth 291 G10
Old Swan Mers 182 C5
Old Swarland Northumb 252 C5
Old Swinford W Mid 133 G8
Old Tame Gtr Man 196 F3
Old Tebay Cumb 222 D2
Old Thirsk N Yorks 215 C8
Old Tinnis Borders 261 D9
Old Toll S Ayrs 257 E9
Oldtown Aberds 293 C7
Aberds 302 G5
Highld 309 L5
Old Town Cumb 211 C11
Cumb 230 C5
Edin 280 G5
E Sus 23 F9
E Sus 38 F2
E Sus 38 F4
E Yorks 218 F3
Herts 104 F4
Scilly 1 G4
Swindon 63 C7
W Yorks 196 B3
Oldtown of Ord Aberds 302 D6
Old Trafford Gtr Man 184 B4
Old Tree Kent 71 G8
Old Tupton Derbys 170 B5
Oldwalls Swansea 56 C3
Old Warden C Beds 104 C2
Old Warren Flint 166 C4
Oldway Swansea 56 D5
Torbay 9 C7
Old Way Som 28 D5
Oldways End Devon 26 B5
Old Weston Cambs 121 B11
Old Wharf Hereford 98 D4
Oldwhat Aberds 303 D8
Old Whittington Derbys 186 G5
Oldwich Lane W Mid 118 C4
Old Wick Highld 310 D7
Old Wimpole Cambs 122 G6
Old Windsor Windsor 66 E3
Old Wingate Durham 234 D3
Old Wives Lees Kent 54 C5
Old Woking Sur 50 B4
Old Wolverton
M Keynes 102 C6
Oldwood Worcs 115 D11
Old Woodhall Lincs 174 B2
Old Woodhouses
Shrops 167 G9
Old Woodstock Oxon 82 B6
Olgrinmore Highld 310 D4
Olive Green Staffs 152 F2
Oliver's Battery Hants 33 B7
Ollaberry Shetland 312 E5
Ollag W Isles 297 G3
Ollerbrook Booth
Derbys 185 D10
Ollerton Ches E 184 F3
Notts 171 B11
Ollerton *continued*
Shrops 150 D2
Ollerton Fold Lancs 194 C6
Ollerton Lane Shrops 150 D3
Olmarch Ceredig 112 F2
Olmstead Green Essex 106 C2
Olney M Keynes 121 G7
Olrig Ho Highld 310 C5
Olton W Mid 134 G2
Olveston S Glos 60 B6
Olwen Ceredig 93 B11
Ombersley Worcs 116 E6
Ompton Notts 171 B11
Omunsgarth Shetland 313 J5
Onchan IoM 192 E4
Onecote Staffs 169 D9
Onehouse Suff 125 F10
Onen Mon 78 C6
Onesacre S Yorks 186 C3
Ongar Hill Norf 157 E11
Ongar Street Hereford 115 D7
Onibury Shrops 115 B9
Onich Highld 290 G2
Onllwyn Neath 76 C4
Onneley Staffs 168 G3
Onslow Village Sur 50 D3
Onthank E Ayrs 267 G8
Onziebust Orkney 314 D4
Openshaw Gtr Man 184 B5
Openwoodgate Derbys 170 F5
Opinan Highld 299 B7
Highld 307 K3
Orange Lane Borders 272 G5
Orange Row Norf 157 E10
Orasaigh W Isles 305 G5
Orbiston N Lanark 268 D4
Orbliston Moray 302 D3
Orbost Highld 298 E2
Orby Lincs 175 B7
Orchard Hill Devon 24 B6
Orchard Leigh Bucks 85 E7
Orchard Portman Som 28 C2
Orcheston Wilts 46 D5
Orcop Hereford 97 F9
Orcop Hill Hereford 97 F9
Ord Highld 295 D8
Ordale Shetland 312 C8
Ordhead Aberds 293 B8
Ordie Aberds 292 C6
Ordiequish Moray 302 D3
Ordiqhill Aberds 302 D5
Ordley Northumb 241 F10
Ordsall Gtr Man 184 B4
Notts 187 E11
Ore E Sus 38 E4
Oreston Plym 7 E10
Oreton Shrops 132 G3
Orford Suff 109 B8
Warr 183 C10
Organford Dorset 18 C4
Orgreave Staffs 152 F3
S Yorks 186 D6
Oridge Street Glos 98 F5
Orlandon Pembs 72 D4
Orlestone Kent 54 G3
Orleton Hereford 115 D9
Worcs 116 D3
Orleton Common
Hereford 115 D9
Orlingbury N Nhants 121 C7
Ormacleit W Isles 297 H3
Ormathwaite Cumb 229 F11
Ormesby Redcar 225 B10
Ormesby St Margaret
Norf 161 G9
Ormesby St Michael
Norf 161 G9
Ormiclate Castle
W Isles 297 H3
Ormidale Lodge Argyll 275 F11
Ormiscaig Highld 307 K3
Ormiston Borders 262 G2
E Loth 271 B8
Ormsaigbeg Highld 288 C6
Ormsaigmore Highld 288 C6
Ormsary Argyll 275 F8
Ormsgill Cumb 210 E3
Ormskirk Lancs 194 F2
Ornsby Hill Durham 233 B9
Orpington London 68 F3
Orrell Gtr Man 194 F4
Mers 182 B4
Orrell Post Gtr Man 194 G4
Orrisdale IoM 192 C4
Orrock Fife 280 D4
Orroland Dumfries 237 E9
Orsett Thurrock 68 C6
Orsett Heath Thurrock 68 D6
Orslow Staffs 150 F6
Orston Notts 172 G3
Orthwaite Cumb 229 E11
Ortner Lancs 202 C6
Orton Cumb 222 D2
N Nhants 120 B6
Staffs 133 D7
Orton Brimbles Pboro 138 D3
Orton Goldhay Pboro 138 D3
Orton Longueville
Pboro 138 D3
Orton Malborne Pboro 138 D3
Orton-on-the-Hill Leics 134 C6
Orton Rigg Cumb 239 G8
Orton Southgate Pboro 138 E2
Orton Waterville Pboro 138 D3
Orton Wistow Pboro 138 D2
Orwell Cambs 123 G7
Osbaldeston Lancs 203 G8
Osbaldeston Green
Lancs 203 G8
Osbaldwick York 207 C8
Osbaston Leics 135 C8
Shrops 148 E6
Telford 149 F11
Osbaston Hollow Leics 135 B8
Osbournby Lincs 155 B11
Oscroft Ches W 167 B8
Ose Highld 298 E3
Osea Island Essex 88 D6
Osehill Green Dorset 29 F11
Osgathorpe Leics 153 F8
Osgodby Lincs 189 C9
N Yorks 207 G8
N Yorks 217 C11
Osgodby Common
N Yorks 207 F8
Osidge London 86 G3
Oskaig Highld 295 B7
Oskamull Argyll 288 E6
Osleston Derbys 152 B4
Osmaston Derby 153 C7
Derbys 170 G2
Osmington Dorset 17 E10
Osmington Mills Dorset 17 E10
Osmondthorpe W Yorks 206 G2
Osmotherley N Yorks 225 F9
Osney Oxon 83 D8
Ospisdale Highld 309 L7
Ospringe Kent 70 G4
Ossaborough Devon 40 E3
Ossemsley Hants 19 B10
Osset Spa W Yorks 197 D9
Ossett W Yorks 197 C9
Ossett Street Side
W Yorks 197 C9
Ossington Notts 172 C3
Ostend Essex 88 F6
Norf 161 C7
Osterley London 66 D6
Oswaldkirk N Yorks 216 D2
Oswaldtwistle Lancs 195 B8
Oswestry Shrops 148 D5
Otby Lincs 189 C10
Oteley Shrops 149 C8
Otford Kent 52 B4
Otham Kent 53 C9
Otham Hole Kent 53 C10
Otherton Staffs 151 G8
Othery Som 43 G11
Otley Suff 126 F4
W Yorks 205 D10
Otterbourne Hants 33 C7
Otterburn Northumb 251 E9
N Yorks 204 B3
Otterburn Camp
Northumb 251 D9
Otterden Place Kent 54 C2
Otter Ferry Argyll 275 E10
Otterford Som 28 E2
Otterham Corn 11 C9
Otterhampton Som 43 E8
Otterham Quay Kent 69 F10
Otterham Station Corn 11 D9
Otter Ho Argyll 275 F10
Ottershaw Sur 66 G4
Otterspool Mers 182 D5
Otterswick Shetland 312 E7
Otterton Devon 15 D7
Otterwood Hants 32 G6
Ottery St Mary Devon 15 B8
Ottinge Kent 55 E7
Ottringham E Yorks 201 C9
Oughterby Cumb 239 F7
Oughtershaw N Yorks 213 C7
Oughterside Cumb 229 C8
Oughtibridge S Yorks 186 C4
Oughtrington Warr 183 D11
Oulston N Yorks 215 E10
Oulton Cumb 238 G6
Norf 160 D2
Staffs 150 E5
Staffs 151 B8
Suff 143 D10
W Yorks 197 B11
Oulton Broad Suff 143 E10
Oultoncross Staffs 151 C8
Oulton Grange Staffs 151 B8
Oulton Heath Staffs 151 B8
Oulton Street Norf 160 D3
Oundle N Nhants 137 F10
Ounsdale Staffs 133 E7
Ousby Cumb 231 E8
Ousdale Highld 311 G4
Ousden Suff 124 F4
Ousefleet E Yorks 199 C10
Ousel Hole W Yorks 205 E8
Ouston Durham 243 G7
Northumb 241 G7
Northumb 242 C3
Outcast Cumb 210 D6
Out Elmstead Kent 55 C8
Outer Hope Devon 8 G3
Outertown Orkney 314 E2
Outgate Cumb 221 F7
Outhgill Cumb 222 E5
Outhill Warks 118 D2
Outhills Aberds 303 D10
Outlands Staffs 150 C5
Outlane W Yorks 196 D5
Outlane Moor W Yorks 196 D5
Outlet Village Ches W 182 G6
Outmarsh Wilts 61 G11
Out Newton E Yorks 201 C11
Out Rawcliffe Lancs 202 E4
Outwell Norf 139 C10
Outwick Hants 31 D10
Outwood Gtr Man 195 F9
Som 28 B4
Sur 51 D10
W Yorks 197 C10
Outwoods Leics 153 F8
Staffs 150 F5
Staffs 152 E4
Warks 134 G4
Ouzlewell Green
W Yorks 197 B10
Ovenden W Yorks 196 B5
Ovenscloss Borders 261 C11
Over Cambs 123 C7
Ches W 167 B10
Glos 80 B4
S Glos 60 C5
Overa Farm Stud Norf 141 F9
Overbister Orkney 314 B6
Over Burrow Lancs 212 D2
Over Burrows Derbys 152 B5
Overbury Worcs 99 D9
Overcombe Dorset 17 E9
Over Compton Dorset 29 D9
Overend W Mid 133 G9
Over End Cambs 137 E11
Derbys 186 G3
Overgreen Derbys 186 G4
Over Green W Mid 134 E3
Over Haddon Derbys 170 B2
Over Hulton Gtr Man 195 F7
Over Kellet Lancs 211 E10
Over Kiddington Oxon 101 G8
Over Knutsford Ches E 184 F3
Over Langshaw
Borders 271 G10
Overleigh Som 44 F3
Overley Staffs 152 F3
Overley Green Warks 117 F11
Over Monnow Mon 79 C8
Overmoor Staffs 169 F7
Over Norton Oxon 100 F6
Over Peover Ches E 184 G3
Overpool Ches W 182 F5
Overs Shrops 131 D7
Overscaig Hotel Highld 309 G4
Overseal Derbys 152 F5
Over Silton N Yorks 225 G9
Overslade Warks 119 C9
Oversland Kent 54 B5
Oversley Green Warks 117 F11
Overstone W Nhants 120 D6
Over Stowey Som 43 F7
Overstrand Norf 160 A4
Over Stratton Som 28 D6
Over Tabley Ches E 184 E2
Overthorpe W Nhants 101 C9
W Yorks 197 D8
Overton Aberdeen 293 B10
Aberds 293 B9
Ches W 183 F8
Dumfries 237 C11
Glos 80 C2
Hants 48 D4
Invclyd 276 G5
Lancs 202 B4
N Yorks 207 B7
Shrops 115 C10
Overton *continued*
Staffs 151 B10
Swansea 56 D3
W Yorks 197 D9
Overton = *Owrtyn* Wrex 166 G5
Overton Bridge Wrex 166 G5
Overtown Lancs 212 D2
N Lanark 268 E6
Swindon 63 D7
W Yorks 197 D11
Over Town Lancs 195 B11
Over Wallop Hants 47 F9
Over Whitacre Warks 134 E5
Over Worton Oxon 101 F8
Oving Bucks 102 G5
W Sus 22 C6
Ovingdean Brighton 36 G5
Ovingham Northumb 242 E3
Ovington Durham 224 C2
Essex 106 C5
Hants 48 G5
Norf 141 C8
Northumb 242 E3
Owen's Bank Staffs 152 D4
Ower Hants 32 D4
Owermoigne Dorset 17 D11
Owlbury Shrops 130 E6
Owlcotes Derbys 170 B6
Owl End Cambs 122 B4
Owler Bar Derbys 186 F3
Owlerton S Yorks 186 D4
Owlet W Yorks 205 F9
Owlpen Glos 80 F4
Owl's Green Suff 126 D5
Owlsmoor Brack 65 G11
Owlswick Bucks 84 D3
Owlthorpe S Yorks 186 E6
Owmby Lincs 200 G5
Owmby-by-Spital Lincs 189 D8
Ownham W Berks 64 E2
Owrtyn = *Overton* Wrex 166 G5
Owslebury Hants 33 C8
Owston Leics 136 B5
S Yorks 198 E5
Owston Ferry N Lincs 199 G10
Owstwick E Yorks 209 G11
Owthorne E Yorks 201 B10
Owthorpe Notts 154 C3
Owton Manor Hrtlpl 234 F5
Oxborough Norf 140 C4
Oxclose S Yorks 186 E6
T&W 243 F7
Oxcombe Lincs 190 F4
Oxcroft Derbys 187 G7
Oxcroft Estate Derbys 187 G7
Oxen End Essex 106 F3
Oxenhall Glos 98 F4
Oxenholme Cumb 211 B10
Oxenhope W Yorks 204 F6
Oxen Park Cumb 210 B6
Oxenpill Som 44 E2
Oxenton Glos 99 E9
Oxenwood Wilts 47 B10
Oxford Oxon 83 D8
Stoke 168 E5
Oxgang E Dunb 278 G3
Oxgangs Edin 270 B4
Oxhey Herts 85 F10
Oxhill Durham 242 G5
Warks 100 B6
Oxlease Herts 86 D2
Oxley W Mid 133 C8
Oxley Green Essex 88 C6
Oxley's Green E Sus 37 C11
Oxlode Cambs 139 F9
Oxnam Borders 262 F5
Oxnead Norf 160 E4
Oxshott Sur 66 G6
Oxspring S Yorks 197 G9
Oxted Sur 51 C11
Oxton Borders 271 E9
Mers 182 D3
Notts 171 E10
N Yorks 206 E6
Oxton Rakes Derbys 186 G4
Oxwich Swansea 56 D3
Oxwich Green Swansea 56 D3
Oxwick Norf 159 D8
Oykel Bridge Highld 309 J3
Oyne Aberds 302 G6
Oystermouth Swansea 56 D6
Ozleworth Glos 80 G3

P

Pabail Iarach W Isles 304 E7
Pabail Uarach W Isles 304 E7
Pabo Conwy 180 F4
Pace Gate N Yorks 205 C8
Pachesham Park Sur 51 B7
Packers Hill Dorset 30 E2
Packington Leics 153 G7
Packmoor Staffs 168 E5
Packmores Warks 118 D5
Packwood W Mid 118 C3
Packwood Gullet
W Mid 118 C3
Padanaram Angus 287 B8
Padbury Bucks 102 E4
Paddington London 67 C9
Warr 183 D10
Paddlesworth Kent 55 F7
Kent 69 G7
Paddock Kent 54 C3
W Yorks 196 D6
Paddockhaugh Moray 302 D2
Paddockhill Ches E 184 F4
Paddockhole Dumfries 248 G6
Paddock Wood Kent 53 E7
Paddolgreen Shrops 149 C10
Padfield Derbys 185 B8
Padgate Warr 183 D10
Padham's Green Essex 87 F10
Padiham Lancs 203 G11
Padney Cambs 123 C10
Padog Conwy 164 E4
Padside N Yorks 205 B9
Padside Green N Yorks 205 B9
Padson Devon 13 B7
Padstow Corn 10 F4
Padworth W Berks 64 F6
Padworth Common
Hants 64 G6
Paganhill Glos 80 D4
Page Bank Durham 233 D10
Page Moss Mers 182 C6
Page's Green Suff 126 D2
Pagham W Sus 22 D5
Paglesham Churchend
Essex 88 G6
Paglesham Eastend
Essex 88 G6
Paibeil W Isles 296 E3
Paible W Isles 305 J2
Paignton Torbay 9 C7
Pailton Warks 135 G9
Painleyhill Staffs 151 C10
Painscastle Powys 96 B3
Painshawfield Northumb 242 E3
Pains Hill Sur 52 C2
Painsthorpe E Yorks 208 B2
Painswick Glos 80 D5
Painter's Forstal Kent 54 B3
Painters Green Wrex 167 G8
Painter's Green Herts 86 B3
Painthorpe W Yorks 197 D10
Paintmoor Som 28 F4
Pairc Shiaboist W Isles 304 D4
Paisley Renfs 267 C9
Pakefield Suff 143 E10
Pakenham Suff 125 D8
Pale Gwyn 147 B9
Pale Green Essex 106 C3
Palehouse Common
E Sus 23 B7
Palestine Hants 47 E9
Paley Street Windsor 65 D11
Palfrey W Mid 133 D10
Palgowan Dumfries 245 G9
Palgrave Suff 126 B2
Pallaflat Cumb 219 C9
Pallington Dorset 17 C11
Pallion T&W 243 F9
Pallister Mbro 225 B10
Palmarsh Kent 54 G6
Palmer Moor Derbys 152 C2
Palmersbridge Corn 11 F9
Palmers Cross Staffs 133 C7
Sur 50 E4
Palmer's Flat Glos 79 D9
Palmers Green London 86 G4
Palmer's Green Kent 53 E7
Palmerstown V Glam 58 F6
Palmersville T&W 243 C7
Palmstead Kent 55 D7
Palnackie Dumfries 237 D10
Palnure Dumfries 236 C6
Palterton Derbys 171 B7
Pamber End Hants 48 B6
Pamber Green Hants 48 B6
Pamber Heath Hants 64 G6
Pamington Glos 99 E8
Pamphill Dorset 31 G7
Pampisford Cambs 105 B9
Pan IoW 20 D6
Orkney 314 G3
Panborough Som 44 D3
Panbride Angus 287 D9
Pancakehill Glos 81 C9
Pancrasweek Devon 24 F3
Pancross V Glam 58 F4
Pandy Gwyn 128 C2
Gwyn 146 F4
Gwyn 147 D7
Mon 96 G6
Powys 129 C8
Wrex 148 B3
Wrex 166 G6
Pandy'r Capel Denb 165 E9
Pandy Tudur Conwy 164 C5
Panfield Essex 106 F4
Pangbourne W Berks 64 D6
Panhall Fife 280 C6
Panks Bridge Hereford 98 B2
Pannal N Yorks 206 C2
Pannal Ash N Yorks 205 C11
Pannel's Ash Essex 106 C5
Panpunton Powys 114 C5
Panshanger Herts 86 C3
Pant Denb 166 E2
Flint 181 G10
Gwyn 144 C4
M Tydf 77 D9
Powys 129 C11
Shrops 148 E5
Wrex 166 D5
Wrex 166 F3
Pantasaph Flint 181 F11
Pantdu Neath 57 C9
Panteg Ceredig 111 E9
Torf 78 F4
Pantersbridge Corn 6 B3
Pant-glas Gwyn 163 F7
Pant-glâs Powys 128 D5
Pant-glas Shrops 148 C5
Pantgwyn Carms 93 F11
Ceredig 92 B4
Pant-lasau Swansea 57 B7
Pantmawr Cardiff 58 C6
Pant Mawr Powys 129 G7
Panton Lincs 189 F11
Pant-pastynog Denb 165 C8
Pantperthog Gwyn 128 C4
Pantside Caerph 78 F2
Pant-teg Carms 93 F9
Pant-y-Caws Carms 92 F3
Pant-y-crûg Ceredig 112 B3
Pant-y-dwr Powys 113 B9
Powys 113 C9
Pant-y-ffridd Powys 130 C3
Pantyffynnon Carms 75 C10
Pantygasseg Torf 78 F3
Pantymwyn Flint 165 C11
Pant-y-pyllau Bridgend 58 C2
Pant-yr-awel Bridgend 58 B2
Pant-y-Wacco Flint 181 F10
Panxworth Norf 161 G7
Papcastle Cumb 229 E8
Papermill Bank Shrops 149 D11
Papigoe Highld 310 D7
Papil Shetland 313 K5
Papley N Nhants 138 F2
Orkney 314 G4
Papple E Loth 281 G11
Papplewick Notts 171 E8
Papworth Everard
Cambs 122 E5
Papworth St Agnes
Cambs 122 E5
Papworth Village Settlement
Cambs 122 E5
Par Corn 5 E11
Paradise Glos 80 C5
Paradise Green Hereford 97 B10
Paramoor Corn 5 F9
Paramour Street Kent 71 G9
Parbold Lancs 194 E3
Parbrook Som 44 F5
W Sus 35 B9
Parc Gwyn 147 C7
Parc Erissey Corn 4 G3
Parc-hendy Swansea 56 B4
Parchey Som 43 F10
Parciau Anglesey 179 E7
Parcllyn Ceredig 110 G4
Parc Mawr Caerph 77 G10
Parc-Seymour Newport 78 G6
Parc-y-rhôs Carms 93 B11
Pardown Hants 48 D5
Pardshaw Cumb 229 G7
Pardshaw Hall Cumb 229 F8
Parham Suff 126 E6
Park Corn 10 G6
Devon 14 B2
Dumfries 247 E10
Som 44 G3
Swindon 63 C7
Park Barn Sur 50 C3
Park Bottom Corn 4 G3
Park Bridge Gtr Man 196 G2
Park Broom Cumb 239 F10

Park Close Lancs 204 E3
Park Corner Bath 45 B9
E Sus 23 C8
E Sus 52 F4
Oxon 65 B7
Windsor 65 C11
Parkend Glos 79 D10
Glos 80 C3
Park End Bedford 121 G9
Cambs 123 E11
Mbro 225 B10
Northumb 241 B9
Som 43 G7
Staffs 168 E3
Worcs 116 C5
Parkengear Corn 5 F8
Parker's Corner W Berks 64 E6
Parker's Green Herts 104 F6
Kent 52 D6
Parkeston Essex 108 E4
Parkfield Corn 6 B6
S Glos 61 D7
W Mid 133 D8
Parkfoot Falk 278 F6
Parkgate Ches E 184 G3
Ches W 182 F3
Cumb 229 B10
Dumfries 248 F2
Essex 87 B11
Kent 53 G11
Sur 51 E8
S Yorks 186 B6
Park Gate Dorset 30 F2
Hants 33 F8
Kent 55 D7
Suff 124 F4
Worcs 117 C8
W Yorks 197 E8
Park Green Essex 105 F9
Parkhall W Dunb 277 G9
Park Hall Shrops 148 C6
Parkham Devon 24 C5
Parkham Ash Devon 24 C5
Parkhead Cumb 230 C2
Glasgow 268 C2
S Yorks 186 E4
Park Head Cumb 231 C7
Derbys 170 E5
W Yorks 197 F7
Parkhill Aberds 303 E10
Invclyd 277 G7
Park Hill Glos 79 F9
Kent 54 G3
Mers 194 G3
Notts 171 E11
N Yorks 214 F6
S Yorks 186 D5
Parkhill Ho Aberds 293 B10
Parkhouse Mon 79 E7
Parkhouse Green
Derbys 170 C6
Parkhurst IoW 20 C5
Parklands W Yorks 206 F3
Park Lane Staffs 133 B7
Wrex 149 B8
Park Langley London 67 F11
Park Mains Renfs 277 G9
Parkmill Swansea 56 D4
Park Mill W Yorks 197 E9
Parkneuk Aberds 293 F9
Fife 279 D11
Park Royal London 67 C7
Parkside C Beds 103 G10
Cumb 219 B10
Durham 234 B4
N Lanark 268 D6
Staffs 151 D8
Wrex 166 D5
Parkstone BCP 18 C6
Park Street Herts 85 E10
W Sus 50 G6
Park Town Luton 103 G11
Oxon 83 D8
Park Village Northumb 240 E5
W Mid 133 C8
Park Villas W Yorks 206 F2
Parkway Hereford 98 D4
Som 29 C9
Park Wood Kent 53 C9
Medway 69 G10
Parkwood Springs
S Yorks 186 D4
Parley Cross Dorset 19 B7
Parley Green BCP 19 B7
Parliament Heath Suff 107 C9
Parlington W Yorks 206 F4
Parmoor Bucks 65 B9
Parnacott Devon 24 F4
Parney Heath Essex 107 E10
Parr Mers 183 C8
Parracombe Devon 41 E7
Parr Brow Gtr Man 195 G8
Parrog Pembs 91 D10
Parsley Hay Derbys 169 C10
Parslow's Hillock Bucks 84 E4
Parsonage Green Essex 88 D2
Parsonby Cumb 229 D8
Parson Cross S Yorks 186 C5
Parson Drove Cambs 139 B7
Parsons Green London 67 D9
Parson's Heath Essex 107 F10
Partick Glasgow 267 B11
Partington Gtr Man 184 C2
Partney Lincs 174 B6
Parton Cumb 228 G5
Cumb 239 G7
Dumfries 237 B8
Glos 99 G7
Hereford 96 B6
Partridge Green W Sus 35 D11
Partrishow Powys 96 G5
Parwich Derbys 169 E11
Pasford Staffs 132 D6
Passenham W Nhants 102 D5
Passfield Hants 49 G10
Passingford Bridge Essex 87 F8
Passmores Essex 86 D6
Paston Norf 160 C6
Pboro 138 C3
Paston Green Norf 160 C6
Pasturefields Staffs 151 D9
Patchacott Devon 12 B5
Patcham Brighton 36 F4
Patchetts Green Herts 85 F10
Patching W Sus 35 F9
Patchole Devon 40 E6
Patchway S Glos 60 C6
Pategill Cumb 230 F6
Pateley Bridge N Yorks 214 F3
Paternoster Heath Essex 88 B6
Pathe Som 43 G11
Pather N Lanark 268 E5
Pathfinder Village Devon 14 C2
Pathhead Aberds 293 G9
E Ayrs 258 G4
Fife 280 C5
Midloth 271 C7
Path Head T&W 242 E5
Pathlow Warks 118 F3
Path of Condie Perth 286 F4
Pathstruie Perth 286 F4
Patient End Herts 105 F8
Patmore Heath Herts 105 F8
Patna E Ayrs 257 G10
Patney Wilts 46 B5
Patrick IoM 192 D3
Patrick Brompton
N Yorks 224 G4
Patricroft Gtr Man 184 B3
Patrington E Yorks 201 C10
Patrington Haven
E Yorks 201 C10
Patrixbourne Kent 55 B7
Patsford Devon 40 F4
Patterdale Cumb 221 B7
Pattiesmuir Fife 279 E11
Pattingham Staffs 132 D6
Pattishall W Nhants 120 G3
Pattiswick Essex 106 G6
Patton Shrops 131 E11
Patton Bridge Cumb 221 F11
Paul Corn 1 D5
Paulerspury W Nhants 102 B4
Paull E Yorks 201 B7
Paul's Green Corn 2 C4
Paulsgrove Ptsmth 33 F10
Paulton Bath 45 B7
Paulville W Loth 269 B9
Pave Lane Telford 150 F5
Pavenham Bedford 121 F9
Pawlett Som 43 E10
Pawlett Hill Som 43 E9
Pawston Northumb 263 C9
Paxford Glos 100 D3
Paxton Borders 273 E8
Payden Street Kent 54 C2
Payhembury Devon 27 G9
Paynes Green Sur 50 F6
Paynter's Cross Corn 7 C7
Paynter's Lane End Corn 4 G3
Paythorne Lancs 204 C2
Payton Som 27 C10
Peacehaven E Sus 36 G6
Peacehaven Heights
E Sus 36 G6
Peacemarsh Dorset 30 B4
Peak Dale Derbys 185 F9
Peak Forest Derbys 185 F10
Peak Hill Lincs 156 F5
Peakirk Pboro 138 B3
Pean Hill Kent 70 G6
Pear Ash Som 45 G9
Pearsie Angus 287 B7
Pearson's Green Kent 53 E7
Peartree Herts 86 C2
Pear Tree Derby 153 C7
Peartree Green Essex 87 F9
Hereford 97 E11
Soton 32 E6
Sur 50 F3
Peas Acre W Yorks 205 E8
Peasedown St John Bath 45 B8
Peasehill Derbys 170 F6
Peaseland Green Norf 159 F11
Peasemore W Berks 64 D3
Peasenhall Suff 127 D7
Pease Pottage W Sus 51 G9
Peas Hill Cambs 139 D8
Peaslake Sur 50 E5
Peasley Cross Mers 183 C8
Peasmarsh E Sus 38 C5
Som 28 E4
Sur 50 D3
Peaston E Loth 271 B8
Peastonbank E Loth 271 B8
Peathill Aberds 303 C9
Peat Inn Fife 287 G8
Peatling Magna Leics 135 E11
Peatling Parva Leics 135 F11
Peaton Shrops 131 G10
Peatonstrand Shrops 131 G10
Peats Corner Suff 126 E3
Pebmarsh Essex 107 E7
Pebsham E Sus 38 F3
Pebworth Worcs 100 B2
Pecket Well W Yorks 196 B3
Peckforton Ches E 167 D8
Peckham London 67 D10
Peckham Bush Kent 53 D7
Peckingell Wilts 62 D2
Pecking Mill Som 44 F6
Peckleton Leics 135 C9
Pedair-ffordd Powys 148 E2
Pedham Norf 160 G6
Pedlars End Essex 87 D8
Pedlar's Rest Shrops 131 G9
Pedlinge Kent 54 F6
Pedmore W Mid 133 G8
Pednor Bottom Bucks 84 E6
Pednormead End Bucks 85 E7
Pedwell Som 44 F2
Peebles Borders 270 G5
Peel Borders 261 B10
IoM 192 D3
Lancs 202 G3
Peel Common Hants 33 G9
Peel Green Gtr Man 184 B2
Peel Hall Gtr Man 184 D4
Peel Hill Lancs 202 G3
Peel Park S Lanark 268 E2
Peene Kent 55 F7
Peening Quarter Kent 38 B5
Peggs Green Leics 153 F8
Pegsdon C Beds 104 E2
Pegswood Northumb 252 F6
Pegwell Kent 71 G11
Peinaha Highld 298 D4
Peinchorran Highld 295 B7
Peingown Highld 298 B4
Peinlich Highld 298 D4
Peinmore Highld 298 E4
Pelaw T&W 243 E7
Pelcomb Pembs 72 B6
Pelcomb Bridge Pembs 72 B6
Pelcomb Cross Pembs 72 B6
Peldon Essex 89 B7
Pelhamfield IoW 21 C7
Pell Green E Sus 52 G6
Pellon W Yorks 196 B5
Pelsall W Mid 133 C10
Pelsall Wood W Mid 133 C10
Pelton Durham 243 G7
Pelton Fell Durham 243 G7
Pelutho Cumb 229 B8
Pelynt Corn 6 D4
Pemberton Carms 75 E8
Gtr Man 194 G5
Pembles Cross Kent 53 D11
Pembre = *Pembrey*
Carms 74 E6
Pembrey = *Pembre*
Carms 74 E6
Pembridge Hereford 115 F7
Pembroke = *Penfro*
Pembs 73 E7
Pembroke Dock = *Doc Penfro* Pembs 73 E7
Pembroke Ferry Pembs 73 E7
Pembury Kent 52 E6
Pempwell Corn 12 F3
Penallt Mon 79 C8
Pen-allt Hereford 97 F11
Penally = *Penalun*
Pembs 73 F10
Penalt Hereford 97 F11
Penalun = *Penally*
Pembs 73 F10
Penare Corn 5 G9
Penarlâg = *Hawarden*
Flint 166 B4
Penarron Powys 130 F2
Penarth V Glam 59 E7
Penarth Moors Cardiff 59 E7
Penbeagle Corn 2 B2
Penbedw Flint 165 B11
Pen-bedw Pembs 92 D4
Penberth Corn 1 E4
Penbidwal Mon 96 G6
Penbodlas Gwyn 144 C5
Pen-bont Rhydybeddau
Ceredig 128 G3
Penboyr Carms 93 D7
Penbryn Ceredig 110 G5
Pencader Carms 93 D8
Pencaenewydd Gwyn 162 G6
Pencaerau Neath 57 B8
Pen-caer-fenny Swansea 56 B4
Pencaitland E Loth 271 B8
Pencarnisiog Anglesey 178 G5
Pencarreg Carms 93 B10
Pencarrow Corn 11 E8
Pencelli Powys 95 F11
Penceilliogi Carms 75 E8
Pen-clawdd Swansea 56 B4
Pencoed Bridgend 58 C3
Pencombe Hereford 115 G11
Pen-common Powys 76 D6
Pencoyd Hereford 97 F10
Pencoys Corn 2 B5
Pencraig Anglesey 179 F7
Hereford 97 G11
Powys 147 D10
Pencroesoped Mon 78 D4
Pencuke Corn 11 C9
Pendas Fields W Yorks 206 F3
Pendeen Corn 1 C3
Pendeford W Mid 133 C7
Penderyn Rhondda 77 D7
Pendine = *Pentywyn*
Carms 74 D2
Pendlebury Gtr Man 195 G9
Pendleton Gtr Man 184 B4
Lancs 203 F11
Pendock Worcs 98 E5
Pendoggett Corn 10 F6
Pendomer Som 29 E8
Pendoylan V Glam 58 D5
Pendre Bridgend 58 C2
Gwyn 110 C2
Powys 95 F10
Pendrift Corn 11 G8
Penegoes Powys 128 C5
Penelewey Corn 4 G6
Penenden Heath Kent 53 B9
Penffordd Pembs 91 G11
Penffordd Lâs = *Staylittle*
Powys 129 E7
Penfro = *Pembroke*
Pembs 73 E7
Pengam Caerph 77 F11
Penge London 67 E11
Pengegon Corn 2 B5
Pengelly Corn 11 E7
Pengenffordd Powys 96 E3
Pengersick Corn 2 D3
Pen-gilfach Gwyn 163 C9
Pengold Corn 11 C8
Pengorffwysfa Anglesey 179 C7
Pengover Green Corn 6 B5
Pen-groes-oped Mon 78 D4
Penguithal Hereford 97 G10
Pengwern Denb 181 F8
Penhale Corn 2 F5
Corn 5 D8
Penhale Jakes Corn 2 D4
Penhallick Corn 3 F7
Corn 4 G3
Penhallow Corn 4 E5
Penhalurick Corn 2 B6
Penhalvean Corn 2 B6
Penhelig Gwyn 128 D2
Penhill Devon 40 G4
Swindon 63 B7
Penhow Newport 78 G6
Penhurst E Sus 23 B11
Peniarth Gwyn 128 B2
Penicuik Midloth 270 C4
Peniel Carms 93 G8
Denb 165 C8
Penifiler Highld 298 E4
Peninver Argyll 255 E8
Penisa'r Waun Gwyn 163 C9
Penistone S Yorks 197 G8
Penjerrick Corn 3 C7
Penketh Warr 183 D9
Penkhull Stoke 168 G5
Penkill S Ayrs 244 D6
Penknap Wilts 45 D11
Penkridge Staffs 151 G8
Pen-lan Swansea 56 B6
Pen-Lan-mabws Pembs 91 F7
Penleigh Wilts 45 C11
Penley Wrex 149 B8
Penllech Gwyn 144 C4
Penllergaer Swansea 56 B6
Penllwyn Caerph 77 F11
Ceredig 128 G3
Penllyn V Glam 58 D3
Pen-llyn Anglesey 178 E4
Pen-lon Anglesey 162 B6
Penmachno Conwy 164 E3
Penmaen Caerph 77 F11
Swansea 56 D4
Penmaenan Conwy 180 F2
Penmaenmawr Conwy 180 F2
Penmaenpool Gwyn 146 F3
Penmaen Rhôs Conwy 180 F5
Penmark V Glam 58 F5
Penmarth Corn 2 B6
Penmayne Corn 10 F4
Pen Mill Som 29 D9
Penmon Anglesey 179 E10
Penmore Mill Argyll 288 D6
Penmorfa Ceredig 110 G6
Gwyn 163 G8
Penmynydd Anglesey 179 G8
Penn Bucks 84 G6
W Mid 133 D7
Pennal Gwyn 128 C4
Pennan Aberds 303 C8
Pennance Corn 4 G4
Pennant Ceredig 111 E10
Conwy 164 D5
Denb 147 C10
Denb 165 E8
Powys 129 D7
Pennant Melangell
Powys 147 D10
Pennar Pembs 73 E7
Pennard Swansea 56 D5
Pennar Park Pembs 72 E6
Penn Bottom Bucks 84 G6
Pennerley Shrops 131 D7
Pennington Cumb 210 D5
Gtr Man 183 B11
Hants 20 C2
Pennington Green
Gtr Man 194 F6
Pennorth Powys 96 F2
Penn Street Bucks 84 F6
Pennsylvania Devon 14 C4
S Glos 61 E8
Penny Bridge Cumb 210 C6
Pennycross Argyll 289 G7
Plym 7 D9
Pennygate Norf 160 E6
Pennygown Argyll 289 E7
Penny Green Derbys 187 F8
Penny Hill Lincs 157 D7
W Yorks 196 D5
Pennylands Lancs 194 F3
Pennymoor Devon 26 E5
Pennypot Kent 54 G6
Penny's Green Norf 142 D3
Pennytinney Corn 10 F6
Pennywell T&W 243 F9
Pen-onn V Glam 58 F5
Penparc Ceredig 92 B4
Pembs 91 E7
Penparcau Ceredig 111 B11
Penpedairheol Caerph 77 F10
Mon 78 E4
Penpergym Mon 78 C4
Penperlleni Mon 78 E4
Penpethy Corn 11 D7
Penpillick Corn 5 D11
Penplas Carms 74 B5
Penpol Corn 3 B8
Penpoll Corn 6 E2
Penponds Corn 2 B4
Penpont Corn 11 G7
Dumfries 247 E8
Powys 95 F9
Penprysg Bridgend 58 C3
Penquit Devon 8 E2
Penrallt Gwyn 145 B7
Powys 129 F9
Penrherber Carms 92 D5
Penrhiw Caerph 78 G2
Penrhiwceiber Rhondda 77 F8
Pen-Rhiw-fawr Neath 76 C2
Penrhiwgarreg Bl Gwent 78 E2
Penrhiw-llan Ceredig 93 C7
Penrhiw-pal Ceredig 92 B6
Penrhiwtyn Neath 57 B8
Penrhos Anglesey 178 E3
Gwyn 144 C6
Hereford 114 F6
Penrhôs Mon 78 C6
Penrhos Mon 78 C6
Powys 76 C3
Pen-rhos Wrex 166 E3
Penrhosfeilw Anglesey 178 E2
Penrhos Garnedd Gwyn 179 G9
Penrhyd Lastra Anglesey 178 C6
Penrhyn Bay = *Bae-Penrhyn*
Conwy 180 E4
Penrhyn Castle Pembs 92 B2
Penrhyn-coch Ceredig 128 G2
Penrhyndeudraeth
Gwyn 146 B2
Penrhynside Conwy 180 E4
Penrhyn side Conwy 180 E4
Penrhys Rhondda 77 F8
Penrice Swansea 56 D3
Penrith Cumb 230 E6
Penrose Corn 10 G3
Corn 11 F7
Penrose Hill Corn 2 D4
Penruddock Cumb 230 F4
Penryn Corn 3 C7
Pensarn Carms 74 B6
Conwy 181 F7
Pen-sarn Gwyn 145 D11
Gwyn 162 G6
Pensax Worcs 116 D4
Pensby Mers 182 E3
Penselwood Som 45 G9
Pensford Bath 60 G6
Pensham Worcs 99 C8
Penshaw T&W 243 G8
Penshurst Kent 52 E4
Pensilva Corn 6 B5
Pensnett W Mid 133 F8
Penston E Loth 281 G8
Penstone Devon 26 G3
Penstraze Corn 4 F5
Pentewan Corn 5 F10
Pentiken Shrops 130 G4
Pentir Gwyn 163 B9
Pentire Corn 4 C5
Pentirvin Shrops 130 C6
Pentlepoir Pembs 73 D10
Pentlow Essex 106 B6
Pentlow Street Essex 106 B6
Pentney Norf 158 G4
Penton Corner Hants 47 D10
Penton Grafton Hants 47 D10
Penton Mewsey Hants 47 D10
Pentonville London 67 C10
Pentowin Carms 74 B3
Pentraeth Anglesey 179 F8
Pentrapeod Caerph 77 E11
Pentre Carms 75 C8
Denb 165 D10
Flint 165 C11
Flint 166 B4
Flint 166 C2
Flint 166 D2
Powys 129 F11
Powys 130 D5
Powys 130 E5
Powys 147 D11
Powys 148 G3
Rhondda 77 F7
Shrops 148 D4
Shrops 149 F7
Wrex 148 B2
Wrex 166 G3
Pentrebach Carms 94 E6
M Tydf 77 E9
Rhondda 58 B5
Swansea 75 D10
Pentre-bâch Ceredig 93 B11
Pentre-bach Powys 95 E8
Pentrebane Cardiff 58 D6
Pentrebeirdd Powys 148 G3
Pentre Berw Anglesey 179 G7
Pentre-bont Conwy 164 E2
Pentre Broughton Wrex 166 E4
Pentre Bychan Wrex 166 F4
Pentrecagal Carms 92 C6
Pentre-celyn Denb 165 E11
Powys 129 B7
Pentre-chwyth Swansea 57 B7
Pentre Cilgwyn Wrex 148 B4
Pentre-clawdd Shrops 148 C5
Pentre-coed Shrops 149 B7
Pentre-cwrt Carms 93 D7
Pentre Dolau-Honddu
Powys 95 C9
Pentredwr Denb 165 F11
Pentre-dwr Swansea 57 B7
Pentrefelin Anglesey 178 C6
Carms 93 G11
Ceredig 94 B2
Conwy 180 G4
Denb 166 G2
Gwyn 145 B10
Pentre-Ffwrndan Flint 182 G3
Pentrefoelas Conwy 164 E5
Pentref-y-groes Caerph 77 F11
Pentre-galar Pembs 92 E3
Pentregat Ceredig 111 G7
Pentre-Gwenlais Carms 75 B10
Pentre Gwynfryn Gwyn 145 D11
Pentre Halkyn Flint 182 G2
Pentreheyling Shrops 130 E4
Pentre Hodre Shrops 114 B6
Pentre Isaf Conwy 164 B5
Pentre Llanrhaeadr
Denb 165 C9
Pentre Llifior Powys 130 D2
Pentrellwyn Ceredig 93 C8
Pentre-llwyn-llwyd
Powys 113 G9
Pentre-llyn Ceredig 112 C2
Pentre-llyn cymmer
Conwy 165 E7
Pentre Maelor Wrex 166 F5
Pentre Meyrick V Glam 58 D3
Pentre-newydd Shrops 148 B5
Pentre-Piod Torf 78 E3
Pentre-Poeth Carms 75 E8
Newport 59 B9
Pentre'r beirdd Powys 148 G3
Pentre'r Felin Conwy 164 B4
Pentre'r-felin Denb 165 B10
Powys 95 E8
Pentre-rhew Ceredig 112 G3
Pentre-tafarn-y-fedw
Conwy 164 C4
Pentre-ty-gwyn Carms 94 D6
Pentreuchaf Gwyn 145 B7
Pentre-uchaf Conwy 180 F5
Pentrich Derbys 170 E5
Pentridge Dorset 31 D8
Pentrisil Pembs 91 E11
Pentwyn Caerph 77 E10
Cardiff 59 C8
Pen-twyn Caerph 78 E2
Pentwyn = *Pendine*
Carms 74 D2
Pen-twyn Carms 75 C9
Mon 79 D8
Torf 78 E3
Pentwyn Berthlwyd
Caerph 77 F10
Pentwyn-mawr Caerph 77 F11
Pentyrch Cardiff 58 C6
Penuchadre V Glam 57 G11
Pen-Uchar Plwyf Flint 181 G11
Penuwch Ceredig 111 E11
Penwartha Corn 4 E5
Penwartha Coombe Corn 4 E5
Penweathers Corn 4 G6
Penwithick Corn 5 D10
Penwood Hants 64 G2
Penwortham Lane
Lancs 194 B4
Penwyllt Powys 76 B5
Pen-y-Ball Top Flint 181 F11
Penybanc Carms 75 C10
Pen-y-banc Carms 93 G8
Carms 94 G2
Pen-y-bank Caerph 77 E10
Penybedd Carms 74 E6
Penybont Ceredig 128 F2
Powys 114 E2
Pen-y-Bont Bl Gwent 78 D2
Carms 92 F6
Gwyn 128 C4
Gwyn 146 D2
Powys 148 E4
Pen y Bont ar ogwr
= *Bridgend* Bridgend 58 C2
Penybontfawr Powys 147 E11
Penybryn Caerph 77 F10
Pen-y-Bryn Gwyn 145 B9
Gwyn 146 F3
Pembs 92 C3
Powys 130 C3
Shrops 148 B6
Wrex 166 G3
Penycae Wrex 166 F3
Pen-y-cae Bridgend 58 C2
Neath 57 D9
Powys 76 C4
Pen-y-cae-mawr Mon 78 F6
Penycaerau Gwyn 144 D3
Pen-y-cefn Flint 181 F10
Pen-y-clawdd Mon 79 D7
Pen-y-coed Shrops 148 E5
Pen-y-coedcae Rhondda 58 B5
Penycwm Pembs 90 G6
Pen-y-Darren M Tydf 77 D9
Penydre Swansea 75 E11
Pen-y-fai Bridgend 57 E11
Carms 75 E7
Pen-y-fan Carms 56 B4
Mon 79 D8
Penyfeidr Pembs 91 F7
Pen-y-felin Flint 165 B11
Penyffordd Flint 166 C4
Pen-y-ffordd Denb 181 F8
Flint 181 E10
Penyffridd Gwyn 163 D8
Pen y Foel Shrops 148 E5
Penygarn Torf 78 E3
Pen-y-garn Carms 93 E11
Ceredig 128 F2
Penygarnedd Powys 148 E2
Pen-y-garnedd
Anglesey 179 F8
Penygelli Powys 130 E2
Pen-y-gop Conwy 164 G6
Penygraig Rhondda 77 G7
Pen-y-graig Gwyn 144 C3
Penygraigwen Anglesey 178 D6
Penygroes Gwyn 163 E7
Pembs 92 D3
Pen-y-groes Carms 75 C9
Pen-y-groeslon Gwyn 144 C4
Pen-y-Gwryd Hotel
Gwyn 163 D11
Pen-y-lan Cardiff 59 D7
Newport 59 B9
V Glam 58 D3
Pen-y-maes Flint 181 F11
Pen-y-Myndd Carms 75 E7
Penymynydd Flint 166 C4
Pen-y-Park Hereford 96 C5
Penyraber Pembs 91 D9
Pen-yr-englyn Rhondda 76 F6
Penyrheol Caerph 58 B6
Swansea 56 B5
Torf 78 F3
Pen-yr-heol Bridgend 58 C2
Mon 78 C6
Pen-yr-Heolgerrig
M Tydf 77 D8
Pen-y-rhiw Rhondda 58 B5
Penysarn Anglesey 179 C7
Pen-y-stryt Denb 165 E11
Penywaun Rhondda 77 E7
Pen-y-wern Shrops 114 B6
Penzance Corn 1 C5
Peopleton Worcs 117 G8
Peover Heath Ches E 184 G3
Peper Harow Sur 50 E2
Peppercombe Devon 24 C5
Pepper Hill Som 43 F7
W Yorks 196 B6
Peppermoor Northumb 264 F6
Pepper's Green Essex 87 C10
Pepperstock C Beds 85 B9
Perceton N Ayrs 267 G7
Percie Aberds 293 D7
Percuil Corn 3 C9
Percyhorner Aberds 303 C9
Percy Main T&W 243 D8
Per-ffordd-llan Flint 181 F10
Perham Down Wilts 47 D9
Periton Som 42 D3
Perivale London 67 C7
Perkhill Aberds 293 C7
Perkinsville Durham 243 G7
Perlethorpe Notts 187 G11
Perranarworthal Corn 3 B7
Perrancoombe Corn 4 E5
Perran Downs Corn 2 C3
Perranporth Corn 4 E5
Perranuthnoe Corn 2 D2
Perranwell Corn 3 B7
Corn 4 E5
Perranwell Station Corn 3 B7
Perran Wharf Corn 3 B7
Perranzabuloe Corn 4 E5
Perrott's Brook Glos 81 D8
Perry Devon 26 F5
Kent 55 B9
W Mid 133 E11
Perry Barr W Mid 133 E11
Perry Beeches W Mid 133 E11
Perry Common W Mid 133 E11
Perry Crofts Staffs 134 C4
Perryfields Worcs 117 C8
Perryfoot Derbys 185 E10
Perry Green Essex 106 G6
Herts 86 B6
Som 43 F9
Wilts 62 B3
Perrymead Bath 61 G9
Perrystone Hill Hereford 98 F2
Perry Street Kent 68 E6
Som 28 F4
Perrywood Kent 54 B4
Pershall Staffs 150 C6
Pershore Worcs 99 B8
Pert Angus 293 G8
Pertenhall Bedford 121 D11
Perth Perth 286 E5
Perthcelyn Rhondda 77 F9
Perthy Shrops 149 C7
Perton Hereford 97 C11
Staffs 133 D7
Pertwood Wilts 45 F11
Pested Kent 54 C4
Peterborough Pboro 138 D3
Peterburn Highld 307 L2
Peterchurch Hereford 96 D6
Peterculter Aberdeen 293 C10
Peterhead Aberds 303 E11
Peterlee Durham 234 C4
Petersburn N Lanark 268 C5
Petersfield Hants 34 C2
Peter's Finger Devon 12 D3
Peter's Green Herts 85 B10
Petersham London 67 E7
Peters Marland Devon 25 E7
Peterstone Wentlooge
Newport 59 C9
Peterston-super-Ely
V Glam 58 D5
Peterstow Hereford 97 G11
Peter Tavy Devon 12 F6
Petertown Orkney 314 F3
Peterville Corn 4 E4
Petham Kent 54 C6
Petherwin Gate Corn 11 D11
Petrockstow Devon 25 F8
Petsoe End M Keynes 103 B7
Pett E Sus 38 E5
Pettaugh Suff 126 F3
Pett Bottom Kent 54 E6
Kent 55 C7
Petteridge Kent 53 E7
Pettinain S Lanark 269 G9
Pettings Kent 68 G6
Pettistree Suff 126 G5
Pett Level E Sus 38 E5
Petton Devon 27 C8
Shrops 149 D8
Petts Wood London 68 F2
Petty Aberds 303 F7
Pettycur Fife 280 D5
Petty France S Glos 61 B9
Pettymuick Aberds 303 G9
Pettywell Norf 159 E11
Petworth W Sus 35 C7
Pevensey E Sus 23 E10
Pevensey Bay E Sus 23 E11
Peverell Plym 7 D9
Pewsey Wilts 63 G7
Pewsey Wharf Wilts 63 G7
Pewterspear Warr 183 E10
Phantassie E Loth 281 F11
Pharisee Green Essex 106 G2
Pheasants Bucks 65 B9
Pheasant's Hill Bucks 65 B9
Pheasey W Mid 133 D11
Pheonix Green Hants 49 B9
Phepson Worcs 117 F8
Philadelphia T&W 243 G8
Philham Devon 24 C3
Philiphaugh Borders 261 D10
Phillack Corn 2 B3
Philleigh Corn 3 B9
Phillip's Town Caerph 77 E10
Philpot End Essex 87 B10
Philpstoun W Loth 279 F10
Phocle Green Hereford 98 F2
Phoenix Green Hants 49 B9
Phoenix Row Durham 233 F9
Phorp Moray 301 D10
Pibsbury Som 28 B6
Pibwrlwyd Carms 74 B6
Pica Cumb 228 G6
Piccadilly S Yorks 187 B7
Warks 134 D4
Piccadilly Corner Norf 142 F5
Piccotts End Herts 85 D9
Pickburn S Yorks 198 F4
Picken End Worcs 98 C6
Pickering N Yorks 216 C5
Pickering Nook Durham 242 F5
Picket Hill Hants 31 F11
Picket Piece Hants 47 D11
Picket Post Hants 31 F11
Pickford W Mid 134 G5
Pickford Green W Mid 134 G5
Pickhill N Yorks 214 C6
Picklenash Glos 98 F4
Picklescott Shrops 131 D8
Pickles Hill W Yorks 204 F6
Pickletillem Fife 287 E8
Pickley Green Gtr Man 195 G7
Pickmere Ches E 183 F11
Pickney Som 27 B11
Pickstock Telford 150 E4
Pickup Bank Blackburn 195 C8
Pickwell Devon 40 E3
Leics 154 G5
Pickwick Wilts 61 E11
Pickwood Scar W Yorks 196 C5
Pickworth Lincs 155 C10
Rutland 155 G9
Picton Ches W 182 G6
Flint 181 E10
N Yorks 225 D8
Pict's Hill Som 28 B6
Piddinghoe E Sus 36 G6
Piddington Bucks 84 G4
Oxon 83 B10
W Nhants 120 G6
Piddlehinton Dorset 17 B10
Piddletrenthide Dorset 17 B10
Pidley Cambs 122 B6
Pidney Dorset 30 F2
Piece Corn 2 B5
Piercebridge Darl 224 B4
Piercing Hill Essex 86 F6
Pierowall Orkney 314 B4
Piff's Elm Glos 99 F8
Pigdon Northumb 252 F5
Pightley Som 43 F8
Pig Oak Dorset 31 G8
Pigstye Green Essex 87 D10
Pike End W Yorks 196 D4
Pikehall Derbys 169 D11
Pike Hill Lancs 204 G3
Pike Law W Yorks 196 D4
Pikeshill Hants 32 F3
Pikestye Hereford 97 B10
Pilford Dorset 31 G8
Pilgrims Hatch Essex 87 F9
Pilham Lincs 188 C5
Pilhough Derbys 170 C3
Pill N Som 60 D4
Pembs 72 D6
Pillaton Corn 7 C7
Staffs 151 G8
Pillerton Hersey Warks 100 B6
Pillerton Priors Warks 100 B5
Pilleth Powys 114 D5
Pilley Glos 81 B7
Hants 20 B2
S Yorks 197 G10
Pilley Bailey Hants 20 B2
Pillgwenlly Newport 59 B10
Pilling Lancs 202 D4
Pilling Lane Lancs 202 D3
Pillmouth Devon 25 C7
Pillowell Glos 79 D10
Pillows Green Glos 98 F5
Pillwell Dorset 30 D3
Pilmuir Borders 261 G11
Pilning S Glos 60 B5
Pilrig Edin 280 F5
Pilsbury Derbys 169 C10
Pilsdon Dorset 16 B4
Pilsgate Pboro 137 B11
Pilsley Derbys 170 C6
Derbys 186 G2
Pilsley Green Derbys 170 C6
Pilson Green Norf 161 G7
Piltdown E Sus 36 C6
Pilton Devon 40 G5
Edin 280 F4
N Nhants 137 G10
Rutland 137 C8
Som 44 E5
Pilton Green Swansea 56 D2
Piltown Som 44 F5
Pimhole Gtr Man 195 E10
Pimlico Herts 85 D9
Lancs 203 E10
London 67 D9
W Nhants 102 C2
Pimperne Dorset 29 F9
Dorset 30 F6
Pinchbeck Lincs 156 D4
Pinchbeck Bars Lincs 156 D3
Pinchbeck West Lincs 156 E4
Pincheon Green
S Yorks 199 D7
Pinckney Green Wilts 61 G10
Pincock Lancs 194 D5
Pineham Kent 55 D10
M Keynes 103 C7
Pinehurst Swindon 63 B7
Pinfarthings Glos 80 E5
Pinfold Lancs 193 E11
Pinfold Hill S Yorks 197 G9
Pinfoldpond C Beds 103 E8
Pinford End Suff 124 F6
Pinged Carms 74 E6
Pingewood W Berks 65 F7
Pin Green Herts 104 F4
Pinhoe Devon 14 C5
Pinkett's Booth W Mid 134 G5
Pink Green Worcs 117 D11
Pinkie Braes E Loth 281 G7
Pinkney Wilts 61 B11
Pinkneys Green Windsor 65 C11
Pinksmoor Som 27 D10
Pinley W Mid 119 B7
Pinley Green Warks 118 D4
Pin Mill Suff 108 D4
Pinminnoch Dumfries 236 D2
S Ayrs 244 E5
Pinmore S Ayrs 244 E6
Pinmore Mains S Ayrs 244 E6
Pinnacles Essex 86 D6
Pinner London 66 B6
Pinner Green London 85 G10
Pinnerwood Park
London 85 G10
Pin's Green Worcs 98 B6
Pinsley Green Ches E 167 F9
Pinstones Shrops 131 F9
Pinvin Worcs 99 B9
Pinwall Leics 134 C6
Pinwherry S Ayrs 244 F5
Pinxton Derbys 171 E7
Pipe and Lyde Hereford 97 C10
Pipe Aston Hereford 115 C9
Pipe Gate Shrops 168 G2
Pipehill Staffs 133 B11
Pipehouse Bath 45 B9
Piperhall Argyll 266 D2
Piperhill Highld 301 D8
Pipe Ridware Staffs 151 F11
Piper's Ash Ches W 166 B6
Piper's End Worcs 98 E6
Piper's Hill Worcs 117 D9
Piper's Pool Corn 11 E11
Pipewell N Nhants 136 G6
Pippacott Devon 40 F4
Pippin Street Lancs 194 C5
Pipps Hill Essex 69 B7
Pipsden Kent 53 G9
Pipton Powys 96 D3
Pirbright Sur 50 B2
Pirbright Camp Sur 50 B2
Pirnmill N Ayrs 255 C9
Pirton Herts 104 E2
Worcs 99 B7
Pisgah Ceredig 112 B3
Stirling 285 G11
Pishill Oxon 65 B8
Pishill Bank Oxon 84 G2
Pismire Hill S Yorks 186 C5
Pistyll Gwyn 162 G4
Pit Mon 78 D5
Pitagowan Perth 291 G10
Pitblae Aberds 303 C9
Pitcairngreen Perth 286 E4
Pitcalnie Highld 301 B8
Pitcaple Aberds 303 G7
Pitchcombe Glos 80 D5
Pitchcott Bucks 102 G5
Pitcher's Green Suff 125 F8
Pitchford Shrops 131 C10
Pitch Green Bucks 84 E3
Pitch Place Sur 49 F11
Sur 50 C3
Pitcombe Som 45 G7
Pitcorthie Fife 280 D2
Fife 287 G9
Pitcot Som 45 D7
V Glam 57 G11
Pitcox E Loth 282 F2
Pitcur Perth 286 D6
Pitfancy Aberds 302 E5
Pitfichie Aberds 293 B8
Pitforthie Aberds 293 F10
Pitgair Aberds 303 D7
Pitgrudy Highld 309 K7
Pithmaduthy Highld 301 B7
Pitkennedy Angus 287 B9
Pitkevy Fife 286 G6
Pitkierie Fife 287 G9
Pitlessie Fife 287 G7
Pitlochry Perth 286 B3
Pitmachie Aberds 302 G6
Pitmain Highld 291 C9
Pitmedden Aberds 303 G8
Pitminster Som 28 D2
Pitmuies Angus 287 C9
Pitmunie Aberds 293 B8
Pitney Som 29 B7
Pitrocknie Perth 286 C6
Pitscottie Fife 287 F8
Pitsea Essex 69 B8
Pitses Gtr Man 196 G2
Pitsford W Nhants 120 D5
Pitsford Hill Som 42 G6
Pitsmoor S Yorks 186 D5
Pitstone Bucks 84 B6
Pitstone Green Bucks 84 B6
Pitstone Hill Bucks 85 C7
Pitt Hants 33 B7
Pittachar Perth 286 E2
Pitt Court Glos 80 F3
Pittendreich Moray 301 C11
Pittentrail Highld 309 J7
Pittenweem Fife 287 G9
Pitteuchar Fife 280 B5
Pittington Durham 234 C2
Pittodrie Aberds 302 G6
Pitton Swansea 56 D2
Wilts 47 G8
Pitts Hill Stoke 168 E5
Pittswood Kent 52 D6
Pittulie Aberds 303 C9
Pittville Glos 99 G9
Pityme Corn 10 F5
Pity Me Durham 233 B11
Pityoulish Highld 291 B11
Pixey Green Suff 126 B4
Pixham Sur 51 C7
Worcs 98 B6
Pixley Hereford 98 D3
Shrops 150 D3
Pizien Well Kent 53 C7
Place Newton N Yorks 217 E7
Plaidy Aberds 303 D7
Corn 6 E5
Plain-an-Gwarry Corn 4 G3
Plain Dealings Pembs 73 B9
Plains N Lanark 268 B5
Plainsfield Som 43 F7
Plain Spot Notts 171 E7
Plain Street Corn 10 F5
Plaish Shrops 131 D10
Plaistow London 68 C2
London 68 E2
W Sus 50 G4
Plaistow Green Essex 106 F6
Plaitford Wilts 32 D3
Plaitford Green Hants 32 C3
Plank Lane Gtr Man 194 G6
Plans Dumfries 238 D3
Plantation Bridge Cumb 221 F9
Plantationfoot Dumfries 248 E4
Plardiwick Staffs 150 E6
Plasau Shrops 149 E7
Plâs Berwyn Denb 165 G11
Plas-canol Gwyn 145 F11
Plas Coch Wrex 166 E4
Plas Dinam Powys 129 F10
Plas Gogerddan Ceredig 128 G2
Plashet London 68 C2
Plashett Carms 74 D3
Plasiolyn Powys 129 C11
Plas Llwyngwern Powys 128 C5
Plas Meredydd Powys 130 D3
Plas Nantyr Wrex 148 B3
Plasnewydd Powys 129 D9
Plaster's Green Bath 60 G4
Plastow Green Hants 64 G4
Plas-yn-Cefn Denb 181 G8
Platt Kent 52 B6
Platt Bridge Gtr Man 194 G6
Platt Lane Shrops 149 B10
Platts Common
S Yorks 197 G11
Platt's Heath Kent 53 C11
Plawsworth Durham 233 B11
Plaxtol Kent 52 C6
Playden E Sus 38 C6
Playford Suff 108 B4
Play Hatch Oxon 65 D8
Playing Place Corn 4 G6
Playley Green Glos 98 E5
Plealey Shrops 131 B8
Pleamore Cross Som 27 D10
Plean Stirling 278 D6
Pleasant Valley Pembs 73 D10
Pleasington Blackburn 194 B6
Pleasley Derbys 171 C8
Pleasleyhill Notts 171 C8
Pleck Dorset 30 D3
Dorset 30 E2
W Mid 133 D9
Pleckgate Blackburn 203 G9
Pleck or Little Ansty
Dorset 30 G3
Pledgdon Green Essex 105 F11
Pledwick W Yorks 197 D10
Plemstall Ches W 183 G7
Plenmeller Northumb 240 E6
Pleshey Essex 87 C11
Plockton Highld 295 B10

Plocrapol W Isles 305 J3
Plot Gate Som 44 G4
Plot Street Som 44 F5
Ploughfield Hereford 97 C7
Plough Hill Warks 134 E6
Plowden Shrops 131 F7
Ploxgreen Shrops 131 C7
Pluckley Kent 54 D2
Pluckley Thorne Kent 54 E2
Plucks Gutter Kent 71 G9
Plumbland Cumb 229 D9
Plumbley S Yorks 186 E6
Plumford Kent 54 B4
Plumley Ches E 184 F2
Plump Hill Glos 79 B11
Plumpton Cumb 230 D5
E Sus 36 E5
W Nhants 101 B11
Plumpton End
W Nhants 102 B4
Plumpton Foot Cumb 230 D5
Plumpton Green E Sus 36 D5
Plumpton Head Cumb 230 E6
Plumstead London 68 D3
Norf 160 C2
Plumstead Common
London 68 D3
Plumstead Green Norf 160 C2
Plumtree Notts 154 C2
Plumtree Green Kent 53 D10
Plumtree Park Notts 154 C2
Plungar Leics 154 C5
Plush Dorset 30 G2
Plusha Corn 11 E11
Plushabridge Corn 12 G2
Plusterwine Glos 79 F9
Plwmp Ceredig 111 G7
Plymouth Plym 7 E9
Plympton Plym 7 D10
Plymstock Plym 7 E10
Plymtree Devon 27 G9
Pobgreen Gtr Man 196 F4
Pochin Houses Caerph 77 E11
Pocket Nook Gtr Man 183 B10
Pockley N Yorks 216 B2
Pocklington E Yorks 208 D2
Pockthorpe
Norf 141 D8
Norf 158 D6
Norf 159 E10
Norf 159 F11
Pode Hole Lincs 156 E4
Podimore Som 29 C8
Podington Bedford 121 E8
Podmoor Worcs 117 C7
Podmore Norf 159 G9
Staffs 150 B5
Podsmead Glos 80 B4
Poffley End Oxon 82 C5
Pogmoor S Yorks 197 F10
Point Corn 3 B8
Point Clear Essex 89 C9
Pointon Lincs 156 C2
Pokesdown BCP 19 C8
Pol a Charra W Isles 297 K3
Polbae Dumfries 236 B4
Polbain Highld 307 H4
Polbathic Corn 7 D7
Polbeth W Loth 269 C10
Polborder Corn 7 C7
Polbrock Corn 5 B10
Polchar Highld 291 C10
Polebrook N Nhants 137 F11
Pole Elm Worcs 98 B6
Polegate E Sus 23 D9
Pole Moor W Yorks 196 D5
Poles Highld 309 K7
Polesden Lacey Sur 50 C6
Poleshill Som 27 C9
Pole's Hole Wilts 45 C10
Polesworth Warks 134 C5
Polgear Corn 2 B5
Polgigga Corn 1 E3
Polglass Highld 307 J5
Polgooth Corn 5 E9
Poling W Sus 35 G8
Poling Corner W Sus 35 F8
Polkerris Corn 5 E11
Polla Highld 308 D3
Polladras Corn 2 C4
Pollard Street Norf 160 C6
Pollhill Kent 53 C11
Poll Hill Mers 182 E3
Pollie Highld 309 H7
Pollington E Yorks 198 D6
Polliwilline Argyll 255 G8
Polloch Highld 289 C9
Pollok Glasgow 267 C10
Pollokshields Glasgow 267 C11
Polmadie Glasgow 267 C11
Polmarth Corn 2 B6
Polmassick Corn 5 F9
Polmear Corn 5 E11
Polmont Falk 279 F8
Polmorla Corn 10 G5
Polnessan E Ayrs 257 G10
Polnish Highld 295 G9
Polopit N Nhants 121 B10
Polpenwith Corn 2 D6
Polpeor Corn 2 B2
Polperro Corn 6 E4
Polruan Corn 6 E2
Polsham Som 44 E4
Polsloe Devon 14 C4
Polstead Suff 107 D9
Polstead Heath Suff 107 C9
Poltalloch Argyll 275 D9
Poltesco Corn 2 F6
Poltimore Devon 14 B5
Polton Midloth 270 C5
Polwarth Borders 272 E4
Polwheveral Corn 2 D6
Polyphant Corn 11 E11
Polzeath Corn 10 F4
Pomeroy Derbys 169 B10
Pomphlett Plym 7 E10
Ponciau Wrex 166 F3
Pond Close Som 27 B10
Ponde Powys 96 D2
Pondersbridge Cambs 138 E5
Ponders End London 86 F5
Pond Park Bucks 85 E7
Pond Street Essex 105 D9
Pondtail Hants 49 C10
Pondwell IoW 21 C8
Poniou Corn 1 B4
Ponjeravah Corn 2 D6
Ponsanooth Corn 3 B7
Ponsford Devon 27 F8
Ponsonby Cumb 219 D11
Ponsongath Corn 3 F7
Ponsworthy Devon 13 G10
Pont Corn 6 E2
Pont Aber Carms 94 G4
Pont Aber-Geirw Gwyn 146 D5
Pontamman Carms 75 C10
Pontantwn Carms 74 C6
Pontardawe Neath 76 E2
Pontarddulais Swansea 75 E9
Pontarfynach = *Devils Bridge* Ceredig 112 B4
Pont-ar-gothi Carms 93 G10
Pont ar Hydfer Powys 95 F7
Pont-ar-llechau Carms 94 G4
Pontarsais Carms 93 F8
Pontblyddyn Flint 166 C3
Pontbren Araeth Carms 94 G3
Pontbren Llwyd Rhondda 76 D6
Pontcanna Cardiff 59 D7
Pont Cyfyng Conwy 164 D2
Pont Cysyllte Wrex 166 G3
Pontdolgoch Powys 129 E10
Pont Dolydd Prysor
Gwyn 146 B4
Pontefract W Yorks 198 C3
Ponteland Northumb 242 C5
Ponterwyd Ceredig 128 G4
Pontesbury Shrops 131 B7
Pontesbury Hill Shrops 131 B7
Pontesford Shrops 131 B8
Pontfadog Wrex 148 B4
Pontfaen Pembs 91 E10
Pont-faen Powys 95 E9
Shrops 148 B5
Pont Fronwydd Gwyn 146 E6
Pont-gareg Pembs 92 C2
Pontgarreg Ceredig 110 G6
Ponthen Shrops 148 F6
Pont-Henri Carms 75 D7
Ponthir Torf 78 G4
Ponthirwaun Ceredig 92 B5
Pont Hwfa Anglesey 178 E2
Pontiago Pembs 91 D8
Pont iets = *Pontyates*
Carms 75 D7
Pontithel Powys 96 D3
Pontllanfraith Caerph 77 F11
Pontlliw Swansea 75 E10
Pont-Llogel Powys 147 F10
Pontllyfni Gwyn 162 E6
Pontlottyn Caerph 77 D10
Pontneddfechan Powys 76 D6
Pontnewydd Torf 78 F3
Pont-newydd Carms 74 D6
Flint 165 B11
Pontnewynydd Torf 78 E3
Pont Pen-y-benglog
Gwyn 163 C10
Pontrhydfendigaid
Ceredig 112 D4
Pont Rhydgaled Powys 128 G6
Pont Rhyd-goch
Conwy 163 C11
Pont-Rhyd-sarn Gwyn 147 D7
Pont Rhyd-y-berry
Powys 95 D9
Pont Rhyd-y-cyff
Bridgend 57 D11
Pontrhydyfen Neath 57 C9
Pont-rhyd-y-groes
Ceredig 112 C4
Pontrhydyrun Torf 78 F3
Pont-Rhythallt Gwyn 163 C8
Pontrilas Hereford 97 F7
Pontrobert Powys 148 G2
Pont-rug Gwyn 163 C8
Pont Senni = *Sennybridge*
Powys 95 F8
Ponts Green E Sus 23 B11
Pontshill Hereford 98 G2
Pont-siôn Ceredig 93 B8
Pont Siôn Norton
Rhondda 77 G9
Pontsticill M Tydf 77 C9
Pont-Walby Neath 76 D5
Pontwgan Conwy 180 G3
Pontyates = *Pont-iets*
Carms 75 D7
Pontyberem Carms 75 C8
Pont-y-blew Shrops 148 B6
Pontyclun Rhondda 58 C4
Pontycymer Bridgend 76 G6
Pontyglasier Pembs 92 D2
Pont-y-gwaith Rhondda 77 G8
Pontymister Caerph 78 G2
Pontymoel Torf 78 E3
Pont-y-pant Conwy 164 E3
Pont y Pennant Gwyn 147 E8
Pontypool Torf 78 E3
Pontypridd Rhondda 58 B5
Pont yr Afon-Gam
Gwyn 164 G2
Pont-yr-hafod Pembs 91 F8
Pont-y-rhyl Bridgend 58 B2
Pont-Ystrad Denb 165 C9
Pont-y-wal Powys 96 D2
Pontywaun Caerph 78 G2
Pooksgreen Hants 32 E5
Pool Corn 4 G3
W Yorks 205 D10
Poolbrook Worcs 98 C5
Poole BCP 18 C6
N Yorks 198 B3
Som 27 C10
Poole Keynes Glos 81 F8
Poolend Staffs 169 D7
Poolestown Dorset 30 D2
Poolewe Highld 307 L3
Pooley Bridge Cumb 230 G5
Pooley Street Norf 141 G11
Poolfold Staffs 168 D5
Poolhead Shrops 149 C9
Pool Head Hereford 115 G11
Pool Hey Lancs 193 D11
Poolhill Glos 98 F4
Poolmill Hereford 97 G11
Pool o' Muckhart Clack 286 G4
Pool Quay Powys 148 G5
Poolsbrook Derbys 186 G6
Poolside Moray 302 E4
Poolstock Gtr Man 194 G5
Pooltown Som 42 F3
Pootings Kent 52 D3
Pope Hill Pembs 72 C6
Pope's Hill Glos 79 C11
Popeswood Brack 65 F10
Popham Devon 41 G8
Hants 48 E5
Poplar London 67 C11
Poplar Grove Lincs 190 B6
Poplars Herts 104 G5
Popley Hants 48 C6
Porchester Nottingham 171 G9
Porchfield IoW 20 C4
Porin Highld 300 D3
Poringland Norf 142 C5
Porkellis Corn 2 C5
Porlock Som 41 D11
Porlockford Som 41 D11
Porlock Weir Som 41 D11
Portachoillan Argyll 255 B8
Port Allen Perth 286 E6
Port Ann Argyll 275 E10
Port Appin Argyll 289 E11
Port Arthur Shetland 313 K5
Portash Wilts 46 G3
Port Askaig Argyll 274 G5
Portavadie Argyll 275 G10
Port Bannatyne Argyll 275 G11
Port Brae Fife 280 C5
Port Bridge Devon 9 D7
Portbury N Som 60 D4
Port Carlisle Cumb 238 E6
Port Charlotte Argyll 254 B3
Portchester Hants 33 F10
Portclair Highld 290 B6
Port Clarence Stockton 234 G5
Port Dinorwic = *Y Felinheli*
Gwyn 163 B8
Port Driseach Argyll 275 F10
Port Dundas Glasgow 267 B11
Porteath Corn 10 F5
Port Edgar Edin 280 F2
Port Ellen Argyll 254 C4
Port Elphinstone Aberds 293 B9
Portencalzie Dumfries 236 B2
Portencross N Ayrs 266 F3
Porterfield Renfs 267 B9
Port Erin IoM 192 F2
Port Erroll Aberds 303 F10
Porter's End Herts 85 B11
Portesham Dorset 17 D8
Portessie Moray 302 C4
Port e Vullen IoM 192 C5
Port-Eynon Swansea 56 D3
Portfield Argyll 289 G9
Som 28 B6
W Sus 22 B5
Portfield Gate Pembs 72 B6
Portgate Devon 12 D4
Port Gaverne Corn 10 E6
Port Glasgow Invclyd 276 G6
Portgordon Moray 302 C3
Portgower Highld 311 H4
Porth Corn 4 C6
Rhondda 77 G8
Porthallow Corn 3 E7
Corn 6 E4
Porthcawl Bridgend 57 F10
Porth Colmon Gwyn 144 C3
Porthcothan Corn 10 G3
Porthcurno Corn 1 E3
Portheiddy Pembs 90 E6
Port Henderson Highld 299 B7
Porthgain Pembs 90 E6
Porthgwarra Corn 1 E3
Porthhallow Corn 3 E7
Porthill Shrops 149 G9
Staffs 168 F5
Port Hill Oxon 65 B7
Porthilly Corn 10 F4
Porth Kea Corn 4 G6
Porthkerry V Glam 58 F5
Porthleven Corn 2 D4
Porthllechog = *Bull Bay*
Anglesey 178 C6
Porthloo Scilly 1 G4
Porthmadog Gwyn 145 B11
Porthmeor Corn 1 B4
Porth Navas Corn 3 D7
Porthoustock Corn 3 E8
Porthpean Corn 5 E10
Porthtowan Corn 4 F3
Porth Tywyn = *Burry Port*
Carms 74 E6
Porth-y-felin Anglesey 178 E2
Porthyrhyd Carms 75 B8
Carms 94 D4
Porth-y-waen Shrops 148 E5
Portico Mers 183 C7
Portincaple Argyll 276 C4
Portington Devon 12 F4
E Yorks 207 G11
Portinnisherrich Argyll 275 B10
Portinscale Cumb 229 G11
Port Isaac Corn 10 E5
Portishead N Som 60 D3
Portkil Argyll 276 E5
Portknockie Moray 302 C4
Port Lamont Argyll 275 F11
Portland Som 44 F3
Portlethen Aberds 293 D11
Portlethen Village
Aberds 293 D11
Portlevorchy Highld 306 D7
Portling Dumfries 237 D10
Port Lion Pembs 73 D7
Portloe Corn 3 B10
Port Logan Dumfries 236 E2
Portlooe Corn 6 E4
Portmahomack Highld 311 L3
Port Mead Swansea 56 B6
Portmeirion Gwyn 145 B11
Portmellon Corn 5 G10
Port Mholair W Isles 304 E7
Port Mor Highld 288 B6
Portmore Hants 20 B2
Port Mulgrave N Yorks 226 B5
Portnacroish Argyll 289 E11
Portnahaven Argyll 254 B2
Portnalong Highld 294 B5
Portnaluchaig Highld 295 G8
Portnancon Highld 308 C4
Port Nan Giùran
W Isles 304 E7
Port nan Long W Isles 296 D4
Portnellan Stirling 285 E8
Stirling 285 F8
Port Nis W Isles 304 B7
Portobello Edin 280 G6
T&W 243 F7
W Mid 133 D9
W Yorks 197 D10
Port of Menteith Stirling 285 G9
Porton Wilts 47 F7
Portpatrick Dumfries 236 D2
Port Quin Corn 10 E5
Portrack Stockton 225 B9
Port Ramsay Argyll 289 E10
Portreath Corn 4 F3
Portree Highld 298 E4
Port St Mary IoM 192 F3
Portscatho Corn 3 B9
Portsea Ptsmth 33 G10
Portsea Island Ptsmth 33 G11
Portskerra Highld 310 C2
Portskewett Mon 60 B4
Portslade Brighton 36 F3
Portslade-by-Sea
Brighton 36 G3
Portslade Village
Brighton 36 F3
Portsmouth Ptsmth 21 B9
W Yorks 196 B2
Port Solent Ptsmth 33 F10
Portsonachan Argyll 284 E4
Portsoy Aberds 302 C5
Port Sunlight Mers 182 E4
Port Sutton Bridge
Lincs 157 E9
Portswood Soton 32 E6
Port Talbot Neath 57 D9
Porttanachy Moray 302 C3
Port Tennant Swansea 57 C7
Portuairk Highld 288 C6
Portvasgo Highld 308 C5
Portway Dorset 18 D2
Glos 98 E5
Hereford 97 B9
Hereford 97 D9
Som 28 B6
Portway *continued*
Som 44 F3
W Mid 133 F9
Worcs 117 C11
Port Wemyss Argyll 254 B2
Port William Dumfries 236 E5
Portwood Gtr Man 184 C6
Portwrinkle Corn 7 E7
Posenhall Shrops 132 C3
Poslingford Suff 106 B5
Posso Borders 260 C6
Postbridge Devon 13 F9
Postcombe Oxon 84 F2
Post Green Dorset 18 C5
Postling Kent 54 F6
Postlip Glos 99 F10
Post Mawr = *Synod Inn*
Ceredig 111 G8
Postwick Norf 142 B5
Potarch Aberds 293 D8
Potash Suff 108 D2
Potbridge Hants 49 C8
Pot Common Sur 50 E2
Potholm Dumfries 249 F9
Potmaily Highld 300 F4
Potman's Heath Kent 38 B5
Potsgrove C Beds 103 F9
Potten End Herts 85 D8
Potten Street Kent 71 F9
Potter Brompton
N Yorks 217 D9
Pottergate Street Norf 142 E3
Potterhanworth Lincs 173 B9
Potterhanworth Booths
Lincs 173 B9
Potter Heigham Norf 161 F8
Potter Hill Leics 154 E4
S Yorks 186 B4
Potterne Wilts 46 B3
Potterne Wick Wilts 46 B4
Potternewton W Yorks 206 F2
Potters Bar Herts 86 E3
Potters Brook Lancs 202 C5
Potters Corner Kent 54 E3
Potter's Cross Staffs 132 G6
Potters Crouch Herts 85 D10
Potter's Forstal Kent 53 D11
Potter's Green E Sus 37 C8
W Mid 135 G7
Pottersheath Herts 86 B2
Potters Hill N Som 60 F4
Potters Marston Leics 135 D9
Potter Somersal Derbys 152 B2
Potterspury W Nhants 102 C5
Potter Street Essex 87 D7
Potterton Aberds 293 B11
W Yorks 206 F4
Pottery Field W Yorks 206 G2
Potthorpe Norf 159 E8
Pottington Devon 40 G5
Potto N Yorks 225 E9
Potton C Beds 104 B4
Pott Row Norf 158 E4
Pott Shrigley Ches E 184 F6
Pouchen End Herts 85 D8
Poughill Corn 24 F2
Devon 26 F5
Poulner Hants 31 F11
Poulshot Wilts 46 B3
Poulton Ches W 166 D5
Glos 81 E10
Mers 182 C4
Mers 182 E4
Poulton-le-Fylde Lancs 202 F2
Pound Som 28 D6
Pound Bank Worcs 98 B5
Worcs 116 C4
Poundbury Dorset 17 C9
Poundffald Swansea 56 C5
Poundfield E Sus 52 G4
Poundford E Sus 37 C9
Poundgate E Sus 37 B7
Poundgreen Wokingham 65 F7
Pound Green E Sus 37 C8
Hants 48 B5
IoW 20 D2
Suff 124 G4
Worcs 116 B5
Pound Hill W Sus 51 F9
Poundland S Ayrs 244 F5
Poundon Bucks 102 F2
Poundsbridge Kent 52 E4
Poundsgate Devon 13 G10
Poundstock Corn 11 B10
Pound Street Hants 64 G3
Pounsley E Sus 37 C8
Poverest London 68 F3
Povey Cross Sur 51 E9
Powburn Northumb 264 F3
Powderham Devon 14 E5
Powder Mills Kent 52 D5
Powers Hall End Essex 88 B4
Powerstock Dorset 16 B6
Powfoot Dumfries 238 D4
Pow Green Hereford 98 C4
Powhill Cumb 238 F6
Powick Worcs 116 G6
Powler's Piece Devon 24 D5
Powmill Perth 279 B10
Pownall Park Ches E 184 E4
Powntley Copse Hants 49 E8
Poxwell Dorset 17 E10
Poyle Slough 66 D4
Poynings W Sus 36 E3
Poyntington Dorset 29 D11
Poynton Ches E 184 E6
Telford 149 F11
Poynton Green Telford 149 F11
Poyntzfield Highld 301 C7
Poyston Pembs 73 B7
Poyston Cross Pembs 73 B7
Poystreet Green Suff 125 F9
Praa Sands Corn 2 D3
Pratling Street Kent 53 B8
Pratt's Bottom London 68 G3
Praze Corn 2 B3
Praze-an-Beeble Corn 2 B4
Predannack Wollas Corn 2 F5
Prees Shrops 149 C11
Preesall Lancs 202 D3
Preesall Park Lancs 202 D3
Prees Green Shrops 149 C11
Preesgweene Shrops 148 B5
Prees Heath Shrops 149 B11
Preeshenlle Shrops 148 C6
Prees Higher Heath
Shrops 149 B11
Prees Lower Heath
Shrops 149 C11
Prees Wood Shrops 149 C11
Prenbrigog Flint 166 C3
Prendergast Pembs 73 B7
Pembs 90 G6
Prenderguest Borders 273 D8
Prendwick Northumb 264 G2
Pren-gwyn Ceredig 93 C8
Prenteg Gwyn 163 G9
Prenton Mers 182 D4
Prescot Mers 183 C7
Prescott Devon 27 E9
Glos 99 F9
Prescott *continued*
Shrops 132 G3
Shrops 149 E8
Presdales Herts 86 C5
Preshome Moray 302 C4
Press Derbys 170 B5
Pressen Northumb 263 B8
Prestatyn Denb 181 E9
Prestbury Ches E 184 F6
Glos 99 G9
Presteigne Powys 114 E6
Presthope Shrops 131 D11
Prestleigh Som 44 E6
Prestolee Gtr Man 195 F9
Preston Borders 272 D5
Brighton 36 F4
Devon 14 G3
Dorset 17 E10
E Loth 281 F11
E Loth 281 G7
E Yorks 209 G9
Glos 81 E8
Glos 98 E3
Herts 104 G3
Kent 70 G4
Kent 71 G8
Lancs 194 B4
London 67 B7
Northumb 264 D5
Rutland 137 C7
Shrops 149 G10
Torbay 9 C7
T&W 243 D8
Wilts 62 D4
Wilts 63 E9
Preston Bagot Warks 118 D3
Preston Bissett Bucks 102 F3
Preston Bowyer Som 27 B10
Preston Brockhurst
Shrops 149 E10
Preston Brook Halton 183 E9
Preston Candover Hants 48 E6
Preston Capes
W Nhants 119 G11
Preston Crowmarsh
Oxon 83 G10
Preston Deanery
W Nhants 120 F5
Prestonfield Edin 280 G5
Preston Fields Warks 118 D3
Preston Grange T&W 243 C8
Preston Green Warks 118 D3
Preston Gubbals Shrops 149 F9
Preston-le-Skerne
Durham 234 G2
Preston Marsh Hereford 97 B11
Prestonmill Dumfries 237 D11
Preston Montford
Shrops 149 G8
Preston on Stour Warks 118 G4
Preston-on-Tees
Stockton 225 B8
Preston on the Hill
Halton 183 E9
Preston on Wye Hereford 97 C7
Prestonpans E Loth 281 G7
Preston Pastures Worcs 100 B3
Preston Plucknett Som 29 D8
Preston St Mary Suff 125 G8
Preston-under-Scar
N Yorks 223 G11
Preston upon the Weald
Moors Telford 150 F3
Preston Wynne Hereford 97 B11
Prestwich Gtr Man 195 G10
Prestwick Northumb 242 C5
S Ayrs 257 D9
Prestwold Leics 153 E11
Prestwood Bucks 84 E5
Staffs 133 F7
Staffs 169 G10
Prey Heath Sur 50 B3
Price Town Bridgend 76 G6
Prickwillow Cambs 139 G11
Priddy Som 44 C4
Pride Park Derbys 153 B7
Priestacott Devon 24 F6
Priestcliffe Derbys 185 G10
Priestcliffe Ditch
Derbys 185 G10
Priest Down Bath 60 G6
Priestfield W Mid 133 D8
Worcs 98 C6
Priesthaugh Borders 249 C11
Priesthill Glasgow 267 C10
Priesthorpe W Yorks 205 F10
Priest Hutton Lancs 211 E10
Priestley Green
W Yorks 196 B6
Prieston Borders 262 D2
Priestside Dumfries 238 D4
Priestthorpe W Yorks 205 F8
Priest Weston Shrops 130 D5
Priestwood Brack 65 F11
Kent 69 G7
Priestwood Green Kent 69 G7
Primethorpe Leics 135 E10
Primrose T&W 243 E8
Primrose Corner Norf 160 G6
Primrose Green Norf 159 F11
Primrosehill Herts 85 E9
Primrose Hill Bath 61 F8
Lancs 193 F11
London 67 C9
W Mid 133 F8
Primrose Valley
N Yorks 218 D2
Primsland Worcs 117 E8
Prince Hill Ches E 168 G2
Prince Royd W Yorks 196 D6
Princes End W Mid 133 E9
Princes Gate Pembs 73 C10
Prince's Marsh Hants 34 B3
Princes Park Mers 182 D5
Princes Risborough
Bucks 84 E4
Princethorpe Warks 119 C8
Princetown Caerph 77 C10
Devon 13 G7
Prinsted W Sus 22 B3
Printstile Kent 52 E5
Prion Denb 165 C9
Prior Muir Fife 287 F9
Prior Park Northumb 273 E9
Prior Rigg Cumb 239 D11
Priors Frome Hereford 97 D11
Priors Halton Shrops 115 B9
Priors Hardwick Warks 119 F9
Priorslee Telford 150 G4
Priors Marston Warks 119 F9
Prior's Norton Glos 99 G7
Priors Park Glos 99 E7
Priorswood Som 28 B2
Priory Pembs 72 D6
Priory Green Suff 107 C8
Priory Heath Suff 108 C3
Priory Wood Hereford 96 B5
Prisk V Glam 58 D4
Pristacott Devon 25 B8
Priston Bath 61 G7
Pristow Green Norf 142 F2
Prittlewell Southend 69 B11
Privett Hants 21 B7
Hants 33 B11
Prixford Devon 40 F4
Probus Corn 5 F7
Proncy Highld 309 K7
Prospect Cumb 229 C8
Prospect Village Staffs 151 G10
Prospidnick Corn 2 C4
Provanmill Glasgow 268 B2
Prowse Devon 26 F4
Prudhoe Northumb 242 E3
Prussia Cove Corn 2 D3
Ptarmigan Lodge
Stirling 285 G7
Pubil Perth 285 C8
Publow Bath 60 G6
Puckeridge Herts 105 G7
Puckington Som 28 D5
Pucklechurch S Glos 61 D7
Pucknall Hants 32 B5
Puckrup Glos 99 D7
Puckshole Glos 80 D4
Puddaven Devon 8 C5
Puddinglake Ches W 168 B2
Pudding Pie Nook Lancs 202 F6
Puddington Ches W 182 G4
Devon 26 E4
Puddle Corn 5 D11
Puddlebridge Som 28 E4
Puddledock Kent 52 C3
Kent 68 E4
Norf 141 E11
Puddletown Dorset 17 C11
Pudleigh Som 28 E4
Pudleston Hereford 115 F11
Pudsey W Yorks 196 B2
W Yorks 205 G10
Pulborough W Sus 35 D8
Pulcree Dumfries 237 D7
Pule Hill W Yorks 196 B5
Puleston Telford 150 E4
Pulford Ches W 166 D5
Pulham Dorset 30 F2
Pulham Market Norf 142 F3
Pulham St Mary Norf 142 F4
Pullens Green S Glos 79 G10
Pulley Shrops 131 B9
Pullington Kent 53 G10
Pulloxhill C Beds 103 E11
Pulverbatch Shrops 131 C8
Pumpherston W Loth 269 B11
Pumsaint Carms 94 C3
Puncheston = *Cas-Mael*
Pembs 91 F10
Puncknowle Dorset 16 D6
Punnett's Town E Sus 37 C10
Purbrook Hants 33 F11
Purewell BCP 19 C9
Purfleet Thurrock 68 D5
Puriton Som 43 E10
Purleigh Essex 88 E4
Purley London 67 G10
Purley on Thames
W Berks 65 D7
Purlogue Shrops 114 B5
Purlpit Wilts 61 F11
Purls Bridge Cambs 139 F9
Purn N Som 43 B10
Purse Caundle Dorset 29 D11
Purslow Shrops 131 G7
Purston Jaglin W Yorks 198 D2
Purtington Som 28 F5
Purton Glos 79 E11
W Berks 64 D3
Wilts 62 B5
Purton Common Wilts 62 B5
Purton Stoke Wilts 81 G9
Purwell Herts 104 F4
Pury End W Nhants 102 B4
Pusey Oxon 82 F5
Putley Hereford 98 D2
Putley Common Hereford 98 D2
Putley Green Hereford 98 D3
Putloe Glos 80 D3
Putney London 67 D8
Putney Heath London 67 E8
Putney Vale London 67 E8
Putnoe Bedford 121 G11
Putsborough Devon 40 E3
Putson Hereford 97 D10
Puttenham Herts 84 C5
Sur 50 D2
Puttock End Essex 106 C6
Puttock's End Essex 87 B9
Putton Dorset 17 E9
Puxey Dorset 30 E3
Puxley W Nhants 102 C5
Puxton N Som 60 G2
Pwll Carms 75 E7
Powys 130 C3
Pwll-clai Flint 181 G11
Pwllcrochan Pembs 72 E6
Pwll-glas Denb 165 E10
Pwllgloyw Powys 95 E10
Pwllheli Gwyn 145 B7
Pwll-Mawr Cardiff 59 D8
Pwll-melyn Flint 181 G11
Pwllmeyric Mon 79 G8
Pwll-trap Carms 74 B3
Pwll-y-glaw Neath 57 C9
Pwllypant Caerph 59 B7
Pye Bridge Derbys 170 E6
Pyecombe W Sus 36 E3
Pye Corner Devon 14 B4
Kent 53 D11
Newport 59 B9
S Glos 60 D6
Pye Green Staffs 151 G9
Pye Hill Notts 170 E6
Pyewipe NE Lincs 201 E9
Pyle IoW 20 F5
Swansea 56 D5
Pyle = *Y Pîl* Bridgend 57 E10
Pylehill Hants 33 D7
Pyle Hill Sur 50 B3
Pyleigh Som 42 G6
Pylle Som 44 F6
Pymore or Pymoor
Cambs 139 F9
Pype Hayes W Mid 134 E2
Pyrford Sur 50 B4
Pyrford Green Sur 50 B4
Pyrford Village Sur 50 B4
Pyrland Som 28 B2
Pyrton Oxon 83 F11
Pytchley N Nhants 121 C7
Pyworthy Devon 24 G4

Q

Quabbs Shrops 130 G4
Quabrook E Sus 52 G2
Quadring Lincs 156 C4
Quadring Eaudike Lincs 156 C4
Quags Corner W Sus 34 C5
Quainton Bucks 84 B2
Quaker's Yard M Tydf 77 F9
Quaking Houses
Durham 242 G5
Quality Corner Cumb 219 B9
Quarhouse Glos 80 E5
Quarley Hants 47 E9
Quarmby W Yorks 196 D6
Quarndon Derbys 170 G4
Quarndon Common
Derbys 170 G4
Quarrelton Renfs 267 C8
Quarrendon Bucks 84 B4
Quarr Hill IoW 21 C7
Quarriers Village
Invclyd 267 B7
Quarrington Lincs 173 G9
Quarrington Hill
Durham 234 D2
Quarrybank Ches W 167 B8
Quarry Bank W Mid 133 F8
Quarryford E Loth 271 B11
Quarryhead Aberds 303 C9
Quarry Heath Staffs 151 G8
Quarryhill Highld 309 L7
Quarry Hill Staffs 134 C4
Quarrywood Moray 301 C11
Quarter S Lanark 268 E4
Quartley Devon 27 B7
Quatford Shrops 132 E4
Quatquoy Orkney 314 E3
Quatt Shrops 132 F5
Quebec Durham 233 C9
W Sus 34 C3
Quedgeley Glos 80 C4
Queen Adelaide Cambs 139 G11
Queenborough Kent 70 E2
Queen Camel Som 29 C9
Queen Charlton Bath 60 F6
Queen Dart Devon 26 D4
Queenhill Worcs 99 D7
Queen Oak Dorset 45 G9
Queen's Bower IoW 21 E7
Queensbury London 67 B7
W Yorks 205 G8
Queen's Corner W Sus 34 B5
Queensferry Edin 280 F2
Flint 166 B4
Queen's Head Shrops 148 D6
Queenslie Glasgow 268 B3
Queen's Park Bedford 103 B10
Blackburn 195 B7
Ches W 166 B6
Essex 87 F11
W Nhants 120 E5
Queenstown Blackpool 202 F2
Queen Street Kent 53 D7
Wilts 62 B4
Queensville Staffs 151 E8
Queenzieburn N Lanark 278 F3
Quemerford Wilts 62 F4
Quendale Shetland 313 M5
Quendon Essex 105 E10
Queniborough Leics 154 G2
Quenington Glos 81 E10
Quernmore Lancs 202 B6
Queslett W Mid 133 E11
Quethiock Corn 6 C6
Quhamm Shetland 312 G6
Quholm Orkney 314 E2
Quick Gtr Man 196 G3
Quick Edge Gtr Man 196 G3
Quicks Green W Berks 64 D5
Quidenham Norf 141 F10
Quidhampton Hants 48 C4
Wilts 46 G6
Quilquox Aberds 303 F9
Quina Brook Shrops 149 C10
Quinbury End W Nhants 120 G2
Quindry Orkney 314 G4
Quinton W Mid 133 G9
W Nhants 120 G5
Quintrell Downs Corn 5 C7
Quixhill Staffs 169 G10
Quoditch Devon 12 B4
Quoig Perth 286 E2
Quoisley Ches E 167 F8
Quoit Corn 5 C8
Quorndon or Quorn
Leics 153 F11
Quothquan S Lanark 259 B11
Quoyloo Orkney 314 D2
Quoynee Highld 310 D6
Quoyness Orkney 314 F2
Quoys Shetland 312 B8
Shetland 313 G6

R

Raasay Ho Highld 295 B7
Rabbit's Cross Kent 53 D9
Rableyheath Herts 86 B2
Raby Cumb 238 G5
Mers 182 F4
Racecourse Suff 108 C3
Racedown Hants 47 E9
Rachan Mill Borders 260 C4
Rachub Gwyn 163 B10
Rack End Oxon 82 E6
Rackenford Devon 26 D5
Rackham W Sus 35 E9
Rackheath Norf 160 G5
Rackley Som 43 C11
Racks Dumfries 238 C2
Rackwick Orkney 314 B4
Orkney 314 G2
Radbourne Derbys 152 B5
Radcliffe Gtr Man 195 F9
Northumb 253 C7
Radcliffe on Trent Notts 154 B2
Radclive Bucks 102 E3
Radcot Oxon 82 F3
Raddery Highld 301 D7
Raddington Som 27 B8
Raddon Devon 26 G6
Radernie Fife 287 G8
Radfall Kent 70 G6
Radfield Kent 70 G2
Radford Bath 45 B7
Nottingham 171 G9
Oxon 101 G8
W Mid 134 G6
Worcs 117 F10
Radfordbridge Oxon 101 G8
Radford Semele Warks 118 E6
Radipole Dorset 17 E9
Radlet Som 43 F8
Radlett Herts 85 F11
Radley Oxon 83 F8
Radley Green Essex 87 D10
Radley Park Oxon 83 F8
Radlith Shrops 131 B8
Radmanthwaite Notts 171 C8
Radmoor Shrops 150 E2
Radmore Green Ches E 167 D9
Radmore Wood Staffs 151 D11
Radnage Bucks 84 F3
Radnor Corn 4 G4
Radnor Park W Dunb 277 G9
Radstock Bath 45 C7
Radstone W Nhants 101 C11
Radway Warks 101 B7
Radway Green Ches E 168 E3
Radwell Bedford 121 F10
Radwell *continued*
Herts 104 D4
Radwinter Essex 106 D2
Radwinter End Essex 106 D2
Radyr Cardiff 58 C6
Raehills Dumfries 248 E3
Raera Argyll 289 G10
Rafborough Hants 49 B11
Rafford Moray 301 D10
Raga Shetland 312 D6
Ragdale Leics 154 F3
Ragdon Shrops 131 E9
Raggalds W Yorks 205 G7
Ragged Appleshaw
Hants 47 D10
Raginnis Corn 1 D5
Raglan Mon 78 D6
Ragmere Norf 141 E11
Ragnal Wilts 63 E10
Ragnall Notts 188 G4
Rahane Argyll 276 D4
Rahoy Highld 289 D8
Raigbeg Highld 301 G8
Rails S Yorks 186 D3
Rainbow Hill Worcs 117 F7
Rainford Mers 194 G3
Rainford Junction Mers 194 G3
Rainham London 68 C4
Medway 69 F10
Rainhill Mers 183 C7
Rainhill Stoops Mers 183 C8
Rainow Ches E 185 F7
Rainowlow Ches E 185 F7
Rain Shore Gtr Man 195 D11
Rainsough Gtr Man 195 G10
Rainton Dumfries 237 D8
N Yorks 215 D7
Rainton Bridge T&W 234 B2
Rainton Gate Durham 234 B2
Rainworth Notts 171 D9
Raisbeck Cumb 222 D2
Raise Cumb 231 B10
Rait Perth 286 E6
Raithby Lincs 190 E4
Raithby by Spilsby Lincs 174 B5
Rake W Sus 34 B4
Rake Common Hants 34 B3
Rake End Staffs 151 F11
Rake Head Lancs 195 C10
Rakes Dale Staffs 169 G9
Rakeway Staffs 169 G8
Rakewood Gtr Man 196 E2
Raleigh Devon 40 G5
Ralia Lodge Highld 291 D9
Rallt Swansea 56 C4
Ram Carms 93 B11
Ram Alley Wilts 63 G8
Ramasaig Highld 297 G7
Rame Corn 2 C6
Corn 7 F8
Rameldry Mill Bank
Fife 287 G7
Ram Hill S Glos 61 D7
Ram Lane Kent 54 D3
Ramnageo Shetland 312 C8
Rampisham Dorset 29 G9
Rampside Cumb 210 F4
Rampton Cambs 123 D8
Notts 188 F3
Ramsbottom Gtr Man 195 D9
Ramsburn Moray 302 D5
Ramsbury Wilts 63 E9
Ramscraigs Highld 311 G5
Ramsdean Hants 34 C2
Ramsdell Hants 48 B5
Ramsden London 68 F3
Oxon 82 B5
Worcs 99 B8
Ramsden Bellhouse
Essex 88 G2
Ramsden Heath Essex 88 F2
Ramsden Wood
W Yorks 196 C2
Ramsey Cambs 138 F5
Essex 108 E4
IoM 192 C5
Ramseycleuch Borders 261 G7
Ramsey Forty Foot
Cambs 138 F6
Ramsey Heights Cambs 138 F5
Ramsey Island Essex 89 D7
Ramsey Mereside
Cambs 138 F5
Ramsey St Mary's
Cambs 138 F5
Ramsgate Kent 71 G11
Ramsgill N Yorks 214 E2
Ramshaw Durham 232 B5
Durham 233 F8
Ramsholt Suff 108 C6
Ramshorn Staffs 169 F9
Ramsley Devon 13 C8
Ramslye Kent 52 F5
Ramsnest Common Sur 50 G2
Ranais W Isles 304 F6
Ranby Lincs 190 F2
Notts 187 E11
Rand Lincs 189 F10
Randwick Glos 80 D4
Ranfurly Renfs 267 C7
Rangag Highld 310 E5
Rangemore Staffs 152 E3
Rangeworthy S Glos 61 B7
Rankinston E Ayrs 257 G11
Rank's Green Essex 88 B3
Ranmoor S Yorks 186 D4
Ranmore Common Sur 50 C6
Rannerdale Cumb 220 B3
Rannoch Lodge Perth 285 B9
Rannoch Station Perth 285 B8
Ranochan Highld 295 G10
Ranskill Notts 187 D11
Ranton Staffs 151 E7
Ranton Green Staffs 150 E6
Ranworth Norf 161 G7
Rapkyns W Sus 50 G6
Raploch Stirling 278 C5
Rapness Orkney 314 B5
Rapps Som 28 D4
Rascal Moor E Yorks 208 F2
Rascarrel Dumfries 237 E9
Rashielee Renfs 277 G9
Rashiereive Aberds 303 G9
Rashwood Worcs 117 D8
Raskelf N Yorks 215 E9
Rassal Highld 299 E8
Rassau Bl Gwent 77 C11
Rastrick W Yorks 196 C6
Ratagan Highld 295 D11
Ratby Leics 135 B10
Ratcliff London 67 C11
Ratcliffe Culey Leics 134 D6
Ratcliffe on Soar Leics 153 D9
Ratcliffe on the Wreake
Leics 154 G2
Ratford Wilts 62 E3
Ratfyn Wilts 47 E7
Rathen Aberds 303 C10
Rathillet Fife 287 E7
Rathmell N Yorks 204 B2
Ratho Edin 280 G2

Ratho Station Edin. 280 G2
Rathven Moray 302 C4
Ratlake Hants 32 C6
Ratley Warks 101 B7
Ratling Kent 55 C8
Ratlinghope Shrops 131 D8
Ratsloe Devon 14 B5
Rattar Highld 310 B6
Ratten Row Cumb 230 B3
Cumb 230 C2
Lancs 202 E4
Norf 157 G10
Rattery Devon 8 C4
Rattlesden Suff 125 F9
Rattray Perth 286 C5
Raughton Cumb 230 B3
Raughton Head Cumb 230 B3
Raunds N Nhants 121 C9
Ravelston Edin. 280 G4
Ravenfield S Yorks 187 B7
Ravenglass Cumb 219 F11
Ravenhead Mers. 183 C8
Ravenhills Green Worcs 116 G4
Raveningham Norf 143 D7
Ravenscar N Yorks 227 E9
Ravenscliffe Stoke 168 E4
W Yorks 205 F9
Ravenscraig Invclyd 276 F5
Ravensdale IoM 192 C4
Ravensden Bedford 121 G11
Ravenseat N Yorks 223 E7
Raven's Green Essex 108 G2
Ravenshall Staffs 168 F3
Ravenshead Notts 171 E9
Ravensmoor Ches E 167 E10
Ravensthorpe Pboro 138 C3
W Nhants 120 C3
W Yorks 197 C8
Ravenstone Leics 153 G8
M Keynes 120 G6
Ravenstonedale Cumb 222 E4
Ravenstown Cumb 211 D7
Ravenstruther S Lanark 269 F8
Ravenswood Village Settlement Wokingham 65 G10
Ravensworth N Yorks 224 D2
Raw N Yorks 227 D8
Rawcliffe E Yorks 199 C7
York 207 C7
Rawcliffe Bridge
E Yorks 199 C7
Rawdon W Yorks 205 F10
Rawdon Carrs W Yorks 205 F10
Rawfolds W Yorks 197 C7
Rawgreen Northumb 241 F10
Raw Green S Yorks 197 F9
Rawmarsh S Yorks 186 B6
Rawnsley Staffs 151 G10
Rawreth Essex 88 G3
Rawreth Shot Essex 88 G3
Rawridge Devon 28 F2
Rawson Green Derbys 170 F5
Rawtenstall Lancs 195 C10
Rawthorpe W Yorks 197 D7
Rawyards N Lanark 268 B5
Raxton Aberds 303 F8
Raydon Suff 107 D11
Raygill N Yorks 204 D4
Raylees Northumb 251 E10
Rayleigh Essex 88 G4
Rayne Essex 106 G4
Rayners Lane London 66 B6
Raynes Park London 67 F8
Reabrook Shrops 131 C7
Reach Cambs 123 D11
Read Lancs 203 G11
Reader's Corner Essex 88 E2
Reading Reading 65 E8
Readings Glos 79 B10
Reading Street Kent 54 G2
Kent 71 F11
Readymoney Corn 6 E2
Ready Token Glos 81 E10
Reagill Cumb 222 B2
Rearquhar Highld 309 K7
Rearsby Leics 154 G3
Reasby Lincs 189 F9
Rease Heath Ches E 167 E10
Reaster Highld 310 C6
Reaulay Highld 299 D7
Reawick Shetland 313 J5
Reawla Corn 2 B4
Reay Highld 310 C3
Rechullin Highld 299 D8
Reculver Kent 71 F8
Red Ball Devon 27 D9
Redberth Pembs 73 E9
Redbourn Herts 85 C10
Redbournbury Herts 85 C10
Redbourne N Lincs 189 B7
N Lincs 200 G3
Redbridge Dorset 17 D11
London 68 B2
Soton 32 E5
Red Bridge Lancs 211 D9
Redbrook Mon 79 C8
Wrex 167 G8
Red Bull Ches E 168 D4
Staffs 150 B4
Redburn Highld 300 C5
Highld 301 E9
Northumb 241 E7
Redcar Redcar 235 G8
Redcastle Angus 287 B10
Highld 300 E5
Redcliff Bay N Som 60 D2
Redcroft Dumfries 237 B9
Redcross Worcs 117 C7
Red Dial Cumb 229 B11
Reddicap Heath W Mid 134 D2
Redding Falk 279 F8
Reddingmuirhead Falk 279 F8
Reddish Gtr Man 184 C5
Warr 183 D11
Redditch Worcs 117 D10
Rede Suff 124 F6
Redenhall Norf 142 G5
Redenham Hants 47 D10
Redesdale Camp
Northumb 251 D8
Redesmouth Northumb 251 G9
Redford Aberds 293 F9
Angus 287 C9
Dorset 29 F10
Durham 233 E7
W Sus 34 B5
Redfordgreen Borders 261 F9
Redgorton Perth 286 E4
Redgrave Suff 125 B10
Redheugh Angus 292 G6
Redhill Aberds 293 C9
Aberds 302 F6
Herts 104 E6
Notts 171 F9
N Som 60 G4
Shrops 131 B9
Shrops 150 G4
Staffs 150 D6
Sur 51 C9
Telford 150 G4
Red Hill BCP 19 B7
Red Hill *continued*
Hants 34 E2
Hereford 97 D10
Kent 53 C7
Leics 135 D10
Pembs 72 B6
Warks 118 F2
Worcs 117 G7
W Yorks 198 B2
Redhills Cumb 230 F6
Devon 14 C4
Redhouse Argyll 275 G9
Red House Common
E Sus 36 C5
Redhouses Argyll 274 G4
Redisham Suff 143 G8
Red Lake Telford 150 G3
Redland Bristol 60 D5
Orkney 314 D3
Redland End Bucks 84 E4
Redlands Dorset 17 E9
Som 44 G3
Swindon 81 G11
Redlane Som 28 E2
Redlingfield Suff 126 C3
Red Lodge Suff 124 C3
Red Lumb Gtr Man 195 D10
Redlynch Som 45 G8
Wilts 32 C2
Redmain Cumb 229 E8
Redmarley D'Abitot Glos 98 E5
Redmarshall Stockton 234 G3
Redmile Leics 154 B5
Redmire N Yorks 223 G10
Redmonsford Devon 24 D4
Redmoor Corn 5 C11
Redmoss Aberds 303 F8
Rednal Shrops 149 D7
W Mid 117 B10
Redpath Borders 262 B3
Red Pits Norf 159 D11
Redpoint Highld 299 C7
Red Post Corn 24 F3
Red Rail Hereford 97 F10
Red Rice Hants 47 E10
Red Rock Gtr Man 194 F5
Red Roses Carms 74 C2
Red Row Northumb 253 D7
Redruth Corn 4 G3
Red Scar Lancs 203 G7
Redscarhead Borders 270 G4
Redstocks Wilts 62 G2
Red Street Staffs 168 E4
Redtye Corn 5 C10
Redvales Gtr Man 195 F10
Red Wharf Bay Anglesey 179 E8
Redwick Newport 60 C2
S Glos 60 B4
Redwith Shrops 148 E6
Redworth Darl 233 G10
Reed Herts 105 D7
Reed End Herts 104 D6
Reedham Lincs 174 D2
Norf 143 C8
Reedley Lancs 204 F2
Reedness E Yorks 199 C9
Reed Point Lincs 174 E2
Reeds Beck Lincs 174 B2
Reedsford Northumb 263 C9
Reeds Holme Lancs 195 C10
Reedy Devon 14 D2
Reen Manor Corn 4 E5
Reepham Lincs 189 G8
Norf 159 E11
Reeth N Yorks 223 F10
Reeves Green W Mid 118 B5
Refail Powys 130 C3
Regaby IoM 192 C5
Regil Bath 60 G4
Regoul Highld 301 D8
Reiff Highld 307 H4
Reigate Sur 51 C9
Reigate Heath Sur 51 C8
Reighton N Yorks 218 D2
Reighton Gap N Yorks 218 D2
Reinigeadal W Isles 305 H4
Reisque Aberds 293 B10
Reiss Highld 310 D7
Rejerrah Corn 4 D5
Releath Corn 2 C5
Relubbus Corn 2 C3
Relugas Moray 301 E9
Remenham Wokingham 65 C9
Remenham Hill
Wokingham 65 C9
Remony Perth 285 C11
Rempstone Notts 153 E11
Remusaig Highld 309 J7
Rendcomb Glos 81 D8
Rendham Suff 126 E6
Rendlesham Suff 126 G6
Renfrew Renfs 267 B10
Renhold Bedford 121 G11
Renishaw Derbys 186 F6
Renmure Angus 287 B10
Rennington Northumb 264 F6
Renshaw Wood Shrops 132 B6
Renton W Dunb 277 F7
Renwick Cumb 231 C7
Repps Norf 161 F8
Repton Derbys 152 D6
Reraig Highld 295 C10
Reraig Cot Highld 295 B10
Rerwick Shetland 313 M5
Rescassa Corn 5 G9
Rescobie Angus 287 B9
Rescorla Corn 5 D10
Resipole Highld 289 C9
Reskadinnick Corn 4 G2
Resolfen =*Resolven*
Neath 76 E4
Resolis Highld 300 C6
Resolven =*Resolfen*
Neath 76 E4
Restalrig Edin 280 G5
Reston Borders 273 C7
Cumb 221 F9
Restronguet Passage Corn 3 B8
Restrop Wilts 62 B5
Resugga Green Corn 5 D10
Reswallie Angus 287 B9
Retallack Corn 5 B8
Retew Corn 5 D8
Retford Notts 188 E2
Retire Corn 5 C10
Rettendon Essex 88 F3
Rettendon Place Essex 88 F3
Revesby Lincs 174 C3
Revesby Bridge Lincs 174 C4
Revidge Blackburn 195 B7
Rew Devon 9 G9
Devon 13 G11
Dorset 29 F11
Rewe Devon 14 B4
Rew Street IoW 20 C5
Rexon Devon 12 D4
Rexon Cross Devon 12 D4
Reybridge Wilts 62 F2
Reydon Suff 127 B9
Reydon Smear Suff 127 B9
Reymerston Norf 141 B10
Reynalton Pembs 73 D9
Reynoldston Swansea 56 C3
Rezare Corn 12 F3
Rhadyr Mon 78 E5
Rhaeadr Gwy =*Rhayader*
Powys 113 D9
Rhandir Conwy 180 G4
Rhandirmwyn Carms 94 C5
Rhayader =*Rhaeadr Gwy*
Powys 113 D9
Rhedyn Gwyn 144 C5
Rhegreanoch Highld 307 H5
Rhemore Highld 289 D7
Rhencullen IoM 192 C4
Rhenetra Highld 298 D4
Rhes-y-cae Flint 181 G11
Rhewl Denb 165 C10
Denb 165 F11
Shrops 148 C6
Wrex 149 B7
Rhewl-fawr Flint 181 E10
Rhewl-Mostyn Flint 181 E11
Rhian Highld 309 H5
Rhicarn Highld 307 G5
Rhiconich Highld 306 D7
Rhicullen Highld 300 B6
Rhidorroch Ho Highld 307 K6
Rhiews Shrops 150 B2
Rhifail Highld 308 E7
Rhigolter Highld 308 D3
Rhigos Rhondda 76 D6
Rhilochan Highld 309 J7
Rhippinllwyd Ceredig 92 C5
Ceredig 110 G6
Rhiroy Highld 307 L6
Rhitongue Highld 308 D6
Rhivichie Highld 306 D7
Rhiw Gwyn 144 D4
Rhiwabon =*Ruabon*
Wrex 166 G4
Rhiwbebyll Denb 165 B10
Rhiwbina Cardiff 59 C7
Rhiwbryfdir Gwyn 163 F11
Rhiwceiliog Bridgend 58 C3
Rhiwderin Newport 59 B9
Rhiwen Gwyn 163 C9
Rhiwfawr Neath 76 C2
Rhiwinder Rhondda 58 B4
Rhiwlas Gwyn 147 B8
Gwyn 163 B9
Powys 148 C3
Rhode Som 43 G9
Rhode Common Kent 54 B5
Rhodes Gtr Man 195 F11
Rhodesia Notts 187 F9
Rhodes Minnis Kent 55 E7
Rhodiad Pembs 90 F5
Rhonadale Argyll 255 D8
Rhondda Rhondda 77 F7
Rhonehouse or Kelton Hill
Dumfries 237 D9
Rhoose V Glam 58 F5
Rhos Carms 93 D7
Rhôs Denb 165 C10
Neath 76 E2
Rhos Powys 148 F5
Rhosaman Carms 76 C2
Rhosbeirio Anglesey 178 C5
Rhoscefnhir Anglesey 179 F8
Rhoscolyn Anglesey 178 F3
Rhôs Common Powys 148 F5
Rhoscrowther Pembs 72 E6
Rhosddu Wrex 166 E4
Rhos-ddû Gwyn 144 B5
Rhosdylluan Gwyn 147 D7
Rhosesmor Flint 166 B2
Rhosfach Pembs 92 F2
Rhos-fawr Gwyn 145 B7
Rhosgadfan Gwyn 163 D8
Rhosgoch Anglesey 178 D6
Powys 96 B3
Rhos-goch Powys 96 B3
Rhosgyll Gwyn 163 G7
Rhos Haminiog Ceredig 111 E10
Rhos-hill Pembs 92 C3
Rhoshirwaun Gwyn 144 D3
Rhos Isaf Gwyn 163 D7
Rhoslan Gwyn 163 G7
Rhoslefain Gwyn 110 B2
Rhosllanerchrugog
Wrex 166 F3
Rhôs Lligwy Anglesey 179 D7
Rhosmaen Carms 94 G2
Rhosmeirch Anglesey 179 F7
Rhosneigr Anglesey 178 G4
Rhosnesni Wrex 166 E5
Rhôs-on-Sea Conwy 180 E4
Rhosrobin Wrex 166 E4
Rhossili Swansea 56 D2
Rhosson Pembs 90 F4
Rhostrehwfa Anglesey 178 G6
Rhostryfan Gwyn 163 D7
Rhostyllen Wrex 166 F4
Rhoswiel Shrops 148 B5
Rhosybol Anglesey 178 D6
Rhos-y-brithdir Powys 148 E2
Rhosycaerau Pembs 91 D8
Rhosygadair Newydd
Ceredig 92 B4
Rhosygadfa Shrops 148 C6
Rhos-y-garth Ceredig 112 C2
Rhosygilwen Pembs 92 C4
Rhos-y-gwaliau Gwyn 147 C8
Rhos-y-llan Gwyn 144 B4
Rhos-y-Madoc Wrex 166 G4
Rhosymedre Wrex 166 G3
Rhos-y-meirch Powys 114 D5
Rhosyn-coch Carms 92 G5
Rhu Argyll 275 G9
Argyll 276 E5
Rhuallt Denb 181 F9
Rhubodach Argyll 275 F11
Rhuddall Heath Ches W 167 C9
Rhuddlan Ceredig 93 C9
Denb 181 F8
Rhue Highld 307 K5
Rhulen Powys 96 B2
Rhunahaorine Argyll 255 C8
Rhyd Ceredig 92 C5
Gwyn 163 G10
Powys 129 C9
Rhydaman =*Ammanford*
Carms 75 C10
Rhydargaeau Carms 93 F8
Rhydcymerau Carms 93 D11
Rhydd Worcs 98 B6
Rhyd-Ddu Gwyn 163 E9
Rhydd Green Worcs 98 B6
Rhydding Neath 57 B8
Rhydfudr Ceredig 111 D11
Rhydgaled Conwy 165 C7
Rhydgaled =*Chancery*
Ceredig 111 B11
Rhydlewis Ceredig 92 B6
Rhydlios Gwyn 144 C3
Rhydlydan Conwy 164 E5
Powys 129 E11
Rhydmoelddu Powys 113 B11
Rhydness Powys 96 C2
Rhydowen Carms 92 F3
Ceredig 93 B8
Rhyd-Rosser Ceredig 111 D11
Rhydspence Hereford 96 B4
Rhydtalog Flint 166 D2
Rhyd-uchaf Gwyn 147 B8
Rhydwen Gwyn 146 F4
Rhydwyn Anglesey 178 D4
Rhyd-y-Brown Pembs 91 G11
Rhyd-y-clafdy Gwyn 144 B6
Rhydycroesau Powys 148 C4
Rhyd-y-cwm Shrops 130 G3
Rhydyfelin Carms 92 D5
Ceredig 111 B11
Powys 129 E11
Rhondda 58 B5
Rhyd-y-foel Conwy 180 F6
Rhyd-y-fro Neath 76 D2
Rhydygele Pembs 91 G7
Rhyd-y-gwin Swansea 75 E11
Rhyd-y-gwystl Gwyn 145 B8
Rhydymain Gwyn 146 E6
Rhyd-y-meirch Mon 78 D4
Rhyd-y-meudwy Denb 165 E10
Rhydymwyn Flint 166 B2
Rhyd-y-pandy Swansea 75 E11
Rhyd-yr-onen Gwyn 128 C2
Rhyd-y-sarn Gwyn 163 G11
Rhydywrach Carms 73 B11
Rhyl Denb 181 E8
Rhymney Caerph 77 D10
Rhyn Wrex 148 B6
Rhynd Fife 287 E8
Perth 286 E5
Rhynie Aberds 302 G4
Highld 301 B8
Ribbesford Worcs 116 C5
Ribblehead N Yorks 212 D5
Ribble Head N Yorks 212 D5
Ribbleton Lancs 203 G7
Ribby Lancs 202 G4
Ribchester Lancs 203 F8
Riber Derbys 170 D4
Ribigill Highld 308 D5
Riby Lincs 201 F7
Riby Cross Roads Lincs 201 F7
Riccall N Yorks 207 F8
Riccarton E Ayrs 257 B10
Richards Castle
Hereford 115 D9
Richborough Port Kent 71 G10
Richings Park Bucks 66 D4
Richmond London 67 E7
N Yorks 224 E3
S Yorks 186 D6
Richmond Hill W Yorks 206 G2
Richmond's Green
Essex 106 F2
Rich's Holford Som 42 G6
Rickard's Down Devon 24 B6
Rickarton Aberds 293 E10
Rickerby Cumb 239 F10
Rickerscote Staffs 151 E8
Rickford N Som 44 B3
Rickinghall Suff 125 B10
Rickleton T&W 243 G7
Rickling Essex 105 E9
Rickling Green Essex 105 F10
Rickmansworth Herts 85 G9
Rickney E Sus 23 D10
Riddell Borders 262 E2
Riddings Derbys 170 E6
Riddlecombe Devon 25 E10
Riddlesden W Yorks 205 E7
Riddrie Glasgow 268 B2
Ridgacre W Mid 133 G10
Ridge Bath 44 B5
Dorset 18 D4
Hants 32 D4
Herts 86 E2
Lancs 211 G9
Som 28 F3
Wilts 46 G3
Ridgebourne Powys 113 E11
Ridge Common Hants 34 C2
Ridge Green Sur 51 D10
Ridgehill N Som 60 G4
Ridge Hill Gtr Man 185 B7
Ridge Lane Warks 134 E5
Ridgemarsh Herts 85 G8
Ridge Row Kent 55 E8
Ridgeway Bristol 60 D6
Derbys 170 E5
Derbys 186 E6
Kent 54 E5
Newport 59 B9
Pembs 73 D10
Som 45 D8
Staffs 168 E5
Ridgeway Cross Hereford 98 B4
Ridgeway Moor Derbys 186 E6
Ridgewell Essex 106 C4
Ridgewood E Sus 23 B7
Ridgmont C Beds 103 D9
Ridgway Shrops 131 F7
Sur 50 B4
Riding Gate Som 30 B2
Riding Mill Northumb 242 E2
Ridley Kent 68 G6
Northumb 241 E7
Ridley Stokoe Northumb 250 F6
Ridleywood Wrex 166 E6
Ridlington Norf 160 C6
Rutland 136 C6
Ridlington Street Norf 160 C6
Ridsdale Northumb 251 G10
Riechip Perth 286 C4
Riemore Perth 286 C4
Rienachait Highld 306 F5
Rievaulx N Yorks 215 B11
Riff Orkney 314 E4
Riffin Aberds 303 E7
Rifle Green Torf 78 D3
Rift House Hrtlpl 234 E5
Rigg Dumfries 239 D7
Riggend N Lanark 278 G5
Rigsby Lincs 190 F6
Rigside S Lanark 259 B9
Riley Green Lancs 194 B6
Rileyhill Staffs 152 F2
Rilla Mill Corn 11 G11
Rillaton Corn 11 G11
Rillington N Yorks 217 E7
Rimac Lincs 191 C7
Rimington Lancs 204 D2
Rimpton Som 29 C10
Rimswell E Yorks 201 B10
Rimswell Valley
E Yorks 201 B10
Rinaston Pembs 91 F9
Rindleford Shrops 132 D4
Ringasta Shetland 313 M5
Ringford Dumfries 237 D8
Ringing Hill Leics 153 F9
Ringinglow S Yorks 186 E3
Ringland Newport 59 B11
Norf 160 G2
Ringles Cross E Sus 37 C7
Ringlestone Kent 53 B9
Kent 53 B11
Ringley Gtr Man 195 F9
Ringmer E Sus 36 E6
Ringmore Devon 8 F3
Ring o' Bells Lancs 194 E3
Ringorm Moray 302 E2
Ring's End Cambs 139 C7
Ringsfield Suff 143 F8
Ringsfield Corner Suff 143 F8
Ringshall Herts 85 C7
Suff 125 G10
Ringshall Stocks Suff 125 G10
Ringstead N Nhants 121 B9
Norf 176 E2
Ringtail Green Essex 87 B11
Ringwood Hants 31 F11
Ringwould Kent 55 D11
Rinmore Aberds 292 B6
Rinnigill Orkney 314 G3
Rinsey Corn 2 D3
Rinsey Croft Corn 2 D4
Riof W Isles 304 E3
Ripe E Sus 23 C8
Ripley Derbys 170 E5
Hants 19 B9
N Yorks 214 G5
Sur 50 B5
Riplingham E Yorks 208 G5
Ripon N Yorks 214 E6
Ripper's Cross Kent 54 E3
Rippingale Lincs 155 D11
Ripple Kent 55 D10
Worcs 99 D7
Ripponden W Yorks 196 D4
Rireavach Highld 307 K5
Risabus Argyll 254 C4
Risbury Hereford 115 G10
Risby E Yorks 208 G6
Lincs 189 C10
Suff 124 D5
Risca Caerph 78 G2
Rise E Yorks 209 E9
Rise Carr Darl 224 B5
Riseden E Sus 52 G6
Kent 53 F8
Rise End Derbys 170 D3
Risegate Lincs 156 D4
Riseholme Lincs 189 F7
Risehow Cumb 228 E6
Riseley Bedford 121 E10
Wokingham 65 G8
Rise Park London 87 G8
Nottingham 171 F9
Rishangles Suff 126 D3
Rishton Lancs 203 G10
Rishworth W Yorks 196 D4
Rising Bridge Lancs 195 B9
Risingbrook Staffs 151 E8
Risinghurst Oxon 83 D9
Rising Sun Corn 12 G3
Risley Derbys 153 B9
Warr 183 C10
Risplith N Yorks 214 F4
Rispond Highld 308 C4
Rivar Wilts 63 G10
Rivenhall Essex 88 B4
Rivenhall End Essex 88 B4
River Kent 55 E9
W Sus 34 C6
River Bank Cambs 123 D10
Riverhead Kent 52 B4
Rivers' Corner Dorset 30 E3
Riverside Cardiff 59 D7
Plym 7 D8
Stirling 278 C6
Worcs 117 D10
Riverside Docklands
Lancs 194 B4
Riverton Devon 40 G6
Riverview Park Kent 69 E7
Rivington Lancs 194 E6
Rixon Dorset 30 E3
Rixton Warr 183 C11
Roach Bridge Lancs 194 B5
Roaches Gtr Man 196 G3
Roachill Devon 26 C4
Roade W Nhants 120 G5
Road Green Norf 142 E5
Roadhead Cumb 240 C2
Roadmeetings S Lanark 269 F7
Roadside Highld 310 C5
Roadside of Catterline
Aberds 293 F10
Roadside of Kinneff
Aberds 293 F10
Roadwater Som 42 F4
Road Weedon W Nhants 120 F2
Roag Highld 298 E2
Roa Island Cumb 210 G4
Roast Green Essex 105 E9
Roath Cardiff 59 D7
Roath Park Cardiff 59 D7
Roberton Borders 261 G10
S Lanark 259 D10
Robertsbridge E Sus 38 C2
Robertstown Moray 302 E2
Rhondda 77 E8
Roberttown W Yorks 197 C7
Robeston Back Pembs 73 B9
Robeston Cross Pembs 72 D5
Robeston Wathen Pembs 73 B9
Robeston West Pembs 72 D5
Robhurst Kent 54 G2
Robin Hill Staffs 168 D6
Robin Hood Derbys 186 G3
Lancs 194 E4
W Yorks 197 B10
Robinhood End Essex 106 D4
Robin Hood's Bay
N Yorks 227 D9
Robins W Sus 34 B4
Robinson's End Warks 134 E6
Roborough Devon 7 C10
Devon 25 D9
Rob Roy's House Argyll 284 F5
Robroyston Glasgow 268 B2
Roby Mers 182 C6
Roby Mill Lancs 194 F4
Rocester Staffs 152 B2
Roch Pembs 91 G7
Rochdale Gtr Man 195 E11
Roche Corn 5 C9
Roche Grange Staffs 169 C7
Rochester Medway 69 F8
Northumb 251 D8
Rochford Essex 88 G5
Worcs 116 D2
Roch Gate Pembs 91 G7
Rock Caerph 77 F11
Corn 10 F4
Devon 28 G3
Neath 57 C9
Northumb 264 E6
Som 28 C4
Worcs 116 C4
W Sus 35 E10
Rockbeare Devon 14 C6
Rockbourne Hants 31 D10
Rockcliffe Cumb 239 E9
Dumfries 237 D10
Flint 182 G3
Lancs 195 C11
Rockcliffe Cross Cumb 239 E8
Rock End Staffs 168 D5
Rock Ferry Mers 182 D4
Rockfield Highld 311 L3
Mon 79 C7
Rockford Devon 41 D9
Hants 31 F11
Rockgreen Shrops 115 B10
Rockhampton S Glos 79 G11
Rockhead Corn 11 E7
Rockhill Shrops 114 B5
Rockingham N Nhants 137 E7
Rockland All Saints
Norf 141 D9
Rockland St Mary Norf 142 C6
Rockland St Peter Norf 141 D9
Rockley Notts 188 G2
Wilts 63 E7
Rockley Ford Som 45 C8
Rockness Glos 80 F4
Rockrobin E Sus 52 G6
Rocksavage Halton 183 E8
Rocks Park E Sus 37 C7
Rockstowes Glos 80 F3
Rockville Argyll 276 C4
Rockwell End Bucks 65 B9
Rockwell Green Som 27 C10
Rocky Hill Scilly 1 G4
Rodbaston Staffs 151 G8
Rodborough Glos 80 E4
Rodbourne Swindon 62 C6
Wilts 62 C2
Rodbourne Bottom Wilts 62 C2
Rodbourne Cheney
Swindon 62 B6
Rodbridge Corner
Essex 107 C7
Rodd Hereford 114 E6
Roddam Northumb 264 E2
Rodden Dorset 17 E8
Rodd Hurst Hereford 114 E6
Roddymoor Durham 233 D9
Rode Som 45 C10
Rodeheath Ches E 168 B5
Rode Heath Ches E 168 D3
Rode Hill Som 45 C10
Roden Telford 149 F11
Rodford S Glos 61 C7
Rodgrove Som 30 C2
Rodhuish Som 42 F4
Rodington Telford 149 G11
Rodington Heath
Telford 149 G11
Rodley Glos 80 C2
W Yorks 205 F10
Rodmarton Glos 80 F6
Rodmell E Sus 36 F6
Rodmer Clough
W Yorks 196 B3
Rodmersham Kent 70 G2
Rodmersham Green Kent 70 G2
Rodney Stoke Som 44 C3
Rodsley Derbys 170 G2
Rodway Som 43 F9
Telford 150 F3
Rodwell Dorset 17 F9
Roebuck Low Gtr Man 196 F3
Roecliffe N Yorks 215 F7
Roe Cross Gtr Man 185 B7
Roedean Brighton 36 G4
Roe End Herts 85 B8
Roe Green Gtr Man 195 G9
Herts 86 D2
Herts 104 E6
Roehampton London 67 E8
Roe Lee Blackburn 203 G9
Roesound Shetland 312 G5
Roestock Herts 86 D2
Roffey W Sus 51 G7
Rogart Highld 309 J7
Rogart Station Highld 309 J7
Rogate W Sus 34 C4
Roger Ground Cumb 221 F7
Rogerstone Newport 59 B9
Rogerton S Lanark 268 D2
Roghadal W Isles 296 C6
Rogiet Mon 60 B3
Rogue's Alley Cambs 139 B7
Roke Oxon 83 G10
Rokemarsh Oxon 83 G10
Roker T&W 243 F10
Rollesby Norf 161 F8
Rolleston Leics 136 C4
Notts 172 E2
Rollestone S Yorks 186 E5
Wilts 46 E5
Rollestone Camp Wilts 46 E5
Rolleston-on-Dove
Staffs 152 D4
Rolls Mill Dorset 30 E3
Rolston E Yorks 209 D10
Rolstone N Som 59 G11
Rolvenden Kent 53 G10
Rolvenden Layne Kent 53 G11
Romaldkirk Durham 232 G5
Romanby N Yorks 225 G7
Roman Hill Suff 143 E10
Romannobridge Borders 270 F3
Romansleigh Devon 26 C2
Rome Angus 293 G7
Romesdal Highld 298 D4
Romford Dorset 31 F9
Kent 52 E6
London 68 B4
Romiley Gtr Man 184 C6
Romney Street Kent 68 G4
Rompa Shetland 313 L6
Romsey Hants 32 C5
Romsey Town Cambs 123 F9
Romsley Shrops 132 G5
Worcs 117 B9
Romsley Hill Worcs 117 B9
Ronachan Ho Argyll 255 B8
Ronague IoM 192 E3
Rondlay Telford 132 B4
Ronkswood Worcs 117 G7
Rood End W Mid 133 F10
Rookby Cumb 222 C6
Rook End Essex 105 E11
Rookhope Durham 232 C4
Rooking Cumb 221 B8
Rookley IoW 20 E6
Rookley Green IoW 20 E6
Rooks Bridge Som 43 C11
Rooksey Green Suff 125 G8
Rooks Hill Kent 52 C5
Rooksmoor Glos 80 E4
Rook's Nest Som 42 G5
Rook Street Wilts 45 G10
Rookwith N Yorks 214 B4
Rookwood W Sus 21 B11
Roos E Yorks 209 G11
Roose Cumb 210 F4
Roosebeck Cumb 210 F5
Roosecote Cumb 210 F4
Roost End Essex 106 C4
Rootham's Green
Bedford 122 F2
Rooting Street Kent 54 D3
Rootpark S Lanark 269 E9
Ropley Hants 48 G6
Ropley Dean Hants 48 G6
Ropley Soke Hants 49 G7
Ropsley Lincs 155 C9
Rora Aberds 303 D10
Rorandle Aberds 293 B8
Rorrington Shrops 130 C5
Rosarie Moray 302 E3
Roscroggan Corn 4 G3
Rose Corn 4 E5
Roseacre Kent 53 B9
Lancs 202 F4
Rose-an-Grouse Corn 2 B2
Rose Ash Devon 26 C3
Rosebank E Dunb 278 G3
S Lanark 268 F6
Rosebery Midloth 270 D6
Rosebrae Moray 301 C11
Rosebrough Northumb 264 D4
Rosebush Pembs 91 F11
Rosecare Corn 11 B9
Rosedale Herts 86 E4
Rosedale Abbey
N Yorks 226 F4
Roseden Northumb 264 E2
Rosedinnick Corn 5 B8
Rosedown Devon 24 C3
Rosefield Highld 301 D8
Rose Green Essex 107 F8
Suff 107 C9
Suff 107 D8
W Sus 22 D6
Rose Grove Lancs 204 G2
Rosehall Highld 309 J4
N Lanark 268 C4
Rosehaugh Mains
Highld 300 D6
Rosehearty Aberds 303 C9
Rosehill Blackburn 195 C8
Corn 4 E5
Corn 5 C10
Gtr Man 184 D3
London 67 F9
Pembs 72 B5
Shrops 150 C3
T&W 243 D8
Rose Hill Bucks 66 C2
Derbys 153 B7
E Sus 23 B7
Gtr Man 195 F8
Lancs 204 G2
Oxon 83 E8
Suff 108 C3
Sur 51 D7
Roseisle Moray 301 C11
Roseland Corn 6 C5
Roselands E Sus 23 E10
Rosemarket Pembs 73 D7
Rosemarkie Highld 301 D7
Rosemary Lane Devon 27 E11
Rosemelling Corn 5 D10
Rosemergy Corn 1 B4
Rosemount Perth 286 C5
Rosenannon Corn 5 B9
Rosenithon Corn 3 E8
Roser's Cross E Sus 37 C9
Rose Valley Pembs 73 E8
Rosevean Corn 5 D10
Rosevear Corn 2 E5
Roseville W Mid 133 E8
Rosevine Corn 3 B9
Rosewarne Corn 2 B4
Corn 4 G2
Rosewell Midloth 270 C5
Roseworth Stockton 234 G4
Roseworthy Corn 2 B4
Corn 4 F5
Roseworthy Barton Corn 2 B4
Rosgill Cumb 221 B10
Rosherville Kent 68 E6
Roshven Highld 289 B9
Roskear Croft Corn 4 G3
Roskhill Highld 298 E2
Roskill House Highld 300 D6
Roskorwell Corn 3 E7
Rosley Cumb 230 B2
Roslin Midloth 270 C5
Rosliston Derbys 152 F4
Rosneath Argyll 276 E5
Ross Borders 273 C9
Dumfries 237 E8
Northumb 264 B4
Perth 285 E11
Rossett Wrex 166 D5
Rossett Green N Yorks 206 C2
Ross Green Worcs 116 E5
Rossie Ochill Perth 286 F4
Rossie Priory Perth 286 D6
Rossington S Yorks 187 B10
Rosskeen Highld 300 C6
Rossland Renfs 277 G8
Rossmore BCP 19 C7
Ross-on-Wye Hereford 98 G2
Roster Highld 310 F6
Rostherne Ches E 184 E2
Rostholme S Yorks 198 F5
Rosthwaite Cumb 220 C5
Cumb 220 G4
Roston Derbys 169 G10
Rosudgeon Corn 2 D3
Rosyth Fife 280 E2
Rotchfords Essex 107 E8
Rotcombe Bath 44 B6
Rothbury Northumb 252 C3
Rotherbridge W Sus 35 C7
Rotherby Leics 154 F3
Rotherfield E Sus 37 B9
Rotherfield Greys Oxon 65 C8
Rotherfield Peppard
Oxon 65 C8
Rotherham S Yorks 186 C6
Rotherhithe London 67 D11
Rothersthorpe
W Nhants 120 F4
Rotherwas Hereford 97 D10
Rotherwick Hants 49 B8
Rothes Moray 302 E2
Rothesay Argyll 275 G11
Rothiebrisbane Aberds 303 F7
Rothiemay Crossroads
Moray 302 E5
Rothiemurchus Lodge
Highld 291 C11
Rothienorman Aberds 303 F7
Rothiesholm Orkney 314 D6
Rothley Leics 153 G11
Northumb 252 F2
Rothley Plain Leics 153 G11
Rothley Shield East
Northumb 252 E2
Rothmaise Aberds 302 F6
Rothwell Lincs 189 B11
N Nhants 136 G6
W Yorks 197 B10
Rothwell Haigh
W Yorks 197 B10
Rotsea E Yorks 209 C7
Rottal Angus 292 G5
Rotten End Essex 106 F4
Suff 127 D7
Rotten Green Hants 49 B9
Rotten Row W Berks 64 E5
W Mid 118 B3
Rottingdean Brighton 36 G5
Rottington Cumb 219 C9
Rotton Park W Mid 133 F10
Roud IoW 20 E6
Rougham Norf 158 E6
Suff 125 E8
Rougham Green Suff 125 E8
Rough Bank Gtr Man 196 E2
Roughbirchworth
S Yorks 197 G9
Roughburn Highld 290 E5
Rough Close Staffs 151 B8
Rough Common Kent 54 B6
Roughcote Staffs 168 G6
Rough Haugh Highld 308 E7
Rough Hay Staffs 152 E4
Roughlee Lancs 204 E2
Roughley W Mid 134 D2
Roughmoor Som 28 B2
Swindon 62 B6
Roughrigg N Lanark 278 G6
Roughsike Cumb 240 B2
Roughton Lincs 174 C2
Norf 160 B4
Shrops 132 E5
Roughton Moor Lincs 174 C2
Roughway Kent 52 C6
Roundbush Essex 88 E5
Round Bush Herts 85 F10
Roundbush Green Essex 87 C9
Round Green Luton 103 G11
Roundham Som 28 F6
Roundhay W Yorks 206 F2
Round Maple Suff 107 C9
Round Oak Shrops 131 G7
W Mid 133 F8
Round's Green W Mid 133 F9
Roundshaw London 67 G10
Round Spinney
W Nhants 120 D5
Roundstonefoot
Dumfries 248 B4
Round Street Kent 69 F7
Roundstreet Common
W Sus 35 B9
Roundswell Devon 40 G4
Roundthorn Gtr Man 184 D4
Roundthwaite Cumb 222 E2
Roundway Wilts 62 G4
Roundyhill Angus 287 B7
Rousdon Devon 15 C11
Rousham Oxon 101 G9
Rous Lench Worcs 117 G10
Routenburn N Ayrs 266 C3
Routh E Yorks 209 E7
Rout's Green Bucks 84 F3
Row Corn 11 F7
Cumb 211 B8
Cumb 231 E8
Rowanburn Dumfries 239 B10
Rowanfield Glos 99 G8
Rowardennan Stirling 277 B7
Rowarth Derbys 185 D8
Row Ash Hants 33 E8
Rowbarton Som 28 B2
Rowberrow Som 44 B3
Row Brow Cumb 229 D7
Rowde Wilts 62 G3
Rowden Devon 13 B8
N Yorks 205 B11
Rowe Head Cumb 210 D5
Rowen Conwy 180 G3
Rowfoot Northumb 240 E5
Rowford Som 28 B2
Row Green Essex 106 G4
Row Heath Essex 89 B10
Rowhedge Essex 107 G10
Rowhill Sur 66 G4
Rowhook W Sus 50 G6
Rowington Warks 118 D4
Rowington Green
Warks 118 D4
Rowland Derbys 186 G2
Rowlands Castle Hants 34 E2
Rowlands Gill T&W 242 F5
Rowland's Green
Hereford 98 D3
Rowledge Sur 49 E10
Rowlestone Hereford 97 F7
Rowley E Yorks 208 G5
Shrops 130 B6
Rowley Green London 86 F2
Rowley Hill W Yorks 197 E7
Rowley Park Staffs 151 E8
Rowley Regis W Mid 133 F9
Rowley's Green W Mid 134 G6
Rowling Kent 55 C9
Rowly Sur 50 E4
Rownall Staffs 169 F7
Rowner Hants 33 G9
Rowney Green Worcs 117 C10
Rownhams Hants 32 D5
Row-of-trees Ches E 184 F4
Rowrah Cumb 219 B11
Rowsham Bucks 84 B4
Rowsley Derbys 170 B3
Rowstock Oxon 64 B3
Rowston Lincs 173 D9
Rowthorne Derbys 171 C7
Rowton Ches W 166 C6
Shrops 149 G7
Telford 150 F2
Rowton Moor Ches W 166 C6
Row Town Sur 66 G4
Roxburgh Borders 262 C5
Roxburgh Mains
Borders 262 D5
Roxby N Lincs 200 D2
N Yorks 226 B5
Roxeth London 66 B6
Roxton Bedford 122 G3
Roxwell Essex 87 D10
Royal British Legion Village
Kent 53 B8
Royal Leamington Spa
Warks 118 D6
Royal Oak Darl 233 G10
Lancs 194 G2
N Yorks 218 D2
Royal's Green Ches E 167 G10
Royal Tunbridge Wells
=*Tunbridge Wells* Kent 52 F5
Royal Wootton Bassett
Wilts 62 C5
Roybridge Highld 290 E4
Royd S Yorks 197 G8
Roydhouse W Yorks 197 E8
Royd Moor S Yorks 197 G8
W Yorks 198 E2
Roydon Essex 86 D6
Norf 141 G11
Norf 158 E4
Roydon Hamlet Essex 86 D6
Royds Green W Yorks 197 B11
Royston Glasgow 268 B2
Herts 105 C7
S Yorks 197 E11
Royston Water Som 28 E2
Royton Gtr Man 196 F2
Ruabon =*Rhiwabon*
Wrex 166 G4

Ruaig Argyll 288 E2
Ruan High Lanes Corn 3 B10
Ruan Lanihorne Corn 5 G7
Ruan Major Corn 2 F6
Ruan Minor Corn 2 F6
Ruarach Highld 295 C11
Ruardean Glos 79 B10
Ruardean Hill Glos 79 B10
Ruardean Woodside Glos 79 B10
Rubery Worcs 117 B9
Rubha Ghaisinis W Isles 297 G4
Rubha Stoer Highld 306 F5
Ruchazie Glasgow 268 B3
Ruchill Glasgow 267 B11
Ruckcroft Cumb 230 C6
Ruckhall Hereford 97 D9
Ruckinge Kent 54 G4
Ruckland Lincs 190 F4
Rucklers Lane Herts 85 E9
Ruckley Shrops 131 C10
Rudbaxton Pembs 91 G9
Rudby N Yorks 225 D9
Ruddington Notts 153 C11
Ruddle Glos 79 C11
Rudford Glos 98 G5
Rudge Shrops 132 D6
Som 45 C10
Rudge Heath Shrops 132 D5
Rudgeway S Glos 60 B6
Rudgwick W Sus 50 G5
Rudhall Hereford 98 F2
Rudheath Ches W 183 G11
Rudheath Woods Ches W 184 G2
Rudhja Garbh Argyll 289 E11
Rudley Green Essex 88 E4
Rudloe Wilts 61 E10
Rudry Caerph 59 B7
Rudston E Yorks 217 F11
Rudyard Staffs 169 D7
Ruewood Shrops 149 D9
Rufford Lancs 194 D3
Rufforth York 206 C6
Ruffs Notts 171 F8
Rugby Warks 119 B10
Rugeley Staffs 151 F10
Ruggin Som 27 D11
Ruglen S Ayrs 245 C7
Rugley Northumb 264 G5
Ruilick Highld 300 E5
Ruishton Som 28 C3
Ruisigearraidh W Isles 296 C5
Ruislip London 66 B5
Ruislip Common London 66 B5
Ruislip Gardens London 66 B5
Ruislip Manor London 66 B6
Ruiton W Mid 133 E8
Ruloe Ches W 183 G9
Rumach Highld 295 G8
Rumbling Bridge Perth 279 B10
Rumbow Cottages Worcs 117 B8
Rumburgh Suff 142 G6
Rumbush W Mid 118 B2
Rumer Hill Staffs 133 B9
Rumford Corn 10 G3
Falk 279 F8
Rumney Cardiff 59 D8
Rumsam Devon 40 G5
Rumwell Som 27 C11
Runcorn Halton 183 E8
Runcton W Sus 22 C5
Runcton Holme Norf 140 B2
Rundlestone Devon 13 G7
Runfold Sur 49 D11
Runhall Norf 141 B11
Runham Norf 143 B10
Norf 161 G9
Runham Vauxhall Norf 143 B10
Running Hill Head Gtr Man 196 F4
Runnington Som 27 C10
Running Waters Durham 234 C2
Runsell Green Essex 88 D3
Runshaw Moor Lancs 194 D4
Runswick Bay N Yorks 226 B6
Runwell Essex 88 G2
Ruscombe Glos 80 D4
Wokingham 65 D9
Ruscote Oxon 101 C8
Rushall Hereford 98 E2
Norf 142 G3
Wilts 46 B6
W Mid 133 C10
Rushbrooke Suff 125 E7
Rushbury Shrops 131 E10
Rushcombe Bottom BCP 18 B5
Rushden Herts 104 E6
N Nhants 121 D9
Rushenden Kent 70 E2
Rusher's Cross E Sus 37 B10
Rushey Mead Leicester 136 B2
Rushford Devon 12 F4
Norf 141 G8
Rushgreen Warr 183 D11
Rush Green Essex 89 B11
Herts 86 C5
Herts 104 G4
London 68 B4
Norf 141 B11
Rush-head Aberds 303 E8
Rush Hill Bath 61 G8
Rushington Hants 32 E5
Rushlake Green E Sus 23 B10
Rushland Cross Cumb 210 B6
Rushley Green Essex 106 D5
Rushmere C Beds 103 F8
Suff 143 F9
Rushmere St Andrew Suff 108 B4
Rushmere Street Suff 108 B4
Rushmoor Sur 49 E11
Telford 150 G2
Rushmore Hants 33 E11
Rushmore Hill London 68 G3
Rushock Hereford 114 F6
Worcs 117 C7
Rusholme Gtr Man 184 B5
Rushton Ches W 167 C9
Dorset 18 D3
N Nhants 136 G6
N Yorks 217 C9
Shrops 132 B2
Rushton Spencer Staffs 168 C6
Rushwick Worcs 116 G6
Rushyford Durham 233 F11
Rushy Green E Sus 23 C7
Ruskie Stirling 285 G10
Ruskington Lincs 173 E9
Rusland Cumb 210 B6
Rusling End Herts 104 G4
Rusper W Sus 51 F8
Ruspidge Glos 79 C11
Russel Highld 299 E8
Russell Hill London 67 G10
Russell's Green E Sus 38 E2
Russell's Hall W Mid 133 F8
Russell's Water Oxon 65 B8
Russel's Green Suff 126 C5
Russ Hill Sur 51 E8
Rusthall Kent 52 F5
Rustington W Sus 35 G9
Ruston N Yorks 217 C9
Ruston Parva E Yorks 217 G11
Ruswarp N Yorks 227 D7
Ruthall Shrops 131 F11
Rutherford Borders 262 C4
Rutherglen S Lanark 268 C2
Ruthernbridge Corn 5 B10
Ruthin V Glam 58 D3
Ruthin = Ruthun Denb 165 D10
Ruthrieston Aberdeen 293 C11
Ruthun = Ruthin Denb 165 D10
Ruthven Aberds 302 E5
Angus 286 C6
Highld 291 D9
Highld 301 F8
Ruthven House Angus 287 C7
Ruthvoes Corn 5 C8
Ruthwaite Cumb 229 D10
Ruthwell Dumfries 238 D3
Ruxley London 68 E3
Ruxton Hereford 97 F11
Ruxton Green Hereford 79 B8
Ruyton-XI-Towns Shrops 149 E7
Ryal Northumb 242 C2
Ryal Fold Blackburn 195 C7
Ryall Dorset 16 C4
Worcs 99 C7
Ryarsh Kent 53 B7
Rychraggan Highld 300 F4
Rydal Cumb 221 D7
Ryde IoW 21 C7
Rydens Sur 66 F6
Rydeshill Sur 50 C3
Rydon Devon 14 G3
Rye E Sus 38 C6
Ryebank Shrops 149 C10
Rye Common Hants 49 C9
Ryecroft S Yorks 186 B6
W Yorks 205 F7
Ryecroft Gate Staffs 168 C6
Ryeford Glos 80 E4
Rye Foreign E Sus 38 C5
Rye Harbour E Sus 38 D6
Ryehill E Yorks 201 B8
Ryeish Green Wokingham 65 F8
Ryelands Hereford 115 F9
Rye Park Herts 86 C5
Rye Street Worcs 98 D5
Ryeworth Glos 99 G9
Ryhall Rutland 155 G10
Ryhill W Yorks 197 E11
Ryhope T&W 243 G10
Rylah Derbys 171 B7
Rylands Notts 153 B10
Rylstone N Yorks 204 B5
Ryme Intrinseca Dorset 29 E9
Ryther N Yorks 207 F7
Ryton Glos 98 E4
N Yorks 216 D5
Shrops 132 C5
T&W 242 E5
Warks 135 F7
Ryton-on-Dunsmore Warks 119 C7
Ryton Woodside T&W 242 E4

S

Sabden Lancs 203 F11
Sabine's Green Essex 87 F8
Sackers Green Suff 107 D8
Sacombe Herts 86 B4
Sacombe Green Herts 86 B4
Sacriston Durham 233 B10
Sadberge Darl 224 B6
Saddell Argyll 255 D8
Saddell Ho Argyll 255 D8
Saddington Leics 136 E3
Saddle Bow Norf 158 F2
Saddlescombe W Sus 36 E3
Saddle Street Dorset 28 G5
Sadgill Cumb 221 D9
Saffron's Cross Hereford 115 G10
Saffron Walden Essex 105 D10
Sageston Pembs 73 E9
Saham Hills Norf 141 C8
Saham Toney Norf 141 C8
Saighdinis W Isles 296 E4
Saighton Ches W 166 C6
Sain Dunwyd = St Donats V Glam 58 F2
St Abbs Borders 273 B8
St Abb's Haven Borders 273 B8
St Agnes Corn 4 E4
Scilly 1 H3
St Albans Herts 85 D10
St Allen Corn 4 E6
St Andrews Fife 287 F9
St Andrew's Major V Glam 58 E6
St Andrew's Wood Devon 27 F9
St Annes Lancs 193 B10
St Anne's Park Bristol 60 E6
St Ann's Dumfries 248 E3
Nottingham 171 G9
St Ann's Chapel Corn 12 G4
Devon 8 F3
St Anthony Corn 3 C9
St Anthony-in-Meneage Corn 3 D7
St Anthony's T&W 243 E7
St Anthony's Hill E Sus 23 E10
St Arvans Mon 79 F8
St Asaph = Llanelwy Denb 181 G8
St Athan = Sain Tathon V Glam 58 F4
Sain Tathon = St Athan V Glam 58 F4
St Augustine's Kent 54 C6
St Austell Corn 5 E10
St Austins Hants 20 B2
St Bees Cumb 219 C9
St Blazey Corn 5 E11
St Blazey Gate Corn 5 E11
St Boswells Borders 262 C3
St Breock Corn 10 G5
St Breward Corn 11 F7
St Briavels Glos 79 E9
St Briavels Common Glos 79 E8
St Bride's Pembs 72 C4
St Brides Major = Saint-y-Brid V Glam 57 G11
St Bride's Netherwent Mon 60 B2
St Brides-super-Ely V Glam 58 D5
St Brides Wentlooge Newport 59 C9
Saintbridge Glos 80 B5
St Budeaux Plym 7 D8
Saintbury Glos 100 D2
St Buryan Corn 1 D4
St Catherine Bath 61 E9
St Catherine's Argyll 284 G5
St Catherine's Hill BCP 19 B8
St Chloe Glos 80 E4
St Clears = Sanclêr Carms 74 B3
St Cleer Corn 6 B5
St Clement Corn 4 G6
St Clether Corn 11 E10
St Colmac Argyll 275 G11
St Columb Major Corn 5 C8
St Columb Minor Corn 4 C6
St Columb Road Corn 5 D8
St Combs Aberds 303 C10
St Cross Hants 33 B7
St Cross South Elmham Suff 142 G5
St Cyrus Aberds 293 G9
St David's Perth 286 E3
St David's = Tyddewi Pembs 90 F5
St Day Corn 4 G4
St Decumans Som 42 E5
St Dennis Corn 5 D9
St Denys Soton 32 E6
St Devereux Hereford 97 E8
St Dials Torf 78 G3
St Dogmaels = Llandudoch Pembs 92 B3
St Dominick Corn 7 B8
St Donat's = Sain Dunwyd V Glam 58 F2
St Edith's Wilts 62 G3
St Endellion Corn 10 F5
St Enoder Corn 5 D7
St Erme Corn 4 E6
St Erney Corn 7 D7
St Erth Corn 2 B3
St Erth Praze Corn 2 B3
St Ervan Corn 10 G3
St Eval Corn 5 B7
St Ewe Corn 5 F9
St Fagans Cardiff 58 D6
St Fergus Aberds 303 D10
St Fillans Perth 285 E10
St Florence Pembs 73 E9
St Gennys Corn 11 B8
St George Bristol 60 E6
Conwy 181 F7
St George in the East
London 67 C10
V Glam 58 E5
St Georges N Som 59 G11
St George's Gtr Man 184 B4
Telford 150 G4
V Glam 58 D5
St George's Hill Sur 66 G5
St George's Well Devon 27 F8
St Germans Corn 7 D7
St Giles Lincs 189 G7
London 67 C10
St Giles in the Wood Devon 25 D8
St Giles on the Heath Devon 12 C3
St Giles's Hill Hants 33 B7
St Gluvias Corn 3 C7
St Godwalds Worcs 117 D9
St Harmon Powys 113 C9
St Helena Warks 134 C5
St Helen Auckland Durham 233 F9
St Helens Cumb 228 E6
IoW 21 D8
Mers 183 B8
St Helen's E Sus 38 E4
S Yorks 197 F11
St Helen's Wood E Sus 38 E4
St Helier London 67 F9
St Hilary Corn 2 C2
V Glam 58 E4
Saint Hill Devon 27 F9
W Sus 51 F11
St Ibbs Herts 104 F3
St Illtyd Bl Gwent 78 E2
St Ippollytts Herts 104 F3
St Ishmael's Pembs 72 D4
St Issey Corn 10 G4
St Ive Corn 6 B6
St Ive Cross Corn 6 B6
St Ives Cambs 122 C6
Corn 2 A2
Dorset 31 G10
St James Dorset 30 C5
London 67 C9
Norf 160 E5
St James's End W Nhants 120 E4
St James South Elmham Suff 142 G6
St Jidgey Corn 5 B8
St John Corn 7 E8
St Johns London 67 D11
Warks 118 C5
St John's E Sus 52 G4
IoM 192 D3
Kent 52 B4
Kent 52 E5
Sur 50 B3
Worcs 116 G6
W Yorks 206 F4
St John's Chapel Devon 25 B8
Durham 232 D3
St John's Fen End Norf 157 G10
St John's Highway Norf 157 G10
St John's Park IoW 21 C8
St John's Town of Dalry Dumfries 246 G4
St John's Wells Aberds 303 F7
St John's Wood London 67 C9
St Judes IoM 192 C4
St Julians Herts 85 D10
Newport 59 B10
St Just Corn 1 C3
St Justinian Pembs 90 F4
St Just in Roseland Corn 3 B9
St Katharines Wilts 63 G9
St Katherine's Aberds 303 F7
St Keverne Corn 3 E7
St Kew Corn 10 F6
St Kew Highway Corn 10 F6
St Keyne Corn 6 C4
St Lawrence Corn 5 B10
Essex 89 E7
IoW 20 F6
Kent 71 F11
St Leonards Dorset 31 G10
E Sus 38 F3
S Lanark 268 E2
St Leonard's Bucks 84 D6
St Leonard's Street Kent 53 B7
St Levan Corn 1 E3
St Luke's Derby 152 B6
London 67 C10
St Lythans V Glam 58 E6
St Mabyn Corn 10 G6
St Madoes Perth 286 E5
St Margarets Herts 86 C5
London 67 E7
St Margaret's Hereford 97 E7
St Margaret's at Cliffe Kent 55 E11
St Margaret's Hope Orkney 314 G4
St Margaret South Elmham Suff 142 G6
St Mark's Glos 99 G8
IoM 192 E3
St Martin Corn 2 E6
Corn 6 E5
St Martins Perth 286 D5
St Martin's Shrops 148 B6
St Martin's Moor Shrops 148 B6
St Mary Bourne Hants 48 C2
St Marychurch Torbay 9 B8
St Mary Church V Glam 58 E4
St Mary Cray London 68 F3
St Mary Hill V Glam 58 D3
St Mary Hoo Medway 69 D10
St Mary in the Marsh Kent 39 B9
St Mary's Orkney 314 F4
St Mary's Bay Kent 39 B9
St Maughans Mon 79 B7
St Maughans Green Mon 79 B7
St Mawes Corn 3 C8
St Mawgan Corn 5 B7
St Mellion Corn 7 B7
St Mellons Cardiff 59 C8
St Merryn Corn 10 G3
St Mewan Corn 5 E9
St Michael Caerhays Corn 5 G9
St Michael Church Som 43 G10
St Michael Penkevil Corn 5 G7
St Michaels Kent 53 F11
Torbay 9 C7
Worcs 115 D11
St Michael's Hamlet Mers 182 D5
St Michael's on Wyre Lancs 202 E5
St Michael South Elmham Suff 142 G6
St Minver Corn 10 F5
St Monans Fife 287 G9
St Neot Corn 6 B3
St Neots Cambs 122 E3
St Newlyn East Corn 4 D6
St Nicholas Herts 104 F5
Pembs 91 D7
V Glam 58 E5
St Nicholas at Wade Kent 71 F9
St Nicholas South Elmham Suff 142 G6
St Nicolas Park Warks 135 E7
St Ninians Stirling 278 C5
St Olaves Norf 143 D9
St Osyth Essex 89 B10
St Osyth Heath Essex 89 B10
St Owens Cross Hereford 97 G10
St Pancras London 67 C10
St Paul's Glos 80 B4
St Paul's Cray London 68 F3
St Paul's Walden Herts 104 G3
St Peters Kent 71 F11
St Peter's Glos 99 G8
T&W 243 E7
St Peter South Elmham Suff 142 G6
St Peter The Great Worcs 117 G7
St Petrox Pembs 73 F7
St Pinnock Corn 6 C4
St Quivox S Ayrs 257 E9
St Ruan Corn 2 F6
Saint's Hill Kent 52 E4
St Stephen Corn 5 E8
St Stephens Corn 7 D8
Herts 85 D10
St Stephen's Corn 12 D2
St Teath Corn 11 E7
St Thomas Devon 14 C4
Swansea 57 C7
St Tudy Corn 11 F7
St Twynnells Pembs 73 F7
St Veep Corn 6 E2
St Vigeans Angus 287 C10
St Vincent's Hamlet Essex 87 G9
St Wenn Corn 5 C9
St Weonards Hereford 97 G9
St Winnow Corn 6 D2
Saint y Brid = St Brides Major V Glam 57 G11
St y-Nyll V Glam 58 D5
Saith ffynnon Flint 181 F11
Salcombe Devon 9 G9
Salcombe Regis Devon 15 D9
Salcott-cum-Virley Essex 88 C6
Salden Bucks 102 F6
Sale Gtr Man 184 C3
Saleby Lincs 191 F7
Sale Green Worcs 117 F8
Salehurst E Sus 38 C2
Salem Carms 94 F2
Ceredig 128 G3
Corn 4 G4
Salen Argyll 289 E7
Highld 289 C8
Salendine Nook W Yorks 196 D6
Salenside Borders 261 E11
Salesbury Lancs 203 G9
Saleway Worcs 117 F8
Salford C Beds 103 D8
Gtr Man 184 B4
Oxon 100 F5
Salford Ford C Beds 103 D8
Salford Priors Warks 117 G11
Salfords Sur 51 D9
Salhouse Norf 160 G6
Saligo Argyll 274 G3
Salisbury Wilts 31 B10
Salkeld Dykes Cumb 230 D6
Sallachan Highld 289 C11
Sallachy Highld 295 B11
Highld 309 J5
Salle Norf 160 E2
Salmans Kent 52 E4
Salmonby Lincs 190 G4
Salmond's Muir Angus 287 D9
Salmonhutch Devon 14 B2
Salperton Glos 99 G11
Salperton Park Glos 81 B9
Salph End Bedford 121 G11
Salsburgh N Lanark 268 C6
Salt Staffs 151 D9
Salta Cumb 229 B7
Saltaire W Yorks 205 F8
Saltash Corn 7 D8
Saltburn Highld 301 C7
Saltburn-by-the-Sea Redcar 235 G9
Saltby Leics 155 D7
Salt Coates Cumb 238 G5
Saltcoats Cumb 219 F11
E Loth 281 E9
N Ayrs 266 G4
Saltcotes Lancs 193 B11
Saltdean Brighton 36 G5
Salt End E Yorks 201 B7
Salter Lancs 212 G2
Salterbeck Cumb 228 F5
Salterforth Lancs 204 D3
Salters Heath Hants 48 B6
Saltershill Shrops 150 D2
Salters Lode Norf 139 C11
Salter Street W Mid 118 C2
Salterswall Ches W 167 B10
Salterton Wilts 46 F6
Saltfleet Lincs 191 C7
Saltfleetby All Saints Lincs 191 C7
Saltfleetby St Clement Lincs 191 C7
Saltfleetby St Peter Lincs 190 D6
Saltford Bath 61 F7
Salt Hill Slough 66 C3
Salthouse Cumb 210 F4
Norf 177 E9
Saltley W Mid 133 F11
Saltmarsh Newport 59 C11
Saltmarshe E Yorks 199 C9
Saltness Orkney 314 G2
Shetland 313 J4
Saltney Flint 166 B5
Salton N Yorks 216 D4
Saltrens Devon 25 C7
Saltwell T&W 243 E7
Saltwick Northumb 242 B5
Saltwood Kent 55 F7
Salum Argyll 288 E2
Salvington W Sus 35 F10
Salwarpe Worcs 117 E7
Salwayash Dorset 16 B5
Sambourne Warks 117 E11
Wilts 45 E11
Sambrook Telford 150 E4
Samhla W Isles 296 E3
Samlesbury Lancs 203 G7
Samlesbury Bottoms Lancs 194 B6
Sampford Arundel Som 27 D10
Sampford Brett Som 42 E5
Sampford Chapple Devon 25 G10
Sampford Courtenay Devon 25 G10
Sampford Moor Som 27 D10
Sampford Peverell Devon 27 E8
Sampford Spiney Devon 12 G6
Sampool Bridge Cumb 211 B9
Samuel's Corner Essex 70 B3
Samuelston E Loth 281 G9
Sanachan Highld 299 E8
Sanaigmore Argyll 274 F3
Sanclêr = St Clears Carms 74 B3
Sancreed Corn 1 D4
Sancton E Yorks 208 F4
Sand Highld 307 K4
Shetland 313 J5
Som 44 D2
Sandaig Highld 295 E9
Sandal W Yorks 197 D10
Sandale Cumb 229 C10
Sandal Magna W Yorks 197 D10
Sandavore Highld 294 G6
Sandbach Ches E 168 C3
Sandbach Heath Ches E 168 C3
Sandbank Argyll 276 E3
Sandbanks BCP 18 D6
Kent 70 G4
Sandborough Staffs 152 F2
Sandbraes Lincs 200 G6
Sandend Aberds 302 C5
Sanderstead London 67 G10
Sandfields Glos 99 G8
Neath 57 C8
Staffs 134 B2
Sandford Cumb 222 B4
Devon 26 G4
Dorset 18 D4
Hants 31 G11
IoW 20 E6
N Som 44 B2
Shrops 148 E6
Shrops 149 C11
S Lanark 268 G4
Worcs 99 B7
W Yorks 205 F11
Sandford Batch N Som 44 B2
Sandfordhill Aberds 303 E11
Sandford Hill Stoke 168 G6
Sandford on Thames Oxon 83 E8
Sandford Orcas Dorset 29 C10
Sandford St Martin Oxon 101 F8
Sandgate Kent 55 G7
Sand Gate Cumb 211 D7
Sandgreen Dumfries 237 D7
Sandhaven Aberds 303 C9
Argyll 276 E3
Sandhead Dumfries 236 E2
Sandhill Bucks 102 F4
Cambs 139 F11
S Yorks 198 F2
Sandhills Dorset 29 E11
Dorset 29 G9
Mers 182 C4
Oxon 83 D9
Sur 50 F2
W Yorks 206 F3
Sandhoe Northumb 241 D11
Sandhole Argyll 275 D11
Sand Hole E Yorks 208 F2
Sandholme E Yorks 208 G2
Lincs 156 B6
Sandhurst Brack 65 G10
Glos 98 G6
Kent 38 B3
Sandhurst Cross Kent 38 B3
Sandhutton N Yorks 215 C7
Sand Hutton N Yorks 207 B9
Sandiacre Derbys 153 B9
Sandilands Lincs 191 E8
S Lanark 259 B9
Sandiway Ches W 183 G10
Sandleheath Hants 31 E10
Sandling Kent 53 B9
Sandlow Green Ches E 168 B3
Sandness Shetland 313 H3
Sandon Essex 88 E2
Herts 104 E6
Staffs 151 C8
Sandonbank Staffs 151 D8
Sandown IoW 21 E7
Sandown Park Kent 52 E6
Sandpit Dorset 28 G6
Sandpits Glos 98 F6
Sandplace Corn 6 D5
Sandridge Herts 85 C11
Wilts 62 F2
Sandringham Norf 158 D3
Sands Bucks 84 G4
Sandsend N Yorks 227 C7
Sands End London 67 D9
Sandside Cumb 210 D6
Cumb 211 C9
Orkney 314 F2
Sand Side Cumb 210 C4
Lancs 202 C4
Sandside Ho Highld 310 C3
Sandsound Shetland 313 J5
Sandtoft N Lincs 199 F8
Sandvoe Shetland 312 D5
Sandway Kent 53 C11
Sandwell W Mid 133 F10
Sandwich Kent 55 B10
Sandwich Bay Estate Kent 55 B11
Sandwick Cumb 221 B8
Orkney 314 H4
Shetland 313 L6
Sandwith Cumb 219 C9
Sandwith Newtown Cumb 219 C9
Sandy Carms 75 E7
C Beds 104 B3
Sandybank Orkney 314 C5
Sandy Bank Lincs 174 E3
Sandy Carrs Durham 234 C3
Sandycroft Flint 166 B4
Sandy Cross E Sus 37 C9
Sur 49 D11
Sandy Down Hants 20 B2
Sandyford Dumfries 248 E6
Stoke 168 E5
Sandygate Devon 14 G3
IoM 192 C4
S Yorks 186 D4
Sandy Gate Devon 14 C5
Sandy Haven Pembs 72 D5
Sandyhills Dumfries 237 D10
Sandylake Corn 6 C2
Sandylands Lancs 211 G8
Som 27 C10
Sandylane Swansea 56 D5
Sandy Lane Wilts 62 F3
Wrex 166 G5
W Yorks 205 F8
Sandypark Devon 13 D10
Sandysike Cumb 239 D9
Sandy Way IoW 20 E5
Sangobeg Highld 308 C4
Sangomore Highld 308 C4
Sanham Green W Berks 63 F10
Sankey Bridges Warr 183 D9
Sankyns Green Worcs 116 E5
Sanna Highld 288 C6
Sanndabhaig W Isles 297 G4
W Isles 304 E6
Sannox N Ayrs 255 C11
Sanquhar Dumfries 247 B7
Sansaw Heath Shrops 149 E10
Santon Cumb 220 E2
N Lincs 200 E2
Santon Bridge Cumb 220 E2
Santon Downham Suff 140 F6
Sapcote Leics 135 E9
Sapey Bridge Worcs 116 F4
Sapey Common Hereford 116 E4
Sapiston Suff 125 B8
Sapley Cambs 122 C4
Sapperton Derbys 152 C3
Glos 80 E6
Lincs 155 C10
Saracen's Head Lincs 156 D6
Sarclet Highld 310 E7
Sardis Carms 75 D9
Pembs 73 D10
Sarisbury Hants 33 F8
Sarn Bridgend 58 C2
Flint 181 F10
Powys 130 E4
Sarnau Carms 74 B4
Ceredig 110 G6
Gwyn 147 B9
Powys 95 E10
Powys 148 F4
Sarn Bach Gwyn 144 D6
Sarnesfield Hereford 115 G7
Sarn Meyllteyrn Gwyn 144 C4
Saron Carms 75 C10
Carms 93 D7
Denb 165 C8
Gwyn 163 B8
Gwyn 163 D7
Sarratt Herts 85 F8
Sarratt Bottom Herts 85 F8
Sarre Kent 71 G9
Sarsden Oxon 100 G5
Sarsden Halt Oxon 100 G5
Sarsgrum Highld 308 C3
Sasaig Highld 295 E8
Sascott Shrops 149 G8
Satley Durham 233 C8
Satmar Kent 55 F9
Satran Highld 294 B6
Satron N Yorks 223 F8
Satterleigh Devon 25 C11
Satterthwaite Cumb 220 G6
Satwell Oxon 65 C8
Sauchen Aberds 293 B8
Saucher Perth 286 D5
Sauchie Clack 279 C7
Sauchieburn Aberds 293 G8
Saughall Ches W 182 G5
Saughall Massie Mers 182 D3
Saughton Edin 280 G4
Saughtree Borders 250 D3
Saul Glos 80 D2
Saundby Notts 188 D3
Saundersfoot = Llanussyllt Pembs 73 E10
Saunderton Bucks 84 E3
Saunderton Lee Bucks 84 F4
Saunton Devon 40 F3
Sausthorpe Lincs 174 B5
Saval Highld 309 J5
Savary Highld 289 E8
Saveock Corn 4 F5
Saverley Green Staffs 151 B9
Savile Park W Yorks 196 C5
Savile Town W Yorks 197 C8
Sawbridge Warks 119 D10
Sawbridgeworth Herts 87 B7
Sawdon N Yorks 217 B8
Sawley Derbys 153 C9
Lancs 203 D11
N Yorks 214 F4
Sawood W Yorks 204 G6
Sawston Cambs 105 B9
Sawtry Cambs 138 G3
Sawyers Hill Wilts 81 G8
Sawyer's Hill Som 27 C11
Saxby Leics 154 F6
Lincs 189 D8
W Sus 35 G7
Saxby All Saints N Lincs 200 D3
Saxelbye Leics 154 E4
Saxham Street Suff 125 E11
Saxilby Lincs 188 F5
Saxlingham Norf 159 B10
Saxlingham Green Norf 142 D4
Saxlingham Nethergate Norf 142 D4
Saxlingham Thorpe Norf 142 D4
Saxmundham Suff 127 E7
Saxondale Notts 154 B3
Saxon Street Cambs 124 F3
Saxtead Suff 126 D5
Saxtead Green Suff 126 E5
Saxtead Little Green Suff 126 D5
Saxthorpe Norf 160 C2
Saxton N Yorks 206 F5
Sayers Common W Sus 36 D3
Scackleton N Yorks 216 E2
Scadabhagh W Isles 305 J3
Scaftworth Notts 187 C11
Scagglethorpe N Yorks 216 E6
Scaitcliffe Lancs 195 B9
Scaladal W Isles 305 G3
Scalan Moray 292 B4
Scalasaig Argyll 274 D4
Scalby E Yorks 199 B10
N Yorks 227 G10
Scald End Bedford 121 F10
Scaldwell W Nhants 120 C5
Scaleby Cumb 239 E11
Scalebyhill Cumb 239 E10
Scale Hall Lancs 211 G9
Scale Houses Cumb 231 B7
Scales Cumb 230 F2
Cumb 231 C7
Lancs 202 G5
Scalford Leics 154 E5
Scaling Redcar 226 C4
Scaliscro W Isles 304 F3
Scallasaig Highld 295 D10
Scallastle Argyll 289 F8
Scalloway Shetland 313 K6
Scalpay W Isles 305 J4
Scalpay Ho Highld 295 C8
Scalpsie Argyll 255 B11
Scamadale Highld 295 F9
Scamblesby Lincs 190 F3
Scamland E Yorks 207 E11
Scammadale Argyll 289 G10
Scamodale Highld 289 B10
Scampston N Yorks 217 D7
Scampton Lincs 189 F7
Scaniport Highld 300 F6
Scapa Orkney 314 F4
Scapegoat Hill W Yorks 196 D5
Scar Orkney 314 B6
Scarborough N Yorks 217 B10
Scarcewater Corn 5 E8
Scarcliffe Derbys 171 B7
Scarcroft W Yorks 206 E3
Scarcroft Hill W Yorks 206 E3
Scardroy Highld 300 D2
Scarff Shetland 312 E4
Scarfskerry Highld 310 B6
Scargill Durham 223 C11
Scar Head Cumb 220 G5
Scarinish Argyll 288 E2
Scarisbrick Lancs 193 E11
Scarness Cumb 229 E10
Scarning Norf 159 G9
Scarrington Notts 172 G2
Scarth Hill Lancs 194 F2
Scarthingwell N Yorks 206 F5
Scartho NE Lincs 201 F9
Scarvister Shetland 313 J5
Scarwell Orkney 314 D2
Scatness Shetland 313 M5
Scatraig Highld 301 F7
Scawby N Lincs 200 F3
Scawsby S Yorks 198 G5
Scawthorpe S Yorks 198 F5
Scawton N Yorks 215 C10
Scayne's Hill W Sus 36 C5
Scethrog Powys 96 F2
Scholar Green Ches E 168 D4
Scholemoor W Yorks 205 G8
Scholes Gtr Man 194 F5
S Yorks 186 B5
W Yorks 197 B7
W Yorks 197 F7
W Yorks 204 F6
W Yorks 206 F3
Scholey Hill W Yorks 197 B11
School Aycliffe Durham 233 G11
Schoolgreen Wokingham 65 F8
School Green Ches W 167 C10
Essex 106 E4
IoW 20 D2
W Yorks 205 G8
Schoolhill Aberds 293 D11
School House Dorset 28 G5
Sciberscross Highld 309 H7
Scilly Bank Cumb 219 B9
Scissett W Yorks 197 E8
Scleddau Pembs 91 E8
Scofton Notts 187 E10
Scole Norf 126 B2
Scole Common Norf 142 G2
Scolpaig W Isles 296 D3
Scone Perth 286 E5
Sconser Highld 295 B7
Scoonie Fife 287 G7
Scoor Argyll 274 B5
Scopwick Lincs 173 D9
Scoraig Highld 307 K5
Scorborough E Yorks 208 D6
Scorrier Corn 4 G4
Scorriton Devon 8 B4
Scorton Lancs 202 D6
N Yorks 224 E5
Sco Ruston Norf 160 E5
Scotbheinn W Isles 296 F4
Scotby Cumb 239 G10
Scotch Corner N Yorks 224 E4
Scotches Derbys 170 F4
Scotforth Lancs 202 B5
Scotgate W Yorks 196 E6
Scot Hay Staffs 168 F4
Scothern Lincs 189 F8
Scotland Leics 136 D3
Leics 153 E7
Lincs 155 C10
W Berks 64 F5
Scotland End Oxon 100 E6
Scotland Gate Northumb 253 G7
Scotlands W Mid 133 C8
Scotland Street Suff 107 D9
Scotlandwell Perth 286 G5
Scot Lane End Gtr Man 194 F6
Scotsburn Highld 301 B7
Scotscalder Station Highld 310 D4
Scotscraig Fife 287 E8
Scots' Gap Northumb 252 F2
Scotston Aberds 293 F9
Perth 286 C3
Scotstoun Glasgow 267 B10
Scotstown Highld 289 C10
Scotswood T&W 242 E5
Windsor 66 F2
Scottas Highld 295 E9
Scotter Lincs 199 G11
Scotterthorpe Lincs 199 G11
Scottlethorpe Lincs 155 E11
Scotton Lincs 188 B5
N Yorks 206 B2
N Yorks 224 F3
Scottow Norf 160 E5
Scott Willoughby Lincs 155 B11
Scoughall E Loth 282 E2
Scoulag Argyll 266 D2
Scoulton Norf 141 C9
Scounslow Green Staffs 151 D11
Scourie Highld 306 E6
Scourie More Highld 306 E6
Scousburgh Shetland 313 M5
Scout Dike S Yorks 197 G8
Scout Green Cumb 221 D11
Scouthead Gtr Man 196 F3
Scowles Glos 79 C9
Scrabster Highld 310 B4
Scraesburgh Borders 262 F5
Scrafield Lincs 174 B4
Scragged Oak Kent 69 G10
Scrainwood Northumb 251 B11
Scrane End Lincs 174 G5
Scrapsgate Kent 70 E2
Scraptoft Leics 136 B2
Scrapton Som 28 E3
Scratby Norf 161 F10
Scrayingham N Yorks 216 G4
Scredda Corn 5 E10
Scredington Lincs 173 G9
Screedy Som 27 B9
Scremby Lincs 174 B6
Scremerston Northumb 273 F10
Screveton Notts 172 G2
Scrivelsby Lincs 174 B3
Scriven N Yorks 206 B2
Scronkey Lancs 202 D4
Scrooby Notts 187 C11
Scropton Derbys 152 C3
Scrub Hill Lincs 174 D2
Scruton N Yorks 224 G5
Scrwgan Powys 148 E3
Scuddaborg Highld 298 C3
Scuggate Cumb 239 C10
Sculcoates Hull 209 G7
Sculthorpe Norf 159 C7
Scunthorpe N Lincs 199 E11
Scurlage Swansea 56 D3
Sea Som 28 E4
Seaborough Dorset 28 F6
Seabridge Staffs 168 G4
Seabrook Kent 55 G7
Seaburn T&W 243 F10
Seacombe Mers 182 C4
Seacox Heath Kent 53 G8
Seacroft Lincs 175 C9
W Yorks 206 F3
Seadyke Lincs 156 B6
Seafar N Lanark 278 G5
Seafield Highld 311 L3
Midloth 270 C5
S Ayrs 257 E8
W Loth 269 B10
Seaford E Sus 23 F7
Seaforth Mers 182 B4
Seagrave Leics 154 F2
Seagry Heath Wilts 62 C3
Seaham Durham 234 B4
Seahouses Northumb 264 C6
Seal Kent 52 B4
Sealand Flint 166 B5
Seale Sur 49 D11
Seamer N Yorks 217 C10
N Yorks 225 C9
Seamill N Ayrs 266 F4
Sea Mill Cumb 210 F5
Sea Mills Bristol 60 D5
Corn 10 G4
Sea Palling Norf 161 D8
Searby Lincs 200 F5
Seasalter Kent 70 F5
Seascale Cumb 219 E10
Seathorne Lincs 175 B9
Seathwaite Cumb 220 C4
Cumb 220 F4
Seatle Cumb 211 C7
Seatoller Cumb 220 C4
Seaton Corn 6 E6
Cumb 228 E6
Devon 15 C10
Durham 243 G9
E Yorks 209 D9
Kent 55 B8
Northumb 243 B8
Rutland 137 D8
Seaton Burn T&W 242 C6
Seaton Carew Hrtlpl 234 F6
Seaton Delaval Northumb 243 B8
Seaton Ross E Yorks 207 E11
Seaton Sluice Northumb 243 B8
Seatown Aberds 302 C5
Aberds 303 D11
Dorset 16 C4
Seaureaugh Moor Corn 2 B6
Seave Green N Yorks 225 E11
Seaview IoW 21 C8
Seaville Cumb 238 G5
Seavington St Mary Som 28 E6
Seavington St Michael Som 28 D6
Seawick Essex 89 C10
Sebastopol Torf 78 F3
Sebay Orkney 314 F5
Sebergham Cumb 230 C3
Sebiston Velzian Orkney 314 D2
Seckington Warks 134 B5
Second Coast Highld 307 K4
Second Drove Cambs 139 F10
Sedbergh Cumb 222 G3
Sedbury Glos 79 G8
Sedbusk N Yorks 223 G7
Seddington C Beds 104 B3
Sedgeberrow Worcs 99 D10
Sedgebrook Lincs 155 B7
Sedgefield Durham 234 F3
Sedgeford Norf 158 B4
Sedgehill Wilts 30 B5
Sedgemere W Mid 118 B4
Sedgley W Mid 133 E8
Sedgley Park Gtr Man 195 G10
Sedgwick Cumb 211 B10
Sedlescombe E Sus 38 D3
Sedlescombe Street E Sus 38 D3
Sedrup Bucks 84 C3
Seed Kent 54 B2
Seed Lee Lancs 194 C5
Seedley Gtr Man 184 B4
Seend Wilts 62 G2
Seend Cleeve Wilts 62 G2
Seend Head Wilts 62 G2
Seer Green Bucks 85 G7
Seething Norf 142 D6
Seething Wells London 67 F7
Sefton Mers 193 G11
Segensworth Hants 33 F8
Seggat Aberds 303 E7
Seghill Northumb 243 C7
Seifton Shrops 131 G9

Seighford Staffs 151 D7
Seilebost W Isles 305 J2
Seion Gwyn 163 B8
Seisdon Staffs 132 E6
Seisiadar W Isles 304 E7
Selattyn Shrops 148 C5
Selborne Hants 49 G8
Selby N Yorks 207 G8
Selgrove Kent 54 B4
Selham W Sus 34 C6
Selhurst London 67 F10
Selkirk Borders 261 D11
Sellack Hereford 97 F11
Sellack Boat Hereford 97 F11
Sellafirth Shetland 312 D7
Sellan Corn 1 C4
Sellibister Orkney 314 B7
Sellick's Green Som 28 D2
Sellindge Kent 54 F6
Selling Kent 54 B4
Sells Green Wilts 62 G3
Selly Hill N Yorks 227 D7
Selly Oak W Mid 133 G10
Selly Park W Mid 133 G11
Selmeston E Sus 23 D8
Selsdon London 67 G10
Selsey W Sus 22 E5
Selsfield Common
W Sus 51 G10
Selside Cumb 221 F10
N Yorks 212 D5
Selsley Glos 80 E4
Selsmore Hants 21 B10
Selson Kent 55 B10
Selsted Kent 55 E8
Selston Notts 171 E7
Selston Common Notts 171 E7
Selston Green Notts 171 E7
Selwick Orkney 314 F2
Selworthy Som 42 D2
Semblister Shetland 313 H5
Semer Suff 107 B9
Sem Hill Wilts 30 B5
Semington Wilts 61 G11
Semley Wilts 30 B5
Sempringham Lincs 156 C2
Send Sur 50 B4
Send Grove Sur 50 C4
Send Marsh Sur 50 B4
Senghenydd Caerph 77 G10
Sennen Corn 1 D3
Sennen Cove Corn 1 D3
Sennybridge *= Pont Senni*
Powys 95 F8
Serlby Notts 187 D10
Serrington Wilts 46 F5
Sessay N Yorks 215 D9
Setchey Norf 158 G2
Setley Hants 32 G4
Seton E Loth 281 G8
Seton Mains E Loth 281 F8
Setter Shetland 312 E6
Shetland 313 H5
Shetland 313 J7
Shetland 313 L6
Settiscarth Orkney 314 E3
Settle N Yorks 212 G6
Settrington N Yorks 216 E6
Seven Ash Som 43 G7
Sevenhampton Glos 99 G10
Swindon 82 G2
Seven Kings London 68 B3
Sevenoaks Kent 52 C4
Sevenoaks Common
Kent 52 C4
Sevenoaks Weald Kent 52 C4
Seven Sisters *= Blaendulais*
Neath 76 D4
Seven Springs Glos 81 B7
Seven Star Green Essex 107 F8
Severn Beach S Glos 60 B4
Severnhampton Swindon 82 G2
Severn Stoke Worcs 99 C7
Sevick End Bedford 121 G11
Sevington Kent 54 E4
Sewards End Essex 105 D11
Sewardstone Essex 86 F5
Sewardstonebury Essex 86 F5
Sewell C Beds 103 G9
Sewerby E Yorks 218 F3
Seworgan Corn 2 C6
Sewstern Leics 155 E7
Sexhow N Yorks 225 D9
Sezincote Glos 100 E3
Sgarasta Mhor W Isles 305 J2
Sgiogarstaigh W Isles 304 B7
Sgiwen *= Skewen* Neath 57 B8
Shabbington Bucks 83 D11
Shab Hill Glos 80 B6
Shackerley Shrops 132 B6
Shackerstone Leics 135 B7
Shacklecross Derbys 153 C8
Shackleford Sur 50 D2
Shackleton W Yorks 196 B3
Shacklewell London 67 B10
Shacklford Sur 50 D2
Shade W Yorks 196 C2
Shadforth Durham 234 C2
Shadingfield Suff 143 G8
Shadoxhurst Kent 54 F3
Shadsworth Blackburn 195 B8
Shadwell Glos 80 F3
London 67 C11
Norf 141 G8
W Yorks 206 F2
Shaffalong Staffs 169 E7
Shaftenhoe End Herts 105 D8
Shaftesbury Dorset 30 C5
Shafton S Yorks 197 E11
Shafton Two Gates
S Yorks 197 E11
Shaggs Dorset 18 E3
Shakeford Shrops 150 D3
Shakerley Gtr Man 195 G7
Shakesfield Glos 98 E3
Shalbourne Wilts 63 G10
Shalcombe IoW 20 D3
Shalden Hants 49 E7
Shalden Green Hants 49 E7
Shaldon Devon 14 G4
Shalfleet IoW 20 D4
Shalford Essex 106 F4
Som 45 G8
Sur 50 D4
Shalford Green Essex 106 F4
Shalloch Moray 302 D3
Shallowford Devon 25 B11
Devon 41 E8
Staffs 151 D7
Shalmsford Street Kent 54 C5
Shalstone Bucks 102 D2
Shamley Green Sur 50 E4
Shandon Argyll 276 D5
Shandwick Highld 301 B8
Shangton Leics 136 D4
Shankhouse Northumb 243 B7
Shanklin IoW 21 E7
Shannochie N Ayrs 255 E10
Shannochill Stirling 277 B10
Shanquhar Aberds 302 F5
Shanwell Fife 287 E8
Shanzie Perth 286 B6
Shap Cumb 221 B11
Shapridge Glos 79 B11
Shapwick Dorset 30 G6
Som 44 F2
Sharcott Wilts 46 B6
Shard End W Mid 134 F3
Shardlow Derbys 153 C8
Shareshill Staffs 133 B8
Sharlston W Yorks 197 D11
Sharlston Common
W Yorks 197 D11
Sharmans Cross W Mid 118 B2
Sharnal Street Medway 69 E9
Sharnbrook Bedford 121 F9
Sharneyford Lancs 195 C11
Sharnford Leics 135 E9
Sharnhill Green Dorset 30 F2
Sharoe Green Lancs 202 G6
Sharow N Yorks 214 E6
Sharpenhoe C Beds 103 E11
Sharperton Northumb 251 C11
Sharples Gtr Man 195 E8
Sharpley Heath Staffs 151 B9
Sharpness Glos 79 E11
Sharpsbridge E Sus 36 C6
Sharp's Corner E Sus 23 B9
Sharpstone Bath 45 B9
Sharp Street Norf 161 E7
Sharpthorne W Sus 51 G11
Sharptor Corn 11 G11
Sharpway Gate Worcs 117 D9
Sharrington Norf 159 B10
Sharrow S Yorks 186 D4
Sharston Gtr Man 184 D4
Shatterford Worcs 132 G5
Shatterling Kent 55 B9
Shatton Derbys 185 E11
Shaugh Prior Devon 7 C10
Shavington Ches E 168 E2
Shaw Gtr Man 196 F2
Swindon 62 B6
W Berks 64 F3
Wilts 61 F11
W Yorks 204 F6
Shawbank Shrops 131 G9
Shawbirch Telford 150 G2
Shawbury Shrops 149 E11
Shawclough Gtr Man 195 E11
Shaw Common Glos 98 F3
Shawdon Hall Northumb 264 G3
Shawell Leics 135 G10
Shawfield Gtr Man 195 E11
Staffs 169 C9
Shawfield Head
N Yorks 205 C11
Shawford Hants 33 C7
Som 45 C9
Shawforth Lancs 195 C11
Shaw Green Herts 104 E5
Lancs 194 D4
N Yorks 205 C11
Shawhead Dumfries 237 B10
N Lanark 268 C4
Shaw Heath Ches E 184 F3
Gtr Man 184 D5
Shawhill Dumfries 238 D6
Shawlands Glasgow 267 C11
Shaw Lands S Yorks 197 F10
Shaw Mills N Yorks 214 G5
Shawsburn S Lanark 268 E5
Shaw Side Gtr Man 196 F2
Shawton S Lanark 268 F3
Shawtonhill S Lanark 268 F3
Shay Gate W Yorks 205 F8
Sheandow Moray 302 F2
Shear Cross Wilts 45 E11
Shearington Dumfries 238 D2
Shearsby Leics 136 E2
Shearston Som 43 G9
Shebbear Devon 24 F6
Shebdon Staffs 150 D5
Shebster Highld 310 C4
Sheddens E Renf 267 D11
Shedfield Hants 33 E9
Sheen Staffs 169 C10
Sheepbridge Derbys 186 G5
Sheepdrove W Berks 63 D10
Sheep Hill Durham 242 F5
Sheeplane C Beds 103 E8
Sheepridge Bucks 65 B11
W Yorks 197 D7
Sheepscar W Yorks 206 G2
Sheepscombe Glos 80 C5
Sheepstor Devon 7 B11
Sheepwash Devon 25 F7
Northumb 253 F7
Sheepway N Som 60 D3
Sheepy Magna Leics 134 C6
Sheepy Parva Leics 134 C6
Sheering Essex 87 C8
Sheerness Kent 70 E2
Sheerwater Sur 66 G4
Sheet Hants 34 C3
Shrops 115 C10
Sheets Heath Sur 50 B2
Sheffield Corn 1 D5
S Yorks 186 D5
Sheffield Bottom
W Berks 65 F7
Sheffield Green E Sus 36 C6
Sheffield Park S Yorks 186 D5
Shefford C Beds 104 D2
Shefford Woodlands
W Berks 63 E11
Sheigra Highld 306 C6
Sheildmuir N Lanark 268 D5
Sheinton Shrops 132 C2
Shelderton Shrops 115 B8
Sheldon Derbys 169 B11
Devon 27 F10
W Mid 134 G3
Sheldwich Kent 54 B4
Sheldwich Lees Kent 54 B4
Shelf Bridgend 58 C2
W Yorks 196 B6
Shelfanger Norf 142 G2
Shelfield Warks 118 E2
W Mid 133 C10
Shelfield Green Warks 118 E2
Shelfleys W Nhants 120 F4
Shelford Notts 171 G11
Warks 135 F8
Shell Worcs 117 F9
Shelland Suff 125 E10
Shellbrook Leics 152 F6
Shelley Essex 87 E9
Suff 107 D10
W Yorks 197 E8
Shelley Woodhouse
W Yorks 197 E8
Shell Green Halton 183 D8
Shellingford Oxon 82 G4
Shellow Bowells Essex 87 D10
Shellwood Cross Sur 51 D8
Shelsley Beauchamp
Worcs 116 E4
Shelsley Walsh Worcs 116 E4
Shelthorpe Leics 153 F10
Shelton Bedford 121 D10
Norf 142 E4
Shelton *continued*
Notts 172 G3
Shrops 149 G9
Stoke 168 F5
Shelton Green Norf 142 E4
Shelton Lock Derby 153 C7
Shelton under Harley
Staffs 150 B6
Shelve Shrops 130 D6
Shelvin Devon 27 G11
Shelvingford Kent 71 F8
Shelwick Hereford 97 C10
Shelwick Green
Hereford 97 C10
Shenfield Essex 87 G10
Shenington Oxon 101 C7
Shenley Herts 85 E11
Shenley Brook End
M Keynes 102 D6
Shenleybury Herts 85 E11
Shenley Church End
M Keynes 102 D6
Shenley Fields W Mid 133 G10
Shenley Lodge
M Keynes 102 D6
Shenley Wood
M Keynes 102 D6
Shenmore Hereford 97 D7
Shennanton Dumfries 236 C5
Shennanton Ho
Dumfries 236 C5
Shenstone Staffs 134 C2
Worcs 117 C7
Shenstone Woodend
Staffs 134 C2
Shenton Leics 135 C7
Shenval Highld 300 G4
Moray 302 G2
Shenvault Moray 301 E10
Shepeau Stow Lincs 156 G6
Shephall Herts 104 G5
Shepherd Hill W Yorks 197 C9
Shepherd's Bush London 67 C8
Shepherd's Gate Norf 157 F11
Shepherd's Green Oxon 65 C8
Shepherd's Hill Sur 50 G2
Shepherd's Patch Glos 80 E2
Shepherd's Port Norf 158 C3
Shepherdswell or
Sibertswold Kent 55 D9
Shepley W Yorks 197 F7
Shepperdine S Glos 79 F10
Shepperton Sur 66 F5
Shepperton Green Sur 66 F5
Shepreth Cambs 105 B7
Shepshed Leics 153 F9
Shepton Beauchamp
Som 28 D6
Shepton Mallet Som 44 E6
Shepton Montague Som 45 G7
Shepway Kent 53 C9
Sheraton Durham 234 D4
Sherberton Devon 13 G8
Sherborne Bath 44 B5
Dorset 29 D10
Glos 81 C11
Sherborne St John Hants 48 B6
Sherbourne Warks 118 E5
Sherbourne Street Suff 107 C9
Sherburn Durham 234 C2
N Yorks 217 D9
Sherburn Grange
Durham 234 C2
Sherburn Hill Durham 234 C2
Sherburn in Elmet
N Yorks 206 G5
Shere Sur 50 D5
Shereford Norf 159 D7
Sherfield English Hants 32 C3
Sherfield on Loddon
Hants 49 B7
Sherfin Lancs 195 B9
Sherford Devon 8 G5
Dorset 18 C4
Som 28 C2
Sheriffhales Shrops 150 G5
Sheriff Hill T&W 243 E7
Sheriff Hutton N Yorks 216 F3
Sheriff's Lench Worcs 99 B10
Sheringham Norf 177 E11
Sherington M Keynes 103 B7
Sheringwood Norf 177 E11
Shermanbury W Sus 36 D2
Shernal Green Worcs 117 E8
Shernborne Norf 158 C4
Sherrard's Green Worcs 98 B5
Sherrardspark Herts 86 C2
Sherriffhales Shrops 150 G5
Sherrington Wilts 46 F3
Sherston Wilts 61 B11
Sherwood Nottingham 171 G9
Sherwood Green Devon 25 C9
Sherwood Park Kent 52 E6
Shettleston Glasgow 268 C2
Shevington Gtr Man 194 F4
Shevington Moor
Gtr Man 194 E4
Shevington Vale
Gtr Man 194 F4
Sheviock Corn 7 D7
Shewalton N Ayrs 257 B8
Shibden Head W Yorks 196 B5
Shide IoW 20 D5
Shiel Aberds 292 B4
Shiel Bridge Highld 295 D11
Shieldaig Highld 299 B8
Highld 299 D8
Shieldhall Glasgow 267 B10
Shieldhill Dumfries 248 F2
Falk 279 F7
S Lanark 269 G10
Shield Row Durham 242 G6
Shielfoot Highld 289 C8
Shielhill Angus 287 B8
Invclyd 276 G4
Shifford Oxon 82 E5
Shifnal Shrops 132 B4
Shilbottle Northumb 252 B5
Shilbottle Grange
Northumb 252 B6
Shildon Durham 233 F10
Shillford E Renf 267 D8
Shillingford Devon 27 C7
Oxon 83 G9
Shillingford Abbot Devon 14 D4
Shillingford St George
Devon 14 D4
Shillingstone Dorset 30 E4
Shillington C Beds 104 E2
Shillmoor Northumb 251 B9
Shilton Oxon 82 D3
Warks 135 G8
Shilvington Northumb 252 G5
Shimpling Norf 142 G3
Suff 125 G7
Shimpling Street Suff 125 G7
Shincliffe Durham 233 C11
Shiney Row T&W 243 G8
Shinfield Wokingham 65 F8
Shingay Cambs 104 B6
Shingham Norf 140 C5
Shingle Street Suff 109 C7
Shinner's Bridge Devon 8 C5
Shinness Highld 309 H5
Shipbourne Kent 52 C5
Shipdham Norf 141 B9
Shipdham Airfield Norf 141 B9
Shipham Som 44 B2
Shiphay Torbay 9 B7
Shiplake Oxon 65 D9
Shiplake Bottom Oxon 65 C8
Shiplake Row Oxon 65 D9
Shiplate N Som 43 B11
Shiplaw Borders 270 F4
Shipley Derbys 170 G6
Northumb 264 F4
Shrops 132 D6
W Sus 35 C10
W Yorks 205 F8
Shipley Bridge Sur 51 E10
Shipley Common
Derbys 171 G7
Shipley Shiels Northumb 251 E7
Shipmeadow Suff 143 F7
Shipping Pembs 73 D10
Shippon Oxon 83 F7
Shipston-on-Stour
Warks 100 C5
Shipton Bucks 102 F5
Glos 81 B8
N Yorks 207 B7
Shrops 131 E11
Shipton Bellinger Hants 47 D8
Shipton Gorge Dorset 16 C5
Shipton Green W Sus 22 C4
Shipton Lee Bucks 102 G4
Shipton Moyne Glos 61 B11
Shipton Oliffe Glos 81 B8
Shipton on Cherwell
Oxon 83 B7
Shipton Solers Glos 81 B8
Shiptonthorpe E Yorks 208 E3
Shipton-under-Wychwood
Oxon 82 B3
Shirburn Oxon 83 F11
Shirdley Hill Lancs 193 E11
Shirebrook Derbys 171 B8
Shirecliffe S Yorks 186 C4
Shiregreen S Yorks 186 C5
Shirehampton Bristol 60 D4
Shiremoor T&W 243 C8
Shirenewton Mon 79 G7
Shire Oak W Mid 133 C11
Shireoaks Derbys 185 E9
Notts 187 E9
Shires Mill Fife 279 D10
Shirkoak Kent 54 F2
Shirland Derbys 170 D6
Shirlett Shrops 132 D3
Shirley Derbys 170 G2
Hants 19 B9
London 67 F11
Soton 32 E6
W Mid 118 B2
Shirley Heath W Mid 118 B2
Shirley holms Hants 19 B11
Shirley Warren Soton 32 E5
Shirl Heath Hereford 115 F8
Shirrell Heath Hants 33 E9
Shirwell Devon 40 F5
Shirwell Cross Devon 40 F5
Shiskine N Ayrs 255 E10
Shitterton Dorset 18 C2
Shobdon Hereford 115 E8
Shobley Hants 31 F11
Shobnall Staffs 152 E4
Shobrooke Devon 26 G5
Shoby Leics 154 F3
Shocklach Ches W 166 F6
Shocklach Green
Ches W 166 F6
Shoeburyness Southend 70 C2
Sholden Kent 55 C11
Sholing Soton 32 E6
Sholing Common Soton 33 E7
Sholver Gtr Man 196 F3
Shootash Hants 32 C4
Shooters Hill London 68 D2
Shootersway Herts 85 D7
Shoot Hill Shrops 149 G8
Shop Corn 10 G3
Corn 24 E2
Devon 24 E5
Shop Corner Suff 108 E4
Shopford Cumb 240 C3
Shopnoller Som 43 G7
Shopp Hill W Sus 34 B6
Shopwyke W Sus 22 B5
Shore Gtr Man 196 D2
W Yorks 196 B2
Shore Bottom Devon 28 G2
Shoreditch London 67 C10
Som 28 C2
Shoregill Cumb 222 E5
Shoreham Kent 68 G4
Shoreham Beach W Sus 36 G2
Shoreham-by-Sea
W Sus 36 F2
Shore Mill Highld 301 C7
Shoresdean Northumb 273 F9
Shores Green Oxon 82 D5
Shoreside Shetland 313 J4
Shoreswood Northumb 273 F8
Shoreton Highld 300 C6
Shorley Hants 33 B9
Shorncliffe Camp Kent 55 F7
Shorncote Glos 81 F8
Shorne Kent 69 E7
Shorne Ridgeway Kent 69 E7
Shorne West Kent 69 E7
Shortacombe Devon 12 D6
Shortacross Corn 6 D5
Shortbridge E Sus 37 C7
Short Cross W Mid 133 G9
Shortfield Common Sur 49 E10
Shortgate E Sus 23 B7
Short Green Norf 141 F11
Shorthampton Oxon 100 G6
Shortheath Hants 49 F9
Sur 49 E10
Short Heath Derbys 152 G6
W Mid 133 C9
W Mid 133 E11
Shorthill Shrops 131 B8
Shortlands London 67 F11
Shortlanesend Corn 4 F6
Shortlees E Ayrs 257 B10
Shortmoor Devon 28 G2
Dorset 29 G7
Shorton Torbay 9 C7
Shortroods Renfs 267 B9
Shortstanding Glos 79 C9
Shortstown Bedford 103 B11
Short Street Wilts 45 D10
Shortwood Glos 80 F4
S Glos 61 D7
Shorwell IoW 20 E5
Shoscombe Bath 45 B8
Shoscombe Vale Bath 45 B8
Shotatton Shrops 149 E7
Shotesham Norf 142 D5
Shotgate Essex 88 G3
Shotley N Nhants 137 D8
Suff 108 D4
Shotley Bridge Durham 242 G3
Shotleyfield Northumb 242 G3
Shotley Gate Suff 108 E4
Shottenden Kent 54 C4
Shottermill Sur 49 G11
Shottery Warks 118 G3
Shotteswell Warks 101 B8
Shottisham Suff 108 C6
Shottle Derbys 170 F4
Shottlegate Derbys 170 F4
Shotton Durham 234 D4
Durham 234 F3
Flint 166 B4
Northumb 242 B6
Northumb 263 C8
Shotton Colliery
Durham 234 C3
Shotts N Lanark 269 C7
Shotwick Ches W 182 G4
Shouldham Norf 140 B3
Shouldham Thorpe Norf 140 B3
Shoulton Worcs 116 F6
Shover's Green E Sus 53 G7
Shraleybrook Staffs 168 F3
Shrawardine Shrops 149 F8
Shrawley Worcs 116 E6
Shreding Green Bucks 66 C4
Shrewley Warks 118 D4
Shrewley Common
Warks 118 D4
Shrewsbury Shrops 149 G9
Shrewton Wilts 46 E5
Shripney W Sus 22 C6
Shrivenham Oxon 63 B8
Shropham Norf 141 E9
Shroton or Iwerne Courtney
Dorset 30 E5
Shrub End Essex 107 G9
Shrubs Hill Sur 66 F3
Shrutherhill S Lanark 268 F5
Shucknall Hereford 97 C11
Shudy Camps Cambs 106 C2
Shulishadermor Highld 298 E4
Shulista Highld 298 B4
Shuna Ho Argyll 275 C8
Shurdington Glos 80 B6
Shurlock Row Windsor 65 E10
Shurnock Worcs 117 E10
Shurrery Highld 310 D4
Shurrery Lodge Highld 310 D4
Shurton Som 43 E8
Shustoke Warks 134 E4
Shute Devon 15 B11
Devon 26 G5
Shute End Wilts 31 B11
Shutford Oxon 101 C7
Shut Heath Staffs 151 E7
Shuthonger Glos 99 D7
Shutlanger W Nhants 120 G4
Shutta Corn 6 E5
Shutt Green Staffs 133 B7
Shuttington Warks 134 B5
Shuttlesfield Kent 55 E7
Shuttlewood Derbys 187 G7
Shuttleworth Gtr Man 195 D10
Shutton Hereford 98 F3
Shwt Bridgend 57 D11
Siabost bho Dheas
W Isles 304 D4
Siabost bho Thuath
W Isles 304 D4
Siadar W Isles 304 C5
Siadar Iarach W Isles 304 C5
Siadar Uarach W Isles 304 C5
Sibbaldbie Dumfries 248 F4
Sibbertoft W Nhants 136 G3
Sibdon Carwood Shrops 131 G8
Sibford Ferris Oxon 101 D7
Sibford Gower Oxon 101 D7
Sible Hedingham Essex 106 E5
Sibley's Green Essex 106 F2
Sibsey Lincs 174 E5
Sibsey Fen Side Lincs 174 E4
Sibson Cambs 137 D11
Leics 135 C7
Sibster Highld 310 D7
Sibthorpe Notts 172 F3
Notts 188 G2
Sibton Suff 127 D7
Sibton Green Suff 127 C7
Sicklesmere Suff 125 E7
Sicklinghall N Yorks 206 D3
Sid Devon 15 D8
Sidbrook Som 28 B3
Sidbury Devon 15 C8
Shrops 132 F3
Sidcot N Som 44 B2
Sidcup London 68 E3
Siddal W Yorks 196 C6
Siddick Cumb 228 E6
Siddington Ches E 184 G4
Glos 81 F8
Siddington Heath
Ches E 184 G4
Sidemoor Worcs 117 C9
Side of the Moor
Gtr Man 195 E8
Sidestrand Norf 160 B5
Sideway Stoke 168 G5
Sidford Devon 15 C8
Sidlesham W Sus 22 D5
Sidlesham Common
W Sus 22 C5
Sidley E Sus 38 F2
Sidlow Sur 51 D9
Sidmouth Devon 15 D8
Sidway Staffs 150 B5
Sigford Devon 13 G11
Sigglesthorne E Yorks 209 D9
Sighthill Edin 280 G3
Glasgow 268 B2
Sigingstone *= Tresigin*
V Glam 58 E3
Signet Oxon 82 C2
Sigwells Som 29 C10
Silchester Hants 64 G6
Sildinis W Isles 305 G4
Sileby Leics 153 F11
Silecroft Cumb 210 C2
Silfield Norf 142 D2
Silford Devon 24 B6
Silian Ceredig 111 G11
Silkstead Hants 32 C6
Silkstone S Yorks 197 F9
Silkstone Common
S Yorks 197 G9
Silk Willoughby Lincs 173 G9
Silloth Cumb 238 G4
Sills Northumb 251 C8
Sillyearn Moray 302 D5
Siloh Carms 94 D4
Silpho N Yorks 227 G9
Silsden W Yorks 204 D6
Silsoe C Beds 103 D11
Silton Dorset 30 B3
Silverburn Midloth 270 C4
Silverdale Lancs 211 E9
Staffs 168 F4
Silverdale Green Lancs 211 E9
Silver End Essex 88 B4
W Mid 133 F8
Silvergate Norf 160 D3
Silver Green Norf 142 E5
Silverhill E Sus 38 E3
Silver Hill E Sus 38 B2
Silverhill Park E Sus 38 E4
Silver Knap Som 29 C11
Silverknowes Edin 280 F4
Silverley's Green Suff 126 B5
Silvermuir S Lanark 269 F8
Silverstone W Nhants 102 C3
Silver Street Glos 80 E3
Kent 69 G11
Som 27 C11
Som 44 G4
Worcs 117 B11
Silverton Devon 27 G7
W Dunb 277 F8
Silvertonhill S Lanark 268 E4
Silvertown London 68 D2
Silverwell Corn 4 F4
Silvington Shrops 116 B2
Silwick Shetland 313 J4
Sim Hill S Yorks 197 G9
Simister Gtr Man 195 F10
Simmondley Derbys 185 C8
Simm's Cross Halton 183 D8
Simm's Lane End Mers 194 G4
Simonburn Northumb 241 C9
Simonsbath Som 41 F9
Simonsburrow Devon 27 D10
Simonside T&W 243 E8
Simonstone Lancs 203 G11
N Yorks 223 G7
Simprim Borders 272 F6
Simpson M Keynes 103 D7
Pembs 72 B5
Simpson Cross Pembs 72 B5
Simpson Green W Yorks 205 F9
Sinclair's Hill Borders 272 E6
Sinclairston E Ayrs 257 F11
Sinclairtown Fife 280 C5
Sinderby N Yorks 214 C6
Sinderhope Northumb 241 G8
Sinderland Green
Gtr Man 184 C2
Sindlesham Wokingham 65 F9
Sinfin Derby 152 C6
Sinfin Moor Derby 153 C7
Singdean Borders 250 C3
Singleborough Bucks 102 E5
Single Hill Bath 45 B8
Singleton Lancs 202 F3
W Sus 34 E5
Singlewell Kent 69 E7
Singret Wrex 166 D4
Sinkhurst Green Kent 53 E10
Sinnahard Aberds 292 B6
Sinnington N Yorks 216 B4
Sinton Worcs 116 E6
Sinton Green Worcs 116 E6
Sion Hill Bath 61 F8
Sipson London 66 D5
Sirhowy Bl Gwent 77 C11
Sisland Norf 142 D6
Sissinghurst Kent 53 F9
Sisterpath Borders 272 F5
Siston S Glos 61 D7
Sithney Corn 2 D4
Sithney Common Corn 2 D4
Sithney Green Corn 2 D4
Sittingbourne Kent 70 G2
Six Ashes Staffs 132 F5
Six Bells Bl Gwent 78 E2
Sixhills Lincs 189 D11
Six Hills Leics 154 E2
Sixmile Kent 54 E6
Six Mile Bottom Cambs 123 F11
Sixpenny Handley Dorset 31 D7
Sizewell Suff 127 E9
Skaigh Devon 13 C8
Skail Highld 308 E7
Skaill Orkney 314 C4
Orkney 314 E2
Orkney 314 F5
Skares E Ayrs 258 F2
Skateraw E Loth 282 F4
Skaw Shetland 312 B8
Shetland 312 G7
Skeabost Highld 298 E4
Skeabrae Orkney 314 D2
Skeeby N Yorks 224 E4
Skeete Kent 54 E6
Skeffington Leics 136 C4
Skeffling E Yorks 201 D11
Skegby Notts 171 C7
Notts 188 G3
Skegness Lincs 175 C9
Skelberry Shetland 313 G6
Shetland 313 M5
Skelbo Highld 309 K7
Skelbo Street Highld 309 K7
Skelbrooke S Yorks 198 E4
Skeldyke Lincs 156 B6
Skelfhill Borders 249 C11
Skellingthorpe Lincs 188 G6
Skellister Shetland 313 H6
Skellorn Green Ches E 184 E6
Skellow S Yorks 198 E4
Skelmanthorpe W Yorks 197 E8
Skelmersdale Lancs 194 F3
Skelmonae Aberds 303 F8
Skelmorlie N Ayrs 266 B3
Skelmuir Aberds 303 E9
Skelpick Highld 308 D7
Skelton Cumb 230 D4
E Yorks 199 B9
N Yorks 223 E11
Redcar 226 B3
York 207 B7
Skelton-on-Ure
N Yorks 215 F7
Skelwick Orkney 314 B4
Skelwith Bridge Cumb 220 E6
Skendleby Lincs 174 B6
Skendleby Psalter Lincs 190 G6
Skene Ho Aberds 293 C9
Skenfrith Mon 97 G9
Skerne E Yorks 208 B6
Skerne Park Darl 224 C5
Skeroblingarry Argyll 255 E8
Skerray Highld 308 C6
Skerricha Highld 306 D7
Skerryford Pembs 72 C6
Skerton Lancs 211 G9
Sketchley Leics 135 E8
Sketty Swansea 56 C6
Skewen *= Sgiwen* Neath 57 B8
Skewes Corn 5 B9
Skewsby N Yorks 216 E2
Skeyton Norf 160 D4
Skeyton Corner Norf 160 D5
Skiag Bridge Highld 307 G7
Skibo Castle Highld 309 L7
Skidbrooke Lincs 190 C6
Skidbrooke North End
Lincs 190 B6
Skidby E Yorks 208 G6
Skilgate Som 27 B7
Skillington Lincs 155 D7
Skinburness Cumb 238 F4
Skinflats Falk 279 E8
Skinidin Highld 298 E2
Skinner's Bottom Corn 4 F4
Skinners Green W Berks 64 F2
Skinnet Highld 308 C5
Skinningrove Redcar 226 B4
Skipness Argyll 255 B9
Skippool Lancs 202 E3
Skiprigg Cumb 230 B3
Skipsea E Yorks 209 B9
Skipsea Brough E Yorks 209 C9
Skipton N Yorks 204 C5
Skipton-on-Swale
N Yorks 215 D7
Skipwith N Yorks 207 F9
Skirbeck Lincs 174 G4
Skirbeck Quarter Lincs 174 G4
Skirethorns N Yorks 213 G9
Skirlaugh E Yorks 209 F8
Skirling Borders 260 B3
Skirmett Bucks 65 B9
Skirpenbeck E Yorks 207 B10
Skirwith Cumb 231 E8
Skirza Highld 310 C7
Skitby Cumb 239 D10
Skitham Lancs 202 E4
Skittle Green Bucks 84 E3
Skulamus Highld 295 C8
Skullomie Highld 308 C6
Skyborry Green Shrops 114 C5
Skye Green Essex 107 G7
Skye of Curr Highld 301 G9
Skyfog Pembs 90 F6
Skyreholme N Yorks 213 G11
Slack Derbys 170 C4
W Yorks 196 B3
W Yorks 196 D5
Slackcote Gtr Man 196 F3
Slackhall Derbys 185 E9
Slackhead Moray 302 C4
Slack Head Cumb 211 D9
Slackholme End Lincs 191 G8
Slacks of Cairnbanno
Aberds 303 E8
Slad Glos 80 D5
Sladbrook Glos 98 F5
Slade Devon 27 F10
Devon 40 D4
Kent 54 C2
Pembs 72 B6
Slade End Oxon 83 G9
Slade Green London 68 D4
Slade Heath Staffs 133 B8
Slade Hooton S Yorks 187 D8
Sladen Green Hants 48 C2
Sladesbridge Corn 10 G6
Slades Green Worcs 99 E7
Slaggyford Northumb 240 G5
Slaidburn Lancs 203 C10
Slaithwaite W Yorks 196 E5
Slaley Derbys 170 D3
Northumb 241 F11
Slamannan Falk 279 G7
Slape Cross Som 43 F10
Slapewath Redcar 226 B2
Slapton Bucks 103 G8
Devon 8 G6
W Nhants 102 B2
Slateford Edin 280 G4
Slate Haugh Moray 302 C4
Slatepit Dale Derbys 170 B4
Slattocks Gtr Man 195 F11
Slaugham W Sus 36 B3
Slaughterbridge Corn 11 D8
Slaughterford Wilts 61 E10
Slaughter Hill Ches E 168 D2
Slawston Leics 136 E5
Slay Pits S Yorks 199 F7
Sleaford Hants 49 F10
Lincs 173 F9
Sleagill Cumb 221 B11
Sleap Shrops 149 D9
Sleapford Telford 150 F2
Sleapshyde Herts 86 D2
Sleastary Highld 309 K6
Slebech Pembs 73 B8
Sledge Green Worcs 98 E6
Sledmere E Yorks 217 G8
Sleeches Cross E Sus 52 G5
Sleepers Hill Hants 33 B7
Sleetbeck Cumb 240 B2
Sleet Moor Derbys 170 E6
Sleight Dorset 18 B5
Sleights N Yorks 227 D7
Slepe Dorset 18 C4
Sliabhna h-Airde
W Isles 296 F3
Slickly Highld 310 C6
Sliddery N Ayrs 255 E10
Slideslow Worcs 117 C9
Sligachan Hotel Highld 294 C6
Sligneach Argyll 288 G4
Sligrachan Argyll 276 C3
Slimbridge Glos 80 E2
Slindon Staffs 150 C6
W Sus 35 F7
Slinfold W Sus 50 G6
Sling Glos 79 D9
Gwyn 163 B10
Slingsby N Yorks 216 E3
Slioch Aberds 302 F5
Slip End C Beds 85 B9
Herts 104 D5
Slippery Ford W Yorks 204 E6
Slipton N Nhants 121 B9
Slitting Mill Staffs 151 F10
Slochd Highld 301 G8
Slockavullin Argyll 275 D9
Slogan Moray 302 E3
Sloley Norf 160 E5
Sloncombe Devon 13 D10
Sloothby Lincs 191 G7
Slough Slough 66 D3
Slough Green Som 28 C3
W Sus 36 B3
Slough Hill Suff 125 G7
Sluggan Highld 301 G8
Sluggans Highld 298 E4
Slumbay Highld 295 B10
Sly Corner Kent 54 G3
Slyfield Sur 50 C3
Slyne Lancs 211 F9
Smailholm Borders 262 B4
Smallbridge Gtr Man 196 D2
Smallbrook Devon 14 B3
Glos 79 E9
Smallburgh Norf 160 E6
Smallburn Aberds 303 E10
E Ayrs 258 D5
Smalldale Derbys 185 E11
Derbys 185 F9
Small Dole W Sus 36 E2
Small End Lincs 174 D6
Smalley Derbys 170 G6
Smalley Common
Derbys 170 G6
Smalley Green Derbys 170 G6
Smallfield Sur 51 E10
Smallford Herts 85 D11
Small Heath W Mid 134 F2
Smallholm Dumfries 238 B4
Small Hythe Kent 53 G11
Smallmarsh Devon 25 C10
Smallrice Staffs 151 C9
Smallridge Devon 28 G4
Smallshaw Gtr Man 196 G2
Smallthorne Stoke 168 E5
Small Way Som 44 G6
Smallwood Ches E 168 C4
Worcs 117 D10
Smallwood Green Suff 125 F8
Smallwood Hey Lancs 202 D3
Smallworth Norf 141 G10
Smannell Hants 47 D11
Smardale Cumb 222 D4
Smarden Kent 53 E11
Smarden Bell Kent 53 E11
Smart's Hill Kent 52 E4
Smaull Argyll 274 G3
Smeatharpe Devon 27 E11
Smeaton Fife 280 C5
Smeeth Kent 54 F5
Smeeton Westerby
Leics 136 E3
Smelthouses N Yorks 214 G3
Smercleit W Isles 297 K3
Smerral Highld 310 F5
Smestow Staffs 133 E7
Smethcott Shrops 131 D9
Smethwick W Mid 133 F10
Smethwick Green
Ches E 168 C4
Smirisary Highld 289 B8
Smisby Derbys 152 F6
Smite Hill Worcs 117 F7
Smithaleigh Devon 7 D11
Smithbrook W Sus 34 C6
Smith End Green Worcs 116 G5
Smithfield Cumb 239 D10
Smith Green Lancs 202 C5
Smithies S Yorks 197 F11
Smithincott Devon 27 E9
Smithley S Yorks 197 G11
Smith's End Herts 105 D8
Smiths Green Ches E 184 G4
Smith's Green Ches E 168 E3
Essex 105 G11
Essex 106 C3
Smithston Aberds 302 G5
Smithstown Highld 299 B7
Smithton Highld 301 E7
Smithwood Green Suff 125 G8
Smithy Bridge Gtr Man 196 D2
Smithy Gate Flint 181 F11
Smithy Green Ches E 184 G2
Gtr Man 184 D5
Smithy Houses Derbys 170 F5
Smithy Lane Ends Lancs 194 E2
Smock Alley W Sus 35 D9
Smockington Leics 135 F9
Smoky Row Bucks 84 D4
Smoogro Orkney 314 F3
Smug Oak Herts 85 E10
Smyrton S Ayrs 244 G4
Smythe's Green Essex 88 B6
Snagshall E Sus 38 C3
Snaigow House Perth 286 C4
Snailbeach Shrops 131 C7
Snails Hill Som 29 E7
Snailswell Herts 104 E3
Snailwell Cambs 124 D2
Snainton N Yorks 217 C8
Snaisgill Durham 232 F5
Snaith E Yorks 198 C6
Snape N Yorks 214 C5
Suff 127 F7
Snape Green Lancs 193 E11
Snape Hill Derbys 186 F5
S Yorks 198 G2
Snapper Devon 40 G5
Snaresbrook London 67 B11
Snarestone Leics 134 B6
Snarford Lincs 189 E9
Snargate Kent 39 B7
Snarraness Shetland 313 H4
Snatchwood Torf 78 E3
Snave Kent 39 B8
Sneachill Worcs 117 G8
Snead Powys 130 E6
Snead Common Worcs 116 D4
Sneads Green Worcs 117 D7
Sneath Common Norf 142 F3
Sneaton N Yorks 227 D7
Sneatonthorpe N Yorks 227 D8
Snedshill Telford 132 B4
Sneinton Nottingham 153 B11
Snelland Lincs 189 E9
Snelston Derbys 169 G11
Snetterton Norf 141 E9
Snettisham Norf 158 C3
Sneyd Green Stoke 168 F5
Sneyd Park Bristol 60 D5
Snibston Leics 153 G8
Snig's End Glos 98 F5
Snipeshill Kent 70 G2
Sniseabhal W Isles 297 H3
Snitter Northumb 252 C2
Snitterby Lincs 189 C7
Snitterfield Warks 118 F4
Snitterton Derbys 170 C3
Snitton Shrops 115 B11
Snittongate Shrops 115 B11
Snodhill Hereford 96 C6
Snodland Kent 69 G7
Snods Edge Northumb 242 G3
Snowden Hill S Yorks 197 G9
Snowdown Kent 55 C8
Snow End Herts 105 E8
Snow Hill Ches E 167 E10
W Yorks 197 C10
Snow Lea W Yorks 196 D5
Snowshill Glos 99 E11
Snow Street Norf 141 G11
Snydale W Yorks 198 D2
Soake Hants 33 E11
Soar Anglesey 178 G5
Carms 94 F2
Devon 9 G9
Gwyn 146 B2
Powys 95 E9
Soar-y-Mynydd Ceredig 112 G5
Soberton Hants 33 D10
Soberton Heath Hants 33 E10
Sockbridge Cumb 230 F6
Sockburn Darl 224 D6
Sockety Dorset 29 F7
Sodom Denb 181 G9
Shetland 313 G7
Wilts 62 C4
Sodylt Bank Shrops 148 B6
Soham Cambs 123 C11
Soham Cotes Cambs 123 B11
Soho London 67 C9
Som 45 D7
W Mid 133 F10
Solas W Isles 296 D4
Soldon Cross Devon 24 E4
Soldridge Hants 49 G7
Sole Street Kent 54 D5

Sole Street continued
Kent 69 F7
Solfach =Solva Pembs 90 G5
Solihull W Mid 118 B2
Solihull Lodge W Mid 117 B11
Sollers Dilwyn Hereford 115 F8
Sollers Hope Hereford 98 E2
Sollom Lancs 194 D3
Solva =Solfach Pembs 90 G5
Somerby Leics 154 G5
Lincs 200 F5
Somercotes Derbys 170 E6
Somerdale Bath 61 F7
Somerford BCP 19 C9
Ches E 168 B4
Staffs 133 B7
Somerford Keynes Glos 81 G8
Somerley W Sus 22 D4
Somerleyton Suff 143 D9
Somersal Herbert
Derbys 152 B2
Somersby Lincs 190 G4
Somersham Cambs 123 B7
Suff 107 B11
Somers Town London 67 C9
Ptsmth 21 B8
Somerton Newport 59 B10
Oxon 101 F9
Som 29 B7
Suff 124 G6
Somerton Hill Som 29 B7
Somerwood Shrops 149 G11
Sompting W Sus 35 G11
Sompting Abbotts
W Sus 35 F11
Sonning Wokingham 65 D9
Sonning Common Oxon 65 C8
Sonning Eye Oxon 65 D9
Sontley Wrex 166 F4
Sookholme Notts 171 B8
Sopley Hants 19 B9
Sopwell Herts 85 D11
Sopworth Wilts 61 B10
Sorbie Dumfries 236 E6
Sordale Highld 310 C5
Sorisdale Argyll 288 C4
Sorley Devon 8 F4
Sorn E Ayrs 258 D3
Sornhill E Ayrs 258 C2
Sortat Highld 310 C6
Sotby Lincs 190 F2
Sothall S Yorks 186 E6
Sots Hole Lincs 173 C10
Sotterley Suff 143 G9
Soudley Shrops 131 E9
Shrops 150 D4
Soughley S Yorks 197 G7
Soughton =Sychdyn
Flint 166 B2
Soulbury Bucks 103 F7
Soulby Cumb 222 C4
Cumb 230 F5
Souldern Oxon 101 E10
Souldrop Bedford 121 E9
Sound Ches E 167 F10
Shetland 313 H5
Shetland 313 J6
Sound Heath Ches E 167 F10
Soundwell S Glos 60 D6
Sourhope Borders 263 E8
Sourin Orkney 314 C4
Sourlie N Ayrs 266 G6
Sour Nook Cumb 230 C3
Sourton Devon 12 C6
Soutergate Cumb 210 C4
South Acre Norf 158 G6
South Acton London 67 D7
South Alkham Kent 55 E8
Southall London 66 C6
South Allington Devon 9 G10
South Alloa Falk 279 C7
Southam Cumb 219 C9
Glos 99 F9
Warks 119 E8
South Ambersham
W Sus 34 C6
Southampton Soton 32 E6
South Anston S Yorks 187 E8
South Ascot Windsor 66 F2
South Ashford Kent 54 E4
South Auchmachar
Aberds 303 E9
Southay Som 28 D6
South Baddesley Hants 20 B3
South Ballachulish
Highld 284 B4
South Balloch S Ayrs 245 D8
South Bank Redcar 234 G6
York 207 C7
South Barrow Som 29 B10
South Beach Northumb 243 B8
South Beach =Marian-y-de
Gwyn 145 C7
South Beddington
London 67 G9
South Benfleet Essex 69 B9
South Bents T&W 243 E10
South Bersted W Sus 22 C6
South Blainslie
Borders 271 G10
South Bockhampton BCP 19 B9
Southborough Kent 52 E5
London 67 F7
London 68 F2
Southbourne BCP 19 C8
W Sus 22 B3
South Bramwith
S Yorks 198 E6
South Brent Devon 8 D3
South Brewham Som 45 F8
South Bromley London 67 C11
Southbrook Wilts 45 G10
South Broomage Falk 279 E7
South Broomhill
Northumb 252 D6
Southburgh Norf 141 C9
South Burlingham Norf 143 B7
Southburn E Yorks 208 C5
South Cadbury Som 29 B10
South Cairn Dumfries 236 C1
South Carlton Lincs 189 F7
Notts 187 E9
South Carne Corn 11 E10
South Cave E Yorks 208 G4
South Cerney Glos 81 F8
South Chailey E Sus 36 D5
South Chard Som 28 F4
South Charlton
Northumb 264 E5
South Cheriton Som 29 C11
Southchurch Southend 70 B2
South Church Durham 233 F10
South Cliffe E Yorks 208 F3
South Clifton Notts 188 G4
South Clunes Highld 300 E5
South Cockerington
Lincs 190 D5
South Common Devon 28 G4
Southcoombe Oxon 100 F6
South Cornelly Bridgend 57 E10
South Corriegills
N Ayrs 256 C2
South Corrielaw
Dumfries 248 G5
Southcote Reading 65 E7
Southcott Corn 11 B9
Devon 24 D6
Wilts 47 B7
Southcourt Bucks 84 C4
South Cove Suff 143 G9
South Creagan Argyll 289 E11
South Creake Norf 159 B7
Southcrest Worcs 117 D10
South Crosland
W Yorks 196 E6
South Croxton Leics 154 G3
South Croydon London 67 G10
South Cuil Highld 298 C3
South Dalton E Yorks 208 D5
South Darenth Kent 68 F5
Southdean Borders 250 B4
Southdene Mers 182 B6
South Denes Norf 143 C10
Southdown Bath 61 G8
Corn 7 E8
South Down Hants 33 C7
Som 28 E2
South Duffield N Yorks 207 G9
South Dunn Highld 310 D5
South Earlswood Sur 51 D9
Southease E Sus 36 F6
South Elkington Lincs 190 D3
South Elmsall W Yorks 198 E3
South Elphinstone
E Loth 281 G7
Southend Argyll 255 G7
Bucks 65 B9
Glos 80 F2
London 67 E11
Oxon 83 E9
W Berks 64 D2
W Berks 64 E5
Wilts 63 E7
South End Bedford 103 B10
Bucks 103 F7
Cumb 210 G4
E Yorks 209 E9
Hants 31 D10
South-end Herts 86 B6
South End N Lincs 200 C6
Norf 141 E9
Southend-on-Sea
Southend 69 B11
Southerhouse Shetland 313 K5
Southerly Devon 12 D6
Southernby Cumb 230 D3
Southern Cross Brighton 36 F3
Southernden Kent 53 D11
Southerndown V Glam 57 G11
Southerness Dumfries 237 D11
Southern Green Herts 104 E6
South Erradale Highld 299 B7
Southery Norf 140 E2
Southey Green Essex 106 E5
South Fambridge Essex 88 F5
South Farnborough
Hants 49 C11
South Fawley W Berks 63 C11
South Ferriby N Lincs 200 C3
Southfield Northumb 243 B7
South Field E Yorks 200 B4
Windsor 66 D3
Southfields London 67 E9
Thurrock 69 C7
Southfleet Kent 68 E6
South Flobbets Aberds 303 F7
Southford IoW 20 F6
South Garth Shetland 312 D7
South Garvan Highld 289 B11
Southgate Ceredig 111 A11
London 86 G3
Norf 159 C7
Norf 160 E2
Swansea 56 D5
W Sus 51 F9
South Glendale W Isles 297 K3
South Gluss Shetland 312 F5
South Godstone Sur 51 D11
South Gorley Hants 31 E11
South Gosforth T&W 242 D6
South Green Essex 87 G11
Essex 89 B8
Kent 69 G11
Norf 157 F10
Norf 159 G11
Suff 126 B3
South Gyle Edin 280 G3
South-haa Shetland 312 E5
South Hackney London 67 C11
South Ham Hants 48 C6
South Hampstead London 67 C9
South Hanningfield Essex 88 F2
South Harefield London 66 B5
South Harrow London 66 B6
South Harting W Sus 34 D3
South Hatfield Herts 86 D2
South Hayling Hants 21 B10
South Hazelrigg
Northumb 264 C3
South Heath Bucks 84 E6
Essex 89 B10
South Heighton E Sus 23 E7
South-heog Shetland 312 E5
South Hetton Durham 234 B3
South Hiendley
W Yorks 197 E11
South Hill Corn 12 G2
N Som 43 B10
Pembs 72 C4
South Hinksey Oxon 83 E8
South Hole Devon 24 C2
South Holme N Yorks 216 D3
South Holmwood Sur 51 D7
South Hornchurch
London 68 C4
South Huish Devon 8 G3
South Hykeham Lincs 172 C6
South Hylton T&W 243 F9
Southill C Beds 104 C3
Dorset 17 E9
Southington Hants 48 D4
South Kelsey Lincs 189 B8
South Kensington London 67 D9
South Kessock Highld 300 E6
South Killingholme
N Lincs 201 D7
South Kilvington
N Yorks 215 C8
South Kilworth Leics 136 G2
South Kirkby W Yorks 198 E2
South Kirkton Aberds 293 C9
South Kiscadale N Ayrs 256 D2
South Knighton Devon 14 G2
Leicester 136 C2
South Kyme Lincs 173 F11
South Lambeth London 67 D10
South Lancing W Sus 35 G11
Southlands Dorset 17 F9
South Lane S Yorks 197 F9
Southleigh Devon 15 C10
South Leigh Oxon 82 D5
South Leverton Notts 188 E3
South Littleton Worcs 99 B11
South Lopham Norf 141 G10
South Luffenham
Rutland 137 C8
South Malling E Sus 36 E6
Southmarsh Som 45 G8
South Marston Swindon 63 B7
Southmead Bristol 60 D5
South Merstham Sur 51 C9
South Middleton
Northumb 263 E11
South Milford N Yorks 206 G5
South Millbrex Aberds 303 E8
South Milton Devon 8 G4
South Mimms Herts 86 E2
Southminster Essex 89 F7
South Molton Devon 26 B2
Southmoor Oxon 82 F5
South Moor Durham 242 G5
South Moreton Oxon 64 B5
South Mundham W Sus 22 C5
South Muskham Notts 172 D3
South Newbald E Yorks 208 F4
South Newbarns Cumb 210 F4
South Newington Oxon 101 E8
South Newsham
Northumb 243 B8
South Newton Wilts 46 G5
South Normanton
Derbys 170 D6
South Norwood London 67 F10
South Nutfield Sur 51 D10
South Ockendon Thurrock 68 C5
Southoe Cambs 122 E3
Southolt Suff 126 D3
South Ormsby Lincs 190 F5
Southorpe Pboro 137 C11
South Ossett W Yorks 197 D9
South Otterington
N Yorks 215 B7
Southover Dorset 17 C8
E Sus 36 F6
E Sus 37 B11
South Owersby Lincs 189 C9
Southowram W Yorks 196 C6
South Oxhey Herts 85 G10
South Park Sur 51 D8
South Pelaw Durham 243 G7
South Perrott Dorset 29 F7
South Petherton Som 28 D6
South Petherwin Corn 12 E2
South Pickenham Norf 141 C7
South Pill Corn 7 D8
South Pool Devon 8 G5
South Poorton Dorset 16 B6
Southport Mers 193 D10
South Port Argyll 284 E4
Southpunds Shetland 313 L6
South Quilquox Aberds 303 F8
South Radworthy Devon 41 G9
South Rauceby Lincs 173 F8
South Raynham Norf 159 E7
South Reddish Gtr Man 184 C5
Southrepps Norf 160 B5
South Reston Lincs 190 E6
Southrey Lincs 173 B10
Southrop Glos 81 E11
Oxon 101 E7
Southrope Hants 49 E7
South Ruislip London 66 B6
South Runcton Norf 140 B2
South Scarle Notts 172 C4
Southsea Ptsmth 21 B8
Wrex 166 E4
South Shian Argyll 289 E11
South Shields T&W 243 D9
South Shore Blackpool 202 G2
South Side Durham 233 F8
Orkney 314 D5
South Somercotes Lincs 190 C6
South Stainley N Yorks 214 G6
South Stainmore Cumb 222 C6
South Stanley Durham 242 G5
South Stifford Thurrock 68 D6
Southstoke Bath 61 G8
South Stoke Oxon 64 C6
W Sus 35 F8
South Stour Kent 54 F4
South Street E Sus 36 D5
Kent 54 B5
Kent 68 G6
Kent 69 G10
Kent 70 F6
London 52 B2
South Tawton Devon 13 C9
South Tehidy Corn 4 G3
South Thoresby Lincs 190 F6
South Tidworth Wilts 47 D8
South Tottenham
London 67 B10
Southtown Norf 143 B10
Orkney 314 G4
Som 28 D4
Som 44 F5
South Town Devon 14 E5
Hants 49 F7
South Twerton Bath 61 G8
South Ulverston Cumb 210 D6
South View Hants 48 C6
Southville Devon 8 G4
Torf 78 F3
South Voxter Shetland 313 G5
Southwaite Cumb 230 C4
South Walsham Norf 161 G7
Southwark London 67 D10
South Warnborough
Hants 49 D8
Southwater W Sus 35 B11
Southwater Street
W Sus 35 B11
Southway Plym 7 C9
Som 44 E4
South Weald Essex 87 G9
South Weirs Hants 32 G3
Southwell Dorset 17 G9
Notts 172 E2
South Weston Oxon 84 F2
South Wheatley Corn 11 C10
Notts 188 D3
South Whiteness
Shetland 313 J5
Southwick Hants 33 F10
N Nhants 137 E10
Som 43 D11
T&W 243 F9
Wilts 45 B10
W Sus 36 F2
South Widcombe Bath 44 B5
South Wigston Leics 135 D11
South Willesborough
Kent 54 E4
South Willingham
Lincs 189 E11
South Wimbledon London 67 E9
South Wingate Durham 234 E4
South Wingfield Derbys 170 D5
South Witham Lincs 155 F8
Southwold Suff 127 B10
South Wonford Devon 24 F5
South Wonston Hants 48 F3
Southwood Derbys 153 E7
Hants 49 B10
Norf 143 B7
Som 44 G5
Worcs 116 E4
South Woodford London 86 G6
South Woodham Ferrers
Essex 88 F4
South Wootton Norf 158 E2
South Wraxall Wilts 61 G10
South Yardley W Mid 134 G2
South Yarrows Highld 310 E7
South Yeo Devon 25 G8
South Zeal Devon 13 C9
Soval Lodge W Isles 304 F5
Sowber Gate N Yorks 215 B7
Sowerby N Yorks 215 C8
W Yorks 196 C4
Sowerby Bridge
W Yorks 196 C5
Sowerby Row Cumb 230 D3
Sower Carr Lancs 202 E3
Sowley Green Suff 124 G4
Sowood W Yorks 196 D5
Sowood Green W Yorks 196 D5
Sowton Devon 14 C5
Sowton Barton Devon 14 D2
Soyal Highld 309 K5
Soyland Town W Yorks 196 C4
Spacey Houses N Yorks 206 C2
Spa Common Norf 160 C5
Spalding Lincs 156 E4
Spaldington E Yorks 207 G11
Spaldwick Cambs 122 C2
Spalford Notts 172 B4
Spanby Lincs 155 B11
Spango Invclyd 276 G4
Spanish Green Hants 49 B7
Sparham Norf 159 F11
Sparhamhill Norf 159 F11
Spark Bridge Cumb 210 C6
Sparkbrook W Mid 133 G11
Sparkford Som 29 B10
Sparkhill W Mid 133 G11
Sparkwell Devon 7 D11
Sparl Shetland 312 G5
Sparnon Corn 1 E3
Sparnon Gate Corn 4 G3
Sparrow Green Norf 159 G9
Sparrow Hill Som 44 C2
Sparrowpit Derbys 185 E9
Sparrow's Green E Sus 52 G6
Sparsholt Hants 48 G2
Oxon 63 B10
Spartylea Northumb 232 B3
Spath Staffs 151 B11
Spaunton N Yorks 226 G4
Spaxton Som 43 F8
Spean Bridge Highld 290 E4
Spear Hill W Sus 35 D10
Spearywell Hants 32 B4
Speckington Som 29 C9
Speed Gate Kent 68 F5
Speedwell Bristol 60 E6
Speen Bucks 84 F4
W Berks 64 F3
Speeton N Yorks 218 E2
Speke Mers 182 E6
Speldhurst Kent 52 E5
Spellbrook Herts 87 B7
Spelsbury Oxon 101 G7
Spelter Bridgend 57 C11
Spen W Yorks 197 B7
Spencers Wood
Wokingham 65 F8
Spen Green Ches E 168 C4
Spennells Worcs 116 C6
Spennithorne N Yorks 214 B2
Spennymoor Durham 233 E11
Spernall Warks 117 E11
Spetchley Worcs 117 G7
Spetisbury Dorset 30 G6
Spexhall Suff 143 G7
Speybank Highld 291 C10
Spey Bay Moray 302 C3
Speybridge Highld 301 G10
Speyview Moray 302 E2
Spillardsford Aberds 303 D10
Spilsby Lincs 174 B6
Spindlestone Northumb 264 C5
Spinkhill Derbys 187 F7
Spinney Hill W Nhants 120 E5
Spinney Hills Leicester 136 C2
Spinningdale Highld 309 L6
Spion Kop Notts 171 B9
Spirthill Wilts 62 D3
Spital Mers 182 E4
Windsor 66 D3
Spitalbrook Herts 86 D5
Spitalfields London 67 C10
Spitalhill Derbys 169 F11
Spital Hill S Yorks 187 C10
Spital in the Street
Lincs 189 D7
Spital Tongues T&W 242 D6
Spithurst E Sus 36 D6
Spittal Dumfries 236 D5
E Loth 281 F9
E Yorks 207 C11
Highld 310 D5
Northumb 273 E10
Pembs 91 G9
Stirling 277 D10
Spittalfield Perth 286 C5
Spittal Houses S Yorks 186 B5
Spittal of Glenmuick
Aberds 292 E5
Spittal of Glenshee
Perth 292 F3
Spittlegate Lincs 155 C8
Spixworth Norf 160 F4
Splatt Corn 10 F4
Corn 11 D10
Devon 25 F10
Som 43 F8
Splayne's Green E Sus 36 C6
Splott Cardiff 59 D7
Spofforth N Yorks 206 C3
Spondon Derby 153 B8
Spon End W Mid 118 B6
Spon Green Flint 166 C3
Spooner Row Norf 141 D11
Spoonleygate Shrops 132 D6
Sporle Norf 158 G6
Spotland Bridge
Gtr Man 195 E11
Spott E Loth 282 F3
Spratton W Nhants 120 C4
Spreakley Sur 49 E10
Spreyton Devon 13 B9
Spriddlestone Devon 7 E10
Spridlington Lincs 189 E8
Sprig's Alley Oxon 84 F3
Springbank Glos 99 G8
Spring Bank Cumb 229 G10
Springboig Glasgow 268 C3
Springbourne BCP 19 C8
Springburn Glasgow 268 B2
Spring Cottage Leics 152 F6
Spring End N Yorks 223 F9
Springfield Argyll 275 F11
Caerph 77 F11
Dumfries 239 D8
Essex 88 D2
Fife 287 F7
Gtr Man 194 F5
Highld 300 C6
M Keynes 103 D7
Moray 301 D10
W Mid 133 D8
W Mid 133 F9
W Mid 133 G11
Springfields Stoke 168 G5
Spring Gardens Som 45 D9
Spring Green Lancs 204 E4
Spring Grove London 67 D7
Springhead Gtr Man 196 G3
Springhill E Renf 267 D10
IoW 20 B6
N Lanark 269 D7
Staffs 133 B11
Staffs 133 C9
Spring Hill Gtr Man 196 F2
Lancs 195 B8
W Mid 133 D7
Springholm Dumfries 237 C10
Springkell Dumfries 239 B7
Spring Park London 67 F11
Springside N Ayrs 257 B9
Springthorpe Lincs 188 D5
Spring Vale S Yorks 197 G9
Spring Valley IoM 192 E4
Springwell Essex 105 C10
T&W 243 F7
T&W 243 F9
Springwells Dumfries 248 E3
Sproatley E Yorks 209 G9
Sproston Green Ches W 168 B2
Sprotbrough S Yorks 198 G4
Sproughton Suff 108 C2
Sprouston Borders 263 B7
Sprowston Norf 160 G4
Sproxton Leics 155 E7
N Yorks 216 C2
Sprunston Cumb 230 B3
Spunhill Shrops 149 C8
Spurlands End Bucks 84 F5
Spurstow Ches E 167 D9
Spurtree Shrops 116 D2
Spynie Moray 302 C2
Spyway Dorset 16 C6
Square and Compass
Pembs 91 E7
Squires Gate Blackpool 202 G2
Sraid Ruadh Argyll 288 E1
Srannda W Isles 296 C6
Sronphadruig Lodge
Perth 291 F9
Stableford Shrops 132 D5
Staffs 150 B6
Stacey Bank S Yorks 186 C3
Stackhouse N Yorks 212 F6
Stackpole Pembs 73 F7
Stackpole Quay Pembs 73 F7
Stacksford Norf 141 E11
Stacksteads Lancs 195 C10
Stackyard Green Suff 107 B9
Staddiscombe Plym 7 E10
Staddlethorpe E Yorks 199 B10
Staddon Devon 24 C3
Devon 24 G5
Staden Derbys 185 G9
Stadhampton Oxon 83 F10
Stadhlaigearraidh
W Isles 297 H3
Stadmorslow Staffs 168 D5
Staffield Cumb 230 C6
Staffin Highld 298 C4
Stafford Staffs 151 E8
Stafford Park Telford 132 B4
Stafford's Corner Essex 89 B7
Stafford's Green Dorset 29 C10
Stagbatch Hereford 115 F9
Stagden Cross Essex 87 C10
Stagehall Borders 271 G9
Stagsden Bedford 103 B9
Stagsden West End
Bedford 103 B9
Stag's Head Devon 25 B11
Stain Highld 310 C7
Stainburn Cumb 228 F6
N Yorks 205 D10
Stainby Lincs 155 E8
Staincliffe W Yorks 197 C8
Staincross S Yorks 197 E10
Staindrop Durham 233 G8
Staines Green Herts 86 C3
Staines-upon-Thames
Sur 66 E4
Stainfield Lincs 155 D11
Lincs 189 G10
Stainforth N Yorks 212 F6
S Yorks 198 E6
Staining Lancs 202 F3
Stainland W Yorks 196 D5
Stainsacre N Yorks 227 D8
Stainsby Derbys 170 B6
Lincs 190 G4
Stainton Cumb 211 B10
Cumb 230 F5
Cumb 239 F9
Durham 223 B11
Mbro 225 C9
N Yorks 224 F2
S Yorks 187 C9
Stainton by Langworth
Lincs 189 F9
Staintondale N Yorks 227 F9
Stainton le Vale Lincs 189 C11
Stainton with Adgarley
Cumb 210 E5
Stair Cumb 229 G10
E Ayrs 257 E10
Stairfoot S Yorks 197 F11
Stairhaven Dumfries 236 D4
Staithes N Yorks 226 B5
Stakeford Northumb 253 F7
Stake Hill Gtr Man 195 F11
Stakenbridge Worcs 117 B7
Stake Pool Lancs 202 D4
Stalbridge Dorset 30 D2
Stalbridge Weston
Dorset 30 D2
Stalham Norf 161 D7
Stalham Green Norf 161 E7
Stalisfield Green Kent 54 C3
Stallen Dorset 29 D10
Stallingborough
NE Lincs 201 E7
Stalling Busk N Yorks 213 B8
Stallington Staffs 151 B8
Stalmine Lancs 202 D3
Stalmine Moss Side
Lancs 202 D3
Stalybridge Gtr Man 185 B7
Stambermill W Mid 133 G8
Stamborough Som 42 F4
Stambourne Essex 106 D4
Stambourne Green
Essex 106 D4
Stamford Lincs 137 B10
Stamford Bridge
Ches W 167 B7
E Yorks 207 B10
Stamfordham Northumb 242 C3
Stamford Hill London 67 B10
Stamperland E Renf 267 D11
Stamshaw Ptsmth 33 G10
Stanah Cumb 220 B6
Lancs 202 E3
Stanborough Herts 86 C2
Stanbridge C Beds 103 G9
Dorset 31 G8
Stanbridgeford C Beds 103 G9
Stanbrook Essex 106 F2
Worcs 98 B6
Stanbury W Yorks 204 F6
Stand Gtr Man 195 F9
N Lanark 268 B5
Standburn Falk 279 G8
Standeford Staffs 133 B8
Standen Kent 53 E11
Standen Hall Lancs 203 E10
Standen Street Kent 53 G10
Standerwick Som 45 C10
Standford Hants 49 G10
Standford Bridge
Telford 150 E4
Standingstone Cumb 229 B11
Cumb 229 E7
Standish Glos 80 D4
Gtr Man 194 E5
Standish Lower Ground
Gtr Man 194 F5
Standlake Oxon 82 E5
Standon Hants 32 B6
Herts 105 G7
Staffs 150 B6
Standon Green End
Herts 86 B5
Stane N Lanark 269 D7
Stanecastle N Ayrs 257 B8
Stanfield Norf 159 E8
Stoke 168 E5
Stanford C Beds 104 C3
Kent 54 F6
Norf 141 E7
Shrops 148 G6
Stanford Bishop
Hereford 116 G3
Stanford Bridge Worcs 116 D4
Stanford Dingley
W Berks 64 E5
Stanford End Wokingham 65 G8
Stanford Hills Notts 153 E10
Stanford in the Vale
Oxon 82 G4
Stanford-le-Hope
Thurrock 69 C7
Stanford on Avon
W Nhants 119 B11
Stanford on Soar Notts 153 E10
Stanford on Teme
Worcs 116 D4
Stanford Rivers Essex 87 E8
Stanfree Derbys 187 G7
Stanground Pboro 138 D4
Stanhill Lancs 195 B8
Stanhoe Norf 158 B6
Stanhope Borders 260 D4
Durham 232 D5
Kent 54 E3
Stanion N Nhants 137 F8
Stank Cumb 210 E4
Stanklyn Worcs 117 C7
Stanks W Yorks 206 F3
Stanley Derbys 170 G6
Durham 242 G5
Lancs 194 F3
Notts 171 C7
Perth 286 D5
Shrops 132 G3
Shrops 132 G5
Staffs 168 E6
Wilts 62 E3
W Yorks 197 C10
Stanley Common
Derbys 170 G6
Stanley Crook Durham 233 D9
Stanley Downton Glos 80 E4
Stanley Ferry W Yorks 197 C11
Stanley Gate Lancs 194 G2
Stanley Green BCP 18 C6
Ches E 184 E5
Shrops 149 B10
Stanley Hill Hereford 98 C3
Stanley Moor Staffs 168 E6
Stanley Pontlarge Glos 99 E9
Stanleytown Rhondda 77 G8
Stanlow Ches W 182 F6
Staffs 132 D5
Stanmer Brighton 36 F4
Stanmore Hants 33 B7
London 85 G11
Shrops 132 E4
W Berks 64 D3
Stanner Powys 114 F5
Stannergate Dundee 287 D8
Stannersburn Northumb 250 F6
Stanners Hill Sur 66 G3
Stanningfield Suff 125 F7
Stanningley W Yorks 205 G10
Stannington Northumb 242 B6
S Yorks 186 D4
Stanpit BCP 19 C9
Stansbatch Hereford 114 E6
Stansfield Suff 124 G5
Stanshope Staffs 169 E10
Stanstead Suff 106 B6
Stanstead Abbotts Herts 86 C5
Stansted Kent 68 G6
Stansted Airport Essex 105 G11
Stansted Mountfitchet
Essex 105 G10
Stanthorne Ches W 167 B11
Stanton Glos 99 E11
Mon 96 G6
Northumb 252 F4
Staffs 169 F10
Suff 125 C9
Stantonbury M Keynes 102 C6
Stanton by Bridge
Derbys 153 D7
Stanton-by-Dale Derbys 153 B9
Stanton Chare Suff 125 C9
Stanton Drew Bath 60 G5
Stanton Fitzwarren
Swindon 81 G11
Stanton Gate Notts 153 B9
Stanton Harcourt Oxon 82 D6
Stanton Hill Notts 171 C7
Stanton in Peak Derbys 170 C2
Stanton Lacy Shrops 115 B9
Stanton Lees Derbys 170 C3
Stanton Long Shrops 131 E11
Stanton-on-the-Wolds
Notts 154 C2
Stanton Prior Bath 61 G7
Stanton St Bernard Wilts 62 G5
Stanton St John Oxon 83 D9
Stanton St Quintin Wilts 62 D2
Stanton Street Suff 125 D9
Stanton under Bardon
Leics 153 G9
Stanton upon Hine Heath
Shrops 149 E11
Stanton Wick Bath 60 G6
Stantway Glos 80 C2
Stanwardine in the Fields
Shrops 149 E8
Stanwardine in the Wood
Shrops 149 D8
Stanway Essex 107 G8
Glos 99 E11
Stanway Green Essex 107 G9
Suff 126 C4
Stanwell Sur 66 E5
Stanwell Moor Sur 66 E4
Stanwick N Nhants 121 C9
Stanwick-St-John
N Yorks 224 C3
Stanwix Cumb 239 F10
Stanycliffe Gtr Man 195 F11
Stanydale Shetland 313 H4
Staoinebrig W Isles 297 H3
Stape N Yorks 226 G5
Stapehill Dorset 31 G9
Stapeley Ches E 167 F11
Stapenhill Staffs 152 E5
Staple Kent 55 B9
Som 42 E6
Staplecross E Sus 38 C3
Staple Cross Devon 27 C8
Staplefield W Sus 36 B3
Staple Fitzpaine Som 28 D3
Stapleford Cambs 123 G9
Herts 86 B4
Leics 154 F6
Lincs 172 D5
Notts 153 B9
Wilts 46 F5
Stapleford Abbotts Essex 87 G8
Stapleford Tawney Essex 87 F8
Staplegrove Som 28 B2
Staplehay Som 28 C2
Staple Hill S Glos 61 D7
Worcs 117 C9
Staplehurst Kent 53 E9
Staple Lawns Som 28 D3
Staplers IoW 20 D6
Staples Hill W Sus 35 B8
Staplestreet Kent 70 G5
Stapleton Bristol 60 D6
Cumb 240 C2
Hereford 114 D6
Leics 135 D8
N Yorks 198 D4
N Yorks 224 C5
Shrops 131 C9
Som 29 C7
Stapley Som 27 E11
Staploe Bedford 122 E2
Staplow Hereford 98 C3
Stapness Shetland 313 J4
Star Anglesey 179 G8
Fife 287 G7
Pembs 92 E4
Som 44 B2
Stara Orkney 314 D2
Starbeck N Yorks 206 B2
Starbotton N Yorks 213 E9
Starcross Devon 14 E5
Stareton Warks 118 C6
Stargate T&W 242 E5
Star Hill Mon 79 E7
Starkholmes Derbys 170 D4
Starling Gtr Man 195 E9
Starlings Green Essex 105 E9
Starr's Green E Sus 38 D3
Starston Norf 142 G4
Start Devon 8 G6
Startforth Durham 223 B10
Start Hill Essex 105 G10
Startley Wilts 62 C2
Startop's End Bucks 84 C6
Starveall S Glos 61 B9
Starvecrow Kent 52 D5
Statenborough Kent 55 B10
Statford St Andrew Suff 127 E7
Statham Warr 183 D11
Stathe Som 28 B5
Stathern Leics 154 C5
Station Hill Cumb 229 B11
Station Town Durham 234 D4
Statland Common
Norf 141 D10
Staughton Green Cambs 122 D2
Staughton Highway
Cambs 122 E2
Staughton Moor Cambs 122 E2
Staunton Glos 79 C8
Glos 98 F5
Staunton in the Vale
Notts 172 G4
Staunton on Arrow
Hereford 115 E7
Staunton on Wye
Hereford 97 B7
Staupes N Yorks 205 B10
Staveley Cumb 211 B7
Cumb 221 F9
Derbys 186 G6
N Yorks 215 G7
Staveley-in-Cartmel
Cumb 211 B7
Staverton Devon 8 C5
Glos 99 G7
Wilts 61 G11
W Nhants 119 E10
Staverton Bridge Glos 99 G7
Stawell Som 43 F11
Stawley Som 27 C9
Staxigoe Highld 310 D7
Staxton N Yorks 217 D10
Staylittle Ceredig 128 F2
Staylittle =Penffordd-Lâs
Powys 129 E7
Staynall Lancs 202 E3
Staythorpe Notts 172 E3
Stead W Yorks 205 D8
Steam Mills Glos 79 B10
Stean N Yorks 213 E11
Steanbow Som 44 F5
Stearsby N Yorks 216 E2
Steart Som 29 B9
Som 43 D9
Stebbing Essex 106 G3
Stebbing Green Essex 106 G3
Stechford W Mid 134 F2
Stede Quarter Kent 53 F11
Stedham W Sus 34 C5
Steel Northumb 241 F10
Northumb 251 G9
Steel Bank S Yorks 186 D4
Steel Cross E Sus 52 G4
Steelend Fife 279 C10
Steele Road Borders 250 E2
Steeleroad-end Borders 250 E2
Steel Green Cumb 210 D3
Steel Heath Shrops 149 B10
Steen's Bridge
Hereford 115 F10
Steep Hants 34 B2
Steephill IoW 21 F7
Steep Lane W Yorks 196 C4
Steeple Dorset 18 E4
Essex 88 E6
Steeple Ashton Wilts 46 B2
Steeple Aston Oxon 101 F9
Steeple Barton Oxon 101 G8
Steeple Bumpstead
Essex 106 C3
Steeple Claydon Bucks 102 F3
Steeple Gidding Cambs 138 G2
Steeple Langford Wilts 46 F4
Steeple Morden Cambs 104 C5
Steep Marsh Hants 34 B3
Steeraway Telford 132 B3
Steeton W Yorks 204 E6
Stein Highld 298 D2
Steinmanhill Aberds 303 E7
Stella T&W 242 E5
Stelling Minnis Kent 54 D6
Stelvio Newport 59 B9
Stembridge Som 28 C6
Swansea 56 C3
Stemster Highld 310 C5
Stemster Ho Highld 310 C5
Stenalees Corn 5 D10
Stenaquoy Orkney 314 C5
Stencoose Corn 4 F4
Stenhill Devon 27 E9
Stenhouse Dumfries 247 E8
Edin 280 G4
Stenhousemuir Falk 279 E7
Stenigot Lincs 190 E3
Stennack Corn 2 B5
Stenness Shetland 312 F4
Stenscholl Highld 298 C4
Stenso Orkney 314 D3
Stenson Derbys 152 D6
Stenton E Loth 282 G2
Fife 280 B5
Stentwood Devon 27 F10
Stenwith Lincs 154 B6
Stepaside Corn 5 F9
Pembs 73 D10
Powys 129 F11
Stepping Hill Gtr Man 184 D6
Steppingley C Beds 103 D10
Stepps N Lanark 268 B3
Sterndale Moor Derbys 169 B10
Sternfield Suff 127 E7
Sterridge Devon 40 D5
Stert Wilts 46 B4
Sterte BCP 18 C6
Stetchworth Cambs 124 F2
Stevenage Herts 104 G4
Steven's Crouch E Sus 38 D2
Stevenston N Ayrs 266 G5
Stevenstone Devon 25 D8
Steventon Hants 48 D4
Oxon 83 G7
Shrops 115 C10
Steventon End Essex 105 C11
Stevington Bedford 121 G9
Stewards Essex 87 D7
Steward's Green Essex 87 E7
Stewartby Bedford 103 C10
Stewarton Argyll 255 F7
E Ayrs 267 F8
Stewkley Bucks 103 F7
Stewkley Dean Bucks 102 F6
Stewley Som 28 D4
Stewton Lincs 190 D5
Steyne Cross IoW 21 D8
Steyning W Sus 35 E11
Steynton Pembs 72 D6
Stibb Corn 24 E2
Stibbard Norf 159 D9
Stibb Cross Devon 24 E6
Stibb Green Wilts 63 G8
Stibbington Cambs 137 D11
Stichill Borders 262 B6
Sticker Corn 5 E9
Stickford Lincs 174 D5
Stick Hill Kent 52 E3
Sticklepath Devon 13 C8
Devon 40 G5
Som 28 E4
Som 42 F4
Sticklinch Som 44 F5
Stickling Green Essex 105 E9
Stickney Lincs 174 D4
Stiffkey Norf 177 E7
Stifford's Bridge Hereford 98 B4
Stiff Street Kent 69 G11
Stileway Som 44 E3
Stillingfleet N Yorks 207 E7
Stillington N Yorks 215 F11
Stockton 234 G3
Stilton Cambs 138 F3
Stinchcombe Glos 80 F2
Stinsford Dorset 17 C10
Stiperstones Shrops 131 C7
Stirchley Telford 132 B4
W Mid 133 G11
Stirkoke Ho Highld 310 D7
Stirling Aberds 303 E11
Stirling 278 C5
Stirtloe Cambs 122 D3
Stirton N Yorks 204 C5
Stisted Essex 106 G5
Stitchcombe Wilts 63 F8
Stitchin's Hill Worcs 116 G5
Stithians Corn 2 B6
Stittenham Highld 300 B6
Stivichall W Mid 118 B6
Stixwould Lincs 173 B11
Stoak Ches W 182 G6
Stobhill Northumb 252 G6
Stobhillgate Northumb 252 F6
Stobieside S Lanark 258 B4
Stobo Borders 260 B5
Stoborough Dorset 18 D4
Stoborough Green
Dorset 18 D4
Stobs Castle Borders 250 B2
Stobshiel E Loth 271 C9
Stobswood Northumb 252 E6
Stock Essex 87 F11
Lancs 204 D3
N Som 60 G3
Stockbridge Hants 47 G11
S Yorks 198 F5
W Sus 22 C5
W Yorks 205 E7
Stockbridge Village
Mers 182 C6
Stockbury Kent 69 G10
Stockcross W Berks 64 F2
Stockend Glos 80 D4
Stocker's Head Kent 54 C3
Stockerston Leics 136 D6
Stockfield W Mid 134 G2
Stock Green Worcs 117 F9
Stockheath Hants 22 B2
Stock Hill Suff 125 D9
Stockholes Turbary
N Lincs 199 F9
Stockiemuir Stirling 277 E10
Stocking Hereford 98 E2
Stockingford Warks 134 E6
Stocking Green Essex 105 D11

Stocking Pelham Herts 105 F9
Stockland Devon 28 G2
Stockland Bristol Som 43 E8
Stockland Green Kent 52 E5
W Mid 133 E11
Stockleigh English Devon 26 F5
Stockleigh Pomeroy
Devon 26 G5
Stockley Wilts 62 F4
Stocklinch Som 28 D5
Stockport Gtr Man 184 C5
Stocksbridge S Yorks 186 B3
Stocksfield Northumb 242 E3
Stocks Green Kent 52 D5
Stockstreet Essex 106 G6
Stockton Hereford 115 E10
Norf 143 E7
Shrops 130 C5
Shrops 132 D4
Telford 150 F5
Warks 119 E8
Wilts 46 F3
Stockton Brook Staffs 168 E6
Stockton Heath Warr 183 D10
Stockton-on-Tees
Stockton 225 B8
Stockton on Teme
Worcs 116 D4
Stockton on the Forest
York 207 B9
Stocktonwood Shrops 130 C5
Stockwell Devon 27 G7
Glos 80 C6
London 67 D10
Stockwell End W Mid 133 C7
Stockwell Heath Staffs 151 E11
Stockwitch Cross Som 29 C9
Stockwood Bristol 60 F6
Dorset 29 F9
Stock Wood Worcs 117 F10
Stockwood Vale Bath 60 F6
Stodday Lancs 202 B5
Stodmarsh Kent 71 G8
Stody Norf 159 C11
Stoer Highld 307 G5
Stoford Som 29 E9
Wilts 46 F5
Stoford Water Devon 27 F9
Stogumber Som 42 F5
Stogursey Som 43 E8
Stoke Devon 24 C2
Hants 22 C2
Hants 48 C2
Medway 69 D10
Plym 7 D9
Suff 108 C3
W Mid 119 B7
Stoke Abbott Dorset 29 G7
Stoke Albany N Nhants 136 F6
Stoke Aldermoor
W Mid 119 B7
Stoke Ash Suff 126 C2
Stoke Bardolph Notts 171 G10
Stoke Bishop Bristol 60 D5
Stoke Bliss Worcs 116 E3
Stoke Bruerne
W Nhants 102 B4
Stoke by Clare Suff 106 C4
Stoke-by-Nayland Suff 107 D9
Stoke Canon Devon 14 B4
Stoke Charity Hants 48 F3
Stoke Climsland Corn 12 G3
Stoke Common Hants 33 C7
Stoke Cross Hereford 116 G2
Stoke D'Abernon Sur 50 B6
Stoke Doyle N Nhants 137 F10
Stoke Dry Rutland 137 D7
Stoke Edith Hereford 98 C2
Stoke End Warks 134 D3
Stoke Farthing Wilts 31 B9
Stoke Ferry Norf 140 D4
Stoke Fleming Devon 9 F7
Stokeford Dorset 18 D3
Stoke Gabriel Devon 8 D6
Stoke Gifford S Glos 60 D6
Stoke Golding Leics 135 D7
Stoke Goldington
M Keynes 102 B6
Stokegorse Shrops 131 G11
Stoke Green Bucks 66 C3
Stokeham Notts 188 F3
Stoke Hammond Bucks 103 F7
Stoke Heath Shrops 150 D3
W Mid 135 G7
Worcs 117 D8
Stoke Hill Devon 14 C4
Hereford 98 B2
Stoke Holy Cross Norf 142 C4
Stokeinteignhead Devon 14 G4
Stoke Lacy Hereford 98 B2
Stoke Lane Hereford 116 G2
Stoke Lyne Oxon 101 F11
Stoke Mandeville Bucks 84 C4
Stokenchurch Bucks 84 F3
Stoke Newington
London 67 B10
Stokenham Devon 8 G6
Stoke on Tern Shrops 150 D2
Stoke-on-Trent Stoke 168 F5
Stoke Orchard Glos 99 F8
Stoke Park Suff 108 C3
Stoke Poges Bucks 66 C3
Stoke Pound Worcs 117 D9
Stoke Prior Hereford 115 F10
Worcs 117 D8
Stoke Rivers Devon 40 F6
Stoke Rochford Lincs 155 D8
Stoke Row Oxon 65 C7
Stoke St Gregory Som 28 B4
Stoke St Mary Som 28 C3
Stoke St Michael Som 45 D7
Stoke St Milborough
Shrops 131 G11
Stokesay Shrops 131 G8
Stokesby Norf 161 G8
Stokesley N Yorks 225 D10
Stoke sub Hamdon Som 29 D7
Stoke Talmage Oxon 83 F11
Stoke Trister Som 30 B2
Stoke Wake Dorset 30 F3
Stoke Water Dorset 29 G7
Stoke Wharf Worcs 117 D9
Stokoe Northumb 250 F6
Stolford Som 43 D8
Stondon Massey Essex 87 E9
Stone Bucks 84 C3
Glos 79 F11
Kent 38 B6
Kent 68 E5
Som 44 G5
Staffs 151 C8
S Yorks 187 D9
Worcs 117 B7
Stonea Cambs 139 E9
Stoneacton Shrops 131 E10
Stone Allerton Som 44 C2
Ston Easton Som 44 C6
Stonebow Worcs 99 B8
Stonebridge Essex 70 B2
London 67 C8
Norf 141 E8
Stonebridge *continued*
N Som 43 B11
Sur 51 D7
W Mid 134 G4
Stone Bridge Corner
Pboro 138 C5
Stonebridge Green Kent 54 D2
Stonebroom Derbys 170 D6
Stonebyres Holdings
S Lanark 268 G6
Stone Chair W Yorks 196 B6
Stoneclough Gtr Man 195 F9
Stonecombe Devon 40 E6
Stone Cross E Sus 23 E10
E Sus 37 B8
E Sus 52 G6
Kent 52 F4
Kent 54 F4
Kent 55 B10
W Mid 133 E10
Stonecrouch Kent 53 G7
Stonedge Borders 250 B3
Stone-edge Batch
N Som 60 E3
Stoneferry Hull 209 G8
Stonefield Argyll 289 F11
S Lanark 268 D3
Staffs 151 C7
Stonefield Castle Hotel
Argyll 275 F9
Stonegate E Sus 37 B11
N Yorks 226 D5
Stonegrave N Yorks 216 D3
Stonegravels Derbys 186 G5
Stonehall Kent 55 D9
Worcs 99 B7
Stonehaugh Northumb 241 B7
Stonehaven Aberds 293 E10
Stone Head N Yorks 204 E4
Stone Heath Staffs 151 B9
Stonehill Sur 66 G4
Stone Hill Kent 54 D2
Kent 54 F5
S Glos 60 E6
S Yorks 199 F7
Stonehills Hants 33 G7
Stonehouse Aberds 303 F8
Glos 80 D4
Northumb 240 F5
Plym 7 E9
S Lanark 268 F5
Stone House Cumb 212 B5
Stonehouses Staffs 169 G7
Stone in Oxney Kent 38 B6
Stoneleigh London 67 G8
Warks 118 C6
Stoneley Green Ches E 167 E10
Stonely Cambs 122 D2
Stonepits Worcs 117 F10
Stonequarry W Sus 52 F2
Stone Raise Cumb 230 B4
Stoner Hill Hants 34 B2
Stonesby Leics 154 E6
Stonesfield Oxon 82 B5
Stones Green Essex 108 F3
Stone Street Kent 52 C5
Suff 107 D9
Suff 143 G7
Stonestreet Green Kent 54 F5
Stonethwaite Cumb 220 C5
Stoneton Warks 119 G9
Stonewells Moray 302 C2
Stonewood Kent 68 E5
Stoneyard Green
Hereford 98 C4
Stoneybank E Loth 280 G6
Stoneybreck Shetland 313 N2
Stoneyburn W Loth 269 C9
Stoneycombe Devon 9 B7
Stoneycroft Mers 182 C5
Stoney Cross Hants 32 E3
Stoneyfield Gtr Man 195 E11
Moray 301 D11
Stoneyford Derbys 170 F6
Devon 27 F8
Stoneygate Aberds 303 F10
Leicester 136 C2
Stoney Hill Worcs 117 C9
Stoneyhills Essex 88 F6
Stoneykirk Dumfries 236 D2
Stoneylane Shrops 115 B11
Stoney Middleton
Derbys 186 F2
Stoney Royd W Yorks 196 C5
Stoney Stanton Leics 135 E9
Stoney Stoke Som 45 G8
Stoney Stratton Som 45 F7
Stoney Stretton Shrops 131 B7
Stoneywood Aberdeen 293 B10
Falk 278 E5
Stonganess Shetland 312 C7
Stonham Aspal Suff 126 F2
Stonnall Staffs 133 C11
Stonor Oxon 65 B8
Stonton Wyville Leics 136 D4
Stony Batter Hants 32 B3
Stony Cross Devon 25 B8
Hereford 98 B4
Hereford 115 D10
Stony Dale Notts 172 G2
Stonyfield Highld 300 B6
Stonyford Hants 32 D4
Stony Gate T&W 243 G9
Stony Green Bucks 84 F5
Stony Heap Durham 242 G4
Stony Heath Hants 48 B5
Stony Houghton Derbys 171 B7
Stony Knaps Dorset 28 G5
Stonyland Devon 25 B8
Stony Littleton Bath 45 B8
Stonymarsh Hants 32 B4
Stony Stratford
M Keynes 102 C5
Stoodleigh Devon 26 D6
Stop-and-Call Pembs 91 D8
Stopes S Yorks 186 D3
Stopgate Devon 28 F2
Stopham W Sus 35 D8
Stopper Lane Lancs 204 D2
Stopsley Luton 104 G2
Stoptide Corn 10 F4
Stores Corner Suff 109 B7
Storeton Mers 182 E4
Storiths N Yorks 205 C7
Stormontfield Perth 286 E5
Stormore Wilts 45 D10
Stornoway W Isles 304 E6
Storridge Hereford 98 B4
Storrington W Sus 35 E9
Storrs Cumb 221 G7
S Yorks 186 D3
Storth Cumb 211 C9
Storwood E Yorks 207 E10
Stotfield Moray 302 B2
Stotfold C Beds 104 D4
Stottesdon Shrops 132 G3
Stoughton Leics 136 C2
Sur 50 C3
W Sus 34 E3
Stoughton Cross Som 44 D2
Stoul Highld 295 F9
Stoulton Worcs 99 B8
Stourbridge W Mid 133 G8
Stourpaine Dorset 30 F5
Stourport on Severn
Worcs 116 C6
Stour Provost Dorset 30 C3
Stour Row Dorset 30 C4
Stourton Staffs 133 F7
Warks 100 D5
Wilts 45 G9
W Yorks 206 G2
Stourton Caundle Dorset 30 D2
Stourton Hill Warks 100 D6
Stout Som 44 G2
Stove Orkney 314 C6
Shetland 313 L6
Stoven Suff 143 G8
Stow Borders 271 G9
Lincs 155 B11
Lincs 188 E5
Stow Bardolph Norf 140 B2
Stow Bedon Norf 141 D9
Stowbridge Norf 140 B2
Stow cum Quy Cambs 123 E10
Stowe Glos 79 D9
Hereford 96 B5
Lincs 156 G2
Shrops 114 C6
Staffs 152 G2
Stowe-by-Chartley
Staffs 151 D10
Stowe Green Glos 79 D9
Stowell Glos 81 C9
Som 29 C11
Stowey Bath 44 B5
Stowfield Hereford 79 B9
Stowford Devon 12 B4
Devon 12 D4
Devon 24 E3
Devon 25 B10
Devon 41 E7
Stowgate Lincs 156 G3
Stowlangtoft Suff 125 D9
Stow Lawn W Mid 133 D8
Stow Longa Cambs 122 C2
Stow Maries Essex 88 F4
Stowmarket Suff 125 F10
Stow-on-the-Wold
Glos 100 F3
Stow Park Newport 59 B10
Stowting Kent 54 E6
Stowting Common Kent 54 E6
Stowting Court Kent 54 E6
Stowupland Suff 125 F11
Straad Argyll 275 G11
Strachan Aberds 293 D8
Strachurmore Argyll 284 G5
Stradbroke Suff 126 C4
Stradishall Suff 124 G4
Stradsett Norf 140 C3
Stragglethorpe Lincs 172 E6
Straid S Ayrs 244 E4
Straight Soley Wilts 63 E10
Straith Dumfries 247 F8
Straiton Edin 270 B5
S Ayrs 245 C9
Straloch Aberds 303 G8
Perth 292 G2
Stramshall Staffs 151 B11
Strand Glos 80 C2
London 67 C10
Strands Cumb 210 C3
Strang IoM 192 E4
Strangeways Gtr Man 184 B4
Strangford Hereford 97 F11
Stranghow Redcar 226 B3
Strangways Wilts 46 E6
Stranog Aberds 293 D10
Stranraer Dumfries 236 C2
Strata Florida Ceredig 112 D4
Stratfield Mortimer
W Berks 65 G7
Stratfield Saye Hants 65 G7
Stratfield Turgis Hants 49 B7
Stratford C Beds 104 B3
Glos 99 D7
London 67 C11
Stratford Marsh London 67 C11
Stratford New Town
London 67 C11
Stratford St Andrew
Suff 127 E7
Stratford St Mary Suff 107 E10
Stratford Sub Castle
Wilts 46 G6
Stratford Tony Wilts 31 B9
Stratford-upon-Avon
Warks 118 F3
Strath Highld 299 B7
Highld 310 D6
Strathallan Castle Perth 286 F3
Strathan Highld 295 F11
Highld 307 G5
Highld 308 C5
Strathan Skerray Highld 308 C6
Strathaven S Lanark 268 G4
Strathavon Lo Moray 301 G11
Strathblane Stirling 277 F11
Strathcanaird Highld 307 J6
Strathcarron Highld 299 E9
Strathcoil Argyll 289 F8
Strathcoul Highld 310 D5
Strathdon Aberds 292 B5
Strathellie Aberds 303 C10
Strathgarve Lodge
Highld 300 C4
Strathkinness Fife 287 F8
Strathmashie House
Highld 291 D7
Strathmiglo Fife 286 F6
Strathmore Lodge
Highld 310 E5
Strathpeffer Highld 300 D4
Strathrannoch Highld 300 B3
Strathtay Perth 286 B3
Strathvaich Lodge
Highld 300 B3
Strathwhillan N Ayrs 256 B2
Strathy Highld 300 B6
Highld 310 C2
Strathyre Stirling 285 F9
Stratton Corn 24 F2
Dorset 17 C9
Glos 81 E8
Stratton Audley Oxon 102 F2
Stratton Chase Bucks 85 G7
Stratton-on-the-Fosse
Som 45 C7
Stratton St Margaret
Swindon 63 B7
Stratton St Michael
Norf 142 E4
Stratton Strawless Norf 160 E4
Stravithie Fife 287 F9
Strawberry Bank Cumb 211 B8
Strawberry Hill E Sus 52 F5
London 67 E7
W Yorks 198 C2
Streat E Sus 36 D5
Streatham London 67 E10
Streatham Hill London 67 E10
Streatham Park London 67 E9
Streatham Vale London 67 E9
Streatley C Beds 103 F11
W Berks 64 C5
Street Cumb 222 D2
Lancs 202 C6
N Yorks 226 E4
Som 28 F5
Som 44 F3
Street Ash Som 28 E3
Street Ashton Warks 135 G9
Street Dinas Shrops 148 B6
Street End Hants 33 D9
Kent 54 C6
W Sus 22 D5
Street Gate T&W 242 F6
Streethay Staffs 152 G2
Streethouse W Yorks 197 C11
Street Houses N Yorks 206 D6
Streetlam N Yorks 224 F6
Street Lane Derbys 170 F5
Streetly W Mid 133 D11
Street Lydan Wrex 149 B8
Streetly End Cambs 106 B2
Street of Kincardine
Highld 291 B11
Street on the Fosse Som 44 F6
Strefford Shrops 131 F8
Strelley Notts 171 G8
Strensall York 216 G2
Strensham Worcs 99 C8
Stretch Down Devon 26 E4
Stretcholt Som 43 E9
Strete Devon 8 F6
Stretford Gtr Man 184 C4
Hereford 115 F10
Stretford Court Hereford 115 F8
Strethall Essex 105 D9
Stretham Cambs 123 C10
Strettington W Sus 22 B5
Stretton Ches W 166 E6
Derbys 170 C5
Rutland 155 F8
Staffs 151 G7
Staffs 152 D5
Warr 183 E10
Stretton en le Field
Leics 152 G6
Stretton Grandison
Hereford 98 C2
Stretton-on-Dunsmore
Warks 119 C8
Stretton-on-Fosse
Warks 100 D4
Stretton Sugwas
Hereford 97 C9
Stretton under Fosse
Warks 135 G8
Stretton Westwood
Shrops 131 D11
Strichen Aberds 303 D9
Strines Gtr Man 185 D7
Stringston Som 43 E7
Strixton N Nhants 121 E8
Stroat Glos 79 F9
Strode N Som 60 G4
Strom Shetland 313 J5
Stromeferry Highld 295 B10
Stromemore Highld 295 B10
Stromness Orkney 314 F2
Stronaba Highld 290 E4
Stronachlachar Stirling 285 F8
Stronachullin Lodge
Argyll 275 F9
Stroncreggan Highld 290 F2
Stronchrubie Highld 307 H7
Strone Argyll 255 F7
Argyll 274 G6
Argyll 276 E3
Highld 290 E3
Highld 291 D9
Highld 300 G5
Invclyd 276 G5
Stronelairg Lodge
Highld 291 C7
Stroneskar Argyll 275 C9
Stronmachair Stirling 285 G8
Stronmilchan Argyll 284 E5
Stronord Dumfries 236 C6
Stronsaul Argyll 276 F2
Strontian Highld 289 C10
Stronvar Stirling 285 E9
Strood Kent 53 G11
Medway 69 F8
Strood Green Sur 51 D8
W Sus 35 C8
W Sus 50 G6
Strothers Dale
Northumb 241 F11
Stroud Glos 80 D4
Hants 34 C2
Sur 50 F2
Stroude Sur 66 F4
Stroud Green Essex 88 G5
Glos 80 D4
London 67 B10
Stroul Argyll 276 E4
Stroupster Highld 310 C7
Stroxton Lincs 155 C8
Stroxworthy Devon 24 D4
Struan Highld 294 B5
Perth 291 G10
Strubby Lincs 191 E7
Structon's Heath Worcs 116 D5
Strugg's Hill Lincs 156 B5
Strumpshaw Norf 142 B6
Strutherhill S Lanark 268 F5
Struthers Fife 287 G7
Struy Highld 300 F3
Stryd Anglesey 178 E2
Stryd y Facsen Anglesey 178 E4
Stryt-issa Wrex 166 F3
Stuartfield Aberds 303 E9
Stubb Norf 161 E8
Stubbermere W Sus 22 B3
Stubber's Green
W Mid 133 C10
Stubbings Windsor 65 C10
Stubbing's Green Suff 125 C11
Stubbington Hants 33 G9
Stubbins Lancs 195 D9
Lancs 202 E6
Stubble Green Cumb 219 F11
Stubbles W Berks 64 D5
Stubbs Cross Kent 54 F3
Stubbs Green Norf 143 D7
Stubb's Green Norf 142 D5
Stubhampton Dorset 30 E6
Stub Place Cumb 219 G11
Stubshaw Cross
Gtr Man 194 G5
Stubton Lincs 172 F5
Stubwood Staffs 151 B11
Stuckgowan Argyll 285 G7
Stuckton Hants 31 E11
Studdal Kent 55 D10
Studd Hill Kent 71 F7
Studfold N Yorks 212 E6
Stud Green Ches E 168 C2
Windsor 65 D11
Studham C Beds 85 B8
Studland Dorset 18 E6
Studley Warks 117 E11
Wilts 62 E3
Studley Green Bucks 84 F3
Wilts 45 B10
Studley Roger N Yorks 214 E5
Studley Royal N Yorks 214 E5
Stump Cross Essex 105 C10
Stumps Cross Glos 99 E11
Stuntney Cambs 123 B11
Stunts Green E Sus 23 C10
Sturbridge Staffs 150 C6
Sturford Wilts 45 E10
Sturgate Lincs 188 D5
Sturmer Essex 106 C3
Sturminster Common
Dorset 30 E3
Sturminster Marshall
Dorset 31 G7
Sturminster Newton
Dorset 30 E3
Sturry Kent 71 G7
Stursdon Corn 24 E2
Sturton N Lincs 200 G3
Sturton by Stow Lincs 188 E5
Sturton le Steeple Notts 188 E3
Stuston Suff 126 B2
Stutton N Yorks 206 E5
Suff 108 E3
Styal Ches E 184 E4
Styants Bottom Kent 52 B5
Stydd Lancs 203 F9
Styrrup Notts 187 C10
Suainebost W Isles 304 B7
Suardail W Isles 304 E6
Succoth Aberds 302 F4
Argyll 284 G6
Suckley Worcs 116 G4
Suckley Green Worcs 116 G4
Suckley Knowl Worcs 116 G4
Suckquoy Orkney 314 H4
Sucksted Green Essex 105 F11
Sudborough N Nhants 137 G9
Sudbourne Suff 127 G8
Sudbrook Lincs 173 G7
Mon 60 B4
Sudbrooke Lincs 189 F8
Sudbury Derbys 152 C3
London 67 C7
Suff 107 C7
Sudden Gtr Man 195 E11
Suddie Highld 300 D6
Sudgrove Glos 80 D6
Suffield Norf 160 C4
N Yorks 227 G9
Sugnall Staffs 150 C5
Sugwas Pool Hereford 97 C9
Suisnish Highld 295 D7
Suladale Highld 298 D3
Sulaisiadar W Isles 304 E7
Sulby IoM 192 C4
Sulgrave T&W 243 F8
W Nhants 101 B11
Sulham W Berks 64 E6
Sulhampstead W Berks 64 F6
Sulhampstead Abbots
W Berks 64 F6
Sulhampstead Bannister
Upper End W Berks 64 F6
Sulhamstead W Berks 64 F6
Sulland Orkney 314 B5
Sullington W Sus 35 E9
Sullington Warren
W Sus 35 E9
Sullom Shetland 312 F5
Sullom Voe Oil Terminal
Shetland 312 F5
Sully V Glam 59 F7
Sumburgh Shetland 313 N6
Summerbridge N Yorks 214 G4
Summer Bridge
N Yorks 214 G4
Summercourt Corn 5 D7
Summerfield Kent 55 B9
Norf 158 B5
Worcs 116 C6
Summerfield Park
W Mid 133 F10
Summergangs Hull 209 G8
Summer Heath Bucks 84 G2
Summerhill Newport 59 B10
Pembs 73 D11
Staffs 133 B11
Telford 150 F4
Worcs 116 B6
Wrex 166 E4
Summer Hill E Sus 23 D9
W Mid 133 E9
Summerhouse Darl 224 B4
Summerlands Cumb 211 B10
Som 29 D8
Summerleaze Mon 60 B2
Summerley Derbys 186 F5
Summerscales N Yorks 205 C8
Summersdale W Sus 22 B5
Summerseat Gtr Man 195 E9
Summerston Glasgow 277 G11
Summerstown Bucks 102 G3
London 67 E9
Summertown Oxon 83 D8
Summit Gtr Man 195 E10
Gtr Man 196 D2
Gtr Man 196 F2
Sunbrick Cumb 210 E5
Sunbury Common Sur 66 E5
Sunbury-on-Thames Sur 66 F6
Sundayshill S Glos 79 G11
Sundaywell Dumfries 247 G8
Sunderland Argyll 274 G3
Cumb 229 D9
Lancs 202 B4
T&W 243 F9
Sunderland Bridge
Durham 233 D11
Sundhope Borders 261 D8
Sundon Park Luton 103 F11
Sundridge Kent 52 B3
London 68 E2
Sun Green Gtr Man 185 B7
Sunhill Glos 81 E10
Sunipol Argyll 288 D5
Sunken Marsh Essex 69 C10
Sunk Island E Yorks 201 D9
Sunningdale Windsor 66 F3
Sunninghill Windsor 66 F2
Sunningwell Oxon 83 E7
Sunniside Durham 233 D8
T&W 242 F6
T&W 243 G8
Sunny Bank Gtr Man 195 F10
Sunny Bower Lancs 203 G10
Sunnybrow Durham 233 E9
Sunnyfields S Yorks 198 F4
Sunny Hill Derby 152 C6
Sunnyhurst Blackburn 195 C7
Sunnylaw Stirling 278 B5
Sunnymead Oxon 83 D8
Sunnymeads Windsor 66 D4
Sunnymede Essex 87 G11
Sunnyside S Yorks 187 C7
Sunnyside *continued*
W Sus 51 F11
Sunset Hereford 114 F6
Sunton Wilts 47 C8
Surbiton London 67 F7
Surby IoM 192 E3
Surfleet Lincs 156 D5
Surfleet Seas End Lincs 156 D5
Surlingham Norf 142 B6
Surrex Essex 107 G7
Suspension Bridge
Norf 139 E10
Sustead Norf 160 B3
Susworth Lincs 199 G10
Sutcombe Devon 24 E4
Sutcombemill Devon 24 E4
Sutherland Grove
Argyll 289 E11
Suton Norf 141 D11
Sutors of Cromarty
Highld 301 C8
Sutterby Lincs 190 G5
Sutterton Lincs 156 B5
Sutterton Dowdyke
Lincs 156 C5
Sutton Bucks 66 D4
Cambs 123 B8
C Beds 104 B4
Devon 8 G4
E Sus 23 F7
Kent 55 D10
Lincs 172 E5
London 67 G9
Mers 183 C8
Norf 161 E7
Notts 154 B5
Notts 187 E11
N Yorks 198 B3
Oxon 82 D6
Pboro 137 D11
Pembs 72 B6
Shrops 132 F4
Shrops 149 D7
Shrops 149 G10
Shrops 150 C3
Som 44 G6
Staffs 150 E5
Suff 108 B6
Sur 50 D5
S Yorks 198 E5
W Sus 35 D7
Sutton Abinger Sur 50 D6
Sutton at Hone Kent 68 E5
Sutton Bassett
N Nhants 136 E5
Sutton Benger Wilts 62 D2
Sutton Bingham Som 29 E8
Sutton Bonington
Notts 153 E10
Sutton Bridge Lincs 157 E9
Sutton Cheney Leics 135 C8
Sutton Coldfield W Mid 134 D2
Sutton Corner Lincs 157 D8
Sutton Courtenay Oxon 83 G8
Sutton Crosses Lincs 157 E8
Sutton Cum Lound
Notts 187 E11
Sutton End W Sus 35 D7
Sutton Forest Side
Notts 171 D8
Sutton Gault Cambs 123 B8
Sutton Green Ches W 182 F5
Sur 50 C4
Wrex 166 F6
Sutton Hall Shrops 132 C4
Sutton Heath Mers 183 C8
Sutton Hill Telford 132 C4
Sutton Holms Dorset 31 F9
Sutton Howgrave
N Yorks 214 D6
Sutton in Ashfield Notts 171 D7
Sutton-in-Craven
N Yorks 204 E6
Sutton Ings Hull 209 G8
Sutton in the Elms
Leics 135 E10
Sutton Lakes Hereford 97 B10
Sutton Lane Ends
Ches E 184 G6
Sutton Leach Mers 183 C8
Sutton Maddock Shrops 132 C4
Sutton Mallet Som 43 F11
Sutton Mandeville Wilts 31 B7
Sutton Manor Mers 183 C8
Sutton Marsh Hereford 97 C10
Sutton Mill N Yorks 204 E6
Sutton Montis Som 29 C10
Sutton on Hull Hull 209 G8
Sutton on Sea Lincs 191 E8
Sutton-on-the-Forest
N Yorks 215 G11
Sutton on the Hill
Derbys 152 C4
Sutton on Trent Notts 172 B3
Sutton Poyntz Dorset 17 E10
Sutton Row Wilts 31 B7
Sutton St Edmund Lincs 157 G7
Sutton St James Lincs 157 F7
Sutton St Michael
Hereford 97 B10
Sutton St Nicholas
Hereford 97 B10
Sutton Scarsdale
Derbys 170 B6
Sutton Scotney Hants 48 F3
Sutton Street Suff 108 C6
Sutton under Brailes
Warks 100 D6
Sutton-under-
Whitestonecliffe
N Yorks 215 C9
Sutton upon Derwent
E Yorks 207 D10
Sutton Valence Kent 53 D10
Sutton Veny Wilts 45 E11
Sutton Waldron Dorset 30 D5
Sutton Weaver Ches W 183 F8
Sutton Wick Bath 44 B5
Oxon 83 G7
Swaby Lincs 190 F5
Swadlincote Derbys 152 F6
Swaffham Norf 140 B6
Swaffham Bulbeck
Cambs 123 E11
Swaffham Prior Cambs 123 E11
Swafield Norf 160 C5
Swaile's Green E Sus 38 C3
Swainby N Yorks 225 E9
Swain House W Yorks 205 F9
Swainshill Hereford 97 C9
Swainsthorpe Norf 142 C4
Swainswick Bath 61 F9
Swaithe S Yorks 197 G11
Swalcliffe Oxon 101 D7
Swalecliffe Kent 70 F6
Swallow Lincs 201 G7
Swallow Beck Lincs 173 B7
Swallowcliffe Wilts 31 B7
Swallowfield Wokingham 65 G8
Swallowfields Devon 8 C5
Swallowhurst Cumb 220 G2
Swallownest S Yorks 187 E7
Swallows Cross Essex 87 F10
Swalwell T&W 242 E6
Swampton Hants 48 C2
Swanage Dorset 18 F6
Swanbach Ches E 167 G11
Swanbister Orkney 314 F3
Swanborough Swindon 81 G11
Swan Bottom Bucks 84 D6
Swanbourne Bucks 102 F6
Swanbridge V Glam 59 F7
Swan Green Ches W 184 G2
Suff 126 C5
Swanland E Yorks 200 B3
Swanley Glos 80 F2
Kent 68 F4
Swanley Bar Herts 86 E3
Swanley Village Kent 68 F4
Swanmore Hants 33 D9
IoW 21 C7
Swannay Orkney 314 D2
Swannington Leics 153 F8
Norf 160 F2
Swanpool Lincs 189 G7
Swanscombe Kent 68 E6
Swansea = *Abertawe*
Swansea 56 C6
Swanside Mers 182 C6
Swanston Edin 270 B4
Swan Street Essex 107 F7
Swanton Abbott Norf 160 D5
Swanton Hill Norf 160 D5
Swanton Morley Norf 159 F10
Swanton Novers Norf 159 C10
Swanton Street Kent 53 B11
Swan Village W Mid 133 E9
Swanwick Derbys 170 E6
Hants 33 F8
Swanwick Green Ches E 167 F9
Swarby Lincs 173 G8
Swarcliffe W Yorks 206 F3
Swardeston Norf 142 C4
Swarister Shetland 312 E7
Swarkestone Derbys 153 D7
Swarland Northumb 252 C5
Swarraton Hants 48 F5
Swartha W Yorks 205 D7
Swarthmoor Cumb 210 D5
Swartland Orkney 314 D2
Swathwick Derbys 170 B5
Swaton Lincs 156 B2
Swavesey Cambs 123 D7
Sway Hants 19 B11
Swayfield Lincs 155 E9
Swaythling Soton 32 D6
Sweet Green Worcs 116 E2
Sweetham Devon 14 B3
Sweethaws E Sus 37 B8
Sweethay Som 28 C2
Sweetholme Cumb 221 B11
Sweethouse Corn 5 C11
Sweets Corn 11 B9
Sweetshouse Corn 5 C11
Swefling Suff 126 E6
Swell Som 28 C5
Swelling Hill Hants 49 G7
Swepstone Leics 153 G7
Swerford Oxon 101 E7
Swettenham Ches E 168 B4
Swetton N Yorks 214 E3
Swffryd Caerph 78 F2
Swiftsden E Sus 38 B2
Swift's Green Kent 53 E11
Swilland Suff 126 G3
Swillbrook Lancs 202 G5
Swillington W Yorks 206 G3
Swillington Common
W Yorks 206 G3
Swimbridge Devon 25 B10
Swimbridge Newland
Devon 40 G6
Swinbrook Oxon 82 C3
Swincliffe N Yorks 205 B10
W Yorks 197 B8
Swincombe Devon 41 E7
Swinden N Yorks 204 C3
Swinderby Lincs 172 C5
Swindon Glos 99 G8
Staffs 133 E7
Swindon 63 C7
Swine E Yorks 209 F8
Swinefleet E Yorks 199 C9
Swineford S Glos 61 F7
Swineshead Bedford 121 D11
Lincs 174 G2
Swineshead Bridge
Lincs 174 G2
Swinethorpe Lincs 172 B5
Swiney Highld 310 F6
Swinford Leics 119 B11
Oxon 82 D6
Swingate Notts 171 G8
Swingbrow Cambs 139 F7
Swingfield Minnis Kent 55 E8
Swingfield Street Kent 55 E8
Swingleton Green Suff 107 B9
Swinhoe Northumb 264 D6
Swinhope Lincs 190 B2
Swining Shetland 312 G6
Swinister Shetland 312 E5
Shetland 313 L6
Swinithwaite N Yorks 213 B10
Swinmore Common
Hereford 98 C3
Swinnie Borders 262 F4
Swinnow Moor
W Yorks 205 G10
Swinscoe Staffs 169 F10
Swinside Cumb 229 G10
Swinside Townfoot
Borders 262 F6
Swinstead Lincs 155 E10
Swinton Borders 272 F6
Glasgow 268 C3
Gtr Man 195 G9
N Yorks 214 D4
N Yorks 216 E5
S Yorks 186 B6
Swinton Bridge S Yorks 187 B7
Swinton Hill Borders 272 F6
Swintonmill Borders 272 F6
Swinton Park Gtr Man 195 G9
Swiss Valley Carms 75 E8
Swithland Leics 153 G10
Swordale Highld 300 C5
Highld 309 K6
Swordland Highld 295 F9
Swordly Highld 308 C7
Sworton Heath Ches E 183 E11
Swyddffynnon Ceredig 112 D3
Swynnerton Staffs 151 B7
Swyre Dorset 16 D6
Sycamore Devon 28 F3
Sychdyn = *Soughton*
Flint 166 B2
Sychtyn Powys 129 B9
Sydallt Wrex 166 D4
Syde Glos 81 C7
Sydenham London 67 E11
Oxon 84 E2
Som 43 F10
Sydenham Damerel
Devon 12 F4
Syderstone Norf 158 C6
Sydling St Nicholas
Dorset 17 B8
Sydmonton Hants 48 B3
Sydney Ches E 168 D2
Syerston Notts 172 F2
Syke Gtr Man 195 D11
Sykehouse S Yorks 198 D6
Sykes Lancs 203 C8
Syleham Suff 126 B4
Sylen Carms 75 D8
Symbister Shetland 313 G7
Symington Borders 271 F8
S Ayrs 257 C9
S Lanark 259 B11
Symondsbury Dorset 16 C4
Symonds Green Herts 104 F4
Symonds Yat Hereford 79 B9
Synderford Dorset 28 G5
Synod Inn = *Post Mawr*
Ceredig 111 G8
Synton Borders 261 E11
Synton Mains Borders 261 E11
Synwell Glos 80 G3
Syre Highld 308 E6
Syreford Glos 99 G10
Syresham W Nhants 102 C2
Syster Highld 310 C6
Syston Leics 154 G2
Lincs 172 G6
Sytchampton Worcs 116 D6
Sytch Ho Green Shrops 132 E5
Sytch Lane Telford 150 E2
Sywell N Nhants 120 D6

T

Taagan Highld 299 C10
Tabley Hill Ches E 184 F2
Tabor Gwyn 146 F5
Tàbost W Isles 304 B7
Tabost W Isles 305 G5
Tachbrook Mallory
Warks 118 E6
Tacker Street Som 42 F4
Tackley Oxon 101 G9
Tacleit W Isles 304 E3
Tacolneston Norf 142 D2
Tadcaster N Yorks 206 E5
Tadden Dorset 31 G7
Taddington Derbys 185 G10
Glos 99 E11
Taddiport Devon 25 D7
Tadhill Som 45 D7
Tadley Hants 64 G6
Oxon 64 B4
Tadlow Cambs 104 B5
C Beds 104 B5
Tadmarton Oxon 101 D7
Tadnoll Dorset 17 D11
Tadwick Bath 61 E8
Tadworth Sur 51 B8
Tafarnau-bach
Bl Gwent 77 C10
Tafarn-y-bwlch Pembs 91 E11
Tafarn-y-gelyn Denb 165 C11
Taff Merthyr Garden Village
M Tydf 77 F10
Taff's Well Rhondda 58 C6
Tafolwern Powys 129 C7
Tai Conwy 164 C3
Taibach Neath 57 D9
Tai-bach Powys 148 D3
Taigh a Ghearraidh
W Isles 296 D3
Taigh Bhalaigh W Isles 296 D3
Tai-mawr Conwy 165 G7
Tai-morfa Gwyn 144 D5
Tain Highld 309 L7
Highld 310 C6
Tai-nant Wrex 166 F3
Tainlon Gwyn 162 E6
Tairbeart W Isles 305 H3
Tai'r-Bull Powys 95 F9
Tairgwaith Neath 76 C2
Tai'r-heol Caerph 77 G10
Tai'r-ysgol Swansea 57 B7
Tai-Ucha Denb 165 D8
Takeley Essex 105 G11
Takeley Street Essex 105 G10
Talacharn = *Laugharne*
Carms 74 C4
Talachddu Powys 95 E11
Talacre Flint 181 E10
Talardd Gwyn 147 D7
Talaton Devon 15 B7
Talbenny Pembs 72 C4
Talbot Green Rhondda 58 C4
Talbot Heath BCP 19 C7
Talbot's End S Glos 80 G2
Talbot Village BCP 19 C7
Talbot Woods BCP 19 C7
Tale Devon 27 G9
Talerddig Powys 129 C8
Talgarreg Ceredig 111 G8
Talgarth Powys 96 E3
Talgarth's Well Swansea 56 D2
Talisker Highld 294 B5
Talke Staffs 168 E4
Talke Pits Staffs 168 E4
Talkin Cumb 240 F3
Talladale Highld 299 B9
Talla Linnfoots Borders 260 E4
Tallaminnoch S Ayrs 245 D10
Talland Corn 6 E4
Tallarn Green Wrex 166 G6
Tallentire Cumb 229 D8
Talley Carms 94 E2
Tallington Lincs 137 B11
Talmine Highld 308 C5
Talog Carms 92 F6
Talsarn Carms 94 F5
Tal-sarn Ceredig 111 F10
Talsarnau Gwyn 146 B2
Talskiddy Corn 5 B8
Talwrn Anglesey 179 F7
Wrex 166 F3
Tal-y-bont Ceredig 128 F3
Conwy 164 B3
Gwyn 145 E11
Gwyn 179 G10
Talybont-on-Usk Powys 96 G2
Tal-y-cafn Conwy 180 G3
Tal-y-coed Mon 78 B6
Talygarn Rhondda 58 C4
Talyllyn Powys 96 F2
Tal-y-llyn Gwyn 128 B4
Talysarn Gwyn 163 E7
Tal-y-waenydd Gwyn 163 F11
Talywain Torf 78 E3
Tal-y-wern Powys 128 C6
Tamanabhagh W Isles 304 F2
Tame Bridge N Yorks 225 D10
Tamer Lane End
Gtr Man 194 G6
Tamerton Foliot Plym 7 C9

Tame Water Gtr Man 196 F3
Tamfourhill Falk 279 E7
Tamworth Staffs 134 C4
Tamworth Green Lincs 174 G5
Tancred N Yorks 206 B5
Tandem W Yorks 197 D7
Tanden Kent 54 F2
Tandlehill Renfs 267 C8
Tandridge Sur 51 C11
Tanerdy Carms 93 G8
Tanfield Durham 242 F5
Tanfield Lea Durham 242 G5
Tang N Yorks 205 B10
Tangasdal W Isles 297 M2
Tang Hall York 207 C8
Tangiers Pembs 73 B7
Tangley Hants 47 C10
Tanglwst Carms 92 E6
Tangmere W Sus 22 B6
Tangwick Shetland 312 F4
Tangy Argyll 255 E7
Tan Hills Durham 233 B11
Tan Hinon Powys 129 F7
Tanhouse Lancs 194 F3
Tanis Wilts 62 G3
Tankersley S Yorks 197 G10
Tankerton Kent 70 F6
Tanlan Flint 181 E10
Tan-lan Conwy 164 C3
Gwyn 163 G10
Tanlan Banks Flint 181 E10
Tannach Highld 310 E7
Tannachie Aberds 293 E9
Tannadice Angus 287 B8
Tanner's Green Worcs 117 C11
Tannington Suff 126 D4
Tannington Place Suff 126 D4
Tannochside N Lanark 268 C4
Tan Office Suff 126 E2
Tan Office Green Suff 124 F5
Tansley Derbys 170 D4
Tansley Hill W Mid 133 F9
Tansley Knoll Derbys 170 C4
Tansor N Nhants 137 E11
Tanterton Lancs 202 G6
Tantobie Durham 242 G5
Tanton N Yorks 225 C10
Tanwood Worcs 117 C8
Tanworth-in-Arden
Warks 118 C2
Tan-y-bwlch Gwyn 163 G11
Tanyfron Wrex 166 E3
Tan-y-fron Conwy 165 C7
Tan-y-graig Anglesey 179 F8
Gwyn 144 B6
Tanygrisiau Gwyn 163 F11
Tan-y-groes Ceredig 92 B5
Tan-y-mynydd Gwyn 144 C6
Tan-y-pistyll Powys 147 D11
Tan-yr-allt Denb 181 E9
Gwyn 163 E7
Tanyrhydiau Ceredig 112 D4
Tanysgafell Gwyn 163 B10
Taobh a Chaolais
W Isles 297 K3
Taobh a' Ghlinne
W Isles 305 G5
Taobh a Thuath Loch
Aineort W Isles 297 J3
Taobh a Tuath Loch
Baghasdail W Isles 297 J3
Taobh Siar W Isles 305 H3
Taobh Tuath W Isles 296 C5
Taplow Bucks 66 C2
Tapnage Hants 33 E9
Tapton Derbys 186 G5
Tapton Hill S Yorks 186 D4
Tarbat Ho Highld 301 B7
Tarbert Argyll 255 B7
Argyll 275 G7
Argyll 275 G9
Tarbet Argyll 285 G7
Highld 295 F9
Highld 306 E6
Tarbock Green Mers 183 D7
Tarbolton S Ayrs 257 D10
Tarbrax S Lanark 269 D10
Tardebigge Worcs 117 D10
Tardy Gate Lancs 194 B4
Tarfside Angus 292 F6
Tarland Aberds 292 C6
Tarleton Lancs 194 C3
Tarleton Moss Lancs 194 C2
Tarlogie Highld 309 L7
Tarlscough Lancs 194 E2
Tarlton Glos 81 F7
Tarn W Yorks 205 F9
Tarnbrook Lancs 203 B7
Tarnock Som 43 C11
Tarns Cumb 229 B8
Tarnside Cumb 221 G8
Tarporley Ches W 167 C9
Tarpots Essex 69 B9
Tarr Som 42 G6
Tarraby Cumb 239 F10
Tarrant Crawford
Dorset 30 G6
Tarrant Gunville Dorset 30 E6
Tarrant Hinton Dorset 30 E6
Tarrant Keyneston
Dorset 30 G6
Tarrant Launceston
Dorset 30 F6
Tarrant Monkton Dorset 30 F6
Tarrant Rawston Dorset 30 F6
Tarrant Rushton Dorset 30 F6
Tarrel Highld 311 L2
Tarring Neville E Sus 36 G6
Tarrington Hereford 98 C2
Tarrington Common
Hereford 98 D2
Tarryblake Ho Moray 302 E5
Tarsappie Perth 286 E5
Tarskavaig Highld 295 E7
Tarts Hill Shrops 149 B8
Tarves Aberds 303 F8
Tarvie Highld 300 D4
Perth 292 G2
Tarvin Ches W 167 B7
Tarvin Sands Ches W 167 B7
Tasburgh Norf 142 D4
Tasley Shrops 132 E3
Taston Oxon 101 G7
Tat Bank W Mid 133 F9
Tatenhill Staffs 152 E4
Tatenhill Common
Staffs 152 E3
Tathall End M Keynes 102 B6
Tatham Lancs 212 F2
Tathwell Lincs 190 E4
Tatling End Bucks 66 B4
Tatsfield Sur 52 B2
Tattenhall Ches W 167 D7
Tattenhoe M Keynes 102 E6
Tatterford Norf 159 D7
Tattersett Norf 158 C6
Tattershall Lincs 174 D2
Tattershall Bridge
Lincs 173 D11
Tattershall Thorpe
Lincs 174 D2
Tattingstone Suff 108 D2
Tattingstone White Horse
Suff 108 D2
Tattle Bank Warks 118 E3
Tatton Dale Ches E 184 E2
Tatworth Som 28 F4
Taunton Gtr Man 196 G2
Som 28 C2
Taverham Norf 160 G3
Taverners Green Essex 87 B9
Tavernspite Pembs 73 C11
Tavistock Devon 12 G5
Taw Green Devon 13 B9
Tawstock Devon 25 B9
Taxal Derbys 185 F8
Tay Bridge Dundee 287 E8
Tayinloan Argyll 255 C7
Taymouth Castle Perth 285 C11
Taynish Argyll 275 E8
Taynton Glos 98 G4
Oxon 82 C2
Taynuilt Argyll 284 D4
Tayport Fife 287 E8
Tayvallich Argyll 275 E8
Tea Green Herts 104 G2
Tealby Lincs 189 C11
Tealing Angus 287 D8
Teams T&W 242 E6
Team Valley T&W 242 E6
Teanford Staffs 169 G8
Teangue Highld 295 E8
Teanna Mhachair
W Isles 296 E3
Teasley Mead E Sus 52 F4
Tebay Cumb 222 E2
Tebworth C Beds 103 F9
Tedburn St Mary Devon 14 C2
Teddington Glos 99 E9
London 67 E7
Teddington Hands Worcs 99 E9
Tedsmore Shrops 149 D7
Tedstone Delamere
Hereford 116 F3
Tedstone Wafer
Hereford 116 F3
Teesville Redcar 225 B10
Teeton W Nhants 120 C3
Teffont Evias Wilts 46 G3
Teffont Magna Wilts 46 G3
Tegryn Pembs 92 E4
Teigh Rutland 155 F7
Teigncombe Devon 13 D9
Teigngrace Devon 14 G2
Teignmouth Devon 14 G4
Teign Village Devon 14 E2
Telford Telford 132 B3
Telham E Sus 38 E3
Tellisford Som 45 B10
Telscombe E Sus 36 G6
Telscombe Cliffs E Sus 36 G5
Templand Dumfries 248 F3
Temple Corn 11 G8
Glasgow 267 B10
Midloth 270 D6
Wilts 45 E10
Windsor 65 C10
Temple Balsall W Mid 118 B4
Temple Bar Carms 75 B9
Ceredig 111 G10
W Sus 22 B5
Templeborough
S Yorks 186 C6
Temple Cloud Bath 44 B6
Templecombe Som 30 C2
Temple Cowley Oxon 83 E8
Temple End Essex 106 C6
Suff 124 G3
Temple Ewell Kent 55 E9
Temple Fields Essex 87 C7
Temple Grafton Warks 118 G2
Temple Guiting Glos 99 F11
Templehall Fife 280 C5
Temple Herdewyke
Warks 119 G7
Temple Hill Kent 68 D5
Temple Hirst N Yorks 198 C6
Templeman's Ash Dorset 28 G6
Temple Normanton
Derbys 170 B6
Temple Sowerby Cumb 231 F8
Templeton Devon 26 E5
Pembs 73 C10
W Berks 63 F11
Templeton Bridge Devon 26 E5
Templetown Durham 242 G4
Tempsford C Beds 122 G3
Ten Acres W Mid 133 G11
Tenandry Perth 291 G11
Tenbury Wells Worcs 115 D11
Tenby = Dinbych-y-Pysgod
Pembs 73 E10
Tencreek Corn 6 E4
Tendring Essex 108 G2
Tendring Green Essex 108 F2
Tendring Heath Essex 108 F2
Ten Mile Bank Norf 140 D2
Tenston Orkney 314 E2
Tenterden Kent 53 G11
Terfyn Conwy 180 F6
Gwyn 163 C9
Terhill Som 43 G7
Terling Essex 88 B3
Ternhill Shrops 150 C2
Terpersie Castle Aberds 302 G5
Terras Corn 5 E8
Terregles Banks
Dumfries 237 B11
Terrible Down E Sus 23 B7
Terrick Bucks 84 D4
Terriers Bucks 84 G5
Terrington N Yorks 216 E3
Terrington St Clement
Norf 157 E10
Terrington St John
Norf 157 G10
Terryhorn Aberds 302 F4
Terry's Green Warks 118 C2
Terwick Common W Sus 34 C4
Teston Kent 53 C8
Testwood Hants 32 E5
Tetbury Glos 80 G5
Tetbury Upton Glos 80 F5
Tetchill Shrops 149 C7
Tetchwick Bucks 83 B11
Tetcott Devon 12 B2
Tetford Lincs 190 G4
Tetley N Lincs 199 E9
Tetney Lincs 201 G10
Tetney Lock Lincs 201 G10
Tetsworth Oxon 83 E11
Tettenhall W Mid 133 D7
Tettenhall Wood W Mid 133 D7
Tetworth Cambs 122 G4
Teuchan Aberds 303 F10
Teversal Notts 171 C7
Teversham Cambs 123 F9
Teviothead Borders 249 B10
Tewel Aberds 293 E10
Tewin Herts 86 C3
Tewin Wood Herts 86 B3
Tewitfield Lancs 211 E10
Tewkesbury Glos 99 E7
Teynham Kent 70 G3
Teynham Street Kent 70 G3
Thackley W Yorks 205 F9
Thackley End W Yorks 205 F9
Thackthwaite Cumb 229 G8
Thainston Aberds 293 F8
Thakeham W Sus 35 D10
Thame Oxon 84 D2
Thames Ditton Sur 67 F7
Thames Haven Thurrock 69 C8
Thames Head Glos 81 F7
Thamesmead London 68 C3
Thanington Kent 54 B6
Thankerton S Lanark 259 B11
Tharston Norf 142 E3
Thatcham W Berks 64 F4
Thatto Heath Mers 183 C8
Thaxted Essex 106 E2
The Aird Highld 298 D4
Theakston N Yorks 214 B6
Thealby N Lincs 199 D11
The Alders Staffs 134 C3
Theale Som 44 D3
W Berks 64 E6
The Arms Norf 141 D7
Thearne E Yorks 209 F7
The Bage Hereford 96 C5
The Balloch Perth 286 F2
The Bank Ches E 168 D4
The Banks Gtr Man 185 D7
Wilts 62 D4
The Barony Ches E 167 E11
Orkney 314 D2
The Barton Wilts 62 D5
The Batch S Glos 61 E7
The Beeches Glos 81 E8
The Bell Gtr Man 194 F4
The Bents Staffs 151 C10
Theberton Suff 127 D8
The Blythe Staffs 151 D10
The Bog Shrops 131 D7
The Borough Dorset 30 E2
London 67 D10
The Bourne Sur 49 E10
Worcs 117 F9
The Bows Stirling 285 G11
The Braes Highld 295 B7
The Brampton Staffs 168 F4
The Brand Leics 153 G10
The Bratch Staffs 133 E7
The Breck Orkney 314 F3
The Brents Kent 70 G4
The Bridge Dorset 30 E3
The Broad Hereford 115 E9
The Brook Suff 125 B11
The Brushes Derbys 186 F5
The Bryn Mon 78 D4
The Burf Worcs 116 D6
The Butts Hants 49 F8
Som 45 D9
The Camp Glos 80 D6
Herts 85 D11
The Cape Warks 118 D5
The Chart Kent 52 C3
The Chequer Wrex 167 G7
The Chuckery W Mid 133 D10
The City Bucks 84 F3
The Cleaver Hereford 97 F10
The Close W Sus 22 C5
The Colony Oxon 100 D6
The Common Bath 60 G6
Bucks 102 E5
Dorset 30 E3
Shrops 150 D3
Suff 108 B2
Swansea 56 C4
Wilts 47 G8
Wilts 61 G11
Wilts 62 C4
W Sus 51 G7
The Corner Kent 53 E8
Shrops 131 F8
The Cot Mon 79 F8
The Craigs Highld 309 K4
The Crofts E Yorks 218 E4
The Cronk IoM 192 C4
The Cross Hands Leics 134 C6
The Cwm Mon 79 G7
Theddingworth Leics 136 F3
Theddlethorpe All Saints
Lincs 191 D7
Theddlethorpe St Helen
Lincs 191 D7
The Dell Suff 143 D9
The Delves W Mid 133 D10
The Den N Ayrs 266 E6
The Dene Durham 242 G4
Hants 47 C11
The Down Kent 53 F7
Shrops 132 E3
The Downs Sur 50 F3
The Dunks Wrex 166 E4
The Eals Northumb 251 F7
The Eaves Glos 79 D10
The Fall W Yorks 197 B10
The Fence Glos 79 D8
The Flat Glos 80 B3
The Flatt Cumb 240 B3
The Flourish Derbys 153 B8
The Folly Herts 85 C11
S Glos 61 E8
The Fording Hereford 98 F3
The Forge Hereford 114 F6
The Forstal Kent 54 F4
The Forties Derbys 152 F6
The Four Alls Shrops 150 C3
The Fox Wilts 62 B6
The Foxholes Shrops 132 G2
The Frenches Hants 32 C4
The Frythe Herts 86 C2
The Garths Shetland 312 B8
The Gibb Wilts 61 D10
The Glack Borders 260 B6
The Gore Shrops 131 G11
The Grange Norf 160 E2
N Yorks 225 F11
The Green Cambs 122 D5
C Beds 85 B8
Cumb 210 C3
Cumb 211 D7
Essex 88 B3
Hants 32 B3
M Keynes 103 C7
Norf 141 C11
Norf 159 B11
Oxon 101 F9
Shrops 130 G6
S Yorks 197 G8
Warks 118 F4
Wilts 45 G11
W Nhants 102 C5
The Grove Dumfries 237 B11
Durham 242 G3
Herts 85 F9
Shrops 131 B7
Shrops 131 G8
Worcs 99 C7
The Gutter Derbys 170 F5
The Gutter *continued*
Worcs 117 B9
The Hacket S Glos 61 B7
The Hague Derbys 185 C8
The Hall Shetland 312 D8
The Hallands N Lincs 200 C5
The Ham Wilts 45 C11
The Handfords Staffs 151 E7
The Harbour Kent 53 D10
The Haven W Sus 50 G5
The Headland Hrtlpl 234 E6
The Heath Norf 159 D8
Norf 160 E3
Norf 160 E4
Staffs 151 C11
Suff 108 D2
The Hem Shrops 132 B4
The Hendre Mon 79 C7
The Herberts V Glam 58 E3
The Hermitage Cambs 123 C7
The High Essex 86 C6
The Highlands E Sus 38 F2
The Hill Cumb 210 C3
The Hobbins Shrops 132 E4
The Hollands Staffs 168 D6
The Hollies Notts 172 E4
The Holmes Derbys 153 B7
The Holt Wokingham 65 D10
The Hook Worcs 98 C6
The Hope Shrops 115 B10
The Howe Cumb 211 B9
IoM 192 F2
The Humbers Telford 150 G3
The Hundred Hereford 115 E10
The Hyde London 67 B8
Worcs 98 C6
The Hythe Essex 107 G10
The Inch Edin 280 G5
The Knab Swansea 56 D6
The Knap V Glam 58 F5
The Knapp Hereford 116 G3
S Glos 79 G11
The Knowle W Mid 133 F9
The Laches Staffs 133 B8
The Lake Dumfries 237 E8
The Lakes Worcs 116 B5
The Lawe T&W 243 D9
The Lawns E Yorks 208 G6
Thelbridge Barton Devon 26 E3
The Leacon Kent 54 G3
The Leath Shrops 131 F11
The Lee Bucks 84 E6
The Lees Kent 54 C4
The Leigh Glos 99 F7
The Leys Staffs 134 C4
The Lhen IoM 192 B4
The Ling Norf 142 D6
The Lings Norf 141 B10
S Yorks 199 F7
The Linleys Wilts 61 F11
Thelnetham Suff 125 B10
The Lunt W Mid 133 D9
Thelveton Norf 142 G3
Thelwall Warr 183 D10
The Manor W Sus 22 C4
The Marsh Ches E 168 C4
Hereford 115 F9
Powys 130 D6
Shrops 150 D3
Staffs 150 D6
Suff 125 B11
Suff 126 B2
Wilts 62 C5
Themelthorpe Norf 159 E11
The Middles Durham 242 G6
The Mint Hants 34 B3
The Moor Flint 166 B4
Kent 38 B3
The Moors Hereford 97 E10
The Mount Hants 64 G2
Reading 65 E8
The Mumbles = Y Mwmbwls
Swansea 56 D6
The Murray S Lanark 268 E2
The Mythe Glos 99 E7
The Nant Wrex 166 E3
The Narth Mon 79 D8
The Neuk Aberds 293 D9
Thenford W Nhants 101 C10
The Node Herts 104 G4
The Nook Shrops 149 C11
Shrops 150 E3
The North Mon 79 D8
Theobald's Green Wilts 62 F4
The Oval Bath 61 G8
The Park Glos 99 G8
The Parks S Yorks 198 F6
The Pitts Wilts 31 B9
The Platt Oxon 83 E9
The Pludds Glos 79 B10
The Point Devon 14 E5
The Pole of Itlaw
Aberds 302 D6
The Port of Felixstowe
Suff 108 E5
The Potteries Stoke 168 F5
The Pound Glos 98 E4
The Quarry Glos 80 F2
Shrops 149 G9
The Quarter Kent 53 E11
Kent 53 G11
The Rampings Worcs 99 E7
The Rectory Lincs 156 G2
The Reddings Glos 99 G8
Therfield Herts 104 D6
The Rhos Pembs 73 C8
The Rhydd Hereford 97 E9
The Riddle Hereford 115 E9
The Ridge Wilts 61 F11
The Ridges Wokingham 65 G10
The Ridgeway Herts 86 E3
The Riding Northumb 241 D10
The Riggs Borders 261 C8
The Rink Borders 261 C11
The Rise Windsor 66 F2
The Rock Telford 132 B3
The Rocks Kent 53 B8
S Glos 61 C8
The Roe Denb 181 G8
The Rookery Herts 85 G10
Staffs 168 D5
The Row Lancs 211 D9
The Rowe Staffs 150 B6
The Ryde Herts 86 D2
The Sands Sur 49 D11
The Scarr Glos 98 F4
The Shoe Wilts 61 E10
The Shruggs Staffs 151 C8
The Slack Durham 233 F8
The Slade W Berks 64 F4
The Smeeth Norf 157 G10
The Smithies Shrops 132 D3
The Spa Wilts 62 G2
The Spring Warks 118 C5
The Square Torf 78 F3
The Stocks Kent 38 B6
Wilts 62 G2
The Straits Hants 49 F9
W Mid 133 E8
The Strand Wilts 46 B2
The Swillett Herts 85 F8
The Sydnall Shrops 150 C3
Thetford Lincs 156 F2
Norf 141 G7
The Thrift Cambs 104 D6
The Throat Wokingham 65 F10
The Toft Staffs 151 F8
The Towans Corn 2 B3
The Town Scilly 1 F3
The Twittocks Glos 99 D7
The Tynings Glos 80 B6
The Vale W Mid 133 G11
The Valley Ches E 167 D11
Kent 54 C3
Leics 154 F4
Pembs 73 D10
The Vauld Hereford 97 B10
The Village Newport 78 G4
Windsor 66 E3
W Mid 133 F7
The Walshes Worcs 116 C6
The Warren Kent 54 E3
Wilts 63 F8
The Waterwheel Shrops 131 C7
The Weaven Hereford 97 E10
The Wells Sur 67 G7
The Wern Wrex 166 E3
The Willows NE Lincs 201 F8
The Wood Shrops 148 E6
Shrops 149 D9
The Woodlands Leics 136 D3
Suff 107 C11
Suff 108 D3
The Woods W Mid 133 D10
The Wrangle Bath 44 B4
The Wrythe London 67 F9
The Wyke Shrops 132 B4
The Wymm Hereford 97 B10
Theydon Bois Essex 86 F6
Theydon Garnon Essex 87 F7
Theydon Mount Essex 87 F7
The Yeld Shrops 131 G11
Thicket Mead Bath 45 B7
Thick Hollins W Yorks 196 E6
Thickthorn Hall Norf 142 B3
Thickwood Wilts 61 E10
Thimbleby Lincs 190 G2
N Yorks 225 F9
Thimble End W Mid 134 E2
Thinford Durham 233 E11
Thingley Wilts 61 E11
Thingwall Mers 182 E3
Thirdpart N Ayrs 266 F3
Thirlby N Yorks 215 C9
Thirlestane Borders 271 F11
Thirn N Yorks 214 B4
Thirsk N Yorks 215 C8
Thirtleby E Yorks 209 G9
Thistleton Lancs 202 F4
Rutland 155 F8
Thistley Green Essex 88 B2
Suff 124 B3
Thixendale N Yorks 216 G6
Thockrington Northumb 241 B11
Tholomas Drove Cambs 139 B7
Tholthorpe N Yorks 215 F9
Thomas Chapel Pembs 73 D10
Thomas Close Cumb 230 C4
Thomastown Aberds 302 F5
Rhondda 58 B4
Thompson Norf 141 D8
Thomshill Moray 302 D2
Thong Kent 69 E7
Thongsbridge W Yorks 196 F6
Thoralby N Yorks 213 B10
Thoresby Notts 187 G10
Thoresthorpe Lincs 191 F7
Thoresway Lincs 189 B11
Thorganby Lincs 190 B2
N Yorks 207 E9
Thorgill N Yorks 226 F4
Thorington Suff 127 C8
Thorington Street Suff 107 D10
Thorlby N Yorks 204 C5
Thorley Herts 87 B7
IoW 20 D3
Thorley Houses Herts 105 G9
Thorley Street Herts 87 B7
IoW 20 D3
Thormanby N Yorks 215 E9
Thorn Devon 13 D9
Powys 114 E5
Thornaby on Tees
Stockton 225 B9
Thornage Norf 159 B11
Thornborough Bucks 102 E4
N Yorks 214 D5
Thornbury Devon 24 F6
Hereford 116 F2
S Glos 79 G10
W Yorks 205 G9
Thornby Cumb 239 G7
W Nhants 120 B3
Thorncliff W Yorks 197 E8
Thorncliffe Staffs 169 D8
Thorncombe Dorset 28 G5
Dorset 30 G5
Thorncombe Street Sur 50 E4
Thorncote Green
C Beds 104 B3
Thorncross IoW 20 E4
Thorndon Suff 126 D2
Thorndon Cross Devon 12 C6
Thorne Corn 24 G2
S Yorks 199 E7
Thorne Coffin Som 29 D8
Thornehillhead Devon 24 D6
Thorne Moor Devon 12 D3
Thornend Wilts 62 D3
Thorner W Yorks 206 E3
Thornes Staffs 133 C11
W Yorks 197 D10
Thorne St Margaret Som 27 C9
Thorney Bucks 66 D4
Notts 188 G5
Pboro 138 C5
Som 28 C6
Thorney Close T&W 243 G9
Thorney Crofts E Yorks 201 C8
Thorney Green Suff 125 E11
Thorney Hill Hants 19 B9
Thorney Island W Sus 22 C3
Thorney Toll Pboro 138 C6
Thorneywood Notts 171 G9
Thornfalcon Som 28 C3
Thornford Dorset 29 E10
Thorngrafton Northumb 241 D7
Thorngrove Som 43 G11
Thorngumbald E Yorks 201 B8
Thornham Norf 176 E2
Thornham Fold
Gtr Man 195 F11
Thornham Magna Suff 126 C2
Thornham Parva Suff 126 C2
Thornhaugh Pboro 137 C11
Thornhill Cardiff 59 C7
Cumb 219 D10
Derbys 185 E11
Dumfries 247 D9
Soton 33 E7
Stirling 278 B3
Torf 78 F3
Thornhill *continued*
Wilts 62 D5
W Yorks 197 D9
Thorn Hill S Yorks 186 C6
Thornhill Edge W Yorks 197 D8
Thornhill Lees W Yorks 197 D8
Thornhill Park Hants 33 E7
Thornhills W Yorks 197 C7
Thornholme E Yorks 218 G2
Thornicombe Dorset 30 G5
Thornielee Borders 261 B10
Thornley Durham 233 D8
Durham 234 D3
Thornliebank E Renf 267 D10
Thornly Park Renfs 267 C9
Thornroan Aberds 303 F8
Thorns N Yorks 223 E7
Suff 124 F4
Thornseat S Yorks 186 C2
Thornsett Derbys 185 D8
Thorns Green Ches E 184 E3
Thornthwaite Cumb 229 F10
N Yorks 205 B9
Thornton Angus 287 C7
Bucks 102 D5
E Yorks 207 D11
Fife 280 B5
Lancs 202 E2
Leics 135 B9
Lincs 174 B2
Mbro 225 C9
Mers 193 G10
Northumb 273 F9
Pembs 72 D6
W Yorks 205 G8
Thornton Curtis N Lincs 200 D5
Thorntonhall S Lanark 267 D11
Thornton Heath London 67 F10
Thornton Hough Mers 182 E4
Thornton in Craven
N Yorks 204 D4
Thornton in Lonsdale
N Yorks 212 E3
Thornton-le-Beans
N Yorks 225 G7
Thornton-le-Clay
N Yorks 216 F3
Thornton-le-Dale
N Yorks 216 C6
Thornton le Moor Lincs 189 B9
Thornton-le-Moor
N Yorks 215 B7
Thornton-le-Moors
Ches W 182 G6
Thornton-le-Street
N Yorks 215 B8
Thorntonloch E Loth 282 G4
Thornton Park Northumb 273 F8
Thornton Rust N Yorks 213 B9
Thornton Steward
N Yorks 214 B3
Thornton Watlass
N Yorks 214 B4
Thornwood Common
Essex 87 D7
Thornydykes Borders 272 F2
Thoroton Notts 172 G3
Thorp Gtr Man 196 F2
Thorp Arch W Yorks 206 D4
Thorpe Cumb 230 F5
Derbys 169 E11
E Yorks 208 D5
Lincs 191 E7
Norf 143 D8
Notts 172 F3
N Yorks 213 G10
Sur 66 F4
Thorpe Abbotts Norf 126 B3
Thorpe Acre Leics 153 E10
Thorpe Arnold Leics 154 E5
Thorpe Audlin W Yorks 198 D3
Thorpe Bassett N Yorks 217 E7
Thorpe Bay Southend 70 B2
Thorpe by Water
Rutland 137 D7
Thorpe Common Suff 108 D5
Thorpe Constantine
Staffs 134 B5
Thorpe Culvert Lincs 175 C7
Thorpe Edge W Yorks 205 F9
Thorpe End Norf 160 G5
Thorpe Fendykes Lincs 175 C7
Thorpe Green Essex 108 G3
Lancs 194 C5
Suff 125 G8
Sur 66 F4
Thorpe Hamlet Norf 142 B4
Thorpe Hesley S Yorks 186 B5
Thorpe in Balne
S Yorks 198 E5
Thorpe in the Fallows
Lincs 188 E6
Thorpe Langton Leics 136 E4
Thorpe Larches Durham 234 F3
Thorpe Latimer Lincs 156 B2
Thorpe Lea Sur 66 E4
Thorpe-le-Soken Essex 108 G3
Thorpe le Street
E Yorks 208 E2
Thorpe le Vale Lincs 190 C2
Thorpe Malsor
N Nhants 120 B6
Thorpe Mandeville
W Nhants 101 B10
Thorpe Market Norf 160 B4
Thorpe Marriot Norf 160 F3
Thorpe Morieux Suff 125 G8
Thorpeness Suff 127 F9
Thorpe on the Hill Lincs 172 B6
W Yorks 197 B10
Thorpe Row Norf 141 B9
Thorpe St Andrew Norf 142 B5
Thorpe St Peter Lincs 175 C7
Thorpe Salvin S Yorks 187 E8
Thorpe Satchville Leics 154 G4
Thorpe Street Suff 125 B10
Thorpe Thewles
Stockton 234 G4
Thorpe Tilney Lincs 173 D10
Thorpe Underwood
N Nhants 136 G5
N Yorks 206 B5
Thorpe Waterville
N Nhants 137 G10
Thorpe Willoughby
N Yorks 207 G7
Thorpe Wood N Yorks 207 G7
Thorpland Norf 140 B2
Thorrington Essex 89 B9
Thorverton Devon 26 G6
Thoulstone Wilts 45 D10
Thrandeston Suff 126 B2
Thrapston N Nhants 121 B9
Thrashbush N Lanark 268 B5
Threapland Cumb 229 D9
N Yorks 213 G9
Threapwood Ches W 166 F6
Staffs 169 G8
Three Ashes Hants 64 G6
Hereford 97 G10
Shrops 115 B7
Three Ashes *continued*
Som 45 D7
Three Bridges Argyll 284 F4
Lincs 190 D6
W Sus 51 F9
Three Burrows Corn 4 F4
Three Chimneys Kent 53 F10
Three Cocked Hat Norf 143 D8
Three Cocks = Aberllynfi
Powys 96 D3
Three Crosses Swansea 56 C5
Three Cups Corner
E Sus 37 C10
Three Fingers Wrex 167 G7
Three Gates Dorset 29 F10
Threehammer Common
Norf 160 E6
Three Hammers Corn 11 D10
Three Holes Norf 139 C10
Three Holes Cross Corn 10 G6
Threekingham Lincs 155 B11
Three Leg Cross E Sus 53 G7
Three Legged Cross
Dorset 31 F9
Threelows Staffs 169 F9
Three Maypoles W Mid 118 B2
Three Mile Cross
Wokingham 65 F8
Threemilestone Corn 4 G5
Threemiletown W Loth 279 F11
Three Oaks E Sus 38 E4
Threepwood Borders 271 G10
Three Sisters Denb 165 C9
Threewaters Corn 5 B10
Threlkeld Cumb 230 F2
Threshers Bush Essex 87 D7
Threshfield N Yorks 213 G9
Thrigby Norf 161 G9
Thringarth Durham 232 G4
Thringstone Leics 153 F8
Thrintoft N Yorks 224 G6
Thriplow Cambs 105 B8
Throapham S Yorks 187 D8
Throckenholt Lincs 139 B7
Throcking Herts 104 E6
Throckley T&W 242 D5
Throckmorton Worcs 99 B9
Throop Dorset 18 C2
Throphill Northumb 252 F4
Thropton Northumb 252 C2
Throsk Stirling 279 C7
Througham Glos 80 D6
Throughgate Dumfries 247 G9
Throwleigh Devon 13 C9
Throwley Kent 54 B3
Throwley Forstal Kent 54 C3
Throxenby N Yorks 217 B10
Thrumpton Notts 153 C10
Notts 188 E2
Thrumster Highld 310 E7
Thrunton Northumb 264 G3
Thrupe Som 44 D6
Thrupp Glos 80 E5
Oxon 82 F3
Oxon 83 B7
Thruscross N Yorks 205 B9
Thrushelton Devon 12 D4
Thrussington Leics 154 F2
Thruxton Hants 47 D9
Hereford 97 E8
Thrybergh S Yorks 187 B7
Thulston Derbys 153 C8
Thunder Bridge
W Yorks 197 E7
Thundergay N Ayrs 255 C9
Thunder Hill Norf 161 F8
Thunder's Hill E Sus 23 C9
Thundersley Essex 69 B9
Thundridge Herts 86 B5
Thurcaston Leics 153 G11
Thurcroft S Yorks 187 D7
Thurdon Corn 24 E3
Thurgarton Norf 160 C3
Notts 171 F11
Thurgoland S Yorks 197 G9
Thurlaston Leics 135 D10
Warks 119 C9
Thurlbear Som 28 C3
Thurlby Lincs 156 F2
Lincs 172 C6
Lincs 191 F7
Thurleigh Bedford 121 F11
Thurlestone Devon 8 G3
Thurloxton Som 43 G9
Thurlstone S Yorks 197 G8
Thurlton Norf 143 D8
Thurlton Links Norf 143 D8
Thurlwood Ches E 168 D4
Thurmaston Leics 136 B2
Thurnby Leics 136 C2
Thurne Norf 161 F8
Thurnham Kent 53 B10
Lancs 202 C5
Thurning N Nhants 137 G11
Norf 159 D11
Thurnscoe S Yorks 198 F3
Thurnscoe East S Yorks 198 F3
Thursby Cumb 239 G8
Thursford Norf 159 C9
Thursford Green Norf 159 C9
Thursley Sur 50 F2
Thurso Highld 310 C5
Thurso East Highld 310 C5
Thurstaston Mers 182 E2
Thurston Suff 125 D8
Thurston Clough
Gtr Man 196 F3
Thurston End Suff 124 G5
Thurstonfield Cumb 239 F8
Thurstonland W Yorks 197 E7
Thurton Norf 142 C6
Thurvaston Derbys 152 B2
Derbys 152 B4
Thuxton Norf 141 B10
Thwaite N Yorks 223 F7
Suff 126 D2
Thwaite Flat Cumb 210 E4
Thwaite Head Cumb 220 G6
Thwaites W Yorks 205 E7
Thwaite St Mary Norf 142 E6
Thwaites Brow W Yorks 205 E7
Thwing E Yorks 217 E11
Tibbermore Perth 286 E4
Tibberton Glos 98 G5
Telford 150 E3
Worcs 117 F8
Tibenham Norf 142 F2
Tibshelf Derbys 170 C6
Tibshelf Wharf Notts 171 C7
Tibthorpe E Yorks 208 B5
Ticehurst E Sus 53 G7
Tichborne Hants 48 G5
Tickencote Rutland 137 B9
Tickenham N Som 60 E3
Ticket Wood Devon 8 G4
Tickford End M Keynes 103 C7
Tickhill S Yorks 187 C9
Tickleback Row Brack 65 E11
Ticklerton Shrops 131 E9
Tickmorend Glos 80 F4
Ticknall Derbys 153 E7
Tickton E Yorks 209 E7
Tidbury Green W Mid 117 B11
Tidcombe Wilts 47 B9
Tiddington Oxon 83 E11
Warks 118 F4
Tidebrook E Sus 37 B10
Tideford Corn 6 D6
Tideford Cross Corn 6 C6
Tidenham Glos 79 F9
Tidenham Chase Glos 79 F9
Tideswell Derbys 185 F11
Tidmarsh W Berks 64 E6
Tidmington Warks 100 D5
Tidnor Hereford 97 D11
Tidpit Hants 31 D9
Tidworth Wilts 47 D8
Tiers Cross Pembs 72 C6
Tiffield W Nhants 120 G3
Tifty Aberds 303 E7
Tigerton Angus 293 G7
Tigh-na-Blair Perth 285 F11
Tighnabruaich Argyll 275 F10
Tighnacachla Argyll 274 G3
Tighnafiline Highld 307 L3
Tighness Argyll 284 G6
Tigley Devon 8 C5
Tilbrook Cambs 121 D11
Tilbury Thurrock 68 D6
Tilbury Green Essex 106 C4
Tilbury Juxta Clare
Essex 106 C5
Tile Cross W Mid 134 F3
Tilegate Green Essex 87 D8
Tile Hill W Mid 118 B5
Tilehouse Green W Mid 118 B3
Tilehurst Reading 65 E7
Tilekiln Green Essex 105 G10
Tiley Dorset 29 F11
Tilford Sur 49 E11
Tilford Common Sur 49 E11
Tilford Reeds Sur 49 E11
Tilgate W Sus 51 G9
Tilgate Forest Row
W Sus 51 G9
Tilkey Essex 106 G6
Tilland Corn 6 C6
Tillathrowie Aberds 302 F4
Tillers' Green Glos 98 E3
Tilley Shrops 149 D10
Tilley Green Shrops 149 D10
Tillicoultry Clack 279 B8
Tillietudlem S Lanark 268 F6
Tillingham Essex 89 E7
Tillington Hereford 97 B9
Staffs 151 E8
W Sus 35 C7
Tillington Common
Hereford 97 B9
Tillislow Devon 12 C3
Tillworth Devon 28 G4
Tillyarblet Angus 293 G7
Tillybirloch Aberds 293 C8
Tillycorthie Aberds 303 G9
Tilly Down Hants 47 D10
Tillydrine Aberds 293 D8
Tillyfour Aberds 293 B7
Tillyfourie Aberds 293 B8
Tillygarmond Aberds 293 D8
Tillygreig Aberds 303 G8
Tillykerrie Aberds 303 G8
Tilly Lo Aberds 293 C7
Tillynaught Aberds 302 C5
Tilmanstone Kent 55 C10
Tilney All Saints Norf 157 F11
Tilney cum Islington
Norf 157 G11
Tilney Fen End Norf 157 G10
Tilney High End Norf 157 F11
Tilney St Lawrence
Norf 157 G10
Tilsdown Glos 80 F2
Tilshead Wilts 46 D4
Tilsmore E Sus 37 C9
Tilsop Shrops 116 C2
Tilstock Shrops 149 B10
Tilston Ches W 167 E7
Tilstone Bank Ches W 167 D9
Tilstone Fearnall
Ches W 167 C9
Tilsworth C Beds 103 G9
Tilton on the Hill Leics 136 B4
Tilts S Yorks 198 F5
Tiltups End Glos 80 F4
Tilty Essex 105 F11
Timberden Bottom Kent 68 G4
Timberhonger Worcs 117 C8
Timberland Lincs 173 D10
Timbersbrook Ches E 168 C5
Timberscombe Som 42 E3
Timble N Yorks 205 C9
Timbold Hill Kent 54 B2
Timbrelham Corn 12 E3
Timperley Gtr Man 184 D3
Timsbury Bath 45 B7
Hants 32 C4
Timsgearraidh W Isles 304 E2
Timworth Suff 125 D7
Timworth Green Suff 125 D7
Tincleton Dorset 17 C11
Tindale Cumb 240 F4
Tindale Crescent
Durham 233 F9
Tindon End Essex 106 E2
Tingewick Bucks 102 E3
Tingley W Yorks 197 B9
Tingon Shetland 312 E4
Tingrith C Beds 103 E10
Tingwall Orkney 314 D3
Tinhay Devon 12 E3
Tinkers End Bucks 102 F5
Tinshill W Yorks 205 F11
Tinsley S Yorks 186 C6
Tinsley Green W Sus 51 F9
Tintagel Corn 11 D7
Tintern Parva Mon 79 E8
Tintinhull Som 29 D8
Tintwistle Derbys 185 B8
Tinwald Dumfries 248 G2
Tinwell Rutland 137 B10
Tipner Ptsmth 33 G10
Tippacott Devon 41 D9
Tipper's Hill Warks 134 F5
Tipperty Aberds 302 C6
Aberds 303 G9
Tipple Cross Devon 12 D3
Tipps End Norf 139 D10
Tip's Cross Essex 87 E9
Tiptoe Hants 19 B11
Tipton W Mid 133 E8
Tipton Green W Mid 133 E9
Tipton St John Devon 15 C7
Tiptree Essex 88 B5
Tiptree Heath Essex 88 B5
Tirabad Powys 95 C7
Tiraghoil Argyll 288 G5
Tircanol Swansea 57 B7
Tirdeunaw Swansea 57 B7
Tirinie Perth 291 G10
Tirley Glos 98 F6
Tirley Knowle Glos 98 F6
Tiroran Argyll 288 G6

Tirphil Caerph 77 E10
Tirril Cumb 230 F6
Tirryside Highld 309 H5
Tir-y-berth Caerph 77 F11
Tir-y-dail Carms 75 C10
Tisbury Wilts 30 B6
Tisman's Common
W Sus 50 G5
Tissington Derbys 169 E11
Titchberry Devon 24 B2
Titchfield Hants 33 F8
Titchfield Common Hants 33 F8
Titchfield Park Hants 33 F8
Titchmarsh N Nhants 121 B10
Titchwell Norf 176 E3
Titcomb W Berks 63 F11
Tithby Notts 154 B3
Tithebarn Staffs 169 G9
Tithe Barn Hillock Mers 183 B9
Titley Hereford 114 E6
Titlington Northumb 264 F4
Titmore Green Herts 104 F4
Titsey Sur 52 C2
Titson Corn 24 G2
Tittenhurst Windsor 66 F3
Tittensor Staffs 151 B7
Titterhill Shrops 131 G10
Tittle Row Windsor 65 C11
Tittleshall Norf 159 E7
Titton Worcs 116 D6
Titty Hill W Sus 34 B5
Tiverton Ches W 167 C9
Devon 27 E7
Tivetshall St Margaret
Norf 142 F3
Tivetshall St Mary Norf 142 F3
Tividale W Mid 133 E9
Tivington Som 42 D2
Tivington Knowle Som 42 E2
Tivoli Cumb 228 G5
Tivy Dale S Yorks 197 F9
Tixall Staffs 151 E9
Tixover Rutland 137 C9
Toab Orkney 314 F5
Shetland 313 M5
Toadmoor Derbys 170 E4
Toad Row Suff 143 F10
Tobermory Argyll 289 D7
Toberonochy Argyll 275 C8
Tobha Beag W Isles 296 D5
Tobha Mor W Isles 297 H3
Tobhtarol W Isles 304 E3
Tobson W Isles 304 E3
Toby's Hill Lincs 191 C7
Tocher Aberds 302 F6
Tockenham Wilts 62 D4
Tockenham Wick Wilts 62 C4
Tockholes Blackburn 195 C7
Tockington S Glos 60 B6
Tockwith N Yorks 206 C5
Todber Dorset 30 C4
Todding Hereford 115 B8
Toddington C Beds 103 F10
Glos 99 E10
W Sus 35 G8
Toddlehills Aberds 303 E10
Todd's Green Herts 104 F4
Todenham Glos 100 D4
Todhill Angus 287 D8
Todhills Cumb 239 E9
Durham 233 E10
Todlachie Aberds 293 B8
Todmorden W Yorks 196 C2
Todpool Corn 4 G4
Todrig Borders 261 F10
Todwick S Yorks 187 E7
Toft Cambs 123 F7
Lincs 155 F11
Shetland 312 F6
Warks 119 C9
Toft Hill Durham 233 F9
Lincs 174 C2
Toft Monks Norf 143 E8
Toft next Newton Lincs 189 D8
Toftrees Norf 159 D7
Tofts Highld 310 C7
Toftshaw W Yorks 197 B7
Toftwood Norf 159 G9
Togston Northumb 252 C6
Tokavaig Highld 295 D8
Tokers Green Oxon 65 D8
Tokyngton London 67 C7
Tolastadh a Chaolais
W Isles 304 E3
Tolastadh bho Thuath
W Isles 304 D7
Tolborough Corn 11 F9
Tolcarne Corn 2 B5
Corn 2 C5
Tolcarne Wartha Corn 2 B5
Toldish Corn 5 D8
Tolgus Mount Corn 4 G3
Tolhurst E Sus 53 G7
Tolladine Worcs 117 F7
Tolland Som 42 G6
Tollard Farnham Dorset 30 D6
Tollard Royal Wilts 30 D6
Toll Bar Mers 183 C7
Rutland 137 B10
S Yorks 198 F5
Tollbar End W Mid 119 B7
Toll End W Mid 133 E9
Tollerford Dorset 17 B7
Toller Fratrum Dorset 17 B7
Toller Porcorum Dorset 17 B7
Tollerton Notts 154 C2
N Yorks 215 G10
Toller Whelme Dorset 29 G8
Tollesbury Essex 89 C7
Tollesby Mbro 225 B10
Tolleshunt D'Arcy Essex 88 C6
Tolleshunt Knights Essex 88 C6
Tolleshunt Major Essex 88 C5
Tollie Highld 300 D5
Toll of Birness Aberds 303 F10
Tolm W Isles 304 E6
Tolmers Herts 86 E4
Tolpuddle Dorset 17 C11
Tolskithy Corn 4 G3
Tolvaddon Downs Corn 4 G3
Tolvah Highld 291 D10
Tolworth London 67 F7
Tomaknock Perth 286 E2
Tom an Fhuadain
W Isles 305 G5
Tomatin Highld 301 G8
Tombreck Highld 300 F6
Tombui Perth 286 B2
Tomchrasky Highld 290 B4
Tomdoun Highld 290 C3
Tomich Highld 300 B6
Highld 300 G3
Tomich House Highld 300 E5
Tomintoul Aberds 292 D3
Moray 292 B3
Tomlow Warks 119 E9
Tomnaven Moray 302 F4
Tomnavoulin Moray 302 G2
Tomperrow Corn 4 G5
Tompkin Staffs 168 E6
Tompset's Bank E Sus 52 G2
Tomsleibhe Argyll 289 F8
Tomthorn Derbys 185 F9
Ton Mon 78 F5
Ton Breigam V Glam 58 D3
Tonbridge Kent 52 D5
Tonderghie Dumfries 236 F6
Tondu Bridgend 57 E11
Tone Som 27 C10
Tonedale Som 27 C10
Tone Green Som 27 C11
Tong Kent 53 D10
Shrops 132 B5
W Yorks 205 G10
Tonge Leics 153 E8
Tonge Corner Kent 70 F2
Tonge Fold Gtr Man 195 F8
Tonge Moor Gtr Man 195 E8
Tong Forge Shrops 132 B5
Tong Green Kent 54 C3
Tongham Sur 49 D11
Tongland Dumfries 237 D8
Tong Norton Shrops 132 B5
Tong Park W Yorks 205 F9
Tong Street W Yorks 205 G9
Tongue Highld 308 D5
Tongue End Lincs 156 F3
Tongwell M Keynes 103 C7
Tongwynlais Cardiff 58 C6
Tonmawr Neath 57 B10
Tonna = *Tonnau* Neath 57 B9
Tonnau = *Tonna* Neath 57 B9
Ton-Pentre Rhondda 77 F7
Ton-teg Rhondda 58 B5
Tontine Lancs 194 G4
Tonwell Herts 86 B4
Tonypandy Rhondda 77 G7
Ton-y-pistyll Caerph 77 F11
Tonyrefail Rhondda 58 B4
Toot Baldon Oxon 83 E9
Toothill Hants 32 D5
Swindon 62 C6
W Yorks 196 C6
Toot Hill Essex 87 E8
Staffs 169 G9
Tooting Graveney London 67 E9
Topcliffe N Yorks 215 D8
W Yorks 197 B9
Topcroft Norf 142 E5
Topcroft Street Norf 142 E5
Top End Bedford 121 E10
Top Green Notts 172 F3
Topham S Yorks 198 D6
Topleigh W Sus 34 D6
Top Lock Gtr Man 194 F6
Top of Hebers Gtr Man 195 F11
Top o' th' Lane Lancs 194 C5
Top o' th' Meadows
Gtr Man 196 F3
Toppesfield Essex 106 D4
Toppings Gtr Man 195 E8
Toprow Norf 142 D3
Topsham Devon 14 D5
Top Valley Nottingham 171 F9
Torbeg N Ayrs 255 E10
Torboll Farm Highld 309 K7
Torbothie N Lanark 269 D7
Torbreck Highld 309 J7
Torbrex Stirling 278 C5
Torbryan Devon 8 B6
Torbush N Lanark 268 D6
Torcross Devon 8 G6
Torcroy Highld 291 D9
Tore Highld 300 D6
Torfrey Corn 6 E2
Torgyle Highld 290 B5
Torinturk Argyll 275 G9
Torkington Gtr Man 184 D6
Torksey Lincs 188 F4
Torlum W Isles 296 F3
Torlundy Highld 290 F3
Tormarton S Glos 61 D9
Tormisdale Argyll 254 B2
Tormitchell S Ayrs 244 E6
Tormore Highld 295 E8
N Ayrs 255 D9
Tornagrain Highld 301 E7
Tornahaish Aberds 292 C4
Tornapress Highld 299 E8
Tornaveen Aberds 293 C8
Torness Highld 300 G5
Toronto Durham 233 E9
Torpenhow Cumb 229 D10
Torphichen W Loth 279 G9
Torphin Edin 270 B4
Torphins Aberds 293 C8
Torpoint Corn 7 E8
Torquay Torbay 9 C8
Torquhan Borders 271 F8
Torr Devon 7 E11
Devon 8 C2
Torra Argyll 254 B4
Torran Argyll 275 C9
Highld 298 E5
Highld 301 B7
Torrance E Dunb 278 G2
Torrans Argyll 288 G6
Torranyard N Ayrs 267 G7
Torre Som 42 E4
Torbay 9 C8
Torridon Highld 299 D9
Torridon Ho Highld 299 D8
Torries Aberds 293 B8
Torrin Highld 295 C7
Torrisdale Highld 308 C6
Torrisdale Castle Argyll 255 D8
Torrisdale-Square
Argyll 255 D8
Torrish Highld 311 H3
Torrisholme Lancs 211 G9
Torroble Highld 309 J5
Torroy Highld 309 K5
Torrpark Corn 11 D10
Torry Aberdeen 293 C11
Aberds 302 F4
Torryburn Fife 279 D10
Torsonce Borders 271 G9
Torsonce Mains Borders 271 G9
Torterston Aberds 303 E10
Torthorwald Dumfries 238 B2
Tortington W Sus 35 F8
Torton Worcs 116 C6
Tortworth S Glos 80 G2
Torvaig Highld 298 E4
Torver Cumb 220 G5
Torwood Falk 278 E6
Torwoodlee Mains
Borders 261 B11
Torworth Notts 187 D11
Tosberry Devon 24 C3
Toscaig Highld 295 B9
Toseland Cambs 122 E4
Tosside N Yorks 203 B11
Tostock Suff 125 E9
Totaig Highld 295 C10
Highld 298 D2
Totardor Highld 294 B5
Tote Highld 298 E4
Totegan Highld 310 C2
Tote Hill Hants 32 C4
W Sus 34 C5
Totford Hants 48 F5
Totham Hill Essex 88 C5
Totham Plains Essex 88 C5
Tothill Lincs 190 E6
Tot Hill Hants 64 G3
Totland IoW 20 D2
Totley S Yorks 186 F4
Totley Brook S Yorks 186 E4
Totley Rise S Yorks 186 E4
Totmonslow Staffs 151 B9
Totnell Dorset 29 F10
Totnes Devon 8 C6
Totnor Hereford 97 E11
Toton Notts 153 C10
Totronald Argyll 288 D3
Totscore Highld 298 C3
Tottenham London 86 G4
Tottenham Hale London 67 B10
Tottenhill Norf 158 G2
Tottenhill Row Norf 158 G2
Totteridge Bucks 84 G5
London 86 G2
Totternhoe C Beds 103 G9
Totteroak S Glos 61 C8
Totterton Shrops 131 F7
Totties W Yorks 197 F7
Tottington Gtr Man 195 E9
Norf 141 D7
Tottlebank Cumb 210 C6
Tottleworth Lancs 203 G10
Totton Hants 32 E5
Touchen End Windsor 65 D11
Toulston N Yorks 206 E5
Toulton Som 43 G7
Toulvaddie Highld 311 L2
Tournaig Highld 307 L3
Toux Aberds 303 D9
Tovil Kent 53 C9
Towan Corn 10 G3
Towan Cross Corn 4 F4
Toward Argyll 266 B2
Towcester W Nhants 102 B3
Towednack Corn 1 B5
Towerage Bucks 84 G4
Tower End Norf 158 F3
Tower Hamlets Kent 55 E10
Towerhead N Som 44 B2
Tower Hill Ches E 184 F6
Devon 12 C3
Essex 108 E5
Herts 85 E8
Mers 194 G2
Sur 51 D7
W Mid 133 E11
W Sus 35 B11
Towersey Oxon 84 D2
Tow House Northumb 241 E7
Towie Aberds 292 B6
Aberds 302 G5
Aberds 303 C8
Towiemore Moray 302 E3
Tow Law Durham 233 D8
Town Barton Devon 14 C2
Townend Derbys 185 E9
Staffs 151 B9
W Dunb 277 F8
Town End Bucks 84 F3
Cambs 139 D8
Cumb 211 B7
Cumb 211 C8
Cumb 212 C2
Cumb 220 D6
Cumb 221 E8
Cumb 221 F7
Cumb 231 F8
Derbys 185 F11
E Yorks 207 C10
Mers 183 D7
W Yorks 196 D5
Townfield Durham 232 B5
Town Fields Ches W 167 B10
Towngate Cumb 230 B6
Lincs 156 G2
Town Green Gtr Man 183 B9
Lancs 194 F2
Norf 161 G7
Townhead Argyll 275 G11
Cumb 229 D7
Cumb 230 D6
Cumb 231 E8
Dumfries 237 E8
N Lanark 268 B4
Northumb 251 E9
S Ayrs 244 C6
S Yorks 186 E4
S Yorks 197 G7
Town Head Cumb 220 D6
Cumb 221 E8
Cumb 222 C2
Cumb 222 C3
Cumb 231 F7
Cumb 231 F8
Cumb 231 G8
Cumb 231 G9
Derbys 185 F11
N Yorks 204 B2
N Yorks 212 F5
Staffs 169 F8
W Yorks 204 D6
Townhead of Greenlaw
Dumfries 237 C9
Townhill Fife 280 D2
Swansea 56 C6
Townhill Park Hants 33 E7
Town Kelloe Durham 234 D3
Townlake Devon 12 G4
Townland Green Kent 54 G2
Town Lane Gtr Man 183 B11
Town Littleworth E Sus 36 D6
Town of Lowton Mers 183 B10
Town Park Telford 132 B3
Town Row E Sus 52 G5
Townsend Bath 44 B5
Bucks 84 D2
Devon 25 B10
Herts 85 D10
Oxon 63 B11
Pembs 72 D4
Som 44 C4
Stoke 168 F6
Wilts 45 B11
Wilts 46 B4
Towns End Hants 48 B5
Som 30 D2
Town's End Bucks 102 G2
Dorset 18 B3
Dorset 18 E5
Dorset 29 F9
Som 45 D7
Townsend Fold Lancs 195 C10
Townshend Corn 2 C3
Town Street Glos 98 F6
Townwell S Glos 79 G11
Town Yetholm Borders 263 D8
Towthorpe E Yorks 217 G8
York 207 B8
Towton N Yorks 206 F5
Towyn Conwy 181 F7
Toxteth Mers 182 D5
Toynton All Saints Lincs 174 C5
Toynton Fen Side Lincs 174 C5
Toynton St Peter Lincs 174 C6
Toy's Hill Kent 52 C3
Trabboch E Ayrs 257 E10
Traboe Corn 2 E6
Tracebridge Som 27 C9
Trabrown Borders 271 F10
Tradespark Highld 301 D8
Orkney 314 F4
Trafford Park Gtr Man 184 B3
Traigh Ho Highld 295 F8
Trallong Powys 95 F9
Trallwn Rhondda 77 G9
Swansea 57 B7
Tramagenna Corn 11 E7
Tram Inn Hereford 97 E9
Tranch Torf 78 E3
Tranent E Loth 281 G8
Tranmere Mers 182 D4
Trantlebeg Highld 310 D2
Trantlemore Highld 310 D2
Tranwell Northumb 252 G5
Trapp Carms 75 B11
Traprain E Loth 281 F11
Trap's Green Warks 118 D2
Trapshill W Berks 63 G11
Traquair Borders 261 C8
Trash Green W Berks 65 F7
Travellers' Rest Carms 74 B5
Trawden Lancs 204 F4
Trawscoed Powys 95 E11
Trawsfynydd Gwyn 146 B4
Trawsnant Ceredig 111 D11
Treadam Mon 78 B5
Treaddow Hereford 97 G10
Treal Corn 2 F6
Trealaw Rhondda 77 G8
Treales Lancs 202 G4
Trearddur Anglesey 178 F3
Treaslane Highld 298 D3
Treath Corn 3 D7
Treator Corn 10 F4
Tre-Aubrey V Glam 58 E4
Trebanog Rhondda 77 G8
Trebanos Neath 76 E2
Trebarber Corn 5 C7
Trebartha Corn 11 F11
Trebarwith Corn 11 D7
Trebarwith Strand Corn 10 D6
Trebeath Corn 11 D11
Tre-Beferad V Glam 58 F3
Trebell Green Corn 5 C11
Treberfydd Powys 96 F2
Trebetherick Corn 10 F4
Trebilcock Corn 5 C9
Treble's Holford Som 43 G7
Tre-boeth Swansea 57 B7
Treborough Som 42 F4
Trebudannon Corn 5 C7
Trebullett Corn 12 F2
Treburgett Corn 11 F7
Treburgie Corn 6 C4
Treburley Corn 12 F3
Treburrick Corn 10 G3
Trebyan Corn 5 C11
Trecastle Powys 95 F7
Trecenydd Caerph 58 B6
Trecott Devon 25 G10
Trecwn Pembs 91 E9
Trecynon Rhondda 77 E7
Tredannick Corn 10 G6
Tredaule Corn 11 E10
Tredavoe Corn 1 D5
Treddiog Pembs 91 F7
Tredegar Bl Gwent 77 D10
Trederwen Powys 148 F5
Tre-derwen Powys 148 F4
Tredethy Corn 11 G7
Tredington Glos 99 F8
Warks 100 C5
Tredinnick Corn 1 C4
Corn 5 D10
Corn 6 B3
Corn 6 D4
Corn 10 G4
Tredogan V Glam 58 F5
Tredomen Caerph 77 G10
Powys 96 E2
Tredown Devon 24 D2
Tredrizzick Corn 10 F5
Tredunnock Mon 78 G5
Tredustan Powys 96 E2
Tredworth Glos 80 B4
Treen Corn 1 B4
Corn 1 E3
Treesmill Corn 5 D11
Treeton S Yorks 186 D6
Trefaes Gwyn 144 C5
Trefanny Hill Corn 6 D4
Trefasser Pembs 91 D7
Trefdraeth Anglesey 178 G6
Trefdraeth = *Newport*
Pembs 91 D11
Trefecca Powys 96 E2
Trefechan Ceredig 111 A11
M Tydf 77 D8
Wrex 166 F3
Trefeglwys Powys 129 E9
Trefeitha Powys 96 E2
Trefenter Ceredig 112 D2
Treffgarne Pembs 91 G9
Treffynnon Pembs 90 F6
Treffynnon = *Holywell*
Flint 181 F11
Trefgarn Owen Pembs 91 F7
Trefil Bl Gwent 77 C10
Trefilan Ceredig 111 F11
Trefin = *Trevine* Pembs 90 E6
Treflach Shrops 148 D5
Trefnanney Powys 148 F4
Trefnant Denb 181 G9
Trefonen Shrops 148 D5
Trefor Anglesey 178 E5
Gwyn 162 F5
Treforda Corn 11 E7
Treforest Rhondda 58 B5
Treforgan Ceredig 92 B4
Tre-Forgan Neath 76 D3
Treforys = *Morriston*
Swansea 57 B7
Trefriw Conwy 164 C3
Trefrize Corn 12 F2
Tref y Clawdd = *Knighton*
Powys 114 C5
Trefynwy = *Monmouth*
Mon 79 C8
Tregada Corn 12 E2
Tregadgwith Corn 1 D4
Tregadillett Corn 12 E2
Tre-gagle Mon 79 D8
Tregaian Anglesey 178 F6
Tregajorran Corn 4 G3
Tregamere Corn 5 C8
Tregardock Corn 10 E6
Tregare Mon 78 C6
Tregarland Corn 6 D5
Tregarlandbridge Corn 6 D4
Tregarne Corn 3 E7
Tregaron Ceredig 112 F3
Tregarrick Mill Corn 6 D4
Tregarth Gwyn 163 B10
Tregath Gwyn 163 B10
Tregatillian Corn 5 C8
Tregatta Corn 11 D7
Tregavarah Corn 1 D4
Tregear Corn 2 E5
Tregeare Corn 11 D10
Tregeiriog Wrex 148 C3
Tregele Anglesey 178 C5
Tregellist Corn 10 F6
Tregeseal Corn 1 C3
Tregew Corn 3 C8
Tre-Gibbon Rhondda 77 E7
Tregidden Corn 3 E7
Treginnis Pembs 90 G4
Treglemais Pembs 90 F6
Tregole Corn 11 B9
Tregolls Corn 2 B6
Tregolwyn = *Colwinston*
V Glam 58 D2
Tregona Corn 5 B7
Tregonce Corn 10 G4
Tregonetha Corn 5 C9
Tregonna Corn 10 G4
Tregonning Corn 5 D7
Tregony Corn 5 G8
Tregoodwell Corn 11 E8
Tregorden Corn 10 G6
Tregorrick Corn 5 E10
Tregoss Corn 5 C9
Tregoyd Powys 96 D4
Tregoyd Mill Powys 96 D3
Tregreenwell Corn 11 E7
Tregrehan Mills Corn 5 E10
Tregroes Ceredig 93 C8
Tregullon Corn 5 C11
Tregunna Corn 10 G5
Tregurrian Corn 5 B7
Tregurtha Downs Corn 2 C2
Tre Gwyr = *Gowerton*
Swansea 56 B5
Tregyddulan Pembs 91 D7
Tregynon Powys 129 D11
Tre-gynwr Carms 74 B6
Trehafod Rhondda 77 G8
Trehafren Powys 129 E11
Trehan Corn 7 D8
Treharris M Tydf 77 F9
Trehemborne Corn 10 G3
Treherbert Rhondda 76 F6
Tre-hill V Glam 58 E5
Trehunist Corn 6 C6
Tre-Ifor Rhondda 77 D7
Trekeivesteps Corn 11 G10
Trekenner Corn 12 F2
Trekenning Corn 5 C8
Treknow Corn 11 D7
Trelales = *Laleston*
Bridgend 57 F11
Trelan Corn 2 F6
Tre-lan Flint 165 B11
Trelash Corn 11 C9
Trelassick Corn 5 E7
Trelawnyd Flint 181 F9
Trelech Carms 92 E5
Treleddyd-fawr Pembs 90 F5
Treleigh Corn 4 G4
Treletert = *Letterston*
Pembs 91 F8
Trelew Corn 3 B8
Trelewis M Tydf 77 F10
Treligga Corn 11 E7
Trelights Corn 10 F5
Trelill Corn 10 F6
Trelion Corn 5 E8
Treliske Corn 4 F6
Trelissick Corn 3 B8
Treliver Corn 5 B9
Trellech Mon 79 D8
Trelleck Grange Mon 79 E7
Trelogan Flint 181 E10
Treloquithack Corn 2 D5
Trelowia Corn 6 D5
Trelowth Corn 5 E9
Trelystan Powys 130 C5
Tremadog Gwyn 163 G9
Tremail Corn 11 D9
Tremain Ceredig 92 B4
Tremaine Corn 11 D10
Tremains Bridgend 58 D2
Tremar Corn 6 B5
Trematon Corn 7 D7
Trematon Castle Corn 7 D8
Tremayne Corn 2 B4
Trembraze Corn 6 B5
Tremedda Corn 1 B5
Tremeirchion Denb 181 G9
Tremethick Cross Corn 1 C4
Tremore Corn 5 C10
Tremorebridge Corn 5 C10
Tremorfa Cardiff 59 D8
Tre-Mostyn Flint 181 F10
Trenance Corn 4 C6
Corn 5 B7
Corn 5 C9
Corn 10 G4
Trenant Corn 6 B4
Corn 10 G5
Trenarren Corn 5 F10
Trenay Corn 6 B3
Trench Telford 150 G3
Trench Green Oxon 65 D7
Trench Wood Kent 52 D5
Trencreek Corn 4 C6
Trencrom Corn 2 B2
Trendeal Corn 5 E7
Trenear Corn 2 C5
Treneglos Corn 11 D10
Trenerth Corn 2 B4
Trenewan Corn 6 E3
Trengune Corn 11 C9
Trenhorne Corn 11 F11
Treningle Corn 5 B10
Treninnick Corn 4 C6
Trenoon Corn 2 F6
Trenoweth Corn 3 C7
Trent Dorset 29 D9
Trentham Stoke 168 G5
Trentishoe Devon 40 D6
Trentlock Derbys 153 C9
Trent Vale Stoke 168 G5
Trenwheal Corn 2 C4
Treoes V Glam 58 D2
Treopert = *Granston*
Pembs 91 E7
Treorchy = *Treorci*
Rhondda 77 F7
Treorci = *Treorchy*
Rhondda 77 F7
Treowen Caerph 78 F2
Powys 130 E2
Tre-pit V Glam 58 E2
Trequite Corn 10 F6
Tre'r-ddôl Ceredig 128 E3
Trerhyngyll V Glam 58 D4
Trerise Corn 2 F6
Trer llai = *Leighton*
Powys 130 B4
Trerose Corn 3 D7
Trerulefoot Corn 6 D6
Tresaith Ceredig 110 G5
Tresamble Corn 3 B7
Tresarrett Corn 11 G7
Tresavean Corn 2 B6
Tresawle Corn 5 F7
Tresawsen Corn 4 F5
Trescoll Corn 5 C10
Trescott Staffs 132 D6
Trescowe Corn 2 C3
Tresean Corn 4 D5
Tresevern Croft Corn 2 B6
Tresham Glos 80 G3
Tresigin = *Sigingstone*
V Glam 58 E3
Tresillian Corn 5 F7
Tresimwn = *Bonvilston*
V Glam 58 E5
Tresinney Corn 11 E8
Tresinwen Pembs 91 C7
Treskerby Corn 4 G4
Treskillard Corn 2 B5
Treskilling Corn 5 D10
Treskinnick Cross Corn 11 B10
Treslothan Corn 2 B5
Tresmeer Corn 11 D10
Tresowes Green Corn 2 D3
Tresoweshill Corn 2 D4
Tresparrett Corn 11 C8
Tresparrett Posts Corn 11 C8
Tressady Highld 309 J7
Tressait Perth 291 G10
Tresta Shetland 312 D8
Shetland 313 H5
Treswell Notts 188 F3
Treswithian Corn 4 G2
Treswithian Downs
Corn 4 G2
Tre-Taliesin Ceredig 128 E3
Trethellan Water Corn 2 B6
Trethevy Corn 11 D7
Trethewell Corn 3 B9
Trethewey Corn 1 E3
Trethillick Corn 10 F4
Trethomas Caerph 59 B7
Trethosa Corn 5 E8
Trethowel Corn 5 E10
Trethurgy Corn 5 D10
Tretio Pembs 90 F5
Tretire Hereford 97 G10
Tretower Powys 96 G3
Treuddyn Flint 166 D3
Trevadlock Corn 11 F11
Trevail Corn 4 D5
Trevalga Corn 11 D7
Trevalgan Corn 1 A5
Trevalyn Wrex 166 D5
Trevance Corn 10 G4
Trevanger Corn 10 F5
Trevanson Corn 10 G5
Trevarrack Corn 1 C5
Trevarren Corn 5 C8
Trevarrian Corn 4 B6
Trevarrick Corn 5 G9
Trevarth Corn 4 G4
Trevaughan Carms 73 B11
Carms 93 G7
Tre-vaughan Carms 93 G8
Treveal Corn 1 A5
Trevegean Corn 1 D3
Treveighan Corn 11 F7
Trevellas Corn 4 E4
Trevelmond Corn 6 C4
Trevelver Corn 10 G5
Trevemper Corn 4 D6
Treven Corn 11 D7
Trevena Corn 2 D4
Trevenen Corn 2 D5
Trevenen Bal Corn 2 D5
Trevenning Corn 11 F7
Treveor Corn 5 G9
Treverbyn Corn 5 D10
Corn 6 B4
Treverva Corn 3 C7
Trevescan Corn 1 E3
Trevethin Torf 78 E3
Trevia Corn 11 E7
Trevigro Corn 6 B6
Trevilder Corn 10 G6
Trevilla Corn 3 B8
Trevilson Corn 4 D6
Trevine Corn 10 F5
Trevine = *Trefin* Pembs 90 E6
Treviscoe Corn 5 D8
Treviskey Corn 2 B6
Trevithal Corn 1 D5
Trevoll Corn 4 D6
Trevone Corn 10 F3
Trevor Wrex 166 G3
Trevorrick Corn 10 G4
Trevor Uchaf Denb 166 G2
Trevowah Corn 4 D5
Trevowhan Corn 1 B4
Trew Corn 2 D4
Trewalder Corn 11 E7
Trewarmett Corn 11 D7
Trewartha Corn 2 B2
Corn 3 B10
Trewassa Corn 11 D8
Treween Corn 11 E10
Trewellard Corn 1 C3
Trewen Corn 11 E7
Corn 11 E11
Mon 79 G7
Trewennack Corn 2 D5
Trewennan Corn 11 E7
Trewern Powys 148 G5
Trewetha Corn 10 E6
Trewethen Corn 10 F6
Trewethern Corn 10 F6
Trewey Corn 1 B5
Trewidland Corn 6 D5
Trewindle Corn 6 C2
Trewint Corn 6 C5
Corn 11 B9
Corn 11 E10
Trewithian Corn 3 B9
Trewithick Corn 11 D11
Trewollock Corn 5 G10
Trewoodloe Corn 12 G2
Trewoofe Corn 1 D4
Trewoon Corn 2 F5
Corn 5 E9
Treworga Corn 5 G7
Treworgan Common
Mon 78 D6
Treworlas Corn 3 B9
Treworld Corn 11 C8
Trewornan Corn 10 G5
Treworrick Corn 6 B4
Treworthal Corn 3 B9
Trewyddel = *Moylgrove*
Pembs 92 C2
Trewyn Devon 24 G4
Tre-wyn Mon 96 G6
Treyarnon Corn 10 G3
Treyford W Sus 34 D4
Trezaise Corn 5 D9
Trezelah Corn 1 C5
Triangle Glos 79 E8
Staffs 133 B11
W Yorks 196 C4
Trickett's Cross Dorset 31 G9
Triffleton Pembs 91 G9
Trillacott Corn 11 D11
Trimdon Durham 234 E3
Trimdon Colliery
Durham 234 D3
Trimdon Grange
Durham 234 D3
Trimingham Norf 160 B5
Trimley Lower Street
Suff 108 D5
Trimley St Martin Suff 108 D5
Trimley St Mary Suff 108 D5
Trimpley Worcs 116 B5
Trimsaran Carms 75 E7
Trims Green Herts 87 B7
Trimstone Devon 40 E3
Trinafour Perth 291 G9
Trinant Caerph 78 E2
Tring Herts 84 C6
Tringford Herts 84 C6
Tring Wharf Herts 84 C6
Trinity Angus 293 G8
Devon 27 F7
Edin 280 F4
Trinity Fields Staffs 151 D8
Trisant Ceredig 112 B4
Triscombe Som 43 F7
Trislaig Highld 290 F2
Trispen Corn 4 E6
Tritlington Northumb 252 E6
Troan Corn 5 D7
Trochry Perth 286 C3
Trodigal Argyll 255 E7
Troearhiwgwair
Bl Gwent 77 D11
Troedrhiwdalar Powys 113 G9
Troedrhiwffenyd Ceredig 93 C8
Troedrhiwfuwch Caerph 77 E10
Troedyraur Ceredig 92 B6
Troedyrhiw M Tydf 77 E9
Trofarth Conwy 180 G5
Trolliloes E Sus 23 C10
Tromode IoM 192 E4
Trondavoe Shetland 312 F5
Troon Corn 2 B5
S Ayrs 257 C8
Trooper's Inn Pembs 73 C7
Trosaraidh W Isles 297 K3
Trossachs Hotel Stirling 285 G9
Troston Suff 125 C7
Trostre Carms 56 B4
Trostrey Common Mon 78 E5
Troswell Corn 11 C11
Trotshill Worcs 117 F7
Trotten Marsh W Sus 34 B4
Trottiscliffe Kent 68 G6
Trotton W Sus 34 C4
Trough Gate Lancs 195 C11
Troutbeck Cumb 221 E8
Cumb 230 F3
Troutbeck Bridge Cumb 221 F8
Troway Derbys 186 F5
Trowbridge Cardiff 59 C8
Wilts 45 B11
Trowell Notts 153 B9
Trow Green Glos 79 D9
Trowle Common Wilts 45 B10
Trowley Bottom Herts 85 C9
Trows Borders 262 C5
Trowse Newton Norf 142 B4
Troydale W Yorks 205 G10
Troy Town Kent 52 D2
Kent 54 E5
Medway 69 F8
Truas Corn 11 D7
Trub Gtr Man 195 F11
Trudoxhill Som 45 E8
Trueman's Heath
Worcs 117 B11
True Street Devon 8 C6
Trull Som 28 C2
Trumaisgearraidh
W Isles 296 D4
Trumfleet S Yorks 198 E6
Trumpan Highld 298 C2
Trumpet Hereford 98 D3
Trumpington Cambs 123 F8
Trumpsgreen Sur 66 F3
Trunch Norf 160 C5
Trunnah Lancs 202 E2
Truro Corn 4 G6
Truscott Corn 12 D2
Trusham Devon 14 E3
Trusley Derbys 152 B5
Trussall Corn 2 D5
Trussell Corn 11 D10
Trusthorpe Lincs 191 E8
Truthan Corn 4 E6
Truthwall Corn 2 C2
Trwstllewelyn Powys 130 D3
Tryfil Anglesey 178 E6
Trysull Staffs 133 E7
Trythogga Corn 1 C5
Tubbs Mill Corn 5 G9
Tubney Oxon 82 F6
Tubslake Kent 53 G9
Tuckenhay Devon 8 D6
Tuckermarsh Devon 7 B8
Tuckerton Som 28 B3
Tuckhill Shrops 132 F5
Tuckingmill Corn 4 G3
Corn 11 F7
Wilts 30 B6
Tucking Mill Bath 61 G9
Tuckton BCP 19 C8
Tuddenham Suff 108 B3
Suff 124 C4
Tuddenham St Martin
Suff 108 B3
Tudeley Kent 52 D6
Tudeley Hale Kent 52 D6
Tudhay Devon 28 G4
Tudhoe Durham 233 D11
Tudhoe Grange
Durham 233 E11
Tudor Hill W Mid 134 D2
Tudorville Hereford 97 G11
Tudweiliog Gwyn 144 B4
Tuebrook Mers 182 C5
Tuesley Sur 50 E3
Tuesnoad Kent 54 E2
Tuffley Glos 80 C4
Tufnell Park London 67 B9
Tufton Hants 48 D3
Pembs 91 F10
Tugby Leics 136 C5
Tugford Shrops 131 F11
Tughall Northumb 264 D6
Tulchan Lodge Angus 292 F3
Tullecombe W Sus 34 B4
Tullibardine Perth 286 F3
Tullibody Clack 279 B7
Tullich Argyll 284 F4
Highld 299 E9
Highld 300 G6
Tullich Muir Highld 301 B7
Tulliemet Perth 286 B3
Tulloch Aberds 293 F9
Aberds 303 F8
Highld 290 E5
Perth 286 E4
Tulloch Castle Highld 300 C5
Tullochgorm Argyll 275 D10
Tulloch-gribban Highld 301 G9
Tullochroisk Perth 285 B11
Tullochvenus Aberds 293 C7
Tulloes Angus 287 C9
Tullybannocher Perth 285 E11
Tullybelton Perth 286 D4
Tullycross Stirling 277 D9
Tullyfergus Perth 286 C6
Tullymurdoch Perth 286 B5
Tullynessle Aberds 293 B7
Tulse Hill London 67 E10
Tumble = *Y Tymbl* Carms 75 C8
Tumbler's Green Essex 106 F6
Tumby Lincs 174 D2
Tumby Woodside Lincs 174 D3
Tummel Bridge Perth 285 B11
Tumpy Green Glos 80 E2
Tumpy Lakes Hereford 97 B10
Tunbridge Hill Medway 69 E10
Tunbridge Wells = *Royal Tunbridge Wells* Kent 52 F5
Tunga W Isles 304 E6
Tungate Norf 160 D5
Tunley Bath 45 B7
Glos 80 E6
Tunnel Hill Worcs 98 C6
Tunnel Pits N Lincs 199 G8
Tunshill Gtr Man 196 E2
Tunstall E Yorks 209 G12
Kent 69 G11
Lancs 212 E2
Norf 143 B8
N Yorks 224 F4
Staffs 150 D5
Stoke 168 E5
Suff 127 G7
T&W 243 G9
Tunstead Derbys 185 G10
Gtr Man 196 G4
Norf 160 E5
Tunworth Hants 49 D7
Tupsley Hereford 97 C10
Tupton Derbys 170 B5
Turbary Common BCP 19 C7
Turfdown Corn 5 B11
Turf Hill Gtr Man 196 E2
Turfholm S Lanark 259 B8
Turfmoor Devon 28 G3
Shrops 149 F7
Turgis Green Hants 49 B7
Turin Angus 287 B9
Turkdean Glos 81 B10
Turkey Island Hants 33 E9
W Sus 34 D3
Turkey Tump Hereford 97 F10
Tur Langton Leics 136 E4
Turleigh Wilts 61 G10
Turleygreen Shrops 132 F5
Turlin Moor BCP 18 C5
Turmer Hants 31 F10
Turn Lancs 195 D10
Turnalt Argyll 275 C9
Turnastone Hereford 97 D7
Turnberry S Ayrs 244 B6
Turnchapel Plym 7 E9
Turnditch Derbys 170 F3
Turner Green Lancs 203 G8
Turner's Green E Sus 23 B10
E Sus 52 G6
Warks 118 D3
W Berks 64 F4
Turners Hill W Sus 51 F10
Turners Puddle Dorset 18 C2
Turnerwood S Yorks 187 E8
Turnford Herts 86 E5
Turnhouse Edin 280 G3
Turnhurst Stoke 168 E5
Turnstead Milton
Derbys 185 E8
Turnworth Dorset 30 F4
Turrerich Perth 286 D2
Turriff Aberds 303 D7
Tursdale Durham 234 D2
Turton Bottoms
Blackburn 195 D8
Turves Cambs 138 D6
Turves Green W Mid 117 B10
Turvey Bedford 121 G8
Turville Bucks 84 G3
Turville Heath Bucks 84 G2
Turweston Bucks 102 D2
Tushielaw Borders 261 F8
Tutbury Staffs 152 D4
Tutnall Worcs 117 C9
Tutnalls Glos 79 E10
Tutshill Glos 79 G8
Tutt Hill Kent 54 D3
Tuttington Norf 160 D4
Tutts Clump W Berks 64 E5
Tutwell Corn 12 F3
Tuxford Notts 188 G2
Twatt Orkney 314 D2
Shetland 313 H5
Twechar E Dunb 278 F4
Tweedale Telford 132 C4
Tweeddaleburn Borders 270 E5
Tweedmouth Northumb 273 E9
Tweedsmuir Borders 260 E3
Twelve Heads Corn 4 G5
Twelve Oaks E Sus 37 C11
Twelvewoods Corn 6 B4
Twemlow Green Ches E 168 B3
Twenties Kent 71 F10
Twenty Lincs 156 E3
Twerton Bath 61 G8
Twickenham London 67 E7
Twigworth Glos 98 G6
Twineham W Sus 36 D3
Twineham Green W Sus 36 C3
Twinhoe Bath 45 B8
Twinstead Essex 107 D7
Twinstead Green Essex 106 D6
Twiss Green Warr 183 B11
Twist Devon 28 G3
Twiston Lancs 204 E2
Twitchen Devon 41 G9
Shrops 115 B7
Twitchen Mill Devon 41 G9
Twitham Kent 55 B9
Twitton Kent 52 B4
Two Bridges Devon 13 G8
Glos 79 D11
Two Burrows Corn 4 F4
Two Dales Derbys 170 C3
Two Gates Staffs 134 C4
Two Mile Ash M Keynes 102 D6
W Sus 35 B10
Two Mile Hill Bristol 60 E6
Two Mile Oak Cross Devon 8 B6
Two Mills Ches W 182 G5
Two Pots Devon 40 E4
Two Waters Herts 85 D9
Twr Anglesey 178 E2
Twycross Leics 134 C6
Twydall Medway 69 F9
Twyford Bucks 102 F3
Derbys 152 D6
Dorset 30 D5
Hants 33 C7
Leics 154 G4

Twyford continued
Lincs 155 E8
Norf 159 E10
Oxon 101 D9
Shrops 148 D6
Wokingham 65 D9
Worcs 99 B10
Twyford Common
Hereford 97 D10
Twyn-Allws Mon 78 C3
Twynholm Dumfries 237 D8
Twyning Glos 99 D7
Twyning Green Glos 99 D8
Twynllanan Carms 94 G5
Twynmynydd Carms 75 C11
Twyn Shôn-Ifan Caerph 77 G11
Twynyrodyn M Tydf 77 D9
Twyn-yr-odyn V Glam 58 E6
Twyn-y-Sheriff Mon 78 D6
Twywell N Nhants 121 B9
Tyberton Hereford 97 D7
Tyburn W Mid 134 E2
Tyby Norf 159 D11
Ty-coch Swansea 56 C6
Tycroes Carms 75 C10
Tycrwyn Powys 148 F2
Tyddewi = St Davids
Pembs 90 F5
Tydd Gote Lincs 157 F9
Tydd St Giles Cambs 157 F8
Tydd St Mary Lincs 157 F8
Tyddyn Powys 129 F9
Tyddyn Angharad Denb 165 F9
Tyddyn Dai Anglesey 178 C6
Tyddyn-mawr Gwyn 163 G9
Ty-draw Conwy 164 D5
Swansea 57 C7
Tye Hants 22 C2
Tye Common Essex 87 G11
Tyegate Green Norf 161 G7
Tye Green Essex 87 C10
Essex 87 D7
Essex 87 F11
Essex 105 D11
Essex 105 G10
Essex 106 G5
Tyersal W Yorks 205 G9
Ty-fry Mon 78 F6
Tyganol V Glam 58 E4
Ty-hen Carms 92 G6
Gwyn 144 C3
Ty-isaf Carms 56 B4
Tyla Mon 78 C2
Tylagwyn Bridgend 58 B2
Tyldesley Gtr Man 195 G7
Tyle Carms 94 F3
Tyle-garw Rhondda 58 C4
Tyler Hill Kent 70 G6
Tylers Causeway Herts 86 D3
Tylers Green Bucks 84 G6
Tyler's Green Essex 87 D8
Sur 51 C11
Tyler's Hill Bucks 85 E7
Ty Llwyn Bl Gwent 77 D11
Tylorstown Rhondda 77 F8
Tylwch Powys 129 G9
Ty-mawr Anglesey 179 D7
Ty Mawr Carms 93 C10
Ty-mawr Conwy 181 F7
Ty Mawr Cwm Conwy 164 F6
Tynant Rhondda 58 B5
Ty-nant Conwy 165 G7
Gwyn 147 D8
Tyncelyn Ceredig 112 E2
Tyndrum Stirling 285 D7
Tyne Dock T&W 243 D9
Tyneham Dorset 18 E3
Tynehead Midloth 271 D7
Tynemouth T&W 243 D9
Tyne Tunnel T&W 243 D8
Tynewydd Ceredig 92 B4
Neath 76 D4
Rhondda 76 F6
Ty-Newydd Ceredig 111 D10
Tyning Bath 45 B7
Tyninghame E Loth 282 F2
Tyn-lon Gwyn 163 D7
Tynron Dumfries 247 E8
Tynsfield N Som 60 E4
Tyntetown Rhondda 77 F9
Ty'n-y-bryn Rhondda 58 B4
Tyn-y-celyn Wrex 148 B3
Tyn-y-coed Shrops 148 D4
Ty'n-y-coedcae Caerph 59 B7
Tyn-y-cwm Swansea 75 E10
Tynyfedw Conwy 165 B7
Tyn-y-fedwen Powys 148 C2
Ty'n-y-ffordd Denb 181 G8
Tyn-y-ffridd Powys 148 C2
Ty'n-y-garn Bridgend 57 E11
Tynygongl Anglesey 179 E8
Tynygraig Ceredig 112 D3
Ty'n-y-graig Powys 113 G10
Ty'n-y-groes Conwy 180 G3
Ty'n-y-maes Gwyn 163 C10
Tyn-y-pwll Anglesey 178 D6
Ty'n-yr-eithin Ceredig 112 E3
Tynyrwtra Powys 129 F7
Tyrells End C Beds 103 E9
Tyrell's Wood Sur 51 B7
Ty'r-felin-isaf Conwy 164 C5
Ty Rhiw Rhondda 58 C6
Tyrie Aberds 303 C9
Tyringham M Keynes 103 B7
Tyseley W Mid 134 G2
Ty-Sign Caerph 78 G2
Tythecott Devon 24 D6
Tythegston Bridgend 57 F11
Tytherington Ches E 184 F6
S Glos 61 B7
Som 45 D9
Wilts 46 E2
Tytherleigh Devon 28 G4
Tytherton Lucas Wilts 62 E2
Tyttenhanger Herts 85 D11
Ty-uchaf Powys 147 E10
Tywardreath Corn 5 E11
Tywardreath Highway
Corn 5 D11
Tywyn Conwy 180 F3
Gwyn 110 C2

U

Uachdar W Isles 296 F3
Uags Highld 295 B9
Ubberley Stoke 168 F6
Ubbeston Green Suff 126 C6
Ubley Bath 44 B4
Uckerby N Yorks 224 E4
Uckfield E Sus 37 C7
Uckinghall Worcs 99 D7
Uckington Glos 99 G8
Shrops 131 B11
Uddingston S Lanark 268 C3
Uddington S Lanark 259 C9
Udimore E Sus 38 D5
Udley N Som 60 G3
Udny Green Aberds 303 G8
Udny Station Aberds 303 G9
Udston S Lanark 268 D3
Udstonhead S Lanark 268 F4
Uffcott Wilts 62 D6
Uffculme Devon 27 E9
Uffington Lincs 137 B11
Oxon 63 B10
Shrops 149 G10
Ufford Pboro 137 C11
Suff 126 G5
Ufton Warks 119 E7
Ufton Green W Berks 64 F6
Ufton Nervet W Berks 64 F6
Ugadale Argyll 255 E8
Ugborough Devon 8 D3
Ugford Wilts 46 G5
Uggeshall Suff 143 G8
Ugglebarnby N Yorks 227 D7
Ughill S Yorks 186 C3
Ugley Essex 105 F10
Ugley Green Essex 105 F10
Ugthorpe N Yorks 226 C5
Uidh W Isles 297 M2
Uig Argyll 276 E2
Argyll 288 D3
Highld 296 F7
Highld 298 C3
Uigen W Isles 304 E2
Uigshader Highld 298 E4
Uisken Argyll 274 B4
Ulaw Aberds 303 G9
Ulbster Highld 310 E7
Ulcat Row Cumb 230 G4
Ulceby Lincs 190 G6
N Lincs 200 E6
Ulceby Skitter N Lincs 200 E6
Ulcombe Kent 53 D10
Uldale Cumb 229 D10
Uley Glos 80 F3
Ulgham Northumb 252 E6
Ullapool Highld 307 K6
Ullcombe Devon 28 F2
Ullenhall Warks 118 D2
Ullenwood Glos 80 B6
Ulleskelf N Yorks 206 E6
Ullesthorpe Leics 135 F10
Ulley S Yorks 187 D7
Ullingswick Hereford 97 B11
Ullington Worcs 100 B2
Ullinish Highld 294 B5
Ullock Cumb 229 G7
Cumb 229 G10
Ulnes Walton Lancs 194 D4
Ulpha Cumb 220 G3
Ulrome E Yorks 209 B9
Ulshaw N Yorks 214 B2
Ulsta Shetland 312 E6
Ulva House Argyll 288 F6
Ulverley Green W Mid 134 G2
Ulverston Cumb 210 D5
Ulwell Dorset 18 E6
Umberleigh Devon 25 C10
Unapool Highld 306 F7
Unasary W Isles 297 J3
Under Bank W Yorks 196 F6
Underbarrow Cumb 221 G9
Undercliffe W Yorks 205 G9
Underdale Shrops 149 G10
Underdown Devon 14 D3
Underhill London 86 F3
Wilts 45 G11
Underhoull Shetland 312 C7
Underling Green Kent 53 D9
Underriver Kent 52 C5
Underriver Ho Kent 52 C5
Under the Wood Kent 71 F8
Under Tofts S Yorks 186 D4
Underton Shrops 132 E3
Underwood Newport 59 B11
Notts 171 E7
Pembs 73 C7
Plym 7 D10
Undley Suff 140 G3
Undy Mon 60 B2
Unifirth Shetland 313 H4
Union Cottage Aberds 293 D10
Union Mills IoM 192 E4
Union Street E Sus 53 G8
United Downs Corn 4 G4
Unstone Derbys 186 F5
Unstone Green Derbys 186 F5
Unsworth Gtr Man 195 F10
Unthank Cumb 230 B3
Cumb 230 D5
Cumb 231 C8
Derbys 186 F4
Unthank End Cumb 230 D5
Upavon Wilts 46 C6
Up Cerne Dorset 29 G11
Upchurch Kent 69 F10
Upcott Devon 24 D2
Devon 25 B9
Devon 25 F11
Devon 40 F3
Hereford 114 G6
Som 27 C11
Upend Cambs 124 F3
Up End M Keynes 103 B8
Up Exe Devon 26 G6
Upgate Norf 160 F2
Upgate Street Norf 141 E11
Norf 142 E5
Up Green Hants 65 G9
Uphall Dorset 29 G9
W Loth 279 G11
Uphall Station W Loth 279 G11
Upham Devon 26 F5
Hants 33 C8
Uphampton Hereford 115 E7
Worcs 116 E6
Up Hatherley Glos 99 G8
Uphempston Devon 8 C6
Uphill N Som 43 B10
Uphill Manor N Som 43 B10
Up Holland Lancs 194 F4
Uplands Glos 80 D5
Swansea 56 C6
Uplawmoor E Renf 267 D8
Upleadon Glos 98 F5
Upleadon Court Glos 98 F5
Upleatham Redcar 226 B2
Uplees Kent 70 G3
Uploders Dorset 16 C6
Uplowman Devon 27 D8
Uplyme Devon 16 C2
Up Marden W Sus 34 E3
Upminster London 68 B5
Up Mudford Som 29 D9
Up Nately Hants 49 C7
Upnor Medway 69 E9
Upottery Devon 28 F2
Uppacott Devon 25 B9
Uppat Highld 311 J2
Uppend Essex 105 F9
Upper Affcot Shrops 131 F8
Upper Ardchronie
Highld 309 L6
Upper Ardgrain
Aberds 303 F9
Upper Ardroscadale
Argyll 275 G11
Upper Arley Worcs 132 G5
Upper Armley W Yorks 205 G11
Upper Arncott Oxon 83 B10
Upper Astley Shrops 149 F10
Upper Aston Shrops 132 E6
Upper Astrop
W Nhants 101 D10
Upper Badcall Highld 306 E6
Upper Bangor Gwyn 179 G9
Upper Basildon W Berks 64 D5
Upper Batley W Yorks 197 B8
Upper Battlefield
Shrops 149 F10
Upper Beeding W Sus 35 E11
Upper Benefield
N Nhants 137 F9
Upper Bentley Worcs 117 D9
Upper Bighouse Highld 310 D2
Upper Birchwood
Derbys 170 E6
Upper Blainslie
Borders 271 G10
Upper Boat Rhondda 58 B6
Upper Boddam Aberds 302 F6
Upper Boddington
W Nhants 119 G9
Upper Bogrow Highld 309 L7
Upper Bogside Moray 302 D2
Upper Bonchurch IoW 21 F7
Upper Booth Derbys 185 D10
Upper Borth Ceredig 128 F2
Upper Boyndlie Aberds 303 C9
Upper Brailes Warks 100 D6
Upper Brandon Parva
Norf 141 B10
Upper Breakish Highld 295 C8
Upper Breinton Hereford 97 C9
Upper Broadheath
Worcs 116 F6
Upper Brockholes
W Yorks 196 B5
Upper Broughton Notts 154 D3
Upper Broxwood
Hereford 115 G7
Upper Bruntingthorpe
Leics 136 F2
Upper Brynamman
Carms 76 C2
Upper Buckenhill
Hereford 97 E11
Upper Bucklebury
W Berks 64 F4
Upper Bullington Hants 48 E3
Upper Burgate Hants 31 D11
Upper Burnhaugh
Aberds 293 D10
Upper Bush Medway 69 F7
Upperby Cumb 239 G10
Upper Caldecote
C Beds 104 B3
Upper Cam Glos 80 F3
Upper Canada N Som 43 B11
Upper Canterton Hants 32 E3
Upper Catesby
W Nhants 119 F10
Upper Catshill Worcs 117 C9
Upper Chapel Powys 95 C10
Upper Cheddon Som 28 B2
Upper Chicksgrove Wilts 31 B7
Upper Church Village
Rhondda 58 B5
Upper Chute Wilts 47 C9
Upper Clapton London 67 B10
Upper Clatford Hants 47 E11
Upper Coberley Glos 81 B7
Upper College Shrops 149 C11
Upper Colwall Hereford 98 C5
Upper Common Hants 48 D6
Upper Cotburn Aberds 303 D7
Upper Cotton Staffs 169 F9
Upper Coullie Aberds 293 B9
Upper Cound Shrops 131 C11
Upper Coxley Som 44 E4
Upper Cudworth
S Yorks 197 F11
Upper Culphin Aberds 302 D6
Upper Cumberworth
W Yorks 197 F8
Upper Cwmbran Torf 78 F3
Upperdale Derbys 185 G11
Upper Dallachy Moray 302 C3
Upper Deal Kent 55 C11
Upper Dean Bedford 121 D10
Devon 8 C4
Upper Denby W Yorks 197 D8
W Yorks 197 F8
Upper Denton Cumb 240 D4
Upper Derraid Highld 301 F10
Upper Diabaig Highld 299 C8
Upper Dicker E Sus 23 D9
Upper Dinchope Shrops 131 G9
Upper Dormington
Hereford 97 D11
Upper Dounreay Highld 310 C4
Upper Dovercourt Essex 108 E4
Upper Dowdeswell Glos 81 B8
Upper Druimfin Argyll 289 D7
Upper Dunsforth
N Yorks 215 G8
Upper Dunsley Herts 84 C6
Upper Eashing Sur 50 E3
Upper Eastern Green
W Mid 134 G5
Upper Eathie Highld 301 C7
Upper Edmonton London 86 G4
Upper Egleton Hereford 98 C2
Upper Elkstone Staffs 169 D9
Upper Ellastone Staffs 169 G10
Upper Elmers End
London 67 F11
Upper End Derbys 185 F9
Glos 81 C10
Glos 81 D8
Leics 154 G4
Upper Enham Hants 47 D11
Upper Farmcote Shrops 132 E5
Upper Farringdon Hants 49 F8
Upper Feorlig Highld 298 E2
Upper Fivehead Som 28 C4
Upper Forge Shrops 132 F4
Upper Framilode Glos 80 C3
Upper Froyle Hants 49 E9
Upper Gambolds Worcs 117 D9
Upper Gills Highld 310 B7
Upper Glenfintaig
Highld 290 E4
Upper Godney Som 44 E3
Upper Goldstone Kent 71 G9
Upper Gornal W Mid 133 E8
Upper Gravenhurst
C Beds 104 D2
Upper Green Essex 105 E8
Mon 78 B5
Suff 124 E4
W Berks 63 G11
W Yorks 197 B9
Upper Grove Common
Hereford 97 F11
Upper Guist Norf 159 D10
Upper Hackney Derbys 170 C3
Upper Hale Sur 49 D10
Upper Halistra Highld 298 D2
Upper Halliford Sur 66 F5
Upper Halling Medway 69 G7
Upper Ham Worcs 99 D7
Upper Hambleton
Rutland 137 B8
Upper Hamnish
Hereford 115 F10
Upper Harbledown Kent 54 B6
Upper Hardres Court
Kent 55 C7
Upper Hardwick
Hereford 115 F8
Upper Hartfield E Sus 52 G3
Upper Hartshay Derbys 170 E5
Upper Haselor Worcs 99 C10
Upper Hatton Staffs 150 B6
Upper Haugh S Yorks 186 B6
Upper Hawkhillock
Aberds 303 F10
Upper Hayesden Kent 52 E5
Upper Hayton Shrops 131 G10
Upper Heath Shrops 131 F11
Upper Heaton W Yorks 197 D7
Upper Hellesdon Norf 160 G4
Upper Helmsley
N Yorks 207 B9
Upper Hengoed Shrops 148 C5
Upper Hergest Hereford 114 G5
Upper Heyford Oxon 101 F9
W Nhants 120 F3
Upper Hill Glos 79 F11
Hereford 115 G9
Upper Hindhope
Borders 251 B7
Upper Holloway London 67 B9
Upper Holton Suff 127 B8
Upper Hopton W Yorks 197 D7
Upper Horsebridge
E Sus 23 C9
Upper Howsell Worcs 98 B5
Upper Hoyland
S Yorks 197 G11
Upper Hulme Staffs 169 C8
Upper Hyde IoW 21 E7
Upper Ifold Sur 50 G4
Upper Inglesham Swindon 82 F2
Upper Inverbrough
Highld 301 F8
Upper Kergord Shetland 313 H6
Upper Kidston Borders 270 G4
Upper Kilcott Glos 61 B9
Upper Killay Swansea 56 C5
Upper Killeyan Argyll 254 C3
Upper Kinsham
Hereford 115 D7
Upper Knockando
Moray 301 E11
Upper Lambourn
W Berks 63 C10
Upper Landywood
Staffs 133 B9
Upper Langford N Som 44 B3
Upper Langwith Derbys 171 B8
Upper Layham Suff 107 C10
Upper Leigh Staffs 151 B10
Upper Lenie Highld 300 G5
Upper Littleton N Som 60 G5
Upper Loads Derbys 170 B4
Upper Lochton Aberds 293 D8
Upper Lode Worcs 99 E7
Upper Longdon Staffs 151 G11
Upper Longwood
Shrops 132 B2
Upper Ludstone Shrops 132 D6
Upper Lybster Highld 310 F6
Upper Lydbrook Glos 79 B10
Upper Lyde Hereford 97 C9
Upper Lye Hereford 115 D7
Upper Maes-coed
Hereford 96 D6
Upper Marsh W Yorks 204 F6
Upper Midhope S Yorks 186 B2
Upper Midway Derbys 152 E5
Uppermill Gtr Man 196 F3
Upper Milovaig Highld 297 G7
Upper Milton Oxon 82 B3
Som 44 D4
Upper Minety Wilts 81 G8
Upper Mitton Worcs 116 C6
Upper Moor Worcs 99 B9
Upper Moor Side
W Yorks 205 G10
Upper Morton S Glos 79 G11
Upper Nash Pembs 73 E8
Upper Netchwood
Shrops 132 E2
Upper Newbold Derbys 186 G5
Upper Nobut Staffs 151 B10
Upper North Dean Bucks 84 F4
Upper Norwood London 67 F10
W Sus 34 D6
Upper Obney Perth 286 D4
Upper Ochrwyth Caerph 59 B8
Upper Oddington Glos 100 F4
Upper Ollach Highld 295 B7
Upper Padley Derbys 186 F2
Upper Pickwick Wilts 61 E11
Upper Pollicott Bucks 84 C2
Upper Poppleton York 207 C7
Upper Port Highld 301 G10
Upper Postern Kent 52 D6
Upper Quinton Warks 100 B3
Upper Race Torf 78 F3
Upper Ratley Hants 32 C4
Upper Ridinghill
Aberds 303 D10
Upper Rissington Glos 82 B2
Upper Rochford Worcs 116 D2
Upper Rodmersham Kent 70 G2
Upper Sandaig Highld 295 D9
Upper Sanday Orkney 314 F5
Upper Sapey Hereford 116 E3
Upper Saxondale Notts 154 B3
Upper Seagry Wilts 62 C2
Upper Shelton C Beds 103 C9
Upper Sheringham
Norf 177 E10
Upper Shirley London 67 G11
Soton 32 E6
Upper Siddington Glos 81 F8
Upper Skelmorlie
N Ayrs 266 B4
Upper Slackstead Hants 32 B5
Upper Slaughter Glos 100 G3
Upper Solva Pembs 90 G5
Upper Soudley Glos 79 C11
Uppersound Shetland 313 J6
Upper Stanton Drew
Bath 60 G6
Upper Staploe Bedford 122 F2
Upper Stoke Norf 142 C5
W Mid 135 G7
Upper Stondon C Beds 104 D2
Upper Stowe W Nhants 120 F2
Upper Stratton Swindon 63 B7
Upper Street Hants 31 D11
Norf 142 G3
Norf 160 B5
Upper Street continued
Norf 160 E6
Norf 160 F6
Norf 161 F7
Suff 108 E2
Suff 124 G5
Suff 126 G2
Upper Strensham
Worcs 99 D8
Upper Studley Wilts 45 B10
Upper Sundon C Beds 103 F10
Upper Swainswick Bath 61 F9
Upper Swanmore Hants 33 D9
Upper Swell Glos 100 F3
Upper Sydenham
London 67 E10
Upper Tankersley
S Yorks 186 B4
Upper Tean Staffs 151 B10
Upperthong W Yorks 196 F6
Upperthorpe Derbys 187 E7
N Lincs 199 G9
Upper Threapwood
Ches W 166 F6
Upper Thurnham Lancs 202 C5
Upper Tillyrie Perth 286 G5
Upperton E Sus 23 E10
Oxon 83 G11
W Sus 35 C7
Upper Tooting London 67 E9
Upper Tote Highld 298 D5
Uppertown Derbys 170 C4
Highld 300 F4
Highld 310 B7
Northumb 241 C9
Orkney 314 G4
Upper Town Derbys 170 D3
Derbys 170 E2
Durham 233 D7
Hereford 97 B11
N Som 60 F4
Suff 125 D8
Wilts 62 D3
W Yorks 204 G6
Upper Treverward
Shrops 114 B5
Upper Tysoe Warks 100 C6
Upper Up Glos 81 F8
Upper Upham Wilts 63 D8
Upper Upnor Medway 69 E9
Upper Vobster Som 45 D8
Upper Walthamstow
London 67 B11
Upper Wardington
Oxon 101 B9
Upper Wardley W Sus 34 B4
Upper Weald M Keynes 102 D5
Upper Weedon
W Nhants 120 F2
Upper Welland Worcs 98 C5
Upper Wellingham
E Sus 36 E6
Upper Welson Hereford 114 G5
Upper Westholme Som 44 E5
Upper Weston Bath 61 F8
Upper Weybread Suff 126 B4
Upper Whiston S Yorks 187 D7
Upper Wick Glos 80 F2
Worcs 116 G6
Upper Wield Hants 48 F6
Upper Wigginton
Shrops 148 B6
Upper Winchendon
Bucks 84 C2
Upper Witton W Mid 133 E11
Upper Wolvercote Oxon 83 D7
Upper Wolverton
Worcs 117 G8
Upperwood Derbys 170 D3
Upper Woodend
Aberds 293 B8
Upper Woodford Wilts 46 F6
Upper Woolhampton
W Berks 64 F5
Upper Wootton Hants 48 C5
Upper Wraxall Wilts 61 E10
Upper Wyche Hereford 98 C5
Uppincott Devon 26 G5
Uppingham Rutland 137 D7
Uppington Dorset 31 F8
Shrops 132 B2
Upsall N Yorks 215 B9
Upsher Green Suff 107 C8
Upshire Essex 86 E6
Up Somborne Hants 47 G11
Upstreet Kent 71 G8
Up Sydling Dorset 29 G10
Upthorpe Glos 80 E3
Suff 125 C9
Upton Bucks 84 C3
Cambs 122 B3
Ches W 166 B6
Corn 11 G11
Corn 24 G2
Cumb 230 D2
Devon 8 G4
Devon 27 G9
Dorset 17 E10
Dorset 18 C5
E Yorks 209 C8
Hants 32 D5
Hants 47 B11
IoW 21 C7
Kent 71 F11
Leics 135 D7
Lincs 188 D5
London 68 C2
Mers 182 D3
Mers 183 D7
Norf 161 G7
Notts 172 E2
Notts 188 F2
Oxon 64 B4
Oxon 82 C2
Pboro 138 C2
Slough 66 D3
Som 27 B7
Som 29 B7
Warks 118 F2
Wilts 45 G11
W Nhants 120 E4
W Yorks 198 E3
Upton Bishop Hereford 98 F2
Upton Cheyney S Glos 61 F7
Upton Cressett Shrops 132 E3
Upton Crews Hereford 98 F2
Upton Cross Corn 11 G11
Upton End C Beds 104 E2
Upton Field Notts 172 E2
Upton Green Norf 161 G7
Upton Grey Hants 49 D7
Upton Heath Ches W 166 B6
Upton Hellions Devon 26 G4
Upton Lea Bucks 66 C3
Upton Lovell Wilts 46 E2
Upton Magna Shrops 149 G11
Upton Noble Som 45 F8
Upton Park London 68 C2
Upton Pyne Devon 14 B4
Upton Rocks Halton 183 D8
Upton St Leonards Glos 80 C5
Upton Scudamore Wilts 45 D11
Upton Snodsbury Worcs 117 G8
Upton upon Severn
Worcs 99 C7
Upton Warren Worcs 117 D8
Upwaltham W Sus 34 E6
Upware Cambs 123 C10
Upwell Norf 139 C9
Upwey Dorset 17 E9
Upwick Green Herts 105 G9
Upwood Cambs 138 G5
Uradale Shetland 313 K6
Urafirth Shetland 312 F5
Uragaig Argyll 274 D4
Urchfont Wilts 46 B4
Urdimarsh Hereford 97 B10
Ure Shetland 312 F4
Ure Bank N Yorks 214 E6
Urgashay Som 29 C9
Urgha W Isles 305 J3
Urgha Beag W Isles 305 H3
Urishay Common
Hereford 96 D6
Urlar Perth 286 C2
Urlay Nook Stockton 225 C7
Urmston Gtr Man 184 C3
Urpeth Durham 242 G6
Urquhart Highld 300 D5
Moray 302 C2
Urra N Yorks 225 E11
Urray Highld 300 D5
Ushaw Moor Durham 233 C10
Usk Mon 78 E5
Usselby Lincs 189 C9
Usworth T&W 243 F8
Utkinton Ches W 167 B8
Utley W Yorks 204 E6
Uton Devon 14 B2
Utterby Lincs 190 C4
Uttoxeter Staffs 151 C11
Uwchmynydd Gwyn 144 D3
Uxbridge London 66 C5
Uxbridge Moor London 66 C5
Uyea Shetland 312 D5
Uyeasound Shetland 312 C7
Uzmaston Pembs 73 C7

V

Vachelich Pembs 90 F5
Vadlure Shetland 313 J4
Vagg Som 29 D8
Vaila Hall Shetland 313 J4
Vaivoe Shetland 312 G7
Vale W Yorks 196 B2
Vale Down Devon 12 D6
Vale of Health London 67 B9
Valeswood Shrops 149 E7
Valley = Y Fali Anglesey 178 F3
Valleyfield Dumfries 237 D8
Valley Park Hants 32 C6
Valley Truckle Corn 11 E7
Valsgarth Shetland 312 B8
Valtos Highld 298 C5
Van Caerph 59 B7
Powys 129 F9
Vange Essex 69 B8
Vanlop Shetland 313 M5
Varchoel Powys 148 G4
Varfell Corn 2 C2
Varteg Torf 78 D3
Vassa Shetland 313 H6
Vastern Wilts 62 C5
Vatsetter Shetland 312 E7
Shetland 313 L5
Vatten Highld 298 E2
Vaul Argyll 288 E2
Vauxhall London 67 D10
Mers 182 C4
W Mid 133 F11
Vaynol Hall Gwyn 163 B8
Vaynor M Tydf 77 C8
Veensgarth Shetland 313 J6
Velator Devon 40 F3
Veldo Hereford 97 C11
Velindre Powys 96 D3
Vellanoweth Corn 2 C2
Vellow Som 42 F5
Velly Devon 24 C3
Veness Orkney 314 D5
Venn Devon 8 F4
Venngreen Devon 24 E5
Venn Green Devon 24 E5
Vennington Shrops 130 B6
Venn Ottery Devon 15 C7
Venn's Green Hereford 97 B10
Venny Tedburn Devon 14 B2
Venterdon Corn 12 G3
Vention Devon 40 E3
Ventnor IoW 21 F7
Venton Devon 7 D11
Ventongimps Corn 4 E5
Ventonleague Corn 2 B3
Venus Hill Herts 85 E8
Veraby Devon 26 B3
Vermentry Shetland 313 H5
Vernham Bank Hants 47 B10
Vernham Dean Hants 47 B10
Vernham Row Hants 47 B10
Vernham Street Hants 47 B11
Vernolds Common
Shrops 131 G9
Verwood Dorset 31 F9
Veryan Corn 3 B10
Veryan Green Corn 5 G8
Vicarage Devon 15 D10
Vicarscross Ches W 166 B6
Vickerstown Cumb 210 F3
Victoria Corn 5 C9
S Yorks 197 F7
Victoria Dock Village
Hull 200 B6
Victoria Park Bucks 84 C4
Victory Gardens
Renfs 267 B10
Vidlin Shetland 312 G6
Viewpark N Lanark 268 C4
Vigo W Mid 133 C10
Vigo Village Kent 68 G6
Vinegar Hill Mon 60 B2
Vinehall Street E Sus 38 C3
Vines Cross E Sus 23 B9
Viney Hill Glos 79 D11
Vinney Green S Glos 61 D7
Virginia Water Sur 66 F3
Virginstow Devon 12 C3
Viscar Corn 2 C6
Vobster Som 45 D8
Voe Shetland 312 E5
Shetland 313 G6
Vogue Corn 4 G4
Vole Som 43 D11
Vowchurch Hereford 97 D7
Vowchurch Common
Hereford 97 D7
Voxmoor Som 27 D10
Voxter Shetland 312 F5
Voy Orkney 314 E2
Vron Gate Shrops 130 B6
Vulcan Village Mers 183 C9

W

Waberthwaite Cumb 220 G2
Wackerfield Durham 233 G9
Wacton Hereford 116 F2
Norf 142 E3
Wacton Common Norf 142 F3
Wadbister Shetland 313 J6
Wadborough Worcs 99 B8
Wadbrook Devon 28 G4
Waddesdon Bucks 84 B2
Waddeton Devon 9 D7
Waddicar Mers 182 B5
Waddicombe Devon 26 B5
Waddingham Lincs 189 B7
Waddington Lancs 203 E10
Lincs 173 C7
Waddingworth Lincs 189 G11
Waddon Devon 14 F3
London 67 G10
Wadebridge Corn 10 G5
Wadeford Som 28 E4
Wade Hall Lancs 194 C4
Wadenhoe N Nhants 137 G10
Wades Green Ches E 167 C11
Wadesmill Herts 86 B5
Wadhurst E Sus 52 G6
Wadshelf Derbys 186 G4
Wadsley S Yorks 186 C4
Wadsley Bridge S Yorks 186 C4
Wadswick Wilts 61 F10
Wadwick Hants 48 C2
Wadworth S Yorks 187 B9
Waen Denb 165 B10
Denb 165 C7
Flint 181 G11
Powys 129 E9
Waen Aberwheeler
Denb 165 B9
Waen-fâch Powys 148 F4
Waen Goleugoed Denb 181 G9
Waen-pentir Gwyn 163 B9
Waen-wen Gwyn 163 B9
Wag Highld 311 G4
Wagbeach Shrops 131 C7
Wagg Som 28 B6
Waggersley Staffs 151 B7
Waggs Plot Devon 28 G4
Wainfelin Torf 78 E3
Wainfleet All Saints
Lincs 175 D7
Wainfleet Bank Lincs 175 D7
Wainfleet St Mary Lincs 175 D8
Wainfleet Tofts Lincs 175 D7
Wainford Norf 142 E6
Waingroves Derbys 170 F6
Wainhouse Corner Corn 11 B9
Wain Lee Staffs 168 D5
Wainscott Medway 69 E8
Wainstalls W Yorks 196 B4
Waitby Cumb 222 D5
Waithe Lincs 201 G9
Wakefield W Yorks 197 C10
Wake Green W Mid 133 G11
Wake Hill N Yorks 214 E3
Wake Lady Green
N Yorks 226 F3
Wakeley Herts 104 F6
Wakerley N Nhants 137 D9
Wakes Colne Essex 107 F7
Wakes Colne Green
Essex 107 E7
Walberswick Suff 127 C9
Walberton W Sus 35 F7
Walbottle T&W 242 D5
Walby Cumb 239 E10
Walcombe Som 44 D5
Walcot Bath 61 F9
Lincs 155 B11
N Lincs 199 C11
Oxon 82 B4
Shrops 130 F6
Swindon 63 C7
Telford 149 G11
Worcs 99 B8
Walcote Leics 135 G11
Warks 118 F2
Walcot Green Norf 142 G2
Walcott Lincs 173 D10
Norf 161 C7
Walden N Yorks 213 C10
Walden Head N Yorks 213 C9
Walden Stubbs N Yorks 198 D5
Waldersey Cambs 139 C8
Waldershaigh S Yorks 186 B3
Walderslade Medway 69 G9
Walderton W Sus 34 E3
Walditch Dorset 16 C5
Waldley Derbys 152 B2
Waldridge Durham 243 G7
Waldringfield Suff 108 C5
Waldringfield Heath
Suff 108 B5
Waldron E Sus 23 B8
Waldron Down E Sus 37 C8
Wales Som 29 C9
S Yorks 187 E7
Wales Bar S Yorks 187 E7
Walesby Lincs 189 C10
Notts 187 G11
Walesby Grange Lincs 189 C10
Wales End Suff 106 B5
Waleswood S Yorks 187 E7
Walford Hereford 97 G11
Hereford 115 C7
Shrops 149 E8
Som 28 B3
Staffs 150 C6
Walford Heath Shrops 149 F8
Walgherton Ches E 167 F11
Walgrave W Nhants 120 C6
Walham Glos 98 G6
Walham Green London 67 D9
Walhampton Hants 20 B2
Walkden Gtr Man 195 G8
Walker T&W 243 E7
Walker Barn Ches E 185 G7
Walkerburn Borders 261 B9
Walker Fold Lancs 203 E9
Walkeringham Notts 188 C3
Walkerith Lincs 188 C3
Walkern Herts 104 F5
Walker's Green Hereford 97 B10
Walker's Heath W Mid 117 B11
Walkerville N Yorks 224 F4
Walkford BCP 19 C10
Walkhampton Devon 7 B10
Walkington E Yorks 208 F5
Walkley S Yorks 186 D4
Walkmill Shrops 131 E7
Walk Mill Lancs 204 G3
Walkmills Shrops 131 D9
Wall Corn 2 B4
Northumb 241 D10
Staffs 134 B2
Wallacestone Falk 279 F8
Wallaceton Dumfries 247 F8
Wallacetown S Ayrs 245 C7
S Ayrs 257 E8
Shetland 313 H5
Wallands Park E Sus 36 E6
Wallasey Mers 182 C4
Wallbank Lancs 195 D11
Wall Bank Shrops 131 E10
Wallbrook W Mid 133 E8
Wallcrouch E Sus 53 G7
Wallend London 68 C2
Wall End Cumb 210 C4
Kent 71 G8
Waller's Green Hereford 98 D3
Walley's Green Ches E 167 C11
Wall Heath W Mid 133 F7
Wall Hill Gtr Man 196 F3
Wallingford Oxon 64 B6
Wallington Hants 33 F9
Herts 104 E5
London 67 G9
Wallington Heath
W Mid 133 C9
Wallingwells Notts 187 E9
Wallis Pembs 91 F10
Wallisdown BCP 19 C7
Walliswood Sur 50 F6
Wall Mead Bath 45 B7
Wall Nook Durham 233 B10
Wallow Green Glos 80 F4
Wallridge Northumb 242 B3
Walls Shetland 313 J4
Wallsend T&W 243 D7
Wallston V Glam 58 E6
Wallsuches Gtr Man 195 E7
Wallsworth Glos 98 G6
Wall under Heywood
Shrops 131 E10
Wallyford E Loth 281 G7
Walmer Kent 55 C11
Walmer Bridge Lancs 194 C3
Walmersley Gtr Man 195 E10
Walmgate Stray York 207 C8
Walmley W Mid 134 E2
Walmsgate Lincs 190 F5
Walnut Grove Perth 286 E5
Walnut Tree M Keynes 103 D7
Walnuttree Green Herts 105 G9
Walpole Som 43 E10
Suff 127 C7
Walpole Cross Keys
Norf 157 F10
Walpole Highway Norf 157 G10
Walpole Marsh Norf 157 F9
Walpole St Andrew
Norf 157 F10
Walpole St Peter Norf 157 F9
Walrow Som 43 D10
Walsal End W Mid 118 B4
Walsall W Mid 133 D10
Walsall Wood W Mid 133 C10
Walsden W Yorks 196 C2
Walsgrave on Sowe
W Mid 135 G7
Walsham le Willows
Suff 125 C9
Walshaw Gtr Man 195 E9
Walshford N Yorks 206 C4
Walsoken Cambs 157 G9
Walson Mon 97 G8
Walston S Lanark 269 F11
Walsworth Herts 104 E4
Walters Ash Bucks 84 F4
Walter's Green Kent 52 E4
Walterston V Glam 58 E5
Walterstone Hereford 96 F6
Waltham Kent 54 D6
NE Lincs 201 G9
Waltham Abbey Essex 86 E5
Waltham Chase Hants 33 D9
Waltham Cross Herts 86 E5
Waltham on the Wolds
Leics 154 D6
Waltham St Lawrence
Windsor 65 D10
Waltham's Cross Essex 106 E3
Walthamstow London 67 B11
Walton Bucks 84 C4
Cumb 240 E2
Derbys 170 B5
Leics 135 F11
Mers 182 C5
M Keynes 103 D7
Pboro 138 C3
Powys 114 F5
Shrops 115 B9
Som 44 F3
Staffs 151 C7
Staffs 151 D7
Suff 108 D5
Telford 149 F11
Warks 118 G5
W Yorks 197 D11
W Yorks 206 D4
Walton Cardiff Glos 99 E8
Walton Court Bucks 84 C4
Walton East Pembs 91 G10
Walton Elm Dorset 30 D3
Walton Grounds
W Nhants 101 E10
Walton Heath Hants 33 F10
Walton Highway Norf 157 G9
Walton in Gordano
N Som 60 E2
Walton-le-Dale Lancs 194 B5
Walton Manor Oxon 83 D8
Walton-on-Thames Sur 66 F6
Walton on the Hill
Staffs 151 E9
Sur 51 B8
Walton-on-the-Naze
Essex 108 G5
Walton on the Wolds
Leics 153 F11
Walton-on-Trent
Derbys 152 F4
Walton Pool Worcs 117 B8
Walton St Mary N Som 60 E2
Walton Summit Lancs 194 B5
Walton Warren Norf 158 F4
Walton West Pembs 72 C5
Walwen Flint 181 F10
Flint 181 G11
Flint 182 F2
Walwick Northumb 241 C10
Walworth Darl 224 B4
London 67 D10
Walworth Gate Darl 233 G10
Walwyn's Castle Pembs 72 C5
Wambrook Som 28 F3
Wampool Cumb 238 G6
Wanborough Sur 50 D2
Swindon 63 C8
Wandel Dyke S Lanark 259 D11
Wandle Park London 67 F10
Wandon End Herts 104 G2
Wandsworth London 67 E9
Wangford Suff 127 B9
Wanlip Leics 154 G2
Wanlockhead Dumfries 259 G9
Wannock E Sus 23 E9
Wansford E Yorks 209 B7
Pboro 137 D11
Wanshurst Green Kent 53 D8
Wanson Corn 24 G1

Wanstead London 68 B2
Wanstrow Som 45 E8
Wanswell Glos 79 E11
Wantage Oxon 63 B11
Wants Green Worcs 116 F5
Wapley S Glos 61 D8
Wappenbury Warks 119 D7
Wappenham W Nhants 102 B2
Wapping London 67 C10
Warbleton E Sus 23 B10
Warblington Hants 22 B2
Warborough Oxon 83 G9
Warboys Cambs 138 G6
Warbreck Blackpool 202 F2
Warbstow Corn 11 C10
Warbstow Cross Corn 11 C10
Warburton Gtr Man 184 D2
Warburton Green
Gtr Man 184 E3
Warcop Cumb 222 B4
Warden Kent 70 E4
Northumb 241 D10
Powys 114 E6
Ward End W Mid 134 F2
Warden Hill Glos 99 G8
Warden Point IoW 20 D2
Warden Street C Beds 104 C2
Ward Green Suff 125 E10
S Yorks 197 G10
Ward Green Cross
Lancs 203 F8
Wardhedges C Beds 103 D11
Wardhill Orkney 314 D6
Wardington Oxon 101 B9
Wardlaw Borders 261 F7
Wardle Ches E 167 D10
Gtr Man 196 D2
Wardle Bank Ches E 167 D10
Wardley Gtr Man 195 G9
Rutland 136 C6
T&W 243 E7
W Sus 34 B4
Wardlow Derbys 185 G11
Wardour Wilts 30 B6
Wardpark N Lanark 278 F5
Wardrobes Bucks 84 E4
Wardsend Ches E 184 E6
Wardy Hill Cambs 139 G9
Ware Herts 86 C5
Kent 71 G9
Wareham Dorset 18 D4
Warehorne Kent 54 G3
Warenford Northumb 264 D4
Waren Mill Northumb 264 C4
Warenton Northumb 264 C4
Wareside Herts 86 B5
Waresley Cambs 122 G4
Worcs 116 C6
Ware Street Kent 53 B9
Warfield Brack 65 E11
Warfleet Devon 9 E7
Wargate Lincs 156 C4
Wargrave Mers 183 C9
Wokingham 65 D9
Warham Hereford 97 D9
Norf 176 E6
Warhill Gtr Man 185 B7
Waring's Green W Mid 118 C2
Wark Northumb 241 B9
Northumb 263 B8
Wark Common
Northumb 263 B8
Warkleigh Devon 25 C10
Warkton N Nhants 121 B7
Warkworth Northumb 252 B6
W Nhants 101 C9
Warlaby N Yorks 224 G6
Warland W Yorks 196 C2
Warleggan Corn 6 B3
Warleigh Bath 61 G9
Warley Essex 87 G9
Warley Town W Yorks 196 B5
Warley Woods W Mid 133 F10
Warlingham Sur 51 B11
Warmbrook Derbys 170 E3
Warmfield W Yorks 197 C11
Warmingham Ches E 168 C2
Warminghurst W Sus 35 D10
Warmington N Nhants 137 E11
Warks 101 B8
Warminster Wilts 45 D11
Warminster Common
Wilts 45 E11
Warmlake Kent 53 C10
Warmley S Glos 61 E7
Warmley Hill S Glos 61 E7
Warmley Tower S Glos 61 E7
Warmonds Hill
N Nhants 121 D9
Warmsworth S Yorks 198 G4
Warmwell Dorset 17 D11
Warnborough Green
Hants 49 C8
Warndon Worcs 117 F7
Warners End Herts 85 D8
Warnford Hants 33 C10
Warnham W Sus 51 G7
Warningcamp W Sus 35 F8
Warninglid W Sus 36 B2
Warpsgrove Oxon 83 F10
Warren Ches E 184 G5
Dorset 18 C3
Pembs 72 F6
S Yorks 186 B5
Warrenby Redcar 235 F7
Warren Corner Hants 34 B2
Hants 49 D10
Warren Heath Suff 108 C4
Warren Row Windsor 65 C10
Warren's Green Herts 104 F5
Warren Street Kent 54 C2
Warrington M Keynes 121 G7
Warr 183 D10
Warriston Edin 280 F5
Warsash Hants 33 F7
Warsill N Yorks 214 F4
Warslow Staffs 169 D9
Warsop Vale Notts 171 B8
Warstock W Mid 117 B11
Warstone Staffs 133 B9
Warter E Yorks 208 C3
Warthermarske N Yorks 214 D4
Warthill N Yorks 207 B9
Wartle Aberds 293 C7
Wartling E Sus 23 D11
Wartnaby Leics 154 E4
Warton Lancs 194 B2
Lancs 211 E9
Northumb 252 C2
Warks 134 C5
Warton Bank Lancs 194 B2
Warwick Warks 118 E5
Warwick Bridge Cumb 239 F11
Warwick on Eden
Cumb 239 F11
Warwicksland Cumb 239 B10
Warwick Wold Sur 51 C10
Wasbister Orkney 314 C3
Wasdale Head Cumb 220 D3
Wash Derbys 185 E9
Washall Green Herts 105 E8
Washaway Corn 5 B10
Washbourne Devon 8 E5
Washbrook Som 44 C2
Suff 108 C2
Washbrook Street Suff 108 C2
Wash Common W Berks 64 G3
Wash Dyke Norf 157 F10
Washerwall Staffs 168 F6
Washfield Devon 26 D6
Washfold N Yorks 223 E11
Washford Som 42 E5
Worcs 117 D11
Washford Pyne Devon 26 E4
Washingborough Lincs 189 G8
Washingley Cambs 138 F2
Washington T&W 243 F8
W Sus 35 E10
Washington Village
T&W 243 F8
Washmere Green Suff 107 B8
Washpit W Yorks 196 F6
Wash Water W Berks 64 G3
Washwood Heath
W Mid 134 F2
Wasing W Berks 64 G5
Waskerley Durham 233 B7
Wasperton Warks 118 F5
Wasp Green Sur 51 D10
Wasps Nest Lincs 173 C9
Wass N Yorks 215 D11
Waste Green Warks 118 D4
Wastor Devon 8 F2
Watchet Som 42 E5
Watchfield Oxon 63 B8
Som 43 D10
Watchgate Cumb 221 F10
Watchhill Cumb 229 C9
Watch House Green
Essex 106 G3
Watchill Dumfries 238 D6
Dumfries 248 G3
Watcombe Torbay 9 B8
Watendlath Cumb 220 B5
Water Devon 13 E11
Lancs 195 B10
Waterbeach Cambs 123 D9
W Sus 22 B5
Waterbeck Dumfries 238 B6
Waterdale Herts 85 E10
Waterden Norf 159 B7
Waterditch Hants 19 B9
Water Eaton M Keynes 103 E7
Oxon 83 C8
Waterend Bucks 84 F3
Cumb 229 G8
Glos 80 C3
Herts 86 C2
Water End Bedford 104 B2
C Beds 103 D11
C Beds 104 B5
Essex 105 C11
E Yorks 207 F11
Hants 49 C7
Herts 85 C8
Herts 86 E2
Waterfall Staffs 169 E9
Waterfoot Argyll 255 D9
Cumb 230 G5
E Renf 267 D11
Lancs 195 C10
Waterford Hants 20 B2
Herts 86 C4
Water Fryston W Yorks 198 B3
Water Garth Nook Cumb 210 F3
Watergate Corn 6 E4
Corn 11 E8
Watergore Som 28 D6
Waterhales Essex 87 F8
Waterham Kent 70 G5
Waterhay Wilts 81 G9
Waterhead Angus 292 F6
Cumb 221 E7
Devon 8 F3
Dumfries 248 E5
Waterhead on Minnoch
S Ayrs 245 E9
Waterheads Borders 270 E4
Waterheath Norf 143 E8
Waterhouses Durham 233 C9
Staffs 169 E9
Water Houses N Yorks 213 F7
Wateringbury Kent 53 C7
Waterlane Glos 80 E6
Waterlip Som 45 E7
Waterloo BCP 18 C6
Blackburn 195 B7
Corn 11 G8
Derbys 170 C6
Gtr Man 196 G2
Highld 295 C8
Mers 182 B4
N Lanark 268 E6
Norf 126 B2
Norf 143 E8
Norf 160 F4
Pembs 73 E7
Perth 286 D4
Shrops 149 C9
Waterloo Park Mers 182 B4
Waterloo Port Gwyn 163 C7
Waterlooville Hants 33 F11
Waterman Quarter Kent 53 E10
Watermead Glos 80 B5
Watermeetings
S Lanark 259 G11
Watermill E Sus 38 E2
Watermillock Cumb 230 G4
Watermoor Glos 81 E8
Water Newton Cambs 138 D2
Water Orton Warks 134 E3
Waterperry Oxon 83 D10
Waterrow Som 27 B9
Watersfield W Sus 35 D8
Watersheddings
Gtr Man 196 F2
Waterside Aberds 292 B5
Aberds 303 G10
Blackburn 195 C8
Bucks 85 E7
Cumb 229 B10
Derbys 185 E8
E Ayrs 245 B10
E Ayrs 267 G9
E Dunb 278 G3
E Renf 267 D10
Sur 51 D11
S Yorks 199 E7
Telford 150 F2
Waterslack Lancs 211 D9
Water's Nook Gtr Man 195 F7
Waterstein Highld 297 G7
Waterstock Oxon 83 D10
Waterston Pembs 72 D6
Water Stratford Bucks 102 E3
Waters Upton Telford 150 F2
Waterthorpe S Yorks 186 E6
Waterton Aberds 303 F9
Bridgend 58 D2
Water Yeat Cumb 210 B5
Watford Herts 85 F10
W Nhants 120 D2
Watford Gap Staffs 134 C2
Watford Heath Herts 85 G10
Watford Park Caerph 58 B6
Wath Cumb 222 D3
N Yorks 214 D6
N Yorks 214 F2
N Yorks 216 D3
Wath Brow Cumb 219 C10
Watherston Borders 271 F8
Wath upon Dearne
S Yorks 198 G2
Watledge Glos 80 E4
Watley's End S Glos 61 C7
Watlington Norf 158 G2
Oxon 83 G11
Watnall Notts 171 F8
Watsness Shetland 313 H3
Watten Highld 310 D6
Wattisfield Suff 125 C10
Wattisham Suff 125 G10
Wattisham Stone Suff 125 G10
Wattlefield Norf 142 D2
Wattlesborough Heath
Shrops 149 G7
Watton E Yorks 208 C6
Norf 141 C8
Watton at Stone Herts 86 B4
Watton Green Norf 141 C8
Watton's Green Essex 87 F8
Wattston N Lanark 268 B5
Wattstown Rhondda 77 G8
Wattsville Caerph 78 G2
Wauchan Highld 295 G11
Waulkmill Lodge Orkney 314 F3
Waun Gwyn 163 C9
Powys 148 F4
Waunarlwydd Swansea 56 B6
Waun Beddau Pembs 90 F5
Waunclunda Carms 94 E3
Waunfawr Gwyn 163 D8
Waun Fawr Ceredig 128 G2
Waungilwen Carms 92 D6
Waungron Swansea 75 E9
Waunlwyd Bl Gwent 77 D11
Waun-Lwyd Bl Gwent 77 D11
Waun-y-clyn Carms 75 E7
Waun y Gilfach Bridgend 57 D10
Wavendon M Keynes 103 D8
Wavendon Gate
M Keynes 103 D8
Waverbridge Cumb 229 B10
Waverley S Yorks 186 D6
Waverton Ches W 167 C7
Cumb 229 B10
Wavertree Mers 182 D5
Wawcott W Berks 63 F11
Wawne E Yorks 209 F7
Waxham Norf 161 D8
Waxholme E Yorks 201 B10
Way Kent 71 F10
Waye Devon 13 G11
Wayend Street Hereford 98 D4
Wayfield Medway 69 F9
Wayford Som 28 F6
Waymills Shrops 167 G9
Wayne Green Mon 78 B6
Way's Green Ches W 167 B10
Waytown Devon 24 C5
Devon 40 G5
Way Village Devon 26 E5
Way Wick N Som 59 G11
Wdig = *Goodwick* Pembs 91 D8
Weachyburn Aberds 302 D6
Weacombe Som 42 E6
Weald Oxon 82 E4
Wealdstone London 67 B7
Wearde Corn 7 D8
Weardley W Yorks 205 E11
Weare Som 44 C2
Weare Giffard Devon 25 C7
Wearhead Durham 232 D3
Wearne Som 28 B6
Weasdale Cumb 222 E3
Weasenham All Saints
Norf 158 E6
Weasenham St Peter
Norf 159 E7
Weaste Gtr Man 184 B4
Weatherhill Sur 51 E10
Weatheroak Hill Worcs 117 C11
Weaverham Ches W 183 G10
Weavering Street Kent 53 B9
Weaverslake Staffs 152 F2
Weaverthorpe N Yorks 217 E9
Webbington Som 43 B11
Webheath Worcs 117 D10
Webscott Shrops 149 E9
Wecock Hants 33 E11
Wedderlairs Aberds 303 F8
Wedderlie Borders 272 E2
Weddington Kent 55 B9
Warks 135 E7
Wedhampton Wilts 46 B5
Wedmore Som 44 D2
Wednesbury W Mid 133 D9
Wednesbury Oak
W Mid 133 E9
Wednesfield W Mid 133 C8
Weecar Notts 172 B4
Weedon Bucks 84 B4
Weedon Bec W Nhants 120 F2
Weedon Lois W Nhants 102 B2
Weeford Staffs 134 C2
Week Devon 8 C5
Devon 12 E5
Devon 25 B9
Devon 26 D2
Weeke Devon 26 F3
Hants 48 G3
Week Green Corn 11 B10
Weekley N Nhants 137 G7
Weekmoor Som 27 B10
Weeks IoW 21 C7
Week St Mary Corn 11 B10
Weel E Yorks 209 F7
Weeley Essex 108 G2
Weeley Heath Essex 108 G3
Weelsby NE Lincs 201 F9
Weem Perth 286 C2
Weeping Cross Staffs 151 E8
Weethley Warks 117 F11
Weethley Bank Warks 117 G11
Weethley Gate Warks 117 G11
Weeting Norf 140 F5
Weeton E Yorks 201 C11
Lancs 202 G3
N Yorks 205 D11
Weetwood W Yorks 205 F11
Weetwood Common
Ches W 167 B8
Weetwood Hall
Northumb 264 D2
Weir Essex 69 B10
Lancs 195 B11
Weirbrook Shrops 148 E6
Weir Quay Devon 7 C8
Welborne Norf 159 G11
Welborne Common
Norf 141 B11
Welbourn Lincs 173 E7
Welburn N Yorks 216 C3
Welburn *continued*
N Yorks 216 F4
Welbury N Yorks 225 E7
Welby Lincs 155 B9
Welches Dam Cambs 139 F9
Welcombe Devon 24 D2
Weld Bank Lancs 194 D5
Weldon N Nhants 137 F8
Northumb 252 D4
Welford W Berks 64 E2
W Nhants 136 G2
Welford-on-Avon
Warks 118 G3
Welham Leics 136 E5
Notts 188 E2
Som 45 G7
Welhambridge
E Yorks 207 G11
Welham Green Herts 86 D2
Well Hants 49 D9
Lincs 190 G6
N Yorks 214 C5
Welland Worcs 98 C5
Welland Stone Worcs 98 D6
Wellbank Angus 287 D8
Well Bottom Dorset 30 D6
Wellbrook E Sus 37 B9
Welldale Dumfries 238 D5
Well End Bucks 65 B11
Herts 86 F2
Weller's Town Kent 52 E4
Wellesbourne Warks 118 F5
Well Green Gtr Man 184 D3
Wellheads Aberds 302 F4
Well Heads W Yorks 205 G7
Well Hill Kent 68 G3
Wellhouse W Berks 64 E4
W Yorks 196 E5
Welling London 68 D3
Wellingborough
N Nhants 121 D7
Wellingham Norf 159 E7
Wellingore Lincs 173 D7
Wellington Cumb 219 E11
Hereford 97 B9
Som 27 C10
Telford 150 G3
Wellington Heath
Hereford 98 C4
Wellington Hill W Yorks 206 F2
Wellisford Som 27 C9
Wellow Bath 45 B8
IoW 20 D3
NE Lincs 201 F9
Notts 171 B11
Wellow Wood Hants 32 C3
Well Place Oxon 65 B7
Wellpond Green Herts 105 G8
Wellroyd W Yorks 205 F10
Wells Som 44 D5
Wellsborough Leics 135 C7
Wells Green Ches E 167 E11
Wells-next-the-Sea
Norf 176 E6
Wellsprings Som 28 B2
Well Street Kent 53 B7
Wellstye Green Essex 87 B10
Wellswood Torbay 9 C8
Welltown Corn 6 B2
Well Town Devon 26 F6
Wellwood Fife 279 D11
Welney Norf 139 E10
Welsford Devon 24 C3
Welshampton Shrops 149 B8
Welsh Bicknor Hereford 79 B9
Welsh End Shrops 149 B10
Welsh Frankton Shrops 149 C7
Welsh Harp London 67 B8
Welsh Hook Pembs 91 F8
Welsh Newton Hereford 79 B7
Welsh Newton Common
Hereford 79 B8
Welshpool Powys 130 B4
Welsh St Donats V Glam 58 D4
Welshwood Park Essex 107 F10
Welstor Devon 13 G10
Welton Bath 45 C7
Cumb 230 C3
E Ayrs 258 D2
E Yorks 200 B3
Lincs 189 F8
W Nhants 119 D11
Welton Hill Lincs 189 E8
Welton le Marsh Lincs 175 B7
Welton le Wold Lincs 190 D3
Welwick E Yorks 201 C10
Welwyn Herts 86 B2
Welwyn Garden City
Herts 86 C2
Wem Shrops 149 D10
Wembdon Som 43 F9
Wembley London 67 B7
Wembley Park London 67 B7
Wembury Devon 7 F10
Wembworthy Devon 25 F11
Wemyss Bay Invclyd 266 B3
Wenallt Ceredig 112 C3
Gwyn 146 F4
Gwyn 165 G7
Wendens Ambo Essex 105 D10
Wendlebury Oxon 83 B9
Wendling Norf 159 G8
Wendover Bucks 84 D5
Wendover Dean Bucks 84 E5
Wendron Corn 2 C5
Wendy Cambs 104 B6
Wenfordbridge Corn 11 F7
Wenhaston Suff 127 B8
Wenhaston Black Heath
Suff 127 C8
Wennington Cambs 122 B4
Lancs 212 E2
London 68 C4
Wensley Derbys 170 C3
N Yorks 213 B11
Wentbridge W Yorks 198 D3
Wentnor Shrops 131 E7
Wentworth Cambs 123 B9
S Yorks 186 B5
Wenvoe V Glam 58 E6
Weobley Hereford 115 G8
Weobley Marsh
Hereford 115 G8
Weoley Castle W Mid 133 G10
Wepham W Sus 35 F8
Wepre Flint 166 B3
Wereham Norf 140 C3
Wereham Row Norf 140 C3
Wereton Staffs 168 E3
Wergs W Mid 133 C7
Wern Gwyn 145 B10
Powys 77 B10
Powys 147 G9
Powys 148 E5
Powys 148 G5
Shrops 148 C5
Swansea 56 C4
Wern ddu Shrops 148 D4
Werneth Gtr Man 196 G2
Werneth Low Gtr Man 185 C7
Wernffrwd Swansea 56 C4
Wern-Gifford Mon 96 G6
Wernlas Shrops 148 E6
Wern-olau Swansea 56 B5
Wernrheolydd Mon 78 C5
Wern Tarw Bridgend 58 C3
Wern-y-cwrt Mon 78 D5
Wern-y-gaer Flint 166 B2
Wernyrheolydd Mon 78 C5
Werrington Corn 12 D2
Pboro 138 C3
Staffs 168 F6
Wervin Ches W 182 G6
Wescoe Hill N Yorks 205 D11
Wesham Lancs 202 G4
Wessington Derbys 170 D5
West Aberthaw V Glam 58 F4
Westacott Devon 40 G5
West Acre Norf 158 F5
West Acton London 67 C7
West Adderbury Oxon 101 D9
West Allerdean
Northumb 273 F9
West Allotment T&W 243 C8
West Alvington Devon 8 G4
West Amesbury Wilts 46 E6
West Anstey Devon 26 B5
West Appleton N Yorks 224 G4
West Ardhu Argyll 288 D6
West Ardsley W Yorks 197 B9
West Ardwell Dumfries 236 E2
West Arthurlie E Renf 267 D9
West Ashby Lincs 190 G3
West Ashford Devon 40 F4
West Ashling W Sus 22 B4
West Ashton Wilts 45 B11
West Auckland Durham 233 F9
West Ayton N Yorks 217 C9
West Bagborough Som 43 G7
West Bank Bl Gwent 78 D2
Halton 183 E8
West Barkwith Lincs 189 E11
West Barnby N Yorks 226 C6
West Barnes London 67 F8
West Barns E Loth 282 F3
West Barsham Norf 159 C8
West Bay Dorset 16 C5
West Beckham Norf 160 B2
West Bedfont Sur 66 E5
West Benhar N Lanark 269 C7
Westbere Kent 71 G7
West Bergholt Essex 107 F9
West Bexington Dorset 16 D6
West Bilney Norf 158 F4
West Blackdene Durham 232 D3
West Blackdown Devon 12 E5
West Blatchington
Brighton 36 F3
West Bold Borders 261 B9
West Boldon T&W 243 E9
Westborough Lincs 172 G5
Westbourne BCP 19 C7
Suff 108 B2
W Sus 22 B3
Westbourne Green
London 67 C9
West Bourton Dorset 30 B3
West Bowling W Yorks 205 G9
West Bradford Lancs 203 E10
West Bradley Som 44 F5
West Bretton W Yorks 197 E9
West Bridgford Notts 153 B11
West Brompton London 67 D9
West Bromwich
W Mid 133 E10
Westbrook Hereford 96 C5
Kent 71 E10
Sur 50 E3
Warr 183 C9
W Berks 64 E2
Wilts 62 F3
Westbrook Green Norf 142 G2
Westbrook Hay Herts 85 D8
West Broughton Derbys 152 C2
West Buckland Devon 41 G7
Som 27 C11
West Burnside Aberds 293 F8
West Burrafirth
Shetland 313 H4
West Burton N Yorks 213 B10
W Sus 35 E7
Westbury Bucks 102 D2
Shrops 131 B7
Wilts 45 C11
Westbury Leigh Wilts 45 C11
Westbury-on-Severn
Glos 80 C2
Westbury on Trym Bristol 60 D5
Westbury Park Bristol 60 D5
Westbury-sub-Mendip
Som 44 D4
West Butsfield Durham 233 C8
West Butterwick
N Lincs 199 F10
Westby Lancs 202 G3
Lincs 155 D9
West Byfleet Sur 66 G4
West Caister Norf 161 G10
West Calder W Loth 269 C10
West Camel Som 29 C9
West Carlton W Yorks 205 E10
West Carr Hull 209 G7
N Lincs 199 F8
West Chadsmoor Staffs 151 G9
West Challow Oxon 63 B11
West Charleton Devon 8 G5
West Chelborough Dorset 29 F8
West Chevington
Northumb 252 D6
West Chiltington W Sus 35 D9
West Chiltington Common
W Sus 35 D9
West Chinnock Som 29 E7
West Chirton T&W 243 D8
West Chisenbury Wilts 46 C6
West Clandon Sur 50 C4
West Cliff BCP 19 C7
N Yorks 227 C7
West Cliffe Kent 55 E10
Westcliff-on-Sea
Southend 69 B11
West Clyne Highld 311 J2
Highld 311 J2
West Clyth Highld 310 F6
Highld 310 F6
West Coker Som 29 E8
Westcombe Som 29 B7
Som 45 F7
West Common Hants 32 G6
West Compton Dorset 17 C7
Som 44 E5
West Cornforth Durham 234 E2
Westcot Oxon 63 B10
Westcote Glos 100 G4
Westcotes Leicester 135 C11
Westcott Bucks 84 B2
Devon 27 G8
Shrops 131 C8
Sur 50 D6
Westcott Barton Oxon 101 F8
Westcourt Wilts 63 G8
West Cowick E Yorks 199 C7
West Cranmore Som 45 E7
Westcroft M Keynes 102 E6
W Mid 133 C8
West Cross Kent 53 G10
Swansea 56 D6
West Crudwell Wilts 80 G6
West Cullery Aberds 293 C9
West Curry Corn 11 C11
West Curthwaite Cumb 230 B2
West Darlochan Argyll 255 E7
Westdean E Sus 23 F8
West Dean Wilts 32 B3
W Sus 34 E5
West Deeping Lincs 138 B2
West Denant Pembs 72 C6
Westdene Brighton 36 F3
West Denton T&W 242 D5
West Derby Mers 182 C5
West Dereham Norf 140 C3
West Didsbury Gtr Man 184 C4
West Down Devon 40 E4
Hants 47 F11
Westdown Camp Wilts 46 D4
Westdowns Corn 11 E7
West Downs Corn 5 C10
West Drayton London 66 D5
Notts 188 G2
West Dulwich London 67 E10
West Ealing London 67 C7
West Edge Derbys 170 C4
West Ella E Yorks 200 B4
Westend Oxon 100 G6
S Glos 79 G10
West End Bedford 121 E11
Bedford 121 G9
Brack 65 E11
Brack 66 G2
Caerph 78 F2
Cumb 239 F8
Dorset 30 G6
E Yorks 201 B9
E Yorks 208 G4
E Yorks 209 B9
E Yorks 209 G9
E Yorks 217 G11
Glos 80 F5
Hants 33 E7
Hants 33 F9
Hants 48 F6
Herts 86 D3
Kent 54 B2
Kent 71 F7
Lancs 195 B8
Lancs 211 G8
Leics 153 F8
Lincs 174 F5
Lincs 190 B5
Mon 78 F6
Norf 141 B8
Norf 161 G10
N Som 60 F3
N Yorks 205 B8
N Yorks 206 E6
N Yorks 207 F7
Oxon 64 B5
Oxon 82 E6
S Glos 61 B8
S Lanark 269 F9
Som 44 C5
Som 45 G7
Suff 143 G9
Sur 49 E10
Sur 66 G6
S Yorks 199 F7
Wilts 30 C6
Wilts 31 C7
Wilts 62 D3
Windsor 65 D10
Worcs 99 D11
W Sus 36 D2
W Yorks 197 B7
W Yorks 205 F10
West End = *Marian-y-mor*
Gwyn 145 C7
West End Green Hants 65 G7
Westend Town
Northumb 241 D7
West-end Town V Glam 58 F3
Westenhanger Kent 54 F6
Wester Aberchalder
Highld 300 G5
Wester Arboll Highld 311 L2
Wester Auchinloch
N Lanark 278 G3
Wester Auchnagallin
Highld 301 F10
Wester Balgedie Perth 286 G5
Wester Brae Highld 300 C6
Wester Broomhouse
E Loth 282 F3
Wester Craiglands
Highld 301 D7
Wester Culbeuchly
Aberds 302 C6
Westerdale Highld 310 D5
N Yorks 226 D3
Wester Dalvoult Highld 291 B11
Wester Dechmont
W Loth 269 B10
Wester Deloraine
Borders 261 E8
Wester Denoon Angus 287 C7
Wester Ellister Argyll 254 B2
Wester Essendy Perth 286 C5
Wester Essenside
Borders 261 E10
Wester Feddal Perth 286 G2
Westerfield Shetland 313 H5
Suff 108 B3
Wester Fintray Aberds 293 B10
Westerfolds Moray 301 C11
Wester Galgantray
Highld 301 E8
Westergate W Sus 22 C6
Wester Gospetry Fife 286 G5
Wester Gruinards
Highld 309 K5
Westerham Kent 52 C2
Westerhope T&W 242 D5
Wester Housebyres
Borders 262 B2
Wester Kershope
Borders 261 D9
Wester Lealty Highld 300 B6
Westerleigh S Glos 61 D8
Westerleigh Hill S Glos 61 D8
Wester Lix Stirling 285 E9
Wester Milton Highld 301 D9
Wester Mosshead
Aberds 302 F5
Western Bank Cumb 229 B10
Western Downs Staffs 151 E8
Western Heights Kent 55 E10
Western Hill Durham 233 C11
Western Park Leicester 135 C11
Wester Ord Aberds 293 C10
Wester Parkgate
Dumfries 248 F2
Wester Quarff Shetland 313 K6
Wester Skeld Shetland 313 J4
Wester Strath Highld 300 D6
Westerton Aberds 293 B9
Aberds 302 E5
Angus 287 B10
Durham 233 E10
Moray 302 D3
W Sus 22 B5
Westertown Aberds 303 F7
Wester Watten Highld 310 D6
Westerwick Shetland 313 J4
West Ewell Sur 67 G8
West Farleigh Kent 53 C8
West Farndon
W Nhants 119 G10
West Felton Shrops 148 D6
West Fenton E Loth 281 E9
West Ferry Dundee 287 D8
Westfield Bath 45 C7
Cumb 228 F5
E Sus 38 D4
Hants 21 B10
Hereford 98 B4
Highld 310 C4
N Lanark 278 G4
Norf 141 B9
Redcar 235 G7
Sur 50 B4
S Yorks 186 E6
W Loth 279 G8
W Yorks 197 C8
W Yorks 205 E9
West Field N Lincs 200 D6
York 207 C7
Westfields Dorset 30 F2
Hereford 97 C9
West Fields W Berks 64 F3
Westfields of Rattray
Perth 286 C5
Westfield Sole Kent 69 G9
West Firle E Sus 23 D7
West Fleetham
Northumb 264 D5
West Flodden
Northumb 263 C10
Westford Som 27 C10
West Garforth W Yorks 206 G3
Westgate Durham 232 D4
N Lincs 199 F9
Norf 176 E4
Norf 177 E7
Westgate Hill W Yorks 197 B8
Westgate on Sea Kent 71 E10
Westgate Street Norf 160 E3
West Ginge Oxon 64 B2
West Gorton Gtr Man 184 B5
West Grafton Wilts 63 G8
West Green Hants 49 B8
London 67 B10
S Yorks 197 F11
W Sus 51 F9
West Greenskares
Aberds 303 C7
West Grimstead Wilts 32 B2
West Grinstead W Sus 35 C11
West Haddlesey
N Yorks 198 B5
West Haddon W Nhants 120 C2
West Hagbourne Oxon 64 B4
West Hagley Worcs 133 G8
West Hall Cumb 240 D3
Westhall Aberds 302 G6
Suff 143 G8
West Hallam Derbys 170 G6
Westhall Hill Oxon 82 C3
West Halton N Lincs 200 C2
Westham Dorset 17 F9
E Sus 23 E10
Som 44 D2
West Ham Hants 48 C6
London 68 C2
Westhampnett W Sus 22 B5
West Hampstead London 67 B9
West Handley Derbys 186 F5
West Hanney Oxon 82 G6
West Hanningfield Essex 88 F2
West Hardwick
W Yorks 198 D2
West Harling Norf 141 G9
West Harlsey N Yorks 225 F8
West Harnham Wilts 31 B10
West Harptree Bath 44 B5
West Harrow London 66 B6
West Harting W Sus 34 C3
West Harton T&W 243 E9
West Hatch Som 28 C3
Wilts 30 B6
Westhay Som 44 E2
Westhead Lancs 194 F2
West Head Norf 139 B11
West Heath Ches E 168 C4
Hants 48 B5
Hants 49 B11
London 68 D3
W Mid 117 B10
West Helmsdale Highld 311 H4
West Hendon London 67 B8
West Hendred Oxon 64 B2
West Herrington T&W 243 G8
West Heslerton N Yorks 217 D8
West Hewish N Som 59 G11
Westhide Hereford 97 C11
Westhill Aberds 293 C10
E Yorks 209 F10
Highld 301 E7
West Hill Devon 15 C7
E Sus 38 E4
E Yorks 218 F3
London 67 E8
N Som 60 D3
Som 30 B2
Staffs 151 G9
Wilts 61 F11
W Sus 51 G10
West Hoathly W Sus 51 G11
West Holme Dorset 18 D3
West Holywell T&W 243 C8
Westhope Hereford 115 G9
Shrops 131 F9
West Horndon Essex 68 B6
Westhorp W Nhants 119 G10
Westhorpe Lincs 156 C4
Notts 171 E11
Suff 125 D10
West Horrington Som 44 D5
West Horsley Sur 50 C5
West Horton Northumb 264 C2
West Hougham Kent 55 E9
Westhoughton Gtr Man 195 F7
West Houlland Shetland 313 H4
Westhouse N Yorks 212 E3
Westhouses Derbys 170 D6
West Houses Lincs 174 E4
West Howe BCP 19 B7
West Howetown Som 42 G2
Westhumble Sur 51 C7
West Huntington York 207 B8
West Huntspill Som 43 E10
West Hurn BCP 19 B8
West Hyde Herts 85 G8
West Hynish Argyll 288 F1
West Hythe Kent 54 G6
West Ilkerton Devon 41 D8
West Ilsley W Berks 64 C3
Westing Shetland 312 C7
Westington Glos 100 D2
West Itchenor W Sus 22 C3
West Jesmond T&W 243 D7
West Keal Lincs 174 C5
West Kennett Wilts 62 F6
West Kensington London 67 D8
West Kilbride N Ayrs 266 F4
West Kilburn London 67 C8
West Kingsdown Kent 68 G5
West Kingston W Sus 35 G9
West Kington Wilts 61 D10
West Kington Wick
Wilts 61 D10
West Kinharrachie
Aberds 303 F9
West Kirby Mers 182 D2
West Kirkby Mers 182 D2
West Knapton N Yorks 217 D7
West Knighton Dorset 17 D10
West Knoyle Wilts 45 G11
West Kyloe Northumb 273 G11
West Kyo Durham 242 G5
Westlake Devon 8 E2
West Lambrook Som 28 D6
Westland Argyll 275 G11
Westland Green Herts 105 G8
Westlands Staffs 168 G4
Worcs 117 E7
West Langdon Kent 55 D10
West Langwell Highld 309 J6
West Lavington Wilts 46 C4
W Sus 34 C5
West Layton N Yorks 224 D2
Westlea Northumb 252 G6
Swindon 62 C6
West Lea Durham 234 B4
West Leake Notts 153 D10
West Learmouth
Northumb 263 B9
Westleigh Devon 25 B7
Devon 27 D9
Gtr Man 194 G6
West Leigh Devon 25 F11
Hants 22 B2
Som 42 G6
Westleton Suff 127 D8
West Lexham Norf 158 F6
Westley Shrops 131 B7
Suff 124 E6
Westley Heights Essex 69 B7
Westley Waterless
Cambs 124 F2
West Lilling N Yorks 216 F2
Westlington Bucks 84 C3
Westlinton Cumb 239 E9
West Linton Borders 270 E2
West Liss Hants 34 B3
West Littleton S Glos 61 D9
West Lockinge Oxon 64 B2
West Looe Corn 6 E5
West Luccombe Som 41 D11
West Lulworth Dorset 18 E2
West Lutton N Yorks 217 F8
West Lydford Som 44 G5
West Lydiatt Hereford 97 C11
West Lyn Devon 41 D8
West Lyng Som 28 B4
West Lynn Norf 158 E2
West Mains Borders 271 F11
S Lanark 268 E2
West Malling Kent 53 B7
West Malvern Worcs 98 B5
Westmancote Worcs 99 D8
West Marden W Sus 34 E3
West Marina E Sus 38 F3
West Markham Notts 188 G2
Westmarsh Kent 71 G9
West Marsh NE Lincs 201 E9
West Marton N Yorks 204 C3
West Mathers Aberds 293 G9
West Melbury Dorset 30 C5
West Melton S Yorks 198 G2
West Meon Hants 33 C10
West Meon Woodlands
Hants 33 B10
West Merkland Highld 308 F3
West Mersea Essex 89 C8
Westmeston E Sus 36 E4
Westmill Herts 104 E3
Herts 105 F7
West Milton Dorset 16 B6
Westminster London 67 D10
West Minster Kent 70 E2
West Molesey Sur 66 F6
West Monkseaton T&W 243 C8
West Monkton Som 28 B3
West Moor T&W 243 C7
Westmoor End Cumb 229 D8
West Moors Dorset 31 G9
West Morden Dorset 18 B4
West Morriston Borders 272 G2
West Morton W Yorks 205 E7
West Mudford Som 29 C9
Westmuir Angus 287 B7
West Muir Angus 293 G7
West Myreriggs Perth 286 C6
Westness Orkney 314 D3
West Ness N Yorks 216 D3
West Newham Northumb 242 B3
Westnewton Cumb 229 C8
Northumb 263 C10
West Newton E Yorks 209 F9
Norf 158 D3
Som 28 B3
West Norwood London 67 E10
Westoe T&W 243 D9
West Ogwell Devon 14 G2
Weston Bath 61 F8
Ches E 168 E2
Ches E 184 G5
Devon 15 D9
Devon 27 G10
Dorset 17 G9
Dorset 29 F8
Halton 183 E8
Hants 34 C2
Hereford 115 F7
Herts 104 E5
Lincs 156 D5
Notts 172 B3
N Yorks 205 D9
Pembs 73 C8
Shrops 114 C6
Shrops 131 E11
Shrops 148 D5
Shrops 149 D11
S Lanark 269 F10
Soton 32 E6
Staffs 151 D9
Suff 143 F8
W Berks 63 E11
W Nhants 101 B11
Weston Bampfylde
Som 29 C10

Weston Beggard
Hereford 97 C11
Westonbirt Glos 61 B11
Weston by Welland
N Nhants 136 E5
Weston Colley Hants 48 F4
Weston Colville Cambs 124 G2
Westoncommon Shrops 149 D8
Weston Common Soton 33 E7
Weston Corbett Hants 49 D7
Weston Coyney Stoke 168 G6
Weston Ditch Suff 124 B3
Weston Favell
W Nhants 120 E5
Weston Green Cambs 124 G2
Norf 160 G2
Sur 67 F7
Weston Heath Shrops 150 G5
Weston Hills Lincs 156 E5
Weston in Arden Warks 135 F7
Westoning C Beds 103 E10
Weston-in-Gordano
N Som 60 E2
Weston Jones Staffs 150 E5
Weston Longville Norf 160 F2
Weston Lullingfields
Shrops 149 E8
Weston Manor IoW 20 D2
Weston Mill Plym 7 D9
Weston-on-Avon
Warks 118 G3
Weston-on-the-Green
Oxon 83 B8
Weston-on-Trent
Derbys 153 D8
Weston Park Bath 61 F8
Weston Patrick Hants 49 D7
Weston Point Halton 183 E7
Weston Rhyn Shrops 148 B5
Weston-sub-Edge Glos 100 C2
Weston-super-Mare
N Som 59 G10
Weston Town Som 45 E8
Weston Turville Bucks 84 C5
Weston under Lizard
Staffs 150 G6
Weston under Penyard
Hereford 98 G2
Weston under Wetherley
Warks 119 D7
Weston Underwood
Derbys 170 G3
M Keynes 121 G7
Westonwharf Shrops 149 D8
Westonzoyland Som 43 G11
West Orchard Dorset 30 D4
West Overton Wilts 62 F6
Westow N Yorks 216 F5
Westowe Som 42 G6
Westown Devon 27 F10
Perth 286 E6
West Panson Devon 12 C2
West Park Hrtlpl 234 E5
Hull 200 B5
Mers 183 B7
T&W 243 D9
W Yorks 205 F11
West Parley Dorset 19 B7
West Pasture Durham 232 G4
West Peckham Kent 52 C6
West Pelton Durham 242 G6
West Pennard Som 44 F4
West Pentire Corn 4 C5
West Perry Cambs 122 D2
West Pontnewydd Torf 78 F3
West Poringland Norf 142 C5
West Porlock Som 41 D11
Westport Argyll 255 E7
Som 28 D5
West Portholland Corn 5 G9
West Porton Renfs 277 G8
West Pulham Dorset 30 F2
West Putford Devon 24 D5
West Quantoxhead Som 42 E6
Westquarter Falk 279 F8
Westra V Glam 58 E6
West Rainton Durham 234 B2
West Rasen Lincs 189 D9
West Ravendale
NE Lincs 190 B2
West Raynham Norf 159 D7
West Retford Notts 187 E11
Westridge Green
W Berks 64 D5
Westrigg W Loth 269 B8
Westrip Glos 80 D4
Westrop Wilts 61 E11
Westrop Green W Berks 64 E4
West Rounton N Yorks 225 E8
West Row Suff 124 B3
West Royd W Yorks 205 F9
West Rudham Norf 158 D6
West Ruislip London 66 B5
Westrum N Lincs 200 F4
West Runton Norf 177 E11
Westruther Borders 272 F2
Westry Cambs 139 D7
West Saltoun E Loth 271 B9
West Sandford Devon 26 G4
West Sandwick Shetland 312 E6
West Scholes W Yorks 205 G7
West Scrafton N Yorks 213 C11
West Shepton Som 44 E6
West Sherford Devon 7 E10
West Side Bl Gwent 77 D11
Orkney 314 C5
West Skelston Dumfries 247 F8
West Sleekburn
Northumb 253 G7
West Somerton Norf 161 F9
West Southbourne BCP 19 C8
West Stafford Dorset 17 D10
West Stockwith Notts 188 C3
West Stoke Devon 13 G9
Som 29 D7
W Sus 22 B4
West Stonesdale
N Yorks 223 E7
West Stoughton Som 44 D2
West Stour Dorset 30 C3
West Stourmouth Kent 71 G9
West Stow Suff 124 C6
West Stowell Wilts 62 G6
West Strathan Highld 308 C5
West Stratton Hants 48 E4
West Street Kent 54 C2
Kent 55 C10
Medway 69 D8
Suff 125 C9
West Tanfield N Yorks 214 D5
West Taphouse Corn 6 C3
West Tarbert Argyll 275 G9
West Tarring W Sus 35 G10
West Third Borders 262 B4
West Thirston Northumb 252 D5
West Thorney W Sus 22 C3
Westthorpe Derbys 187 F7
West Thurrock Thurrock 68 D5
West Tilbury Thurrock 69 D7
West Tisted Hants 33 B11
West Tofts Norf 140 E6
Perth 286 D5
West Tolgus Corn 4 G3
West Torrington Lincs 189 E10
West Town Bath 60 G4
Devon 14 B3
Devon 24 C4
Hants 21 B10
Hereford 115 E8
N Som 60 F3
Som 44 F4
W Sus 36 D3
West Tytherley Hants 32 B3
West Tytherton Wilts 62 E2
Westvale Mers 182 B6
West Vale W Yorks 196 C5
West View Hrtlpl 234 D5
West Village V Glam 58 E3
Westville Devon 8 G4
Notts 171 F8
West Walton Norf 157 G9
West Walton Highway
Norf 157 G9
Westward Cumb 229 C11
Westward Ho! Devon 24 B6
West Watergate Corn 6 E4
West Watford Herts 85 F10
Westweekmoor Devon 12 C4
Westwell Kent 54 D3
Oxon 82 D2
Westwell Leacon Kent 54 D3
West Wellow Hants 32 D3
Westwells Wilts 61 F11
West Wemyss Fife 280 C6
Westwick Cambs 123 D8
Durham 223 B11
Norf 160 D5
West Wick N Som 59 G11
West Wickham Cambs 106 B2
London 67 F11
Westwick Row Herts 85 D9
West Williamston Pembs 73 D8
West Willoughby Lincs 173 G7
West Winch Norf 158 F2
West Winterslow Wilts 47 G8
West Wittering W Sus 21 B11
West Witton N Yorks 213 B11
Westwood Devon 14 B6
Devon 14 E5
Kent 55 D7
Kent 71 F11
Notts 171 E7
Pboro 138 D3
S Lanark 268 E2
Wilts 45 B10
Wilts 46 G6
West Woodburn
Northumb 251 F9
West Woodhay W Berks 63 G11
Westwood Heath
W Mid 118 B5
West Woodlands Som 45 E9
Westwood Park Essex 107 E9
Gtr Man 184 B3
Westwoodside N Lincs 188 B3
West Worldham Hants 49 F8
West Worlington Devon 26 E3
West Worthing W Sus 35 G10
West Wratting Cambs 124 G2
West Wycombe Bucks 84 G4
West Wylam Northumb 242 E4
Westy Warr 183 D10
West Yatton Wilts 61 E11
West Yell Shetland 312 E6
West Yeo Som 43 G10
West Yoke Kent 68 F5
West Youlstone Corn 24 D3
Wetham Green Kent 69 F10
Wetheral Cumb 239 G11
Wetheral Plain Cumb 239 F11
Wetherby W Yorks 206 D4
Wetherden Suff 125 E10
Wetherden Upper Town
Suff 125 D10
Wetheringsett Suff 126 D2
Wethersfield Essex 106 E4
Wethersta Shetland 312 G5
Wetherup Street Suff 126 E2
Wetley Rocks Staffs 169 F7
Wetmore Staffs 152 E5
Wettenhall Ches E 167 C10
Wettenhall Green
Ches E 167 C10
Wettles Shrops 131 F8
Wetton Staffs 169 D10
Wetwang E Yorks 208 B4
Wetwood Staffs 150 C5
Wexcombe Wilts 47 B9
Wexham Street Bucks 66 C3
Weybourne Norf 177 E10
Sur 49 D11
Weybread Suff 142 G4
Weybridge Sur 66 G5
Weycroft Devon 16 B2
Weydale Highld 310 C5
Weyhill Hants 47 D10
Weymouth Dorset 17 F9
Weythel Powys 114 F4
Whaddon Bucks 102 E6
Cambs 104 B6
Glos 80 C4
Glos 99 G9
Wilts 31 B11
Wilts 61 G11
Whaddon Gap Cambs 104 B6
Whale Cumb 230 G6
Whaley Derbys 187 G8
Whaley Bridge Derbys 185 E8
Whaley Thorns Derbys 187 G8
Whaligoe Highld 310 E7
Whalley Lancs 203 F10
Whalley Banks Lancs 203 F10
Whalley Range Gtr Man 184 C4
Whalleys Lancs 194 F3
Whalton Northumb 252 G4
Wham N Yorks 212 G5
Whaplode Lincs 156 E6
Whaplode Drove Lincs 156 G6
Whaplode St Catherine
Lincs 156 E6
Wharf Warks 119 G8
Wharfe N Yorks 212 F5
Wharles Lancs 202 F4
Wharley End C Beds 103 C8
Wharmley Northumb 241 D9
Wharncliffe Side
S Yorks 186 C3
Wharram le Street
N Yorks 217 F7
Wharram Percy
N Yorks 217 G7
Wharton Ches W 167 B11
Hereford 115 F10
Lincs 188 C4
Wharton Green
Ches W 167 B11
Whashton N Yorks 224 D3
Whasset Cumb 211 C10
Whatcombe Dorset 30 G4
Whatcote Warks 100 C6
Whatcroft Ches W 167 B11
Whateley Staffs 134 D4
Whatfield Suff 107 B10
Whatley Som 28 F5
Som 45 D8
Whatlington E Sus 38 D3
Whatmore Shrops 116 C2
Whatsole Street Kent 54 E6
Whatstandwell Derbys 170 E4
Whatton Notts 154 B4
Whauphill Dumfries 236 E6
Whaw N Yorks 223 E9
Wheal Alfred Corn 2 B3
Wheal Baddon Corn 4 G5
Wheal Busy Corn 4 G4
Wheal Frances Corn 4 E5
Wheal Kitty Corn 4 E4
Wheal Rose Corn 4 G4
Wheatacre Norf 143 E9
Wheatcroft Derbys 170 D5
Wheatenhurst Glos 80 D3
Wheathall Shrops 131 C9
Wheathampstead Herts 85 C11
Wheathill Shrops 132 G2
Som 44 G5
Wheat Hold Hants 64 G5
Wheatley Devon 14 C4
Hants 49 E9
Oxon 83 D9
S Yorks 198 G5
W Yorks 196 B5
Wheatley Hill Durham 234 D3
Wheatley Hills S Yorks 198 G6
Wheatley Lane Lancs 204 F2
Wheatley Park S Yorks 198 F5
Wheaton Aston Staffs 151 G7
Wheddon Cross Som 42 F2
Wheedlemont Aberds 302 G4
Wheelbarrow Town Kent 55 D7
Wheeler End Bucks 84 G4
Wheelerstreet Sur 50 E2
Wheelock Ches E 168 D3
Wheelock Heath
Ches E 168 D2
Wheelton Lancs 194 C6
Lancs 194 D5
Lancs 194 D6
Wheen Angus 292 F5
Wheldale W Yorks 198 B3
Wheldrake York 207 D9
Whelford Glos 81 F11
Whelley Gtr Man 194 F5
Whelpley Hill Herts 85 E7
Whelpo Cumb 230 D2
Whelp Street Suff 107 B8
Whelston Flint 182 F2
Whempstead Herts 104 G6
Whenby N Yorks 216 F2
Whepstead Suff 124 F6
Wherry Town Corn 1 D5
Wherstead Suff 108 C3
Wherwell Hants 47 E11
Wheston Derbys 185 F10
Whetley Cross Dorset 29 G7
Whetsted Kent 53 D7
Whetstone Leics 135 D11
London 86 G3
Whettleton Shrops 131 G8
Whicham Cumb 210 C2
Whichford Warks 100 E6
Whickham T&W 242 E6
Whickham Fell T&W 242 F6
Whiddon Devon 40 F5
Whiddon Down Devon 13 C9
Whifflet N Lanark 268 C4
Whigstreet Angus 287 C8
Whilton W Nhants 120 E2
Whilton Locks
W Nhants 120 E2
Whimble Devon 24 G5
Whim Farm Borders 270 E4
Whimple Devon 14 B6
Whimpwell Green Norf 161 D7
Whinburgh Norf 141 B10
Whinfield Darl 224 B6
Whinhall N Lanark 268 B5
Whin Lane End Lancs 202 E3
Whinmoor W Yorks 206 F3
Whinney Hill Stockton 225 B7
S Yorks 187 C7
Whinnieliggate
Dumfries 237 D9
Whinnyfold Aberds 303 F10
Whinny Heights
Blackburn 195 B7
Whins of Milton Stirling 278 C5
Whins Wood W Yorks 205 F7
Whipcott Devon 27 D9
Whippendell Botton
Herts 85 E9
Whippingham IoW 20 C6
Whipsiderry Corn 4 C6
Whipsnade C Beds 85 B8
Whipton Devon 14 C5
Whirley Grove Ches E 184 F5
Whirlow S Yorks 186 E4
Whisby Lincs 172 B6
Whissendine Rutland 154 G6
Whissonsett Norf 159 E8
Whisterfield Ches E 184 G4
Whistlefield Argyll 276 C2
Argyll 276 C4
Whistley Green
Wokingham 65 E9
Whistlow Oxon 101 F9
Whiston Mers 183 C7
Staffs 151 G7
Staffs 169 F8
S Yorks 186 D6
W Nhants 120 E6
Whiston Cross Mers 183 C7
Shrops 132 C5
Whitacre Heath Warks 134 E4
Whitbarrow Village
Cumb 230 F4
Whitbeck Cumb 210 C2
Whitbourne Hereford 116 F4
Whitbourne Moor Wilts 45 D10
Whitburn T&W 243 E10
W Loth 269 C8
Whitburn Colliery
T&W 243 E10
Whitby Ches W 182 F5
N Yorks 227 C7
Whitbyheath Ches W 182 F5
Whitchurch Bath 60 F6
Bucks 102 G5
Cardiff 59 C7
Devon 12 G5
Hants 48 D3
Hereford 79 B9
Pembs 90 F5
Shrops 167 G8
Som 30 C2
Whitchurch Canonicorum
Dorset 16 B3
Whitchurch Hill Oxon 64 D6
Whitchurch-on-Thames
Oxon 64 D6
Whitcombe Dorset 17 D10
Whitcombe *continued*
Som 29 C10
Whitcot Shrops 131 E7
Whitcott Keysett Shrops 130 G5
Whiteacen Moray 302 E2
Whiteacre Kent 54 D6
Whiteacre Heath Warks 134 E4
Whiteash Green Essex 106 E5
White Ball Som 27 D9
Whitebirk Blackburn 195 B8
Whitebog Highld 301 C7
Whitebridge Highld 290 B6
Whitebrook Mon 79 D8
Whiteburn Borders 271 F11
Whitebushes Sur 51 D9
Whitecairn Dumfries 236 D4
Whitecairns Aberds 293 B11
Whitecastle S Lanark 269 G10
Whitechapel Lancs 203 E7
London 67 C10
Whitechurch Maund
Hereford 97 B11
Whitecleat Orkney 314 F5
Whitecliff Glos 79 C9
Whiteclosegate Cumb 239 F10
White Colne Essex 107 F7
White Coppice Lancs 194 D6
Whitecote W Yorks 205 F10
Whitecraig E Loth 281 G7
Whitecraigs E Renf 267 D11
Whitecroft Glos 79 D10
Whitecrook W Dunb 267 B10
Whitecross Corn 2 C2
Corn 6 E2
Corn 10 G5
Falk 279 F9
Som 28 C6
Staffs 151 E7
White Cross Bath 44 B5
Bath 44 B6
Corn 2 E5
Corn 5 D7
Hereford 97 C9
Som 43 D10
Wilts 45 G9
White Cross Hill Cambs 123 B9
White End Worcs 98 E5
Whiteface Highld 309 L7
Whitefarland N Ayrs 255 C9
Whitefaulds S Ayrs 245 B7
Whitefield Aberds 303 G7
Dorset 18 C4
Gtr Man 195 F10
Perth 286 D5
Som 27 B9
Whitefield Lane End
Mers 183 D7
Whiteflat E Ayrs 258 D2
Whiteford Aberds 303 G7
Whitegate Ches W 167 B10
White Gate Gtr Man 195 G11
Som 28 F4
White Grit Shrops 130 D6
Whitehall Blackburn 195 C7
Bristol 60 E6
Devon 27 E10
Devon 40 F4
Hants 49 C8
Herts 104 E6
W Sus 35 C10
White Hall Herts 104 G5
Whitehall Village
Orkney 314 D6
Whitehaven Cumb 219 B9
Shrops 148 E5
Whitehawk Brighton 36 G4
Whiteheath Gate W Mid 133 F9
Whitehill E Sus 37 B8
Hants 49 G9
Kent 54 B4
Midloth 271 B7
Moray 302 D5
S Lanark 268 D4
Staffs 168 E3
White Hill Bath 45 B8
Wilts 45 G10
W Yorks 204 E6
Whitehills Aberds 302 C6
S Lanark 268 E2
T&W 243 E7
White Hills W Nhants 120 E4
Whiteholme Blackpool 202 E2
Whitehough Derbys 185 E8
Whitehouse Aberds 293 B8
Argyll 275 G9
White House Suff 108 B2
Whitehouse Common
W Mid 134 D2
Whitehouse Green
W Berks 65 F7
White Houses Notts 188 F2
Whiteinch Glasgow 267 B10
Whitekirk E Loth 281 E10
Whiteknights Reading 65 E8
Whiteknowes Aberds 293 C7
Whitelackington Som 28 D5
White Lackington
Dorset 17 B10
White Ladies Aston
Worcs 117 G8
Whitelaw S Lanark 268 G2
Whiteleaf Bucks 84 E4
Whiteleas T&W 243 E9
Whiteleaved Oak Glos 98 D5
Whitelee Borders 262 C3
Northumb 250 B6
White Lee W Yorks 197 B8
Whitelees S Ayrs 257 C9
White-le-Head Durham 242 G5
Whiteley Bank IoW 21 E7
Whiteley Green Ches E 184 F6
Whiteley Village Sur 66 G5
White Lund Lancs 211 G8
Whitelye Mon 79 E8
Whitemans Green W Sus 36 B4
White Mill Carms 93 G9
Whitemire Moray 301 D9
Whitemoor Corn 5 D9
Nottingham 171 G8
Warks 118 C5
White Moor Derbys 170 F5
Whitemore Staffs 168 C5
Whitenap Hants 32 C5
White Ness Shetland 313 J5
White Notley Essex 88 B3
White Oak Kent 68 F4
Whiteoak Green Oxon 82 C4
White Ox Mead Bath 45 B8
Whiteparish Wilts 32 C2
White Pit Lincs 190 F5
Whitepits Wilts 45 F10
White Post Kent 52 E4
Notts 171 D10
Whiterashes Aberds 303 G8
Whiterigg Borders 262 C3
Whiterock Bridgend 58 D2
White Rocks Hereford 97 G8
White Roding or White
Roothing Essex 87 C9
Whiterow Highld 310 E7
White's Green W Sus 34 B6
Whiteshill Glos 80 D4
S Glos 60 D6
Whiteside Northumb 240 D6
W Loth 269 B9
Whitesmith E Sus 23 C8
Whitespots Dumfries 247 F10
White Stake Lancs 194 B4
Whitestaunton Som 28 E3
Whitestone Aberds 293 D8
Devon 14 C3
Devon 40 D3
Warks 135 F7
White Stone Hereford 97 C11
Whitestones Aberds 303 D8
Whitestreet Green Suff 107 D9
Whitewall Common Mon 60 B2
Whitewall Corner
N Yorks 216 E5
White Waltham Windsor 65 D10
Whiteway Bath 61 G8
Dorset 18 E3
Glos 80 C6
Glos 80 F4
Whitewell Aberds 303 C9
Corn 11 E7
Highld 291 C11
Lancs 203 D9
Wrex 167 G7
Whitewell Bottom
Lancs 195 C10
Whiteworks Devon 13 G8
Whitfield Kent 55 D10
Northumb 241 F7
S Glos 79 G11
W Nhants 102 D2
Whitfield Court Sur 50 B3
Whitfield Hall Northumb 241 F7
Whitford Devon 15 B11
Whitford =Chwitffordd
Flint 181 F10
Whitgift E Yorks 199 C10
Whitgreave Staffs 151 D7
Whithaugh Borders 249 F11
Whithebeir Orkney 314 C5
Whithorn Dumfries 236 E6
Whiting Bay N Ayrs 256 D2
Whitington Norf 140 D4
Whitkirk W Yorks 206 G3
Whitland =Hendy-Gwyn
Carms 73 B11
Whitlaw Borders 271 F9
Whitleigh Plym 7 C9
Whitletts S Ayrs 257 E9
Whitley Gtr Man 194 F5
N Yorks 198 C5
Reading 65 E8
S Yorks 186 C4
Wilts 61 F11
W Mid 119 B7
Whitley Bay T&W 243 C9
Whitley Bridge N Yorks 198 C5
Whitley Chapel
Northumb 241 F10
Whitley Head W Yorks 204 E6
Whitley Heath Staffs 150 D6
Whitley Lower W Yorks 197 D8
Whitley Reed Ches W 183 E10
Whitley Row Kent 52 C3
Whitley Sands T&W 243 C9
Whitley Thorpe N Yorks 198 C5
Whitley Wood Reading 65 F8
Whitlock's End W Mid 118 B2
Whitminster Glos 80 D3
Whitmoor Devon 27 E9
Whitmore Dorset 31 F9
Staffs 168 G4
Whitmore Park W Mid 134 G6
Whitnage Devon 27 D8
Whitnash Warks 118 E6
Whitnell Som 43 F8
Whitney Bottom Som 28 E4
Whitney-on-Wye
Hereford 96 B5
Whitrigg Cumb 229 D10
Cumb 238 F6
Whitriggs Borders 262 F3
Whitsbury Hants 31 D10
Whitslaid Borders 271 G11
Whitsome Borders 273 E7
Whitsomehill Borders 273 F7
Whitson Newport 59 C11
Whitstable Kent 70 F6
Whitstone Corn 11 B11
Whittingham Northumb 264 G3
Whittingslow Shrops 131 F8
Whittington Glos 99 G10
Lancs 212 D2
Norf 140 D4
Shrops 148 C6
Staffs 133 G7
Staffs 134 B3
Staffs 150 C5
Warks 134 D5
Worcs 117 G7
Whittington Moor
Derbys 186 G5
Whittlebury W Nhants 102 C3
Whittleford Warks 134 E6
Whittle-le-Woods
Lancs 194 C5
Whittlesey Cambs 138 D5
Whittlesford Cambs 105 B9
Whittlestone Head
Blackburn 195 D8
Whitton Borders 263 E7
Hereford 115 C8
London 66 E6
N Lincs 200 C2
Northumb 252 C3
Powys 114 D5
Shrops 115 C11
Stockton 234 G3
Suff 108 B2
Whittonditch Wilts 63 E9
Whittonstall Northumb 242 F3
Whittytree Shrops 115 B8
Whitway Hants 48 B3
Whitwell Derbys 187 F8
Herts 104 G3
IoW 20 F6
N Yorks 224 F5
Rutland 137 B8
Whitwell-on-the-Hill
N Yorks 216 F4
Whitwell Street Norf 160 E2
Whitwick Leics 153 F8
Whitwood W Yorks 198 C2
Whitworth Lancs 195 D11
Whixall Shrops 149 C10
Whixley N Yorks 206 B4
Whoberley W Mid 118 B6
Wholeflats Falk 279 E8
Whome Orkney 314 G3
Whorlton Durham 224 C2
N Yorks 225 E9
Whydown E Sus 38 F2
Whygate Northumb 241 B7
Whyke W Sus 22 C5
Whyle Hereford 115 E11
Whyteleafe Sur 51 B10
Wibdon Glos 79 F9
Wibsey W Yorks 205 G8
Wibtoft Leics 135 F9
Wichenford Worcs 116 E5
Wichling Kent 54 B2
Wick BCP 19 C8
Devon 27 G11
Highld 310 D7
S Glos 61 E8
Shetland 313 K6
Som 28 B6
Som 43 C10
Som 43 E8
V Glam 58 E2
Wilts 31 C11
Worcs 99 B9
W Sus 35 G8
Wicken Cambs 123 C11
W Nhants 102 D4
Wicken Bonhunt Essex 105 E9
Wickenby Lincs 189 E9
Wicken Green Village
Norf 158 C6
Wick Episcopi Worcs 116 G6
Wickersley S Yorks 187 C7
Wicker Street Green
Suff 107 C9
Wickford Essex 88 G3
Wickham Hants 33 E9
W Berks 63 E11
Wickham Bishops Essex 88 C4
Wickhambreaux Kent 55 B8
Wickhambrook Suff 124 G4
Wickhamford Worcs 99 C11
Wickham Green Suff 125 D11
W Berks 63 E11
Wickham Heath W Berks 64 F2
Wickham Market Suff 126 F6
Wickhampton Norf 143 B8
Wickham St Paul Essex 106 D6
Wickham's Cross Som 44 G4
Wickham Skeith Suff 125 D11
Wickham Street Suff 124 G5
Suff 125 D11
Wick Hill Brack 65 E11
Kent 53 E10
Wokingham 65 G9
Wickhurst Kent 52 D4
Wicklane Bath 45 B7
Wicklewood Norf 141 C11
Wickmere Norf 160 C3
Wickridge Street Glos 98 F6
Wick Rocks S Glos 61 E8
Wick St Lawrence
N Som 59 F11
Wickstreet E Sus 23 D8
Wick Street Glos 80 D5
Wickwar S Glos 61 B8
Widbrook Wilts 45 B10
Widcombe Bath 61 G9
Widdington Essex 105 E10
Widdrington Northumb 253 D7
Widdrington Station
Northumb 252 E6
Widecombe in the Moor
Devon 13 F10
Widegates Corn 6 D5
Widemarsh Hereford 97 C10
Widemouth Bay Corn 24 G2
Wideopen T&W 242 C6
Widewall Orkney 314 G4
Widewell Plym 7 C9
Widford Essex 87 D11
Herts 86 B6
Widgham Green Cambs 124 F3
Widham Wilts 62 B5
Widley Hants 33 F11
Widmer End Bucks 84 F5
Widmerpool Notts 154 D2
Widmoor Bucks 66 B2
Widmore London 68 F2
Widnes Halton 183 D8
Wierton Kent 53 D9
Wig Powys 130 F2
Wigan Gtr Man 194 F5
Wiganthorpe N Yorks 216 E3
Wigbeth Dorset 31 F8
Wigborough Som 28 D6
Wig Fach Bridgend 57 F10
Wiggaton Devon 15 C8
Wiggenhall St Germans
Norf 157 G11
Wiggenhall St Mary
Magdalen Norf 157 G11
Wiggenhall St Mary the
Virgin Norf 157 G11
Wiggenhall St Peter
Norf 158 G2
Wiggens Green Essex 106 C3
Wiggington Staffs 134 B4
Wigginstall Staffs 169 C9
Wigginton Herts 84 C6
Oxon 101 E7
Shrops 148 B6
Staffs 134 B4
York 207 B7
Wigginton Bottom Herts 84 D6
Wigginton Heath Oxon 101 D7
Wigglesworth N Yorks 204 B2
Wiggonby Cumb 239 G7
Wiggonholt W Sus 35 D9
Wighill N Yorks 206 D5
Wighton Norf 159 B8
Wightwick Manor Staffs 133 D7
Wigley Derbys 186 G4
Hants 32 D4
Wigmarsh Shrops 149 D7
Wigmore Hereford 115 D8
Medway 69 G10
Wigsley Notts 188 G5
Wigsthorpe N Nhants 137 G10
Wigston Leics 136 D2
Wigston Magna Leics 136 D2
Wigston Parva Leics 135 F9
Wigthorpe Notts 187 E9
Wigtoft Lincs 156 B5
Wigton Cumb 229 B11
Wigtown Dumfries 236 D6
Wigtwizzle S Yorks 186 B2
Wike W Yorks 206 E2
Wike Well End S Yorks 199 E7
Wilbarston N Nhants 136 F6
Wilberfoss E Yorks 207 C10
Wilberlee W Yorks 196 E5
Wilburton Cambs 123 C9
Wilby N Nhants 121 D7
Norf 141 F10
Suff 126 C4
Wilcot Wilts 62 G6
Wilcott Shrops 149 F7
Wilcott Marsh Shrops 149 F7
Wilcove Corn 7 D8
Wilcrick Newport 60 B2
Wilday Green Derbys 186 G4
Wildboarclough Ches E 169 B7
Wilden Bedford 121 F11
Worcs 116 C6
Wildern Hants 33 E7
Wildernesse Kent 52 B4
Wilderspool Warr 183 D10
Wilderswood Gtr Man 194 E6
Wilde Street Suff 124 B4
Wildhern Hants 47 C11
Wildhill Herts 86 D3
Wildmanbridge
S Lanark 268 E6
Wild Mill Bridgend 58 C2
Wildmoor Hants 49 B7
Oxon 83 F7
Worcs 117 B9
Wildridings Brack 65 F11
Wildsworth Lincs 188 B4
Wildwood Staffs 151 E8
Wilford Nottingham 153 B11
Wilgate Green Kent 54 B3
Wilkesley Ches E 167 G10
Wilkhaven Highld 311 L3
Wilkieston W Loth 270 B2
Wilkinthroop Som 29 C11
Wilkin Throop Som 29 C11
Wilksby Lincs 174 C3
Willacy Lane End Lancs 202 F5
Willand Devon 27 E8
Som 27 E11
Willand Moor Devon 27 E8
Willard's Hill E Sus 38 C2
Willaston Ches E 167 E11
Ches W 182 F4
Shrops 149 B11
Willen M Keynes 103 C7
Willenhall W Mid 119 B7
W Mid 133 D9
Willerby E Yorks 208 G6
N Yorks 217 D10
Willersey Glos 100 D2
Willersley Hereford 96 B6
Willesborough Kent 54 E4
Willesborough Lees
Kent 54 E4
Willesden London 67 C8
Willesden Green London 67 C8
Willesley Leics 152 G6
Wilts 61 B11
Willett Som 42 G6
Willey Shrops 132 D3
Warks 135 G9
Willey Green Sur 50 C2
Willhayne Som 28 E4
Williamscott Oxon 101 B9
William's Green Suff 107 C9
Williamslee Borders 270 G6
Williamthorpe Derbys 170 B6
Willian Herts 104 E4
Willicote Pastures
Worcs 100 B3
Willingale Essex 87 D9
Willingcott Devon 40 E3
Willingdon E Sus 23 E9
Willingham Cambs 123 C8
Suff 143 G8
Willingham by Stow
Lincs 188 E5
Willingham Green
Cambs 124 G2
Willington Bedford 104 B2
Derbys 152 D5
Durham 233 D9
Kent 53 C9
T&W 243 D8
Warks 100 D5
Willington Corner
Ches W 167 B8
Willington Quay T&W 243 D8
Willisham Suff 125 G11
Willisham Tye Suff 125 G11
Willitoft E Yorks 207 F10
Williton Som 42 E5
Willoughbridge Staffs 168 G3
Willoughby Lincs 191 G7
Warks 119 D10
Willoughby Hills Lincs 174 F4
Willoughby-on-the-Wolds
Notts 154 D2
Willoughby Waterleys
Leics 135 E11
Willoughton Lincs 188 C6
Willowbank Bucks 66 B5
Willow Green Ches W 183 F10
Worcs 116 F5
Willow Holme Cumb 239 F9
Willows Gtr Man 195 F8
Willows Green Essex 88 B2
Willowtown Bl Gwent 77 C11
Will Row Lincs 191 D7
Willsbridge S Glos 61 E7
Willslock Staffs 151 C11
Willstone Shrops 131 D9
Willsworthy Devon 12 E6
Wilmcote Warks 118 F3
Wilmington Bath 61 G7
Devon 15 B10
E Sus 23 E8
Kent 68 E4
Wilmington Green E Sus 23 D8
Wilminstone Devon 12 F5
Wilmslow Ches E 184 E4
Wilmslow Park Ches E 184 E5
Wilnecote Staffs 134 C4
Wilney Green Norf 141 G11
Wilpshire Lancs 203 G9
Wilsden W Yorks 205 F7
Wilsden Hill W Yorks 205 F7
Wilsford Lincs 173 G8
Wilts 46 B6
Wilts 46 F6
Wilsham Devon 41 D9
Wilshaw W Yorks 196 F6
Wilsill N Yorks 214 G3
Wilsley Green Kent 53 F9
Wilsley Pound Kent 53 F9
Wilsom Hants 49 F8
Wilson Hereford 97 G11
Leics 153 E8
Wilsontown S Lanark 269 D9
Wilstead Bedford 103 C11
Wilsthorpe Derbys 153 C9
Lincs 155 G11
Wilstone Herts 84 C6
Wilstone Green Herts 84 C6
Wilthorpe S Yorks 197 F10
Wilton Borders 261 G11
Cumb 219 C10
Hereford 97 G11
N Yorks 217 C7
Redcar 225 B11
Som 28 C2
Wilts 46 G5
Wilts 63 G9
Wilton Park Bucks 85 G7
Wiltown Devon 27 D11
Som 28 C5
Wimbish Essex 105 D11
Wimbish Green Essex 106 D2
Wimblebury Staffs 151 G10
Wimbledon London 67 E8
Wimble Hill Hants 49 D10
Wimblington Cambs 139 E8
Wimboldsley Ches W 167 C11
Wimbolds Trafford
Ches W 182 G6
Wimborne Minster
Dorset 18 B6
Wimborne St Giles
Dorset 31 E8
Wimbotsham Norf 140 B2
Wimpole Cambs 104 B6
Wimpson Soton 32 E5
Wimpstone Warks 100 B4
Wincanton Som 30 B2
Winceby Lincs 174 B4
Wincham Ches W 183 F11
Winchburgh W Loth 279 G11
Winchcombe Glos 99 F10
Winchelsea E Sus 38 D6
Winchelsea Beach E Sus 38 D6
Winchester Hants 33 B7
Winchestown Bl Gwent 77 C11
Winchet Hill Kent 53 E8
Winchfield Hants 49 C9
Winchfield Hurst Hants 49 C9
Winchmore Hill Bucks 84 G6
London 86 G4
Wincle Ches E 169 B7
Wincobank S Yorks 186 C5
Winder Cumb 219 B10
Windermere Cumb 221 F8
Winderton Warks 100 C6
Windhill Highld 300 E5
S Yorks 198 G3
W Yorks 205 F9
Wind Hill Cumb 210 E5
Pembs 73 F9
Windhouse Shetland 312 D6
Winding Wood W Berks 63 E11
Windle Hill Ches W 182 F4
Windlehurst Gtr Man 185 D7
Windlesham Sur 66 G2
Windley Derbys 170 F4
Windmill Corn 10 G3
Flint 181 G11
Flint 182 G2
Windmill Hill Bristol 60 E5
E Sus 23 C10
Halton 183 E9
Kent 69 F10
Som 28 D4
Worcs 99 B8
W Yorks 197 D11
Windrush Glos 81 C11
Windsor N Lincs 199 E9
Windsor 66 D3
Windsoredge Glos 80 E4
Windsor Green Suff 125 G7
Windwhistle Som 28 F5
Windy Arbor Mers 183 D7
Windy Arbour Warks 118 C5
Windydoors Borders 261 B10
Windygates Fife 287 G7
Windyharbour Ches E 184 G4
Windy Hill Wrex 166 E4
Windyknowe W Loth 269 B9
Windy Nook T&W 243 E7
Windywalls Borders 263 C7
Windy-Yett E Ayrs 267 E9
Wineham W Sus 36 C2
Winestead E Yorks 201 C9
Winewall Lancs 204 E4
Winfarthing Norf 142 F2
Winford IoW 21 E7
N Som 60 F4
Winforton Hereford 96 B5
Winfrith Newburgh
Dorset 18 E2
Wing Bucks 103 G7
Rutland 137 C7
Wingate Durham 234 D4
Wingates Gtr Man 195 F7
Northumb 252 D4
Wingerworth Derbys 170 B5
Wingfield C Beds 103 F10
Suff 126 B4
S Yorks 186 B6
Wilts 45 B10
Wingfield Green Suff 126 B4
Wingfield Park Derbys 170 E5
Wingham Kent 55 B8
Wingham Green Kent 55 B8
Wingham Well Kent 55 B8
Wingmore Kent 55 D7
Wingrave Bucks 84 B5
Winkburn Notts 172 D2
Winkfield Brack 66 E2
Winkfield Place Brack 66 E2
Winkfield Row Brack 65 E11
Winkhill Staffs 169 E9
Winkhurst Green Kent 52 D3
Winkleigh Devon 25 F10
Winksley N Yorks 214 E5
Winkton BCP 19 B9
Winlaton T&W 242 E5
Winlaton Mill T&W 242 E5
Winless Highld 310 D7
Winllan Powys 148 E4
Winmarleigh Lancs 202 D5
Winmarleigh Moss
Lancs 202 D4
Winnal Hereford 97 E9
Winnal Common Hereford 97 E9
Winnall Hants 33 B7
Worcs 116 D6
Winnard's Perch Corn 5 B8
Winnersh Wokingham 65 E9
Winnington Ches W 183 G10
Staffs 150 B4
Winnington Green
Shrops 148 G6
Winnothdale Staffs 151 B10
Winscales Cumb 228 F6
Winscombe N Som 44 B2
Winsdon Hill Luton 103 G11
Winsford Ches W 167 B10
Som 42 G2
Winsham Devon 40 F3
Som 28 F5
Winshill Staffs 152 E5
Winsh-wen Swansea 57 B7
Winsick Derbys 170 B6
Winskill Cumb 231 D7
Winslade Devon 24 D5
Hants 49 D7
Winsley N Yorks 214 G4
Wilts 61 G10
Winslow Bucks 102 F5
Winslow Mill Hereford 98 D2
Winson Glos 81 D9
Winson Green W Mid 133 F10
Winsor Hants 32 E4
Winstanley Gtr Man 194 G5
Winstanleys Gtr Man 194 F5
Winster Cumb 221 G8
Derbys 170 C2
Winston Durham 224 B2
Suff 126 E3
Winstone Glos 81 D7
Winston Green Suff 126 E3
Winswell Devon 25 E7
Winterborne Bassett
Wilts 62 E6
Winterborne Came
Dorset 17 D10

Winterborne Clenston
Dorset 30 G4
Winterborne Herringston
Dorset 17 D9
Winterborne Houghton
Dorset 30 G4
Winterborne Kingston
Dorset 18 B3
Winterborne Monkton
Wilts 62 E6
Winterborne Muston
Dorset 18 B3
Winterborne Stickland
Dorset 30 G4
Winterborne Tomson
Dorset 18 B3
Winterborne Whitechurch
Dorset 30 G4
Winterborne Zelston
Dorset 18 B3
Winterbourne Kent 54 B5
S Glos 60 C6
W Berks 64 E3
Winterbourne Abbas
Dorset 17 C8
Winterbourne Bassett
Wilts 62 E6
Winterbourne Dauntsey
Wilts 47 G7
Winterbourne Down
S Glos 61 D7
Winterbourne Earls Wilts 47 G7
Winterbourne Gunner
Wilts 47 F7
Winterbourne Monkton
Dorset 17 D9
Winterbourne Steepleton
Dorset 17 D8
Winterbourne Stoke
Wilts 46 E5
Winterbrook Oxon 64 B6
Winterburn N Yorks 204 B4
Winterfield Bath 45 B7
Winter Gardens Essex 69 C9
Winterhay Green Som 28 D5
Winterhead N Som 44 B2
Winteringham N Lincs 200 C2
Winterley Ches E 168 D2
Wintersett W Yorks 197 D11
Wintershill Hants 33 D8
Winterton N Lincs 200 D2
Winterton-on-Sea Norf 161 F9
Winter Well Som 28 C3
Winthorpe Lincs 175 B9
Notts 172 D4
Winton BCP 19 C7
Cumb 222 C5
E Sus 23 E8
Gtr Man 184 B3
N Yorks 225 F8
Wintringham N Yorks 217 E7
Winwick Cambs 138 G2
Warr 183 C10
W Nhants 120 C2
Winwick Quay Warr 183 C10
Winyard's Gap Dorset 29 F7
Winyates Worcs 117 D11
Winyates Green Worcs 117 D11
Wirksworth Derbys 170 E3
Wirksworth Moor
Derbys 170 E4
Wirswall Ches E 167 G8
Wisbech Cambs 139 B9
Wisbech St Mary Cambs 139 B8
Wisborough Green
W Sus 35 B8
Wiseton Notts 188 D2
Wishanger Glos 80 D6
Wishaw N Lanark 268 D5
Warks 134 E3
Wisley Sur 50 B5
Wispington Lincs 190 G2
Wissenden Kent 54 E2
Wissett Suff 127 B7
Wistanstow Shrops 131 F8
Wistanswick Shrops 150 D3
Wistaston Ches E 167 E11
Wistaston Green
Ches E 167 E11
Wiston Pembs 73 B8
S Lanark 259 C11
W Sus 35 E10
Wiston Mains S Lanark 259 C11
Wistow Cambs 138 G5
Leics 136 D2
N Yorks 207 F7
Wiswell Lancs 203 F10
Witcham Cambs 139 G9
Witchampton Dorset 31 F7
Witchford Cambs 123 B10
Witcombe Som 29 C7
Withacott Devon 24 D6
Witham Essex 88 C4
Witham Friary Som 45 E8
Witham on the Hill
Lincs 155 F11
Witham St Hughs Lincs 172 C5
Withcall Lincs 190 E3
Withdean Brighton 36 F4
Witherenden Hill E Sus 37 B10
Withergate Norf 160 D5
Witheridge Devon 26 E4
Witheridge Hill Oxon 65 C7
Witherley Leics 134 D6
Withermarsh Green
Suff 107 D10
Withern Lincs 190 E6
Withernsea E Yorks 201 B10
Withernwick E Yorks 209 E9
Withersdale Street Suff 142 G5
Withersdane Kent 54 D5
Withersfield Suff 106 B3
Witherslack Cumb 211 C8
Witherwack T&W 243 F9
Withial Som 44 F5
Withiel Corn 5 B9
Withiel Florey Som 42 G3
Withielgoose Corn 5 B10
Withielgoose Mills Corn 5 B10
Withington Glos 81 B8
Gtr Man 184 C5
Hereford 97 C11
Shrops 149 G11
Staffs 151 B10
Withington Green
Ches E 184 G4
Withington Marsh
Hereford 97 C11
Withleigh Devon 26 E6
Withnell Lancs 194 C6
Withnell Fold Lancs 194 C6
Withybed Green Worcs 117 C10
Withybrook Som 45 D7
Warks 135 G8
Withybush Pembs 73 B7
Withycombe Som 41 F11
Som 42 E4
Withycombe Raleigh
Devon 14 E6
Withyditch Bath 45 B8
Withyham E Sus 52 F3
Withy Mills Bath 45 B7
Withymoor Village
W Mid 133 F8
Withypool Som 41 F10
Withystakes Staffs 169 F7
Withywood Bristol 60 F5
Witley Sur 50 F2
Witnells End Worcs 132 G5
Witnesham Suff 126 G3
Witney Oxon 82 C5
Wittensford Hants 32 E3
Wittering Pboro 137 C11
Wittersham Kent 38 B5
Witton Angus 293 F7
Norf 142 B6
W Mid 133 E11
Worcs 117 E7
Witton Bridge Norf 160 C6
Witton Gilbert Durham 233 B10
Witton Hill Worcs 116 E5
Witton-le-Wear Durham 233 E8
Witton Park Durham 233 E9
Wiveliscombe Som 27 B9
Wivelrod Hants 49 F7
Wivelsfield E Sus 36 C4
Wivelsfield Green E Sus 36 C5
Wivenhoe Essex 107 G10
Wivenhoe Cross Essex 107 G10
Wiveton Norf 177 E8
Wix Essex 108 F3
Wixams Bedford 103 C10
Wixford Warks 117 G11
Wixhill Shrops 149 D11
Wixoe Suff 106 C4
Woburn C Beds 103 E8
Woburn Sands
M Keynes 103 D8
Wofferwood Common
Hereford 116 G3
Wokefield Park W Berks 65 F7
Woking Sur 50 B4
Wokingham Wokingham 65 F10
Wolborough Devon 14 G3
Woldhurst W Sus 22 C5
Woldingham Sur 51 B11
Woldingham Garden Village
Sur 51 B11
Wold Newton E Yorks 217 E10
NE Lincs 190 B2
Wolfclyde S Lanark 260 B2
Wolferd Green Norf 142 D5
Wolferlow Hereford 116 E3
Wolferton Norf 158 D3
Wolfhampcote Warks 119 D10
Wolfhill Perth 286 D5
Wolf's Castle Pembs 91 F9
Wolfsdale Pembs 91 G8
Wolfsdale Hill Pembs 91 G8
Woll Borders 261 E11
Wollaston N Nhants 121 E8
Shrops 148 G6
W Mid 133 G7
Wollaton Nottingham 153 B10
Wollerton Shrops 150 C2
Wollerton Wood Shrops 150 C2
Wollescote W Mid 133 G8
Wollrig Borders 261 E11
Wolsingham Durham 233 D7
Wolstanton Staffs 168 F5
Wolstenholme
Gtr Man 195 D11
Wolston Warks 119 B8
Wolsty Cumb 238 G4
Wolterton Norf 160 C3
Wolvercote Oxon 83 D7
Wolverham Ches W 182 F6
Wolverhampton W Mid 133 D8
Wolverley Shrops 149 C9
Worcs 116 B6
Wolverstone Devon 27 G10
Wolverton Hants 48 B5
Kent 55 E9
M Keynes 102 C6
Shrops 131 F9
Warks 118 E4
Wilts 45 G9
Wolverton Common
Hants 48 B5
Wolvesnewton Mon 79 F7
Wolvey Warks 135 F8
Wolvey Heath Warks 135 F8
Wolviston Stockton 234 F5
Womaston Powys 114 E5
Wombleton N Yorks 216 C3
Wombourne Staffs 133 E7
Wombridge Telford 150 G3
Wombwell S Yorks 197 G11
Womenswold Kent 55 C8
Womersley N Yorks 198 D4
Wonastow Mon 79 C7
Wonderstone N Som 43 B10
Wonersh Sur 50 D4
Wonford Devon 14 C4
Wonson Devon 13 D9
Wonston Dorset 30 F2
Hants 48 F3
Wooburn Bucks 66 B2
Wooburn Green Bucks 66 B2
Wood Pembs 91 G7
Som 28 D4
Woodacott Devon 24 F5
Woodacott Cross Devon 24 F5
Woodale N Yorks 213 D10
Woodbank Argyll 255 F7
Ches W 182 G5
Shrops 131 F11
Woodbastwick Norf 160 F6
Woodbeck Notts 188 F3
Wood Bevington
Warks 117 G11
Woodborough Notts 171 F10
Wilts 46 B6
Woodbridge Dorset 30 D5
Dorset 30 E2
Glos 81 C8
Northumb 253 F7
Suff 108 B5
Woodbridge Hill Sur 50 C3
Woodbridge Walk Suff 109 B7
Wood Burcote
W Nhants 102 B3
Woodburn Common
Bucks 66 B2
Woodburn Moor Bucks 84 G6
Woodbury Devon 14 D6
Woodbury Salterton
Devon 14 D6
Woodchester Glos 80 E4
Woodchurch Kent 54 G2
Mers 182 D3
Woodcock Wilts 45 E11
Woodcock Heath
Staffs 151 D11
Woodcock Hill Herts 85 G9
W Mid 133 G10
Woodcombe Som 42 D3
Woodcot Hants 33 G9
Woodcote London 67 G10
Oxon 64 C6
Sur 51 B8
Telford 150 F5
Woodcote Green London 67 G9
Worcs 117 C8
Woodcott Hants 48 C2
Woodcroft Glos 79 F8
Woodcutts Dorset 31 D7
Wood Dalling Norf 159 D11
Woodditton Cambs 124 F3
Woodeaton Oxon 83 C8
Wood Eaton Staffs 150 F6
Wooden Pembs 73 D10
Woodend Ches E 185 D7
Cumb 219 C10
Cumb 220 F3
Cumb 229 F10
Cumb 229 G7
Essex 87 C9
Fife 280 B4
Notts 171 C7
Staffs 152 D3
W Loth 279 F11
W Nhants 102 B2
W Sus 22 B4
Wood End Bedford 103 B10
Bedford 121 D11
Bedford 121 F11
Bucks 102 E5
C Beds 103 C9
Gtr Man 196 F2
Hereford 98 C2
Herts 104 F6
Warks 118 C2
Warks 134 D4
Warks 134 F5
Windsor 66 E2
W Mid 133 C8
W Mid 135 G7
Wood Enderby Lincs 174 C3
Woodend Green Essex 105 F11
W Nhants 102 B2
Wood End Green London 66 C5
Woodend Ho Argyll 275 G11
Woodfalls Wilts 31 C11
Woodfield Glos 80 F2
Oxon 101 G11
S Ayrs 257 E8
Wood Field Sur 51 B7
Woodford Corn 24 E2
Devon 8 E5
Glos 79 F11
Gtr Man 184 E5
London 86 G6
N Nhants 121 B9
Plym 7 D10
Som 42 F5
Som 44 E4
Woodford Bridge London 86 G6
Woodford Green London 86 G6
Woodford Halse
W Nhants 119 G10
Woodford Wells London 86 G6
Woodgate Devon 27 D10
Norf 159 F10
W Mid 133 G9
Worcs 117 D9
W Sus 22 C6
Wood Gate Staffs 152 D3
Woodgate Hill Gtr Man 195 E10
Woodgates End Essex 105 F11
Woodgates Green
Worcs 116 C2
Woodgate Valley
W Mid 133 G10
Woodgreen Hants 31 D11
Oxon 82 C5
Wood Green Essex 86 E6
London 86 G4
Norf 142 E4
W Mid 133 D9
Worcs 116 D6
Woodhall Herts 86 C2
Invclyd 276 G6
N Yorks 207 G9
N Yorks 223 G9
Wood Hall Essex 105 E9
Woodhall Hills
W Yorks 205 F10
Woodhall Spa Lincs 173 C11
Woodham Bucks 84 B2
Durham 233 F11
Sur 66 G4
Woodham Ferrers Essex 88 F3
Woodham Mortimer
Essex 88 E4
Woodham Walter Essex 88 D4
Woodhatch Sur 51 D9
Woodhaven Fife 287 E8
Wood Hayes W Mid 133 C8
Woodhead Aberds 303 F7
Woodheads Borders 271 F10
Woodhey Gtr Man 195 D9
Mers 182 D4
Woodhey Green Ches E 167 E9
Woodhill Essex 88 E3
N Som 60 D3
Shrops 132 G4
Som 28 B5
Woodhorn Northumb 253 F7
Woodhouse Cumb 211 C10
Cumb 219 B9
Hants 47 D11
Leics 153 F10
N Lincs 199 F9
S Yorks 186 D6
W Yorks 196 C6
W Yorks 197 C11
W Yorks 205 E7
W Yorks 205 F11
Wood House Lancs 203 C10
Woodhouse Down S Glos 60 B6
Woodhouse Eaves
Leics 153 G10
Woodhouse Green
Staffs 168 C6
Woodhouselee Midloth 270 C4
Woodhouselees
Dumfries 239 C9
Woodhouse Mill
S Yorks 186 D6
Woodhouse Park
Gtr Man 184 D4
Woodhouses Ches W 183 F8
Cumb 239 G8
Gtr Man 184 C3
Gtr Man 196 G2
Staffs 133 B11
Staffs 152 F3
Woodhurst Cambs 122 B6
Woodingdean Brighton 36 F5
Woodington Hants 32 C4
Woodkirk W Yorks 197 C9
Woodlake Dorset 18 C3
Woodland Cumb 210 B4
Devon 8 B5
Devon 8 D2
Durham 233 F7
Kent 54 E6
Woodland Head Devon 13 B11
Woodlands Aberdeen 293 B10
Aberds 293 D9
Aberds 303 G8
Dorset 31 F9
Dumfries 238 B3
Gtr Man 185 B7
Hants 32 E4
Highld 300 C5
Kent 68 G5
London 67 D7
N Yorks 206 C2
Som 43 E7
Som 44 F4
S Yorks 198 F4
Wokingham 65 C9
W Yorks 196 B5
Woodlands Common
Dorset 31 F9
Woodlands Park
Windsor 65 D11
Woodlands St Mary
W Berks 63 E10
Woodlane Shrops 150 D3
Staffs 152 E2
Wood Lane Shrops 149 C8
Staffs 168 E4
Wood Lanes Ches E 184 E6
Woodleigh Devon 8 F4
Woodlesford W Yorks 197 B11
Woodley Gtr Man 184 C6
Hants 32 C5
Wokingham 65 E9
Woodley Green
Wokingham 65 E9
Woodleys Oxon 82 B6
Woodlinkin Derbys 170 F6
Woodloes Park Warks 118 D5
Woodmancote Glos 80 F3
Glos 81 D8
Glos 99 F8
Worcs 99 C8
W Sus 22 B3
W Sus 36 E2
Woodmancott Hants 48 E5
Woodmansey E Yorks 209 F7
Woodmansgreen W Sus 34 B5
Woodmans Green E Sus 38 D3
Woodmansterne Sur 51 B9
Woodmill Staffs 152 E2
Woodminton Wilts 31 C8
Woodnesborough Kent 55 B10
Woodnewton N Nhants 137 E10
Woodnook Lancs 195 B9
Lincs 155 C8
Wood Norton Norf 159 D10
Worcs 99 B10
Woodplumpton Lancs 202 G6
Woodram Som 28 D2
Woodrising Norf 141 C9
Wood Road Gtr Man 195 E9
Woodrow Bucks 84 F6
Cumb 229 B10
Dorset 30 E3
Dorset 30 F2
Worcs 117 B7
Worcs 117 D11
Wood Row W Yorks 197 B11
Woods Hereford 96 B5
Woods Bank W Mid 133 D9
Wood's Corner E Sus 23 B11
Woodsden Kent 53 G9
Woodseats Derbys 185 C7
Wood Seats S Yorks 186 B4
Woodseaves Shrops 150 C3
Staffs 150 D5
Woodsend Pembs 72 C5
Wilts 63 D8
Woods End Gtr Man 184 B2
Woodsetton W Mid 133 E8
Woodsetts S Yorks 187 E9
Woodsfield Worcs 98 B6
Woodsfold Lancs 202 F5
Woodsford Dorset 17 C11
Wood's Green E Sus 52 G6
Woodside Aberdeen 293 C11
Aberds 303 E10
Bedford 121 G11
Brack 66 E2
C Beds 85 B9
Ches E 167 C10
Ches W 183 G8
Derbys 170 G5
Derbys 187 G7
Dumfries 238 B2
Durham 233 F9
Essex 87 E7
Fife 287 G8
Hants 20 C2
Hereford 98 E4
Herts 85 E10
Herts 86 D3
IoW 20 C6
London 67 F10
N Lincs 199 G8
Perth 286 D6
Shrops 130 G6
Telford 132 C3
W Mid 133 F8
W Yorks 196 B6
Woodside Green Essex 87 B8
Kent 54 C2
Woodside of Arbeadie
Aberds 293 D9
Woodside Park London 86 G3
Woods Moor Gtr Man 184 D6
Woodspeen W Berks 64 F2
Woodspring Priory
N Som 59 F10
Wood Stanway Glos 99 E11
Woodstock Kent 70 G2
Oxon 82 B6
Pembs 91 F10
Woodston Pboro 138 D3
Wood Street Norf 161 E7
Sur 50 C3
Wood Street Village Sur 50 C3
Woodthorpe Derbys 187 G7
Leics 153 F10
Lincs 190 E6
Notts 171 G9
York 207 D7
Woodton Norf 142 E5
Woodtown Devon 24 C6
Devon 25 B7
Woodvale Mers 193 E10
Woodville Derbys 152 F6
Dorset 30 C4
Woodville Feus Angus 287 C10
Woodwall Green Staffs 150 C5
Wood Walton Cambs 138 G4
Woodway Oxon 64 C4
Woodway Park W Mid 135 G7
Woodwell N Nhants 121 B9
Woodwick Orkney 314 D3
Woodworth Green
Ches E 167 D9
Woodyates Dorset 31 D8
Woody Bay Devon 41 D7
Woofferton Shrops 115 D10
Wookey Som 44 D4
Wookey Hole Som 44 D4
Wool Dorset 18 D2
Woolacombe Devon 40 E3
Woolage Green Kent 55 D8
Woolage Village Kent 55 C8
Woolaston Glos 79 F9
Woolaston Common Glos 79 E9
Woolaston Slade Glos 79 E9
Woolaston Woodside
Glos 79 E9
Woolavington Som 43 E10
Woolbeding W Sus 34 C5
Wooldale W Yorks 197 F7
Wooler Northumb 263 D11
Woolfall Heath Mers 182 C6
Woolfardisworthy Devon 26 F4
Woolfardisworthy or
Woolsery Devon 24 C4
Woolfold Gtr Man 195 E9
Woolfords Cottages
S Lanark 269 D10
Woolford's Water Dorset 29 F11
Woolgarston Dorset 18 E5
Woolgreaves W Yorks 197 D10
Woolhampton W Berks 64 F5
Woolhope Hereford 98 D2
Woolhope Cockshoot
Hereford 98 D2
Woolland Dorset 30 F3
Woollard Bath 60 G6
Woollaston Staffs 151 F7
Woollaton Devon 25 E7
Woollensbrook Herts 86 C5
Woolley Bath 61 F8
Cambs 122 C3
Corn 24 D3
Derbys 170 C5
Wilts 61 G10
W Yorks 197 E10
Woolley Bridge Gtr Man 185 B8
Woolley Green Wilts 61 G10
Windsor 65 C11
Woolmere Green Worcs 117 E9
Woolmer Green Herts 86 B3
Woolmer Hill Sur 49 G11
Woolmersdon Som 43 G9
Woolminstone Som 28 F6
Woolpack Corner Kent 53 F11
Woolpit Suff 125 E9
Woolpit Green Suff 125 E9
Woolpit Heath Suff 125 E9
Woolridge Glos 98 G6
Woolsbridge Dorset 31 F9
Woolscott Warks 119 D9
Woolsery or
Woolfardisworthy
Devon 24 C4
Woolsgrove Devon 26 G3
Woolsington T&W 242 D5
Woolstanwood Ches E 167 D11
Woolstaston Shrops 131 D9
Woolsthorpe Lincs 155 E8
Woolsthorpe by Belvoir
Lincs 154 C6
Woolsthorpe-by-
Colsterworth Lincs 155 E8
Woolston Corn 6 B5
Devon 8 G4
Shrops 131 F8
Shrops 148 E6
Som 29 B9
Som 42 F5
Soton 32 E6
Warr 183 D10
Woolstone Glos 99 E9
M Keynes 103 D7
Oxon 63 B9
Woolston Green Devon 8 B5
Woolton Mers 182 D6
Woolton Hill Hants 64 G2
Woolvers Hill N Som 59 G11
Woolverstone Suff 108 D3
Woolverton Som 45 C9
Woolwell Devon 7 C10
Woolwich London 68 D2
Woolwich Ferry London 68 D2
Woon Corn 5 D10
Woonton Hereford 115 E10
Hereford 115 G7
Wooperton Northumb 264 E2
Wooplaw Borders 271 G9
Woore Shrops 168 G2
Wooton Shrops 115 C11
Shrops 132 F5
Wootten Green Suff 126 C4
Wootton Bedford 103 B10
Hants 19 B10
Hereford 97 D11
Hereford 114 G6
IoW 20 C6
Kent 55 D8
N Lincs 200 D5
Oxon 82 B6
Oxon 83 E7
Shrops 115 B9
Shrops 148 D6
Staffs 150 D6
Staffs 169 F10
W Nhants 120 F5
Wootton Bourne End
Bedford 103 B9
Wootton Bridge IoW 20 C6
Wootton Broadmead
Bedford 103 C10
Wootton Common IoW 20 C6
Wootton Courtenay Som 42 E2
Wootton Fitzpaine Dorset 16 B3
Wootton Green C Beds 103 C9
W Mid 118 B4
Wootton Rivers Wilts 63 G7
Woottons Staffs 151 B11
Wootton St Lawrence
Hants 48 C5
Wootton Wawen Warks 118 E3
Worbarrow Dorset 18 F3
Worcester Worcs 117 F7
Worcester Park London 67 F8
Wordsley W Mid 133 F7
Wordwell Suff 124 C6
Worfield Shrops 132 D5
Worgret Dorset 18 D4
Work Orkney 314 E4
Workhouse Common
Norf 161 E7
Workhouse End Bedford 122 G2
Workhouse Green Suff 107 D8
Workhouse Hill Essex 107 E9
Workington Cumb 228 F5
Worksop Notts 187 F9
Worlaby Lincs 190 F4
N Lincs 200 E4
Worlds End Hants 33 E10
W Mid 134 G2
World's End Bucks 84 D5
London 86 F4
Suff 125 F9
W Berks 64 D3
W Sus 36 D4
Worle N Som 59 G11
Worlebury N Som 59 G10
Worleston Ches E 167 D11
Worley Glos 80 F4
Worlingham Suff 143 F8
Worlington Devon 40 G3
Suff 124 C3
Worlingworth Suff 126 D4
Wormadale Shetland 313 J5
Wormald Green
N Yorks 214 G6
Wormbridge Hereford 97 E8
Wormbridge Common
Hereford 97 E8
Wormegay Norf 158 G3
Wormelow Tump
Hereford 97 E9
Wormhill Derbys 185 G10
Wormingford Essex 107 E8
Worminghall Bucks 83 D10
Wormington Glos 99 D10
Worminster Som 44 E5
Wormiston Ho Fife 287 G10
Wormit Fife 287 E7
Wormleighton Warks 119 G8
Wormley Herts 86 D5
Sur 50 F2
Wormleybury Herts 86 D5
Wormley West End Herts 86 D4
Worms Ash Worcs 117 C8
Wormshill Kent 53 B11
Worms Hill Kent 53 F8
Wormsley Hereford 97 B8
Wornish Nook Ches E 168 B4
Worplesdon Sur 50 C3
Worrall S Yorks 186 C4
Worrall Hill Glos 79 C10
Worsbrough S Yorks 197 G11
Worsbrough Bridge
S Yorks 197 G11
Worsbrough Common
S Yorks 197 F10
Worsbrough Dale
S Yorks 197 G11
Worsham Oxon 82 C3
Worsley Gtr Man 195 G8
Worsley Hall Gtr Man 194 F5
Worsley Mesnes
Gtr Man 194 G5
Worstead Norf 160 D6
Worsthorne Lancs 204 G3
Worston Devon 7 E11
Lancs 203 E11
Worswell Devon 7 F10
Worten Kent 54 E3
Worth Kent 55 B10
Som 44 D4
W Sus 51 F9
Worth Abbey W Sus 51 G10
Wortham Suff 125 B11
Worthen Shrops 130 C6
Worthenbury Wrex 166 F6
Worthing Norf 159 F9
W Sus 35 G10
Worthington Leics 153 E8
Worth Matravers Dorset 18 F5
Worthy Som 41 D11
Worthybrook Mon 79 C7
Worting Hants 48 C6
Wortley Glos 80 G3
S Yorks 186 B4
W Yorks 205 G11
Worton N Yorks 223 G9
Oxon 83 C7
Wilts 46 B3
Wortwell Norf 142 G5
Wotherton Shrops 130 C5
Wothorpe Pboro 137 B10
Wotter Devon 7 C11
Wotton Glos 80 B4
Sur 50 D6
Wotton-under-Edge
Glos 80 G3
Wotton Underwood
Bucks 83 B11
Woughton on the Green
M Keynes 103 D7
Woughton Park
M Keynes 103 D7
Wouldham Kent 69 G8
Woundale Shrops 132 E5
Wrabness Essex 108 E3
Wraes Aberds 302 F5
Wrafton Devon 40 F3
Wragby Lincs 189 F10
W Yorks 198 D2
Wragholme Lincs 190 B5
Wramplingham Norf 142 B2
Wrangaton Devon 8 D3
Wrangbrook W Yorks 198 E3
Wrangham Aberds 302 F6
Wrangle Lincs 174 E6
Wrangle Bank Lincs 174 E6
Wrangle Lowgate Lincs 174 E6
Wrangle Low Ground
Lincs 174 E6
Wrangway Som 27 D10
Wrantage Som 28 C4
Wrawby N Lincs 200 F4
Wraxall Dorset 29 G9
N Som 60 E3
Som 44 F6
Wray Lancs 212 F2
Wray Common Sur 51 C9
Wraysbury Windsor 66 E4
Wrayton Lancs 212 E2
Wrea Green Lancs 202 G3
Wreaks End Cumb 210 B4
Wreath Som 28 F4
Wreay Cumb 230 B4
Cumb 230 G4
Wrecclesham Sur 49 D10
Wrekenton T&W 243 F7
Wrelton N Yorks 216 B5
Wrenbury Ches E 167 F9
Wrenbury cum Frith
Ches E 167 F9
Wrench Green N Yorks 217 B9
Wreningham Norf 142 D3
Wrentham Suff 143 G9
Wrenthorpe W Yorks 197 C10
Wrentnall Shrops 131 C8
Wressle E Yorks 207 G10
N Lincs 200 F3
Wrestlingworth C Beds 104 B5
Wretham Norf 141 F8
Wretton Norf 140 D3
Wrexham Wrex 166 E4
Wreyland Devon 13 E11
Wribbenhall Worcs 116 B5
Wrickton Shrops 132 F2
Wrightington Bar Lancs 194 E4
Wrights Green Warr 183 E10
Wright's Green Essex 87 B8
Wrinehill Staffs 168 F3
Wringsdown Corn 12 D2
Wrington N Som 60 G3
Wrinkleberry Devon 24 C4
Writhlington Bath 45 C8
Writtle Essex 87 D11
Wrockwardine Telford 150 G2
Wrockwardine Wood
Telford 150 G4
Wroot N Lincs 199 G8
Wrose W Yorks 205 F9
Wrotham Kent 52 B6
Wrotham Heath Kent 52 B6
Wroughton Swindon 62 C6
Wroxall IoW 21 F7
Warks 118 C4
Wroxeter Shrops 131 B11
Wroxhall Warks 118 C4
Wroxham Norf 160 F6
Wroxton Oxon 101 C8
Wyaston Derbys 169 G11
Wyatt's Green Essex 87 F9
Wybers Wood NE Lincs 201 F8
Wyberton Lincs 174 G4
Wyboston Bedford 122 F3
Wybunbury Ches E 168 F2
Wychbold Worcs 117 D8
Wych Cross E Sus 52 G2
Wychnor Staffs 152 F3
Wychnor Bridges Staffs 152 F3
Wyck Hants 49 F9
Wyck Rissington Glos 100 G3
Wycliffe Durham 224 C2
Wycoller Lancs 204 F4
Wycomb Leics 154 E5
Wycombe Marsh Bucks 84 G5
Wyddial Herts 105 E7
Wydra N Yorks 205 C10
Wye Kent 54 D5
Wyebanks Kent 54 C2
Wyegate Green Glos 79 D9
Wyesham Mon 79 C8
Wyfordby Leics 154 F5
Wyke Dorset 30 B3
Shrops 132 C2
Sur 50 C2
W Yorks 197 B7
Wyke Champflower Som 45 G7
Wykeham Lincs 156 D5
N Yorks 216 D6
N Yorks 217 C9
Wyken Shrops 132 E5
W Mid 135 G7
Wyke Regis Dorset 17 F9
Wykey Shrops 149 E7
Wykin Leics 135 D8
Wylam Northumb 242 E4
Wylde Hereford 115 D9
Wylde Green W Mid 134 E2
Wyllie Caerph 77 G11
Wylye Wilts 46 F4
Wymans Brook Glos 99 G8
Wymbush M Keynes 102 D6
Wymering Ptsmth 33 F10
Wymeswold Leics 154 E2
Wymington Bedford 121 E9
Wymondham Leics 155 F7
Norf 142 C2
Wymondley Bury Herts 104 F4
Wymott Lancs 194 C4
Wyndham Bridgend 76 G6
Wyndham Park V Glam 58 D5
Wynds Point Hereford 98 C5
Wynford Eagle Dorset 17 B7
Wyng Orkney 314 G3
Wynn's Green Hereford 98 B2
Wynyard Village
Stockton 234 F4
Wyre Piddle Worcs 99 B9
Wysall Notts 154 D2
Wyson Hereford 115 D10
Wythall Worcs 117 B11
Wytham Oxon 83 D7
Wythburn Cumb 220 C6
Wythenshawe Gtr Man 184 D4
Wythop Mill Cumb 229 F9
Wyton Cambs 122 C5
E Yorks 209 G9
Wyverstone Suff 125 D10
Wyverstone Green
Suff 125 D10
Wyverstone Street
Suff 125 D10
Wyville Lincs 155 D7
Wyvis Lodge Highld 300 B4

Y

Yaddlethorpe N Lincs 199 F11
Yafford IoW 20 E4
Yafforth N Yorks 224 G6
Yair Borders 261 C11
Yalberton Torbay 9 D7
Yalding Kent 53 C7
Yanley N Som 60 F5
Yanworth Glos 81 C9
Yapham E Yorks 207 C11
Yapton W Sus 35 G7
Yarberry N Som 43 B11
Yarborough NE Lincs 201 F9
Yarbridge IoW 21 D8
Yarburgh Lincs 190 C5
Yarcombe Devon 28 F2
Yard Som 42 F5
Yarde Som 42 F5
Yardhurst Kent 54 E3
Yardley W Mid 134 F2
Yardley Gobion
W Nhants 102 C5
Yardley Hastings
W Nhants 121 F7
Yardley Wood W Mid 118 B2
Yardro Powys 114 F4
Yarford Som 28 B2
Yarhampton Worcs 116 D5
Yarhampton Cross
Worcs 116 D5
Yarkhill Hereford 98 C2
Yarlet Staffs 151 D8
Yarley Som 44 D4
Yarlington Som 29 B11
Yarlside Cumb 210 F4
Yarm Stockton 225 C8
Yarmouth IoW 20 D3
Yarnacott Devon 40 G6
Yarnbrook Wilts 45 C11
Yarnfield Staffs 151 C7
Yarningale Common
Warks 118 D3
Yarnscombe Devon 25 C9
Yarnton Oxon 83 C7
Yarpole Hereford 115 E9
Yarrow Borders 261 D9
Northumb 250 F6
Som 43 D11
Yarrow Feus Borders 261 D8
Yarrowford Borders 261 C10
Yarsop Hereford 97 B8
Yarwell N Nhants 137 D11
Yate S Glos 61 C8
Yateley Hants 65 G10
Yate Rocks S Glos 61 C8
Yatesbury Wilts 62 E5
Yattendon W Berks 64 E5
Yatton Hereford 115 D8
N Som 60 F2
Yatton Keynell Wilts 61 D11
Yaverland IoW 21 D8
Yawthorpe Lincs 188 C5
Yaxham Norf 159 G10
Yaxley Cambs 138 E3
Suff 126 C2
Yazor Hereford 97 B8
Y Bala = Bala Gwyn 147 B8
Y Bont Faen = Cowbridge
V Glam 58 E3
Y Borth = Borth Ceredig 128 E2
Yeabridge Som 28 D6
Yeading London 66 C6
Yeadon W Yorks 205 E10
Yealand Conyers Lancs 211 E10
Yealand Redmayne
Lancs 211 D10
Yealand Storrs Lancs 211 D9
Yealmbridge Devon 7 E11
Yealmpton Devon 7 E11
Yearby Redcar 235 G8
Yearngill Cumb 229 C8
Yearsley N Yorks 215 E11
Yeaton Shrops 149 F8
Yeaveley Derbys 169 G11
Yedingham N Yorks 217 D7
Yelden Bedford 121 D10
Yeldersley Hollies
Derbys 170 G2
Yeldon Bedford 121 D10
Yelford Oxon 82 E5
Yelland Devon 40 G3
Yelling Cambs 122 E5
Yelsted Kent 69 G10
Yelvertoft W Nhants 119 B11
Yelverton Devon 7 B10
Norf 142 C5
Yenston Som 30 C2
Yeoford Devon 13 B11
Yeolmbridge Corn 12 D2
Yeo Mill Devon 26 B4
Yeo Vale Devon 24 C6
Yeovil Som 29 D9
Yeovil Marsh Som 29 D8
Yeovilton Som 29 C8
Yerbeston Pembs 73 D9
Yesnaby Orkney 314 E2
Yetlington Northumb 252 B2
Yetminster Dorset 29 E9
Yett N Lanark 268 D5
Yettington Devon 15 D7
Yetts o' Muckhart Clack 286 G4
Yew Green Warks 118 D4
Yewhedges Kent 54 B3
Yew Tree Gtr Man 185 B7
W Mid 133 D10
Yewtree Cross Kent 55 E7
Y Fali = *Valley* Anglesey 178 F3
Y Felinheli = *Port Dinorwic*
Gwyn 163 B8
Y Ferwig Ceredig 92 B3
Y Ffôr Gwyn 145 B7
Y-Ffrith Denb 181 E8
Y Gors Ceredig 112 B2
Y Gribyn Powys 129 E8
Yieldshields S Lanark 269 E7
Yiewsley London 66 C5
Yinstay Orkney 314 E5
Y Mwmbwls = *The Mumbles*
Swansea 56 D6
Ynus-tawelog Swansea 75 D10
Ynys Gwyn 145 B11
Ynysboeth Rhondda 77 F9
Ynysddu Caerph 77 G11
Ynysforgan Swansea 57 B7
Ynysgyfflog Gwyn 146 G2
Ynyshir Rhondda 77 G8
Ynys-isaf Powys 76 C3
Ynyslas Ceredig 128 E2
Ynysmaerdy Neath 57 B8
Rhondda 58 C4
Ynysmeudwy Neath 76 D2
Neath 76 D2
Ynys Tachwedd Ceredig 128 E2
Ynystawe Swansea 75 E11
Ynyswen Powys 76 C4
Rhondda 77 F7
Ynysybwl Rhondda 77 G9
Ynysygwas Neath 57 C9
Yockenthwaite N Yorks 213 D8
Yockleton Shrops 149 G7
Yodercott Devon 27 E9
Yokefleet E Yorks 199 C10
Yoker W Dunb 267 B10
Yonder Bognie Aberds 302 E5
Yondertown Devon 7 D11
Yopps Green Kent 52 C6
York Lancs 203 G10
York 207 C7
Yorkletts Kent 70 G5
Yorkley Glos 79 D10
Yorkley Slade Glos 79 D10
York Town Sur 65 G11
Yorton Shrops 149 E10
Yorton Heath Shrops 149 E10
Yottenfews Cumb 219 D10
Youlgrave Derbys 170 C2
Youlstone Devon 24 D3
Youlthorpe E Yorks 207 B11
Youlton N Yorks 215 G9
Youngsbury Herts 86 B5
Young's End Essex 88 B2
Young Wood Lincs 189 G10
Yoxall Staffs 152 F2
Yoxford Suff 127 D7
Y Pîl = *Pyle* Bridgend 57 E10
Yr Hôb = *Hope* Flint 166 D4
Ysbyty Cynfyn Ceredig 112 B5
Ysbyty Ifan Conwy 164 F4
Ysbyty Ystwyth Ceredig 112 C4
Ysceifiog Flint 181 G11
Ysgeibion Denb 165 D9
Yspitty Carms 56 B5
Ystalyfera Neath 76 D3
Ystrad Rhondda 77 F7
Ystrad Aeron Ceredig 111 F10
Ystradfellte Powys 76 C6
Ystradffin Carms 94 B5
Ystradgynlais Powys 76 C3
Ystradmeurig Ceredig 112 D4
Ystrad-mynach Caerph 77 G10
Ystradowen Carms 76 C2
V Glam 58 D4
Ystrad Uchaf Powys 129 C11
Ystumtuen Ceredig 112 B4
Ythanbank Aberds 303 F9
Ythanwells Aberds 302 F6
Ythsie Aberds 303 F8
Y Tymbl = *Tumble* Carms 75 C8
Y Waun = *Chirk* Wrex 148 B5

Z

Zeal Monachorum Devon 26 G2
Zeals Wilts 45 G9
Zelah Corn 4 E6
Zennor Corn 1 B5
Zoar Corn 3 F7
Zouch Notts 153 E10

County and unitary authority boundaries

Ordnance Survey National Grid

The blue lines which divide the Navigator map pages into squares for indexing match the Ordnance Survey National Grid and correspond to the small squares on the boundary map below. Each side of a grid square measures 10km on the ground.

The National Grid 100-km square letters and kilometre values are indicated for the grid intersection at the outer corners of each page. For example, the intersection SE6090 at the upper right corner of page 215 is 60km East and 90km North of the south-west corner of National Grid square SE.

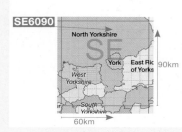

Using GPS with Navigator mapping

Since Navigator Britain is based on Ordnance Survey mapping, and rectified to the National Grid, it can be used with in-car or handheld GPS for locating identifiable waypoints such as road junctions, bridges, railways and farms, or assessing your position in relation to any of the features shown on the map.

On your receiver, choose British Grid as the location format and for map datum select Ordnance Survey (this may be described as Ord Srvy GB or similar, or more specifically as OSGB36). Your receiver will automatically convert the latitude/longitude co-ordinates transmitted by GPS into compatible National Grid data.

Positional accuracy of any particular feature is limited to 50–100m, due to the limitations of the original survey and the scale of Navigator mapping.

For further information see www.gps.gov.uk

Greater London

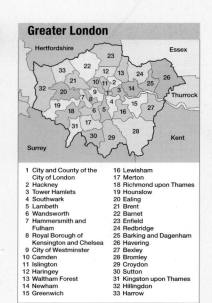

1 City and County of the City of London
2 Hackney
3 Tower Hamlets
4 Southwark
5 Lambeth
6 Wandsworth
7 Hammersmith and Fulham
8 Royal Borough of Kensington and Chelsea
9 City of Westminster
10 Camden
11 Islington
12 Haringey
13 Waltham Forest
14 Newham
15 Greenwich
16 Lewisham
17 Merton
18 Richmond upon Thames
19 Hounslow
20 Ealing
21 Brent
22 Barnet
23 Enfield
24 Redbridge
25 Barking and Dagenham
26 Havering
27 Bexley
28 Bromley
29 Croydon
30 Sutton
31 Kingston upon Thames
32 Hillingdon
33 Harrow

1 Central Scotland

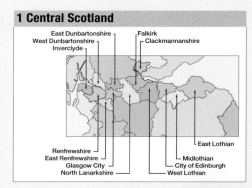

2 Northern England

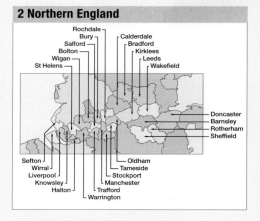

3 West Midlands

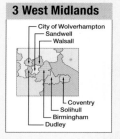

4 South Wales and Bristol area

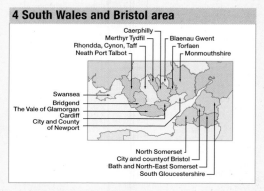

5 Thames Valley

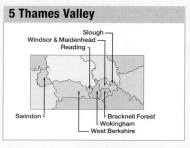

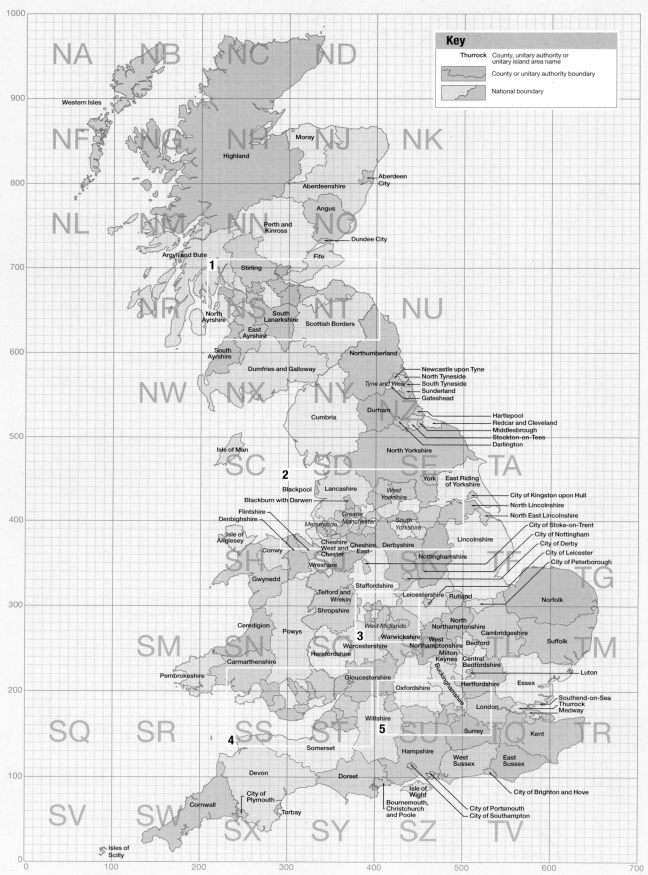

Key

Thurrock — County, unitary authority or unitary island area name

— County or unitary authority boundary

— National boundary